22nd Conferencia Iberoamericana on Software Engineering (CIbSE 2019)

La Habana, Cuba
22-26 April 2019

Editors:

Beatriz Marín
Isabel Sofia Brito
Miguel Katrib Mora
Andreia Malucelli
Estefanía Serral
Giovanni Giachetti
João Araújo
Miguel Goulão
Claudia P. Ayala
Marcela Genero
Vítor E. Silva Souza

ISBN: 978-1-5108-8795-4

Printed from e-media with permission by:

Curran Associates, Inc.
57 Morehouse Lane
Red Hook, NY 12571

Some format issues inherent in the e-media version may also appear in this print version.

Printed by Curran Associates, Inc. (2019)

For permission requests, please contact CIbSE - IberoAmerican Conference on Software Engineering at the address below.

CIbSE - IberoAmerican Conference on Software Engineering
c/o Luca Cernuzzi
Universidad Católica "Nuestra Seóra de la Asunción",
Campus Universitario, Asunción
Barrio Santa Ana, C.C.1683, C.P. 1364
Asunción - Paraguay

Phone: +595 21 334650
Fax: +595 21 310587

lcernuzz@uca.edu.py

Additional copies of this publication are available from:

Curran Associates, Inc.
57 Morehouse Lane
Red Hook, NY 12571 USA
Phone: 845-758-0400
Fax: 845-758-2633
Email: curran@proceedings.com
Web: www.proceedings.com

XXII Ibero-American Conference on Software Engineering
XXII Congreso Iberoamericano en Ingeniería de Software XXII
Congresso Ibero-Americano em Engenharia de Software

CIbSE 2019

April 22- 26, 2019 – La Habana, Cuba

Proceedings of XXII Ibero-American Conference on Software Engineering - CIbSE 2019
April 22-26th, 2019. La Habana, Cuba.

Editors

Beatriz Marín (Universidad Diego Portales, Chile)

Isabel Sofia Brito (Instituto Politécnico de Beja, Portugal)

Miguel Katrib Mora (Universidad de La Habana, Cuba)

Andreia Malucelli (UFPR, Brasil)

Estefanía Serral (KU Leuven, Belgium)

Giovanni Giachetti (Universidad Tecnológica de Chile INACAP, Chile)

João Araújo (Universidade Nova de Lisboa, Portugal)

Miguel Goulão (Universidade Nova de Lisboa, Portugal)

Claudia P. Ayala (Technical University of Catalunya, Spain)

Marcela Genero (Universidad de Castilla-La Mancha, España)

Vítor E. Silva Souza (Universidade Federal do Espírito Santo, Brasil)

Sponsors

Preface

Welcome to the 22nd Ibero-American Conference on Software Engineering (CIbSE'19)!

CIbSE'19 brought a vibrant community of software engineering researchers, educators, students and industrial practitioners together in Habana, Cuba, from April 22 to 26, 2019. Habana is glad to receive this event by the second time, first IDEAS'02 and now CIbSE'19.

CIbSE has distinct characteristics as it welcomes contributions in three languages: Portuguese, Spanish or English. It is backed by 21 previous conferences held in various countries:

Brazil-Torres (IDEAS'98),
San Jose, Costa Rica (IDEAS'99),
Cancun, Mexico (IDEAS'00),
Heredia, Costa Rica (IDEAS'01),
Habana, Cuba (IDEAS'02),
Asunción, Paraguay (IDEAS'03),
Arequipa, Peru (IDEAS'04),
Valparaiso, Chile (IDEAS'05),
La Plata, Argentina (IDEAS'06),
Isla Margarita, Venezuela (IDEAS'07),
Recife, Brazil (IDEAS'08),
Medellín, Colombia (IDEAS09),
Cuenca, Ecuador (CIbSE'10),
Rio de Janeiro, Brazil (CIbSE'11),
Buenos Aires, Argentina (CIbSE'12),
Montevideo, Uruguay (CIbSE'13),
Pucon, Chile (CIbSE'14),
Lima, Peru (CIbSE'15),
Quito, Ecuador (CIbSE'16),
Buenos Aires, Argentina (CIbSE'17),
Bogotá, Colombia (CIbSE'18).

CIbSE is an evolution of the successful IDEAS (Iberoamerican Workshop on Environments and Software Requirements Engineering) which began in 1998. It was strengthened with the integration of two specialized events: the Workshop on Requirements Engineering (WER) in 2010 and the Experimental Software Engineering Latin American Workshop (ESELAW) in 2011. As a result, CIbSE consists of three main tracks: Experimental Software Engineering Latin American Workshop (ESELAW), Requirements Engineering Track (RET) and Software Engineering Track (SET). Last year CIbSE also added an Ibero-American School on Software Engineering (EIbAIS), a natural evolution of the CIbSE tutorials and short courses. EIbAIS aims to promote a forum for discussions regarding software engineering and its related technologies and theoretical foundations, allowing the participation of practitioners, undergraduate and graduate students and researchers in the activities. CIbSE also hosts a Doctoral Symposium for Ph.D. students whose research area includes topics of Software Engineering, Requirements Engineering or Experimental Software Engineering.

In line with CIbSE's spirit, a plural program was prepared, including keynote speeches by influential researchers of the software engineering community, an Industrial Panel composed of prestigious practitioners from Cuba and, a Poster&Mojito session to present emergingideas. This year, we received 154 submissions (145 to the main scientific tracks and 9 to the doctoral symposium) from authors of 26 different countries. All submissions were reviewed by at least three members of the program committee, and an open electronic discussion was held post-review period to assure sufficient quality for the accepted contributions.

The keynote speakers were among the main conference highlights. Len Bass (Software Engineering Institute (SEI) - Pittsburgh, Pennsylvania, United States) keynote for SET, addressed challenges for MicroServices in his enlightening talk "Don't forget about deployment and operations". Marcela Genero (University of Castilla-La Mancha (UCLM), Ciudad Real, Spain) keynote for ESELAW, provided an insightful speech on "Empirical Software Engineering: Where have we come from, and where do we go from here?". Xavier Franch (Universitat Politècnica de Catalunya (UPC-BarcelonaTech)) keynote for RET, discussed the relevance of data in his enlightening talk "The Road to Data-driven Requirements Engineering".

We are grateful to the Program Committee track and Publicity chairs, members and additional reviewers provided excellent support in reviewing the papers. We are also grateful to all speakers, authors, and session chairs for their time and effort that helped to make CIbSE'19 a success. We thank the CIbSE Steering Committee members for the guidance and support in the organization process.

Special thanks to all the people of the organization team for making CIbSE'19 a pleasant experience that will remain in the memories of the participants for years to come.

Beatriz Marín
Isabel Sofia Sousa Brito
General Program Chairs

Miguel Katrib
General Organizer Chair

April, 2019
La Habana, Cuba

Program Committee

Ademar Aguiar	University of Porto
Fernanda Alencar	Universidade Federal de Pernambuco
Leandro Antonelli	LIFIA, Facultad de Informática, UNLP
Nathalie Aquino	Universidad Católica "Nuestra Señora de la Asunción"
Joao Araujo	Universidade NOVA de Lisboa
Marco Antonio Pereira Araújo	IF Sudeste MG
Hugo Arboleda	Universidad Icesi
Hernan Astudillo	Universidad Tecnica Federico Santa María
Claudia Ayala	Universitat Politècnica de Catalunya
Clara Ayora	Tree Technology S.A.
Monalessa Barcellos	UFES
Jorge Barreiros	ISEC / NOVA-LINCS
Judith Barrios Albornoz	University of Los Andes
María Cecilia Bastarrica	Universidad de Chile
David Benavides	University of Seville
Nelly Bencomo	Aston University
Dan Berry	University of Waterloo
Veronica Andrea Bollati	CONICET - UNIVERSIDAD TECNOLÓGICA NACIONAL
Regina Braga	UFJF
Fernando Brito	Instituto Universitário de Lisboa (ISCTE-IUL)
Antonio Brogi	University of Pisa
Agustina Buccella	GIISCO Research Group - Facultad de Informática - Dpto de Ingeniería de Sistemas - Universidad Nacional del Comahue
Nelio Cacho	UFRN
Danilo Caivano	Department of Informatics - University of Bari
Juan Pablo Carvallo	Universidad del Azuay
Alejandro Catala	CiTIUS, University of Santiago de Compostela
Luca Cernuzzi	DEI - Universidad Católica
Carlos Cetina	San Jorge University
Nelly Condori-Fernández	Universidade da Coruña
Fabio Costa	Federal University of Goias
Dolors Costal	Universitat Politècnica de Catalunya
Yania Crespo	University of Valladolid
Jose Antonio Cruz-Lemus	University of Castilla-La Mancha
Jácome Cunha	University of Minho
Luiz Marcio Cysneiros	York University, Toronto
Breno de França	UNICAMP
Jose Luis de la Vara	University of Castilla-La Mancha
Juan De Lara	Universidad Autonoma de Madrid
Andrea Delgado	Instituto de Computación, Facultad de Ingeniería, Universidad de la República
Arilo Claudio Dias-Neto	Federal University of Amazonas
Oscar Dieste	Universidad Politécnica de Madrid
Adler Diniz De Souza	COPPE / UFRJ / UNIFEI
Kleinner Farias	University of Vale do Rio dos Sinos
Alberto Fernández	Universidad

Eduardo Figueiredo	Federal University of Minas Gerais
Brenda L. Flores-Rios	UABC
Efraín R. Fonseca C.	Universidad de las Fuerzas Armadas ESPE
Xavier Franch	Universitat Politècnica de Catalunya
Nestor Garay-Vitoria	University of the Basque Country
Kelly Garces Pernett	Universidad de los Andes
Alejandra Garrido	LIFIA-Facultad de Informatica-UNLP
Marcela Genero	Universidad Castilla-La Mancha
Giovanni Giachetti	INACAP
Roxana Giandini	LIFIA, Facultad de Informática, UNLP
Fáber Danilo Giraldo Velásquez	none
Daniela Godoy	ISISTAN Research Institute
Omar Gomez	Technical School of Chimborazo
Miguel Goulao	Universidade NOVA de Lisboa
Renata Guizzardi	Universidade Federal do Espirito Santo
Gonzalo Génova	Knowledge Reuse Group, Universidad Carlos III de Madrid
Graciela Dora Susana Hadad	Universidad Nacional del Oeste
Clemente Izurieta	Montana State University
Marcos Kalinowski	Pontifical Catholic University of Rio de Janeiro (PUC-Rio)
Gladys Kaplan	UNLaM
Uirá Kulesza	UFRN
Raúl Lapeña	SVIT Research Group, Universidad San Jorge
Julio Cesar Leite	PUC-Rio
Lidia Lopez	Universitat Politècnica de Catalunya
Marcia Lucena	UFRN
Ivan Machado	UFBA - Federal University of Bahia
Andreia Malucelli	PUCPR
Marcelo Martin Marciszack	UTN FRC
Beatriz Marin	Facultad de Ingeniería y Ciencias – Universidad Diego Portales
Luiz Eduardo Galvão Martins	UNIFESP
Silverio Martínez-Fernández	Fraunhofer
Beatriz Marín	Universidad Diego Portales
Santiago Matalonga	University of the West of Scotlannd
Gerardo Matturro	Universidad ORT Uruguay
Emilia Mendes	Blekinge Institute of Technology and Oulu University
Andre Menolli	Universidade Estadual do Norte do Paraná - UENP
Cleviton Monteiro	Universidade Federal Rural de Pernambuco
Miguel Ehécatl Morales Trujillo	University of Canterbury
Ana Moreira	Universidade NOVA de Lisboa
Lourdes Moreno	Universidad Carlos III de Madrid
Daniel Méndez Fernández	Technical University of Munich
Elena Navarro	University of Castilla-La Mancha
Toacy Oliveira	COPPE/UFRJ
Luis Olsina	GIDIS_Web, Engineering School, UNLPam
Roberto Avila Paldes	Centro Universitário de Brasília
Cristina Palomares	Universitat Politècnica de Catalunya
Marco Antonio Paludo	PUCPR - Pontifícia Universidade Católica do Paraná
Jose Ignacio Panach Navarrete	University of Valencia

César Pardo	EAFIT University
Vicente Pelechano	Universitat Politècnica de València
Ernesto Pimentel	University of Malaga
Maria Pinto-Albuquerque	ISCTE-IUL - Instituto Universitário de Lisboa, Portugal
Claudia Pons	Universidad Nacional de La Plata
Rafael Prikladnicki	PUCRS
Fabio Q. B. Da Silva	Federal University of Pernambuco
Carme Quer	Universitat Politècnica de Catalunya
Sheila Reinehr	PUCPR
Marcela Ridao	INTIA UNICEN
António Rito Silva	Universidade de Lisboa
Luis Rivero	UFMA
Abel Rodríguez Morffi	Universidad Central Marta Abreu de Las Villas
Daniel Romero	Universidad Nacional de Asunción
José Raúl Romero	University of Cordoba
Gustavo Rossi	LIFIA-F. Informatica. UNLP
Jenny Ruiz	University of Holguin
Marcela Ruiz	Utrecht University
Juan Sanchez	Valencia University of Technology
Claudio Sant'Anna	Federal University of Bahia
Victor Santander	Universidad Estadual do Oeste do Paraná
Gleison Santos	UNIRIO
Eugenio Scalise	Universidad Central de Venezuela
Estefanía Serral	Katholieke Universiteit Leuven
Diego Sevilla	Universidad de Murcia
Carla Silva	Universidade Federal de Pernambuco
Lyrene Silva	Universidade Federal do Rio Grande do Norte
Vitor E. Silva Souza	Universidade Federal do Espírito Santo
Denis Silveira	Universidade Federal de Pernambunco
Martin Solari	Universidad ORT Uruguay
Isabel Sofia Sousa Brito	Instituto Politécnico de Beja
Vitor E. Silva Souza	Federal University of Espírito Santo, Brazil
Ernest Teniente	Universitat Politècnica de Catalunya
Victoria Torres	Universitat Politècnica de València
Guilherme Travassos	COPPE/UFRJ
Juan Pablo Ucán Pech	UADY
Joselaine Valaski	PUCPR
Pedro Valderas	Universitat Politècnica de València
Pedro Valderas	UPV
Natasha Malveira Costa Valentim	UFPR - Universidade Federal do Paraná
Diego Vallespir	Facultad de Ingeniería, Universidad de la República
Davi Viana	Federal University of Maranhão
Pablo Villarreal	CIDISI - Universidad Tecnológica Nacional - Facultad Regional Santa Fe
Raul Wazlawick	UFSC
Vera Werneck	Universidade do Estado do Rio de Janeiro – UERJ-IME
Roel Wieringa	University of Twente

Krzysztof Wnuk Department of Software Engineering, Blekinge Institute of Technology

Additional Reviewers

Albuquerque, Diogo
Alves, Johnatan
Becker, Pablo
Castro, John W.
Diaz, Javier Gustavo
Diniz, Joao Paulo
Ferreira, Fischer
Granda Juca, Maria Fernanda
Lima, Josias
Menolli, Andre
Moreno, Silvana
Muñoz, Juan Carlos
Pachón, Álvaro
Paludo, Marco
Pereira, Igor
Reinehr, Sheila
Rivera, Belén
Silva, Odair
Valaski, Joselaine
Villanes, Isabel

Author Index

Table of Contents

Software Engineering Track (SET)

SET Best paper

SET Agile Development

SET Software Projects

SET Software Development

SET Software Engineering Education

SET Emergent technologies

SET Model Driven Development

ESELAW Primary Studies

ESELAW Secondary Studies

Doctoral Symposium (DS)

DS Proposals

Emerging Ideas

SET Keynote 2019
Don't forget about deployment and operations

Len Bass[1]

[1] Software Engineering Institute of Carnegie Mellon
USA

Abstract. Standard definitions of software engineering suggest that the software engineer's job is done when the code is omitted. The definitions assume that deployment and operations are problems that belong to other people. In the modern world, this is no longer true. Software engineers must manage their code through to deployment and, frequently, are the first responders when a problem occurs. Without designing for deployment many different types of errors can occur during deployment. Without designing for first response, error correction can take a long time. Microservice architecture is a design style that reduces the errors during deployment, speeds up deployment, and supports error detection after code is placed into production. This talk will describe how microservice architectures perform these miracles and at what cost.

Hybrid Composition of Microservices with EUCalipTool

Pedro Valderas, Victoria Torres, Vicente Pelechano

PROS Research Centre
Universitat Politècnica de València
Camí de Vera s/n, E-46022, Spain
{pvalderas, vtorres, pele}@pros.upv.es

Abstract. In order to provide complex and elaborated functionalities, Microservices may cooperate with each other either by following a centralized (orchestration) or decentralized (choreography) approach. It seems that the decentralized nature of Microservices makes the choreography approach more appropriate to achieve such cooperation, where lighter solutions based on events and message queues are used. However, orchestration through the usage of a process engine provides many advantages both sides, in the modeling and deployment of business process models and also in the realization of such Microservice cooperation. In order to benefit from the goodness of these two approaches, this paper presents a hybrid solution based on the choreography of business process pieces that are internally orchestrated by microservices. To support this solution EUCalipTool and an execution infrastructure are presented.

1 Introduction

Companies such as Amazon, Airbnb, Twitter, Netflix, Apple, Uber and many others are shifted towards a Microservices architecture with the objective of being more agile in doing their business. The technology and functionality independence acquired when applying this architecture allows companies to replace, scale, and upgrade their applications easily and very fast [1], [2], [3]. However, in order to provide their customers with valuable services, developer teams are forced to build microservice compositions due to the small granularity level in which these operate [4]. The definition of such compositions is being made by many organizations programmatically ad-hoc. The major problem when creating compositions in this way is that complexity grows, turning more difficult visualizing, understanding, and maintaining the underlying composition. This complexity has forced many companies, even not software development companies, to build their own solution to compose microservices. Among these solutions we find Zeebe (the evolution of the Camunda project to orchestrate microservices), Netflix Conductor, ING Baker or Uber Cadence. Apart from Zeebe, the other solutions have been developed by non-software companies to deal with the growing number of microservices handled by each company to develop their business. In general, to achieve microservices compositions we can find two major different approaches, these are choreographies and orchestration.

On the one hand, when building compositions with the choreography approach, microservices would act autonomously based on the occurrence of events that are observed in the environment. The distributed nature of this approach introduces benefits and tradeoff. While this can have a positive effect on the speed and on the agility in the composition evolution/adaptation (microservices can be added/deleted to the flow easily), it also rises the composition complexity since the control flow is distributed across microservices. For instance, let us consider a process designed to place orders in a web shop which is supported by four microservices: Customers, Payment, Inventory, and Shipment. The sequence of steps to place an order is the following (see Fig. 1):

1. A client places an order in the web shop, which therefore issues an "Order created" event.
2. The *Customers microservice* is listening to an "Order created" event, based on which reacts by checking the customer data and issuing, when data is correct, a "Customer accepted" event.
3. The *Payment microservice*, which is listening to a "Customer accepted" event, starts to collect the money and once this is done, it issues a "Money collected" event.
4. As soon as the "Money collected" event is issued, the *Inventory microservice* starts to fetch the ordered items.
5. Finally, once the items are fetched, the *Shipping microservice* delivers the order to the client.

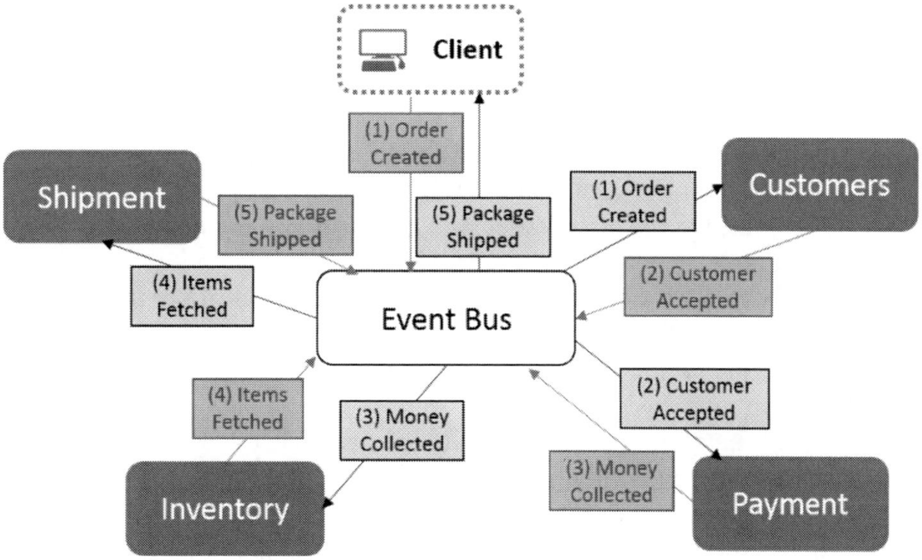

Fig. 1. Microservice collaboration through Choreography

Let us now suppose that our company wants to provide a special treatment to its VIP customers, so they can proceed with the payment by the end of the process. To maintain these low-coupled microservices, this small change would imply the introduction of several changes in different microservices: the *Customers microservice* should generate a different event depending on the type of customer in order to allow the participation of either the *Payment microservice* (regular customers) or the *Inventory microservice* (VIP customers); in the same way, the *Shipment microservice* should generate a different event in order to proceed with the payment or on the contrary the delivery of the order to the customer; and the *Payment microservice* should be also modified in order to deliver the order in case of VIP customers. Note how a single change requires the modification of several microservices and the need of having a clear picture of how microservices participate within the process. The major problem with this approach is that if an engineering decision needs to be taken, it is difficult to analyze processes when they are hard-coded and distributed along multiple microservices.

On the other hand, when building compositions with the orchestration approach, a central controller is in charge of managing all the interactions required to achieve the given composition. The major benefit of this approach is that it is easier to control the flow of the composition. However, this approach introduces coupling and dependences into the composition which may limits flexibility and decoupling. For example, the processing of the composition will stop if the central controller is down. Fig. 2 depicts graphically in a BPMN process model how microservices collaborate when we apply the orchestration approach.

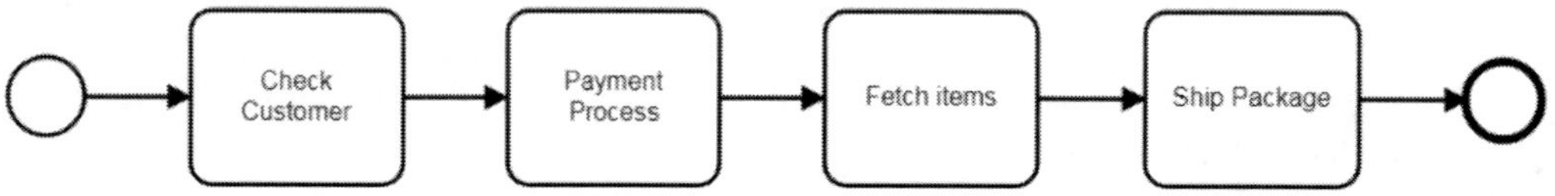

Fig 2. Microservice collaboration through Orchestration

However, in addition to these two major approaches, we can also find hybrid solutions that would fit better when the interaction required to achieve the composition involves synchronous blocks and asynchronous activities. A mixed solution allows us to benefit from the goodness of these two approaches. In this line, this work presents a hybrid solution that combines choreography with the orchestration of process pieces. On the one hand, we want to obtain the flexibility and decoupling that provide event-based choreographies. On the other hand, we want to obtain the possibility of having a central point with the big picture of the whole process for discussions or requirements engineering. In addition, we want to provide developers with tools that facilitate the modelling of a whole process and its distribution among the implicated microservices in order to obtain the desired orchestration of process pieces. To achieve this, we propose the following:

(1) EUCalipTool, an authoring tool to define microservices compositions through a Domain Specific Modelling Language (DSML) that facilitates the modelling activity. Developers can design the whole composition using constructors that are easier to use than business modeling elements. This tool also supports the transformation of an EUCalipTool description into a BPMN specification, the split of it into pieces, and the deployment of each piece into the corresponding microservice. This facilitates further maintenance and evolution of the microservice composition.
(2) A tool-supported architecture to perform distributed executions of microservice compositions through multiples microservices. We take a typical microservice architecture and introduce those components required to integrate EUCalipTool into the architecture and perform an event-based orchestration of business process pieces.

The remainder of the paper is structured as follows. Section 2 outlines the hybrid solution proposed in this work to achieve microservice compositions with the EUCalipTool authoring tool. Section 3 presents the architecture designed to support the solution and the role played by EUCalipTool to achieve microservice collaboration. Section 4 presents the DSML in which EUCalipTool is based on to model microservices compositions. Then, Section 5 explains how the microservice composition defined by designers with EUCalipTool is transformed to be deployed in the proposed microservice architecture. Finally, Section 6 concludes the paper and provides insights of directions for future work.

2 Hybrid Approach to Compose Microservices

In this section we present the proposed approach which is based on the distribution of responsibilities. Following this strategy, a process is split into different pieces whose execution responsibility is delegated to the different participating microservices. As representative example, Fig. 3 shows a little more complex version of the business process introduced previously in section 1.

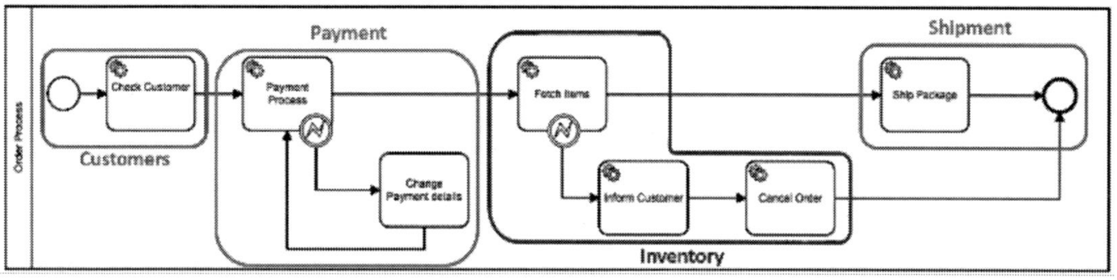

Fig 3. Microservice orchestration split into different fragments

As Fig. 3 shows, the process is split into four pieces that must be executed by different microservices: Customers, Payment, Inventory, and Shipment. Each microservice is in charge of executing its process fragment and to inform the other microservices following an event-based orchestration in order to complete the process (see Fig. 4).

Note that current business process management (BPM) tools provide little support to create a business process model and split it into pieces that can be deployed into different microservices. There is also little help to implement the communication mechanisms that are required to coordinate the execution of the different pieces to complete a process. In addition, there is some misconceptions within the microservice community that can make the adoption of this solution difficult:

- Many times, the task of process modelling is considered as an overhead for a software project.
- BPM tools are considered to be heavyweight and to take weeks to setup.

We think that the contribution that we present in the paper can alleviate these problems since the hybrid solution that we propose facilitates the modelling of a whole process and the distribution of the execution responsibilities among different microservices.

Next sections introduce the two main pillars of our approach: (1) the supporting architecture and (2) EUCalipTool and its DSML.

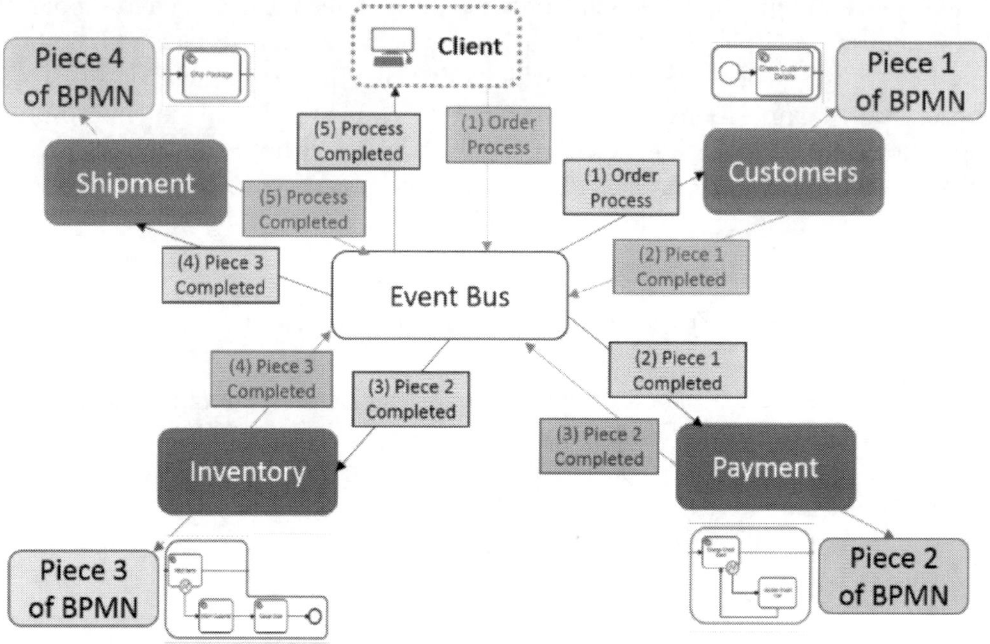

Fig. 4. Event-based Microservice Orchestration

3 Supporting Architecture

In a microservice architecture, applications are structured as a collection of loosely coupled services, which implement the business capabilities of a system. Apart from those business microservices, it is usual to find in this type of architecture other microservices that are focused on supporting infrastructure issues. Examples of this type of microservices are the *Service Registry* that gives support to service discovery, containing the network locations of microservice instances; an *API Gateway* that provides addressability capabilities; an *Authentication Server* that is in charge of controlling the access to the microservices; and a *Configuration Server* that manages microservice configuration on the cloud. In addition, it is also common the use of tools to monitor microservices' status and log their executions, as well as to deploy a message queue to manage asynchronous communication among microservices. Finally, microservices are usually complemented with a client-side load balancer and some library that implements the circuit breaker pattern to support fault tolerance.

Microservices architectures have already been used to build business process modeling and analysis tools [5]. In this work, we extend the typical microservice architecture with three main elements (see red elements in Fig. 5):

1. *EUCalipTool Composer.* It is an authoring tool to create microservices compositions through a DSML based on change patterns [7]. In addition, this tool is in charge of transforming the compositions created through the DSML

into a BPMN executable specification, splitting it into BPMN pieces or fragments, and sending them to the *EUCalipTool Server*.

2. *EUCalipTool Server*. It is a microservice in charge of the following responsibilities:
    a. Receiving the split BPMN processes sent by the *EUCalipTool Composer*, registering them into a process repository, and distributing the pieces among the different microservices. To achieve this, it uses the HTTP end-points published by the *EUCalipTool Client* for each microservice.
    b. Publishing end-points in order to launch each process through the HTTP protocol. The published end-points can be accessed either directly or through the API Gateway.
    c. Launching the execution of each process by triggering the first BPMN piece and delegating the responsibility of continuing the process to the corresponding microservice. To achieve this, a message queue is used.
    d. Providing the *EUCalipTool Composer* with the list of available microservices and their operations. It stores the list of microservices and their operations into a repository and publishes them through an HTTP end-point. To achieve this, microservices must be registered into this server by means of the *EUCalipTool Client*.
3. *EUCalipTool Client*. A client library that contains a lightweight BPMN engine and that is included within each microservice. It also creates an HTTP end-point to properly participate in the orchestration of BPMN pieces. In addition, when including this library into a microservice, it is automatically registered into the *EUCalipTool Server*.

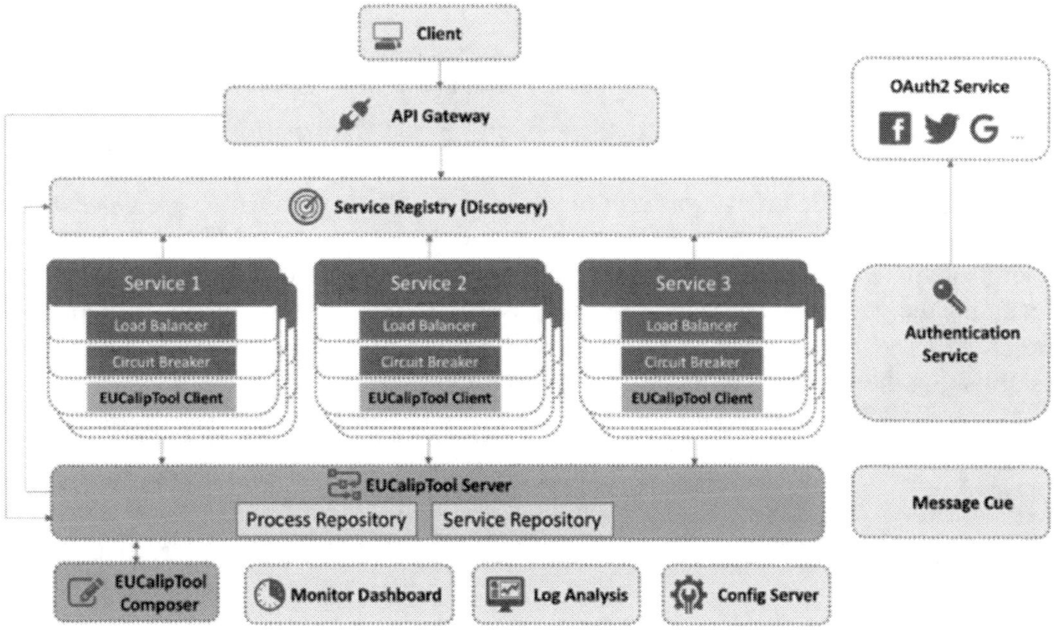

Fig. 5. Overview of the proposed architecture

4 Specifying Microservices Compositions

EUCalipTool is an authoring tool that was designed initially to facilitate the composition of services using a visual interface from a mobile device [6]. To achieve such objective, the design of this tool has been based on the *Change patterns* [7] developed within the context of the process of process modelling. Change patterns are high-level abstractions aimed at achieving flexible and easy adaptations of business process. These abstractions are defined in terms of high-level change operations (e.g., the creation of a parallel branch) which are based on the execution of a set of change primitives (e.g., add/delete activity). As opposed to change primitives, change pattern implementations typically guarantee model correctness after each transformation [9] by associating pre/post conditions with high-level change operations. Usually, process modeling environments supporting the correctness-by-construction principle (e.g., [10]) just provide process modelers with those change patterns that transform a sound process model into another sound one [8]. For this purpose, structural restrictions on process models (e.g., block structuredness) are imposed. In addition, a correct usage of change patterns allows speeding up the creation of the composition.

In this work we take as basis from [5] a small subset of change patterns to allow users to create all main control flow constructs (i.e., sequences, parallel branches, conditional branches, and loops). This set includes: AP1 (Insert Process Fragment) with its two variants, i.e., Serial and Parallel Insert, AP2 (Delete Process Fragment), AP8 (Embed Fragment in Loop), and AP10 (Embed Process Fragment in Conditional Branch).

Our main goal is to provide designers with a tool that facilitate the creation of process models and mitigate the perception of being an overhead.

4.1 DSML Abstract Syntax

This section presents the abstract syntax of the Domain Specific Modelling Language (DSML) that has been designed to allow microservice composition in a high level of abstraction (see Fig. 6). Inspired by the set of patterns introduced above, a microservice *Composition* is made up of *ComposiotionElement*s of two types which are *Operations* (of a *MicroService*) and *Fragments*. A *ComposiotionElement* is defined through the composite pattern, which facilitate the creation of user interfaces that help designers to focus on the definition of either the composition main sequence or the content of a fragment. The *previousElement* relationship between *CompositionElement*s allows establishing the sequence order between operations and fragments.

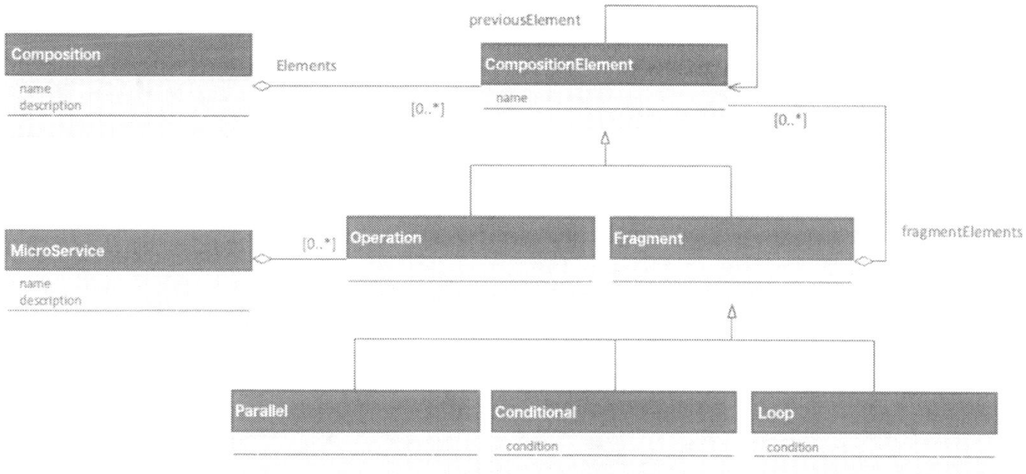

Fig. 6. Domain Specific Language designed for EUCalipTool

In order to better understand the concepts of this metamodel, Fig. 7 identifies them in a process that is composed of a sequence of four operations followed by a parallel fragment. In turn, this latter fragment is made up of a conditional fragment and two operations that are executed in parallel to it.

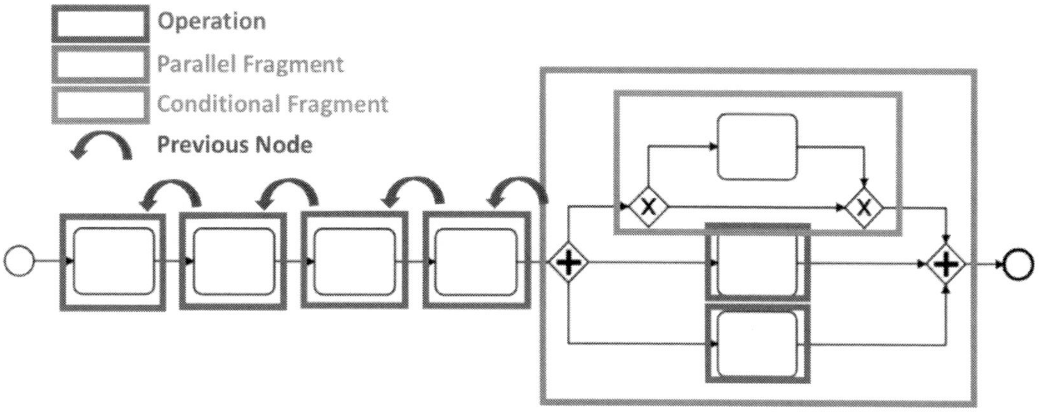

Fig. 7. DSL Concepts applied in an example

4.2 DSML Concrete Syntax

In order to create a composition of microservices we have defined an interface based on the "adding element" metaphor where designers just need to add a set of operations or fragments to a composition.

To exemplify this interface, Fig. 8 shows some of the screens needed to define the *Payment piece* marked in green in Fig. 3. Fig. 8A shows the composition after adding the *checkCustomer* operation of the microservice *Customers*. In order to add more elements, designers just need to click on the "+" symbol. Operations" tab, loops and parallel fragments can be selected from the "Block of Operation" tab.

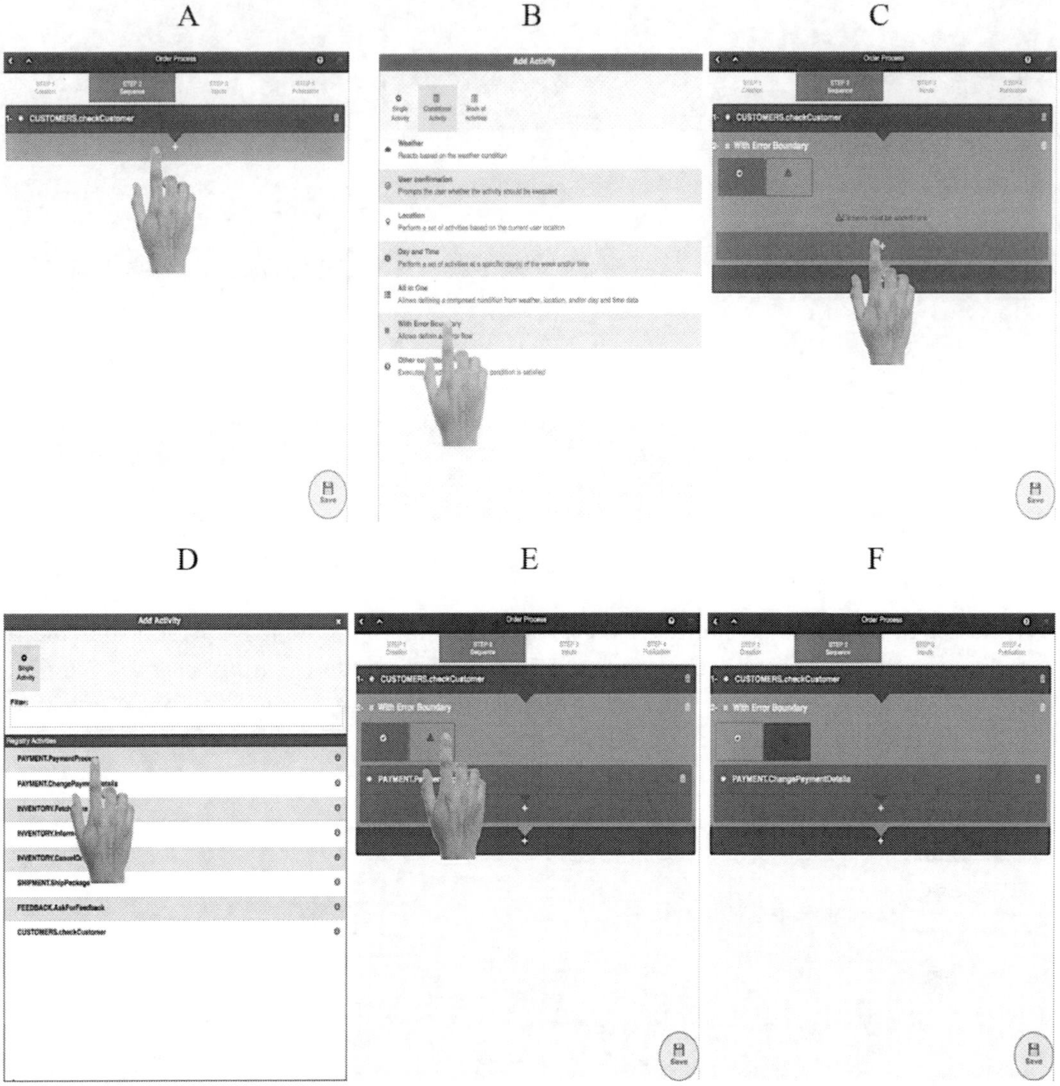

Fig. 8. Example of the DSML Concrete Syntax to create microservice compositions

The type of elements that can be added to a composition are *single operations*, *conditional operations*, and *other blocks of operations*. While conditions can be selected from the "Conditional. Fig. 8B shows a list of predefined conditional operations that are ready to be used in the current composition. In this case, the designer is selecting a special type of condition that will allow him to specify what happens when an error occurs. As a result, a conditional fragment is included after the first operation (see Fig. 8C). Here, the designer should specify two things, the major operation to perform and the compensation operation in case the major activity fails. In this case, the designer selects the *paymentProcess* operation offered by the Payment microservice as the major activity (see Fig. 8D). This is offered as a single operation from the available catalogue. The selection of this single operation results in the screen shown in Fig. 8E. At this point, the designer still has to specify what to do when the major activity of this conditional fragment fails. This can be specified by selecting the tab labelled with the warning icon, and proceeding similarly to the definition of the major operation. In this case, the designer selects the operation *ChangePaymentDetails*. With this action, the second element of the composition is already completed (see Fig. 8F). At this point, the designer should continue by selecting the most appropriate operations or fragments from the catalogue until the composition is completely defined.

5 Supporting the execution of Split BPMN processes

Once a microservice composition is defined with the *EUCalipTool Composer* three main stages are followed to distribute the responsibility of the process execution:

(1) The composition is transformed into a set of BPMN pieces.
(2) BPMN pieces are registered into the *EUCalipTool Server* and deployed into the corresponding microservices.
(3) Each microservice participates in the process through an event-based orchestration.

5.1 Generating BPMN pieces

The *EUCalipTool Composer* analyzes each process defined with its DSML and creates groups of actions according to the microservices that support them. Each of these groups will be transformed into a BPMN piece. If we consider the running example presented in section 1, we can see how four groups of actions are detected (see Fig. 9). In this example, only one group is detected per microservices since all their actions are defined sequentially.

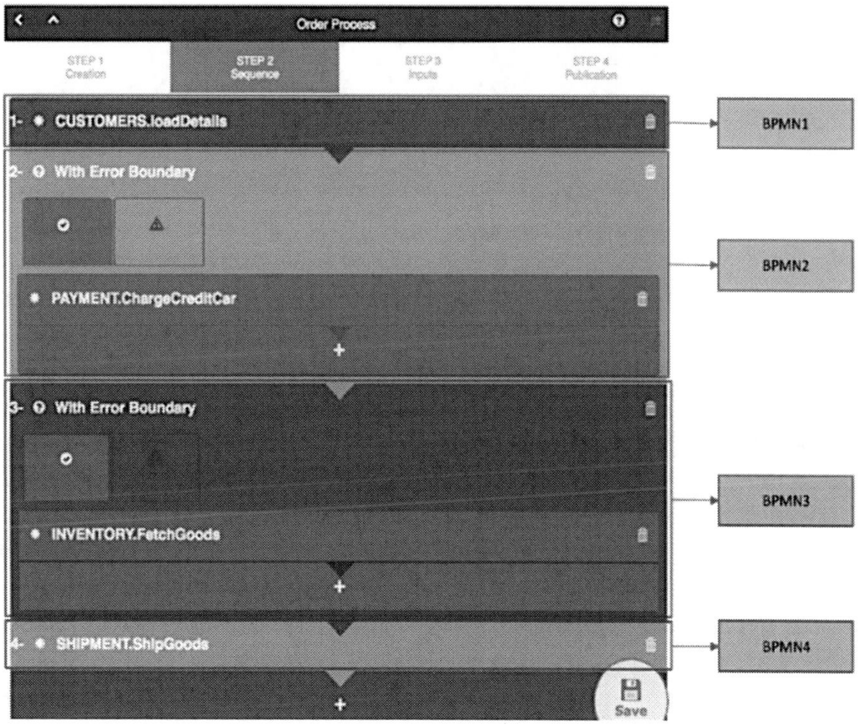

Fig. 9. Identification of BPMN pieces

For each piece of BPMN, the *EUCalipTool Composer* generates a specification with the BPMN tasks to be performed as well as additional tasks to trigger the events that must manage the orchestration. For instance, let us consider the operations that must perform the microservice *Inventory* (third piece of BPMN). This microservice must fetch the items of the order and, in case of error, inform the user and cancel the order. Fig. 10 shows the definition built with the *EUCalipTool Composer* and the generated BPMN process model. As we can see, there are two additional BPMN tasks that are in charge of 1) triggering an Ok event in case there is no error, and 2) a fail event, if some problem occurs. These tasks are preconfigured to publish the event in a message queue.

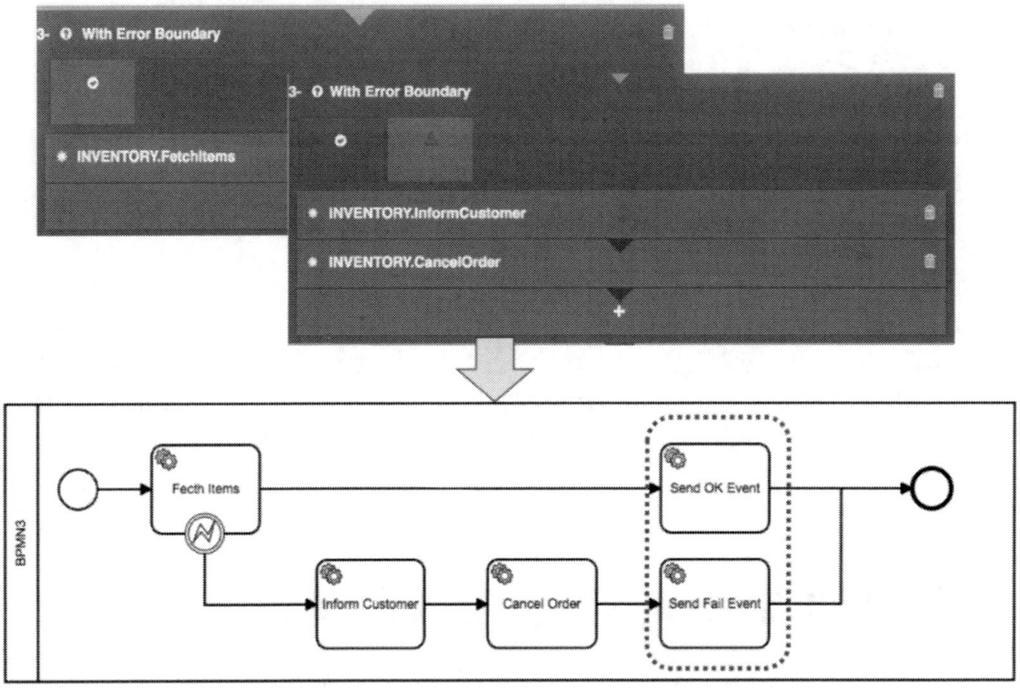

Fig 10. Genereated piece of BPMN

5.2 Distributing BPMN pieces to be orchestrated

Once the set of BPMN pieces has been generated, the *EUCalipTool Composer* sends them to the *EUCalipTool Server*. To do so, the latter publishes an HTTP end-point that accepts this data through POST connections.

When the *EUCalipTool Server* receives a split process from the Composer, it performs the following actions (see Fig. 11):

(1) Register the process into its repository and create a HTTP end-point to launch it.
(2) Deploy each piece of BPMN into the corresponding microservice.
(3) Define an event to launch the first piece of BPMN and configure the first microservice to listing to it.
(4) For each event generated by a piece of BPMN, configure the microservice that must execute the next piece in order to listen to this event.

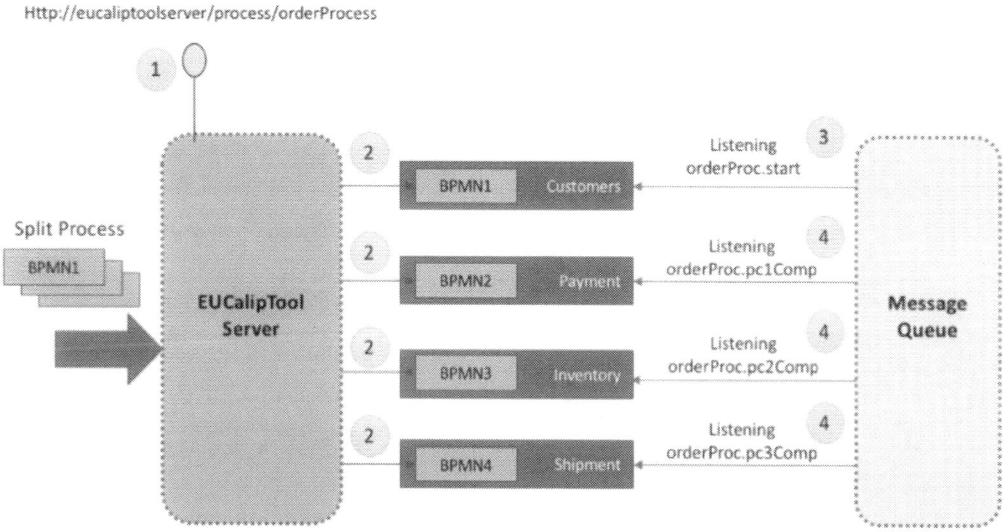

Fig. 11. Actions done by EUCalipTool Server

Note that the *EUCalipTool Server* must interact with the microservices in order to deploy each piece of BPMN as well as to configure the microservice to listen to specific events. This can be done using a set of HTTP end-points that each microservice has available when including the *EUCalipTool Client* (see Fig. 12).

5.3 Orchestrating the BPMN pieces

The orchestration of a split BPMN process is done as follows (see Fig. 12):

(1) A client accesses the end-point published by the *EUCalipTool Server*.
(2) The *EUCalipTool Server* launches the start event for this process.
(3) The microservice that is listening to this event executes the first piece of BPMN. This execution finishes by triggering an event that indicates that the execution of the first BPMN piece is completed.
(4) The microservice that is listening to the event that indicate the execution of the first BPMN piece launches its own BPMN piece (the second one) and when it is executed, generates another event that indicates that the execution of the second BPMN piece is completed.
(5) The microservice that is waiting for the event that indicate the execution of the second BPMN piece does the same as the previous one.
(6) And so on until the process is completed.

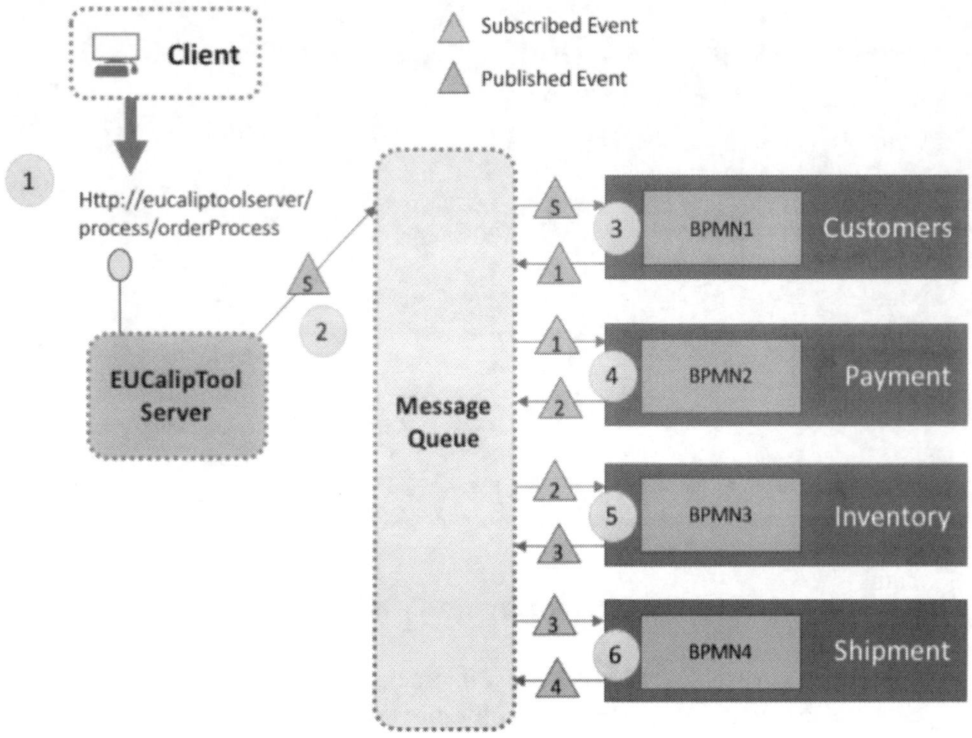

Fig. 12. Event based orchestration of a split BPMN process

6 Conclusions

In this work, we have presented a hybrid solution that combines the choreography and orchestration approaches to deal with microservice compositions with the use of EUCalipTool. The main reason to follow such a hybrid solution is that we want to take advantage of the goodness of each approach. This is, we want to maintain the flexibility and decoupling nature offered in choreographies but also want to keep the composition global vision and management offered by an orchestration approach. For this purpose, EUCalipTool is integrated in a typical microservice architecture to provide: 1) tool support to the specification of microservices compositions and 2) mechanisms to automate the distributed deployment of microservice compositions.

As future work we plan to enrich EUCalipTool with goal-oriented capabilities. In this way, instead of specifying compositions explicitly, developers would just need to state the goals that a composition must satisfy. Then, based on them, EUCalipTool would propose an initial composition intended to satisfy the stated goals.

References

[1] Newman, S.: Building Microservices, USA:O'Reilly Media Inc., February 2015.

[2] Bucchiarone, A., Dragoni, N., Dustdar, S., Larsen, S. T., and Mazzara, M.: From Monolithic to Microservices: An Experience Report from the Banking Domain. *IEEE Software*, vol. 35, no. 3, pp. 50-55, 2018.

[3] Shadija, D., Rezai, M., Hill, R.: Towards an understanding of microservices. ICAC 2017: 1-6

[4] Dragoni, N, Giallorenzo, S., Lluch-Lafuente, A., Mazzara, M., Montesi, F., Mustafin, R., Safina, L.: Microservices: Yesterday, Today, and Tomorrow. Present and Ulterior Software Engineering2017: 195-216

[5] Alpers, S., Becker, C., Oberweis, A., Schuster, T.: Microservice Based Tool Support for Business Process Modelling. EDOC Workshops 2015: 71-78

[6] Valderas, P., Torres, T., Mansanet, M., Pelechano, V.: A mobile-based solution for supporting end-users in the composition of services. Multimedia Tools Appl. 76(15): 16315-16345 (2017)

[7] Weber, B., Reichert, M., Rinderle, S.: Change Patterns and Change Support Features - Enhancing Flexibility in Process-Aware Information Systems. Data and Knowledge Engineering 66 (2008) 438-466

[8] Barbara Weber, Jakob Pinggera, Victoria Torres, Manfred Reichert: Change Patterns in Use: A Critical Evaluation. CoRR abs/1511.04059 (2015)

[9] Casati, F.: Models, Semantics, and Formal Methods for the design of Workflows and their Exceptions. PhD thesis, Milano (1998)

[10] Dadam, P., Reichert, M.: The ADEPT project: a decade of research and development for robust and flexible process support. Comp Scie - R&D 23 (2009) 81-97

BlackSheep: Dynamic Effort Estimation in Agile Software Development using Machine Learning

Rafik Mas'ad[1], Ricardo Ñanculef[1], and Hérnan Astudillo[1]

Department of Informatics, Universidad Técnica Federico Santa María, Chile
rmasad@nursoft.cl, jnancu@inf.utfsm.cl, hernan@inf.utfsm.cl

Abstract. Effort estimation is an important task in software engineering. Inaccurate estimations cause delays in project scheduling, increase cost, and can lead to project failure. Unfortunately, current methods for effort estimation in the agile context are not very accurate, require large amounts of historical data, and/or are not designed to provide estimations after the development process starts.
In this article, we present Blacksheep, a novel technique for project effort estimation in agile contexts. As a learning-oriented method, Blacksheep relies on data to improve effort predictions. However, it combines three key ideas to overcome the problems of current methods. First, it learns from other user stories as soon as they get closed in the project, reducing its dependency on historical data. Second, it uses an ensemble of predictors that are combined to obtain a global effort estimate. Third, it relies on an instance selection procedure designed to dynamically choose training data on the basis of its relevance for the prediction task. All these three components are integrated into a framework that allows predictions at different stages of the development process.
The proposed system is assessed using real data from eleven software projects conducted by a Chilean software company between September 2016 and August 2018. Among other results, we found that using just two closed projects as historical data, BlackSheep achieves an relative absolute error lower than 0.25 in around 78% of the cases, improving on Planning Poker (the current method) by a significant margin.

Keywords: Software development effort estimation · Agile Software Development · Dynamic estimation · Machine learning.

1 Introduction

Delays and cost overruns are usual in software development. According to [6], one of every six projects has a budget overrun of 200% and a schedule overrun of almost 70%. To overcome these problems, at least partly, requires more accurate software development effort estimation (SDEE) techniques, that is, methods to predict the amount of person-hours (or money) required to develop a software system.

Diverse SDEE techniques have been investigated in the last decades [3,2,15,11]. Unfortunately, many of these approaches assume that a classic methodology, e.g.

waterfall, is going to be used by the development team. However, during the last years, agile software development (ASD) methodologies have been most widely adopted in the community due to their effectivity [8]. This paradigm [1], encourages continuous software delivery, is based on short development iterations (2-5 weeks), allows requirements to change over time and aids self-organizing development teams. All these distinctive features have an impact on SDEE and make many classic techniques innacurate and difficult to apply. In particular, they suggest focusing on effort predictions for small parts of a project (e.g. user stories or sprints) rather than the entire project at once.

Currently, SDEE in agile contexts is often done by project teams using expertise-based methods based on user story points (USP), such as Planning Poker [4,7]. Even if these methodologies tend to produce inaccurate predictions and may be inconsistent in time [15], they are frequently preferred on learning-oriented methods proposed more recently. The reason is that learning-oriented methods typically require large amounts of data from similar projects and/or detailed documentation at the beginning of the development process to produce accurate estimations. These requirements can be unrealistic for small development companies (with few projects by year) and teams used to improve documentation as a continuous process. The nature of agile methodologies suggests indeed that SDEE should not only be a disaggregated process, but a dynamic one, capable to continuously revise predictions and learn from data arising after development starts.

To overcome the limitations of current SDEE methods in agile contexts, we present BlackSheep, a learning-oriented framework for SDEE, devised to provide effort estimates at different steps of an ASD project. As other techniques, our method leverages on the ability of machine learning to extract patterns from data. However, our technique is designed to require few amounts of historical data, i.e. data available before the project starts. This is achieved by combining three key ideas: (i) BlackSheep marks a user story as potentially useful as soon as it gets closed in the corresponding project, (ii) it includes an instance selection criterion that dynamically choose chunks of data depending on the time step at which the predictions are required, and (iii) it combines several predictions to produce a global effort estimate. To accommodate standard machine learning algorithms at this point, BlackSheep employs a descriptor of the state of a user story at a given time step. This descriptor includes information regarding the size, productivity and code corresponding to a user story at a given time stamp.

The rest of this paper is organized as follows. In section 2, we state the problem addressed in this paper and the goals of this research. In section 3, we briefly discuss some previous work related to our proposal. Section 4 introduces some concepts and tools used in the rest of the paper, including a short description of the machine learning approaches used by BlackSheep. Our SDEE technique is presented in section 5. In section 6, we assess the proposed method an discuss the obtained results. Section 7 closes the article pointing out the main conclusions of this work.

2 Problem Statement

Even if SDEE techniques based on expert judgment are often inaccurate and may be inconsistent in time, they represent the most widely used approach in practice both by agile and traditional development teams [15]. The main reason is that expertise based methods are simple and do not require to register, store and review data from previous projects [16] to be deployed. On the other hand, as most software companies are small and develop few software projects annually, requiring several dozens, up to hundreds, of data from similar projects to perform estimation can be very unrealistic and make a SDEE technique infeasible in practice. On the other hand, since ASD allows adaptation at virtually any point in a project, a lot of information may not be available in a useful form at the beginning of an agile development cycle. In particular, documentation in ASD projects is a continuous process, and thus requiring more and more accurate documentation at the beginning, as asked by many SDEE techniques, may lead a team to abandon a data-driven approach in favor of a more simple expertise based method that fulfils better the initial uncertainty characterising ASD projects.

The main aim of this work is to develop a data-driven SDEE technique requiring few information at the beginning of the development process, but feeding continuously from data generated during the same project's life cycle. Since both user requirements as well as team efficiency can evolve during the project's life, we hypothesise that a data-driven method focused on project evolution and constant re-estimation not only accommodates better the needs of ASD projects but can also improve the accuracy of alternative methods. We have focused on this problem as part of a collaboration with a real software company where the proposed estimation methodology will be adopted.

3 Related work

Effort estimation is one of the more challenging tasks in software engineering [3] and therefore, there is a bunch of works in the literature devoted to this problem. At least three groups clearly emerge after a review: expertise-based, model-based and learning-oriented techniques.

Expertise-based methods rely on expert knowledge and judgmental processes, involving one or many actors, that compare new projects or functionalities with older ones. For instance, Planning Poker [15] is a method, widely used among ASD teams, in which an effort estimation is obtained as a consensus among individual judgments, reached after a series of discussion and re-estimation rounds. Unfortunately, expertise-based methods like this, tend to be inaccurate, in part due to the technical uncertainty characterizing development of a new software product, but mainly due to the bias of human judgments and their sensitivity to pressure from internal and external groups interested in meeting certain cost targets [14]. This issue makes predictions based on expert judgment often to underestimate effort and duration [15].

Model-based methods perform predictions using simple models defined by a small, fixed and carefully designed set of parameters. In this category, we found classic methods such as CoCoMO [3], SLIM and Function Points Analysis. In principle, these methods allow a certain degree of adjustment to reflect the tendencies of the industry or the peculiarities a given company. However, due to the last technological changes (e.g. the large amount of software reuse supported by modern frameworks) these models are becoming obsolete.

Learning-oriented SDEE techniques are those employing machine learning algorithms to build a predictive model whose functional form is inferred from data. In contrast to model-based SDEE, these approaches rely on more flexible parametric models such as linear regression, semi-parametric methods such as artificial neural networks, or non-parametric techniques including support vector machines and regression trees to perform predictions. Since these techniques estimate the model form *and* its parameters, they typically require more data to be reliable[11]. In the literature, there are works presenting approaches that do not require hundreds of previous projects as training data but, unfortunately, they do not allow continuous predictions [10,12].

4 Theoretical Background

Story Points & Development Speed In ASD projects, it is common to estimate effort using *User Story Points* (USP), a measurement unity that allows expressing the *relative* size of a user story or software feature. Assigning two story points to a user story states that it should take twice as much effort as a user story that is assigned one story point [4]. In this context, the *speed* v of a user story is computed as $v = x/t$, where x is the estimated size of x in USP and t is the actual effort required to complete it. As to obtain a progress measure proportional to the effort, we define the *inverse of the development speed* as v^{-1}.

Moving Averages. In this work, we use metrics to describe the progress of a project in time. Given a sequence of scores $(x_t) = x_1 x_2 \ldots x_T$, it is often convenient to consider a smoothed version of (x_t), such as the *exponential moving average* (EMA) and the *simple moving average* (SMA), defined as

$$\text{EMA}_t = \frac{\sum_{i=0}^{t}(1-\alpha)^i \cdot x_{t-i}}{\sum_{i=0}^{t}(1-\alpha)^i}, \quad \text{SMA}_t = \frac{1}{n}\sum_{i=0}^{n-1} x_{t-i}, \tag{1}$$

where α, n are parameters known as the *smoothing factor* and the *window size* respectively. The smoothing factor is often reparametrized as $\alpha = \exp\left(log(0.5)/H\right)$, where H is referred to as the *half-life*.

Machine Learning Algorithms. Broadly speaking, machine learning is a set of techniques devised to allow a program to automatically improve with experience. In the last years, this technology has been succesfully applied to a number of problems in different fields, including software engineering.

In the case of SDEE, learning-oriented approaches often correspond to the application of supervised learning algorithms, i.e. methods to estimate the functional relationship between variables of interest [13] using explicit examples of this relationship. Among the most popular methods, we have Support Vector Regression and Regression Trees.

Given an input pattern x and a target response y, Support Vector Regression implements a predictor of the form $f(x) = \sum_{\ell} \alpha_{\ell}\, y^{(\ell)} k(x^{(\ell)}, x)$, where $(x^{(\ell)}, y^{(\ell)})_{\ell=1}^{L}$ is a set of examples of the map $x \to y$. The pairwise function k, referred to as *the kernel*, can be regarded as the similarity function of the input pattern space and allows processing different data types, including vectors, images and text. The parameters α_{ℓ} are learnt to minimize a cost function that tolerates small deviations between the predictions and the ground truth data and penalizes the complexity of the obtained predictor.

Regression Trees learns a predictor of the form $f(x) = \sum_{k} y_{\ell}\, R_k(x)$, where $R_k(x)$ is a membership function checking if the input pattern x belongs to a given region $\mathcal{R}_k$ of the input pattern space and y_k is a prototype response associated to that region. The collection of regions $\{\mathcal{R}_k\}_{k=1}^{M}$ in which the input space is partitioned follows a hierarchical top-down pattern, which allows the decision mechanism to be organized as a tree. The set of regions $\{\mathcal{R}_k\}_{k=1}^{M}$ as well as the responses y_k are learnt to minimize a tradeoff between the empirical prediction error and the complexity of the obtained tree (e.g. depth).

Different from the previous techniques, AdaBoost does not learn a *single* predictor, but a *set* of predictors that are then combined to obtain point estimates. The method proceeds in a series of rounds. At each round, it fits a new predictor by weighting the training data in such a way that data points on which previous predictors incurred a large error get more weight. This principle is often combined with sampling, that is, at each round, the training data is drawn from the original dataset using selection probabilities proportional to the weights. In principle, AdaBoost can accomodate different methods to learn the individual predictors (e.g. Support Vector Regression or Regression Trees) and may also incorporate mechanisms, other than data re-weighting, to guarantee the complementarity/diversity of the individual predictions.

5 BlackSheep

At a given time step t, BlackSheep estimates the effort required to finish a project by predicting the effort needed to complete each user story still open in the project. These individual predictions are then aggregated to obtain a project effort estimation. Now, the effort required by a user story s at time t is predicted by training a machine learning model with data from other user stories at time steps $\tau < t$ corresponding to a state similar to the current state of s. This approach requires: (i) a *descriptor* of the state of a user story at a given time step, (ii) a method for *selecting* training data from previous projects and the same project at previous time steps, and (iii) a supervised machine learning model. These components interact as depicted in Fig.1 and are discussed below.

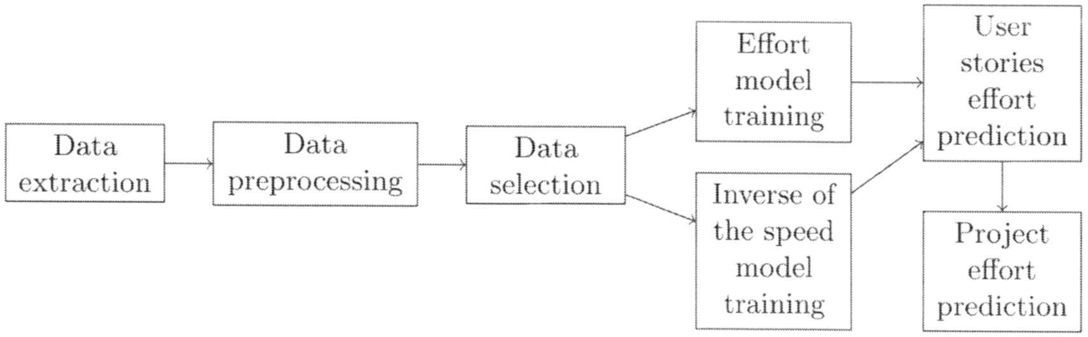

Fig. 1. Process of building a project effort prediction.

5.1 Data Sources

BlackSheep's learning abilities as well as its capacity to provide continuous predictions depend, of course, on data obtained from other projects and from reports regarding the ongoing target project. Concretely, we assume access to the following resources, for each project used to feed BlackSheep (they are available in most ASD contexts):

- **Project's Metadata:** General information regarding active and past projects, such as development stages, user stories, tasks an USP assigned by the team.
- **Effort reports:** provided by the members of the development team regarding the effort incurred in the different projects they participate.
- **Code:** generated by the members of the development team and stored in GIT repositories.

5.2 Data Descriptors

From the data sources identified above, we define a set of metrics aimed to describe the size, productivity and code corresponding to a user story at a given time stamp. The computation of these metrics on the different user stories $\mathcal{S}_p$ that compose a project p at different time stamps $\mathcal{T}$ produces a data frame (or table) X with $|\mathcal{S}_p| \cdot |\mathcal{T}|$ rows and K columns, where K is the size of the proposed descriptor.

Metrics describing the size of a user story include: (1) **Project ID:** Unique ID of the project the user story belongs to. (2) **User story size:** size (in USP) assigned to the user story by the development team. (3) **User story size by role:** size (in USP) assigned to the user story by different members of the development team, grouped by role (back-end, front-end, design). (4) **Milestone size:** size (in USP) of the project's phase the user story belongs to. (5) **Milestone ratio:** ratio of the *user story size* and the *milestone size*. (6) **Project size:** size (in USP) of the project the user story belongs to.

Productivity metrics include: (1) **Days from start:** number of days passed from the first report corresponding to the entity. (2) **SMA of the inverse speed** with $n = 180$ (see Sec.4 for SMA and EMA definitions). (3) **EMA of the inverse speed** with $H = 30$. (4) **Current effort:** Effort (in HH) incurred on the user story up to a given time step. (5) **Advance:** ratio of closed USP and the planned USP. (6) **Rework-ratio:** ratio of the reworking effort and the total effort. (7) **Bimonthly rework-ratio:** ratio of the reworking effort and the total effort in the last two months. (8) **Active user story:** number of active user stories at a given time step. (9) **Delay:** total delay with respect to the prediction obtained using Planning Poker.

Finally, metrics describing the code include: (1) **LOC counts:** number of code lines added and removed in the last week, as well as their sum. (2) **Normalized LOC ratio:** number of code lines added and removed, normalized by the effort incurred the last week. (3) **SMA of LOC counts** with $n = 180$. (4) **EMA of LOC counts** with $H = 30$. (5) **SMA of normalized LOC ratio** with $n = 180$. (6) **EMA of normalized LOC ratio** with $H = 30$. (7) **Active file ratios:** proportion of active files (w.r.t. the total number of files) in the last 30 days. (8) **SMA of Active files ratio** with $n = 180$. (9) **EMA of Active files ratio** with $H = 30$. (10) **Recurrent files ratio:** number of times a file is modified more than once (w.r.t. the total number of files) in the last 30 days. (11) **SMA of Recurrent files ratio** with $n = 180$. (12) **EMA of Recurrent files ratio** with $H = 30$. (13) **File-wise Churn metric:** number of files than are modified more than once (w.r.t. the total number of files) in the last 30 days. (14) **SMA of Churn metric of file** with $n = 180$. (15) **EMA of Churn metric of file** with $H = 30$.

The proposed metrics can be computed with respect to a user story, a project, all the active projects in the company, people working in a project, or all the people working at the company. Table 1 explains the target of each metric. To introduce the metrics computed on people as features of a given user story at a given time step (row of a project's data frame), we compute a weighted average among people's metrics using weights proportional to the effort incurred by these people in the project or all the active projects.

5.3 Data selection

A key component of the proposed system is a method to dynamically select data from other projects to train/fit the predictive models. Since the ultimate goal is to accurately predict project effort at different stages of the development process, our data selection method is based on the level of progress achieved on

	Company	Project	Person	Person in project	User story
Size metrics					(1) to (6)
Productivity metrics	(1) to (3), (6), (7), (9)	(1) to (3), (5) to (7), (9)	(1), (2), (3), (6), (7)	(2), (3), (6), (7)	
Code metrics	(1) to (6)	(1) to (15)			

Table 1. Target of the metrics proposed to describe a user story at a given time step.

a project at a given time step. For instance, if a project we need to predict was assigned 100 USP and, at a give time step, we have completed 30 USP, we may train the predictive models with data from user stories at time steps when they had a progress of around 30%. We note however that, since the velocity in a project is influenced by many factors, the real effort spent on a project or user story at a given time step is, in general, a non-linear function of the fraction of the USP. Hence, we propose to first model this relationship using a function referred to as *relative advancement curve* (RAC) that, given a fraction of effort spent at a given time step, say u_t, computes the fraction of USP completed at this stage $e_t = \mathrm{RAC}(u_t)$. Conducting preliminary experiments, we found that a suitable model is the integral incomplete beta function with parameters $(4, 4)$ that is, $e_t = \mathrm{ibeta}(u_t; 4, 4)$, as depicted in Fig. 2.

Having modeled the RAC, our data selection method works as follows. If, at a given time step, we have completed a fraction e_t of the USP assigned to a user story we want to predict, we train/fit the machine learning model with descriptors corresponding to closed user stories at time steps where the fraction of real spent effort was $\mathrm{RAC}^{-1}(e_t) \pm 0.1$. For instance, if $e_t = 0.1$, we select descriptors corresponding to a relative progress between 18% and 38% of real effort ($\mathrm{RAC}^{-1}(0.1) \approx 0.28$). An key advantage of this method is that it allows to include more training data for stages at which velocity is low. As depicted in Fig. 2, this happens at earlier and later stages of development.

5.4 Model training and effort prediction

Blacksheep estimates project effort by first predicting the effort required to complete each user story still open in the project, and then summing up these individual predictions. More formally, if $\{s_{i,t}^{(p)}\}_i$ denotes the set of active user stories of a project p at time t, the effort required to finish project p at this time step is estimated as $e_t^{(p)} = \sum_i e_{i,t}^{(p)}$, where $e_{i,t}^{(p)}$ denotes the effort prediction for $s_{i,t}^{(p)}$. The

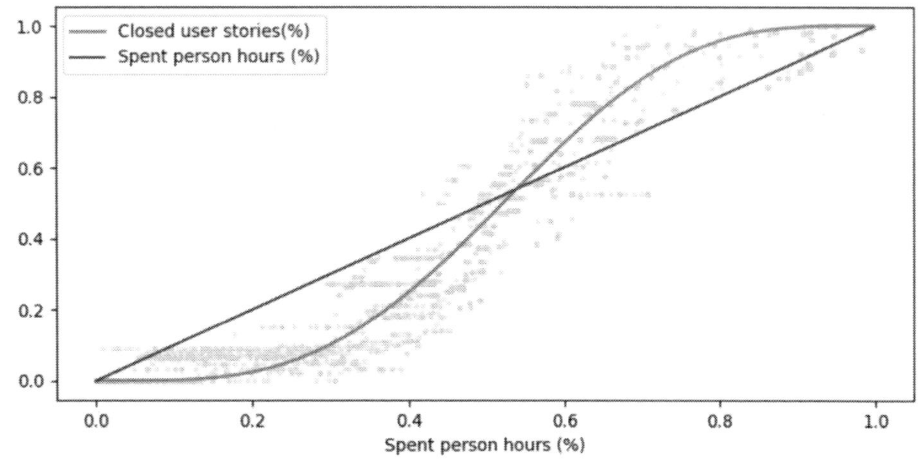

Fig. 2. *Relative advancement curve (RAC).* Percentage of advance (closed USP) on percentage of person hours used.

latter estimate is obtained using a machine learning model trained with the data selection method presented in section 5.3 and the data descriptors introduced in section 5.2. More specifically, we (i) collect the descriptors $x_{j,\tau}^{(n)}$ corresponding to all the user stories (from any project n) that were closed at times steps $\tau < t$ and match the data selection criterion, (ii) get the real effort $y_{j,\tau}^{(n)}$ that was required to finish these stories, and (iii) train a machine learning algorithm to approximate the map $x_{j,\tau}^{(n)} \to y_{j,\tau}^{(n)}$. The effort prediction $e_{i,t}^{(p)}$ is thus obtained as $f(x_{i,t}^{(p)})$ where $x_{i,t}^{(p)}$ is the descriptor corresponding to $s_{i,t}^{(p)}$ at time step t and f is the trained model.

To implement the machine learning model, we propose a combination of two approaches. The first trains a machine learning algorithm to directly predict effort. The second trains the algorithm to predict the inverse of the development speed. In this case, and, as mentioned in section 4, we can compute effort as $e_i = v_i^{-1} \cdot p_i$, where v_i^{-1} is the predicted inverse-speed of a user story (at a given time step) and p_i denotes its size in USP. The direct prediction and the speed-based prediction are aggregated using a simple average. This criterion is motivated by results reported in related works [9,11], which conclude that the combination of models tends to improve the accuracy of learning-oriented approaches, mainly in the case of small datasets, as ours.

For the same reason above, the machine learning algorithm adopted to predict development speed and effort is AdaBoost. As discussed in section 4 this method does not rely on a single predictor, but on a set of predictors that are obtained by training a base learner with slightly different samples. In the case of development speed, we use Support Vector Regression as base learner. In the case of effort instead, we adopt Regression Trees. These techniques were selected on the basis of their current use in the literature and results observed in preliminary experiments.

As a final criterion, we refine the effort prediction obtained for a user story as follows: if the predicted effort is lower than the effort already incurred in the user story, the prediction is replaced by the latter. This criterion will be referred to as *underestimation correction*.

5.5 Performance metrics

There are three main criteria to assess SDEE techniques: mean magnitude relative error (MMRE), mean magnitude of error relative to the estimate (MMER) and percentage relative error deviation (PRED). These metrics have the advantage of being independent of the measurement unit. Both MMRE and PRED are based on the magnitude relative error (MRE).

As BlackSheep is used to perform predictions at different stages of the project, the metrics above will be computed at different time steps t. In this case, the metrics should be normalized with respect the remaining effort at time t and not the total project effort. Since only the remaining effort is uncertain, this criterion produces a more conservative and, in our opinion, realistic error estimate. To state it more clearly, MRE at time t will be computed as follows:

$$\mathrm{MRE}^{(p,t)} = \frac{\left|Y^{(p,t)} - \hat{Y}^{(p,t)}\right|}{Y^{(p,t)} - \mathrm{CUS}^{(p,t)}}, \tag{2}$$

where $Y^{(p,t)}$ is the real effort, $\hat{Y}^{(p,t)}$ is the predicted effort at time t and $\mathrm{CUS}^{(p,t)}$ is the real effort corresponding to the user stories already closed. MMRE and PRED at time t are computed as:

$$\mathrm{MMRE}^{(t)} = \frac{1}{n}\sum_{t=0}^{n} \mathrm{MRE}^{(p,t)}, \text{ and } \mathrm{PRED}^{(t)}(x) = \frac{1}{n}\sum_{p=0}^{n} I(\mathrm{MRE}^{(p,t)} \leq x), \tag{3}$$

where $I(\cdot)$ is an indicator function, n is the number of projects and x is a parameter typically set to 0.25 or 0.3 [11]. Analogously, MMER is defined as follows:

$$\mathrm{MMER}^{(t)} = \frac{1}{n}\sum_{t=0}^{n} \left(\frac{\left|Y^{(p,t)} - \hat{Y}^{(p,t)}\right|}{\hat{Y}^{(p,t)} - \mathrm{CUS}^{(p,t)}} \right). \tag{4}$$

Please note that $\mathrm{MMRE}^{(0)}$, $\mathrm{MMER}^{(0)}$, $\mathrm{PRED}^{(0)}(0.25)$ and $PRED^{(0)}(0.30)$ are exactly the definitions of MMRE, MMER, PRED(0.25) and PRED(0.30) used to assess non-incremental SSDE methods. Note finally that a single estimate of the performance of an incremental method in time can be obtained by aggregating the values of $\mathrm{MMRE}^{(t)}$, $\mathrm{MMER}^{(t)}$, $\mathrm{PRED}^{(t)}(0.25)$ and $\mathrm{PRED}^{(t)}(0.30)$ at different times steps t using some measure of central tendency. Here, we propose to use the mean corresponding to time steps $t \in \{0, 0.1, 0.2, \ldots, 0.9\}$.

6 Validation

In this section, we evaluate the proposed system using real historical data corresponding to 11 projects of a Chilean custom software development company, Nursoft. The data corresponds to projects executed between September/2016 and August/2018, is composed of 301 user stories totaling 1325 USP, and was carried out by 18 people, totaling 8578.9 person-hours. The code corresponding to these projects was stored in 81 GIT repositories, totaling 3,803,259 code lines (LOC).

Experimental Setting. For training and evaluating BlackSheep in time, only the 2 oldest projects were reserved as historical data (training data available before evaluation starts). The other 9 were used to simulate a realistic scenario in which a software company is developing various projects, new projects start, and some projects get closed. In this simulation, the real start/end date of a project was employed to decide when it became active/closed. We denote by $t = t_0$ the oldest project start date and $t = t_f$ the latest project end date. BlackSheep was used to estimate the effort required by each project during the entire interval $[t_0, t_f]$ with a periodicity of $\Delta t = 2$ days. In total, 1310 predictions were made considering all the projects throughout their execution.

Baseline. As mentioned before, expertise-based methods are widely used in the industry. Therefore, besides comparing our final results with related work, we introduce a baseline estimator based on Planning Poker. For this purpose, the prediction made by Planning Poker for a user story i of a project p at time t is defined to be $e_{i,t}^{(p)} = v_0^{-1} \cdot p_i$, where p_i denotes the story's size (in USP) and v_0^{-1} is the inverse of the speed considered for the team. This implies that the predictions made by the baseline estimator are obtained by assuming a constant development speed that, for this experiment, is set to $5 \frac{Hours}{USP}$. These predictions are refined using the same underestimation correction criterion adopted for BlackSheep: if the predicted effort is lower than the effort already incurred in the project, the prediction is replaced by the latter. Predictions for a project p are obtained by summing up the predictions corresponding to all its open user stories.

6.1 Experimental Results

Experimental results corresponding to BlackSheep's predictions before development starts are presented in Table 2. The results corresponding to BlackSheep's predictions during the entire development process $[t_0, t_f]$ were computed as discussed in the previous section and can be found in Table 3. In both cases, we report the results obtained using the predictor trained to directly predict effort, the predictor based on the inverse-velocity, and our proposed combined predictor (referred to as 'Ensemble'). It can be seen that the ensemble is slightly less precise than the best of the individual predictors but, as a result of its robustness, it is a more stable option.

	$MMRE^{(0)}$	$MMER^{(0)}$	$PRED^{(0)}(0.25)$	$PRED^{(0)}(0.30)$
Planning Poker	0.29	0.47	0.33	0.67
Ensemble	0.15 (-0.14)	0.17 (-0.30)	0.78 (0.45)	0.89 (0.21)
Direct Effort Predictor	0.11 (-0.18)	0.12 (-0.35)	1.00 (0.67)	1.00 (0.33)
Inverse-velocity Predictor	0.19 (-0.10)	0.22 (-0.25)	0.78 (0.45)	0.78 (0.21)

Table 2. Performance metrics computed at the beginning of the development time frame. In parentheses, the improvement (difference) of the proposed technique with respect to the team prediction (planning poker).

	$MMRE^{(T)}$	$MMER^{(T)}$	$PRED^{(T)}(0.25)$	$PRED^{(T)}(0.30)$
Planning Poker	0.18	0.26	0.73	0.83
Ensemble	0.13 (-0.05)	0.13 (-0.13)	0.81 (0.08)	0.86 (0.03)
Direct Effort Predictor	0.14 (-0.04)	0.13 (-0.13)	0.83 (0.10)	0.90 (0.07)
Inverse-velocity Predictor	0.15 (-0.03)	0.16 (-0.10)	0.82 (0.09)	0.87 (0.04)

Table 3. Performance metrics computed throughout all the development process of the projects. In parentheses, the improvement (difference) of the proposed technique with respect to the team prediction (planning poker).

It should be noted that, according to the criteria given by Conte et al. [5], BlackSheep is an accurate SDEE both as regards its initial predictions and those made during the development process. This is because it has an MMRE < 0.25 and a PRED(0.25) > 0.75.

6.2 Comparison of Results

BlackSheep presents an improvement over other SDEE techniques, since it (i) achieves an accurate prediction, (ii) requires little training data before being used for the first time and (iii) makes predictions throughout the entire development process. Similar works, using as dependent variables the size of the project in USP and the development speeds, achieve results close to the proposed technique such as [12] (which reports MMRE = 0.16 and PRED(0.25) = 0.86) or [10] (which reports MMRE = 0.15). These methods do not make predictions during the entire development process.

Pospieszny et al. [11] used a different unit to measure the size of the projects (Funtion Points) and employed a database of 1192 projects for training and evaluation. This technique, similar to BlackSheep, performs an average of various machine learning models, continuously predicting the development effort. Since their results were computed using 3-fold cross-validation, we can conclude that the models were trained using data from around 800 projects. Despite the large size of the datasets used to fit the models, their results are less accurate than ours: MMRE = 0.17, MMER = 0.42, PRED(0.25) = 0.69 and PRED(0.30) = 0.75.

Finally, an important comparison regards the accuracy of BlackSheep with respect to an expertise-based method, such as Planning Poker, which are the most used in the industry. Comparing with the baseline defined at the beginning of this section, we can observe, in Table 2 and Fig.3, a substantive advantage of the proposed techniques at the beginning of the development process, where few training data is available ($|\Delta MMRE| = 0.14$ and $|\Delta PRED(0.25)| = 0.45$). This advantage is preserved till around the first half of the estimation horizon. When analyzing the average results in the entire time frame $[t_0, t_f]$ (Table 3), the margins are narrowed: $|\Delta\text{MMRE}| = 0.05$ and $|\Delta\text{PRED}(0.25)| = 0.08$. As

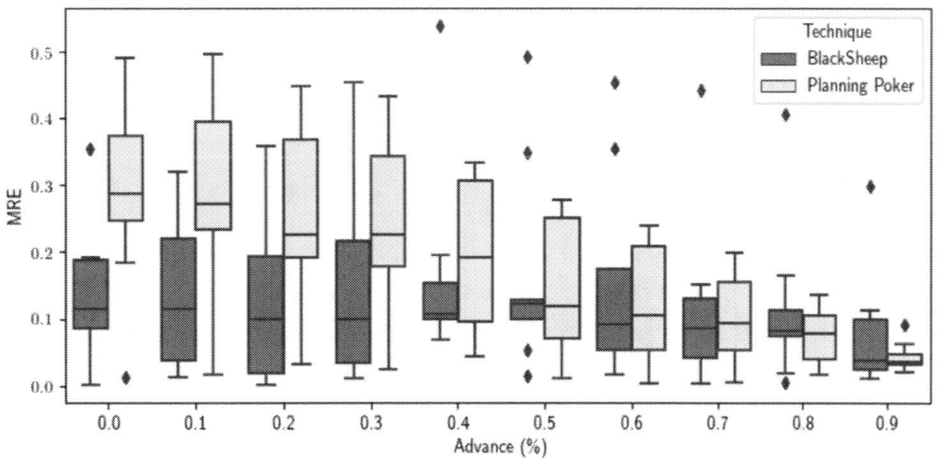

Fig. 3. Boxplot of the MMRE at different prediction stages (% of the total effort).

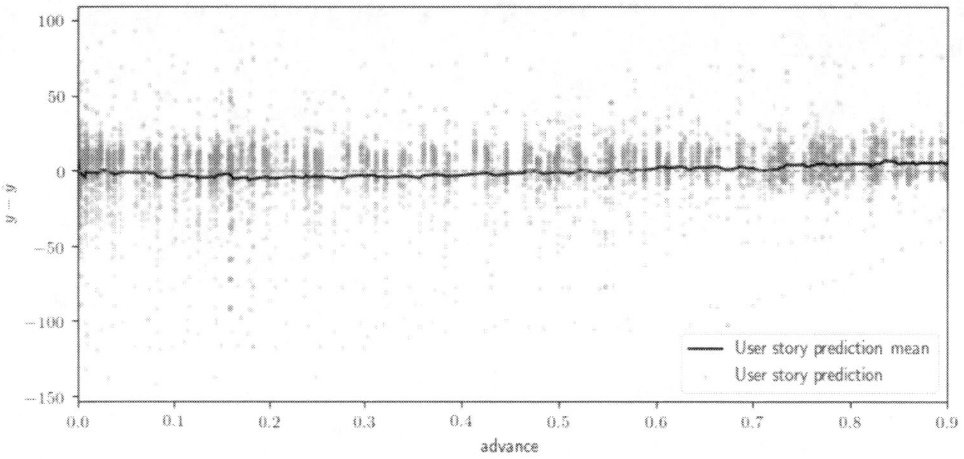

Fig. 4. Graph of the difference between the real values and BlackSheep's predictions for all the user stories ($y - \hat{y}$). In black, we depict the (smoothed) curve corresponding to the average value at different prediction stages (percentages of the total effort).

shown in Fig. 3, this result is due to the fact that the error rate of BlackSheep's predictions remains relatively constant as a project progresses while that of Planning Poker improves. Probably this happens because, as expertise-based methods tend to underestimate effort, Planning Poker benefits more from the underestimation correction method defined in section 5.4.

Note that the individual errors of effort predictions at the dimension of user stories are, on average, greater than the errors for a project as a whole. This is because, when summing up the values of the predictions for user stories, the errors tend to cancel out as can be seen in Fig. 4. This also explains why, although the individual predictions improve during the progress of the project, the accuracy obtained by aggregating them can remain relatively constant. As the number of user stories increases, the average error tends to decrease because there is a better chance that positive errors cancel out negative errors.

Acknowledgment

Dr. Astudillo's work has been partially supported by CONICYT through Basal FB0821 CCTVal.

7 Conclusion

In this work we have presented a learning-oriented technique for SDEE in agile contexts that requires few projects as training data and can provide effort estimates at different time steps. Experiments on real data from 11 software projects demonstrate that this method is accurate both, at the beginning and during the entire development process (more than 75% of the predictions correspond to a relative error lower than 25%), being substantially more accurate than Planning Poker during the first half of the prediction period.

The obtained results are due to the use of human-friendly metrics to define an user story descriptor, the exploitation of data from user stories as soon as they are closed in the project, the dynamic selection of training data to build the estimators, the use of robust machine learning algorithms, and the approach of disaggregating the SDEE task into smaller estimation problems associated with the user stories.

In future work we will analyze the impact of entering data from technologies and design patterns used in the user story to the predictor. We hope to obtain better estimations and determine the elements in a functionality that can lead to a delay.

References

1. Kent Beck et al. Manifesto for agile software development, 2001.
2. Barry Boehm et al. Software development cost estimation approaches—a survey. *Annals of software engineering*, 10(1-4):177–205, 2000.
3. Barry W Boehm et al. *Software engineering economics*, volume 197. Prentice-hall Englewood Cliffs (NJ), 1981.
4. Morakot Choetkiertikul et al. A deep learning model for estimating story points. *IEEE Transactions on Software Engineering*, 2018.
5. S. D. Conte et al. *Software Engineering Metrics and Models*. Benjamin-Cummings Publishing Co., Inc., Redwood City, CA, USA, 1986.
6. Bent Flyvbjerg and Alexander Budzier. Why your IT project may be riskier than you think. https://bit.ly/1Qwn6do, 2011 (accessed February 8, 2019).
7. James Grenning. Planning poker or how to avoid analysis paralysis while release planning. *Hawthorn Woods: Renaissance Software Consulting*, 3:22–23, 2002.
8. Shane Hastie and Stéphane Wojewoda. Standish group 2015 chaos report - q&a with jennifer lynch, Oct 2015.
9. Dinesh R Pai et al. Software effort estimation using a neural network ensemble. *Journal of Computer Information Systems*, 53(4):49–58, 2013.
10. Aditi Panda et al. Empirical validation of neural network models for agile software effort estimation based on story points. *Procedia Computer Science*, 57:772 – 781, 2015.
11. Przemyslaw Pospieszny et al. An effective approach for software project effort and duration estimation with machine learning algorithms. *Journal of Systems and Software*, 137:184–196, 2018.
12. Shashank Mouli Satapathy and Santanu Kumar Rath. Empirical assessment of machine learning models for agile software development effort estimation using story points. *Innov. Syst. Softw. Eng.*, 13(2-3):191–200, September 2017.
13. Sumeet Kaur Sehra et al. Research patterns and trends in software effort estimation. *Information and Software Technology*, 91:1 – 21, 2017.
14. I Thamarai and S Murugavalli. Competitive advantage of using differential evolution algorithm for software effort estimation. *Communication and Power Engineering*, 62, 2017.
15. Muhammad Usman et al. Effort estimation in agile software development: a survey on the state of the practice. In *Proceedings of the 19th International Conference on Evaluation and Assessment in Software Engineering*, page 12. ACM, 2015.
16. Robert K. Wysocki. *Effective Project Management: Traditional, Agile, Extreme, 7th Edition*. Wiley, 2013.

A Catalog of Bad Agile Smells for Agility Assessment

Ulisses Telemaco[1], Toacy Oliveira[1], Paulo Alencar[2], and Don Cowan[2]

[1] System Engineering and Computing Science Program,
Federal University of Rio de Janeiro, Brazil
{utelemaco,toacy}@cos.ufrj.br
[2] David R. Cheriton School of Computer Science,
University of Waterloo, Ontario, Canada
{palencar,dcowan}@csg.uwaterloo.ca

Abstract. Background: The adoption of Agile methods has grown significantly and now almost all software companies state that they are using some aspects of Agile in their software processes. However, the introduction of Agile methods into a software development environment is not a straightforward process. Thus, Agility Assessment (AA) is an important tool that supports the evaluation of how well a company has adopted the agile approach.
Problem: Agility Assessment is usually a manual process and there are few automatic steps during the various phases. Part of this limitation arises because the requirements to check the agility of a project/company are still described in natural language and spread across many sources of documents such as manifestos and company policies.
Aim: The aim of this paper is to organize the body of knowledge related to Agile Methods and identify a set of requirements that can be used in an Agility Assessment process. We extend the metaphor of a bad smell to an Agility Assessment context and propose the term Bad Agile Smell to describe an early warning signal that something in an agile project may need to be adjusted.
Method: A literature review, as well a survey with practitioners, were conducted to identify a set of Agility Bad Smells. The resulting set of identified Agility Bad Smells is presented as a structured catalog.
Result: We identified a set of 20 Bad Agile Smells for agile methods that were considered relevant according to research criteria. The Bad Agile Smells are presented in a structured catalog.

1 Introduction

The adoption of Agile approaches has increased significantly in recent years. Almost all software companies claim they are *Agile* at some level and they are using aspects of agile methods in their software processes [52]. Indeed, being *Agile* has become a critical issue for the Software Industry. Among the benefits of Agile are the acceleration of software delivery, the ability to manage requirement changes and productivity increments.

However, the adoption of an agile methodology is not straightforward. There are many challenges in adopting agile practices such as [20]: 1. An organizational culture at odds with agile values; 2. General organizational resistance to change; 3. Lack of skills/experience with agile methods; 4. Insufficient training and education to move to agile methods; 5. Inconsistent processes and practices across teams; 6. Pervasiveness of traditional development methods.

Agility Assessment (AA) is an important tool to mitigate the challenges related to adopting agile practices. In a nutshell, an AA evaluates how agile a project/organization is and identifies potential gaps that should be resolved to improve the adoption of agile approaches in a project/organization [3].

Due to the multitude of agile methods, the requirements used to evaluate the agility of a project/organization are typically described in natural language and spread across many documents including: manifestos, manuals, books and blogs. There is no standardized catalog of requirements to guide an AA. Although there are many contributions to AA such as tools and methods, there is no study that proposes a collection of agile requirements. A systematic review conducted by Adali et al [3] that aimed at evaluating AA tools confirmed that there is no set of requirements to guide AA.

This paper attempts to identify a set of requirements for AA and organize these requirements in a structured catalog. We extend the metaphor of "bad smells" popularized by Fowler and Becker [18] to the context of Agility Assessment. For Fowler and Becker, a *Code Smell* is an early signal that may indicate that something needs to be refactored in the code. The authors introduced the term as a strategy to mitigate the occurrence of a potential non-compliance in the source code. Thus, in this paper we introduce the term *Agility Bad Smells* to denote signals that indicate a potential point of improvement in the adoption of an agile practice.

To identify a relevant set of Bad Agile Smells, we conducted a literature review that included peer-reviewed academic publications and "grey" literature and allowed us to identify a set of *Bad Agile Smells*. These bad smells were submitted to a survey to reveal their relevance and importance to the industry. The surveys were conducted with specialists in agile methodologies. The most ranked *Bad Agile Smells* were organized as a catalog using a predefined structure.

This study tries to answer the following research question:

RQ: What are the relevant Bad Agile Smells for Agility Assessment?

The aim of this question is to identify a set of *Bad Agile Smells* that meet the following criteria: (a) *are relevant* to Agility Assessment and (b) can be verified during an AA process. As this is an exploratory question, no hypothesis is provided.

The remainder of this paper is organized using the following structure: The study methodology is presented in Section 2. The Subsections 2.1 and 2.2 describe, respectively, the literature review and the survey conducted in this study.

Section 2.3 describes the catalog design and presents a subset of the resulting catalog. Section 3 discusses the related work. Section 4 presents some discussions and threats to the validity of this study and Section 5 concludes the paper.

2 Study Methodology

The aim of this study is to answer the research question (RQ) and identify a set of Bad Agile Smells that are relevant and possible to verify during an Agility Assessment process. The main challenges for identifying such a set are the number of existing Agile Methods and determining what is a Bad Agile Smell and which one is relevant and can be verified in real-world scenarios. To address these challenges, we conducted the study in three phases: *Elicitation*, *Confirmation* and *Cataloging* as shown in Figure 1.

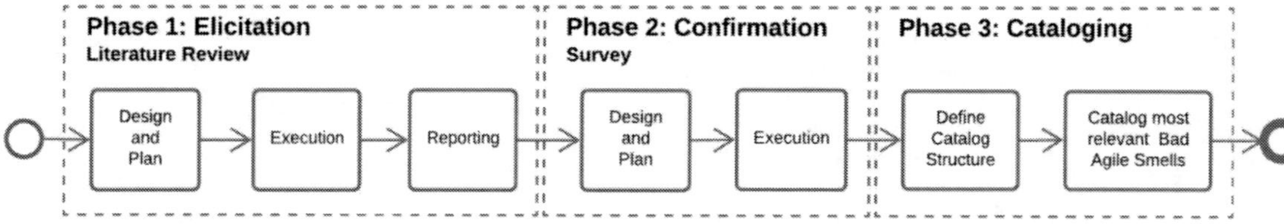

Fig. 1. Methodology for elicitation, confirmation and cataloging of Bad Agile Smells (in BPMN notation [40])

Phase 1 - Elicitation: The elicitation started with the design and planning of the exploratory study. The elicitation phase includes a literature review described in the Section 2.1.

Phase 2 - Confirmation: In the confirmation phase, we conducted surveys with industry practitioners to reveal the relevance of the Bad Agile Smells identified in the elicitation phase. The surveys are described in Section 2.2

Phase 3 - Cataloging: In the cataloging phase, the most relevant Bad Agile Smells were organized in a structured format that we named *Catalog of Bad Agile Smells.*

2.1 Elicitation Phase

In the elicitation phase, we conducted a literature review (LR) that aimed at exploring the existing body of knowledge and focused on identifying a set of Bad Agile Smells. This phase produced a preliminary version of the Catalog of Bad Agile Smells that was used in the survey in the confirmation phase.

Literature Review Characterization and Methodology A conventional literature review (CLR) or a systematic literature review (SLR) are study experiments that aim at collecting evidence about a research area and include only primary studies published in an academic forum. On the other hand, a multivocal literature review (MLR) is a form of an SLR which includes "grey" literature (non-published, nor peer-reviewed sources of information) in addition to the published (formal) literature. We decided to include "grey" literature in this study since the body of knowledge about the research area (Agile Methods) is mainly created by software engineering (SE) practitioners. Unfortunately, a large majority of software practitioners do not publish in academic forums [22] and ignoring "grey" literature may lead this study to limit the insights into the "state of the practice" in SE. So, the LR presented is considered an MLR and includes "grey literature". As this is an exploratory study designed to organize a research area (Bad Agile Smells) and there is no baseline for comparison of the results obtained, the presented literature review is also considered a *quasi-systematic review (QSR)* [51]. In summary, the presented LR is an MLR (since it includes "grey" literature) and a QSR, since there is no baseline for comparison purposes.

The methodology of the LR was based on the method proposed by Kitchenham et al [28] and consists of three main phases: *planning*, *execution* and *reporting*.

Literature Review Planning The aim of the literature review was to identify, in the formal and "grey" literature, a set of Bad Agile Smells that can likely be verified during an Agility Assessment process. Since the literature does not use the term "Bad Smell", we extracted the "Bad Agile Smells" from agile best practices, rules, constraints or restrictions. The research question for this LR was derived from the main RQ (presented in Section 1) and can be summarized as: *What practices are likely to impair the adoption of agility in software projects?*

The scope of this review was defined according to the population, intervention, comparison and outcome (PICO [41]) approach. The *Population* is the set of software development projects. The *Intervention* is the collection of agile software development processes. There is no comparison. The outcome is a set of agile rules, constraints, practices and techniques that are prone to formal verification. Three papers obtained from a previous conventional literature reviews were used as a control: [34], [1] and [30]. The keywords for *Population* are "software projects", "software systems", "software development" and "software engineering". The keywords for *Intervention* are "agile methods", "agile processes", "agile approaches", "agile methodologies", "agile development", "agile software development" and "agile projects". The keywords for *Outcome* are "rules", "constraints", "practices" and "techniques". The sources are collected from the following digital databases, including the conferences, journals and technical reports indexed by IeeeXplore, Web of Science, Scopus and the ACM digital library. The search string taken as the basis for all search engines, structured according to Pai et al. [41] was: *("software process" or "software project" or "software systems" or "software development" or "software engineering") and ("agile methods" or "agile processes" or "agile approaches" or "agile methodologies" or "agile development") and ("rules" or "constraints" or "restrictions" or "practices" or "techniques" or "classification")*

In the selection of "grey" literature, we used documentation for the main agile methods. The agile methods included in the LR were selected according to the criteria presented by Abrahamsson [1]. As a result, the following methods were included in this study: *Extreme Programming (XP)* ([8], [9] and [14]), *Scrum* ([44], [45], [4] and [10]), *Crystal Family* ([13]), *Feature Driven Development (FDD)* ([42] and [31]), *Dynamic Systems Development Method* ([47]), *Adaptive Software Development* ([24]) and *OpenUp* ([1]).

This review includes all article returned by the protocol that meets at least one of the following inclusion criteria (IC): (IC1) Documents must address one or more agile methods; (IC2) Documents must discuss practices, characteristics, rules or constraints related to any agile method.

Publications that satisfy at least one of the following exclusion criteria (EC) were excluded: (EC1) Documents not written in English; (EC2) Documents whose full text is not available; (EC3) Documents clearly dealing with topics irrelevant to the purpose of this review; (EC4) Documents merely reporting the use of individual software processes in development projects; (EC5) If the same study has been published more than once, the most relevant version (i.e., the one explaining the study in greatest detail) will be used and the others will be excluded.

The following information was extracted from each paper selected after running the selection process: *document title, author(s), source, year of publication, agile method* and *description of the bad agile smell.* The results were tabulated. Analysis was carried out to identify duplication. The frequency in which each rule has been reported by different authors was considered. If authors wrote more than one paper, repeated counts were avoided.

Literature Review Execution After the planning phase, the execution phase was applied. The searches returned 1774 references, published between 2001 and 2017. All the controls were retrieved. Repetitions were eliminated and after the application of the inclusion and exclusion criteria, the number of papers selected for full consideration was reduced to 43. The selected documents were fully read in order to find bad agile smells (practices, suggestions, constraints or restrictions prone to formal verification). The assessment of this criterion was made based on the personal experience of the authors. In order to minimize potential threats to the validity of this strategy, we submitted the selected bad agile smells to a survey with practitioners. The survey is described in Section 2.2.

Literature Review Reporting Following the criteria established in the research protocol, 20 Bad Agile Smells were extracted from 35 documents (formal papers and "grey" literature) [1], [34], [30], [6], [33], [12], [37], [15], [23], [5], [43],

[2], [7], [16], [53], [36], [27], [50], [11], [25], [46], [32], [38], [8], [9], [14], [44], [45], [4], [10], [13], [42], [31], [47] and [24] and tabulated in Table 1.

After analyzing the data extracted in the literature review execution, we identified the 20 Bad Agile Smells presented in the Table 1.

2.2 Confirmation Phase

In order to confirm results from the literature review, we conducted a survey based on semi-structured interviews [26] with practitioners to find the relevance of the identified Agile Smells from an industry perspective. The remainder of this section presents the survey that was based on the protocol presented by Oishi [39]. The survey is composed of three main phases: *planning*, *execution* and *reporting*.

Survey Planning The aim of the survey was to evaluate the relevance of the Bad Agile Smells identified in the literature review. The research questions for the Survey are: (RQ1) Which Bad Agile Smells (present in the given catalog) are relevant and prone to validation? (RQ2) Is the evaluation strategy in the catalog consistent with industry practice?

The material used in the survey included an online questionnaire developed using *Google Sheets* and divided into three sections: (1) *Subject Characterization*, (2) *Organization Characterization* and (3) *Bad Agile Smells*. In the *Subject Characterization* and *Organization Characterization* Sections, the participants should provide information about these topics and their companies. The *Bad Agile Smells* Section contained a list of the 20 Bad Agile Smells collected in the literature review. The Agile Smells were displayed in alphabetical order according to the following structure: *Name*, *Short Description* and *Evaluation Strategy*. To assure the construct validity of the questionnaire, the participants should indicate, for each rule: (Answer 1) the relevance of the Agile Smell; (Answer 2) the relevance of the automatic checking/verification of the Agile Smell. The questionnaire accepts the following answers: (a) *No relevance (0 pts)*, (b) *Slightly relevant (1 pt)*, (c) *Very relevant (2 pts)* and (d) *Absolutely relevant (3 pts)*. As each answer has an associated score that varies from 0 to 3 according to its degree of relevance, the most relevant Agile Smell achieves a 6-point score and the least relevant Agile Smell has 0-point score.

We applied convenience sampling [21] and participants were selected from the professional and academic networking connections of the authors. The criteria for the selection of participants were: (a) the participant should have experience (at least 5 years) as Project Manager or Quality Assurance Consultant and (b) the participant should work (or have worked) in an organization that adopts a software process based on agile methods. We avoid selecting participants that are aware of this research (so we excluded co-authors and co-workers).

During the planning phase, we conducted a preliminary test using subjects from inside our research group. The data from this test was not considered in the final results. Our goal during this preliminary test was to collect feedback from the participants and assess the interview plan.

Table 1. 20 Bad Agile Smells extracted from Literature Review (part 1: Elicitation)

01. Complex Tasks: The *Complex Tasks* smell occurs when there are complex tasks in the project/iteration. The definition of "task complexity" may vary from project to project but is usually related to the effort estimated to complete the task.
02. Dependence on Internal Specialists: This smell occurs when a member of the development team is the only specialist who can apply a feature or technology.
03. Shared Developers: A *Shared Developers* smell may be detected when a Developer is working on more than one project at the same time or when she/he is frequently switching between different projects.
04. Unplanned Work: The *Unplanned Work* smell occurs when there are tasks in the iteration plan that where not planned during the iteration planning meeting. Unplanned Work (i.e. tasks included in the iteration plan after iteration planning) may indicate two problems: (a) the unplanned tasks are not related to the iteration goal and thus, they should be avoided, or (b) there is a planning failure since the tasks should have been included in the iteration during the iteration planning.
05. Concurrent Iterations: This smell occurs when there are two (or more) open iterations in the same project.
06. Not Frequent Deliveries: The *Not Frequent Deliveries* smell is detected when the development team does not deliver a new version of the software frequently.
07. Not Test-driven Development: The *Not Test-driven Development* smell is detected when the development team does not apply the technique TDD (Test Driven Development) during the development of the software.
08. Large Development Team: This smell is detected when the development team is larger than the recommended size. The *Large Development Team* smell derives from an agile practice that states the development team should be small to be efficient and effective.
09. Finishing an Iteration with Open Tasks: This smell occurs when an iteration is closed even with open tasks (i.e not completed tasks).
10. Iterations with different length: This smell occurs when two iterations from the same project do not have the same duration.
11. Not Timeboxed Iteration: The *Not Timeboxed Iteration* smell typically occurs when an iteration is extended in order to finish work.
12. Iteration without a deliverable: The occurrence of this smell is detected when an iteration does not have a deliverable (i.e. a functional new version of the software).
13. Iteration without an Iteration Planning: This smell occurs when an iteration does not have an iteration planning.
14. Iteration without an Iteration Retrospective: This smell occurs when an iteration does not have an iteration retrospective.
15. Iteration without an Iteration Review: This smell occurs when an iteration does not have an iteration review.
16. Iteration Tasks started without an estimated effort: This smell is detected when an iteration starts without the effort for all tasks being estimated.
17. Not Timeboxed Meeting: The *Not Timeboxed Meeting* smell derives from an agile best practice that states the process meetings (iteration planning, review, retrospective, etc) should have a pre-defined duration and the duration should preferably be the same during the entire software project.
18. Goals not defined: This smell is detected when the iteration or the project does not have a defined goal
19. Lower priority tasks executed first: The occurrence of this smell indicates the development team is not working on the highest priority tasks.
20. Break between Iterations: This smell occurs when there is an interval between two consecutive iterations

36

Survey Execution During the execution phase, 10 candidate subjects were chosen to be interviewed. We focused on practitioners with relevant experience working on agile projects. The selected subjects included 7 Software Project Managers and 3 Quality Assurance Consultants.

Survey Reporting In the last phase, the collected data was analyzed and a degree of relevance was attributed to each Bad Agile Smell using the previously presented criteria.

2.3 Cataloging Phase

The aim of the third and last phase, *Cataloging Phase*, was to consolidate, complement and organize the results obtained in the previous phases and present them as a structured catalog. The Bad Agile Smells previously identified in the *Literature Review* and submitted to the *Survey* were ranked according to the following criteria: (a) number of papers that cited the Agile Smell (obtained in Literature Review) and (b) degree of relevance (obtained in the survey). Table 2 shows the Bad Agile Smells sorted by their relevance.

Table 2. Ranked Bad Agile Smells

Id	Bad Agile Smell
AS01	Lower priority tasks executed first
AS02	Not Frequent Deliveries
AS03	Iteration without a deliverable
AS04	Iteration without an Iteration Retrospective
AS05	Goals not defined
AS06	Not Timeboxed Meeting
AS07	Iteration without an Iteration Planning
AS08	Complex Tasks
AS09	Unplanned Work
AS10	Dependence on Internal Specialists
AS11	Not Timeboxed Iteration
AS13	Iteration Tasks started without an estimated effort
AS14	Shared Developers
AS15	Not Test-driven Development
AS16	Finishing an Iteration with Open Tasks
AS17	Iterations with different length
AS18	Large Development Team
AS19	Break between Iterations
AS20	Concurrent Iterations

Regarding the catalog structure, the identified smells were organized following a template adapted from [19] and shown in Table 3.

Table 3. Bad Agile Smell Template

Id	Smell's Unique Identifier
Name	Smell's Name
Description	A short description of the Agile Smell
Agile Methods	A discussion on how the analyzed agile methods mention the smell
Industry Perspective	A discussion of relevant aspects of the smell from the industry perspective
Evaluation Strategy	A short description of the evaluation strategy
Parameters	A short description of the evaluation strategy's parameters

Because of space limitations, we have selected the 2 most ranked Agile Smells to be presented in the paper: *AS01: Lower priority tasks executed first* (Table 4) and *AS02: Not Frequent Deliveries* (Table 5). The full catalog can be accessed in Telemaco et al [49].

Table 4. AS01: Lower priority tasks executed first

Id	**AS01**
Name	**Lower priority tasks executed first**
Description	The occurrence of the *AS01* smells indicates the Development Team is not working on the highest priority tasks.
Agile Methods	Four agile method explicitly state that higher priority tasks must be executed first: Scrum, Crystal Methods, DSDM and OpenUP. For Scrum, the whole team should focus on Sprint goal. In Crystal methods, the project leader should prioritize the goals which allow developers to focus on particular areas. In DSDM, to fulfill the principles *Focus on the Business Need* and *Deliver On Time*, DSDM teams must focus on business priorities. OpenUP teams must self-organize around how to accomplish iteration objectives and commit to delivering the results.
Industry Perspective	All survey participants confirmed that working on higher priority tasks is an important rule. However, a participant mentioned that exceptions are tolerated in situations where it is not possible to work on high priority tasks. As example, he cited a situation where an available worker does not have the required skills to perform a high-priority task. In this case, the worker is allowed to work on a less important tasks.
Evaluation Strategy	The occurrence of this smell could be detected by assessing the tasks execution history.
Parameters	No parameter was identified for this evaluation strategy.

3 Related Work

Studies that aim at consolidating the body of knowledge around Agile Methods are in some level related to this paper. Abrantes and Travassos [2] conducted a study to identify the most commonly used agile practices. The authors identified a set of 12 practices: *test driven development*, *continuous integration*, *pair programming*, *planning game*, *onsite customer*, *collective code ownership*, *small*

Table 5. AS02: Not Frequent Deliveries

Id	**AS02**
Name	**Not Frequent Deliveries**
Description	The *Not Frequent Deliveries* smell is detected when the Development Team does not deliver a new version of the software frequently. The occurrence of this smell may indicate that an agile rule that states a Software Project should have frequent deliveries has been violated. The concept of continuous and frequent deliveries is very important to agile methods and this rule is almost a mantra among agile software developers.
Agile Methods	All analyzed agile methods state that deliveries should be frequent. XP divides the work in Small and Short Releases. In Scrum the work is broken in Sprints which are timeboxed periods (approximately 30 days) where the team produces a new executable version of the software. In Crystal methods the development is also incremental and the release times depend on the length of the project. While in Crystal Clear delivery internals are periods of two to three months, in Crystal Orange the increments can be extended to four months. In FDD iterations should take from a few days to a maximum of two weeks. DSDMs philosophy states best business value emerges when projects are aligned to clear business goals, deliver frequently and involve the collaboration of motivated and empowered people. In ADS the project is broken in units called Adaptive Development Cycles that typically last between four and eight weeks. OpenUP divides the project into iterations that take a few weeks.
Industry Perspective	All participants indicated - with different levels - that the detection of this smell is relevant for an Agility Assessment. No additional comment was given.
Evaluation Strategy	An approach to detect the occurrence of this smell is assessing the interval between two Iterations with deliverables.
Parameters	A *Desirable Delivery Interval* parameter could be used to customize the detection of this smell.

releases, *metaphor*, *refactoring*, *sustainable pace*, *simple design* and *coding standards*.

Miller [34] also proposed a set of characteristics to agile processes that includes: *modularity on development process*, *iterative with short cycles*, *time-bound with iteration cycles from one to six weeks*, *parsimony in development processes removing unnecessary activities*, *adaptive with possible emergent new risks*, *incremental process approaches that allow functioning application building in small steps*, *convergent (and incremental) approach* and *people-oriented*.

Although many others papers aim at mapping agile practices [54], [17], [35], [48], [29] and [32], to the best of our knowledge, there is no study that investigated agile methods from the perspective of this study, namely, trying to identify a set of Bad Agile Smells that are relevant and prone to formal validation during an Agility Assessment.

4 Discussion

The study identified an initial set of 20 Agile Smells that was subject of a survey that aimed at characterizing the Agile Smells according to their relevance. It was observed that most of the items were considered relevant according to the personal opinion of the survey participants. The exceptions were the smells *Shared Developers*, *Iterations with different length* and *Large Development Team* that were considered not relevant by some participants. Among the arguments, participants said that these smells derive from rules that are highly prescriptive for agile projects or that affect important organizational policies and therefore are not applicable in real scenarios.

Regarding the relevance of the explicit smell's identification (i.e. whether the identification of the agile smell is useful for an AA), it was also observed that the smells whose occurrence depends on individual workers are more prone to be considered important to explicit identification. For example, the explicit identification of the *Iteration without an Iteration Planning* smell was considered not relevant (although the practice that originated it has been mentioned by all analyzed agile methods). Participants argued that *Iteration Planning* is such a dynamic embedded in their software process and depends on almost the whole development team that the formal identification of its presence is not necessary at all. On the other hand, the identification of the *Lower priority tasks executed first* smell - that was mentioned by only two methods - was considered relevant by all participants. They argued that the choice of which task should be selected from Iteration Backlog usually depends on workers individual decision and therefore the identification of this smell could make a possible compliance violation explicit. Other smells that typically depend on individual workers include *Dependence on Internal Specialists* and *Unplanned Work.*

As threats to validity of this study we can mention:

- The identification of Agile Smells in the literature review and the assessment of what Agile Smell is prone to identification were made initially by the authors through a literature review. In order to mitigate the bias of this strategy, the results were submitted to a survey with specialists in software project management and quality assurance to assess their relevance;
- The survey was conducted with a sampling that is not representative enough to allow us to affirm that the set of identified smells represent the most relevant.

5 Conclusion

This study aimed at identifying a set of Bad Agile Smells that are relevant and prone to verification from the perspective of Agility Assessment. First, we selected an initial set of 20 Bad Agile Smells extracted from a literature review. The identified smells were the subject of a survey that aimed at characterizing them according to their relevance. The 2 most relevant Agile Smells were presented in this paper. The identified smells are presented in the catalog with the following structure: identification, name, description, which agile method mentioned the smell, the industry perspective and strategies for formal verification and parametrization.

Although the Agile Smells have been extracted from agile practices and characteristics, the catalog is not intended to describe practices and characteristics of agile methods. In fact, the catalog aims at presenting a set of Agile Smells that were considered relevant and whose formal identification supports an Agility Assessment process. Thus, the catalog can be used for researchers and industry practitioners who intend to execute an Agility Assessment of a Project or Organization. Making Agility Assessment requirements explicit through a structured catalog is a prelude to an automatic and immediately applicable approach to support AA.

In future work, we can consider: (a) extending the catalog including software development rules present in traditional (or non-agile) processes; (b) identifying the most relevant rules through a more comprehensive survey with a more representative sampling; (c) applying a Controlled Natural Language (CNL) framework to standardize rule descriptions.

References

1. Abrahamsson, P., Salo, O., Ronkainen, J., Warsta, J.: Agile software development methods - Review and analysis. Tech. Rep. 478, VTT Publications (2002)
2. Abrantes, J.F., Travassos, G.H.: Common Agile Practices in Software Processes. In: 2011 International Symposium on Empirical Software Engineering and Measurement. pp. 355–358 (Sept 2011)
3. Adalı, O.E., Özcan-Top, Ö., Demirörs, O.: Evaluation of agility assessment tools: A multiple case study. In: International Conference on Software Process Improvement and Capability Determination. pp. 135–149. Springer (2016)
4. Alliance, S.: Learn About Scrum (2016), https://www.scrumalliance.org/why-scrum
5. Alzoabi, Z.: Agile software: Body of knowledge. Software Design and Development: Concepts, Methodologies, Tools, and Applications: Concepts, Methodologies, Tools, and Applications p. 96 (2013)
6. Anand, R.V., Dinakaran, M.: Popular agile methods in software development: Review and analysis. International Journal of Applied Engineering Research **11**(5), 3433–3437 (2016)
7. Barlow, J.B., Giboney, J., Keith, M.J., Wilson, D., Schuetzler, R.M., Lowry, P.B., Vance, A.: Overview and guidance on agile development in large organizations. Communications of the Association for Information Systems **29**(2), 25–44 (2011)
8. Beck, K.: Embracing change with extreme programming. Computer **32**(10), 70–77 (1999)
9. Beck, K.: Extreme Programming Explained: Embrace Change. Addison-Wesley Longman Publishing Co., Inc., Boston, MA, USA (2000)
10. Berteig, M.: Rules of Scrum (2015), http://www.agileadvice.com/rules-of-scrum/
11. Cao, L., Ramesh, B.: Agile Software Development: Ad hoc practices or sound principles? IT professional **9**(2) (2007)
12. Chagas, L.F., de Carvalho, D.D., Lima, A.M., Reis, C.A.L.: Systematic literature review on the characteristics of agile project management in the context of maturity models. In: International Conference on Software Process Improvement and Capability Determination. pp. 177–189. Springer (2014)
13. Cockburn, A.: Agile Software Development. Addison-Wesley Longman Publishing Co., Inc., Boston, MA, USA (2002)
14. Cunningham, W.: Extreme Programming, http://wiki.c2.com/?ExtremeProgramming
15. Diebold, P., Dahlem, M.: Agile practices in practice: a mapping study. In: Proceedings of the 18th International Conference on Evaluation and Assessment in Software Engineering. p. 30. ACM (2014)

16. Dingsøyr, T., Dybå, T., Moe, N.B.: Agile software development: An introduction and overview. In: Agile Software Development, pp. 1–13. Springer (2010)
17. Dingsøyr, T., Nerur, S., Balijepally, V., Moe, N.B.: A Decade of Agile Methodologies. J. Syst. Softw. **85**(6), 1213–1221 (jun 2012)
18. Fowler, M., Beck, K., Brant, J., Opdyke, W., Roberts, D.: Refactoring: improving the design of existing code. Addison-Wesley Professional (1999)
19. Gamma, E., Helm, R., Johnson, R., Vlissides, J.: Design Patterns: elements of reusable object-oriented software. Pearson Education India (1995)
20. Gandomani, T.J., Zulzalil, H., Ghani, A.A.A., Sultan, A.B.M., Nafchi, M.Z.: Obstacles in moving to agile software development methods; at a glance. Journal of Computer Science **9**(5), 620 (2013)
21. Ghazi, A.N., Petersen, K., Reddy, S.S.V.R., Nekkanti, H.: Survey Research in Software Engineering: Problems and Strategies. arXiv preprint arXiv:1704.01090 (2017)
22. Glass, R.L., DeMarco, T.: Software Creativity 2.0. developer.* Books (2006)
23. Hamed, A.M.M., Abushama, H.: Popular agile approaches in software development: Review and analysis. In: Computing, Electrical and Electronics Engineering (ICCEEE), 2013 International Conference on. pp. 160–166. IEEE (2013)
24. Highsmith, III, J.A.: Adaptive Software Development: A Collaborative Approach to Managing Complex Systems. Dorset House Publishing Co., Inc., New York, NY, USA (2000)
25. Joseph, M.: Software engineering: Agile manifesto. Elektron Journal-South African Institute of Electrical Engineers **22**(9), 70 (2005)
26. Kajornboon, A.B.: Using interviews as research instruments. E-journal for Research Teachers **2**(1), 1–9 (2005)
27. Kautz, K., Pedersen, C.F., Monrad, O.: Cultures of agility–agile software development in practice. In: 20th Australasian Conference on Information Systems. Melbourne (2009)
28. Kitchenham, B., Charters, S.: Guidelines for performing systematic literature reviews in software engineering. Tech. rep., Keele University and University of Durham (Jul 2007)
29. Ktata, O., Lévesque, G.: Agile Development: Issues and Avenues Requiring a Substantial Enhancement of the Business Perspective in Large Projects. In: Proceedings of the 2nd Canadian Conference on Computer Science and Software Engineering. pp. 59–66. C3S2E '09, ACM, New York, NY, USA (2009)
30. Lindvall, M., Basili, V.R., Boehm, B.W., Costa, P., Dangle, K., Shull, F., Tesoriero, R., Williams, L.A., Zelkowitz, M.V.: Empirical Findings in Agile Methods. In: Proceedings of the Second XP Universe and First Agile Universe Conference on Extreme Programming and Agile Methods - XP/Agile Universe 2002. Springer-Verlag, London, UK, UK (2002)
31. Luca, J.D.: Feature Driven Development FDD, http://www.featuredrivendevelopment.com/
32. Martin, R.C.: Agile Software Development: Principles, Patterns, and Practices. Prentice Hall PTR, Upper Saddle River, NJ, USA (2003)
33. Meyer, B.: Agile: The good, the hype and the ugly
34. Miller, G.G.: The Characteristics of Agile Software Processes. In: Proceedings of the 39th International Conference and Exhibition on Technology of Object-Oriented Languages and Systems (TOOLS39). TOOLS '01, IEEE Computer Society, Washington, DC, USA (2001)

35. Misra, S.C., Kumar, V., Kumar, U.: Identifying Some Important Success Factors in Adopting Agile Software Development Practices. J. Syst. Softw. **82**(11), 1869–1890 (nov 2009)
36. Mnkandla, E.: Agile software engineering. Handbook of Research on Software Engineering and Productivity Technologies: Implications of Globalization: Implications of Globalization p. 28 (2009)
37. Moran, A.: Agile software development. In: Agile Risk Management, pp. 1–16. Springer (2014)
38. Newkirk, J.: Introduction to agile processes and extreme programming. In: Proceedings of the 24th International Conference on Software Engineering. ICSE 2002. pp. 695–696 (May 2002). https://doi.org/10.1145/581441.581450
39. Oishi, S.: How to Conduct In-Person Interviews for Surveys. SAGE Publications Inc. (2003)
40. OMG: Business Process Model and Notation (BPMN). Final specification, OMG (jan 2011), http://www.omg.org/spec/BPMN/2.0/
41. Pai, M., McCulloch, M., Gorman, J., Pai, N., Enanoria, W., Kennedy, G., Tharyan, P., Colford, J.: Systematic reviews and meta-analyses: an illustrated, step-by-step guide. The Medical Journal of India (2004)
42. Palmer, S.R., Felsing, M.: A Practical Guide to Feature-Driven Development. Pearson Education, 1st edn. (2001)
43. Rao, K.N., Naidu, G.K., Chakka, P.: A study of the agile software development methods, applicability and implications in industry. International Journal of Software Engineering and its applications **5**(2), 35–45 (2011)
44. Schwaber, K.: SCRUM Development Process. In: Business Object Design and Implementation, pp. 117–134. Springer London (1997)
45. Schwaber, K., Beedle, M.: Agile Software Development with Scrum. Prentice Hall PTR, Upper Saddle River, NJ, USA, 1st edn. (2001)
46. Simmons, G., Dillon, T.: Open source development and agile methods. In: The 7th International Conference on Software Engineering and Applications (2003)
47. Stapleton, J.: Dynamic Systems Development Method: The Method in Practice. Addison-Wesley Longman Publishing Co., Inc., Boston, MA, USA (1997)
48. Subramaniam, V., Hunt, A.: Practices of an Agile Developer: Working in the Real World. Pragmatic Bookshelf, Raleigh, NC (2006)
49. Telemaco, U., Oliveira, T., Mesquita, R., Melo, G., Alencar, P.: A catalog of software development rules for agile methods. Tech. rep., Cheriton School of Computer Science - University of Waterloo (dec 2017)
50. Thomas, J.: Introducing agile development practices from the middle. In: Engineering of Computer Based Systems, 2008. ECBS 2008. 15th Annual IEEE International Conference and Workshop on the. pp. 401–407. IEEE (2008)
51. Travassos, G.H., d. Santos, P.S.M., Mian, P.G., Neto, A.C.D., Biolchini, J.: An Environment to Support Large Scale Experimentation in Software Engineering. In: 13th IEEE International Conference on Engineering of Complex Computer Systems (iceccs 2008). pp. 193–202 (March 2008). https://doi.org/10.1109/ICECCS.2008.30
52. VersionOne: The 12th Annual State of Agile Report™ 2018 (2018), http://stateofagile.versionone.com, accessed: 2018-10-01
53. Williams, L.: Agile software development methodologies and practices. In: Advances in Computers, vol. 80, pp. 1–44. Elsevier (2010)
54. Yu, X., Petter, S.: Understanding Agile Software Development Practices using Shared Mental Models Theory. Information and Software Technology **56**(8), 911–921 (2014)

A Metamodel to represent Agile Software Development Projects

Ulisses Telemaco[1], Toacy Oliveira[1], Paulo Alencar[2], and Don Cowan[2]

[1] System Engineering and Computing Science Program, Federal University of Rio de Janeiro, Brazil
{utelemaco,toacy}@cos.ufrj.br
[2] David R. Cheriton School of Computer Science, University of Waterloo, Ontario, Canada
{palencar,dcowan}@csg.uwaterloo.ca

Abstract. Agile Software Development is an important paradigm in the software engineering community and a significant movement in the software industry. According to Version One Survey 2018[28], 97% of the surveyed organizations are using some aspect of agile practices. However, the adoption of agile practices is not a straightforward task and there are many open questions related to agile methods that the academic community is trying to answer. One of the challenges of academic research related to Agile Software Development is the lack of metamodels to support the representation of agile projects. A preliminary investigation conducted in this study revealed that existing software development metamodels focus on representing elements related to software process definition and neglect aspects related to software project execution such as Iterations, Deliveries and Task Instances.

This study aims at investigating how existing software development metamodels support the representation of agile software development projects and how they can be extended to fill possible gaps.

To achieve this goal, we first identified a set of concepts, entities, and information related to agile projects. Then, we investigated how existing software development metamodels represent the identified elements. Finally, we proposed a metamodel, that we named Agile Software Development Project Metamodel (ASDPM), which contains the elements necessary to represent agile software development projects.

1 Introduction

In 2001, a group of software practitioners and consultants published the Agile Software Development Manifesto [5] as an answer to a business community asking for lighter-weight software development processes. The manifesto was guided by four main principles:

1. **Individuals and interaction** over process and tools;
2. **Working software** over comprehensive documentation;
3. **Customer collaboration** over contract negotiation;

4. **Respond to change** over following a plan.

.

Since this manifesto, Agile Software Development has been one of the most important software development paradigms of the Software Engineering community. Agile evangelists argue that agile methodologies bring benefits such as: improvement in development productivity and quality, faster deliveries and decreasing risks during software development. However, the adoption of agile practices is not a straightforward task and there are many open questions related to agile development that the academic community is investigating. According to the 2018 Version One Survey [28], only 4% of companies state they have fully integrated agile practices into their software development process.

Motivated by another study (in progress) that investigated how Agility Assessment can be automated in organizations, we analyzed the state-of-the-art on software development representation and realized that a metamodel that enables the representation of agile software development projects may still be missing. Mainly because most of the existing metamodels focus on the static perspective of software development or software process definition and neglect providing information related to execution elements. A metamodel that combines process definition elements and project execution elements is necessary to provide a reasonable representation of agile software development projects.

In this study, we contribute to research related to agile development by presenting a metamodel to represent agile software development projects. The proposed metamodel can be used in a wide range of research related to Agile Software Development, although the motivation to identify such a metamodel came initially from a study related to Agility Assessment.

The identification of such a metamodel followed a three-step process. First, we identified a set of concepts, entities and information related to agile software development projects. Second, we investigated how existing metamodels for software development support the representation of the identified elements. Finally, we proposed a metamodel, that we named Agile Software Development Project Metamodel (ASDPM), that contains the elements necessary to represent an agile software development project.

The research questions that guided this study were:

RQ1: What are the main concepts and information necessary to represent an agile software development project?

RQ2: Which software development metamodels contain or partially contain the information necessary to represent an agile software development project?

To answer RQ1, we used a Catalog of Agile Software Development Rules identified by the authors in a previous study [24]. A literature review conducted to answer RQ2 revealed that there is no metamodel that fully represents the information identified in RQ1. To fill this gap, this study investigates how the metamodels can be combined and extended.

As a result, this paper proposes a metamodel that combines elements from the *Process Definition* and *Process Execution* perspectives and includes entities such as *Project*, *Iteration*, *Case* and *Task* as core concepts.

The remainder of this paper is structured as follows. In Section 2, we identify the concepts typically necessary to represent agile software development projects. A literature review to identify how existing metamodels represent the identified information is presented in Section 3. Section 4 presents the proposed Agile Software Development Project Metamodel. An example of an agile project is shown in Section 5 and Section 6 concludes the paper.

2 Concepts necessary to represent agile software development projects

The goal of this section is to answer the research question RQ1 and identify a set of concepts necessary to represent agile software development projects. As our initial motivation was the representation of agile projects for Agility Assessment [2], we used as source of information the Catalog of Agile Software Development Rules proposed by the authors in a previous study [24]. The authors described, in a structured catalog, 20 Agile Software Development Rules extracted from a literature review and confirmed through surveys of industry practitioners. A summary of these rules is presented in alphabetical order in Table 1.

To identify a set of relevant concepts, we applied an iterative and incremental method and for each rule in the catalog, we analyzed its description and noted the main concepts as *codes*. As more data was collected, and re-reviewed, codes were grouped into concepts. Repeated tagged-with-codes concepts, concepts or elements became apparent. At the end of this method, the following concepts composed the basis of the proposed metamodel: *Project*, *Iteration*, *Case* and *Task*.

Project: The *Project* concept is the core entity of the Agile Software Development Project Metamodel and all other entities are in some way related to it. Some rules directly mention this concept. For example, the *"Goals should be clear and well-defined"* rule states that:

> *The **Project's** and Iterations' goals should be clear and well-defined.*

Other rules mention the *Project* concept implicitly, as for example, the *"Every Iteration should be timeboxed"* rule that defines:

> *All Iterations [of the **Project**] should have a fixed time duration.*

Table 1. Summary of Agile Software Rules proposed in [24]

	Rule Name	Short Description
01	Avoid Complex Tasks	Complex Tasks should be avoided. Complex Tasks should be decomposed into simpler Tasks
02	Avoid Dependence on Internal Specialists	A Developer Team should avoid having a single member become the only specialist in a feature or technology in order to avoid dependency on that member
03	Avoid Shared Developers	Developers should work on one Project at a time and be assigned to it for at least two days (or another predefined period) before being switched to another Project. Developer immersion is preferable over having the same Developer shared between Projects
04	Avoid Unplanned Work	A Developer Team should focus on the planned work and unplanned work should be avoided
05	Concurrent Iterations are not allowed	A Software Project should not have concurrent Iterations. An Iteration should start after the end of the previous Iteration
06	Deliveries should be frequent	A Software Project should have frequent deliveries
07	Development should be Test-driven	Test cases should be defined first, then code should be developed to pass the tests
08	Development Team should be small	The Developer Teams should be small to be efficient and effective
09	Do not finish an Iteration with open Tasks	An Iteration should not be finished if there are open Tasks. In this case, Open Tasks can be transferred to another Iteration or to a Product Backlog
10	Every Iteration should be the same length	Every Iteration should have the same duration
11	Every Iteration should be timeboxed	An Iteration should not be extended in order to finish work. If needed, break the problem into smaller, more manageable pieces so that this balance can be achieved
12	Every Iteration should have a deliverable	An Iteration should not be extended in order to finish work. If needed, break the problem into smaller, more manageable pieces so that this balance can be achieved
13	Every Iteration should have an Iteration Planning	Every Iteration should be planned just before its start. Normally an Iteration Plan is elaborated with the main Stakeholders (developer team and customer) that together decide what should be developed in the Iteration
14	Every Iteration should have an Iteration Retrospective	Every Iteration should have an Iteration Retrospective for Team feedback on the Process
15	Every Iteration should have an Iteration Review	Every Iteration should have an Iteration Review for Stakeholder feedback on the Product
16	Every Iteration Tasks must be estimated before starting Iteration	An Iteration should only start after all Tasks are estimated. By estimating the Tasks, the team formally makes a commitment with Iteration goals and deadlines
17	Every meeting should be timeboxed	All the process events such as Iteration Planning, Review, and Retrospective should have a duration defined before they start and the duration preferably should be the same during the entire Software Project
18	Goals should be clear and well-defined	The Project's and Iterations' goals should be clear and well-defined
19	Higher priority tasks must be executed first	The Developer Team should work on the higher priority Tasks first
20	There should be no break between Iterations	An interval between two consecutive Iterations should be avoided

Iteration: The *Iteration* element represents a development cycle that usually produces a portion of the software. Several rules refer to the *Iteration* concept. For example, the *"Every Iteration should be timeboxed"* rule states:

> *All **Iterations** should have a fixed time duration. Thus, an **Iteration** should not be extended or shortened to fit planned or unplanned features.*

Another example is the *"Every Iteration should have a deliverable"* rule that defines:

> *The team should deliver a new version of the software at the end of each **Iteration***

Case: The *Case* entity represents an instance of a software development process. A *Case* may denote many terms in different methodologies. For example, in RUP [16], the development of a *Use Case* could be perceived as a *Case* since it typically follows a small waterfall process: requirement elucidation, design, coding and testing. For some agile methods [1], whose development is *User Story* oriented, the development of a *User Story* could be represented by a *Case* in the Agile Software Development Metamodel.

The *Case* concept was extracted from rules such as *"Avoid Dependence on Internal Specialists"* that states:

> *A Developer Team should avoid making a single member the only specialist in a **feature** or technology so as not to become dependent on that member's knowledge.*

In this analysis, the *Feature* concept was translated to *Case*.

Task: The *Task* element denotes a unit of work. It typically has information about its execution such as start and end dates, duration, who performed the task and which artifacts were consumed/produced. The *Task* concept was extracted from rules such as *"Higher priority tasks must be executed first"* that states:

> *The Team must work on the highest priority **Tasks** first.*

Another example is the *"Avoid Complex Tasks"* rule that states

> *Complex **Tasks** should be avoided. During Iteration planning, the Team should try to break complex **Tasks** into simpler **Tasks**.*

It is important to note that a *Task* element is an instance of a *Task Definition* defined by a Software Development Process. To avoid confusion, in the remainder of this text we will use the term *Task* to denote a *task instance* and *TaskDef* to denote a *task definition*.

3 Literature Review

The literature review (LR) conducted in this study aimed at exploring the existing body of knowledge and investigating how software development metamodels proposed in indexed studies represent (or partially represent) the concepts identified in the previous section. As this is an exploratory study designed to organize a research area (metamodels to support the representation of agile software development projects) and there is no baseline for comparison of the results obtained, the presented literature review is considered a *Quasi-Systematic Review (QSR)* [27]. The methodology of the LR was based on the method proposed by Kitchenham et al [15] and consists of three main phases: *planning*, *execution* and *reporting*.

Literature Review Planning The research question for this LR was derived from the main RQ2 and can be summarized as: *Which Software Development Metamodels contain (or partially contain) the information necessary to represent an agile software development project?*

The scope of this review was defined according to the population, intervention, comparison and outcome PICO [21] approach. The *Population* is the set of software development projects. The *Intervention* is the agile methodologies and software processes. There is no *Comparison*. The *Outcome* is a set of metamodels to represent software development. Three papers obtained from a previous conventional literature review were used as control ([23], [7] and [13]). The keywords for *Population* are "software projects", "software systems", "software development" and "software engineering". The keywords for *Intervention* are "agile methods", "agile processes" and "software processes". The keyword for *Outcome* is "metamodel". The search string taken as the basis for all search engines, structured according to Pai et al. [21] was: *("software project" or "software systems" or "software development" or "software engineering") AND ("agile methods" or "agile processes" or "agile approaches" or "software processes") AND ("metamodel").*

We chose an incremental approach for the study selection. The final set of publications is a combination of automated search strategies and "snow-balling" procedures. Due to the nature of the area of investigation, and the missing standardized terminology, a pure QSLR would be inefficient. The sources were collected from the following digital databases, including the conferences, journals and technical reports indexed by IeeeXplore, Web of Science, Scopus and ACM digital library.

This review includes every article returned by the protocol that addresses one or more software development/process metamodel. Publications that satisfy at least one of the following exclusion criteria (EC) were excluded: (EC1) Documents not written in English; (EC2) Documents whose full text is not available; (EC3) Documents clearly dealing with topics irrelevant to the purpose of this review; (EC4) Documents merely reporting the use of individual software processes in development projects; (EC5) If the same study has been published more than once, the most relevant version, that is the one explaining the study in greatest detail, will be used and the others will be excluded.

The following information was extracted from each paper selected after running the selection process: *document title*, *author(s)*, *source*, *year of publication*, *concepts* and *elements* described in the metamodels.

The overall goal of the literature-review was to select contributions that propose any metamodel related to Software Process and analyze the metamodels in order to investigate how they represent the concepts presented in Section 2. Other characteristics, such as the metamodel relevance, adoption by industry, process ecosystem and supportive tools were not considered in this study. Henderson-Sellers et al [13], Kuhrmann et al [17] and Bendraou et al [7] are some examples of comprehensive studies about Software Process Metamodel Languages (SPML).

Literature Review Execution The search with the aforementioned engines returned 119 references, published between 2001 and 2017. All the controls were retrieved. Repetitions were eliminated and after the application of the inclusion and exclusion criteria, the number of papers selected for full reading was 15. The selected documents were used to extract the main concepts of the metamodel.

Literature Review Reporting Following the criteria established in the research protocol, 12 metamodels were selected from the 15 documents. These metamodels in in alphabetical order are:

1. *APM^3* [22]; 2. *Ayed's approach* [4]; 3. *Chou's approach* [8]; 4. *DiNitto's approach* [19]; 5. *ISO/IEC 24744 (SEMDM)* [14]; 6. *MetaMe* [9]; 7. *OOSPICE* [12]; 8. *OPF* [10]; 9. *PROMENADE* [11]; 10. *SPEM* [20]; 11. *UML4SPM* [6]; 12. *V-Modell XT* [26] [25].

One approach retrieved from the procedure was discarded, the *LiveNet* approach (referenced by Henderson-Sellers et al [13])) was not available.

In the reporting phase, we analyzed the selected metamodels in order to investigate how they represent the entities presented in Section 2.

The most well-established metamodel for specifying Software Process is SPEM (*Software & Systems Process Engineering Metamodel*) [20]. The last specification, SPEM 2.0, was launched in 2008 by the OMG Group and is focused on defining software and systems development processes and their components without adding specific features for particular development domains or disciplines such as project management. The goal is to enable the specification of a large range of development methods and processes of different styles, levels of formalism, life-cycle models and areas without imposing predefined modeling concepts. To achieve this, the SPEM specification is divided into two main packages: *Method Content* and *Process with Methods*. The *Method Content* package defines the core concepts such as *Task*, *Role* and *Work Product*, while the *Process with Methods* package supports the definition of software process models as nested activities that embody essentially the predefined elements in the *Method Content* package.

The main limitation of SPEM in representing agile software development projects is that the metamodel is focused on software process definition and neglects project execution elements, which Henderson-Seller et al [13] call *methodology layer* and *project layer*. Although elements such as *Task*, *Activity*, *Step*, *Role*, *Artifact* and *Iteration* are present in the metamodel, they do not have the same meaning as the elements presented in the previous section. For example, the *Task* element in SPEM represents a task definition and not a task instance. *Task* element has fields to describe general characteristics of a task such as description, predecessor tasks and successor tasks.

Other analyzed metamodels such as (*Chou's approach*, *DiNitto's approach*, *MetaMe*, *OOSPICE*, *OPF*, *PROMENADE*, *UML4SPM* and *V-Modell XT* are similar to SPEM, in that they focus on the methodology layer and neglect the representation of the project layer. These approaches have the elements *Activity*, *Role*, *Artifact* and *Tool* as a basis for software process definition. No or little information about process execution is addressed by these metamodels. The exception is the *MetaME* metamodel that represents the concept *Project*. Metamodels *APM*^{3} and *Ayed's approach*, on the other hand, focus on the project layer of Software Development and do not represent elements related to Process Definition. The only metamodel that supports the representation of both process and project layer is the *ISO/IEC 24744 (SEMDM)* metamodel that has elements corresponding to the concepts *Iteration*, *Task*, *Worker*, *TaskDef*, *RoleDef* and *ArtifactDef*.

Tables 2, 3 and 4 present a summary of the analyzed software development metamodels.

4 A metamodel for representing agile software development projects

By identifying concepts (Section 2) and using them as inputs for a literature review (Section 3), a need for a metamodel that contains the necessary elements to represent agile software development projects was revealed. This section aims

Table 2. Software Process Metamodels (subset 1) and their corresponding elements

	APM^3	Ayed	Chou	Di Nittos
Project	-	-	-	-
Iteration	Stage	Stage	-	-
Iteration Interval	-	-	-	-
Case	-	-	-	-
Task	Work-unit	Task	-	-
Delivery	Product	Deliverable	-	-
Delivery Interval	-	-	-	-
Worker	Role, Responsibility	Producer	-	-
TaskDef	-	-	Activity	Activity, Humam Activity
RoleDef	-	-	-	-
ArtifactDef	-	-	Document	Artifact

Table 3. Software Process Metamodels (subset 2) and their corresponding elements

	ISO 24744	MetaME	OOSPICE	OPF
Project	-	Project	-	-
Iteration	StageWithDuration	-	-	-
Iteration Interval	-	-	-	-
Case	-	-	-	-
Task	WorkUnit, Task	-	-	-
Delivery	-	-	-	-
Delivery Interval	-	-	-	-
Worker	Producer, Person, Team, Role	-	-	-
TaskDef	WorkUnitKind	Process, Activity, Task, ActionStep	Technique, Task, Action	WorkUnit, Activity, Task, Subtask, Technique
RoleDef	ProducerKind, RoleKind	Role	-	Role
ArtifactDef	WorkProductKind	Artifact	WorkProduct	WorkProduct

Table 4. Software Process Metamodels (subset 3) and their corresponding elements

	Promenade	SPEM	UML4SPM	V-Modell XT
Project	-	-	-	-
Iteration	-	-	-	-
Iteration Interval	-	-	-	-
Case	-	-	-	-
Task	-	-	-	-
Delivery	-	-	-	-
Delivery Interval	-	-	-	-
Worker	-	-	-	-
TaskDef	Task	Activity, Task, Definition	Software Activity	Activity, SubActivity, Step
RoleDef	Role	RoleUse, RoleDefinition	Responsible Role	Role
ArtifactDef	Document	WorkProduct	WorkProduct	Product, Subject, Topic

at presenting a proposal for a metamodel - that we named ASDPM (Agile Software Development Project Metamodel) - to support the representation of agile software development projects. Figure 1 shows the resulting metamodel. The metamodel representation and its description are conceptually divided in two parts: *Process Definition* and *Project Execution*.

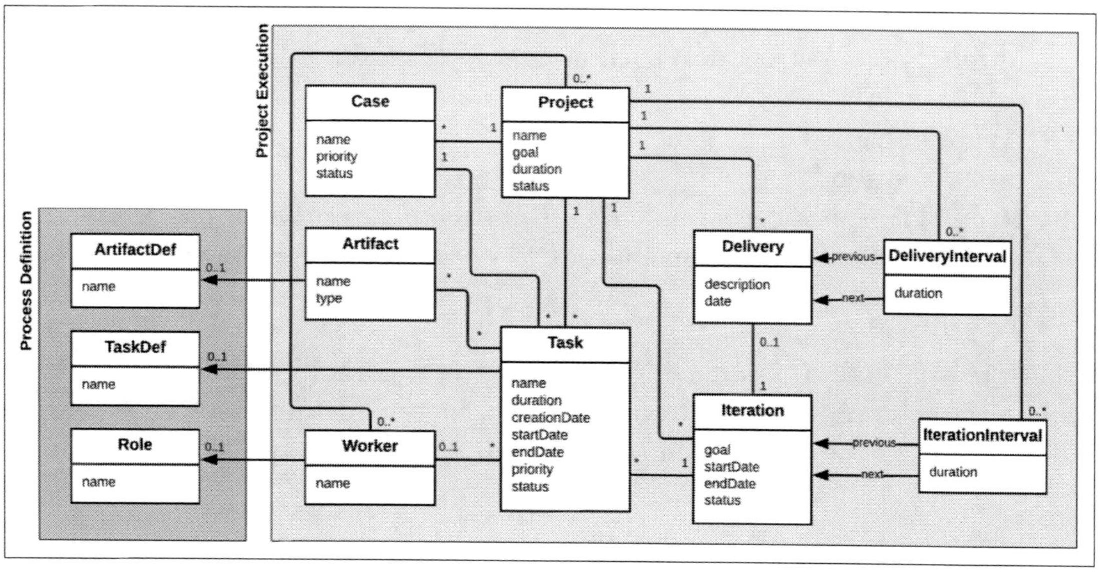

Fig. 1. Agile Software Development Project Metamodel

- **Project**: The core entity of the model represents the software project. The *Project* is associated with *Iterations*, *Cases*, *Tasks*, *Deliveries* and *Delivery Intervals*. It is a singleton entity, thus, a model has only one *Project* instance.
- **Iteration**: An *Iteration* denotes a cycle of development that typically produces a part of the software. It has a duration, a start and an end date, a status and other fields. Some agile methods such as Scrum [3] use the term *Sprint*. FDD methods [18] use the term *Cycle*. As the main associations, an *Iteration* has a list of *Tasks*.
- **Case**: A *Case* represents a small instance of a software process (or an execution of a software process). It could be a software feature, the development of a Use Case or a software module. A *Case* usually has its own flow, which typically has requirement, development and test tasks. A *Case* may be divided among many *Iterations* (see the example in Figure 2).
- **Task**: A *Task* represents a unit of work that is performed during software development. It may be associated with a *Case*, associated with an *Iteration* and assigned to a *Worker*. A *Task* in this perspective has information related to process execution, such as start and end dates, estimated effort, status, time spent on task and worker assigned. A *Task* could also be associated with a *TaskDef*, and, in this case, the *Task* is an instance of the *TaskDef*.
- **Delivery**: A *Delivery* represents the software product delivered at the end of an *Iteration*.
- **DeliveryInterval**: The interval between two consecutive *Deliveries*.
- **Worker**: A team member who executes *Tasks* during an *Iteration*. A *Worker* could have an associated *Role*.
- **Artifact**: *Artifacts* are software products produced and consumed by *Tasks*. It could include: a *requirement specification*, *source code*, *test cases* and *management reports*. An *Artifact* could be associated with an *ArtifactDef*, and, in this case, the *Artifact* is an instance of an *ArtifactDef*.
- **TaskDef**: The specification of a *Task* from the perspective of process definition. Some metamodels such as SPEM [20] and [10] use the term *Activity* or *WorkUnit*.
- **ArtifactDef**: The specification of an *Artifact* from the perspective of process definition.
- **Role**: The specification of a *Role* from the perspective of process definition. A *Role* defines the responsibilities of workers that take part in the software process.

Note that the *Development Team* concept, although presented in several rules, was not represented by an element in the metamodel. This concept is represented by the association between the *Project* and the *Worker* elements.

5 Software Development Instance

This section presents, as an example, a fragment of an agile software development project that illustrates the relation between the core concepts *Project*, *Iteration*,

Case and *Task*. The fragment of the project *MyProject* shown in Figure 2 is composed by 10 cases and 34 tasks that are distributed in 4 iterations. Some cases, such as *Case 1*, *Case 5* and *Case 6*, are fully executed in just one iteration, which means that all tasks that compose the case are planned for a unique iteration: The tasks *T1*, *T2* and *T3* of *Case 1* are executed in *Iteration 1*. The tasks *T16*, *T17* and *T18* of *Case 5* are executed in *Iteration 2*. The tasks *T19* and *T20* of *Case 6* are executed in *Iteration 3*. Other cases, such as *Case 2*, *Case 3* and *Case 7* have their tasks distributed among more than one iteration. The *Case 2*, for example, is executed in two iterations: while Tasks *T4* and *T5* are planned for *Iteration 1*, Tasks *T5* and *T6* are planned for *Iteration 2*. *Case 3* started in *Iteration 1* and ended in *Iteration 3*. No tasks of *Case 3* are executed in *Iteration 2*. The most fragmented case, *Case 7*, has its tasks distributed over 3 iterations: *T21* and *T22* in *Iteration 1*, *T23* and *T24* in *Iteration 2* and *T25* and *T26* in *Iteration 3*.

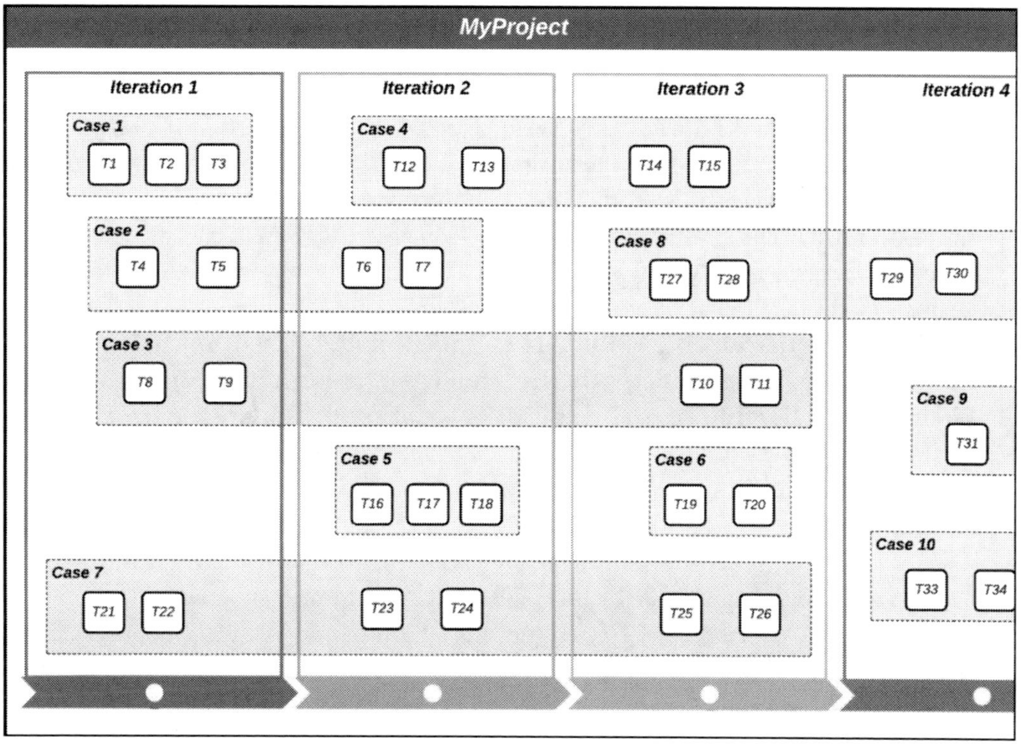

Fig. 2. An agile software development project example

6 Conclusion

This study proposed a metamodel that we named ASDPM (Agile Software Development Project Metamodel) and aims at providing the elements necessary to represent Agile Software Development Projects. Two research questions guided the study: RQ1, which aimed at identifying the concepts required for representing typical Agile Software Development Projects and RQ2 that investigated how existing metamodels represent the identified concepts. To answer RQ1, we applied an iterative and incremental method that used as input a catalog of Agile Software Development Rules proposed by the authors in a previous study [24]. For each rule in the catalog, we analyzed its description and identified the main concepts. These identified concepts were subject of a literature review that aimed at answering RQ2. The literature review revealed that most of the evaluated metamodels focused on the software process definition layer and that the elements related to project execution were under represented. To fulfill this gap, a metamodel that contains elements from both perspectives (process definition and project execution) was proposed. The main concepts that compose the metamodel are: *Project*, *Iteration*, *Case* and *Task*. The metamodel is almost stable, however, as we still working on other research that uses the metamodel, some adjustments in the ASDPM may be necessary.

References

1. Abrahamsson, P., Salo, O., Ronkainen, J., Warsta, J.: Agile software development methods - Review and analysis. Tech. Rep. 478, VTT Publications (2002)
2. Adalı, O.E., Özcan-Top, Ö., Demirörs, O.: Evaluation of agility assessment tools: A multiple case study. In: International Conference on Software Process Improvement and Capability Determination. pp. 135–149. Springer (2016)
3. Alliance, S.: Learn About Scrum (2016), https://www.scrumalliance.org/why-scrum
4. Ayed, H., Vanderose, B., Habra, N.: A metamodel-based approach for customizing and assessing agile methods. In: Quality of Information and Communications Technology (QUATIC), 2012 Eighth International Conference on the. pp. 66–74. IEEE (2012)
5. Beck, K., Beedle, M., van Bennekum, A., Cockburn, A., Cunningham, W., Fowler, M., Grenning, J., Highsmith, J., Hunt, A., Jeffries, R., Kern, J., Marick, B., Martin, R.C., Mellor, S., Schwaber, K., Sutherland, J., Thomas, D.: Manifesto for Agile Software Development (2001), http://www.agilemanifesto.org/
6. Bendraou, R., Gervais, M.P., Blanc, X.: Uml4spm: A uml2.0-based metamodel for software process modelling. In: Briand, L., Williams, C. (eds.) Model Driven Engineering Languages and Systems. pp. 17–38. Springer Berlin Heidelberg, Berlin, Heidelberg (2005)
7. Bendraou, R., Jezequel, J.M., Gervais, M.P., Blanc, X.: A Comparison of Six UML-Based Languages for Software Process Modeling. IEEE Transactions on Software Engineering **36**(5), 662–675 (sep 2010)
8. Chou, S.C.: A process modeling language consisting of high level uml diagrams and low level process language. Journal of Object- Oriented Programming **1**(4), 137–163 (2002)
9. Engels, G., Sauer, S.: A Meta-Method for Defining Software Engineering Methods. In: Graph transformations and model-driven engineering, pp. 411–440. Springer (2010)
10. Firesmith, D., Henderson-Sellers, B.: The OPEN Process Framework: An Introduction. Addison-Wesley (2002)

11. Franch, X., M. Rib, J.: Promenade: A modular approach to software process modelling and enaction (05 1999)
12. Gonzalez-Perez, C., McBride, T., Henderson-Sellers, B.: A metamodel for assessable software development methodologies. Software Quality Journal **13**(2), 195–214 (Jun 2005). https://doi.org/10.1007/s11219-005-6217-7, https://doi.org/10.1007/s11219-005-6217-7
13. Henderson-Sellers, B., Gonzalez-Perez, C.: A comparison of four process metamodels and the creation of a new generic standard. Information and Software Technology **47**(1), 49 – 65 (2005). https://doi.org/https://doi.org/10.1016/j.infsof.2004.06.001, http://www.sciencedirect.com/science/article/pii/S0950584904000850
14. ISO/IEC 24744:2014 - Software Engineering Metamodel for Development Methodologies (SEMDM). Standard, International Organization for Standardization, Geneva, CH (Nov 2014)
15. Kitchenham, B., Charters, S.: Guidelines for performing systematic literature reviews in software engineering. Tech. rep., Keele University and University of Durham (Jul 2007)
16. Kruchten, P.: The Rational Unified Process: An Introduction. Addison-Wesley Professional (2004)
17. Kuhrmann, M., Fernández, D.M., Steenweg, R.: Systematic software process development: Where do we stand today? In: Proceedings of the 2013 International Conference on Software and System Process. pp. 166–170. ICSSP 2013, ACM, New York, NY, USA (2013)
18. Luca, J.D.: Feature Driven Development FDD, http://www.featuredrivendevelopment.com/
19. Nitto, E.D., Lavazza, L., Schiavoni, M., Tracanella, E., Trombetta, M.: Deriving executable process descriptions from uml. In: Proceedings of the 24th International Conference on Software Engineering. ICSE 2002 (May 2002)
20. OMG: Software Process Engineering Metamodel (SPEM) 2.0 Specification. Final specification, OMG (apr 2008), http://www.omg.org/spec/SPEM/2.0/PDF/
21. Pai, M., McCulloch, M., Gorman, J., Pai, N., Enanoria, W., Kennedy, G., Tharyan, P., Colford, J.: Systematic reviews and meta-analyses: an illustrated, step-by-step guide. The Medical Journal of India (2004)
22. Sadi, M.H., Ramsin, R.: APM3: A Methodology Metamodel for Agile Project Management. In: SoMeT. pp. 367–378 (2009)
23. Steenweg, R., Kuhrmann, M., Méndez Fernández, D.: Software engineering process metamodels–a literature review. Technische Universität München, Tech. Rep. TUM-I1220 (2012)
24. Telemaco, U., Oliveira, T., Mesquita, R., Melo, G., Alencar, P.: A catalog of software development rules for agile methods. Tech. rep., Cheriton School of Computer Science - University of Waterloo (dec 2017)
25. Ternite, T.: Variability of Development Models. Ph.D. thesis, Clausthal University of Technology (2010)
26. Ternit, T., Kuhrmann, M.: Das v-modell xt 1.3 metamodell. Standard, Technische Universitt Mnchenn, Germany (2009)
27. Travassos, G.H., d. Santos, P.S.M., Mian, P.G., Neto, A.C.D., Biolchini, J.: An Environment to Support Large Scale Experimentation in Software Engineering. In: 13th IEEE International Conference on Engineering of Complex Computer Systems (iceccs 2008). pp. 193–202 (March 2008). https://doi.org/10.1109/ICECCS.2008.30
28. VersionOne: The 12th Annual State of Agile Report™ 2018 (2018), http://stateofagile.versionone.com, accessed: 2018-10-01

Neutrosophic Cognitive Map for a Multi-Objective Decision Making in Software Projects

Salah H. Al-subhi[1], Gaafar S. Mahdi[1], Iliana P. Pupo[1], Pedro P. Pérez [1], and Maikel L. Vázquez [2]

[1] Grupo de Investigaciones en Gestión de Proyectos, Universidad de las Ciencias Informáticas, Carretera a San Antonio km 2 ½, CP 54830, La Habana, Cuba

[2] Universidad de Guayaquil, Facultad de Ciencias Matemáticas y Físicas, Guayaquil, Ecuador

[1] {salahcuba@yahoo.com, gaafarsadeq@yahoo.com, iperez@uci.cu, ppp@uci.cu}, [2]mleyvaz@gmail.com

Abstract. There are many organizations focused on software development projects. These projects are often considered as high-risk projects, and usually, affected by uncertainty and their high dependence on human resources perceptions. This paper aims at creating a new decision making tool from a multi-objective approach (diagnosis, decision and prediction) during the execution of software projects. The suggested model is based on Neutrosophic Cognitive Maps (NCMs) with a neutrosophic set in map's connections. The proposed model constitutes a suitable tool for making comprehensive decisions in software projects characterized by uncertainty, vagueness, imprecision and indetermination. Finally, the NCM model has been compared with a traditional FCM-based model for decision making in software projects in terms of efficacy.

Keywords: Software Projects, Neutrosophic Cognitive Maps, Fuzzy Cognitive Maps, Single Valued Triangular Neutrosophic Numbers.

1 Introduction

There are many organizations focused on software development since software products are present in all areas in modern societies. Software projects are often considered as high-risk projects, and usually, characterized by a high level of uncertainty, their great dependence on human resources, and their dynamic nature. Hence the low percent of success in software projects as show the reports of the Standish Group International Incorporated [1] and the New Zealand Project Management report issued in 2017 [2].

Poor decisions constitute one of the most common reasons of software project's failure [3]. A report issued by Project Management Institute (PMI) in 2015 [4] indicated that nearly half of unsuccessful projects are impacted by poor decision making, and stated that decision making requires more attention.

In this context, project management schools such as PMBOK [5], ISO 21500 [6], CMMI [7], MPS.BR [8] and other authors [9], [10], [11] have provided guidelines and recommendations for software project management. Although the aforementioned guides and authors recognize the importance of decision making process in software projects [12], they still have the following drawbacks:

- The techniques they propose for decision making in software projects do not deal enough with the uncertainty, ambiguity and impression.
- They do not consider the indeterminacy relations presented in decision making during software development projects.
- They do not address decision making from a multi-objective approach (diagnosis, decisions and prediction) during the control of software projects milestones.

We consider that decision making in software projects can be improved by using soft computing techniques, since they are efficient for modeling complex and dynamic systems with presence of ambiguity, imprecision and uncertainty [13], [14], [15]. Soft computing is based on techniques such as artificial neural networks, genetic algorithms, bayesian networks, case-based reasoning and fuzzy cognitive maps.

In order to select the soft computing technique for modeling decision making process in software projects, the following requirements were considered:

- There are different perceptions of multiple experts involved in software development projects which should be aggregated for decision making process.
- Decision making in software projects is based not only on quantitative indicators, but also on qualitative indicators such as quality assessment, human resource motivations and risk analysis.
- Decision making process should be understood by all stakeholders, this is a principle of total quality in software projects.
- It is important to consider all the interrelationships between concepts and their effects, including feedback relationships, and time influence.

Fuzzy Cognitive Maps (FCMs) introduced by Kosko in 1986 [16] is a suitable tool that meets the aforementioned requirements. FCMs provide a good solution in terms of interpretability of simulation results, experts' perception aggregation simplicity, feedback representation capacity and topology change flexibility [17], [18], [19]. Nevertheless, FCMs have the limitation of not representing indeterminacy relations which are frequently presented in software project decisions. For example, it is known that the decision of increasing control impacts highly on increasing SPI indicator. However, there is an indeterminacy relation between this decision and human resource motivation, since the decision of increasing control may or may not impact on human resource motivation. Therefore, this relation is not represented by FCMs, see left part of Fig. 1.

Neutrosophic sets (NSs) introduced by F. Smarandache in 1995 [20] is able to represent true degree, falsity degree and indeterminacy [21]. Neutrosophic Cognitive Maps (NCMs) introduced by Vasantha & Smarandache in 2003 [22] are an integration of FCMs in neutrosophic environment. This technique overcomes the drawback of not representing indeterminacy relations found in FCMs, see right part of Fig. 1.

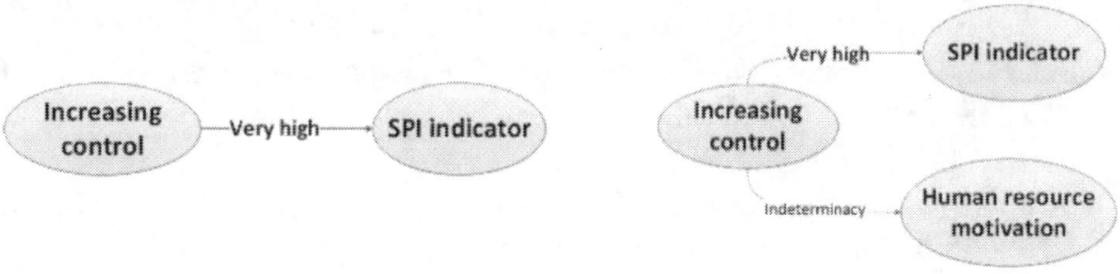

(a) (b)

Fig. 1. (a) A traditional fuzzy cognitive map without indeterminacy relations. (b) A neutrosophic cognitive map with indeterminacy relations between concepts.

NCMs were employed in many scenarios [23], [24], [25], [26]. However, literature consulted revealed only two papers associated to the use of NCMs in software projects. The first one proposed a method for modeling risk interdependencies in projects [27], and the second paper employed NCMs for the identification of success factors in software projects [28]. Nevertheless, the aforementioned papers represent the indeterminacy relations by using the letter *I* without exploiting the potentialities of neutrosophic sets. In the present paper, authors suggest a new approach to represent the indeterminacy relations between concepts.

This paper aims at developing a model based on NCM for making comprehensive decisions from a multi-objective approach (diagnosis, decision and prediction) during the execution of software projects. The rest of this paper is organized as follows: section 2 describes preliminary concepts and notation of Neutrosophic theory. In section 3, authors proposed a model based on NCM for decision making in software projects. Section 4 stands for analysis and discussion. Section 5 is devoted to the conclusion and future research topics.

2 Neutrosophic cognitive maps, concepts and notion

Neutrosophic sets (NSs) is the generalization of Fuzzy Sets (FSs) introduced by Zadeh in 1965 [29] and Intuitive Fuzzy Sets (IFSs) suggested by Atanassov in 1986 [30]. Nevertheless, both FSs and IFSs fail to deal with indeterminacy relations [31]. In contrast, NSs consider the degree of membership, non-membership and indeterminacy.

Definition 1. Let X be a space of points and $x \in X$ [32]. A neutrosophic set in X is defined by a truth-membership function $T_A(x)$, an indeterminacy-membership function $I_A(x)$, and a falsity-membership function $F_A(x)$. $T_A(x)$, $I_A(x)$ and $F_A(x)$ are real standard or real nonstandard subsets of $]^{-}0, 1^{+}[$. That is $T_A(x)$: $X \rightarrow]^{-}0, 1^{+}[$, $I_A(x)$:$X \rightarrow]^{-}0, 1^{+}[$, and $F_A(x)$:$X \rightarrow]^{-}0, 1^{+}[$. There is no restriction on the sum of $T_A(x)$, $I_A(x)$, and $F_A(x)$, so $0^{-} \leq \sup T_A(x) + \sup I_A(x) + \sup F_A(x) \leq 3^{+}$.

Single valued neutrosophic set (SVNS) is an instance of a neutrosophic set which can be used in real scientific and engineering applications [33].

Definition 2. Let X be a universe of discourse. A single valued neutrosophic set over X is an object taking the form $=\{\langle x, T_A(x), I_A(x), F_A(x), \rangle : x \in X\}$, where $T_A(x)$:$X \rightarrow [0, 1]$, $I_A(x)$:$X \rightarrow [0, 1]$, and $F_A(x)$:$X \rightarrow [0, 1]$ with $0 \leq T_A(x) + I_A(x) + F_A(x) \leq 3$ for all $x \in X$. The intervals $T_A(x)$, $I_A(x)$, and $F_A(x)$ represent the truth-membership degree, the indeterminacy-membership degree, and the falsity membership degree of x to X, respectively. For convenience, a SVN number is represented by = (a, b, c), where a, b, $c \in [0, 1]$ and $a + b + c \leq 3$.

However, a combination of triangular fuzzy number with SVNS can be used for handling uncertainty embedded in decision making problems [34].

Definition 3. The single valued triangular neutrosophic number, $\tilde{a} = \langle (a_1, a_2, a_3); \propto_{\tilde{a}}, \theta_{\tilde{a}}, \beta_{\tilde{a}} \rangle$, is a neutrosophic set on the real line set R [35], whose truth, indeterminacy and falsity membership functions are as follows:

$$T_{\tilde{a}}(x) = \begin{cases} \propto_{\tilde{a}} \left(\frac{x-a_1}{a_2-a_1}\right) & (a_1 \leq x \leq a_2) \\ \propto_{\tilde{a}} & (x = a_2) \\ \propto_{\tilde{a}} \left(\frac{a_3-x}{a_3-a_2}\right) & (a_2 < x \leq a_3) \\ 0 & \text{otherwise} \end{cases} \quad (1)$$

$$I_{\tilde{a}}(x) = \begin{cases} \frac{(a_2-x+\theta_{\tilde{a}}(x-a_1))}{(a_2-a_1)} & (a_1 \leq x \leq a_2) \\ \theta_{\tilde{a}} & (x = a_2) \\ \frac{(x-a_2+\theta_{\tilde{a}}(a_3-x))}{(a_3-a_2)} & (a_2 < x \leq a_3) \\ 1 & \text{otherwise} \end{cases} \quad (2)$$

$$F_{\tilde{a}}(x) = \begin{cases} \frac{(a_2 - x + \beta_{\tilde{a}}(x - a_1))}{(a_2 - a_1)} & (a_1 \leq x \leq a_2) \\ \beta_{\tilde{a}} & (x = a_2) \\ \frac{(x - a_2 + \beta_{\tilde{a}}(a_3 - x))}{(a_3 - a_2)} & (a_2 < x \leq a_3) \\ 1 & \text{otherwise} \end{cases} \quad (3)$$

Where $\propto_{\tilde{a}}, \theta_{\tilde{a}}, \beta_{\tilde{a}} \in [0,1]$ and $a_1, a_2, a_3 \in R$, $a_1 \leq a_2 \leq a_3$. The different operations with triangular neutrosophic numbers are described in [35].

3 Neutrosophic cognitive map for a multi-objective decision making in software projects

In this section, we develop a new model based on NCM for making comprehensive decisions from a multi-objective approach (diagnosis, decision and prediction) during the execution of software projects. The maps' connections in the proposed model are represented by triangular neutrosophic sets. The NCM model was built and executed based on the following algorithm:

Algorithm 1:

```
1. t = 1
2. Selection of k Experts
```

3. Identification of Concepts involved in decision making process
4. Assignation of fuzzy linguistic variables
5. Construction of individual maps by each expert
6. Aggregation of individual maps
7. For each case to be evaluated in the aggregated map do
8. Load initial vector A^1 (Indicators nodes)
9. While equilibrium state is not reached do
10. $A_i^{t+1} = f\left(A_i^t + \sum_{i=1}^{n} W_{ji} \cdot A_j^t\right)$ // W_{ji} is the relationship between nodes i,j of the aggregated map
11. $t = t + 1$
12. End while loop
13. Generate case output
14. End for loop

The algorithm 1 is described in next subsections.

3.1 Experts selection

To build the NCM model, a heterogeneous group of five experts was selected considering as criterion a profound knowledge in software projects. Each expert creates, individually, an NCM for decision making in software projects.

3.2 Concepts Identification

Each NCM consists of four types of nodes. The first type represents indicators which reflect the current state of software projects. The second type stands for diagnosis during software project evaluation. The third type are decision concepts that represent possible decisions to be made in order to correct deviations from the software project plan. Finally, prediction concepts allow to know the evolution of software projects according to decisions made. Experts ultimately identified 32 nodes as shown in Table 1.

Table 1. NCM's nodes.

Type	Nodes	Description
Indicator concepts	SPI	Scheduling performance indicator.
	CPI	Cost performance indicator.
	EFPI	Efficacy performance indicator, representing the quality of project.
	LPI	Logistic performance indicator.
	DQPI	Data quality performance indicator.
	HRCPI	Human resource correlation performance indicator.
	HREPI	Human resource efficacy performance indicator.
	HREFI	Human resource efficiency performance indicator.
Diagnosis concepts	F1	Defects on quality of software control.
	F2	Defects on control of tasks and delays.

	F3	Defects on human resource efficiency.
	F4	Defects on human resource efficacy.
	F5	Defects on requirements analysis.
	F6	Defects on cost scheduling.
Decision concepts	D1	Increase the control of software quality.
	D2	Leave project manager.
	D3	Increase control milestones.
	D4	Reward human resources.
	D5	Penalize human resources.
	D6	Hire more human resources.
	D7	Re-scheduling of requirement elicitation process.
	D8	Extra hours scheduling.
	D9	Refine requirements.
Prediction concepts	P1	Improve software quality.
	P2	Recover software project delays.
	P3	Improve requirements definition.
	P4	Increase perceived quality.
	P5	Increase human resource motivation.
	P6	Decrease quality.
	P7	Increase software development delays.
	P8	Increase requirements defects.
	P9	Decrease human resource motivation.

3.3 Assignation of fuzzy linguistic variables

Interconnection influence of concepts is represented by triangular neutrosophic sets, see definition 3. Influence of one concept over another is interpreted as a linguistic variable in the interval [-1, 1] with positive, negative causalities or indeterminacy, as illustrated in Table 2.

Table 2. Triangular neutrosophic sets to represent map's relations.

Linguistic terms	Neutrosophic set based on triangular functions
Negative highest (NHST)	(-0.83, -1.0, -1.0, 0.95, 0.45, 0.15)
Negative very high (NVH)	(-0.67, -0.83, -1.0, 0.95, 0.45, 0.15)
Negative high (NH)	(-0.5, -0.67, -0.83, 0.95, 0.45, 0.15)
Negative mean (NM)	(-0.33, -0.5, -0.67, 0.95, 0.45, 0.15)
Negative low (NL)	(-0.17, -0.33, -0.5, 0.95, 0.45, 0.15)
Negative very low (NVL)	(0, -0.17, -0.33, 0.95, 0.45, 0.15)
None (N)	(0, 0.07, 0.17, 0.95, 0.45, 0.15)
Very low (VL)	(0, 0.17, 0.33, 0.95, 0.45, 0.15)
Low (L)	(0.17, 0.33, 0.5, 0.95, 0.45, 0.15)
Mean (M)	(0.33, 0.5, 0.67, 0.95, 0.45, 0.15)
High (H)	(0.5, 0.67, 0.83, 0.95, 0.45, 0.15)
very high (VH)	(0.67, 0.83, 1.0, 0.95, 0.45, 0.15)
Highest (HST)	(0.83, 1.0, 1.0, 0.95, 0.45, 0.15)
Indeterminacy	(0, 0, 0, 0.1, 0.9, 0.1)

3.4 Maps construction

Each expert builds his own map establishing maps' relations by using the triangular neutrosophic sets illustrated in Table 2. The individual maps are then aggregated as follow:

Let $\tilde{a}_1, \tilde{a}_2 \ldots \tilde{a}_n$ to be experts' preferences, being $\tilde{a}_1 = \langle (a_{11}, a_{12}, a_{13}); \propto_{\tilde{a}_1}, \theta_{\tilde{a}_1}, \beta_{\tilde{a}_1} \rangle$ then the aggregation of preferences is performed with *Agg* operator in equation 4:

$$Agg\ (\tilde{a}_1, \tilde{a}_2, \ldots \tilde{a}_n) = \left(\frac{\sum_{i=1}^{n} a_{i1}}{n}, \frac{\sum_{i=1}^{n} a_{i2}}{n}, \frac{\sum_{i=1}^{n} a_{i3}}{n}, T(\propto_{\tilde{a}_i}), S_1(\theta_{\tilde{a}_i}), S_2(\beta_{\tilde{a}_i}) \right) \quad \textbf{(4)}$$

Being T a t-norm function T: [0,1] x [0,1] → [0,1] for example (min), and S1, S2: s-norm functions S: [0,1] x [0,1] → [0,1] for example (max) [36].

The relationships of the aggregated map are shown in the following tables.

Table 3. Relations between indicators and diagnosis concepts which represent the initial diagnostic.

	F1	F2	F3	F4	F5	F6
SPI	VL	VH	VH	L	VH	M
CPI	VL	VH	VH	N	M	VH
EFPI	HST	M	N	VH	M	N
LPI	L	L	VL	VL	L	VL
DQPI	H	M	VL	H	N	N
HRCPI	VL	VL	H	L	VH	VL
HREPI	VH	M	VL	VH	N	N
HRFPI	VL	H	VH	VL	H	VL

Table 4. Relations between diagnosis and decisions concepts which represent the decision process.

	D1	D2	D3	D4	D5	D6	D7	D8	D9
F1	HST	L	M	VL	L	VL	L	L	M
F2	M	HST	HST	L	L	VL	M	L	M
F3	VL	VH	M	VH	VH	H	M	H	M
F4	VH	H	M	VH	VH	L	M	M	H
F5	M	H	HST	L	L	L	VH	L	H
F6	VL	HST	L	VL	VL	VL	VH	VL	VH

Table 5. Relations between decisions and prediction concepts that represent the prediction process, which include indeterminacy relations.

	P1	P2	P3	P4	P5	P6	P7	P8	P9
D1	VH	NL	L	VH	VL	NVH	NM	NHST	L
D2	M	M	I	M	M	L	NH	VL	L
D3	H	VH	H	I	L	NVH	VL	L	L
D4	H	H	I	H	VH	NH	NVH	L	VL
D5	M	M	M	M	L	M	H	M	M
D6	L	H	L	I	L	VH	M	VH	L
D7	H	VH	H	L	M	I	NM	L	L

D8	M	VH	H	M	L	I	NVH	VL	M
D9	H	VH	H	L	M	L	NVH	M	L

Table 6. Relations between prediction and diagnosis concepts in which feedback relations are represented.

	F1	F2	F3	F4	F5	F6
P1	VL	L	L	VL	L	L
P2	N	VL	VL	L	VL	VL
P3	N	VL	VL	VL	VL	VL
P4	VL	M	VL	L	VL	VL
P5	VL	VL	VL	L	L	L
P6	HST	HST	L	VH	M	L
P7	L	VH	VH	H	VH	H
P8	HST	VH	M	HST	H	M
P9	H	HST	VH	HST	H	M

NCM was built by using the concepts defined by experts in Table 1, and relations illustrated in Tables 3, 4, 5 and 6, see Fig. 2.

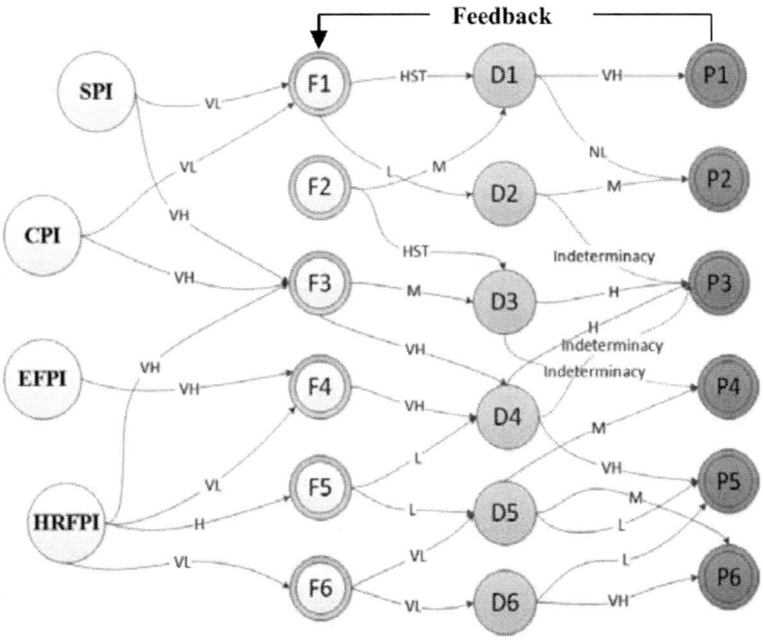

Fig 2. Partial representation of the aggregated NCM, in which Map's connections are represented by triangular neutrosophic sets.

The construction process of NCM by experts was a hard task, taking into account the high number of nodes and interrelationships between them. It is part of our future work to build NCMs by mean of machine learning techniques.

3.5 Simulation process

In simulation process, users can exploit the map, using it for making comprehensive decisions in software projects from a multi-objective approach (diagnosis, decision and prediction). The process is started with the activation of some indicator concepts during the execution of a software project by using equations 5 and 6, bringing about the activation of the rest of the map's concepts. This process terminates when it reaches an equilibrium state [17].

The initial vector A_i^{t+1} at the instant t+1 would be computed as:

$$A_i^{t+1} = f\left(A_i^{\mathrm{t}} + \sum_{i=1}^{n} \mathrm{W_{ji}} \cdot \mathrm{A_j^{t}} \right) \tag{5}$$

Where $f(x)$ is the transformation function and Wji stands for causal links between concepts, which is represented by a triangular neutrosophic set instead of by a single value, as in both traditional FCM and NCMs-based approaches referred to in section 1.

The hyperbolic tangent is one of the most common transformation function used in FCM simulation process to normalize the concept value into the range [-1,1], this function uses λ as a constant for function slope [37]:

$$f(x) = \tanh(x) = \frac{e^{\lambda x} - e^{-\lambda x}}{e^{\lambda x} + e^{-\lambda x}} \tag{6}$$

4 Analysis and discussion

In order to validate the neutrosophic cognitive map (NCM), proposed in this paper, it was compared with a traditional FCM-based model for decision making in software projects. During validation process, the database DPME6 from the Research Database Repository provided by the University of Informatics Science [38] was used. This database contains 5890 records that represent 553 different software projects. Each record describes the project real state in a certain moment of its life. DPME6 contains 3038 records in which projects are evaluated as "bad performance", 605 records where projects are evaluated as "regular performance", and 2247 records belong to projects that are evaluated as "correct performance". Each record has 8 input attributes that correspond to project indicators, and outputs attributes that stand for diagnosis, decision, and prediction respectively.

In terms of efficacy, we introduced a metric success C to evaluate the two maps as follows: Let ρ be a model, a metric success C is defined in (7) as a percentage of records classified as experts do, where n represents the number of records. This equation was applied in order to evaluate the result of diagnosis, decision and prediction processes of both FCM and NCM.

$$C\,(\rho) = 100 \frac{\sum_{i=0}^{n} S_i(\rho)}{n} \tag{7}$$

$$S_i(\rho) = \begin{cases} 0 & \text{if not coincidence with experts} \\ 1 & \text{if coincidence with experts} \end{cases}$$

Authors introduced precision $P(\rho)$ (8) and recalls $R(\rho)$ (9) metrics to evaluate the models capacity for detecting the indeterminacy as follows:

$$P(\rho) = 100\frac{|Z(\rho) \cap I|}{Z(\rho)} \quad \textbf{(8)}$$

$$R(\rho) = 100\frac{|Z(\rho) \cap I|}{I} \quad (9)$$

$Z(\rho)$ is the set of records that a model ρ detects with high indeterminacy and I is the set of records with true high indeterminacy.

For validation process, algorithm 1 was applied for both models NCM and FCM. The FCM was constructed by using the concepts defined by experts in Table 1 and relations illustrated in Tables 3, 4, 5 and 6, without considering indeterminacy relations. Influence of one concept over another is interpreted as a linguistic variable in the interval [-1, 1] with only positive and negative causalities, as illustrated in Table 7.

Table 7. Linguistic terms to represent FCM's relations.

Linguistic terms	Relation's values
Negative highest (NHST)	-1.0
Negative very high (NVH)	-0.83
Negative high (NH)	-0.67
Negative mean (NM)	-0.5
Negative low (NL)	-0.33
Negative very low (NVL)	-0.17
None (N)	0.07
Very low (VL)	0.17
Low (L)	0.33
Mean (M)	0.5
High (H)	0.67
very high (VH)	0.83
Highest (HST)	1.0

Respecting successful evaluation in diagnosis, decision and prediction processes, NCM reported better results than FCM, as shown in Table 8. Regarding precision on indeterminacy detection (*P*) and recall of indeterminacy detection (*R*), NCM reported good results. FCM did not report any results in this aspect since it does not consider indeterminacy relations between concepts.

Table 8. The comparison results between FCM and NCM.

Algorithm	FCM	NCM
Successful diagnosis $C(\text{diagnosis})$	87%	96,98
Successful decision $C(\text{decision})$	92%	99%

Successful prediction $C(\text{prediction})$	83,3%	95,25%
Precision on indeterminacy detection $P(\text{diagnosis})$	-	62%
Precision on indeterminacy detection $P(\text{decisions})$	-	77%
Precision on indeterminacy detection $P(\text{prediction})$	-	71%
Recall on indeterminacy detection $R(\text{diagnosis})$	-	99%
Recall on indeterminacy detection $R(\text{decisions})$	-	99.4%
Recall on indeterminacy detection $R(\text{prediction})$	-	96%

Besides, simulation results revealed that the main problems in diagnosis process were "defects on requirements analysis", "defects on control of tasks and delays", and "defects on human resource efficiency". The main decisions suggested by NCM-based model were: "refine the requirements" and "reward human resources".

In addition, the NCM-based model was applied in a case study on a software project that aimed at developing the following modules:

- Procedures management module for Office 1.
- Procedures management subsystem for Office 2.
- Accounting and financial management subsystem.

The application of the proposed model led to identify the following defects in diagnosis process: defects on control of tasks and delays (F2), and defects on requirements analysis (F5). Only 4 out of the 10 stakeholders involved in the software project were satisfied with the project state. In order to correct the software project's deviations, the model suggested the following decisions: re-scheduling of requirement elicitation process (D7), refine requirements (D9) and hire more human resources (D6).

The project managers decided to re-schedule requirement elicitation (D7); the new elicitation process was scheduled in 21 days, 7 days more than the initial plan of elicitation. The second decision was to redefine requirements (D9) but focused on four modules, one module less than the modules identified in diagnosis process. Besides, team managers decided to hire 6 specialists more (D6).

Map's decisions helped to improve software quality, requirements definition and to increase perceived quality. Therefore, the majority of stakeholders expressed their satisfaction with the project state after the decisions were made, as shown in Fig. 3. Finally, software project finished successfully.

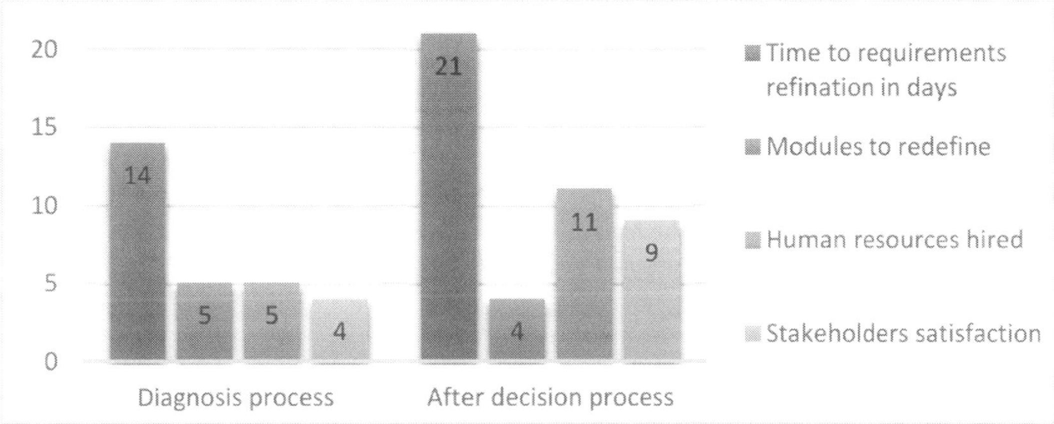

Fig. 3. Graphical representation of the results of diagnosis and decision processes on software project.

5 Conclusion and future work

In this paper, we presented a new decision making model based on Neutrosophic Cognitive Map (NCM) for making comprehensive decisions from a multi-objective approach (diagnosis, decision and prediction) in software projects. The NCM's connections were represented by triangular neutrosophic sets. NCMs have the same advantages of traditional FCMs beside the advantage of handling better vagueness and uncertainty since they consider indeterminacy relations. Such characteristic makes the proposed model more robust by considering all decision aspects (true, false and not sure). In addition, the suggested model was compared with a traditional FCM-based model for decision making in software projects, showing its superiority regarding successful evaluation in diagnosis, decision and prediction. Finally, the model was applied in a case study on a software project leading to improve the project outcomes. In the future, we shall research on the application of machine learning techniques for NCMs construction.

References

1. Johnson, J.: *CHAOS Report: Decision Latency Theory: It Is All About the Interval*. The Standish Group (2018).
2. KPMG's Advisory Group: *Driving business performance, Project Management Survey 2017*. KPMG, New Zealand (2017).
3. Whitney, K.M.; Daniels, C.B.: The Root Cause of Failure in Complex IT Projects: Complexity Itself. *Procedia Computer Science*, Vol. 20, pp. 325–330 (2013).
4. Project Management Institute: Capturing the Value of Project Management Through Decision Making. *Pulse of the Profession*, (2015).
5. Project Management Institute: *A Guide to the Project Management Body of Knowledge (PMBOK® Guide)*. Project Management Institute (2017).

6. Brioso, X.: Integrating ISO 21500 guidance on project management, lean construction and PMBOK. *Procedia Engineering*, Vol. 123, pp. 76–84 (2015).
7. Chrissis, M.B.: *CMMI Para el desarrollo, versión 1.3: Guía para la integración de procesos y la mejora de productos*. Editorial Universitaria Ramón Areces, Madrid (2012).
8. SOFTEX: *MPS.BR - Mejora de Proceso del Software Brasileño, Guía General MPS de Software*. (2012).
9. Paula Filho, W. de P.: *Engenharia de software: fundamentos, métodos e padrões*. Grupo Gen - LTC, Rio de Janeiro (2009).
10. Bocco, M.G.; Velthuis, M.G.P.: *Métodos de investigación en ingeniería del software*. Ra-Ma S.A. Editorial y Publicaciones (2014).
11. Pressman, R.S.; Maxim, B.: *Software Engineering: A Practitioner's Approach*. McGraw-Hill Education, New York, NY (2014).
12. Cunha, J.A.O.G.; Moura, H.P.; Vasconcellos, F.J.S.: Decision-making in Software Project Management: A Systematic Literature Review. *Procedia Computer Science*, Vol. 100, pp. 947–954 (2016).
13. Ibrahim, D.: An Overview of Soft Computing. *Procedia Computer Science*, Vol. 102, pp. 34–38 (2016).
14. Burney, S.M.A.; Ali, S.M.; Burney, S.: A survey of soft computing applications for decision making in supply chain management. In: *2017 IEEE 3rd International Conference on Engineering Technologies and Social Sciences (ICETSS)*, pp. 1–6 (2017).
15. Perez, Y.F.; Corona, C.C.; Galdeano, J.L.V.: A New Model Based on Soft Computing for Evaluation and Selection of Software Products. *IEEE Latin America Transactions*, Vol. 16, pp. 1186–1192 (2018).
16. Kosko, B.: Fuzzy cognitive maps. *International Journal of Man-Machine Studies*, Vol. 24, pp. 65–75 (1986).
17. Papageorgiou, E.I.: *Fuzzy Cognitive Maps for Applied Sciences and Engineering: From Fundamentals to Extensions and Learning Algorithms*. Springer Science & Business Media (2014).
18. Jamshidia, A.; Ait-Kadib, D.; Ruizc, A.: An advanced dynamic risk modeling and analysis in projects management. *Journal of Modern Project Management*, Vol. 5, pp. 6–11 (2017).
19. Nápoles, G.; Espinosa, M.L.; Grau, I.; Vanhoof, K.; Bello, R.: Fuzzy Cognitive Maps Based Models for Pattern Classification: Advances and Challenges. In: *Soft Computing Based Optimization and Decision Models*, Springer, Cham, pp. 83–98 (2018).
20. Smarandache, F.: A Unifying Field in Logics: Neutrosophic Logic. In: Perez, M. (ed.) *Philosophy*, American Research Press, pp. 1–141 (1999).
21. Abdel-Basset, M.; Gunasekaran, M.; Mohamed, M.; Smarandache, F.: A novel method for solving the fully neutrosophic linear programming problems. *Neural Computing and Applications*, (2018).
22. Kandasamy, W.B.V.; Smarandache, F.: *Fuzzy Cognitive Maps and Neutrosophic Cognitive Maps*. Xiquan, Phoenix (2003).
23. Devadoss, A.V.; Anand, M.C.J.; Felix, A.: A Study on the Impact of Violent Video-Games playing among Children in Chennai using Neutrosophic Cognitive

Maps (NCMs). *International Journal of Scientific & Engineering Research*, Vol. 3, (2012).
24. William, M.A.; Devadoss, A.V.; Sheeba, J.J.: A study on Neutrosophic cognitive maps (NCMs) by analyzing the Risk Factors of Breast Cancer. *International Journal of Scientific & Engineering Research*, Vol. 4, (2013).
25. Pramanik, S.; Chackrabarti, S.: A Study on Problems of Construction Workers in West Bengal Based on Neutrosophic Cognitive Maps. *International Journal of Innovative Research in Science, Engineering and Technology*, Vol. 2, (2013).
26. Monda, K.; Pramanik, S.: A Study on Problems of Hijras in West Bengal Based on Neutrosophic Cognitive Maps. *Neutrosophic Sets and Systems*, Vol. 5, (2014).
27. Ameirys Betancourt-Vázquez; Maikel Leyva-Vázquez; Karina Perez-Teruel: Neutrosophic cognitive maps for modeling project portfolio interdependencies. *Critical Review*, Vol. x, (2015).
28. Bhutani, K.; Kumar, M.; Garg, G.; Aggarwal, S.: Assessing it Projects Success with Extended Fuzzy Cognitive Maps & Neutrosophic Cognitive Maps in Comparison to Fuzzy Cognitive Maps. *Neutrosophic Sets and Systems*, Vol. 12, (2016).
29. Zadeh, L.A.: Fuzzy sets. *Information and Control*, Vol. 8, pp. 338–353 (1965).
30. Atanassov, K.T.: Intuitionistic fuzzy sets. *Fuzzy Sets and Systems*, Vol. 20, pp. 87–96 (1986).
31. Leyva-Vázquez, M.; Smarandache, F.: *Neutrosofía: Nuevos avances en el tratamiento de la incertidumbre*. (2018).
32. Abdel-Basset, M.; Mohamed, M.: The role of single valued neutrosophic sets and rough sets in smart city: Imperfect and incomplete information systems. *Measurement*, Vol. 124, pp. 47–55 (2018).
33. Wang, H.; Smarandache, F.; Zhang, Y.; Sunderraman, R.: Single valued neutrosophic sets. *Multispace and Multistructure*, Vol. 4, pp. 410–413 (2010).
34. Biswas, P.; Pramanik, S.; Giri, B.: Aggregation of triangular fuzzy neutrosophic set information and its application to multi-attribute decision making. *Neutrosophic Sets and Systems*, Vol. 12, (2016).
35. Abdel-Basset, M.; Mohamed, M.; Smarandache, F.: An Extension of Neutrosophic AHP–SWOT Analysis for Strategic Planning and Decision-Making. *Symmetry*, Vol. 10, p. 116 (2018).
36. Starczewski, J.T.: *Advanced Concepts in Fuzzy Logic and Systems with Membership Uncertainty*. Springer (2012).
37. Bueno, S.; Salmeron, J.L.: Benchmarking main activation functions in fuzzy cognitive maps. *Expert Systems with Applications*, Vol. 36, pp. 5221–5229 (2009).
38. Pérez, P.P.; Pupo, I.P.; Hechavarría, C.C.R.; Lusardo, C.R.; Sosa, R.G.; López, S.T.: Repositorio de datos para investigaciones en gestión de proyectos. *Revista Cubana de Ciencias Informáticas*, Vol. 13, pp. 176–191 (2019).

Estado de la Usabilidad en el Proceso de Desarrollo Global de Software: Un Mapeo Sistemático de Literatura

John W. Castro[1], Efraín R. Fonseca C.[2], Karina Páez[1], and Victor E. Urbina[1]

[1]Departamento de Ingeniería Informática y Ciencias de la Computación, Universidad de Atacama, Copiapó, Chile
[2]Departamento de Ciencias de la Computación, Universidad de las Fuerzas Armadas ESPE, Sangolquí, Ecuador

john.castro@uda.cl
erfonseca@espe.edu.ec
karina.paez.13@alumnos.uda.cl
victor.urbina@postgrados.uda.cl

Resumen *Contexto:* El Desarrollo Global de Software (DGS) es una práctica de la Ingeniería de Software en la cual los equipos de trabajo se encuentran distribuidos geográficamente, muy útil para abaratar los costos de producción y desarrollar sistemas complejos. Sin embargo, ha evidenciado problemas como coordinación, comunicación, control, sincronización y calidad del producto final. Dado que la usabilidad es una característica de calidad clave, su evaluación resulta un factor determinante.*Objetivo:* Este estudio pretende determinar cómo la usabilidad está siendo incorporada en el DGS y a través de qué técnicas. *Método de Investigación:* Se desarrolló un mapeo sistemático de literatura (SMS), para lo cual realizamos una búsqueda en 6 bases de datos digitales (Scopus, IEEE Xplore, ACM Digital Library, ScienceDirect, Web Of Science y Wiley InterScience). Además, realizamos una búsqueda *backward snowballing* a partir de los estudios primarios identificados en el SMS. *Results:* Encontramos un total de 7 estudios primarios (5 estudios con el SMS y 2 más con la búsqueda *backward snowballing*). Sólo uno de los estudios reporta el uso de técnicas de usabilidad (Perfiles de Usuario, Personas, Escenarios de Tareas, Especificaciones de Usabilidad, Prototipos, Información Post-Test y Pensar en Voz Alta). *Conclusiones:* Parece que la usabilidad está siendo poco considerada en el DGS, ya que identificamos en la literatura pocos estudios que reporten experiencias de su incorporación en este tipo de desarrollos. La usabilidad ha quedado relegada a una investigación académica, pero no a la práctica real del DGS.

Keywords: Desarrollo Global de Software, Usabilidad, Systematic Mapping Study

1 Introducción

El desarrollo global de software (DGS) se ha consolidado como uno de los aspectos más relevantes en la investigación y en la práctica de la Ingeniería de

Software en los últimos años [40]. Este tipo de desarrollos se caracteriza porque las partes interesadas se encuentran en diferentes lugares geográficos, y ofrece diferentes beneficios entre los que se encuentran: (i) mejorar la comercialización y la productividad, (ii) reducir los costos y el tiempo de desarrollo, (iii) compartir conocimiento, y (iv) acceder a un grupo más grande y mejor calificado de desarrolladores [40]. Sin embargo, esta distancia geográfica podría ocasionar una falta de comunicación informal (es decir, la que escapa de reuniones y encuentros formales como por ejemplo, la que se hace día a día en el trabajo con colegas al corregir o hacer observaciones sobre el trabajo de otro) [15][7], problemas de intercambio de información [17] y dificultades de gestión del conocimiento [15], entre otros problemas relacionados con la colaboración entre los miembros del equipo que trabajan en el mismo proyecto pero separados por distancias físicas y temporales [37]. La distancia temporal puede ser impuesta por la diferencia en las zonas horarias [49]. Los problemas que se enfrentan debido a la distancia temporal por ejemplo, son la comunicación síncrona restringida y el retraso en la retroalimentación [7].

Como el DGS implica numerosos desafíos, la ejecución y gestión de proyectos de software distribuidos globalmente es una tarea compleja [24] que podría implicar eventualmente la pérdida de control sobre la calidad del software desarrollado por un equipo proveniente de diferentes lugares y culturas, que tienen diferentes habilidades y responsabilidades [40]. Además, debido a que la usabilidad es una característica clave de calidad, su evaluación resulta un factor determinante en la calidad de un producto software [27]. El estándar ISO 9241 [22] define a la usabilidad como el nivel en el que un producto software puede ser usado por determinados usuarios para lograr objetivos concretos con efectividad, eficiencia y satisfacción en un contexto de uso definido. La carencia de usabilidad ocasiona fallas en los productos software que conducen a pérdidas monetarias sustanciales, insatisfacción del usuario, falta de productividad del equipo de desarrollo y pérdida de tiempo [27]. Por tanto, es importante considerar la usabilidad en el proceso de desarrollo.

En la literatura hemos encontrado una gran cantidad de revisiones sistemáticas sobre diferentes aspectos del DGS, como por ejemplo: (i) sus prácticas de gestión del conocimiento [1], (ii) la estimación del esfuerzo [10], (iii) los retos y recomendaciones para diseñar y realizar cursos de ingeniería de software global [11], (iv) factores de éxito y barreras para la mejora de procesos de software [28]. Sin embargo, no tenemos evidencia de la existencia de una revisión sistemática relacionada directamente con la usabilidad en el DGS. En el estudio empírico de Jiménez y otros [25], los autores realizan una revisión sistemática de literatura sobre los desafíos y mejoras a realizar en el DGS en la que clasifican los estudios primarios en términos de los procesos en el ciclo de vida del software y asignan mejoras, analizan los factores de éxito y áreas a mejorar. Esta clasificación es realizada de acuerdo con la norma ISO/IEC 12207 [23], y los resultados mostraron que no existe en la literatura estudios relacionados con la usabilidad en el DGS, que es uno de los procesos definidos por dicha norma. Por tanto, parece ser que la usabilidad es una línea de investigación que no ha sido considerada a fondo.

La presente investigación tiene por objetivo identificar cómo la usabilidad está siendo incorporada en el DGS y comprender cuales técnicas de usabilidad están siendo aplicadas. Además, conocer el nivel de la usabilidad de las herramientas utilizadas en este tipo de desarrollos porque esta característica de calidad es una de las más importantes que debería tener una herramienta de colaboración [25]. Para identificar, evaluar e interpretar toda la investigación relevante disponible en la literatura relacionada con la usabilidad en el DGS realizaremos un mapeo sistemático de literatura [30].

Lo que resta del artículo está organizado de la siguiente manera. La Sección 2 describe el método de investigación. En la Sección 3 se presentan los resultados. En la Sección 4 realizamos propuestas de adaptaciones que faliciten el uso de técnicas de usabilidad en el DGS. La Sección 5 describe las amenazas a la validez. Finalmente, la Sección 6 reporta nuestras conclusiones.

2 Mapeo Sistemático de Literatura

Un SMS es una metodología que consiste en investigar la literatura sobre un área de interés particular, con el objetivo de determinar la naturaleza, el alcance y la cantidad de estudios primarios publicados [9]. Los SMS categorizan los estudios primarios, mostrando una visión sintetizada del área de investigación que está siendo considerada. Para reportar el SMS seguimos las guías de Kitcheham y Charters [29]. El objetivo de nuestro SMS es responder las siguientes preguntas de investigación (RQ de las siglas en inglés de Research Question):

- **RQ1:** ¿Cómo el Desarrollo Global de Software está considerando la usabilidad en su proceso?
- **RQ2:** ¿Qué técnicas de usabilidad están siendo incorporadas en el Desarrollo Global de Software?
- **RQ3:** ¿Cómo es la usabilidad de las herramientas que se utilizan en el Desarrollo Global de Software?

2.1 Bases de Datos y Estrategia de Búsqueda

El SMS se inició con la identificación de las palabras clave y la cadena de búsqueda, construidas a partir de las preguntas de investigación. Inicialmente se realizó una búsqueda tradicional, a partir de la cual se obtuvieron, en consenso con los investigadores participantes algunos trabajos relacionados con las preguntas de investigación. Estos trabajos fueron estudiados para determinar los términos de búsqueda más apropiados para el SMS. Los términos de búsqueda fueron validados y completados por dos investigadores expertos en el área. La cadena de búsqueda está compuesta por dos componentes. El primero relacionado con el DGS y el segundo con la usabilidad. En la Tabla 1 se encuentra la cadena de búsqueda definida.

Las bases de datos utilizadas fueron *Scopus*, *IEEE Xplore*, *ACM Digital Library*, *ScienceDirect*, *Web Of Science (WoS)* y *Wiley InterScience*, la mayoría

Tabla 1: Cadena de Búsqueda

Componentes de la Cadena		
"global software development" **OR** "global software engineering" **OR** "distributed software development" **OR** "distributed software engineering" **OR** "global-SDLC"	**AND**	usability **OR** "user centered design" **OR** "user experience" **OR** "human computer interaction" **OR** "interaction design"

recomendadas por Brereton y otros [9] para la realización de revisiones sistemáticas. La cadena de búsqueda fue adaptada y aplicada a cada una de las BBDD anteriores, fijando como fecha límite de publicación de los artículos el 16 de mayo de 2018. Es importante mencionar que antes de realizar la búsqueda en estas BBDD con la cadena previamente definida, se determinaron los campos que deberían ser utilizados en cada una de ellas. Los campos de búsqueda fueron establecidos de acuerdo con las características propias de cada BBDD. En todas las BBDD el campo utilizado fue el *Abstract*, excepto en *Web of Science* donde se realizo la búsqueda en el campo *Abstract, Title and Keywords*, porque esta base de datos no permite buscar solamente en el resumen. Para determinar los estudios primarios que tienen relación con las preguntas de investigación, se utilizaron los criterios de inclusión y exclusión listados a continuación.

Criterios de inclusión. El artículo: (i) Describe cómo se considera o cómo se debiera considerar la usabilidad en el proceso de DGS, (ii) reporta herramientas utilizadas en el proceso de DGS, midiendo, además, su usabilidad, (iii) describe las actividades, técnicas o métodos utilizados para evaluar la usabilidad de un sistema desarrollado mediante un proceso de DGS.

Criterios de exclusión. El artículo: (i) Se centra en otras dimensiones propias de este tipo de desarrollo, como la coordinación o la sincronización entre los miembros del equipo de trabajo, (ii) reporta una herramienta que es útil para el DGS, pero no evalúa su usabilidad, (iii) define al DGS como un mecanismo para desarrollar software aplicable al mercado global (que se pueda adaptar a diferentes culturas), (iv) esta escrito en un idioma diferente al inglés.

2.2 Selección de Artículos

La selección de estudios se realizó en dos etapas, la primera mediante la aplicación de los criterios de inclusión y exclusión al título, el resumen y las palabras clave de todos los artículos encontrados. Esta labor la realizó cada investigador por separado, y luego en conjunto para ver inconsistencias y discutir las impresiones del aporte de cada artículo. Denominamos a este grupo como "Artículos Preseleccionados". Luego, se eliminaron los duplicados, y de este ejercicio resultaron 8 artículos, grupo al cual se denominó "Artículos Preseleccionados Diferentes". En la segunda etapa, cada investigador realizó una lectura de cada uno de los artículos pertenecientes al grupo de "Artículos Preseleccionados Diferentes", aplicando los criterios de inclusión y exclusión al texto completo. Posteriormente, se realizó una reunión para discutir los desacuerdos en los artículos seleccionados. Finalmente, el nuevo grupo obtenido con estos artículos ha sido denominado "Estudios Primarios". La Tabla 2 presenta un resumen para cada BBDD del número de artículos obtenidos al aplicar la cadena de búsqueda, así como el número de artículos obtenidos en cada uno de los grupos ("Encontrados","Artículos Preseleccionados", "Artículos Preseleccionados Diferentes", "Estudios Primarios").

Dada la baja cantidad de estudios primarios, se decidió realizar una búsqueda complementaria mediante el método *backward snowballing*, de manera que cada investigador por separado analizó las referencias de los 5 estudios primarios [44][46][5][39][14], y replicando el proceso de revisión anterior se obtuvieron 2 artículos [6][25], obteniendo así un total de 7 estudios primarios.

Tabla 2: Número Total de Artículos Obtenidos en cada BBDD

BBDD	Encontrados	Preselecc.	Preselecc. Dftes	Estudios Primarios
IEEE Xplore	6	2	2	2
ACM Digital Libr.	3	2	2	0
ScienceDirect	2	0	0	0
Scopus	20	4	1	1
Web of Science	9	4	2	2
Wiley InterScience	2	0	0	0
TOTAL	**42**	**12**	**7**	**5**

3 Resultados

Esta sección presenta los resultados obtenidos en el SMS, los cuales están divididos en dos partes: Generalidades de los estudios primarios y las respuestas a las preguntas de investigación. La primera parte se encuentra resumida en la Figura 1, la cual presenta una visión sintética de los estudios primarios identificados. En esta figura, los resultados han sido segmentados en dos áreas. La primera (lado izquierdo), consiste básicamente en dos gráficos (parte superior e inferior) de dispersión XY con burbujas en las intersecciones de las categorías tipo-año de publicación (lado izquierdo - parte superior) y tipo de publicación-tópico estudiado (lado izquierdo - parte inferior). Los tipos de publicación son conferencias y revistas. El tamaño de cada burbuja está determinado por el número de estudios primarios que se han clasificado como pertenecientes a cada categoría. La segunda área (lado derecho) de la Figura 1, presenta el número de estudios primarios por año de publicación. Como se observa en la parte superior del lado derecho de la Figura 1, el interés en la usabilidad en el DGS ha sido muy bajo en el periodo 2005-2013, y en los últimos 5 años no encontramos ningún estudio primario.

La segunda parte de esta sección presenta la síntesis del análisis de los estudios primarios, a partir del cual se respondieron las preguntas de investigación.

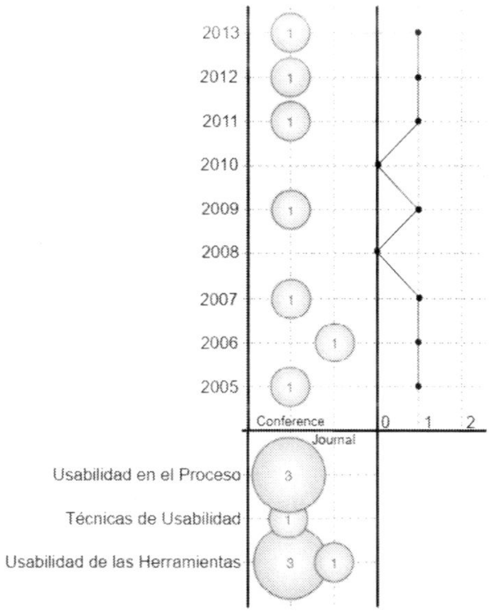

Fig. 1: Mapeo con la distribución de estudios primarios según el tópico, incluyendo tipo y año de publicación.

RQ1: ¿Cómo el Desarrollo Global de Software está considerando la usabilidad en su proceso?

En el trabajo de Milewski y otros [39], esta característica se considera en la medida que el trabajo se divide en dos grandes áreas: HCI/Experiencia de Usuario e Implementación del sistema software. Los autores describen un proyecto en el aula que buscaba brindarles a los estudiantes de pre-grado en ingeniería de software experiencias para ejercer habilidades en el área de HCI. El proyecto proporcionó experiencia en el DGS al formar equipos de estudiantes inscritos en un curso de HCI en la Universidad de Monmouth (Nueva Jersey, EE.UU.) con estudiantes que tomaron un curso de desarrollo de software en la Universidad de Atilim (Ankara, Turquía). Los integrantes del proyecto siguieron las siguientes etapas.

- Perfil de Usuario/Personas: Definir las características del usuario de la aplicación con base en discusiones realizadas en el aula.
- Tareas Críticas: Definir un conjunto de tareas que representan el trabajo más importante y/o más frecuente realizado por los usuarios.
- Metas de Usabilidad/Experiencia del Usuario: Definir aspectos medibles de la usabilidad y/o la experiencia del usuario.
- Modelo Conceptual del Usuario: Realizar dos modelos conceptuales de usuario diferentes para la aplicación. Por ejemplo, podrían ser geo-espaciales, tabulares, gráficos, etc.; podrían basarse en actividades de búsqueda, exploración o conversación.
- Diseño de dos Prototipos de Baja Fidelidad: Crear un prototipo de baja fidelidad no interactivo de cada uno de los modelos conceptuales del usuario.

– "Evaluación rápida y sucia": Realizar una entrevista con una persona a quien se le muestra los dos prototipos de baja fidelidad, se le da parte del contexto de la tarea y se le pide su opinión sobre la utilidad y usabilidad de ambos prototipos.
– Diseño de un Prototipo de Mayor Fidelidad: De acuerdo con los resultados del paso anterior, se selecciona uno de los modelos mentales del usuario y se crea un prototipo de mayor fidelidad utilizando una herramienta de diseño (AxureTM o DroidDrawTM). Comparado con el primer prototipo, este prototipo fue mejor en claridad, estética e integridad en cuanto al contenido del diseño, aún cuando la mayoría de cosas no funcionaban. Este prototipo mostró no sólo visualizaciones estáticas, sino también cómo se esperaba que el sistema reaccionara a las interacciones de los usuarios.
– Prueba de Escenario: Utilizando el prototipo final, realizar una prueba de escenario con dos o más usuarios.
– Iterar al menos una vez: Se analizan los problemas descubiertos en la etapa anterior, se modifica el diseño y se realiza de nuevo la prueba con dos usuarios adicionales.

Dado que las etapas anteriores corresponden a una variante del modelo de Ciclo de Vida de la Ingeniería de Usabilidad propuesto por Mayhew (1999), son actividades ampliamente aceptadas.

Douglas [14] propone un prototipo de un repositorio global de conocimiento de pruebas de usabilidad, y utilizarlo para ayudar a validar mejor las pautas y patrones de diseño. En el estudio empírico realizado por Jiménez y otros [25], los autores realizan una revisión de literatura cuyo objetivo consiste en identificar los mejores procedimientos, modelos y estrategias empleados en el DGS, y determinar los factores de mejora más importantes para los principales problemas encontrados. En esta investigación, los autores clasifican los temas encontrados de acuerdo a la norma ISO 12207. Esta norma establece las actividades que pueden llevarse a cabo durante el ciclo de vida del software, que se agrupan en: Procesos principales, procesos de soporte y procesos generales. Dentro de esos procesos de soporte, se encuentra la usabilidad. Los resultados obtenidos indican que los mayores esfuerzos se centran en los recursos humanos, la gestión organizativa, la infraestructura, la gestión de proyectos, y los autores no han encontrado trabajos que estudien la usabilidad.

RQ2: ¿Qué técnicas de usabilidad están siendo incorporadas en el Desarrollo Global de Software?

De los estudios primarios, solo uno [39] reporta información para dar respuesta a esta pregunta. A continuación, describimos las técnicas de usabilidad que identificamos han sido incorporadas en el DGS.

– Perfil de Usuario/Personas. Son usadas dos técnicas para el análisis del usuario: Perfil de Usuario y Personas. El objetivo de estas técnicas es definir aquel usuario potencial, para diseñar la aplicación con esa persona en mente.
– Escenarios de Tareas. A partir de la discusión de los miembros del equipo de HCI se realizan 2-3 escenarios clave para uso de la aplicación propuesta.

- Especificaciones de Usabilidad. Se realiza una lista de 2 a 4 elementos que se consideren metas medibles que definen la usabilidad y/o la experiencia del usuario (dependiendo de la aplicación) [39].
- Prototipado. De esta técnica se aplican dos de sus variaciones: Prototipo de papel y prototipo de alta fidelidad.
- Información Post-Test. A un usuario se le da parte del contexto de una tarea, y en una entrevista se le piden sus opiniones sobre la utilidad y usabilidad de los prototipos de baja fidelidad.
- Pensar en Voz Alta. Se le asignan a los usuarios tareas comunes que deben realizar, y se les pide que piensen en voz alta mientras las realizan. Esto permitió a los integrantes del grupo de HCI buscar cuellos de botella y confusiones en el uso de la aplicación.

RQ3: ¿Cómo es la usabilidad de las herramientas que se utilizan en el Desarrollo Global de Software?

Beecham y otros [6], proponen una herramienta llamada GT-DSS para apoyar el proceso de toma de decisiones en equipos distribuidos globalmente y realizan su evaluación de usabilidad, de la cual obtuvieron una retroalimentación altamente positiva. Luego, al año siguiente, Beecham y otros [5] reportan los resultados de una segunda evaluación de usabilidad, en la que 12 expertos en GSD evaluaron el sistema. Cada experto probó individualmente y completó un breve cuestionario de usabilidad. Los expertos identificaron muchas áreas que podrían mejorarse. En la evaluación, participaron tanto expertos como investigadores, brindando diferentes perspectivas sobre lo que se debería hacer para mejorar la herramienta. Esta herramienta ha sido diseñada para ayudar a los administradores de software a examinar recomendaciones en la literatura sobre el DGS y el GTM (Modelo de Equipo Global, por sus siglas en inglés). El GT-DSS captura detalles sobre la organización de desarrollo y adapta las prácticas de GTM para que se ajusten a necesidades empresariales y organizativas específicas.

En el trabajo de Seyff y otros [44], los autores evalúan la usabilidad de una aplicación móvil denominada ARENA-M que hace uso del enfoque *EasyWinWin* (propuesto en la misma investigación), basado en el modelo de negociación *Win-Win* [8]. ARENA-M es una aplicación web ASP.NET que utiliza un navegador móvil, y permite a un equipo de *stakeholders* obtener y negociar requisitos de manera distribuida y asíncrona, guiándolos durante la elaboración de acuerdos mutuamente satisfactorios (por ejemplo, mediante el cálculo automático de los resultados de una votación). En su evaluación de usabilidad, los autores compararon esta herramienta con su par para equipos de escritorio, y considerando que son entornos totalmente distintos, el estudio mostró que no hay diferencias significativas en cuanto a usabilidad.

EGRET es una herramienta propuesta por Sinha y otros [46] que tiene como objetivo apoyar los requerimientos de comunicación y gestión en equipos distribuidos. Los usuarios potenciales de la herramienta incluyen a analistas de negocio y arquitectos que interactúan con el cliente y obtienen requisitos de alto nivel. Además, incluye a ingenieros de sistemas, evaluadores y otros miembros de equipos de desarrollo distribuidos que ayudan a refinar estos requisitos y definen criterios de validación para los mismos. Para evaluar su usabilidad, se realiza la presentación de un prototipo a varios grupos de usuarios potenciales, incluidos profesionales de IBM (la organización a la cual pertenecen los investigadores), obteniendo críticas muy positivas.

4 Propuestas de Adaptaciones para Facilitar el Uso de Técnicas de Usabilidad en el DGS

La incorporación de técnicas de usabilidad en los procesos de desarrollo no es una tarea fácil. Existen trabajos que estudian, por ejemplo cómo incorporar la usabilidad en los desarrollos ágiles [34][35][36], y en *Open Source Software* (OSS) [32][33][31]. Estos trabajos concluyen que es necesario reconceptualizar las técnicas de usabilidad bajo el enfoque y características de cada uno de estos tipos de desarrollo. Para el caso del DGS, realizar esta reconceptualización también requiere identificar cuáles son los impedimentos que presentan las técnicas de usabilidad para su incorporación. Estos impedimentos están relacionados directamente con las características del proceso de DGS. El DGS se caracteriza principalmente por la distribución geográfica de: (i) los equipos de desarrollo [16][41][19][25], (ii) *stakeholders* [37], y (iii) usuarios [18]. La participación de los usuarios es fundamental en algunas técnicas de usabilidad pero, como comentamos anteriormente, en el DGS los usuarios están distribuidos geográficamente. Existen dos grupos de técnicas donde son necesarios los usuarios.

En el primer grupo, se encuentran aquellas técnicas donde es necesaria la participación del usuario, pero donde no se requiere que varios usuarios participen simultáneamente, como es el caso por ejemplo de las técnicas grabación de video [20] e información post-test [12]. La grabación de video es una técnica de recolección de datos que permite capturar todo lo que ocurre mientras el usuario realiza una tarea con la aplicación que se pretende evaluar [20]. La técnica información post-test consiste de una entrevista que se realiza a cada usuario después de finalizar la prueba de usabilidad. La entrevista tiene por objetivo solicitar al usuario retroalimentación y sugerencias tanto de la prueba realizada como de la aplicación que estaba siendo evaluada [12]. Con el objetivo de solucionar este impedimento, proponemos que la participación de los usuarios se realice de manera remota, por ejemplo dando su opinión en foros o a través de chats o correos electrónicos a los desarrolladores, y realizando pruebas al software -desde su casa- antes de su liberación.

En el segundo grupo, encontramos las técnicas que exigen que varios usuarios se encuentren físicamente reunidos en el mismo lugar. Las técnicas Focus Groups [42] y tormenta de ideas visual [43] son ejemplos de técnicas de este tipo. En un focus groups, se reúne a un grupo de entre seis y nueve usuarios para discutir nuevos conceptos e identificar temas relevantes en un período de unas dos horas. Las reuniones permiten evaluar las necesidades de los usuarios y sus sensaciones, tanto antes de que sea diseñada la interfaz de usuario como después de un tiempo de uso. La tormenta de ideas visual permite explorar diseños alternativos y validarlos en reuniones donde participan los usuarios. Una vez creados los diseños iniciales, las ideas pueden ser desarrolladas en mayor profundidad con la elaboración de cartulinas que representan el diseño. Estos diseños son evaluados con los usuarios [43]. En estos casos (es decir, técnicas que requiere la participación de varios usuarios reunidos físicamente), proponemos que las reuniones sean: (i) realizadas virtualmente a través de chats, (ii) sean reemplazadas por una wiki, o (iii) o sean llevadas a cabo *online*, utilizando herramientas que permitan la comunicación de texto, voz y vídeo sobre internet. Es importante mencionar que estas propuestas de transformación han sido realizadas sobre técnicas de usabilidad que se han incorporado exitosamente en algunos proyectos OSS [48][33]. Como en OSS el desarrollo es distribuido al igual que en el DGS, consideramos que estas propuestas también serían de utilidad para aplicar técnicas en este tipo de desarrollos.

5 Amenazas a la Validez

Esta sección provee una discusión sobre la validez de los resultados presentados. En cuanto a la validez interna, la cadena de búsqueda constituye en sí una amenaza a la validez, dado que el DGS es un concepto que se ha utilizado en años anteriores para designar el proceso de desarrollo dedicado a producir software para un mercado globalizado, y por esta misma razón, la cadena de búsqueda ha proporcionado artículos relacionados a esta área y no exclusivamente a la que es de nuestro interés. Para reducir esta amenaza hemos incluido otros sinónimos en la cadena de búsqueda para referirnos a este tipo de desarrollos (es decir DGS). Además, puede se hayan dejado fuera artículos relevantes al filtrar por título y resumen, dado que no evidenciaban información útil en dichos campos de acuerdo a los criterios de inclusión definidos.

Con respecto a la validez externa, es decir, la posibilidad de generalizar los resultados, este trabajo es limitado en dos aspectos. El primero es que los pocos artículos encontrados en nuestro estudio empírico, pueden no ser suficientes para generalizar los hallazgos. Es esta la razón por la cual se decidió emplear la búsqueda por *backward snowballing*. El segundo es el año de publicación de los artículos, cerca del 60% tiene 9 o más años de haber sido publicados. Para contrarrestar estos inconvenientes, hemos utilizando una gran cantidad de bases de datos en nuestro SMS. Además, hemos realizado un *backward snowballing*. Sin embargo, es posible que la cantidad y el año de publicación de los estudios primarios sea reflejo de la realidad, en la medida de que no existan prácticas recientes relacionadas con la usabilidad en el DGS.

6 Conclusiones

Este trabajo describe el estado actual de la usabilidad en el DGS. Encontramos un total de 7 estudios primarios referentes a esta temática. A pesar de que no se limitó el rango de años que comprendió el SMS, el número de estudios primarios identificados fue muy bajo. Identificamos algunas técnicas de usabilidad que están siendo incorporadas en una variante del modelo de ciclo de vida de la ingeniería de usabilidad [38]. Estas técnicas son: Perfiles de usuario, Personas, Escenarios de Tareas, Especificaciones de Usabilidad, Prototipado, Información Post-Test, y Pensar en Voz Alta. Es importante mencionar que estas técnicas de usabilidad han sido incorporadas en el contexto de una asignatura de Ingeniería de Software. Sin embargo, ilustra que es posible la aplicación de técnicas de usabilidad en el DGS cuando los equipos se encuentran distribuidos.

Las características del DGS presentan ciertos desafíos para incorporar técnicas de usabilidad. En este trabajo, identificamos que la distribución geográfica de los equipos de desarrollo, y los usuarios es un impedimento para aplicar ciertas técnicas que requieren de la presencia física de los usuarios. Además, estas técnicas no están pensadas para ser incorporadas en este tipo de desarrollos. Consideramos, que una posible solución a este problema consiste en la reconceptualización de las técnicas de usabilidad. Tenemos evidencias de que esta reconceptualización ha permitido aplicar ciertas técnicas de usabilidad en otros tipos de desarrollo (por ejemplo, OSS).

El DGS está expuesto a una gran variedad de riesgos. Uno de los más grandes es la pérdida de control sobre la calidad del software, y dado que la usabilidad es una característica clave de calidad, su evaluación resulta un factor determinante en la calidad de un sistema. Sin embargo, este trabajo ha detectado que la usabilidad no parece tener la relevancia que conlleva ya que, como comentábamos anteriormente, son pocos los estudios que se centran en ella y en los últimos 5 años nuestro SMS no encontró estudios primarios. Además, en este ámbito, la usabilidad ha quedado relegada a una investigación académica, pero no a la práctica real del DGS. Creemos que la baja cantidad de estudios primarios identificados se debe a que el DGS está dirigiendo sus esfuerzos en intentar resolver otras problemáticas relacionadas con: (i) la comunicación [26][37], (ii) la gestión de requisitos [2][21], (iii) la asignación de tareas [45][4], y (iv) la gestión del conocimiento [3][47][13].

Debido al bajo interés en el estudio de la usabilidad en el DGS, se hace necesario realizar más esfuerzos de investigación. Consideramos que estos esfuerzos deben estar orientados a: (i) identificar las prácticas o técnicas de usabilidad que están siendo incorporadas en las empresas que siguen este tipo de desarrollos, (ii) determinar de qué manera están evaluando la usabilidad de los sistemas software que desarrollan, (iii) identificar que otras características del DGS pueden dificultar la incorporación de técnicas de usabilidad, (iv) analizar conjuntamente los tipos de desarrollo OSS y DGS puesto que comparten características similares que dificultan la gestión de usabilidad, de esta manera se dispondría de una mayor base de estudios primarios para identificar técnicas de usabilidad incorporables a casos de desarrollo distribuido como el DGS.

Referencias

1. de Aguiar Beninca, R., Huzita, E., Galdamez, E., Lapasini Leal, G.C., Balancieri, R., Massago, Y.: Knowledge management practices in gsd - a systematic literature review update. ICEIS 2015 - 17th International Conference on Enterprise Information Systems, Proceedings 2, 365–373 (2015)

2. Alferillo, V., Lund, M.I., Matturro, G.: Use case technique for requirements modeling in distributed development environments: A mapping study. In: 2015 Latin American Computing Conference (CLEI). pp. 1–9 (2015)
3. Anwar, R., Rehman, M., Wang, K.S., Amin, A., Akbar, R.: Conceptual framework for implementation of knowledge sharing in global software development organizations. In: 2017 IEEE Symposium on Computer Applications Industrial Electronics (ISCAIE). pp. 174–178 (2017)
4. Aslam, W., Ijaz, F.: A quantitative framework for task allocation in distributed agile software development. IEEE Access 6, 15380–15390 (2018)
5. Beecham, S., Carroll, N., Noll, J.: A decision support system for global team management: Expert evaluation. In: 2012 IEEE Seventh International Conference on Global Software Engineering Workshops. pp. 12–17 (2012)
6. Beecham, S., Noll, J., Richardson, I., Dhungana, D.: A decision support system for global software development. In: 2011 IEEE Sixth International Conference on Global Software Engineering Workshop. pp. 48–53 (2011)
7. Bird, C., Nagappan, N., Devanbu, P., Gall, H., Murphy, B.: Does distributed development affect software quality? an empirical case study of windows vista. In: 2009 IEEE 31st International Conf. on Software Engineering. pp. 518–528 (2009)
8. Boehm, B., Bose, P., Horowitz, E., Lee, M.J.: Software requirements negotiation and renegotiation aids: A theory-w based spiral approach. In: 1995 17th International Conference on Software Engineering. pp. 243–243 (1995)
9. Brereton, P., Kitchenham, B.A., Budgen, D., Turner, M., Khalil, M.: Lessons from applying the systematic literature review process within the software engineering domain. J. Syst. Softw. 80(4), 571–583 (2007)
10. Britto, R., Freitas, V., Mendes, E., Usman, M.: Effort estimation in global software development: A systematic literature review. In: 2014 IEEE 9th International Conference on Global Software Engineering. pp. 135–144 (2014)
11. Clear, T., Beecham, S., Barr, J., Daniels, M., McDermott, R., Oudshoorn, M., Savickaite, A., Noll, J.: Challenges and recommendations for the design and conduct of global software engineering courses: A systematic review. In: Proceedings of the 2015 ITiCSE on Working Group Reports. pp. 1–39. ITICSE-WGR '15, ACM, New York, NY, USA (2015)
12. Constantine, L.L., Lockwood, L.A.D.: Software for Use: A Practical Guide to the Models and Methods of Usage-centered Design. ACM Press/Addison-Wesley Publishing Co., New York, USA (1999)
13. Dorairaj, S., Noble, J., Malik, P.: Knowledge management in distributed agile software development. In: 2012 Agile Conference. pp. 64–73 (2012)
14. Douglas, I.: Testing object management (TOM): A prototype for usability knowledge management in global software. In: Usability and Internationalization. HCI and Culture. pp. 297–305. Springer Berlin Heidelberg, Berlin, Heidelberg (2007)
15. Ebert, C.: Blocks and enablers for global soft. engineering projects. In: 2006 IEEE International Conf. on Global Software Engineering (ICGSE'06). pp. 29–29 (2006)
16. Espinosa, J., Slaughter, S., Kraut, R., Herbsleb, J.: Team knowledge and coordination in geographically distributed software development. J. Manage. Inf. Syst. 24(1), 135–169 (2007)
17. Gumm, D.C.: Distribution dimensions in software development projects: A taxonomy. IEEE Software 23(5), 45–51 (2006)
18. Hanisch, J., Corbitt, B.J.: Requirements engineering during global software development: Some impediments to the requirements engineering process - a case study. In: European Conference on Information Systems (ECIS). pp. 1–13 (2004)

19. Herbsleb, J.D., Moitra, D.: Global software development. IEEE Software 18(2), 16–20 (2001)
20. Hix, D., Hartson, H.R.: Developing User Interfaces: Ensuring Usability Through Product & Process. John Wiley & Sons, Inc., New York, NY, USA (1993)
21. Hussain, W., Buchan, J., Clear, T.: Managing requirements in globally distributed cots customization. In: 2014 IEEE International Conference on Global Software Engineeering Workshops. pp. 33–38 (2014)
22. ISO-9241-11: Ergonomic Requirements for Office Work with Visual Display Terminals (VDTs)-Part 11: Guidelines on Usability. ISO (1998)
23. ISO/IEC-12207:2002: AMENDMENT 1: Information technology-Software life cycle processes. ISO, International Standard Organization (2002)
24. Jain, R., Suman, U.: A systematic literature review on global software development life cycle. SIGSOFT Softw. Eng. Notes 40(2), 1–14 (2015)
25. Jiménez, M., Piattini, M., Vizcaíno, A.: Challenges and improvements in distributed soft. development: A systematic review. Adv. Soft. Eng. pp. 3:1–16 (2009)
26. Jusoh, Y.Y., Nor, R.N.H., Mahmood, B.A., Wafeeq, M.T., Ali, M.A., Jusoh, M.N.B.: Communication management in global software development projects. In: 2018 Fourth International Conference on Information Retrieval and Knowledge Management (CAMP). pp. 1–7 (2018)
27. Kabir, M.A., Rehman, M.U., Majumdar, S.I.: An analytical and comparative study of software usability quality factors. In: 2016 7th IEEE International Conference on Software Engineering and Service Science (ICSESS). pp. 800–803 (2016)
28. Khan, A.A., Keung, J.: Systematic review of success factors and barriers for software process improvement in global software development. IET Software 10(5), 125–135 (2016)
29. Kitchenham, B., Charters, S.: Guidelines for performing Systematic Literature Reviews in Software Engineering. Tech. rep., Keele University and Department of Computer Science University of Durham (2007)
30. Kitchenham, B.: Procedures for Performing Systematic Reviews. Tech. rep., Keele University (2004)
31. Llerena, L., Rodriguez, N., Castro, J., Acuña, S.: How to incorporate a usability technique in the open source software development process. In: Proceedings of the International Conference on Software Engineering and Knowledge Engineering, SEKE. pp. 182–187 (2018)
32. Llerena, L., Castro, J.W., Acuña, S.T.: A pilot empirical study of applying a usability technique in an open source software project. Information and Software Technology 106, 122 – 125 (2019)
33. Llerena, L., Rodriguez, N., Castro, J.W., Acuña, S.T.: Adapting usability techniques for application in open source software: A multiple case study. Information and Software Technology 107, 48 – 64 (2019)
34. Magües, D.A., Castro, J.W., Acuna, S.T.: Hci usability techniques in agile development. In: 2016 IEEE International Conference on Automatica (ICA-ACCA). pp. 1–7 (2016)
35. Magües, D.A., Castro, J.W., Acuña, S.T.: Usability in agile development: A systematic mapping study. In: 2016 XLII Latin American Computing Conference (CLEI). pp. 677–684 (2016)
36. Magües, D., Castro, J., Acuña, S.: Requirements engineering related usability techniques adopted in agile development processes. In: Proceedings of the International Conference on Software Engineering and Knowledge Engineering, SEKE. pp. 537–542 (2016)

37. Malik, B., Faroom, S., Ali, M., Shehzad, N., Yousaf, S., Saleem, H.: Geographical distance and communication challenges in global software development: A review. International Journal of Advanced Computer Science and Applications 9(5), 406–414 (2018)
38. Mayhew, D.J.: The Usability Engineering Lifecycle: A Practitioner's Handbook for User Interface Design. Morgan Kaufmann Publishers Inc., San Francisco, CA, USA, 1st edn. (1999)
39. Milewski, A.E., Serce, F.C., Swigger, K.: Quantitative and qualitative analysis of globally distributed team collaboration in design and development of software. In: 2013 6th International Conference on Human System Interactions (HSI). pp. 443–450 (2013)
40. Misra, S., Adewumi, A., Maskeliūnas, R., Damaševičius, R., Cafer, F.: Unit testing in global software development environment. In: Data Science and Analytics. pp. 309–317. Springer Singapore, Singapore (2018)
41. Monasor, M.J., Vizcaino, A., Piattini, M., Caballero, I.: Preparing students and engineers for global software development: A systematic review. In: 2010 5th IEEE International Conference on Global Software Engineering. pp. 177–186 (2010)
42. Nielsen, J.: Usability Engineering. Morgan Kaufmann Publishers Inc., San Francisco, CA, USA (1993)
43. Preece, J., Rogers, Y., Sharp, H., Benyon, D., Holland, S., Carey, T.: Human-Computer Interaction. Addison Wesley, 1st edn. (1994)
44. Seyff, N., Hoyer, C., Kroiher, E., Grunbacher, P.: Enhancing GSS-based requirements negotiation with distributed and mobile tools. In: 14th IEEE International Workshops on Enabling Technologies: Infrastructure for Collaborative Enterprise (WETICE'05). pp. 87–92 (2005)
45. Simão Filho, M., Pinheiro, P.R., Albuquerque, A.B.: Analysis of task allocation in distributed software development through a hybrid methodology of verbal decision analysis. Journal of Software: Evolution and Process 29(7) (2017)
46. Sinha, V., Sengupta, B., Chandra, S.: Enabling collaboration in distributed requirements management. IEEE Software 23(5), 52–61 (2006)
47. Stapel, K., Schneider, K.: Managing knowledge on communication and information flow in global software projects. Expert Systems 31(3), 234–252 (2014)
48. Terry, M., Kay, M., Lafreniere, B.: Perceptions and Practices of Usability in the Free/Open Source Software (FOSS) Community. In: Proceedings of the 28th Conf. on Human Factors in Computing Systems. pp. 999–1008. CHI'10, ACM (2010)
49. Ågerfalk, P.J., Fitzgerald, B., Holmström, H., Lings, B., Lundell, B., Conchúir, E.Ó.: A framework for considering opportunities and threats in distributed software development. In: Proceedings of the International Workshop on Distributed Software Development. Austrian Computer Society. pp. 47–61 (2005)

Towards a healthier collaboration at the business-development interface

Caique Garutti Moreira and Breno Bernard Nicolau de França

Instituto de Computação - Universidade Estadual de Campinas
caiquemor@gmail.com e breno@ic.unicamp.br

Abstract. Many studies have been conducted on the collaboration between software development and operation deployment (DevOps), but few have considered the interface between business strategy and software development (BizDev). The lack of a good connection between business and development may lead to problems such as misunderstanding of requirements, mismatch of expectations, fail to fulfill deadlines and waste of time and resources. Motivated by that, this study aims at defining roles, responsibilities, and practices concerned with the business-development interface, as well as assessing positive impacts of some practices and drawbacks of the disconnection, so that we can define directions on how to create a healthy interface. For this research, we performed a literature review to gather information on how agile methods have defined roles that act on this interface and to gather information on how practices related to this interface can impact on a project. Aiming a practical understanding regarding the impacts of this interface on real enterprises and organizations, we conducted qualitative research based on interviews. We performed a set of interviews in the IT department of a university, for which the customer was the administrative sector. The interviews were further analyzed using Grounded Theory practices. Relevant practices inserted on the business-development interface stood out, such as customer-on-site, production support, continuous maintenance of requirement lists, and frequent re-prioritization of requirements. We envision further investigations at other organizations targeting different cultures and profiles.

Keywords: Agile Software Development, BizDev, business-development interface.

1 Introduction

As business models evolve and organizations need to adapt to the dynamic and fast time-to-market, software development methodologies also need to be improved regarding value delivery capability and meeting of customer expectations. For doing so, organizations are targeting a wider and healthier collaboration among its functional areas. In this context, the interface between business and development includes all the interactions between the IT and the business sectors within an organization and its partners. While the well-disseminated term DevOps is used to describe the downstream collaboration between software development and its operational deployment and administration [13], the term BizDev can be used to name the upstream collaboration between business strategy and development [10].

The business sector of an organization may be composed of teams focused on content, requirement, administration and even by the final customer. The business area in this interface behaves as a customer for the technology area, establishing demands, specifications, deadlines, and expectations. This way, the technology area acts as the productive force, but it is not limited to it, being possible for it to participate alongside with the business area in activities such as requirements prioritization and establishment of deadlines.

One direct consequence of bad performance at the business-development interface is communication problems, leading to a bad understanding of requirements, mismatch of expectations, fail to fulfill deadlines and waste of time and resources.

Motivated by this scenario, this study aims at gathering information that allow a better definition and categorization of the business-development interface, by raising information on the roles that are involved on this interface, together with their responsibilities and adopted practices. Another objective regards the analysis on how efficient are the practices adopted by companies and organizations regarding this interface, qualitatively comparing them, taking into account the different practices adopted and their level of importance to the interface.

The knowledge resulting from this study should benefit practitioners from both business and development areas, allowing them to achieve a better comprehension of the existing relations around them. Through this understanding they should be able to improve the projects they work on, either by directly applying the analyzed practices inside their teams or by disseminating the understanding and critical insights acquired to the rest of the company or organization.

The remaining sections are organized as follows: Section 2 presents the adopted research methods for this study. Section 3 presents the theoretical foundation used as a base for defining the goals of the qualitative study and how it would be conducted. Section 4 describes the results that emerged from the interviews performed for the qualitative study. Section 5 presents the limitations and threats to validity. Finally, Section 6 presents the concluding remarks and future work.

2 Research Methods

This study is organized into two phases: a literature review and the application of qualitative research through a set of interviews, with further analysis applying Grounded Theory procedures [9].

2.1 Literature Review

Initially, we performed an *ad-hoc* literature review regarding agile methodologies and their definitions for roles, responsibilities, and practices related to the business-development interface. The first analyzed works discuss practices and responsibilities present in different agile methodologies, especially in Scrum

[1][2][4][6]. We decided not focusing on any particular methodology, but rather focus on collecting what each one defines for the interface between business and development, identifying differences and similarities.

Additionally, we analyzed case studies conducted on different companies [3][7][8]. From these studies, it was possible to raise instances on the importance of the BizDev interface and also about the effectiveness of the applied practices. We synthesized and discussed the reviewed literature (see Section 3) to define the scope of this study as well as the objective and script of the interviews.

2.2 Qualitative Research

After the literature review, we began the qualitative study by defining a broad research goal, so it could be sent along with other research details as an invitation to organizations interested in collaborating with data collection (interviews). Such goal summarizes the focus of the study, allowing companies and organizations that accepted to participate to identify practitioners to contribute. Therefore, this study aims at raising practices adopted by those who work at the interface between business and development and identifying their roles and responsibilities, as well as their relationship with the adopted practices. Another goal is to analyze how the adopted practices contribute to a healthier relationship between business and development.

Next, we worked on the development of the interview scripts, based on [5]. Given the research goal, it is important to interview both technical and business profiles. For this reason, two distinct scripts were developed. The scripts (Appendix A) contain open questions, some in common for both profiles and some specific for each area.

The case reported in this paper is the IT department of a public university. For this case, we contacted the director of the IT department and sent the scripts and a term of consent to the interviewed people.

At the time the interviews were conducted, the entire IT department was working on the migration of a legacy COBOL system. This migration task force had been ongoing for several months and changed the way teams organized their tasks. Before the migration, all teams followed an adaptation of the Scrum agile methodology, organizing their work on 2-week sprints. Each sprint contained a set of stories that had been scored during planning poker sessions. The teams also attended the regular meetings defined by Scrum: plannings, retrospectives, and dailies. In order to track the status of the sprint and to estimate if all the stories would be completed before the deadline, the teams used a burndown chart. When the migration task force started, they stopped following the Scrum methodology and started using Kanban. The sprints with fixed story sets were removed, and all teams started working on continuous releases: code would be deployed to production as soon as it was tested, without following specific timelines.

A total of six interviews was conducted. The interviewed group is composed of three requirement analysts, two development leaders, and one regular developer. All the interviews followed a semi-structured format, in which the script acted as guide, but was not followed rigorously. The interviews took 35 minutes on average.

All interviews were recorded and transcripted. The transcriptions were using Grounded Theory procedures [9]. During the open coding, segments of the interview were selected and associated with specific codes to better organize and relate relevant information. Then, codes were all categorized iteratively. Better categorization is development on the axial coding [9]. The QDA Miner Lite tool supports the analysis of the transcribed interviews.

3 Theoretical Foundation

3.1 Agile Roles, Responsibilities and Practices

We analyzed different agile development methodologies as described in [2]. We aimed at identifying roles inserted in the BizDev interface, as well as their practices and responsibilities. Not all methodologies analyzed defined roles involved at this interface, and we identified roles with similar responsibilities but different names.

In eXtreme Programming, the Customer is responsible for writing stories, functional tests, defining when a requirement is satisfied and prioritizing requirements. Scrum's Product Owner is responsible for the product backlog. It should make stories visible to everyone through the product backlog, estimate delivery time for backlog items and translate backlog items into a definition of features to be developed. The Customer and the Team should participate in the creation and maintenance of the Product Backlog.

The Crystal methodology defines the Business Expert, which should possess knowledge about the business context, being responsible for the business plan. It should keep track of which requirements are changing and which are stable. The Business Analyst-Designer should communicate and negotiate with users, and specify requirements and interfaces based on that communication. In Feature Driven Development, the Domain Expert is a role that can be performed by a user, customer, sponsor or business analyst. The Domain Expert should possess knowledge about what are the goals for every requirement, and pass this knowledge to the developers in order to ensure that they will deliver a good system.

Finally, Dynamic System Development Method defines the Ambassador User, which is responsible for bringing knowledge from the user community to the project. It should also disseminate information from the project to the user community and guarantee that enough feedback is obtained from it. The Visionary should guarantee that essential requirements are discovered at the beginning of the project and that the project is always fulfilling these essential requirements.

3.2 Impacts of business involvement on the development process

When requirements are solely created by the business people, they tend to be written in a way developers cannot comprehend, creating the necessity of further clarification [3]. Also, developers may encounter technical constraints that make the complete fulfillment of a requirement unfeasible, creating the need for reporting the problem to the business area and waiting for a decision. This scenario indicates that development projects would benefit from good and constant communication between business and technology teams. However, business people tend to be constantly busy and unavailable, creating large waiting times for the development teams, even leading to leading to situations when the development team is forced to make product decisions without business basis to meet deadlines [3].

Other impacts from having the business area neglecting participation in the development process regard problems with requirement prioritization and limited feedback [3]. In some cases, it is not possible to deliver all requirements on the agreed deadline, so it is needed to focus on delivering as much value as possible. If the development team lacks business knowledge needed to prioritize tasks, the business area should provide support and be available for the development process. When there is no such support, business people neglect participation at important meetings like presentations at the end of sprints, limiting the provided feedback, and decreasing the improvement capacity of a product [3].

According to Beck [11], in eXtreme Programming, a "real customer" should be interested in the project, making itself available for the development team to answer questions and solve disputes. This practice is described as "on-site customer". The impact of having the customer on site was studied on [4]. Perceived benefits of this practice include the transfer of business knowledge to the development team, faster feedback from the customer during the development process and increased quality to the product [4]. However, the benefits of having the customer on-site were only perceived on the team in which the customer behaved actively and was more involved in the development process [4]. When the customer behaves passively, the price of applying this practice was too high and it did not pay out [4].

Two reasons leading to little involvement from the business area on the development process are traditional project organization and isolation of development budget under the IT sector [3]. On traditional project organization, the business area participates actively only on the initial phase, creating many documents containing requirements, definitions, and deadlines. After such initial phase is finished, the business area almost withdraws from the process, understanding its participation on the project is over. When the cost of paying extra hours for developers is paid only by the IT sector, the business area feels less responsible and sympathetic when a project fails, since it had not invested resources on the development process [3].

Making business people involved in more project stages helps to create a sense of ownership and belonging about the project and towards the development team [3]. As result, people from the business area start to feel like they have more control about the project progress and that the project becomes more predictable. For this reason, they are more eager to collaborate with the development team [3].

4 Results

4.1 Organizing the BizDev Interface

Based on similarities between the responsibilities of the analyzed roles (Section 3.1), we proposed three distinct fronts. A front means a set of strongly connected practices and responsibilities. The fronts do not have responsibility intersections among them, but one role may be associated with more than one front, which means that one role may possess responsibilities of more than one front. The union of the responsibilities of the three fronts comprises all the responsibilities gathered during the analysis that are involved in the BizDev interface.

Business Tracker. Comprises all activities regarding the creation and continuous maintenance of a requirement list, such as user stories, product backlogs, and feature lists. The Business Tracker should guarantee that project development is always guided by the requirement list. Those associated with this front should define requirements alongside with their importance and risk for the project, being able to prioritize them. It is also expected that a Business Tracker is able to define when a requirement is satisfied.

The following roles have one or more tasks and responsibilities on this front: Customer (XP and Scrum), Product Owner (Scrum), Team (Scrum) and Visionary (DSDM). Customer role does not refer to the final customer necessarily. This role is played by someone who has interest in the project and that possess sufficient business knowledge to define requirements.

Business Ambassador. Comprises all activities related to translating users' needs into business requirements and translating these requirements into features to be developed. Other activities include negotiating deadlines with the customer. It is expected from the Business Ambassador to be capable of explaining technical constraints and resource allocation so that customers can understand demands to fulfill each deadline. Ambassadors should inform developers regarding the priority of each requirement, so they can invest effort towards maximizing value delivery.

All activities comprised in this front focus on communication. It is required for those acting in this front to understand and clarify poorly defined requirements created by the customers, as well as to minimally understand technical jargon.

The following roles have one or more tasks and responsibilities on this front: Product Owner (Scrum), Business Analyst-Designer (Crystal), Domain Expert (FDD) and Ambassador User (DSDM).

Business Expert. This front does not comprise well-defined tasks, it is rather defined by one responsibility: having deep knowledge about the business domain, becoming a source of requirements. Those who act in this front should be available during many different stages of the project, reducing time to get additional information and clarifications regarding requirements. Customers usually act on this front, even when they are not considered part of the team. Team members may also act on this front when they have deep knowledge of the business.

The following roles have one or more tasks and responsibilities on this front: Business Expert (Crystal) and Domain Expert (FDD).

4.2 Understanding BizDev in the Field

The interview process described in Section 2 took three days. People from the IT sector worked together at the same open place, while the administrative sector was located at a different building. The administrative sector acted as both internal customer and end user. Other end users include professors and students of the university. The working teams are composed of five to six people. All the teams have at least one requirement analyst, and one of the teams also had a customer allocated as a part-time analyst. The remaining members of the team are one development leader and a variable number of developers.

For the last couple of months before the interviews, the entire IT sector was allocated on a task force to migrate large-scale legacy systems written in Cobol. For a long period, the migration task happened alongside with improvements to the system, but due to a deadline imposed by external factors, it was decided that the improvements would be performed at a later time and that all teams would focus on the migration. Since the projects' organization significantly changed for this migration task force, we focused on getting information from both earlier and current state. Before the migration project, each team was responsible for specific modules and submodules of the system (such as student registration, grading, and discipline scheduling). During the migration task, the teams kept the same members, but lost responsibilities over specific modules and started participating in a shared backlog.

Before the migration, teams used to attend specific meetings defined by Scrum, such as planning, daily and retrospectives. Team members also mentioned another recurrent meeting, called status report, attended by one member from each team (usually the development leader), by the IT and the administrative directors.

During the analysis of the interviews, important practices and behaviors upon the BizDev interface stood up. They are described in the next subsections, in which the terms "business area" and "customer" refer exclusively to the administrative sector. When we want to emphasize end users, other terms appear. The term "team" is used to describe teams located inside the IT sector, which are composed of developers and requirements analysts.

Customer-on-Site. The business area selected two teams from the IT department to participate in an initiative for reengineering business processes, guided by one external consulting company. The lead developer of one of those teams mentioned that the decision of having the customer being allocated inside the development team came during this initiative. Initially, the customer was allocated full time on the development team. However, it is currently allocated as part-time, working half period on the administrative sector, half period with the development team.

The lead developer working along with this on-site customer reported some benefits of this practice. Being closer to the developers, the customer started seeing the difficulties they had for understanding requirements written by the business area. Thus, the customer started to provide additional details about the requirements before handing them off to the development team. Another perceived benefit is increased productivity due to fewer interruptions and needs for clarifying requirements. Because of her participation on the process of gathering requirements and on the specification of use cases, the customer-on-site can act as a local source of business knowledge for the developers, eliminating the need to wait for external communication. As a result of the axial coding, these interactions and activities are depicted in Figure 1.

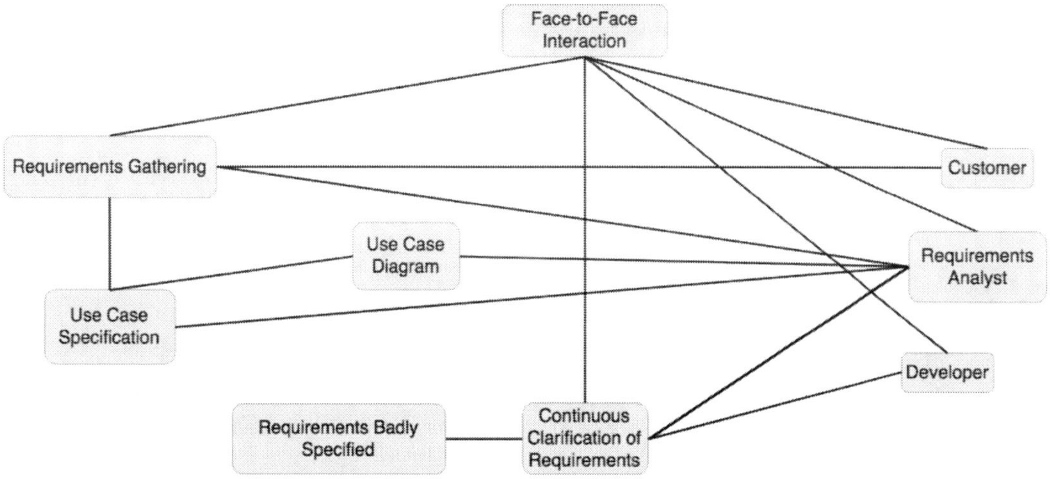

Fig 1. Activities and Interactions of the Customer-on-Site

The customer-on-site is empowered with the authority of making business decisions, which made the re-prioritizing process more natural to the development team. This happens because the customer can understand better technical limitations and how they are affecting tasks by lowering their priority. The customer-on-site never had the obligation to report to the business area before making decisions, which evidences his/her empowerment.

One unexpected behavior reported by the lead developer experiencing the customer-on-site is that a new type of conflict was created with the business area. It regards that some people from the business area started seeing the customer-on-site as someone exclusively from the development team, as an outsider. We observed this conflict on comments saying the customer-on-site has biased opinions due to its proximity to the development team, claiming that its opinion is based on some kind of protective behavior and not on technical or business knowledge. The lead developer is concerned with the possibility of such conflict to decrease the power the customer-on-site has for making decisions for the business area.

Requirements Analysts inside Development Teams. The fact that all teams contained at least one requirement analyst is a sign of approximation between business and development. The three analysts interviewed had a technical background, which allowed them to write the requirements sent to the developers in a very detailed way, even by referring to table and column names from the database.

Previously, the analysts gathered requirements from the customers. During the migration task force, the requirements are extracted directly from the legacy systems, in a reverse engineering process. As analysts write new use cases, developers implement the use cases previously specified, in parallel. It is the analysts' responsibility to homologate implemented use cases and inform existing problems to the development team. When developers encounter problems on understanding any requirement, they ask the analysts for clarification. In cases when the requirements analyst also needs more information on a requirement, they contact the business area and ask for information. In this scenario, the requirements analysts are in constant communication with both business and development people.

One of the interviewed analysts reported the attendance at planning meetings of the developers, helping to detail requirements and their priorities. He/she also reported that after some time the whole development team was invited to take part in meetings with the business area, usually attended by requirements analysts only. As the collaboration improved, he/she started taking part in daily meetings, explaining what he/she was working on and what use cases were currently under tests.

List of Use Cases and Re-Prioritization. Prior to the migration task force, demands were passed to the developers through a requirement list in the form of use cases. The entire team could participate in the prioritization and re-prioritization of those use cases. Besides, teams worked on two-week sprints, engaging on planning and retrospective meetings. On both meetings, the current priorities were discussed and re-evaluated. From these meetings, the priority of use cases could change. For priority changes considered to be small, the team was allowed to take decisions by itself. Otherwise, when changes are critical or involve many dependencies, one specific meeting would be planned, with participation from members of the business area. The list of use cases was not fixed or closed, but rather an open artifact, receiving continuous updates.

Currently, the backlog of the IT sector is composed by a list of "applications", where each "application" is defined as one entire system flow. This list of applications has no details about the flow, and for this reason one of the responsibilities of the requirements analysts is to generate detailed use cases from the applications, using the legacy system as the source of information.

Production Support. Production support involves all the work made to maintain systems already released and used in production. Existing activities are bug fixes, failure analysis and answering users' and customers' questions. Some bugs are detected automatically and reported through the Redmine tool, while others are reported directly by end users or by the business area, through the creation of issues at the Redmine tool or through other means of contact (phone, email, direct contact). There is no team allocated exclusively to work on production support, so every team has to engage frequently on this kind of activity. It is the lead developer's responsibility to pull production support tasks to their team, prioritizing it against the team's current priorities. However, one of the teams reported that developers also helped on this prioritization, pushing tasks to themselves based on their knowledge about how critical the support task is.

As one of the interviewed lead developers mentioned production support tasks are frequent and do interfere on planned deadlines. Due to the academic nature of the systems, there are certain periods of the year such as beginning and ending of semesters when demands for production support grows significantly. At these periods, not only the number of tasks increase but their criticity increase as well, demanding faster attention and solution from the development teams.

One practice adopted by one of the interviewed teams to reduce the impact of the production support on planned deadlines is to allocate a fixed amount of items for the sprint. In this case, three stories (~15 hours) are held for ongoing support tasks and, for this reason, the amount of stories regarding feature implementations is reduced. This team's lead developer considered that this practice worked fine, even though sometimes production support tasks continued to impact planned deadlines. Another practiced adopted by this team is to create new stories (besides the three already reserved) for production support tasks that began on the previous sprint but had not finished yet, still demanding effort from the team. This practice is applied on the critical periods of the academic year, as described before.

Situating BizDev Fronts. Through the use of coding procedures from Grounded Theory, we identified in which fronts the analyzed roles were inserted. For example, an interview segment describing how team members would discuss the priority of backlog items during planning meetings coded as both "re-prioritization of backlog items" and "developer", indicating the "developer" role performs this practice when playing on the Business Tracker front.

We were able to identify benefits of having people acting in the Business Expert front through interview segments coded as "Constant clarification of use cases". Being more available to the development team, the customer-on-site was able to reduce significantly the amount of time spent with clarification of requirements. The customer-on-site allocated in one of the interviewed teams worked alongside with the requirements analyst, and due to his/her business knowledge, he/she was able to write more detailed requirements.

The presence of requirements analysts inside development teams indicates how pertinent and relevant is the Business Ambassador front. Interview segments coded as "technical background" indicated how requirement analysts have no complications in communicating with developers. Since requirements analysts had a technical background, they are able to understand and communicate well with both developers and customers, even being able to write requirements adding technical details. The requirements analysts work as a bridge between developers and the business area, gathering requirements from customers and translating them into user stories or use cases that developers can understand, and also by communicating questions from the development team for the business area to answer.

All roles analyzed in the qualitative study have one activity associated with the Business Tracker front: the continuous re-prioritization of backlog items. The requirements analysts and the customer-on-site also acted at this front by creating and detailing the use cases that compose the backlog. Even though all roles participated at the Business Tracker front, we were not able to identify anyone having the specific responsibility of guaranteeing that all the development process is always guided by the requirements list (backlog).

5 Threats to Validity

Mainly, this qualitative research is limited to the adopted investigation methods, namely an *ad-hoc* literature review and a set of interviews with practitioners. In this sense, we discuss the threats to validity under a pragmatic worldview [12].

5.1 Theoretical Validity

We started by identifying roles, responsibilities, and practices proposed and well-documented in the literature. Then, we synthesized those elements to reach a perspective that is agnostic to any particular agile method. It allowed us to structure two interviews scripts (instruments) to collect information regarding the BizDev interface. As far as we could identify, these instruments provided a large spectrum of the intended phenomenon, with no bias to any specific reference on how the BizDev interface should be.

5.2 Generalizability

Although the definition of the BizDev fronts (Section 4.1) intends to be general, we understand it as a first version for characterizing this interface. Internally, i.e., within the teams and the observed organization, we understand it fully captures the roles, responsibilities, and practices. However, we also recognize that more instances are required, i.e., we need to further investigate the BizDev interface externally, observing different teams and organizations, with different cultures and development processes.

5.3 Descriptive Validity

Apart from the instruments intending to be agnostic to particular agile methods, we understand the data collected using interview scripts as free from bias as participants were free to answer as much as they need with no time constraints and also aware of the importance on collaborating for this research. The interviews were audio recorded and transcribed in full with no synthesis or intervention by the researchers. Finally, the analysis of the interview data was performed using Grounded Theory procedures for coding the data, namely the Constant Comparative Method, using conceptualization and abstraction. Thus, we understand the current state of our codebook as an authentic abstraction of the raw data.

5.4 Interpretive Validity

Qualitative analysis naturally faces subjectivity due to interpretive synthesis and conceptualization. However, we understand the reasoning leading to our findings can be traced back to raw data in a reasonable way through the generated codes and categories in the codebook. Two researchers performed and constantly reviewed the analysis to reduce possible bias.

6 Final Remarks

This paper presented a study concerning a better characterization of the BizDev interface. For that, we conducted a literature review and a qualitative study to gather information considering the consolidated knowledge available in the literature and the state of the practice by conducting a set of interviews.

The information gathered so far indicates that a healthy interface between business and development can benefit software projects. Closer communication with the business area can improve the productivity of development teams by reducing the time spent waiting for requirements clarification. Also, to have additional business knowledge inside the development teams enables major flexibility through a better re-prioritization process.

As future works, we envision to conduct further investigation on other organizations and cultures with different profiles. For that, we plan to review the interview scripts aiming at improving the data collection efficiency without compromising their current effectiveness, as we experienced a great effort to transcribe all the interviews and some data was not relevant for the research goals.

References

1. Agile Manifesto, http://agilemanifesto.org. Access at: 2018/02/07.
2. Abrahamsson, P., Salo, O., Ronkainen, J., Warsta, J.: Agile software development methods: Review and analysis, VTT publication 478, Espoo, Finland (2002)
3. van Waardenburg, G., vans Vliet, H.: When Agile Meets Enterprise. Journal Information and Software Technology, Volume 55, Issue 12, 2154-2171 (2013).
4. Conboy, K.: Agility from first principles: reconstructing the concept of agility in information systems development. J. Inf. Systems Research 20 (3), 317-480 (2009).
5. Stuart Weiss, R.: Learning from Strangers: The Art and Method of Qualitative Interview Studies. Free Press, New York (1995).
6. Schwaber, K.: Agile Project Management With Scrum. Microsoft Press (2004).
7. Bass, J. M.: Agile Method Tailoring in Distributed Enterprises: Product Owner Teams. In: 8th Intl. Conf. on Global Software Engineering (ICGSE), p. 154-163. IEEE, Bari (2013).
8. Gregorio, D. D.: How the Business Analyst Supports and Encourages Collaboration on Agile Projects. In: Systems Conference (SysCon), IEEE International. p. 1-4. IEEE, Vancouver (2012).
9. Corbin, J., Strauss, A. L: Basics of Qualitative Research - Techniques and Procedures for Developing Grounded Theory. 4th ed. SAGE Publications (1990).
10. Fitzgerald, B., Stol, K.: Continuous Software Engineering: A Roadmap and Agenda. Journal of Systems and Software, Volume 123, p. 176-189 (2015).
11. Beck, K. Extreme Programming Explained: Embrace Change. 2nd. ed. Addison-Wesley (2000).
12. Petersen, K., Gencel, C.: Worldviews, research methods, and their relationship to validity in empirical software engineering research. In: International Workshop on Software

Measurement and the Eighth International Conference on Software Process and Product Measurement (IWSM-MENSURA), pp. 81-89. IEEE, Ankara, Turkey (2013).
13. de França, B. B. N., Jeronimo Junior, H., Travassos, G. H.: Characterizing DevOps by Hearing Multiple Voices. In: Proceedings of the 30th Brazilian Symposium on Software Engineering, pp. 53-62. ACM, Maringá, Brazil (2016).

Appendix A - Interview Scripts

1. Common Questions

Warm Up:

- For how long have you been in the company?
- How many people are part of your team? (or teams, in cases when the interviewed works in more than one)

About the Job Description:

- What is the name of the interviewed position?
- What are the interviewed responsibilities?

Requirement Managing:

- How are the product's features defined?
    - Where does the information needed to decide these features come from? Customer inputs? Are there specific meetings on the business team for that purpose?
- Is there any requirement list?
    - How is it build? How are updates made to it? How is it exposed to the development team? And for the business team?
    - How are requirements translated into features to be developed?
    - How far does it plan? Months? A year?
- How are the requirements prioritized? Who participates on this process?
- Can requirements be re-prioritized?
    - Case positive: How often does this happen? Does the interviewed believe this is beneficial?
    - Case negative: For what reason do the priorities keep stable? Does the interviewed think having reprioritization would be beneficial?

2. Specific Questions for Technical Profile

Task Division:

- How is the definition of the tasks the team will work on through the week?

Feature Delivery:

- How is a task defined as done?
- Do you make any tests with the final customer? Case positive, how is it done and who participates on this process?
- How is the delivery of a feature made?
- Is there any follow up after the features are delivered?

- How do you get to know whether the delivery fulfilled the requirement of the customer and business area?

Communication With Business Area and With Customers:

- Is there any planned meeting? Like daily, weekly, post-sprint presentations.
  - Case Positive: How are these meetings? Who participates on them? How long they last? What is discussed?
- What happens when developers have business questions during the process?
  - How hard is it for the development team to talk to customers and to the business area?
- Are there conflicts between the business and development areas? (Get specific examples)
- How does the development team communicate problems encountered to the business area?
  - What happens when the development team realizes that it won't be able to reach a deadline? How are expectations managed?
- How is communication itself? Is it needed for the development team to translate technical jargons? How is the experience of explaining technical obstacles and problems for the business area?
  - Does communication problems like fail to comprehend requirements happen?

3. Specific Questions for Business Profile

Requirement Managing:

- How are the product's features defined?
  - Where does the information needed to decide these features come from? Customer inputs? Are there specific meetings on the business team for that purpose?

Communication With the Development Team:

- How are product requirements transmitted to the development team?
  - How often does this communication happen? (Formal and informal)
- How is the tracking of development made? How do you know if everything will end on the planned time?
- Do you happen to find it hard to understand the technical team? For example, many technical jargons, many unknown technologies being used.
- Do you usually involve someone technical in any type of business meetings?

Communication with the customer:

- How do you gather feedback from the customer about delivered products?
- Are there any tests made with the customers?
- How are bugs detected?
  - After a bug is detected, what actions are taken?

Get Your Spreadsheets Under (Version) Control

José Nuno Macedo[13], Ricardo Moreira[24], Jácome Cunha[14], and João Saraiva[13]

[1] Universidade do Minho, Portugal
[2] Universidade NOVA de Lisboa, Portugal
[3] HASLab/INESC TEC, Portugal
[4] NOVA LINCS, Portugal
a72424@alunos.uminho.pt rm.moreira@campus.fct.unl.pt
{jacome,saraiva}@di.uminho.pt

Abstract. Spreadsheets play a pivotal role in many organizations. They serve to store and manipulate data or forecasting, and they are often used to help in the decision process, thus directly impacting the success, or not, of organizations.

As the research community already realized, spreadsheets tend to have the same problems "professional" software contain. Thus, in the past decade many software engineering techniques have been successfully proposed to aid spreadsheet developers and users. However, one of the most used mechanisms to manage software projects is still lacking in spreadsheets: a version control system. A version control system allows for collaborative development, while also allowing individual developers to explore different alternatives without compromising the main project.

In this paper we present a version control system, named SheetGit, oriented for end-user programmers. It allows to graphically visualize the history of versions (including branches), to switch between different versions just by pointing and clicking, and to visualize the differences between any two versions in an animated way. To validate our approach/tool we performed an empirical evaluation which shows evidence that SheetGit can aid users when compared to other tools.

Keywords: Spreadsheets · Version Control System

1 Introduction

Spreadsheet systems are a success example in the history of software systems. They have achieved an astonishing usage both in terms of the number of users (55 million of end-users programmers in 2012 just in the USA alone [13]) and the variety of domains in which they are nowadays used. Moreover, they are used both by professional programmers at large worldwide organizations, and by non-professional programmers in small family-run businesses. In fact, spreadsheet systems are installed in 90% of all computers globally [3] .

Spreadsheet systems offer end users a high level of flexibility, making it easier to get started working with them. Although spreadsheets start as a single user, simple software artifact, as any other software system, they tend to quickly evolve into a large and complex system! Moreover, in the age of cloud-based software development, spreadsheets tend to be maintained in a collaborative environment.

In such a context, software is nowadays developed by relying on version control systems that help collaboratively building complex systems. A version control mechanism helps teams to manage changes to the same source code over time. These systems usually track and provide control over changes in software files and implicitly allow developers to return to any earlier stage of the software.

Although the spreadsheet research community has done considerable work, for instance, in defining abstractions for complex spreadsheets [7, 6, 4] or developing testing frameworks [1, 2], unfortunately, little work has been done in supporting version control based spreadsheet development. As a consequence, version control in spreadsheet development is rare, still! There are several reasons for this situation. First, spreadsheet users, usually non-professional programmers, are not familiar with systems for version control software. Second, spreadsheets are easy to share - usually a single file artifact which has to be under version control, thus making it difficult to control and maintain their integrity. Third, version control systems, such as Git[5], work very well for text-based languages, but they cannot be directly applied to the visual-representation of spreadsheets.

Although, version control systems are rarely used in spreadsheet development, research shows that version control does help end users [11]. Because the traditional version control systems cannot be directly applied to (visual) spreadsheets, end users perform their own versioning manually by adding a suffix/prefix to a file name with the file's version number! This can be seen even in large companies such as Enron [9], where they often sent updated spreadsheets through email. However, manual versioning holds numerous risks, as it is possible for a user to receive an email with a wrong or already outdated version, which would cause a problem whose root can be difficult to trace.

The goal of our work is three-fold: First, to bring version control to spreadsheet end-users developers in an intuitive manner. Second, to incorporate yet another modern software development methodology into the spreadsheet realm. Third, to help end users to create, manage, and comprehend complex spreadsheets. For this purpose, we created an add-in for Microsoft Excel, named SheetGit, which automatically commits changes, creates branches when needed, allows the user to change between versions, and see the spreadsheet differences between versions. Because, the control version is to be used by end users, our user interface has been carefully designed: an history slider is presented in our plug-in allowing end-users to return/see any earlier version of their spreadsheet. A new version of a spreadsheet is added to the control version by just pressing a button (or by configuring such a commit to occur when a given number of cells have been updated). This will be detailed in Section 3.2.

To evaluate SheetGit we performed an empirical evaluation with 18 participants, doing two different kinds of tasks in two different spreadsheets. Evidence show SheetGit helped end users being faster and more correct in most cases. Section 4.5 presents this study in detail.

---

[5] https://git-scm.com

2 Related work

In this paper we present a version control system, named SheetGit. The initial ideas that motivated the development of this tool were presented in a preliminary workshop paper [12]. We now present in great detail SheetGit, we extend the visual interface of the tool, and we present a validation of our approach and tool.

Microsoft Excel's official approach, which they simply call *History*, is available solely on the Windows platform. However, it is limited to spreadsheets hosted on Microsoft Sharepoint, so one cannot make use of it without being online, but it does allow collaboration between users. Versions are saved automatically when the user saves the document; Excel will either create a completely new version or merge the changes with the last one, with unknown criteria.

One of the important features in version control is the ability to see the differences between versions of a file, but Excel does not have such a feature.

It is worth noting that Microsoft has actually developed an official tool to detect spreadsheet differences called *Spreadsheet Compare*[6] that comes alongside some versions of Excel 2013 and 2016 in Windows. It works as an external tool and can function without having Excel itself open, having no integration with Excel's version control system. In *Spreadsheet Compare*, spreadsheets are displayed side-by-side without their formatting, and depending on the type of change, have specific colors highlight the altered cells. Unfortunately, there is no easy way to detect changes to entire rows and columns, as sometimes the program's algorithm merely sees them as regular changed cell values. While that is indeed correct, it is not very useful for users as it does not represent what happened in reality. When it does detect row/column changes, it adds them to the list of all changes, but does not specifically show that in the spreadsheets.

Coopy[7] is a spreadsheet version control tool which supports showing differences, patching, merging and conflict resolution on spreadsheets and database tables. It is separated from spreadsheet programs, and focuses on keeping data in synchronization with various people across multiple spreadsheet technologies by converting the worksheets to an intermediate format called CSVS. This CSVS format is based on the well known CSV format but with support for multiple worksheets per file, unambiguous header rows, and a clear representation of NULL. While Coopy does have a large feature-set, its interface is aimed more towards professional programmers with its use of concepts, information and syntax probably difficult for end users to know.

The revision history system of Google Sheets[8] is very powerful. It begins functioning immediately upon creating a new spreadsheet and automatically commits a new version whenever a new change is made. If various changes are done in a short period of time, Google Sheets may aggregate the changes into a single commit. In the Revision History page, one is able to see a list of all

[6] https://support.office.com/en-us/article/overview-of-spreadsheet-compare-13fafa61-62aa-451b-8674-242ce5f2c986

[7] http://share.find.coop

[8] https://www.google.com/sheets/about/

versions right next to the actual spreadsheet, each having the list of people who edited the spreadsheet in that particular version and their unique color. Upon clicking one of the versions, the spreadsheet will change to show that particular point in history but in a gray-scale color scheme; the cells that were edited in some fashion will be tinted with the unique color of their author.

XLTools[9] is a suite of various utilities for Microsoft Excel all in one VSTO add-in, one of them being called Version Control. This tool can create a local Git repository for the active workbook, where committing can be done either manually or automatically when saving; commit messages can also be added. The user also has access to the list of revisions, where they can choose to compare or save individual worksheets. However, there is no option to directly restore to a previous version. One has to save the file somewhere and then overwrite the original when Excel is closed, as the original cannot be overwritten while Excel and the add-on are open. Despite using Git, the system is fully local and has no collaboration features. Spreadsheet comparing can only be applied to one worksheet at a time. This will open a new Excel window with both old and new spreadsheets, having the new cell values tinted in red and its text in bold. The tool does not detect formatting changes and merely detects the actual cell value, and since formatting when comparing sheets is not changed, if one is unfortunate enough to have the same red cell formatting as the add-on uses, edited cells in the document may be confused with cells that were never touched.

Xltrail[10] is a recently created program that provides version control in spreadsheets. It is not directly integrated with Excel, it instead functions by creating a folder in the operating system that will be monitored by the program. Any spreadsheets placed in it become versioned, and when they are edited, the program will detect the changes and create a new version appropriately. It can also work through the cloud by detecting changes on Dropbox or Sharepoint accounts. In this case one would not need to download their personal client. Versions are kept in a linear format, much like Microsoft Excel. The service provides diffing, in a similar way to Coopy's highlighter format. Xltrail does not work without an internet connection nor does it support branching and merging.

Table 1 presents an overview of the features implemented by all tools.

Table 1. Table comparing SHEETGIT features with existing tools

Tool	Commit	Diff	Merge	Branch	Collaboration	Offline
SHEETGIT	yes	yes	yes	yes	yes	yes
Microsoft Excel	yes	no	no	no	yes	no
Spreadsheet Compare	no	yes	no	no	no	no
Coopy	no	yes	yes	no	no	yes
Google Sheet	yes	yes	no	no	yes	no
XLTools	yes	yes	no	no	no	yes
xltrail	yes	yes	no	no	yes	no

[9] https://xltools.net

[10] http://xltrail.com

3 The SheetGit Tool

In this section we describe several features for version control for spreadsheets and introduce SHEETGIT. We have created our solution as an Excel add-in to keep it as closely knit to Excel as possible, as this potentially increases its acceptance among spreadsheet developers as opposed to have to be run as an external tool. This will also enable us to present information directly in the active spreadsheet, and grant us access to Excel's proprietary file formats.

3.1 Technological Choices

There are two main types of add-ins for Excel: *i)* the *Visual Studio Tools for Office* (VSTO), add-ins made with C# or Visual Basic, and *ii)* the new type Microsoft calls *Office add-ins*. The latter are simply web pages that can interact with the documents using an API in Javascript. They are sandboxed and less closely integrated with Office, making them more restrictive than VSTO add-ins, but in exchange, they would also work in Excel for browsers.

We chose to create an VSTO add-in instead of using the new Javascript API, because we find the API not powerful enough for what we intend to create. We ultimately want the add-in to start immediately when Excel is ran so there is no risk of the users forgetting to enable the add-in, possibly losing data as a result, something that is not possible in the Javascript add-ins due to their sandboxed nature. As a result, our solution will only support Microsoft Excel in the Windows platforms.

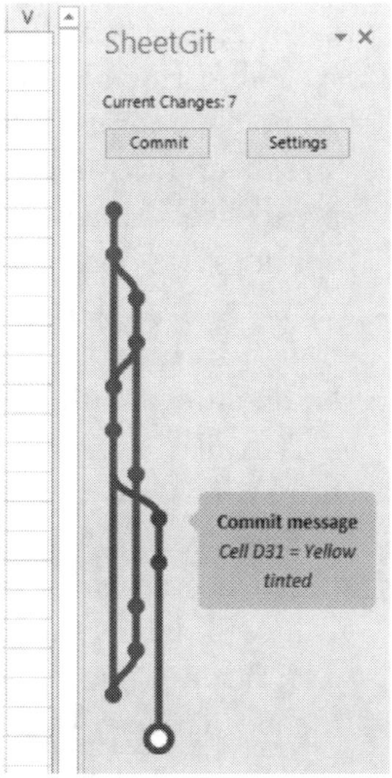

Fig. 1. SHEETGIT's task pane, displaying various commits

The add-in consists of a self-contained task pane, as seen in Figure 1, that includes an embedded browser to allow us to make use of Javascript, while retaining the advantages of VSTO add-ins. Our version tree is created using Gitgraph.js[11], a Javascript library. We use Bitbucket[12] in the background to actually manage the different versions of the spreadsheet, that is, each commit is actually stored in a private Bitbucket repository as a new file.

3.2 SheetGit Capabilities

We implemented a set of fundamental features: committing versions, switching between commits/versions, the option to see the actual differences between two versions, merge two different commits, and sharing these between various people.

[11] http://gitgraphjs.com

[12] https://bitbucket.org

Committing One of the most important features of a version control system is to organize the history of the commits done by the different users. In our particular case a *commit* is a set of changes in a workbook that occurred since the last commit until the next one. These commits can be done automatically (each time the user saves the file), or manually (when the user decides to commit the changes). A commit can also be called a *version* of the spreadsheet.

The list of commits, or versions, is displayed in a tree format, as shown in Figure 1. We use a tree because of its simplicity and adaptability, allowing for an intuitive graphical representation of many version control functions such as branches and merges. Very popular version control services such as Github[13] or Bitbucket also make use of a tree structure to display their version lists. The commits are placed chronologically, with the topmost being the oldest and the bottom most the youngest.

The large white commit is the currently active version, meaning it is the spreadsheet the user is seeing. A user can click in a desired commit in the tree, and the workbook will change so it is in the state of the particular version selected. In this case, the user restored his spreadsheet to a previous version, so it is not the most recent version of the spreadsheet.

By default, commits are generated automatically, reducing the burden on the user. By using metrics such as time since last edit and amount of data entered into the workbook, we combine various commits into blocks such that the end result may be indifferent to the user. In fact, Google Sheets has a similar behavior. An option to enable manual commits has also been added, for more experienced users who know better when to actually commit changes.

Each commit is associated with an optional commit message, auto-generated version number, and an automatically generated summary of the changes, which is shown upon hovering a commit dot in the tree as illustrated in the text box displayed in Figure 1.

Even though these messages are automatically generated, the user has always the possibility of editing such message by clicking and directly editing it. Next we list some of the messages shown for particular changes (the message should be self explanatory, c being a cell address, v a value, *col* a column letter, *row* a row number, and *color* a color): Cell $c = v$; Deleted cell c content; Deleted column *col*; Inserted row *row*; Cell $c =$ *color* tinted.

Note that the formatting changes are also recorded and displayed. This is necessary in spreadsheets as they are naturally visual tools. This is a feature none of the professional version control systems hold.

Showing Differences Between Commits To make an easy to understand comparison in complex spreadsheets, SheetGit presents a slider between two consecutive commits. Dragging the slider from one commit to the other displays the individual differences (e.g. cell changes) between them, one at a time. This allows the user to see the differences step-by-step rather than being overwhelmed

[13] https://github.com

with all of them at the same time. This scales well with spreadsheet size and complexity as long as the user controls the speed of traversing the timeline. An option to skip to certain cells of the comparison also helps in this regard. The differences that are shown as the user moves through the timeline are also appropriately highlighted in the spreadsheet as one needs to be able to tell it apart from the rest of the spreadsheet. This can be done for example by changing the affected areas color or by drawing a circle around it.

In SheetGit, the Diff Pane, as shown in Figure 2, contains all functionality related to viewing differences between two versions.

The slider moves through each cell that has differences between the two versions. The two directional buttons move the slider up and down, one step at a time, for when more precision is required and because some users may favor clicking buttons rather than dragging the slider.

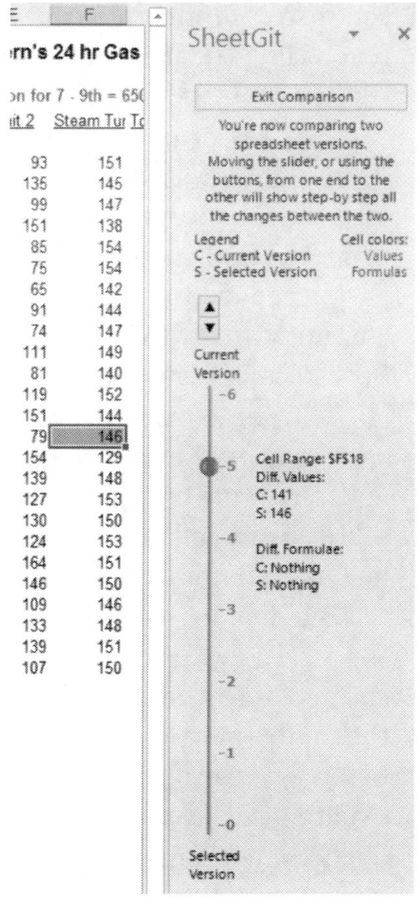

Fig. 2. Comparison between two versions in SheetGit

Collaborative Development Version control systems are a great incentive for collaborative work. Thus, the visualization of the commits must reflect the changes introduced by the different users. To do so, our tree has a different color for each user working in a particular spreadsheet.

Moreover, in order to organize the collaborative development, each user gets his own branch so such particular development can be done without interfering with the main development. Branches other than the main one are thus colored with the user's color, signaling the respective author's ownership. Thus, the commits are shown as colored dots in the tree, each color uniquely representing the commit's author. This can be seen in Figure 1, where two different colors signal that two different authors collaborated on the same spreadsheet.

Each user can have more than one branch. For instance, if the user begins to edit the spreadsheet from an older version (recall the last version is the bottom dot in the line), it will be created a new branch for the forthcoming commits.

Merging Since each user has its own branch, at some point she/he may desire to integrate her/his changes in the main branch. When done, this will be displayed in the tree structure in an analogous way to the new branch, as illustrated in Figure 1, where the red author performed merges twice over the development cycle. These merges are signaled by the red line joining the main branch.

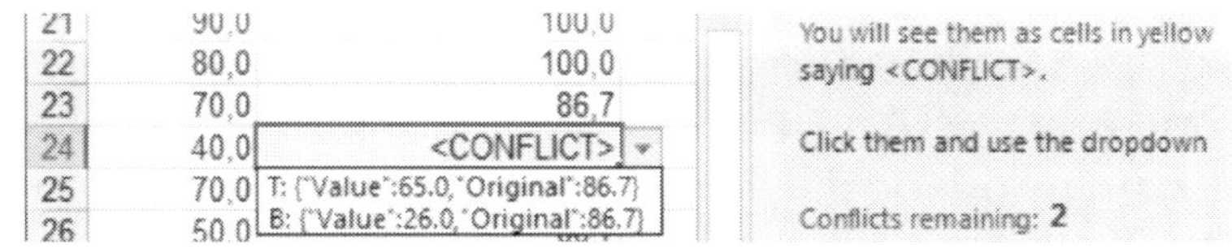

Fig. 3. Example of conflict when merging with SheetGit: When a new branch was created the original value of the conflicting cell was 86.7. Then, in the new branch (B) that cell changed to 26.0, while it was also changed in the main branch/trunk (T) to 65.0. Thus, a conflict occurs when merging the branches.

To make the development process easier for end user, we decided that it is not possible to merge changes between branches from different users. Nevertheless, it is possible to merge branches from the same user.

In some cases, conflicts may happen when merging to the main branch. In these cases two situations may occur. First, if there are concurrent changes to cells, the user must solve the conflicts by hand, that is, he/she must decide which version goes to the main branch. SheetGit will show the possible solutions, allowing the user to choose the intended one, as displayed in Figure 3. The second situation occurs when the changes are in different cells. In this case, all the cells will be integrated in the spreadsheet without the need for user intervention.

SheetGit is available at http://spreadsheetsunl.github.io/sheetgit.

4 Empirical Evaluation

The aim of our study is to evaluate the effectiveness and efficiency of users using SheetGit when compared to the use of Excel and Spreadsheet Compare.

4.1 Study Design

Hypotheses. With this study we intend to test two hypotheses:

1. In order to perform a given set of tasks, users spent less time when using SheetGit instead of using only Excel and Spreadsheet Compare.
2. Spreadsheets used with the support of SheetGit have a correctness grade higher than using only Excel and Spreadsheet Compare.

Formally, the two hypotheses being tested are: H_T for the time that is needed to perform a given set of tasks, and H_C for the correctness grade found in different types of spreadsheets. They are respectively formulated as follows:

1. **Null hypothesis**. H_{T_0}. The time to perform a given set of tasks using SheetGit is not less than that taken using Excel and Spreadsheet Compare. $H_{T_0} : \mu_d \leq 0$, where μ_d is the expected mean of the time differences.
   Alternative hypothesis. $H_{T_1} : \mu_d > 0$. The time to perform a given set of tasks using SheetGit is less than using Excel and Spreadsheet Compare.
   Measures needed. Time taken to perform the tasks.

2. **Null hypothesis**. H_{C_0}. The correctness grade in spreadsheets when using SheetGit is not smaller than using Excel and Spreadsheet Compare. H_{C_0} : $\mu_d \leq 0$, where μ_d is the mean difference of the correctness grades.
   Alternative hypothesis. $H_{C_1} : \mu_d > 0$. The correctness grade when using SheetGit is smaller than when using only Excel and Spreadsheet Compare.
   Measures needed. Correctness grade for each spreadsheet.

The independent variables are, for H_T, the time to perform the tasks (efficiency), and for H_C, the correctness grades (effectiveness).

Subjects and Objects. The study was performed with freshmen computer science students from the NOVA University of Lisbon. They were chosen because they are likely to have minimal experience with Excel and not enough programming experience to know about version control. To provide incentive for participation, we decided to raffle a voucher with the value of fifty Euro for a retail store. From the 18 subjects, 16 were male and 2 were female. All of the subjects were below 20 years old. 62% of the subjects had experience with Excel and only 25% have had experience with version control.

The objects of this study are three spreadsheets. The spreadsheet used as a tutorial, termed Southpoint, calculates the total gas usage when given input values. It was used to explain how to use SheetGit to half of the participants, and Spreadsheet Compare to the other half. The second spreadsheet, termed Grades, manages and calculates grades for students of an university course. The third spreadsheet, termed Markets, calculates the income of Enron's global markets. The spreadsheets were retrieved from two widely used spreadsheet repositories: EUSES [8] and VEnron [5].

Instrumentation. After the tutorial phase, each participant received two spreadsheets: the Grades and the Markets. For each spreadsheet, the participants received two tasks. The first task asks users to correct an error in a spreadsheet that sprouted in a recent version, but was correct some time ago. So users would have to *diff* the multiple versions to find out where the error occurred, and then correct it in a new version. The second task asks users to unite two versions of a spreadsheet that have diverged from a common ancestor. Users would then have to compare the three spreadsheets (the ancestor and the two different children) and then perform a three-way merge. During the study a pre-questionnaire a post-questionnaire were given to participants.

Participants were randomly split between two groups as to have an equal amount of people with and without SheetGit. Some participants started with the Markets spreadsheet and others with the Grades spreadsheet. This is important as during the tasks performed with their first spreadsheet, participants are still learning and will gradually improve, so when they reach the second spreadsheet, they will have more experience than they had at the start. Concentration levels also begin to decrease over a period of time, which could influence the time spent on each task.

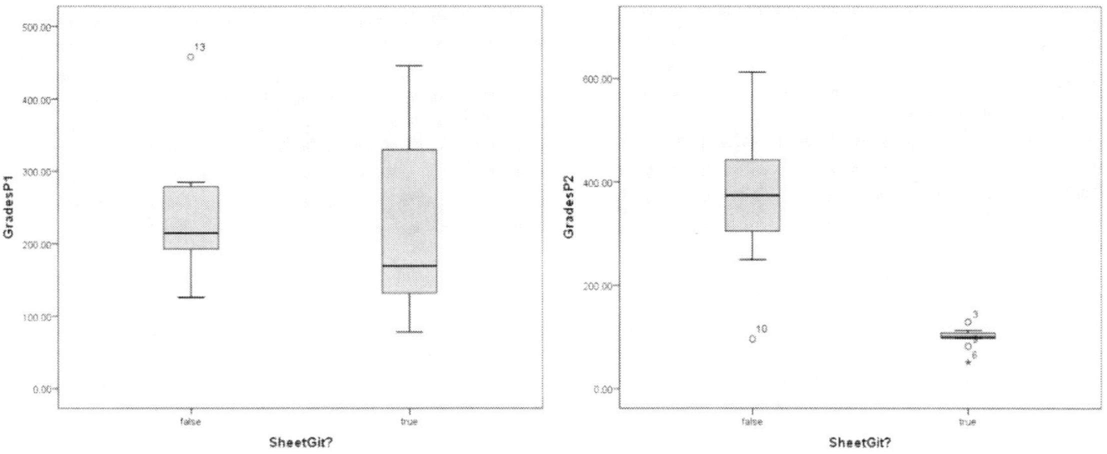

Fig. 4. Box plots for the Grades tasks time (first/second task on the left/right chart).

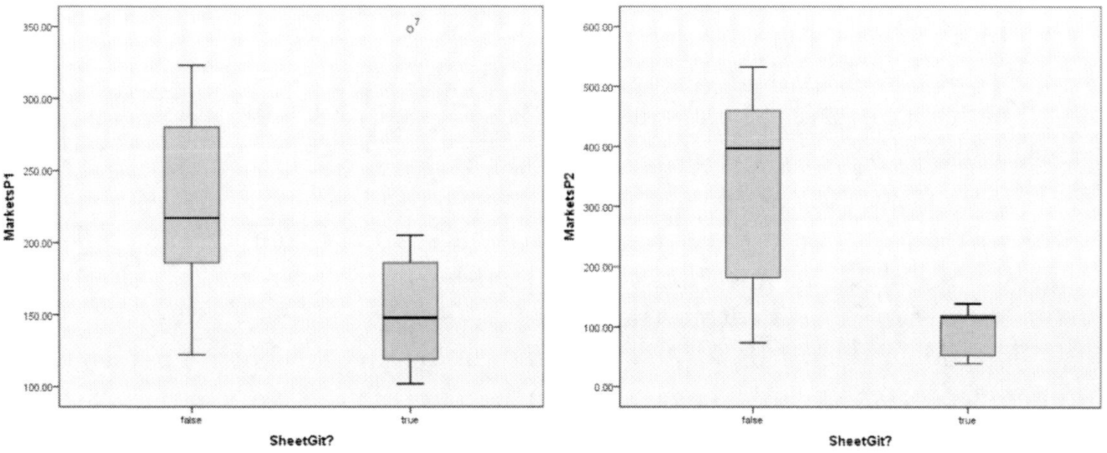

Fig. 5. Box plots for the Markets tasks time (first/second task on the left/right chart).

4.2 Results Analysis

Time spent (efficiency). There are noticeable differences in the time the participants used to perform the study. Figure 4 shows the time it took for the participants to perform Grades spreadsheet tasks. The Y axis contains the time in seconds and the X axis defines if SheetGit (box with label *true*) or Spreadsheet Compare was used (box with label *false*).

Figure 5 presents the times for the Markets spreadsheet.

Correctness grade (effectiveness). In regards to correctness, we divided the type of errors participants could perform into two categories: having incorrect values inputted in the correct version and inputting the correct values in a wrong version. As such, the bar chart in Figure 6a shows the number of participants who committed the former error, while Figure 6b the latter. The charts show all the spreadsheets' results together.

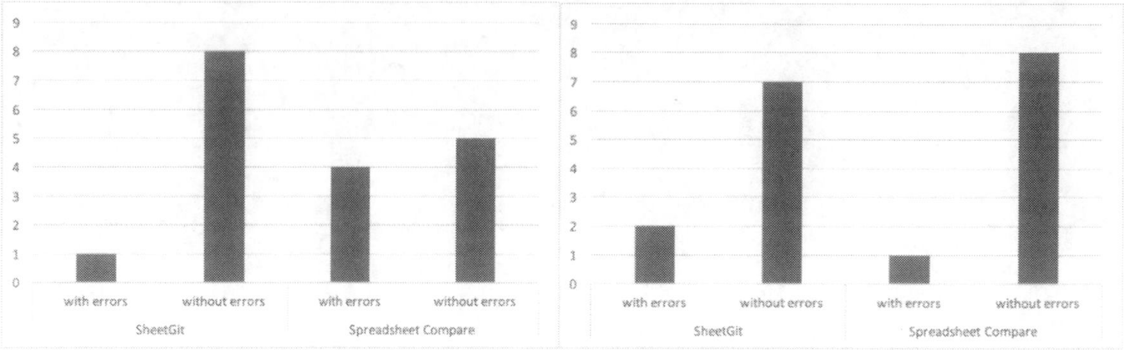

(a) Wrong values in the right version. (b) Correct values in wrong version.

Fig. 6. Errors produced by the participants.

Hypothesis Testing. To test our hypothesis on efficiency, we ran a Welch unequal variances t-test to determine if there is any statistical significance [10].

For Grades task 1, $p = 0.682$, task 2, $p = 0.001$, and for Markets task 1, $p = 0.116$, task 2, $p = 0.004$.

We also calculated Cohen's d to determine our effect size [10].

For Grades task 1 the results if 0.196974, task 2 2.499612, and for Markets task 1 0.784395, task 2 1.819253.

Comparison of times. From the t-test results we can deduce that only task 2 has statistical significance for both spreadsheets. For the task 1, there was no statistical significance within the study.

Through Cohen's d we can see that in task 2 for both spreadsheets the difference between the two means can be classified as very large (> 0.8). So SheetGit in these tasks helped the participants in a scale of more than one standard deviation, which is very impressive.

Comparison of correctness. A couple of different tests were conducted, such as the Pearson Chi-Square and Fisher's Exact Test but no statistical relevance could be found, mostly due to the low count of errors in both cases.

4.3 Results Interpretation

The results from the analysis suggest that SheetGit does improve user performance while performing these tasks. The second task, related to merging in version control, had strong statistical relevance, being noticeably superior over not using SheetGit. This is likely because SheetGit actually introduces a new method that directly aids users in the merging process. An example would be how it pinpoints conflicting cells while the counterpart users would have to search for them manually. SheetGit also automates parts of the merging process when possible to perform decisions without user input, which helps greatly lower the time, difficulty and possibility of errors within the task.

Regarding the first task, related to diffing and correcting errors, there was no statistical significance found, though the average time required to solve the task was inferior for SheetGit users. This is likely because while SheetGit allows one to move between versions and diff without changing windows, it is not that much faster than performing a diff with Spreadsheet Compare. Even if the interface proves to be simpler, both sides of the participants received tutorials for their tools, so provided they understood the tool, it would be likely for the difference to be small. The results can also be attributed to the fact that there were few versions to compare, which can provide an edge to Spreadsheet Compare, which displays all differences between two versions instantaneously. SheetGit instead shows the changes one by one, though it can group changes from multiple versions in a single diff. In this scenario, SheetGit would likely be even faster because those without it would have to navigate through menus several times to change the versions to compare.

While no statistical relevance was obtained from analyzing the correctness of the tasks, SheetGit had less errors in terms of wrong values overall. This may be because of the unified interface, all inside Excel, which keeps the users focused and can lead to less human error. The lower average time when performing the tasks would also help in terms of focus. It is interesting to note that SheetGit did indeed have more errors when it comes to users inputting the correct values, but in wrong versions. What this means is that they corrected what error they had to find, but in an old version. So the new resulting version did not have any of the changes that occurred between that old version and the latest. All of these errors occurred in the exact version where the error had, which means the users just did not return to the latest version to correct it there.

4.4 Threats to validity

A few threats to validity deserve being analyzed.

Regarding internal validity, in order to minimize any effects on the independent variables that would reflect on the causality, several actions were taken. First, half the participants started with the Markets spreadsheet, and the other half with Grades. This would minimize any learning effects from happening throughout the session. Second, the study was intentionally short in order to prevent the participants from losing focus while performing their tasks. Third, the study was performed over two sessions, one in which half the participants used SheetGit and the other where the latter half did not. Fourth, all participants executed the exact same tasks, so no group received special treatment.

For conclusion validity, a concern is the low amount of participants, which leads to a lower statistical power for the study. When calculating the correctness grade, we grouped the tasks' errors together to increase the statistical power.

As for construct validity, participants were informed beforehand that they were not under any sort of evaluation to guarantee they would not be affected by the study itself. The tasks we asked the participants to perform are common issues that are solved by the use of version control, either with or without our tool, such as merging and diffing spreadsheets. By choosing these sort of tasks, our study construct can evaluate whether or not users are more effective and efficient while using SheetGit.

Finally, regarding external validity, related to the strength to generalize the results of this study to industrial practice, we have selected two spreadsheets from the real-world: one from an actual company and another from the EUSES corpus, which in turn retrieved it from a Google search as part of a real-world example. Although the spreadsheets are real-world spreadsheets, the environment is not. Nevertheless, the participants represent a wide range of spreadsheet users, and thus, we believe that results are generalizable.

4.5 Discussion

The empirical study we conducted reveals promising results for SheetGit. Most participants wrote on the post-questionnaire that SheetGit helped them greatly in performing their tasks and that they thought it was a necessary tool.

Despite that participants had a short amount of time to learn a completely new perspective on managing backups and versions with our add-in, they accomplished their tasks on average faster than those that did not use SheetGit. Even if the first task did not achieve statistical significance, the users did in fact finish on average faster than those without SheetGit, which is impressive if one considers that they had to learn a new interface and perspective on Excel. That said, it could be faster by, for example, giving ahead of time a small highlight to every cell that would be changed. This way, users have a much better notion of the version in its entirety and the train of thought behind the changes.

Regarding errors, most found were related to users correcting errors on versions that were not the latest. This may be due to a lack of understanding or just an honest mistake due to the seamless nature of the interface, as this sort of situation happened even with users that finished both tasks fairly fast and otherwise correctly. A warning could be shown in case changes are attempted on versions that are not the latest to prevent this sort of error. The version tree could also be better labeled, much like SheetGit's diff tab, which has a detailed explanation of its functionality and appearance directly on the interface.

5 Conclusion

Spreadsheets are the most used programming environment in the world. However, they still lack many of the advanced features that modern programming environments offer, and in particular lack a proper version control system. We chose to alleviate this problem by bringing SheetGit to Excel. SheetGit functions as an integrated add-in for Excel and aids users by providing various functionalities of version control, such as automated version creation, collaboration, version comparison, and uniting two versions together in one spreadsheet. We offer all these features directly in Excel in a graphical and intuitive manner.

The empirical validation we performed showed that SheetGit does improve the users' efficiency when performing some tasks, while receiving praise from the participants for its concept, ease of use and necessity in the spreadsheet world.

Version control systems still have some features which were not included in SheetGit such as cherry picking, rebase and many others. But careful consideration must be put into these more advanced control versions features as they must be abstracted and adapted to spreadsheets and their end-user developers. Otherwise the user interface will just become more complex which is against the original purpose of the application. As future work we plan to study how such advanced features can be incorporated to SheetGit.

References

1. Abraham, R., Erwig, M.: Autotest: A tool for automatic test case generation in spreadsheets. In: Proceedings of the 2006 IEEE Symposium on Visual Languages and Human-Centric Computing (VL/HCC '06). pp. 43–50. IEEE CS (2006)
2. Abraham, R., Erwig, M.: Mutation operators for spreadsheets. IEEE Trans. Software Eng **35**(1), 94–108 (2009), http://dx.doi.org/10.1109/TSE.2008.73
3. Bradley, L., McDaid, K.: Using bayesian statistical methods to determine the level of error in large spreadsheets. In: 31st International Conference on Software Engineering. pp. 351–354. IEEE (2009)
4. Cunha, J., Fernandes, J.P., Mendes, J., Saraiva, J.: Embedding, evolution, and validation of model-driven spreadsheets. IEEE Transactions on Software Engineering **41**(3), 241–263 (March 2015). https://doi.org/10.1109/TSE.2014.2361141
5. Dou, W., Xu, L., Cheung, S., Gao, C., Wei, J., Huang, T.: Venron: A versioned spreadsheet corpus and related evolution analysis. In: 2016 IEEE/ACM 38th International Conference on Software Engineering Companion. pp. 162–171 (2016)
6. Engels, G., Erwig, M.: Classsheets: Automatic generation of spreadsheet applications from object-oriented specifications. In: Procs. of the 20th IEEE/ACM Int. Conf. on Automated Software Engineering. pp. 124–133. ACM (2005)
7. Erwig, M., Burnett, M.: Adding apples and oranges. 4th Int. Symp. on Practical Aspects of Declarative Languages pp. 173–191 (2002)
8. Fisher, M., Rothermel, G.: The euses spreadsheet corpus: A shared resource for supporting experimentation with spreadsheet dependability mechanisms. SIGSOFT Softw. Eng. Notes **30**(4), 1–5 (2005)
9. Hermans, F., Murphy-Hill, E.: Enron's spreadsheets and related emails: A dataset and analysis. In: Proceedings of the 37th International Conference on Software Engineering. pp. 7–16. ICSE '15, IEEE Press, Piscataway, NJ, USA (2015)
10. Kitchenham, B., Madeyski, L., Budgen, D., Keung, J., Brereton, P., Charters, S., Gibbs, S., Pohthong, A.: Robust statistical methods for empirical software engineering. Empirical Software Engineering **22**(2), 579–630 (Apr 2017)
11. Kuttal, S.K., Sarma, A., Rothermel, G.: On the benefits of providing versioning support for end users: An empirical study. ACM Trans. Comput.-Hum. Interact. **21**(2), 9:1–9:43 (Feb 2014). https://doi.org/10.1145/2560016
12. Moreira, R.: Sheetgit: A tool for collaborative spreadsheet development. In: Milazzo, P., Varró, D., Wimmer, M. (eds.) Software Technologies: Applications and Foundations. pp. 415–420. Springer International Publishing, Cham (2016)
13. Scaffidi, C., Shaw, M., Myers, B.: Estimating the numbers of end users and end user programmers. In: Visual Languages and Human-Centric Computing, 2005 IEEE Symposium on. pp. 207–214 (Sept 2005). https://doi.org/10.1109/VLHCC.2005.34

La gestión de reutilización de software en el Modelo de la Calidad para el Desarrollo de Aplicaciones Informáticas en Cuba

Leanet Tamayo Oro[1], Yoandy Lazo Alvarado[2], José Felipe Ramírez Pérez[3]

[1] Departamento de Consultoría y Evaluación a Procesos
Centro Nacional de Calidad de Software (CALISOFT) (Cuba)
leanet.tamayo@calisoft.cu
[2] Departamento de Consultoría y Evaluación a Procesos
Centro Nacional de Calidad de Software (CALISOFT) (Cuba)
yoandy.lazo@calisoft.cu
[3] Centro de Informática Médica,
Universidad de las Ciencias Informáticas (UCI) (Cuba)
framirez@uci.cu

Resumen. La competitividad del mercado de la industria del software exige a las empresas elaborar productos en menos tiempo de desarrollo, con bajos costos y una alta calidad. En este contexto se han definido normas y modelos de referencias, que presentan una estrategia de trabajo progresiva para la maduración del proceso de desarrollo de software. Aplicar buenas prácticas de gestión de reutilización de software en el desarrollo del producto trae consigo ventajas competitivas en indicadores de rendimiento de los procesos como son la disminución del tiempo de desarrollo y aumentar la calidad en el producto final. En Cuba no es viable para la mayoría de las organizaciones desarrolladoras de software, la implantación de estos modelos y normas por el alto costo que representan. La presente investigación propone un conjunto de buenas prácticas de la gestión de reutilización identificadas mediante una revisión bibliográfica, sintetizadas en requisitos y procesos de Desarrollo de la solución técnica y proceso de Gestión de Procesos de la Organización del Modelo de Calidad para el Desarrollo de Aplicaciones Informáticas. La propuesta incluye una descripción gráfica y textual de los procesos de diseño del producto y gestión de reutilización, que facilita el cumplimiento de los requisitos, así como los roles involucrados. Este proceso fue sometido a grupos focales y a pilotos para comprobar que es una propuesta apta para extender a la industria de aplicaciones y servicios informáticos.

Palabras clave: proceso de desarrollo, gestión de reutilización, diseño del producto.

1. Introducción

La competitividad del mercado de la industria del software exige a las empresas elaborar productos que satisfagan al cliente en menos tiempo de desarrollo, bajos costos y una alta calidad [1-4]. Para alcanzar estos propósitos se adoptan modelos y normas internacionales, los cuales ofrecen una estrategia de trabajo progresiva que contribuyen, a largo plazo, a mejorar los indicadores de rendimiento de los procesos de desarrollo de software [4-11]. Cuba cuenta con un Modelo de la Calidad para el Desarrollo de Aplicaciones Informáticas (MCDAI) el cual tiene como propósito que sea fácil de entender y aplicar, y que sirva este de base para alcanzar evaluaciones futuras en otros modelos de referencia internacional [12].

Los modelos y normas internacionales proponen un conjunto de buenas prácticas entre la que se encuentra la reutilización de activos de software. Un estudio realizado por los autores de esta investigación permitió identificar que la reutilización es considerada como una posible respuesta a las exigencias del mercado de: productos fiables, con bajos costos y entregados a tiempo; y empresas con elevados índices de productividad [2, 4, 13-16].

La reutilización de software es el proceso de crear sistemas de software a partir de software existente [14, 17]. El enfoque de la reutilización ha transitado desde una perspectiva individual, donde se reutiliza código fuente cuando es necesario; por una oportunista, donde se cuenta con un repositorio de componentes que son reutilizados una vez surja una necesidad; hasta una gestionada, donde el proceso de creación de componentes reutilizables se realiza de manera institucionalizada, sistemática, planificada y mejorada con el fin de obtener óptimos resultados en el proceso de desarrollo de software [13, 14, 17]. Esta evolución ha permitido a organizaciones reconocidas como: Hewlett-Packard, Cummins, Inc., General Motors, CelsiusTech, Rockwell-Collins, Motorola, Philips, Nokia, Boeing, Raytheon y Salion, Inc., adopten un enfoque de línea de productos para sus sistemas de software [4, 15].

Una línea de productos de software es un conjunto de sistemas de software que comparten un conjunto común y gestionado de características que satisfacen las necesidades específicas de un segmento de mercado o misión particular y que se desarrollan a partir de un conjunto común de activos principales de forma prescrita [13].

El enfoque de reutilización en Cuba por lo general no está dirigido al desarrollo de líneas de producto de software. Un diagnóstico realizado en el 2014 a una muestra de catorce (14) organizaciones desarrolladoras de software, identificó que el 66,98% de las mismas dirigen su producción a un segmento de mercado, sin embargo, las buenas prácticas de gestión de la reutilización, identificadas en [6, 7, 13, 18], no se implementan en el 49% y se implementan parcialmente en el 33%. Los resultados del diagnóstico también permitieron identificar que el 52,24% de los proyectos se entregaron fuera de tiempo, el 16,42% no cumplieron la totalidad de los requisitos pactados con el cliente, el 50% no analizan alternativas de solución a partir de componentes reutilizables y el 65% no registra las principales decisiones arquitectónicas [19].

Los autores de esta investigación, en noviembre de 2017 aplicaron encuestas y entrevistas a 24 jefes de proyecto y 16 arquitectos de 8 organizaciones desarrolladoras de software en Cuba, con la finalidad de profundizar en el comportamiento de la gestión de reutilización. Los resultados permitieron identificar que: el 92% no define una arquitectura de dominio que tenga en cuenta los elementos comunes y variantes, el 97% no evalúa la arquitectura, el 69% no aplica un programa que gestione el desarrollo de activos reutilizables, el 65% no evalúa las oportunidades de reutilización a partir de activos de dominio desarrollados, ni identifican los esfuerzos de adaptación, creación o adquisición de nuevos activos y el 90% no cuenta con un repositorio de activos reutilizables. En abril de 2018, también se aplicó una encuesta a 15 especialistas con más de 10 años de experiencia en el desarrollo de software, lo que permitió concluir que el enfoque de reutilización más utilizado es el oportunista.

Por lo antes descrito se define como objetivo de esta investigación desarrollar un proceso de diseño y gestión de la reutilización para el Modelo de la Calidad para el Desarrollo de Aplicaciones Informáticas que permita aumentar el rendimiento del proceso de desarrollo de software en Cuba en cuanto a la reducción del tiempo de desarrollo y el aumento del cumplimiento de los requisitos.

2. Materiales y métodos

Los autores de esta investigación realizaron una revisión bibliográfica con el propósito de identificar las buenas prácticas del desarrollo de software para la reutilización en los artículos [13-17, 20, 21] y en los siguientes modelos y normas: ISO/IEC/IEEE 12207:2017 [9], ISO/IEC/IEEE 15288:2015 [10], CMMI-DEV [7], MoProSoft [11], MPS.Br [6] y COMPETISOFT [22]. En la Tabla 1 se muestra un resumen de este análisis, constituyendo esta la base para la propuesta de la presente investigación.

Tabla 1. Buenas prácticas del desarrollo de software para la realización (fuente: elaboración propia).

Buena práctica	**CMMI-DEV**	**MPS.Br**	**MoProSoft**	**COMPETISOFT**	**ISO/IEC /IEEE**	
					12207	**15288**
Desarrollar y seleccionar soluciones alternativas y los criterios de selección	x	x		x		x
Diseñar y documentar el producto o componente de producto	x	x	x	x	x	x
Diseñar interfaces internas y externas	x	x	x	x	x	x
Realizar análisis sobre si hacer-reutilizar o comprar	x	x		x		x
Implementar el producto o componente de producto	x	x	x	x	x	x
Desarrollar documentación de soporte	x	x	x	x		
Definir Estrategia de integración	x	x	x	x	x	x
Gestionar un programa de gestión de reutilización		x			x	x
Gestionar la biblioteca de activos reutilizables.		x			x	x
Definir Modelo de dominio teniendo en cuenta los elementos comunes y variantes		x			x	x
Definir la arquitectura de dominio teniendo en cuenta los elementos comunes y variantes		x			x	x
Desarrollar activos para la reutilización		x			x	x

En el caso de los modelos CMMI-DEV, MoProSoft y COMPETISOFT presentan las bases para desarrollar con reutilización, pero no tienen el enfoque gestionado de la reutilización. Las normas ISO/IEC/IEEE 12207 y 15288, proponen un proceso de gestión del conocimiento que impulsa la gestión de reutilización de activos de software.

El modelo MPS.Br propone un área de gestión de reutilización y una de desarrollo para la reutilización donde se separan las actividades de gestión, infraestructura y alineación estratégica con los objetivos de negocio con las actividades ingenieriles necesarias para el desarrollo de activos reutilizables.

La mayoría de los modelos y normas antes mencionados poseen períodos de implementación extensos y están acompañados de grandes esfuerzos para su asimilación, además de elevados costos de consultoría y evaluación, elemento que dificulta su adopción en Cuba.

Teniendo en cuenta lo antes descrito se decidió realizar una propuesta propia que indique “qué” hacer para gestionar la reutilización y ejemplifique “cómo” ponerla en práctica mediante un proceso que contiene actividades, roles asociados, técnicas y herramientas.

Para la elaboración de la propuesta se convocaron 12 especialistas de más de 4 años de experiencia en los roles de Jefe de proyecto, Arquitecto y Desarrollador. Posteriormente se realizó un análisis, basado en el método grupo focal, con el propósito de definir los requisitos que debería tener el MCDAI respecto a la reutilización, teniendo en cuenta las buenas prácticas identificadas (ver tabla 1) y las incidencias de estas sobre los problemas detectados. Los requisitos identificados fueron agrupados por los niveles de madurez Básico, Intermedio y Avanzado [12], lo cual permite que la propuesta pueda ser adoptada de forma escalonada, incorporando pequeñas mejoras en las organizaciones.

3. Resultados

Se decidió incorporar las buenas prácticas de gestión de reutilización en varias áreas del conocimiento del MCDAI, la gestión de la biblioteca y el programa de gestión de reutilización el cual se encarga de gestionar el proceso de reutilización de software en las organizaciones, concebir proyectos para la familia de productos alineados a las políticas, estrategia de la organización y al modelo de negocio definido. A continuación, se muestra un gráfico con la representación de la incorporación de las buenas prácticas en el modelo MCDAI.

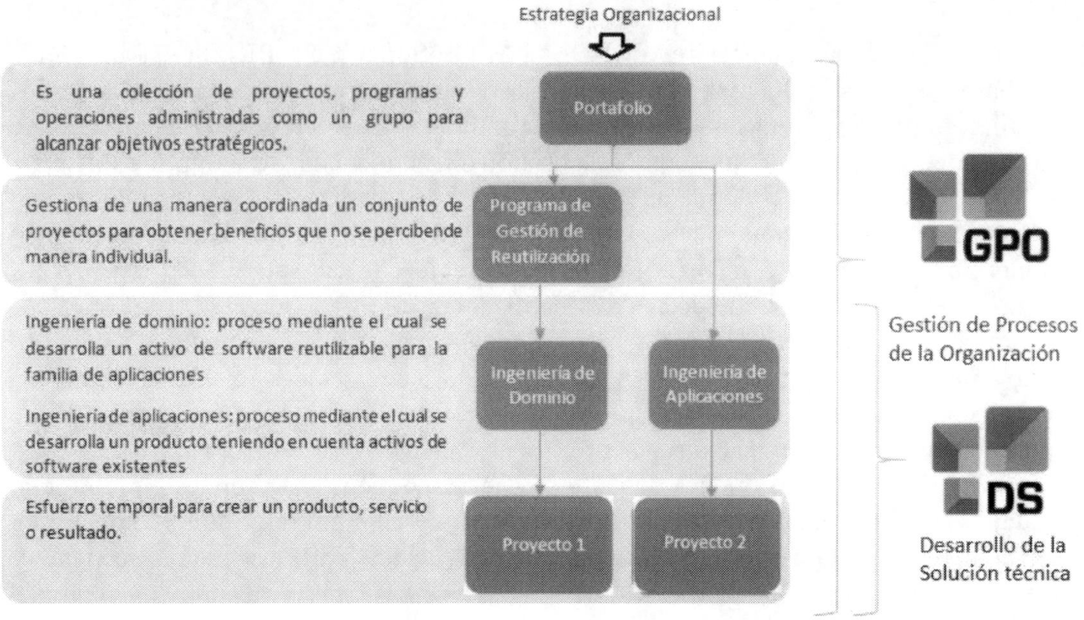

Fig. 1. La gestión de la reutilización en el MCDAI (Fuente: elaboración propia).

Se elaboró el proceso de Gestión de Procesos de la Organización (GPO), que tiene como propósito definir los procesos de la organización y crear un marco de trabajo que, siguiendo los procesos establecidos, permita conducir a la organización al cumplimiento de su misión y objetivos estratégicos. Gestionar los recursos y concebir los proyectos de desarrollo de software. Gestionar el ciclo de vida de los activos reutilizables.

Se elaboró el proceso base Desarrollo de la Solución Técnica (DS), que tiene como propósito: seleccionar y evaluar soluciones a partir de alternativas existentes. Diseñar, implementar y ensamblar los componentes que forman parte de la solución para dar cumplimiento a los requisitos. Identificar oportunidades de reutilización sistemática de activos de software y desarrollar activos a partir de ingeniería de dominios.

Para cumplir con este propósito se definieron los siguientes requisitos separados por niveles de madurez.

Tabla 2. Directrices de los procesos GPO y DS (Fuente: elaboración propia).

Nivel	GPO	DS
Directrices del nivel Básico	D 1 Definir el plan estratégico de la organización.	D 1 Identificar soluciones.
	D 2 Definir y mantener el/los modelo(s) de negocio.	D 2 Diseñar el producto o el componente de producto.
	D 5 Definir roles.	D 4 Implementar el producto o el componente de producto.
	D 6 Proveer recursos.	D 6 Desarrollar la documentación de soporte de producto.
	D 7.1 Concebir proyecto.	D 7 Empaquetar y entregar el producto.
Directrices del nivel Intermedio	D 3 Definir y mantener el/los modelo(s) y estándares del entorno de trabajo.	D 1.1 Evaluar las posibles soluciones aplicables.
	D 4 Institucionalizar procesos.	D 2.1 Definir y describir interfaces.

Nivel	GPO	DS
	D 5.1 Definir competencias.	D 3 Definir estrategia de integración.
	D 7 Gestionar portafolio.	D 5 Integrar el producto.
	D 7.2 Utilizar modelos y datos históricos.	
Directrices del nivel Avanzado	D 8 Orientar la organización hacia la reutilización.	D 1.2 Evaluar las posibles soluciones aplicables a partir de activos reutilizables.
	D 8.1 Gestionar los activos reutilizables.	D 8 Desarrollar en función de la reutilización de activos de dominio.

3.1. Relación entre los procesos base de GPO y DS

A continuación, se muestra un gráfico que representa la relación entre el proceso base de DS y GPO teniendo en cuenta las prácticas de gestión de reutilización.

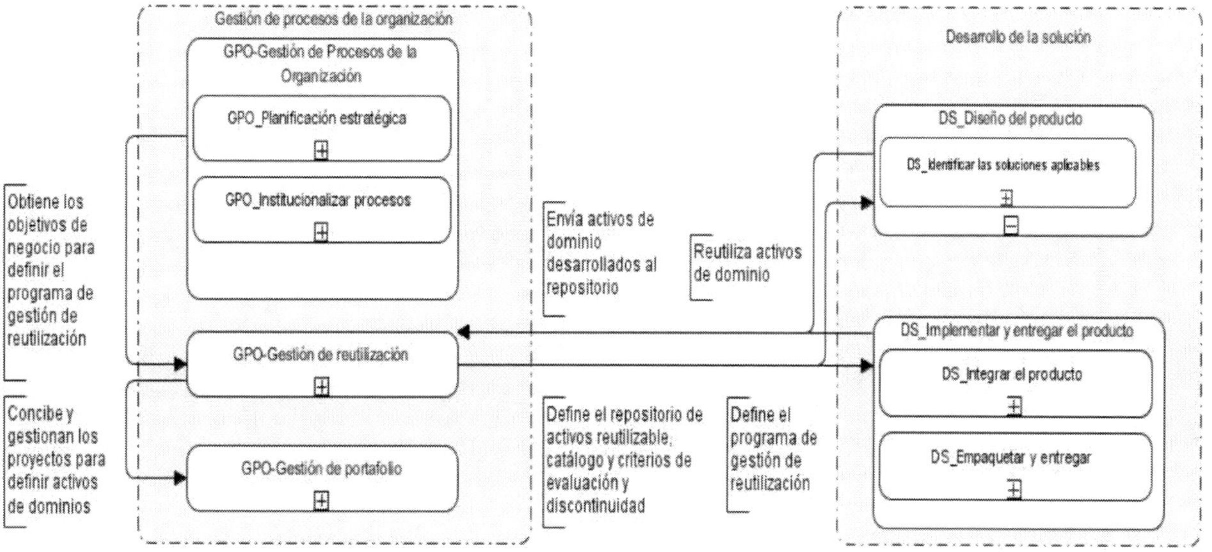

Fig. 2. Relación DS y GPO teniendo en cuenta la gestión de reutilización. (Fuente: elaboración propia).

3.1. El desarrollo para la reutilización de software en el Proceso base de Diseño del Producto

Como parte de la solución se propone dos procesos macro (Diseño del producto) que facilita a las entidades la implementación de los requisitos; no es de obligatorio cumplimiento sino una guía que se puede adecuar a las condiciones de cada entidad. Debido a la amplitud de la solución propuesta se muestra a continuación una breve descripción del proceso de Diseño del Producto.

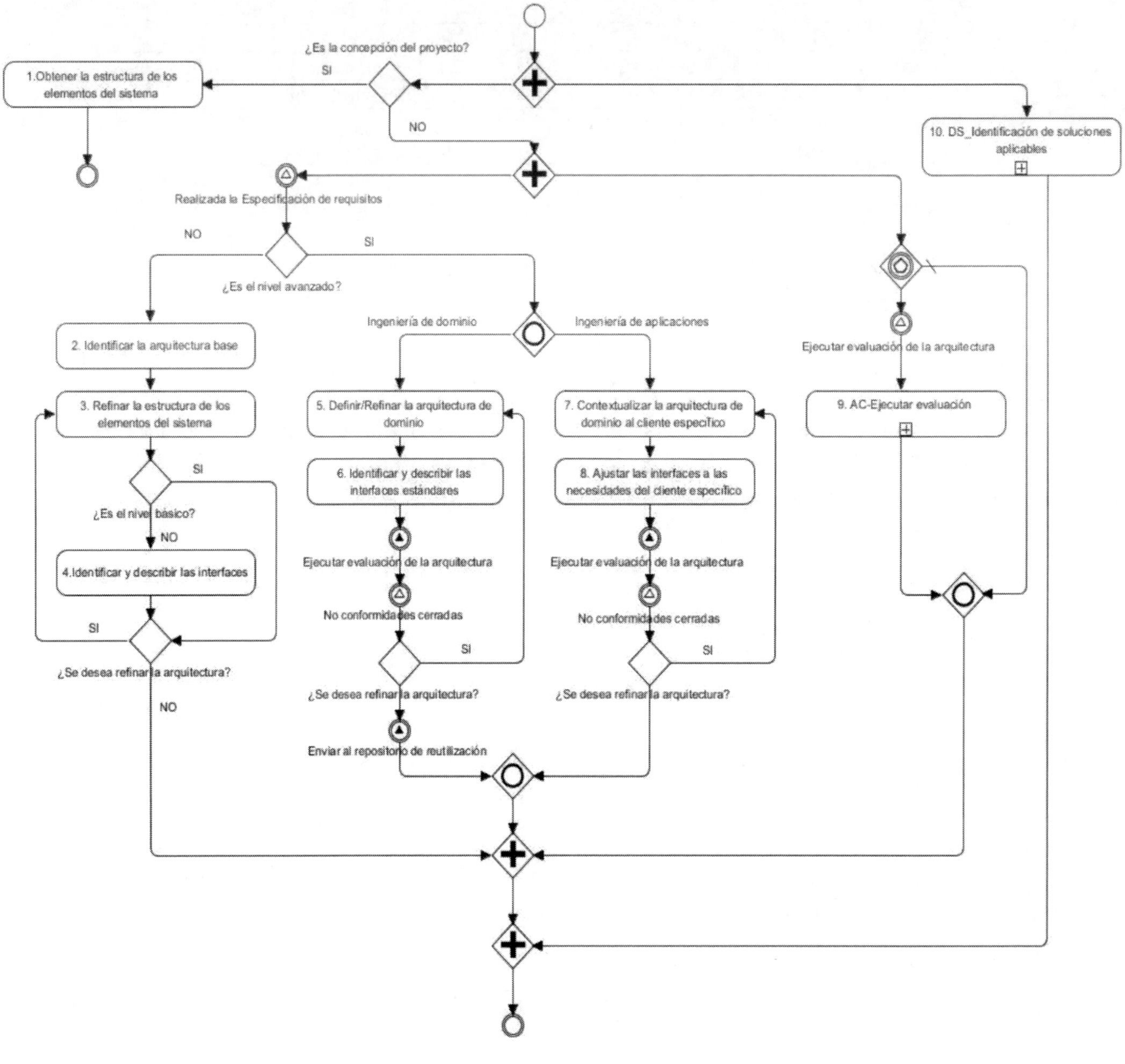

Fig. 3. Descripción gráfica del proceso Diseño del producto.

Descripción textual del proceso

Actividad 1: Obtener la estructura de los elementos del sistema.

El Comité técnico / Arquitecto teniendo en cuenta las necesidades, el alcance y los objetivos del proyecto definidos en la "Oferta" y/o "Proyecto técnico": Identifica los principales componentes del producto y realiza su representación estructural a un alto nivel de abstracción, determinando las relaciones existentes entre los elementos que lo componen. Se obtiene como resultado de la ejecución de esta actividad la "Oferta" y/o "Proyecto técnico" / Propuesta técnica inicial (actualizada).

Actividad 2: Identificar la arquitectura base.

El Arquitecto teniendo en cuenta la propuesta técnica inicial definida en la "Oferta" y/o "Proyecto técnico" y la "Especificación de requisitos": Define los atributos de la calidad y requisitos funcionales que impactan en la arquitectura. Realiza la priorización de las unidades funcionales. Determinan los componentes que funcionan como plataforma del sistema que será desarrollado y que sirve como base para futuras implementaciones. Se obtiene como resultado de la ejecución de esta actividad la "Arquitectura del sistema".

Actividad 3: Refinar la estructura de los elementos del sistema.

El Arquitecto teniendo en cuenta la propuesta técnica inicial definida en la "Oferta" y/o "Proyecto técnico", la "Especificación de requisitos", y las partes interesadas identificadas: Refina la descomposición del sistema en módulos o componentes, en dependencia del tamaño y complejidad del mismo y teniendo en cuenta las soluciones aplicables como son las tecnologías, estilos arquitectónicos, patrones entre otros. Determina los datos persistentes que se necesitan manejar en el sistema e identifica el modelo de datos. Define la estructura de los nodos físicos como apoyo al despliegue del sistema. Se obtiene como resultado de la ejecución de esta actividad la "Arquitectura del sistema" / Estructura de los elementos del sistema

Actividad 4: Identificar y describir las interfaces.

A partir de la "Especificación de requisitos" y la "Arquitectura del sistema": El Arquitecto define y describen las interfaces entre los componentes del sistema (internas), y las interfaces con componentes externos al mismo para controlar los elementos de entrada-salida y garantizar la integración con elementos externos y con el resto de los componentes del sistema. El Diseñador identifica y describe las interfaces con los usuarios del sistema de manera tal que se cumplan los requisitos de usabilidad aplicables. Se obtiene como resultado de la ejecución de esta actividad la "Arquitectura del sistema" / Descripción de interfaces (actualizada).

Actividad 5: Definir/Refinar la arquitectura de dominio.

En el nivel Avanzado, el Comité técnico / Arquitecto teniendo en cuenta la propuesta técnica inicial definida en la "Oferta" y/o "Proyecto técnico", la "Especificación de requisitos", las partes interesadas identificadas, el estilo arquitectónico estándar y la plataforma tecnológica definidas en la "Arquitectura de dominio": Determina las vistas arquitectónicas que se van a desarrollar, de acuerdo a los puntos de vista necesarios para satisfacer a las partes interesadas en posibles entornos específicos. Define/Refina la estructura estándar del sistema e identifica los componentes que van a ser comunes y variantes, opcionales u obligatorios para toda la familia de aplicaciones. Determina los datos persistentes que se necesitan manejar en el sistema y se apoya en el "Modelo conceptual" para definir el modelo de datos estándar. Se obtiene como resultado de la ejecución de esta actividad la "Arquitectura del dominio" / Vista arquitectónicas (creadas).

Actividad 6: Identificar y describir las interfaces estándares.

A partir de la "Especificación de requisitos" y la "Arquitectura del dominio": El Arquitecto define y describe las interfaces estándares entre los componentes de la familia de aplicaciones (internas), y las interfaces con componentes externos, donde se especifica los elementos comunes y variantes, opcionales u obligatorios. El Diseñador identifica y describe las interfaces para posibles usuarios de la familia de aplicaciones como un marco de trabajo común, de manera que se cumplan los requisitos de usabilidad aplicables. Se obtiene como resultado de la ejecución de esta actividad la "Arquitectura de dominio" / Vista de integración (creada) / Vista de Presentación (creada).

Actividad 7: Contextualizar la arquitectura de dominio al cliente específico.

El Arquitecto teniendo en cuenta la propuesta técnica inicial definida en la "Oferta" y/o "Proyecto técnico", la "Especificación de requisitos", el "Modelo de dominio" y las partes interesadas identificadas: En función de las vistas arquitectónicas definidas en la "Arquitectura de dominio", determina las vistas que se van a modificar o desarrollar, de acuerdo a los puntos de vista necesarios para satisfacer a las partes interesadas en un entorno específico. En función de los elementos variantes identificados en el "Análisis de los componentes de la solución que se van a hacer/reutilizar/adquirir" y siguiendo el estilo arquitectónico estándar; se modifican los elementos necesarios en los componentes variantes y/o se incorporan nuevos competentes, para satisfacer las necesidades del cliente específico. Identifica nuevos datos persistentes en relación al "Modelo de datos" identificados en la "Arquitectura de dominio". Define la estructura de los nodos físicos como apoyo al despliegue del sistema. Se obtiene como resultado de la ejecución de esta actividad la "Arquitectura del sistema" / Vistas arquitectónicas.

Actividad 8: Ajustar las interfaces a las necesidades del cliente específico.

A partir de la "Especificación de requisitos", "Arquitectura del dominio" y la "Arquitectura del sistema": El Arquitecto identifica y describe las interfaces internas y externas que se modificarán o agregarán, para controlar los elementos de entrada-salida y garantizar la integración con el resto de los componentes. El Diseñador identifica y describe las modificaciones a las interfaces para los usuarios del sistema, de manera que se cumplan los requisitos de usabilidad aplicables. Se obtiene como resultado de la ejecución de esta actividad la "Arquitectura de dominio" / Vista de integración (creada) / Vista de Presentación (creada).

Actividad 9: AC-Ejecutar evaluación.

El Equipo de evaluación, teniendo en cuenta los atributos de la calidad aplicables y los requisitos arquitectónicamente significativos, verifica que el diseño se encuentre técnicamente correcto guiado por el subproceso AC-Ejecutar Evaluación (AC es la sigla del proceso base Aseguramiento de la Calidad del MCDAI).

Actividad 10: DS_Identificación de Soluciones Aplicables.

El Comité técnico / Arquitecto identifica las soluciones aplicables al producto como lo plantea el sub-proceso DS-Identificación de Soluciones Aplicables.

3.2. La gestión de reutilización de software como proceso del Proceso base Gestión de Procesos de la Organización

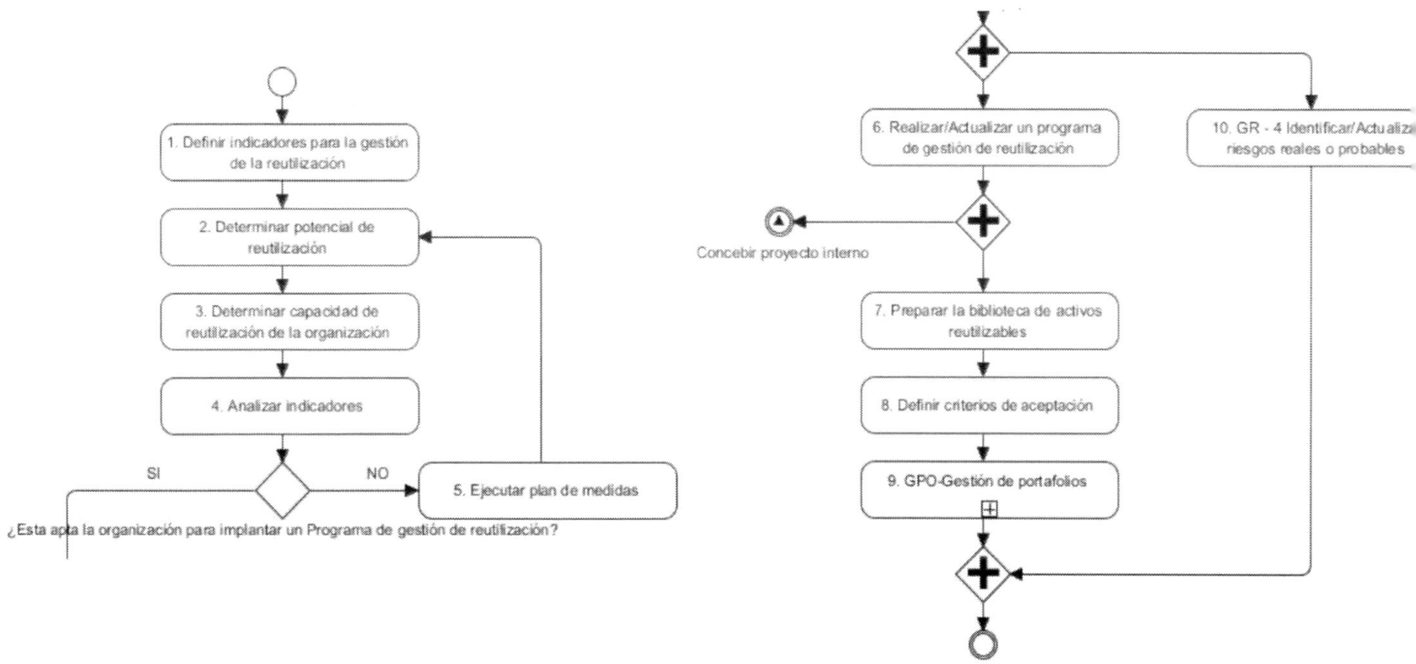

Fig. 4. Descripción gráfica del proceso Gestión de reutilización.

Descripción textual del subproceso GPO-Gestión de reutilización

Actividad 1: Definir indicadores para la gestión de la reutilización.

La Dirección define los indicadores "Potencial de reutilización de los dominios de aplicación" y "Capacidad de reutilización de la organización" a medir en el diagnóstico a la organización como establece el subproceso MyM-Definición de la medición y análisis (MyM es la sigla del proceso base Medición y Mejora del MCDAI).

- Para concebir el indicador "Potencial de reutilización de los dominios de aplicación" se tienen en cuenta aspectos como: componentes reutilizables existentes, importancia del dominio en términos de proyectos futuros, estudio de mercado, la madurez y estabilidad de los componentes reutilizables, entre otros.
- Para concebir el indicador "Capacidad de reutilización de la organización" se tienen en cuenta aspectos como: disponibilidad de recursos humanos y financieros, dinámica de trabajo en la organización, potencial de reutilización de los dominios (esto puede implicar una inversión mayor o menor por lo que influye en los estados financieros), entre otros.

Se obtiene como resultado los Indicadores definidos.

Actividad 2: Determinar potencial de reutilización.

El Grupo de expertos, teniendo en cuenta el indicador "Potencial de reutilización de los dominios de aplicación", el Registro de proyectos de la organización y los expedientes de proyecto, determina el potencial de reutilización de cada dominio de aplicación. Se obtiene como resultado el Informe de diagnóstico de la organización / Listado de dominios con el potencial de reutilización.

Actividad 3: Determinar capacidad de reutilización de la organización.

La Dirección, teniendo en cuenta el indicador "Capacidad de reutilización de la organización", el Listado de dominios con el potencial de reutilización y el Plan estratégico de la organización, determina la capacidad que la misma posee para adoptar un programa de gestión de reutilización. Se obtiene como resultado el Informe de diagnóstico de la organización / Capacidad de reutilización.

Actividad 4: Analizar indicadores.

La Dirección analiza el resultado de los indicadores con el fin de determinar si la organización tiene la capacidad de adoptar un Programa de gestión de reutilización, en el caso tenerla; realiza un análisis de los recursos con los que cuenta la organización, la planificación estratégica y los dominios de aplicación con mayor potencial de reutilización con el objetivo de identificar y priorizar los dominios en los que se pretende realizar un programa de gestión de reutilización. En caso de no tener la capacidad, elabora un plan de acciones para alcanzar la capacidad deseada. Se obtiene como resultado el Informe de diagnóstico de la organización / Análisis de los indicadores, en caso de ser necesario un Plan de acción.

Actividad 5: Ejecutar plan de medidas.

La Dirección, ejecuta las actividades planificadas en el Plan de medidas con el fin de que la organización alcance la capacidad necesaria para implementar un Programa de gestión de reutilización.

Actividad 6: Realizar/Actualizar un Programa de gestión de reutilización.

La Dirección a partir del análisis del Informe de diagnóstico y el Plan de estratégico de la organización, elabora/actualiza un Programa de gestión de reutilización. El mismo contiene el alcance, conformado por los portafolios en los que se va a trabajar y los activos de dominios que se desarrollarán o modificarán; las metas, describe los resultados específicos que se quieren logar; los recursos necesarios; las actividades a desarrollar, y el monitoreo que se va a realizar, alineado a la planificación de los portafolios contenida en el Plan estratégico de la organización. Se obtiene como resultado el Programa de gestión de reutilización.

Actividad 7: Preparar la biblioteca de activos reutilizables.

El Administrador de la configuración teniendo en cuenta el Programa de gestión de reutilización identifica la o las herramientas necesarias que funcionen como una biblioteca de activos de dominio de la organización (Se apoya en la minería de texto, en herramientas de búsqueda, repositorios, herramientas de integración continua, entre otras). Diseña la estructura de la biblioteca en base a las herramientas seleccionadas. Las herramientas y el diseño permiten: catalogar, almacenar, buscar y recuperar los activos de dominio, registrar los consumidores de los activos y notificar a estos sobre sus actualizaciones. Despliega la biblioteca. Se obtiene como resultado la biblioteca de activos preparada.

Actividad 8: Definir criterios de aceptación.

Un Grupo de expertos determina los criterios de aceptación, certificación, discontinuidad y evaluación de los activos. Se obtiene como resultado los criterios de los activos reutilizables identificados.

Actividad 9: GPO-Gestión de portafolios.

La Dirección, teniendo en cuenta el Programa de gestión de reutilización y el Plan estratégico de la organización, gestiona los portafolios involucrados de acuerdo al subproceso GPO-Gestión de portafolios (GPO es la sigla del Proceso base Gestión de Procesos de la Organización del MCDAI).

Actividad 10: GR - 4 Identificar/Actualizar riesgos reales o probables.

La Dirección revisa el Programa de gestión de reutilización e identifica los riesgos que puedan influir en su cumplimiento. Se obtiene como resultado el Registro de riesgos y tratamientos con el Listado riesgos identificados como establece el proceso GR - Gestión de riesgos (GR es la sigla del Proceso base Gestión de Riesgos del MCDAI).

4. Validación

Con la intención de validar los requisitos que componen el proceso de GPO y DS asociados a la gestión de reutilización, se realizaron grupos focales, la cual constituye una técnica valiosa y muy utilizada en la última década para obtener información. Para su conformación se tuvo en cuenta los criterios emitidos por Méndez y Aigneren [23, 24], al decir que el tamaño del grupo debe oscilar entre cuatro (4) y doce (12) participantes; asegurando que todos puedan emitir sus criterios y que haya riqueza de ideas. Además, debe ser homogéneo y determinado por el propósito del estudio.

Para cumplir con lo antes expuesto se ha invitado a especialistas de la industria de servicios y aplicaciones informáticas, dedicados a realizar tareas relacionadas con el diseño y desarrollo de software, para analizar los resultados de esta investigación en siete (7) encuentros. Las entidades que participaron fueron: CALISOFT con tres (3) especialistas, XETID (2), UCI (1), Cedipad (1), Joven Club (1), OSRI (1), Etecsa (1), SICS/MITRANS (2) y en total sumaron 12 profesionales.

Los acuerdos tomados en las sesiones de trabajo derivaron en mejoras a los procesos base que fueron valiosas para que se lograran procesos refinados y alineados con las características de la industria de servicios y aplicaciones informáticas.

En el último encuentro al exponer el resultado final de los procesos base DS y GPO fueron aprobados por todo el equipo participante. En dicho encuentro predominó el criterio: "Los procesos base son una propuesta que se ajusta a las necesidades de la industria de servicios y aplicaciones informáticas. Los elementos de apoyo que lo componen, como son: la descripción gráfica y textual del proceso, facilitarán la implantación de los requisitos en cada entidad sin necesidad de invertir mucho tiempo y recursos."

Los procesos base de DS y GPO, se aplicaron en cuatro (4) empresas (DESOFT, TRANSOFT, DATYS Y AICROS) a través de proyectos pilotos. La composición de dichas empresas es variada en tamaños y características. Hay empresas que tienen implantadas normas de calidad y otras que solo usan los modelos, normas, estándares y/o guías de calidad como referencia [25].

Se aplicó la técnica IADOV para evaluar el nivel de satisfacción de los usuarios con los procesos propuestos. La técnica fue aplicada a 20 especialistas con un promedio de 10 años de experiencia desempeñando roles de jefe de proyecto, arquitecto y programador. Los resultados obtenidos fueron que el 75% de los usuarios muestran una clara satisfacción con la propuesta presentada, el 15% más satisfecho que insatisfecho y el 10% no definido o contradictorio. Además, no se contó con usuarios insatisfechos, por los que se obtuvo un Índice de Satisfacción Grupal de 0.85, en base a 1, lo que indica la satisfacción de los usuarios con los procesos de DS y GPO.

También se aplicó un estudio de caso donde se recopiló información de los indicadores de rendimiento de los procesos, antes y después de aplicar la propuesta, a partir de esta información en cinco proyectos, de tres meses de duración, de desarrollo web (ver tabla 3). A continuación, se especifican los indicadores que fueron evaluados en el caso de estudio:

T = tiempo dedicado al desarrollo.

CR = cumplimiento de requisitos arquitectónicamente significativos.

Pi = Proyectos del 1 al 5 que aplicaron la propuesta.

Tabla 3. Caso de estudio. Rendimiento del proceso. Fuente: elaboración propia

Antes (Sin aplicar la propuesta)	Indicadores		Después (Aplicada la propuesta)	Indicadores	
	T	CR		T	CR
P1	500 h	0.66	P1	350 h	0.98
P2	400 h	0.94	P2	250 h	0.98
P3	200 h	0.55	P3	130 h	0.95
P4	210 h	0.48	P4	120 h	0.75
P5	300 h	0.68	P5	250 h	0.99

En la tabla 2 se pudo apreciar una mejoría en los indicadores de rendimiento, una vez aplicada la propuesta, mediante la reducción de tiempo, así como un aumento del índice de cumplimiento de requisitos arquitectónicamente significativos.

5. Conclusiones

El análisis crítico de los modelos CMMI-DEV, MPS.Br, MoProSoft, COMPETISOFT y las normas ISO/IEC/IEEE 12207 y 15288, permitió identificar los requisitos necesarios para poder realizar la gestión de reutilización de software desde un enfoque de gestión a un enfoque ingenieril.

La propuesta de los procesos de DS y GPO del MCDAI incorpora buenas prácticas de gestión de reutilización desde dos perspectivas diferentes para complementar ambas propuestas y fomentar la reutilización en las organizaciones desarrolladoras de software.

Se definieron las descripciones gráficas de los procesos separados por niveles de madurez para cumplir con los requisitos propuestos y facilitar la adopción de los mismos, que permiten entender las buenas prácticas seleccionadas para GPO y DS.

La validación de la propuesta, con el objetivo de garantizar la confiabilidad en los resultados, constató la convergencia de los resultados obtenidos y evidenció que la solución propuesta es adecuada y resuelve la necesidad de la investigación.

6. Referencias

1. Medina, E., A.J. Solís, I.P.T. de Andalucía, *La necesidad de un sistema de la calidad para prevenir y controlar los problemas. Parque tecnológico de Andalucía.* 2006.
2. Bastarrica, C., *Productividad en la Industria TIC. Bits, Ciencia y Sociedad.* 2011.

3. Regaliza, P., et al., *Proyectos software desde una perspectiva cibernética*, in *in IX Congreso de Ingeniería de Organización: Gijón, 8-9 Septiembre de 2005.* . 2005.
4. Salazar Labrada, L., *Desarrollo del proceso Solución Técnica para los proyectos de desarrollo de la Universidad de la Ciencias Informáticas*. 2017, UNIVERSIDAD DE LAS CIENCIAS INFORMÁTICAS.
5. Aguilar, L.F., *Gobernanza.* El nuevo proceso de gobernar. Publicado por Fundación Friedrich Naumann para la Libertad, México, 2010.
6. SOFTEX, *MPS.BR - Mejora de Proceso del Software Brasileño. Guía de Implementación - Parte 5: Fundamentos para Implementación del Nivel C del MR-MPS.* 2009.
7. SEI, S.E.I., *CMMI para Desarrollo, Versión 1.3.* 2010.
8. CYTED, C.y.T.p.e.D., *COMPETISOFT-Mejora de Procesos para Fomentar la Competitividad de la Pequeña y Mediana Industria del Software de Iberoamérica. Versión 0.2.* 2006.
9. ISO, I., IEEE, *12207 Systems and software engineering-software life cycle processes.* International Organization for Standardization, Geneva, Switzerland, 2017.
10. ISO, I., IEEE, *15288. Systems and software engineering-System life cycle processes.* 2015.
11. Oktaba, H., *Modelo de Procesos para la Industria de Software-MoproSoft-Versión 1.3, Agosto de 2005.* 2005, NMX-059/01-NYCE-2005.
12. Pérez, D.M., *Guía general para un modelo cubano de desarrollo de aplicaciones informáticas*, in *Universidad de las Ciencias Informáticas(UCI)*. 2014.
13. Northrop, L., et al., *A framework for software product line practice, version 5.0.* SEI.–2007–http://www. sei. cmu. edu/productlines/index. html, 2012.
14. Manso, M.M. and F.J.P. García *Medición en la Reutilización Orientada a Objetos.* 2013.
15. Bergey, J.K., et al., *Fourth DoD Product Line Practice Workshop Report.* 2001.
16. Alam, M.M., A.I. Khan, and A. Zafar, *A Comprehensive Study of Software Product Line Frameworks.* International Journal of Computer Applications, 2016. **151**(3).
17. Martinez, J., T. Ziadi, and T.F. Bissyandé, *Bottom-Up Adoption of Software Product Lines - A Generic and Extensible Approach.* 2015: p. http://dx.doi.org/10.1145/2791060.2791086.
18. SOFTEX, *MPS.BR - Mejora de Proceso del Software Brasileño. Guía de Implementación - Parte 3: Fundamentos para Implementación del Nivel E del MR-MPS.* 2009.
19. CALISOFT, C.N.d.C.d.S., *CS-03-D (14-001) LIBRO DE DIAGNÓSTICO.* 2014.
20. Krueger, C., *New methods behind a new generation of software product line successes.* KC Kang, V. Sugumaran, and S. Park,"Applied Software Product Line Engineering", Auerbach Publications, 2010: p. 39-60.
21. Bosch, J. *Maturity and evolution in software product lines: Approaches, artefacts and organization.* in *International Conference on Software Product Lines*. 2002. Springer.
22. COMPETISOFT, *COMPETISOFT-Mejora de Procesos para Fomentar la Competitividad de la Pequeña y Mediana Industria del Software de Iberoamérica. Versión 0.2.* Diciembre, 2006.
23. Méndez, A.L.d., *La entrevista y los grupos focales.* 2007.
24. Aigneren, M., *La técnica de recolección de información mediante grupos focales. La Sociología en sus escenarios.* 2009.
25. Deborat Pérez, D.A., *Evolución del modelo de calidad para el desarrollo de aplicaciones informáticas.* XVII Convención y Feria Internacional Informática 2016, 2016.

Architectural Tactics for Scalability

Cristian Orellana[1], Mónica M. Villegas[2] and Hernán Astudillo[3]

Universidad Técnica Federico Santa María
Toeska Research Group
Valparaíso, Chile
[1]cristian.orellanae@usm.cl,
[2]monica.villegas@usm.cl,
[3]hernan@inf.utfsm.cl

Abstract. Scalability is the ability to handle increased workload by repeatedly applying a cost-effective strategy for extending a systems capacity. Architectural tactics have been proposed as a way to systematically organize design decisions to provide quality attributes (QA), and many have been published for performance, availability, security and so on. Scalability-related tactics have usually been included in catalogs of performance and availability tactics, or for specific contexts like big data, but proper understanding of their aspects and trade-offs requires a specific catalog. This article surveys scalability tactics proposed in the literature; compares and homologates them into a smaller set; proposed to consider "workload" as their stimulus; and organizes them into a taxonomy addressing (workload) detection, reaction, and prediction. This proposal is a first step towards giving scalability first-class status as an addressable quality attribute.

Keywords: Scalability · Quality attributes · Software architecture · Architectural tactics

1 Introduction

Nowadays, designing systems that can handle an increased workload and high demands of resources has become a requirement, mostly in IoT and Big Data ecosystems. For software architects making the right decisions to provide a robust and efficient solution that adapts to high demand conditions at runtime without impacting other quality attributes (such as availability or performance) becomes challenging. For non-expert architects, the existence of multiple decisions while designing a system can be a complex process. Thus, having a reference catalog becomes helpful as a reference point for making decisions based on specific scenarios and the tactics that can solve them.

The concept of scalability provides an architectural driver that allows a system to continue operating on a regular basis when service requests are increased, and there is an impact on the workload that the system must process, being a critical aspect for the correct operation of the system. To achieve this goal, it is necessary to understand preliminarily what is scalability and how it is possible to identify risk situations that could potentially compromise the scalability of a system.

Architectural tactics have been proposed as a mechanism to pack and reuse architectural knowledge that addresses specific quality attributes. Architectural tactics have been proposed for several quality attributes like Performance, Security and son, but none for Scalability; indeed, we found that tactics that address scalability have been included in catalogs Availability or Performance tactics, thus impairing consideration of trade-offs [7] among scalability decisions as such.

Our approach is to identify and characterize design decisions that impact scalability, and which may be easy for experienced architects but could be entirely neglected by novice architects due to their smaller methodological and lived repertoir of techniques to detect, prevent and mitigate scalability problems. To identify and organized scalabilitty tactics, we followed a simple process: (1) search related work; (2) select tactics catalogs available in the literature; (3) identify scalability tactics from these catalogs; and (4) map proposed tactics to scalability concepts, like AFK scale cube and horizontal/vertical scalability.

The reminder of this document is structured as follows: Section 2 gives background scalability; Section 3 summarizes previous efforts and related work; Section 4 presents the steps followed to identify, filter and homologate tactics; Section 5 presents the resulting taxonomy of scalability tactics; Section 6 illustrates the proposed tactics catalog with a practical case based on an actual system; and finally, Section 7 summarizes and concludes.

2 Scalability

Scalability is a topic that has been addressed numerous times in the literature. Books such as [11] [6] [8] that describe this quality attribute in detail, and numerous articles describe it and relate scalability with other quality attributes such as performance [4].

Scalability is usually defined regarding workload, which Elnaffar et al. [16] define as a set of requests presented to the system. Weinstock et al. [14] propose two definitions for scalability: (1) "the ability to handle increased workload," i.e. a system is scalable if it can handle a large demand of resources and still work in a stable manner; and (2) "the ability to handle increased workload by repeatedly applying a cost-effective strategy for extending a system's capacity," i.e. a system would need a repeatedly addition of resources for its correct behavior. Since a system requires more resources to improve its behavior, the literature [13] distinguises *horizontal scalability*, also called "scaling out" and related to adding resources to logical units in a system; and *vertical scalability*, also called "scaling up," related to adding resources to physical units.

Since scalability implies the addition of resources, Abbott et al. [9] specify the AFK (AFK Consulting Group: Abbot, Fisher and Keeven) scale cube (see Fig. 2), describing its X, Y and Z-Axis in terms of scalability. The AFK scale cube covers the cloning and replication actions for each axis and showing the importance of such actions for this quality attribute.

The X-Axis (scaling out) is related to the addition of resources to logical units in a system, in other words, clone resources. The Y-Axis, aims to split the system by functionality and the Z-Axis describes that data is splitted and replicated for workload balance. Abbott et al.'s definitions [9] are centered on databases also apply to any system that needs replication of resources, specifically when it has an increased workload and needs more resources to handle it.

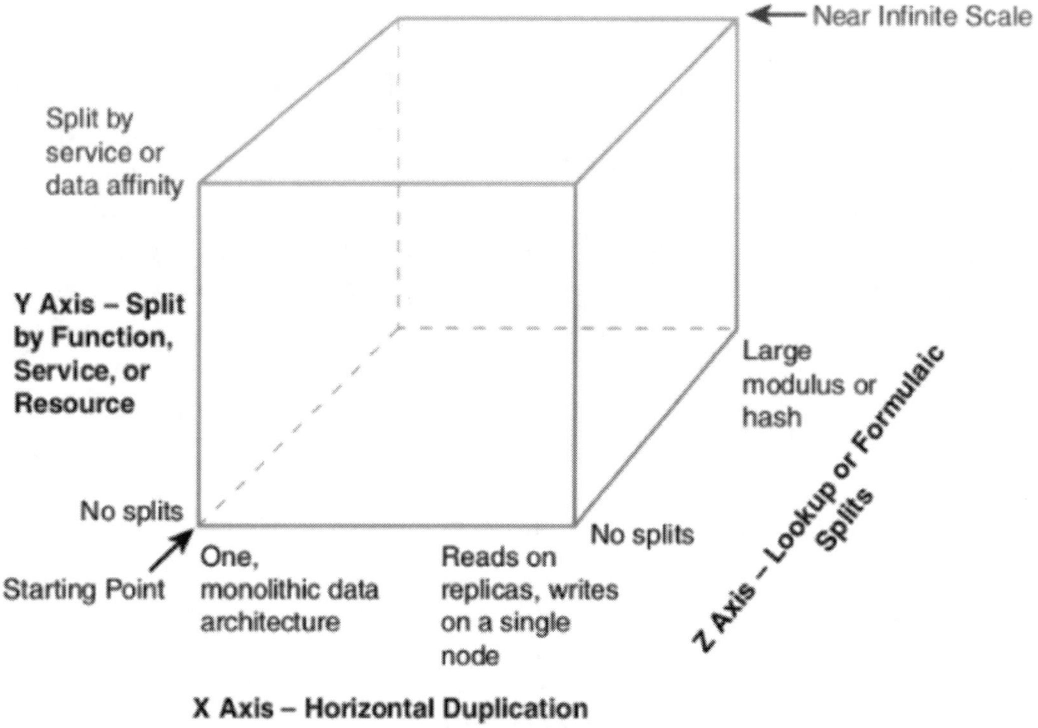

Fig. 1. AFK Scale Cube [9]

Since workload is one of the critical aspects of a system when we are talking about scalability, we can say that a scalability problem starts when a threshold of resources usage is reached, and the system is not able to continue processing requests properly as it did when the workload was lower. When this happens, a performance problem arises (as shown in response time, latency and other metrics), and subsequently, if the problem is not identified and managed appropriately, it will lead to a availability problem, since there will be no resources available to attend requests. See Rozanski's [4] performance or knee curve (see Fig. 2), which describes the way workload impacts the average response time: when workload increases, the average response time gets to a peak (knee in the curve) and then grows infinitely. Thus, this is the first symptom that there is a scalability problem in the system.

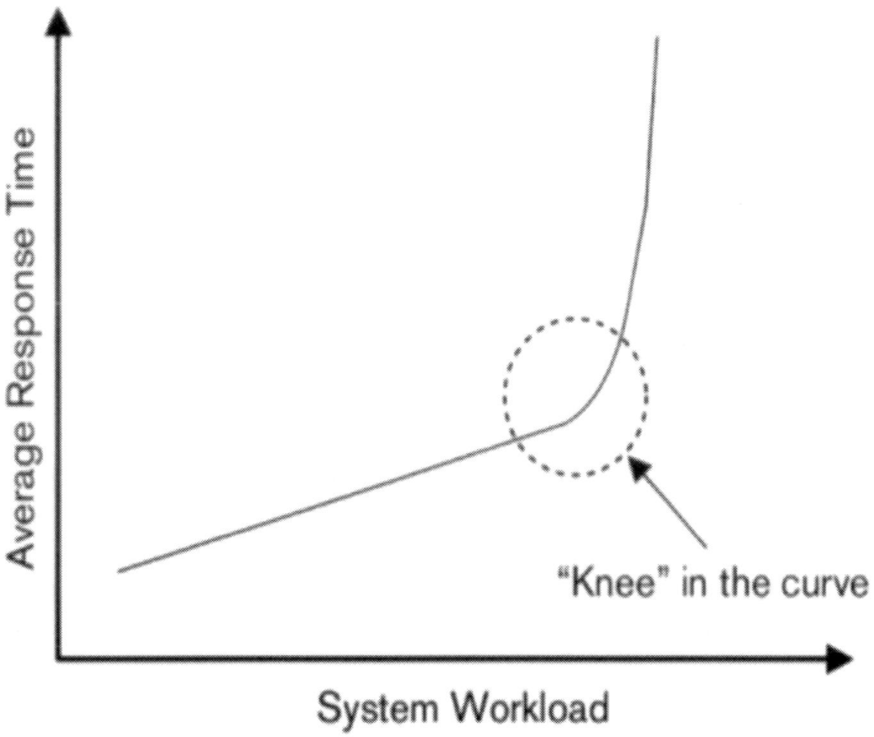

Fig. 2. Performance or knee curve [10]

3 Scalability Tactics

A software system is built taking several design decisions regarding its overall shape, components, technologies, and so on. For large software systems, the key decisions address the non-functional properties (or quality attributes) that the system must exhibit.

Bass, Clements and Kazman [10] defined (first in 2003 and later on refined) *architectural tactics* as design decisions that influence the achievement of a quality attribute response. By cataloging tactics, they provided a way of making the design more systematic within some limitations. In literature, there are several catalogs [1] [4] [10] that cover quality attributes such as performance, availability, security, modifiability, etc.

Gorton et al. [1] describe the challenges of "Big Data" systems that confront software architects, and proposed tactics for scalability (see Fig. 3) to address increased workload, showing how distributed software architecture QA's are tightly linked to both data and deployment architectures.

Duboc et al. [2] present a goal-oriented approach for eliciting, modeling and reasoning about scalability requirements. The approach consists of systematically identifying scalability-related obstacles to the satisfaction of goals, assessing the likelihood and severity of these obstacles, and generating new goals to deal with them. This work is oriented to identify obstacles related to scalability but not related to define or specify scalability tactics.

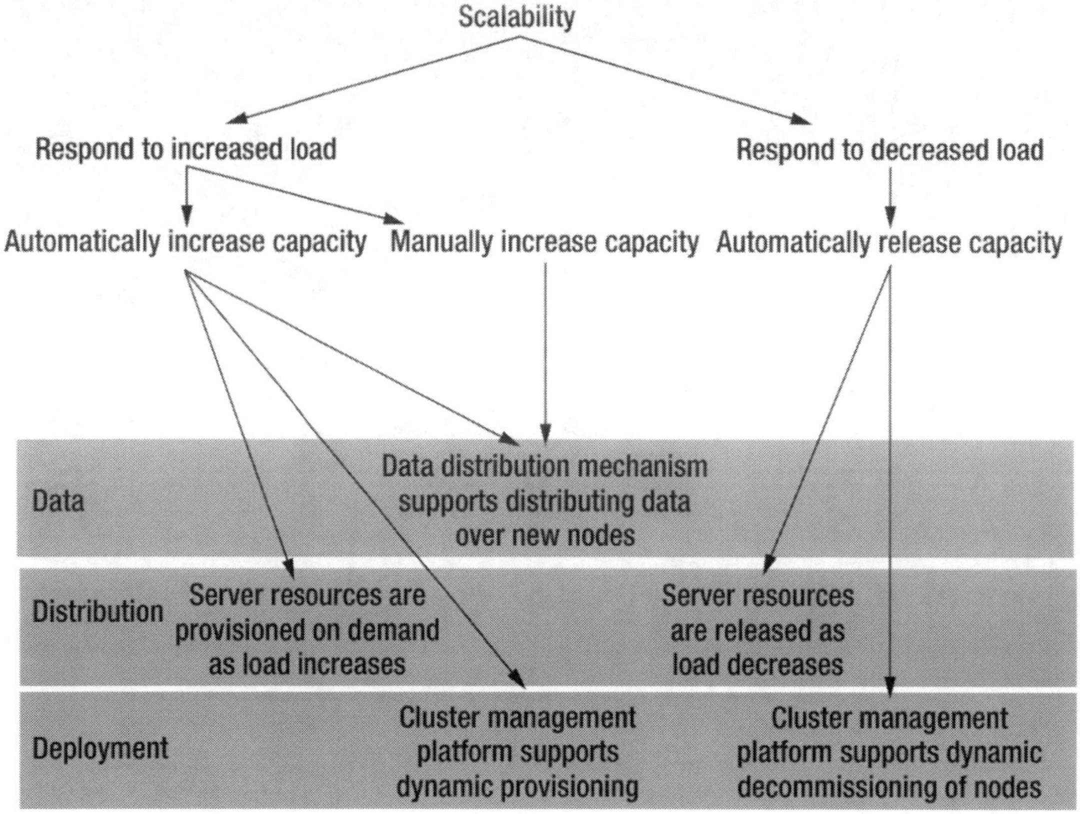

Fig. 3. Scalability tactics proposed by Gorton et al. [1].

Kazman et al. [3] show how architecture design and analysis techniques rest on a small number of foundational principles, and how those principles can be instantiated as a core set of techniques, which can be re-combined for new purposes addressing problems of ever-increasing scale, and specifically the highly complex problems of analyzing software-intensive ecosystems.

Rozanski et al. [4] propose some tactics based on the relation between performance and scalability problems: *optimize repeated processing*, *reduce contention via replication*, *prioritize processing*, *consolidate related workload*, *distribute processing over time*, *minimize the use of shared resources*, *reuse resources and results*, *partition and parallelize*, *scale up or scale out*, *degrade gracefully*, *use asynchronous processing*, *relax transactional consistency*, *make design compromises.* Rozanski's proposal describes individual tactics instead of a classification regarding to design decisions, so this wouldn't be an exact guide for an early architect who would like to know what decisions to make to mitigate scalability problems.

Bass et al. [10] exposes tactics for quality attributes such as *availability* and *performance*, this tactics can be related to scalability in a way where some of them could trigger scalability problems. After analyzing these tactics, we detected a close link between performance and scalability regarding to the tactics of: *increase resources*, *increase resource efficiency*, *introduce concurrency*, *sched-*

ule resources, *maintain multiple copies of computations*, and *maintain multiple copies of data*; and between availability and scalability regarding to the tactics of: *active redundancy*, *passive redundancy* and *degradation*.

Abbott et al. [9] present a set of 50 scalability rules classified into 12 categories. These rules are intended for architects to have in considerations certain principles when designing a system for it to deal with scalability. Abbott's work is focused on presenting principles but not specific tactics for scalability, but this principle could be used for the definition of tactics, or at least a certain part of them could be related directly to scalability tactics definitions.

Hull [12] describes a set of 20 obstacles of scalability that are usually active in large systems. This obstacles show aspects such as *lack of cache*, *slow data transmission*, *weak communication*, *lack of documentation*, *lack of logs*, *growing technical debt*, and *insufficient monitoring*. Hull's work shows obstacles on systems that are related to scalability, aspects that could be taken in consideration for the definition of tactics that could mitigate them during the design decisions making.

Ahluwalia [5] exposes a set of patterns that are intended to be used to make a system scalable. The patterns describe by Ahluwalia are: introduce scalability, optimize algorithm, add hardware, introduce parallelism, optimize decentralization, control shared resources, add intra-process parallelism, add inter-process parallelism, add hybrid parallelism, and automate scalability. The main difference of Ahluwalia's work and our proposal, is that our intention is to define a set of tactics based on several considerations instead of patterns itself.

Gorton et al. [1] define *scalability tactics* to address increased workload in big data systems, focusing on the elasticity concept of cloud systems. They omit design decisions like workload detection and workload management tactics like scheduling, which also provide strategies to minimize workload and enhance a system scalability.

Bass et al. [10] present separate *performance tactics*, that address *events* as stimulus focusing on control resource demand and manage resources, and *scalability tactics*, that address *workload* as stimulus, and as these tactics are focused on performance, we could use some of them in our proposal. We could use performance tactics related to scalability, in the way it aims to deal with workload before it compromises the availability of a system, and the availability of a system is compromised when the performance presents alterations and misbehaviors. The tactics catalog proposed by Rozanski et al. [4] is focused on performance and scalability tactics, but the most of these tactics presented are in fact design principles and not tactics specifically. Also, some of the tactics exposed could impact some other quality attribute tactics, such as, relax transactional consistency, which could have a negative impact on the integrity of the system.

4 Homologation of Existing Scalability Tactics

As seen above, several architectural tactics for scalability have been proposed by several authors: some appear in several proposals, and few appear in just one. To elaborate this taxonomy, a simple process was followed: (1) search related work (summarized in Section 3); (2) select tactics catalogs available in the literature (see Section 3); (3) identify scalability-related tactics in these catalogs; and (4) map proposed tactics to scalability concepts relevant. The end results is a consolidated taxonomy of tactics with three main branches: *workload detection*, *workload reaction*, and *workload prediction*; see details in Section 5.

4.1 Tactics Catalog Selection

The first step was to review and analyze the existing catalogs of architectural tactics related to scalability and performance. Besides scalability tactics, we looked for performance tactics, since performance is closely related to scalability and workload increases can quickly lead to scalability problems.

Our analysis derived that availability problems may appear from a system inability to scale; some conclusions are that:

1. A performance problem will derive at some point in a problem of availability if the workload that originates it increases without being properly managed.
2. If a system can manage workload and its impact on performance, then it will not have availability problems.

This does not imply that all availability problems necessarily involve a performance problem, but only that availability problems triggered by an excessive workload in systems designed to be scalable have an initial impact on performance and later on availability. From this we conclude that solving the performance problem can mitigate or prevent the related availability problem.

This led to the selection of catalogs for "Scalability tactics" proposed by Gorton et al. [1], the "Performance and Scalability Tactics" by Rozanski et al. [4], and the "Tactics of performance,' by Bass et al. [10]. The "Availability Tactics" by Bass et al. [10] were excluded because the availability problems caused by unmanaged workload can be prevented with performance and scalability tactics.

4.2 Tactics Filtering

From the selected catalogs, we exclude elements presented as tactics but corresponding to design principles [11]. Specifically, from Rozanski's catalog [4] of performance and scalability tactics we excluded "reuse resources and results," "use asynchronous processing," "make design compromises" and "consolidate related workload".

On the other hand we excluded the "Degrade gracefully" tactic [4] (or *Degradation* [10]), which is classic in the literature, it also appears in multiple catalogs, sometimes as a principle and sometimes as a tactic for performance or availability. It is a powerful tactic, perhaps even bio-inspired (considering that the human body executes a similar technique to protect heart and brains in critical conditions such as hypothermia or sepsis). But under our concept of scalability, this tactic could not only impact functionality negatively (which is not critical) but also compromise other quality attributes (such as performance), since functionalities are excluded and the system does not operate under its complete state and the main idea of scalability is that the system keeps responding correctly even when the workload increases.

4.3 Tactics Homologation

The tactics homologation step (summarized in Table 1) combined scalability tactics proposed by Gorton et al. [1], performance and scalability tactics proposed by Rozanski et al. [4], and performance tactics proposed by Bass et al. [10]. All found tactics were mapped to relevant scalability concepts, such as the AFK scale cube (in Fig. 2), scaling up, scheduling resources, and request queueing. This mapping yield the *Manage workload* branch in the tactics taxonomy, shown in Fig. 4. Unlike *Manage workload*, the branches *Detect workload* and *Predict workload* were not homologated from existing tactics, since it was not possible to find the concept of "tactics" as a architectural construct to propose design decisions in these aspects in the literature that we explore. Instead, we use concepts, techniques and proposals to define a set of tactics that address these aspects.

5 Proposed Taxonomy of Scalability Tactics

This section organizes in a taxonomy the scalability tactics resulting from the steps in Section 4. The tactics are organized (see Fig. 4) around the three key decisions that a software architect must take to provide a software system with capabilities to address scalability concerns: (1) *detect workload*, i.e. early detection of situations that could compromise the scalability of a system; (2) *react to workload*, i.e. mitigation measures to effectively manage a scalability issue; and (3) *predict workload*, i.e. ability predict the incidence of a scalability problem.

5.1 Detect Workload

These tactics monitor resources to detect when workload approaches critical thresholds (predefined, presumably near the max supported by the system). There is significant literature on workload analysis; see [18] and [22] for application to cloud and database engines.

- Define Alarms for Critical Event Notification: The purpose of generating alarms is to characterize a risk situation that could trigger a scalability problem. This is useful since it allows taking actions that require human intervention and also provides indicators to evaluate the frequency of such events.

Table 1. Tactics Homologation

Proposed Tactic	**"Scalability tactics" (Gorton [1])**	**"Performance and scalability tactics" (Rozanski & Woods [4])**	**"Performance tactics" (Bass, Clements, Kazman [10])**
Scale Out Resources (X Axis)	Automatically increase capacity	Scale up or scale out	Maintain multiple copies of computations
	Manually increase capacity	Reduce contention via replication	Maintain multiple copies of data
Split Resources (Y Axis)	-	Partition and parallelize	-
Sharding (Z Axis)	-	-	-
Scale Up Resources	Automatically increase capacity		Increase resources
	Manually increase capacity		
Schedule Resources	-	Prioritize processing	Schedule resources
		Distribute processing over time	
Queue Requests	-	-	Bound Queue Sizes
Relax Transactional Consistency	-	Relax Transactional Consistency	-

- Real-Time CPU Usage Monitoring: Having appropriate instrumentation to monitor system resources allows predicting a potential scalability event as the utilization of these resources increases due to the workload generated by responding to new requests. Monitoring CPU usage can help identify whether the amount of workload is significant to generate a problem to serve future requests.
- Real-Time Memory Usage Monitoring: Monitor the use of memory to identify early an overload in the system that could impact on excessive response times or unavailability to meet customer requests.
- Threshold-based Event Triggering: Establish resource usage levels that must be met before the system begins executing a scalability strategy.
- Log Events: Log critical events to audit them later.

5.2 Manage Workload

Several tactics address how to provide the system with capabilities for managing the excessive workload when it happens.

- Scale Out Resources: Add resources to logical units in a system, i.e. clone resources.

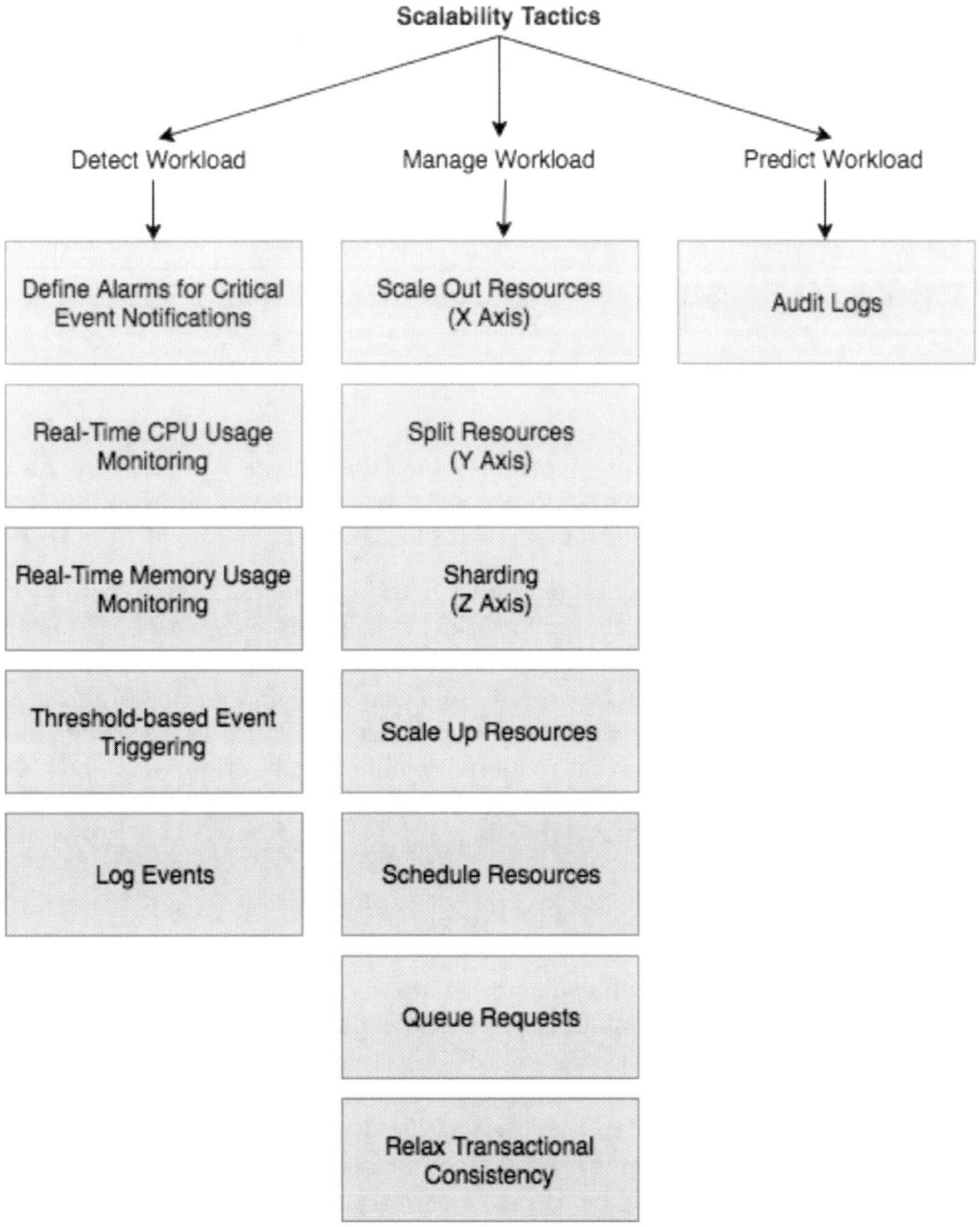

Fig. 4. The proposed taxonomy of Scalability Tactics

- Split Resources: Split resources by functionality to manage their workload.
- Sharding: Split and replicate data for workload balance.
- Scale Up Resources: Increase the available system resources in terms of main memory, disk space and processor, in order to be able to serve a greater demand of requests when a predefined threshold is reached. This operation

should not be performed if the scalability requirements are met with the resources available at the time the threshold is reached.

- Schedule Resources: Define the behavior, organization and prioritization of system resources to efficiently handle requests in instances of overhead.
- Queue Requests: Manage workload through processing queues.
- Relax Transactional Consistency: This tactic allows to relax the rules of consistency inherent to atomic operations traditionally produced by databases. Usually, in environments that use distributed databases or NoSQL databases, there is an application instance of this tactic. When using this tactic it must be considered that there is an important trade-off with the integrity of the data.

5.3 Predict Workload

Although there is significant literature on workload prediction [17] [19] [20] [21] [23] [15], we found only one architectural tactic in the literature (namely, log auditing, which is also used to detect workloads).

- Audit Logs: A fundamental aspect to identify a scalability event is to be able to trace its cause and the impact that it could have in case of happening. Performing log analysis allows to identify recurrent events and risk factors that predict their occurrence [16], allowing to define alarms and schedule mitigation actions. The log analysis will allow to know the behavior of the system during an event that requires scalability and in this way to be able to detect typical patterns that can anticipate an increased workload that must be managed efficiently by the system.

6 Illustrative Case

These tactics catalog was implemented in a practical case. The system that was designed is a prediction system that generates data to predict future events in the urban transport vehicles context. This system was mainly composed of (1) a driver data capture module, involving both vehicle and driver data, (2) an environmental and road data capture module, (3) a data processing module to generate the predictions; and (4) a system for hosting the generated prediction data, that eventually would be used to create reports that the parties would use for detailed information related to future events . Considering that it is a large scale system due to the number of vehicles and data to be processed, the tactics from the proposed tactics catalog were used during the design of the system architecture. The tactics used were:

1. Real-Time Memory Usage Monitoring: this tactic was used in the design, because the system requires to handle buffers and large amount of memory for capturing and processing data in real-time.
2. Log Events: this tactic was used in the design, because the system requires to register events constantly, for the early detection of malfunctioning features in the system.

3. Scale Out Resources: this tactic was used in the design, because the system requires to manage eventually the addition of databases, servers or processing resources in runtime.
4. Queue Requests: this tactic was used in the design, because the system requires to be able to manage large amounts of data with queuing in this case.

These tactics allowed the company designers (which for confidentiality reasons we are not allowed to identify) to follow a catalog of tactics as a guide for the design of the architecture of the system.

7 Conclusions and Future Work

Scalability is the system ability to respond to large workloads without affecting its performance or availability. The design of large-scale systems requires addressing scalability, and architectural tactics are a design knowledge reuse technique that can support this task. Although scalability is well addressed in the literature, there is little documentation on actual tactics and the existing tactics catalogs are partial or subsumed in performance or availability taxonomies.

This article gathered proposed tactics for scalability, and organized them in a taxonomy according to whether they address workload detection, reaction or prevention. This tactics can be used by architects in early stages to support decision making to improve the system scalability.

Ongoing work is mapping existing technologies with tactics in the catalog, to support architects in selecting combinations of technologies, products and frameworks that enable incorporation of the desired tactics in actual systems.

Acknowledgments

This work has been partially supported by Comisión Nacional de Investigación Científica (CONICYT) under grants PCHA/Doctorado Nacional/2017-21171506 and PCHA/Doctorado Nacional/2017-21171351, Universidad Técnica Federico Santa María (under PIIC, Programa de Incentivos a la Iniciación Científica), and CONICYT PIA (Basal FB0821 CCTVal).

References

1. I. Gorton and J. Klein, "Distribution, Data, Deployment: Software Architecture Convergence in Big Data Systems," in IEEE Software, vol. 32, no. 3, pp. 78-85, May-June 2015.
2. L. Duboc, E. Letier and D. S. Rosenblum, "Systematic Elaboration of Scalability Requirements through Goal-Obstacle Analysis," in IEEE Transactions on Software Engineering, vol. 39, no. 1, pp. 119-140, Jan. 2013.
3. R. Kazman, M. Gagliardi and W. Wood, "Scaling up software architecture analysis," Journal of Systems and Software, Volume 85, Pages 1511-1519, 2012.

4. N. Rozanski, E. Woods, "Software Systems Architecture: Working with Stakeholders Using Viewpoints and Perspectives", Addison-Wesley, 2011.
5. K. S. Ahluwalia, "Scalability Design Patterns", In Proceedings of the 14th Conference on Pattern Languages of Programs (PLOP '07). ACM, New York, NY, USA, Article 2, 8 pages, 2007.
6. I. Gorton, "Essential Software Architecture Second Edition", Springer, 2011.
7. I. Mistrik, N. Ali, R. Kazman, J. Grundy, B. Schmerl, "Managing Trade-offs in Adaptable Software Architectures", Morgan Kaufmann, 2017.
8. H. H. Liu, "Software Performance and Scalability, a Quantitative Approach", Wiley, 2009.
9. M. L. Abbot, M. T. Fisher, "Scalability Rules: 50 Principles for Scaling Web Sites", Addison-Wesley Professional, 2011.
10. L. Bass, P. Clements, R. Kazman, "Software Architecture in Practice Third Edition", Addison-Wesley Professional, 2013.
11. M. L. Abbott, M. T. Fisher, "The Art of Scalability: Scalable Web Architecture, Processes, and Organizations for the Modern Enterprise", Addison-Wesley Professional, 2010.
12. S. Hull, "20 Obstacles to Scalability", Acmqueue, Volume 11, issue 7, 2013.
13. Belson, H., and Ho, J. Scalability. Dalam D. C. Rajapakse, "A Fresh Graduate's Guide to Software Development Tools and Technologies", Comp.nus.edu.sg, https://www.comp.nus.edu.sg/ seer/book/2e/, 2012.
14. C. B. Weinstock, J. B. Goodenough, "On System Scalability", 2006
15. M. Zaman, A. Ahmadi, Y. Makris, "Workload characterization and prediction: A pathway to reliable multi-core systems," 2015 IEEE 21st International On-Line Testing Symposium (IOLTS), Halkidiki, pp. 116-121, 2015
16. S. Elnaffar, P. Martin, "Techniques and a Framework for Characterizing Computer Systems' Workloads," 2006 Innovations in Information Technology, Dubai, pp. 1-5, 2006.
17. B. Mozafari, C. Curino, S. Madden, "DBSeer: Resource and Performance Prediction for Building a Next Generation Database Cloud", CIDR, 2013 .
18. S. Singh, I. Chana, "Metrics based Workload Analysis Technique for IaaS Cloud", CoRR, abs/1411.6753, 2014.
19. J. Yang, C. Liu, Y. Shang, Z. Mao, J. Chen, "Workload Predicting-Based Automatic Scaling in Service Clouds", 2013 IEEE Sixth International Conference on Cloud Computing, Santa Clara, CA, pp. 810-815, 2013.
20. J. Duggan, U. Cetintemel, O. Papaemmanouil, E. Upfal, "Performance Prediction for Concurrent Database Workloads", In Proceedings of the 2011 ACM SIGMOD International Conference on Management of data (SIGMOD '11). ACM, New York, NY, USA, 337-348, 2011 .
21. S. Elnikety, S. Dropsho, E. Cecchet, W. Zwaenepoel, "Predicting Replicated Database Scalability from Standalone Database Profiling", In Proceedings of the 4th ACM European conference on Computer systems (EuroSys '09). ACM, New York, NY, USA, 303-316, 2009.
22. B. Mozafari, C. Cuerino, A. Jindal, S. Madden, "Performance and Resource Modeling in Highly-Concurrent OLTP Workloads", In Proceedings of the 2013 ACM SIGMOD International Conference on Management of Data (SIGMOD '13). ACM, New York, NY, USA, 301-312, 2013.
23. D. Gmach, J. Rolia, L. Cherkasova, A. Kemper, "Workload Analysis and Demand Prediction of Enterprise Data Center Applications", 2007 IEEE 10th International Symposium on Workload Characterization, Boston, MA, pp. 171-180, 2007.

Viewing an ERP as an SPL: Exploratory study

Yenisei Delgado Verdecia and María Cecilia Bastarrica

Computer Science Department, University of Chile
{ydelgado,cecilia}@dcc.uchile.cl

Abstract Software Product Lines have been established as one of the best ways to promote reuse. Enterprise Resource Planning (ERP) are systems composed of a set of functional modules, whose implementation involves their configuration and customization in order to satisfy a customer's needs. This paper focuses on integrating both concepts by viewing an ERP as an SPL by proposing an approach to extract an SPL from an existing ERP. To this end, we conducted an exploratory study of the Odoo ERP suite, illustrating how our approach is applied. As a result, we could recover the ERP domain artifacts and we could derive ERP implementations. Although the proposed approach was able to configure ERP implementations, we found that it cannot be used to customize assets or to define reusable assets not yet considered as part of the existent ERP.

Keywords: Software Product Line, SPL, Enterprise Resource Planning, ERP, Open Source ERP, Odoo ERP

1 Introduction

The need for integrated support for the operational management of an organization motivates the evolution of business information systems towards comprehensive solutions called Enterprise Resource Planning that integrate and facilitate, through a platform, the management of an organization [2, 6, 17, 22]. This platform is composed of interdependent units called modules that support the processes that are carried out in each department of the organization [3, 13]. The process of selecting and integrating the modules to meet the needs of the organization is known as ERP implementation. In this way, ERP systems can be implemented either altogether or addressing incrementally different functions, departments or modules of the organization operation.

A product line is a set of products that together address a particular market segment or fulfill a particular mission. In that sense, a Software Product Line (SPL) allows for the generation of a set of software products for a specific domain, based on the reuse of a well-defined infrastructure of core assets [20]. Core assets constitute all reusable elements of the SPL, *e.g.,* features, software components, architecture, performance modeling and analysis, test cases, test plans, and documentation. This massive asset reuse reduces cost and time required for building each software product.

The work presented in this paper is motivated by the idea of viewing an ERP as an SPL and thus take advantage of the SPL product derivation strategy for implementing an ERP. Therefore, our main objective in this paper is to explore to what extent an ERP can be considered as an SPL. For this, we defined an approach to extract the core assets defined for any SPL from an existing ERP. To illustrate the feasibility of the proposed approach, we conducted an exploratory study using Odoo, an open source ERP. We found that our approach can manage ERP configuration but not other implementation operations such as customization or bolt-ons. However, it is worth stating that these modifications are not directly addressed by SPLs either.

The paper is organized as follows. Section 2 addresses the basic concepts of SPL and ERP. Section 3 describes our approach. We present the exploratory study in Section 4, its application and its results. Some related work is discussed in Section 6. Finally, Section 7 concludes our work and suggests future work.

2 Background Concepts

In this section we detail mainly those background concepts of SPL and ERP that are relevant for a clear understanding of the presented approach.

2.1 Software Product Line (SPL)

A SPL is a strategy for developing related systems from a set of common assets. Clements and Northrop [5], focus on the software product family:

> *"a set of software-intensive systems sharing a common, managed set of features that satisfy the specific needs of a particular market segment or mission and that are developed from a common set of core assets in a prescribed way".*

Pohl, Klaus and Böckle [18] define SPL as activity:

> *"a paradigm to develop software applications (software-intensive systems and software products) using platforms and mass customization".*

Here "platform" refers to a base of technologies on which other technologies or processes are built [18] and "mass customization" is the large-scale production of goods tailored to individual customers' needs [7]. In the SPL context, platform is a collection of reusable assets that are used in a consistent and systematic way to build products and to facilitate mass customization.

Reusable assets include different kinds of software development artifacts, such as requirements models, architectural models, software components, test plans, and test designs, among others. In order to allow for the development of custom applications that reuse predefined assets, the variability of the domain needs to be identified. In SPL, *common* features are part of every product, in exactly the same form, and *variable* features are only part of some products.

To build a robust platform as well as creating specific applications, SPL define two processes [12, 18]: Domain engineering and Application engineering.

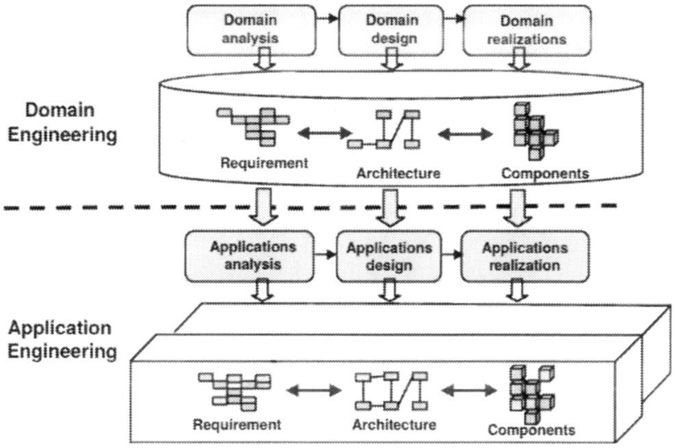

Figure 1. Software Product Line (Adapted from [18])

Domain Engineering [18] is the process that establishes the reuse infrastructure (upper part of Figure 1). Its main goals are: (1) To state the scope of the SPL; (2) To ensure that the variability is appropriately identified in order to generate all the products within the defined scope, and (3) To define and build the mandatory and reusable assets. This process is in turn involves three sub-processes:

Domain analysis: covers all the activities required to document the common and variable features as well as their relationships.

Domain design: establishes a high-level structure for the SPL, *i.e.*, common and variable components for the development of specific applications based on a reference architecture.

Domain realization: provides the detailed design and the implementation of reusable software assets, based on the reference architecture.

There must be a correspondence between features, architecture components and implemented components, but this might not be exhaustive. For example, not all components defined in the reference architecture need to be realized upfront, they can be implemented only when needed and then they can be reused.

Application Engineering [18] Also know as product engineering, is the process that elicits specific requirements from end user and develops the product by reusing assets developed in the domain engineering (bottom part of Figure 1). Its main goals are: (1) To achieve the highest possible reuse of the domain assets, exploiting the commonalities and the variability of the SPL, and (2) To document the application artifacts, *i.e.*, application requirements, architecture, components, and tests, and relate them to the domain artifacts. It involves three sub-processes:

Application analysis: covers all activities to define an application requirements specification. All deltas between application requirements and the available capabilities are identified.

Application design: encompasses the activities for producing the application architecture. This sub-process selects and configures the variable parts of the reference architecture and also incorporates application specific adaptations.

Application realization: uses reusable and application specific assets to build the intended application. Its main concerns are to select and configure reusable components and to realize application specific assets.

2.2 Enterprise Resource Planning (ERP)

An ERP is a set of information systems that allows for the integration of the operations of an organization such as management control, inventory, human resources and so forth. According to Jacobs and Bendoly [10], ERP can be defined as both a concept and a system. The conceptual definition refers to the integration of business processes within an organization. However, the definition of the ERP as a system is the technological infrastructure designed to support and take advantage of the capabilities of the tools used by an organization [10]. In this sense, an ERP considered as a system can be characterized as packaged software developed to meet the general needs of organizations [3, 13].

Basically, an ERP combines several functions of management by means of packages related to the main areas of the organization. So ERP systems are designed to be modular, allowing for the gradual installation of packages. In this sense, the packages can be classified into three types:

(i) Basic or elementary packages: those that must be installed (mandatory) since they are necessary for any implementation of the ERP to work.
(ii) Additional or optional packages: selected depending on the specific needs of the organization complementing the basic packages.
(iii) Tailor-made packages: designed to meet specific organizational needs that are not contemplated in the basic or additional packages.

When an ERP system is implemented in the organization, ERP system packages are selected according to the characteristics of the organization and the processes that need support. In addition, some modifications to the ERP system may be necessary, *e.g.,* customization, configuration or costume-made packages. We now briefly describe these three types of ERP modifications:

(i) Customization: implies the modification of an ERP software package to match the existing business processes of the organization. Therefore, changes to the functionality or the source code of the ERP packages are made [9, 19].
(ii) Configuration: involves configuration of parameters in the packages, to choose between different executions of processes and functions. In this type of modification, the ERP system code is not modified [3, 9].
(iii) Costume-made: are extensions to the ERP, developed by either the implementers of an independent software provider to satisfy the needs of a particular client. In particular, when these packages are implemented by third parties, they are called bolt-ons [3, 8].

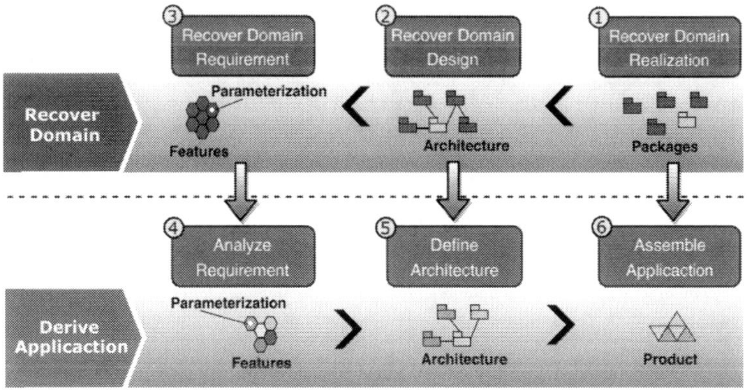

Figure 2. Overview of our approach

3 Approach

Our purpose is to conceptualize the ERP as an SPL. The starting point is a particular ERP in the form of source code, whose structure is in principle not known. Therefore, it is necessary to reconstruct the architecture of the ERP to derive applications tailored to the specific customers' needs. With this aim, our approach, as visualized in Figure 2, defines two processes: Recover domain and Derive application. We next describe each of these processes.

3.1 Recover Domain (RD)

RD process (upper part of Figure 2) conceptualizes the ERP as an SPL in order to build the Domain Engineering. Thus, this process aims to reconstruct the reusable assets *i.e.*, software components, architecture, features and the involved variability. To this end, we defined three sub-processes:

Recover domain realization: uses reverse engineering to reconstruct the software modules involved in the ERP system. It involves two phases:

1. Identify packages: set of packages that group the functionalities of the ERP modules. In this phase, the names of the packages are associated to the names of the ERP modules.

2. Differentiate generic and specific packages: define which ERP modules are generic and specific. In this phase, the elementary ERP modules are mapped to common packages in the SPL and optional ERP modules that are mapped to packages that may not exists in all products. Therefore, it is necessary to review the basic documentation of the ERP, in order to know how the ERP packages are organized and what are the basic and optional ERP packages.

Recover domain design: identifies software packages and their dependencies using a module viewtype [1]. This is the starting point for recovering the product line architecture (PLA). Its elements are modules *i.e.*, the implementation of software units that provide a coherent set of responsibilities. It also considers three types of relationships: *is part of, depends on,* and *is a.* The mandatory and variable packages identified in the Recover domain realization need to be mapped to mandatory and variable modules in the PLA. To carry out this step, it may be useful to check the ERP documentation whenever available.

Recover domain requirements: identifies and describes the features that the products address. These features may be either mandatory or variable, and they must be consistent with the variability identified for the PLA. In this sub-process the scope of the domain, as well as the parameterizations points, are also identified. We defined two phases for this sub-process:

(i) Identify major features: identifies the scope of the domain. To express variability in terms of common and variable features, we may use different notations such as feature models [4] or OVM [15], among others, even though it is common in industry to use just spreadsheets. In this work we use feature models. We thus determine two key points to define the feature model:
   - *Feature Relationship:* to identify relations between features, especially hierarchy, order, and grouping.
   - *Constraints:* to identify restrictions among features and represent valid feature combinations, *e.g.,* 'feature X requires feature Y' and 'feature X excludes feature Y'.

   Considering these key points, the feature diagram is built, so the results of this phase is a feature model.

(ii) Identify parameterization[1]: recognizes the features that can be parameterized taking into account the characteristics of the organization. The result of this phase is the location of the parameterization point of the feature as well as the definition of the corresponding parameters.

3.2 Derive Applications (DA)

DA process (bottom of Figure 2) describes how to develop applications based on the recovered domain. To achieve that purpose we defined three sub-processes:

Analyze requirements: map the customer's requirements to those identified earlier during Recover domain requirements. Thus, the requirements analysis includes the selection of existing features, setting parameters, modifying features that do not match exactly what is needed, and identifying features not considered yet. This results in a valid application within the SPL scope.

Define architecture: use the PLA to instantiate the application architecture. In this phase the selected and parameterized features are mapped to the corresponding modules in the PLA. The result of this phase is the specific application architecture.

[1] ERP characteristic that allows that allows the system to adjust to the terminology of the business rules of each organization *e.g.,* language: the parameterization of the product when defining *e.g.,* the Spanish language.

Assemble application: compose the product assembling the packages obtained in the Recover domain process. Thus, a product can be assembled using reusable artefacts associated with the obtained architecture. The result of this phase is the product.

4 Exploratory study

We conducted an exploratory study that is defined in three phases: i) selecting the ERP to apply our approach, ii) recover domain of the ERP and iii) derive applications based on the recovered domain.

4.1 Phase 1 - ERP selection

Currently in the market we find two types of ERP systems: proprietary and open source ERP. Among proprietary ERPs we can find Oracle, SAP and Microsoft Dynamics. There are also several open source ERP systems, flexible and rich in functions, such as Adempiere, Openbravo or Odoo.

We selected Odoo for our exploratory study that is an open source ERP system. It was created by Odoo S.A. (formerly OpenERP S.A.) founded in 2004. It has an active community of developers, technical documentation and a cycle of publication of new versions of 12 months. It is a modular system that has official modules and others developed by third parties. It allows for the implementation and integration of costume-made modules to be able to adapt it to the specific needs of the organization. Its main modules are Sales, Customer Relationship Management, Human Resources, Purchase, Inventory, Manufacturing, Point of Sale, Accounting, Project, Timesheet, Payroll and Website.

In this exploratory study, we use Odoo 11.0, in its Community Edition[2]. It is developed in Python 3.5 and uses PostgreSQL 9.5 as a database management system. Odoo uses a client/server architecture in which clients are web browsers accessing the Odoo server via RPC Protocol[3]. This architecture permits that the business logic and extensions are generally performed on the server side, although supporting features can be added to the client, *e.g.*, new data representation such as interactive maps. Moreover, it is designed to be multi-platform, *e.g.*, Windows, Linux or Mac. It also follows the Model-View-Controller (MVC) architectural pattern. Then, Odoo modules contain in its directory, the models that define the data structure, the views that define the user's interfaces and the controllers that support the business logic of the applications.

Odoo has a modular structure, where each module adds new features or modifies existing ones for building applications. In Odoo, modules are called *'addon'* and each one is defined in a directory that in turn contains a number of directories described in Table 1. In addition, an Odoo module is declared by its manifest or descriptor file, called **__manifest__.py**, which specifies the module

[2] Official Community packages with all relevant dependency requirements are available at `https://www.odoo.com/es_ES/page/download`

[3] See `https://www.odoo.com/documentation/11.0/webservices/odoo.html`

Table 1. Composition of Odoo module

Directories		**Description**
Basic	data	Contains demo and data xml
	models	Contains models definition
	controllers	Contains controllers (HTTP routes)
	views	Contains the views and templates
	static	Contains the web assets, separated into css/, js/, img/, lib/
Optional	wizard	Regroups the transient models and their views
	report	Contains the reports (models based on SQL views (for reporting)), Python objects and XML views
	tests	Contains the Python/YML tests

metadata. The manifest file[4] contains a single Python dictionary, where each key specifies module metadata.

4.2 Phase 2 - Recover domain

The main objective of the Recover domain process is to reconstruct the reusable assets of the domain engineering *e.g.*, components, PLA and features. As stated in Section 3, we first recover the realization, then the design and finally the requirements model.

Realization recovery: First, we identify packages based on the Odoo source code. According to the Odoo documentation, addons folder contains all ERP modules. We found 292 addons in that directory. Each module is classified by functional categories (defined in the 'category' key of the manifest file). In total, Odoo defines 29 functional categories to organize modules in areas of interest[5].

As it can be seen in Figure 3, Accounting is a functional category that contains several addons inside. The relations between the addons were defined taking into account the 'depends' key of the manifest file of the module *account*. It depends on the *product, analytic, portal, base-setup* and *web-planner* modules. In turn, each of these modules has their own dependencies.

Our second objective is to identify generic and specific packages. According to Odoo documentation, the only generic module *i.e.*, mandatory, is the so called base module. All other modules are considered as specific *i.e.*, optional.

Design recovery: At this point, dependencies between packages are identified. In Odoo, when a module is installed, all of its dependencies are also installed, and

[4] Each manifest fields is described in detail at `https://www.odoo.com/documentation/11.0/reference/module.html#reference-module-manifest`

[5] The functional categories are defined at `https://github.com/odoo/odoo/blob/11.0/odoo/addons/base/module/module_data.xml`

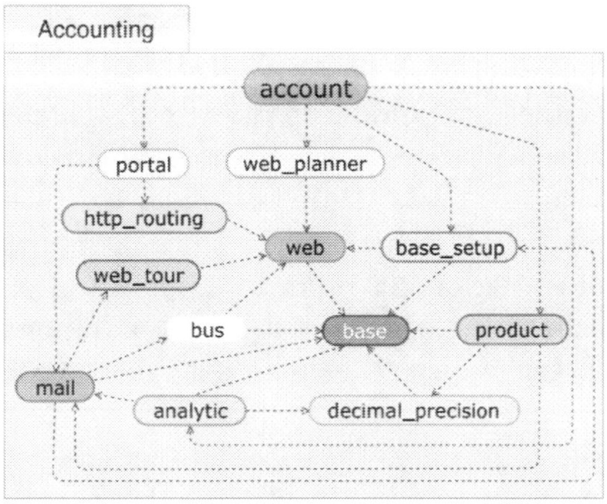

Figure 3. Module view Accounting

similarly during module loading. The 'depends' key in the manifest file defines existing dependencies between Odoo modules.

We selected only some areas of interest defined by Odoo for the exploratory study *e.g.,* Accounting, Sales, Purchase, Inventory and Subscriptions. However, we will not consider Subscriptions for our case study as it is a module of the Odoo Enterprise Edition that includes 20% more modules.

Based on the manifest file corresponding to addons of the selected areas of interest, we can start to build the PLA. Figure 4 illustrates how we obtain a part of the PLA and shows the Module view of a part the PLA.

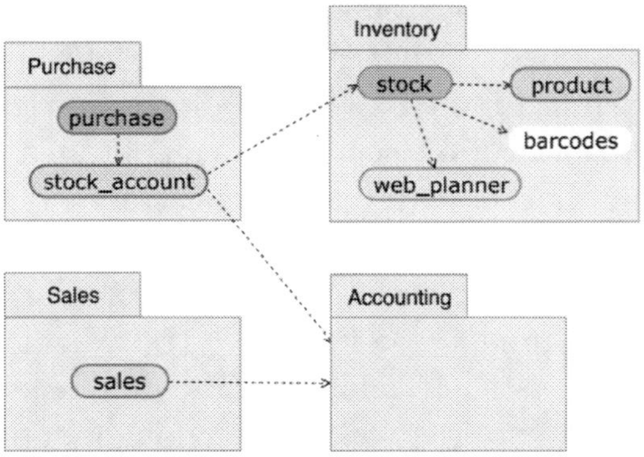

Figure 4. Relations view between areas of interest selected

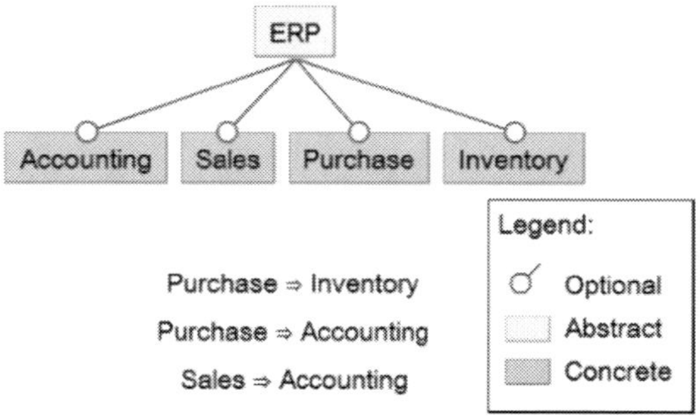

Figure 5. Feature model example

Requirements recovery: The first objective of this phase is to identify features, variability and constraints in terms of a feature model. This, in turn, defines the set of valid products. For this, we considered the areas of interest shown in Figure 4. To create a feature diagram we used the FeatureIDE[6] tool [23]. Figure 5 depicts the feature model created. In the tree, nodes represent features and edges describe relations. A single root node, here ERP, represents the domain concept being modeled. Optional features are decorated with a hollow circle, *e.g.,* Accounting. In this case, three constraints were defined, *e.g.,* the first one, Purchase ⇒ Inventory, reads 'Purchase requires Inventory'. Similarly, for the other constraints.

The second objective of this phase is to identify the parameterization points. Depending on the business, there are different parameterizations to be made *e.g.,* customer terminologies, local codes, formats (separators, date and time), currency structure, *etc.* These parameterization points are directly related to the features. In Odoo, coin, date, time formats or language correspond to general parameterization points applied to all modules. This level of parameterization is defined in two types of files .po and .pot which are in the I18n folder of each module. The .po files are the actual translation files whereas .pot is the template for the translation.

4.3 Phase 3 - Derive application

The main goal of this phase is to derive applications based on the recovered domain. So, our first objective is to map the application requirements (the ERP implementation) to the features of the domain and select features needed for a customized software system, resulting in a configuration. To exemplify this phase, we select Purchase as an area of interest to derive an implementation of the ERP (as SPL).

As an application configuration is a decision process to get a valid feature combination, where the interdependencies of all features are considered [18], we used the FeatureIDE editor to configure an application according to the feature model. For this, we start from the obtained feature model (see Figure 6.①), which has a configuration view as shown in Figure 6.②, that allows an iterative feature (de)selection. Hence, based on the features selected, we can obtain a valid product that complies with the combinations of features and constraints defined in a feature model *e.g.,* the configuration of Purchase shown in Figure 6.③.

Our second objective is to obtain the concrete architecture of the application. Based on the application configuration obtained (see Figure 7.①), we can map features to architecture modules as well as their relationships. So, we derive the architecture presented in Figure 7.②. Note that relations among modules is obtained from the PLA recovered during *Design Recovery* (see Figure 4).

The final objective is to compose the product. Considering the modules identified as part of the architecture -in this case for Purchase- their realization is taken into account for assembling the application. Table 2 describes all the components that form part of these modules. Similarly, modules correspond to those identified during *Realization Recovery* (see Figures 3 and 4).

[6] FeatureIDE is an open-source framework for feature-oriented software development (FOSD) based on Eclipse. See `https://featureide.github.io/`

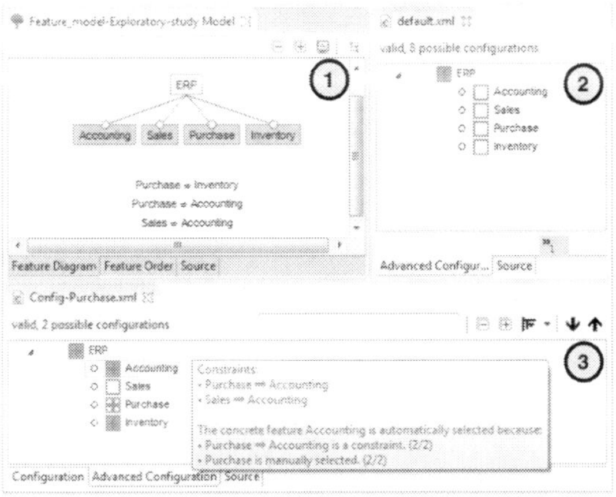

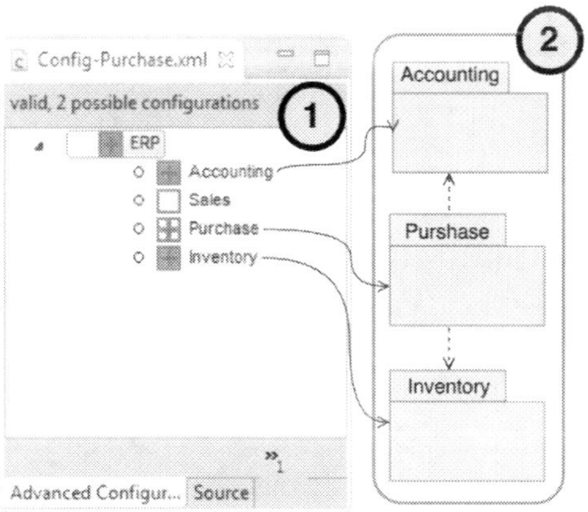

Figure 6. Derive application: ① Feature model, ② Feature model configuration view and ③ Configuration of Purchase

Figure 7. Architecture of Configuration Purchase: ① Configuration of Purchase and ② Architecture of Purchase

Table 2. Components included in the actual application

Modules	Components
Purchase	purchase, stock_account
Inventory	stock, product, barcodes, web_planner
Accounting	account, portal, web, base, mail, product, web_planner, web_tour, http_routing, bus, base_setup, analytic, decimal_precision

5 Discussion

We now present the result of the case study and discuss some threats to validity.

5.1 Results

Mapping the functional areas of the ERP with features as well as defining the constraints, allow us to verify if a particular set of features are valid in the SPL. Constraints were defined based on the existing dependencies between modules corresponding to the functional areas considered in the Derive application phase. However, if a customer's requirement cannot be mapped to one or more existing features, some strategy should be followed: either using an existing bolt-on that covers these needs or building a new module, but our approach does not address this issue yet. Moreover, once the feature model is conceptualized, it is easy to derive the product by reusing the defined product line architecture. Additionally, the traceability of the analysis, design and implementation elements is established by construction, and thus the derivation of particular products is straightforward whenever the feature model contains all the desired requirements.

5.2 Threats to validity

As in any exploratory study, there are limitations that must be considered when interpreting its results. We are aware that our study only considered one ERP, thus generalization will require further case studies. Furthermore, we used a particular type of ERP, in this case, an open source ERP (Odoo 11.0), thereby others ERP *e.g.,* proprietary, could have lead to different results. Also, the possibility of properly recovering the elements of the domain depends to a large degree on the quality of the ERP documentation, both in identifying the modules implemented and in determining the variability. Fourth, identify at a code level, the definition of modules dependencies was crucial in view of being able to derive the architecture. In addition, the dependencies indicate the order of component implementation and; Fifth, the constraints defined are based on existing dependencies among modules corresponding to functional areas. However, despite limitations of our study, our results demonstrate that is possible viewing an ERP as an SPL.

6 Related work

Most studies relating ERP focus on modeling, but very few on considering ERP implementation as an SPL process. We have observed that publications on ERP modeling are quite old while SPL is still an area of intense research and interest. However, there are a few recent works that relate these two topics [14, 16].

Nöbauer *et al.* [16] present an industrial case study to evaluate a semi-automatic tool-based approach to identify reusable features in customized ERP products. Here, customers' requirements are defined as reusable features that are used to customize ERP systems but not subsequent phases.

Wu *et al.* [24] define industry-oriented ERP (IERP) as an ERP software designed for specific industry sectors. They present a framework for developing IERP where business process modeling and software reuse are primary methods to improve the operation of component-based IERP. The framework consists of server layer, teamwork supporting layer, IERP construction and customization layer, reusable assets and tool-set layer, and the IERP system instance layer. In this sense, ERP and SPL concepts are implicitly related.

Soffer *et al.* [21] present a generic reverse engineering process, for modeling the alternatives at different application levels of an ERP system. They suggest that this generic process serves for comprehensive ERP modeling, as well as for obtaining a model of other process-supportive off-the-shelf systems that are of generic and configurable nature. This work focuses on implementing process variants based on the values of certain attributes of the ERP database. We do not claim to be as general as this work, but we also include application derivation.

Kouamou [11] presents the implementation of a service oriented ERP. He uses reverse engineering for reusing software and migrate the ERP towards service oriented architecture (SOA). The purpose is to implement a software package that respects the principles of SOA by reusing the existing solution. Here, SPL concepts are implicit and product derivation is not addressed.

Mani *et al.* [14] propose an approach for automatically generating the domain-specific rules based on user requirements by using the feature model. The feature model bridges the concepts of a domain model in ontology form and the business process. Again, the focus is only at the feature level.

7 Conclusion

In this paper, we defined the processes to reuse an ERP for deriving new products. For this, our approach proposes two processes: Recover domain and Derive applications which are composed of sub-processes. Our first process Recover domain conceptualizes the ERP as an SPL in order to build the Domain Engineering of the ERP and our second process Derive applications describes how to develop applications based on the recovered domain, *i.e.*, the Application engineering. In an effort to illustrate how our approach can be put into practice, we conducted an exploratory study. We selected the Odoo ERP and we showed how each process defined in our approach can be carried out.

In summary, the results of this exploratory case study show that only an ERP can be seen as a product line following this approach if its code is accessible. Besides, the implementation of an ERP generally involves, not only the configuration of existing modules and the use of bolt-ons. It also requires internal customizations of the modules to add or modify functionality. This customization of modules in turn could eventually be considered as an SPL for each module, which adds a level of complexity: SPL of SPLs.

Although the automatic assembly of a specific product through the selection of features is a great challenge because it must guarantee the adequate integration of the components associated with the features, it still requires to formally model all SPL artifacts involved as well as the traceability among them.

References

1. L. Bass, P. Clements, and R. Kazman. *Software Architecture in Practice.* Addison-Wesley Professional, third edition, 2012.
2. I. Bose, R. Pal, and A. Ye. ERP and SCM systems integration: The case of a valve manufacturer in China. *Information & Management*, 45(4):233–241, 2008.
3. L. Brehm, A. Heinzl, and M. L. Markus. Tailoring ERP systems: a spectrum of choices and their implications. In *Proceedings of the 34th Annual Hawaii International Conference on System Sciences*, pages 9–pp. IEEE, Jan 2001.
4. K. C. Kang, S. Cohen, J. A. Hess, W. Novak, and A. Spencer Peterson. Feature-Oriented Domain Analysis (FODA) feasibility study. Technical Report CMU/SEI-90-TR-21, SEI, Carnegie Mellon University, November 1990.
5. P. Clements and L. Northrop. *Software product lines: practices and patterns*, volume 3. Addison-Wesley Reading, 2002.
6. T. H. Davenport. Putting the Enterprise into the Enterprise System. *Harvard Bus. Rev.*, 76(4):121–131, July 1998.
7. M. Davis Stanley. *Future Perfect.* Addison-Wesley, Reading, MA, 1987.

8. A. Gupta. Enterprise resource planning: the emerging organizational value systems. *Industrial Management & Data Systems*, 100(3):114–118, 2000.
9. D. Hislop. The client role in consultancy relations during the appropriation of technological innovations. *Research Policy*, 31(5):657 – 671, 2002.
10. F. R. Jacobs and E. Bendoly. Enterprise resource planning: developments and directions for operations management research. *European Journal of Operational Research*, 146(2):233–240, 2003.
11. G. E. Kouamou. Building a Service-Oriented ERP from an Open Source Software. In *2009 Fourth International Conference on Software Engineering Advances*, pages 33–38, Sept 2009.
12. F. J. v. d. Linden. Software product families in Europe: the Esaps and Cafe projects. *IEEE Software*, 19(4):41– 49, Aug 2002.
13. W. Luhttps and D. M. Strong. A framework for evaluating ERP implementation choices. *IEEE Transactions on Engineering Management*, 51(3):322–333, 2004.
14. N. Mani, M. Helfert, and C. Pahl. A Domain-specific Rule Generation Using Model-Driven Architecture in Controlled Variability Model. In *Knowledge-Based and Intelligent Information & Engineering Systems: Proceedings of the 21st International Conference KES-2017*, volume 112, pages 2354 – 2362, 2017.
15. A. Metzger and K. Pohl. Variability Management in Software Product Line Engineering. In *29th International Conference on Software Engineering (ICSE 2007), Minneapolis, MN, USA, May 20-26, 2007, Companion Volume*, pages 186–187. IEEE Computer Society, 2007.
16. M. Nöbauer, I. Groher, and N. Seyff. Feature-Based Reuse in the ERP Domain: An Industrial Case Study. In *22nd International Systems and Software Product Line Conference (SPLC'2018)*, volume 1, pages 170–178, 2018.
17. K. Park and A. Kusiak*. Enterprise resource planning (ERP) operations support system for maintaining process integration. *International Journal of Production Research*, 43(19):3959–3982, 2005.
18. K. Pohl, G. Böckle, and F. J. v. d. Linden. *Software Product Line Engineering: Foundations, Principles and Techniques*. Springer-Verlag, Berlin, Heidelberg, 2005.
19. M. Rothenberger and M. Srite. An Investigation of Customization in ERP System Implementations. *IEEE Transactions on Engineering Management*, 56(4):663–676, 2009.
20. SEI. Arcade Game Maker pedagogical product line. `http://www.sei.cmu.edu/productlines/ppl/`, 2018. Online; accessed 21/05/2018.
21. P. Soffer, B. Golany, and D. Dori. ERP modeling: a comprehensive approach. *Information Systems*, 28(6):673 – 690, 2003.
22. Y.-f. Su and C. Yang. Why are enterprise resource planning systems indispensable to supply chain management? *European Journal of Operational Research*, 203(1):81–94, 2010.
23. T. Thüm, C. Kästner, F. Benduhn, J. Meinicke, G. Saake, and T. Leich. FeatureIDE: An Extensible Framework for Feature-oriented Software Development. *Science of Computer Programming*, 79:70–85, Jan 2014.
24. S. L. Wu, L. Xu, and W. He. Industry-oriented enterprise resource planning. *Enterprise Information Systems*, 3(4):409–424, 2009.

Test Adequacy Criteria Based on Inductive Inference of the Specification

Jorge Triñanes and Diego Vallespir

Universidad de la República, Uruguay
{triniane, dvallesp}@fing.edu.uy

Abstract. We defined test adequacy criteria that only depend on the specification. They state that a test suite is adequate if an inductive inference machine is able to infer a correct program. We chose a software tool to use as inductive inference machine and applied it to evaluate a series of test suites developed for a specific program. This application showed that the information content relevant to the specification of a test suite has impact on its effectiveness in fault detection. Theoretical analysis showed that this result has general validity.

Keywords: Black-box test acceptance criteria · Inductive inference · Defect detection effectiveness · Information relevant to the specification.

1 Introduction

Testing is an essential activity in software engineering and it consumes a significant amount of resources [3, 12]. Acceptance criteria for test case selection play an important role in test effectiveness [3].

Formally, test criteria C are a decision predicate defined on triples (P, RM, T) where P is a program, RM is a reference model related to P and T is a set of test cases. When C (P, RM, T) holds it is said that T satisfies the criteria C for P and RM [2].

Test criteria can be used in a proactive way to guide test case selection so that when the selection terminates the criteria are automatically fulfilled or can be used after the fact to determine if the set of test cases anyhow else selected is sufficient [2].

There are two major groups of selection techniques of test cases and acceptance criteria: those based on the code, which are called white-box, and those based on the specification, called black-box [2]. There are other types of techniques [2, 18] but for the aim of this work they are not relevant. We exclude from the scope of our analysis the black-box techniques of combinatorial testing.

It is recognized the need to develop additional research that provides analytical, statistical or empirical evidence of the effectiveness of test case selection techniques in revealing defects [3]. Empirical evaluation of the effectiveness in defect detection of black-box test case selection techniques has not provided clear results[8].

There are software tools that can determine if a set of test cases satisfies or not white-box adequacy criteria, in contrast to the evaluation of black-box criteria that requires human intervention. White-box criteria may be empirically evaluated using automated procedures while empirical evaluation of black-box criteria is based on the human application of the techniques[8]. This fact rises experiment costs, significantly increases the number of factors that need to be controlled and makes experiment replication more difficult.

In experimental settings in which several subjects apply a test case selection technique to evaluate its effectiveness in defect detection the results of this application should be evaluated in order to exclude those that are not adequate [4]. This evaluation is both time consuming and potentially controversial. An automated procedure to evaluate black-box test cases would be a significant aid. Also, teaching and learning black-box techniques presents several challenges [9]. Automatic evaluation of test cases could help, providing learners with adequate feedback.

In this work we propose black-box adequacy criteria that we name Inductive Inference of the Specification (IIS). The proposal is based on previous work of Weyuker [15] and Zhu [17, 16] that relates inductive inference to testing. We present IIS criteria and a first and simple example of its application. We observe that test suites that satisfy IIS are more effective in defect detection than those that do not satisfy IIS. We generalize the observed results from a theoretical perspective. Finally we devise a heuristic-based procedure that aims to build a test suite that points to satisfy IIS for programs that can be expressed as a simple function that calls itself.

The remainder of this paper is organized as follows. Section 2 defines IIS, Section 3 presents the application of IIS to evaluate a set of test suites developed for a specific program. Section 4 analyzes and evaluates that application. Section 5 is devoted to the development of a heuristic-based procedure to build a set of test cases that satisfy IIS for a specific category of programs. Section 6 discusses related work and section 7 presents conclusions and future work.

2 IIS Criteria

2.1 Inductive Inference

The term "inductive inference" (sometimes also called "inductive programming") refers to the process of establishing the hypothesis of a general rule derived from examples. For instance, given the sequence: 011, 00000011, 00111, 00001, 0011 it could be assumed that the elements of the sequence follow the rule *any number of 0s followed by any number of 1s.* If the source of elements of the sequence continues to generate values, the new elements might or might not comply with that rule. Induction is a way of reasoning that enables to pass from particular to general [1].

In the induction process it is possible to develop different models and several criteria have been proposed to choose from them. A particularly important one is model *simplicity* [1].

In order to apply IIS we need an Inductive Inference Machine (IIM) capable of inferring a program from a test suite (TS).

Definition 1: IIS criteria. Given an IIM M, a specification S and a test suite T, T satisfies IIS if M generates a program P' by inductive inference of T and P' is correct with respect to S.

Currently there are many tools that make it possible to infer a program from a test suite, but in general those tools are only capable of inferring programs that comply with certain restrictions. Kitzelman makes a review of different approaches and types of tools and classifies them in three categories: functional analytical approach, logical inductive programming and approaches based on functional generation and testing [10].

In functional generation and testing approaches input and output examples are not used in program construction, instead they are used to evaluate generated programs. Program generation is done, for example, by genetic programming [11]. Systems based on genetic programming maintain populations of candidate solutions and generate new ones by means of stochastic methods such as reproduction, mutation, cross-over and selection to maximize function fitness.

POLYGP and ADATE systems are examples of this approach. Kitzelman considers ADATE the most powerful inductive programming system, especially designed to evolve recursive programs [10].

2.2 ADATE System

ADATE is an evolutionary system that maintains a population of programs (kingdom in terms of ADATE) and makes a guided search through a fitness function. The collection of programs that ADATE generates and maintains starts with only one individual and then expands with evolution progression. ADATE performs transformations of the individuals to get new individuals.

The programs are represented in ADATE-ML, a subset of Standard ML [14]. Standard ML is a mostly functional programming language strongly and statically typed [13].

ADATE provides a set of data types already created for which it is not necessary to define those data types and associated functions. ADATE enables to infer programs from test cases, but it is not capable of inferring new data types, so they have to be provided together with test cases [14].

A specification in ADATE contains definitions of data types that describe input and output, primitive and other auxiliary functions to be used in program synthesis, example input values and input-output values for the example input values.

2.3 Use of ADATE to apply IIS

ADATE can be used as an inductive inference machine to apply IIS. However, some of the traits of ADATE demand the definition of an acceptance/rejection protocol. ADATE does not generate a sole program from test cases, it generates many programs and it does not have a stop mechanism, it continues to run endlessly. At any time it is possible to obtain information about the "best" program generated so far.

From the definition of IIS a test suite satisfies IIS using ADATE if ADATE generates a candidate program that is correct with respect to the specification. Additional criteria must be defined to determine when we will be able to say that IIS is not satisfied with ADATE. Therefore the definition of the criteria is adjusted so as to take into consideration ADATE peculiarities.

Definition 2: IIS criteria for ADATE. Given a specification S, a positive integer E and a test suite T, T satisfies IIS for ADATE if ADATE generates a program P' from T that is correct with respect to S. If this requirement is not met and if ADATE generates at least a candidate program P" that satisfies all the cases of T and none of the generated programs is correct, and after E additional evaluations after the generation of P" ADATE does not find a better candidate program, it is said that T does not satisfy IIS for ADATE. The value E could depend on the complexity of the program.

Below IIS for ADATE is applied to test suites for a program that receives as input a list of integer values and returns a list with the input values sorted in non-decreasing order. In a relatively arbitrary way the value of E for this program was set to twenty million.

We present test suites for this program as a list of cases separated by a slash. Each case is presented as a pair [input data], [output data]. List values are separated by commas.

The test suites are:

a) [] , [] / [1,2,3] , [1,2,3] / [3,2,1] , [1,2,3]
b) [] , [] / [1,2,4] , [1,2,4] / [1,3,2] , [1,2,3] / [2,1,2] , [1,2,2] / [2,1,-3] , [-3,1,2].

In order to quickly detect incorrect programs generated by ADATE we use **TS CORR**:

[], [] / [1], [1] / [3,1], [1,3] / [1,2,3], [1,2,3] / [1,3,2], [1,2,3] / [2,1,3], [1,2,3] / [2,3,1], [1,2,3] / [3,1,2], [1,2,3] / [3,2,1], [1,2,3] / [1,3,3], [1,3,3] / [3,1,3], [1,3,3] / [3,3,1], [1,3,3] / [1,1,3], [1,3,3] / [1,3,1], [1,1,3] / [3,1,1], [1,1,3] / [3,3,3], [3,3,3] / [7,5,6,5,4,1], [1,4,5,5,6,7].

ADATE generated multiple programs that satisfy all test cases from TS (a), but none of those programs is correct. The best of them, among other defects, returns wrong outputs for inputs [1,3,2] and [2,3,1]. ADATE continued generating programs and did not find any better than this one after more than 44 million additional evaluations. So TS (a) does not satisfy IIS for ADATE.

ADATE also generated multiple programs from TS (b) and after little more than 17,000 evaluations generated a program that satisfies TS CORR. We proved by mathematical induction that this program properly sorts lists of any length, therefore TS (b) satisfies IIS.

3 Application of IIS

In order to assess the usefulness of IIS in the evaluation of test suites obtained by applying a black box technique, we applied IIS to evaluate test suites generated by 11 subjects in an experiment in which they used the techniques equivalence partition and boundary value analysis. As part of the experiment all subjects received training in the techniques. Then they used these techniques to build test suites for a program that receives a list of integers as input and returns the list of integers sorted in ascending order.

We used ADATE System as the IIM. For each test suite developed by the subjects we created an ADATE specification file and executed ADATE System.

In many cases the test suites included incorrect input values (not integers). Standard ML is strongly typed and type control is done at compilation time, therefore these cases were not included in the generation.

Test cases with invalid types can be evaluated separately with a text type input. In the specification of test cases the expected output could have the values "Valid" or "Not Valid". In this evaluation every test case should be included. IIS would be satisfied for non-valid types if the IIM was capable of generating a correct validation program of input types. The implementation of this approach is out of the scope of this work.

We executed ADATE System version 0.50 running under Linux Crunchbang in a virtual machine with 1385 MB of allocated memory defined in Oracle Virtual Box with Windows 7 with 2,75 GB of usable memory as host in a PC with an AMD Phenom II X4 B95 3.00 GHz processor. We used Mlton 20041109-1.i386 SML compiler. We tested generated programs in the interactive environment provided by Standard ML of New Jersey v110.74 running in Windows.

ADATE runs endlessly and its termination has to be forced so in each execution we had to wait for ADATE to create a candidate program that satisfied every test case included in the specification file.

In the generation process, ADATE generates and evaluates a large number of programs, many of which are only good for genetic evolution and are not candidate solutions. From now on the term "generated program" by ADATE will only be used to name those programs that ADATE identifies as candidate solutions.

3.1 IIS satisfaction

For eight out of eleven test suites (those corresponding to subjects 1,2,3,4, 5,6,9,10) none of the generated programs was correct, even though they did satisfy all input-output pairs. Furthermore ADATE could not generate a correct program after E additional evaluations, so those test suites do not satisfy IIS. For three other test suites (subjects 7, 8, 11), the generated programs verified TS CORR and then we proved by mathematical induction on the length of the input lists that those programs are correct. So these three test suites satisfy IIS.

Following is the code generated by ADATE with TS 7 as input.

```
PG7
fun f Xs =
  case Xs of
    nill => Xs
  | cons( V1927, V1928 ) =>
  case f( V1928 ) of
    nill => Xs
  | cons( V3350, V3351 ) =>
  case ( V1927 < V3350 ) of
    false => cons( V3350, f( cons( V1927, V3351 ) ) )
  | true => cons( V1927, f( V1928 ) )
```

Instance 10 contains a test case in which the result is inconsistent with the input, given that for the input list [-1,-2,1] the written expected output is the same list, being [-2,-1,1] the correct result. For this instance, it can be said that the set of test cases is not appropriate.

For the remaining instances (1,2,3,4,5,6,9) it cannot be known for sure if ADATE could not generate a correct program with more running time. We analyze below the characteristics of the test suites that made it possible to generate a correct program and of those that did not.

Test cases cover the categories empty list, input with one element (except instance 11), disordered input and ordered input. Table 1 presents the number of cases corresponding to each of these categories. The atypical instance 10 is not included. Instances appear arranged from higher to lower number of total test cases with disordered values and, for those with the same value, for the total number of cases.

Table 1. Case categories

Instance	Empty	One element	Dis-ordered	Ordered	List Lengths	Correct
8	1	3	17	13	0,1,2,3,4	Y
7	1	1	5	1	0,1,2,3,5,6	Y
11	1		3	1	0,3	Y
2	1		2	2	0,4,5	N
9	1	1	2	1	0,1,5,13	N
3	1	1	1	1	0,1,6	N
4	1	1	1	1	0,1,2,4	N
1	1		1	1	0,3	N
5	1		1		0,5	N
6	1		1		0,4	N

In table 1 the three instances for which ADATE generated a correct program are grouped at the top. Instances 1, 3, 4, 5 and 6 only have one case each with disordered input values.

4 Analysis and Evaluation of IIS

4.1 IIS satisfaction and defect detection in the case study

A way to evaluate test suites created with a black-box technique for specification S consists of using them to detect defects in incorrect programs such as those generated by ADATE from test suites that do not satisfy IIS. In the process of evaluating IIS satisfaction we obtained a set of incorrect programs, a set of test suites that satisfy IIS and a set of test suites that do not satisfy IIS. We tested those incorrect programs with both sets of test suites.

There are three test suites from the experiment that satisfy IIS: TS 7, TS 8, TS 11. On the other hand, there are test suites that do not satisfy IIS. Table 2 presents the number of revealed failures by each of those test suites in each incorrect program generated by ADATE. The first column contains the test suite identification, the second column contains the total number of test cases in the test suite. The next eight columns contain the number of cases of the test suite in which each program fails. The last column contains the total number of programs that fail with each test suite.

Table 2. Program failures for each TS

TS	# Cases	Prg 1	Prg 2	Prg 3	Prg 4	Prg 5	Prg 6	Prg 9	Prg 10	# Prg Fail
7	8	3	3	2	5	5	4	3	6	8
8	34	7	3	3	23	23	25	3	30	8
11	5	1	1	1	4	4	4	1	4	8
1	3	0	0	0	2	2	1	0	1	4
2	5	1	0	0	4	4	4	0	4	5
3	4	1	0	0	2	2	2	0	2	3
4	4	0	0	0	0	2	2	0	2	3
5	2	1	0	0	1	0	1	0	1	4
6	2	0	0	0	1	1	0	0	1	3
9	5	1	0	0	3	2	2	0	3	5
10	2	0	0	0	1	1	1	0	1	4

Test suites that satisfy IIS detect defects in every incorrect program generated by ADATE. In contrast test suites that do not satisfy IIS can at most detect defects in 5 out of 8 incorrect programs.

4.2 IIS satisfaction and defect detection, theoretical analysis

The previous result will be analyzed from a theoretical perspective. A simple definition of the complexity is the length of the program in bytes. A shorter program is simpler and a longer program is more complex. Lets assume that IIM M has the simplest hypothesis property as defined by Zhu [16].

Definition 3: Simplest hypothesis property. M is said to have the simplest hypothesis property if it always produces the simplest program consistent with the input instances.

We use the notation |P| to denote the complexity of program P.

Lemma 1: Given a test suite T consistent with specification S, and a program P' generated by M from test suite T. Then T reveals a failure respect to S in every program P" simpler than P' |P"| < |P'|.

Proof: If P" does not fail in at least one case of T then P" is simpler than P' and satisfies T in contradiction with the simplest hypothesis property of M.

The relation between test suites related to specification S, "M infers from test suite X a program with same complexity as the program inferred by M from test suite Y" is an equivalence relation stated in the set of test suites for specification S. So it partitions the set in equivalence classes. Any test suite from one of these classes reveals at least one defect in every program of less complexity.

It should be noted that programs with same complexity may give different outputs for the same input.

Theorem 1: Given a test suite T that satisfies IIS for specification S with M, so exists a program P' generated by M from test suite T and P' is correct respect to S. Then T reveals a failure in every program P" simpler than P' |P"| < |P'|.

Proof: By direct application of Lemma 1.

Theorem 2: Given programs P' and P" generated by M respectively from test suites T and T'. If P' and P" are both correct respect to specification S, then P' and P" have the same complexity |P'| = |P"|.

Proof: If $|P'| \neq$ |P"| we name P_0 the simplest from P' and P" and P_1 the other one and we name T_0 and T_1 the corresponding test suites. By Lemma 1 T_1 detects at least one defect in P_0 in contradiction with the hypothesis that P_0 is correct respect to S.

Theorem 1 and theorem 2 state that every program simpler than a correct program inferred by M is incorrect and that test suites that satisfy IIS reveal at least one defect in all of them. Those theorems explain the difference observed in defect detection effectiveness between test suites that satisfy IIS and those that do not.

The fact that an IIM generates an incorrect program from a test suite can be interpreted as lack of information in the test suite. This is why the simplest program that can be inferred corresponds to another (and simpler) specification. A relation between the amount of information relevant to the specification provided by a test suite and the complexity of the specification is hereby stated.

As all the programs inferred by M that are correct respect to specification S have the same complexity we may take the complexity of a simplest correct program as the complexity of the specification. Also we may take as test suite T complexity the complexity of the inferred program P. If P is correct respect to S the complexities of T and S will be the same. If P is not correct respect to S then it corresponds to specification S' which is not more complex than S.

5 Heuristics to build a test suite that satisfies IIS

IIS is difficult to apply because it requires to prove that an inferred program is correct respect to the specification. In this section we present a procedure that aims to build a test set that satisfies IIS. It is suitable for the family of programs that can be expressed as a simple function that calls itself.

5.1 Same information relevant to the specification

Definition 4: No constant property. An IIM M is said to have the no constant property if when the input test suite is composed of a sole test case M does not infer a program that returns a constant value for all the program domain.

Constant programs are the simplest programs that satisfy a test suite with a sole test case. Those programs in general only satisfy that sole test case. With the no constant property the inferred programs from test suites with a sole test case will satisfy other test suites with a sole test case. Lets assume that IIM M has the no constant property.

Definition 5: Test cases that provide the same information relevant to a specification. Given IIM M, specification S and test cases consistent with S C_0 and C_1, test suite T_0 composed of C_0 and test suite T_1 composed of C_1, program P_0 generated by M from T_0 and program P_1 generated by M from T_1. If $P_0(X) = P_1(X)$ for all X in program domain as stated by S we say that C_0 and C_1 provide the same information relevant to specification S.

The previous definition states that two test cases provide the same information relevant to the specification if the corresponding inferred programs are equivalent. Note that a program is equivalent to itself. It is easy to see that the relation "provide the same information relevant to the specification" is an equivalence relation in the domain of test cases.

For the program under study two test cases in which the inputs are lists of the same length with elements with the same relative order provide exactly the same information relevant to the specification. For example test cases A := [1,-3,5] , [-3,1,5] and B := [7,1,9] , [1,7,9] provide exactly the same information to the IIM. We take as representative of the input part of the test cases the list formed by the minimal value 0 and the subsequent consecutive values for the different ordered values in the case. For example, the list [7,10,3,10,5,2,7] contains the different values (2,3,5,7,10). We substitute these values by (0,1,2,3,4) and form the list [3,4,1,4,2,0,3]. For test cases A and B the normal value is N:= [1,0,2], [0,1,2]. For the sorting program two test cases with the same normal value provide the same information relevant to the specification.

5.2 Simplest program that satisfies a Test Case

All the proofs included in the theoretical analysis are indirect proofs so, given a specification S, there is no certitude about the effective existence of a program that satisfies a test suite consistent with S and that is simpler than the simplest correct program. In order to shed light to this issue we will analyze simplest programs that satisfy test suites with only one test case for the sorting program. We are interested in simplest programs that satisfy a test case and the whole class of test cases that provide the same information relevant to the specification. Without loss of generality we restrict the analysis to the normal cases as in 5.1.

The simplest programs that satisfy the cases empty list [] and a list with one element [a] are Identity (I) and constant programs [] and [a]. There are 3 normal lists with two elements: [0,0],[0,1],[1,0]. Again the simplest program for the first two of them is I, and for the last one is a swap of elements 1 and 2 which we represent by Swap(1,2). Other simplest programs are the respective expected outputs as constants: [0.0], [0,1], [0,1]. There are 13 normal lists of three elements. Table 3 presents them with the corresponding simplest program. The third column contains an alternative constant program. A constant program may be simpler than a Swap or even than I, but it is only valid for one case of the class. For example, a program that always returns [0,0,1] satisfies a test case with [0,1,0] as input but neither satisfies any other input of the same class, i.e. [0,3,0], nor from any different class i.e. [0,1,0,0]. For this reason we will exclude constant programs from the rest of this analysis.

Table 3. Simplest Program for normal cases of list length 3

Test Case	Simplest Program	Constant Program
[0,0,0]	I	[0,0,0]
[0,0,1]	I	[0,0,1]
[0,1,0]	Swap(2,3)	[0,0,1]
[0,1,1]	I	[0,1,1]
[1,0,0]	Swap(1,3)	[0,0,1]
[1,0,1]	Swap(1,2)	[0,1,1]
[1,1,0]	Swap(1,3)	[0,1,1]
[0,1,2]	I	[0,1,2]
[0,2,1]	Swap(2,3)	[0,1,2]
[1,0,2]	Swap(1,2)	[0,1,2]
[1,2,0]	Swap(1,3)Swap(2,3)	[0,1,2]
[2,0,1]	Swap(1,2)Swap(2,3)	[0,1,2]
[2,1,0]	Swap(1,3)	[0,1,2]

There are 6 simplest programs for test cases of list length 3. For sufficiently great list length simplest programs will become recursive.

5.3 Heuristics towards IIS satisfaction

The program under study is a recursive function. We saw that a test suite that satisfies IIS does not need to cover neither the different normal cases for certain list size nor all the simplest programs. By contrast, if we have a program that has not recursion/iteration, i.e. a program that is only composed of case structures and without recursion, to satisfy IIS requires to cover all the simplest programs and all the border conditions. Without this coverage the inference of a correct program is not possible.

In the program under study it is easy to identify test cases that provide the same information relevant to the specification. In programs that manipulate data structures the information content relevant to the specification is explicit. But there are recursive functions for which this identification may be rather difficult. Take for example the Euclidean algorithm to find the greatest common divisor of two integers a and b. The information content relevant to the specification is implicit in the values of a and b and is associated with the level of recursion needed to terminate the algorithm.

The analysis of simplest programs becomes more difficult as list size increases so it is less clear if two test cases are independent or if they are satisfied by a tiny recursive program. If we work with short list lengths we may evaluate if a possible new test case is satisfied by a simplest program different from those that satisfy the test cases previously selected. The following procedure points to build a test suite that satisfies IIS for programs that can be expressed as a simple function that calls itself.

First we try to simplify the problem taking normal values like in 5.1. Then we execute the following steps:

1. Select the minimum level of recursion that is not trivial (list length 3 for the sorting program).

2. For that level of recursion identify all the different simplest programs that satisfy the normal test cases of that level. Each different simplest program corresponds to a class of test cases that provide the same information relevant to the specification. Create a test case for each one of those programs.

3. If the total number of test cases is very low (less than five), select the next level of recursion and repeat step 2.

4. Include test cases that cover all the simplest programs for the trivial levels of recursion (list lengths 0, 1 and 2 for the sorting program).

The analysis of table 1 suggests that three test cases with different information relevant to the specification very likely will enable IIS satisfaction. In step 3 of the procedure we require an additional test to increase the likelihood of IIS satisfaction.

5.4 Limitations

The main limitation of IIS has to do with its dependence on an IIM and its capabilities. The need to prove that the inferred program is correct may be circumvented testing the program with random input. If an oracle is available the evaluation of IIS may be automated. If the program has any failure IIS is not satisfied. If it does not fail at all IIS will be satisfied with certain likelihood.

The main difficulty to apply IIS is the running time needed for an IIM as ADATE to generate a program. Some of the generations done with the list sorting program, which is very simple, ran for more than 24 hours.

It is not clear whether this approach can escalate to more complex programs. ADATE has a mechanism by which components that can be used in the generation are supplied, so that a gradual generation by components is conceivable, but it has not been evaluated yet. Furthermore, the ADATE system currently has serious limitations as far as the user interface is concerned.

The application of IIS considering input data with non-valid types, even though it does not appear to present major difficulties, is pending.

6 Related work

In 1983, Weyuker proposed adequacy criteria of sets of test cases according to which both the program and the specification should be inferred from the set of test cases. Since these criteria are very difficult to apply, she considered two less demanding variations regarding the scope of the inference: to only infer the program or to only infer the specification [15]. IIS corresponds to a slightly relaxed version of the second variation since the specification does not need to be directly inferred. It is enough to infer a program that is correct regarding the specification. Note that this relaxation is not free, it comes at the price of having to prove that the inferred program is correct.

Fraser and Walkinshaw suggest a mechanism to automatically build a model of a program that consists of several steps [6]. This proposal has something to do with the definition of IIS to the extent that it uses an IIM to infer a program from a test suite, but with a very different objective: to build an approximate model of the program.

Zhu shows that the testing process can be seen as an inductive inference process in which whoever tests a program tries to deduce its properties for the whole input space from the observation of program behavior in a limited set of cases [17, 16]. Zhu defines a conceptual device M capable of performing an inductive inference of a program P from a set of test cases T. Then he defines adequacy criteria which he calls *Inductive Inference in M* according to which T satisfies the criteria if M allows to inductively infer P (the program under test) from T [16]. IIS are similar to Zhu's criteria but the inferred program in IIS needs not to be (and usually is not) the program under test. IIS are independent of the program under test and may be applied before its existence. The inferred program usually will be quite different from the program under test and it will be even coded in a different language (ADATE-ML if the IIM is ADATE).

Several adequacy criteria based on the specification were proposed based on different types of formal specification [18, 7]. IIS may be used with any type of specification.

Czemerinski, Braberman and Uchitel propose adequacy criteria for test suites obtained through a black-box technique, oriented to the test of components that present non-trivial requirements regarding the order in which their methods or procedures should be invoked. These criteria are based on an abstraction of the semantics associated with the expected behavior[5]. It is the only precedent of adequacy criteria oriented to black-box techniques and not dependent on formal methods that we know of, but these are suitable to certain types of components under test and IIS are of more general validity.

7 Conclusions and future work

7.1 Conclusions

We defined acceptance criteria IIS for test suites that only depend on the specification and that do not depend on the code. IIS require an IIM. We presented a way that ADATE System can be used as an IIM to implement IIS.

We applied IIS in the evaluation of test suites generated by different subjects as part of an experiment. Test suites that met the criteria turned out to be significantly better than those that did not, taking into account its characteristics and the diversity of the cases considered.

We showed that an IIM enables to generate incorrect programs respect to the specification and that they can be used in test suite evaluation. The test suites that satisfy IIS revealed defects in all the incorrect programs generated by the IIM.

We proved that, assuming that the IIM has the property of simplest hypothesis, a test suite that satisfies IIS (for which the IIM generated a correct program P) reveals at least one fault in every program that is simpler than P. We think that this result is of great importance from a theoretical point of view and can lead to practical developments. To our knowledge it is the first time that it is stated a relation between the information content of a test suite relevant to the specification and its effectiveness in fault detection.

We introduced the idea of a correspondence between the amount of information relevant to the specification contained in a test suite and the complexity of the program generated by the IIM. If the IIM infers from a test suite a program that is incorrect with respect to the specification we need to supply additional information so that the correct program is the simplest program that can be inferred. A triple relation arose between the complexity of a specification S, the information content of the simplest program P that satisfies specification S and the information content relevant to the specification of a test suite T that satisfies IIS.

We showed a way to use in test case selection the simplest program that satisfies a test case.

7.2 Future work

We will evaluate IIS usefulness as an aid to teach black-box test case selection techniques. We will explore the application of IIS to more complex programs by means of exploiting the capability that has ADATE to try user-defined functions in program synthesis. We will also implement the treatment of non-valid types.

We will work on the automated evaluation of IIS satisfaction based on the failure rate of the inferred programs with random input and on the definition of a degree of IIS satisfaction.

We will further analyze heuristics to build test suites that satisfy IIS, the relation between IIS and other adequacy criteria and we will try to apply the ideas behind IIS to combinatorial testing.

References

1. Angluin, D., Smith, C.H.: Inductive inference: theory and methods. ACM Computing Surveys **15**(3), 237–269 (Sep 1983)
2. Bertolino, A.: Software testing research and practice. In: Proceedings of the abstract state machines 10th international conference on Advances in theory and practice. pp. 1–21. Springer-Verlag, Berlin, Heidelberg (2003)
3. Bertolino, A.: Software testing research: achievements, challenges, dreams. In: Proceedings FOSE'07 Future of Software Engineering. pp. 85–103. IEEE CS, Washington DC (2007)
4. Briand, L.C.; Di Penta, M.L.Y.: Assessing and improving state-based class testing: A series of experiments. IEEE Transactions on Software Engineering **30**(11), 770–783 (Nov 2004)
5. Czemerinski, H., Braberman, V., Uchitel, S.: Behaviour abstraction coverage as black-box adequacy criteria. In: 2013 IEEE Sixth International Conference on Software Testing, Verification and Validation. pp. 222–231. IEEE (2013)
6. Fraser, G., Walkinshaw, N.: Behaviourally adequate software testing. In: 2012 IEEE Fifth International Conference on Software Testing, Verification and Validation. pp. 300–309. IEEE (2012)
7. Fraser, G., Wotawa, F., Ammann, P.: Testing with model checkers: A survey. Journal of Software Testing Verification and Reliability, **19**(3), 215–261 (September 2009)
8. Juristo, N; Moreno, A.: Reviewing 25 years of testing technique experiments. Empirical Software Engineering **9**(1-2), 7–44 (2004)
9. Kaner, C.; Bach, J.P.B.: Lessons learned in software testing: A context-driven approach. In: Proceedings of the 20th Conference on Software Engineering Education & Training CSEET '07. pp. 157–166. IEEE Computer Society, Washington DC (2007)
10. Kitzelmann, E.: Inductive programming: a survey of program synthesis techniques, Lecture Notes in Computer Science, vol. 5812. Springer-Verlag, Berlin (2010)
11. Koza, J.R.: Genetic Programming: On the Programming of Computers by Means of Natural Selection (Complex Adaptive Systems). MIT Press, Cambridge, MA (1992)
12. Orso, A., Rothermel, G.: Software testing: a research travelogue (2000-2014). In: Proceedings FOSE 2014 Future of Software Engineering. pp. 117–132. ACM, New York (2014)
13. Pucella, R.: Notes on programming standard ml of new jersey (version 110.0.6) (Jan 2001), http://www.cs.cornell.edu/riccardo/prog-smlnj/notes-011001.pdf, last accessed July 30, 2018
14. Vattekar, G.: Adate user manual (March 2006), http://www-ia.hiof.no/~rolando/ML/ADATE/AdateManual.pdf, last accessed July 30, 2018
15. Weyuker, E.J.: Assessing test data adequacy through program inference. ACM Transactions on Programming Languages and Systems **5**(4), 641–655 (Oct 1983)
16. Zhu, H.: A formal interpretation of software testing as inductive inference. Software Testing, Verification and Reliability **6**(1), 3–31 (Mar 1996)
17. Zhu, H., Hall, P., May, J.: Inductive inference and software testing. Software Testing, Verification and Reliability **2**(2), 69–81 (Jul 1992)
18. Zhu, H., Hall, P., May, J.: Software unit test coverage and adequacy. ACM Computing Surveys **29**(4), 366–427 (Dec 1997)

Teaching of formal methods: evidence of its inclusion in curricula, results, and difficulties

Silvana Moreno[1], Diego Vallespir[1], and Álvaro Tasistro[2]

[1] Universidad de la República, Uruguay
{smoreno,dvallesp}@fing.edu.uy
[2] Universidad ORT, Uruguay
{tasistro}@ort.edu.uy

Abstract. Formal methods aim at ensuring that both the operation and performance of the program are correct under any situation. As software complexity and security and safety risks grow, the teaching of these methods in universities becomes really important. However, teaching these methods is difficult and the best way to include them in the curricula is not clear. So, our aim is to get to know the evidence of the inclusion and results of formal methods in computing curricula. In order to achieve this, we conducted a Systematic Literature Review. We found that 10 universities have published works on the inclusion of formal methods in their curricula. The proposals present different ways of including formal methods (e.g., teaching them in only one course vs. teaching them in different courses, teaching at an undergraduate level vs. teaching at a graduate level), the results obtained, and the difficulties that arose. The results of this review are valuable to improve the teaching of formal methods in universities.

Keywords: formal methods education, computing curricula, software engineering education

1 Introduction

Nowadays, software controls countless systems that affect practically every aspect of our daily activity, many of them critical. The incorrect performance or the lack of performance of some part of these systems may produce high costs, but can also entail serious economic risks or even threaten people's health or lives. There are numerous software development processes, methods, techniques, and tools that aim at increasing the quality of the products and reducing the time to market.

Formal methods (FM) are a particular set of techniques to specify, develop, and verify software systems. FMs aim to ensure that both the operation and performance of the program are correct in any situation. This is a type of method that has very good results as it develops products with a low number of defects and that are easily maintainable [14].

It is necessary for software engineers to have enough theoretical knowledge in the area to apply FMs in their companies [13, 16, 17].

Since last decade, new languages and tools have been developed to support FMs in order to verify and validate systems [26]. Furthermore, numerous projects in the software industry have used these methods successfully [3, 36, 23, 35], also increasing the quality of the systems and the productivity of the development [1, 20, 24]. However, there are arguments against FMs: they are "too mathematical" and only trained people can use them [2], and the lack of engineers qualified in the use of FMs is one of the reasons why they have not been used widely [4] and also the main obstacle in its adoption [8].

In spite of the above mentioned problems, several organizations encourage the teaching of FMs. Scientific associations such as the Association for Computer Machinery (ACM), the Computer Society of the Institute of Electronic and Electrical Engineering (IEEE) [38], and the British Computer Society (BCS) consider FMs as one of the concepts that the undergraduate curriculum in Computer Sciences (CS) should include. Furthermore, the Software Engineering Education Knowledge (SEEK) includes FMs as a topic [6].

Lichtenberger [21] finds that FM education in a typical undergraduate curriculum is in a "sad state" and suggests the development of a curriculum for software engineering that changes the way FMs are taught. His proposal consists of deleting classic math teaching (calculus, algebra) and putting an emphasis on the problem-solving process (formal specification, developing problem-solving algorithms, and correctness testing). Other works understand that there is still a division between the FM and software engineering (SE) disciplines, which causes problems when teaching FM in SE degrees[7, 27].

This situation leads us to say that additional education, and also a different type of education, on formal methods is necessary. The only way to achieve the effective transfer of FMs to the industry is through training [37].

In order to improve the teaching of FMs, we need to consider the evidence of its inclusion in university curricula. Therefore, we planned and executed a systematic literature review (SLR). SLRs are used to find, evaluate, and add all the evidence present in the relevant research articles with reference to a specific research question [19].

In this article, we present the evidence found for the inclusion of formal methods in computing curricula (computer science, software engineering, computer engineering, information technology, and information systems).

The rest of the document is structured in the following way: section 2 explains the research method and describes the systematic literature review; section 3 shows the results of the research; in section 4 we discuss the findings and their connection to the objectives of the work; section 5 explains the threats to validity; and finally, section 6 summarizes the conclusions and future work.

2 Method of the Systematic Review

The aim of this systematic review is to get evidence on the inclusion of FMs in university curricula and the results obtained as a consequence of such inclusion. We carried it out following the process suggested by Kitchenham [19].

The SLR was conducted by only one researcher (the first author of the paper).

2.1 Research questions

The following are the research questions of the SLR:
RQ1:What proposals are published about the inclusion of FMs in computing curricula?
RQ2: Is the inclusion proposed at an undergraduate or graduate level?
RQ3: What is the form of inclusion (in the first years/throughout the curricula)?
RQ4: How many courses are included in the curriculum?
RQ5: What languages and tools are used to teach?
RQ6: What are the difficulties the inclusion presents, if any?
RQ7: What are the results obtained?

2.2 Data Sources and Search Strategy

We used the Scopus database to carry out the search. Scopus indexes the papers published by IEEE, ACM and others. Kitchemham argues that IEEE and ACM cover the most important software engineering journals and conference proceedings [19].

The search string is divided into three parts. The first part refers to the topic of interest (formal methods). The second presents possible synonyms of "curriculum". Finally, the third part refers to different nomenclature a computing degree can have. Some of the synonyms related to the terms "curriculum" and "software engineering" were obtained from Dieste [9].
("formal method") AND ("curriculum" OR "curricula" OR "syllabus" OR "education" OR "career") AND ("software engineering" OR "computer science" OR "computer engineering" OR "informatics" OR "information technology" OR "information system")

2.3 Selection of studies

The articles that fulfill both of the following conditions were included:

- The article focuses on formal methods within an engineering curriculum.
- The article answers at least one of the research questions

The articles that were not written in English were excluded.

2.4 Data extraction and synthesis

In this research project, we read each article completely in order to answer the research questions, since analyzing the abstracts was not enough.

We made a qualitative synthesis, using the methods of narrative synthesis and vote counting[19].

3 Results

The search was performed on September 2018, using Scopus. We applied the search string in titles and abstracts and found 98 articles from 1986 to 2018. For each of the 98 articles, we read title and abstract to decide whether it should be considered for a full text read or not. We discarded 50 articles in this stage. For the remaining 48 articles, we read the full text and selected 15 articles for the data extraction, discarding the others.

We extracted the data from 10 of the 15 articles resulting from the search. The reason for this decision is that we obtained 5 articles by Ann Kelly Sobel and 2 articles by Garlan published in different years that include the same curricula. This is why we selected only one article written by each author, dismissing the remaining 5. The references of the discarded ones are: [10, 32, 31, 33, 29]. The article we selected by each author is the one that describes the curriculum in more detail.

Due to the number of papers we found, we decided to exclude the quality assessment step of the SLR process.

The results of the SLR are presented in the following subsections.

3.1 Results for RQ1

This subsection presents the results of RQ1:What proposals are published about the inclusion of FMs in computing curricula?

Table 1 presents the 10 articles resulting from the review sorted in ascending order by date of publication, country, and objectives of the proposals. The geographical distribution of the universities gives us a first impression of the low inclusion of FM (four in USA, three in Europe, and three in Asia).

3.2 Results for RQ2, RQ3 and RQ4

This subsection presents the results of RQ2: Is the inclusion proposed at undergraduate or graduate level?, RQ3: What is the form of inclusion? and RQ4: How many courses are included in the curriculum?

Table 2 presents the level of inclusion (LI) and the number of FM courses proposed in the curricula. If the inclusion is proposed for undergraduate students, we use the letter U, for graduate the letter G, and for both we use U/G.

Some authors claim that students should be motivated with FMs at early stages. In these cases, the authors propose the inclusion in undergraduate curricula (proposals ID 2, 3, 6, 8, 10). Other authors (proposals 1, 4 and 9) prefer

Table 1. Date of publication, country and objectives

Id	Date	Ref.	Country	Objectives
1	1995	[11]	USA	Incorporate FM throughout the curriculum
2	1998	[30]	USA	Incorporate FM throughout the curriculum
3	2000	[34]	Greece	Teaching formal specification but in a detailed way
4	2000	[5]	Korea	Debate on which is the most effective way of teaching FM
5	2003	[25]	USA	Teach the students the importance of modeling mathematical tools to evaluate software components and techniques
6	2008	[28]	USA	The reason for the inclusion is not presented
7	2008	[12]	France	Incorporate problem-based learning techniques throughout the curriculum
8	2009	[22]	Japan	Motivate the students to use FM in the industry
9	2015	[18]	Japan	Discusses their experience with FM education
10	2015	[15]	Germany	Describes how to include FM in a foundational SE course

Table 2. Level, number of courses

Id	LI	# courses
1	G	5 compulsory courses, set of optional courses and final project
2	U	2 new courses and 4 existing courses
3	U	1 new course
4	G	1 new course
5	U/G	1 new course
6	U	1 new course
7	U/G	several courses
8	U	several courses and final project
9	G	44 lecture classes and a final project
10	U	1 new course

to orient the inclusion in graduate curricula, with more mature students capable of applying FMs easily in industrial projects. Proposals 5 and 7 propose courses that can be included both in undergraduate and graduate curricula.

Besides the levels of inclusion of the FMs (U, G, U/G), proposals vary in the number of courses proposed. Proposals 3, 4, 5, 6 and 10 choose to approach FM teaching in only one course. In contrast, 1, 2, 7, 8 and 9 prefer several courses throughout the curriculum so as to gradually gain experience. The author of proposal 1 particularly criticizes the approach of introducing FMs in only one course, since this tends to isolate their use in the traditional activities of software development.

Regardless of the level of inclusion and the number of proposed courses, some authors claim that students should be motivated with formal methods from an early stage. In these cases, authors propose inclusion in the curriculum during the first few years of the degree (proposals 1, 2, 3, 8 and 10). In the other proposals, it is not made clear at what stage of the curriculum it should be taught.

3.3 Results for RQ5

This subsection presents the results of RQ5: What languages and tools are used to teach?

Table 3 presents the formal methods and tools used for each proposal. Formal language Z is used in several proposals (1, 3, 5 and 6). In 1 and 3, the students produce formal specifications in Z from requirements in natural language. Furthermore, in 3, they also do the reverse work: they interpret the specifications from Z to natural language. In proposal 1, some courses are based on support tools. However, it does not mention which ones. In 3, the article does not mention the use of tools.

Table 3. Formal methods and tools

Id	FM	Tools
1	VDM and Z	based on tools, but they are not described
2	some FM	PVS
3	Z	does not appear in this article
4	Coloured Petri Net and Statecharts	Tool of Coloured Petri Net and STATEMATE
5	Z	Z/EVES
6	Z and JML	Z/EVES-jml compiler and RAC
7	It does not appear in the article	does not appear in this article
8	VDM and SOFL	IFAD VDM or SOFL GUI
9	VDM, B-Method, Event-B and Coq	SPIN, SMV, LTSA, CSP and UPPAAL
10	DSL	GEAR model checking

In proposal 5, apart from learning to specify using Z, they also learn refinement and proofs. In the first years this course was taught, the proofs were done manually; in later versions, they started to use the ORA's Z/EVES.

The course of proposal 6, similarly to the previous ones, proposes at first the use of Z language to specify formally, and the Z/EVES tool to check the syntax and the correctness of the program. After teaching this course for some years, the authors decided to change the language and the tool. In the last years of the course, they teach JML as a formal specification language, and the JML compiler and RAC to check the assertions in execution time. The reason for this decision, according to the authors, is that Z is not a good language to integrate with languages and development contexts.

Proposal 2 incorporates a formal operational method, but it does not specify which one. The operational FM is based on the specification and verification of software components. In this case, the selected tool was PVS, which makes it possible to conduct an analysis of the specifications. The method and tool to be used in this case depend on the criterion of the person implementing the proposal.

Proposals 8 and 9 introduce VDM. Proposal 8 uses VDM to formally specify the first two years of the curriculum, and SOFL for the third and fourth years, teaching more complex expressions. In this proposal, the authors decide to use the tools only in the final project (4th year). They argue that the tools are not always effective, and it is better for the students to learn to specify and understand the specifications at hand. The use of tools by students leaves the solutions to tools rather than to students themselves. In a first class of mathematical logic, proposal 9 introduces set theory, predicate logic, hoare logic, and temporal logic. In another 12 classes, the formal specification (6 classes) and model checking (6 classes) topics are introduced. In each class, a method (VDM, B, SPIN, among others) and basic aspects of verification and validation using tools are taught.

Proposal 10 introduces process-modeling languages using Domain Specific Language (DSL). In order to convey the idea of property-based correctness and compliance, they directly introduce temporal logics and model checking as a formal verification technique on the (process-) model level, together with a corresponding tool. This proposal chooses to include lightweight formal methods, and the authors wanted to provide scalable approaches with a low threshold for adoption.

Finally, proposal 4 teaches by using small-scale but realistic practical examples. Throughout this course, they must learn and apply the formal Petri Net and Statecharts methods, and they can optionally use any other ones. In this case, they use type-checking tools, code generation, and performance simulation tools in an interactive way.

3.4 Results for RQ6

This subsection presents the results of RQ6: What are the difficulties the inclusion presents, if any?

Table 4 presents the difficulties found by the authors of each proposal.

Table 4. Difficulties found

Id	Difficulties founds
1	Lack of appropriate textbooks to teach and lack of tools
2	Lack of textbooks
3	Difficulty for the professor to revise
4	Difficulties with the Coloured Petri Net and STATEMATE tool
5	Lack of tools/documentation. Student frustration when demonstrated formally
6	Tools do not provide technical support. Interfaces are not very intuitive for students
7	Persuade others that the teaching approach works
8	Tools that were visually unattractive and not very amusing for students
9	Students felt the classes formal specification and model checking were difficult
10	The proposal does not mention difficulties

Almost all the proposals presented difficulties when they introduced FM in the curriculum. The lack of textbooks and the lack of, or problems in the use of support tools are the most mentioned difficulties. Proposals 1 and 2 state that the few textbooks available are not appropriate for the students. Therefore, professors must devote a lot of time to the preparation of all the study material.

The support tools are also questioned in several proposals (1, 4, 5, 6 and 8). The authors argue that the tools are generally designed to be used in research and not by the students. Because of this, the tools do not have user manuals, documentation, and are not visually appropriate to be used by students.

In proposal 9, 38.8% of students mentioned difficulties in the formal specification lessons because they are unfamiliar with logic expressions. Model checking was more difficult to understand (71.4% of students). The authors believe that the difficulties mentioned in model checking were due to a more complex set of exercises.

Finally, proposal 5 mentions difficulties the students face when building the proofs. They consider that "stronger" students were the ones who managed to complete the test with difficulty, while "weaker" students were unable to complete the test and gave up.

Figure 1 presents the evolution through time of the three most mentioned difficulties (text books, support tools, and the use of FMs). These difficulties are presented according to the characteristics (lack, difficulty) mentioned in the proposals.

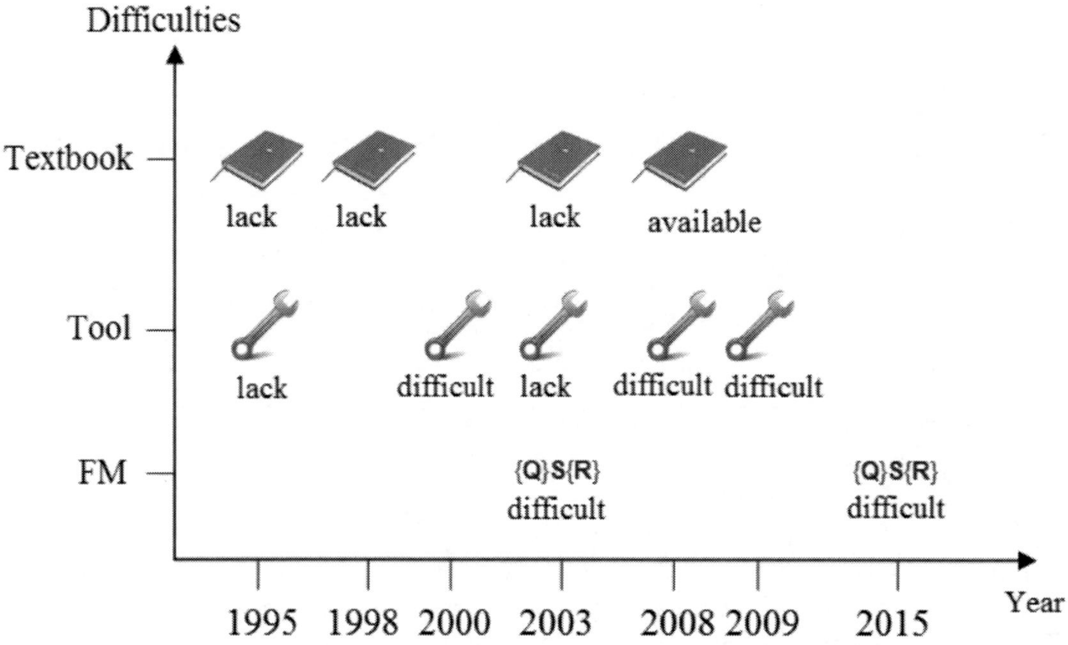

Fig. 1. Evolution of difficulties

It can be seen that the lack of textbooks is mentioned by proposals 1, 2 and 5 between 1995 and 2008. After this date, lack of textbooks does not appear among the difficulties found in any of the proposals, therefore, we might think there was some progress in the availability of FM textbooks. In contrast, in proposal 6 (2008), the authors mention that there are a number of text and reference books available.

Regarding support tools, a technological evolution can be observed over a few years. Proposals 1 and 5 (1995 and 2003) mention the lack of tools, while the authors of proposals 4, 6 and 8 (2000, 2008 and 2009) mention the use of the tools as a difficulty.

Finally, in proposals 5 and 9, students find difficulties in both specifications and formal demonstrating.

The results described by the different proposals are qualitative in general. Normally, in the proposals, students were motivated and willing to learn and apply FMs in the future. Furthermore, they expressed (in several proposals) that they obtained benefits when applying FMs, and that they would continue to use them in other courses or in the industry.

3.5 Results for RQ7

This subsection presents the results of RQ7: What are the results obtained? Table 5 presents the results obtained by the authors of each proposal.

Table 5. Results obtained by the authors

Id	Results
1	Students learn to approach the use of FMs with an open mind and a willingness to discover ways to exploit them for practical problems.
2	Students get better results in exams, shorter programs with fewer errors
3	External examiners and student surveys make positive comments
4	Students express that they felt capable of better understanding the performance of the system. The authors find that teaching FMs is difficult and takes time
5	Students can learn formal techniques as an integral part of software engineering. They suggest that they will continue using formal techniques in the future
6	Provides the students with a radically different overview of software development.
7	The introduction of FMs in the study plan through problems was successful.
8	Students with work experience find FMs easier to learn and use than students without experience
9	Students find FMs applicable
10	There is an improvement in SW development skills in students

Proposal 2 reveals some quantitative data on the application of FMs. In this proposal, some students followed the traditional curriculum while others followed the FM curriculum. At the end of three of the six courses of the curriculum, it has been observed that FM students score 16% higher in exam results. Based on the evaluation made by the professors, the programming tasks of FM students tend to be smaller (LOCs), present fewer defects (mainly due to omissions in the requirements) and focus on a general solution to a problem.

The remaining proposals present their conclusions based on the students and professors' feedback, or the researcher's own perception. The students seem enthusiastic about FMs, willing to discover ways of exploiting them for practical and realistic problems (1 and 5), and being capable of better understanding the performance of the system (4).

In proposal 9, a student survey reveals that most of them find FMs applicable. Specifically, 50% stated "somewhat applicable", 40% stated "mostly applicable", 10% stated "fully applicable", while no students marked the "not very applicable" category.

The students' feedback in proposal 3 indicates that their knowledge and skills have increased compared to other courses taken at the same time (Java Programming, Logics, Operating Systems).

The authors of proposal 7 consider that the problem-based approach is successful, but they must convince their colleagues that it really works. They explain that, in general, their colleagues demand evidence that is difficult to provide.

In 8, the authors conclude that it is not important whether FMs can be used directly as an efficient software engineering technique, since the result will be that students will be well-trained and disciplined.

The authors of proposal 10 observe differences in SW development skills between the students who take the curriculum prior to the introduction of the course and the students who take the curriculum with the new FM course. The students of the curriculum without the FM course were more confident in architectural issues and coding skills, while those who take the FM course have a more intuitive confidence with application development and with mastering a number of different technologies. In addition to this, the authors are confident that teaching lightweight formal methods should be part of software engineering education.

4 Discussion

The results obtained from the systematic review provide knowledge regarding the inclusion of FMs in computing curricula. The differences found regarding the ways of teaching FMs -such as in one or several courses, which formal method to teach, or the support tools used- prove that a consensus has not yet been reached on how to teach them.

In general, the results of the proposals do not show an effect on FM teaching nor in the curriculum or skills acquired by students. The only proposal that evaluates the effects of the introduction of FMs is the software created by the students of proposal 2. The rest of the proposals mention the opinions of students, teachers, and researchers. We understand this might be due to the fact that there is still a maturation process for the way in which research in software engineering education is conducted. A way to increase inclusion of, and interest in, FMs, is to submit results of the effects the teaching of these methods has on software development.

In this review, we found only 10 universities have reported the inclusion of FMs in their curricula, and they vary in different aspects. Some chose inclusion at an undergraduate level, others in the graduate level, while others may be applied in an undergraduate and/or graduate level. The arguments in favor of the inclusion at the undergraduate level indicate that FMs should be taught at early stages. The arguments in favor of the inclusion at the graduate level suggest that the more advanced students, who have more training, tend to learn and apply FMs in a better way. As we already mentioned, it is not clear which of these options is better.

Moreover, half of the proposals opt for only one course, while the other half opt for several courses distributed throughout the curriculum. We understand that teaching FMs from the early stages and as a part of the software development process seems to be more appropriate, with the purpose of training professionals that are able to develop quality software. However, as stated before, more studies are needed in order to shed light on this matter.

Throughout the years, there has been an increase in the availability of textbooks and support tools. However, the tools are still unattractive for use among students.

The results of FMs inclusion in curricula are positive. The 10 proposals confirmed, in spite of the difficulties, that it is possible to introduce FMs in curricula. In the majority of the proposals, the feedback from the students revealed that they feel motivated, capable of exploiting FMs and intend to use them in the future.

We agree with several authors [2, 4] on the importance of improving education of FMs in curricula. We invite the community to present their proposals and results regarding the inclusion of FMs in the curricula.

5 Threats to validity

We identified the following threats to the validity of our work. Firstly, the scope of the review was restricted to the Scopus search engine. Although this search engine has a wide coverage of publications and indexes, and several publication catalogues (including IEEE, ACM, Springer and Elsevier), some articles may have been omitted.

Secondly, we noticed that in several articles it was impossible to find an answer for all the defined questions. Therefore, it was impossible for us to get complete data for all the articles we found. In order to reduce this threat, we intend to contact the authors of the works published and consult them on the missing data.

Finally, we believe that the amount of papers collected is not a significant sample of reality. We propose as future work to expand this research with a survey to several universities to be able to find information not reported.

6 Conclusions

The aim of this research was to obtain information on the inclusion of FMs in computing curricula and its results.

The results obtained show that 10 universities have reported the inclusion of FMs in their curricula. These proposals made it possible for us to learn about the existence of different ways of teaching FMs. As mentioned above, strategies for teaching FMs were found through one or various courses, applying one or several FMs, with or without support tools, among others.

Concerning the number of proposals found, we can conclude that they do not reflect the reality of the FM inclusion in computing curricula. We are aware of several universities in Latin America and Europe that include FMs in their curricula. This review exposes the flaws of the community in publishing results of FM teaching. We believe that an increase in research and communication of the results by the community would encourage their teaching and use.

The results of this work helps us understand the benefits of the inclusion of FMs in the curricula and gives us an overview with different forms of inclusion, their results, and their problems. Also, this SLR helped us improve our SLR protocol and extraction spreadsheet.

Regarding future work, it would be interesting to carry out a survey in several universities to find more information about their undergraduate and graduate curricula. This means, we would collect more data on the universities that include FMs as part of their curricula, even though it is not reported. We plan to extend our SLR considering other digital libraries as well. Collecting this evidence will help us improve the teaching of these methods.

References

1. Abrial, J.: Formal methods: Theory becoming practice. Journal of Universal Computer Science **13**(5), 619–628 (May 2007)
2. Baldwin, D., Henderson, P.B.: The importance of mathematics to the software practitioner. IEEE Software **19**(2), 112–111 (March 2002)
3. Best, D.W., Kress, C.E., Mykris, N.M., Russell, J.D., Smith, W.J.: An advanced-architectur cmos/sos microprocessor. IEEE Micro **2**(3), 10–26 (August 1982)
4. Bjørner, D., Havelund, K.: 40 years of formal methods. In: Jones, C., Pihlajasaari, P., Sun, J. (eds.) FM 2014: Formal Methods. pp. 42–61. Springer International Publishing, Cham (2014)
5. Cha, S.: Pet formalisms versus industry-proven survivors: Issues on formal methods education. Journal of Research and Practice in Information Technology **32**(1), 39–45 (December 2000)
6. Joint Task Force on Computing Curricula, A.f.C.M.A., Society, I.C.: Computer Science Curricula 2013: Curriculum Guidelines for Undergraduate Degree Programs in Computer Science. ACM, New York, NY, USA (2013), 999133
7. Cowling, J.: The role of modelling in teaching formal methods for software engineering. In: Formal Methods in Software Engineering Education and Training. pp. 11–18 (2015)
8. Davis, J.A., Clark, M., Cofer, D., Fifarek, A., Hinchman, J., Hoffman, J., Hulbert, B., Miller, S.P., Wagner, L.: Study on the barriers to the industrial adoption of formal methods. In: Pecheur, C., Dierkes, M. (eds.) Formal Methods for Industrial Critical Systems. pp. 63–77. Springer Berlin Heidelberg, Berlin, Heidelberg (2013)

9. Dieste, O., Padua, A.G.: Developing search strategies for detecting relevant experiments for systematic reviews. In: First International Symposium on Empirical Software Engineering and Measurement (ESEM 2007). pp. 215–224 (September 2007)
10. Garlan, D.: Formal methods for software engineers: Tradeoffs in curriculum design. Software Engineering Education pp. 131–142 (October 1992)
11. Garlan, D.: Making formal methods education effective for professional software engineers. Information and Software Technology **37**(5), 261 – 268 (1995)
12. Gibson, J.P.: Weaving a formal methods education with problem-based learning. In: Margaria, T., Steffen, B. (eds.) Leveraging Applications of Formal Methods, Verification and Validation. pp. 460–472. Springer Berlin Heidelberg, Berlin, Heidelberg (2008)
13. Gries, D.: The need for education in useful formal logic; an invitation to formal methods. IEEE Computer pp. 29–30 (1996)
14. Groote, J., Osaiweran, A., Wesselius, J.: Benefits of applying formal methods to industrial control software. Formal Methods (2005)
15. H. Bordihn, A. Lamprecht, T.M.: Foundations of semantics and model checking in a software engineering course. In: proceedings of the first workshop on formal methods in software engineering education and training (2015)
16. Hinchey, M.G., Bowen, J.: To formalize or not to formalize? IEEE Computer **29**, 18–19 (April 1996)
17. Holloway, M., Butler, R.: Impediments to industrial use of formal methods. Computer (1996)
18. Ishikawa, F., Yoshioka, N., Tanabe, Y.: Keys and roles of formal methods education for industry: 10 year experience with top se program. In: Proceedings First Workshop on Formal Methods in SEE and Training. (2015)
19. Kitchenham, B., Budgen, D., Brereton, P.: Evidence-based software engineering and systematic reviews, vol. 4. CRC Press (2015)
20. Kurita, T., Nakatsugawa, Y.: The application of vdm to the industrial development of firmware for a smart card ic chip. International Journal of Software and Informatics **3**, 343–355 (January 2009)
21. Lichtenberger, F.: Making formal methods popular: The crux is math education! In: Formal Methods in Software Engineering Education and Training. pp. 27–34 (2015)
22. Liu, S., Takahashi, K., Hayashi, T., Nakayama, T.: Teaching formal methods in the context of software engineering. ACM SIGCSE Bulletin **41**(2), 17–23 (2009)
23. Miller, S., Srivas, M.: Formal verification of the aamp5 microprocessor: A case study in the industrial use of formal methods. In: Proceedings of the 1st Workshop on Industrial-Strength Formal Specification Techniques. pp. 2–. WIFT '95, IEEE Computer Society, Washington, DC, USA (1995)
24. Osaiweran, A., Schuts, M., Hooman, J., Groote, J.F., van Rijnsoever, B.: Evaluating the effect of a lightweight formal technique in industry. International Journal on Software Tools for Technology Transfer **18**(1), 93–108 (February 2016)
25. Perry, A.: Integrating formalism into undergraduate software engineering. Journal of Systems and Software **74**(2), 147 – 154 (2003)
26. Perry, W.E.: Effective methods for software testing: Includes complete guidelines, Checklists, and Templates. John Wiley & Sons (2007)
27. Robinson, K.: Embedding formal development in software engineering. In: International Conference on Technical Formal Methods. pp. 203–213. Springer (2004)

28. Sebern, M., Welch", H.: "formal methods in the undergraduate software engineering curriculum". In: "2008 Annual Conference & Exposition". "ASEE Conferences", "Pittsburgh, Pennsylvania" (June 2008)
29. Sobel, A.E.K.: A software engineering curriculum incorporating formal methods: a progress report. In: 27th Annual Frontiers in Education Conference. vol. 2, pp. 872 vol.2– (November 1997)
30. Sobel, A.E.K.: Applying an operational formal method throughout software engineering education. Information and Software Technology **40**(4), 233–238 (1998)
31. Sobel, A.E.K.: A software engineering curriculum incorporating an operational formal method. In: 28th Annual Frontiers in Education Conference. vol. 2, pp. 807–810 vol.2 (November 1998)
32. Sobel, A.E.K.: Final results of incorporating an operational formal method into a software engineering curriculum. Frontiers in Education Conference **2**, 13a3–18 – 13a3–22 (1999)
33. Sobel, A.E.K., Clarkson, M.R.: Formal methods application: an empirical tale of software development. IEEE Transactions on Software Engineering **28**(3), 308–320 (March 2002)
34. Sotiriadou, A., Kefalas, P.: Teaching formal methods in computer science undergraduates. In: International Conference on Applied and Theoretical Mathematics (2000)
35. Srivas, M., Miller, S.: Applying formal verification to a commercial microprocessor. Proceedings of the Asia and South Pacific Design Automation Conference (August 1995)
36. Srivas, M., Miller, S.: Formal verification of an avionics microprocessor. Tech. rep., NASA (1995)
37. Toledo, B.: Introduction of the formal methods in software engineering training. Revista Antioqueña de las Ciencias Computacionales y la Ingeniería de Software pp. 25–32 (2013)
38. Tucker, B., Robert, R., Keith, B.: Computing curricula 1991: Report of the acm/ieee-cs joint curriculum task force. Tech. rep., ACM/IEEE-CS, New York, NY, USA (1991)

Soft skills in software engineering in higher education. An initial study of its state in Latin America

Gerardo Matturro[1[0000-0001-6432-1223]], Martín Solari[1[0000-0001-5532-3227]]

[1] Universidad ORT Uruguay, Montevideo, Uruguay
matturro@uni.ort.edu.uy, martin.solari@ort.edu.uy

Abstract. Soft skills, though prized by software companies when hiring new professional, are not usually included as an active teaching topic in university careers in software engineering, information systems or computer science. In this article we report the main results of a survey on the state of soft skills teaching in software engineering in higher education institutions in Latin America. We found several university programs that include specific courses on soft skills. The respondents consider that combining soft skills in technical courses is a valid didactical approach, in addition to specific courses on soft skills. While the results cannot be generalized by virtue of the size of the sample, respondents have a favorable opinion regarding that the teaching of these skills should be included in the curricula of those careers, and there is also a high interest in creating a community of professors and researchers to work together in researching and dissemination of initiatives in teaching soft skills in software engineering.

Keywords: soft skills, software engineering, higher education, Latin America.

1 Introducción

El desarrollo de software es una actividad altamente técnica que requiere personas capaces de realizar diversas funciones en proyectos de software, y con conocimientos y experiencia en diversas metodologías, herramientas y técnicas.

Las empresas de software, cuando forman equipos de proyectos o cuando contratan nuevos profesionales, a menudo tienden a enfatizar el conocimiento y las habilidades técnicas de los posibles candidatos. Sin embargo, cuando las personas trabajan juntas en un proyecto de software, también se necesitan otras habilidades y capacidades relacionadas con la realización de actividades tales como comunicarse e interactuar con otros miembros del equipo y con los interesados en el proyecto, administrar el tiempo, presentar el avance del proyecto, negociar con el cliente, resolver problemas y tomar decisiones, entre otras.

Este tipo de habilidades se conocen como “habilidades blandas” o “habilidades no técnicas”, y pueden definirse como la combinación de destrezas, actitudes, y hábitos que permiten a las personas desempeñarse mejor en el lugar de trabajo, complementando las habilidades técnicas necesarias para hacer su trabajo, e influyendo en la forma en que se comportan e interactúan con los demás [1], [2], [3].

Capretz y Ahmed afirman que en la actualidad muy pocos cursos en los programas de estudio de ingeniería de software tocan los temas del trabajo en equipo y la evaluación de las habilidades blandas [4]. Según estos autores, incluso es difícil encontrar una universidad que tenga un curso completo sobre los aspectos humanos de la ingeniería de software, y consideran que es desafortunado que las habilidades blandas están lejos de ser parte de la educación de ingeniería de software convencional.

Jones Morel y Griffiths, por su parte, afirman que, si bien un grado universitario, tal como una Licenciatura, se considera un paso necesario para el progreso profesional, hay una brecha creciente entre lo que necesitan las organizaciones y las habilidades y destrezas que realmente proporciona una licenciatura. A medida que se automatizan más habilidades técnicas, los empleadores les dan mayor importancia a las habilidades interpersonales y de equipo de los graduados universitarios que contratan. Esta brecha entre lo que quieren las empresas y lo que ofrecen las universidades ha crecido a medida que el lugar de trabajo se vuelve cada vez más digital, global y ocupado por la generación de los *millenials* [5].

El propósito de este artículo es reportar el proceso seguido y los resultados obtenidos de una encuesta sobre la enseñanza de habilidades blandas en ingeniería de software en educación superior en América Latina.

La realización de esta encuesta forma parte de un proyecto más amplio denominado *ESSISAL: Enseñanza de Soft Skills en Ingeniería de Software en América Latina.* Nuestro objetivo es conocer el estado actual de la enseñanza de habilidades blandas en carreras de grado universitario relativas a ingeniería y desarrollo de software en universidades e instituciones de educación superior en América Latina, con la finalidad de promover una iniciativa regional colaborativa para la enseñanza y el desarrollo de este tipo de habilidades en los futuros gradados.

Los resultados de este trabajo son de interés para investigadores interesados en la enseñanza de los aspectos humanos de la ingeniería de software, así como para responsables y diseñadores de planes de estudio de carreras universitarias relacionadas a la ingeniería y desarrollo de software.

El resto de este artículo está organizado de la siguiente manera. En la sección 2 se hace una revisión del término "habilidades blandas", se exponen tres enfoques habituales para caracterizar el concepto, y se aborda la importancia y la necesidad de incorporar la enseñanza de estas habilidades en los planes de estudio. La sección 3 explica el diseño metodológico del estudio, donde se exponen las preguntas de investigación y los procedimientos de recolección y preparación de datos. En la sección 4 se presentan los principales resultados obtenidos, mientras que en la sección 5 se expone la discusión de estos resultados. La sección 6 aborda las amenazas a la validez de este estudio y en la sección 7 se presentan las conclusiones y se esbozan los trabajos futuros.

2 Antecedentes

En esta sección presentamos una breve revisión de la literatura general (no limitada al área de ingeniería de software) sobre el concepto de "habilidades blandas". Destacamos la ausencia de una definición única, y revisamos tres enfoques típicos para conceptualizar el término a fin de desarrollar una definición de trabajo para este estudio. Además, discutimos sobre la relevancia de las habilidades blandas en la práctica de la ingeniería de software y en la educación superior.

2.1 Las habilidades blandas en la literatura general

Según Dell'Aquila y colegas las "habilidades blandas" son un concepto amplio que abarca muchas dimensiones del desarrollo de la esfera personal, que involucra una combinación de componentes emocionales, de comportamiento y cognitivos [6].

En la literatura sobre el tema se pueden encontrar tres enfoques amplios para definir o caracterizar el concepto de "habilidades blandas": dar una definición explícita, dar ejemplos de habilidades blandas específicas, y comparándolas con las denominadas habilidades técnicas "duras".

Algunas definiciones tomadas de la literatura general indican que las habilidades blandas son "habilidades personales respaldadas por nuestra inteligencia emocional que nos ayudan a comportarnos de una manera socialmente aceptable y nos adaptamos a un entorno social" [2], "un compendio de varios componentes como actitud, habilidades, hábitos y prácticas que se combinan hábilmente para maximizar la efectividad en el trabajo" [1], y como "habilidades interpersonales que demuestran la capacidad de una persona para comunicarse de manera efectiva y establecer relaciones con otros en interacciones personales así como en grupos y equipos" [7].

Debido a la vaguedad de las definiciones anteriores y la dificultad de una definición unificada, algunos autores caracterizan este tipo de habilidades mediante ejemplos de lo que consideran "habilidades blandas". Así, las habilidades blandas abarcan habilidades tan variadas como la comunicación, la gestión de conflictos, la negociación, el trabajo en equipo [7], el liderazgo, la motivación, la gestión del tiempo, las habilidades de realizar presentaciones [8], la resolución de problemas, el pensamiento analítico, la flexibilidad, la asertividad [9], establecimiento de relaciones comerciales, la comunicación no verbal y lenguaje corporal [10], la capacidad personal para funcionar en armonía con los demás, la apertura a aprender nuevas ideas, y la tolerancia a situaciones no tan agradables y diferencias de opinión [2], por solo nombrar algunas.

El tercer enfoque utilizado por algunos autores para caracterizar las habilidades blandas es contrastarlas con las denominadas "habilidades duras". Este término generalmente refiere a la capacidad técnica y al conocimiento factual necesario para hacer el trabajo [3], las competencias técnicas que un individuo posee a través del aprendizaje y la aplicación práctica [9], que generalmente se asocian con conocimientos técnicos y comprensión de un proceso [11].

Para este estudio, nos referiremos a "habilidades blandas" como la combinación de habilidades, actitudes, hábitos y rasgos de personalidad que permiten a las personas desempeñarse mejor en el lugar de trabajo, complementando las habilidades técnicas necesarias para hacer su trabajo e influyendo en la forma en que se comportar e interactúa con los demás [12].

2.2 Las habilidades blandas en la educación superior en ingeniería de software

Diversos autores han discutido sobre la relevancia de las habilidades blandas en la práctica de la ingeniería de software y la necesidad de incorporar este tema en el currículo de ingeniería de software en la educación superior.

En este sentido, Zurita y colegas afirman que en la actualidad existe una necesidad cada vez mayor de que los estudiantes desarrollen no solo competencias técnicas, sino también las llamadas "habilidades blandas" para realizar actividades profesionales de manera efectiva y eficiente en un mundo globalizado [13]. Radermacher y Walia presentan un estudio realizado para determinar en qué áreas los estudiantes que se gradúan con mayor frecuencia no alcanzan las expectativas de la industria o el mundo académico. Una de esas áreas es, precisamente, la de las habilidades blandas, entre las que destacan la comunicación oral y escrita, el trabajo en equipo, la resolución de problemas, el pensamiento crítico, la ética y el liderazgo como ejemplos de este tipo de habilidades [14].

Más recientemente, Capretz y Ahmed [4] consideran que un "eslabón perdido" en la ingeniería de software es el conjunto de habilidades blandas que son esenciales en el proceso de desarrollo de software. Bajo esta consideración, si bien las habilidades blandas se encuentran entre los aspectos más importantes en la creación de software, a menudo son pasados por alto por los educadores y profesionales. Estos autores coinciden en que incluso las últimas guías para la enseñanza y el aprendizaje de la ingeniería de software, a saber, SWEBOK V3.0 y la Guía del plan de estudios IEEE/ACM, destacan las competencias técnicas y otorgan una consideración marginal a las vagamente caracterizadas habilidades no técnicas.

A nivel latinoamericano, el interés en las habilidades blandas, o competencias genéricas como también se les suele llamaren la región, también está en la agenda de diversas instituciones vinculadas a la enseñanza superior.

Así, por ejemplo, el Consejo Federal de Decanos de Facultades de Ingeniería (CONFEDI) de la República Argentina elaboró un documento sobre Competencias Genéricas de Egreso del Ingeniero Iberoamericano [15], que ha sido adoptado por la Asociación Iberoamericana de Instituciones de Enseñanza de la Ingeniería (ASIBEI) [16]. De las 10 competencias genéricas definidas en este documento, las siguientes corresponden a las denominadas Competencias sociales, políticas y actitudinales: competencia para desempeñarse de manera efectiva en equipos de trabajo, competencia para comunicarse con efectividad, competencia para actuar con ética, responsabilidad profesional y compromiso social, competencia para aprender en forma continua y autónoma, y competencia para actuar con espíritu emprendedor.

La Comisión Nacional de Acreditación de Chile también ha enfatizado la necesidad de que los planes de estudio de la educación superior incluyan el desarrollo de competencias transversales o genéricas tales como comunicación oral y escrita, pensamiento crítico, solución de problemas, desarrollo de relaciones interpersonales, y trabajo en equipo, entre otras [17].

Asimismo, el Proyecto Tuning para América Latina también resalta la importancia de las habilidades blandas en la formación de los futuros profesionales en el área de Informática en educación superior [18].

Este tipo de habilidades son relevantes para otro aspecto de importancia para los futuros graduados y refiere a lo que se denomina "empleabilidad". Hillage y Pollar definen el concepto de empleabilidad como una construcción multidimensional que incluye: la capacidad de asegurar el primer empleo; la capacidad de un individuo para transferir posiciones entre el mismo empleador; y la capacidad de asegurar el empleo de una nueva organización [19]. En un estudio presentado por Finch y colegas con respecto a los factores que influyen en la empleabilidad de los nuevos graduados, encontraron que de los 17 factores de empleabilidad individuales medidos, cinco de los seis factores mejor clasificados pertenecían a la categoría de habilidades blandas. Además, sus hallazgos ilustran que, al contratar a nuevos graduados, los empleadores le dan mayor importancia en las habilidades blandas y menos importancia a la reputación académica [20].

Por este motivo, en opinión de Rao, debe haber una coordinación efectiva entre la academia, los estudiantes, la industria y los directores de las instituciones educativas para mejorar este tipo de habilidades entre los estudiantes [21], habilidades que en su opinión mejoran la empleabilidad de los profesionales.

3 Diseño metodológico

En esta sección se presenta el diseño metodológico de este estudio, para el que hemos seguido el modelo propuesto por Punch [22], y que incluye el enunciado de las preguntas de investigación planteadas, la descripción de la muestra seleccionada, el cuestionario utilizado, y los procedimientos para la recolección y el análisis de los datos.

3.1 Preguntas de investigación

Para este trabajo se plantearon las siguientes cuatro preguntas de investigación:

- RQ1: ¿Cuáles son las habilidades blandas que se enseñan en las carreras de grado mediante cursos o asignaturas específicas?
- RQ2: ¿Cuán importante se considera incorporar a los planes de estudio alguna asignatura para la enseñanza de habilidades blandas?
- RQ3: ¿Qué modalidad o enfoque didáctico se considera más adecuado para la enseñanza de habilidades blandas?
- RQ4: ¿Cuál es el nivel de interés de los directores o responsables académicos en conformar una Red latinoamericana para la enseñanza de habilidades blandas?

3.2 La muestra

La encuesta se envió a directores, coordinadores o responsables académicos de 115 carreras de grado universitario en ingeniería o licenciatura en ingeniería de software, informática, computación, sistemas o sistemas de información de 85 Universidades pertenecientes a 15 países de América Latina.

Se trata de una muestra no probabilística en la que las 85 universidades consideradas fueron elegidas mediante el criterio de estar afiliadas o académicamente vinculadas a las dos principales comunidades de investigación en ingeniería de software en América Latina: CLEI (Centro Latinoamericano de Estudios en Informática) y CIbSE (Congreso Iberoamericano en Ingeniería de Software).

CLEI (clei.org) es una institución sin fines de lucro que reúne a las Universidades y Centros de Investigación Latinoamericanos más importantes y prestigiosos en el área de investigación y docencia en Informática. CIbSE (cibseconference.org) es un congreso anual internacional de ingeniería de software cuyo principal objetivo es promover la investigación científica de alta calidad en países de Iberoamérica y, así, dar apoyo a los investigadores en esta comunidad en la publicación y discusión de su trabajo.

Para el caso de CLEI, las universidades seleccionadas son las que figuran como instituciones miembros en su página web (www.clei.org/instituciones-miembro/). Para el caso de CIbSE, se seleccionaron aquellas universidades latinoamericanas a las que estuvieran afiliados los miembros de los comités de programa de la edición XXI del congreso (2018).

Para cada universidad seleccionada se buscó en su sitio web información sobre carreras de ingeniería o licenciatura en ingeniería de software, informática, computación, sistemas o sistemas de información, u otra denominación que indicara estar vinculada a la ingeniería y el desarrollo de software. A su vez, para cada carrera identificada, se buscó el nombre de su director, coordinador, o responsable académico y su dirección de e-mail. En varios casos fue significativo no encontrar ninguna información de contacto, lo cual impidió enviarle la encuesta a la persona responsable de la carrera.

3.3 El cuestionario

Para la recolección de datos se elaboró un cuestionario con una serie de preguntas dirigidas a obtener los datos necesarios para dar respuesta a las preguntas de investigación.

El cuestionario está organizado en las siguientes secciones:

- Datos demográficos de los respondientes: Nombre, dirección de e-mail para futuros contactos, universidad y país.
- Nombre de la carrera de grado que dirige y vínculo académico del respondiente.
- Asignaturas en los planes de estudio de las carreras, específicamente enfocadas en la enseñanza de alguna habilidad blanda.

- Opinión sobre la importancia de incorporar alguna asignatura para la enseñanza de habilidades blandas en la carrera mencionada.
- Opinión sobre el enfoque didáctico más adecuado para la enseñanza y el desarrollo de habilidades blandas en ingeniería de software en los estudiantes de la carrera mencionadas.
- Interés de los respondientes en formar parte de una Red latinoamericana de docentes e investigadores para promover y desarrollar técnicas y herramientas para enseñar habilidades blandas en ingeniería de software.

3.4 Procedimiento de recolección de datos

La distribución del cuestionario a los encuestados se realizó mediante envío de correo electrónico personalizado donde se incluyó el enlace a la versión en línea, que se podía completar directamente y devolverlo una vez completado. El cuestionario se elaboró y distribuyó usando las funcionalidades de Google Forms.

La encuesta se realizó en dos períodos: 8 al 30 de Junio y 8 al 30 de Octubre de 2018.

3.5 Procedimiento para el análisis de los datos

Los datos recopilados fueron extraídos de cada formulario completado, y tabulados en diferentes planillas Excel para facilitar su análisis y dar estructura a la presentación de resultados y poder, así, responder a las preguntas de investigación planteadas.

Las respuestas a las preguntas cerradas fueron tabuladas para contar la cantidad de respuestas en cada opción, y las respuestas a las preguntas abiertas fueron analizadas en busca de datos faltantes o incorrectos para luego identificar categorías en las que clasificar las respuestas completas y correctas recibidas.

4 Resultados obtenidos

En esta sección presentamos los resultados obtenidos y las respuestas a las preguntas de investigación.

4.1 Respondientes y orígenes de las respuestas

La Tabla 1 muestra la distribución, por país, de las cantidades de universidades y carreras encuestadas y que respondieron. Son varias las universidades que ofrecen más de una carrera en el área, con diferentes denominaciones y perfiles profesionales.

Tabla 1. Universidades y carreras encuestadas y que respondieron

País	Encuestadas		Respondieron	
	Universidades	Carreras	Universidades	Carreras
Argentina	12	15	4	4
Bolivia	1	1	0	0
Brasil	16	26	5	10
Chile	8	12	5	5
Colombia	13	13	7	7
Costa Rica	7	8	3	4
Cuba	2	2	0	0
Ecuador	7	9	3	3
El Salvador	1	1	0	0
México	1	3	1	1
Panamá	3	5	2	4
Paraguay	3	5	2	3
Perú	3	4	3	3
Uruguay	4	7	3	6
Venezuela	4	4	2	2
Totales	**85**	**115**	**40 (47%)**	**52 (45%)**

En consecuencia, hemos recibido respuestas del 47 % de las universidades consideradas y del 45% por las carreras encuestadas.

Con respecto a quienes respondieron la encuesta, la Tabla 2 muestra los diferentes vínculos funcionales con las carreras:

Tabla 2. Vínculos funcionales y académicos de los respondientes

Vínculo con la carrera	Cantidad	Porcentaje
Director/a de carrera	26	50
Coordinador/a académico/a de la carrera	12	23
Responsable académico/a de la carrera	4	8
Catedrático/a de área	1	2
Vicedecano/a de Facultad	1	2
Director/a de departamento	2	4
Docente e investigador	1	2
Profesor de área	5	10
Total	**52**	**100%**

Los casos de “Docente e investigador” y de “Profesor de área” corresponden a respondientes a quienes el directores o coordinadores de carrera que recibieron el cuestionario y delegaron la respuesta.

4.2 Respuesta a las preguntas de investigación 1 y 2

Tal como expusimos en la sub-sección 3.1, las preguntas de investigación 1 y 2 son las siguientes:

- RQ1: ¿Cuáles son las habilidades blandas que se enseñan en las carreras de grado mediante cursos o asignaturas específicas?

- RQ2: ¿Cuán importante se considera incorporar a los planes de estudio alguna asignatura para la enseñanza de habilidades blandas?

Para responder a estas dos preguntas de investigación es necesario hacer la distinción entre quienes indicaron que el plan de estudios de su carrera ya incluye alguna asignatura relativa a habilidades blandas y quienes indicaron que no incluyen ninguna.

Para esto, en el cuestionario se incluyó la siguiente pregunta de verificación: *¿Hay alguna asignatura en el plan de estudios de la carrera, "específicamente" enfocada en la enseñanza de algunas habilidades blandas?*

La Tabla 3 muestra la distribución de respuestas:

Tabla 3. Respuestas a si la carrera incluye o no alguna asignatura "específica"

Opción	Cantidad	Porcentaje
Si	33	63%
No	19	37%
Total	**52**	**100%**

Para quienes respondieron "Si" a la pregunta de verificación, el cuestionario bifurcaba a la siguiente pregunta: *Indique el nombre de esa o esas asignaturas (uno por línea), y el semestre o cuatrimestre en el que se dicta(n).* Las respuestas esperadas en el cuestionario eran el o los nombres de las asignaturas (o materias) y el semestre o cuatrimestre en el que están ubicadas en el respectivo plan de estudios (en algunos casos no fue indicado el semestre).

Para responder, entonces, la pregunta de investigación RQ1 se agruparon las respuestas en las siguientes categorías de habilidades blandas:

- **Habilidades de comunicación**: Comunicación oral y escrita (semestre 1), Expresión oral y escrita I y II, Expresión oral y escrita (semestre 1), Español (semestre 2), Comunicación (Semestre 2), Comunicación integral (semestre 2), Oratoria (semestre 6), Comunicación I (semestre 1), Comunicación II (semestre 2), Competencias comunicativas, Comunicación (semestre 1), Comunicación oral y escrita (cuatrimestre 2).
- **Habilidades interpersonales**: Psicología social (semestre 1), Relaciones humanas (semestre 1).
- **Trabajo en equipo**: Trabajo en equipo y liderazgo (semestre 2), Habilidades de equipo en desarrollo de software (semestre 7).
- **Liderazgo**: Liderazgo personal (semestre 4), Liderazgo, Liderazgo (semestre 7), Trabajo en equipo y liderazgo (semestre 2), Curso de liderazgo (extracurricular).
- **Ética**: Ética profesional, Ética en ciencia de la computación (semestre 8), Ética y argumentación crítica (semestre 1), Ética, legislación y comunicación profesional (semestre 3), Ética general y profesional (semestre 9), Ética y legislación (Optativa; cualquier nivel), Ética profesional (semestre 7).
- **Gestión de conflictos**: Gestión de comunicación y conflictos en equipos (Semestre 7).

- ***Otras***: Género y cultura (semestre 4), Marketing personal, Pensamiento inductivo/deductivo, Ciudadanía e interculturalidad.

Los casos de nombres duplicados corresponden a asignaturas de igual nombre en universidades o carreras diferentes.

A pesar de que la pregunta del cuestionario refiere a alguna asignatura o curso *"específicamente" enfocada en la enseñanza de algunas habilidades blandas*, se recibieron 9 respuestas en las que se mencionan asignaturas que, por su nombre, no parecen corresponder a específicas sobre habilidades blandas, tales como Fundamentos de ingeniería de software, Formación de empresas de base tecnológica, Planeación estratégica de sistemas, Algoritmos y programación, Sistemas de bases de datos, Sistemas de información, Problemas económicos nacionales, Apreciación Artística y literaria, y Arquitectura de software por nombrar algunas.

Al considerar que estas respuestas no responden correctamente a la pregunta específica formulada, las cifras rectificadas de la Tabla 3 se muestran ahora en la Tabla 4:

Table 4. Carreras CON y SIN asignaturas específicas

Opción	Cantidad	Porcentaje
Carreras CON asignaturas específicas	24	46%
Carreras SIN asignaturas específicas	28	54%
Total	**52**	**100%**

Por su parte, para quienes respondieron "No" a la pregunta de verificación, el cuestionario bifurcaba a la siguiente pregunta: *¿Cuán importante considera incorporar alguna asignatura para la enseñanza de habilidades blandas en la carrera mencionada?* La Tabla 5, que responde a la pregunta de investigación RQ2, muestra la distribución de las 19 respuestas:

Table 5. Importancia de incorporar alguna asignatura al plan de estudios

Opción	Cantidad	Porcentaje
1 – No importante	3	16
2 – Poco importante	2	11
3 – Neutral	3	15
4 – Importante	4	21
5 – Muy Importante	7	37
Total	**19**	**100%**

En conjunto, las opiniones "Importante" y "Muy importante" representan el 58% de las respuestas recibidas.

4.3 Respuesta a la pregunta de investigación 3

Tal como expusimos en la sub-sección 3.1, la pregunta de investigación RQ3 es ¿Qué modalidad o enfoque didáctico considera más adecuado para la enseñanza de habilidades blandas?

La Tabla 6 muestra la distribución de las 52 respuestas en base a las tres opciones de modalidades consultadas.

Table 6. Preferencia de modalidad de enseñanza de habilidades blandas

Modalidad o enfoque didáctico	Cantidad	Porcentaje
Cursos específicos sobre determinadas habilidades blandas	0	0
Incorporar su enseñanza y desarrollo en cursos de otras asignaturas	17	33
Las dos modalidades anteriores	33	64
Otra modalidad	2	4
Totales	**52**	**100%**

En "otra modalidad o enfoque didáctico" se recibieron las siguientes propuestas: "*las dos anteriores más el resolver problemas reales en apoyo a pequeños empresarios*" y "*a través de asignaturas donde se trabaja el desarrollo de proyectos reales*".

4.4 Respuesta a la pregunta de investigación 4

La pregunta de investigación RQ4 es ¿Cuál es el nivel de interés de los directores o responsables académicos en conformar una Red latinoamericana para la enseñanza de habilidades blandas?

En el cuestionario, la pregunta específica fue: "*Indique su interés en formar parte de una Red latinoamericana de docentes e investigadores para promover y desarrollar técnicas y herramientas para enseñar habilidades blandas en ingeniería de software, así como para intercambiar experiencias y generar difusión de iniciativas sobre la temática.*".

La Tabla 7 muestra la distribución de respuestas en base a las tres opciones de grado o modalidad de participación consultadas.

Table 7. Interés en participar en una red latinoamericana

Grado de interés	Cantidad	Porcentaje
No estoy interesado	1	2
Interesado en recibir novedades	9	17
Interesado en participar	42	81
Total	**52**	**100%**

5 Discusión

En este trabajo hemos presentado los resultados de una encuesta a directores, coordinadores y responsables académicos de 115 carreras de grado universitario en ingeniería o licenciatura en ingeniería de software, informática, computación, sistemas o sistemas de información de 85 Universidades pertenecientes a 15 países de América Latina. El propósito es conocer algunos aspectos del estado actual de la enseñanza de habilidades blandas a los estudiantes de esas carreras, en el entendido de que estas habilidades son de relevancia para la práctica profesional de la ingeniería de software y un elemento de importancia para la empleabilidad de los futuros graduados.

De las carreras respecto de las cuales se recibieron respuestas, casi la mitad incluyen cursos específicos sobre determinadas habilidades blandas, según se mostró en la Tabla 4. Los cursos o materias específicas corresponden principalmente a Habilidades de comunicación, Trabajo en equipo, Liderazgo, Etica profesional, y Gestión de conflictos. Sin embargo, hay otras habilidades blandas consideradas relevantes para la práctica de la ingeniería de software, tales como habilidades de presentación, negociación, resolución de problemas, interés por aprender, autonomía, y otras [23] que no han sido mencionadas por los respondientes.

La cuestión discutible aquí es si este tipo de habilidades se pueden enseñar o desarrollar con cursos específicos o si, por el contrario, su desarrollo en los estudiantes debe formar parte de cursos generales de otras áreas de conocimiento en los que estén embebidos aspectos del desarrollo de ciertas habilidades. Según Clarkson [24], los programas tradicionales de capacitación en el aula son insuficientes para el desarrollo de habilidades y, más bien, una combinación de sesiones en el aula, oportunidades para practicar comportamientos en entornos auténticos, y los comentarios de expertos y la reflexión sobre esas sesiones de práctica son los principales elementos para un programa de capacitación exitoso en habilidades no técnicas.

Por otra parte, ciertas habilidades blandas están íntimamente relacionadas a otras habilidades, y no parece adecuado enseñarlas o desarrollarlas por separado como si fueran habilidades independientes. Así, por ejemplo, las "habilidades de presentación" (las habilidades necesarias para brindar una presentación efectiva a diversas audiencias) requieren "habilidades de organización" para preparar y organizar lo que se debe entregar en la presentación, "habilidades interpersonales" para crear empatía con la audiencia, "habilidades de toma de decisiones" para decidir qué material incluir en la presentación, y "habilidades de comunicación" para transmitir adecuadamente lo que se pretende presentar. De manera similar, el manejo de conflictos requiere habilidades de negociación y resolución de problemas, así como habilidades de comunicación oral y de escucha activa.

Por esto, consideramos que cada habilidad o conjunto interrelacionado de habilidades requiere un tipo particular de enfoque o modalidad de enseñanza y desarrollo, así como estudiar si mejor forma de desarrollarlas es mediante cursos específicos o incorporadas a otras asignaturas. Los resultados mostrados en la Tabla 6 indican que la combinación de ambas modalidades cuenta con la preferencia mayoritaria de las opiniones de los respondientes.

Finalmente, en cuanto al interés en participar en una red latinoamericana de docentes e investigadores para fomentar la enseñanza y desarrollo de habilidades blandas, 8 de cada 10 respondientes lo hizo favorablemente. Esto denota un muy alto interés por parte de directores y coordinadores académicos de las carreras en promover la investigación en el tema, así como en la difusión de iniciativas y en el intercambio de experiencias académicas.

6 Amenazas a la validez

La principal amenaza a la validez de este estudio refiere a que la muestra de universidades y carreras encuestadas no puede considerarse como representativa de las universidades y carreras de grado universitario en ingeniería o licenciatura en ingeniería de software, informática, computación, sistemas o sistemas de información que se imparten en América Latina. El documento del Proyecto Tuning para América Latina [18] menciona que hay 6.257 universidades en 12 de los países que participaron del proyecto, pero no menciona cuantas universidades ofrecen carreras de grado ni cuantas carreras de las de interés se ofrecen. En base a esa cantidad global de universidades, las consideradas en este trabajo son apenas el 0,01% lo cual, claramente, impide hacer cualquier tipo de generalización estadística de los resultados.

7 Conclusiones y trabajo futuro

La enseñanza y el desarrollo de habilidades blandas en carreras de grado universitario en ingeniería de software es un aspecto de importancia para los futuros graduados en cuanto a que contribuyen a mejorar sus posibilidades de empleabilidad. También para su desarrollo profesional, atendiendo a que estas habilidades son consideradas relevantes para la industria del software y demandadas por las empresas de este sector industrial.

El presente estudio muestra, en este sentido, que hay opinión favorable de los responsables académicos de las carreras relevadas en cuanto a la importancia de su enseñanza, y de incluir el tema en los planes de estudios de las carreras. Este interés está alineado con las recomendaciones de organismos de acreditación de carreras universitarias y con los resultados del Proyecto Tuning para América Latina, tal como se comentó en la sección 2.

Atendiendo a este interés, como trabajo futuro nos planteamos extender la realización de la encuesta a otras universidades de América Latina y, junto con las que han respondido, crear una comunidad de práctica para intercambiar y difundir experiencias de enseñanza de habilidades blandas. Esta comunidad permitirá avanzar en la investigación conjunta sobre las maneras más adecuadas de incluir estas habilidades en los planes de estudio de las carreras y en la evaluación de resultados, así como en identificar aquellas habilidades más relevantes para la práctica profesional.

Referencias

1. Ramesh, G. y Ramesh, M., The ACE of soft skills. Attitude, communication and etiquette for success. New Delhi: Dorling Kindersley, 2010.
2. Verma, S., Soft skills for the BPO sector. New Delhi: Dorling Kindersley, 2009.
3. Klaus, P., The hard truth about soft skills. Workplace lessons smart people wish they'd learned sooner. Harper Collins, 2008.
4. Capretz L. F. y Ahmed, F., A Call to Promote Soft Skills in Software Engineering, Psychol Cogn Sci Open J, vol. 4, n.º 1, 2018.

5. N. Jones Morel y B. Griffiths, Redefining Competency Based Education: Competence for Life. New York: NY: Business Expert Press, 2018.
6. Dell'Aquila, E., Marocco, D., Ponticorvo, M., di Ferdinando, A., Schembri, M., y Miglino, O., Educational Games for Soft-Skills Training in Digital Environments. Switzerland: Springer, 2017.
7. Kamin, M., Soft skills revolution. A guide for connecting with compassion for trainers, teams, and leaders. Pfeiffer, 2013.
8. Rao, M. S., Soft skills enhancing employability. New Delhi: I. K. International Publishing House, 2010.
9. Bhatnaga, N., Effective communication and soft skills. New Delhi: Dorling Kindersley, 2012.
10. Goldberg, D. M. y Rosenfeld, M., People-Centric Skills. Interpersonal and communication skills for auditors and business professionals. Hoboken: NJ: Wiley, 2014.
11. Prince, E. S., The advantage. The 7 soft skills you need to stay one step ahead. Financial Times Press, 2013.
12. Matturro, G., Raschetti, F. y Fontán, C., A Systematic Mapping Study on Soft Skills in Software Engineering, J. Univers. Comput. Sci., (Accepted for publication), 2019.
13. Zurita, G., Baloian, N., Pino, J., y Boghosian, M., Introducing a Collaborative Tool Supporting a Learning Activity Involving Creativity with Rotation of Group Members, J. Univers. Comput. Sci., vol. 22, n.º 10, pp. 1360-1379, 2016.
14. Radermacher, A. y Walia, G., Gaps Between Industry Expectations and the Abilities of Graduates, en Proceeding of the 44th ACM Technical Symposium on Computer Science Education (SIGCSE 2013), Denver, 2013, pp. 525-530.
15. CONFEDI, Competencias en ingeniería. Mar del Plata: Universidad FASTA Ediciones, 2014.
16. ASIBEI, Competencias y perfil del ingeniero iberoamericano, formación de profesores, y desarrollo tecnológico e innovación. Bogotá: ASIBEI, 2016.
17. CNA-Chile - Comisión Nacional de Acreditación, Criterios de Evaluación para Carreras y Programas de Pregrado, 2015. [En línea]. Disponible en: https://www.cnachile.cl/Criterios%20y%20Procedimientos/DJ%20009-4%20Criterios.pdf.
18. Contreras Véliz, J. L. (Editor), Proyecto Tuning América Latina. Educación Superior en América Latina: reflexiones y perspectivas en Informática. Bilbao: Universidad de Deusto, 2013.
19. Hillage, J. y Pollard, E., Developing a framework for policy analysis, No. 85. Institute for Employment Studies, UK Department of Education and Employment, 1998.
20. Finch, D., Hamilton, L., Baldwin, R., y Zehner, M., An exploratory study of factors affecting undergraduate employability, Education+Training, vol. 55, n.º 7, pp. 681-704, 2013.
21. Rao, M. S., Enhancing employability in engineering and management students through soft skills, Ind. Commer. Train., vol. 46, n.º 1, pp. 42-48, 2014.
22. Punch, K., Survey research. The basics. London: Sage Publications, 2003.
23. Matturro, G., Raschetti, F. y Fontán, C., Soft Skills in Software Development Teams, presentado en 8th International Workshop on Cooperative and Human Aspects of Software Engineering, Florencia, 2015, pp. 101-104.
24. Clarkson, M., Developing IT staff. A practical approach. London: Springer-Verlag, 2001.

Ingeniería de Software Aplicada a Telemática: Rediseñando el Curso de Conmutación y Enrutamiento

Adriana Collaguazo-Jaramillo[0000-0002-0707-0226], Mónica Villavicencio[0000-0002-2601-2638], Verónica Moreira, y Paolo Lara

Escuela Superior Politécnica del Litoral, ESPOL
Facultad de Ingeniería en Electricidad y Computación, FIEC
Campus Gustavo Galindo Km 30.5 Vía Perimetral, P.O. Box 09-01-5863
Guayaquil, Ecuador
{acollag, mvillavi, mavemore, pslara}@espol.edu.ec
http://www.espol.edu.ec

Resumen El 92 % de las materias de formación profesional de la carrera de Ingeniería en Telemática a nivel de pregrado en la Escuela Superior Politécnica del Litoral, Ecuador, se enfoca en el desarrollo de interfaces de usuario para presentar datos sensados por dispositivos de red. Sin embargo, el énfasis de estas materias radica en el hardware, dejando a un lado el componente de desarrollo de software. Esto conlleva a la producción de software de baja calidad y sin posibilidades de reutilización. Este artículo, presenta una propuesta de mejora para el dictado del curso de Conmutación y Enrutamiento incorporando horas para el aprendizaje de temáticas de Ingeniería de Software. Como resultado, rediseñamos el curso, incluyendo Scrum, nociones de arquitectura de software, estándares de codificación, analizadores de código y casos de pruebas de aceptación. Con 21 horas de entrenamiento, logramos que todos los sistemas desarrollados sean entregados a tiempo, con un código fácil de mantener, y que uno de ellos cumpla con el 100 % de las especificaciones dadas.

Palabras clave: Ingeniería de Software · Telemática · Scrum · Conmutación y Enrutamiento · Rediseño de curso.

1. Introducción

La Telemática es una de las especialidades tecnológicas emergentes que se origina de la fusión de dos grandes disciplinas: telecomunicaciones e informática. Entre las áreas de competencia del profesional de Telemática, se encuentran: Networking, infraestructura tecnológica, y programación de sistemas [1]. Específicamente, en el área de Networking, se desarrollan sistemas que optimizan las tareas rutinarias de esta rama, tales como configuración de plantillas en los dispositivos de red y de generación de archivos de configuración de respaldo. La carrera de pregrado de Ingeniería en Telemática en la Escuela Superior Politécnica del Litoral (ESPOL) cuenta con 24 materias de formación profesional, y tan sólo dos de estas (8 %) son de programación: Programación Orientada a Objetos y Programación de Sistemas. Adicionalmente, los estudiantes toman Fundamentos de Programación como materia de formación básica en su primer año de estudios.

Con dichas materias los estudiantes se encuentran en la capacidad de desarrollar software en el 92 % de las materias de formación profesional. Sin embargo, los estudiantes no cuentan con una instrucción formal de la disciplina de Ingeniería de Software. Esta disciplina se encarga del estudio del desarrollo de software de manera sistematizada y organizada, desde la especificación de requerimientos, pasando por el diseño e implementación, hasta el diseño de pruebas para la verificación y validación del producto final para garantizar la calidad del software [13]. La falta de integración de conocimientos de Networking y de Ingeniería de Software en el programa de Telemática ha conllevado a la producción de software de baja calidad y sin posibilidades de reutilización. Esta situación, nos motivó a analizar las falencias del software producido por los estudiantes del curso de Conmutación y Enrutamiento y, a proponer el rediseño del curso incorporando el uso de la metodología ágil Scrum como marco de gestión de proyectos. Nuestro objetivo es fomentar el desarrollo de aplicaciones de software de calidad que faciliten la configuración de dispositivos de red, tales como conmutadores y enrutadores [2]. El curso de Conmutación y Enrutamiento se dicta en el séptimo semestre de la malla curricular de Ingeniería en Telemática, tiene una duración de 64 horas distribuidas en 16 semanas. El objetivo general del curso es analizar tecnologías de conmutación y enrutamiento usando requerimientos específicos de hardware, software y modelos de estructura para redes de datos.

Este artículo se encuentra organizado de la siguiente forma: la sección 2 presenta trabajos relacionados; la sección 3 explica la metodología de investigación; la sección 4 explica las falencias identicadas durante el desarrollo de software; la sección 5 describe los cambios realizados al curso para mejorar la calidad del software producido; la sección 6 presenta los resultados obtenidos, y finalmente la sección 7 presenta las conclusiones del artículo.

2. Trabajos Relacionados

En la búsqueda de publicaciones que conjuguen la enseñanza de ingeniería de software en cursos de pregrado de la carrera de Telemática, no tuvimos éxito, pues no hallamos artículos relacionados. Sin embargo, encontramos artículos que muestran la incorporación de temáticas de ingeniería de software en cursos de sistemas embebidos [6], los cuales consideramos como trabajos relacionados puesto que los dispositivos de red son sistemas embebidos [7].

Según Koopman, profesor del curso de sistemas embebidos ofrecido por la Universidad Carnegie Mellon, la aplicación de una metodología de desarrollo incrementa notablemente la tasa de éxito de los proyectos desarrollados por los estudiantes, pues éstos cumplen con las funcionalidades solicitadas al final del semestre [7].

En el Instituto Brasileño de Tecnología Aeronáutica, se desarrolló una experiencia académica aplicando pruebas de software en sistemas integrados críticos en tiempo real. Siendo la mayor contribución la mejora en la calidad del software y la optimización del tiempo para realizar las pruebas unitarias y de integración [8].

Otro ejemplo, es la experiencia de enseñanza de desarrollo de software para sistemas embebidos en la Universidad de Minho, donde se enfatiza en la arquitectura y lenguajes de programación para sistemas embebidos [3].

En la Universidad de Calgary se desarrollaron trabajos de investigación que consistían en realizar pruebas, por medio de las cuales determinaron dos factores que afectan la adopción de metodologías ágiles en sistemas embebidos. Estos factores son: 1) la falta de soporte completo para el ciclo de vida y 2) falta de soporte de herramientas; es decir, que las aplicaciones incrustadas tienen un ciclo de vida diferente al de las aplicaciones de escritorio. Por lo tanto, los procesos de producción ágil requieren modificaciones significativas para satisfacer las demandas de este nuevo entorno. [12]

En EE.UU., Camboya, India y Senegal, grupos de estudiantes desarrollaron proyectos de sistemas embebidos usando Scrum, destacando la importancia de las herramientas para apoyar las actividades de aseguramiento de la calidad de las aplicaciones [10].

En la Escuela de Sistemas Electrónicos y de Computación (SECS) de la Universidad de Cincinnati, se rediseñó el curso de sistemas embebidos, incorporando técnicas de modelado de software en el diseño de un sistema en tiempo real desarrollado por estudiantes como parte de un proyecto multidisciplinario. [14]

Una experiencia similar se vivió en el dictado de cursos de sistemas embebidos en el Instituto Tecnológico de Aeronáutica de Brasil, puesto que los estudiantes generaron el prototipo de un sistema embebido (SETRAIF)) adoptando Scrum y MDD (Model Driven Development o Desarrollo Dirigido por Modelos por sus siglas en inglés). La comunicación y colaboración de los estudiantes permitió una interacción valiosa para lograr trabajo cooperativo, vivir una experiencia profesional y entregar el prototipo esperado a tiempo [4].

3. Metodología

La metodología utilizada para realizar el presente trabajo consta de 3 etapas:

1. Identificación de las falencias en el desarrollo de software producido por los estudiantes del curso de Conmutación y Enrutamiento.
2. Rediseño del curso de Conmutación y Enrutamiento, incorporando la enseñanza y aplicación de conceptos claves de Ingeniería de Software.
3. Análisis de los resultados obtenidos luego de impartir la nueva versión del curso.

Para la identificación de las falencias más comunes se revisaron los proyectos realizados por los estudiantes, haciendo énfasis en el código fuente, en el modelamiento de la red, y la implementación de protocolos de red.

Las revisiones periódicas nos permitieron identificar las falencias en la guía del proyecto proporcionada por la profesora, en la documentación de la arquitectura, en la escritura del código fuente y en la gestión de la información. Estas revisiones se llevaron a cabo en el segundo semestre del año 2017.

Además, diseñamos un instrumento de autoevaluación para los estudiantes, el cual consiste de una encuesta de 17 preguntas distribuidas en 4 secciones. Los objetivos de la encuesta son: a) Identificar el grado de conocimiento previo de ingeniería de software, b) Obtener información sobre la manera en que los estudiantes gestionan sus proyectos, c) Identificar los aspectos que afectan el desarrollo del proyecto del curso, y d) Determinar qué prácticas contribuyen a mejorar el resultado final de los proyectos. La encuesta se aplicó en los dos semestres académicos del año 2017.

Una vez identificadas las falencias, rediseñamos el curso de Conmutación y Enrutamiento; para lo cual trabajamos con una docente de la carrera de Ingeniería en Computación, quien nos capacitó y guió en la selección de temas de ingeniería de software. Posteriormente, una docente de la carrera de Ingeniería en Telemática, dictó la nueva versión de la materia de Conmutación y Enrutamiento durante el primer término 2018 con la guía de la profesora de ingeniería de software.

4. Identificación de Falencias

La encuesta de autoevaluación fue respondida por 28 estudiantes, de los cuales el 100 % tenía conocimientos previos sobre desarrollo de software que fueron adquiridos en las materias: Fundamentos de Programación, Programación Orientada a Objetos y Programación de Sistemas. Sin embargo, el 61 % de los estudiantes no tenía conocimientos de Ingeniería de Software.

Respecto a la gestión de los proyectos del curso, la Tabla 1 muestra los resultados de la autoevaluación realizada por los estudiantes. En esta tabla se denota que los estudiantes reconocen que no planifican adecuadamente las actividades de sus proyectos (54 %); sin embargo, manifestaron que conocen como realizar diagramas de Gantt. Consideramos que la inadecuada planificación (68 %) se puede derivar de la falta de comprensión de los requisitos del sistema [5].

Tabla 1. Identificación de falencias en el proyecto mediante la autoevaluación de los estudiantes.

Id	Falencia	Porcentaje
AU-FAL1	No se comprende claramente lo que deben desarrollar.	68 %
AU-FAL2	No se planifican todas las actividades del proyecto, ni se las asigna equitativamente a los participantes del grupo.	54 %
AU-FAL3	Desconocen como manipular datos usando bases de datos.	11 %
AU-FAL4	Estimación inadecuada de tiempo para realizar actividades del proyecto.	11 %
AU-FAL5	Entrega imcompleta del proyecto.	54 %

En la autoevaluación de los aspectos que afectan el desarrollo del proyecto del curso, los estudiantes manifestaron que esto se debe a: la falta de disponibilidad de horarios para acceder a los laboratorios, falta de tiempo para reunirse en grupo y no complementar las tareas individuales asignadas como parte del proyecto. Por último, las prácticas que contribuyeron a mejorar el resultado final de los proyectos fueron: tener un líder en el equipo, reunirse frecuentemente entre los miembros del equipo para aclarar dudas, mostrar avances a la profesora y planificar las próximas actividades.

Como mencionamos anteriormente, a partir de las múltiples revisiones de los avances de los proyectos, identificamos otras falencias, adicionales a las manifestadas por los estudiantes a través de la encuesta de autoevaluación, las cuales se muestran en la Tabla 2. A continuación, una breve explicacion de dichas falencias:

Tabla 2. Identificación de falencias en las revisiones de avances del proyecto.

Id	Falencias	Porcentaje
RE-FAL1	Requisitos no especificados	67 %
RE-FAL2	Código difícil de mantener	100 %
RE-FAL3	Ausencia de la documentación de despliegue de aplicación	100 %
RE-FAL4	Falta de gestión de información a través de bases de datos	33 %
RE-FAL5	Falta de organización archivos del proyecto	67 %
RE-FAL6	El sistema entregado no cumple con las especificaciones dadas	67 %

1. *Requisitos no especificados.* La forma utilizada para especificar los requisitos del sistema en el curso era mediante una descripción general del sistema y de las funcionalidades requeridas para administrar los enrutadores o conmutadores en una red de datos, enfocándose en un protocolo de la capa de enlace de datos, de red y de transporte del modelo OSI. Dicha descripción estaba conformada por un par de párrafos explicativos de la solución esperada, descripción que no era suficientemente clara para los estudiantes.
2. *Código difícil de mantener.* Durante la revisión de los proyectos, observamos los siguientes problemas de mantenibilidad de código: 1) uso de nombres genéricos para nombrar las variables utilizadas en el sistema (por ejemplo: *lista1, ventana, objeto*); 2) falta de modularización (por ejemplo: las clases que incluyen sus funcionalidades junto a las acciones de la interfaz gráfica); 3) escasez de comentarios en el código; 4) ausencia de estándares de codificación y 5) código repetido y poco eficiente.
3. *Ausencia de la documentación de despliegue de aplicación.* En todos los proyectos revisados encontramos esta falencia, pues no encontramos documentación de la arquitectura a fin de conocer el ambiente necesario para desplegar la aplicación (recursos requeridos y dependencias).
4. *Falta de gestión de información a través de bases de datos.* Esta falencia se puede dividir en dos problemas. El primero es la falta de uso de bases de datos. La mayoría de los proyectos revisados almacenaban la información del programa en archivos de texto. Por otro lado, aquellos proyectos que sí utilizaban bases de datos, no poseían documentación de cómo se encontraba estructurada, ni existía un diccionario de datos.

5. *Falta de organización de archivos del proyecto.* Notamos en algunos proyectos que todos los archivos del proyecto se encontraban en una sola carpeta. Además, habían archivos con nombres genéricos, lo que dificultaba conocer qué funcionalidades se encontraban dentro de ellos.
6. *El sistema entregado no cumple con las especificaciones dadas.* Los sistemas estaban incompletos o no funcionaban como se esperaba.

A partir de las falencias identificadas, procedimos a seleccionar las prácticas de Ingeniería de Software necesarias para mitigarlas, en especial aquellas que aporten a la mejora en la gestión de los proyectos, a la comprensión de requisitos del sistema y a la mantenibilidad del código.

5. Rediseño del curso de Conmutación y Enrutamiento

La materia de Conmutación y Enrutamiento es teórico-práctica. Las prácticas se realizan en el laboratorio de sistemas telemáticos. En el curso se desarrollaron 3 proyectos, uno por cada grupo de estudiantes. La Tabla 3 contiene las temáticas y los lenguajes de programación utilizados en los proyectos.

Tabla 3. Proyectos desarrollados utilizando Ingeniería de Software.

Id	Temática del Proyecto	Lenguaje
PROY1	Sistema de respaldos diarios automáticos de los archivos de configuración de inicio de los dispositivos de red como enrutadores y conmutadores	Java
PROY2	Sistema de aprovisionamiento de VLAN, "Virtual Routing and Forwarding" (VRF) y direccionamiento IP para la activación de una empresa en la red de un ISP	Java
PROY3	Sistema de configuración del protocolo de enrutamiento BGP para la interconexión entre empresas o ISP	Python

Para el rediseño del contenido del curso, incorporamos 21 horas con temáticas de Ingeniería de Software, las cuales se muestran en la Tabla 4; además, en la tabla se observa la semana en que se impartió la temática, el tiempo invertido, y la falencia que se desea eliminar en los proyectos.

Los tópicos de Ingeniería de Software y la forma en que estos fueron incorporados, se explica a continuación:

1. Elaboración de Historias de Usuarios y Criterios de Aceptación: Como paso inicial, la profesora de la materia redactó las historias de usuarios y los criterios de aceptación (5 criterios en promedio por cada historia de usuario). Esto se hizo, puesto que en la encuesta, los estudiantes indicaron que no comprendían claramente lo que debían desarrollar. Inicialmente, las historias de usuario se redactaron con lenguaje muy técnico y poseían de 2 a 3 criterios de aceptación. Luego, se modificaron a un lenguaje natural para facilitar su comprensión. En total, 8 revisiones fueron necesarias para depurar los requerimientos iniciales de los proyectos.

Tabla 4. Contenido y planificación de horarios del curso con el rediseño aplicando Ingeniería de Software.

Semana	Horas	Falencias	Tópicos
1	4		Introducción al diseño de redes
2	4		Modelo de Arquitectura empresarial Evaluación de redes
3	3	RE-FAL1 AU-FAL2 AU-FAL5	Historias de Usuarios y Criterios de Aceptación. Introducción a Metodología Scrum
4	4		Entorno conmutado
5	3		Revisión de proyectos (Sprint Reviews)
6	4	RE-FAL2 RE-FAL3 RE-FAL4 RE-FAL5	Estándares de codificación, analizadores de código y técnicas de refactorización. Presentación de los recursos para el desarrollo de software y uso de GitHub. Diseño de componentes de arquitectura
7	4		Resolución de problemas en el conmutador
8	3		Revisión de proyectos (Sprint Reviews)
9	4		Protocolo de árbol de expansión
10	4		Tendencias de Tecnologías WAN
11	4		Revisiones de proyectos (Sprint Reviews)
12	4		Características y funcionamiento de protocolos de enrutamiento avanzados. Algoritmo DUAL y SFP
13	4		Atributos de ruta de BGP
14	7		Arquitectura de VPN MPLS. Modelo de enrutamiento de MPLS VPN
15	4	RE-FAL6	Revisiones de proyectos (Sprint Reviews). Validación de las funcionalidades con pruebas de aceptación
16	4		Redes con recursos limitados. Traducción de direcciones (NAT)

A continuación, se presenta un ejemplo de historias de usuario y criterios de aceptación del proyecto "Sistema de configuración del protocolo de enrutamiento BGP para la interconexión entre empresas o ISP":
Historia de usuario de Configurar Sistema Autónomo (AS): Como Ingeniero de Networking puedo seleccionar el nombre de la empresa, nombre del dispositivo y los AS públicos entre 1 a 64512 de los dispositivos de red local y remoto, para el establecimiento de una interconexión entre empresas o ISP usando el protocolo de enrutamiento BGP.
Criterios de aceptación:

- Dado a que el usuario selecciona el nombre de la empresa local, nombre del dispositivo local, número de AS para el dispositivo local entre 1 a 64512 y selecciona el nombre de la empresa remota, nombre del dispositivo remoto, número de AS para el dispositivo remoto entre 1 a 64512 cuando da click en configurar AS entonces se muestra el mensaje "Se ha configurado el AS [#_local] local en el dispositivo local y el AS [#_remoto] en el dispositivo remoto", se almacena en la base de datos los números de AS local y remoto con los nombres del dispositivos correspondientes, y se crean las sesiones BGP con los AS en los dispositivos local y remoto.

- Dado a que el usuario no selecciona el nombre de la empresa local, o el nombre del dispositivo local, o el número de AS para el dispositivo local entre 1 a 64512 o no selecciona el nombre de la empresa remota, o el nombre del dispositivo remoto, o el número de AS para el dispositivo remoto entre 1 a 64512 cuando da click en configurar AS entonces se muestra el mensaje de error "Falta información, inténtelo de nuevo".
- Dado que el usuario selecciona el nombre de la empresa local, nombre del dispositivo local, número de AS para el dispositivo local entre 1 a 64512 o selecciona el nombre de la empresa remota, nombre del dispositivo remoto, número de AS para el dispositivo remoto entre 1 a 64512 pero ocurre un error de conectividad con los dispositivos local o remoto cuando da click en configurar AS entonces se le muestra el mensaje de error "Falla en la conexión con el dispositivo [local o remoto], inténtelo más tarde", se crea una archivo con los intentos fallidos de configuración de AS que contiene la fecha/hora, nombre del dispositivo local o remoto, y los números de AS.

2. Introducción a Scrum: Debido a que los estudiantes manifestaron que tenían problemas para planificar las actividades de su proyecto, se los capacitó en el uso de Scrum como marco de trabajo para gestionar proyectos de forma ágil. La herramienta de planificación utilizada fue Asana por su facilidad de aprendizaje y uso libre de costo. Los estudiantes aprendieron: los principios ágiles; qué son las historias de usuarios y los criterios de aceptación; los roles, documentos y prácticas de Scrum [11]; y como usar Asana para la gestión del proyecto.
3. Estándares de Codificación, analizadores de código y técnicas de refactorización: Para asegurar la mantenibilidad del código es necesario utilizar estándares de codificación para normar la creación de comentarios, la denominación de variables, el espaciado para asegurar la legibilidad y para evitar la repetición del código. Para el análisis de código se utilizaron Pylint para Python y Checkstyle para Java.
4. Presentación de los recursos para el desarrollo de software y uso de GitHub. Distintas herramientas de software en línea fueron presentadas a los estudiantes; por ejemplo, Lucidchart para la elaboración de los diagramas de arquitectura, GitHub para la gestión y control de versiones del código fuente, Pylint y Checkstyle para la revisión de la calidad del código fuente, GNS3 para la simulación de la red propuesta, y MySQL como gestor de bases de datos.
5. Diseño de componentes de arquitectura: Debido a que los proyectos de Telemática no tenían documentación de la arquitectura del sistema, se solicitó a los estudiantes que diseñaran 3 diagramas utilizando UML:

   - Diagrama de red: Este diagrama es generalmente usado en proyectos de Telemática para mostrar las interconexiones entre los componentes físicos y lógicos de la red. En la Figura 1 se muestra el diagrama de red del proyecto de "Sistema de configuración del protocolo de enrutamiento BGP para la interconexión entre empresas o ISP".

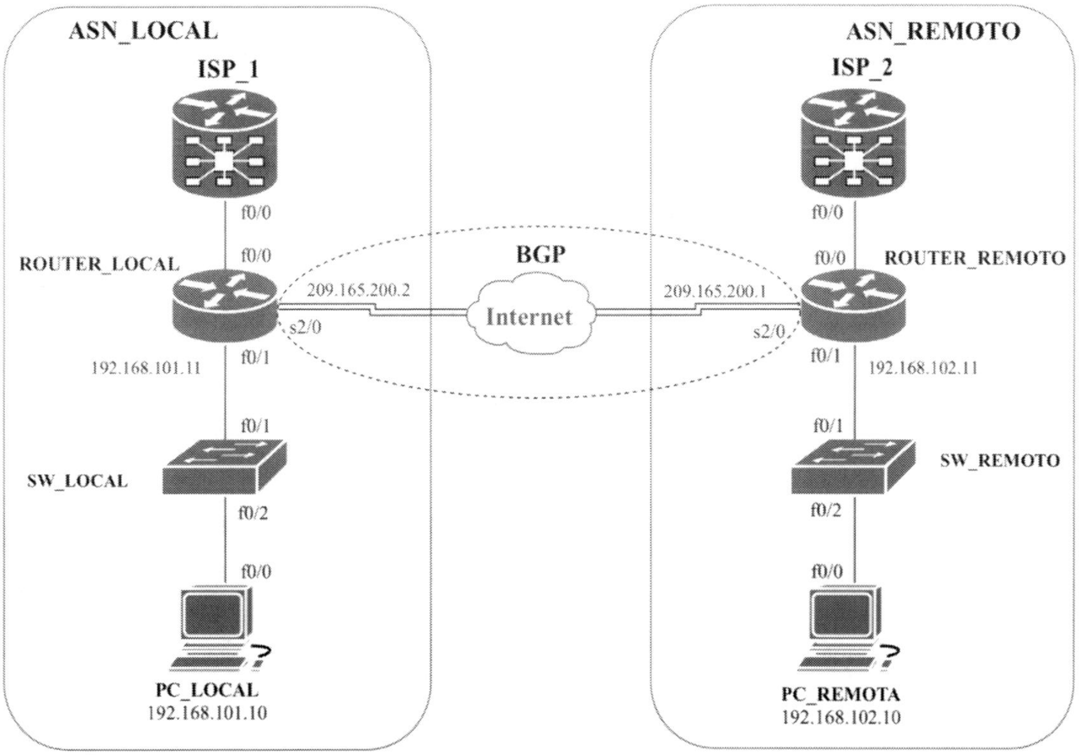

Figura 1. Diagrama de red de un proyecto.

- Diagrama de despliegue: Este diagrama es necesario para mostrar la interacción entre los componentes de hardware y software que actúan en el sistema.
- Diagrama de entidad-relación. Este diagrama permite conocer como se encuentra estructurada la base de datos.

6. Revisiones planificadas: Para mejorar la calidad del producto final se realizaron revisiones cada 2 a 3 semanas, en las cuales se revisaba el código fuente y la documentación.
7. Validación de las funcionalidades con pruebas. Una vez que los estudiantes terminaron el desarrollo de sus proyectos, se ejecutaron casos de pruebas basados en los criterios de aceptación. De esta manera, pudimos corroborar en que medida cumplieron los requerimientos planteados en los proyectos.

En la Tabla 5 se muestran las prácticas de ingeniería de software que se realizaron en el curso. Cada práctica fue diseñada para reducir las falencias identificadas y mejorar los proyectos de los estudiantes, tal como se muestra en la Tabla 6.

Tabla 5. Prácticas de Ingeniería de Software.

Id	Prácticas
PRAC1	Especificación de requerimientos con historias de usuarios y criterios de aceptación
PRAC2	Scrum
PRAC3	Calidad de código: Estándares de codificación y analizadores de código
PRAC4	Diseño de componentes de arquitectura
PRAC5	Presentación de los recursos para el desarrollo de software y uso de GitHub
PRAC6	Pruebas de software

Tabla 6. Prácticas de Ingeniería de Software utilizadas para mitigar falencias.

Falencia	PRAC1	PRAC2	PRAC3	PRAC4	PRAC5	PRAC6
AU-FAL1	x	x				
AU-FAL2		x				
AU-FAL3				x		
AU-FAL4		x				
AU-FAL5	x	x				x
RE-FAL1	x					
RE-FAL2			x		x	
RE-FAL3				x		
RE-FAL4				x		
RE-FAL5					x	
RE-FAL6						x

6. Análisis de Resultados

Luego de realizar las prácticas de Ingeniería de Software analizamos los resultados obtenidos, los cuales se resumen a continuación:

1. Cumplimiento de especificaciones del sistema: Hasta el año 2017, no se había logrado el cumplimiento total de los proyectos, pues los estudiantes no comprendían claramente los requerimientos de los sistemas a desarrollar. Esto a su vez generaba retrasos en la entrega de los proyectos por la falta de comprensión de las funcionalidades esperadas. Adicionalmente, los estudiantes acudían frecuentemente a la oficina de la profesora para aclarar dudas sobre las funcionalidades esperadas del sistema. A partir del 2018 y con los requerimientos definidos por medio de historias de usuarios y criterios de aceptación, los requerimientos del proyecto estuvieron más claros y los estudiantes consultaron a la profesora, máximo dos veces en el semestre.
2. Gestión del proyecto: Previo a la ejecución de esta investigación, se realizaban 2 revisiones de avances de los proyectos, a mitad y al final del semestre; lo cual dificultaba identificar el progreso obtenido por los estudiantes. Por eso, se implementaron prácticas de Scrum y en cada grupo se asignaron los roles de Product Owner y Scrum Master [9]. Los sprints tenían duraciones de 2 a 3 semanas, al final de los cuáles se realizaban Sprint Reviews con la pro-

fesora de la materia de Conmutación y Enrutamiento. Los Scrum Meetings se realizaban solo una vez cada semana, cuando los estudiantes se reunían para elaborar el proyecto. Como herramienta de gestión de proyectos, se utilizó Asana para asignar tareas a los responsables de las tareas del Sprint y monitorear el seguimiento de sus avances.

3. Calidad del código: Anteriormente, el concepto de calidad del código era ignorado, pues en las revisiones de los avances de los proyectos solo se consideraba la funcionalidad del sistema, más no como había sido desarrollado. Con el uso de está práctica, se obtuvo un código fuente más legible y por lo tanto mantenible, pues contiene comentarios que describen sus funcionalidades y se utilizan nombres descriptivos para las variables y funciones. Se modularizó el código y las funcionalidades se separaron; sin embargo, el analizador de código no presentó una mejora notable. Esto se debe a que, a pesar de que los estudiantes añadieron comentarios para describir las funciones, incluyendo los argumentos que reciben y los resultados, éstos no estaban escritos de la manera que pide el estándar de programación de docstring para Python y Javadoc para Java.
4. Diseño de componentes de arquitectura: El diagrama de red ya era conocido por los estudiantes de Telemática, dado que realizaban simulaciones en GNS3. Para la elaboración del diagrama de red utilizaban Microsoft Visio. Posteriormente, se utilizó la aplicación web Lucichard, en lugar de Microsoft Visio. En la elaboración de los diagramas de despliegue, de entidad-relación (ER) fue necesario realizar correcciones en varias ocasiones, dado a que estos diagramas eran nuevos para los estudiantes. En el diagrama de despliegue, los estudiantes tuvieron dificultad en reconocer los elementos que debían presentar en conjunto con los dispositivos de conmutación y enrutamiento. Además, los estudiantes no reciben la materia de Sistema de Bases de Datos, por lo cual desconocían el diagrama de ER. En la Figura 2 se muestra el diagrama de despliegue de uno de los proyectos.
   Respecto a los resultados de los componentes de arquitectura, en promedio se realizaron 2 correcciones en los diagramas de red, 3 correcciones en el diagrama de despliegue y 2 correcciones en el diagrama de entidad-relación. La mayor dificultad se encontró en realizar el diseño de las tablas necesarias para almacenar la información ingresada en las aplicaciones. A pesar de las revisiones que se realizaron, un grupo de estudiantes cometió el error de crear una tabla para los dispositivos enrutadores y otra tabla para los dispositivos conmutadores, ambas con los mismos campos. Por tanto, fue necesario sugerirles la creación de la tabla "dispositivo"para guardar la información de los enrutadores, conmutadores, e incluir un campo para diferenciar el tipo de dispositivo.
5. Recursos para el desarrollo de software y uso de GitHub: En versiones previas del curso, los estudiantes entregaban los documentos (manual técnico, manual de usuario y el código fuente) impresos en papel. En la actualidad, el código fuente de los proyectos es almacenado en GitHub y los manuales en repositorios, lo cual facilitó la identificación de las versiones del código

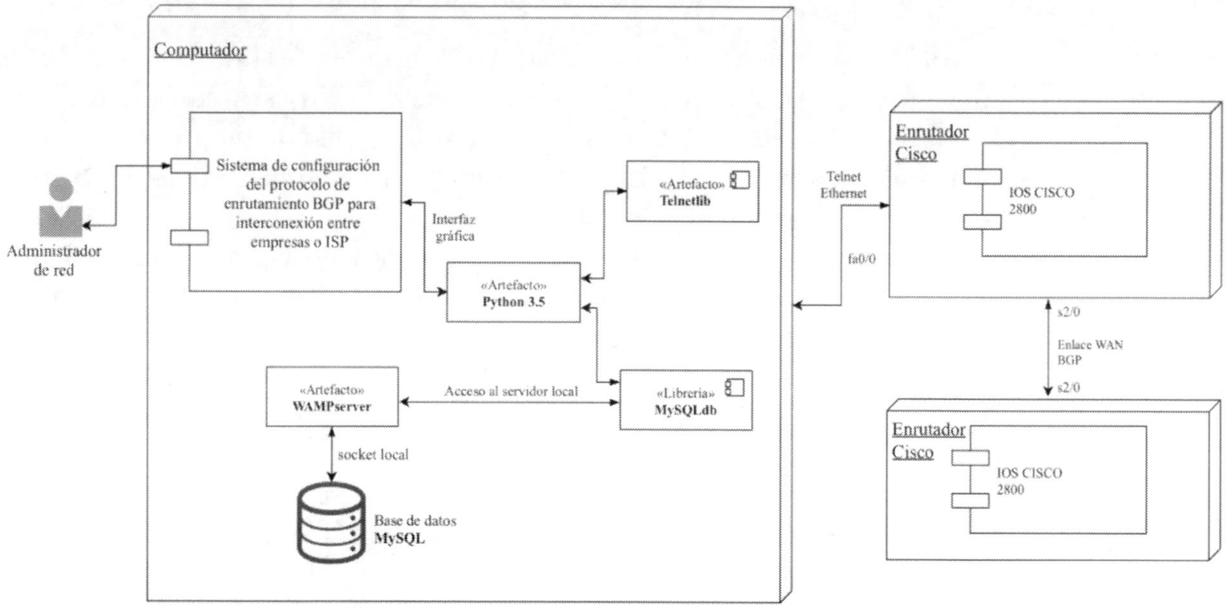

Figura 2. Diagrama de despliegue de un proyecto.

y mejoró notablemente la organización de la documentación digital. A los estudiantes se les proporcionó un manual de GitHub en versión electrónica para el auto-aprendizaje de dicha herramienta. Sin embargo, la falta de conocimiento y del manejo de GitHub se evidenciaron cuando se utilizaron los analizadores de código. En cursos futuros, pensamos incluir videos y ejemplos sobre el uso de GitHub.

6. Pruebas de software: Anteriormente, no se efectuaban casos de pruebas de aceptación sobre los proyectos. Con el uso de esta práctica, diseñamos casos de pruebas de aceptación para comprobar el cumplimiento de los requisitos del sistema y validar su apropiado funcionamiento. Durante las revisiones brindamos retroalimentación sobre las funcionalidades mostradas y en el último sprint ejecutamos todos los casos de prueba. En la Tabla 7 se muestran los resultados de las validaciones de las funcionalidades con pruebas efectuadas en cada proyecto. Como se observa, un proyecto cumplió con todas las especificaciones dadas y el 100 % de las pruebas resultaron exitosas.

Tabla 7. Resumen de pruebas realizadas con proyectos realizados.

Proyecto	Historias de Usuario	Pruebas exitosas	Total de pruebas	% Pruebas exitosas
PROY1	4	10	19	52.63 %
PROY2	4	22	28	78.57 %
PROY3	3	24	24	100.00 %

Al finalizar el curso, los estudiantes realizaron presentaciones para demostrar la funcionalidad de los sistemas en producción con los dispositivos de red.

Además, presentaron los documentos del proyecto como diagramas de red, despliegue y entidad-relación, manuales técnico, de usuario y el código fuente en GitHub. A manera de ejemplo se presenta el enlace del proyecto 3 (ver enlace en https://github.com/acollaguazo/1T2018-SISTEMA-DE-CONFIGURACION-DEL-PROTOCOLO-BGP-PROYECTO-G3.git).

7. Conclusiones

En los proyectos de gestión para dispositivos de red como conmutadores y enrutadores, al no contar con una educación formal sobre las buenas prácticas a seguir durante el desarrollo de software, se obtiene un producto con código ilegible y muchas veces incompleto. Se pudo observar que aplicando Ingeniería de Software en un curso de Conmutación y Enrutamiento se solucionaron algunos problemas presentes en el desarrollo de este tipo de proyectos.

Para aplicar Scrum en el curso, optamos por un manejo de tiempos límites para las tareas asignadas y, además, un control del proyecto por medio de un Product Owner y un Scrum Master. La duración de los sprints tuvo que ser acomodada al tiempo transcurrido entre cada entregable que se pedía en el curso. Además, fue necesario rediseñar el curso para incluir la explicación de conceptos y herramientas para el desarrollo de software y gestión del proyecto.

Por otro lado, usando historias de usuario y criterios de aceptación especificamos los requerimientos de forma clara, lo cuál consideramos fue uno de los puntos claves para obtener mejoras de los proyectos. Cabe mencionar, que en dicha especificación no participaron los estudiantes, pues la intención era que ellos comprendieran bien los requerimientos y no que los formularan.

Además, para el diseño de los componentes de arquitectura decidimos utilizar 3 diagramas: de red, de despliegue y de entidad-relación, dado que los proyectos involucraban dispositivos de red como enrutadores y conmutadores, y el uso de bases de datos. Respecto al diagrama de entidad-relación no pudo ser profundizado, ya que los estudiantes no reciben la materia de Sistema de Bases de Datos, lo que compromete habilidades y competencias para el uso y modelado de sistemas. En cuanto a la calidad del código, se pudo mejorar su mantenibilidad al obtener como producto final un código legible y documentado. Sin embargo, el uso de analizadores de código no fue fructífero debido a problemas en el uso de estándares de codificación.

Cabe mencionar que, al momento de realizar las revisiones de los proyectos, los estudiantes ponían más énfasis en presentar los avances relacionados a los dispositivos de conmutación y enrutamiento y relegaban el componente de desarrollo de software, pues percibían que estos conocimientos eran adicionales y no parte del curso. Por esto, a futuro presentaremos el contenido completo del curso, incluyendo los temas de Ingeniería de Software a ser cubiertos.

Como trabajo futuro, pensamos incorporar Scrum y el resto de prácticas de Ingeniería de Software en los proyectos que se realicen con el sector empresarial, específicamente en sistemas desarrollados para dispositivos de red en proveedores de Internet, y así medir los resultados obtenidos.

Referencias

1. CEPROEM: Encuesta de seguimiento a graduados. http://seguimiento.ceproem.espol.edu.ec/index.php/formulario/graduados (2019)
2. Collaguazo-Jaramillo, A., Alcivar, R., Pesantez, J., Ponguillo, R.: Cost effective test-bed for comparison of sdn network and traditional network. IPCCC 2018 - 37th IEEE – International Performance Computing and Communications Conference (2018)
3. Fernandes, J.M., Machado, R.J.: Teaching embedded systems engineering in a software-oriented computing degree. Proceedings - Frontiers in Education Conference, FIE pp. 5–10 (2007). https://doi.org/10.1109/FIE.2007.4417949
4. d. Freitas, R.C., d. Oliveira, J.A., Hino, F.Y.A., Neto, J.S., Vicente, L.M., d. Cunha, A.M., Dias, L.A.V.: Applying interdisciplinarity and agile methods in the development of an embedded system. In: 2014 11th International Conference on Information Technology: New Generations. pp. 645–646 (April 2014). https://doi.org/10.1109/ITNG.2014.44
5. GoogleDrive: Encuesta sobre la metodología del proyecto de conmutación y enrutamiento. https://forms.gle/SL5UgzzSZDU1Mvn48 (2017)
6. Könnölä, K., Suomi, S., Mäkilä, T., Rantala, V., Lehtonen, T.: Can embedded space system development benefit from agile practices? EURASIP Journal on Embedded Systems **2017**(1), 3 (Jul 2016). https://doi.org/10.1186/s13639-016-0040-z, `https://doi.org/10.1186/s13639-016-0040-z`
7. Koopman, P., Smailagic, A., Steenkiste, P., Thomas, D.E., Wang, C., Choset, H., Gandhi, R., Krogh, B., Marculescu, D., Narasimhan, P., Paul, J.M., Rajkumar, R., Siewiorek, D.: Undergraduate embedded system education at carnegie mellon **4** (2005). https://doi.org/10.1145/1086519.1086522, `http://portal.acm.org/citation.cfm?doid=1086519.1086522`
8. Loubach, D.S., Nobre, J.C., Da Cunha, A.M., Dias, L.A., Nascimento, M.R.: Testing critical software: A case study for an aerospace application. AIAA/IEEE Digital Avionics Systems Conference - Proceedings (May 2014) (2006). https://doi.org/10.1109/DASC.2006.313741
9. Martini, A., Pareto, L., Bosch, J.: A multiple case study on the inter-group interaction speed in large, embedded software companies employing agile **28** (2015)
10. Scharff, C.: Guiding Global Software Development Projects using Scrum and Agile with Quality Assurance (2011)
11. Shen, M., Yang, W., Rong, G., Shao, D.: Applying agile methods to embedded software development: A systematic review. In: 2012 Second International Workshop on Software Engineering for Embedded Systems (SEES). pp. 30–36 (June 2012). https://doi.org/10.1109/SEES.2012.6225488
12. Smith, M., Miller, J., Huang, L., Tran, A.: A more agile approach to embedded system development. IEEE Software **26**(3), 50–57 (May 2009). https://doi.org/10.1109/MS.2009.57
13. Sommerville, I.: Ingeniería del software (2012)
14. Subbian, V., Purdy, C.: Redesigning an advanced embedded systems course: A step towards interdisciplinary engineering education. ISEC 2013 - 3rd IEEE Integrated STEM Education Conference pp. 1–4 (2013). https://doi.org/10.1109/ISECon.2013.6525231

Insights about Educational Resources for Software Engineers: The Perspective of Ecuadorian Professionals

Mónica Villavicencio, Angely Oyola, Edgar Izquierdo
Facultad de Ingeniería en Electricidad y Computación (FIEC)
Escuela Superior Politécnica del Litoral (ESPOL)
Campus Gustavo Galindo, Km 30.5 vía Perimetral, Guayaquil-Ecuador
{mvillavi, ajoyola, eizquier}@espol.edu.ec

Abstract. As in other disciplines, the software engineering profession demands continuous learning. One way of dealing with this demand is the use of available educational resources like books, videos, online courses, amongst others. This paper is aimed at getting insights about the training needs of software professionals and their expectations regarding educational resources. A survey was administered to 85 of these professionals working, either for a software development company or within an IT department of public or private organizations in Ecuador. Results indicate that online courses are the preferred educational resources. Also, gender and age are key demographic characteristics distinguishing the professionals' preferences about such resources. Men are willing to devote up to 5 hours per week for training using educational resources while women, being more flexible in this regard, may spend up to 10 hours. In addition, professionals, 30 years old or younger, favor resources related to the software architecture topic while those older than 30 years prefer the agile development topic instead. We argue that the findings of the study are valuable for educators and trainers interested in better developing software engineering educational resources.

Keywords: Software Engineering; Training Needs; Educational Resources, Continuous Learning; Software Professional Needs

1 Introduction

As in other disciplines, the software engineering profession demands continuous learning. This is a crucial task not only for practitioners responsible for in-house software development but also for companies in the software industry. Failure to attach to continuous learning may result in an ineffective participation in a business-related context. This may explain why professionals commonly opt to take courses, offered by universities as continuing education programs, either open or not, as well as by other organizations in the software engineering arena. It is understandable, however, that open educational resources (OERs) seem to be the preferred option for learning purposes, not only for university students but also for employees related to the software industry.

In fact, during the last years, OERs have become an alternative for professionals to learn topics of their interest as these resources are characterized for their openness and possibility to share and reuse their content [1], which gives a differential advantage to OERs compared to any other type of educational resource. However, previous research provides evidence of a limited amount of computer science OERs addressing software engineering topics, mostly in English [2]. The study just mentioned highlighted the existence of 24 OERs regarding software engineering from a total of 370 in the field of computer science, being 70% of them offered in the English language. This situation is an indication that more work needs to be done to provide greater alternatives, either open or not, related to the software engineering domain. Also, the language in which they are presented is as important in the sense that they can be beneficial to a larger audience worldwide.

Certainly, the language, in which educational resources (including OERs amongst other alternatives) are offered, might be a barrier for Spanish-speaking people looking for learning topics of their interest by their own [4]–[8]. This can be so as the English proficiency in Latin America is lower than Europe and Asia according to the EF English Proficiency Index [9]. This is an important consideration for the present research as the study was conducted among practitioners in Ecuador. The reduced offer of educational resources, more accentuated for Spanish-speaking population together with the lack of English proficiency in Latin American countries, suggest that research should be aimed at identifying the needs and expectations of software engineering professionals. To fill this gap, the study seeks to answer the following questions: what kind of educational resources do software engineering professionals prefer for self-learning purposes? What are the topics that they would like to learn? What are the main features they expect from educational resources?

The rest of this paper is structured as follows: Section II describes related works; Section III explains the methodology of the study; Section IV presents the results; and Section V concludes the article.

2 Related Work

Previous research has reported a great variety of educational resources that can be open, for profit or free, which include: curriculum, maps, course materials, streaming videos, multimedia applications, podcasts, games, books and other resources, designed for teaching and learning purposes [10]. A particular case of an educational resource is an OER, concept originally adopted in 2002 at the UNESCO Open Courseware (OCW) Forum. Since then, OERs have gained increasing attention among universities worldwide, becoming a subject of main interest for educational purposes. Initially, OERs were thought as complementary educational resources or guidelines for learners. Currently, their use has become more widespread around the world [1], [35], [36].

Another case of an educational resource is a MOOC although it is not normally open, it can be free. A MOOC is a course delivered through a web platform, in which educational material is provided, including quizzes and assignments, commonly graded [3]. MOOCs are available for independent and self-directed studies [11]; mainly aimed at an adult audience, such as students and employees.

For university students, on the one hand, previous work has focused on educational resources and their characteristics with the idea of giving them a solid structure in a way that facilitates learning [12], [13]. For workers (i.e. software professionals in our study), on the other hand, research has been oriented to identify problems along the software development process and their possible causes which leads to the conclusion that training is needed [14], [15].

Regardless of the audience to which educational resources (open or not, for profit or free) are addressed, their availability to self-learning and to gaining current knowledge and tools can have a positive effect in releasing quality products associated to the software industry. On the contrary, it is apparent to expect that the lack of educational resources does not contribute to this aim. In fact, the extant literature reveals that companies face the problem of hiring professionals with little experience to develop functional software according to requirements [16]. In addition, Lehtinen et al. refer to the lack of abilities exhibited by professionals to develop quality software [17].

From the above discussion, one can argue that some problems faced by software companies seem to come from deficiencies originated in university education. To solve these issues, Martins et al. suggest that university courses should focus on the importance of requirements and their traceability, as these are the basis for developing quality products [18]. Additionally, recommendations concern the use of software testing in an educational venue, so that upcoming professionals can get a clear understanding of its importance.

Beyond the proper management of requirements and software testing, Alarifi et al. recommend upgrading the syllabus of software engineering courses, making them more practical and well-focused on solving industry problems [19]. Also, these authors emphasize the lack of practical experience of university students in applying agile methodologies. This may explain why they finish their education without being able to develop skills to deal with changing requirements. Unterkalmsteiner et al. also stress that usually students do not get aware of the benefits of testing and costs incurred as a result of delivering poor quality software [20].

Other authors argue that many software engineering activities are performed by people without the necessary background while the required skills in their duties commonly change throughout their professional careers [21], [22]. This suggests that professionals in an early stage of their careers need a mix of competences, which can be instilled in them through educational resources as means of continuous learning.

Going in this direction, previous studies have reported the use of educational resources for professional training. One of them is of Stamatis Karnouskos in which the relationship between a MOOC and employee competencies and innovation has been examined. The author stresses that both corporations and individual employees are interested in continuously enhancing existing knowledge. In this sense, MOOCs are educational resources oriented to enhance employees' competencies [6]. Also, Wendt et al. point out that professionals are more likely to enroll in non-credit online short courses (SPOC) rather than in those that offer credits, valuable to reach a degree in Computer Science or Software Engineering [23].

Certainly, the availability of educational resources, either open or not, for profit or free, is an important contribution to knowledge acquisition and to learning new topics and tools in the software engineering field. Yet, to be better effective in these regards, we contend that the point of view of professionals, working on areas related to software development, should be considered. This means that their inputs are of great relevance when designing and implementing educational resources as a way of meeting their learning needs and expectations. Previous research, however, has not addressed these demands, which sets the motivation for the present study.

3 Methodology

To gather information for this study, we designed a survey instrument based on the recommendations presented in the following articles: [16], [17], [19], [24]–[26]. The survey, administered in Ecuador the first trimester of 2017, included a set of 20 questions split into four sections: 1) Participant information; 2) Company information; 3) Issues faced by software professionals; and 4) Their training needs.
As mentioned, the first two sections asked respondents about their profile and the company' general information. Questions in Section 3 were designed to get insights about the underlying causes of problems encountered by companies in the process of developing software. In addition, respondents were inquired to indicate about the negative impact as a result of these problems, including: software released with faults or delays; software developing costs exceeding the initial budget; and unsatisfied customers; amongst others. To formulate these questions, we took into consideration the results of [15], [17], [18], [34]. Section 4 aimed at knowing the learning needs and preferences of respondents regarding the software engineering field.

The questionnaire was pilot tested with 38 practitioners in October 2016. Results of this test allowed us to identify ambiguity in the wording of questions and their multiple-choice answers.

The final version of the questionnaire was administered by using Google forms. The link of the survey instrument (https://goo.gl/forms/ED1AwEll6dCCeRnX2) was sent via email to a list of organizations obtained from a database of the ESPOL's University Office in charge of facilitating recruitment of students for companies in such database. This way, a total of nearly 1000 private and public organizations were considered and a random sample of 400 organizations was drawn from the population. Next, potential respondents from the organizations in the sample were contacted, either software professionals working for a software development company or employees working at an IT department of public or private organizations producing software for in-house use. Two reminders to fill out the survey were sent via e-mail, and by the end of the data collection process, eighty-five responses were received.

4 Results

The demographic characteristics of participants are shown in Table 1. It can be observed that most of respondents were male (76.5%), which is not uncommon in science, technology, engineering, and mathematics (STEM) careers. The two most representative groups in the sample were between 25 to 30 and 31 to 40 years old. Regarding the role of participants within their organizations, 38.8% of them work as programmers, while 21.2% as business analysts. Important to highlight is that men are mainly in leading positions, such as chief technology officer (CTO) and owner of a software development company. The percentage of men in these two leading positions is higher compared to women (i.e. 3.2 times for CTOs and 2.4 times for owners). Also, an interesting finding is that no women in the sample were working as software architects nor test engineers.

With respect to the field of study of respondents, we found that nearly 89% has a computer science background, 4.8% in telecommunications and 7% in other disciplines.

Table 1. Demographics of respondents

Characteristics	%
Sex	
Male	76.5
Female	23.5
Age	
18 – 24	14.1
25 – 30	35.3
31 – 40	32.9
41 – 60	16.5
61 or over	1.2
Field of study	
Computer Science	88.2
Telecommunications	4.8
International Business	2.4
Marketing	1.2
Industrial Engineering	1.2
Others	2.2
Role in the organization	
Programmer	38.8
Business Analyst	21.2
Project Manager	14.1
CTO	10.6
Owner	9.4
Software Architect	3.5
Software Test Engineer	2.4

The second section gathered information about the characteristics of organizations in the study. Table 2 shows that 56.5% represents software development companies and 43.5% corresponds to IT departments producing software for own use. Table 2 also shows the number of employees working in software development, type of industry in which software is being used, and the target market (i.e. local, national or international).

As shown, most of the organizations have software development departments with less than 20 employees. Software being produced is mainly used in banks or financial institutions, followed by government and manufacturing organizations. Most of the companies producing software sell their products locally within the Ecuadorian territory.

Table 2. Characteristics of organizations

Characteristics	%
Number of employees	
1 - 9	51.2
10 - 19	28.1
20 - 29	4.9
30 - 39	8.5
40 or over	7.3
Company/Department	
Software development company	56.5
In-house development (IT department)	43.5
Users of software (organizations)	
Banks and Financial organizations	35.5
Governmental institutions	10.4
Manufacturing companies	8.2
Educational institutions	6.0
Health service organizations	4.9
Others	35.0
Target market	
Local	31.8
National	50.4
International	17.8

When inquired about the issues faced during the software development process, respondents mentioned three main problems, closely related to customers as illustrated in Table 3. They are as follows: lack of customer involvement; unrealistic planning; customers are not clear about their needs; and, requirements are not properly prioritized. These results are in line with the studies conducted by [17], [27], confirming that the main drawbacks during software development are associated to requirements and testing.

As a negative impact of the issues presented in Table 3, 76.5% of participants indicated that projects are usually finished with delays, 45.9% mentioned that software is delivered with faults, 41.2% reported customer dissatisfaction, and 17.6% stated that projects commonly exceed the budget.

For gathering information about the training needs of participants, the survey instrument included a question with seven possible answers, defined according to [18], [28], [29]. Regardless of gender, Table 4 shows that agile development was the preferred topic (58.8%) followed by software architecture (52.9%) and testing (49.4%). The topics most commonly specified by participants were agile development, agile project management, Scrum, Kanban, cloud application architecture, microservices, Docker, effective test cases, automated testing, and requirements elicitation and prioritization techniques.

Table 3. Identified issues during the development process (multiple choices apply)

Issues *	% choice count **	choice count **
Lack of customer involvement	18.1	58
Unrealistic planning	16.2	52
Customers are not clear about their needs	13.4	43
Requirements are not properly prioritized	13.4	43
Lack of abilities, experience and knowledge	11.2	36
Insufficient testing	9.0	29
Inadequate design	7.8	25
Lack of organization in the team	5.0	16
Lack of communication among team members	4.4	14
Other	1.9	6
TOTAL		**321**

Number of respondents = 85

* Total number of responses= 321; x^2 (13) = 84.43; $p<0.001$

** Choice count was calculated over the 321 responses of the 85 respondents.

When considering the gender aspect, however, differences become visible among female and male respondents regarding their training needs. On the one hand, the top three preferred topics for female participants are as follows: testing (60.0%), agile development (55.0%) and software architecture and software maintenance (45.0%). These females' preferences may be explained by the fact that none of them works as software architects or testing engineers. In other words, they seem to be preferably interested in subjects in which they acknowledge that they are lacking. As found in this sample, females mostly work as business analysts, programmers and project managers.

On the other hand, the training needs expressed by males are the following: agile development (60.0%); software architecture (55.4%) and testing (46.2%). According to these results, males' preferences seem to be oriented to reinforce knowledge for performing their current roles. In this sample, males are mainly owners of software development companies, CTOs, programmers, and architects, amongst other roles.

The age aspect also makes the difference among respondents. The top three topics for professionals, aged 30 years or less, are: software architecture (59.5%); testing (54.8%); and agile development (52.4%). For respondents between 31 and 40 years old, the most desirable training needs include: agile development (71.4 %); software architecture (50.0 %); and requirements (50.0%). The most preferred topics for professionals older than 40 years are: agile development (53.3%), testing (53.3%) and requirements (46.7%).

Besides, participants were asked to indicate their preferences about the type of educational resources to meet their training needs. Table 5 shows that the option chosen the most concerns online courses (92.9%) while the rest in the list are much less preferred.

Table 4. Training desired by professionals (Multiple choices apply)

A	B	C	D	E	F	G	H
*	**		***	***	****	****	****
Agile development	22.6	58.8	55.0	60.0	52.4	71.4	53.3
Software architecture	20.4	52.9	45.0	55.4	59.5	50.0	40.0
Testing	19.0	49.4	60.0	46.2	54.8	39.3	53.3
Requirements	16.7	43.5	40.0	44.6	38.1	50.0	46.7
Software maintenance	10.4	27.1	45.0	21.53	26.2	25.0	33.3
Refactoring	9.1	23.5	20.0	24.6	30.9	14.3	20.0
Other	1.8	4.7	0.0	6.2	2.4	3.6	13.3

A: Desired training, B: % choice count, C: % of respondents, D: % females, E: % males, F: $<$ 3 years, G: 30$\leq$ years$\leq$40, H: $>$ 40 years

Number of respondents= 85; * Total number of responses= 221; x2 (6) = 51.49; $p<0.001$

** Choice count was calculated over the 221 responses of the 85 respondents

*** % calculated over all females/males in the sample

**** % calculated over all respondents in the interval

Note: This was a multiple-choice question. An independent frequency analysis was performed for each variable (column) of the table, e.g. % males who chose "Agile development" as the most desired training was calculated over all males in the sample (39/65= 60.0%). Similarly, the % choice count for "Software maintenance" was calculated over all 221 responses (23/221= 10.4%).

Regardless of gender, the findings indicate that time is an important issue in the sense that "the less the better". That is, 50.6% of respondents expressed their willingness to dedicate less than 5 hours a week for learning topics related to software engineering by using educational resources; while 44.7% would spend between 5 to 10 hours. Only few of them (4.7%) would devote more than 10 hours a week for the training purpose. Looking at gender differences, most of women (55.0%) would be willing to get trained by using educational resources requiring 5 to 10 hours a week, while most of men (52.3%) would like to dedicate less than 5 hours. This means that females are more flexible in terms of dedication time to learning new topics. With respect to age, professionals less than 40 years old (57.1%) are in favor of educational resources designed to demand up to 5 hours a week.

Thanks to the massive access to Internet nowadays, many educational resources are freely available online; however, not all of them can be categorized as of good quality [13]. Certainly, this is the main risk that people face when choosing freely available resources. To avoid this risk, it is crucial to define certain characteristics so that an educational resource becomes pedagogical and suitable for facilitating students' learning. In this commitment, we asked participants to choose from a list of characteristics considered as critical for software engineering educational resources. We developed a list of desirable features based on the work reported in [13], [30]–[33].

As shown in Table 6, software professionals look for resources easy to understand, available any time, and those giving them practical advice to be applied in their workplace (i.e. very practical information including tips). Moreover, we found that a high percentage of professionals are willing to spend time in learning by using freely available resources whether these are topic-specific (i.e. resources that provide the specific knowledge base without including other less important content; very concise theoretical basis).

Looking at gender differences, both men (73.9%) and women (90.0%) agreed that the main expected feature must be in the sense that the topics should be easy to understand. In addition, they also agree in the less important feature (i.e. interaction among learners and teacher), 30.0% for females and 44.6% for males. By considering the age of respondents, younger than 40 years old (77.1%) prefer educational resources easy to understand. In contrast, those between 41 and 60 years old (92.9%) prefer to have practical tips, useful for their duties at work.

Table 5. Preferred type of educational resources (Multiple choices apply)

A *	B **	C	D ***	E ***	F ****	G ****	H ****
Online courses	50.3	92.9	95.0	92.3	95.2	89.3	93.3
Videos	21.4	41.2	40.0	41.5	35.7	53.6	33.3
Books	25.1	40.0	35.0	41.5	35.7	42.9	46.7
Educational games	3.2	5.9	10.0	4.6	9.5	0.0	6.7

A: Preferred Educational Resources, B: %choice count, C: % of respondents, D: % females, E: % males, F: < 30 years, G: 30<=40 years, H: > 40 years

Number of respondents=85

* Total number of responses= 406; x2 (3) = 182.75; p<0.001

** Choice count was calculated over the total 406 responses (from 85 respondents)

*** % calculated over all females/males in the sample

**** % calculated over all respondents in the interval

Table 6. Expected features of educational resources (Multiple choices apply)

Expected features*	**%choice count** **	**choice count** **
Easy to understand	15.1	66
Content always available online	12.8	56
With practical tips useful to my work	11.9	52
Specific to the topic I want to learn	11.0	48
Flexible, to go at my own pace	10.6	46
Contributing for a better performance at work	10.6	46
Offered from prestigious universities	10.3	45
Suggesting other sources of information	9.4	41
Facilitating interaction among learners and teacher	8.0	35
Other	0.2	1
TOTAL		**436**

Number of respondents= 85
* Total number of responses= 436; x2 ( ) = ; p<0.
** Choice count was calculated over all the 436 responses (from 85 respondents)

5 Conclusions

This article presents the results of a survey administered to software professionals, aimed at identifying their training needs related to software engineering as well as the expected features of educational resources. As discussed, the main training needs of software practitioners concern agile development, cloud application architecture, microservices, automated testing, and requirements elicitation and prioritization techniques.

Results also indicate that gender and age of professionals are relevant demographic characteristics, influential in their preferences for learning (i.e. type of an educational resource, time devoted for learning, and expected features of those resources).

In addition, we found that professionals are mostly inclined towards online courses rather than books or other type of educational resources. It is also evident that the lack of available time is an issue for continuous education activities as software professionals can only spend less than 5 hours per week. Besides, they look for resources allowing them to learn with ease as well as those that offer tips for applying the learnt topics in their duties at work. Although the results presented in this article are only based on the opinions of software professionals, we contend that the information gathered through the survey instrument is valuable for educators and trainers interested in developing educational resources for the software engineering field. On the one hand, knowing the preferences for software engineering topics, the type of resource and its expected features can facilitate the development of proper content and approach of resources for the software engineering discipline. On the other hand, the findings give scholars clues in terms of what the focus should be when building resources for continuous learning. Finally, the approach followed in this study is also useful for researchers as to have a means to get insights about the specificities of training needs of professionals from other disciplines.

Important to mention is that the present work is the first part of a two-step study. This way, the next release is intended to contribute with free educational resources for Spanish-speaking professionals.

References

1. A. Marcus-Quinn and Y. Diggins, "Open educational resources", Procedia - Social and Behavioral Sciences, vol 93, pp 243 – 246, 2013.
2. R. Navarrete, S. Luján-Mora, and M. Peñafiel, "Use of open educational resources in E-learning for higher education," in eDemocracy & eGovernment (ICEDEG), 2016 Third International Conference on, 2016, pp. 164–170.
3. S. Karnouskos, "Massive open online courses (MOOCs) as an enabler for competent employees and innovation in industry," Comput. Ind., vol. 91, pp. 1–10, 2017.

4. J. Willems and C. Bossu, "Equity considerations for open educational resources in the glocalization of education," Distance Educ., vol. 33, no. 2, pp. 185–199, 2012.
5. I. F. Silveira and K. O. Villalba-Condori, "An Open Perspective for Educational Games," J. Inf. Technol. Res. JITR, vol. 11, no. 1, pp. 18–28, 2018.
6. H. Gore, "Massive open online courses (MOOCs) and their impact on academic library services: Exploring the issues and challenges," New Rev. Acad. Librariansh., vol. 20, no. 1, pp. 4–28, 2014.
7. D. Badarch, S. Kanyazeva, and A. Lane, "Introducing the Opportunities and Challenges of OER; The Case of Commonwealth Independent Baltic States," Glenne J Harley K Butch. N Van Wyk, 2012.
8. P. von Böselager and J. Neumann, "OER World Map Web Application." [Online]. Available: https://oerworldmap.org,. [Accessed: 06-Oct-2017].
9. EF, "EF English Proficiency," 2018. [Online]. Available: https://www.ef.com.ec/epi/regions/latin-america/. [Accessed: 29-Nov-2018].
10. N. Butcher, "A Basic Guide to Open Educational Resources (OER)." United Nations Educational, Scientifi c and Cultural Organization, 2015.
11. D. Vila-Viñas, D. Araya, and P. Bouchard, "Educación: recursos educativos abiertos," in Buen Conocer-FLOK Society. Modelos sostenibles y políticas públicas para una economía social del conocimiento común y abierto en el Ecuador, Asociación aLabs, 2015, pp. 61–142.
12. E. Hu, Y. Li, J. Li, and W.-H. Huang, "Open educational resources (OER) usage and barriers: a study from Zhejiang University, China," Educ. Technol. Res. Dev., vol. 63, no. 6, pp. 957–974, 2015.
13. I. E. Allen and J. Seaman, "Opening the Curriculum: Open Educational Resources in US Higher Education, 2014.," Babson Surv. Res. Group, 2014.
14. M. Geogy and A. Dharani, "A Scrutiny of the Software Requirement Engineering process," Procedia Technol., vol. 25, pp. 405–410, 2016.
15. M. H. N. Nasir and S. Sahibuddin, "Critical success factors for software projects: A comparative study," Sci. Res. Essays, vol. 6, no. 10, pp. 2174–2186, 2011.
16. Y. Shen, "Software Engineering Challenges in Small Companies," Univ. Hels., 2008.
17. T. O. Lehtinen and M. V. Mantyla, "What are problem causes of software projects? Data of root cause analysis at four software companies," in Empirical Software Engineering and Measurement (ESEM), 2011 International Symposium on, 2011, pp. 388–391.
18. L. E. G. Martins and T. Gorschek, "Requirements engineering for safety-critical systems: A systematic literature review," Inf. Softw. Technol., vol. 75, pp. 71–89, 2016.
19. A. Alarifi, M. Zarour, N. Alomar, Z. Alshaikh, and M. Alsaleh, "SECDEP: Software engineering curricula development and evaluation process using SWEBOK," Inf. Softw. Technol., vol. 74, pp. 114–126, 2016.
20. M. Unterkalmsteiner, T. Gorschek, R. Feldt, and E. Klotins, "Assessing requirements engineering and software test alignment—Five case studies," J. Syst. Softw., vol. 109, pp. 62–77, 2015.
21. P. O. Antonino, A. Morgenstern, and T. Kuhn, "Embedded-Software Architects: It's Not Only about the Software," IEEE Softw., vol. 33, no. 6, pp. 56–62, 2016.
22. C. Ebert and S. Counsell, "Toward Software Technology 2050," IEEE Softw., vol. 34, no. 4, pp. 82–88, 2017.
23. K. D. Wendt, K. Reily, and M. P. Heimdahl, "First Steps towards Exporting Education: Software Engineering Education Delivered Online to Professionals," in Software Engineering Education and Training (CSEET), 2016 IEEE 29th International Conference on, 2016, pp. 241–245.
24. C. C. Vidal, N. A. Segura, S. P. Campos, and S. Sánchez-Alonso, "Quality in learning objects: evaluating compliance with metadata standards," in Research Conference on Metadata and Semantic Research, 2010, pp. 342–353.
25. J. Segal and C. Morris, "Developing software for a scientific community: some challenges and solutions," Handb. Res. Comput. Sci. Eng. Theory Pract., pp. 177–196, 2011.

26. V. Garousi, K. Petersen, and B. Ozkan, "Challenges and best practices in industry-academia collaborations in software engineering: A systematic literature review," Inf. Softw. Technol., vol. 79, pp. 106–127, 2016.
27. S. A. Kumar and T. A. Kumar, "Study the impact of requirements management characteristics in global software development projects: an ontology based approach," Int. J. Softw. Eng. Appl., vol. 2, no. 4, p. 107, 2011.
28. M. Villavicencio, H. V. Revelo, and J. Pincay, "Towards the evaluation of open educational resources for learning software engineering," in Computing Conference (CLEI), 2016 XLII Latin American, pp. 1–9, 2016.
29. J. A. Guzmán-Luna, C. A. Vélez-Carvajal, and S. A. G. Arias, "Un modelo de procesamiento de lenguaje natural para la detección de errores en requisitos de software," Rev. Virtual Univ. Católica Norte, no. 46, pp. 169–186, 2015.
30. J. M. Pawlowski and M. Bick, "Open educational resources," Bus. Inf. Syst. Eng., vol. 4, no. 4, pp. 209–212, 2012.
31. A. M. Arendt and B. E. Shelton, "Incentives and disincentives for the use of OpenCourseWare," Int. Rev. Res. Open Distrib. Learn., vol. 10, no. 5, 2009.
32. Q. Chen and S. Panda, "Needs for and utilization of OER in distance education: a Chinese survey," Educ. Media Int., vol. 50, no. 2, pp. 77–92, 2013.
33. E. Tovar Caro and I. Lesko, "Analysis of successful modes for the implementation and use of Open Course Ware (OCW) & Open Educational Resources (OER) in higher education. the virtual mobility case," RIED Rev. Iberoam. Educ. Distancia, vol. 17, no. 1, 2014.
34. Lohnson, J. The Standish Group, "Chaos report: Decision Latency Theory", Retrieved Dec 12, 2018 from https://www.standishgroup.com/store/services/10-chaos-report-decision-latency-theory-2018-package.html, 2018.
35. S. Abramovich, M. McBride, "Open education resources and perceptions of financial value", The Internet and Higher Education, vol 39, pp 33-38, 2018.
36. Chen S.H., Nasongkhla J., Donaldson J. A., "From Vision to Action – A Strategic Planning Process Model for Open Educational Resources", Procedia - Social and Behavioral Sciences, volume 174, pp 3707-3714, 2015.

Conceptualizing the Domain of Automated Feedback for Learners

Estefanía Serral[1] and Jenny Ruiz[2], Jan Elen[1], Monique Snoeck[1]

[1] KU Leuven, Naamestraat 69, 3000 Leuven, Belgium
{estefania.serralasensio; jan.elen; monique.snoeck}@kuleuven.be
[2] University of Holguin, XX Anniversary Ave, 80100 Holguin, Cuba
jruizp@uho.edu.cu

Abstract. Achieving high-quality automated feedback that helps and guides students in their learning process is one of the most pursued challenges within the field of technology-enhanced learning (TEL). However, there is no theoretical foundation that conceptualizes what automated feedback consists of in order to understand what must be considered to automatically design and deliver feedback. Based on a critical review of the literature, this paper presents a framework that identifies and defines the most important factors to characterise automated feedback. The framework can 1) help to better frame scientific contributions on automated feedback, which will facilitate their application and validation; and 2) serve researchers and developers as guidance in the design and implementation of quality automated feedback within TEL environments.

Keywords: automated feedback; framework; technology-enhanced learning.

1 Introduction

Feedback has always been viewed as a critical factor for improving the acquisition of knowledge and skills [1], however, students report deficits in the amount and quality of the external feedback they receive [2]. For this reason, automated feedback has become one of the most pursued challenges within the field of technology-enhanced learning (TEL). Studies report that teachers appreciate the ways these environments can supplement their instruction, especially when they have little time to provide the needed individualized guidance to their increasingly large classrooms of students [4]. Therefore, software engineering techniques need to be investigated to develop TEL environments that provide personalized support for learners by including automatic guidance and feedback based on their needs [3].

For the research presented in this paper, we define the term *automated feedback* as "feedback addressed to learners that considers their needs and that is automatically generated and delivered by a TEL environment".

Automated feedback for learners has been highly researched topic by different research communities, where authors refer to the same aspects using many different terms. This cacophony of terms is a symptom of the lack of theoretical foundation that clarifies the terminology and compiles what must be considered in order to design and deliver high-quality automated feedback. This paper elaborates a framework to conceptualizing the research on automated feedback. Specifically, the framework identifies and clarifies the most important factors to consider for automating feedback. It can serve researchers: 1) to better delineate their scientific contributions and experiments in a way that allows for comparison with other scientific work and facilitates the application of their findings and the understanding of research gaps, and 2) as guidance in the design and implementation of software engineering techniques to provide quality automated feedback within TEL environments.

In order to develop the framework, we performed a critical review of the literature on external educational feedback and feedback automation through the lenses of the authors' respective expertise domains of educational science and computer science. A total of 87 papers were finally selected and completely analysed.

The rest of the paper is organized as follows. Section 2 explains the method we used to perform the literature review. Section 3 presents the proposed framework describing all the important factors for automated feedback. Section 4 evaluates the framework and identifies future work. Finally, conclusions are provided in Section 5.

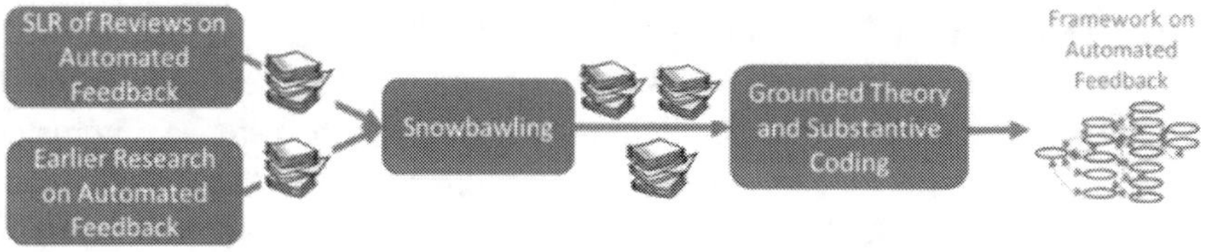

Fig. 1. Review method overview.

2 Method

Due to the lack of common terminology around automated feedback and the ambiguity of the terms *automated* and *feedback*, we decided to follow the search approach shown in Fig. 1. First, we undertook a systematic literature review using *Scopus*, focusing on *reviews* on automated feedback performed in the past 10 years. We use the following search string: (TITLE-ABS-KEY (("computer-based" OR "tutoring system" OR "digital system" OR "virtual system" OR "learning environment" OR "digital environment" OR "virtual environment" OR "Model-tracing tutor" OR technology OR technologies OR "computer tutor" OR "on-line educational platform" OR "learning system" OR "blending learning" OR "blended learning" OR e-learning OR "online learning") AND (feedback) AND (learner OR student OR learners OR students))) AND PUBYEAR > 2006 PUBYEAR < 2017 AND (LIMIT-TO (DOCTYPE, "re")) AND (LIMIT-TO (LANGUAGE , "English")).

While the use of feedback to improve learning is a well-researched topic in the literature, the results of the search revealed that only few reviews have been performed for analysing the automatic construction and delivery of feedback using a TEL environment. A total of 167 reviews were found, and only the following 9 out of them were relevant to this research: [6]–[14]. Different reviews identify one or a few interesting factors, but none of them propose a framework that compiles all. Second, we applied snowballing starting with these 9 review papers as well related papers found through earlier research [15]. A final set of 87 articles were completely analysed to build the framework. Third, we applied grounded theory and substantive coding [16] to analyse the selected papers with the purpose of forming the automated feedback framework. Essential factors for automated feedback and their different alternatives were identified through open (descriptive) coding and we iterated through the set of papers and refined the categories until saturation was reached. The criteria for selecting a concept as factor was that 1) it appears in the set of considered papers and 2) we consider it relevant for automated feedback according to our experience in the subject. The selected factors were then clustered for a better comprehension of the results (see Section 3).

3 Framework for Automated Feedback

As a result of this literature review, we propose a framework for automated feedback. It identifies the terminology of relevant factors for automated feedback and facilitates sharing a precise meaning of the terminology used in the domain. The factors have been grouped into 6 core factors, which are, as much as possible, mutually orthogonal:

- Content Design: what factors are relevant for automatically designing the feedback content and which are their alternatives?
- Delivery: what factors are relevant for automatically delivering feedback and which are their alternatives?
- Context: what contextual factors are relevant for automated feedback?
- Usage: what are the different possible usages of feedback by learners?
- Impact: what factors can be measured or observed to determine the impact of automated feedback?
- Technique: what are the different techniques, algorithms, technologies, etc. used or implemented for automating feedback?

These factors are further grouped into three main categories (see Fig. 2). The first three factors (Content Design, Delivery and Context) are relevant when "designing feedback". Next, Usage and Impact represent factors of "feedback results". The factor Technique refers to the means used for automatically creating and delivering the feedback.

In the remainder, all the identified factors are discussed. For each factor, we provide a name and possible synonyms a definition and a description. For some of the factors, the literature presents a clear further classification into different alternatives. These have been added as an extra level in Fig. 2. For other factors, literature does not present such clear-cut further classification or the nature of the factor does not allow it (e.g., domain). The number shown in brackets next to each factor is the number of analysed papers where that factor appears.

3.1 Content Design

Feedback content refers to the information made available to the learners in the feedback message. A careful design may maximize the feedback's effect [7]. The content depends on the *purpose* of the feedback, the *level* at which is provided, its *nature*, and the *domain knowledge* to which it refers.

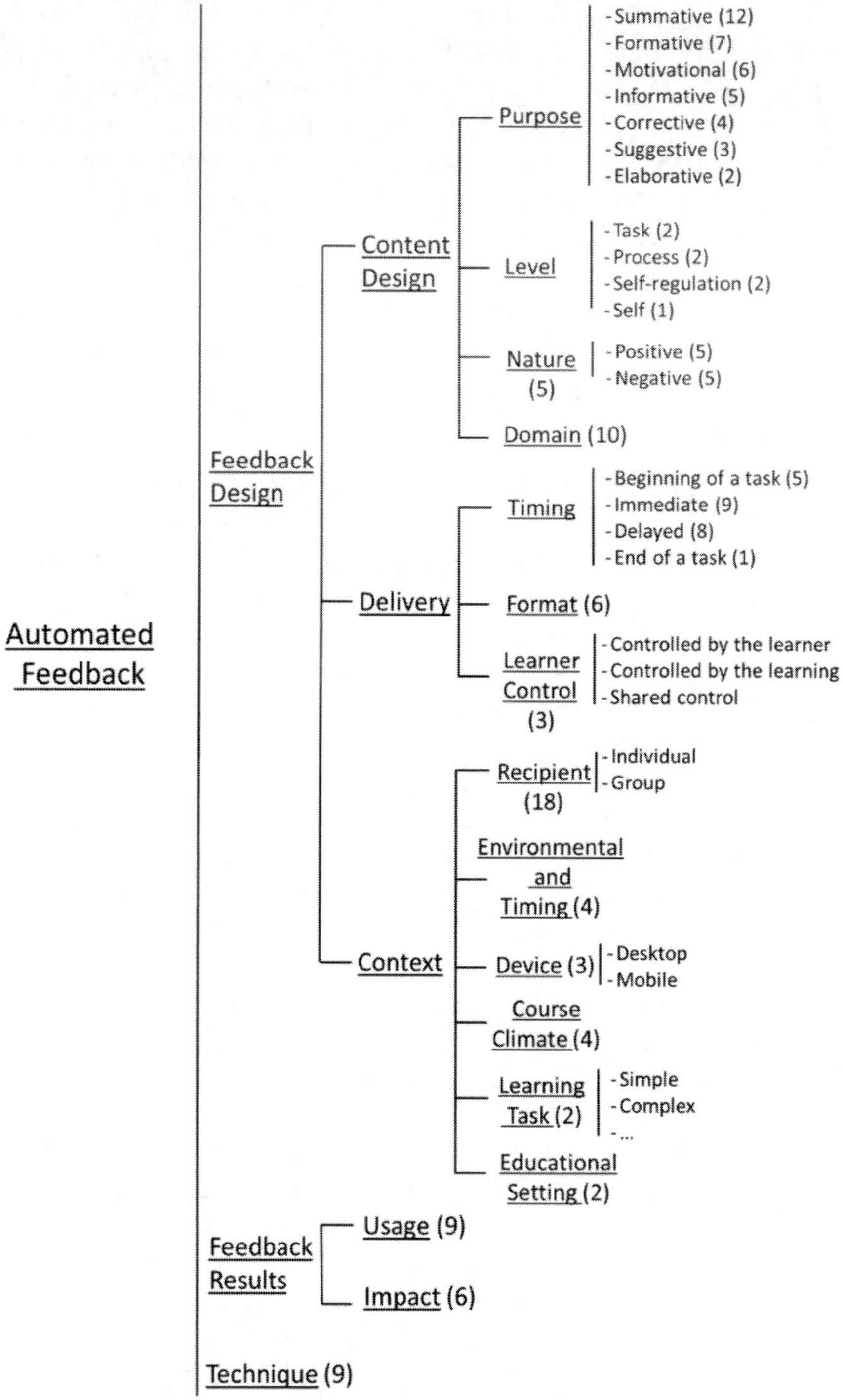

Fig. 2. Overview of the factors that characterize automated feedback.

Purpose (synonyms: scope, goal, type or function). The purpose of feedback is the reason or objective for which it is created. The following purposes (which are not mutually exclusive in most cases) are recognized in the literature:

Summative Purpose: It evaluates the learner with regard to a set of criteria and presents up-to-date success or failure information. This feedback communicates the results of summative assessment, made for the purpose of assigning grades to students and helps students retrospectively [17].

Formative or instructional Purpose: It provides learners with information and guidelines to improve their answers to a particular task while it is still being performed or completed. Formative feedback is usually effective in knowledge and skills acquisition, and it is more appreciated by students than summative feedback [17].

Motivational Purpose [18]–[20]: It usually provides positive or negative reinforcement to promote engagement. Examples of motivational indicators and strategies include: usage statistics to summarize achievements or engagement in terms of persistence, feedback from peers or more capable partners, the use of awards, etc.

Informative Purpose: This feedback provides an elaborate picture of where a learner stands in reference to others, certain criteria or their previous results. Research suggests that informative feedback is more effective in teaching desirable outcomes, and is perceived as more valuable by learners [21].

Verification and Corrective Purpose: This feedback assesses whether the answer is correct or not (verification). Besides the verification of the answer, corrective feedback adds knowledge about the correct response (e.g. "This concept is not correct").

Suggestive Purpose: This feedback includes advice on how to proceed and invites the learner to explore, expand or improve an idea. Similarly, *reflective* feedback is used by Stone (2012) to make students reflect on specific problems, ideas, or solutions.

Elaborative Purpose: It provides explanation, examples guidance that can help the learner to improve her/his answer and errors. Its definition is very close to informative feedback. The latter focuses on comparisons while *elaborative* focuses on the answer.

The most common and studied types of feedback are summative and formative, the rest are less investigated in the literature or can be subsumed by these 2 options.

Level. The level at which feedback is provided can be defined as the object of the feedback. Level of feedback was introduced by Hattie and Timperley [24] as an important factor to classify feedback and it is very well accepted in the education research community. This classification distinguishes the following 4 feedback levels:

Task-level feedback addresses how well tasks are understood, performed or accomplished. It focuses on faults in the interpretation of the task or in the outcome produced. It is considered to be very effective; however, too much task-level feedback may lead students to focus on the immediate goal and use trial-and-error strategies.

Process level feedback addresses the process that needs to be executed to understand or perform tasks. Such feedback is related to the student's own error-detection strategies, and has to serve as an 'advance-organizer', giving cues to lead to more effective information search or to better strategies.

Self-regulation level feedback refers to the regulatory or metacognitive process level. This feedback is triggered by students' learning behaviour and not by the accuracy of their responses [23]. It´s about students' capabilities of self-monitoring, directing, and regulating of actions.

Self-level feedback addresses issues of personal evaluations and affect of the learner, including features such as praise and judgment. The impact of this feedback is yet not clear, however, it is likely to better enhance self-efficacy if the feedback is related to the learner effort, self-regulation, or processes relating to the tasks and its performance.

In the last two levels, the learner characteristics (e.g., commitment, confidence, capability to create internal feedback, etc.; see Section 3.3) have a bigger influence on the effect of the provided feedback, since it is intended to create internal feedback.

Nature (synonym: valence). It is the tone of the message that is provided to the learner. It can be positive or negative [20], [24], [25]. Positive feedback is provided when a learner has met or exceeded a specific criterion; while negative feedback is provided when the target behaviour has fallen short of that criterion. There is no clear indication to choose between one or the other: commonly accepted, positive feedback is used to enhance motivation, while negative feedback may be accepted as a challenge and may trigger self-regulation [26].

A balance in the proportion of both types of feedback is crucial [27]. Positive feedback motivates learners to continue using their existing strategies and the absence of positive feedback can frustrate them. Negative feedback is key to provide information for improvement [24].

Domain knowledge. *Domain knowledge* can be defined as the content or knowledge to be taught, as well as the relationships between the domain elements [27]–[31][32]. It represents all the information related to the specific course or learning module for which the feedback is provided, e.g.: information regarding the specific learning objects that are used (tasks, assessment exercises, etc.); the specific and general goals, and the assessment criteria; the methods and processes for performing a task; the competences or skills that students will acquire; etc.

To be comprehensible for students and provide relevant information for improving their learning, feedback must provide the relevant domain knowledge. For instance, Ludvigsen et al. state that for feedback to be effective, students need to know the goals of a course, compare the goals to their own work, and take action to close the gap between the students' current performance and the desired one [31]. To design the feedback content in an automated way, the domain knowledge must be represented in a machine-understandable format and be accurately interlinked.

3.2 Delivery (synonym: presentation)

Feedback delivery, i.e., how the feedback is presented to the learner, may have a big impact on the effect of feedback since it can, e.g., make a student pay more attention to it [33]. The most important aspects to consider when delivering feedback are: timing, presentation format, and learner control over the feedback.

Timing. It refers to the moment when feedback is delivered to a learner. Providing feedback at the right moment is very important to allow students improving their performance, change their strategies or reconsider their thinking about the problem to be solved [34]. Deciding which is the best timing to deliver feedback is critical as it needs to be associated with an event or state and should not be intrusive for the students. The most common moments to provide feedback are:

From the beginning of a learning task/process, available anytime: the feedback is given at the beginning of a task or a process and can be available anytime on demand.

Immediate, just-in-time, or in-action feedback: the feedback is provided right after a student faces a learning problem or has responded to an item, task, process, or test. The aim of immediate feedback is enabling the learner to adapt instantly.

Delayed: the feedback is given after a certain time, usually indicated in relative terms, i.e., provided a while (minutes, hours, weeks) after a student faces a learning problem or has completed an item, task, process, or test.

At the end of a learning task/process (also called About-action feedback): this feedback informs learners after finishing a task how they performed key skills and enables them to monitor their progress and adapt accordingly in subsequent tasks[35].

Presentation format (synonym: modality). Different formats for presenting feedback to learners can be used. The most important ones are written, visual, or aural format. We can further also distinguish more specific ones, such as: shown in an external window independent from the learning environment interface or embedded in it, chat dialogues with the teacher, blogs, text messages, emails, etc. [22].

Learner control. Learner control refers to the decisions the learners take regarding the feedback they want to receive, e.g., how often, for which domain knowledge, etc. In a TEL environment, three general options are possible regarding who has the control over these decisions; the feedback can be controlled by the learner, by the learning environment, or by both (shared control) [36]. The level of learner control will affect whether and to what extent feedback is delivered.

3.3 Context

Context is a complex term that covers many aspects. Verbert et al. (2012) analyse different context definitions that are relevant for learning environments and tried to define a common simple classification of context information that is relevant to applications in TEL [37]. We refine and extend this classification to focus on automated feedback. We consider context to be the factors that can influence the content, delivery, usage, or impact of feedback, but also the factors that lead to the decision of giving feedback. The most important aspects to take into account as feedback context are: the recipient, environment and timing information, the interaction device used to interact with the TEL environment and, the classroom climate and the educational context.

It is important to note that designing feedback according to its context may have a significant influence on the feedback's effectiveness [17], [38], [39]. The richer the context information available, the more precise the provided feedback can be.

Recipient (synonym: receiver). The recipient of feedback is the person (or persons) that gets it. Being aware of relevant information about the feedback recipient is essential to personalize feedback and therefore maximize its effect. Personalized feedback has a high impact on students: they value it because it makes their learning processes easier and motivates them not to give up [19].

The individual's interpretation of feedback is key to developing self-efficacy and leading to further learning [24]. [32], [40], proposed a learner model for specifying the learner´s information that can be relevant in an educational domain, and specifically for Adaptive Learning Environments (ALE).

When feedback is automated, the feedback recipient is either an individual learner or a group of learners. It is important that in the latter case, each learner still perceives the feedback as pertaining to him/her, otherwise, the feedback can be just considered as irrelevant [24]. For both, individual or group feedback, it is important to take into account several elements, such as: answers and scores, information on accessibility, previous and current interactions with the system, affective state, learner´s location, and learner´s base line characteristics.

Environmental and timing context (synonym: physical and temporal conditions). Information about the environment is information about the location where the students are. Common measures are temperature, noise or light. Such measures must be considered to understand the interaction between the learner and the TEL environment, and to construct and provide effective feedback accordingly [3], [41].

An example can be derived from the timing of the interaction, i.e., when the interaction takes place: part of the day, day of the week, month, season, etc. Also, how often students interact with the TEL environment may be an indication to provide or not feedback. For instance, if a student only starts to do the homework exercises just before the deadline [42], feedback might be appropriate to help her/him to understand that that is not the most appropriate learning strategy.

Interactive device. The rapid progress of technology development has enabled the creation of many devices on which a TEL environment can be used. Knowing which device is used to interact with the environment and to provide feedback offers valuable context information to determine how feedback must be designed and delivered.

A main subdivision of devices is desktop or mobile (e.g., smartphone, tablet, laptop). The first one implies that the mobility and location of the learner will be static and therefore the environmental context will infrequently change; while in the second one, the learner can be moving or interacting with the TEL environment in many different locations and the environmental context will frequently change.

For instance, information about the interaction device that is important to consider for automated feedback is: operating system, screen size, available interaction resources (e.g., vibration, sound, touch interface…), performance and response time, etc. This information is sometimes referred to as computing context [37].

Course climate (synonym: classroom climate and classroom atmosphere). It refers to the tone or mood that is perceived by the learners of the course, be it on-site or online. Feedback is dependent on a learning environment that fosters continual improvement and creates opportunities for knowledge seeking and application by students. Thus, the course climate may influence automated feedback, above all if the learner has control over feedback and therefore feedback is on demand. It can even make feedback welcome or not welcome by students [24].

Learning task. van Merriënboer et al. define simple-to-complex categories of learning tasks [43]. Learning tasks within a particular category are equivalent, i.e., they can be performed on the basis of the same body of generalized knowledge (e.g., mental models, cognitive strategies, or other cognitive schemas). We can find the following learning task categories in the literature:

- Simple tasks: associated with low intrinsic cognitive load to process few elements.
- Complex tasks: aim at the integration of knowledge, skills, and attitudes; it requires more cognitive effort to process numerous elements and their interactions.

Van Merriënboer et al. also identify the following types of learning tasks:

- Conventional tasks: present a problem and its context, and ask for a solution.
- Worked-out examples: present the task to study a solved problem.
- Completion tasks: present a problem, its context, and part of a solution.

- Goal-free tasks: present a non-specific goal in a specific context, and ask to define the goal and to find a solution.
- Reverse tasks: present both a goal and a solution, and invite the learner to give situations where the solution may be helpful to reach the goal.

Educational setting. The educational setting refers to how the course and its content is situated in the context of the educational system, for instance, at what educational level the course is taught (primary education, secondary education, university (bachelor, master), doctorate, in-company training; or whether the course is taught through distance learning (online, blended) or classroom learning (onsite).

3.4 Usage (synonym: follow up)

When studying feedback practices, it is vital to examine how students engage with and use feedback in their own learning [31]. There are studies on how students like or experience feedback, although not automated. These studies agree that most students seem happy to receive feedback [27], [31], [33], [44]–[46].

Not all students have fruitful strategies for dealing constructively with feedback. Instead of using it in an active way, e.g., by writing down points to remember for future assignments or making reflective analyses of the comments [33], students usually rather adopt ad hoc procedures or refer to diffuse strategies, such as having to "work harder". Consequently, a number of students use the feedback *passively* [45], [46]; or *not at all.*

In [27][31], how learners use feedback is studied. In [27], the study explores student perceptions of feedback. A majority of students said that feedback was useful for: motivation purposes; keeping encouraged to improve; improving their coursework; reflecting on what they have learned; boosting their confidence in the case of positive comments; etc. In [31] the following feedback usages are identified: check if their learning is on track; address difficult concepts with their peers or teacher; adjust and focus the material to study; identify difficult topics; identify wrong applied learning strategies.

3.5 Impact (synonym: feedback effect)

The impact of feedback refers to how learning is affected by feedback, i.e., how students change their learning behaviour after receiving feedback. For instance, if their scores are higher or lower, whether they need more or less time to complete tasks, etc. The impact is directly linked with the purpose for which feedback was created and how the students really use it, but also depends on the other factors previously explained. To understand the impact, it is important to understand what students do when receiving feedback and whether it really helps them to improve. This becomes easier to study when feedback is automatically provided in a TEL environment, since this environment can be used to measure the use and impact of the feedback.

In [10], a model for evaluating the effects of feedback is defined distinguishing between cognitive, meta-cognitive, and motivational feedback effects. The model provides a list of indicators to measure feedback effects, such as number of errors corrected, number of trials until de answer was correct, time spent processing feedback, assessment of task difficulty, degree of satisfaction of self-performance, etc.

Table 1. Applying the framework for characterizing research contributions

Factor/Contribution	(Craig, Sullins, & Craig, 2015)	(Rosmalen et al, 2015)
Content		
Purpose	Summative: Current scores and attempts for solving a task (progress feedback)	Formative
Level	Task level	Task level
Nature		
Domain		Presentation and debating skills
Delivery		
Format	Visual	Textual and visual
Timing	Immediate	In action / about action
Leaner control		
Context		
Recipient	Individual. It takes into account the learner characteristics and behaviour	Individual
E/T		From May 9. 2007 to June 6, 2007
Device	Desktop	Desktop
Climate		
Learning task		
Educational setting	University	Training for youth parliament members
Usage		
Impact	Measured by student´s scores	
Technique	Natural language: extended weighted keyword matching and latent semantic analysis	Sensors for capturing the interaction with the TEL environment: speech, visible movement tracking and video signals

3.6 Technique

In order to achieve automated feedback, techniques or algorithms that analyse the relevant information and automate its design and delivery are needed:

1) Design: when constructing the feedback content, algorithms can automatically take into account or decide on the purpose of the feedback, the level, the nature, and which domain knowledge will appear in the feedback.
2) Delivery: algorithms should ideally deliver the feedback to the learner automatically at the appropriate moment, considering the selected learner control over the feedback, and using the most appropriate modality for that specific situation.

In order to automate feedback, appropriate techniques or algorithms need to be implemented: the context information must be identified and captured, appropriately represented in a machine-understandable format, and automatically analysed for determining which feedback content and delivery is the best for that particular context.

Some context elements, such as the learners' baseline characteristics, can be considered rather stable data, while other context elements might be very dynamic and constantly changing over time. Appropriate techniques are needed for each type of data.

The advances in mobile computing, wireless communication, and sensing technologies have already enabled the development of context-aware ubiquitous learning environments, environments that can take into account the context information and the real-world learning status of the students. Some of these environments even take advantage of the interaction of the students with the real-world to provide innovative ways of learning and improve the learning process of a specific subject [3].

With a TEL environment, learner's behaviour can be automatically logged through their interaction with the environment. These logs can then be automatically processed by learning analytics that can drive the delivery of the most appropriate feedback.

Finally, while checking the use and impact of feedback can be hard, time-consuming, or even impossible in a manual way, technologically-supported learning environments provide many interesting opportunities to develop techniques or algorithms that do this in an automatic way, e.g., by logging student behaviour and developing learning analytics that can help to understand the actual use of feedback and measure its impact.

4 Discussion and Further Work

Although very challenging, automated feedback is necessary to deal with current learning needs. While examining the literature, it became apparent that, although the research on feedback is very vast, the domain lacks a unified terminology. While some works are highly cited [24], there is also an abundance of different terms used for similar or even identical concepts by many authors: e.g., what some authors call elaborative feedback, others call formative feedback; or the term 'nature' may be known as 'valence' instead. The disparity in, and in some cases absence of, terminology makes it very hard to compare and consolidate contributions to a global theory on automated feedback. The creation of a framework offers a uniform terminology as a first step in organizing the vast amount of research on feedback into a global theory. See Table 1 as an example, where two relevant articles in the area of automated feedback are compared using the framework. The table shows the framework factors as rows, and the selected papers as columns. Besides framing the contributions of each article to automated feedback, the framework also facilitates to identify missing information (empty cells in the table) that may have been very useful for better understanding and contextualizing the articles' contribution and applying the articles' findings in the future.

For a preliminary validation, the current framework was presented to 30 professors in higher education in 2 different tutorials at the conferences ER 2018 and CAiSE 2018. The attendants were positive and highlighted the usefulness of the framework for understanding the different types of feedback available and the aspects that are needed to consider to provide it. Further research is however needed to formally assess the framework's practical utility. To that end, we plan to extend JMermaid [5], a tool that has been used for more than 10 years for teaching conceptual modeling by means of simulation enriched with feedback. The limited current feedback options that JMermaid provides will be extended with different kinds of feedback, and their usage and impact in different contexts will be evaluated by means of experimental evaluations.

Many links can be found among the presented factors. A few illustrative examples are as follows. Rosmalen et al. affirm that the combination of in- and about-action feedback (delivery timing) supports the enhancement of the learners' meta cognitive skills, such as self-monitoring, and self-regulation (self-regulation level) [35]. According to [24], the stage in the learning process (timing context) may be relevant according to the purpose of the feedback: if the purpose is to motivate learners to spend more effort in order to reach success, then early stages in the learning process may be more adequate to provide feedback. Presenting a complete overview of such relationships and how they contribute to the effectiveness of feedback would be a complement to the proposed framework, but is beyond the scope of this paper. Although this article does not provide a review of *all* literature on automated feedback, the framework provides a very ample theoretical foundation that contributes to better comprehend this area.

The application of the framework using a simple table (see Table 1) is a first approach, but can be considerably improved. The table can be the basis in future research of a semantic database that implements the framework in a machine-understandable format. Such database would allow the current literature on automated feedback to be appropriately represented and easily analysed in an automatic way. This can be further used to identify research gaps in the literature, e.g., lack of experimental evaluation to determine if a specific type of feedback is useful. Using the database, further research can be performed to find combinations of feedback design and delivery that are recommended in the literature for each specific context to increase its use and impact.

5 Conclusion

This paper has proposed a framework for automated feedback as an attempt to unify terminology, to provide theoretical foundation, and to provide an analytical tool that helps researchers and educators to better characterize and frame their research on automated feedback. The framework identifies and explains in detail a total of 6 core factors about feedback design, feedback results, and delivery means, finally subdivided into 16 subfactors with their corresponding alternatives that are important to be considered for automating feedback in a TEL environment. In addition, the framework can also serve as guidance to construct, deliver and test automated feedback in TEL environments. The benefits of such approach, however, still need to be measured and demonstrated in further developments and experiments.

References

[1] V. J. Shute, "Focus on formative feedback," *Rev. Educ. Res.*, 78, 1, pp. 153–89, 2008.

[2] D. Boud and E. Molloy, "Rethinking models of feedback for learning: the challenge of design," *Assess. Eval. High. Educ.*, 38, 6, pp. 1–15, 2012.

[3] G.-J. Hwang, "Definition , framework and research issues of smart learning environments - a context-aware ubiquitous learning perspective," *Smart Learn. Environ.*, 1,1, pp. 1–14, 2014.

[4] L. Gerard, C. Matuk, K. McElhaney, and M. C. Linn, "Automated, adaptive guidance for K-12 education," *Educ. Res. Rev.*, vol. 15, pp. 41–58, 2015.

[5] J. Ruiz, E. Serral, and M. Snoeck, "Technology Enhanced Support for Learning Interactive Software Systems," In MODELSWARD, 2018, pp. 185–210.

[6] A. Devi and K. Revathi, "A review of technology choice for teaching language skills and areas in the CALL literature," *ReCALL*, vol. 3, no. 0975-2935, pp. 262–268, 2016.

[7] J. Yuan and C. Kim, "Effective feedback design using free technologies," *J. Educ. Comput.*

Res., vol. 52, no. 3, pp. 408–434, 2015.
[8] T. Srivastava, L. S. Waghmare, and S. J. Vagha, "Revisiting feedback practices in formative assessment of Indian Medical Schools," *Natl. J. Physiol. Pharm. Pharmacol.*, vol. 5, no. 1, pp. 1–4, 2015.
[9] S. Gedye, "Formative assessment and feedback: A review," *Planet*, 23, 1, pp. 40–45, 2010.
[10] S. Narciss, "Designing and evaluating tutoring feedback strategies for digital learning environments on the basis of the interactive tutoring feedback model," *Digit. Educ. Rev.*, vol. 23, no. 1, pp. 7–26, 2013.
[11] M. D. M. Sánchez-Vera, J. T. Fernández-Breis, D. Castellanos-Nieves, F. Frutos-Morales, and M. P. Prendes-Espinosa, "Semantic Web technologies for generating feedback in online assessment environments," *Knowledge-Based Syst.*, vol. 33, pp. 152–165, 2012.
[12] J. W. Gikandi, D. Morrow, and N. E. Davis, "Online formative assessment in higher education: A review of the literature," *Comput. Educ.*, vol. 57, no. 4, pp. 2333–2351, 2011.
[13] F. M. Van Der Kleij, C. F. Timmers, and T. J. H. M. Eggen, "The effectiveness of methods for providing written feedback through a computer-based assessment for learning: A systematic review," *Cadmo*, vol. 19, no. 1, pp. 21–38, 2011.
[14] S. Hepplestone, G. Holden, B. Irwin, H. Parkin, and L. P. Thorpe, "Using technology to encourage student engagement with feedback: a literature review," *Res. Learn. Technol.*, vol. 19, no. 2, pp. 117–127, 2011.
[15] E. Serral and M. Snoeck, "Conceptual framework for feedback automation in SLEs, " *SEEL* 2016, Springer.
[16] J. A. Holton, "The coding process and its challenges," in *The Sage handbook of grounded theory*, & K. C. A. Bryant, Ed. Thousand Oaks, CA: Sage. nges., 2007, pp. 265–289.
[17] D. S. Campos, A. J. Mendes, M. J. Marcelino, D. J. Ferreira, and L. M. Alves, "A multinational case study on using diverse feedback types applied to introductory programming learning," *42nd Frontiers in Education Conference - FIE'12*, 2012, pp. 1–6.
[18] A. Jones *et al.*, "Creating Coherent Incidental Learning Journeys on Smartphones Using Feedback and Progress Indicators," *Int. J. Mob. Blended Learn.*, 6, 4, pp. 75–92, 2014.
[19] M. J. Martínez-Argüelles, D. Plana-Erta, C. Hintzmann-Colominas, M. Badia-Miró, and J. M. Batalla-Busquets, "Usefulness of feedback in e-Learning from the students' perspective," *ECEL*, pp. 283–292, 2013.
[20] Z. Tanes, K. E. Arnold, A. S. King, and M. A. Remnet, "Using Signals for appropriate feedback: Perceptions and practices," *Comput. Educ.*, vol. 57, no. 4, pp. 2414–2422, 2011.
[21] J. L. Owen and J. E. Dudley, "A Content Analysis of the Treatment of Informative and Reinforcing Feedback in Contemporary Communication Theory Textbooks," 9, 4, 2007.
[22] J. A. Stone, "Using reflective blogs for pedagogical feedback in CS1," in *SIGCSE*, 2012, pp. 259–264.
[23] I. Roll, V. Aleven, B. M. McLaren, and K. R. Koedinger, "Improving students' help-seeking skills using metacognitive feedback in an intelligent tutoring system," *Learn. Instr.*, vol. 21, no. 2, pp. 267–280, 2011.
[24] J. Hattie and H. Timperley, "The power of feedback," *Rev. Educ. Res.*, 77, 1, pp. 16–7, 2007.
[25] A. Mitrovic, S. Ohlsson, and D. Barrow, "The effect of positive feedback in a constraint-based intelligent tutoring system," *Comput. Educ.*, vol. 60, no. 1, pp. 264–272, 2013.
[26] P. Black and D. Wiliam, "Developing the theory of formative assessment," *Educ.*

Assessment, Eval. Account., vol. 21, no. 1, pp. 5–31, 2009.

[27] M. R. Weaver, "Do students value feedback? Student perceptions of tutors' written responses," *Assess. Eval. High. Educ.*, vol. 31, no. 3, pp. 379–394, 2006.

[28] Y. H. P. Iskandar, L. Gilbert, G. B. Wills, and N. Basir, "The Development of Semantic Feedback for Teaching and Learning in Physical Education," in *ICALT*, 2013, pp. 385–387.

[29] A. Pears, J. Harland, M. Hamilton, and R. Hadgraft, "What is feedback? connecting student perceptions to assessment practices," in *LaTiCE 2013*, 2013, 2015, pp. 106–113.

[30] Andreu Grimalt-reynes Mark Inverno, "Designing Educational Social Machines for Effective Feedback," in *International Conference e-Learning*, 2014, pp. 239–248.

[31] K. Ludvigsen, R. Krumsvik, and B. Furnes, "Creating formative feedback spaces in large lectures," *Comput. Educ.*, vol. 88, pp. 48–63, 2015.

[32] M. Vandewaetere, P. Desmet, and G. Clarebout, "The contribution of learner characteristics in the development of computer-based adaptive learning environments," *Comput. Human Behav.*, vol. 27, no. 1, pp. 118–130, 2011.

[33] A. Jonsson, "Facilitating productive use of feedback in higher education," *Act. Learn. High. Educ.*, vol. 14, no. 1, pp. 63–76, 2013.

[34] I. Rasmussen, A. Lund, and O. Smørdal, "Visualisation of trajectories of participation in a wiki: A basis for feedback and assessment?," *Nord. J. Digit. Lit.*, pp. 20–35, 2012.

[35] P. Van Rosmalen, D. Börner, J. Schneider, O. Petukhova, and J. Van Helvert, "Feedback Design in Multimodal Dialogue Systems," in *CSEDU*, 2015, pp. 209–217.

[36] D. R. Pridemore and J. D. Klein, "Control of Feedback in Computer-Assisted Instruction," *Educ. Technol. Res. Dev.*, vol. 39, no. 4, pp. 27–32, 2013.

[37] K. Verbert *et al.*, "Context-aware recommender systems for learning: a survey and future challenges," *IEEE Trans. Learn. Technol.*, vol. 5, no. 4, pp. 318–335, 2012.

[38] J. Segedy, J. S. Kinnebrew, and G. Biswas, "Supporting student learning using conversational agents in a teachable agent environment," in *ICLS,* 2012, pp. 251–255.

[39] G. Gibbs, "The importance of context in understanding teaching and learning: reflections on thirty five years of pedagogic research," in *Keynote at the International Society for the Scholarship of Teaching and Learning*, 2012.

[40] S. Bull, M. D. Johnson, C. D. Epp, D. Masci, M. Alotaibi, and S. Girard, "Formative Assessment and Meaningful Learning Analytics," in *14th ICALT*, 2014, pp. 327–329.

[41] P. Lehsten, R. Zender, U. Lucke, and D. Tavangarian, "A service-oriented approach towards context-aware mobile learning management systems," in *PERCOM Workshops*, 2010, pp. 268–273.

[42] G. Sedrakyan, J. De Weerdt, and M. Snoeck, "Process-mining enabled feedback: 'Tell me what I did wrong' vs. 'tell me how to do it right,'" *Comput. Human Behav.*, vol. 57, pp. 352–376, Apr. 2016.

[43] J. J. G. van Merriënboer, P. A. Kirschner, and L. Kester, "Taking the Load Off a Learner's Mind: Instructional Design for Complex Learning," *Educ. Psychol.*, 38, 1, pp. 5–13, 2003.

[44] C. Furnborough and M. Truman, "Adult beginner distance language learner perceptions and use of assignment feedback.," *Distance Educ.*, vol. 30, no. 3, pp. 399–418, 2009.

[45] K. Holmes and G. Papageorgiou, "Good, bad and insufficient: Students' expectations, perceptions and uses of feedback," *J. Hosp. Leis. Sport Tour. Educ.*, 8, 1, pp. 85–96, 2009.

[46] H. Pokorny and P. Pickford, "Complexity, cues and relationships: Student perceptions of feedback," *Act. Learn. High. Educ.*, vol. 11, no. 1, pp. 21–30, 2010.

Mantenibilidad y productividad en la enseñanza de la Ingeniería del Software: análisis cuantitativo de un enfoque práctico*

Yania Crespo González-Carvajal[1], Margarita Gonzalo Tasis[1], and Esperanza Manso Martínez[1]

Departamento de Informática, Universidad de Valladolid, España
{yania,marga,manso}@infor.uva.es

Resumen El desarrollo del software de fácil mantenimiento controlando la deuda técnica es cada vez más valorado en las empresas. Esto requiere entornos integrados que incluyan herramientas de medida, que proporcionan al desarrollador información relevante para que pueda mejorar el producto durante el desarrollo. A partir de esta idea se ha implantado una experiencia en la enseñanza relacionada con el desarrollo de proyectos software, cuyos objetivos han sido conocer y mejorar la productividad, el trabajo en equipo y la calidad del desarrollo fundamentalmente en cuanto a mantenibilidad, todo ello soportado por un entorno integrado de herramientas que faciliten dichos objetivos. Este trabajo presenta la evolución y adaptación de la experiencia, durante cuatro años, analizada desde el punto de vista de un estudio cuantitativo de la calidad, en cuanto a mantenibilidad, del trabajo realizado por los estudiantes y del control de su productividad. Los resultados nos muestran que al incorporar `SonarQube` se mejora la mantenibilidad y al incorporar `GitLab Issue Tracker` se aumenta el control de la productividad.

Keywords: Educación de Ingeniería del Software · productividad · mantenibilidad · estudio de casos ·

1. Introducción

En la actualidad, la demanda de software a gran escala, la transformación de espacios de producción en equipos de trabajo geográficamente distribuidos, la necesidad de reducir el tiempo de salida al mercado del producto desarrollado y la satisfacción del cliente han ido generando una multitud de tecnologías que se han tornado imprescindibles para el desarrollo de software.

En el curso 2014-2015 se introdujo en el plan de estudios del Grado de Ingeniería Informática de la Universidad de Valladolid la asignatura "Tecnologías para el Desarrollo de Software" para dotar al alumno de técnicas y herramientas que permiten agilizar la producción de software con garantías de calidad. Esta asignatura se ha sometido a un proceso de mejora continua, a lo largo de

* Este trabajo ha sido parcialmente financiado por los Proyectos de Innovación Docente de la Universidad de Valladolid PID2017/2018-28, PID2018/2019-38 y PID2018/2019-39.

cuatro cursos, con el objetivo de ayudar al alumno a mejorar su aprendizaje, interiorizando las mejores prácticas en el desarrollo de software, en particular en entornos de desarrollo *Agile*. Se hace énfasis en *Test Driven Development* (TDD) y el llamado ciclo *Red-Green-Refactor*, integración continua, entrega continua, gestión de la configuración, *pair programming*, etc.

Como resultado de este proceso, se propuso la implantación en los estudios de un entorno profesional (*on premises*) en el que se integran una serie de herramientas variadas para que el alumno pueda, entre otras cosas, mejorar su productividad, el cumplimiento de guías de estilo y de diseño, así como la gestión de la configuración y en particular el control de versiones. Las herramientas `GitLab` y `SonarQube` forman parte de esta solución en la actualidad.

En este trabajo se describe el proceso de mejora continua de la asignatura, y las mejoras que esta evolución ha supuesto en el desempeño práctico de los alumnos, mediante un análisis cuantitativo de un estudio de casos.

El artículo se organiza de la siguiente forma: en la Sección 2 se presenta el contexto: temas, secuenciación de la asignatura y evolución. A continuación en la Sección 3 se describen algunos trabajos relacionados. Posteriormente en la Sección 4 se presentan los objetivos y preguntas de investigación que nos hemos planteado. A continuación, en la Sección 5 se detalla el diseño del estudio realizado para posteriormente en la Sección 6 describir la forma en la que se llevó a cabo. En la Sección 7 se analizan los resultados obtenidos. Finalmente en la Sección 8 se presentan las amenazas a la validez y las conclusiones del estudio.

2. Contexto

"Tecnologías para el Desarrollo de Software" es una asignatura de tercer curso optativa de la mención de Ingeniería del Software. En el curso 2014-2015 se definieron sus contenidos y secuenciación de la siguiente forma:

Tema 1 Desarrollo basado en frameworks: Tipos, técnicas y ejemplos prácticos. Frameworks de aplicación vs Frameworks de dominio. Frameworks de caja blanca vs Frameworks de caja negra. Caja gris. Técnicas: método plantilla, anotaciones, lenguajes específicos de dominio. Lenguajes de la familia XML. XML vs JSON. Ejemplos prácticos. JAXP: The Java API for XML Processing. JSR: The Java API for JSON Processing. JUnit.

Tema 2 Prácticas Ágiles y TDD. El ciclo *Red-Green-Refactor*: Programación por pares. *Red*: TDD y *Test First*. Pruebas unitarias, automatización. Pruebas en aislamiento mediante *Mock Objects*. Otros casos especiales: Pruebas de aplicaciones que acceden a bases de datos, pruebas con documentos XML.

Tema 3 *Green*. Desarrollo y Depuración: Autodocumentación. Gestión de la Configuración. Repositorios. Control de Versiones. Configuración de Proyectos y Gestión de Dependencias. Integración continua y entrega continua. Cobertura y monitorización.

Tema 4 *Refactor*: Las Ws de Refactoring (What? When? Where? How?) Operaciones de Refactoring más utilizadas. Refactoring Scripts.

En su desarrollo práctico, en el 14-15, se utilizó Java, JUnit, EasyMock, `git`, (Atlassian) `Bitbucket`, Ant, Maven, Eclipse y sus plugins: EclEmma, Eclipse Metrics, Eclipse Refactoring.

2.1. Evolución

En el curso inicial, **2014-2015**, se pidió a los alumnos que llevasen una bitácora con la carga de horas (en horas-hombre) dedicadas a la asignatura, haciendo especial énfasis en las prácticas. Adicionalmente se solicitó que obtuviesen con el apoyo de Eclipse Metrics y EclEmma algunas métricas de tamaño, de calidad de los tests, etc. de cada práctica realizada y lo reflejasen en un archivo README.md conjuntamente con la cantidad de horas-hombre que había representado el desarrollo de la práctica. Por último se hizo énfasis en documentar mediante javadoc para mejorar la comprensibilidad de su desarrollo.

Sin embargo, se constató que, salvo en casos excepcionales, la documentación javadoc, si la había, era escasa y de poca calidad. Además, al revisar las entregas de los alumnos, se advirtió que pocas tenían el archivo README.md y de tenerlo, en aún menos casos se indicaban las mediciones solicitadas.

Se realizó una encuesta anónima, voluntaria y offline entre los estudiantes. Respondieron 18 de los 28 matriculados. De dicha encuesta se obtuvo la siguiente información. La media de las horas dedicadas a las prácticas de la asignatura fue de $78,67$ horas. Los estudiantes registraron varias propuestas de mejora entre las que destaca repetidas veces: (a) "Relajar" los contenidos de XML, si bien lo consideran necesario por la naturaleza de los lenguajes específicos de dominio con los que se trabaja, (b) introducir antes en el temario el control del versiones y (c) profundizar más en temas de integración continua y automatización.

Teniendo en cuenta esto, para el curso **2015-2016** se trabajó, por una parte, en introducir en asignaturas del año inferior (segundo) todo lo necesario para que llegasen a ésta dominando mejor el uso de javadoc y lo básico de JUnit. Con esto y, aligerando el contenido de los lenguajes de la familia XML, se consiguió más tiempo para profundizar en la integración continua y la automatización.

Se realizó la misma encuesta que el curso anterior, pero sólo 9 de los 24 matriculados respondieron. Se piensa que influyó el cambio del calendario académico en la escasa participación. El segundo cuatrimestre comenzó demasiado pronto y los estudiantes ya estaban inmersos en ello cuando se pasó la encuesta. La media de horas dedicadas a las prácticas, según los encuestados, fue de $84,29$. Entre las propuestas de mejora volvía a destacar la sugerencia de introducir lo primero de todo el control de versiones para poder realizar todas las prácticas desde el principio utilizándolo e ir puliendo su uso a lo largo del desarrollo de la asignatura.

De esta forma, a lo largo del curso **2016-2017** se introdujeron mejoras en las prácticas, y se fue trabajando en modificar la secuenciación de los contenidos y de los objetivos de las mismas. En concreto en este curso se introduce el concepto de Deuda Técnica [1]; el uso de PMD como plugin de Eclipse para analizar la calidad del código y se incluyó en el enunciado que los alumnos preparen un objetivo ant llamado "medidas" en el que se pide obtener medidas de tamaño, complejidad ciclomática, etc. Se introduce el uso de una herramienta de time tracking para controlar el tiempo dedicado a las prácticas. Los alumnos en una encuesta realizada indican que no les ha gustado utilizar esta herramienta.

Finalmente, para el curso **2017-2018** se introdujo como **Tema 0**, la **gestión básica de la configuración y el control de versiones**. El uso de `git` como control de versiones en local, `GitLab` *on premises* como repositorio remoto, `Bitbucket` como mirror, y `GitLab Issue Tracker` como su nombre indica como parte de la gestión de la configuración y el control de la productividad. En este curso se introdujo el uso de `SonarQube` para el control de la calidad de sus prácticas 3 y 4 como parte de un pipeline de integración continua preparado en `GitLab` basado en objetivos Ant y Maven. Se introdujeron las medidas del modelo SQALE [4] relacionadas con la Deuda Técnica y soportadas por `SonarQube`.

El enunciado de las prácticas evolucionó de tal forma que el propio documento que describe el enunciado contiene: la descripción del supuesto a realizar pero también una guía precisa de lo que se espera, los criterios de evaluación desglosados y una recopilación de problemas frecuentes a ser evitados por los estudiantes, de forma tal que el propio enunciado es un documento que facilita el aprendizaje y la autoevaluación.

En los enunciados de las prácticas 1 y 2 se indica que la gestión de la configuración (issue tracker y control de versiones) se exige pero no se evalúa. De esta forma los estudiantes se ven motivados a hacerlo y van aprendiendo hasta llegar las prácticas 3 y 4 donde ya sí se evalúa cómo se realiza el control de versiones. Concretamente se evalúa la forma en la que se realiza la estrategia "rama por tarea", realizando fusiones (merges) y resolución de conflictos.

El objetivo principal de la práctica 2 es realizar en parejas la fase *Red* del ciclo TDD. En la práctica 3, a partir de lo diseñado en la práctica 2 y la especificación descrita en el javadoc así como en los tests ("la especificación está en los tests"), se realiza la fase *Green* del ciclo TDD. Finalmente en la práctica 4 se realiza de forma individual un desarrollo de pequeño tamaño abordando una iteración del ciclo TDD completo *Red-Green-Refactor*. El control de versiones se evalúa, pero además se utiliza para revisitar el desarrollo de los alumnos y comprobar que se ha realizado en este orden: TDD y *Test First*, desarrollar el código más simple que pasa los tests, mejorar los test para aumentar la cobertura y, finalmente, buscar oportunidades de mejora del código mediante refactoring. Siempre teniendo en cuenta que un proceso de refactoring debe abordarse sólo si los tests pasan en verde.

3. Trabajos relacionados

En una línea similar a nuestro trabajo se encuentra [5]. Los sujetos del estudio son 100 estudiantes de Ingeniería de Sistemas, sin especificar el contexto de alguna asignatura, y los objetos son 40 aplicaciones escritas en distintos lenguajes de programación. El objetivo es utilizar análisis estático del código fuente para identificar qué métricas pueden ayudar a mejorar la calidad de las aplicaciones cuando se está escribiendo código. Las métricas utilizadas tienen que ver principalmente con la complejidad, problemas potenciales y deuda técnica. Se utiliza `SonarQube` para recoger las métricas de diferentes tipos, y el estándar y guías utilizados son ISO 9126 y SQALE. El estudio concluye que el uso de estándares, guías y modelos de calidad, mejoran las características que forman parte de la deuda técnica. Además, en los casos en que esto se ha obviado ha sido a expensas de incrementar sensiblemente la deuda técnica.

El uso de `GitHub` como plataforma de aprendizaje se analiza en [3]. Los sujetos son estudiantes de dos asignaturas, una de grado y una de posgrado. De los posibles 50 sujetos finalmente participan 19. Se recoge información de los estudiantes mediante una encuesta y se dan recomendaciones a los diseñadores de `GitHub` sobre cambios a tener en cuenta en sus características para mejorar su aplicabilidad en un entorno educativo. Adicionalmente se brindan recomendaciones para utilizar de forma más efectiva `GitHub` en la enseñanza. En [6] también se estudia el uso de `GitHub` y `SonarQube` analizando el feedback recibido de los estudiantes mediante una encuesta que indica que los estudiantes se sienten motivados por el uso de este entorno.

El trabajo que se presenta en [2] es el que tiene más puntos en común con este estudio. En él se analiza la evolución en diferentes semestres, estudia diferentes aspectos de los proyectos. En particular comenta sobre la información de deuda técnica obtenida con `SonarQube` y la cantidad de issues de diferentes niveles de seguridad.

Nuestro estudio mejora los anteriores principalmente en los siguientes puntos: (a) se estudian métricas de producto relacionadas con mantenibilidad y de productividad; (b) el tipo de estudio es longitudinal, i.e, hay un proceso de recogida de información a lo largo de diferentes años, que permite estudiar los cambios que se producen en la calidad final de los proyectos, cuando los alumnos disponen de diferentes métricas-guía en el desarrollo e implementación; (c) se realiza un estudio descriptivo y exploratorio de la información para extraer conclusiones útiles; y (d) es el único que hemos encontrado que utiliza `GitLab` *on premises* lo cual tiene ventajas en un entorno educativo porque se soluciona la gestión de usuarios, la protección de datos y la privacidad. Al igual que [5] utilizamos SQALE pero en el marco de la evolución de ISO 9126 a 25000 (SQuaRE).

4. Objetivos del estudio

El objetivo de este estudio es analizar si el proceso de mejora continua implantado en la asignatura contribuye al desempeño práctico de los alumnos en cuanto a desarrollar con mejor calidad, desde el punto de vista de la mantenibilidad, tanto el código como las pruebas automatizadas, y en cuanto al control de su productividad. Son dos aspectos esenciales en los que se hace énfasis en esta asignatura y les sirven de base para el resto de su vida académica y laboral.

La familia de normas ISO/IEC 25000, conocida como SQuaRE (System and Software Quality Requirements and Evaluation), tiene como objetivo la creación de un marco de trabajo común para evaluar la calidad del producto software y es el resultado de la evolución de otras normas anteriores, especialmente de las normas ISO/IEC 9126. En concreto ISO/IEC 25010 describe el modelo de calidad para el producto software presenta las características y subcaracterísticas de calidad frente a las cuales evaluarlo. La característica de calidad Mantenibililidad de este modelo es importante en este trabajo porque a lo largo de las asignaturas de programación anteriores y en ésta se hace énfasis en desarrollar software para que sea más mantenible.

Así, las preguntas de investigación que nos plantearemos son las siguientes:

Q1: ¿Los cambios introducidos mejoran el control de la productividad de los alumnos?

Q2: ¿Los cambios introducidos mejoran la mantenibilidad del software desarrollado por los alumnos?

Curso	Sujetos	Proyectos par.	Proyectos indiv.	Herramientas	Mejoras
14-15	28	15	22	`git`, `Bitbucket`, Ant, Maven, Eclipse+plugins: EclEmma, Eclipse Metrics, Eclipse Refactoring	README.md con anotaciones de horas-hombre
15-16	24	12	20	ídem	test unitarios y JUnit se introducen en asignatura de curso anterior, se profundiza en integración continua y automatización
16-17	25	12	25	ídem + pmd + time tracking	se introduce el concepto de deuda técnica, se pide registrar tiempo con time tracking, se pide explícitamente en prácticas realizar objetivo ant "medidas"
17-18	24	12	19	ídem + `GitLab` + `SonarQube` (incluye PMD as plugin) + `GitLab Issue Tracker`	tema 0 control de versiones y gestión básica de la configuración, se pide registrar tiempo con `GitLab Issue Tracker`, se vincula deuda técnica con SQALE, se cambia el objetivo ant "medidas" para obtener el análisis de `SonarQube`

Tabla 1. Esquema de la cronología del estudio

5. Diseño y ejecución del estudio

En esta sección se describe el diseño y ejecución del estudio, qué se ha hecho y cómo se ha realizado. La Tabla 1 muestra de forma resumida el contexto y la evolución de la asignatura comentados en la Sección 2 que sirve como guía para el diseño del estudio de casos. A partir de ahí se describen en los siguientes apartados las variables independientes y dependientes a tener en cuenta, los sujetos participantes, objetos y herramientas del estudio.

5.1. Variables dependientes e independientes

Las variables **independientes** son las condiciones en las que han realizado los alumnos las prácticas cada curso, en cuanto a herramientas utilizadas, contenidos impartidos y enunciados de las prácticas. Las dos últimas columnas de la Tabla 1 lo reflejan. Eliminando todo lo que es común, las variables independientes serían variables booleanas cuyos valores para cada curso se muestran en forma de vector: $v_{pmd} = [0, 0, 1, 1]$, $v_{timetracking} = [0, 0, 1, 1]$, $v_{gitlab} = [0, 0, 0, 1]$, $v_{gitlabIssueTracker} = [0, 0, 0, 1]$, $v_{sonarqube} = [0, 0, 0, 1]$ en cuanto a herramientas; $v_{technicaldebt} = [0, 0, 1, 1]$, $v_{sqale} = [0, 0, 0, 1]$ en cuanto a contenidos; y $v_{ant\_medidas} = [0, 0, 1, 1]$ y $v_{malaspracticas} = [0, 0, 0, 1]$ en cuanto a enunciado.

Para responder a Q1, productividad y control del tiempo, la variable **dependiente** v_{hh} mide las horas-hombre empleadas en la resolución de las prácticas. Por otra parte, el control de la productividad por parte de los alumnos se mide analizando cuántos registros de datos de horas-hombre empleadas en la resolución de cada práctica se tienen en cada curso. Se estudia con más detalle el control del tiempo registrado mediante `GitLab Issue Tracker` en el último curso.

Para responder a Q2 las variables **dependientes** serán métricas con escala de ratio para evitar limitaciones en el uso de recursos para valorar los datos observados. Se prefieren porcentajes y ratios a valores absolutos.

Se tomaron las métricas *lines*, *lines of code*, *classes* que indica la cantidad de clases, *complexity* que calcula la complejidad ciclomática para medir la cantidad de caminos diferentes desde la entrada hasta la salida, es decir, un recuento de estos caminos y *branches to cover* que recuentan las condiciones que deben ser cubiertas por los tests. Estas métricas, todas absolutas, se incluyeron para caracterizar los proyectos y poder constatar que se trata de proyectos comparables en cuanto a tamaño y dificultad a la hora de conseguir altos niveles de cobertura.

En las prácticas de esta asignatura solamente se permiten comentarios javadoc en el código. Se explica el principio "si tienes necesidad de escribir un comentario, escribe una función". Se evalúa la calidad de los comentarios javadoc de cara a mejorar la comprensibilidad y por tanto la mantenibilidad. De ahí que se consideró como medida interesante a tener en cuenta la cantidad de líneas de comentarios (métrica *comment lines*) lo que nos permite calcular la ratio densidad de comentarios *comment lines/lines of code*.

Dentro de la Mantenibilidad se encuentran diferentes subcaracterísticas. Una de ellas es la que se denomina "capacidad de ser probado" (*testability*). En esta asignatura se trabaja mucho este aspecto. Para medir *testatibility* se usan, por una parte, número de tests (métrica *tests*) como base para calcular la tasa conocida como *code-to-tests=tests/lines of code*, porcentaje de éxito de los tests (*unit test success*) y medidas de cobertura. Las métricas de cobertura (*coverage*) se calculan de forma tal que se realiza una combinación de *lines_ coverage* y *branch_ coverage*. La métrica *lines_ coverage* no es interesante en este estudio porque es muy fácil obtener altos niveles de este tipo de cobertura en proyectos de tamaño pequeño. Por tanto incluimos en el estudio *branch_ coverage* que es la componente que hace la diferencia. Las métricas de cobertura son porcentajes.

De cara a evaluar la Mantenibilidad es importante detectar la presencia de *Code Smells*. Por ello se incluye la métrica *code smells* que calcula la cantidad total de éstos presentes en el código. A partir de esta cantidad absoluta se calculará la densidad de smells como *smells density = code smells/lines of code*. Precisamente en relación con esto, y según SQALE, se consideraran las métricas *technical debt* que representa el tiempo acumulado para resolver los problemas de calidad en el código; y *technical debt ratio* que, como su nombre indica, es una ratio respecto del total de líneas desarrolladas. No se incluye la métrica *technical debt*, porque su valor absoluto no sirve para comparar proyectos de diferentes tamaños. Se incluye en el estudio *technical debt ratio*. En SQALE se define la métrica *maintainability rating* (conocida precisamente como SQALE). Se decide **no** incluir ésta como variable en el estudio porque todos los proyectos dan el mismo resultado para esta métrica ya que son desarrollos demasiado pequeños como para poder diferenciarse en cuanto a las categorías (intervalos) con las que se define ésta. Por la misma razón **no** se incluye *effort to reach maintainability rating A* porque casi todos están en el mismo rating.

En resumen, las variables dependientes serán las métricas: *comment density = comment lines/lines of code*, *code to test = tests/lines of code*, *unit test success*, *branch_coverage*, *smells density = code smells/lines of code* y *technical debt ratio*.

5.2. Sujetos participantes y objetos del estudio

Los sujetos participantes son los alumnos matriculados en la asignatura a lo largo de 4 cursos: 28+24+25+24=91 alumnos en total sin repeticiones. Son alumnos de tercero de grado de la mención en Ingeniería del Software y habitualmente antes de realizar esta asignatura ya han cursado: Fundamentos de Programación, Paradigmas de Programación, Programación Orientada a Objetos, Estructuras de Datos y Fundamentos de Ingeniería del Software.

Las prácticas 3 y 4 serán los objetos de estudio. Es en ellas donde puede analizarse tanto la calidad del código como de los tests, y, por otro lado, los alumnos ya llegan entrenados en el uso del `GitLab Issue Tracker` estimando y anotando el tiempo empleado en cada tarea. La práctica 3, como las anteriores 1 y 2, se realizan en parejas (aplicando *pair programming*). La práctica 4 es individual y se utiliza en sustitución del examen. Los sujetos participantes son los que se presentaron a esta modalidad. Se recogen datos de las prácticas 3 y 4 de los cuatro cursos 2014-2015, 2015-2016, 2016-2017 y 2017-2018.

6. Ejecución del estudio

En esta sección se describe cómo se ha llevado a cabo el estudio, la automatización y recogida de datos y la obtención de mediciones.

6.1. Obtención de las medidas de Productividad

Se realizó un recuento manual de los archivos README.md entregados con las prácticas en los cursos 14-15, 15-16 y 16-17, y se buscó en cada uno de ellos si se había indicando la cantidad de horas-hombre dedicadas. Se tomó nota de los valores encontrados y se obtuvieron medias. De las encuestas realizadas los cursos 14-15 y 15-16 se recogieron lo que los encuestados aportan como horas dedicadas a las prácticas.

Para el curso 17-18 se descargó la información anotada en el `GitLab Issue Tracker` de 28 proyectos y se procesó para obtener los totales del tiempo en horas-hombre empleado. De éstos, 10 corresponden a la práctica 3 y 18 corresponden a la práctica 4. Se recogió toda esta información y se anonimizó.

De estos proyectos, uno (etiquetado como 'P4.13') no anota ni la estimación del tiempo ni el tiempo empleado, y por tanto se saca del estudio. Otros dos proyectos ('P4.1' y 'P4.12') no anotan finalmente el tiempo empleado en cada tarea, quizás por falta de tiempo al llegar a la fecha de entrega, aunque sí realizan estimaciones. Pero se deciden sacar del estudio debido a los ceros en el tiempo empleado. En el resto de proyectos queda alguna tarea sin anotar pero muchas anotadas por lo que se mantienen en el estudio los 25 restantes.

Curso	Parejas (p3)	Individual (p4)
2014-2015	15	22
2015-2016	12	20
2016-2017	12	25
2017-2018	12	19
Total	51	86

Tabla 2. Proyectos recogidos en SonarQube automáticamente

Curso	Parejas (p3)	Individual (p4)
2014-2015	15	22
2015-2016	11	20
2016-2017	12	20
2017-2018	10	18
Total	48	80

Tabla 3. Proyectos incluidos finalmente en el estudio.

6.2. Obtención de las medidas de Mantenibilidad

Las medidas para las métricas como variables dependientes se obtuvieron con SonarQube. El servidor SonarQube utilizado calcula 139 métricas identificadas con nombre, clave o identificador y el tipo de la métrica. En https://docs.sonarqube.org/display/SONARQUBE56/Metric+Definitions se puede consultar la documentación de las métricas. La versión del servidor SonarQube utilizada es la 5.6.6. Dado que era la que teníamos instalada cuando la utilizaron los estudiantes el curso 17-18 en las prácticas 3 y 4 (https://sonarqube2.inf.uva.es).

Se automatizó la recogida de datos de todos los proyectos. Para esto se definió un pom file que responde al arquetipo maven-quickstart. Este arquetipo era el que debían utilizar los alumnos al desarrollar las prácticas p3 y p4 en todos los cursos. De ahí que la estructura de todos los proyectos era la misma. Se introdujeron en el pom file todas las dependencias necesarias para todos los proyectos a lo largo de los 4 cursos. En el pom file también se configuraron todos los plugins necesarios para producir los informes de ejecución de los tests, el análisis de cobertura, así como los análisis de calidad con SonarQube. De esta forma se pudo tratar a todos los proyectos por igual y automatizar los análisis, aunque no se hubiese usado SonarQube más que en el curso 17-18.

Se anonimizaron los proyectos y todos los pom files de todas las prácticas se sustituyeron mediante un script del shell por el pom file preparado, generando un identificador de proyecto único para cada una siguiendo un patrón que permite distinguir curso y práctica. Con esta automatización se subieron 137 proyectos al servidor SonarQube cuya distribución por curso y práctica se puede consultar en la Tabla 2.

A partir de este punto toda la automatización se realizó utilizando R. Se lanzaron peticiones http al servidor SonarQube para obtener mediciones de las métricas elegidas para todos los proyectos. Sin embargo, para un grupo de proyectos no fue posible obtener dichas métricas. Se detectó que eran proyectos para los que no se podían obtener *branches to cover* o *complexity* porque a los autores no les dio tiempo de terminar la práctica y no habían podido llegar a implementar todos los métodos. Dado que la aproximación a seguir en estas prácticas se basa en "TDD" & "Test first", estos proyectos tenían un conjunto de tests para producir los *stubs* y la especificación de las clases ("TDD") y los tests de caja negra ("Test first"), es decir, la parte Red, pero no llegaban a implementar los *stubs* para poder llegar a Green y, por tanto, tampoco a Refactor. Estos proyectos se excluyen del estudio. Finalmente participan un total de 128 proyectos cuya distribución por curso y práctica se puede consultar en la Tabla 3.

Id	Time.Estimate	Time.Spent
P3.1	9.000000	12.666667
P3.2	28.833333	31.883333
P3.3	5.250000	5.380556
P3.4	8.833333	10.133333
P3.5	102.166667	35.068333
P3.6	10.500000	4.533333
P3.7	21.250000	30.000000
P3.8	21.500000	23.000000
P3.9	9.833333	8.450000
P3.10	35.666667	36.143056

Id	Time.Estimate	Time.Spent
P4.2	23.916667	19.983333
P4.3	24.583333	24.500000
P4.4	13.500000	13.683333
P4.5	14.000000	10.500000
P4.6	4.233333	3.236389
P4.7	19.500000	20.166667
P4.8	28.500000	26.666667
P4.9	22.750000	24.666667
P4.10	23.000000	21.266667
P4.11	9.250000	9.283333
P4.14	33.000000	27.600000
P4.15	11.000000	10.833333
P4.16	14.766667	13.766667
P4.17	25.833333	34.319444
P4.18	5.083333	5.166667

Summary

		P3		P4	
Projects		Time.Estimate	Time.Spent	Time.Estimate	Time.Spent
Total:25	Min.:	5.250	4.533	4.233	3.236
P3: 10	1st Qu.:	9.208	8.871	12.250	10.667
P4: 15	Median:	15.875	17.833	19.500	19.983
	Mean:	25.283	19.726	18.194	17.709
	3rd Qu.:	27.000	31.413	24.250	24.583
	Max.:	102.167	36.143	33.000	34.319

Tabla 4. Estimaciones y tiempos empleados en los proyectos en el curso 2017-2018 registrados utilizando `GitLab Issue Tracker`.

7. Análisis de Resultados

En cuanto a Q1, control de productividad, se han recogido los siguientes datos v_{hh} totales en las 4 prácticas de la asignatura. Se muestran a continuación indicando la fuente de la que se ha obtenido.

curso	14-15	15-16	16-17	17-18
fuente	encuesta	encuesta	-	issue tracker
medias	78,67	84,29	-	69

Para las prácticas p3 y p4 de los tres cursos anteriores al 17-18 solamente se ha podido obtener de los README.md un registro para la práctica 4 frente a los 10 de p3 y 15 de p4 del 17-18. En la Tabla 4 se observan los totales por proyecto del tiempo estimado y el empleado así como los estadísticos más habituales, media, mediana, entre otros, de las prácticas 3 y 4 del curso 17-18. 'P3.5' es un outlier en estimación. Tal parece que no se intentó estimar sino que simplemente se indicaron tiempos muy grandes. 'P3.3', 'P4.6' y 'P4.18' son outliers porque solamente anotaron la estimación y el tiempo de algunas de las tareas.

La introducción de `GitLab Issue Tracker` ha tenido como consecuencia que prácticamente todas las entregas de prácticas en 17-18 mantienen un issue tracker y anotan para cada tarea el tiempo estimado y el tiempo empleado en realizarla. Todo un éxito comparado con los cursos anteriores.

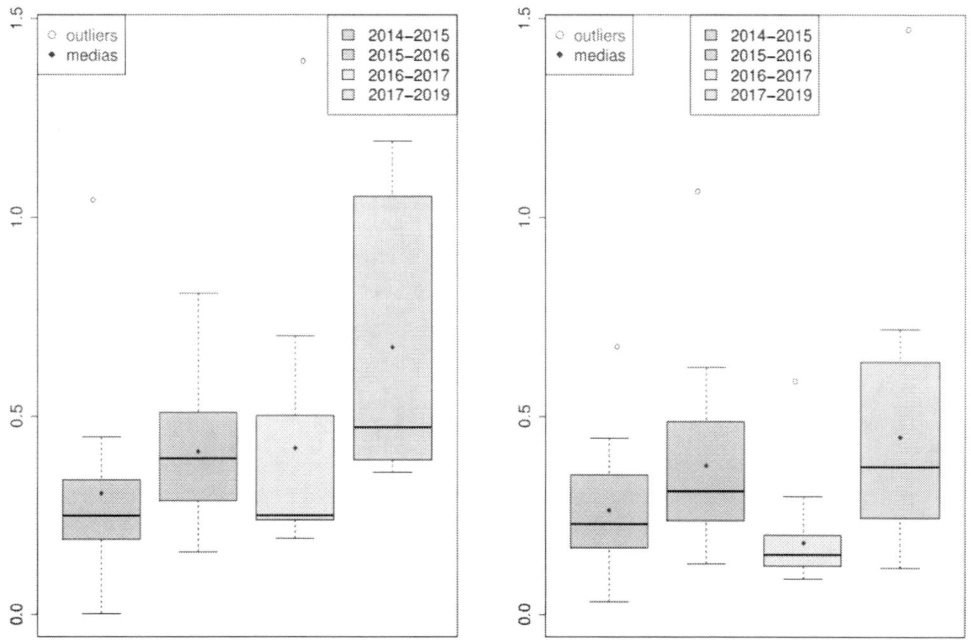

Figura 1. Evolución de la ratio code to test mediante boxplots: práctica por parejas (p3) a la izquierda y práctica individual (p4) a la derecha.

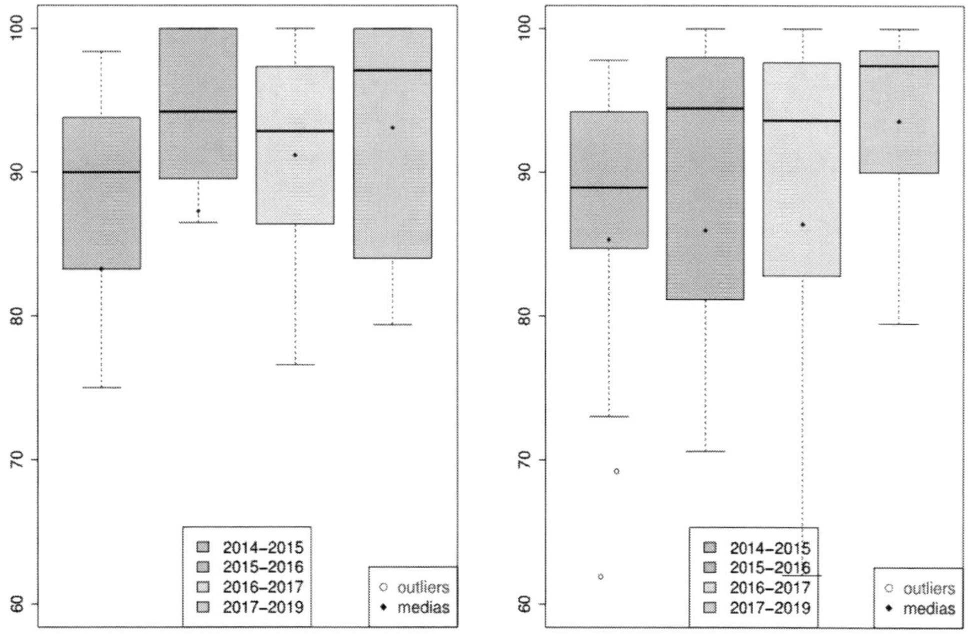

Figura 2. Evolución de branch_coverage mediante boxplots: práctica por parejas (p3) a la izquierda y práctica individual (p4) a la derecha.

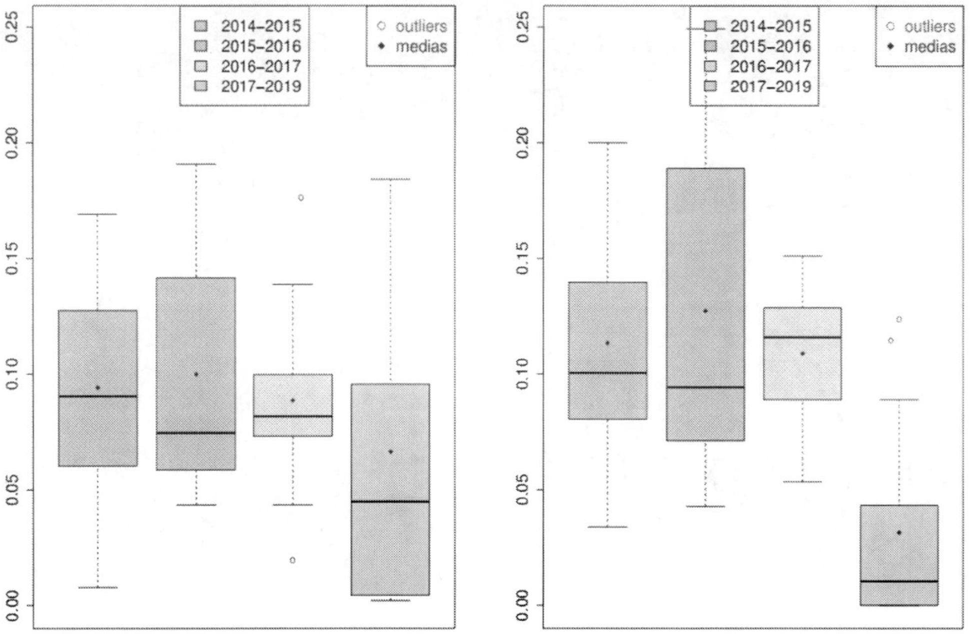

Figura 3. Evolución de la densidad de *Code Smells* según las reglas comprobadas por `SonarQube` mediante boxplots: práctica por parejas (p3) a la izquierda y práctica individual (p4) a la derecha.

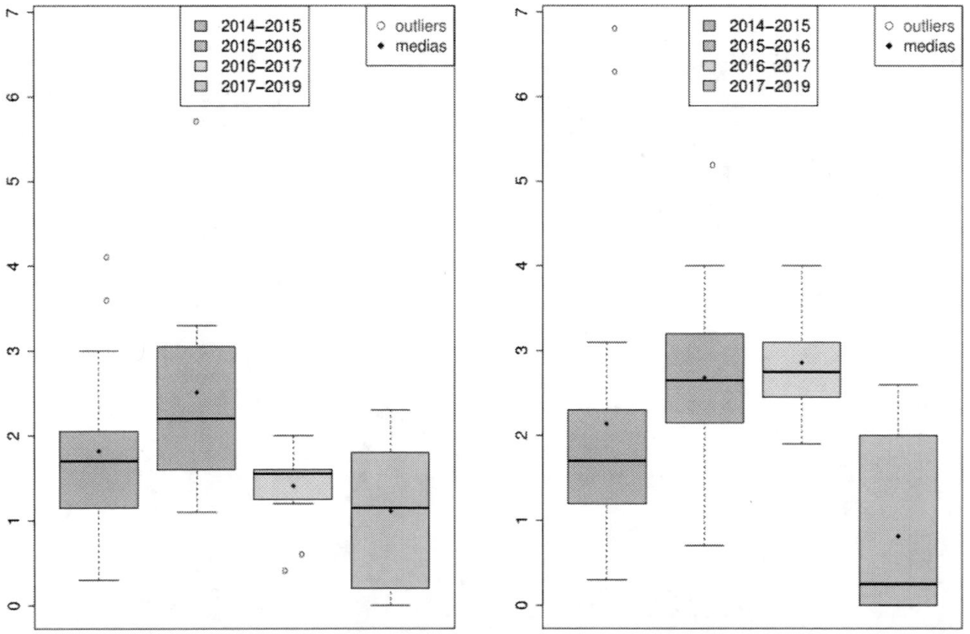

Figura 4. Evolución de las medidas relativas a la ratio de deuda técnica mediante boxplots: práctica por parejas (p3) a la izquierda y práctica individual (p4) a la derecha.

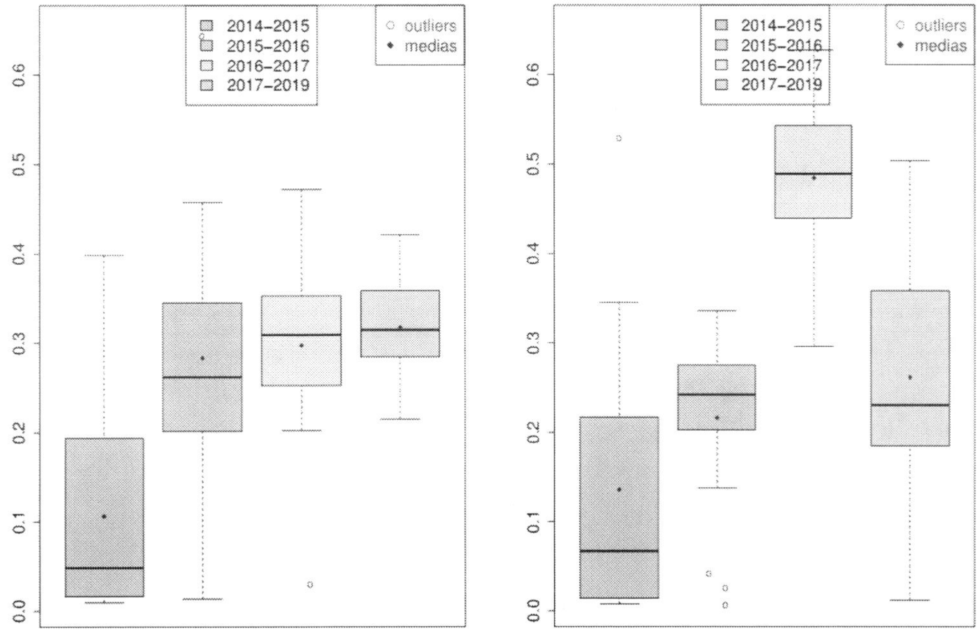

Figura 5. Evolución de la densidad de comentarios mediante boxplots: práctica por parejas (p3) a la izquierda y práctica individual (p4) a la derecha.

En cuanto a Q2, Mantenibilidad, Los resultados obtenidos se muestran en boxplots enriquecidos con rombos azules para indicar los valores de la media y círculos rojos que muestran *outliers*. Se presentan en paralelo siempre dos gráficos, el primero para las prácticas por parejas (P3) y el segundo para las individuales (P4). En la Figura 1 se puede ver cómo se incrementa la ratio de cantidad de tests por funcionalidad desarrollada (medida en líneas de código) siendo mucho mayor en el 17-18, tanto en P3 como en P4. En la Figura 2 se observa que la métrica branch_coverage en el curso 17-18 es mejor en media, mediana y también se comportan mejor los cuartiles inferior y superior tanto para P3 como para P4.

La densidad de *Code Smells* detectados en el curso 17-18 (Figura 3) es menor en el curso 17-18 tanto en P3 como en P4, aunque en P4 la diferencia con los otros años es mayor. Este resultado es muy importante para los objetivos del estudio porque refleja que, antes de usar `SonarQube`, en el último paso del ciclo TDD (fase *Refactor*), los estudiantes iban a ciegas buscando oportunidades de refactoring para mejorar su código. Sin embargo, el 17-18 se aprecia en P4 que en esta fase refactorizan eliminando la presencia de *Code Smells* y reduciendo así la deuda técnica como se ve también en la Figura 4.

En la Figura 5 se muestra una evolución positiva de la densidad de comentarios en P3, aunque en P4 es mejor el 16-17 que el 17-18. Si bien cantidad no es calidad, se aprecia el esfuerzo por mejorar la documentación pública del API.

8. Conclusiones y amenazas a la validez

La mejora del entorno de desarrollo de software realizada durante cuatro años, en el ámbito de la enseñanza, se ha completado en el último curso 17-18 incorporando `GitLab` y `SonarQube` como herramientas de medida y control que han incrementado la calidad de los proyectos desarrollados. Adicionalmente, la mejora de los enunciados de las prácticas así como el cambio en la secuenciación de la asignatura parece tener un efecto positivo como indudablemente ha tenido un efecto motivador y muy positivo el uso de `GitLab Issue Tracker` en el control de la productividad. A los alumnos les ha servido para ir practicando en realizar estimaciones de tareas no muy grandes descomponiéndolas en subtareas más pequeñas, y se ha conseguido finalmente que casi todos lleven un registro del tiempo, lo cual les sirve para reflexionar sobre su productividad. Según los criterios de evaluación, la parte correspondiente a usar el issue tracker (estimar el tiempo y registrar el tiempo empleado) es mínima. Sin embargo, los estudiantes manifiestan sentirse motivados por el uso de este entorno.

En el caso del estudio sobre productividad, la validez se amenaza porque la medida horas-hombre no estaba disponible en muchos casos. Por otra parte, en el estudio sobre Mantenibilidad, los resultados obtenidos son dependientes de la versión de `SonarQube` y de los algoritmos que usan para obtener las métricas. Además, en el caso de ambos estudios, los alumnos son diferentes en cada curso, así que los resultados pueden estar sesgados por el conocimiento que tienen los alumnos de cada año. Esta amenaza se podría evitar evaluando a los alumnos para clasificarlos por dicha evaluación. En cuanto a los objetos del estudio, los proyectos varían de un año a otro, pero en este caso la amenaza se ve paliada porque el grado de dificultad es similar lo cual queda corroborado por las medidas de complejidad y tamaño de los mismos.

Referencias

1. Allman, E.: Managing technical debt. Communications of ACM **55**(5) (May 2012)
2. Delgado, D., Velasco, A., Aponte, J., Marcus, A.: Evolving a project-based software engineering course: a case study. In: The 30th IEEE Conference on Software Engineering Education and Training. pp. 77–86 (2017)
3. Feliciano, J., Storey, M., Zagalsky, A.: Student experiences using github in software engineering courses: A case study. In: 2016 IEEE/ACM 38th International Conference on Software Engineering Companion (ICSE-C). pp. 422–431 (May 2016)
4. Letouzey, J.L., Ilkiewicz, M.: Managing technical debt with the SQALE method. IEEE Software **29** (2012)
5. Quezada Sarmiento, P., Guaman, D., Barba Guamán, L.R., Enciso, L., Cabrera, P.: Sonarqube as a tool to identify software metrics and technical debt in the source code through static analysis. In: Proceedings of 2017 the 7th International Workshop on Computer Science and Engineering. pp. 171–175 (07 2017)
6. Raibulet, C., Arcelli Fontana, F.: Collaborative and teamwork software development in an undergraduate software engineering course. The Journal of Systems & Software **144**, 409 – 422 (2018)

The RoCS Framework to Support the Development of Autonomous Robots

Leonardo Ramos, Gabriel Divino, Breno Bernard Nicolau de França, Leonardo Montecchi, and Esther Colombini

Universidade Estadual de Campinas
Campinas, SP, Brazil
leo.o.rms@gmail.com, gabriel.lg.divino@gmail.com,
{breno,leonardo,esther}@ic.unicamp.br

Abstract. With the expansion of autonomous robotics and its applications (e.g. medical, competition, military), the biggest hurdle in developing mobile robots lies in endowing them with the ability to interact with the environment and to make correct decisions so that their tasks can be executed successfully. However, as the complexity of robotic systems grows, the need to organize and modularize software for their correct functioning also becomes a challenge, making the development of software for controlling robots a complex and intricate task. In the robotics domain there is a lack of reference software architectures and, although most robot architectures available in the literature facilitate the creation process with their modularity, existing solutions do not provide development guidance on reusing existing modules. Based on the well-known IBM Autonomic Computing reference architecture (known as MAPE-K), this work defines a refined architecture following the Robotics perspective. To explore the capabilities of the proposed refinement, we implemented the RoCS (Robotics and Cognitive Systems) framework for autonomous robots. We successfully tested the framework under simulated robotics scenarios that mimic typical robotics tasks. Finally, we understand the proposed framework needs experimental evaluation as well as assessments on real-world scenarios.

Keywords: Robotics, Software Architecture, Autonomous Computing.

1 Introduction

With the expansion of autonomous robotics and its applications (e.g. medical, competition, military), the biggest hurdle in developing mobile robots lies in endowing them with the ability to interact with the environment and to make correct decisions so that their tasks can be executed successfully.

Typically operating in the real world — of continuous, unknown, and often unpredictable nature — it is expected that robots act through their perception, reasoning, planning, and decision-making process to accomplish their goals. With the expansion of cooperative, distributed and assistive robotics and the widespread utilization of bipedal, aerial, and aquatic robots, other challenges were incorporated, such as multiple robot coordination, human-robot interaction, and three-dimensional control and navigation. These new scenarios demand more complex algorithms and the interaction of various AI techniques.

As the complexity of robotic systems grows, the need to organize and modularize software for their correct functioning also becomes a challenge, as information to be processed becomes distributed in space and time. The most desirable qualities for robotics software are: modularity, portability, robustness, and reusability for different kinds of robotics applications.

Several architectures and frameworks oriented to robotic systems are available in the literature, e.g., see [5, 10, 11, 13–16, 18, 21, 23]. Nevertheless, when considering heterogeneous robot architectures and applications, it is still an arduous and costly job to reuse existing software, either in partial or complete form, as most are ad-hoc solutions. Furthermore, it is almost impossible to perform fair comparisons of specialized algorithms (e.g., navigation, vision) in a real scenario, when a modular architecture is not available.

In this work we define RoCS, a development framework to support the current state of autonomous robotics, targeting easier reuse and portability of modules. The framework's architecture instantiates the Autonomic Computing Architecture defined by IBM [1], known as MAPE-K, under a robotics perspective.

The remaining sections are organized as follows. Section 2 presents the background and relevant concepts from the robotics domain. Section 3 discusses related work. Section 4 presents our instantiation to the MAPE-K reference architecture. Section 5 presents the RoCS Framework for autonomous robots. Section 6 presents the framework evaluation for an usual robotics scenario. Finally, Section 7 presents the final remarks and future work.

2 Background

2.1 Service robotics

Robotics has migrated from industrial applications to service robots, where robots help or replace humans in services [3]. In this new scenario, robots are usually autonomous or semi-autonomous, and they have to interact with each other and with humans in dynamic environments efficiently and securely.

The increased complexity of these new applications requires developing new robot platforms and coordinating several modules to accomplish the tasks proposed, as well as measuring the degree of success. Moreover, robots are often very expensive and their batteries have a short autonomy, two factors that limit the feasibility of extensive physical testing. High-fidelity simulation is commonly applied; hence, approaches supporting a smooth transition from the simulated environment to the real robot are mandatory.

To foster advancements in service robots, the RoboCup Federation [4] has proposed a set of challenges for evaluating the success of developments in a variety of domains. From playing soccer to assisting in typical tasks at home, these autonomous robots need to coordinate a variety of elements to succeed.

Although RoboCup standardizes the tasks that will be addressed, how they will be evaluated, and, in few cases, which robot platforms are allowed, the job of defining the software and hardware components of the robots is left open. A quick look at different domains [4] such as the *playing soccer task*, where robots can vary from humanoids and wheeled, to those with a standard platform , or the assistive robots in *home tasks*, show the variety of solutions that are applied in the software domain to solve the problems.

Because teams that work in RoboCup challenges participate in various editions, and because the code is necessarily shared among groups after the competition, solutions from some teams become widely used, such as the B-Human [2] framework. However, reuse of this framework mostly happens due to the quality of specific algorithms that it implements for solving certain problems, rather than the flexibility and organization of the code itself. We aim instead at defining a framework that can guide the user in structuring and reuse its code.

2.2 Robotic Programming Paradigms

The development of control paradigms for robots in dynamic environments has been the subject of research in the field of robotics. The approaches proposed in the literature are usually divided into three paradigms: **deliberative** [5], **reactive** [8, 20], and **hybrid** [7, 9].

In the *deliberative paradigm*, the robot uses the available sensory information and its knowledge of the world to reason about and create a plan. A search is conducted on possible scenarios, to find the one that best fulfills the task. This requires the robot to look ahead, and think about the consequences of each action, which can take a long time. When enough time is available, this approach allows the robot to act accordingly. However, it may not be practical if the robot has to react quickly to environmental changes.

The *reactive paradigm* tightly couples sensory inputs to actuation. It allows the robots to react almost instantaneously to environmental changes and it expects that intelligence emerges from the collective conjunction of very simple behaviors. Typically, the information acquired by sensors is directly used for actuation and it is not retained as internal memory. For this reason, internal representation of the environment is limited, which prevents long-term planning.

In the *hybrid paradigm*, which is what most of the current architectures classify as, there is a combination of the responsiveness, robustness, and flexibility of reactive systems with more traditional deliberative approaches where reasoning is mandatory. The challenge in this kind of paradigm is solving conflicts between the two different natures, and the organization of components.

3 Related Work

Several works suggest a structured approach to the control of robots.

The Robot Operating System (ROS) [18] is a set of software libraries and tools for robot development, which provides the functionality typical of an operating system for a heterogeneous cluster of robots. ROS has gained popularity because it abstracts the hardware devices, thus being compatible with multiple simulators and robot models. However, it provides the basic software components of a robot without necessarily prescribing an architecture, also limited to Unix-compatible platforms. Other framework that adopt a similar approach are frameworks such as Player, [11], ORCA [15] and OPRos [10].

The Task Control Architecture (TCA) [23] consists of *task*-specific modules connected to a central *control* module. The task modules perform all the required processing and communicate with the control via messages. The control routes these messages to their destination and maintains task control information. The architecture defines control constructs to support both deliberative and reactive behaviors. TCA provides a set of commonly needed mechanisms, such as task decomposition, resource management, execution monitoring and error recovery. Although the TCA facilitates the modular and incremental design of complex robot systems, the centralized control can easily become the bottleneck.

To dilute the centralization problem, *layered architectures* were proposed [13,21]. Three to four layers are typically used, depending on the implementation. In practice, layers are organized differently, based on the kind of robot and kind of task, which leads to large variety in architectures and prevents reuse.

The *4D/RCS* reference architecture provides a theoretical foundation for engineering software for unmanned vehicle systems [5]. The architecture consists of a multi-layered hierarchy of computational nodes, each having the capability of world observing, self-orientation, decision-making, and autonomous action. This decision cycle is mostly known as the OODA-loop: observe, orient, decide and act. It is realized by five elements for each node: *sensory processing*, *world modeling*, *value judgment*, *behavior generation*, and *knowledge database*. The behavior generation module of a node is connected to those of the adjacent nodes, creating a command tree. Furthermore, each robot is partitioned into *subsystems*, that in turn are partitioned in *primitives* and then in *servo* computational nodes. This granularity, while feasible in specific scenarios, poses a problem when the robot's components are not unambiguously separable.

4 Framework Architecture

The lack of reference software architectures for autonomous robots led us to base our work on the more general Autonomic Computing reference architecture, known as MAPE-K [1], which is summarized in Section 4.1. Then, Section 4.2 discusses the details of our architecture and the choices that we made in its definition. Finally, Section 4.3 discusses the hybrid robotics paradigm.

4.1 The MAPE-K Reference Architecture

Autonomic, or *self-adaptive*, systems are intended to continuously adjust its operation in response to changes perceived in themselves or the environment, with minimal outside intervention. To do this, in MAPE-K, systems are composed by autonomic managers and the associated managed resources (Figure 1).

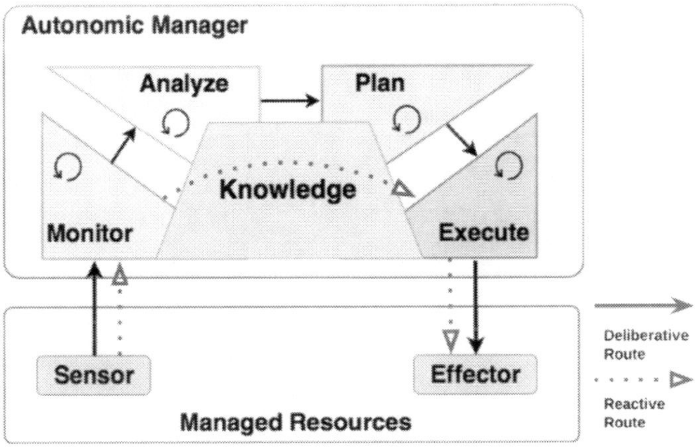

Fig. 1: Autonomic Manager in the MAPE-K Architecture (adapted from [1]).

According to the MAPE-K architecture [1], the autonomic manager should be composed of five basic building blocks (Figure 1): *Monitor*, *Analyze*, *Plan*, *Execute*, and *Knowledge*. Besides them, the Sensor and Actuator (Effector) touch-points work as supporting components for sensing (data collection) and acting upon the managed resources, respectively.

This reference architecture was designed to deal mostly with IT systems, like business information systems, distributed services and web applications. Later, MAPE-K extensions for adaptive systems such as FORMS [24] and ActivFORMS [12, 17] have been proposed. However, although the authors of these works use robotics scenarios, their proposal advocates an extension that allows the agent to adapt itself to a changing environment, rather than addressing the typical problems of autonomous service robotics presented in Section 1. Accordingly, there is a gap when applying MAPE-K concepts to robotic systems.

4.2 Detailed RoCS Architecture

In this section, we present the instantiation from the MAPE-K reference architecture (Section 4.1) building blocks considering the robotic perspective.

The **Monitor** block (Figure 2a) gathers and interprets raw data incoming from Sensors. One or more `SensorDriver` interact directly with physical sensing devices through the `monitor` port. The `RawDataInterpreter` translates raw data into final values, e.g., voltage from a temperature sensor into the actual temperature value. Finally, the `MonitorPublisher` module is the one responsible for publishing the interpreted data through the `publish` port.

Observed data from Sensors can be of diverse types, structures, and dynamics. The sensors can be either real or simulated, and their communication protocol and data nature (e.g. analogical vs. digital) may vary enormously. Regardless of sensors characteristics, a Monitor block must rapidly organize, interpret and forward the data for being analyzed.

The **Analyze** block (Figure 2b) filters, processes, and aggregates the data received from the Monitor block to determine if a change in the world has happened. It is where complex algorithms like time-series forecasting, queuing models, and advanced filtering can be executed to analyze the monitored data.

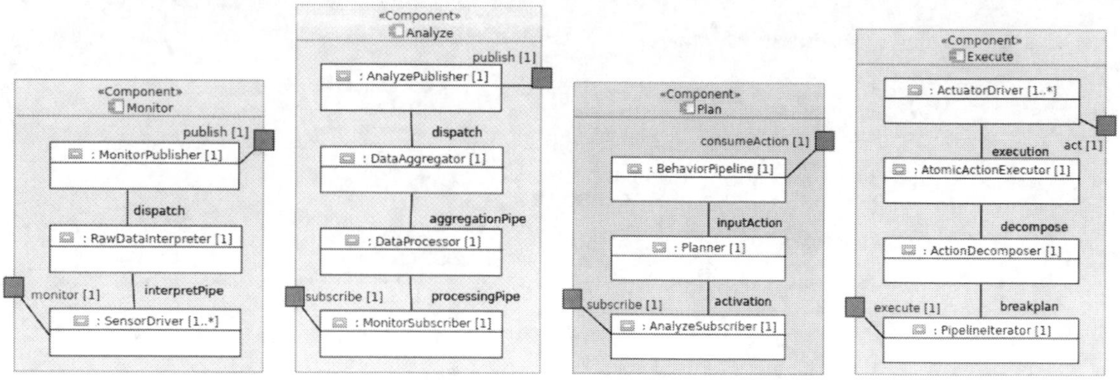

(a) (b) (c) (d)

Fig. 2: Representation of the internal structures of the Monitor (a), Analyze (b), Plan (c) and Execute (d) components.

The `MonitorSubscriber` block receives data from the `subscribe` port. The `DataProcessor` module runs data processing algorithms to search for alterations with respect to the known world state. The `DataAggregator` module translates the results in application-level concepts, possibly fusing the results of multiple data processing algorithms. Finally, if a relevant change in the world is perceived, the `AnalyzePublisher` sends this information to the next block, which can elaborate a response accordingly.

The **Plan** block (Figure 2c) creates, selects, and forwards behaviors to be executed by the `Execute` block. Specific changes trigger the generation of new behavior. The realization of this block may range from simple Finite State Automatas to complex Cognitive Systems fine-tuned for specific tasks.

First, the block receives changes detected by the `Analyze` block via its `subscribe` port, which is delegated to the `AnalyzeSubscriber` module. Their received change is sent to the `Planner` module, which is the module that decides which behaviors the robot should execute based on the tasks at hand and occurred changes. Lastly, this new behavior is sent to a pipeline (`BehaviorPipeline`) that will be read by the Execute block.

In the **Execute** block (Figure 2d), a planned behavior gets transformed into real robot actions like head movement or team communication. Once the next behavior has been decided, multiple actions might be needed to actually change the world state and realize the intended behavior.

The `Plan` block sends the desired behavior in the pipeline, which the `Execute` block has to iterate over. This is done by the `PipelineIterator` module, which is directly connected to the `execute` port. Whenever a behavior is received, it has to be decomposed in a sequence of atomic actions (`ActionDecomposer`). Then, each of these actions is executed by the `AtomicActionExecutor`, which is in charge of sending the correct message to the specific actuator drivers. One or more `ActuatorDriver` modules then directly communicate with the physical actuators. This is repeated until no atomic actions are left, after which the next behavior is extracted from the pipeline. This block is also responsible for any outgoing communication to other robots, via TCP, UDP, or other protocols.

A **Knowledge** source is a grouping of data structures designed with the sole purpose of providing access to the world information to all the building blocks. Information in the `Knowledge` block is organized in four structures.

The `WorldModel` represents any data that the robot can perceive from the world, such as the temperature, a map of the robot's surroundings, or the position of other robots. The `RobotModel` deals with information about the robot structure and internal configuration, such as the parameters of its actuators, kinematics and inverse kinematics. The `StrategyModel` is a mapping of predefined strategies (if any) from which the robot can choose for executing its tasks and behaviors, e.g., the "defender" or "attacker" roles in case of a football competition. Finally, the `ReactiveModel` is responsible for storing the rules that trigger a reactive action by the `Execute` block.

In robot swarms or other cooperative scenarios, agents would share this `Knowledge` source, or part of it, among all of them. Each robot would be responsible for sending any new acquired world information to the other robots it knows, until all robots share a common database.

4.3 Design for the Hybrid Paradigm

For the architecture to be consistent with robotics practices, it has to obey one of the Robotics Programming Paradigms (Section 2.2). We designed our architecture to support the *hybrid* paradigm, as it represents the current state of the art, and it is the most flexible solution. In the following, we discuss how our architecture supports both the *deliberative* and the *reactive* routes.

Deliberative Route. To implement a deliberative system, an agent has to go through the following phases: sensory input acquisition, task generation and behavior filtering, action selection, and action execution. In the proposed architecture, the first step is performed by the `Monitor` and the `Analyze` blocks. Meanwhile, the `Plan` block is responsible for generating the task plan, filtering the robot's behavior, and selecting the actions to be performed. Finally, the `Execute` block executes them. Therefore, the full MAPE-K classical cycle (solid arrows in Figure 1) works as a Deliberative System.

Reactive Route. A reactive robot system tightly couples perception to action without the use of intervening abstract representations or history [6]. The selection of the reaction to the sensory input is done in an inhibitory way, in which a hierarchy of behaviors is defined and then enacted by actuators.

Such mechanism can be defined in our architecture, although a different abstraction is needed. There are two ways of implementing a reactive system within the the MAPE-K architecture: i) implementing a high-priority reactive layer in the `Plan` block, or ii) capturing a low-level view of the world in the `Knowledge`, based on which a reactive action can be triggered immediately.

Biologically, a reactive action, like the reflex arc, is processed by a neural pathway that can act on an impulse without the assistance of the brain. That is, the response to specific stimuli does not need conscious thought. From the computational point of view, the deliberative planning and the reactive behavior will run independently, at different frequencies, and based on different data.

Therefore, the first abstraction (high-priority module in the `Plan`) could not be interpreted as biologically correct, as the sensory input reaches the `Plan` block, which can be thought as the robot's conscious brain. The second abstraction, instead, considers the `Knowledge` Source as that neural pathway, connecting the receptors (the `Monitor` block), to the effectors (the `Execute` block). The `Execute` block thus triggers one of the many pre-defined reflexes once a specific change in the `Knowledge` Source occurs (dashed arrows in Figure 1).

5 The RoCS Framework

Based on the software architecture described in Section 4, we designed and implemented the *RoCS Framework*, a concrete framework to guide robot developers in structuring their code. The framework has been implemented in C++, which is one of the most popular languages in the robotics domain, and its source code is available on the GitHub platform [19]. The structure of the framework is shown in the Class Diagram in Figure 3 and is described in the following.

5.1 Framework Structure

The core of the framework consists of one class for each of the five main blocks of the architecture: `Monitor`, `Analyze`, `Plan`, `Execute`, and `Knowledge`, depicted with their respective colors in Figure 3, as in Section 4.

While there may exist, in general, multiple independent instances of the Monitor and Analyze blocks, this is not the case for Plan, Execute, and Knowledge, and for this reason they apply the *Singleton* pattern. It is reasonable to constrain the framework user to have i) a single consistent knowledge base (`Knowledge`), ii) a single place where robot reasoning is performed, to avoid the production of conflicting plans (`Plan`), and iii) a single engine responsible for executing the planned actions (`Execute`).

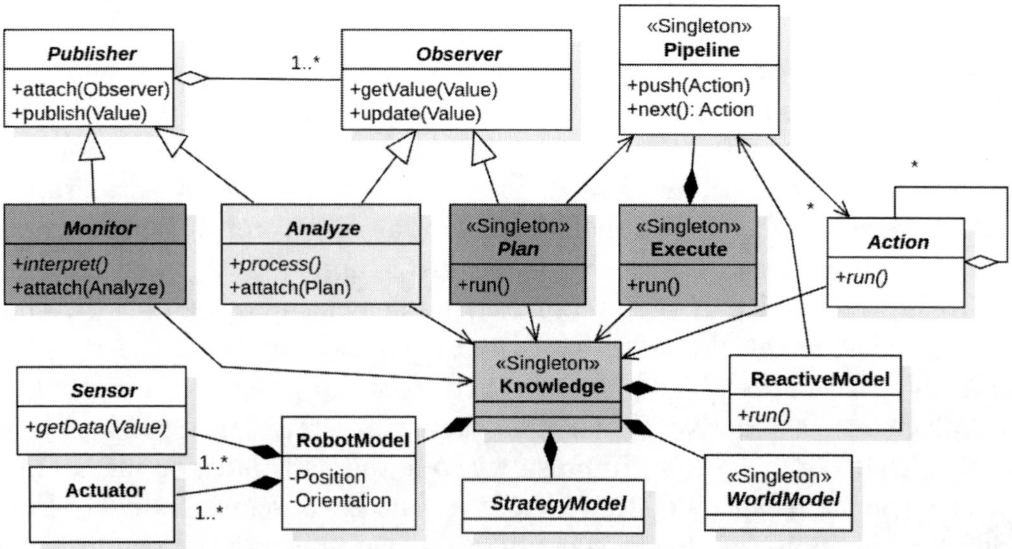

Fig. 3: Class Diagram of the RoCS Framework.

The Monitor, Analyze, and Plan classes communicate using a publish/subscribe messaging pattern. As such, each of them extends the `Publisher` and/or `Observer` abstract classes, which realize communication channel. However, it should be noted that the `attach` operation, which is needed to register an observer in the list of recipients of a publisher, is not present in the `Publisher` class itself. Instead, the more specific `attach(Analyze)` and `attach(Plan)` methods are added to the `Monitor` and `Analyze` classes, respectively. This choice constrains the framework user to follow the proposed architecture, preventing him from connecting blocks in an arbitrary way. Otherwise, with a generic `attach(Observer)` it would be possible to make the Plan observe the Analyze, or even an Analyze to observe itself.

Communication between the `Plan` and the `Execute` occurs through a queue, implemented by the `Pipeline` class. This queue contains a list of actions that are meant to be executed, as objects of type `Action`. Because the possible actions depend on the kind of robot and scenario at hand, the `Action` class is abstract and is meant to be extended by users of the framework. The queue is actually a *priority queue*, to allow the reactive behavior to override the decisions taken by the Plan block (deliberative behavior), by submitting actions of a higher priority. The `Execute` class owns the Pipeline, which is also a *Singleton*.

The `Knowledge` class maintains a knowledge base that is shared among all the other blocks. It is composed of four main parts. The `WorldModel` class contains a representation of the world as known to the robot. It is also a *Singleton*, to avoid inconsistencies. We just provide an abstract class to be extended by the user, since this is application-specific. The `StrategyModel` class is meant to contain pre-defined strategies, if they exist, to be accessed by the Plan block. Its usage is optional and also widely dependent from the target application. As such, we provide an abstract class to be extended by the user.

The `RobotModel` class contains a description of the physical structure and status of the robot, in terms of its position (coordinates), orientation, as well as the available sensors and actuators. The information about available sensors and actuators is maintained by aggregation with objects of type `Sensor` or `Actuator`. These two classes are also abstract.

The `Sensor` class has a `getData(Value)` method, which is used to read the data from the sensor. `Sensor` is a C++ *template* class, parameterized with the `Value` type, in order to support sensors returning different kinds of data. Implementation of the `getData` method is however specific for each kind of sensor. A Monitor block may monitor the value of one or more sensors (e.g., a group of sensors of the same type), as represented by the association between the `Monitor` and `Sensor` classes. In general, the opposite is also true: the value of a sensor can be used for multiple different purposes requiring different processing paths.

The `ReactiveModel` class represents a portion of reactive behavior, that is, a known deterministic mapping between input observed at sensor and actions to be executed by the robot. In general, the `Knowledge` may contain multiple instances of `ReactiveModel`, each one addressing a specific aspect of the robot's behavior, e.g., a reactive model to avoid falling, and another one to avoid obstacles. The

ReactiveModel class accesses sensors via the Knowledge class and, when specific thresholds are exceeded, it issues actions to the Pipeline.

5.2 Control Flow

In the *initialization* phase, the setup of the robot configuration is performed. This involves creating instances of the required blocks, that is, the Knowledge (and consequently its parts), the Execute, the Plan, and a certain number of Sensor, Actuator, Analyze, and Plan instances, according to the physical structure of the robot and the target application.

Then, the required associations are established, which means: i) associating each Monitor with the Sensors it will monitor, ii) subscribing each Analyze to the publishing channel of one or more Monitor, and subscribing the Plan to the publishing channel of one or more Analyze.

The *execution* is multi-threaded, that is, there is a thread running for each instance of the main blocks of the architecture: Monitor, Analyze, Plan, and Execute. All of these threads may access the Knowledge to read or write information from/to the knowledge base, typically the WorldModel or the RobotModel. A separate thread is also running for each existing ReactiveBehavior.

A Monitor thread cyclically runs the interpret abstract method, in which it is supposed to read the sensors to which it is connected, and return the value to be published to its observers. The implementation of this function is of course dependent of the application and should be implemented by the user. The publishing part is instead handled by the framework, transparently to the user.

An Analyze thread cyclically runs the process abstract method. In this method the data values received from the Monitor instances should be merged and processed to return a high-level information, which is then published towards the Analyze. Also in this case the publishing part is handled by the framework.

The Plan thread cyclically runs the run abstract method, which is meant to be implemented by the user of the framework. In this method the actual planning is performed, based on data received from the various Analyze instances. The results of planning is one or more Action objects, which are enqueued to the Pipeline. An Action can be atomic, when its behavior is entirely defined in its class, or can be composed of a sequence of other simpler actions (macro-action).

The Execute thread cyclically runs the run method. In this case the concrete implementation of this method is provided by the framework, and Execute is a concrete class. The behavior is simple: at each iteration it gets the next Action in the pipeline and executes it, by calling the act method. This method is abstract and its implementation depends on the concrete kind of action. A macro-action would typically call the act operation on its children according to a specific sequence, possibly complementing it with additional behavior.

Finally, threads corresponding to ReactiveModel instances also run periodically, executing the run operation. At each iteration the reactive model reads the value of the sensors of its interest (e.g., a gyroscope to avoid falling) and, in case specific conditions are met, it issues a new high-priority Action that is added to the Pipeline. Such conditions are again application-dependent.

5.3 Extension Points

The user of the framework may extend the provided classes to implement the behavior of a specific robot. We consider four kinds of extension points: *mandatory*, *deliberative*, *reactive*, and *optional*.

Mandatory. The user must extend the `Sensor` and `Actuator` abstract classes, implementing concrete classes based on the specific scenario. It must provide an implementation of the `getData` method in `Sensor`, and a method to control the `Actuator`. The user must also extend the `Action` abstract class with concrete classes, based on the kinds of actions that are possible in the considered scenario, and provide an implementation of the `act` method for each of them.

Deliberative. These are extension points that must be used when the robot should implement a deliberative behavior. In this case, the user must extend the `Monitor` and `Analyze` classes and implement the `intepret` and `process` methods, respectively. The user may create a hierarchy of classes, in case different data should be monitored or analyzed separately. To implement deliberative behavior, the user must also extend the `Plan` class and implement the `run` method.

Reactive. These are extension points that must be used when the robot should implement a reactive behavior. In this case, the user must extend the `ReactiveModel` class and implement the `run` method. The user may create a hierarchy of classes extending `ReactiveModel`, in case different of reactive behaviors should be executing concurrently.

Optional. If needed: i) the `RobotModel` class can be extended to contain further properties that reflect the current status of the robot; ii) the `WorldModel` class can be extended to contain properties that reflect the current status of the world as known to the robot; and iii) the `StrategyModel` abstract class can be extended to contain predefined strategies to be accessed by the Plan. Whether these extensions are needed or not depends on the application.

6 Evaluation

To assess the application of the framework in a typical robotics task, we deployed a Pioneer P3DX robot in the V-REP [22] simulator running the framework. The robot has the following configuration. As **sensors**, it uses 16 range sensors (sonars) distributed around the robot circumference, 1 position and 1 orientation sensor that act as entities that are aware of the real position (x, y, z) and orientation (θ) of the robot. This special kind of sensors are provided by the simulator; in a real deployment they would be replaced by a localization algorithm running in the `Analyze`. As **actuators**, it uses two rotate motors responsible for driving the differential robot in the scene. In terms of actions, we consider two **atomic actions** and three **macro-actions** (see Table 1).

To evaluate the capability of the framework of supporting a hybrid approach, we defined a task where both deliberative and reactive routes can be activated. The robot task is *to reach a specific position in the environment (origin 0,0) while avoiding collisions*. It is important to mention that the robot is not aware of the

Table 1: Actions included in the experiment and their decomposition.

Action	Decomposition
`SetWheelSpeed`	*atomic*
`TurnAngle`	*atomic*
`AvoidCollision`	`TurnAngle; SetWheeelSpeed`
`GoToOrigin`	`TurnToPosition; SetWheeelSpeed`
`TurnToOrigin`	`TurnAngle`

existence of obstacles while it computes its plan to reach the goal. Therefore, the "avoid the obstacle" behavior will be executed in a reactive fashion. At the same time, another robot with a simple 'explore the world' behavior (not implemented using the framework) is running in the environment to add more complexity to the scene.

Figure 4a presents the simulated environment. In this scene, the robot starts in the top of the environment, close to the walls and the box, and it should reach the origin of the system, defined as a point with coordinates (0,0). Figure 4 depicts the resulting trajectory performed by the robot and the macro-actions enqueued in the `Pipeline`. Each small dot represents an action, while the squares indicate a change in the executing paradigm (deliberative or reactive). As the pipeline is cleared once the reactive action route is active, the robot has to re-plan based on the information on its new position.

6.1 Implementation of Extension Points

To accomplish the task described in Section 6, the following extension points (see Section 5.3) were implemented according to the Diagram presented in Figure 5.

Each sensor described earlier was implemented through the extension of either `Sensor` or one of its heirs, like `Range`. The same applies to `WheelVREP`, which implements the motion of robot wheels and is the concrete implementation of an `Actuator` in our scenario. Three `Monitors` were created, one for watch-

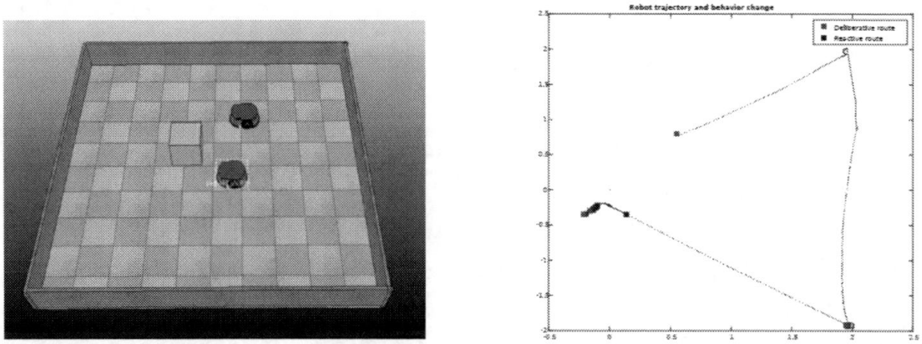

(a) (b)

Fig. 4: Simulated environment for the experiment (a) with two robots deployed. The robot at the bottom is the secondary robot that is not running the framework. (b) the resulting trajectory with the corresponding active paradigm for the robot that implements the framework. A video with the resulting simulation can be found at: https://youtu.be/fbZCgmZIjqg

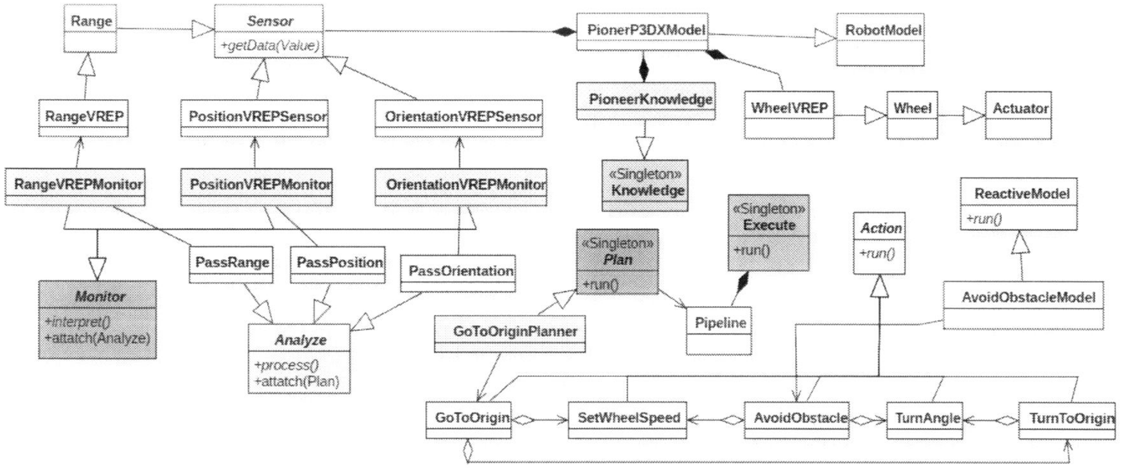

Fig. 5: Implementation using the RoCS framework for the proposed scenario. Associations that can be inferred from Figure 3 have been omitted for simplicity.

ing each type of `Sensor`, and three correspondly `Analyzers`: `PassOrientation`, `PassPosition` and `PassRange`.

The `GoToOriginPlanner` is responsible for defining which actions should be sent to the queue, whereas `AvoidObstacle`, `GoToOrigin`, `SetWheelSpeed`, `TurnAngle` and `TurnToOrigin` represent the actual actions that will be performed and transformed into actuators commands. Finally, `AvoidObstacleModel` and `PioneerP3DXModel` are the extensions of the `ReactiveModel` and of the `RobotModel`, respectively.

It is important to remember that one of the requirement of the framework is to facilitate the transfer from the simulated robot to the real one. In this case, we would only have to change the concrete Sensor and Actuator classes, which facilitates enormously such work.

7 Final Remarks

We presented an instantiation to the MAPE-K reference architecture towards the Robotics perspective, mainly for service robots applications with heterogeneous physical platforms. From this, we developed the RoCS framework to support the development of autonomous robots under a known architecture. We understand this approach can assist students or novices in robot development, and help experienced developers focus on their specific problems like machine learning algorithms for computer vision, sensor fusion techniques, and locomotion for robot models using particular physical devices (e.g., wheels, legs, propulsion). Initially, the RoCS framework was evaluated in a simple but usual scenario for service robots as proof of concept. For future work, we envision the development of robots using the RoCS framework for competitions such as the RoboCup Humanoid Soccer Teen Size League and RoboCup Flying Robots Competition.

References

1. An architectural blueprint for autonomic computing. Tech. rep., IBM (Jun 2005)

2. B-human team homepage (2018), https://www.b-human.de/index.html
3. International federation of robotics (2018), https://ifr.org/
4. The robocup federation (2018), http://www.robocup.org
5. Albus, J.S., Lumia, R., Fialaa, J., Wavering, A.: NASREM: The NASA/NBS Standard Reference Model for Telerobot Control System Architecture. In: Proceedings of 20th Int. Symposium on Industrial Robots. pp. 1412–1419 (October 1989)
6. Arkin, R.C.: Behavior-Based Robotics. MIT Press (1998)
7. Bayouth, M., Nourbakhsh, I.R., Thorpe, C.E.: A hybrid human-computer autonomous vehicle architecture. In: Third ECPD International Conference on Advanced Robotics, Intelligent Automation and Control (1998)
8. Brooks, R.: Intelligence without representation. Artificial Intelligence **47**, 139–159 (1991)
9. Chan, Y.J., Yow, K.C.: A strategy-driven framework for multi-robot cooperation system. In: Control, Automation, Robotics and Vision, 2006. ICARCV'06. 9th International Conference on. pp. 1–6. IEEE (2006)
10. Choulsoo, J., et al.: OPRoS: A New Component-Based Robot Software Platform. ETRI Journal **32**(5), 646–656 (2010)
11. Collett, T.H.J., Macdonald, B.A.: Player 2.0: Toward a practical robot programming framework. In: in Proc. of the Australasian Conference on Robotics and Automation (ACRA) (2005)
12. De La Iglesia, D.G., Weyns, D.: MAPE-K Formal Templates to Rigorously Design Behaviors for Self-Adaptive Systems. ACM Transactions on Autonomous and Adaptive Systems **10**(3), 15:1–15:31 (2015)
13. Jeong, I.B., Kim, J.H.: Multi-layered architecture of middleware for ubiquitous robot. In: Systems, Man and Cybernetics 2008. pp. 3479–3484 (October 2008)
14. Kim, D., et al.: SHAGE: A Framework for Self-managed Robot Software. In: Proceedings of the 2006 International Workshop on Self-adaptation and Self-managing Systems (SEAMS'06). pp. 79–85 (2006)
15. Makarenko, A., Brooks, A., Kaupp, T.: On the benefits of making robotic software frameworks thin. In: IROS Proceedings (2007)
16. Malek, S., et al.: An Architecture-driven Software Mobility Framework. Journal of Systems and Software **83**(6), 972–989 (2010)
17. Qasim, A., Kazmi, S.A.R.: MAPE-K Interfaces for Formal Modeling of Real-Time Self-Adaptive Multi-Agent Systems. IEEE Access **4**, 4946–4958 (2016)
18. Quigley, M., et al.: ROS: an open-source Robot Operating System. In: ICRA Workshop on Open Source Software (2009)
19. Ramos, L., Divino, G., de França, B.B.N., Montecchi, L., Colombini, E.: RoCS GitHub Repository (2018), https://github.com/oramleo/RoCS
20. Ranganathan, A., Koenig, S.: A reactive robot architecture with planning on demand. In: Proceedings of the IEEE/RSJ International Conference on Intelligent Robots and Systems (IROS 2003). pp. 1462–1468 (2003)
21. Rauch, C., et al.: A concept of a reliable three-layer behaviour control system for cooperative autonomous robots. In: 35th German Conference on Artificial Intelligence. pp. 24–27. Germany (September 2012)
22. Rohmer, E., Singh, S.P.N., Freese, M.: V-REP: a Versatile and Scalable Robot Simulation Framework. In: IROS Proceedings (2013)
23. Simmons, R., Mitchell, T.: A task control architecture for autonomous robots. In: Proc. Third Annual Workshop on Space Oper. Auto. and Robotics (July 1989)
24. Weyns, D., Malek, S., Andersson, J.: FORMS: A Formal Reference Model for Self-adaptation. In: Proceedings of the 7th International Conference on Autonomic Computing (ICAC'10). pp. 205–214. ACM (2010)

Towards an Architecture for Human Computer Interaction within the Internet of Things and Ambient Assisted Living Domain

Xavier Maita-Tepán, Xavier Garnica-Bautista, Priscila Cedillo
Department of Computer Science, University of Cuenca,
Cuenca, Ecuador
{xavier.maita, xavier.garnica, priscila.cedillo}@ucuenca.edu.ec

Abstract. The Internet of Things (IoT) is part of the fourth industrial revolution; nowadays, it is common to find regular objects connected to Internet. Here, the connectivity should be transparent to users; however, the interactions that are involved between people and things should be natural and appropriate to each profile and need. In this context, this paper proposes an architecture named AALIIoT (Ambient Assisted Living Interactions for IoT), which supports the design of IoT solutions for Ambient Assisted Living (AAL) environments in order to facilitate the interaction between users with special needs and the IoT artifacts (i.e., sensors, actuators). Also, this architecture contemplates different modes of interaction (e.g., gestural, auditory, visual, cerebral) to allow the communication between devices and people for everyday activities, which may be difficult for them. Finally, a system prototype based on AALIIoT has been implemented, which takes into account specific needs of a user profile. Then, for the evaluation of the proposed architecture, a quasi-experiment was executed, which allowed to analyze the architecture and the perceived efficacy from the point of view of 5 systems engineers and undergraduate students. The results show that the participants perceived AALIIoT to be easy to use, useful, and also expressed their intention to use the architecture in the future.

Keywords: Software Architecture, Human-Computer Interaction, Internet of Things, Ambient Assisted Living.

1 Introduction

Human-Computer Interaction (HCI) represents a channel of direct communication between people and technological applications [1]. This communication is focused on providing solutions that support the daily activities that integrate individuals from different targets [2]. Besides, new technologies have emerged lately, such as Ambient Assisted Living (AAL) and Internet of Things (IoT), which used together, provide support in the improvement of the quality of life for people with special needs (e.g., elderly people, people with disabilities). However, it is necessary to take into account the interaction between technologies and people in an appropriate manner, considering the context and users' needs [3]. Such needs are related to the forms of interaction, such as the use of the movement of eyes, speech commands, gestures or, in extreme cases, through the use of brain interfaces that help them in overcoming physical and cognitive barriers [4]. In this context, AAL refers to a way to guarantee better living conditions for seniors, who have chronic diseases proper of their age, through the development of innovative technologies and services [5].

On the other hand, the world is ageing rapidly, and governments are paying attention to the vulnerable sectors of the population. The United Nations Population Fund (UNFPA) [6] states that people aged 60 and older make up the 12.3% of the global population, and by 2050, that number will rise to almost 22%. Also, there are factors that support the improvement of the life expectancy (e.g., better nutrition, sanitation, health care, education, economic well-being) [6]. These reasons promote the creation of technological solutions that support the daily activities of elderly people. Those solutions help in monitoring the health and sensing the environments for seniors with different disabilities or constraints proper of their age.

Currently, there are several studies related to architectures for IoT applications that may be present in AAL [7], [8], [9]. Rahman and Hossain in [7] presents an architecture of a virtual caregiver that tries to satisfy the needs of an elderly person within their home. However, that solution does not consider different profiles, nor the user interaction needs. On the other hand, Jagadish et al. [8] proposes a system architecture to analyze brain signals and extract commands to control IoT-enabled environments. However, the contribution is specifically directed at the brain-computer interfaces and does not consider other forms of interaction. In addition, Errobidart et al. in [9] it presents a user interface and a communication platform for a modular home automation system aimed at users who suffer some type of disability. However, his contribution is only focused on the use of voice commands. It is noted that most of the existing solutions focus on a single type of interaction for a very specific group of users or do not take into account all the requirements for people with different interaction needs and their coexistence. Consequently, this paper proposes an architecture named ALLIoT for the construction of solutions that facilitate the interaction between a wide spread of users with different special needs and devices, sensors or actuators connected to the Internet in AAL environments, which supports the improvement of the quality of life of people. Also, this solution is illustrated by means of a prototype that presents a scenario that is built by using the proposed architecture.

Finally, this paper is structured as follows: Section 1 presents a brief introduction to the contribution; in Section 2, the related studies are discussed; Section 3 shows the theoretical foundations of the areas of the proposed architecture; section 4 presents the software architecture and the description of its main components; Section 5 presents the implementation of a prototype of a system based on the proposed architecture; Section 6 presents an evaluation method to empirically validate the proposed architecture through a quasi-experiment; Section 7, the execution and discussion of the quasi-experiment results and, Section 8 presents the conclusions and future work.

2 Related work

In the literature, several proposals for architectures have been found for IoT applications in the domain of health care; some are related to hardware and communication aspects; others are related to the interactions between users and the system; however, they all are focused on a single type of interaction for a specific group of people or are not oriented to the AAL domain. Thus, Ahmed and Fischer [10] present an IoT architecture for AAL via Information-Centric Networking (ICN) approach, which seeks the improvement of the performance of communication between the heterogeneous device and services integrated in IoT-AAL; however, they do not consider the interaction with the users. In addition, Ray [11] presents a survey on IoT architectures that summarizes the current state in several domains. In the field of medical care, this study addresses works related to home health care, electronic health, ubiquitous health and hospital management. Here, the author analyzes the contributions related to the platforms that pursue various medical facilities integrated with sensors. Also, Ray [12] presents H3IoT, a new architectural framework for IoT to monitor the health of older people at home. However, this architecture does not take into account the interactions between users and the environment. Also, the collection of Internet of Things solutions oriented to the health care has given way to the Internet of Medical Things (IoMT) [13] which ensures the availability and processing of healthcare data through smart medical devices and web, which main feature is monitoring in real time the signals coming from people; however, in this field, few information is oriented to provide information about user interactions with the things.

Consequently, there is a lack of architectures that provide natural interactions between users and the IoT solutions that are located in AAL environments, by means of different and various modes of interactions, taking into account the needs of users.

3 Theoretical foundations

3.1 Ambient Assisted Living

Ambient Assisted Living (AAL) is a concept in which technology is used as a way to improve the well-being and independence of the elderly and people with disabilities [14]. The technology used in AAL has been designed so these group of people can live independently, helping them to perform daily tasks that, in general, cannot be performed properly by themselves [15]. In this way, an environment is created in which people can continue to be self-sufficient.

3.2 Human Interactions for Ambient Assisted Living

With the emergence of environmental intelligence systems, the traditional interaction between man and computer through graphic interfaces is becoming a thing of the past, preventing the user to be constantly indicating to the system each action to be performed [16] and it is beginning to adopt interactions similar to human-human communication, which represent the most natural way to interact [17].

Natural interactions between people and environment refers to the execution of commands, taking the intentions of users as inputs [18]. Users request the execution of actions by means of natural commands, being able to use gestures, voice, vision, thoughts or monitoring of their vital signs, activities and the environment through sensors [19].

Considering the AAL systems, in which elderly people are involved, traditional interactions through graphical interfaces of users, tend to be tedious and difficult because not all of them have the necessary skills to visualize a screen, move a pointer, or use a touch device [20]. Here, natural interactions take an important role in the AAL domain by using the interaction that most closely matches the capabilities that each user has. In this sense, among the natural interactions frequently used, it can find interactions through gestures [7], [21], [22], vision [23], [24], voice [9], [25], [26], brain interfaces [8], [27], [28] and sensor-based and context sensitive interactions [29].

4 Proposed architecture

The proposed software architecture (see Fig. 1) is named AALIIoT and is designed to support IoT-based solutions, which are deployed in Ambient Assisted Living environments (e.g., home, nursing homes, hospitals). The main objective of this solution is to address aspects related to the users' interactions, and include them into a solution, where different types of devices, sensors or actuators are located.

Those components are connected to the internet in order to provide assistance to users with specific needs (i.e., elderly and people with disabilities). On this instance, users can either intervene or not in the control of the things. Each one of these possibilities is specified as follows:

- *Control without the user intervention*: when the devices or sensors execute certain actions based on the interpretation of the data collected from the environment. For example, a device that measures the temperature and regulates it automatically according to the ambient temperature.
- *Control with the user intervention*: refers to the situation in which, the devices or sensors need a user command or interaction to perform an action. For example, opening a door when a person makes a specific gesture with a hand.

AALIIoT considers the most frequent types of natural interaction in AAL environments mentioned in the previous section: i) vocal interaction, ii) visual interaction, iii) gestural interaction, iv) mental interaction, vi) sensor-based interaction, in addition to the traditional forms of interaction: vii) interaction with graphical user interfaces. Those interactions are integrated with devices, sensors and actuators that are part of the applications that are responsible to support for a better users' quality of life.

4.1 Main components about interactions

User Management Module (1). This module is responsible for identifying each user within the environment and enabling the appropriate interactions for him. Also, it is based on a set of personal data and preferences, which are stored in two repositories: i) a user information repository, and ii) a repository of users' profiles. Each component of this module is described as follows:

- *User identifier (1.1):* Identifies the user who will interact with the AAL environment using some kind of authentication.

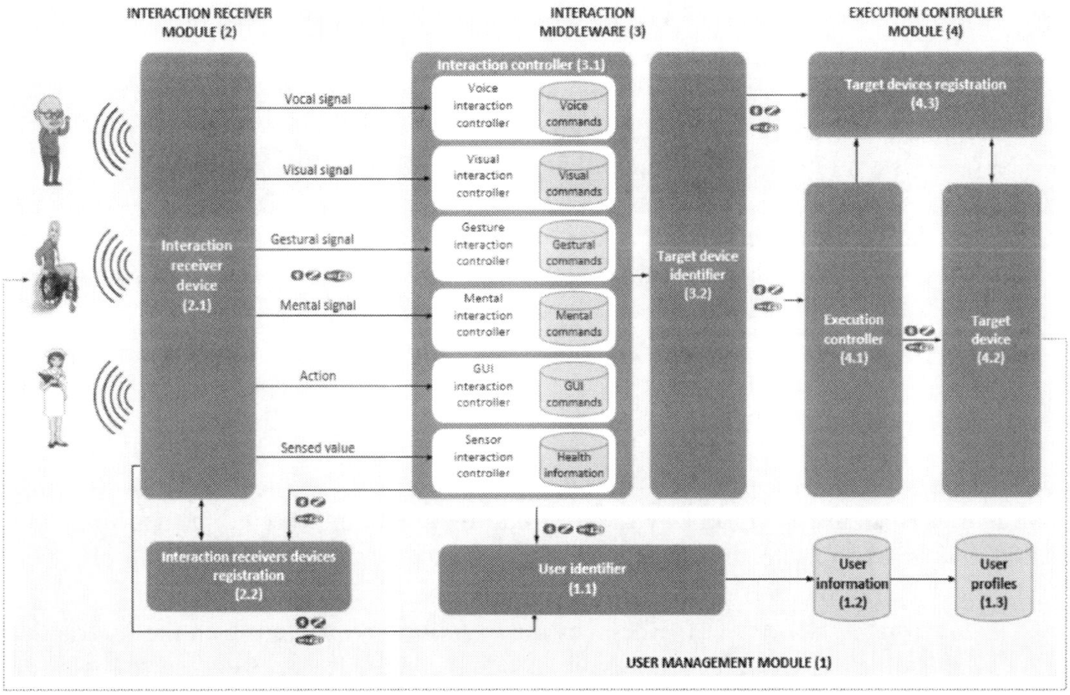

Fig. 1. Static view of AALIIoT software architecture.

- *User information repository (1.2):* It stores the personal information of a user and the necessary data to validate the authentication.
- *Repository of user profiles (1.3):* It stores user profiles that will be assigned to the people who will use the system within the environment, so that each user can interact with the system using the interactions specified in their assigned profile. A user profile is a digital representation of the data belonging to a particular user or group of users [30]; stores information entered manually (personal information, habits, preferences, interests) or by inference of unobservable information related to the actions, thoughts or behaviors of users [31] in order to determine the appropriate interaction for the users and the components with which they will interact.

Interaction Receiving Module (2). This module is responsible for recognizing the implicit or explicit users' commands, through interaction receiving devices or sensors for their later execution. The components of this module are the following:

- *Interaction receiving devices (2.1):* They are formed by the set of devices capable of capturing the users' interactions with the environment, either through gestures, auditory signals, eye movements, mental commands, actions performed on devices with GUIs, or values measured by sensors. The data collected represent the requests made by the user in order to carry out a specific action.
- *Interaction receiving devices registration (2.2):* It refers to the specification and detail of the properties of each of the interaction receiving devices available in the environment.

Interaction Middleware (3). This module is responsible for interpreting the signals sent by the Interaction Receiving Module (2). Also, it identifies the device(s) that will execute the action requested by the user. The components of the Interaction Middleware (3) are described below:

- *Interaction controller (3.1):* This component processes and interprets the received commands based on specific algorithms and command repositories, which are available for each form of interaction.
- *Target device identifier (3.2):* Component that identifies the device to which the command sent by the user is directed.

Also, it is important to consider that the architecture supports several types of interaction. Therefore, if it is necessary to include other interaction controllers, they can be added easily by means of software components (e.g., Application Programming Interfaces – APIs, web services). Thus, the architecture is considered flexible interoperable with other solutions and extensive.

4.2 Main components about IoT

Execution Controller Module (4). This module is responsible for waiting for the commands that have been sent by the user and that were interpreted in the Interaction Middleware (3) to perform a requested action. Each device or actuator will change a state according to the user's request. It has the following components:

- *Execution controller (4.1):* Receives the execution requested from the Interaction Middleware (3); also, it prepares and sends the action to be executed to the target device or actuator.
- *Target device (4.2):* It represents the devices that can be controlled by the user through some kind of interaction (e.g., light bulb, electric door, electric shutter, electric window).
- *Target device registration (4.3):* This component specifies and registers the properties of each device, sensor or actuator located in the environment (e.g., IP address, allowed commands, current status).

AALIIoT is not limited to the use of a particular communication and data transmission protocol like Zigbee, Bluetooth, HTTP. This will depend on the functional requirements of the system which are defined by the team of analysts and software developers according to the characteristics of the environment.

5 Illustrating the AALIIoT architecture

This section presents the implementation and deployment of a system prototype based on the software architecture presented in this paper.

5.1 Scenario and description of system functionality

The proposed scenario is as follows: there is a person, his name is Richard, he is 70 years old and has a physical disability; therefore, he uses a wheelchair to move. During the night, he usually gets up to drink water; thus, he needs an easy way to turn on/off the light with a simple interaction.

Thus, it is necessary to include an Interaction Receiving Device (i.e., sensor) that captures the signals sent by the user, an Interaction Middleware that processes the received signals and an Execution Controller (i.e, actuator) that converts signals into observable actions on the light bulb which is connected to a network. Also, Richard's asks for the following system features: 1) Turn on/off the light using hand gestures. 2) Turn on/off the light using a graphical use interface (GUI).

5.2 Implementation of the system prototype

The modules of the system were developed with different programming languages (i.e., Python, Java, Arduino). The communication between each module was carried out by using the HTTP protocol and its methods GET and POST. There is a client device that communicates with a server using the invocation of a Uniform Resource Locator (URL). Finally, the server processes the request and returns an HTTP response code. Below is a brief description of the implementation of the different components.

Interaction receiving module. This module contains the devices that capture the signals made by Richard for processing and interpretation.

- *Receiving device of GUI interaction:* GUI interaction has created a graphical user interface for a mobile application that is installed on smartphones with Android operating system (Fig. 2).
- *Receiving device of gestural interaction:* this component uses an infrared video camera to gather the user's interactions in a dark environment The captured signal is sent to the gestural interaction handler for processing (Fig. 3).

Interaction middleware. This module was implemented using Java.

- *GUI interaction controller:* This component was implemented as an internal service of the interaction middleware. It receives the actions generated on the graphic interface, and presents it to the user for control of the IoT devices.
- *Gesture interaction controller:* This controller acts as an external service for the middleware. Also, the controller is attached to the middleware by means of HTTP requests and responses.

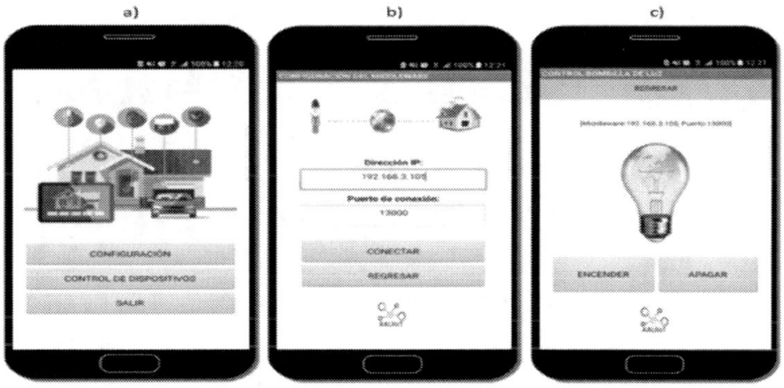

Fig. 2. Mobile application that works as a receiving device of GUI interaction.
a) Main GUI, b) Network configuration GUI, c) Control of the light bulb GUI.

The algorithm that executes the Interaction Controller to process gestural signals was programmed in Python, and makes use of OpenCV library. In Fig. 3, the process of gesture detection is illustrated; here, the system detects the contour of the hands (Fig. 3a, 3b) and counts the four vertices between the five fingers of the open hand (Fig 3c). In this way, it is possible to identify the number of fingers shown in the photo. Here, the open hand represents the "ON" and the close hand represents the "OFF" commands.

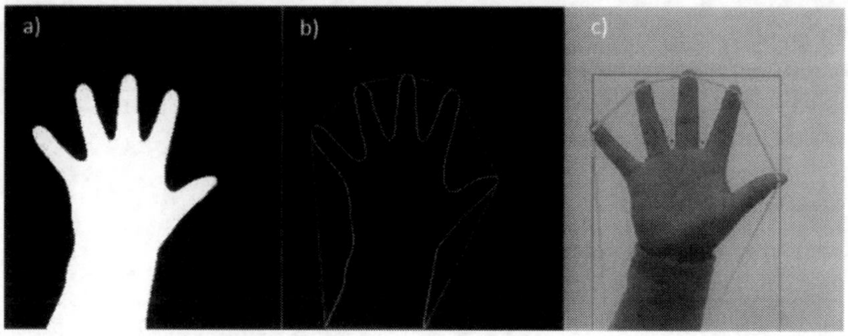

Fig. 3. Gesture detection process using the OpenCV library with Python.

Execution controller module. This module includes the device that will be controlled by the user (light bulb) and the execution controller that will operate said device.

- *Execution controller:* The ESP8266 chip works as a router, meaning that the chip provides a Wi-Fi network connection with Internet access within the home and assigns IP addresses to all devices connected to that network. This component is a server that exposes different services for the reception of HTTP requests from the Interaction Middleware.
- *Target device:* This device corresponds to a 60W light bulb connected to the electrical wiring of the environment and to the NodeMCU module through a relay device that works as a switch.
- *Target device registration:* The information of the devices is stored in an XML file, and the Execution Controller can execute the commands sent by the user.

Deployment of a system prototype. The prototype of the system was deployed on an environment for testing with real users. All components must be connected at the same wireless network. Finally, as shown in Fig. 4, the user begins to interact with the system and the GUI by gestural signals and actions to control the light bulb.

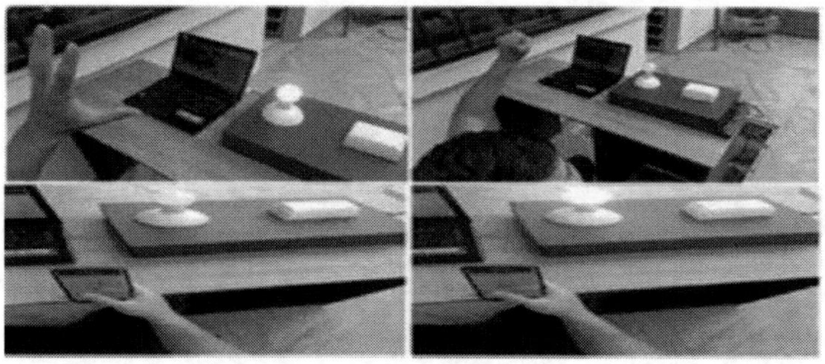

Fig. 4. User controlling the light bulb using gestures and a GUI

6 Evaluation method

The method used for evaluating this solution is based on the adaptation of Method Evaluation Model (MEM) [32], which provides mechanisms to determine the current performance, acceptance and possible technological adoption in practice by measuring variables such as efficiency, effectiveness and user perceptions [33].

The MEM has been adapted for use in software architectures; this adaptation consists on determining the specific aspects of the software architecture that will be evaluated. In this case, the efficiency, effectiveness and perceptions of the user were measured when configuring the components and modules of the AALIIoT software architecture for the creation of systems through a set of tasks proposed in specific scenarios. The variables based on performance are measured by evaluating current efficiency and effectiveness:

- *Current effectiveness:* degree to which each component of the architecture has been correctly configured in each module in a specific task.
- *Current efficiency:* summation of the times used in the accomplishment of each task executed by the participants.

The variables based on perception are measured using a questionnaire that presents a series of questions aimed at evaluating the perceived ease of use (PEOU), perceived utility (PU) and intention to use (ITU). This evaluation instrument is available in http://bit.ly/2QhobvZ.

6.1 A case study design to evaluate the AALIIoT architecture

The objective of this evaluation to predict the efficacy of the software architects during the system design activity based on the selection of the components that are part of the AALIIoT architecture, to solve a specific problem. For this, two research questions have been raised:

- RQ1: Is the AALIIoT architecture perceived as easy to use, useful and it is considered as a solution to be used in the future?
- RQ2: How was the software architects' efficacy when designing a solution for a specific scenario?

The first research question can be answered by means of the following hypotheses:

- $H1_0$: The AALIIoT architecture is perceived as difficult to use, $H1_0 = \neg H1_1$
- $H2_0$: The AALIIoT architecture is not perceived as useful, $H2_0 = \neg H2_1$
- $H3_0$: There is no intention to use AALIIoT architecture in the future, $H3_0 = \neg H3_1$

The second research question can be answered by means of the effectiveness and the efficiency of users solving the tasks raised.

6.2 The planning of the evaluation

Context selection. The context is determined by: i) the AALIIoT software architecture; in which, the specific activity to be evaluated is the design of a system that selects the appropriate components of the architecture to be used in order to fulfill the requirements of users in a particular scenario; and, ii) the participants involved in the evaluation were five professionals in the area of Systems Engineering who develop software for several organizations located in Cuenca-Ecuador.

Experimental tasks. The main tasks consist of the resolution of three exercises set in specific scenarios, each exercise has four tasks, described below:

- Task 1: The selection of the appropriate interaction with the receiving devices performed by the Interaction Receiver Module that will capture the user's commands, considering the interaction needs identified in the proposed scenario.

- Task 2: The selection of interaction drivers and the identification of the devices that the Interaction Middleware must have to process the signals sent by the interaction receiving devices chosen in Task 1.
- Task 3: The selection of execution controllers and devices that the user can control in the Execution Controller Module.
- Task 4: The selection of the type of identification of users and the necessary devices to carry out this action in the User Identification Module.

Variables. Table 1 shows the variables based on the users' perception. These variables are measured by using a Likert scale questionnaire of 5 points in a set of 14 questions. The measurement value of each variable was calculated as the arithmetic mean of the answers to the questions associated with these variables. Table 2 shows the variables based on the performance and the measurement function used to determine the values, where m represents the number of proposed exercises, n the number of tasks that each exercise contains, *task rating* represents the hits (i.e., 1) or errors (i.e., 0) when subjects execute a task.

Table 1. Dependent variables based on perceptions

Variable	Description
Perceived Ease of Use (PEOU)	The degree to which participants believe that learning and using the proposed architecture will be effort-free.
Perceived Utility (PU)	The degree to which participants believe that using the proposed architecture will increase their performance.
Intention to Use (ITU)	The degree to which participants intend to use the proposed architecture in the future.

Table 2. Dependent variables based on performance

Variable	Equation
Effectiveness	$\frac{\sum_{j=1}^{m}(\sum_{i=1}^{n} task\_rating_{ij})}{m * n}$
Efficiency	$\sum_{j=1}^{m}\left(\sum_{i=1}^{n} task\_time_{ij}\right)$

7 The execution of the evaluation

Before the final evaluation, a 60-minute training session was held with the 5 participants, in order to explain the concepts related to: 1) AAL, HCI, IoT concepts (30 mins), 2) AALIIoT software architecture, an explanation of the experimental material and a demonstrative example (30 mins).

7.1 Analysis of the users' perceptions

Fig. 5 shows the box-plots for each perception variable where it is observed that the mean of each variable is greater than 3, which represents the neutral value of the Likert scale.

The boxplots figure shows some abnormal data-points (i.e., participant_id=2), it is a participant who cannot attend the training session. Therefore, he was removed from the subsequent analysis in order to avoid outliers' values.

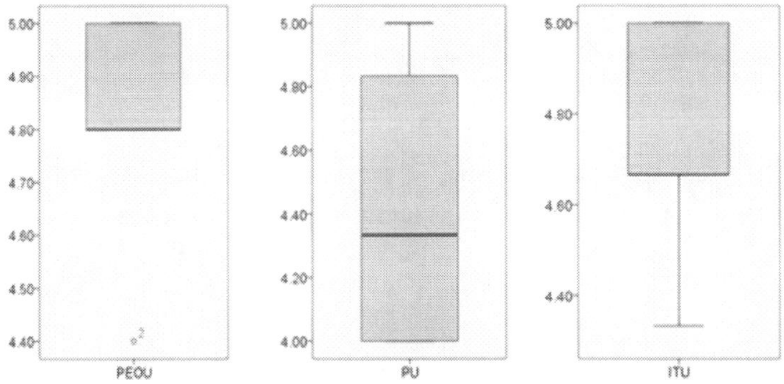

Fig. 5. Box-plots for PEOU, PU and ITU variables.

7.2 Analysis of results

Table 3 shows the results of the Shapiro-Wilk normality test, to analyze the distribution of the variables. The variables PEOU, PU and ITU were measured using the Likert scale of 5 points. Tests have been applied to verify the hypothesis by comparing the mean of the answers to the questions related to a neutral variable.

The variables PEOU, PU and ITU, have a normal distribution ($p > 0.05$), the hypothesis has been tested by applying the one-tailed t-test with a test value of 3, since this value corresponds to the neutral value of the Likert scale of the questionnaire. The results allow to reject the null hypotheses $H1_0$, $H2_0$ and $H3_0$; thus, the participants perceive the proposed software architecture as easy to use, useful and also expressed their intention to use the architecture in the future.

Table 3. Shapiro-Wilk test for PEOU, PU and ITU.

Var	Min	Max	Media	Std. Dev	Std E.	1-T. p-value	Shapiro-Wilk test p-value
PEOU	4.40	5.00	4.8	0.24495	0.10954	0.000<0.001	0.146>0.05
PU	4.00	5.00	4.4333	0.46547	0.20817	0.002<0.001	0.246>0.05
ITU	5.33	5.00	4.7333	0.27889	0.12472	0.000<0.001	0.314>0.05

7.3 Analysis of user performance

A measurement of the effectiveness and efficiency of the participants was made when designing systems for specific scenarios using the modules and components of the AALIIoT software architecture in practice. Table 4 shows the values of descriptive statistics for the effectiveness and efficiency variables. The participants had an average of 86.25% of effectiveness when completing the experimental exercises. The efficiency was calculated as the effort required in minutes to solve the experimental exercises. The participants had an efficiency that was from 8.25 to 11.85 minutes.

Table 4. Variables based on User Performance

Variable	Min	Max	Mean	Std. Dev
Effectiveness	0.71	1	0.8625	0.10464
Efficiency	8.25	11.85	10.20	1.49615

7.4 Discussion

To answer the first research question RQ1, the results of the evaluation allow to reject the null hypotheses $H1_0$, $H2_0$ and $H3_0$ accepting their alternatives hypotheses, this means that the software architecture was perceived as useful, easy to use and the users have the intention to use it in the future if there is a need to design and build systems belonging to the HCI, IoT and AAL domain.

In response to the second research question RQ2, it is concluded that the participants completed their activities with an average effectiveness of 86.25% and efficiency ranging from 8.25 to 11.85 minutes; However, these results could be even more favorable as the experience and understanding of the users increases in the use of the different components and modules of the architecture, in addition to the domain in which it works.

8 Conclusion and further work

In this paper the AALIIoT software architecture has been presented. This approach is based on Human-Computer Interaction (HCI) in environments that the Internet of Things (IoT) systems or applications are involved into Ambient Assisted Living environments (AAL). AALIIoT considers several ways of interaction between elderly people and environments that contains technology to improve their quality of life. However, this architecture can be used also by people with several disabilities that need different ways of interaction (i.e., gestural, vocal, visual, brain, with sensors).

In addition, a prototype of a system that uses the modules and components of the AALIIoT architecture was presented. The prototype of the system fulfills the requirements of a user within a specific scenario in which an elderly person with a physical disability is allowed to turn on and off a light bulb by using two types of interactions (i.e., gestures, a mobile application deployed on a smartphone).

Also, an evaluation with software architects has been performed. Considering the results that evaluation, it can be concluded that, in all cases, the software architecture is perceived as easy to use, useful and that the participants intend to use it in the future. Regarding the effectiveness, an average of about 86% was achieved, with an efficiency ranging from 8.25 to 11.85 minutes.

As future work, it is important to consider the creation of a domain specific language (DSL) for representing the AALIIoT architecture. Also, it is important to create ways to collect the requirements for representing the interactions in a methodological manner. Finally, about the empirical evaluation, it is intended to perform realistic validations applied in real industrial environments to carry out case studies or controlled experiments with a greater number of participants. Another aspect to be considered for evaluating the study in the future, is to include potential users of AAL environments, and to measure their satisfaction and the effectiveness of the interactions implemented by following AALIIoT.

Acknowledgment

This research is supported by the research project: DIUC-XVII - "Fog computing applied to monitor devices used in assisted living environments; case study: platform for the elderly people".

References

1. Dix, A.: "Human-computer interaction," in *Encyclopedia of database systems*. Springer, 2009, pp. 1327–1331.
2. Hoenig, H.; Taylor Jr, D. H.; and Sloan, F. A.: "Does assistive technology substitute for personal assistance among the disabled elderly?", in *American Journal of Public Health*, vol. 93, no. 2, pp. 330–337, 2003.
3. Dohr, A.; Modre-Opsrian, R.; Drobics, M.; Hayn, D.; Schreier, G.: "The internet of things for ambient assisted living," in *Information technology: new generations (ITNG)*, 2010 seventh international conference on. IEEE, 2010, pp. 804–809.
4. Abascal, J.: "Human-computer interaction in assistive technology: from" patchwork" to" universal design"," in *Systems, Man and Cybernetics*, 2002 IEEE International Conference on, vol. 3. IEEE, 2002, pp. 6–pp.
5. Mainetti, L.; Manco, L.; Patrono, L.; Secco, A.; Sergi, I.; Vergallo, R.: "An ambient assisted living system for elderly assistance applications," in *Personal, Indoor, and Mobile Radio Communications (PIMRC)*, 2016 IEEE 27th Annual International Symposium on. IEEE, 2016, pp. 1–6
6. U. N. P. Fund, Ageing, https://www.unfpa.org/, 2016.
7. Rahman M. A.; Hossain, M. S.: "A cloud-based virtual caregiver for elderly people in a cyber-physical iot system," *Cluster Computing*, pp. 1–14, 2018.
8. Jagadish, B., Kiran, M.; Rajalakshmi, P.: "A novel system architecture for brain controlled iot enabled environments," in *e-Health Networking, Applications and Services (Healthcom)*, 2017 IEEE 19th International Conference on. IEEE, 2017, pp. 1–5.
9. Errobidart, J.; Uriz, A. J.; Gonzalez, E.; Gelosi, I. E.; Etcheverry, J. A.: "Offline domotic system using voice comands," in *Embedded Systems (CASE)*, 2017 Eight Argentine Symposium and Conference on. IEEE, 2017, pp. 1–6.
10. Hail, M. A.; Fischer, S.: "Iot for aal: An architecture via information-centric networking," in *Globecom Workshops (GC Wkshps)*, 2015 IEEE. IEEE, 2015, pp. 1–6.
11. Ray, P. P.: "A survey on internet of things architectures," in *Journal of King Saud University-Computer and Information Sciences*, 2016.
12. Ray, P. P.: "Home health hub internet of things (h 3 iot): An architectural framework for monitoring health of elderly people," in *Science Engineering and Management Research (ICSEMR)*, 2014 International Conference on. IEEE, 2014, pp. 1–3.
13. S. for information Organization, 9th. Int. Conf. on the Applications of Digital Information and Web Technologies (ICADIWT 2018), https://www.socio.org.uk/icadiwt/iomt/, 2018.
14. Rosas, J.; Camarinha-Matos, L. M.; Carvalho, G.; Oliveira, A. I.; Ferrada, F.: "Development of an ecosystem for ambient assisted living," in *International Summer Workshop on Multimodal Interfaces*. Springer, 2013, pp. 200–227.
15. Kuneva, M.; Dozsa, C.; Mann, E.; Miles, I.; Parent, A.; Vasconcelos, D.: "Interim

evaluation of the ambient assisted living joint programme: Unlocking innovation in ageing well," Report of High-Level Expert Panel, appointed by the European Commission/DG Information Society & Media, vol. 77, 2010.
16. Valli, A.: "The design of natural interaction," in *Multimedia Tools and Applications*, vol. 38, no. 3, pp. 295–305, 2008.
17. Reeves, B.; Nass, C. I.: The media equation: How people treat computers, television, and new media like real people and places. Cambridge university press, 1996.
18. Schmidt, A.; "Implicit human computer interaction through context," in *Personal technologies*, vol. 4, no. 2-3, pp. 191–199, 2000.
19. Cantoni, V.; Cellario, M.; Porta, M.: "Perspectives and challenges in e-learning: towards natural interaction paradigms," in *Journal of Visual Languages & Computing*, vol. 15, no. 5, pp. 333–345, 2004.
20. Pires, C. G.; Pinto, F.; Teixeira, V. D.; Freitas, J.; Dias, M. S.: "Living home center–a personal assistant with multimodal interaction for elderly and mobility impaired e-inclusion," Proc. PROPOR. Coimbra, 2012.
21. Starner, T.; Auxier, J.; Ashbrook, D.; Gandy, M.: "The gesture pendant: A self-illuminating, wearable, infrared computer vision system for home automation control and medical monitoring," in *Wearable Computers, the 4th Int. Symp.* IEEE, 2000, pp. 87–94.
22. Bhuiyan, M.; Picking, R.: "Gesture-controlled user interfaces, what have we done and what's next," in *Proceedings of the Fifth Collaborative Research Symposium on Security, ELearning, Internet and Networking* (SEIN 2009), Darmstadt, Germany, 2009, pp. 25–29.
23. Kraichan, C.; Pumrin, S.: "Face and eye tracking for controlling computer functions," in *Electrical Engineering/Electronics, Computer, Telecommunications and Information Technology (ECTI-CON)*, 2014 11th International Conference on. IEEE, 2014, pp. 1–6.
24. Lee, M.-S.; Trajkovic, M.; Dagtas, S.; Gutta, S.; Brodsky, T.; Philomin, V.; Lin, Y.-T.; Strubbe, H.; Cohen-Solal, E.: "Computer vision based elderly care monitoring system," Mar. 27 2003, uS Patent App. 10/189,272.
25. Portet, F.; Vacher, M.; Golanski, C.; Roux, C.; Meillon, B.: "Design and evaluation of a smart home voice interface for the elderly: acceptability and objection aspects," Personal and Ubiquitous Computing, vol. 17, no. 1, pp. 127–144, 2013.
26. Moritz, N.; Goetze, S.; Appell, J.-E.: "Ambient voice control for a personal activity and household assistant," in *Ambient Assisted Living. Springer*, 2011, pp. 63–74.
27. Bianchi, V.; De Munari, I.; Ciampolini P. et al.: "Controlling AAL environments through BCI," in *Mechatronic and Embedded Systems and Applications (MESA)*, 2014 IEEE/ASME 10th International Conference on. IEEE, 2014, pp. 1–6.
28. Mora, N.; Bianchi, V.; De Munari, I.; Ciampolini, P.: "A BCI platform supporting AAL applications," in *Int. Conf. on Universal Access in HCI*. Springer, 2014, pp. 515–526.
29. Hossain M. A.; Ahmed, D. T.: "Virtual caregiver: an ambient-aware elderly monitoring system," in *IEEE Trans. on Inf. Tech. in Biomedicine*, vol. 16, no. 6, pp. 1024–1031, 2012.
30. Skillen, K.-L.; Chen, L.; Nugent, C. D.; Donnelly, M. P.; Burns, W.; Solheim, I.: "Ontological user profile modeling for context-aware application personalization," in *Int. Conference on Ubiquitous Computing and Ambient Intelligence*, 2012, pp. 261–268.
31. Zukerman, I.; Albrecht, D. W.: "Predictive statistical models for user modeling," in *User Modeling and User-Adapted Interaction*, vol. 11, no. 1-2, pp. 5–18, 2001.
32. Dawson, D.; Desmarais, R.; Kienle, H. M.; Müller, H. A.: "Monitoring in Adaptive Systems Using Reflection," in *Int. Workshop on Soft. Eng. for Adaptive and self-managing Systems.*, 2008, pp. 81–88.
33. Moody, D.: A Practical Method for Representing Large Entity Relationship Models. PhD thesis, 2001.

Towards using Memoization for Saving Energy in Android *

Rui Rua[13], Marco Couto[13], Adriano Pinto[24], Jácome Cunha[14], and João Saraiva[14]

[1] Universidade do Minho, Portugal
[2] Universidade NOVA de Lisboa, Portugal
[3] HASLab/INESC TEC, Portugal
[4] NOVA LINCS, Portugal

{rui.a.rua,marco.l.couto}@inesctec.pt ab.pinto@campus.fct.unl.pt
{jacome,saraiva}@di.uminho.pt

Abstract. Over the last few years, the interest in the analysis of the energy consumption of Android applications has been increasing significantly. Indeed, there are a considerable number of studies which aim at analyzing the energy consumption in the Android ecosystem, such as measuring/estimating the energy consumed by an application or block of code, or even detecting energy expensive coding patterns or APIs.
In this paper, we present an initial study of the impact of memoization in the energy consumption of Android applications. We compare implementations of 18 methods from different applications, with and without using memoization, and measure the energy consumption of both of them. The results show that using memoization can be a good approach for saving energy, since 13 of those methods decreased their energy consumption.

Keywords: Android · Energy · Memoization

1 Introduction

The Android ecosystem is evolving at an impressive pace. Since this system can run on a wide variety of devices, from smartphones to tablets of several manufacturers, to wearables, its widespread usage in the last decade is notorious.

This proliferation of Android devices increased the interest in a particular research area: energy consumption analysis of software applications. It has been an intensive research topic in the last few years, greatly motivated not only by the mobile development area, characterized by powerful computing systems, yet energy-harvesting, which run over batteries with limited capacity, but also by the growing interest of developers in knowing more about how to develop software in a energy-saving manner [24].

* Work financed by the ERDF - European Regional Development Fund through the Operational Programme for Competitiveness and Internationalisation - COMPETE 2020 Programme and by National Funds through the Portuguese funding agency, Fundação para a Ciência e a Tecnologia, project POCI-01-0145-FEDER-016718.

Several research works focused on detecting or predicting the energy consumption that is triggered by a software artifact [11, 12]. For instance, some works presented techniques for monitoring and classifying energy consumption of blocks of code, such as lines of code [18], methods [7], API calls [20–23], or code patterns [17, 27]. Even the energy consumed at the testing phase can be a concern [19], as well as the display of visual elements in the application views [8].

Nevertheless, the amount of information provided about an application that can be used by developers to reduce its energy consumption at the development phase, is still very low [24]. In this paper we study the influence of incremental computation, obtained via method memoization, on the energy consumption in the context of the Android ecosystem. We present a systematic study that shows the energy gains of applying memoization techniques to Android applications. Memoization is widely used in the context of functional programming to speedup the execution time of programs: calls of a function are cached/memoized, and next calls to that function with the same arguments are obtained from the cache, so that the function is not call again. In order to be able to perform method memoization we consider side-effect free methods, only. That is, methods that implement functions and as consequence are prone to memoization [30]. After computing such methods (i.e., functions) in the application's source code, we refactor it into a semantically equivalent one which memoize/reuses its calls. To study the impact in performance of our memoization refactoring, we monitor the energy consumption while executing the non-incremental and the incremental versions of several Android applications with the same inputs. Our first experimental results show that memoization can greatly improve the energy efficiency of an Android application, considering that such application is prone to it, without threatening its normal functioning and/or efficiency.

To summarize, we intend to answer to the following research question: *Can memoization help reduce energy consumed by Android applications?*

This paper is organized as follows. Section 2 introduces the concept of memoization for Android applications and describes in detail our experimental setting. We present the results of the experiment in Section 3, which are discussed in Section 4, where we also answer our research question. Section 5 presents the threats to the validity of this work. Related approaches are describeded in Section 6. Finally, Section 7 presents our conclusions and future work directions.

2 Experimental Study

In this section, we start by explaining how to decide if a Java/Android method can be memoized. We then describe in detail our memoization technique for Android applications, along with the empirical study used for validation.

2.1 What Can be Memoized?

Yang et al. [29] proposed a set of three pre-conditions to classify a Java method as memoizable:

1. The method must be pure, that is, it must be a function;
2. The arguments must be immutable;
3. The return value cannot depend on static fields, public member fields nor publicly exposed member fields.

In our particular case, we have simplified the application of pre-condition (2) and used only methods that have as arguments primitive types or the *Context* object of an application (since it is immutable).

In the next section we will describe in detail the experimental study we conducted: the methods analyzed, the conditions under which such methods were tested, and the full procedure to actually run the tests and obtain results.

2.2 Experimental Setup

This section describes the study conducted, describing the Android applications and methods used, how methods were refactored, and the experiment setup.

Android applications and methods analysis: We used two Android applications from the MUSE repository[5] (`Pixate Freestyle`[6] and `android-demos`) and another one from F-Droid[7] (`Chanu`[8]). The distribution of methods analyzed from each of these applications is described in Table 1.

`Pixate Freestyle` is a free framework that lets users style his native Android views with stylesheets and is very much based on the graphical component. This application contains 219 classes. `android-demos` is a very specific application from the repository and contains 34 classes. `Chanu` is a well-known application with 538 classes. Basically, it is the code of the 4chan site application where users can browse images of various contents. This is the largest application among the three and so it was where we most applied the technique of memoization.

Since our goal is to test each method prone to memoization individually, we decided that it was best suited to extract such methods from these application and run our experiments in a controlled manner. In order to do so, we created our own application only with such methods which we literally copied from their applications. After this process, we duplicated the application, and in the second version all the 18 methods were using our memoization technique.

Methods Refactoring: We manually analyzed the methods for the three selected applications. After finding memoizable methods, we created an application to encompass all those methods. We have then created two versions of the same application: one with all methods in their original form and the other with the memoized ones.

Our memoization technique consisted of storing the input of the methods as a key in a `HashMap` and its output as the value. So, if the method had already

[5] https://opencatalog.darpa.mil/MUSE.html.
[6] https://github.com/Pixate/pixate-freestyle-android
[7] https://f-droid.org
[8] https://f-droid.org/en/packages/com.chanapps.four.activity

Method	Input	Output	Application
createIntent	Context,String,String	Intent	Chanu
countLines	String	int	Chanu
replyText	Long[]	String	Chanu
join	List<String>, String	String	Chanu
threadSubject	String, String	String	Chanu
textViewFilter	String, boolean	String	Chanu
getUrl	Context, String	String	Chanu
planifyText, quoteText, exifText	String	String	Chanu
getNumeral	String, String	String	Pixate Freestyle
removeLocaleInfoFromFloat, addNegativeSign, addPositiveSign	String	String	Pixate Freestyle
isMobile	String	boolean	android-demos
readableFileSize	long	String	android-demos
dip2px; px2dip	Context,float	int	android-demos

Table 1: Characterization of methods used in experiments.

been called for a particular input, then we just accessed its value on the map and returned it. Otherwise, a new entry was created on the map and the result returned. In cases where the methods only received a single input parameter, this was directly the key of the map. However, there were cases in which more than one argument was passed as parameter. Table 1 presents a characterization of the methods used in our experiments, containing for each method, the respective name, application, input and output parameters. In this table, some of such examples can be observed. For instance, the method name *getURL* from the Chanu application receives two distinct objects as an argument. For the multi-parameter cases, a library called javatuples [29] was used. In this way, the input values were saved in tuples which became the `HashMap` key.

Experiments execution: In order to test the energy impact of memoization in these methods, we defined a usage scenario for them, consisting of invoking a method 50 times with different parameters passed to it. This resulted in inserting 50 entries in the method's map structure. To take advantage of memoization, this procedure was repeated 10, 20, 30, 40, and 50 times, and each of this repetition sets are what we consider our *test cases.*

To obtain a representative number of measurements, each test case was repeated 25 times for each method in both the original and the memoized versions (alternatively), using a Nexus 4 running Android version 5.1.1 - API level 22. In order to perform energy monitoring, we used the Trepn Profiler [9], an accurate Energy profiler developed by Qualcomm. Before running each iteration, we performed the initial set up, where the previously installed version of the application under test was removed, the new version was installed and switched on (as well as the Trepn app), and a warm-up of 5 seconds was considered. After this set up, Trepn started profiling at the same time that the test was executed. When the test finished, the energy results were recorded and both the app and Trepn were switched off.

[9] https://developer.qualcomm.com/software/trepn-power-profiler

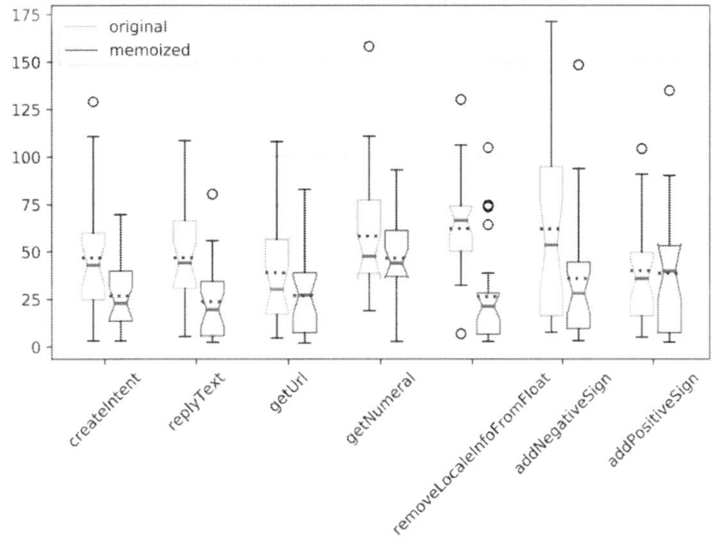

Fig. 1: Methods favoring memoization with consumption between 0 and 175 mJ.

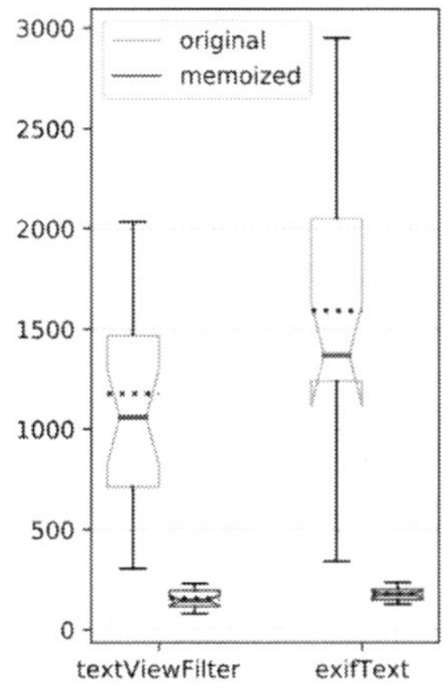

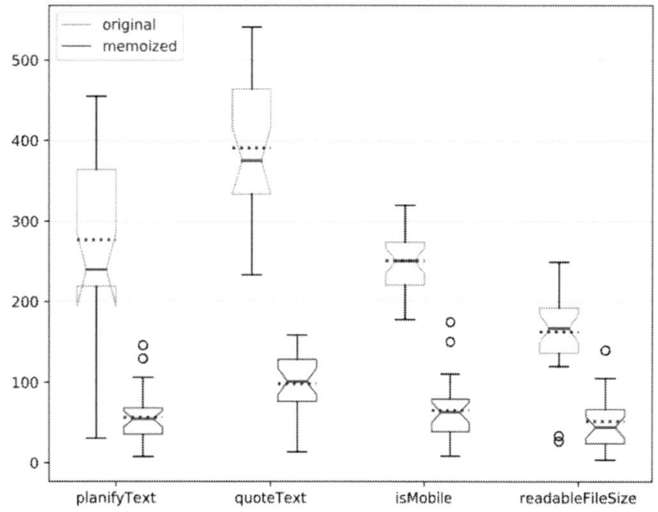

Fig. 2: Methods in favor of memoization with consumption between 0 and 3000 mJ (left hand-side chart) and between 0 and 600 mJ (right hand-side chart).

3 Results

In this section we present in detail the results obtained from the experiment described in the previous section. Figures 1 and 2 display a box plot for each of the 13 methods we could find a statistically significant difference between the energy consumption of the original method and the energy consumption of the memoized one in favor of the memoization, that is, when the memoized method consumed less energy than the original version[10].

[10] We divided the methods in different charts because they have different scales of values and to have them all in the same one would not allow to properly see the details.

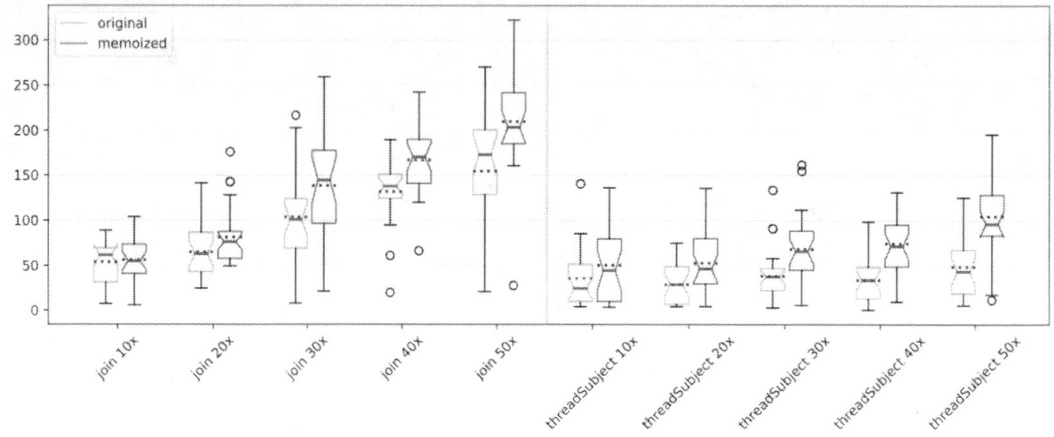

Fig. 3: Box plots representing the energy spent by the original and memoized methods, considering 10-50 executions of the tests, where the original version spent less energy.

Each box plot represents the energy measurements, in millijoules (mJ), of the 25 executions of the corresponding method showing the minimum and maximum values (marked by the whiskers), possible outliers (marked by small circles), the 1st and 3rd quartiles (bottom and top of the box), the median (marked by the red horizontal filled in line), and the average (marked by the blue horizontal dashed line). Each yellow/green pair represents the original/memoized version of the method. We also show the notch because it can be seen as an informal test of the null hypothesis that the medians are equal, that is, if two notches overlap, then it is not possible to reject the null hypothesis with a 95% confidence [4]. In Section 4 we will present formal verification of the statistical differences of the energy measurements.

Note these charts show the energy values for 10 executions of the test suite, the first being with new values, and the remaining with repeated ones. In Section 4 we will detail more the analysis of different numbers of executions.

In Figure 3 we show the box plots with the energy consumption of the only two methods where the energy consumed by the memoized versions is statistically different from the original methods, but in favor of the original ones. Once more, we refer to Section 4 to test executions greater than 10 times.

Figure 4 presents once more box plots, but now for the three methods where no statistical difference was found for original and memoized methods. For these three methods we executed the same test suite, but now running it 10, 20, 30, 40, and 50 times. The goal was to take more advantage of the memoization and understand if this would turn the method better or worst the original one. Each increment of 10 executions only makes the memoized method read the stored values, while the original version needs to run entirely. Indeed it may be the case the overhead of the memoization (another method call, plus the map) makes the gain negligible. However, what we recorded for these methods is that sometimes the memoized version is better, but sometimes the original one also is. We will come back to this discussion in Section 4.

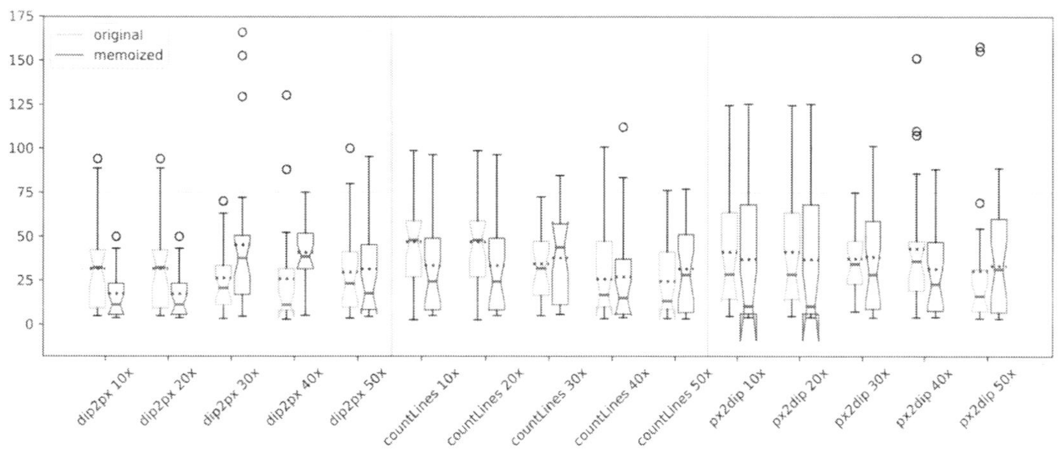

Fig. 4: Box plots representing the energy spent by the original and memoized methods, considering 10 to 50 executions of the tests with no statistical difference.

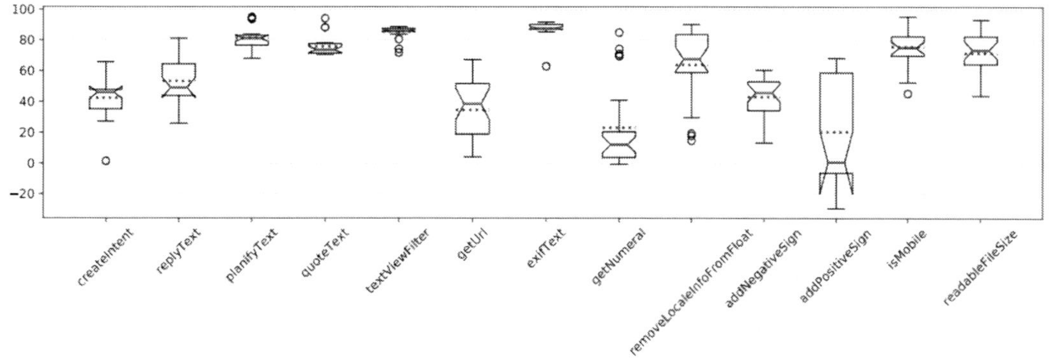

Fig. 5: Energy losses from the original method to the memoized one of the methods that have positive results.

The results presented until now seem to indicate that there is a positive effect in the energy consumption when memoizing method calls. In Figure 5 we present the percentage of losses in the energy spent from the original version of the method to the memoized one, considering the methods where memoization produces positive results (the methods represented in Figures 1 and 2). For each method, we calculated the percentage of energy decrease as follows. For each of the 25 executions, we sorted, independently, the original and the memoized values of energy consumption. We then calculated the losses of energy from the use of the original version to the memoized one using the formula $\frac{original - memoized}{original} \times 100$. Positive values represent the fact that there is indeed a loss of energy from the original to the memoized, thus supporting the use of memoization, and negative values imply an increase in the energy spent, thus pointing situations where memoization does not consumes less energy.

As we can see, the gains are fairly positive. Note once more we are only showing the results for running the test suite 10 times, as this already points to quite positive results. We will discuss these gains further on in the Section 4.

method	10x	20x	30x	40x	50x
exifText	(87, 90)	(92, 95)			
textViewFilter	(85, 88)	(94, 94)			
planifyText	(77, 83)	(86, 89)			
quoteText	(71, 78)	(88, 92)			
isMobile	(70, 82)	(84, 96)			
readableFileSize	(64, 82)	(82, 89)			
removeLocaleInfoFromFloat	(59, 84)	(66, 71)			
replyText	(44, 64)	(-9, 17)	(41, 76)	(41, 71)	(48, 76)
createIntent	(35, 48)	(-21, 6)	(35, 54)	(21, 43)	(49, 66)
addNegativeSign	(34, 53)	(62, 80)	(61, 75)	(68, 94)	(71, 86)
getUrl	(19, 52)	(32, 66)	(45, 57)	(37, 56)	(49, 62)
getNumeral	(4, 21)	(-21, 2)	(9, 30)	(27, 45)	(60, 75)
addPositiveSign	(-6, 59)	(40, 48)	(51, 65)	(36, 57)	(10, 26)
join	(-11, 11)	(-40, -8)	(-46, -18)	(-30, -22)	(-36, -19)
px2dip	(-55, 0)	(2, 60)	(-27, 53)	(4, 52)	(-82, 5)
threadSubject	(-62, 1)	(-99, -54)	(-92, -75)	(-280, -101)	(-219, -102)
countLines	(-84, -7)	(16, 62)	(-17, 6)	(-15, 21)	(-53, 16)
dip2px	(-161, -60)	(24, 47)	(-71, -35)	(-281, -62)	(-21, 17)

Table 2: 1st (on the left hand-side of the column) and 3rd (on the right) quartiles of the energy losses from the use of the original method to the use of the memoized version.

To increase the reading of these results we present in Table 2 the percentage of the energy not spent, comparing the memoized method to the original one of the 1st and 3rd quartiles. This follows from the box plots, complementing the information and giving central values of the losses.

Finally, Table 3 shows the percentage of times the energy spent by the memoized method is lower than the original one, considering the 25 runs of each method, for the 5 test cases. Note the underlined values are the ones where we could not find statistical significant difference between the original and memoized measurements. For all the other methods there is statistical significant difference between the energy consumption of the original and the memoized method. Values in **bold** indicate when more than 50% of the 25 runs spend more energy in the memoized methods than the original ones. The values with no special formatting have statistical significance in favor of the memoized versions.

4 Discussion

The first observation is the most obvious one: memoization has a clear impact on energy consumption in Android applications. In fact, for the majority of situations the impact is fairly positive. Considering the 18 tested methods, the energy consumption for 13 of them has consistently decreased when using memoization (as can be seen in Figures 1 and 2). For those methods, we can observe that the average consumption of the 25 measurements is always lower when using memoization, as well as the minimum and maximum values, and the values for the 1st and 3rd quartile. Figure 2 shows the methods that had the biggest impact.

These values allow us to answer to the research question: can memoization be used to reduce energy consumption in Android applications?

	10x	20x	30x	40x	50x
createIntent	72	56	68	68	72
getUrl	60	72	68	76	76
replyText	68	52	84	92	84
getNumeral	56	56	64	68	84
addNegativeSign	56	88	84	100	100
addPositiveSign	56	72	80	84	80
planifyText	100	100	-	-	-
quoteText	100	100	-	-	-
textViewFilter	100	100	-	-	-
exifText	100	100	-	-	-
removeLocaleInfoFromFloat	80	88	-	-	-
isMobile	100	100	-	-	-
ReadableFileSize	88	100	-	-	-
join	48	**32**	28	**28**	**24**
threadSubject	**40**	36	**20**	**12**	**20**
countLines	**36**	68	48	**44**	44
dip2px	**24**	68	**32**	**28**	56
px2dip	**40**	56	48	64	**44**

Table 3: Percentage (of the 25 runs) that the memoized version consumes less energy than the original one (For each method and for each test setting). Underlined values have statistical significance; bold values represent more than 50% of the 25 runs spend more energy in the memoized methods than the original ones.

To make these results more meaningful, we want to know if there is statistical evidence behind these observations, that is, if the energy consumed by the memoized version of these methods is consistently lower than the original one. Thus, we tested the following hypothesis:

$\boldsymbol{H}_0 : P(A > B) = 0.5$
$\boldsymbol{H}_1 : P(A > B) \neq 0.5$

where B and A represent the act of randomly drawing a value from the set of 25 measurements, with and without using memoization, respectively. Hence, $P(A > B)$ represents, when drawing from both A and B, the probability of getting a value from A (without memoization) larger than the one drawn from B (using memoization). Our null hypothesis is then obtaining a probability of 50%, while obtaining one different than 50% is the alternative hypothesis.

To understand if there is an overall significant relevance between the distributions of A and B, we ran the Wilcoxon signed-rank test, with a two-tail p-value considering $\alpha = 0.01$[11]. The test was repeated for the 13 methods where the use of memoization led to improvements in energy consumption. At the end, the test produced significant relevance, with the p-value < 0.01 for 11 of the 13 cases. The exceptions where `getUrl` and `addPositiveSign`, both with parametric distributions, which we will exclude for now and explain later. To calculate a non-parametric effect size, Field [10] suggests using Rosenthal's formula [25, 26]

[11] All the values obtained for this test, for the 18 methods, are available at https://goo.gl/WHXQeA.

to compute a correlation, and compare the correlation values against Cohen's [5] suggested thresholds: 0.1 for small, 0.3 for medium and 0.5 for large significance.

From the 11 scenarios, 8 were non-parametric, and the values obtained were: 0.4 (medium) for `createIntent` and `replyText` methods, and 0.6 (large) for the remaining methods. For the remaining 3 methods, a D'Agostino and Pearson's test [9] revealed that we were dealing with normal distributions, and so we should calculate the Cohen's d coefficient to determine the magnitude of the effect size. According to Sawilowsky [28], the reference thresholds and their respective effect size should be 0.01 (very small), 0.2 (small), 0.5 (medium), 0.8 (large), 1.2 (very large), and 2 (huge significance).

We obtained values of 0.4 for the `getNumeral`, 0.6 for `addNegativeSign`, and 1.4 for the method `removeLocaleInfoFromFloat`. Considering these reference values, we have statistical support to say that, for these methods, using memoization does lead to energy savings.

The effect size values calculated so far were only for the scenario where each method was called 10 times in each measured test. It may happen that, for methods with lower significance values, repeating the experience with an increasing number of calls could lead to results more or less supportive. Thus, we repeated the experience with 20, 30, 40 and 50 invocations, calculated the significance values and the effect size (see Table 3). We observe that all 13 aforementioned methods continue to have more than 50% of the 25 tests in favor of memoization and, although in some specific cases the statistical experiment resulted in no significance, the percentage of memoization favorable tests kept increasing with the increasing number of calls for all of them, and the same happened with the significance. Such cases were the previously excluded `getUrl` and `addPositiveSign` method. Hence, we categorized these 13 methods as *prone to memoization*.

The use of memoization, however, does not always mean saving energy. In some cases, it is not possible to determine whether memoization results in energy saving or not. In our experiments, we found 3 methods fitting such criteria. The results of such experiments are shown in Figure 4, in which the methods where called 10 times on each test. As we can see by examining the box plots, the values for the original version and the version using memoization are very similar.

By running the same statistical experiment performed for the 13 methods were memoization actually decreased energy consumption, we observed that the results for `dip2px`, `px2dip`, and `countLines` methods were not statistically significant. This means that the reason behind the energy consumption being lower is not related to the use of memoization, neither to the use of the original version of the method. Similarly, the percentage of tests in favor of memoization was mostly around 50%, dropping or increasing a few percentage levels unpredictably when increasing the number of invocations. Therefore, we categorized these methods as *unpredictable*.

For the remaining 2 methods (`threadSubject` and `join`), we observed that the energy consumption actually increased in the majority of cases while using memoization. In fact, if we examine Table 3, we see that for such methods the percentage of times where the memoized version consumes less energy is always lower than 50%, for all test scenarios. We ran the same statistical test as before to check if the values were consistently worse for the memoized version, and we obtained significant relevance for all of them, except `px2dip`. However, the effect size varied from "small significance" to "medium significance". Thus, these methods are then categorized as *unfit for memoization*.

The most interesting observations can, however, be seen in Table 2. The data presented there shows the calculated gains (positive values) or losses (negative values) when using memoization. To obtain these values, we first sorted, for each method, the energy consumed by the original and memoized version, in order to compare the lower/higher energy consumption values of one version with the lower/higher values of the other. Then, we calculated the gains pairwise and arranged them in a box plot. The first element of the pair in each table cell is the gain calculated for the 1st quartile of the box plots, while the second element is the gain considering the 3rd quartile. With this, we try to show the gains/losses are independent of the energy consumption measured absolute value. Each column contains the gains/loses for the obtained results of running the same experiment, but varying the number of times each method is invoked.

As expected, we see that the majority of the values are positive, that is, memoization is, in the majority of cases, a suitable technique to save energy. In the first 7 methods, the impact is more notorious since in all the 25 measurements the memoized version has a significantly lower energy consumption, and when we repeated the experiment for 20 invocations per test, the impact is even greater. Also, the significance values kept increasing, so we stopped measuring and categorized them as *strongly prone to memoization* methods.

If we look only to the pairs with both positive gains in the column for 10 invocations (methods *prone to memoization*), the gains can go from 3% to 90%. Theses values tend to increase if we increase the number of invocations: for these same methods, considering 20 invocations, if we exclude the ones with negative values, since they were the cases with no statistical significance (see Table 3), they go from 31% to 96%. For the other scenarios (30, 40 or 50 invocations), the values are always positive, as the significance keeps being maintained.

For the *unpredictable* methods, the gains are also unpredictable: the 3rd quartile value is negative (loss), but the 1st is positive (gain). Even so, in that scenario the statistical test showed there was no significance for both the methods, as we increase the number of invocations and tend to decrease proportionally.

5 Threats to Validity

Measuring the energy consumption of a mobile device is complex [3]. This is mostly due to the fact that it is quite difficult to fully isolate the code or application under measurement. To address this issue, we executed our application 25 times, thus giving it enough slack to have in average results that correspond to the truth and with as low side effects as possible. Moreover, we executed the application in a factory-reseted device, in airplane mode and with the lowest brightness level, to ensure the energy consumed by the display was as low as possible. Because, our memoization reuses the results of previously computed (memoized) method calls, thus, we reduce the computations/work needed by a program. We focus our evaluation in measuring the energy savings of the CPU. However, a detail study on how the energy of the screen and communication mechanisms (two known energy greedy aspects in mobile devices) are also affected by memoization is needed.

To assure the data retrieved were consistent, both the memoized and non-memoized applications were run in the same environment, half of the times starting with the memoized version, and the other half with the non-memoized one. Thus, this gives us confidence the differences we found between the two versions are only due to the usage or not of memoization.

The energy consumption values were obtained by using Trepn, a tool developed by Qualcomm, a manufacturer of processors and chipsets of mobile devices. As Trepn obtains the power values directly from the PMIC (Power Management Integrated Circuit) present in the chipsets, the values obtained through this tool are accurate [14], and has been used in several works [13, 15, 16].

Our experimentation occurred only in one smartphone and one version of the operating system. It is expected to find different absolute values in different smartphones and Android versions, but the differences between the memoized versions and original ones are quite consistent and thus it is not expected to see significant changes in the differences if changing the evaluation settings.

Another possible issue is the executed tests. Indeed, it is usually difficult to find tests for Android applications [6–8]. Thus, we created a test suite for each method we wanted to analyze and execute it a different number of times to understand when using memoization is beneficial. We have shown that for most cases to read 9 times a memoized value is sufficient. If a method is called most of the times with different values, than memoization will not be useful.

6 Related Work

Yang et al. proposed a technique and tool to determine the functional purity of Java methods [29]. In particular, if a method is a pure function, then it can be memoized. In their evaluation they were able to successfully memoize several methods from 3 different Java libraries and to reduce its execution time. As expected the memory usage increased due to the memo table.

A quite similar approach has also been proposed by Agosta et al. [1], since in their work they have also defined which Java methods can be memoized based on their functional purity. They defined a theoretical model to predict the effectiveness of the memoization in terms of energy consumption, but their approach has been applied to a particular set of computations in a desktop computer. In our experiments we have had a similar result. The most important difference is that we have shown that memoization has also a positive impact in the energy consumption in mobile devices.

Banerjee and Roychoudhury proposed a set of guidelines to improve energy consumption of mobile devices related to the use of energy-intensive resources such as the GPS or the camera [2]. Based on these guidelines they propose a set of refactorings to ensure the guidelines are followed within an application. They have shown that this technique allows to spent between 3% and 29% less energy. Our solution can be combined with this one as they address different issues, possibly achieving even greater gains.

Cruz and Abreu have also proposed a set of refactorings based on performance guidelines to improve the energy consumption of Android applications [8]. They have shown that these refactorings improve the energy consumption, although this does not occur for all applications and refactorings.

7 Conclusions

In this work we have explored the use of memoization in Android applications, focusing on its impact in the energy consumption. We selected 18 methods from 3 different applications and designed an experiment to evaluate the energy consumption of such methods, as well as their memoized versions. The results from this experiment show that indeed the use of memoization promotes energy saving in most cases. These are our first experimental results, and we will further study the impact of these energy savings in the overall consumption of the applications.

The goal of this paper was to show the impact of memoization on energy consumption. However, it will be also interesting to relate these results to the execution time and energy consumption obtained with our memoization refactoring. We will pursue this topic in future work.

References

1. Agosta, G., Bessi, M., Capra, E., Francalanci, C.: Automatic memoization for energy efficiency in financial applications. Sustainable Computing: Informatics and Systems **2**(2), 105–115 (2012), IEEE Int. Green Computing Conference (IGCC'11)
2. Banerjee, A., Roychoudhury, A.: Automated re-factoring of android apps to enhance energy-efficiency. In: Proceedings of the International Conference on Mobile Software Engineering and Systems. pp. 139–150. ACM, New York, NY, USA (2016)
3. Banerjee, A., Roychoudhury, A.: Future of mobile software for smartphones and drones: Energy and performance. In: Proceedings of the 4th International Conference on Mobile Software Engineering and Systems. pp. 1–12. IEEE Press (2017)
4. Chambers, J.M., Cleveland, W.S., Kleiner, B., Tukey, P.A.: Graphical Methods for Data Analysis. Chapman and Hall/CRC (2017)
5. Cohen, J.: Statistical power analysis for the behavioral sciences . hilsdale. NJ: Lawrence Earlbaum Associates **2** (1988)
6. Couto, M., Cunha, J., Fernandes, J.P., Pereira, R., Saraiva, J.: GreenDroid: A tool for analysing power consumption in the android ecosystem. In: Scientific Conf. on Informatics, 2015 IEEE 13th International. pp. 73–78 (Nov 2015)
7. Couto, M., T., C., Cunha, J., Fernandes, J.P., Saraiva, J.: Detecting anomalous energy consumption in android applications. In: Quintão Pereira, F.M. (ed.) Programming Languages, LNCS, vol. 8771, pp. 77–91. Springer Int. Publishing (2014)
8. Cruz, L., Abreu, R.: Performance-based guidelines for energy efficient mobile applications. In: 4th Conf. on Mobile Software Eng. and Systems. pp. 46–57 (2017)

9. D'Agostino, R.B.: An omnibus test of normality for moderate and large size samples. Biometrika **58**(2), 341–348 (1971)
10. Field, A.: Discovering statistics using SPSS. Sage publications (2009)
11. Hao, S., Li, D., Halfond, W.G.J., Govindan, R.: Estimating mobile application energy consumption using program analysis. In: Proc. of 35th Int. Conf. on Software Engineering (ICSE) (May 2013)
12. Hao, S., Li, D., Halfond, W., Govindan, R.: Estimating android applications' cpu energy usage via bytecode profiling. In: Green and Sustainable Software (GREENS), 2012 First Int. Workshop on. pp. 1–7 (June 2012)
13. Hegde, N., Melanson, E.L., Sazonov, E.: Development of a real time activity monitoring android application utilizing smartstep. In: Proceedings of the 38th IEEE Int. Conf. of the Engineering in Medicine and Biology Society. pp. 1886–1889 (2016)
14. Hoque, M.A., Siekkinen, M., Khan, K.N., Xiao, Y., Tarkoma, S.: Modeling, profiling, and debugging the energy consumption of mobile devices. ACM Comput. Surv. **48**(3), 39:1–39:40 (Dec 2015)
15. Hu, Y., Yan, J., Yan, D., Lu, Q., Yan, J.: Lightweight energy consumption analysis and prediction for android applications. Science of Computer Programming (2017)
16. Jabbarvand, R., Sadeghi, A., Garcia, J., Malek, S., Ammann, P.: EcoDroid: An approach for energy-based ranking of android apps. In: Procs. of the 4th Int. Workshop on Green and Sustainable Software. pp. 8–14. IEEE Press (2015)
17. Li, D., Halfond, W.G.J.: An investigation into energy-saving programming practices for android smartphone app development. In: Proc. of 3rd Int. Workshop on Green and Sustainable Software. pp. 46–53. GREENS 2014, ACM (2014)
18. Li, D., Hao, S., Halfond, W.G.J., Govindan, R.: Calculating source line level energy information for android applications. pp. 78–89. ISSTA 2013, ACM (2013)
19. Li, D., Jin, Y., Sahin, C., Clause, J., Halfond, W.G.J.: Integrated energy-directed test suite optimization. pp. 339–350. ISSTA 2014, ACM (2014)
20. Linares-Vásquez, M., Bavota, G., Bernal-Cárdenas, C., Oliveto, R., Di Penta, M., Poshyvanyk, D.: Mining energy-greedy api usage patterns in android apps:an empirical study. In: 11th Conf. on Mining Software Repositories. pp. 2–11 (2014)
21. Liu, K., Pinto, G., Liu, Y.D.: Data-oriented characterization of application-level energy optimization. In: Egyed, A., Schaefer, I. (eds.) Fundamental Approaches to Software Engineering, LNCS, vol. 9033, pp. 316–331. Springer (2015)
22. Pereira, R., Couto, M., Cunha, J., Fernandes, J.P., Saraiva, J.: The influence of the java collection framework on overall energy consumption. In: Proc. of 5th Int. Workshop on Green and Sustainable Software. pp. 15–21. ACM (2016)
23. Pinto, G., Castor, F.: Characterizing the energy efficiency of java's thread-safe collections in a multi-core environment. In: Proc. of SPLASH'2014 workshop on Software Engineering for Parallel Systems (SEPS), SEPS. vol. 14 (2014)
24. Pinto, G., Castor, F., Liu, Y.D.: Mining questions about software energy consumption. In: 11th Conf. on Mining Software Repositories. pp. 22–31. ACM (2014)
25. Rosenthal, R.: Meta-analytic procedures for social research, vol. 6. Sage (1991)
26. Rosenthal, R., Cooper, H., Hedges, L.: Parametric measures of effect size. The handbook of research synthesis pp. 231–244 (1994)
27. Sahin, C., Pollock, L., Clause, J.: How do code refactorings affect energy usage? In: Symp. on Empirical Sw Engineering and Measurement. pp. 36:1–36:10 (2014)
28. Sawilowsky, S.: New effect size rules of thumb **8**, 597–599 (11 2009)
29. Yang, J., Hotta, K., Higo, Y., Kusumoto, S.: Towards purity-guided refactoring in Java. In: Int. Conf. on Software Maintenance and Evolution. pp. 521–525 (2015)
30. Yang, J., Hotta, K., Higo, Y., Kusumoto, S.: Revealing purity and side effects on functions for reusing Java libraries. pp. 314–329. ICSR 2014, Cham (2014)

Desarrollo de un Software de Análisis de RNA con Integración de Mecanismos Interactivos

Wilson CASTILLO-ROJAS, Cristian VALDIVIA-ARAYA[1[1530000]] y Fernando MEDINA-QUISPE[2[1100000]]

[1] Universidad de Atacama, Av. Copayapu 485, Copiapó, Chile
[2] Universidad Arturo Prat, Av. Arturo Prat 2120, Iquique, Chile
wilson.castillo@uda.cl

Abstract. El desarrollo de software moderno exige por parte de los usuarios, cada vez más prestaciones acorde a la tecnología existente, en particular al que proveen los lenguajes de programación. Es así, como integrar mecanismos interactivos se ha convertido en una herramienta importante en la construcción de software. Una técnica muy utilizada en análisis de datos masivos son las Redes Neuronales Artificiales (RNA), las cuales se basan en el principio de emular el modo de aprendizaje del sistema neuronal humano, y son reconocidas como útiles para el análisis de datos complejos. Sin embargo, es muy difícil entender cómo las RNA generan sus patrones debido a la complejidad de su arquitectura. Para abordar esto, el artículo presenta el diseño y desarrollo de un software, como un entorno visual, con integración de Mecanismos de Interacción (MI), que permitan al usuario conocer el funcionamiento interno y organización de una RNA, en particular para el caso del tipo Perceptrón Multi-Capa (PMC). Lo anterior, permite analizar las componentes (neuronas) del modelo RNA a través de la disposición de visualizaciones antes, durante y posterior al proceso de análisis de la RNA. Esta investigación puede servir como trabajo inical, para medir la efectividad de los MI seleccionados y aplicados en el software, y que aporten en el entendimiento del comportamiento del modelo RNA y en la interpretación de los resultados (patrones) obtenidos.

Keywords: Desarrollo de software, Interacción humano computador, Análisis de redes neuronales artificiales.

1 Introducción

En la sociedad del conocimiento el rol social de la informática se ha convertido en un agente de cambio tecnológico importante. Esto también ha sido influenciado por el desarrollo del hardware y de las telecomunicaciones. Por esto, el desarrollo del software ha tenido que enfrentar nuevos desafíos en su proceso de diseño e implementación. Uno de estos desafíos es la usabilidad del software, que considera características de: facilidad de uso, capacidad intuitiva, ubicuidad, inclusividad, idiomática, aspectos culturales y sociológicos, estándares de usabilidad, diseño gráfico, MI y de adaptación, etc. Estas características tienen relación directa con la Interacción Humano-Computador (IHC) del software, lo cual refuerza el hecho de considerar la participación de los usuarios en las primeras etapas del diseño y construcción de las interfaces del software.

Por lo anterior, la IHC se trata de un área donde convergen muchas otras, y requiere de un equipo multidisciplinario. En el desarrollo de proyectos de software, muchas veces no se da la importancia a la IHC, esto se ve reflejado en la Ingeniería de Software (IS), debido a la ausencia del tratamiento del diseño y construcción de la interfaz de usuario, en los métodos de desarrollo de software más comunes. Antes quizás esto no era relevante, sin embargo, actualmente y debido a la importancia de la IHC, se torna necesario contar con métodos que integren el desarrollo de software con el desarrollo de la interfaz de usuario, considerando las características de la IHC [1].

Este trabajo de investigación aborda los aspectos señalados anteriormente, aplicándolos en el desarrollo de un software de análisis de RNA. En particular, se centra en la integración de distintos MI y visualizaciones complementarias, que permiten facilitar el entendimiento del funcionamiento interno del modelo RNA generado al usuario analista de datos.

Las RNA se basan en el principio de emular el modo de aprendizaje del sistema neuronal humano, y son reconocidas como muy útiles para el análisis de datos complejos. A diferencia de los métodos estadísticos tradicionales, las RNA no se basan en un modelo específico para analizar los datos [2]. Sin embargo, es muy difícil entender como las RNA generan sus patrones debido a la complejidad de su arquitectura [3].

El resultado de este trabajo corresponde al diseño e implementación de un software como entorno visual de RNA, en particular para el caso del tipo PMC. Esto, permite analizar las componentes (neuronas) del modelo RNA a través de la disposición de visualizaciones complementarias y MI ad-hoc; antes (sobre los datos), durante (sobre el modelo) y posterior (sobre los patrones) al proceso de análisis de la RNA.

2 Marco Conceptual

2.1 Concepto de RNA

Los modelos de RNA, están compuestos por gran número de unidades simples de procesamiento llamadas neuronas, y conectadas entre sí a través de una topología definida. Normalmente, las neuronas se agrupan en capas comenzando con una capa de entrada, desde donde se obtienen los datos, y termina con una capa de salida para devolver los resultados. Cada topología o arquitectura, responde a un tipo de problema concreto que se requiere resolver [4].

La topología define el tipo de red neuronal concreta, y los pesos son los parámetros que se ajustan para codificar la información contenida en un conjunto de datos de entrenamiento que definen el problema. Esto permite a la red, aprender y generalizar el conocimiento aprendido. En la tarea de interpretación de patrones y sus conexiones de la RNA, han surgido varios enfoques para ayudar en el entendimiento del funcionamiento de esta técnica, desde algoritmos que permiten extraer conocimiento simbólico a través de su arquitectura y de sus pesos [3], hasta modelos de visualización para el diseño y análisis de RNA [5, 6, 7].

El diseño de la topología de una RNA, es una tarea fundamental porque generalmente están constituidas por muchas unidades de procesamiento (neuronas) interconectadas, lo que las hace difíciles de inspeccionar y analizar para conseguir los resultados esperados. Por lo general, la topología se diseña de forma experimental y luego continúa iterando con distintas variaciones internas, hasta conseguir el patrón que entregue un rendimiento dentro de los parámetros esperados. Existen distintos de modelos RNA, pero este trabajo se centra fundamentalmente en el tipo PMC.

Una de las formas de disminuir la complejidad, para el análisis e identificación de los modelos en los datos, es a través de su representación visual. Las capacidades de percepción visual humana se pueden utilizar como apoyo en la detección de patrones, que quizás no son evidentes o detectables por métodos automatizados de análisis de datos. Al comprender cómo trabaja el modelo, se puede mejorar la interpretación de patrones o reglas generadas.

El apoyo visual en la interpretación de un modelo RNA puede generar sinergia, que combine las facultades de percepción visual humana con el poder de procesamiento computacional. Para lograr conseguir una técnica de visualización apropiada, se pueden incorporar métricas que permitan comparar las distintas componentes (neuronas), y utilizar MI apropiados para poder recorrer el modelo a través de estas componentes, y así obtener información adicional del modelo.

2.2 Perceptrón MultiCapa

El PMC es una generalización del perceptrón simple, y surgió como consecuencia de las limitaciones de dicha arquitectura en lo referente al problema de separabilidad no lineal [3]. La arquitectura de estas redes se caracteriza porque tienen neuronas agrupadas en diferentes capas. Cada una de las capas está conformada por un conjunto de neuronas y se distinguen tres tipos de capas diferentes: la capa de entrada, las capas ocultas y la capa de salida. Un ejemplo generalizado de esta estructura se puede ver en la Figura 1.

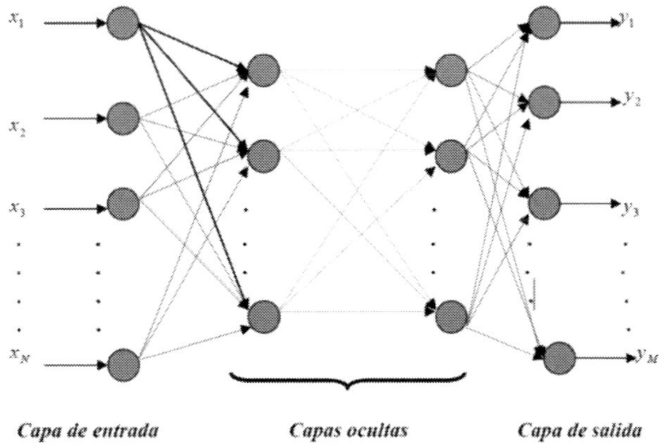

Fig. 1. Arquitectura del PMC.

Las neuronas de la capa de entrada, no realizan procesamiento solo se limitan a recibir los datos de entrada, y propagarlos a las siguientes capas. La capa de salida, se encarga de entregar el resultado final del procesamiento de la red. Las neuronas de las capas ocultas, se encargan de realizar el procesamiento no lineal de los patrones recibidos por las neuronas de entrada, o por otras neuronas de las capas ocultas.

Las conexiones del PMC siempre están dirigidas hacia adelante, por lo que reciben el nombre de redes "feedforward". Las conexiones entre neuronas llevan asociado un número real llamado peso de la conexión. La activación se propaga por la red a través de los pesos, desde la capa de entrada hacia la capa intermedia, donde se aplica una función de activación a las entradas que le llegan, entonces la activación se propaga a través de los pesos hacia la capa de salida. Todas las neuronas de la red llevan asociado un umbral que se trata como una conexión, y tiene como entrada la constante 1.

2.3 Mecanismos de Interacción

Para lograr una exploración exhaustiva de los datos en una interfaz de usuario, es necesario utilizar MI integrados. Los MI, permiten al usuario interactuar con visualizaciones y cambiarlas dinámicamente, de acuerdo con los objetivos de exploración. Adicionalmente, los MI permiten relacionar y combinar múltiples visualizaciones independientes [8]. El proceso de visualización de información, es el apoyo para la formación de una imagen mental de los datos. Esta imagen mental no es un esquema o una descripción estructural de los datos, pero es una comprensión de la potencial historia detrás de los datos, y esencialmente transforma un cúmulo de datos en información. Según Ware [9], la formación de una imagen mental puede ser aumentada al permitir que el usuario interactúe con los datos.

Los MI, se pueden clasificar en base a los efectos que tienen en el despliegue final en la interfaz y los datos. Por ejemplo, las técnicas de navegación se centran en la modificación de la proyección de los datos en la pantalla, utilizando métodos manuales o automatizados. Los métodos de vistas realzadas, permiten a los usuarios ajustar el nivel de detalle sobre una parte o toda la visualización, y modificar el mapeo para enfatizar algún subconjunto de los datos. Las técnicas de selección, proporcionan a los usuarios la capacidad de aislar un subconjunto de los datos desplegados para operaciones tales como el resaltado, filtrado, y análisis cuantitativo. La selección se puede realizar directamente en la visualización (manipulación directa) o a través de cuadros de diálogos y otros mecanismos de consulta (manipulación indirecta) [8].

Otra distinción importante, está entre interacción discreta y continua. Por ejemplo, haciendo una selección de un menú o siguiendo un enlace hipertexto es una típica interacción discreta, donde la acción del usuario produce una respuesta del sistema. La interacción continua se puede considerar como una forma especial de interacción discreta, donde un flujo de acciones del usuario produce un flujo de respuestas del sistema. Si el flujo de salida se fusiona en una percepción continua, la interacción se percibe como continua.

Este MI es importante para las interfaces de manipulación-directa (o manual), donde generalmente se persigue la ilusión de estar en contacto directo con los datos. Shneiderman [10], descubre la aparición de un patrón en el diseño de interfaces de usuario para visualizaciones de información. Este patrón es "vista-resumida primero, acercamiento (zoom) y filtro, después detalle bajo demanda", y se conoce ampliamente como "Mantra Búsqueda de Información Visual". Aunque, siguiendo este mantra no garantiza la entrega de una interfaz de usuario siempre exitosa.

Ware en [9], modela los MI en visualización de información con tres ciclos: resolviendo-problemas, exploración, y bajo-nivel de interacción. El movimiento de los modelos del ciclo de exploración, en espacio de información con analogías y metáforas de la navegación física, y el ciclo de bajo-nivel de interacción abarca la selección y manipulación de datos. La taxonomía de Shneiderman [10], lista siete MI que los usuarios desean realizar:

- Vista General (Overview): vista de la colección total.
- Enfoque (Zoom): vista de un sólo ítem en un objeto o nivel de atributo.
- Filtro: eliminación de ítems no deseados del conjunto desplegado.
- Detalle-bajo-demanda: obtener detalles de un grupo de datos seleccionados.
- Relación: vista de relaciones entre un grupo seleccionado, subgrupo o ítem.
- Historia: acciones de: deshacer, ejecutar de nuevo, y refinar usando un almacenamiento de información histórica.
- Extracción: la extracción de una sub-colección y parámetros de un conjunto.

2.4 Métodos Ágiles de Desarrollo

Los métodos tradicionales de desarrollo de IS se centran en el diseño y arquitectura del software, dejando relegado el tratamiento del diseño y construcción de la interfaz de usuario o de la IHC, muchas veces siendo esto de manera improvisada o en manos de la experticia de algún programador o diseñador gráfico. Justamente, la ausencia de la integración del proceso de IS y la IHC, ha provocado la aparición y masificación del uso de métodos desarrollo de software modernos como los Métodos Ágiles (MÁ) [11, 14].

El desarrollo de software ágil establece los siguientes principios: individuos e interacciones sobre procesos y herramientas, software de trabajo sobre documentación completa, colaboración del cliente sobre negociación de contrato y respuesta a cambios sobre un plan. Este enfoque desafía los métodos tradicionales como cascada, en los que una actividad comienza solo cuando termina la anterior, y donde se requiere documentación extensa y bien fundamentada. Debido a esto, las versiones de la filosofía ágil como eXtreme Programming, Scrum, Crystal Clear, Feature Driven Development o Unified Process prevalecen actualmente entre otras [11].

Los MÁ ayudan a minimizar la probabilidad de fracaso en lo relacionado a tiempo, costos y funcionalidades de los proyectos de software. Este enfoque permite ir adaptando el proceso de desarrollo a un contexto dinámico, realizando ajustes acordes con la realidad del proyecto, lo que implica realizar iteraciones sucesivas para lograr los objetivos en cada etapa [12].

2.5 IS e IHC

Uno de los métodos para integrar las disciplinas de IS e IHC, es el uso de Patrones de Interacción (PI). Un PI describe una solución exitosa a un problema recurrente concerniente a la interfaz de usuario, en un contexto dado. Un PI es un medio de comunicación que expresa una solución de interfaz en una forma textual y gráfica, a fin de ser entendida por otras personas, con diferentes formaciones profesionales. Estos capturan la experiencia y conocimiento de expertos, quienes han producido soluciones exitosas a problemas, a fin de que esas soluciones queden a disposición de personas con menos experiencia; sin embargo, los patrones no proveen siempre las soluciones definitivas, algunas veces los usuarios de patrones deben adaptar, utilizar, instanciar o implementar un patrón [1].

Otro método para lograr integrar la IS y la IHC, es utilizar el Diseño Centrado en el Usuario (DCU), que es el enfoque dominante en el área de IHC, e involucra al usuario final en un proceso de desarrollo multidisciplinario iterativo, basado en el diseño y evaluación, por lo que el diseñador entiende las necesidades y tareas del usuario [11]. Pero, al igual que las metodologías tradicionales o pesadas, el DCU necesita que todos los requisitos se reúnan y evalúen antes que se puedan implementarse. Un aspecto importante de DCU es la colaboración entre usuarios y desarrolladores para crear soluciones de software, de modo que cada grupo aporte su propia experiencia. Según Norman [13], primero es necesario identificar y modelar las necesidades de los usuarios, y luego involucrarlos en evaluaciones iterativas del producto. Por lo tanto, el propósito es mejorar la facilidad de uso del producto para: reducir errores, satisfacer a los usuarios y facilitar su aprendizaje y uso.

Tanto DCU como los MÁ se centran en el usuario/cliente, y aplican un proceso de desarrollo iterativo con pruebas continuas. Estas propuestas contrastan con los procesos de desarrollo basados en la arquitectura tradicional, que están dirigidos por desarrolladores cuyo primer objetivo es lograr una buena implementación. Sin embargo, el DCU y los MÁ muestran grandes diferencias relacionadas con la forma en que actúan y cuáles son sus intereses [14]. Por un lado, la recomendación de flexibilidad ágil en la acción para enfrentar cambios está en desacuerdo con el principio DCU del diseño de interfaz antes de la implementación. Por otro lado, DCU desarrolla un producto holístico, mientras que el proceso ágil es incremental y da como resultado subproductos. Mientras que los MÁ se centran en el desarrollo de código, los métodos DCU se centran en el diseño de los MI en las que los usuarios estarán involucrados.

Finalmente, ambos enfoques buscan satisfacer las necesidades de los usuarios, pero de maneras diferentes. Los MÁ involucran a los usuarios en la verificación de la implementación correcta de la funcionalidad; mientras que DCU registra la opinión de los usuarios sobre otros aspectos de toda la aplicación, como la satisfacción o la eficiencia de uso. DCU se centra en cómo los usuarios finales trabajan con el sistema, mientras que a los MÁ le preocupa más cómo se debe construir el software.

3 Revisión de Trabajos Relacionados

Dentro de la revisión de trabajos relacionados con el que se describe en este artículo, destacan los siguientes:

Neuroph [15], es un framework implementado en lenguaje Java de código abierto para desarrollar arquitecturas de RNA. Contiene una biblioteca de clases base que corresponden con los elementos básicos de RNA. También posee un editor gráfico que soporta la creación, entrenamiento y almacenamiento de estructuras de RNA. Neuroph se puede utilizar para diversas tareas como clasificación, reconocimiento, predicción, aproximación de funciones y modelado. Actualmente, Neuroph soporta las redes: Adaline, Perceptron, PMC con Backpropagation, Hopfield, Konhonen, Hebbian, Maxnet, Aprendizaje Competitivo, Instar, Outstar, BAM, RBF y NFR.

Otro trabajo corresponde al de Simbrain [16], que es un software para el diseño y análisis de RNA con una interfaz gráfica de usuario que se compone de elementos que se pueden acoplar entre sí. Los paneles de red permiten a los usuarios construir redes y observar la dinámica cambiante de las neuronas, junto con cambios correspondientes en gráficos, tablas y entornos virtuales. La interfaz gráfica u otros objetos se pueden deshabilitar para aumentar la velocidad computacional y la eficiencia de la simulación. El código lógico de Simbrain está separado de su código GUI (Graphical User Interface), y puede ser utilizado como una biblioteca independiente de la GUI.

Sevarac en [15], integra a través de un framework diversos tipos de arquitecturas de RNA, no obstante, los mecanismos de interacción son insuficientes y limitados. No incluye vistas complementarias para contribuir a la comprensión del modelo de forma complete, y que permitan realizar una comparación de componentes.

Tosi y Yoshimi en [16], proponen la vinculación de los distintos componentes y vistas, lo que facilita una mejor interacción y comprensión del modelo a nivel macro, sin embargo, no se observa un estudio a nivel individual de cada elemento de la red que permita examinar y conocer lo que sucede dentro de cada una de estas unidades.

El último trabajo revisado trata de TensorFlow Playground [17], y es un entorno visual web interactivo, que permite al usuario experimentar a través de la manipulación directa de RNA, en lugar de programar completamente la red, lo que posibilita la construcción rápida e intuitiva de las RNA. Además, facilita visualización de las características de cada unidad de la red simultáneamente. Proporciona una variedad de posibilidades para el cambio rápido de parámetros, y examinar inmediatamente los efectos de esos cambios. Este es uno de los entornos visuales más interactivos respecto a los demás trabajos analizados, y en el cual se basa el trabajo que presenta este artículo, principalmente en los MI incorporados en el desarrollo del software.

4 Prototipo para Análisis de RNA

4.1 Modelo Conceptual

Varios factores deben ser considerados al diseñar un entorno visual apropiado en una tarea de análisis de datos masivos. Uno de estos factores son las limitaciones de la tecnología de reproducción de imágenes, que apoya solamente entre uno y tres millones de pixeles, mientras que los conjuntos de datos típicos contienen centenares de bytes hasta terabyte de información. La dispersión/densidad de los datos es otro punto por considerar, en este caso los datos pueden requerir preprocesamiento computacional con uso de interpolación [18].

Otro factor que determina la efectividad de una visualización es la tarea de exploración. Actualmente no existen esquemas de visualización de datos multidimensionales que respondan adecuadamente a este tipo de datos. Algunas visualizaciones son mejores para mostrar estructuras jerárquicas en los datos otras para desplegar clústeres o valores fuera de rango, y para desplegar dos o tres formas de correlaciones. Algunas visualizaciones pueden manejar conjuntos grandes de datos y otras se adaptan mejor para pocos datos. Esto significa que un sistema visual de análisis de datos masivos, debe incluir diferentes visualizaciones para ser aplicables a todos los casos de exploración de datos. No hay actualmente una herramienta que satisfaga esta condición, dado que la mayoría utilizan un subconjunto específico de métodos de visualización [19].

Considerando los aspectos definidos anteriormente, se presenta el diseño e implementación de un entorno visual web a nivel de prototipo, que integra los MÁ de desarrollo con MI, aplicado al análisis de modelos RNA, específicamente para el tipo PMC, El modelo conceptual de este prototipo se puede observar en la Figura 2, el cual tiene las siguientes características:

- Vista Minable; es el componente que actúa como principal insumo del sistema, el cual presenta los datos preprocesados, transformados y adaptados, con la capacidad de aplicar visualizaciones e interacciones que permitan explorar estos datos con un mayor nivel de detalle.
- Generación visual del modelo RNA; en este contexto ocurre la mayor interacción del usuario a través de diversas herramientas que le proveen la capacidad de modificar parámetros, visualizar, seleccionar y aplicar métricas, además de utilizar una técnica descriptiva de Minería de Datos (MD) que apoye en la comprensión más completa del modelo.
- Modelo RNA Ajustado; con los ajustes previos y la selección de parámetros adecuados se obtiene un modelo más completo que permite obtener resultados fiables y que además retroalimenta al sistema con los elementos necesarios para producir modelos más robustos y eficientes en las nuevas iteraciones.

En el proceso de construcción del modelo de RNA ajustado se utilizan una serie de herramientas que permiten interactuar y visualizar los elementos que lo componen, con el propósito de realizar las adaptaciones necesarias y así generar un modelo más preciso y ajustado conjunto de datos. A continuación, se presentan estas herramientas:

- Artefactos Gráficos; que permitan facilitar la interpretación de los datos de manera más rápida y visual. Representan la relación entre los elementos de forma conceptual, haciendo destacar los patrones y tendencias que aportan información relevante al modelo.
- Mecanismos de Interacción; que proporcionen instrumentos para que el usuario recorra el modelo y sus componentes (neuronas), retroalimente el modelo basado en transformaciones visuales, y que permita el ajuste de parámetros.
- Métricas; que facilitan la medición y análisis de la correspondencia entre las diferentes variables o atributos.
- Técnica Descriptiva de MD; que permite analizar la distribución, asociaciones o patrones relevantes en los datos.

La Figura 2, representa el modelo conceptual del prototipo, donde se indica como interactúan sus componentes principales. La entrada al sistema es la vista minable que corresponde a los datos transformados y ajustados para el análisis, por otro lado, la salida es el modelo RNA ajustado como resultado de todo el proceso. Los rectángulos representan los módulos que corresponden a una división conceptual del sistema, como una agrupación de funciones relacionadas que representan un servicio. El óvalo simboliza el caso de uso como requerimiento funcional del sistema. Las flechas, representan los flujos de datos en el proceso entre: la entrada (Vista minable), proceso (Generación visual del modelo RNA), y salida (Modelo RNA Ajustado). Finalmente, las líneas desde y hacia los rectángulos ó módulos del sistema, representan las asociaciones de conexión, indicando si se presenta algún tipo de interacción entre esos componentes.

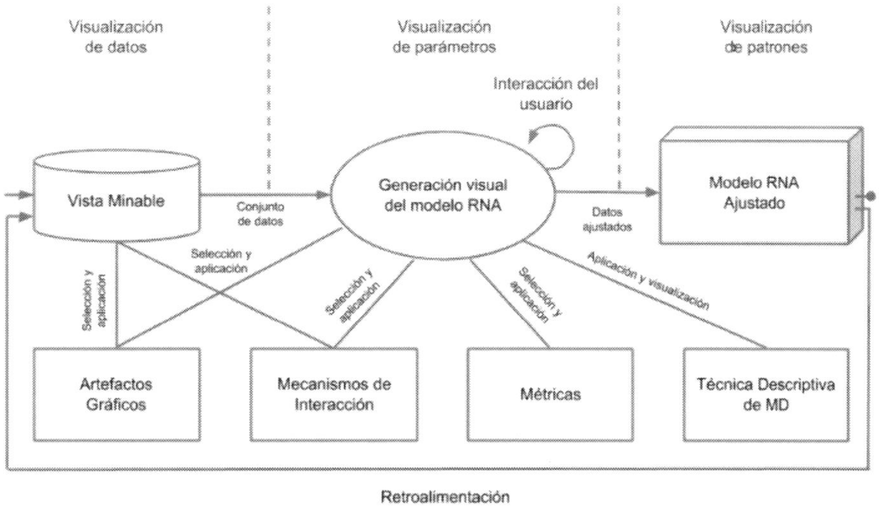

Fig. 2. Modelo conceptual del prototipo propuesto.

4.2 Arquitectura

El entorno visual para análisis de RNA-PMC, se desarrolla en un ambiente web utilizando la MÁ de desarrollo, y por tanto, debe cumplir con ciertas normas utilizadas para este propósito, como la utilización del protocolo HTTP para las peticiones (request) y las respuestas (response). En esta arquitectura cliente-servidor, el cliente se encarga de la interacción del usuario con las visualizaciones y parámetros para generar las peticiones hacia el servidor, el cual las procesa, accede a los datos solicitados y ejecuta los algoritmos necesarios para devolver la respuesta en un formato estándar (XML o JSON), para cualquier cliente (navegador web) pueda interpretarlo y generar las vistas necesarias.

A nivel lógico se utiliza el patrón Modelo-Vista-Controlador (MVC) para separar los datos, la lógica de la aplicación y la gestión de los eventos. Para esto se definen los tres elementos que la componen:

- El modelo; presenta la estructura de los datos, es la única fuente de información, se encarga de proporcionar los datos a la vista y al controlador.

- El controlador; escucha los eventos y envía las peticiones hacia el modelo, luego ejecuta las acciones apropiadas para retornar los datos a la vista.
- La vista; se encarga de presentar los datos del modelo al usuario, por lo general a través de la interfaz gráfica.

Se utilizan herramientas de alto nivel que permiten el desarrollo ágil mediante el uso de librerías y/o funcionalidades estándares. Para cargar los modelos y ejecutar los algoritmos se utiliza TensorFlow [17], que es un framework de código abierto desarrollado por Google, y proporciona capacidades para construir y entrenar modelos de RNA. Para las visualizaciones se utiliza la librería de JavaScript D3.js que permite generar gráficos interactivos y dinámicos con la ventaja de tener mayor control sobre los resultados y presentación de los datos. La Figura 3 presenta la arquitectura de tres capas utilizada para el desarrollo de este entorno visual.

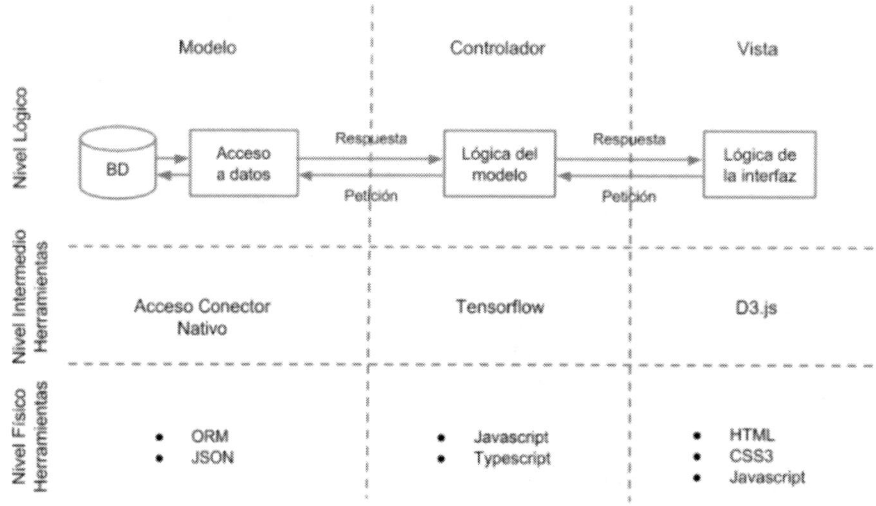

Fig. 3. Arquitectura de tres capas del prototipo.

4.3 Patrón de Diseño de IHC

Para el diseño y construcción de las IHC del prototipo, se utilizó como base los fundamentos de usabilidad de algunos autores ([1], [11], y [14]). Se ha puesto especialmente atención al trabajo de caracterización y MI, basado en el enfoque PI. La estructura del entorno visual, esta diseñada en base al esquema entrada-proceso-salida que representa un orden lógico e intuitivo y así permite un flujo de trabajo simple. La Figura 4 presenta el diseño de la interfaz principal del prototipo, y es utilizada para representar todos los elementos que componen el entorno visual para análisis de RNA-PMC propuesto.

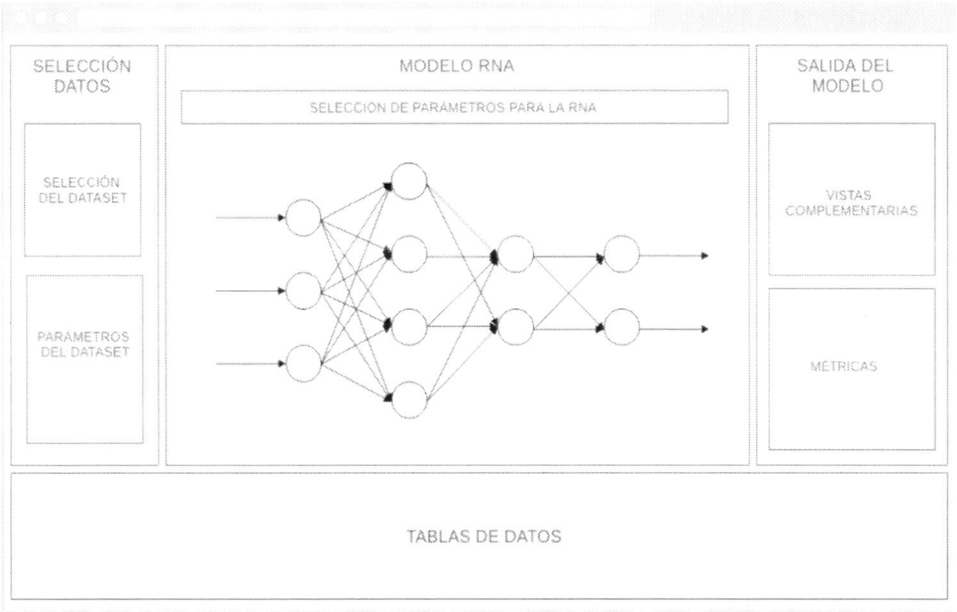

Fig. 4. Diseño de la interfaz gráfica del prototipo.

La descripción de los elementos o áreas que componen este diseño es la siguiente:

- Selección de datos; corresponde a la entrada del modelo donde se carga un conjunto de datos, en este caso la vista minable o analizar, y además es posible ajustar ciertos parámetros de este.
- Modelo RNA; es la pieza fundamental del entorno, donde se puede seleccionar los parámetros para el modelo, interactuar y visualizar todos sus elementos
- Salida del modelo; es el lugar donde se visualizan elementos adicionales, con la particularidad de medir ciertos resultados además de complementar el conocimiento extraído a través del modelo.
- Tablas de datos graficados; que permiten examinar datos particulares de los elementos del modelo, a través de gráficas para datos multidimensionales.

4.4 Implementación

A nivel físico se utilizaron herramientas estándares para el desarrollo web, tales como ORM y JSON para el acceso a datos. También se utilizó el lenguaje de programación JavaScript para ejecutar las consultas y generar los resultados. Así como HTML5, CSS3, y también JavaScript, para la presentación e implementación de la interfaz gráfica del usuario. En las Figuras 5 y 6, se muestran algunas de las interfaces gráficas del entorno visual, y donde se pueden observar las componentes descritas en el modelo conceptual.

En ambos casos, se presenta en el sector izquierdo de la interfaz, el área de carga de datos y configuración de parámetros iniciales, así como la selección del tipo de gráfica para datos multidimensionales que se presenta en la parte inferior de la pantalla. Para esto último, se han implementado dos: coordenadas paralelas y mapa de calor. También, se proyecta implementar métricas que permitan comparar componentes del modelo RNA.

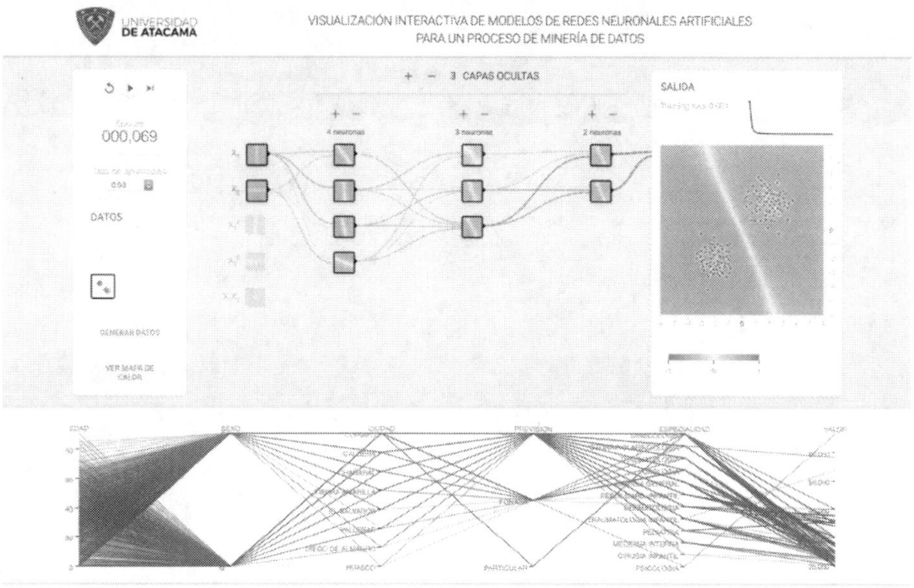

Fig. 5. Interfaz gráfica con gráfica coordenadas paralelas.

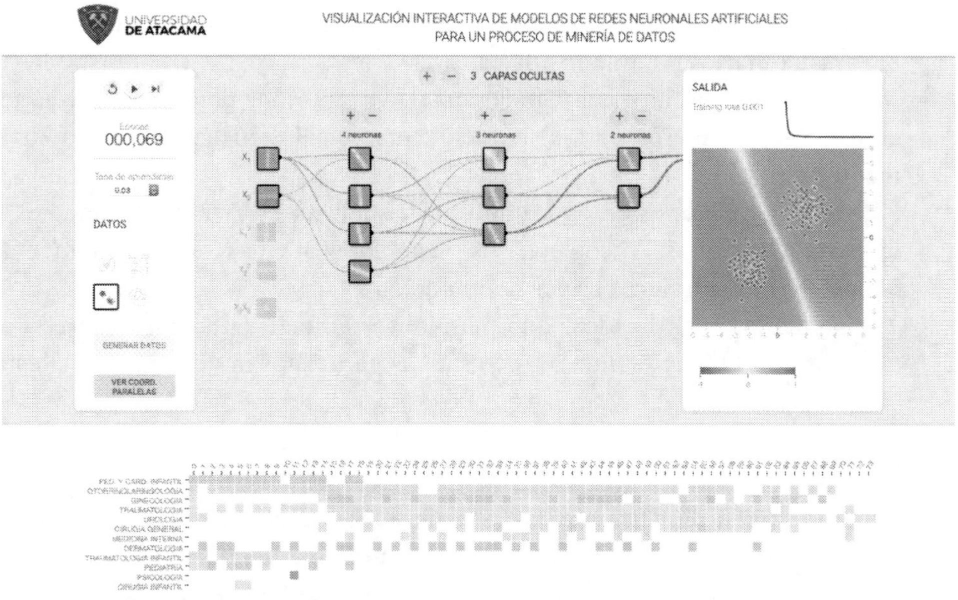

Fig. 6. Interfaz gráfica con gráfica mapa de calor.

En el centro de la interfaz, se ha dejado el área de trabajo para el análisis de la RNA-PMC. En esta área, fundamentalmente se han implementado distintos MI que le permiten al usuario recorrer las componentes del modelo RNA (neuronas), ver el valor del peso de cada una, así como aumentar o disminuir el nivel de capas del modelo, lo cual es provisto por el framework TensorFlow [17]. También se han integrado MI en las gráficas de coordenadas paralelas y mapa de calor. Finalmente, en el sector derecho de la interfaz, se presentan vistas complementarias que sirven para el análisis, en particular, para ambas figuras se muestra una gráfica de clusterización de las neuronas del modelo. Falta eso sí, implementar artefactos gráficos adicionales, los cuales están en fase de pruebas. Además, se considera una parte para mostrar métricas, ha implementar, que permitan comparar componentes (neuronas) del modelo.

Conclusiones y Trabajo Futuro

Las conclusiones preliminares que se han logrado obtener en este trabajo son las siguientes:

- El diseño y desarrollo del software para el análisis de RNA-PMC, ha sido abordado de manera apropiada, incorporando los aspectos descritos en el marco conceptual, esto es considerando: integración de IS e IHC a través del uso de PI, incorporación de MI ad-hoc que permiten al usuario recorrer el modelo RNA, y de este modo favorecer el entendimiento del modelo.
- Se ha logrado establecer un diseño de interfaces con vistas complementarias, con el enfoque entrada-proceso-salida:
  - En el área selección de datos que cubre la entrada permite la carga, parametrización, selección de gráficas y el análisis exploratorio del conjunto de datos o vista minable. Las gráficas para datos multidimensionales seleccionadas de esta área, se visualizan en la parte inferior de la interfaz de usuario y también incorporan MI.
  - Para el proceso, se establece el área modelo RNA que permite visualizar y recorrer de manera interactiva el modelo RNA-PMC, a través de sus capas y componentes (neuronas), a través de la disposición de MI que facilitan esta labor.
  - Finalmente, en el área salida del modelo se disponen vistas complementarias, tales como; visualizaciones de clusterizaciones del conjunto de datos, y métricas para comparar componentes del modelo.
- Se logra como resultado, un entorno visual que dispone de herramientas bastantes útiles y con características de usabilidad adecuadas y simples, basadas en un PI diseñado, que permite el análisis de conjuntos de datos de alto volumen y dimensionalidad, y que facilitan el análisis de RNA-PMC.
- Se tienen seleccionadas y definidas, un conjunto de métricas para comparar las componentes del modelo RNA-PMC.

Como trabajos futuros se consideran los siguientes:

- Validar el entorno visual prototipo con analistas de datos que utilicen modelos RNA, y obtener sus evaluaciones subjetivas respecto a los elementos que contiene, y sobre aspectos de usabilidad, MI, etc.
- Implementar las métricas para la comparación de componentes del modelo RNA-MPC.

- Incorporar vistas complementarias a través de artefactos gráficos adicionales, que aporten en el análisis de modelos de RNA-PMC.
- Explorar la posibilidad de generalizar el entorno visual para otros tipos de modelo de RNA.

Referencias

1. Acosta, A., Zambrano, N.: Importancia, problemas y soluciones en el diseño de la Interfaz de Usuario. Revista SABER Universidad Oriente de Venezuela, ISSN: 1315-0162, volumen 18, nro. 2(5), 174–182 (2006).
2. Isasi, P.: Redes de Neuronas Artificiales: Un enfoque práctico. Editorial Pearson (2004).
3. Castellanos, A.: Algoritmos para la Minería de Datos con Redes de Neuronas (2013).
4. Gutiérrez, J.: Redes Probabilísticas y Neuronales en las Ciencias Atmosféricas (2004).
5. Zachary, T.: Simbrain 3.0: A flexible, visually-oriented neural network simulator (2016).
6. Abadi, M.: TensorFlow: Large-Scale Machine Learning on Heterogeneous Distributed Systems (2015).
7. Goodman, Dan.: Brian: a simulator for spiking neural networks in Python (2008).
8. Berthold, M. Hand, D.: Intelligent Data Analysis: An Introduction, 2a ed., Alemania - Springer. ISBN-10: 3540430601. ISBN-13: 9783540430605 (2007).
9. Ware, C.: Information Visualization: Perception for Design (2nd. ed.). San Francisco, Morgan Kaufman Publishers. ISBN: 1-55860-819-2 (2004).
10. Shneiderman, B.: The eyes have it: A task by data type taxonomy for information visualizations. In VL'96: Proceedings of the IEEE Symposium on Visual Languages (pp. 336–343). IEEE Computer Society (1996).
11. Losada B., Urretavizcaya, M., Fernández-Castro, I.: A guide to agile development of interactive software with a ''User Objectives''- driven methodology. Science of Computer Programming 78 (2013), pp 2268–2281. Elsevier B.V. All rights reserved (2012).
12. Navarro, A., Fernández, J., Morales, J.: Revisión de metodologías ágiles para el desarrollo de software. Prospect. Vol. 11, No. 2, págs. 30-39 (2013).
13. Norman, D.A.: The invisible Computer, MIT Press, Cambridge MA, (1998).
14. Ferreira, J.: Interaction Design and Agile Development: A Real-World. Pers. (2007).
15. Sevarac, Z.: Neuroph-Java neural network framework (2012).
16. Tosi, Z., Yoshimi, J.: Simbrain 3.0: A flexible, visually-oriented neural network simulator. Neural Networks Volume 83, Pages 1-10 (2016).
17. Wongsuphasawat, K., Smilkov, D., Wexler, J., Wilson, J., Mané, D.: Visualizing Dataflow Graphs of Deep Learning Models in TensorFlow. IEEE Transactions on Visualization and Computer Graphics ,Volume: 24 , Issue: 1 (2017).
18. Grinstein, G., Ward, M. O.: Introduction to Data Visualization, in: Fayyad U., Grinstein G. G., Wierse A. (eds.), Information Visualisation in Data Mining and Knowledge Discovery, Morgan Kaufmann Publishers, San Francisco, pp. 21-45 (2002).
19. Hoffman, P. E., Grinstein, G. G.: A Survey of Visualizations for High-Dimensional Data Mining, in: Fayyad U., Grinstein G. G., Wierse A. (eds.), Information Visualisation in Data Mining and Knowledge Discovery, Morgan Kaufmann Publishers, San Francisco, pp. 47-85 (2002).

Model-driven development of multi-agent systems: A systematic mapping

Nemury Silega[1], Antonio Hernández[1], Yury Kravchenko[2], Gilberto F. Castro[3, 4] and Diana M. López[5]

[1]Universidad de Ciencias Informáticas, Habana, Cuba
{nsilega, ahdominguez}@uci.cu
[2]Southern Federal University, Rostov-on-Don, Russia
krav-jura@yandex.ru
[3]Universidad Católica Santiago de Guayaquil, Guayaquil, Ecuador
gilberto.castro@ucsg.edu.ec
[4]Universidad de Guayaquil, Guayaquil, Ecuador
gilberto.castro@ug.edu.ec
[5]Universidad Tecnológica ECOTEC, Guayaquil, Ecuador
dlopez@ecotec.edu.ec

Abstract.

Context: Model-Driven Development (MDD) and Multi-Agent Systems (MAS) are two challenging research areas in software engineering. MDD is about improving software development whilst Multi-Agent Systems (MASs) are systems in which many intelligent autonomous entities (agents) interact with each other for solving their selfish or common problems, and to achieve certain goal. Hence examining the available proposals in the literature to use MDD when developing MAS may be insightful.

Objective: This work aims at assessing the state of the art in MDD for MAS. It mainly focuses on: what are the characteristics of MDD approaches that support MAS; what types of MAS are supported and what is the impact of these approaches in the quality of both the development process and system.

Method: We carried out a mapping study following a formal guide. We applied a search string over the set of three popular browsers (Scopus, IEEE and ACM). Consequently, 78 papers were selected and analyzed with respect to the defined classification criteria derived from the research questions.

Results: The analysis allows us to answer the research questions. We remark: 1) predominance of papers from academic environment and written by researchers only; 2) predominance of top-down transformation in software development activities; 3) inexistence of consolidated methods; 4) significant percentage of works without tool support; 5) wide variety of modeling notation and languages; 6) lack of empirical evidences to demonstrate the actual impact of the approaches; 8) limited application in real cases.

Conclusion: This study provides the state of the art in the topic and identifies problems that deserve investigations in the future, for instance the significant percentage of works without tool support or the lack of real case studies.

Keywords: multi-agent systems, MDD, systematic mapping

1 Introduction

In recent years the use of Multi agent systems (MASs) has grown more and more as a software engineering paradigm for designing and developing complex software systems. In MASs, applications are designed and developed in terms of autonomous software entities (agents) that can flexibly achieve their objectives by interacting with one another in terms of high-level protocols and languages [1]. An autonomous agent is a computational entity that can perceive, reason, act, and communicate [2].

On the other hand, Model Driven Development (MDD) is a paradigm for the software development, which defines models as the primary artifact. There are evidences that confirm that the adoption of MDD based approaches increases productivity of the software development as well as the quality of the systems. Model Driven Architecture (MDA) is an OMG specific implementation of MDD. MDA defines three types of models: Computing Independent Models (CIM), Platform Independent Models (PIM) and Platform Specific Models (PSMs). MDA aims to tackle the complexity of software development through four aspects: standardization, automation, raising the abstraction level and separation of concerns [3]. Increasing the abstraction level improves the communication and understanding among software developers [4].

The adoption of MDD based approaches in the context of MASs may deliver interesting engineering methods, which could tackle some reported issues. For example the complexity for the MAS developer due to the diversity of agent-oriented methodologies as well as the insufficient reutilization during the development of a MAS due to an incorrect separation of concerns according to the abstraction level. In fact, OMG fosters technologies to support the development of MASs, HTM5 is an OMG MDA based multi-view metamodel for agent-oriented development of cloud robotic system.

Although it is possible to find several MDD based approaches to support the development of MASs, we only found one work [5] that examines the characteristics of these approaches. Kardas made a survey of 11 approaches, which are evaluated according to five criteria defined by the author. In spite of the extensive discussion about the 11 approaches, the low number of approaches analyzed makes it difficult to identify the trends of the works that apply MDD in the development of MASs.

Therefore, the goal of this work is to explore the characteristics of these approaches. This paper presents a systematic mapping to know the state of art in the application of MDD based approaches in the development of MASs. A mapping study provides an overview of a research area through classification and counting contributions in relation to the categories of that classification [6]. The structure of the paper is as follows: Section 2 explains the research method used. Section 3 presents the results of the mapping. Section 4 concludes the paper.

2 Method

To carry out the mapping we have used the guide defined by Pettersen [6], which describes the main steps to execute a systematic mapping as well as the aspects to report: *Research question, Search, Study selection and Quality assessment, Data ex-*

traction, Analysis and classification and finally discussion about the results of the mapping. In the next section, the results for each step are presented.

2.1 Research question

Pettersen states that research questions may be classified in two categories: *focused on common elements or focused on the topic area* [6]. The first and the last questions that we defined belong to the first category whilst the remainder questions are focused on the study topic. To define the questions focused on the MDD topic, we adopted some ideas of the study by Ameller et al [7].Table 1 shows the research questions.

In RQ1, we expect to obtain an overall description of the approaches by means of popular metadata that are common in every research publications, such as year, venue, research type and research method. In RQ2, we are interested in getting the details of the approaches in terms of the main specifications of MDD: methods, characteristics, input and output models, languages as well as tools to support these approaches.

With RQ3, we want to know the characteristics of the MASs supported by MDD approaches; for example, we are interested in getting the domain of these MASs and exactly what elements are supported by the MDD approaches. In RQ4, we check the existence of empirical evidences about the impact of MDD approaches to develop MASs. We focused on both product and process attributes.

Table 1. Research questions of the mapping study

RQ 1. – Which approaches adopt MDD specifications in the development of MASs?
RQ 1.1 – How has the number of publications evolved over the years?
RQ 1.2 – In which type of venue are articles mostly published?
RQ 1.3 – What research types and research methods have been applied?
RQ 2. – What are the main characteristics of MDD approaches that support MASs?
RQ 2.1. — Which methods are applied by these approaches?
RQ 2.2. — What are the main characteristics of the MDD process?
RQ 2.3. — What are the input and the output of the MDD approaches?
RQ 2.4. — What notations or languages do the MDD approaches regard?
RQ 2.5. — How do the MDD approaches carry out the transformations?
RQ 2.6. — Do the approaches report tools?
RQ 3. – What type of MASs are supported by MDD?
RQ 3.1. — What types of MAS are generated by the MDD approach?
RQ 4. – What is the impact of the approaches?
RQ 4.1 – What process quality attributes are improved with these approaches?
RQ 4.2 – What product quality characteristics are improved with these approaches?

2.2 Search

We are interested in the investigations that relate MDD and MAS areas. Hence, the search string is a conjunction of the two populations.

$$Search\ population = \text{MDD population}\ and\ MAS\ population$$

Regarding the MDD population, we have considered the most popular expressions to refer to this paradigm. As result, the string is:

$$MDD\ population\ = \text{MDD or Model driven development or Model} - \text{driven development or MDA or Model Driven Architecture}$$

Concerning to MAS population, we considered common expressions to refer to this topic. As result, the string is:

$$MAS\ population = MAS\ or\ Multi\ agent\ Systems\ or\ Multi - agent\ systems\ or\ Multiagent\ systems$$

To make the search, we chose SCOPUS, IEEE Xplore and ACM; three of the most suitable databases to find scientific literature [8]. We used the search string to execute the search. We adopted the tool EndNote X6 to manage the large number of references and to delete duplicates. The first row of Table 2 shows the search results.

2.3 Study selection and quality assessment

We used the approach of Ameller [7] to select the papers for the study. This approach consists of five steps. Bellow, we describe the results for each step.

Step 1. *Basic search.* This step consists of searching on the selected databases with the search string. We mentioned the results of this step in the previous section.

Step 2. *Topic area considered.* We exploited the features of the search tools to refine the resulting list and to consider only the references related to computer science.

Step 3. *Title and abstract considered.* In this step, we review the title and abstract of the works then the papers that are not evidently related to the topic are discarded. In this step we applied the inclusion/exclusion (see Table 3) criteria to filter the papers. In the case of doubt, we kept the paper to the next step.

Step 4. *Fast reading.* In this step, a fast reading of the papers was made. The papers that clearly met the exclusion criteria were discarded. The cases of doubt where discussed between two authors and a decision was made to include or not the paper.

Step 5. *Full reading.* The full text of the remainder works were reviewed and evaluated again using the exclusion/inclusion criteria. The execution of these five steps increases the probability of selecting a correct sample of papers. Table 2 shows the papers that was filtered after each step. Finally, we analyzed 78 works [2, 9-83].

Table 2. Results of applying five steps to select

	Scopus	ACM	IEEE	Total
Search results	300	85	756	1141
Topic	130	59	155	344
Title + Abstract (Duplicates)	93	8 (44 duplicated)	39 (8 duplicated)	140
Fast reading	82	8	25	115
Full reading	60	2	16	78
Selected papers	60	2	16	78

Table 3. Inclusion/Exclusion criteria

Criteria	Description
Inclusion	The paper describes an MDD-based approach to develop MAS, either a whole system or a concrete aspect of a system
Inclusion	The paper describes the adoption of some MDD specifications (Metamodels, transformation rules, MDD tools) to carry out some activities in the context of MAS
Exclusion	The work is about MAS but is not related with MDD
Exclusion	The work only argues that a MAS could be developed with MDD, but no real approach in this direction is described
Exclusion	The work is a review about the state of the art about the relation of MAS and MDD
Exclusion	The work is not a research paper
Exclusion	The work describes the results of either evaluation or validation of a proposal that is not well described in the paper

2.4 Data extraction

The data extraction was performed by the third and fourth authors and reviewed by the first and second authors. This is a suitable strategy to ensure the data extraction process [6]. A form in an excel sheet to tabulate the extracted information was created. The form has some fields to identify the article (Id, title, authors) and fields to tabulate the information according to the defined classification scheme.

2.5 Analysis and classification

We followed the recommendations by Pettersen [6] to distinguish between topic-independent classification and topic-specific classification. For the first type, we considered the venue, research type and research method [6]. For the topic-independent classification, we used ideas from the mapping developed by Ameller [7], specifically related with the MDD topic. We used ISO/IEC 9126-1 [84] to classify the product characteristics that could be improved. We describe these classifications bellow.

RQ 1. – Which works adopt MDD specifications for the development of MASs?

For the classification of the venues as well as the research type and research method, we used the schemes recommended by Pettersen. The scheme for the venues is based on the proposal of the ministry of education of Finland. The scheme for the research type and research method is based on the work made by Weringa et al [85].

RQ 2. – What are the characteristics of MDD approaches that support MASs?

For the characteristics, we followed the same classfication of Ameller [7]. For the criterion *method* (RQ 2.1), the values may be: *Proposes new method*, *Adapts existing method* or *No method*. In case of *Adapts existing method,* we record the *Method name.*

In this study the verified characteristics (RQ 2.2) of the MDD process are *type of transformations* and *type of activities*. Transformations may be *top-down, bottom-up or horizontal*. Type of activities may be: *Engineering, Development, Specification, Integration, Migration, Others.* The criteria for the input and output (RQ 2.3) are

Input model type and Output model type. We also record the reminder of notations or modeling languages (RQ 2.4) that each approach adopts.

In order to describe the transformations (RQ 2.5), we record *transformation language name* and the *transformation type* (either *ModelToModel*, *ModelToText* or *TextToModel*). For automatic (or semi) transformations, we record the *tool* as well.

Regarding to the tools (RQ 2.6), we considered two types of tools: *tools to support the metamodeling* and *tools for modeling*. For both types, we record *Tool name.*

We are interested to know the domains where these approaches have been applied (RQ 3.1); hence we record the *domain name.*

To know the impact of these approaches we record the processes quality attributtes (RQ 4.1) that are improved. We only considered the cases where empirical evidences are presented. The attributes are *productivity, efficiency, eficacy* and *cost.* We are also interested to know the impact in the product quality (RQ 4.2). Based on the ISO/IEC 9126-1 [84], we check the impact in *functionality, reliability, usability, efficiency, maintainability* and *portability.*

3 Results of the mapping

3.1 Question1 (RQ 1)

Fig.1 shows that 2013 is the year with the highest number of works (11) while 2004 is the year with the lowest number of works (only 1). For the remainder years, the number of works has been steady between four and seven.

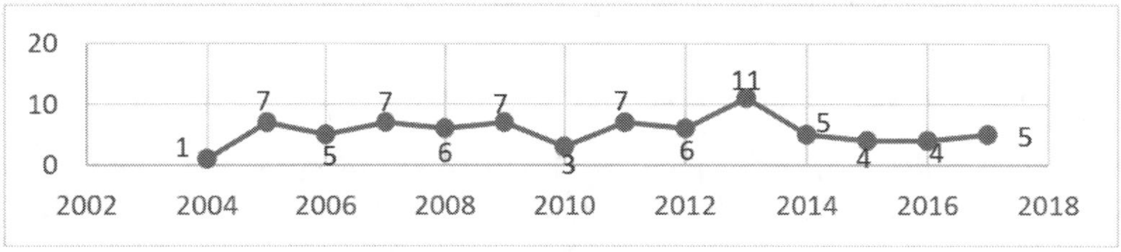

Fig. 1. Publications by year

Regarding the type of venue, Fig.2 depicts that the most common are the conference paper publications [2, 9, 11, 12, 14-16, 18-22, 24-31, 33, 35-37, 41-44, 46-53, 55, 57-62, 65-67, 71, 72, 74, 76-79, 82] with the 72 % of the analyzed works while the journal papers[13, 16, 17, 23, 32, 34, 38-40, 45, 54, 56, 63, 64, 68-70, 73, 75, 80, 83] represent the 27 % of the analyzed works and one paper is a book section[10]. Only the journals Autonomous Agents and Multi-Agent Systems, International Arab Journal of Information Technology and International Journal of Agent-Oriented Software Engineering have two works; the remainder journals have only one paper.

Regarding the research type, it is noteworthy that 72 papers are classified as Solution proposals while only four are Evaluation researches and two are Validation researches. On the other hand, the Validation researches applied the research methods Academic case study and Laboratory experiments. The evaluation researches applied Action research, Industrial Case study (2 works), and Laboratory experiments. This confirms the lack of evidences that demonstrate the actual impact of the proposals.

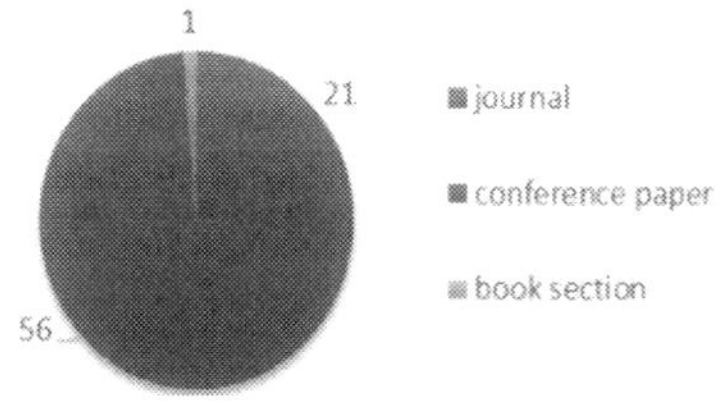

Fig. 2. Type of publications

3.2 Question 2 (RQ2)

Regarding the MDD based method applied, 33 works define a new method while 45 adopt an already existent method. The most adopted method, as we expected, was MDA with 43 works. This confirms that MDA is the most prominent method that implements MDD. A reason for this fact could be that MDA is fostered by OMG, which is the most important organization in the definition of standards for the industry. Hence, their proposals receive the attention of the community.

We also recorded information about the type of activities and the type of transformation. Fig.3 a) depicts that the 62 % (48) of the proposals adopt MDD based approaches to Develop while the 32 % (25) adopts these approaches to Specify.

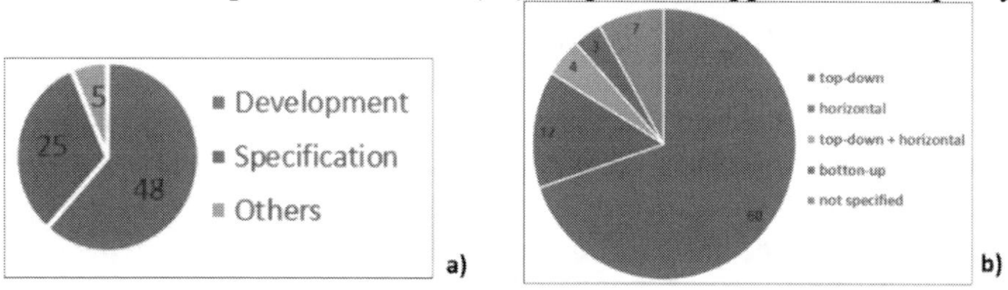

Fig. 3. a) Type of activities b) Type of transformations

Fig. 3 b) shows that 70 % (60) of the works executes the top-down transformation and 14 % (12) executes horizontal transformations. The approaches usually start in the PIM level. The analysis yielded that 73 % (57) of the works starts in the PIM level while only the 26 % (20) considers the CIM level. This demonstrates a lack of the MDD based approaches. This could be due to the difficulty to obtain good CIM models. Therefore, the transformation from CIM to PIM is another open issue.

The 62 % (48) of the works ends with the generation of code. The code generation is a promise of MDD; it could enhance the productivity and reduce mistakes. On the other hand, 14 and 12 works finish with PIM and PSM respectively.

As we expected, the most popular transformation languages are ATL, QVT and MOF script which have been applied in 11, 5 and 3 works respectively. MOF script is used for model to text transformations while ATL and QVT are applied in model to model transformations. It is noteworthy that only 16 works adopt some of these languages which are considered the *de facto* transformation languages. Nevertheless, the 52 % (41) of the works specifies the transformations with natural language. Furthermore, some works apply their own approaches to specify the transformations. The adoption of a transformation language is crucial to ensure the quality of the transformation rules as well as to exploit a tool to execute the transformations. Hence, the use of languages is an issue that has to be considered in the MDD based approaches.

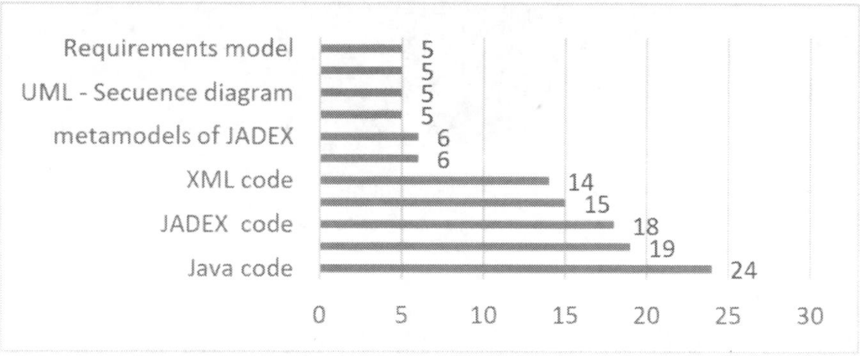

Fig. 4. Type of models

On the other hand, the analysis of the models that are included in the selected papers demonstrated the variety of languages and notations adopted. It is noteworthy that a wide number of works describe models without clarifying the notation or language that conform them. This is an evident issue that has to be considered for the papers that describe MDD based approaches. Hence, we recorded the name of every model that is included in the papers even whether modeling notation or language is not specified. We identified 279 different models. We considered the code for a platform or a language as a model too. The requirements models are the most common models in the CIM level while the models that conform the PIM4Agents Metamodel are the most usual in the PIM level. Finally, the models for the framework Jade are the most used in the PSM level. Regarding the code, the most usual is the generation of Java code as well as code for the frameworks Jade and Jadex. Fig.5 depicts the most common type of models.

Regarding the tools, the 33 % of works uses the Eclipse platform to carry out the modeling or the transformations activities. Furthermore, several works use their own tools. It is important to remark that several works describe specific tools but some of them are developed as plugins for Eclipse, for example Ingenias Development Kit.

3.3 Question 3 (RQ3)

The approaches usually have not been adopted in real industrial environments. However, the works usually describe an example of application. Hence, we take the domain of the examples as the potential application domains. We found examples in the following domains: crisis management, e-commerce, chat systems, game industry, car reservation management, flight and hotel arrangements, air traffic control, etc.

3.4 Question 4 (RQ4)

We found few evidences about the real impact of the analyzed approaches. Usually the papers mention potential benefits but they do not provide empirical evidences. For example, the papers describe that the approaches could improve the productivity, reduce costs and avoid human mistakes. However they do not apply scientific methods to prove it. As we remarked in section 4.1, the lack of works that provide empirical evaluations is one of the problems that have to be addressed in the area of MMD. We only found the following evidences:

- One work proves the impact in the performance of the system.
- One work proves the impact in the productivity during the development process.
- One work demonstrates the impact in the maintainability of the systems.
- One work proves the reduction of the time to understand agent-based simulations.

4 Conclusions

As conclusions of the analysis, we would like to remark some aspects. Few papers apply scientific methods to provide evidences about the real impact of the proposals. The transformation rules have to be specified by means of transformation languages instead of natural language. The use of formal transformation languages enables the validation of the rules as well as the automatic transformation. During the description of the MDD based approaches the languages or metamodels have to be specified. It is difficult to evaluate the proposals without these specifications. Perhaps, a proposal to standardize the description of the MDD based approaches could be useful to homogenize the descriptions. The descriptions have to include an analysis of the impact in the product (or process) quality attributes. There is a great variety of models and usually have a poor justification. Furthermore, the support tools are poorly described as well.

5 References

1. Zambonelli, F., N. Jennings, and M. Wooldridge: *Developing multiagent systems: The Gaia methodology.* ACM Trans. Softw. Eng. Methodol. **12**(3), 317-370 (2003).
2. Mani, N., V. Garousi, and B.H. Far. *A UML-Based Conversion Tool for Monitoring and Testing Multi-agent Systems.* In *2008 20th IEEE International Conference on Tools with Artificial Intelligence.* (2008).
3. Hahn, C., et al., *Meta-models, models, and model transformations: towards interoperable agents*, in *Proceedings of the 4th German conference on Multiagent System Technologies*. 2006.
4. OMG, *MDA Guide Version 1.0.1.* 2003.
5. Kardas, G.: *Model-driven development of multiagent systems: a survey and evaluation.* The Knowledge Engineering Review **28**(4), 479-503 (2013).
6. Petersen, K., S. Vakkalanka, and L. Kuzniarz: *Guidelines for conducting systematic mapping studies in software engineering: An update.* Information and Software Technology **64**(Supplement C), 1-18 (2015).
7. Ameller, D., et al.: *Development of service-oriented architectures using model-driven development: A mapping study.* Information and Software Technology **62**(Supplement C), 42-66 (2015).

8. Dyba, T., T. Dingsoyr, and G. Hanssen. *Applying systematic reviews to diverse study types: An experience report*. In *Empirical Software Engineering and Measurement, 2007. ESEM 2007.* (2007).
9. Zinnikus, I., et al., *A model driven approach to agent-based service-oriented architectures*, in *Proceedings of the 4th German conference on Multiagent System Technologies*. 2006, Springer-Verlag: Erfurt, Germany. p. 110-122.
10. Zhu, H. and L. Shan, *Caste-centric modelling of multi-agent systems: The CAMLE modelling language and automated tools*, in *Model-Driven Software Development*. 2005, Springer Berlin Heidelberg. p. 57-89.
11. Yiwei, L., B. Kerong, and H. Zhiyong. *A model driven agent-oriented self-adaptive software development method*. In *2015 12th International Conference on Fuzzy Systems and Knowledge Discovery (FSKD)*. (2015).
12. Xinjun, M., Z. Jianming, and W. Ji, *Engineering adaptive multi-agent systems with ODAM methodology*. 2009. p. 380-385.
13. Xiao, L. and D. Greer: *Towards agent-oriented model-driven architecture*. European Journal of Information Systems **16**(4), 390-406 (2007).
14. Xiao, L., J. Fox, and H. Zhu. *An agent-oriented approach to support multidisciplinary care decisions*.pp. 8-17. IEEE Computer Society (2013).
15. Vazquez, J., et al. *ALIVE: A Model-Driven Framework to Develop Dynamic, Flexible, Distributed Service-Oriented Systems*. In *12th International Symposium on Symbolic and Numeric Algorithms for Scientific Computing*. (2010).
16. Trencansky, I. and R. Cervenka: *Agent Modeling Language (AML): A comprehensive approach to modeling MAS*. Informatica **29**(4), 391-400 (2005).
17. Tello-Leal, E., O. Chiotti, and P.D. Villarreal: *Process-oriented integration and coordination of healthcare services across organizational boundaries*. Journal of Medical Systems **36**(6), 3713-3724 (2012).
18. Graþanin, D., S.A. Bohner, and M. Hinchey, *Towards a Model-Driven Architecture for Autonomic Systems*, in *Proceedings of the 11th IEEE International Conference and Workshop on Engineering of Computer-Based Systems*. 2004, IEEE Computer Society. p. 500.
19. Taveter, K. and L. Sterling, *An expressway from agent-oriented models to prototypes*. 2008. p. 147-163.
20. Stuit, M., N. Szirbik, and H. Wortmann. *Building Agent-Based Simulations Using Structural and Process Mental Models*. In *Ninth International Symposium on Symbolic and Numeric Algorithms for Scientific Computing (SYNASC)*. (2007).
21. Stoyanov, S., et al. *Service-oriented and agent-based approach for the development of InfoStation eLearning intelligent system architectures*. In *2008 4th International IEEE Conference Intelligent Systems*. (2008).
22. Spanoudakis, N. and P. Moraitis. *Modular JADE Agents Design and Implementation Using ASEME*. In *2010 IEEE/WIC/ACM International Conference on Web Intelligence and Intelligent Agent Technology*. (2010).
23. Silverman, B.G., et al.: *Rich socio-cognitive agents for immersive training environments: case of NonKin Village*. Autonomous Agents and Multi-Agent Systems **24**(2), 312-343 (2012).

24. Silva, M., D. Lopes, and Z. Abdelouahab, *A remote IDS based on multi-agent systems, Web Services and MDA*, in *International Conference on Software Engineering Advances, ICSEA'06*. 2006.
25. Silva, C., et al. *Support for aspectual modeling to Multiagent system architecture*. In *2009 ICSE Workshop on Aspect-Oriented Requirements Engineering and Architecture Design*.pp. 38-43 (2009).
26. Schatten, M., et al., *Agents as bots – An initial attempt towards model-driven MMORPG gameplay*, Y. Demazeau, et al., Editors. 2017, Springer Verlag. p. 246-258.
27. Santos, F., I. Nunes, and A.L.C. Bazzan. *Supporting the Development of Agent-Based Simulations: A DSL for Environment Modeling*. In *2017 IEEE 41st Annual Computer Software and Applications Conference (COMPSAC)*. (2017).
28. Sansores, C. and J. Pavón, *Agent-based simulation replication: A model driven architecture approach*, in *4th Mexican International Conference on Artificial Intelligence, MICAI 2005*. 2005. p. 244-253.
29. Rougemaille, S., et al., *ADELFE design, AMAS-ML in action: A case study*, in *9th International Workshop on Engineering Societies in the Agents World, ESAW 2008*. 2009. p. 105-120.
30. Rekik, M., et al., *Modeling secure mobile agent systems*, in *6th KES International Conference on Agent and Multi-Agent Systems: Technologies and Applications, KES-AMSTA 2012*. 2012. p. 330-339.
31. Poveda, G. and R. Schumann, *An ontology-driven approach for modeling a multi-agent-based electricity market*, in *14th German Conference on Multiagent System Technologies, MATES 2016*. 2016.
32. Perini, A. and A. Susi: *Agent-oriented visual modeling and model validation for engineering distributed systems.* Computer Systems Science and Engineering **20**(4), 319-329 (2005).
33. Penserini, L., et al., *From stakeholder intentions to software agent implementations*. 2006, Springer Verlag. p. 465-479.
34. Pavón, J., C. Sansores, and J.J. Gómez-Sanz: *Modelling and simulation of social systems with INGENIAS.* International Journal of Agent-Oriented Software Engineering **2**(2), 196-221 (2008).
35. Pantoja, C.E. and R. Choren, *A MDA methodology to support multi-agent system development*, in *5th International Conference on Agents and Artificial Intelligence, ICAART 2013*. 2013. p. 393-396.
36. Okouya, D., et al., *Designing MAS organisation through an integrated MDA/ontology approach?*, in *1st International Workshop on Transforming and Weaving Ontologies in Model Driven Engineering, TWOMDE*. 2008.
37. Nunes, I. and M. Luck, *Softgoal-based plan selection in model-driven BDI agents*, in *13th International Conference on Autonomous Agents and Multiagent Systems, AAMAS 2014*. 2014, International Foundation for Autonomous Agents and Multiagent Systems (IFAAMAS). p. 749-756.
38. Nouzri, S. and A. Fazziki: *Towards an MDA-based multi-agent system.* International Journal of Reasoning-based Intelligent Systems **3**(3-4), 181-193 (2011).

39. Nouzri, S. and A. El Fazziki: *A mapping from BPMN model to JADEX model.* International Arab Journal of Information Technology **12**(1), 77-85 (2015).
40. Nagrath, V., et al.: *Peer to peer trade in HTM5 meta model for agent oriented cloud robotic systems.* Peer-to-Peer Networking and Applications **9**(2), 328-343 (2016).
41. Missaoui, E., et al., *NCRIO: A normative holonic metamodel for multi-agent systems*, in *12th International Conference on Hybrid Artificial Intelligent Systems, HAIS 2017*, H. Quintian, et al., Editors. 2017, Springer Verlag. p. 638-649.
42. Maalal, S. and M. Addou, *A model design of multi-agent systems*, in *International Conference on Multimedia Computing and Systems, ICMCS'11*. 2011.
43. Lafi, L., et al., *Towards generic semi-automatic transformation process in MDA*, in *4th International Conference on Information and Communication Technology and Accessibility, ICTA 2013*. 2013, IEEE Computer Society.
44. Kuster, C., et al. *Model-driven development and validation of multi-agent systems in JIAC v with the agent world editor.* In *5th International Conference on Ambient Systems, Networks and Technologies, ANT 2014*.pp. 920-927. Elsevier (2014).
45. Kardas, G., et al.: *Model driven development of semantic web enabled multi-agent systems.* International Journal of Cooperative Information Systems **18**(2), 261-308 (2009).
46. Kardas, G., et al., *Modeling tools for platform specific design of multi-agent systems*, in *7th German Conference on Multiagent System Technologies, MATES 2009*. 2009. p. 202-207.
47. Kallel, S., et al., *MDA-based approach for implementing secure mobile agent systems*, in *13th International Workshop on Agent-Oriented Software Engineering XIII, AOSE 2012*. 2013. p. 56-72.
48. Jung, Y., J. Lee, and M. Kim, *Multi-agent based community computing system development with the model driven architecture*, in *5th international joint conference on Autonomous agents and multiagent systems*. 2006.
49. Judith, P.F. and E. Kirubakaran. *Domain specific modeling framework for agent development.* In *2013 Fourth International Conference on Computing, Communications and Networking Technologies (ICCCNT)*.pp. 1-5 (2013).
50. Jarraya, T. and Z. Guessoum, *Towards a model driven process for multi-agent system*, in *5th International Central and Eastern European Conference on Multi-Agent Systems, CEEMAS 2007*. 2007. p. 256-265.
51. Kirby, J. *Model-Driven Agile Development of Reactive Multi-Agent Systems.* In *30th Annual International Computer Software and Applications Conference (COMPSAC'06)*.pp. 297-302 (2006).
52. Huamonte, J. and K. Smith. *The use of roles to model agent behaviors for model driven architecture.* In *IEEE SoutheastCon, 2005.*,pp. 594-598 (2005).
53. Hellingrath, B. and P. Küppers, *Model-driven development of multi-agent based collaborative planning concepts for heterarchical supply chains*, in *5th International Conference on Industrial Applications of Holonic and Multi-Agent Systems, HoloMAS 2011*. 2011. p. 153-164.

54. Harbouche, A., M. Erradi, and A. Mokhtari: *Deriving multi-agent system behavior.* International Journal of Software Engineering and its Applications **7**(4), 137-156 (2013).
55. Hahn, C., et al. *Integration of Multiagent Systems and Semantic Web Services on a Platform Independent Level.* In *2008 IEEE/WIC/ACM International Conference on Web Intelligence and Intelligent Agent Technology*.pp. 200-206 (2008).
56. Hahn, C., C. Madrigal, and K. Fischer: *A platform-independent metamodel for multiagent systems.* Autonomous Agents and Multi-Agent Systems **18**(2), 239-266 (2009).
57. Hahn, C., S. Jacobi, and D. Raber, *Enhancing the interoperability between multiagent systems and service-oriented architectures through a model-driven approach*, in *IEEE/WIC/ACM International Conference on Intelligent Agent Technology, IAT 2010*. 2010. p. 415-422.
58. Hahn, C. and K. Fischer, *Service composition in holonic multiagent systems: Model-driven choreography and orchestration*, in *3rd International Conference on Industrial Applications of Holonic and Multi-Agent Systems, HoloMAS*. 2007.
59. Graja, Z., A. Regayeg, and A.H. Kacem, *ForMAAD: Towards a model driven approach for agent based application design*, in *11th International Workshop on Agent-Oriented Software Engineering XI, AOSE 2010*. 2011.
60. Goncalves, J. and A. Krishna. *Dynamic Non -functional Requirements Based Model -Driven Agent Development.* In *2015 24th Australasian Software Engineering Conference*.pp. 128-137 (2015).
61. Glake, D., et al. *Modeling through model transformation with MARS 2.0.* In *Agent-Directed Simulation Symposium, ADS 2017*.pp. 13-24. The Society for Modeling and Simulation International (2017).
62. George, B., et al., *Requirements Capture for Cougaar Model-Driven Architecture System*, in *Proceedings of the 29th Annual IEEE/NASA on Software Engineering Workshop*. 2005, IEEE Computer Society. p. 109-117.
63. García-Magariño, I. and C. Gutiérrez: *Agent-oriented modeling and development of a system for crisis management.* Expert Systems with Applications **40**(16), 6580-6592 (2013).
64. García-Magariño, I.: *Towards the integration of the agent-oriented modeling diversity with a powertype-based language.* Computer Standards and Interfaces **36**(6), 941-952 (2014).
65. García-Magariño, I. *A set of method fragments for developing multi-agent systems assisted with model transformations.* In *2011 11th International Conference on Intelligent Systems Design and Applications*.pp. 30-35 (2011).
66. Garcia, E., E. Argente, and A. Giret, *A modeling tool for service-oriented open multiagent systems*, in *12th International Conference on Principles of Practice in Multi-Agent Systems, PRIMA 2009*. 2009. p. 345-360.
67. Fischer, K., et al., *Model Driven Design of Multiagent Systems*, in *3rd International Conference on Agents and Artificial Intelligence, ICAART*. 2013.
68. Fischer, K., C. Hahn, and C. Madrigal-Mora: *Agent-oriented software engineering: a model-driven approach.* International Journal of Agent-Oriented Software Engineering **1**(3-4), 334-369 (2007).

69. Fernández, E., et al.: *Agent-based monitoring service for management of disruptive events in supply chains.* Computers in Industry **70**, 89-101 (2015).
70. Elammari, M. and Z. Issa: *Using Model Driven architecture to develop Multi-Agent Systems.* International Arab Journal of Information Technology **10**(4). 2013.
71. El Fazziki, A., S. Nouzri, and M. Sadgal, *A multi-agent development approach based on the MDA for modelling information systems*, in *International Conference for Internet Technology and Secured Transactions, ICITST 2009.* 2009.
72. Demirkol, S., et al. *SEA_L: A Domain-specific Language for Semantic Web enabled Multi-agent Systems.* In *2012 Federated Conference on Computer Science and Information Systems (FedCSIS).*pp. 1373-1380 (2012).
73. Cirilo, E., et al.: *Automating the product derivation process of multi-agent systems product lines.* Journal of Systems and Software **85**(2), 258-276 (2012).
74. Chtourou, W. and L. Bouzguenda, *Towards an interaction protocols adaptation and management system for coordination in crisis business processes*, G. Jezic, et al., Editors. 2016, Springer Science and Business Media Deutschland. p. 139-150.
75. Challenger, M., et al.: *On the use of a domain-specific modeling language in the development of multiagent systems.* Engineering Applications of Artificial Intelligence **28**, 111-141 (2014).
76. Cabac, L., D. Mosteller, and M. Wester-Ebbinghaus, *Modeling organizational structures and agent knowledge for mulan applications*, M. Koutny, A. Yakovlev, and S. Haddad, Editors. 2014, Springer Verlag. p. 62-82.
77. Cabac, L., et al., *Agent models for concurrent software systems*, in *6th German Conference on Multiagent System Technologies, MATES 2008.* 2008. p. 37-48.
78. Bircan, E., M. Challenger, and G. Kardas. *Interoperability of MAS DSMLs via horizontal model transformations.* In *2016 Federated Conference on Computer Science and Information Systems (FedCSIS).*pp. 1555-1564 (2016).
79. Ayala, I., M. Amor, and L. Fuentes, *Towards the automatic derivation of malaca agents using MDE*, in *11th International Workshop on Agent-Oriented Software Engineering XI, AOSE 2010.* 2011. p. 128-147.
80. Ashamalla, A., G. Beydoun, and G. Low: *Model driven approach for real-time requirement analysis of multi-agent systems.* Computer Languages, Systems and Structures **50**, 127-139 (2017).
81. Amor, M., L. Fuentes, and A. Vallecillo. *Bridging the gap between agent-oriented design and implementation using MDA.* In *5th International Workshop on Agent-Oriented Software Engineering V, AOSE 2004.*pp. 93-108 (2005).
82. Agüero, J., et al., *Developing pervasive systems as service-oriented multi-agent systems*, in *7th International ICST Conference on Mobile and Ubiquitous Systems, MobiQuitous 2010.* 2012. p. 78-89.
83. Agüero, J., et al.: *Towards the development of agent-based organizations through MDD.* International Journal on Artificial Intelligence Tools **22**(2) (2013).
84. Coallier, F.: *Software engineering–Product quality–Part 1: Quality model.* International Organization for Standardization: Geneva, Switzerland (2001).
85. Wieringa, R., et al.: *Requirements engineering paper classification and evaluation criteria: a proposal and a discussion.* Requirements Engineering **11**(1), 102-107 (2006).

A Metrics-driven Inspection Framework for Model Transformations

Maria Fernanda Granda[1], Otto Parra[1], and Nelly Condori-Fernández[2,3]

[1] Department of Computer Science, University of Cuenca, Cuenca, Ecuador
{fernanda.granda, otto.parra}@ucuenca.edu.ec
[2] Department of Computer Science, University of A Coruña, Spain
n.condori.fernandez@udc.es
[3] Vrije Universiteit Amsterdam, The Netherlands
n.condori-fernandez@vu.nl

Abstract. [Context] Model transformations are key elements of Model-driven Engineering. They allow querying, synthesizing and transforming models into other models or code. [Problem] However, as with other software development artefacts, they are not free from anomalies and thus require both verification and validation techniques. [Objective] The objective of this study is to define a semi-automated framework for inspecting the correctness (notions of type and correspondence) of model transformations, by means of detecting and locating anomalies in the transformation rules. [Method] In order to compare the correctness of source and target models, we assume that operational behaviour can be compared by metrics applied on projections from the source model to the target (with deliberate loss of information), which should be preserved by the transformation. [Results] We demonstrate the applicability of our framework for inspecting the correctness of a model-to-model transformation required in a model-driven testing approach. The main result of the study highlights the advantages of metrics for detecting any missing, incorrect or unnecessary transformation rules that have an impact on the correctness of the model transformations. From the research perspective, the feedback produced by the implemented tool will be useful for future research.

Keywords: Model Transformations, Type-Correctness, Correspondence Correctness, Inspection, Metrics.

1 Introduction

Models are the main artefacts in Model-Driven Engineering (MDE) and efforts are focused on their creation, testing and evolution at different levels of abstraction through model transformations. However, as with other software development artefacts, model transformations are not anomalies-free and so must be systematically verified and validated [1]. Otherwise, anomalies introduced by the transformations will be propagated and may produce more anomalies in the subsequent MDE activities.

Verification and validation are independent procedures that are used together for checking that a product (i.e. software artefact) meets requirements and specifications and that it fulfills its intended purpose. However, verifying a transformation that transforms one artefact into another is fundamentally more complex than verifying an individual artefact itself [2]. Thus, some researchers argue that specialist techniques are required [1][2][3] to this task. The inspection is used in researches to validate a software artefact, which is analysed against predetermined criteria of entry or against the specifications which were used to build the artefact. Applying inspection technique to the model transformation validation, one has the documentation of the target model as predetermined criterion, which will be compared with the produced model. These models (i.e. source and target model) are considered the entries, so that the comparisons are done. The goal of our research is to make both *type-correctness* property and *correspondence correctness* of model transformations measurable.

But, what is a "correct" transformation? We considered some of the different notions of correctness summarized by Rahim and Whittle [1]. These authors claim that a transformation satisfies the *type-correctness* property if its target models is conforming to the abstract syntax of the target language. A transformation is said to be correct with respect to *static semantics* if the target models satisfy the well-formedness constraints of the target metamodel. A transformation is correct with respect to *dynamic semantics* if the target models preserve a given property of the source model (these could be domain properties of the source model such as security, application-specific properties, or properties relating to the semantics of the source modelling language, e.g., run-to-completion semantics for UML state machines). A transformation can also be deemed correct if the target model contains the expected target elements corresponding to the source elements in the source model. They refer to this aspect of correctness as *correspondence correctness*. They also acknowledge that some approaches focus on semantics of model transformation properties of the transformation itself—such as termination, confluence of transformation rules, and executability.

In this paper, we present a semi-automated metrics-driven inspection framework to measure both *type-correctness* property and *correspondence correctness* of a complex model transformation used in the context of Model-Driven Engineering. With the purpose of demonstrating the applicability of our framework, it was used in an model-driven testing approach named CoSTest [4][5]. The main contributions of this paper are:

- A semi-automated process defined for inspecting the correctness of model transformations.
- Automated tool to support some activities of such process (i.e. model transformation and report generation).
- A set of metrics defined to predict the quality properties we propose to measure (i.e. *type-correctness* property and *correspondence correctness*). These metrics are evaluated at the instance level, meaning that each execution of the transformations is measured.

This paper is structured as follows: Section 2 summarizes the work related. Section 3 presents the framework and the set of proposed metrics to measure the model transformation correctness. In section 4, we demonstrate the applicability of our framework using an illustrative example. Finally, Section 5 outlines the conclusions and future work.

2 Related Work

Research in validation using metrics and inspection is still at an early stage, where the research focuses on establishing metrics and mapping them to relevant quality attributes of model transformations such as maintainability, testability, performance. A survey [1] summarizes 57 approaches for verifying model transformations and classify them along two dimensions. Firstly, the authors present a coarse-grained classification based on the technical details of the approach (i.e., testing, theorem proving, graph theory, model checking, inspection and metrics). Secondly, they present a finer-grained classification which categorizes approaches according to criteria such as technique, effort, tooling, properties verified and type of transformation.

From these results, we can summarize that only eight approaches are related to inspection and metrics of model transformations (see Table 1). In most of them (7 out of 8 approaches), the technique is applied on the transformation rules (i.e. direct technique) instead of verifying the properties of the generated output (i.e. indirect technique). Column 3 in Table 1 shows that only 4 approaches have a tool support. Some works (3 out of 8 approaches, see column Property in Table 1) are focussed in the preservation of static semantics of models, one approach does not report the property and others (4 of 7 approaches) addressed the preservation of dynamic semantics of models. About the types of transformation for which the related work is applicable, the survey reported 5 of 8 approaches addressing model-to-model (M2M) transformation, 1 approach for model-to-code (M2C) transformation and 2 approaches for both type of transformations (see fifth column in Table 1).

Table 1. Categorization of inspection approaches taken from [1]

Approach	Technique	Tool	Property	Transformation Type	Metrics-driven
[6]	Indirect	No	-	M2C	No
[7]	Direct	Yes	Termination, confluence, executability	M2M	Yes
[8]	Direct	Yes	Termination, confluence, executability	Both	No
[9]	Direct	Yes	Termination, confluence, executability	M2M	No
[10]	Direct	No	Dynamic semantics of models	Both	Yes
[11]	Direct	No	Dynamic semantics of models	M2M	Yes
[12]	Direct	Partial	Dynamic semantics of models	M2M	Yes
[13]	Direct	No	Dynamic semantics of models	M2M	Yes
Our proposal	Indirect	Partial	Correctness of type and correspondence	M2M	Yes

Currently indirect approaches using theorem proving are focused on verifying M2M transformations, and these approaches require the translation of the target model into a formalism (e.g. semantic model) that can be handled by a theorem prover [1]. Theorem provers are either used to prove that the model transformations can generate target models with certain properties or compare the target models with oracles [1].

In contrast to this type of indirect techniques that use theorem proving, we proposed a semi-automated framework for verifying and inspecting the correctness of type and correspondence for M2M transformations, which consists of (i) a tool to generate a report and support the manual intervention to inspect the target model comparing with the expected model (oracle); (ii) set of proposed metrics providing a measure of the model transformation correctness achieved. These values then will be used to locate the anomalies in transformation rules and correct them. Next section we present the details of our approach.

3 Framework for inspecting the Correctness of Type and Correspondence of Model Transformations

A conceptual overview for a model-to-model transformation (M2M) from a modelling language A to B is given in Fig. 1. Two important elements must be stuck out in this context: (1) ***Metamodel*** constitutes the definition of a modelling language, which provides the constructor and the relations with constraints for describing the whole class of models that can be represented by that language with a valid semantic. (2) A ***transformation*** defines a correspondence relation (e.g. transformation rules) between elements in a source metamodel A and elements in a target metamodel B. Therefore, executing transformation A2B helps build a group of elements in target models to conform (well-formed) to their metamodels, using the information from a set of elements in source models, which must also agree with their metamodels.

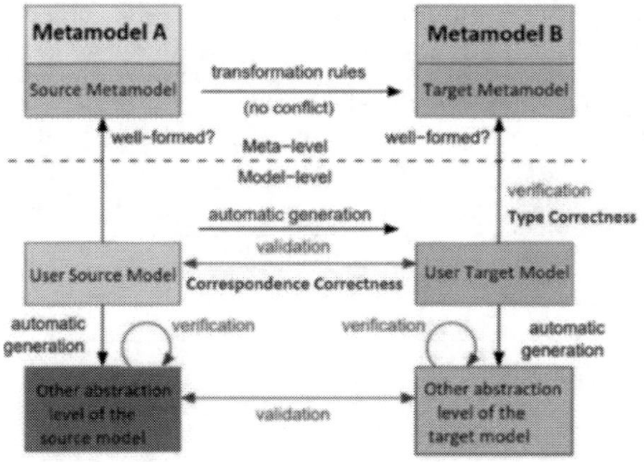

Fig. 1. Model transformation adapted from [14]

Our inspection framework focuses on two aspects: type-correctness and correspondence correctness for model transformations. For the *type-correctness*, we verify whether a model transformation can generate well-formed target models. Well-formedness is verified by checking whether the target model conforms to OCL constraints of the target metamodel. For the *correspondence correctness*, we compare (i.e. inspect) the structural correspondence between the expected (i.e. oracle) and target models. Therefore, we applied an indirect technique. Fig. 2 shows an overview on how our framework operates, its (manual and automatic) activities, input and output artefacts. A description of each activity of our proposed framework is as follows:

1. Defining precisely each modelling languages (both A and B) based on metamodeling. It is required include traceability information in target metamodel (see Section 4.1 for an example).
2. Defining the model transformation using a specific set of structural correspondence rules (i.e. non-conflicting mappings or transformation rules) to transform the source model into target model (A2B transformation).
3. Deriving and verifying the target model. For any specific (but arbitrary) well-formed model instance of the source language A, we derive and check if the corresponding B target model satisfies the well-formedness constraints of the target metamodel (static semantics) by automatic transformation (e.g., using ATL [15]).
4. Traversing the models and collecting the cross-links (i.e. model attributes) to trace source elements with the corresponding target elements.
5. Measuring the correctness (type and correspondence) of the model transformation by applying inspection and the proposed metrics.
6. Taking a decision, although the approach can indicate the correctness level of the model transformation, the inspector (expert) is who takes a decision for considering if the target model is correct. If so, then indirectly the transformation and its rules can be considered are correct as well.
7. In another case, the transformation rules have to be adjusted and the evaluation process has to be executed again. For this purpose, the report generated in the step 4 helps to locate the anomalies in the transformation rules.

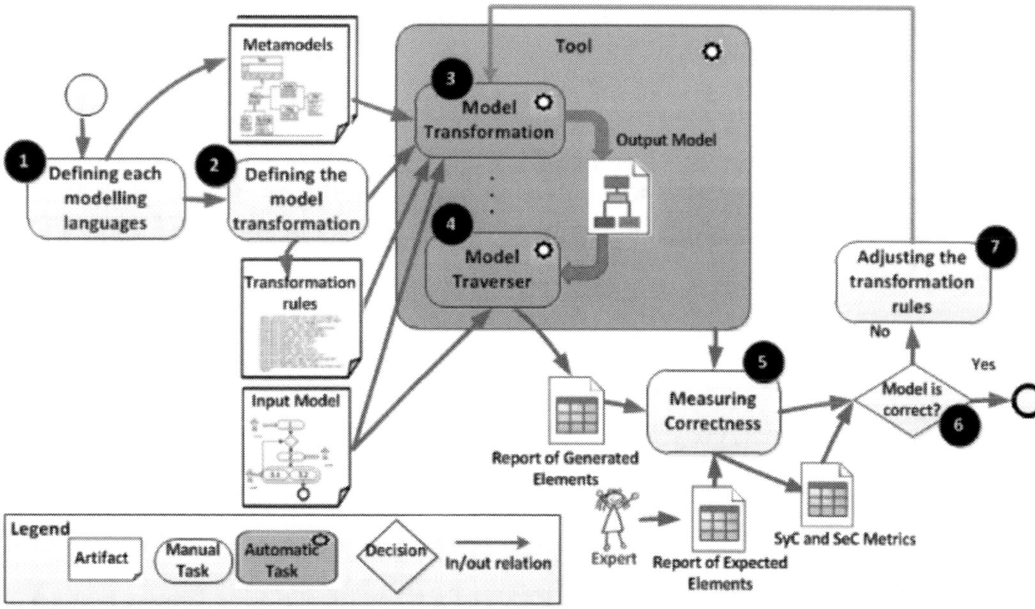

Fig. 2. Overview of our framework for inspecting the correctness of a M2M transformation

3.1 Automated tool for inspecting the target model and traversing the models

The M2M transformation with its transformation rules can be evaluated by performing a simple depth-first search on the model instances. Our tool gives support to both third and fourth activities of our framework (See Fig. 2), by automating the model transformation and generating reports with the trace of the relationship between the source and target elements of the models. The model transformations were implemented using an ATL (ATLAS Transformation Language) [15] and metamodels in Meta Object Facility –MOF [16], the Eclipse Modelling Framework -EMF [17] that employs constraints using Object Constraint Language -OCL [18] to precisely describe their invariants.

3.2 Metrics for evaluating the model transformation correctness

As shown in Fig. 2 the report of generated elements (outcome of the tool) are input of the correctness measurement activity. In this sub-section, we present the metrics with scope of both transformation and rule proposed to measure the type correctness and correspondence correctness of model transformations.

Definition of Basic and Derived Metrics with Transformation scope.

The ***type-correctness*** of a transformation (TC_T) is measured by the metric value achieved by the respective rules in the target model. *ATrule* measures the correctness of an atomic rule (it does not contain any reference to any rule including self-reference, while *Crule* measures the correctness of the composite rule (*CompositeRule*), because its result depends on two values (1) outcome of its nested rules, which generates elements on target model that need others nested rules; and (2) the own *ATrule* value.

If an atomic rule generates a correct element, then its *ATRule* value is 1; otherwise its value is 0. Since target model can have a hierarchical structure, TC_T is calculated starting from the most nested level of the structure up to the highest level. These derived metrics are as follows:

- **Type-Correctness for rule *i*,** the Crule*i* value is calculating using the average of the sum of its ATrule*i* values plus the average of its k element values corresponding to Crule*l* or ATrule*l* of the nested rules.

$$Crulei = \left(\text{ATrule}i + \frac{\sum_{l=1}^{k} \text{Crule}l\,|\,\text{ATrule}l}{k}\right)/2 \qquad (1)$$

- **Type-Correctness of the model Transformation** (TC_T) corresponds to the ACrule value in the top level of the model. This value is multiplied by 100 to obtain the percentage of the type-correctness of the transformation.

$$\text{TC\_T} = \text{Crule}i * 100\% \qquad (2)$$

For ***Correspondence Correctness*** (CC_T) of a transformation, a similar pattern to that for metrics on Type-Correctness is followed. However, we only consider one value for correspondence correctness of a *CCrule*, if the rule is a *CompositeRule*, we take the composite *CCrule* value; otherwise we take the *ATRule* value. The metrics that can be used in both transformations are as follows:

- **Correspondence Correctness for rule *i*,** the CCrule*i* value is calculated using the average of the sum of its k element values corresponding to CCrule*l* or ATrule*l* of the nested rules.

$$CCrulei = \frac{\sum_{l=1}^{k}[\text{CCrule}l \mid \text{ATrule}l]}{k} \qquad (3)$$

- **Correspondence Correctness of the model Transformation** (CC_T) corresponds to CCrule value in the top level of the model. Both values are multiplied by 100 to obtain the percentage of the correspondence correctness of the transformation.

$$\text{CC\_T} = CCrulei * 100\% \qquad (4)$$

Definition of Basic and Derived Metrics with Rule scope.

The basic metrics with rule scope are shown in Table 2. Expected elements are provided by the expert. On the other hand, the elements generated by each rule are retrieved from the target model using the information of traceability (i.e. rule used) stored in each model element. This report is supported by our tool. The respective derived metrics (ratio values) are listed in Table 3. The values of these metrics are only at the element level, so that they do not consider the contained elements. The contained elements are considered in the next metrics with transformation scope.

Table 2. Basic metrics to calculate the Correctness of Type and Correspondence of a Rule

Metric	Definition
N_EG*j*	Total number of elements generated by the rule j
N_CEG*j*	Total number of Correct Elements generated by the rule j
N_EE*j*	Number of expected elements to be generated by the rule j

Table 3. Derived metrics to calculate the Correctness of Type and Correspondence of a Rule

Metric	Definition	Formula
TC_*rulej*	Type-Correctness reached by the rule j	N_CEG*j* / N_EG*j* (5)
CC_*rulej*	Correspondence Correctness reached by the rule j	N_EG*j* / N_EE*j* (6)

Thanks to the measures (outcome of the correctness measurement activity), the inspector (expert) has the information to realize on the differences between the obtained model and the expected one. These differences could mean: a) there are unnecessary rules in the M2M transformation that generate additional elements of the expected ones, b) there are missing rules because the elements were not generated as expected, or c) the rule is incorrect, the expected output may be different from the actual output because an existing rule is not correctly implemented. However, these measures do not to allow knowing if the errors are serious or insignificant. In this paper, we considered all errors with the same severity, but we could define a weight for each rule type in order to classify the error relevance.

In the following section, we illustrate each activity of our metrics-driven inspection framework in the context of model-driven testing, where test case models are automatically derived from requirements models.

4 Application of the inspection framework

We present (an extract of) a complex model transformation from Communicational Analysis (CA) Model [19] to CoSTest's Test Model (TM) [4] (denoted as CA2TM) in order to demonstrate the applicability of our framework for measuring the correctness of model transformations. We selected this transformation (CA2TM) because during the development phase of the CoSTest tool, we were challenged to measure the correctness of the model transformations implemented in the tool. Therefore, we collected the process and data followed for inspecting and measuring the M2M transformation, which are reported in this paper.

4.1 Defining modelling languages

CA Model as the source modelling language. CA is used to specify the requirement models and includes a Communicative Event (CE) and the message structures as main artefacts for specifying the functional requirements. Fig. 3 shows the main CA artefacts based on the Sudoku system [20], which defines the functionality for managing different users, playing with their sudokus and generating new ones.

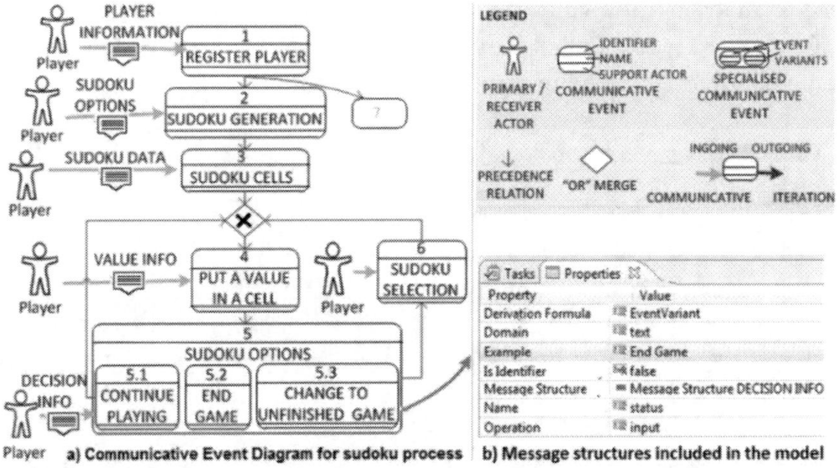

Fig. 3. Excerpt from a CA model for Sudoku CS, adapted from [20]

CoSTest's TM as the target modelling language. CoSTest's TM is used to capture the semantics of the test model available in the CoSTest tool. A precise metamodeling treatment of CoSTest's TM was discussed in [4]. However, we have updated this metamodel including in Element class the traceability information of each one of them (i.e. location and transformation rule attributes) in order to measure the proposed correctness metrics. Now, we briefly revisit the metamodel and the operational semantics of CoSTest's TM in Fig. 4, it includes the rules that generate the different target model elements.

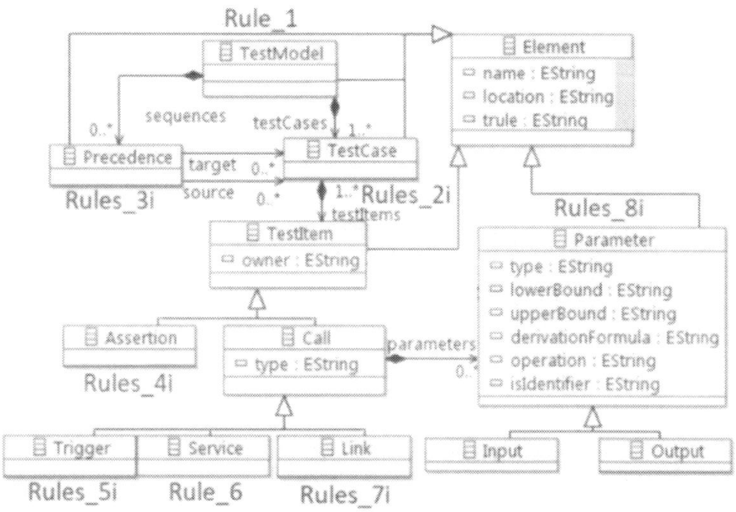

Fig. 4. CoSTest metamodel for our transformation example (taken from [4])

4.2 Defining the CA2TM model Transformation

For the sake of readability, we use concrete syntax to describe instances of requirements model (see Fig. 5a) and test model (see Fig. 5b) with two test scenarios (i.e. TS1 and TS2) for our example, Sudoku system. As in the CA to TM, model transformation can be used to generate a target model of a certain structure (TM) from a source model of a different structure CA. Specific structural configurations in the source model (such as an Communicative Event node in the CA model, (see Fig. 5) produce specific structural configurations in the target model (such as a Test Case in the TM).

The rules to accomplish the structural transformations may be simple (i.e. the mapping correspondence is 1 to 1) or complicated (i.e. the mapping correspondence is 1 to n) (see some examples in Table 4).

In essence, we expect that the correspondence conditions are independently specified for a model transformation, and an independent tool checks if these conditions are satisfied by the instance models, after the model transformation has been executed. We also require that the model transformation builds up a structure for bookkeeping the mapping between the source and target models (e.g. using cross-link attributes as the Element class shown in Fig. 4).

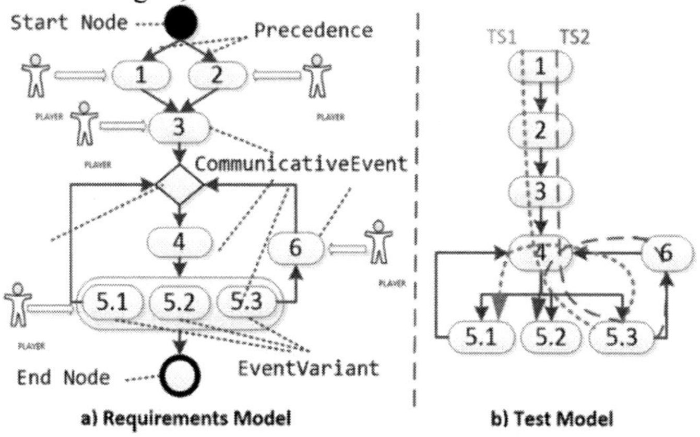

Fig. 5. Examples using graphical concrete syntax of (a) CA model, (b) CoSTest's TM

Table 4. Some transformations and mapping correspondences used in our CA2TM case study

CA	TM	mapping correspondence
Model	Test Model	1:1
Precedence	Precedence	1:n
Communicative Event	Test Case	1:1
	Assertion	1:1
Textual Requirement	Assertion	1:1
Iteration	Link	1:n
Node (End, Start)	-	Informational
Logical node (And, Or)	-	Informational
Organisational actor	-	Not used

4.3 Deriving and Verifying the Target Model

The transformation rules previously defined are formalized using ATL language, an XMI (XML Metadata Interchange) [16] representation then is generated automatically, which would yield the target model (Fig. 5b) as the output when supplying (the XMI representation of) the Sudoku's CA model (Fig. 3) as the input.

The target model can be checked automatically to prove any model property using existing model checker tools or invariants in the same transformation tool (see an example of invariants in Fig. 6). Fig. 6 shows some OCL invariants used as the static semantics that are checking when the target model (TM) in our CA2TM transformation is derived. These example of constraints include that names must be unique within their respective contexts, classes must have a name and the multiplicity constraints for relations, and so on.

```
context TestModel inv TC_mult1: self.testCases->size()>0;
context Element inv Element_name: self.name<>null;
context Element inv Element_location: self.Location<>null;
context Element inv Element_trule: self.trule<>null;
context Precedence inv Precedence_Name: self->forAll(e1,e2 | e1.name = e2.name implies e1=e2);
context Precedence inv Preced_TC: self.target<>null or self.source<>null;
context TestCase inv TestCase_Name: self->forAll(e1,e2 | e1.name = e2.name implies e1=e2);
context TestCase inv TI_mult1: self.testItems->size()>0;
context TestItem inv TestItem_owner: self-> forAll(e|e.oclIsKindOf(Link) = false implies e.owner<>null);
```

Fig. 6. Some OCL invariants used for the target model of the CA2TM transformation

If the verification succeeds, then we conclude that the model transformation is correct with respect to static semantic of the pair (p, q) of properties for the specific pairs of source and target models having semantics defined by a set of transformation rules. Otherwise, property p is not preserved by the model transformation and debugging can be initiated based upon the error trace(s) retrieved by the model checker. As before, this debugging phase may fix problems in the model transformation or in the specification of the target language. However, there are anomalies on transformation rules that are difficult to detect such as elements that have type-correctness problems (e.g. element names are syntactically incorrect) as well as correspondence correctness problems (e.g. missing or unnecessary elements). Therefore, in the Section 3.2, we present a set of metrics that will help to detect this kind of problems.

4.4 Traversing the Models

Since the metamodels of both the source and target models are available with the transformations, and the trace information (i.e. *name*, *location* and *trule* in the *Element* class, see Fig. 4) is included in the target metamodel, we have implemented the code of a model traverser in our tool to trace source elements with the corresponding target elements, and generate a report for inspection. This trace information needs to be analysed each time the rules specification changes. We call the model traverser at the end of each execution of the transformation, supplying to it the source and target model instances with the trace information (see example presented in Section 4.1).

4.5 Measuring the Correctness of the CA2TM model Transformation

To show how metrics measure the correctness in a model, we will use the data of a partial test model TM1 of our illustrative example (i.e. Sudoku system), with four test cases (i.e. TC1 – TC4) and one precedence Pr1.

Firstly, we used the report of the elements obtained by the M2M transformation using the tool (see Tables 5 and 6). Second, the expert compares that the report of elements is equal to the expected report otherwise it has to be completed with the missing elements before calculating the metrics (e.g. row highlighted in Table 5 is added because it is a missing element in the output model). Third, the expert checks the output model with expected model and assign the values ATrulei for each model element. In our example, there are some elements that have type-correctness problems (e.g. parameter and trigger names are syntactically incorrect because they include spaces) as well as correspondence correctness problems (e.g. unnecessary elements). This can be clearly evaluated by assigning to these elements the value 0 to ATrulei, such as some values in Table 5 and Table 6 are shown.

Table 5. Report generated with our tool to calculate the metric TC_T for our illustrative example

TEST MODEL	Rule	Crulei (1)	ATrulei	Crule/	Element (Precedence or Test Case)	Rule	Crulei (1)	ATrulei	Crule/	Test Items (Assertion, Service, Trigger, Link)	Rule	Crulei (1)	ATrulei	Crule/	Parameters	Rule	Crulei (1)	ATrulei
TM1	R1	0,97	1	0,94	Test case TC1	R2.1	1,00	1	1,00	Service S1	R6.1	1,00	1	1,00	parameter P1	R8.1	1	1
					Test case TC2	R2.1	1,00	1	1,00	Service S2	R6.1	1,00	1	1,00	parameter P1	R8.1	1	1
					Test case TC3	R2.1	0,78	1	0,56	Trigger T1	R5.2	0,67	1	0,33	parameter P1	R8.1	1	1
															parameter P2	R8.1	0	0
		TC_T= Crule1*100 TC_T= 97% (2)													parameter P3	R8.1	0	0
										Trigger T2	R5.2	0,50	1	0,00	parameter P1	R8.3	0	0
										Trigger T3	R5.2	0,50	1	0,00	parameter P1	R8.3	0	0
															parameter P2	R8.3	0	0
					Test case TC4	R2.1	0,92	1	0,83	**Trigger T1**	**R5.2**	**0**	**0**	**0,00**	**parameter P1**	**R8.3**	**0**	**0**
										Link L1	R7.2	1,00	1	1,00	parameter P1	R7.2	1	1
															parameter P2	R7.2	1	1
										Link L2	R7.1	1,00	1	1,00	parameter P1	R7.1	1	1
															parameter P2	R7.1	1	1
										Service S1	R6.1	1,00	1	1,00	parameter P1	R8.1	1	1
															parameter P2	R8.1	1	1
															parameter P3	R8.1	1	1
															parameter P4	R8.1	1	1
										Assertion A1	R4.4	1,00	1					
										Assertion A2	R4.4	1,00	1					
					Precedence Pr1	R3.1	1,00	1										

From these results, Table 5 shows that the Type-Correctness of the transformation (TC_T) is 0.97=97%, we applied the metrics (1) and (2). In similar way, Table 6 shows that the Correspondence Correctness of the transformation (CC_T) is 0.92=92%, we applied the metrics (3) and (4).

Then, we calculate the TC_rulej and CC_rulej metric values for each transformation rule by comparing the number of elements generated with the number of expected elements. Table 7 shows the results of calculating the metrics (5) and (6) for our transformation example using the data from Table 5 and Table 6.

From these results, we see that the rules 5.2 and 8.3 are incorrect (see values of TC_rulej column in Table 6) because they are generating elements with type-correctness anomalies (e.g. names with spaces). In the similar way, we see that the rules 6.2 and 7.2 are generating missing or unnecessary elements (see values of CC_rulej column in Table 6 and the anomalies identified in Table 5); therefore, these metrics are less than 100%. Since the rule 8.1 being nested in rule 6.2, which generates a missing element (see row of the missing trigger in Table 6), so its value also does not reach 100%.

Table 6. Report generated using our tool to calculate the metric CC_T for our illustrative example

TEST MODEL	Rule	CCrulei (3)	Element (Precedence or Test Case)	Rule	CCrulei (3)	Test Items (Assertion, Service, Trigger, Link)	Rule	CCrulei (3)	Parameters	Rule	CCrulei (3)	Atrulei	Anomaly
TM1	R1	0,92	**Test case TC1**	**R2.1**	**1,00**	Service S1	R6.1	1,00	parameter P1	R8.1	1	1	
			Test case TC2	**R2.1**	**1,00**	Service S2	R6.1	1,00	parameter P1	R8.1	1	1	
CC_T= CCrule1*100 CC_T= 92% (4)			**Test case TC3**	**R2.1**	**0,75**	Trigger T1	R5.2	1,00	parameter P1	R8.1	1	1	
									parameter P2	R8.1	1	1	
									parameter P3	R8.1	1	1	
						Trigger T2	R5.2	1,00	parameter P1	R8.3	1	1	
						Trigger T3	R5.2	1,00	parameter P1	R8.3	1	1	
									parameter P2	R8.3	1	1	
						Service S1	**R6.2**	**0,00**	parameter P1	R8.1	0	0	Missing Trigger
			Test case TC4	**R2.1**	**0,83**	**Trigger T1**	**R5.2**	**1,00**	parameter P1	R8.3	1	1	
						Link L1	**R7.2**	**0,00**	**parameter P1**	**R7.2**	**0**	**0**	Unnecessary Link
									parameter P2	**R7.2**	**0**	**0**	
						Link L2	**R7.1**	**1,00**	parameter P1	R7.1	1	1	
									parameter P2	R7.1	1	1	
						Service S1	**R6.1**	**1,00**	parameter P1	R8.1	1	1	
									parameter P2	R8.1	1	1	
									parameter P3	R8.1	1	1	
									parameter P4	R8.1	1	1	
						Assertion A1	**R4.4**	**1,00**				1	
						Assertion A2	**R4.4**	**1,00**				1	
			Precedence Pr1	**R3.1**	**1,00**							1	

Table 7. Values of TC_rule*j* and CC_rule*j* calculated for our example

CA2TM Transformation rule	TC_rulej (1)	CC_rulej (2)	CA2TM Transformation rule	TC_rulej (1)	CC_rulej (2)
1	1/1= 100%	1/1=100%	6.2	-	**0/1= 0%**
2.1	4/4 = 100%	4/4 = 100%	7.1	3/3=100%	3/3=100%
3.1	1/1 = 100%	1/1 = 100%	7.2	3/3=100%	**0/3=0%**
4.4	2/2= 100%	2/2 =100%	8.1	**9/10=90%**	**9/10=0.90%**
5.2	**3/4=0.75%**	4/4=100%	8.3	**0/4=0%**	4/4=100%
6.1	3/3=100%	3/3=100%			

4.6 Taking a decision

The differences found allowed us to take corrective actions to adjust our M2M transformation, so that for the next iteration the problems identified in the transformation rules were fixed, achieving 100% in the correctness of type and correspondence.

4.7 Adjusting the transformation rules

By using the report generated by our tool, we located easily the anomalies in the transformation rules, which facilitated the correction process.

Our framework was applied to CA2TM transformations with ten CA source models. Each CA source model contained a variety of characteristics that allowed us to test the functioning of the different transformation rules defined for CA2TM transformation under review. Due to severe page limitations, we can only provide an overview of a illustrative example of the CA2TM transformation, the reader is referred to URL (https://costestproject2017.wordpress.com/) for a more detailed information of the other CA2TM transformations. Then, the differences found in each iteration allowed us to take corrective actions to adjust the M2M transformation, so that for the next iteration the problems identified in the transformation rules were fixed. Achieving a correctness (type and correspondence) of 100% from the 5th CA2TM transformation.

5 Conclusions and Future Work

In this paper, we proposed a semi-automated metrics-driven framework to inspect if a model transformation preserves the type correctness and correspondence correctness. For this purpose, we have defined a set of basic and derived metrics, which can be computed and used to inspect the target model comparing with the expected model (oracle). The metrics-driven inspection is supported with a report implemented in the tool containing the elements of target and source models.

We demonstrated the applicability of our framework for inspecting the correctness of a complex model transformation from a requirements model (i.e. Communicational Analysis model) to test models (i.e. CoSTest's test model). We found that the defined metrics were useful for identifying and locating anomalies (i.e. incorrect, missing and redundant rules) in the transformation rules, which improved the effectiveness of the model transformation under inspection. Our framework also measures the correctness of M2M transformation without having to transform them into any other formalism or to abstract any of their features. Naturally, we will continue our research focusing on the tool's scalability and cost (inspection effort) as well as defining weights to classify the severity of the founded errors.

References

1. Rahim, L., Whittle, J.: A survey of approaches for verifying model transformations. Softw. Syst. Model. 14, 1003–1028 (2015).
2. Stürmer, I., Conrad, M., Fey, I., Dörr, H.: Model Transformation Testing Challenges. In: Int. Workshop on Soft. Engineering for Automotive systems (SEAS '06). pp. 45–52 (2006).

3. Küster, J.M., Heckel, R., Engels, G.: Defining and validating transformations of UML models. In: Proceedings - 2003 IEEE Symposium on Human Centric Computing Languages and Environments, HCC 2003. pp. 145–152 (2003).
4. Granda, M.F., Condori-Fernandez, N., Vos, T.E.J., Pastor, O.: Towards the automated generation of abstract test cases from requirements models. In: 1st International Workshop on Requirements Engineering and Testing. pp. 39–46. IEEE, Karlskrona, Sweden (2014).
5. Granda, M.F., Condori-fernández, N., Vos, T.E.J., Pastor, Ó.: CoSTest : A tool for Validation of Requirements at Model Level. In: 25th International Requirements Engineering Conference - Tool Demo (2017).
6. Stürmer, I., Conrad, M., Fey, I., Dörr, H.: Experiences with model and autocode reviews in model-based software development. Proc. 2006 Int. Work. Softw. Eng. Automot. Syst. - SEAS '06. 45 (2006).
7. Van Amstel, M.F., Lange, C.F., Brand, M.G.: Using metrics for assessing the quality of ASF+SDF model transformations. In: 2nd International Conference on Theory and Practice of Model Transformations. pp. 239–248 (2009).
8. Amstel, V., Van Den Brand, M.G.J.: Model Transformation Analysis: Staying ahead of the maintenance nightmare. In: 4th Int. Conf. on Theory and Practice of Model Transformations. pp. 108–122 (2011).
9. Van Amstel, M., Bosems, S., Kurtev, I., Pires, L.F.: Performance in Model Transformations: Experiments with ATL and QVT. Lect. Notes Comput. Sci. 6707, 198–212 (2011).
10. Saeki, M., Kaiya, H.: Measuring Model Transformation in Model Driven Development. In: Int. Conference on Advanced Information, Systems Engineering. pp. 77–80 (2007).
11. Vignaga, A.: Metrics for Measuring ATL Model Transformations, Tech. rep., Universidad de Chile. (2009).
12. Kapová, L., Goldschmidt, T., Becker, S., Henss, J.: Evaluating maintainability with code metrics for model-to-model transformations. In: 6th Int. conference on Quality of Software Architectures: research into Practice–Reality and Gaps, QoSA'10. pp. 151–166 (2010).
13. Rahimi, S., Lano, K.: Integrating goal-oriented measurement for evaluation of model transformation. In: Int. Symp. on Computer Science and Soft. Eng. pp. 129–134 (2011).
14. Varró, D., Pataricza, A.: Automated Formal Verification of Model Tranformations. In: Critical Systems Development in UML. pp. 63–78 (2003).
15. Jouault, F., Allilaire, F., Bézivin, J., Kurtev, I.: ATL: A model transformation tool. Sci. Comput. Program. 72, 31–39 (2008).
16. OMG: MOF 2.0/XMI Mapping Specification, v2.1, https://www.omg.org/spec/XMI/2.1/.
17. Steinberg, D., Budinsky, F., Paternostro, M., Merks, E.: EMF: Eclipse Modeling Framework. , Amsterdam (2008).
18. Object Management Group: OCL : Object Constraint Language. (2014).
19. España, S., González, A., Pastor, Ó.: Communication Analysis: A Requirements Engineering Method for Information Systems. In: 21st International Conference on Advanced Information Systems Engineering. pp. 530–545 (2009).
20. Tort, A., Olivé, A.: Case Study: Conceptual Modeling of Basic Sudoku, http://guifre.lsi.upc.edu/Sudoku.pdf.

Desarrollo de Interfaces de Usuario basado en MDD: un mapeo sistemático

Juan Carlos Mejias [1], Nemury Silega[1] and Manuel Noguera[2]

[1] Universidad de las Ciencias Informáticas. Carretera a San Antonio de los Baños km 2 ½, Reparto Torrens, La Lisa, La Habana, Cuba. C.P.: 19370
{jmejias, nsilega}@uci.cu
[2] Universidad de Granada. C/. Cortadura del Valle s/n Zip: 51001 Ceuta, España.
mnogera@ugr.es

Abstract. El Desarrollo de Interfaces de Usuario Dirigido por Modelos (MDUID) tiene el objetivo de ofrecer un entorno en el que los desarrolladores pueden diseñar e implementar interfaces de usuario de una forma profesional, consistente y sistemática. La adopción de propuestas basadas en MDUID ha mejorado el desarrollo de software en diversos aspectos como el aumento de la productividad, la reutilización y la calidad. En este trabajo se presentan los resultados de un estudio de mapeo sistemático para identificar los elementos más relevantes relacionados con el MDUID durante el período 2004-2017. Como resultado de este trabajo, se clasificaron las investigaciones seleccionadas y se identificaron nuevas líneas de investigación que pueden ser aprovechadas por la comunidad científica internacional.

Keywords: Mapeo sistemático, interfaz de usuario, MDUID, IU, MDD.

1 Introducción

En la actualidad, los usuarios son más exigentes con la calidad de las aplicaciones que demandan, en gran medida su opinión respecto a las mismas está fundamentada en su experiencia con la Interfaz de Usuario (IU) [1,2]. En consecuencia, los requisitos que se imponen a la IU son mayores (soporte multiplataforma, acceso remoto, soporte multiusuario, usabilidad, eficiencia) y por lo tanto, el esfuerzo dedicado a obtener la interfaz de las aplicaciones es también elevado, llegando a representar según Rosson y Myers [3] alrededor del 48% del código generado y el 50% del tiempo empleado para su desarrollo. Estos aspectos han sido corroborados y respaldados por Meixner et al [4] y Martin et al [5] en trabajos más recientes.

El Desarrollo Dirigido por Modelos (MDD) surge como un nuevo paso hacia una verdadera industrialización de la producción de software. En tal sentido, el Desarrollo Dirigido por Modelos de Interfaces de Usuario (MDUID) intercepta dos subáreas del desarrollo de software: el MDD y el Desarrollo de Interfaz de Usuario (UID).

MDUID provee un entorno en el que los desarrolladores pueden diseñar e implementar interfaces de usuario de una forma profesional, consistente y sistemática [6, 7,

8, 9]. Se basa en la idea de que la IU puede ser definida por un conjunto de modelos declarativos tales que cada uno de ellos trata facetas particulares como las tareas y la presentación. Esos modelos guían el ciclo de vida del desarrollo de la interfaz y conforman la base para la generación automática de diversos productos de software, entre ellos, el código fuente de la interfaz. Pinheiro da Silva [6] distingue las siguientes ventajas derivadas del uso de modelos de interfaces de usuario:

- Proveen una descripción más abstracta de una IU que las descripciones de interfaces de usuario provistas por las herramientas tradicionales de desarrollo de IU.
- Facilitan la creación de métodos para diseñar e implementar una IU de manera sistemática ya que permiten: Modelar IU a distintos niveles de abstracción, Refinar los modelos de manera incremental y Reutilizar especificaciones de IU.
- Proveen la infraestructura requerida para automatizar las tareas relacionadas con el diseño de la IU y los procesos de implementación.

Teniendo en cuenta las ventajas de MDD para la industria del software [10,11,12,13], diversas soluciones se han propuesto para el MDUID. Sin embargo en su mayoría presentan carencias respecto a su fiabilidad y su capacidad de demostrar los beneficios de su adopción.

En este trabajo se presentan los resultados de un estudio de mapeo sistemático para identificar las evidencias existentes del MDUID durante el período 2004-2017. Las motivaciones principales del presente estudio pueden resumirse de la siguiente forma: i) Ofrecer una visión general del estado de la cuestión en la literatura relacionada acerca de los enfoques MDUID, que facilite la comprensión de este dominio de investigación. ii) Identificar y clasificar los diferentes resultados que se encuentren, sirviendo de punto de partida para futuras investigaciones, agilizando y facilitando la orientación del investigador principiante en el dominio de MDUID.

El documento se estructura de la siguiente forma: la próxima sección describe el método usado para conducir el mapeo y se detallan las actividades realizadas. A continuación se presenta un análisis de las propuestas y se discuten los resultados alcanzados con el mapeo. Finalmente se presentan las conclusiones y los trabajos futuros.

2 Método de investigación

Un estudio de mapeo sistemático ("systematic mapping") tiene como objetivo construir un esquema de clasificación y estructurar un campo de interés en la Ingeniería del Software [14]. Permite organizar las propuestas y resultados de investigación sobre un dominio, y por tanto se encuentra dirigido al análisis temático y a la identificación de los principales foros de publicación. Su utilización permite categorizar los resultados publicados hasta el momento en un área determinada y está considerado como, un paso previo para decidir en qué áreas del campo es interesante abordar una revisión sistemática más detallada [15].

El proceso de mapeo sistemático consiste en las siguientes etapas [16]: *Pregunta(s) de investigación, Búsqueda, Selección de estudios y evaluación de calidad, Extracción de datos, Análisis y clasificación y Validez de la evaluación.* A continuación se describen los resultados de la ejecución de estas actividades.

2.1 Definición de las preguntas de investigación

Las preguntas de investigación se definen conforme a los objetivos principales del estudio. Se recomienda [17, 18] que en su definición se consideren cuatro partes:

1. **Población:** Profesionales interesados en realizar el desarrollo de las IU siguiendo el paradigma de desarrollo MDUID.
2. **Factor de estudio:** Estado actual del MDUID en el desarrollo de software.
3. **Intervención en la comparación:** Entornos de desarrollo, metodologías, herramientas basadas en el MDUID para el desarrollo de software.
4. **Resultado:** Características fundamentales de las propuestas MDUID encontradas.

Estos elementos permitieron definir las siguientes preguntas de investigación (PI):

Preguntas específicas del área de estudio:

PI1: ¿Qué atributos de calidad del proceso de desarrollo de software se benefician con estas investigaciones?

PI2: ¿Qué características de la calidad del producto han sido más analizadas?

PI3: ¿Cuáles son las tecnologías más utilizadas en las propuestas analizadas?

PI4: ¿Cuáles son los modelos y/o metamodelos más usuales?

PI5: ¿Qué propuestas centradas en aspectos metodológicos existen?

Preguntas independientes del área de estudio:

PI6: ¿Qué tipo de investigación y método de investigación es el más usual en propuestas basadas en MDUID para el desarrollo de software?

PI7: ¿Qué entornos, académicos o industriales, son los más utilizados en el momento de aplicar la investigación?

2.2 Ejecución de la búsqueda

Para realizar una búsqueda exitosa es necesario seleccionar las fuentes de datos y definir una estrategia de búsqueda. Las fuentes seleccionadas fueron Google Scholar, ACM, IEEE, Springer y Scopus. Google Scholar, motor de búsqueda líder en el seno de la comunidad científica de investigadores, indexa un amplio número de fuentes de documentación, entre las que se encuentran ACM, IEEE, Springer y Scopus. Por otra parte, Google Scholar recupera documentos que no aparecen en bibliotecas digitales, y que, sin embargo forman parte del acervo científico de las distintas disciplinas, por lo que es complemento en la elaboración de mapeos y revisiones sistemáticas [18].

En las búsquedas se utilizaron términos relacionados con el tema de la investigación así como su combinación. Los términos claves fueron *user interface*, *model driven user interface development* y *software*. La cadena se conformó con estos términos (y sinónimos) y con operadores booleanos, resultando finalmente la siguiente:

("user interface" OR "graphical user interface" OR GUI) AND ("model driven user interface development" OR "model-driven user interface development" OR MDUID) AND (software OR "software development")

En cada una de las fuentes, las búsquedas se realizaron considerando los campos *palabras clave*, *título* y *resumen*. La búsqueda se acotó al período 2004 – 2017 porque el 2004 es el año en que el MDUID alcanza su mayor auge [19]. Los resultados de ejecutar la cadena de búsqueda en Google Scholar fueron 115 artículos, que incluyen, tanto publicaciones indizadas en las bibliotecas digitales más importantes en el área de Ingeniería del Software (incluidas ACM, IEEE, Springer y Scopus) como literatura gris publicada en las Webs de las universidades (informes, tesis).

El segundo paso de búsqueda consistió en adaptar la cadena de búsqueda a las características de los buscadores específicos de ACM Digital Library, IEEE Xplore Digital Library, Springer y Scopus. La ejecución de la búsqueda en estos motores específicos arrojó 45631 resultados (ACM) de los cuales se pudo comprobar que a partir del 102 no se relacionaban con los aspectos definidos en la búsqueda, 40 resultados (IEEE), 10538 resultados (Springer) y 57 resultados (Scopus) respectivamente.

Debido a que los cuatro buscadores ordenan los resultados por la relevancia de la publicación, se analizaron los 100 resultados más relevantes de ACM y Springer, los 40 resultados arrojados por IEEE y los 57 resultados de Scopus. La búsqueda en Google Scholar arrojó 115 resultados y todos fueron analizados. En total se analizaron 412 publicaciones. Asimismo, se eliminaron los trabajos duplicados para garantizar una mayor precisión. En la Tabla 1 se presenta un resumen de estos datos.

Tabla 1. Resultados de la búsqueda.

Buscador	**Google Scholar**	**ACM**	**IEEE**	**Springer**	**Scopus**	**Total**
Total de Trabajos	115	45631	40	10538	57	56381
Trabajos analizados	115	100	40	100	57	412
Trabajos candidatos	28	22	13	33	36	132
Trabajos seleccionados	20	12	10	20	12	74

Con el objetivo de obtener una buena muestra y reducir la posibilidad de que trabajos relevantes para el estudio quedaran fuera de los resultados arrojados por los buscadores a partir de la cadena de búsqueda hemos combinado la estrategia de buscar con otra estrategia. En este caso hemos aplicado una variante de "*snowballing process*". Para la ejecución de esta estrategia se recomienda partir de un conjunto representativo de artículos. En este caso partimos de los 28 trabajos seleccionados en Scopus, los 12 seleccionados más los 16 que aparecían en Scopus pero que ya lo habíamos analizado de otros buscadores. Para agilizar la búsqueda y aumentar la probabilidad de encontrar artículos de interés decidimos buscar los artículos que citan a los 28 artículos de Scopus. Para ejecutar este procedimiento explotamos las facilidades del buscador de Scopus que permite obtener las citas de un conjunto de artículos.

Esta estrategia mejora el mapeo en dos sentidos, en primer lugar refuerza la pertinencia de los artículos seleccionados que, al ser citados por otros trabajos que también se relacionan con el tema en cuestión, resulta una medida precisa de su idoneidad para el estudio. En segundo lugar, se puede enriquecer la muestra de trabajos analizados con artículos que por algún motivo pudieron quedar fuera de los resultados arrojados por los buscadores y que sí se relacionan con la temática del estudio.

La búsqueda de artículos que citan los 28 de Scopus arrojó 103 resultados. Como resultado interesante se puede resaltar el hecho de que la mayoría de los 28 trabajos de los que se partió estaban dentro de estos 103, lo que demuestra su relación con la temática. También aparecieron trabajos que ya se habían analizado cuando se realizó la búsqueda en otros buscadores. Del resto de los trabajos se analizaron los que tenían alguna cita, de los que se tomaron 18 candidatos y finalmente se seleccionaron para el mapeo 11 trabajos. La suma de este último conjunto de artículos con los 74 que ya se habían seleccionado permite que finalmente se hayan seleccionado para el mapeo un total de 85 trabajos.

2.3 Filtrado de estudios

La selección de los estudios se ha formulado basada en los siguientes criterios de inclusión/exclusión:

Inclusión: libros y artículos de revistas, congresos, y conferencias que describan propuestas basadas en MDUID para el desarrollo de software.

Exclusión:

1) Documentos y trabajos técnicos que tratan sobre la adopción de MDUID.
2) Trabajos que no ofrezcan solución a un problema determinado.
3) Artículos no disponibles para ser descargados.

Para la selección de los trabajos se utilizó primeramente el criterio de inclusión. Para ello el análisis se realizó sobre el título, resumen y palabras claves de cada uno de los trabajos filtrados en la búsqueda, obteniendo así la mayor cantidad de investigaciones basadas en postulados de MDUID para el desarrollo de software. En segunda instancia se utilizó el criterio de exclusión, centrado fundamentalmente en el resumen, introducción y conclusiones. En caso de ser necesario, se revisaron con mayor profundidad los trabajos que lo requerían para poder resolver la duda de si incluirlos o excluirlos atendiendo a los criterios de inclusión/exclusión definidos anteriormente.

El proceso de filtrado se dividió en tres etapas secuenciales. En la primera etapa, cada revisor aplicó los criterios de inclusión y exclusión basándose en el título y resumen de los trabajos asignados aleatoriamente. Seguidamente, cada revisor aplicó los mismos criterios a un conjunto de artículos que se le asignaron, que ahora incluye la introducción, las conclusiones y las citas que haya tenido, obtenido así el conjunto de trabajos candidatos. En la tercera etapa, fueron analizados nuevamente los trabajos candidatos para así obtener los trabajos seleccionados para realizar el mapeo. La cantidad de trabajos candidatos y seleccionados se puede apreciar en la Tabla 1. El conjunto de trabajos seleccionados para el mapeo se pueden encontrar en el **Apéndice 1**.

Fiabilidad de los criterios de inclusión/exclusión

Para evaluar la fiabilidad de los criterios de inclusión/exclusión de los trabajos analizados, y por tanto, incrementar la fiabilidad de los resultados independientes del revisor, se seleccionó una sub-muestra de la población consistente en las 50 primeras referencias arrojadas por la búsqueda inicial en Google Scholar. Esta sub-muestra representa un 43,48% del total de los resultados arrojados por este buscador, y un 40% de los resultados de este buscador finalmente seleccionados para el análisis.

Tras el establecimiento de los criterios de revisión, el título y el resumen de las referencias, fueron utilizados para clasificar los trabajos de manera independiente por dos revisores R1 y R2 (ver Tabla 2). La fiabilidad inter-revisor se calculó mediante el estadístico Kappa de Cohen [20]. El grado de fiabilidad arrojado por el estadístico fue satisfactorio (KA=0.71). Este grado indica la existencia de una base de criterios suficientemente clara y que no denota divergencias significativas entre revisores [21].

Tabla 2 Distribución de artículos por revisor y respuesta.

		R2		TOTAL
		+	-	
R1	+	26	4	30
	-	3	17	20
TOTAL		29	21	**50**

2.4 Definición del esquema de clasificación

Luego de tener seleccionadas las publicaciones relevantes se definieron cinco tipos de clasificaciones atendiendo a los objetivos que tiene este estudio:

Calidad del proceso: se refiere a los atributos de calidad del proceso de desarrollo que se benefician con las propuestas basadas en MDUID. Estos se clasificaron en: productividad, eficacia, eficiencia y costos.

Calidad del producto: se refiere a las características de la calidad del producto que han sido más analizadas en las investigaciones. Considerando lo que especifica la norma ISO/IEC 9126-1, las características de calidad se clasificaron en: funcionalidad, fiabilidad, usabilidad, eficiencia, mantenibilidad y portabilidad [22].

Propuesta metodológica: se refiere a los trabajos centrados en aspectos metodológicos. Pueden ser Total (cuando definen actividades a realizar, roles involucrados y artefactos) o Parcial (cuando definen actividades a realizar, roles o artefactos).

Tecnologías o herramientas más utilizadas: Se refiere a las tecnologías utilizadas en los trabajos analizados. Las mayormente mencionadas son XML, UsiXML, UML, ATL, XIML, QVT, IFML, CTT, Eclipse Modeling Framework, Eclipse Plugins, Webratio, Herramienta IdealXML y CTT Environment.

Modelos\metamodelos: Se refiere a los modelos y/o metamodelos propuestos en los trabajos analizados. Los más usuales son Modelo de tarea, Modelo de dominio, Modelo de usuario, Modelo de IU Abstracta y Modelo de IU Concreta.

Tipo de investigación y método de investigación: Esta clasificación se basa en el esquema descrito por Petersen [16] y basado en el trabajo de Wieringa et al [23]. Pueden ser: *Propuesta de Solución*, *Investigación de evaluación* empleando los métodos de investigación *Estudio de caso industrial* o *Experimento controlado con practicantes* e *Investigación de validación* empleando el método *Estudio de caso académico*.

Entorno de aplicación: esta clasificación hace referencia al entorno donde se desarrolla la investigación, o donde determinan los autores su aplicación. Pueden ser Entornos académicos (proponen realizar nuevas investigaciones y/o desarrollo de nuevas ideas), o Entornos industriales (son aplicadas en alguna organización).

De cada estudio relevante se recopiló información sobre el Año y el Tipo de publicación (si fue publicado en una revista, en una conferencia, en un libro, como tesis de grado, maestría o doctoral). La Fig. 1 presenta el esquema de clasificación completo.

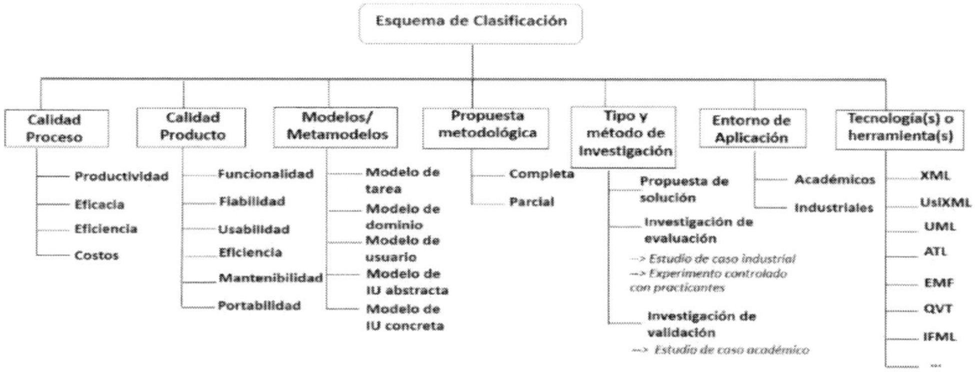

Fig. 1. Esquema de clasificación

2.5 Validación de las amenazas.

Ante las posibles amenazas que pudieran restar validez al mapeo sistemático que se presenta, se realizaron las siguientes acciones de mitigación:

• **Definición de preguntas de investigación**. Para minimizar el riesgo de que las preguntas no abarquen todos los aspectos relevantes que caracterizan la investigación, se realizaron tormentas de ideas para definirlas con la participación de todos los autores del estudio. Además, se refinó el conjunto inicial de preguntas, especialmente en el paso de lectura rápida, con las similitudes detectadas en los trabajos seleccionados.

• **Identificación de estudios primarios**. Dado que las palabras clave de ingeniería de software no están estandarizadas, es posible que las palabras clave seleccionadas y la cadena de búsqueda no puedan capturar todas las publicaciones relevantes. Para evitar la inadecuación de nuestra cadena de búsqueda, agregamos un paso de análisis de referencia a nuestra estrategia de búsqueda para verificar si se habían omitido trabajos relevantes a los que se hace referencia en los documentos seleccionados.

Los documentos que fueron objeto de lectura completa fueron examinados mediante un proceso de seguimiento de las referencias, en busca de trabajos que podrían haberse evadido de nuestro análisis. Más precisamente, la estrategia de búsqueda presentada en la Sección 2.2 fue el resultado de un conjunto de iteraciones.

• **Identificación de fuentes bibliográficas**. La pertinencia de las fuentes bibliográficas también se validó a través del seguimiento de las referencias, mencionado anteriormente. Este análisis mostró que no faltaba ninguna fuente relevante.

• **Selección de estudios primarios**. Para evitar el riesgo de que la selección de documentos esté sesgada por juicios personales, los criterios de inclusión y exclusión guiaron la selección. Los criterios fueron evaluados (Sección 2.3.1), para así incrementar las posibilidades de obtener resultados fiables e independientes del revisor.

• **Identificación de valores para los criterios de clasificación**. Con respecto a los criterios de tipo **Calidad del producto**, se definieron los valores posibles de las características de calidad del producto de software propuestas por norma ISO/IEC 9126-1. El criterio de los tipos de investigación y método de investigación se especificó de acuerdo al esquema descrito por Petersen [16] y en el trabajo de Wieringa et al [23]. Para mayor información puede consultar la Sección 2.4.

• **Extracción de datos**. El proceso de extracción de datos consistió en completar una hoja de cálculo para cada uno de los documentos seleccionados con la información más relevante. Tener una visión general de todos los documentos seleccionados nos ayudó a analizar los resultados después. Cada uno de los criterios a clasificar estaba acompañado de una descripción y la lista de posibles valores en caso de que los valores fueran cerrados. De este modo, todos los revisores utilizaron los mismos criterios y evaluaron el estado de las investigaciones tal y como han sido publicadas. Además como plantea Kitchenham et al. [24] así como Brereton et al. [25] se encontró útil que los datos extraídos fueran revisados. Para reducir el sesgo, un primer revisor evaluó todas las extracciones realizadas por un segundo revisor.

3 Resultados

El último paso del mapeo sistemático consiste en la extracción de datos y el proceso de mapeo de las distintas dimensiones. La Fig. 2 muestra el comportamiento de las publicaciones por año. El número de publicaciones en esta área de conocimiento se han mantenido estables entre 6 y 9 en el periodo 2007-2014 lo que demuestra el interés de la comunidad, incluso en el 2015 se evidencia un aumento de las publicaciones demostrando que todavía este es un tema de interés para la comunidad científica. Sin embargo, sería interesante analizar las causas de la notable disminución de trabajos sobre la temática en 2016 y 2017.

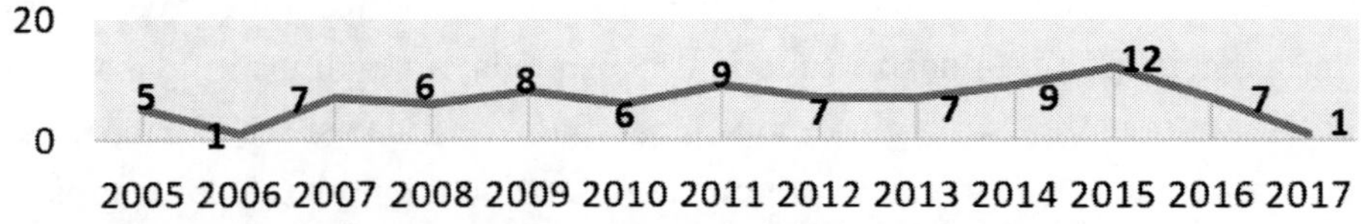

Fig. 2 Cantidad de publicaciones seleccionadas para el mapeo por año

A continuación damos respuesta a las preguntas formuladas en la Sección 2.1.

PI1: *¿Cuáles de los atributos de la calidad del proceso se han beneficiado con estas investigaciones?*

Después del análisis de los resultados, se puede apreciar que los atributos de calidad del proceso que más han sido abordados en investigaciones basadas en MDUID son Productividad (45.88%), Costos (4.71%), Eficiencia (1.18%) y Eficacia (1.18%).

Uno de los trabajos analizados [20] demuestra que su propuesta mejora en un 90% la productividad en el desarrollo de interfaces de usuario utilizando un enfoque basado en MDUID. Sin embargo, comúnmente, los trabajos carecen de evidencias empíricas que demuestren el impacto de las propuestas en las variables relacionadas, tanto con la calidad del producto, como con el proceso de desarrollo. Estos elementos indican la necesidad de realizar estudios que apliquen métodos científicos para demostrar en la práctica las implicaciones de la adopción de propuestas basadas en MDUID.

PI2: *¿Qué características de la calidad del producto han sido más analizadas?*

La *usabilidad* (64.71%), *funcionalidad* (29.41%) y *mantenibilidad* (11.76%) son las características de calidad del producto más investigadas en el MDUID. El resto de las características han sido estudiadas en menor escala. Al igual que en la respuesta a la pregunta anterior se manifiesta la carencia de evidencias empíricas. Por lo tanto se demuestra la necesidad de trabajos que evalúen empíricamente los beneficios de soluciones basadas en MDUID. La Fig. 3 ilustra el resultado de ambas preguntas.

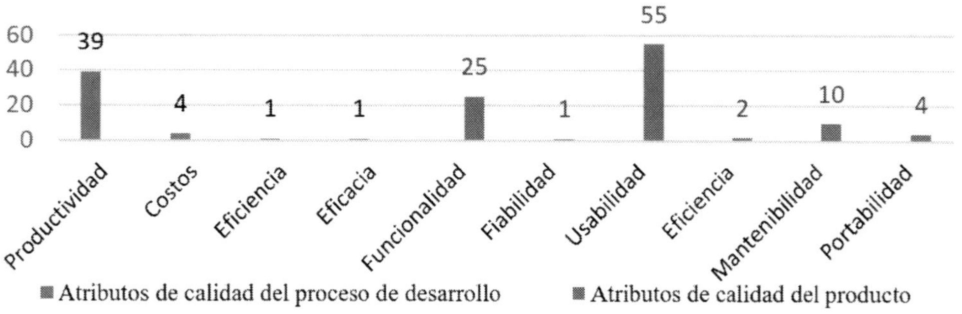

Fig. 3 Trabajos según calidad del proceso de desarrollo y calidad del producto

PI3: *¿Cuáles son las tecnologías y/o herramientas más utilizadas en las propuestas basadas en el MDUID?*

En las investigaciones analizadas se utilizan diversas tecnologías y herramientas. Hay investigaciones [21,22,25,26,27] que proponen tecnologías y herramientas propias. Otros trabajos utilizan las tecnologías y herramientas más difundidas como UsiXML, UML, ATL. Se pudo confirmar que no existe un estándar que indique características especiales para su selección.

Debido a la variedad de tecnologías, sólo se mencionan las más utilizadas: XML (31.76%), UsiXML (25.88%), UML (17.65%), Eclipse Modeling Framework - EMF (16.47%), ATL (10.59%), CTT (9.41%), QVT (8.24%), IFML (8.24%) destacándose

Webratio como herramienta de soporte a este lenguaje, Eclipse Plugins (5.88%), XUL (3.53%), Herramienta IdealXML (3.53%), CTT Environment – CCTE (3.53%).

PI4: *¿Cuáles son los modelos y/o metamodelos más usuales?*

Se pudo constatar que predomina el uso de los Modelos de tarea (30.59%), Modelos de dominio (23.53%), Modelos de usuario (7.06%), Modelos de IU abstracta (37.65%), Modelos de IU concreta (28.24%). Existen investigaciones [28,29,30,31] que proponen modelos y meta-modelos propios. Mientras otras adoptan modelos meta-modelos definidos por investigadores reconocidos en el área [32,33].

PI5: *¿Qué propuestas centradas en aspectos metodológicos existen?*

De los trabajos seleccionados, solo el 55.29% (47 trabajos) constituyen investigaciones que abordan de cierta manera aspectos metodológicos. De ellas el 100% fueron clasificadas como parciales, pues detallan sólo ciertos aspectos metodológicos. No se encontró ningún trabajo que detalle los roles involucrados, las actividades a realizar por cada rol y los artefactos a obtener en cada actividad de una forma clara y precisa.

Los aspectos metodológicos no han recibido la misma atención que otros, por ejemplo los aspectos tecnológicos. Esta idea ratifica la necesidad de hacer propuestas en ese sentido, incluso puede ser un tópico a revisar en un estudio en profundidad.

PI6: *¿Qué tipo de investigación y método de investigación es el más usual en propuestas basadas en MDUID para el desarrollo de software?*

Las *propuestas de solución* (96.46%) resulta ser el tipo de investigación con mayor predominio en los trabajos basados en el MDUID para el desarrollo de software. Por otro lado, se encontró que dos trabajos (2.36%) resultó ser *investigación de evaluación* y un trabajo (1.18%) es una *investigación de validación*. De las investigaciones de evaluación un trabajo empleó el método de investigación Experimento controlado con practicantes y otro el Estudio de caso industrial. La investigación de validación utilizó el Estudio de caso académico.

PI7: *¿Qué entorno es el más utilizado al momento de aplicar la investigación, entornos académicos o entornos industriales?*

El 95% de los trabajos son aplicados en entornos académicos, y sólo un 5% es aplicado en entornos industriales. Estos datos evidencian que, pese a que MDUID posee buena aceptación en el entorno académico, todavía su adopción en la industria del software es insuficiente. Por lo tanto, es necesario revisar qué factores influyen en este elemento. Probablemente la resistencia al cambio sea un factor relevante.

4 Evaluación del proceso de mapeo

Petersen [16] describe 26 acciones que considera relevantes para llevar a cabo en los estudios de mapeos sistemáticos. En nuestro mapeo sistemático se aplicaron 15, para una relación del 57.69%. Este porciento nos permite afirmar que se desarrollaron la mayoría de las acciones propuestas por Petersen lo que se puede considerar un indicador de completitud y correctitud del estudio.

5 Conclusiones y trabajos futuros

En este trabajo se presentan los resultados de un mapeo sistemático de estudios (85 investigaciones) para identificar los elementos más relevantes relacionados con el MDUID durante el período 2004-2017. De los trabajos seleccionados, el 64.70% (55 trabajos) forma parte de memorias de conferencias científicas y eventos, el 29.41% (25 artículos) han sido publicados en revistas, el 4.71% (4 investigaciones) se han publicado como libro y el 1.18% está asociado a una tesis doctoral.

Los trabajos se seleccionaron mediante los criterios de inclusión/exclusión definidos, cuya fiabilidad se evaluó mediante el estadístico Kappa de Cohen. Cada investigación seleccionada fue revisada y clasificada según el esquema de clasificación, permitiendo recopilar la información para responder las preguntas de investigación.

En el análisis realizado se demostró que comúnmente los trabajos carecen de evidencias empíricas que demuestren el impacto de las propuestas en las variables relacionadas, tanto con la calidad del producto, como con el proceso de desarrollo. Estos elementos indican la necesidad de realizar estudios que apliquen métodos científicos para demostrar en la práctica, las implicaciones de la adopción de propuestas basadas en MDUID. Estas deficiencias detectadas constituyen líneas de investigación que pueden ser explotadas por la comunidad científica internacional.

Por otro lado, llama la atención los resultados tan dispares encontrados en función de la aplicación de los estudios en entornos académicos o industriales. El 95% de los trabajos seleccionados se aplican en entornos académicos, y sólo un 5% es aplicado en entornos industriales, demostrando que pese a la buena aceptación del MDUID en el entorno académico, todavía su adopción en la industria del software es insuficiente, siendo necesario revisar qué factores están influyendo en este aspecto.

Por último, resulta de especial relevancia no encontrar una propuesta que detalle los aspectos metodológicos fundamentales asociados al MDUID (roles involucrados, actividades a realizar y artefactos a obtener) de una forma clara y precisa. Solo el 55.29% (47 trabajos) constituye investigaciones que abordan de cierta manera aspectos metodológicos, pero de una forma muy breve, evidenciando la poca atención prestada por los investigadores y la necesidad actual de hacer propuestas en este sentido.

Referencias

[1] Granollers, T. 2004. Características y Fases de MPIu+a. MPIu+a Modelo de Proceso de la Ingeniería de la usabilidad y de la accesibilidad. [En línea] 2004. Disponible en: http://www.grihotools.udl.cat/mpiua/fases-mpiua/ [Consultado el 11/03/2017].

[2] Hassan Montero, Yusef and Ortega Santamaría, Sergio. 2009. Informe APEI sobre usabilidad. Gijón: APEI, 2009. 978-84-692-3782-3.

[3] Rosson, Mary Beth and Myers, Brad A. 1992. Survey on user interface programming. Computer/Human Interaction. 1992.

[4] Meixner, Gerrit, Patern`o, Fabio and Vanderdonckt, Jean. 2011. Past, present, and future of model-based user interface development. 2011. págs. 2-11.

[5] Martin, Christopher and Braune, Annerose. 2017. Integration of a Template System into Mod-el-Based User Interface Development Workflows. Lecture Notes in Computer Science (includ-ing subseries Lecture Notes in Artificial Intelligence and Lecture Notes in Bioinformatics). 480-495.

[6] Pinheiro da Silva, Paulo. 2001. User interface declarative models and development environments: A survey. Heidelberg: Springer Berlin, 2001. págs. 207–226.
[7] Mohammed Gomaa, Akram Salah and Rahman, Syed. 2005. Towards a better model based user interface development environment: A comprehensive survey. s.l.: Proceedings of MICS, 2005.
[8] Meixner, Gerrit, Patern`o, Fabio and Vanderdonckt, Jean. 2011. Past, present, and future of model-based user interface development. 2011. págs. 2-11.
[9] Meixner, Gerrit, Calvary, Gaelle and Vanderdonckt, J. 2010. Introduction to model-based user interfaces. Technical report, MBUI working group. 2010.
[10] Hutchinson, J. E. 2011. An empirical assessment of model driven development in industry. Lancaster: Tesis de doctorado, School of Computing and Communications. Lancaster University, 2011.
[11] Martínez, Y., Cachero, C. and Meliá Beigbeder, S. 2011. Evidencia empírica sobre mejoras en productividad y calidad en enfoques MDD: un mapeo sistemático. Madrid: ATI, 2011. 1885-4486.
[12] Mohagheghi, Parastoo, et al. 2011. Where does model-driven engineering help? Experiences from three industrial cases. s.l.: Springer-Verlag, 2011.
[13] Mohagheghi, Parastoo, et al. 2013. An empirical study of the state of the practice and acceptance of model-driven engineering in four industrial cases. s.l.: Margaret-Anne Storey, 2013.
[14] K. Petersen, R. Feldt, S. Mujtaba, and M. Mattsson, "Systematic Mapping Studies in Software engineering," in EASE '08: Proceedings of the 12th International Conference on Evaluation and Assessment in Software Engineering. University of Bari (Italy), June 26 - 27, pp. 71-80, 2008.
[15] Mujtaba, S., Petersen, K., Feldt, R. and Mattsson, M., "Software product line variability: A systematic mapping study", School of Engineering, Blekinge Inst. of Technology, 2008. Disponible en: sites.google.com/site/drfeldt/mujtaba_apsec08_sysmap_spl_variabili.pdf.
[16] Petersen, K., Vakkalanka, S. and Kuzniarz, L. Guidelines for conducting systematic mapping studies in software engineering: An update. Information and Software Technology, 64, 1–18, 2015.
[17] Kitchenham, B. and Charters, S., Guidelines for performing systematic literature reviews in software engineering. Technical Report EBSE-2007-01, School of Computer Science and Mathematics, Keele University, Inglaterra, 2007.
[18] Noruzi, A., "Google Scholar: The new generation of citation indexes", Libri/Copenhagen Journal, vol. 55, nº 4, pp. 170-180, 2005.
[19] Akiki, Pierre A, Bandara, Arosha K and Yu, Yijun. 2015. Adaptive model-driven user inter-face development systems. ACM Computing Surveys (CSUR), 2014, vol. 47 no 1, p. 9.
[20] K. Gwet, "Inter-rater reliability: dependency on trait prevalence and marginal homogeneity," Statistical Methods for Inter-Rater Reliability Assessment Series, vol. 2, pp. 1-9, 2002.
[21] Fleiss, J.L., Statistical methods for rates and proportions, John Wiley, 1981.
[22] ISO/IEC 9126-1, Software engineering - Product quality Part 1: Quality model, ISO, 2001.
[23] R. Wieringa, N. Maiden, N. Mead, C. Rolland, Requirements engineering paper classification and evaluation criteria: a proposal and a discussion, Requirements Eng. 11 (1) 102–107, 2006.
[24] B. Kitchenham, O. Pearl Brereton, D. Budgen, M. Turner, J. Bailey, S. Linkman, Systematic literature reviews in software engineering–a systematic literature review, Inf. Softw. Technol. 51 (1) (2009) 7–15.
[25] P. Brereton, B.A. Kitchenham, D. Budgen, M. Turner, M. Khalil, Lessons from applying the systematic literature review process within the software engineering domain, J. Syst. Softw. 80 (4) (2007) 571–583.
[26] Schramm, Arne, et al. 2010. Rapid UI Development for Enterprise Applications: Combining Manual and Model-Driven Techniques. Berlin: Springer, 2010.
[27] Hennig, Stefan, et al. User Driven Evolution of User Interface Models - the FLEPR Approach. s.l.: Springer, 2011.
[28] Sousa, Kenia et al. User Interface Development Life Cycle for Business-Driven Enterprise Applications. Louvain-la-Neuve, Belgium: Springer, 2009.
[29] Pires da Silva, Luís and Brito e Abreu, Fernando. Model-Driven GUI Generation and Navigation for Android BIS Apps. Lisboa, Portugal: IEEE, 2014.

[30] Di Santo, Giuseppe and Zimeo, Eugenio. Reversing GUIs to XIML Descriptions for the Adaptation to Heterogeneous Devices. Italia: ACM, 2007.
[31] Witt, Hendrik et al. The WUI-Toolkit: A Model-Driven UI Development Framework for Wearable User Interfaces. Alemania: IEEE, 2007.
[32] Ben, Ammar et al. Dealing with Usability in Model-Driven Development Method. s.l.: Springer, 2014.
[33] Figueroa Martinez, Jose, et al. Enriching UsiXML language to support awareness require-ments. s.l.: ScienceDirect, 2012.

Apéndice 1 Investigaciones seleccionadas para el mapeo

Título	Autores	Año
Towards Method Engineering of Model-Driven User Interface Development	Sousa, Mendonça y Vanderdonckt	2007
Picture-Driven User Interface Development for Applications on Multi-platforms	Nguyen y otros	2014
Using Profiles to Support Model Transformations in the Model-Driven Development of User Interfaces	Aquino y otros	2009
Usability Evaluation of User Interfaces Generated with a Model-Driven Architecture Tool	Abrahão y otros	2008
Dealing with Usability in Model-Driven Development Method	Ammar y otros	2014
A Model-Driven Engineering Approach for the Usability of Plastic User Interfaces	Sottet y otros	2008
Model-Driven Privacy and Security in Multi-modal Social Media Uis	Tesoriero y otros	2012
An empirical evaluation of a usability measurement method in a Model Driven Framework	Ammar y Mahfoudhi	2013
Reflection of a Year Long Model-Driven Business and UI Modeling Development Project	Sukaviriya y otros	2009
Model-Driven Engineering of Workflow User Interfaces	Guerrero y otros	2009
Accelerated Development for Accessible Apps – Model Driven Development of Transportation Apps for Visually Impaired People	Krainz, Feiner y Fruhmann	2016
Model-Driven Development Based on OMG's IFML with WebRatio and Mobile Platform	Acerbis y otros	2015
Research of Model-Driven Interactive Automatic / Semi-automatic Form Building	Ding y Li	2007
HCI Design Patterns as a Building Block in Model-Driven Engineering	Seffah	2015
MDA Applied: A Task-Model Driven Tool Chain for Multimodal Applications	Heinrich otros	2007
User Driven Evolution of User Interface Models – The FLEPR Approach	Hennig y otros	2011
USIXML: A Language Supporting Multi-path Development of User Interfaces	Limbourg y otros	2005
User Interface Development Life Cycle for Business-Driven Enterprise Applications	Sousa, Mendonça y Vanderdonckt	2009
A MDA-Compliant Environment for Developing User Interfaces of Information Systems	Vanderdonckt	2005
Megamodeling and Metamodel-Driven Engineering for Plastic User Interfaces MEGA-UI	Sottet y otros	2009
A case study in automated GUI generation for multiple devices	Raneburger y otros	2013
Applying MDA Approach to Create Graphical User Interfaces	Monte-Mor y otros	2011
Semi-automatic user interface generation considering pointing granularity	Kavaldjian y otros	2009
A model-driven approach for generating RIA interfaces using IFML and ontologies	Laaz y Mbarki	2016
A model driven approach to generate graphical user interfaces for Rich Internet Applications using Interaction Flow Modeling Language	Roubi, Erramdani y Mbarki	2015
Model-driven GUI generation and navigation for Android BIS apps	Pires y Brito	2014
Generating Android graphical user interfaces using an MDA approach	Lachgar y Abdali	2014
A Model-Driven Methodology for Developing Secure Data-Management Applications	Basin, Clavel y Egea	2014
Model-Driven Instrumentation of Graphical User Interfaces	Funk, Hoyer y Link	2009
Focusing Graphical User Interfaces in Model-Driven Software Development	Link y otros	2008
Generative pattern-based design of user interfaces	Vanderdonckt y Montero	2010
An Abstract Interaction Model for a MDA Software Production Method	Valverde, Panach y Pastor	2007
Transformation templates adding flexibility to model-driven engineering of user interface	Aquino y otros	2010
Reversing GUIs to XIML descriptions for the adaptation to heterogeneous devices	Di Santo y Zimeo	2007
Designing user interface adaptation rules with T XML	López y otros	2009
The UI pilot a model-based tool to guide early interface design	Puerta y otros	2005
A model-driven approach for generating interfaces from user interaction diagrams	Zeferino y Vilain	2014
Interactive model driven graphical user interface generation	David Raneburger	2010
Generating User Interface from Conceptual, Presentation and User models with JMermaid in a learning approach	Ruiz, Sedrakyan y Snoeck	2015

A model-driven approach to generating user interfaces	Kavaldjian	2007
Implementing adaptive interfaces a user model for the development of usability in interactive systems	Mejía y otros	2012
Towards virtualization of user interfaces based on UsiXML	Molina y otros	2005
Adaptive Model-Driven User Interface Development Systems	Akiki, Bandara y Yu	2015
Model-driven UI Development integrating HCI Patterns	Yigitbas y otros	2015
Model-driven User Interface Development with the Eclipse Modeling Project	Wolff y Forbrig	2010
Enriching UsiXML language to support awareness requirements	Figueroa y otros	2012
Integrating Human-Centered and Model-Driven Methods in Agile UI Development	Fischer y otros	2015
Customized UI Development Through Context-Sensitive GUI Patterns	Yigitbas y Sauer	2016
Enactment of User Interface Development Methods in Software Life Cycles	Khaddam y otros	2016
CIAT-GUI: A MDE-compliant environment for developing Graphical User Interfaces of information systems	Molina, Giraldo y Gallardo	2012
Deriving User Interfaces from Task Models	Wolff y Forbrig	2012
The WUI-Toolkit: A Model-Driven UI Development Framework for Wearable User Interfaces	Witt, Nicolai y Kenn	2007
Model-based Reengineering of User Interfaces	Wolff y Forbrig	2005
User Interface Derivation from Business Processes: A Model-Driven Approach for Organizational Engineering	Sousa y otros	2008
T:XML: A Tool Supporting User Interface Model Transformation	López y otros	2011
Towards Methodological Guidance for User Interface Development Life Cycle	Cano y Vanderdonckt	2011
A Model-Driven Interactive System	Wu y Hua	2013
Lightweight Low-Level Query-Centric User Interface Modeling	Kis y Bogdan	2013
User-Centered Reverse Engineering	Montero y otros	2013
Model and framework for multimodal and adaptive user interfaces generation in the context of business processes development	Zappia	2014
Rapid UI Development for Enterprise Applications: Combining Manual and Model-Driven Techniques	Schramm,Preußner, Heinrich y Vogel	2010
Engineering Context-Adaptive UIs for Task-Continuous Cross-Channel Applications	Yigitbas y Sauer	2016
Towards a domain-specific language to design adaptive software: the DMLAS Approach	Bocanegra y otros	2016
Automatic Adaptation of User Workflows within Model-Based User Interface Generation during Runtime on the Example of the SmartMote	Breiner, Bizik, Rauch y otros	2011
Efficient Generation of Ambient Intelligent User Interfaces	Breiner y otros	2011
A Concerted Model-driven and Pattern-based Framework for Developing User Interfaces of Interactive Ubiquitous Applications	Engel, Märtin y Forbrig	2015
Adapt-First: a MDE transformation approach for supporting User Interface Adaptation	Khaddam y otros	2015
Metamodel-driven definition of a visual modeling language for specifying interactive groupware applications: An empirical study	Molina, Gallardo, Redondo y otros	2012
Automated WIMP-UI Behavior Generation: Parallelism and Granularity of Communication Units	Raneburger y otros	2011
Consistency in use through Model based User Interface Development	Trapp y Schmettow	2006
Equivalent representations of multimodal user interfaces	Hees y Engelen	2012
A Model-Based Framework for Multi-Adaptive Migratory User Interfaces	Yigitbas, Sauer y Engels	2015
A model-driven and task-oriented method for the development of collaborative systems	Gallardo y otros	2013
Self-adaptive UIs: Integrated Model-Driven Development of UIs and Their Adaptations	Yigitbas y otros	2017
Challenges to the Model-Driven Generation of User Interfaces at Runtime for Ambient Intelligent Systems	Adam, Breiner, Mukasa y Trapp	2008
Task Models for Safe Software Evolution and Adaptation	Bergh, Sahni y Coninx	2010
Model-Driven Development of Security-Aware GUIs for Data-Centric Applications	Basin, y otros	2011
AME: an Adaptive Modelling Environment as a Collaborative Modelling Tool	García y otros	2014
Enhancing the Usability of BPM-Solutions by Combining Process and User-Interface Modelling	Trætteberg y Krogstie	2008
A User Interface Stereotype to build Web Portals	da Costa y Lopes	2014
A Multi-Viewpoint Approach to Support Collaborative User Interface Generation	García y otros	2015
UIPLML: Pattern-based Engineering of User Interfaces of Multi-Platform Systems	Thanh-Diane y otros	2016
Combining MDE and Scrum on the rapid prototyping of web information systems	Basso y Mainardi	2015
Model-driven Development and Evolution of Customized User Interfaces	Pleuss y otros	2013
Towards Task-Based Development of Enterprise Mashups	Tietz y otros	2011

Mutants for Metric Temporal Logic Formulas

Ariel Gonzalez[1], Maximiliano Cristiá[2], and Carlos Luna[3]

[1] Universidad Nacional de Río Cuarto, Río Cuarto, Argentina
agonzalez@dc.exa.unrc.edu.ar
[2] CIFASIS, Universidad Nacional de Rosario, Rosario, Argentina
cristia@cifasis-conicet.gov.ar
[3] Universidad de la República, Montevideo, Uruguay
cluna@fing.edu.uy

Abstract. This paper presents a work that continues previous works by the authors. The work integrates DEVS, a formalism for modeling and simulation of discrete event systems, temporal logic, model-checking and mutation, model-based testing. Properties of a DEVS model are described in temporal logic and checked with a model-checker. Then, we propose some mutants for these temporal logic formulas. The model checker is used again to generate counter examples for the mutant formulas. These counter examples could be used as the basis for the test cases with which the implementation of the DEVS model is tested.

Keywords: Temporal logic, Devs, Model-based testing, Mutation.

1 Introducción

Las pruebas de software constituyen una parte muy importante del proceso de desarrollo de sistemas. Se estima que el 50% del esfuerzo total está dedicado a pruebas y depuración [3, 7, 18]. Muchas veces en la industria las pruebas se realizan de manera *ad hoc*, con escasos fundamentos teóricos de base. La disponibilidad de una especificación formal hace posible convertir las pruebas en un proceso bien definido con una teoría sólida. Una especificación formal proporciona una descripción precisa de los requerimientos de un sistema, que facilita la aplicación e implementación de técnicas de verificación automática. Por ejemplo, el chequeo de modelos (*model checking* - MC) [11], en donde un sistema se comprueba algorítmicamente frente a requisitos codificados en una lógica temporal; o el testing basado en modelos, en donde la especificación formal se usa para obtener casos de prueba con los cuales testear la implementación [32].

Si bien la verificación formal puede garantizar la corrección de la implementación, en general es aplicable a sistemas de tamaño limitado y no es posible, en general, la automatización completa. Sin embargo, MC ofrece muchas posibilidades de automatizar la verificación de propiedades de programas. En este contexto, la Lógica Temporal Lineal (*Linear Temporal Logic* - LTL) [24] es una lógica ampliamente aceptada y muy expresiva, que permite especificar propiedades de sistemas no triviales. Además, es compatible con los chequeadores de modelos más utilizados, como SPIN [17] y Uppaal [4]. LTL permite razonar sobre las transiciones entre estados de un sistema, es decir, sobre las computaciones realizadas. Consecuentemente, los programas se modelan como sistemas de transiciones y sus propiedades como fórmulas LTL y, a través de la técnica de MC, es posible demostrar automáticamente que un programa verifica una propiedad LTL. Además, si el programa no verifica la propiedad, el chequeador de modelos devuelve un *contraejemplo*—es decir, una secuencia de transiciones que llevan el programa a un estado donde la propiedad es falsa.

Por otra parte, varias etapas y actividades del proceso de testing de software pueden automatizarse y no requieren recursos humanos del más alto nivel técnico. Sin embargo, el testing solo puede aumentar la confianza en la corrección del programa; no sirve para *demostrar* su corrección. El testing basado en especificaciones formales (*Model-Based Testing* - MBT) combina las bondades de los métodos formales con la del testing tradicional. Usando MBT se busca determinar (automáticamente) si una implementación dada cumple con su especificación, donde la noción de "cumplimiento" no garantiza la corrección pero es mucho más rigurosa que en los contextos clásicos de testing.

Tanto cuando se trabaja con MC como con MBT es necesario contar con una especificación formal del programa que se quiere verificar. En este trabajo utilizamos el lenguaje de especificación de sistemas de eventos discretos (*Discrete Event System Specification* - DEVS) [9, 33]. DEVS es un formalismo modular y jerárquico para modelar y analizar sistemas de diversos tipos, en particular, sistemas de eventos discretos, sistemas de ecuaciones diferenciales (o sistemas continuos) y sistemas híbridos continuos y discretos. Está basado en la teoría de sistemas y los modelos son de naturaleza jerárquica, es decir, se componen de modelos atómicos y modelos acoplados con el fin de construir diseños con distintos niveles de abstracción. El mecanismo de verificación de propiedades de un sistema modelado en DEVS se basa en simulaciones.

Una de las ventajas de DEVS es que permite especificar sistemas que deben verificar requisitos temporales complejos, aunque DEVS no posee un lenguaje que permita describir la propiedad a verificar. Es decir, mediante DEVS es posible especificar un sistema de transiciones temporizadas pero no es posible describir propiedades temporales que ese sistema debe verificar. En este sentido, nosotros proponemos utilizar la Lógica Temporal Métrica (*Metric Temporal* Logic - MTL) [20]. MTL es una de varias extensiones de LTL que permite expresar restricciones temporales cuantitativas sobre sistemas complejos de tiempo real [23]. Entonces, dado un modelo DEVS (M), una propiedad MTL que éste debe verificar (P) y una implementación de M (I), en este trabajo proponemos combinar el MC con el MBT para verificar tanto M como I respecto de P, mediante testing. Esto permitiría a los desarrolladores DEVS contar con una técnica automatizable para testear sus modelos e implementaciones.

1.1 Propuesta y contribuciones

Proponemos utilizar patrones de especificación de propiedades de requisitos temporales (i.e. P) y mutación de especificaciones para obtener los elementos esenciales con los cuales generar simulaciones para verificar el modelo DEVS (i.e. M) y casos de prueba con los que testear su implementación (i.e. I). Un patrón de especificación de propiedad es una descripción general de un requisito que ocurre comúnmente en las secuencias de estados permitidas en un modelo. Los patrones de especificaciones ayudan a los desarrolladores que no conocen en profundidad la especificación de propiedades temporales puesto que les sugieren propiedades generales y recurrentes de los sistemas [13]. Una primera contribución de este artículo consiste en una serie de patrones de especificaciones de propiedades expresadas en MTL.

Una vez que el desarrollador DEVS ha escrito P utilizando uno de los patrones que proponemos, puede utilizar mutación de especificaciones para generar los elementos esenciales para definir simulaciones y casos de prueba. La técnica de mutación de especificaciones se inspira en el testing por mutación (*mutation testing*) [12]. La mutación de especificaciones es más reciente y se relaciona con MBT. Por ejemplo, Stocks y Carrington la usan para generar casos de prueba a partir de especificaciones Z [27]. Más recientemente, la mutación de especificaciones se ha aplicado a modelos de máquinas de estados finitos [5]. En este sentido, una segunda contribución de este trabajo es la propuesta de operaciones de mutación para especificaciones MTL dadas en términos los patrones definidos.

Este trabajo complementa y extiende resultados de [15, 16], en donde se propone la especificación de sistemas reactivos con restricciones temporales a través de una representación gráfica, mediante una variante de las máquinas de estados de UML [25]. A través de una transformación de modelos se obtiene un modelo DEVS con el objetivo de validar el comportamiento del sistema involucrado mediante simulaciones. También se define la generación de código C++ a partir de un modelo DEVS para la herramienta PowerDevs [6].

1.2 Organización del trabajo

En la Sección 2 se presentan, sucintamente, las nociones básicas involucradas en el trabajo. Posteriormente, en la Sección 3 se incluye el análisis y la formulación de patrones de requisitos basados en características del formalismo DEVS mediante MTL. En la Sección 4 se proponen posibles mutaciones de los patrones MTL relevantes. En la Sección 5 se presenta un caso de estudio con el fin de validar nuestra propuesta. Finalmente, las conclusiones y los trabajos futuros se describen en la Sección 6.

2 Nociones Preliminares

2.1 Testeo por Mutación

Las pruebas basadas en mutación [22] constituyen un enfoque, propuesto por DeMillo, Lipton y Sayward [12], para evaluar la calidad de un conjunto de casos de prueba y detectar errores en una implementación. En mutaciones basadas en código un mutante es una copia de un programa en la que se ha insertado un pequeño cambio. Este cambio se aplica al código fuente del software y comúnmente en una sola sentencia del código. Los mutantes generados al introducir exactamente un cambio en un programa se conocen como mutantes de primer orden [21]. Los mutantes con más de un cambio se conocen como mutantes de orden superior. Debido a un efecto de acoplamiento es probable que los mutantes de orden superior sean detectados por los casos de prueba para mutantes de primer orden. Por lo tanto, en general solo se generan mutantes de primer orden en pruebas de mutaciones. Luego se ejecuta cada caso de prueba y se determinan cuántos de ellos *matan* uno o más mutantes. Matar un mutante significa que el caso de prueba produce un resultado diferente al del programa original.

En testing por mutación basado en modelos, los casos de prueba son generados desde el modelo o especificación del comportamiento de un sistema. Mediante la aplicación de cambios en los operadores del lenguaje de modelado se obtienen modelos erróneos, a fin de generar trazas que distingan el comportamiento esperado del real y de esta forma revelar errores en la implementación. Un mutante de la especificación representa la especificación que el desarrollador pensó que tenía que implementar. Luego, como los casos se generan para distinguir las dos especificaciones; si la implementación corresponde al modelo mutado el caso de prueba retornará un valor que corresponde al modelo mutado y no al original.

El testing por mutación de propiedades temporales de un sistema es una propuesta de los últimos años [8, 29, 31]. En este contexto, los mutantes son generados por cambios en las fórmulas de una lógica temporal (e.g. LTL) que la máquina de estados debe verificar en lugar de cambios en la máquina de estados misma. De esta forma, se testea si la implementación verifica o no la propiedad temporal que el sistema debe cumplir. Luego, a través de técnicas como MC se generan trazas de modelos inválidos.

2.2 Formalismo DEVS

Orientado a los problemas de modelado y simulación de sistemas discretos, en la década del '70 Bernard Zeigler propuso un marco teórico y una metodología para modelado y simulación de sistemas, dando surgimiento al formalismo DEVS [33]. DEVS es un formalismo de modelado con una sólida semántica, fundado en una base teórica de sistemas. Este formalismo, a veces caracterizado como universal, permite describir sistemas dinámicos orientados a eventos discretos. Por su capacidad para modelar sistemas complejos y por su simplicidad, DEVS es actualmente uno de los formalismos más utilizados para el modelado de sistemas guiados por eventos discretos.

Definition 1. *Un modelo atómico DEVS se define como* $\langle X, Y, S, \delta_{ext}, \delta_{int}, \lambda, ta \rangle$*, donde* X *es el conjunto de eventos de entrada;* Y *el conjunto de eventos de salida;* S *el conjunto de estados;* $ta : S \rightarrow \Re^{+}_{0,\infty}$ *la función avance de tiempo (tiempo de permanencia en un estado);* $\delta_{int} : S \rightarrow S$ *es la función de transición interna;* $\delta_{ext} : Q \times X \rightarrow S$ *la función de transición externa, con* $Q = \{(s, e) \,|s \in S, 0 \leq e \leq ta\,(s)\}$ *el conjunto de estados total y* e *el tiempo transcurrido desde la última transición;* $\lambda : S \rightarrow Y$ *la función de salida.*

Un sistema que está en un estado $s \in S$, permanecerá en dicho estado por un tiempo $ta(s)$ excepto que, habiendo transcurrido un tiempo e menor o igual que $ta(s)$, ocurra un evento de entrada con valor $x \in X$. En tal caso, el sistema experimentará una *transición externa* y cambia al estado $s' = \delta_{ext}(s, e, x)$. En cambio, si el tiempo transcurrido e es igual a $ta(s)$ sin que se hayan producido eventos externos, un evento interno ocurrirá dando lugar a una *transición interna*. Esto producirá un evento de salida con valor $y = \lambda(s)$ y un cambio a un nuevo estado $s' = \delta_{int}(s)$. En ambos casos, el sistema permanecerá en el nuevo estado, por el tiempo que ta lo determine o hasta que otra vez ocurra un evento externo. La función de *avance de tiempo*, ta, admite asociar un tiempo entre 0 e ∞ a un estado $s \in S$. En el primer caso, cuando se alcance s (llamado *estado transitorio*) inmediatamente sucederá una transición interna generando un evento de salida y un cambio de estado. Por otra parte, cuando el sistema alcance un estado s cuyo tiempo asociado sea ∞ (llamado *estado pasivo*), no tendrán lugar transiciones internas y permanecerá por siempre en este estado, salvo que un evento externo ocurra.

El formalismo DEVS permite definir modelos compuestos, formados por otros modelos DEVS, atómicos o compuestos. Sin embargo, es posible obtener a partir de un modelo DEVS acoplado un modelo atómico equivalente.

2.3 Metric Temporal Logic (MTL)

La Lógica Temporal Métrica (MTL) es una extensión de LTL que permite expresar propiedades temporales cuantitativas [19]. Por ejemplo, la formula $\Box(a \rightarrow \Diamond_{[0,3]} b)$ expresa que siempre que ocurra a se debe satisfacer b en a lo sumo en 3 unidades de tiempo.

Definition 2. *Dado un conjunto de proposiciones atómicas P, las fórmulas MTL son construidas desde P usando conectores lógicos y versiones de restricción de tiempo del operador $\cup$ (*until*): $\alpha ::= p \mid \neg\alpha \mid \alpha \wedge \alpha \mid \alpha \vee \alpha \mid \alpha \cup_I \alpha$, donde $p \in P$ e $I \subseteq [0, \infty]$ es un intervalo.*

El operador $\phi \cup_I \alpha$ significa: ϕ debe cumplirse desde ahora hasta algún punto dentro de I unidades de tiempo, cuando α comienza a satisfacerse. Podemos definir el operador $\Diamond_I$ (*finally*) como: $\Diamond_I \alpha \equiv true \cup_I \alpha$; y el operador $\Box_I$ (*globally*) de la siguiente forma: $\Box_I \alpha \equiv \neg\Diamond_I \neg\alpha$. Por simplicidad, la ausencia del intervalo asociado a un operador modal representa el intervalo $[0, \infty]$ ($\cup \equiv \cup_{[0,\infty]}$).

3 Patrones de especificaciones de requisitos temporales

Los modelos representan abstracciones de sistemas e ignoran muchos detalles de implementación. Este trabajo se focaliza en sistemas especificados con el formalismo DEVS y propiedades especificadas con MTL. En este contexto, tenemos un modelo DEVS M, su implementación I y una propiedad MTL P que tanto M como I deben verificar. Como DEVS permite especificar sistemas con requisitos temporales complejos, tanto los modelos como las implementaciones suelen contener errores vinculados a la temporización. En este trabajo asumimos que las fórmulas MTL que describen las propiedades temporales que deben verificarse son correctas y corresponden a una formalización apropiada de los requisitos temporales que la implementación debe verificar. En este sentido, nuestra propuesta apunta a detectar errores de temporización en M e I realizando un cierto análisis sobre P, que se detalla en la Sección 4. Para mejorar las posibilidades de que P sea correcta primero proponemos patrones de especificaciones de requisitos temporales para fórmulas MTL. De esta forma, los desarrolladores podrán dar sus fórmulas MTL partiendo de patrones de requisitos temporales que aparecen recurrentemente en esta clase de sistemas.

Los patrones de propiedades de requisitos temporales que proponemos están basados en [13]. Un patrón de especificación de propiedad es una descripción general de un requisito que ocurre comúnmente en las secuencias de estados permitidas en un modelo. Los patrones definidos están inspirados en los formalismos que admiten la especificación literal del tiempo. En particular, los modelos DEVS admiten la especificación del tiempo de permanencia en sus estados. Para mejorar la comprensión de la propuesta consideramos como ejemplo un semáforo simple que alterna entre tres estados, pasando de verde a amarillo, de amarillo a rojo y de este último a verde. En verde y rojo el sistema permanece un tiempo fijo de 20 segundos, mientras que en amarillo está exactamente 3 segundos.

- *Precedencia.* Las propiedades de precedencia ocurren a menudo en especificaciones de sistemas reactivos. Refieren a situaciones en donde un estado activa la ocurrencia de otro. Siguiendo el ejemplo del semáforo, el color amarillo debe seguir inmediatamente después de estar 20 segundos en verde: $\Box(verde \rightarrow (verde \cup_{[20,20]} amarillo))$.
  Patrón: $\Box(P \rightarrow (P \cup_{[x,y]} S))$
- *Seguridad/Ausencia.* Una propiedad P nunca ocurre a partir de un determinado momento. En nuestro ejemplo, nunca el semáforo puede estar en dos colores al mismo tiempo: $\Diamond_{[0,0]}(\Box\neg(x \wedge y))$, donde x e y son dos colores distintos.
  Patrón: $\Diamond_{[x,y]}(\Box(\neg P)) \equiv$
- *Ocurre entre.* Una propiedad P ocurre entre O y R. Por ejemplo, un semáforo siempre estará (durante un cierto tiempo) en amarillo entre el verde y rojo: $\Box(verde \rightarrow (verde \cup_{[20,20]} amarilla \wedge (amarilla \cup_{[3,3]} rojo))))$.
  Patrón: $\Box(O \rightarrow (O \cup_{[x,y]} P \wedge (P \cup_{[u,t]} R))))$
- *Respuesta, antes que.* Una propiedad P ocurre antes de R, o una propiedad R ocurre en respuesta a P. Si consideramos un algoritmo de exclusión mutua, por ejemplo cada vez que existe una solicitud de acceso a una variable compartida luego de un tiempo no mayor a x, el acceso debe otorgarse: $\Box(solicitud\_acceso \rightarrow \Diamond_{[0,x]} acceso\_concedido)$.
  Patrón: $\Box(P \rightarrow \Diamond_{[x,y]} R)$

Si bien estos patrones no cubren todas las propiedades temporales que se pueden especificar en MTL, constituyen una muestra expresiva y representativa de requisitos temporales muy usuales.

4 Mutantes para fórmulas MTL

Esta sección describe el análisis que proponemos efectuar sobre fórmulas MTL (P) con el fin de detectar si un modelo DEVS (M) y su implementación (I) las verifican (o no). Si M o I no verifican P significa que verifican alguna otra propiedad P_e. Si fuese posible generar una simulación para M o un caso de prueba para I tal que distingan P de P_e, sabríamos que se ha modelado o implementado una propiedad equivocada. Entonces, es necesario definir un mecanismo que permita generar las fórmulas P_e que se habrían implementado en lugar de P. El mecanismo que proponemos se basa en mutación de fórmulas MTL. Es decir, proponemos generar mutantes de P mediante cambios, usando operadores de mutación, en los elementos que intervienen en la fórmula. Las mutaciones sobre estos requisitos temporales generan mutantes (propiedades inválidas) que pueden ser utilizados para generar casos de prueba para verificar si la implementación detecta los cambios (mata al mutante).

4.1 Trabajos relacionados

En la actualidad existen aproximaciones sobre mutaciones para algunos formalismos, como las máquinas de estados [30] y las redes de Petri [14], entre otros. En el caso de las máquinas de estados, algunos operadores de mutación consideran, por ejemplo, la eliminación o cambio de destino de una transición, la eliminación de un estado o la negación de las guardas. Generalmente, las mutaciones sobre modelos no son muchas, de tal manera que las comprobaciones de adecuación de las pruebas resultan factibles. En [2, 26] se han estudiado mutaciones basadas en modelos orientadas a la implementación; formulan nuevas mutaciones sobre los modelos que van más allá de lo que se puede lograr con las pequeñas mutaciones sintácticas tradicionales. Es un tipo de mutación basada en la semántica.

Las mutaciones sintácticas se basan en aplicar pequeños cambios de alguna entidad u operador para inyectar un posible error de tipeo. Normalmente son mutaciones de primer orden y es común que se apliquen a código y modelos. Mientras que las mutaciones basadas en la semántica inyectan cambios (uno o varios) de tal manera que el código, modelo o propiedad donde se apliquen generen un posible error de interpretación. Las malas interpretaciones son en gran medida dependientes del contexto. Este contexto debe usarse para determinar qué mutantes semánticos deben producirse. Por lo tanto, estas últimas se aplican normalmente a modelos o propiedades, aunque existen trabajos que las aplican sobre código [10].

También existen trabajos que proponen mutaciones sobre propiedades de modelos. Büchler et al. [8] proponen mutaciones sobre propiedades de seguridad y autenticación en protocolos de comunicación, definidas en *High Level Protocol Specification Language* (HLPSL). En [29], los autores proponen un marco de trabajo para generar casos de prueba basados en mutación de especificaciones LTL. La estrategia consiste en generar un conjunto finito de trazas de longitud acotada, a partir de trazas de longitud posiblemente infinita y desde un conjunto de trazas posiblemente infinito. Para ello, definen criterios y métricas de cobertura de propiedades y en base a mutaciones muy limitadas generan casos de prueba con un MC. Trakhtenbrot [31] define mutantes a partir de patrones de especificación con LTL. En dicho artículo se toman como referencia los patrones propuestos en [13] y se consideran solo mutaciones basadas en la semántica. Este trabajo describe posibles variantes (mutantes) de un patrón a partir de una descripción del requisito en lenguaje natural; no obstante, no se consideran aplicaciones o casos de estudio que permitan validar el enfoque.

En el presente trabajo las mutaciones propuestas son más específicas que las consideradas en los trabajos referidos. Las especificaciones en MTL permiten declarar no solo el orden en el que ciertos estados de un sistema deben aparecer sino también cuándo deben suceder. Por ejemplo, los mutantes generados desde LTL pueden no ser *matados* dado que la implementación puede seguir el orden correcto de los cambios de estados pero los momentos en que se dan estos cambios podrían ser incorrectos. En el ejemplo del semáforo (mencionado en la sección anterior), la secuencia de cambios de color podría estar implementada correctamente pero las duraciones temporales en cada estado podrían diferir de la especificación. Trazas generadas a partir de un mutante MTL con cambios en los valores temporales podrían detectar estos errores de implementación.

4.2 Mutaciones propuestas

A continuación se listan mutaciones que consideran cambios de operadores de la lógica MTL y de valores temporales admitidos.

Cambio de Intervalo MTL admite la especificación del tiempo sobre los operadores modales $\cup_{[x,y]}$, $\Diamond_{[x,y]}$ y $\Box_{[x,y]}$. Posibles mutantes se pueden obtener generando cambios en los valores x e y. En los modelos DEVS es común definir $ta(s) = 0$ para expresar salidas inmediatas y $ta(s) = \infty$ para los estados pasivos. Las implementaciones suelen tener errores en relación a esto. La generación de mutantes a través de cambios en los intervalos en las propiedades ayudaría a detectarlos al generar trazas de ejecución (simulaciones o casos de prueba, según el contexto) que distinguen mutantes de originales. Se consideran los siguientes cambios en los valores del intervalo $[x, y]$ asociado a los operadores modales:

- Inserta el valor 0 al inicio del intervalo $\rightarrow [0, y]$.
- Inserta el valor 0 al inicio y final del intervalo $\rightarrow [0, 0]$.
- Inserta el valor ∞ al final del intervalo $\rightarrow [x, \infty]$.
- Inserta el valor ∞ al inicio y final del intervalo $\rightarrow [\infty, \infty]$.
- Inserta un valor inferior próximo a x al inicio del intervalo.
- Inserta un valor superior próximo a y al final del intervalo.

Cambio de Operadores Se aplican los mutantes clásicos por cambio de operadores lógicos. Por ejemplo, negar una propiedad o intercambiar el operador $\wedge$ por $\vee$ y viceversa. Las mutaciones por cambio de los operadores modales son más limitadas en la práctica, dado que un cambio de operador puede producir una propiedad irrelevante para un testeo. Se permiten hacer cambios sobre los tres operadores modales pero guiados por la semántica de los patrones.

Mutación de patrones Si bien se admite que cualquier operador modal puede ser insertado, eliminado o reemplazado por otro, solo vamos a obtener algunas propiedades mutadas que representen posibles errores de implementación. Se analizan los patrones definidos en la Sección 3 y posibles mutantes relevantes. En las mutaciones se consideran, en algunos casos, posibles combinaciones de cambios de intervalo y operadores (lógicos y modales). En lo que sigue, las variables x e y corresponden a aquellas usadas en los patrones de la Sección 3.

- *Precedencia*: $\Box(P \rightarrow (P \cup_{[x,y]} S))$
  1. Ocurre P pero luego deja de ocurrir y más tarde, entre x e y, ocurre S.
     Mutante: $\Box(P \rightarrow (\neg P \cup_{[x,y]} S))$.
  2. Si $x > 0$, S ocurre al mismo tiempo que P.
     Mutante: $\Box(P \rightarrow (P \cup_{[0,0]} S))$.
  3. Si $y \neq \infty$, S podría no ocurrir.
     Mutante: $\Box(P \rightarrow (P \cup_{[\infty,\infty]} S))$.
- *Seguridad/Ausencia*: $\Diamond_{[x,y]}(\Box(\neg P))$
  1. Si $x \neq 0$, P no ocurre desde el inicio.
     Mutante: $\Diamond_{[0,0]}(\Box(\neg P))$.
  2. P ocurre en x y luego no ocurre más.
     Mutante: $\Diamond_{[s,y]}(\Box(\neg P)$, donde s es próximo a x $(s > x)$.
- *Ocurre entre*: $\Box(O \rightarrow (O \cup_{[x,y]} P \wedge (P \cup_{[u,t]} R))))$
  1. Ocurre O, luego P, pero P puede dejar de ocurrir y posteriormente ocurre R.
     Mutante: $\Box(O \rightarrow (O \cup_{[x,y]} P \wedge (\Diamond_{[u,t]} R))))$.
  2. Si $u > 0$, ocurren P y R al mismo tiempo.
     Mutante: $\Box(O \rightarrow (O \cup_{[x,y]} P \wedge (P \cup_{[0,0]} R))))$.
  3. Si $u > 0$ y $y > 0$, ocurren O, P y R al mismo tiempo.
     Mutante: $\Box(O \rightarrow (O \cup_{[0,0]} P \wedge (P \cup_{[0,0]} R))))$.
- *Respuesta, antes que*: $\Box(P \rightarrow \Diamond_{[x,y]} R)$
  1. No siempre hay una respuesta para cada solicitud.
     Mutante: $\Diamond_{[0,\infty]}(P \rightarrow \Diamond_{[x,y]} R)$.
  2. La respuesta nunca llega en intervalo esperado.
     Mutante: $\Box(P \rightarrow \Box_{[x,y]} \neg R)$.
  3. Si $x > 0$, la respuesta puede llegar antes de lo esperdo.
     Mutante: $\Diamond_{[0,\infty]}(P \rightarrow \Diamond_{[0,u]} R)$, donde u es próximo a x $(u < x)$.

Si un desarrollador contara con una herramienta que (al menos) lo asistiera en generar trazas a partir de estos mutantes, contaría con una metodología sistemática y cuantificable para analizar los principales requerimientos o propiedades que su sistema debería verificar.

4.3 Generación de trazas

Los MC son herramientas adecuadas, no solo para verificar que una propiedad se satisface, sino para generar contraejemplos que puede ser utilizados como casos de prueba para una implementación [8, 29]. En la actualidad no hay herramientas de este tipo que admitan la lógica MTL, sino solo aproximaciones (como [28]). Nuestra propuesta consiste en utilizar un MC a fin de generar casos de prueba considerando la semántica *pointwise* de MTL que es decidible [23]. Con los MC las trazas pueden ser generadas como sigue: Sea P una propiedad MTL válida del sistema y P' una mutación de ésta que no se satisface, es decir: $M \models_{MC} P$ y $M \models_{MC} \neg P'$. Una traza de ejecución que distinga P de P' es generada por $M \models_{MC} P' \wedge \neg P$. De esta forma se obtienen trazas (por contraejemplos) que se corresponden con el mutante y no con la propiedad original.

5 Caso de estudio

Esta sección ejemplifica nuestra propuesta con un sistema de alarmas para vehículos (SAV) basado en [1] y extendido con características actuales de estos sistemas. Se exhiben algunas propiedades relevantes y críticas, y mutantes que representan posibles errores de interpretación de los desarrolladores.

Los SAV consisten en una computadora central que controla los sensores instalados en un auto; por ejemplo, si la alarma está armada, en el momento que se detecta un movimiento se activan las señales visuales y sonoras. Los controles están implementados por software embebido y éstos deben funcionar correctamente. Un fallo en el software podría generar que la alarma no suene cuando debería hacerlo, o producir algún accidente si se corta el combustible cuando la alarma está desactivada. A continuación se describen brevemente las características generales del SAV considerado: *Armado de la alarma*: una vez que el vehículo se encuentra cerrado y la alarma es activada, en 20 segundos ésta debería armarse; *Activación*: si una apertura de puerta sucede cuando la alarma está armada, las luces de parpadear y el sonido (a través de una sirena especial o las bocinas) deben activarse; *Desactivado*: la alarma puede ser desactivada en cualquier momento; *Corte de combustible*: si la alarma fue activada y el motor es puesto en marcha, luego de 60 segundos se debe cortar el sistema de paso de combustible a fin de evitar un robo.

El sistema se modela a través del acoplamiento de dos modelos DEVS atómicos, uno para la alarma y otro para el motor. Utilizamos la notación gráfica definida en [15] para describir cada modelo atómico tal como lo muestra la Figura 1. Cada estado de los modelos atómicos describe un estado del vehículo como sigue. *Alarma*: `A_S1` (abierto y alarma desactivada); `A_S2` (cerrado y alarma desactivada), `A_S3` (alarma activada y abierto), `A_S4` (alarma activada y cerrado), `A_S5` (alarma armada), `A_S6` (alarma disparada con sonido y luces intermitentes), `A_S7` (alarma disparada con luces intermitentes). *Motor*: `M_S1` (motor detenido y alarma desactivada), `M_S2` (motor detenido y alarma activada), `M_S3` (motor en marcha y alarma activada), `M_S4` (motor en marcha y alarma desactivada), `M_S5` (motor en marcha y el paso del combustible desactivado).

Los distintos sensores envían señales de apertura y cierre de una puerta, activado y desactivado de una alarma, y encendido y detención del motor.

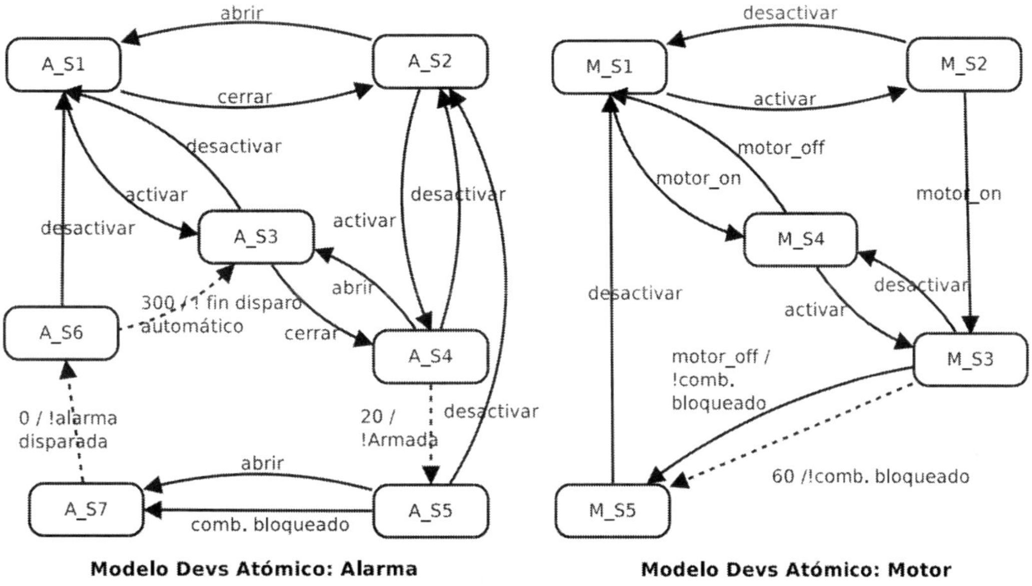

Fig. 1. Modelo DEVS acoplado del sistema de alarma de un vehículo.

A continuación se presentan algunas propiedades que debe cumplir el sistema, basadas en los patrones y posibles mutantes relevantes que no satisfacen el sistema y se desean considerar en la etapa de testeo.

- Propiedad de *Seguridad*: *Nunca ocurre que la alarma está armada, el motor en marcha y no es posibile cortar el combustible en 60 segundos.*
  $\Diamond_{[0,0]} \Box(\neg(A\_S5 \wedge M\_S4)) \equiv \Box(\neg(A\_S5 \wedge M\_S4))$
  Mutante: *El vehículo se encuentra a 60 segundos del corte del combustible y la alarma no está armada.*
  $\Box\neg A\_S5 \vee M\_S4$
- Propiedad de *Respuesta*: *Cada vez que la alarma es activada y el vehículo esté cerrado, si la alarma no se desactiva o se abre una puerta en el lapso de 20 segundos entonces la alarma debe armarse.*
  $\Box(A\_S4 \rightarrow (\Diamond_{[0,y]}(A\_S3 \vee A\_S2) \vee \Diamond_{[20,20]} A\_S4)$, con $y < 20$
  Mutante 1: *La alarma podría no armarse nunca luego de 20 segundos si no se desactiva o se abre una puerta antes.*
  $\Box(A\_S4 \rightarrow (\Diamond_{[0,y]}(A\_S3 \vee A\_S2) \vee \Diamond_{[20,\infty]} A\_S4)$
  Mutante 2: *La alarma podría activarse antes de 20 segundos.*
  $\Box(A\_S4 \rightarrow (\Diamond_{[0,y]}(A\_S3 \vee A\_S2) \vee \Diamond_{[0,20]} A\_S4)$
- Propiedad de *Precedencia*: *Siempre que la alarma esté armada y el motor se encuentre en marcha, o bien se desactiva la alarma o, en a lo sumo 60 segundos, se debe cortar el paso del combustible.*
  $\Box(A\_S5 \wedge M\_S3 \rightarrow A\_S5 \wedge M\_S3 \cup_{[0,60]} (A\_S2 \vee M\_S5))$
  Mutante: *Todo ocurre al mismo tiempo.*
  $\Box(A\_S5 \wedge M\_S3 \rightarrow A\_S5 \wedge M\_S3 \cup_{[0,0]} (A\_S2 \vee M\_S5))$
- Propiedad *Ocurre entre*: *El sonido de la alarma se activará inmediantamente después que se enciendan las luces de intermitencia y en a lo sumo 300 segundos dejará de sonar.*

$\Box(A\_S7 \rightarrow (A\_S7 \cup_{[0,0]} A\_S6 \wedge (A\_S6 \cup_{[0,300]} \neg A\_S6)))$
Mutante: *La alarma se dispara pero el sonido nunca se activa.*
$\Box(A\_S7 \rightarrow (A\_S7 \cup_{[0,0]} \neg A\_S6 \wedge (\neg A\_S6 \cup_{[0,300]} \neg A\_S6)))$

Las propiedades descriptas representan características de comportamientos comunes (patrones) a los SAV's; por otro lado, los mutantes que surgen de estas características representan fallos vinculados a la temporización cuantitativa. En algunos casos el no cumplimiento del tiempo en la implementación podría conducir en la práctica a situaciones críticas no deseables.

6 Conclusiones y Trabajo Futuro

Este trabajo complementa [15, 16], en donde el formalismo DEVS se usa para modelar el comportamiento de sistemas, dado su poder expresivo y aplicación en la industria. En particular, existen herramientas de simulación disponibles que se utilizan en la práctica. Aunque las simulaciones permiten recrear ciertos comportamientos de un sistema, éstas no son adecuadas para generar casos de prueba basados en propiedades. Por tal motivo se presenta aquí un mecanismo basado en mutaciones de propiedades que permite generar pruebas con un MC.

Algunos trabajos recientes consideran aproximaciones para la generación de casos de pruebas por mutación basada en propiedades. Sin embargo, presentamos aquí una estrategia, aún no abordada, que permitiría encontrar errores en las implementaciones que difieren de su versión correcta en variaciones de los requisitos temporales. Las mutaciones definidas para las fórmulas MTL están, de alguna manera, influenciadas por las características del formalismo DEVS. Sin embargo, éstas pueden ser aplicadas también a otros formalismos basados en autómatas finitos. Además, permiten generar mutantes con variaciones en los intervalos temporales que, en combinación con cambios de los operadores lógicos y modales, determinan propiedades que representan comportamientos que podrían suceder en momentos no deseados, o comportamientos que no ocurren en intervalos de tiempo donde deberían ocurrir.

El proceso completo propuesto, que contempla desde los primeros avances en [15, 16] hasta la ejecución de los casos de prueba en las implementaciones, tiene por objetivo otorgar a los programadores herramientas que les permitan mejorar sus sistemas por medio de aproximaciones progresivas, con mayor rigurosidad y formalidad. La propuesta integral es la principal contribución de esta investigación. Como principal trabajo futuro planeamos estudiar la eficacia de la técnica propuesta en términos del número de errores que descubre. El análisis de casos de estudio de porte industrial nos permitirá validar la propuesta en cada etapa, más allá del ejemplo considerado en este artículo.

Referencias

1. Aichernig, B.K., Brandl, H., Jöbstl, E., Krenn, W.: Uml in action: A two-layered interpretation for testing. SIGSOFT Softw. Eng. Notes **36**(1), 1–8 (Jan 2011), http://doi.acm.org/10.1145/1921532.1921559

2. Aichernig, B.K., Brandl, H., Jöbstl, E., Krenn, W., Schlick, R., Tiran, S.: Killing strategies for model-based mutation testing. Softw. Test. Verif. Reliab. **25**(8), 716–748 (Dec 2015), http://dx.doi.org/10.1002/stvr.1522
3. Bass, L., Clements, P., Kazman, R.: Software Architecture in Practice. Addison-Wesley Longman Publishing Co., Inc., Boston, MA, USA, 2 edn. (2003)
4. Behrmann, G., David, A., Larsen, K.G.: A tutorial on uppaal. In: Bernardo, M., Corradini, F. (eds.) SFM. LNCS, vol. 3185, pp. 200–236. Springer (2004), http://dblp.uni-trier.de/db/conf/sfm/sfm2004.html#BehrmannDL04
5. Belli, F., Budnik, C.J., Hollmann, A., Tuglular, T., Wong, W.E.: Model-based mutation testing-approach and case studies. Sci. Comput. Program. **120**(C), 25–48 (May 2016), https://doi.org/10.1016/j.scico.2016.01.003
6. Bergero, F., Kofman, E.: Powerdevs: A tool for hybrid system modeling and real-time simulation. Simulation **87**(1-2), 113–132 (Jan 2011), http://dx.doi.org/10.1177/0037549710368029
7. Brooks, Jr., F.P.: The mythical man-month (anniversary ed.). Addison-Wesley Longman Publishing Co., Inc., Boston, MA, USA (1995)
8. Büchler, M., Oudinet, J., Pretschner, A.: Security mutants for property-based testing. In: Gogolla, M., Wolff, B. (eds.) TAP. LNCS, vol. 6706, pp. 69–77. Springer (2011), http://dblp.uni-trier.de/db/conf/tap/tap2011.html#BuchlerOP11
9. Châne, F., Giambiasi, N., Paillet, J.: From DEVS model to timed automata. In: Arabnia, H.R., Reza, H. (eds.) Proceedings of the International Conference on Software Engineering Research and Practice, SERP '04, June 21-24, 2004, Las Vegas, Nevada, USA, Volume 2. pp. 498–504. CSREA Press (2004)
10. Clark, J.A., Dan, H., Hierons, R.M.: Semantic mutation testing. Science of Computer Programming **78**(4), 345 – 363 (2013), http://www.sciencedirect.com/science/article/pii/S0167642311000992, special section on Mutation Testing and Analysis (Mutation 2010) - Special section on the Programming Languages track at the 25th ACM Symposium on Applied Computing
11. Clarke, E.M., Henzinger, T.A., Veith, H., Bloem, R. (eds.): Handbook of Model Checking. Springer (2018), https://doi.org/10.1007/978-3-319-10575-8
12. DeMillo, R.A., Lipton, R.J., Sayward, F.G.: Hints on test data selection: Help for the practicing programmer. Computer **11**(4), 34–41 (Apr 1978), http://dx.doi.org/10.1109/C-M.1978.218136
13. Dwyer, M.B., Avrunin, G.S., Corbett, J.C.: Patterns in property specifications for finite-state verification. In: Boehm, B.W., Garlan, D., Kramer, J. (eds.) ICSE. pp. 411–420. ACM (1999), http://dblp.uni-trier.de/db/conf/icse/icse99.html#DwyerAC99
14. Fabbri, S.C.P.F., Maldonado, J.C., Masiero, P.C., Delamaro, M.E., Wong, W.E.: Mutation testing applied to validate specifications based on petri nets. In: von Bochmann, G., Dssouli, R., Rafiq, O. (eds.) FORTE. IFIP Conference Proceedings, vol. 43, pp. 329–337. Chapman - Hall (1995), http://dblp.uni-trier.de/db/conf/forte/forte1995.html#FabbriMMDW95
15. Gonzalez, A., Luna, C., Daniele, M., Cuello, R., Perez, M.: Towards an automatic model transformation mechanism from UML state machines to DEVS models. CLEI Electron. J. **18**(2) (2015), http://www2.clei.org/cleiej/paper.php?id=334
16. Gonzalez, A., Luna, C.D., Abella, R.: UML state machine as modeling language for DEVS formalism. In: XLII Latin American Computing Conference, CLEI 2016, Valparaíso, Chile, October 10-14, 2016. pp. 1–12. IEEE (2016), https://doi.org/10.1109/CLEI.2016.7833350

17. Holzmann, G.J.: The model checker spin. IEEE Trans. Softw. Eng. **23**(5), 279–295 (May 1997), https://doi.org/10.1109/32.588521
18. Jones, C., Bonsignour, O.: The Economics of Software Quality. Addison-Wesley (2011), http://books.google.com.ar/books?id=_t5l5Cn0NBEC
19. Koymans, R.: Specifying real-time properties with metric temporal logic. Real-Time Systems **2**(4), 255–299 (Nov 1990)
20. Koymans, R.: Specifying real-time properties with metric temporal logic. Real-Time Systems **2**(4), 255–299 (Nov 1990). https://doi.org/10.1007/BF01995674, https://doi.org/10.1007/BF01995674
21. Offutt, A.J.: Investigations of the software testing coupling effect. ACM Trans. Softw. Eng. Methodol. **1**(1), 5–20 (Jan 1992), http://doi.acm.org/10.1145/125489.125473
22. Omar, E., Ghosh, S., Whitley, D.: Homaj: A tool for higher order mutation testing in aspectj and java. In: Proceedings of the 5th International Workshop on Mutation Analysis (MUTATION'14). Cleveland, USA (31 March 2014)
23. Ouaknine, J., Worrell, J.: On the decidability of metric temporal logic. In: 20th IEEE Symposium on Logic in Computer Science (LICS 2005), 26-29 June 2005, Chicago, IL, USA, Proceedings. pp. 188–197 (2005), https://doi.org/10.1109/LICS.2005.33
24. Pnueli, A.: The temporal logic of programs. In: 18th Annual Symposium on Foundations of Computer Science, Providence, Rhode Island, USA, 31 October - 1 November 1977. pp. 46–57. IEEE Computer Society (1977), https://doi.org/10.1109/SFCS.1977.32
25. Rumbaugh, J., Jacobson, I., Booch, G.: Unified Modeling Language Reference Manual, The (2Nd Edition). Pearson Higher Education (2004)
26. Silva, R.A., do Rocio Senger de Souza, S., de Souza, P.S.L.: A systematic review on search based mutation testing. Information and Software Technology **81**, 19 – 35 (2017), http://www.sciencedirect.com/science/article/pii/S0950584916300167
27. Stocks, P., Carrington, D.: A Framework for Specification-Based Testing. IEEE Transactions on Software Engineering **22**(11), 777–793 (Nov 1996)
28. Sukvanich, P., Thongtak, A., Vatanawood, W.: Translating basic metric temporal logic formulas into promela. In: 7th Information Science and Applications (ICISA). pp. 1035–1043. pringer, Singapore (2016), https://doi.org/10.1007/978-981-10-0557-299
29. Tan, L., Sokolsky, O., Lee, I.: Specification-based testing with linear temporal logic. In: Zhang, D., Grègoire, E., DeGroot, D. (eds.) IRI. pp. 493–498. IEEE Systems, Man, and Cybernetics Society (2004), http://dblp.uni-trier.de/db/conf/iri/iri2004.html#TanSL04
30. Trakhtenbrot, M.: Implementation-oriented mutation testing of statechart models. In: ICST Workshops. pp. 120–125. IEEE Computer Society (2010), http://dblp.uni-trier.de/db/conf/icst/icstw2010.html#Trakhtenbrot10
31. Trakhtenbrot, M.B.: Mutation patterns for temporal requirements of reactive systems. In: ICST Workshops. pp. 116–121. IEEE Computer Society (2017), http://dblp.uni-trier.de/db/conf/icst/icstw2017.html#Trakhtenbrot17
32. Utting, M., Legeard, B.: Practical Model-Based Testing: A Tools Approach. Morgan Kaufmann Publishers Inc., San Francisco, CA, USA (2006)
33. Zeigler, B.P., Vahie, S.: Devs formalism and methodology: Unity of conception/diversity of application. In: Proceedings of the 25th Conference on Winter Simulation. pp. 573–579. WSC '93, ACM, New York, NY, USA (1993), http://doi.acm.org/10.1145/256563.256724

Responsibility Modeling and Tracking against Process Performance Indicators*

Cristina Cabanillas and Jan Mendling

Vienna University of Economics and Business, Austria
{cristina.cabanillas,jan.mendling}@wu.ac.at

Abstract. Human resources are assigned responsibilities over process activities (e.g. performing the work or approving the outcome). The responsibility assignments must be enforced so that suitable resources are engaged in the process at runtime. Moreover, organizations define Process Performance Indicators (PPIs) that help to monitor the progress w.r.t. target values related to the activities (e.g. execution times). Controlling how PPIs depend on resources is crucial for process managers especially when things go wrong (e.g. to alert people or adapt target values). However, this is still usually done manually. This paper presents a two-fold contribution: (i) a graphical representation of responsibilities in process models, and (ii) a procedure to automatically identify how resources are involved in the PPIs of a process. The work is driven by a use case found in industry for which a prototype has been implemented.
Keywords: automated analysis, business process management, key performance indicators, resource assignment, responsibility modeling

1 Introduction

Human resources (for short resources) play a key role in the completion of business processes by executing or supervising the work to be done. Specifically, resources are assigned to process activities with different types of responsibilities, which include, among others, being *responsible* for the execution of the work, being *accountable* for the outcome produced, or being *informed* about the work progress. Specifically, resources are assigned these responsibilities by defining constraints that restrict the set of resources that can hold them. For example, the person responsible for activity A may have a specific skill, the person accountable for the activity may hold a specific position in the organization, and the person being informed may belong to a specific department. Furthermore, the constraints defined for a responsibility associated with an activity may be related to responsibilities associated with other activities. For instance, the person responsible for activity B cannot be the same person that was responsible for activity A (i.e. A and B must be executed by different resources – separation of

* This work was funded by the EU H2020 programme under MSCA-RISE agreement 645751 (RISE_BPM) and by the Austrian Science Fund (FWF) Elise Richter programme under agreement V 569-N31 (PRAIS).

duties [1]) but the person accountable for activity B has to be the same person that was accountable for activity A (i.e. A and B must be approved by the same resource – binding of duties [1]). In addition to responsibility management, organizations are concerned with performance measurement, either because they work under the influence of norms and regulations that impose restrictions, or because they need to optimize their processes due to the big market competition. To do so, Process Performance Indicators (PPIs)– generically called Key Performance Indicators (KPIs)– are defined [2]. Such PPIs may affect several process activities at once. For example, a PPI may measure how long the completion of activities A and B takes because there is a rule stating that the two activities should be executed in maximum 5 days. The fulfillment of the PPI might greatly depend on the performance of the resources involved in the activities.

Therefore, in this context it is crucial to understand who is in charge of what, especially when things go wrong because, for instance, a resource is unexpectedly unavailable or the process is being delayed. Having automated support for understanding which resources holding responsibilities for process activities are related to the PPIs defined for a process would help the managers with that time-consuming and error-prone task. However, our experience in industry reveals a lack of support in this direction. Specifically, checking the correlation of resource assignments and PPIs is usually done manually by the process managers and there is not a systematic way of tracking resource responsibilities w.r.t. the PPIs in place. This is influenced by the fact that responsibilities and resource assignments are rarely specified within process models due to the limited support provided by the process modeling notations.

In this paper, we deal with two research challenges found in such a scenario: (i) the modeling of the large casuistry involved in responsibility assignment along with process models, resulting in *responsibility-aware process models*; and (ii) the automatic identification of dependencies between resources and PPIs by analysing the responsibility-aware process models w.r.t. the PPIs defined upon them. Following the design science research methodology [3], we have designed a conceptual solution driven by a use case from the scientific paper publication domain and we have validated its feasibility by developing a proof-of-concept implementation that can be extended for including further features.

Section 2 explains the motivation to conduct this work and delimits its scope. Section 3 presents our approach. Section 4 describes our proof-of-concept implementation, and Section 5 remarks the conclusions drawn and next steps planned.

2 Motivation

This work is motivated by a real scenario and the lack of existing support to address the issues identified in it, as described next.

2.1 Use Case Scenario

The use case presented here belongs to a well-known paper publishing company. Fig. 1 shows the Business Process Model and Notation (BPMN) [4] model of a

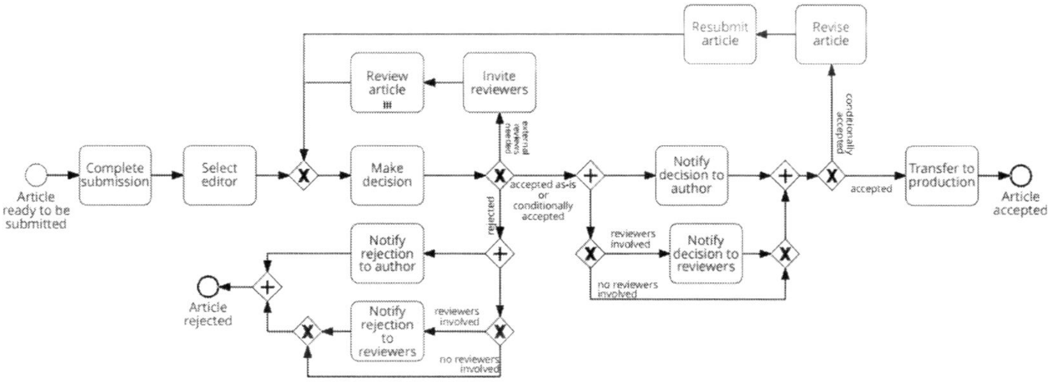

Fig. 1: Journal article review process

slightly simplified version of the article review process for a scientific journal. An author first uploads all the submission files onto the system. That may require help from the support team of the journal. Once everything is correctly uploaded, the author is notified. An editor is then allocated to the paper by the journal manager and takes over the rest of the review steps. The editor has a look at the paper and makes a first decision about it. It may be directly rejected, in which case the author is just informed; it may be accepted as-is and sent to production; it may require revisions as specified by the editor (conditionally accepted); or it may require a thorough review by one or more external reviewers. Most of the times the paper must go under a peer-review. This starts with the invitation of reviewers to review the paper. The reviewers then have limited time to submit their review with their feedback. With that information, the editor again makes a decision, which is notified to the author and the reviewers. In case of conditional acceptance, the author is given some time to revise the paper with the input received from the reviewers and the editor. The new version is then made available in the system and checked again by the editor, who proceeds like before. After one or more review rounds, the paper is eventually rejected or accepted for publication. In case of critical problems during the execution of the process, these escalate to the journal manager and the publisher manager, in this order. Table 1 collects the responsibilities associated with the process in a specific type of Responsibility Assignment Matrix (RAM) called RASCI matrix [5]. The rows of the table are the process activities and the columns are the organizational roles involved in them. The cells indicate the responsibility held by each role for each activity, where *R (responsible)* performs the work, *A (accountable)* approves the work, *S (support)* provides help for work completion when required, *C (consulted)* may help by giving input or feedback, and *I (informed)* should be notified in relation to activity execution.

Several deadlines are defined within the article review process so that a final decision is made in a limited time period. In order to track the process execution and make sure that such deadlines are met, a set of PPIs are defined by the publisher manager, including those in Table 2. These PPIs are measured by aggregating the total execution times of the activities affected by them.

	Author	Editor	Reviewer	Journal manager	Support team	Publisher manager
Business process				R		A
Complete submission	R, I				S, C	A
Select editor		I		R		A
Make decision		R		A		
Notify refection to author	I	R		A		
Notify rejection to reviewers		R	I	A		
Invite reviewers		R	I	A		
Review article		A	R			
Notify decision to author	I	R		A		
Notify decision to reviewers		R	I	A		
Revise article	R	A				
Resubmit article	R, I	A			S, C	
Transfer to production		R		A		

Table 1: RASCI matrix for the article review process

PPI	Description	Target	Activities
$PPI_{SubmissionTime}$	Time from the initiation of the submission to its completion	$\leq$ 3 days	Complete submission
$PPI_{DeskReject}$	Time from the end of submission until the author is notified of rejection without invited reviewers	$\leq$ 2 weeks	- Select editor - Make decision - Notify rejection to author
$PPI_{DeskAccept}$	Time from the end of submission until the author is notified of acceptance without invited reviewers	$\leq$ 2 weeks	- Select editor - Make decision - Notify decision to author
$PPI_{RevisionTime}$	Time on revision and resubmission for conditionally accepted papers	$\leq$ 8 weeks	- Revise article - Resubmit article

Table 2: Subset of the PPIs defined for the journal article review process

Monitoring the PPIs is of utmost importance to the publishing company as their reputation depends on their efficiency and effectiveness performing article reviews. Their aim is to increase the number of articles processed per year per journal, which can be achieved either with a faster throughput or with a larger number of submissions. Two questions arise here regarding PPI tracking: *(Q1) who contributes to a PPI?* and *(Q2) who can redefine a PPI?* The first question implies checking who are the resources that may influence performance (i.e. the resources involved in the activities). Those resources will be alerted to problems with the PPIs they are related to. The second question affects a higher responsibility level and implies checking who are the resources accountable for the PPI. They will be blamed if things go wrong and they usually have authority to redefine the PPIs or their target values within a limited scope.

So far there is no system support that automatically provides these insights. In fact, the actual situation is as follows. The process model the company has is used for activity execution monitoring but it does not contain information about responsibilities and the resources associated with them. The specification (meta data) of responsibilities, change or access-control is maintained in Excel sheets. The PPI monitoring is software-supported but only includes PPI calculation. It thus shows data analytics for the activities and PPIs (e.g. average execution times) but disregards the resource angle, being unable to identify how the PPIs depend on the resources in terms of the two aforementioned questions. An integrated definition of responsibilities and process models as well as automated support for answering Q1 and Q2 against the PPIs defined by the company would help to anticipate to problems and hence, save time and potential costs.

2.2 Related Work

The work related to this paper tackles responsibility modeling and automated PPI analysis in business processes.

Responsibility Modeling in Business Processes. In the last years, a number of languages for defining resource assignment constraints for process activities have been designed (e.g. [1, 6–9]) with the aim of improving the expressiveness provided by existing process modeling notations. The expressiveness of a resource assignment language is typically evaluated against the acknowledged *creation patterns*, a subset of the *workflow resource patterns* [10] that defines constraints on human resources, including: Direct, Role-based, Capability-based, History-based, Organizational and Deferred Distribution; Separation of Duties; Case Handling; and Retain Familiar (a.k.a. binding of duties). Current notations, like BPMN or UML Activity Diagrams, support a limited set of patterns or do not have semantics enabling automated analysis or execution. Similarly, most of the new approaches (i) focus on specific patterns (e.g. those related to access-control constraints [1, 8]); (ii) are ad-hoc to specific modeling notations [1, 7–9]; (iii) do not provide a full graphical representation of the patterns supported [7–9]; or (iv) are not formally defined [4]. The RALph visual notation [11] was designed to overcome such limitations. RALph supports all the creation patterns, some of them with explicit constructs (e.g. direct, role-based and capability-based distribution) and others with constructs that aggregate several types of constraints (e.g. RALph history connectors enable the specification of binding and separation of duties within the same or different process instances[1]). To define a constraint that determines the assignment of resources to an activity, the respective RALph symbol (construct) is associated to the activity with a connector. For instance, to indicate that activity A is assigned to resources with role R, a role symbol labeled with R is connected to activity A in the model. Moreover, RALph is independent of any process modeling language and it has a formal semantics defined as a semantic mapping to Resource Assignment Language (RAL) [6], formally defined in description logics.

Still, none of these approaches considers the various responsibilities associated with an activity, like those defined in the RASCI model [5]. Instead, the constraints defined on the activities are assumed to determine who can execute them (i.e. responsible). The inclusion of responsibilities has been addressed by adding the RASCI responsibilities as new BPMN activities [12] with textual resource assignments, which are hidden as activity properties in the BPMN model.

On the other hand, RAMs in general are not expressive enough to model some creation patterns (e.g. separation or binding of duties) so their decoupled use as-is with existing process modeling notations remains insufficient, too.

[1] Due to space limitations, we refer to [11] for a detailed description of RALph.

Therefore, the graphical modeling of responsibilities along with the organizational perspective of business processes taking into consideration all the aforementioned aspects is still an open challenge, which we address in this paper.

Automated Analysis of PPIs. PPIs are quantifiable metrics that allow the evaluation of the efficiency and effectiveness of business processes [2]. They can be measured directly by data that is generated within the process flow, such as activity duration or data objects. Several approaches have been developed for integrating PPI definitions with business process models by means of graphical notations [13] and templates [2, 14]. PPI modeling has been widely studied and is not an objective in this paper.

More interesting to the problem at hand is the work related to the automated analysis of PPIs and how that relates to the responsibilities of the resources involved in them. The work in [15] enables the design-time analysis of PPIs but the responsibility concepts are out of scope. An extension to include the RASCI model was later developed [16]. However, the analysis performed is purely focused on the calculation of the PPIs (i.e. whether they are fulfilled) and does not consider checking the dependencies with the resources that contribute to them. That characteristic is shared by other approaches dealing with PPI definition and analysis [17, 18]. Hence, the existing approaches could be adapted and integrated with our approach for further completeness but do not address the problem introduced in this paper. To the best of our knowledge, support for automatically identifying dependencies between PPIs and resources in business processes in terms of questions Q1 and Q2 (cf. Section 2.1) is still missing.

3 Our Approach

We have developed a solution for the problems identified under the specifications of the real use case scenario studied. The contribution is two-fold: a graphical definition of responsibilities in process models (cf. Section 3.1), which is achieved by extending RALph to model all kinds of responsibilities, resulting in R-RALph; and a two-step procedure for automatically analyzing PPIs on top of a responsibility-aware process model (cf. Section 3.2), which involves translating an R-RALph-aware BPMN model to an extended (and more expressive) version of a RAM, and the subsequent automated analysis of the output RAL-aware RAM along with the PPIs defined, to answer Q1 and Q2.

3.1 Responsibility-aware RALph (R-RALph)

We rely on RALph for graphically representing responsibilities (e.g. RASCI) because of its expressiveness, its graphical support and its easy integration with BPMN models. Therefore, we adapt the definition of RALph from [11] to our specific context and extend it to make it responsibility-aware. Note that driven by the use case scenario (cf. Section 2.1), some assumptions are considered in the extension: (1) the possible resource assignments include role-based assignments, position-based assignments and history-based assignments within the same process instance; and (2) there can be only one assignment per responsibility per process element (i.e. no alternative or multiple assignments). A third assumption is derived from (1), namely (3) an organizational model is a set of roles and positions (for short organizational entities) and resources with unique names.

Definition 1 (Process model). *A process model is a tuple* $PM = (A, G, E, D, SF, IF)$, *where* A *is a set of activities,* G *is a set of gateways*[2], E *is a set of events (where* e_{start} *is the start event),* D *is a set of data objects,* $SF \subset (A \cup G \cup E) \times (A \cup G \cup E)$ *is a sequence flow relation, and* $IF \subset (A \times D) \cup (D \times A)$ *is a data association relation.*

Definition 2 (R-RALph-aware Process Model). *An R-RALph-aware process model is a tuple* $RRPM = (PM, OE, RM, BD, AE, RAC, HC_{ini}, HC_{end}, lbl_{sr}, lbl_{rm})$, *where:*

- PM *is a process model,*
- $OE \subset S \cup P$ *is a set of organizational entities – roles* (S) *and positions* (P),
- RM *is a set of responsibility magnets, which represent responsibilities,*
- BD *is a set of binding-of-duty entities referring to the same process instance,*
- $AE \subset A \cup e_{start}$ *are assignable process elements,*
- $RAC \subset (AE \times RM) \cup (RM \times OE)$ *are resource assignment connectors,*
- $HC_{ini} \subset RM \times BD$ *are the initial part of history connectors,*
- $HC_{end} \subset BD \times RM$ *are the final part of history connectors,*
- $lbl_{sr} : OE \rightarrow (L_{sr} \cup \epsilon)$ *labels organizational entities either with the empty string* (ϵ) *or with the name of a specific role or position* (L_{sr}),
- $lbl_{rm} : RM \rightarrow L_{rm}$ *labels responsibility magnets with the responsibility names.*

In short, the extension of RALph to R-RALph consists of introducing a responsibility magnet between the process element (activity or start event) and the resource assignment (RALph symbol) that is generic (i.e. it can be used to model any responsibility, defined as a label). In this work, we use the responsibilities of the RASCI model. Note that derived from the use case scenario, there can be resource assignments at the process level (e.g. responsible and accountable). We have decided to link those assignments to the start event of the process. The following functions are defined for R-RALph-aware process models:

- $responsibilities : AE \rightarrow \mathcal{P}(RM)$ returns the responsibilities associated to a process activity or start event.
  $responsibilities(ae) = rm \in RM, \forall RAC(ae, rm)$.
- $assignment : (AE \times RM) \rightarrow RALExpr$ returns the RAL expression[3] associated to a specific responsibility for a process activity or start event.

An example is provided in Fig. 2. For that model, responsibilities("Select editor") = {"R", "A", "I"}; assignment("Select editor", "I") = {"HAS ROLE Editor"}, which indicates that the person informed as a result of the activity

[2] We use the vocabulary of BPMN 2.0 [4].

[3] We remind that RALph is the graphical representation of RAL (textual).

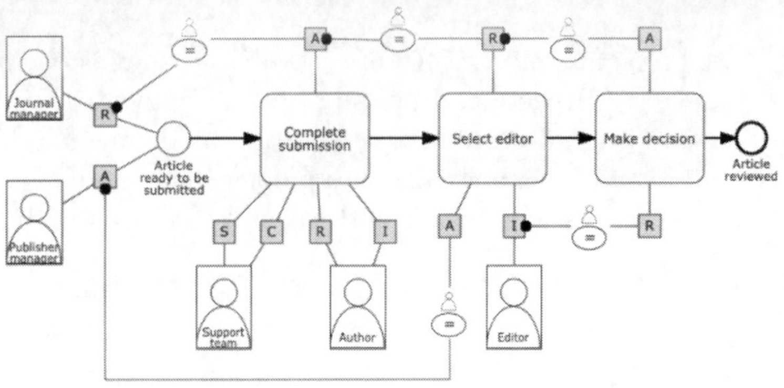

Fig. 2: R-RALph-aware BPMN model

Algorithm 1 (extractRRAM). It extracts a RAL-aware RAM from an R-RALph-aware BPMN model. **IN:** *RRPM*; **OUT:** *RRAM*

```
RRAM ← ∅
for all ae ∈ AE do
    for all resp ∈ responsibilities(ae) do
        ralExpr ← assignment(ae, resp)
        cell_RRAM ← (ae, resp, ralExpr)
        RRAM ← RRAM ∪ cell_RRAM
    end for
end for
return RRAM
```

must have the role *Editor*; and assignment("Make decision", "A") = {"IS PERSON responsible for ACTIVITY Select editor"}, which expresses a binding of duties between the person accountable for the latter and the person responsible for the former (i.e. the same journal manager that selected the editor is accountable for the decision made upon the paper acceptance).

3.2 Analyzing PPIs against Responsibility-aware Process Models

To reply to Q1 and Q2 (cf. Section 2.1), we have developed a two-step procedure. The input knowledge comprises an R-RALph-aware process model and a list of PPIs related to the process. The details of the approach follow next.

Extract the RAL-aware RAM. The first element we need is a RAM matrix able to collect expressive resource assignments for a set of responsibilities.

Definition 3 (RAL-aware RAM). *A RAL-aware RAM is a matrix where cells* $RRAM_{AE,RM} : AE \times RM \rightarrow RALExpr$ *contain RAL resource assignment expressions for the responsibilities (e.g. RASCI) associated to process activities.*

Function $entity : RALExpr \times RRAM \rightarrow OE$ returns the organizational entity of the potential holders of a responsibility from a RAL expression and a RAL-aware RAM. The latter is required for solving the binding of duties constraints.

Algorithm 1 has been designed for extracting a RAL-aware RAM from an R-RALph-aware process model. To do so, we go through all the activities of the process (*line 2*) and for each of them, in turn, we go through every associated responsibility (*line 3*) and find the respective resource assignment (*line 4*). With the activity, the responsibility and the RAL expression corresponding to the resource assignment, a new cell is added to the RAL-aware RAM (*lines 5-6*).

Identify the Access Rights for each PPI. To identify the dependencies between PPIs and resources we need to know the activities affected by each PPI. As external assistance is nonetheless required for this, we assume that the PPI descriptions already contain the associated lists of activities.

Definition 4 (PPI). *A PPI is a function* $PPI : \mathcal{P}(A) \times \mathbb{R}$ *that returns the value resulting from a calculation on a specific metric (e.g. duration) for a set of process activities.*

Two functions are defined for a PPI:

- $PPI\_input : PPI \rightarrow \mathcal{P}(A)$ returns the set of activities affected by a PPI. For instance, PPI_input$(PPI_{SubmissionTime})$ = {"Complete submission"} and PPI_input$(PPI_{DeskReject})$ = {"Select editor", "Make decision", "Notify rejection to author"}.
- $|PPI\_input(ppi)|$ returns the number of activities affected by a PPI. For example, $|PPI\_input(PPI_{DeskReject})| = 3$.

With the RAL-aware RAM and such a description of PPIs, Q1 and Q2 can be answered. Before describing Algorithms 2 and 3, let us explain what the two questions technically mean according to the needs found in our use case. The resources that contribute to a PPI (Q1) are those who hold the same responsibility in all the activities affected by the PPI. This, in our case, includes RASCI responsibilities R, A, S and C. That is, if, for example, a resource is responsible (R) for executing all the activities affected by a PPI, the PPI is dependent on that resource and hence, the resource should be alerted in case something is going wrong during process execution. In terms of access rights, we say that the PPI must be *visible* to the resource as their cooperation might be required. However, only a subset of those resources has the authority to edit the PPI description (Q2). In particular, only a resource accountable for all the activities affected by the PPI is allowed to modify its definition for adapting it to new circumstances. In terms of access rights, we say that the PPI is *editable* by the resource. In case nobody meets the visibility or edition requirements for a PPI given the R-RALph-aware process model, the problem escalates, which means the resource responsible or accountable for the whole process will take over (cf. Table 1). In a real environment, the person responsible for a process is usually called (operational) process manager, while the person accountable for it can be seen as a strategic manager of the organizational unit. The PPI will be visible to both resources and editable by the latter one.

Definition 5 (PPI-RAM). *A PPI-RAM is a matrix where cells* $PPIRAM_{PPI,AR} : PPI \times AR \rightarrow \mathcal{P}(OE)$ *specify which organizational entities have specific access rights for a PPI. For us,* AR = *{"Visible", "Editable"} are the possible access rights that an organizational entity can have on a PPI.*

Algorithm 2 (discoverAccessRights). It infers the visibility and edition rights for a set of PPIs defined for a process from the respective RAL-aware RASCI matrix.
IN: $PPI, RRAM$; **OUT:** $PPIRAM$

```
1: PPIRAM ← ∅
2: for all ppiActivities ∈ PPI_input(PPI) do
3:    for all respType ∈ {"R", "A"} do
4:       PPIRAM ← insertData(e_start, respType, RRAM, PPIRAM)
5:    end for
6:    if |ppiActivities| = 1 then
7:       a ← ppiActivities[0] // first activity
8:       for all respType ∈ {"R", "A", "S", "C"} do
9:          PPIRAM ← insertData(a, respType, RRAM, PPIRAM)
10:      end for
11:   else
12:      for all respType ∈ {"R", "A", "S", "C"} do
13:         count ← 0
14:         resSet ← ∅ // duplicates not allowed
15:         for all a ∈ ppiActivities do
16:            ralExpr ← assignment(a, respType)
17:            if ralExpr ≠ ∅ then
18:               ent ← entity(ralExpr, RRAM)
19:               if ent ≠ ∅ then
20:                  resSet ← resSet ∪ ent
21:               end if
22:               count ← count + 1
23:            end if
24:         end for
25:         if |resSet| = 1 AND count = |ppiActivities| then
26:            cellA_PPIRAM ← (PPI, resSet[0], "Visible") // first resource
27:            PPIRAM ← PPIRAM ∪ cellA_PPIRAM
28:            if restType = "A" then
29:               cellA_PPIRAM ← (PPI, resSet[0], "Editable") // first resource
30:               PPIRAM ← PPIRAM ∪ cellA_PPIRAM
31:            end if
32:         end if
33:      end for
34:   end if
35: end for
36: return PPIRAM
```

Algorithm 2 has been designed to find out the access rights of the resources of an organization over the PPIs defined for a process based on their activities. We go through the set of PPIs (*line 1*) performing the following steps for each of them. First, we include the PPI as visible for the resource responsible for the process, and as visible and editable for the resource accountable for the process (*lines 3-5*). This is done for all the PPIs. Once the visibility and edition permissions have been added at the process level, we check whether the PPI we are processing affects one or more activities (*line 6*). If only one activity is affected, the PPI is visible to the resources with responsibilities R, A, S and C; and editable by the resource with responsibility A (*lines 7-10*). If, on the contrary, the PPI affects several activities, we apply the metric described above. For each R, A, S and C responsibility (*line 12*) we go through the activities of the PPI storing the resource assigned to them (*lines 13-24*). If all of the activities have the same resource holding a responsibility, a new cell is created and added to the PPI-RAM with visibility permissions (*lines 25-27*). Moreover,

Algorithm 3 (insertData). This auxiliary function inserts new data in a PPI-RAM.
IN: $x \in AE, rm \in RM, RRAM, PPIRAM$; **OUT:** $PPIRAM$

1: $ralExpr \leftarrow assignment(x, rm)$
2: **if** $ralExpr \neq \emptyset$ **then**
3:     **if** $ent \leftarrow entity(ralExpr, RRAM) \neq \emptyset$ **then**
4:         $cell_{PPIRAM} \leftarrow (PPI, ent, \text{``}Visible\text{''})$
5:         $PPIRAM \leftarrow PPIRAM \cup cell_{PPIRAM}$
6:         **if** rt = "A" **then**
7:             $cellA_{PPIRAM} \leftarrow (PPI, ent, \text{``}Editable\text{''})$
8:             $PPIRAM \leftarrow PPIRAM \cup cellA_{PPIRAM}$
9:         **end if**
10:     **end if**
11: **end if**
12: **return** $PPIRAM$

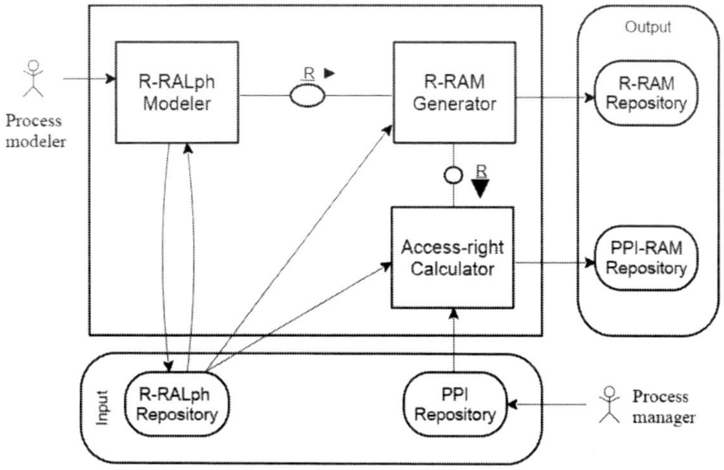

Fig. 3: Responsibility Control System architecture

if the responsibility is A, another cell with edition permissions is created and inserted (*lines 28-31*). The algorithm returns the PPI-RAM generated (*line 36*).

To collect some repeating steps to create and insert cells in the resulting PPI-RAM, Algorithm 3 has been defined. Such an algorithm obtains the RAL expression associated to a specific responsibility for a specific activity (*line 1*) from the RAL-aware RAM previously extracted (cf. Algorithm 1). Then, it searches the resource assigned based on the RAL expression (*line 3*), and it creates and adds a new cell with visibility access for that resource w.r.t. that PPI in the PPI-RAM (*lines 4-5*). If the responsibility relates to accountability, another cell is created and added with edition permission (*lines 6-9*).

4 Implementation

To test the feasibility of our approach, we have developed a proof-of-concept implementation. Fig. 3 illustrates the architecture of the system with a Fundamental Modeling Concepts (FMC)[4] Block Diagram. In the following, we describe the main components and the way in which they have been implemented.

[4] `http://www.fmc-modeling.org/`

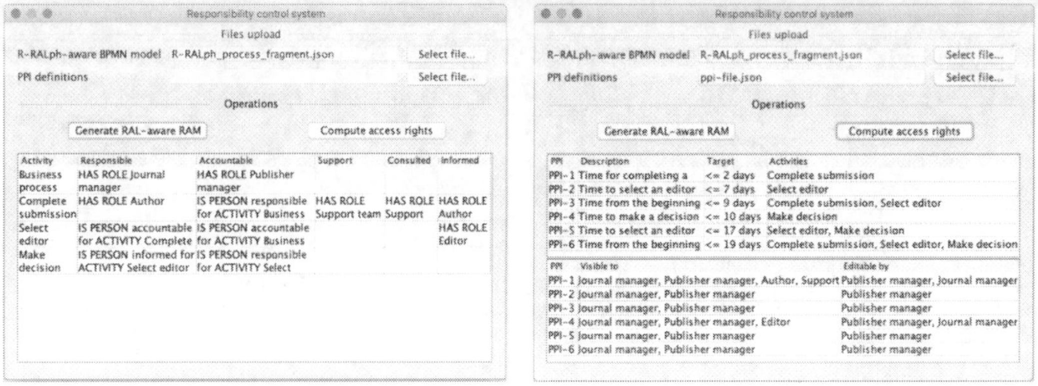

(a) R-RAM Generator (b) Access-right Calculator

Fig. 4: Examples of outputs for the process in Fig. 2

R-RALph Modeler. This component provides support for creating R-RALph-aware BPMN models that are stored in a repository for potential updates. Such models are a necessary input of the other components of the system.

R-RAM Generator. This component implements Algorithm 1, extracting a RAL-aware RAM from an R-RALph-aware BPMN model defined with the R-RALph Modeler. The matrix is stored in a repository for future consultations.

Access-right Calculator. This component implements Algorithms 2 and 3 for which the previously defined R-RALph-aware BPMN model is required as well as a list of the PPIs in place that includes the activities contributing to each PPI. The output matrix is also stored in a specific repository.

We have developed the R-RALph Modeler by extending the Oryx editor[5] with a stencil that allows for the integration of R-RALph assignments in the BPMN models. The result are models like the one in Fig. 2 stored in the JSON format. The implementation of the RAL-aware RAM Generator and the Access-right Calculator as well as the Graphical User Interface (GUI) has been done in Java. For homogeneity, the PPI files are also defined in JSON. Screencasts of the results obtained for the process model fragment of Fig. 2 are shown in Fig. 4. Specifically, Figure 4a shows the respective RAL-aware RAM. As can be seen, the rows are the process activities, the columns are the responsibilities (RASCI) and the cells contain RAL expressions defining the constraints to assign resources to responsibilities. Fig. 4b shows the PPI-RAM generated by the Access-right Calculator. On top of it, it includes an outline of the PPIs related to the process, uploaded as an input. In the running example, which has only three activities[6], we have defined the PPIs on possible groupings of the activites. With the PPI-RAM, when a PPI is running late, we directly know the resources that are behind them in order to alert them (visibility access right); as well as who is authorized to redefine the PPI, if more flexibility is required (edition access right).

[5] `https://bpt.hpi.uni-potsdam.de/Oryx/`

[6] Note that we had to simplify the running example w.r.t. the use case described in Section 2.1 due to the space limitations.

5 Conclusions

This paper introduces a novel approach for jointly handling resource assignments and PPIs in business processes with a two-fold contribution addressing a modeling and an analytical problem. It contributes to the conceptual design principles of a Process- and Resource-Aware Information System (PRAIS) [19]. The approach is driven by a real problem identified in industry and exemplified in a use case scenario of the scientific paper publication domain. Similar problems have been encountered in other domains related, for instance, to ticketing systems. The conceptual approach has been implemented and applied to a running example, which demonstrates its feasibility. Nevertheless, we want to remark two aspects of this work that reveal potential future extensions, which we plan to address as next steps to complement the solution presented in this paper.

First, as aforementioned the solution has been designed for a real problem encountered in an organization considering the specification given for a use case, determined by the organization as a representative description of the problem but whose scope is limited. On the one hand, assumptions 1-3 (cf. Section 3.1) restrict the types of resource assignments that can be defined for the process activities as well as the entities that are part of the organizational model. However, we believe that including other concepts, like organizational units and resource capabilities, is not a big deal and that extension still fits well into our current approach. Considering more advanced resource assignments (e.g. hierarchy-based and data-driven) would need to be explored more thoroughly. On the other hand, the metrics used for calculating the visibility and edition rights w.r.t. the PPIs (cf. Section 3.2) are restrictive. We believe in other domains it could be necessary to implement more flexible metrics that do not force a resource to hold the same responsibility in all the activities evaluated. For instance, a variation could be to consider that a PPI is visible to a resource if they participate (with any R, A, S or C responsibility) in N of the activities that are affected by the PPI, where N can be configured as a threshold value (e.g. ≥50% of the activities). This modification does not change the conceptual problem and solution presented in the paper but could constitute an extension of the algorithms designed.

Second, we have developed a design-time solution for the problem. The RAL-aware RAM generated can be used both at design time and at run time but at run time, the PPI-RAM should point at specific resources instead of at entities like roles or positions. This could be achieved either by having runtime data that we did not have access to or by running simulations. The difference with the design-time output lies in the fact that the RAL expressions included in the RAL-aware RAM would be solved with the actual resource allocation data in order to build the PPI-RAM. That is, however, not a research challenge anymore, as the operation of solving RAL assignments has already been implemented [6].

References

1. M. Strembeck and J. Mendling, "Modeling process-related RBAC models with extended UML activity models," *Inf. Softw. Technol.*, vol. 53, pp. 456–483, 2011.

2. A. del Río-Ortega, M. Resinas, A. Duran, and A. Ruiz-Cortés, "Using templates and linguistic patterns to define process performance indicators," *Enterprise Information Systems*, vol. 10, no. 2, pp. 159–192, 2016.
3. K. Peffers, T. Tuunanen, M. Rothenberger, and S. Chatterjee, "A Design Science Research Methodology for Information Systems Research," *Journal of Management Information Systems*, vol. 24, no. 3, pp. 45–77, 2007.
4. OMG, "BPMN 2.0," recommendation, OMG, 2011.
5. C. Doglione, "Understanding Responsibility Assignment Matrix (RACI Matrix)." `http://project-management.com/understanding-responsibility-assignment-matrix-raci-matrix/`. Last access in August 2018.
6. C. Cabanillas, M. Resinas, A. del Río-Ortega, and A. Ruiz-Cortés, "Specification and Automated Design-Time Analysis of the Business Process Human Resource Perspective," *Information Systems*, vol. 52, pp. 55–82, 2015.
7. L. J. R. Stroppi, O. Chiotti, and P. D. Villarreal, "A BPMN 2.0 Extension to Define the Resource Perspective of Business Process Models," in *Congreso Iberoamericano en Software Engineering (CIbSE)*, 2011.
8. C. Wolter and A. Schaad, "Modeling of Task-Based Authorization Constraints in BPMN," in *BPM'07*, vol. 4714, pp. 64–79, 2007.
9. W. M. P. van der Aalst and A. H. M. ter Hofstede, "YAWL: Yet Another Workflow Language," *Information Systems*, vol. 30, no. 4, pp. 245–275, 2005.
10. N. Russell, W. M. P. van der Aalst, A. H. M. ter Hofstede, and D. Edmond, "Workflow Resource Patterns: Identification, Representation and Tool Support," in *Conf. on Advanced Inf. Syst. Engineering (CAiSE)*, pp. 216–232, 2005.
11. C. Cabanillas, D. Knuplesch, M. Resinas, M. Reichert, J. Mendling, and A. Ruiz-Cortés, "RALph: A Graphical Notation for Resource Assignments in Business Processes," in *Conf. on Advanced Inf. Syst. Eng. (CAiSE)*, vol. 9097, pp. 53–68, 2015.
12. C. Cabanillas, M. Resinas, and A. Ruiz-Cortés, "A template-based approach for responsibility management in executable business processes," *Enterprise Information Systems*, vol. 12, no. 5, pp. 550–586, 2018.
13. B. Korherr and B. List, "Extending the EPC and the BPMN with Business Process Goals and Performance Measures," in *Int. Conf. on Enterprise Information Systems (ICEIS)*, 2007.
14. M. Castellanos, F. Casati, S. Ming-Chien, and D. Umeshwar, "iBOM: a platform for intelligent business operation management," in *IEEE Int. Conf. on Data Engineering (ICDE)*, 2005.
15. A. del Río-Ortega, M. Resinas, C. Cabanillas, and A. Ruiz-Cortés, "On the definition and design-time analysis of process performance indicators," *Information Systems*, vol. 38, no. 4, pp. 470–490, 2013.
16. A. del Río-Ortega, M. Resinas, C. Cabanillas, and A. Ruiz-Cortés, "Defining and Analysing Resource-Aware Process Performance Indicators," in *Conf. on Advanced Inf. Syst. Engineering (CAiSE) Forum*, vol. 998, pp. 57–64, 2013.
17. C. Momm, M. Gebhart, and S. Abeck, "A Model-Driven Approach for Monitoring Business Performance in Web Service Compositions," in *Int. Conf. on Internet and Web Applications and Services (ICIW)*, 2009.
18. C. Pedrinaci, D. Lambert, B. Wetzstein, T. van Lessen, L. Cekov, and M. Dimitrov, "SENTINEL: a semantic business process monitoring tool," in *Int. Workshop on Ontology-Supported Business Intelligence (OBI)*, 2008.
19. C. Cabanillas, "Process- and Resource-Aware Information Systems," in *Int. Conf. on Enterprise Distributed Object Computing (EDOC)*, pp. 1–10, 2016.

eBPSim: A Simulation Tool for Testing Elasticity Strategies in Cloud-based Business Process Solutions

Diego Cocconi[1], Jorge Roa[2], and Pablo Villarreal[3]

[1] Universidad Tecnológica Nacional (UTN) Facultad Regional San Francisco, Av. de la Universidad 501, San Francisco (Córdoba) 2400, Argentina
[2] CIDISI, UTN Facultad Regional Santa Fe, Lavaisse 610, Santa Fe (Santa Fe Province) 3000, Argentina
[3] CIDISI / CONICET, UTN Facultad Regional Santa Fe, Lavaisse 610, Santa Fe (Santa Fe Province) 3000, Argentina
[1] dcocconi@sanfrancisco.utn.edu.ar
[2,3] {jroa, pvillarr}@frsf.utn.edu.ar

Abstract. In the design and deployment of cloud-based applications, elasticity is an important issue. Quantifying and evaluating the performance of elasticity strategies for provisioning resources in a real Cloud computing environment is challenged, tedious, time-consuming, and therefore it is not cost-effective. Such limitations lead to the use of a simulation tool. Although there are several simulators for Cloud environments, they do not allow the evaluation of the efficiency of different elasticity strategies for cloud-based applications for process execution. In this work a simulation tool is proposed to allow the simulation of BPaaS solutions along with the comparison of different elasticity strategies for the business processes to execute. The tool extends the Cloud simulator CloudSim Plus, and allows defining an elasticity controller (via a Strategy design pattern) and a load balancer in the same way, besides the definition of the processes to simulate. The tool could also be used by service providers to: (1) get an estimation of computing resources required during different executions of process scenarios, to know the QoS level that can be offered to the clients; (2) test different resource allocation policies and load balancing techniques.

Keywords: Cloud computing, business process, BPaaS, elasticity, simulator.

1 Introduction

With the consolidation of the Cloud computing technology to deliver ubiquitous and on-demand services through the Internet, organizations can rely on a new way of exploiting software. This technology is realizable by means of different service and deployment models. The three basic service models are: *IaaS* (*Infrastructure-as-a-Service*), *PaaS* (*Platform-as-a-Service*) and *SaaS* (*Software-as-a-Service*) [1]. A particular type of SaaS is the *Business Process as a Service* (BPaaS) model, where business processes can be defined, deployed, executed, and accessed over the Internet [2].

Independently of the Cloud service model, the design and deployment of any cloud-based application have to consider Cloud environment specific issues. *Elasticity (on-demand scaling)*, also known as *redeploying* or *dynamic provisioning* of applications, is one of the most important issues. Elasticity enables real-time acquisition/release of computing resources to scale the applications up and down in order to meet their run-time requirements or demands, while letting application owners pay only for the resources used [3]. Elasticity management also depends of the application features, therefore evaluation of different strategies is required. In the context of BPaaS, elasticity is for improving performance and reducing costs of the Cloud services that execute the processes.

Quantifying the performance of different elasticity strategies for provisioning resources in a real Cloud computing environment (such as Amazon EC2[1], Microsoft Azure[2], Google App Engine[3]) for different applications and service models is extremely challenging because: (1) clouds exhibit varying demands, supply patterns, system sizes, and resources (hardware, software, network); (2) users have heterogeneous, dynamic, and competing QoS requirements; and (3) applications have varying performance, workload, and dynamic scaling requirements [4]. So it is difficult to determine and evaluate an elasticity strategy considering these issues.

The use of real Cloud infrastructures for benchmarking the applications performance (response times, cost benefits) under variable conditions (availability, workload patterns) is often constrained by the rigidity of the infrastructure. Further, it is tedious and time-consuming to re-configure benchmarking parameters across a Cloud computing infrastructure over multiple test runs. Such limitations lead to a more viable alternative: the use of simulation tools [4].

Today exist several simulators for Cloud environments [5]. Most of them are focused on the representation of physical components present in a datacenter, for modeling and simulating IaaS services. New approaches were also proposed to simulate BPaaS environments [6], but they are based on a unique elasticity approach, avoiding the evaluation of the efficiency of different elasticity strategies.

Therefore, in this work a simulation tool is proposed with the aim to allow the simulation of a BPaaS solution along with the comparison of different elasticity strategies, to determine the best one according to the business process scenario to implement and execute. The tool extends the Cloud simulator *CloudSim Plus* [7] to get a toolkit suitable for business processes. The tool could also be used by service providers to: (1) get an estimation of computing resources required during different executions of process scenarios, knowing the QoS level that can be offered to the clients; and (2) test different resource allocation policies and load balancing techniques.

To this end, the tool is structured in a way that allows defining an elasticity controller (via a Strategy design pattern) and a load balancer in the same way. The tool supports representing business processes and their tasks as an input for the simulation. Then this structure is mapped to representations of physical resources and the simula-

---

[1] https://aws.amazon.com/ec2/

[2] https://azure.microsoft.com/

[3] https://cloud.google.com/appengine/

tion takes place. Finally, simulation results are mapped again to a structure suitable for representing execution results of business processes instances (and tasks). Multiple indicators are generated to evaluate the process execution efficiency in terms of performance and costs.

This work is organized as follows. Section 2 presents a background related to BPaaS and elasticity. Section 3 describes the simulation tool for elasticity strategies for BPaaS. Section 4 summarizes experimentation and results. Section 5 discusses related work. Conclusions and future works are given in Section 6.

2 Background

2.1 Business Processes as a Service (BPaaS)

Cloud computing is a new paradigm for creating distributed systems based on the Internet [8]. From a business point of view, Cloud computing could be seen as a model for delivering on-demand services, where shared resources and applications are provided through the Internet.

There are three service models for Cloud computing: SaaS (Software-as-a-Service), PaaS (Platform-as-a-Service), and IaaS (Infrastructure-as-a-Service) [1]. Cloud computing has also different deployment models, such as *private cloud*, *community cloud*, *public cloud*, and *hybrid cloud* [9].

Related to Cloud computing and the *Business Process Management* (BPM) domain, a new service model has emerged: *Business Process as a Service* (BPaaS). BPaaS is defined as the delivery of *Business Process Outsourcing* (BPO) services that are sourced from the Cloud and constructed for multi-tenancy. Like computational services, their execution is regulated by *Service Level Agreements* (SLAs) and supported by specific software, usually *Process-Aware Information Systems* (PAISs). As a Cloud service, processes can be executed and accessed over the Internet by means of BPaaS [10].

2.2 Elasticity in Cloud Computing

In Cloud computing, elasticity (on-demand scaling) defines the degree to which a system is able to adapt to workload changes by provisioning and de-provisioning resources in an autonomic manner, such that at each time the available resources match the current demand as closely as possible [11].

There are mainly two elasticity models: (1) *reactive* and (2) *proactive* (or *predictive*). The reactive approach reacts to the current load and uses thresholds of resource utilization or of SLA violations to trigger the need for additional capacity. In proactive approaches, the system anticipates the change of load, and acts before reactive ones [12]. There are also several scaling strategies, but two are mostly used: (1) *scale-out/scale-in* or *horizontal elasticity* (*replication*); and (2) *scale-up/scale-down* or *vertical elasticity* [12-13]. Scale-out/scale-in allows adding/removing machine instances or processing nodes of the same type based on the quota agreed in the SLAs [14].

Scale-up/scale-down consists of adding/removing resources (e.g. processing, memory, and storage) from a virtual instance, or directly moving from small nodes to more powerful nodes with better processor, memory, or storage (or vice versa) [12].

A very popular approach used by Web servers deployed on Cloud providers such as Amazon EC2 is a scale-out/scale-in reactive elasticity model with threshold-based rules or policies. The simplicity and intuitive nature of these policies make them very appealing to Cloud clients. However, setting the corresponding metrics and thresholds is a per-application task and requires a deep understanding of workload trends. The number of virtual instances will vary according to a set of rules, typically two: one for scaling up/out (Eq. 1) and another for scaling down/in (Eq. 2) [15].

$$\begin{aligned}&\text{if } x_1 > thrU_1 \text{ and/or } x_2 > thrU_2 \text{ and/or } \ldots\\&\quad\text{for } durU \text{ seconds then}\\&\qquad n = n + s \text{ and}\\&\qquad \text{do nothing for } inU \text{ seconds}\end{aligned} \tag{1}$$

$$\begin{aligned}&\text{if } x_1 < thrL_1 \text{ and/or } x_2 < thrL_2 \text{ and/or } \ldots\\&\quad\text{for } durL \text{ seconds then}\\&\qquad n = n - s \text{ and}\\&\qquad \text{do nothing for } inL \text{ seconds}\end{aligned} \tag{2}$$

Each rule has two parts: the condition and the action to be executed when the condition is met. The condition part uses one or more performance metrics (x_1, x_2, ...), such as the input request rate or average response time. Each performance metric has upper (*thrU*) and lower (*thrL*) thresholds. If the condition is met for a given time (*durU* or *durL*), then the corresponding action will be triggered. For horizontal scaling, the application manager should define a fixed amount *s* of instances to be acquired or released (being *n* the current number in use), while for vertical scaling *s* refers to an increase or decrease of resources such as CPU or RAM. After executing an action, the rule inhibits itself for a small cool down period defined by *inU* and *inL*) [15]. Typical metrics for this approach are Web requests per second for horizontal scaling of Web servers [16] and the throughput for vertical scaling in database servers [17].

Testing elasticity approaches using real Cloud environments (such as an IaaS Cloud provider like Amazon) can be hard to perform due to several factors: (1) an specific interface (or even the complete Cloud application) has to be built for interacting with the Cloud IaaS platform; (2) it can be a highly time consuming task testing with real load, because it has to be done in real time, with real virtual instances being created, loaded, executing the scheduled load, and destroyed; (3) the use of the IaaS service will incur in costs (except if the IaaS environment is a private Cloud platform); (4) it is impossible (or very complex) to reproduce the same results of testing under the same conditions.

To overcome all those difficulties, several Cloud simulators have been built [18], trying to emulate real IaaS providers, with representative components such as physical servers, virtual machines (VMs), network connections, and that offer results in terms of energy consumption, response times, costs, etc. They are general enough to allow the simulation of any kind of Cloud solution. However, the simulation of the load and resources in scenarios with specific applications, such as PAISs, requires domain context information and entities to specify and evaluate the model to simulate. Thus, the extension of existing Cloud simulators is an alternative to this problem. The simulator proposed in this work is based on the Cloud simulation framework known as *CloudSim Plus*[4].

3 eBPSim: Simulator for Elasticity Strategies in BPaaS

The simulator described in this work is intended to test the performance of different elasticity strategies in BPaaS scenarios deployed on a Cloud IaaS environment. Thus, it allows simulating business process loads to be executed in the Cloud and evaluating the performance of elasticity methods in terms of execution time and cost.

The simulator extends the CloudSim Plus framework, which is based on another popular IaaS simulation framework called *CloudSim*[5]. CloudSim Plus adds several features to CloudSim that are used in eBPSim: (1) load creation in simulation time; (2) interaction with the simulation clock, allowing calling methods for monitoring or listening on each clock tick; (3) a basic elasticity mechanism for VMs, which can be used as reference for comparing other strategies; and (4) an automatic mechanism for destroying VMs when they are idle, which simplify the design of the elasticity mechanism that scales down.

The eBPSim simulator enables the simulation of a BPaaS environment, i.e. it emulates a Cloud service that offers business process execution in the Cloud. To this end, it supports the creation of VM nodes required for the execution of process instances and the specification of hardware profiles for these nodes. Besides the hardware representation via VMs, physical servers, storage, etc., there is required an adequate structure for representing business process entities necessary to build a BPaaS environment. The tool provides entities for representing process models (which contain task definitions) and also executed cases, consisting of sequences of task instances already executed. These task instances have attached the real workload, simulating the invocation and execution of software applications. This means that all the business process structure must be mapped to a workload set to be directly executable by entities representing the IaaS environment. Once executed, the workload is mapped back again to the structure representing business processes, but in terms of execution measures of cases (e.g. execution times, costs, delays, etc.). This mapping allows linking the execution details with the process models, which enables the comparison of the theoretical expected behavior against the real execution. Several indicators and graphs are shown after simulation, based on these entities.

Even though the tool is intended to test different allocation algorithms for distributing load among the nodes besides testing algorithms for elasticity, only the part related to elasticity is fully described in this work. In the following subsections

4 http://cloudsimplus.org/

5 http://www.cloudbus.org/cloudsim/

CloudSim Plus framework and the architecture, design, and implementation of the eBPSim tool are described in details.

3.1 CloudSim and CloudSim Plus

The eBPSim simulator makes use of the CloudSim Plus architecture, which on turn is based on the CloudSim framework. CloudSim provides support for the modeling and simulation of virtualized cloud-based data center environments including interfaces for VMs, memory, storage, and bandwidth. It also manages issues such as provisioning of hosts to VMs, application execution, and monitoring. By extending the basic entities of CloudSim, a Cloud application developer can generate a mix of workload request distributions and application configurations, model different Cloud scenarios, and perform tests based on the custom configurations [4].

CloudSim Plus project was initiated as an independent fork of CloudSim, pursuing the improvement of the class hierarchy and code, increasing the application of reusability principles; improving the code documentation, re-structuring of project modules and packages in order to simplify usage, and adding the new set of features described before in Section 3 [7].

3.2 eBPSim Architecture

The architecture of eBPSim is shown in Fig. 1. eBPSim makes use of the CloudSim Plus structure as base and it has its own layer distribution. The first layer (*Infrastructure*) is intended to model all physical hardware entities (datacenter, hosts, etc.) and the entities that represent software that will be executed by the hardware, such as VMs and executable tasks, called *cloudlets* in CloudSim Plus. These entities of eBPSim inherit from entities of CloudSim Plus. Thus, by means of this layer eBPSim becomes independent of the Cloud simulation framework used.

The second layer (*Platform*) models the main aspects to provide a BPaaS service, so besides general entities such as nodes, load balancer, elasticity controller, executable load, etc., entities for business processes are provided.

Finally, the third layer (*Simulation*) is the simulator application layer, which defines the user's application to simulate, shows appropriate forms and lists for the user interface to configure hardware properties, costs, process models, cases, elasticity criteria, and supports several output indicators and graphs.

3.3 Design and Implementation of eBPSim

This section describes the entities/classes involved on each layer that are the building blocks of eBPSim. *CloudEnvironment* is the main class, which represents the Cloud (simulation) environment, being responsible for managing and orchestrating the execution of simulation events. This class inherits from the *CloudSim* class of CloudSim Plus.

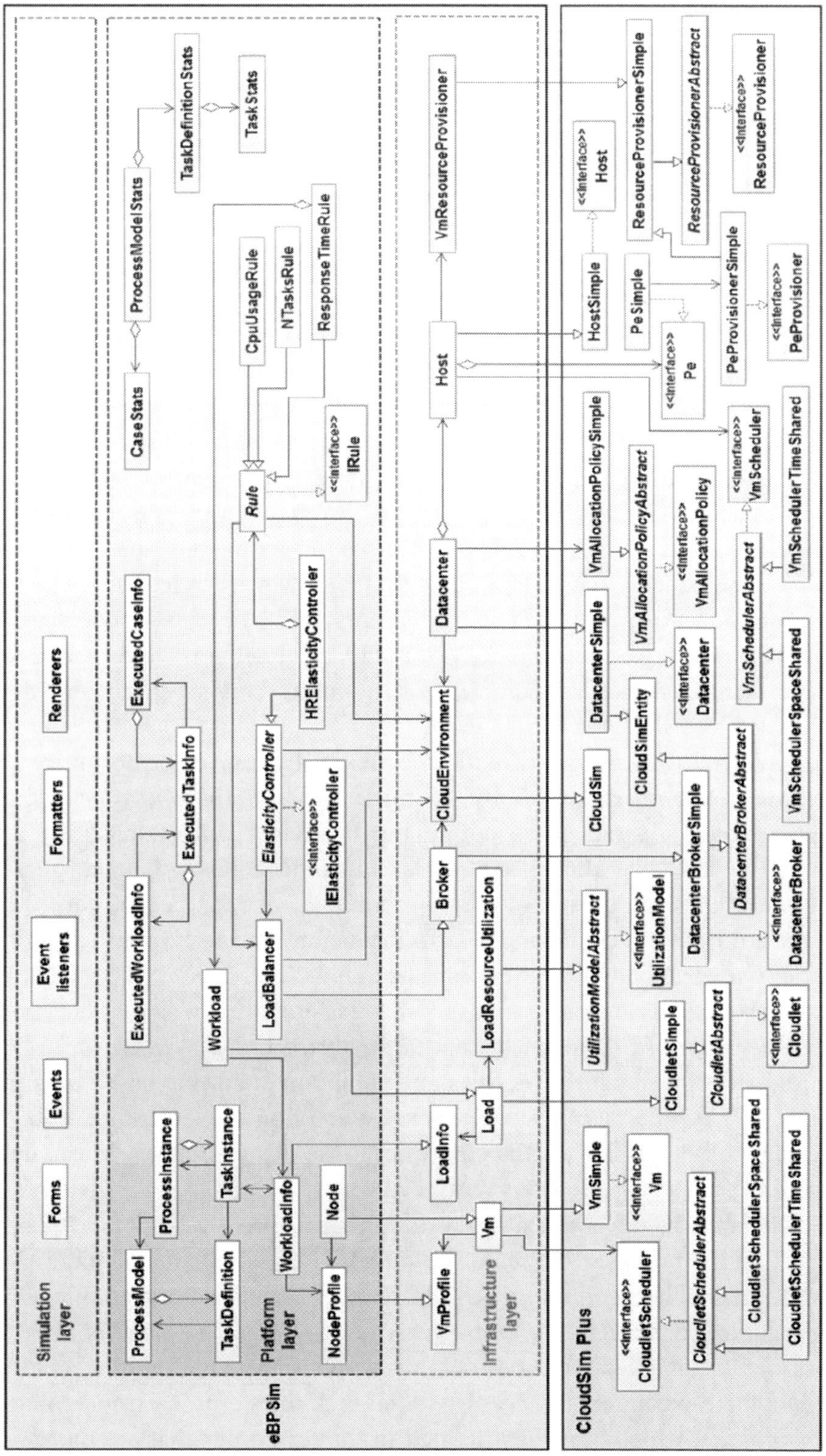

Fig. 1. Architecture and class diagram of eBPSim.

Datacenter class models the infrastructure-level services (hardware) that a Cloud provider offers. It encapsulates a set of hosts with their own hardware configurations (memory, cores, capacity, and storage). This class inherits from the *DatacenterSimple* class of CloudSim Plus, which is an implementation of the *Datacenter* interface.

Host class models a physical resource such as a server. It inherits from the *HostSimple* class of CloudSim Plus, which is an implementation of the *Host* interface.

Broker class models the broker responsible for discovering suitable Cloud service providers for allocation of resources/services that can meet the application's QoS needs. This class inherits from *DatacenterBrokerSimple*, an implementation of the *DatacenterBroker* interface of CloudSim Plus.

Load class models the cloud-based application services in terms of computational requirements. All the computational information is specified by means of the auxiliary class *LoadInfo*. *Load* class inherits from the *CloudletSimple* class of CloudSim Plus, a class that implements the interface *Cloudlet*.

Vm class models a VM, which defines accessible memory, processor, storage size, and the VMs internal provisioning policy for executing load. This class inherits from the *VmSimple* class of CloudSim Plus, which implements the interface *Vm* and uses the *VmProfile* auxiliary class for specifying the resources of the VM.

The Platform layer of eBPSim joins up classes in four groups: load balancing, elasticity, nodes, and process. Under the load balancing category is defined a basic load balancer: *LoadBalancer* class. This class inherits from the *Broker* class and uses its services for distributing a given amount of load to a given number of active VMs that can execute them. As load balancing is not the main focus of this work, the default model provided by CloudSim Plus is used.

Classes referred to elasticity provide the flexibility and extensibility required for implementing a customized elasticity controller. *IElasticityController* interface and *ElasticityController* abstract class define the behavior that an elasticity controller must have. The interface allows to define any kind of elasticity controller and the class is a partial implementation of the common behavior that a customized elasticity controller should have. This design allows extension via the Strategy design pattern. Any elasticity mechanism at a global or individual VM scope is supported. Reactive and horizontal elasticity techniques based on rules are already supported via *HRElasticityController* class, *IRule* interface, and *Rule* abstract class. *HRElasticityController* contains a set of rules. Each rule defines an evaluation condition based on a particular metric (e.g.: CPU usage, response time, etc.), specifying the thresholds to be checked for triggering the rule. This way, the controller is the responsible to determine if a rule was triggered and if a scale out/in is required.

Node class is under the node category and inherits directly from the *Vm* class, representing a specific purpose VM node. *NodeProfile* class is the equivalent to *VmProfile* class. *Node* enables representing a VM with a particular configuration for a specific set of applications, such as a Web Server node or a database server node.

Process classes include all entities that allow the representation of a process model structure and their execution. *ProcessModel* class defines a process and contains a list of *TaskDefinitions*, which have data related to the task types that are part of the process. *ProcessInstance* class allows specifying a concrete case of a *ProcessModel*; *TaskInstance* does the same for *TaskDefinition*. Each *TaskInstance* is linked to a *WorkloadInfo* class instance, which have the information about the computational resources required for the task execution. During the simulation this structure is mapped to a set of *Workload* classes, representing software tasks that can be directly executed by the nodes. After simulation, results are mapped back to another process structure containing the information of the execution. *ExecutedCaseInfo* class represents a case instance of a process model, which has a list of *ExecutedTaskInfo*. *ExecutedTaskInfo* instances represent the execution of a task instance belonging to a case and have an *ExecutedWorkloadInfo* instance, the result of the simulated workload. All of these classes allow to reconstruct the original process structure, but in terms of instances already executed. Another group of classes (*ProcessModelStats*, *CaseStats*, *TaskDefinitionStats*, *TaskStats*) allow to organize statistical information of the process structure already simulated in order to infer aggregate data, such as execution time mean/min/max, total cost, etc., of a process or task. Information of process classes enables the building of tables and graphs in the user interface layer (Simulation layer).

Finally, entities of Simulation layer are forms, event listeners, and lists of entities of Platform layer, allowing interaction with the user, performing the simulation, and showing its results, in several tables and graphs.

4 Experimentation and Results

As an example for illustrating simulation capabilities of eBPSim, the process model illustrated in the diagram of Fig. 2 is considered. This model served as input for *BIMP simulator*, an online business process simulator, to generate the cases and task instances, according to different scenarios. Scenario 1 consists of 30 process instances, with fixed arrival time at 100 seconds and fixed task durations too. Scenario 2 also consists of 30 process instances, but with Normal distribution arrival and tasks durations. Finally, scenario 3 has 60 process instances, with exponential arrival time and task durations. This way, BIMP generates the workload used by eBPSim, which consists of an XML file according to the MXML (*Mining eXtensible Markup Language*) format. This format enables registering events product of the simulation, specifying the time of occurrence.

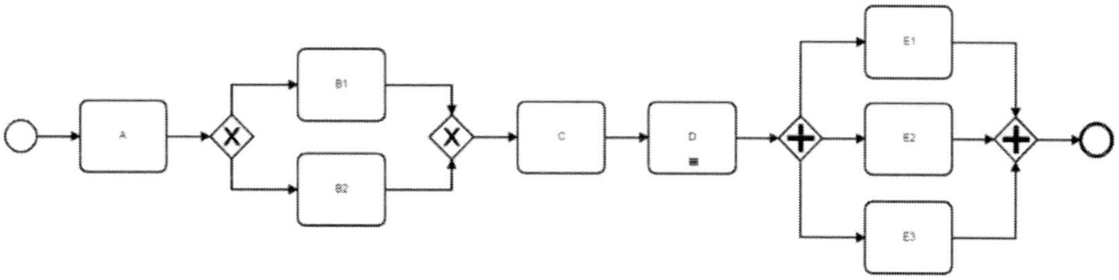

Fig. 2. Process model for testing purposes.

In eBPSim, once the file is loaded, it is created a process model with task definitions (using *ProcessModel* and *TaskDefinition* classes) and cases with their task instances, which consists of the real workload (via the *ProcessInstance*, *TaskInstance* and *WorkloadInfo* classes). Start times for process and task instances are directly read from the XML file, fetching the tag that records the creation event of these instances. Durations of task instances are calculated using the tags that record the creation and completion events of them.

By means of the entities provided by eBPSim for implementing an elasticity controller, a horizontal reactive one was implemented (using the class *HRElasticityController*), which defines three different rules in this case (via the *Rule* class and *IRule* interface) for testing their performance. The first one is a regular case of a CPU usage rule. The other two are combined and take into account as metrics the max number of process tasks that a node is executing at a given time and the response time of the task execution (the allowable percent that a task can exceed its theoretical duration). Then three settings of these different elasticity strategies were configured in eBPSim, as summarized in Table 1. To make results in term of costs more easily understanding, a costing model such as the cost model of Amazon is used, which is based on a cost per active node. Each node that will be created uses a profile similar to the *t3.medium* Linux instance of Amazon (and it has a cost per second similar too).

The first setting (Setting 1) has elasticity disabled. Setting 2 utilizes elasticity with the rule of CPU usage. Parameter "*Min duration for triggering the rule*" specifies the min time that the rule condition has to be met before triggering the rule (i.e. *durU* in Eq. 1). "*Stabilization time*" represents the time that, after triggered the rule, it inhibits itself for the cool down period (i.e. *inU* in Eq. 1). Rules for scale down are not implemented in this case, because it is used the basic mechanism of CloudSim Plus to shutdown VMs when they are idle: if the node is not used during a "*Node destruction delay*" period, the node is powered down automatically. The threshold of the rule has the same meaning as *thrU* in Eq. 1. Setting 3 combines the other two rules, the one based on the max number of process tasks that a node is capable to handle at a given time and the allowable percent that a task can exceed its theoretical duration.

Table 1. eBPSim settings for simulating the process model of Fig. 2.

	Parameters		Values
General configurations	Costing model		Active nodes
	Cost per second of active node [$]		0.0000115
	Node profile	Number of CPUs	2
		CPUs speed [MIPS]	2000
Setting 1: without elasticity	Elasticity options	Elasticity type	Without elasticity
Setting 2: horizontal reactive strategy (CPU usage metric)	Elasticity options	Elasticity type	Horizontal reactive
		Min duration for triggering the rule [s] (*durU* in Eq. 1)	5.0
		Stabilization time [s] (*inU* in Eq. 1)	10.0
		Node destruction delay [s]	10.0
	Rule options	Metric	CPU usage [%]
		Threshold (*thrU* in Eq. 1)	70.0

Setting 3: horizontal reactive strategy (process-specific metrics)	Elasticity options	Elasticity type	Horizontal reactive
		Min duration for triggering the rule [s] (*durU* in Eq. 1)	5.0
		Stabilization time [s] (*inU* in Eq. 1)	10.0
		Node destruction delay [s]	10.0
	Rule 1 options	Metric	Max number of tasks
		Threshold (*thrU* in Eq. 1)	2
	Rule 2 options	Metric	Allowable percent that a task can exceed its theoretical duration [%]
		Threshold (*thrU* in Eq. 1)	10.0

Each one of the three workload scenarios was tested under the tree configuration settings. Results of simulation are shown in Table 2.

Table 2. eBPSim simulation results for different scenarios under settings of Table 1 (one simulation run).

Scenarios		1			2			3		
eBPSim settings		1	2	3	1	2	3	1	2	3
Sim. time window [s]		3480.0			3421.0			7750.0		
Total time of active nodes [s]		3480.6	3255.8	3140.7	3421.6	3140.5	3139.4	7750.1	3258.8	4215.7
Nodes created		1	82	23	1	54	39	1	146	125
Total cost [$]		0.040	0.069	0.066	0.039	0.075	0.062	0.089	0.096	0.111
Mean case duration [s]		227.7			223.2			225.5		
Cases simulation	Mean exec. time [s]	555.3	276.3	244.9	504.3	232.0	248.7	4089.1	396.4	355.2
	Min exec. time [s]	252.6	220.6	220.4	238.4	215.5	215.3	160.9	112.6	106.9
	Max exec. time [s]	742.6	530.1	348.2	689.4	412.4	335.8	7151.5	1129.2	885.2
	Mean exceeded time from estimated duration [s]	327.7	54.1	17.2	281.1	9.4	25.5	3863.6	161.6	119.7
Cases time exceedance from theoretical duration	Exceedance range [%]	Percentage of cases that exceed they duration [%]								
	0% - 10%	3.3	83.3	80.0	3.3	96.7	63.3	0.0	2.0	3.3
	10% - 50%	6.7	0.0	13.3	10.0	0.0	36.7	1.7	49.0	51.7
	50% - 100%	13.3	0.0	6.7	16.7	0.0	0.0	0.0	24.5	38.3
	>100%	76.7	16.7	0.0	70.0	3.3	0.0	98.3	24.5	6.7

As it can be expected, setting 1 has the worst performance in terms of execution time in all scenarios, but the best in terms of cost because only one node is used. A lot of cases have exceeded their estimated duration, with an amount even equal or above 100% (76.7%, 70.0%, and 98.3% for settings 1, 2, and 3, respectively, according to the last four rows of Table 2). Settings 2 and 3 illustrate that the behavior can be different, according to the metric chosen and the nature of the process. In general, setting 3 seems to be more cautious on creating node instances than setting 2, which is an advantage because in real Cloud environments there is an initialization time for each node that is created, degrading the real response of the rule. In terms of costs, setting 3 is better for the scenarios with fixed and normal distributions (scenarios 2 and 3, respectively), but becomes more expensive for the scenario with exponential distributions. Execution times show better performance for setting 3 using fixed and exponential distributions (scenarios 1 and 3, respectively), but not for the process with normal distributions (scenario 2).

These examples show that for reaching a conclusion about which strategy is better, several target processes have to be tested, considering the distributions that emulate their instances behavior better and using a representative number of instances. Then several runs of the simulation should be carried out to get average values.

5 Related Work

Nowadays there are several proposals of Cloud simulators. Most of them are focused on the modeling and simulation of IaaS services. In [5] an evaluation of the most popular simulators for Cloud IaaS environments is provided, and it was concluded that CloudSim [4] is the most suitable. CloudSim leaves to the user the implementation of his own resource provisioning, allocation, and software that will make use of the subjacent architecture. The user has to create code according to the application area, because CloudSim is a general purpose Cloud simulator. Besides, if the user would like to test different elasticity strategies, he will have to build its own elasticity controller. CloudSim Plus [7], a project from a group different from the original authors, was intended for redesigning CloudSim conserving all of its features and adding others, such us the listeners used in this work for monitoring elasticity.

Several simulators have taken CloudSim as a base to simulate SaaS services, for example [18]. However, they are not specifically designed taking into account business process execution requirements, their timing constraints (start times and execution times of process and task instances), and the allocation of resources for the tasks.

A recent approach in the area of BPaaS was proposed in [6]; nonetheless, this simulator, as well as the above mentioned ones, do not offer the possibility of testing and evaluating different elasticity strategies for a particular cloud-based business process scenario. In contrast, this work is focused on simulating process instances over a Cloud environment and verifying the performance of different elasticity strategies, considering time and cost.

6 Conclusions and Future Works

In this work a simulation tool (eBPSim) was proposed to allow the simulation of BPaaS solutions along with the comparison of different elasticity strategies (and also load balancing techniques, but left out of the scope of this paper) for a particular business process scenario to implement and execute in the Cloud. The tool extends the Cloud simulator CloudSim Plus by enabling the users to define and implement a specific elasticity controller (via a Strategy design pattern) and a load balancer in the same way, besides the definition of the processes to simulate.

eBPSim provides an already implemented elasticity controller for horizontal reactive elasticity strategies, which are the most used in real Cloud environments due to their simplicity and easy understanding. The users can define any rule based on the desired metrics, and they also can combine these rules. Therefore, they can evaluate the performance of the rules according to the execution time of process and task instances, and the cost in terms of computing resources used.

Based on the eBPSim tool, a clear and agile methodology could be followed to simulate BPaaS scenarios. The workload required to execute the business processes from a given scenario (cases and task start times and durations) can be derived from a previous simulation in a process simulation tool such as BIMP. The process traces that results are imported into eBPSim and then mapped into executable load, which then is simulated on a Cloud environment by the tool, under different elasticity and load balancing conditions. After finished the simulation, information of execution results (execution times, costs, etc.) are shown via several graphs and tables.

As an example of the utility of this simulator, experimentation with several scenarios from a process model was carried out. It allowed showing that the performance and cost of an elasticity strategy is not the same for all the scenarios, which requires to evaluate each strategy for each particular scenario to determine the best option.

Besides its testing purposes, another potential use of the simulator is the use for estimation of clients QoS requirements of the BPaaS service offered by the provider.

Future work is focused on enhancing the simulator to support non automated tasks usually involved in a process model, such as user tasks, which have different behavior than service tasks (they use only a portion of computational resources along their duration). Other future step is oriented to use the tool for validating Cloud designs for offering BPaaS on collaborative business process contexts (i.e., considering a given workload of collaborative processes, and been able to perform a previous simulation to know the resources required, the most appropriate elasticity criteria, etc.).

References

1. Grefen, P. (2013). "Networked business process management". *International Journal of IT/Business Alignment and Governance (IJITBAG)*, 4(2), 54-82.
2. del–Río–Ortega, A., Gutiérrez, A. M., Durán, A., Resinas, M., & Ruiz–Cortés, A. (2015, June). "Modelling service level agreements for business process outsourcing services". In *International Conference on Advanced Information Systems Engineering* (pp. 485-500). Springer, Cham.

3. Han, R., Ghanem, M. M., Guo, L., Guo, Y., & Osmond, M. (2014). "Enabling cost-aware and adaptive elasticity of multi-tier cloud applications". *Future Generation Computer Systems*, 32, 82-98.
4. Buyya, R., Ranjan, R., & Calheiros, R. N. (2009, June). "Modeling and simulation of scalable Cloud computing environments and the CloudSim toolkit: Challenges and opportunities". In *High Performance Computing & Simulation, 2009. HPCS'09. International Conference on* (pp. 1-11). IEEE.
5. Ahmed, A., & Sabyasachi, A. S. (2014, February). "Cloud computing simulators: A detailed survey and future direction". In *Advance Computing Conference (IACC), 2014 IEEE International* (pp. 866-872). IEEE.
6. Ahmed-Nacer, M., Suri, K., Sellami, M., & Gaaloul, W. (2017, June). "Simulation of configurable resource allocation for cloud-based business processes". In *Services Computing (SCC), 2017 IEEE International Conference on* (pp. 305-313). IEEE.
7. Silva Filho, M. C., Oliveira, R. L., Monteiro, C. C., Inácio, P. R., & Freire, M. M. (2017, May). "CloudSim plus: a cloud computing simulation framework pursuing software engineering principles for improved modularity, extensibility and correctness". In *Integrated Network and Service Management (IM), 2017 IFIP/IEEE Symposium on* (pp. 400-406). IEEE.
8. Pallis, G. (2010). "Cloud computing: the new frontier of internet computing". *IEEE internet computing*, 14(5), 70-73.
9. Cocconi, D., Roa, J., & Villarreal, P. D. (2017). "Cloud-based platform for collaborative business process management". In *Simposio Latinoamericano de Procesos de Negocio, Arquitecturas y Sistemas Organizacionales (SLPNASO)-JAIIO 46* (Córdoba, 2017).
10. Yu, D., Zhu, Q., Guo, D., Huang, B., & Su, J. (2015, June). "jBPM4S: A multi-tenant extension of jBPM to support BPaaS". In *Asia-Pacific Conference on Business Process Management* (pp. 43-56). Springer International Publishing.
11. Herbst, N. R., Kounev, S., & Reussner, R. H. (2013, June). "Elasticity in Cloud Computing: What It Is, and What It Is Not". In *ICAC* (Vol. 13, pp. 23-27).
12. Coutinho, E. F., de Carvalho Sousa, F. R., Rego, P. A. L., Gomes, D. G., & de Souza, J. N. (2015). "Elasticity in cloud computing: a survey". *Annals of telecommunications-annales des télécommunications*, 70(7-8), 289-309.
13. Farokhi, S., Jamshidi, P., Lucanin, D., & Brandic, I. (2015, July). "Performance-based vertical memory elasticity". In *Autonomic Computing (ICAC), 2015 IEEE International Conference on* (pp. 151-152). IEEE.
14. Hwang, K., Bai, X., Shi, Y., Li, M., Chen, W. G., & Wu, Y. (2016). "Cloud performance modeling with benchmark evaluation of elastic scaling strategies". *IEEE Transactions on parallel and distributed systems*, 27(1), 130-143.
15. Lorido-Botran, T., Miguel-Alonso, J., & Lozano, J.A. (2014). "A review of auto-scaling techniques for elastic applications in cloud environments". *Journal of grid computing*, 12(4), 559-592.
16. Lesch, V., Bauer, A., Herbst, N., & Kounev, S. (2018, March). "FOX: Cost-Awareness for Autonomic Resource Management in Public Clouds". In *Proceedings of the 2018 ACM/SPEC International Conference on Performance Engineering* (pp. 4-15). ACM.
17. Das, S., Nishimura, S., Agrawal, D., & El Abbadi, A. (2011). "Albatross: lightweight elasticity in shared storage databases for the cloud using live data migration". *Proceedings of the VLDB Endowment*, 4(8), 494-505.
18. Aslanpour, M. S., & Dashti, S. E. (2016, April). "SLA-aware resource allocation for application service providers in the cloud". In *Web Research (ICWR), 2016 Second International Conference on* (pp. 31-42). IEEE.

Especificación del Modelo de Proceso para una Revisión Sistemática de Literatura

Guido Tebes, Denis Peppino, Pablo Becker y Luis Olsina
GIDIS_Web, Facultad de Ingeniería, UNLPam, General Pico, LP, Argentina
{guido.tebes92, denispeppino92}@gmail.com;{beckerp, olsinal}@ing.unlpam.edu.ar

Abstract. La Revisión Sistemática de Literatura (RSL) es una metodología de investigación destinada a obtener evidencia desde artículos científicos almacenados en repositorios digitales, la cual debe ser sistemática, reproducible y auditable para formular preguntas de investigación sobre un área temática o fenómeno de interés y para buscar, seleccionar, analizar y comunicar toda la investigación relevante, básica o aplicada, necesaria para responder a dichas preguntas. La RSL se puede realizar sobre estudios primarios o secundarios. En cualquier caso, se requiere de procesos y métodos bien establecidos. Si bien existen guías del proceso de la RSL para Ingeniería de Software, las cuales indican los pasos a seguir en las tres fases del proceso propuesto por Kitchenham, consideramos que sería un aporte para la comunidad científica el robustecer la especificación de su proceso. Para este fin, empleando perspectivas de modelado de proceso, documentamos la especificación del proceso de RSL usando principalmente el lenguaje SPEM. En tanto desarrollamos el trabajo, ejemplificamos aspectos del proceso usando una RSL piloto sobre ontologías de testing de software ya realizada.

Keywords: RSL (SLR en Inglés), Perspectivas de modelado de proceso, Perspectiva funcional, informacional y de comportamiento, SPEM.

1 Introducción

A partir de que Kitchenham publicó en 2004 el informe técnico [8] sobre revisiones sistemáticas de literatura –basado en investigaciones previas aplicadas al dominio de medicina-, el empleo de las RSL en las diversas comunidades científicas de Ingeniería de Software (IS) se ha tornado más y más frecuente para obtener evidencias mayoritariamente de estudios primarios, y en menor medida de secundarios. La salida producida al aplicar el proceso de RSL sobre estudios primarios se denomina *estudio secundario*, en tanto que el documento resultante de aplicar dicho proceso sobre estudios secundarios se denomina *estudio terciario*.

Por citar sólo unos pocos ejemplos, los autores en [15, 16, 17] documentan estudios secundarios sobre distintas temáticas en IS, en tanto que los autores en [6, 11] documentan estudios terciarios. Mayoritariamente los investigadores han reutilizado los procedimientos y guías propuestas por Kitchenham en 2004 [8], las cuales fueron revisadas primero en 2005 por Biolchini *et al.* [3], y luego actualizadas por Kitchenham y sus colegas en 2007 [4, 10]. Más recientemente, en 2013, mediante la realización de una

RSL, Kitchenham *et al.* [9] evaluaron y sintetizaron estudios publicados por investigadores de IS (incluyendo distintos tipos de estudios, no sólo primarios) que tratan sobre sus experiencias en realizar RSL y sus propuestas en mejorar el proceso de la RSL.

La Fig. 1 muestra la especificación del proceso de dichos autores, y adoptado o adaptado ligeramente por el resto de la comunidad de IS hasta el presente. Básicamente el proceso propuesto para la RSL [4] describe qué hacer mediante sus fases y pasos, o en otras palabras del dominio de proceso [2], mediante sus procesos, actividades y tareas. Sin embargo, el objetivo inicial del proceso no debería ser cómo realizar cada actividad o tarea por medio de métodos. Notar que una estrategia bien establecida, ya sea de evaluación [13], de testing, de RSL, entre otras, debería integrar tres capacidades, a saber: un marco conceptual de dominio, especificaciones de perspectivas de proceso y especificaciones de métodos.

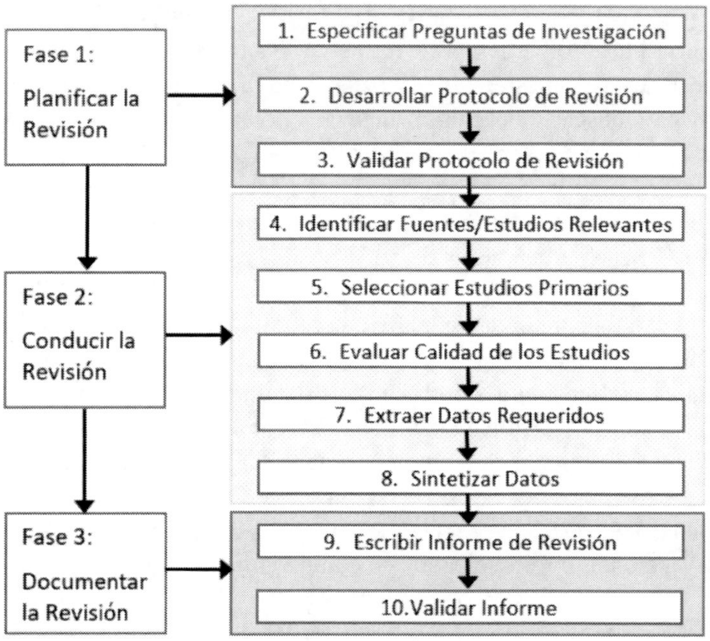

Fig. 1. Proceso de RSL propuesto por Kitchenham *et al.* (traducido al español del original [4])

Focalizándonos sólo en el aspecto del proceso (y no en el de especificación de métodos), observamos una posibilidad de mejora de la vista especificada en la Fig. 1, si tuviéramos en cuenta los principios de modelado de proceso propuestos por Curtis *et al.* [5], y empleados por ejemplo en [1].

Curtis *et al.* describen cuatro vistas o perspectivas en la que un proceso puede ser modelado, a saber: *funcional*, la cual describe qué actividades se deben llevar a cabo y qué flujo de entidades de información (artefactos) es importante para realizar las actividades y tareas; *de comportamiento*, que especifica cuándo deben ejecutarse las actividades, por lo que incluye identificar secuencias, paralelismos, iteraciones, etc.; *informacional*, la cual se centra en la estructura de los artefactos producidos o consumidos por las actividades, en sus interrelaciones, etc.; y *organizacional*, que tiene como fin mostrar dónde y quiénes son los agentes (en cumplimiento de roles) que intervienen en la realización de las actividades. Además de estas cuatro vistas, en [12] se define una perspectiva *metodológica*, la cual especifica particularmente qué constructores centrados en modelos (esto es, métodos) se asignan a las descripciones de actividades.

Entre los beneficios de usar modelado de proceso para robustecer a las especificaciones de un proceso en general, y para robustecer a un proceso de RSL en particular, podemos indicar el de *facilitar el entendimiento y la comunicación*, lo cual implica que el modelo de proceso (con la riqueza que proporciona las representaciones gráficas) sea entendible para la comunidad interesada; el de *dar soporte a la mejora de procesos*, ya que se identifican todas las perspectivas fundamentales del modelo de proceso, lo cual favorece a la reutilización y a la evaluación de impactos ante potenciales cambios en el proceso; el de *dar soporte a la gestión del proyecto*, esto es, a la planificación, asignación de recursos, monitoreo y control; el de *permitir la automatización de procesos* lo que ayuda a proporcionar herramientas de soporte y mejorar el rendimiento; el de *favorecer la verificación y validación de las perspectivas del proceso* lo que redundará en consistencia, repetitividad y auditabilidad de proyectos.

Por lo tanto, el principal aporte del presente trabajo consiste en robustecer al proceso de RSL actualmente utilizado por las comunidades científicas, considerando con mayor rigor los principios y beneficios de modelado de proceso antes descriptos. Para tal fin, usaremos sólo tres perspectivas a saber *funcional*, *informacional* y *de comportamiento*, por razones de espacio. Además, ilustraremos aspectos del proceso de RSL empleando un estudio piloto sobre ontologías de testing de software recientemente realizado [14].

El resto del artículo se organiza de la siguiente manera. En la sección 2 se discute la motivación y los trabajos relacionados a nuestra investigación. La sección 3 especifica el proceso de RSL y discute aspectos de las perspectivas de modelado. En la sección 4 se ilustra una RSL con el caso aplicado a ontologías de testing de software. Por último, la sección 5 resume conclusiones y líneas de avance.

2 Motivación y Trabajos Relacionados

Una de las motivaciones para modelar el proceso de RSL surgió de ciertas dificultades que enfrentamos (todos los autores del presente trabajo) al llevar a cabo el proceso de un estudio piloto de RSL (sobre ontologías de testing de software [14]), el cual no estaba explícitamente especificado en los procesos existentes, tal como el mostrado en la Fig. 1. El objetivo general de esta prueba era poder refinar y mejorar aspectos del diseño del protocolo, tales como las preguntas de investigación, el protocolo de búsqueda, los criterios de selección y de calidad, y/o los formularios de extracción de datos seleccionando una muestra de estudios primarios y ejecutando esta iteración no en la actividad de planificación (o diseño de la RSL, en la cual se pueden validar algunos artefactos) sino en la de conducción (o ejecución). Además, observamos aspectos débilmente especificados en los procesos de RSL existentes desde el punto de vista de perspectivas de modelado de proceso (tal como analizaremos en la sección 3), y a veces una débil separación de preocupaciones entre qué hacer (proceso) y cómo hacerlo (métodos).

Así, la primera representación gráfica del proceso de RSL propuesto por Kitchenham *et al.* [4] fue realizada en 2007 (teniendo en cuenta trabajos previos de los mismos autores [8] y de otros como [3]), el cual fue adoptado o adaptado ligeramente por el resto de la comunidad de IS hasta el presente. Si analizamos a la Fig. 1, en todos los procesos de RSL empleados recientemente se observa que tienen en común las fases de Planificar (o Diseñar Revisión, actividad A1, en Fig. 2), de Conducir (o Ejecutar Revisión, actividad A2), y de Documentar (o Analizar y Documentar Revisión, actividad

A3). A pesar que a nivel de fase se preservan en general las mismas tres (por ejemplo, en [15, 16, 17], por citar unos pocos trabajos), a nivel de pasos (sub-actividades y tareas) difieren unos de otros. Por lo tanto, si comparamos los tres pasos para la fase 1 de la Fig. 1, en [16] se modelizan también tres, a saber: paso 1) Necesidad de la RSL; paso 2) Formulación de las preguntas de investigación; y paso 3) Formulación del protocolo de revisión. En tanto que en [15] se representan cinco pasos: 1) Meta y necesidad de la RSL; 2) Definir las preguntas de investigación; 3) Definir cadena de búsqueda; 4) Definir criterios de inclusión/exclusión; y 5) Validar protocolo.

La misma falta de consenso en nombrar e incluir pasos se observa entre dichos trabajos para la fase 2. Por ejemplo, se incluye el paso "Selección y extracción piloto" en [15], que podría ser semejante al paso "Selección de estudios primarios potenciales" en [16]. Sin embrago, la selección y extracción piloto no itera o retroalimenta a la fase 1, la cual podría ayudar a mejorar aspectos del diseño de la RSL, como proponemos en la siguiente sección.

Por último, otras adaptaciones o variaciones del proceso propuesto por Kitchenham *et al.* se observan en [6, 7]. En [7] se enfatiza el uso de dos métodos denominados *backward* y *forward snowballing*, en tanto que en [6] se incluye la actividad de *snowballing* en el proceso de revisión.

En definitiva, como hipótesis subyacente, la brecha existente en la falta de estandarización del proceso de RSL utilizado actualmente por las comunidades científicas se podría achicar, si consideráramos con mayor rigor los principios y beneficios de modelado de proceso indicados en la sección introductoria. A seguir su desarrollo.

3 Especificación del Modelo de Proceso de RSL

Considerando que aún no existe un consenso generalizado en la terminología utilizada en el dominio de proceso, es necesario introducir el significado de algunos términos a usar antes de enfocarnos en la especificación del modelo de proceso de RSL. Cabe acotar que los términos considerados a continuación (resaltados en itálica) están tomados de la ontología de proceso propuesta en [2].

En este trabajo un *proceso* está compuesto por actividades y una *actividad* está formada por un conjunto de *tareas*, siendo este último un elemento atómico (es decir, que no se puede descomponer). Teniendo presente que una actividad se puede descomponer en actividades de menor nivel de granularidad que no llegan a ser tareas, en [2] se ha incluido el concepto *sub-actividad.* Además, proceso, actividad y tarea son considerados *definiciones de trabajo*, las cuales indican "qué" hacer. Toda definición de trabajo (proceso/actividad/tarea) consume y modifica y/o produce *productos de trabajo.* Un tipo particular de producto de trabajo son los *artefactos* (por ejemplo, diagramas y documentos). Por último, los *métodos* son *recursos* que indican "cómo" llevar a cabo la *descripción* de una *definición de trabajo.*

Respecto a la discusión central de esta sección, la Fig. 2 ilustra, desde la perspectiva de comportamiento, al proceso de RSL propuesto. Como se puede apreciar, este proceso, al igual que el proceso original [4], cuenta con tres actividades principales: (A1) Diseñar Revisión, (A2) Ejecutar Revisión y (A3) Analizar y Documentar Revisión. A su vez, estas actividades agrupan sub-actividades y tareas.

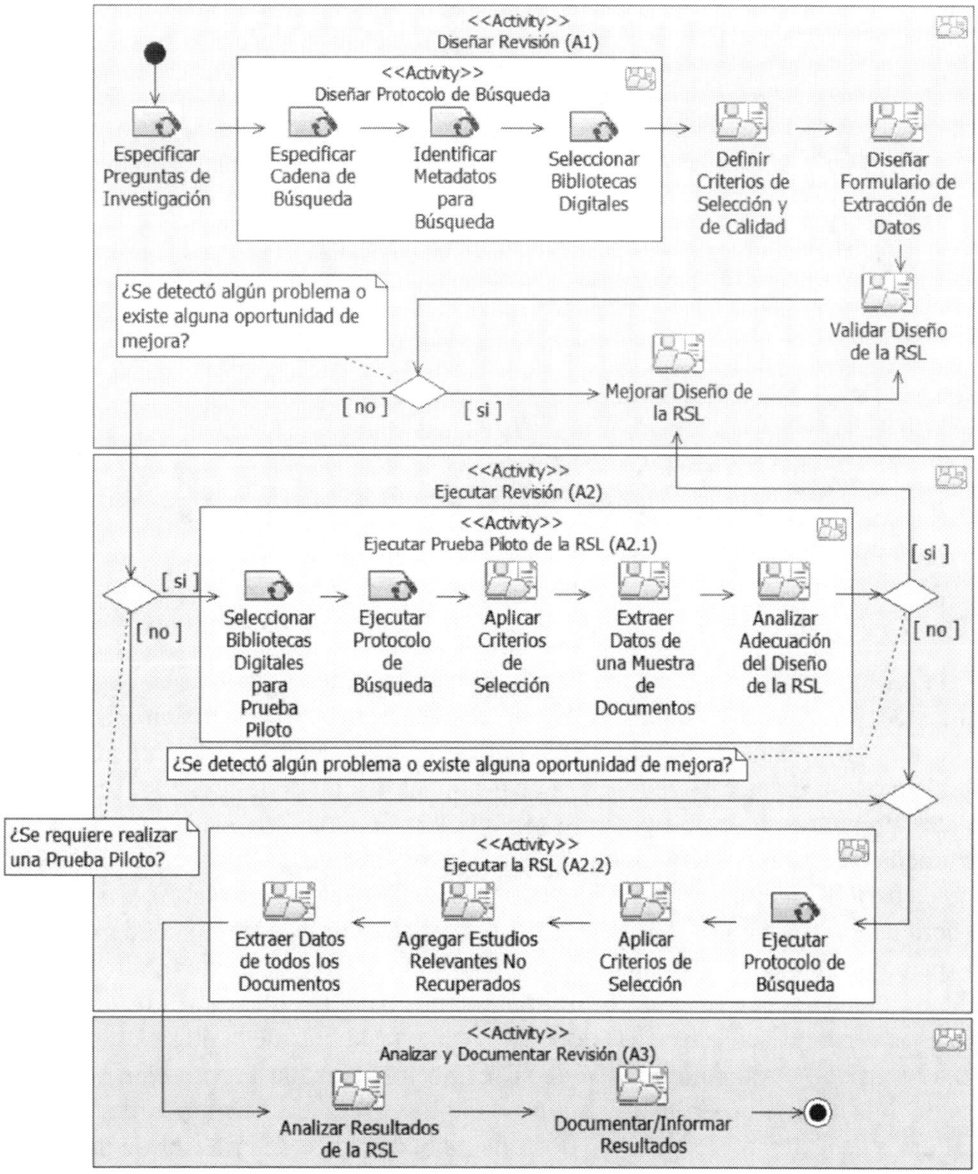

Fig. 2. Perspectiva de comportamiento del proceso de RSL propuesto

Notar que, por ejemplo, para la sub-actividad Diseñar Protocolo de Búsqueda se muestran las tareas que la misma involucra mientras que para el resto de las sub-actividades de A1 no. Esto está hecho *ex profeso* con el fin de comunicar al lector que las sub-actividades tienen tareas, pero al mismo tiempo no dar el detalle de todas para preservar la legibilidad del diagrama. En las siguientes sub-secciones se describen con más profundidad las tres actividades principales y en algunos casos se utilizan las perspectivas funcional e informacional para enriquecer la especificación del proceso.

3.1 Diseñar Revisión (A1)

La actividad A1 tiene como objetivo principal diseñar el protocolo de la RSL. Para ello se deben llevar a cabo las tareas y actividades de la Fig. 3 teniendo en cuenta el flujo y los artefactos de entrada y salida allí indicados.

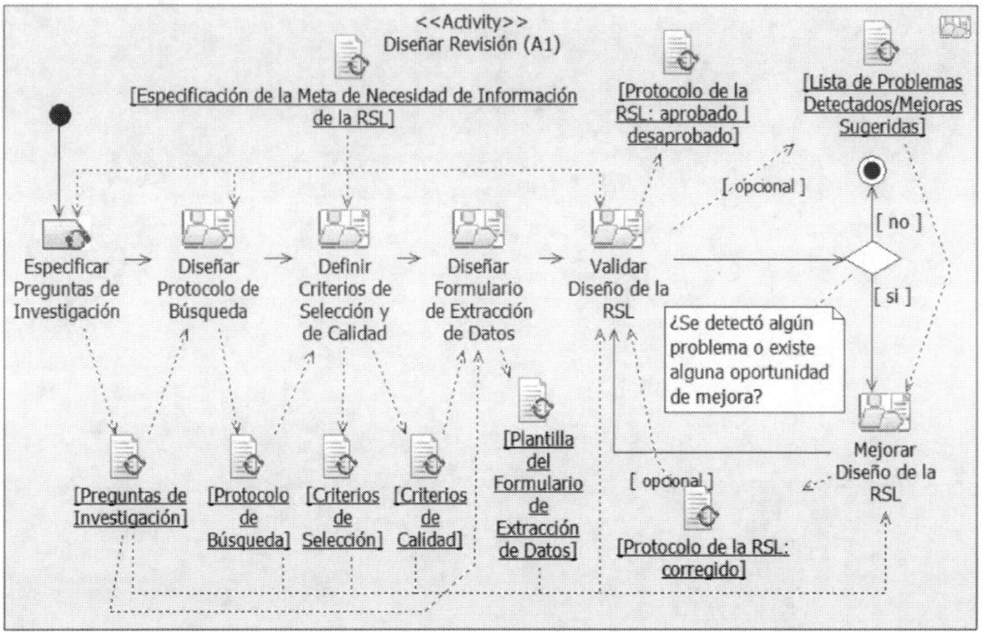

Fig. 3. Perspectiva funcional y de comportamiento para la actividad Diseñar Revisión (A1)

Tal como se observa en dicha figura, la primera tarea a realizar es Especificar Preguntas de Investigación la cual consume el documento "Especificación de la Meta de Necesidad de Información de la RSL". Este artefacto contiene la declaración de la meta establecida por los investigadores, la cual guía al diseño de la revisión. Luego, a partir de las "Preguntas de Investigación" se lleva a cabo la actividad Diseñar Protocolo de Búsqueda, la cual involucra las tareas Especificar Cadena de Búsqueda, Identificar Metadatos para Búsqueda y Seleccionar Bibliotecas Digitales (ver Fig. 2). Como resultado se obtiene el "Protocolo de Búsqueda", el cual se compone de una cadena (string) de búsqueda formada por términos y operadores lógicos, los metadatos sobre los cuales se aplicará dicha cadena (por ej., título, resumen y palabras clave) y, por último, las bibliotecas digitales seleccionadas donde se realizará la búsqueda de artículos.

A partir del "Protocolo de Búsqueda" es posible ejecutar la actividad Definir Criterios de Selección y de Calidad. Esta produce los artefactos "Criterios de Selección" y "Criterios de Calidad". El primero documenta el conjunto de criterios de inclusión y de exclusión, es decir las características que determinan si un artículo es considerado o no en la revisión. El segundo documenta características que permitan en A2 evaluar en cierta medida la calidad de los estudios recuperados como así también identificar aspectos relevantes o deseables para los investigadores.

Como se observa en la Fig. 3, la siguiente actividad es Diseñar Formulario de Extracción de Datos. Como salida se obtiene la "Plantilla del Formulario de Extracción de Datos" cuyos campos son definidos a partir de las "Preguntas de Investigación" y de los "Criterios de Calidad". Esta será utilizada en A2 para recopilar información sobre cada uno de los artículos recuperados. Luego se deben validar todos los documentos producidos hasta ese momento. Validar Diseño de la RSL consiste en revisar tales documentos con el fin de detectar problemas u oportunidades de mejora. Esta actividad suele ser llevada a cabo por investigadores con experiencia en RSL. Como resultado se obtiene el documento "Protocolo de la RSL", el cual contiene todos los artefactos antes producidos, tal como se observa mediante la perspectiva informacional en la Fig. 4.

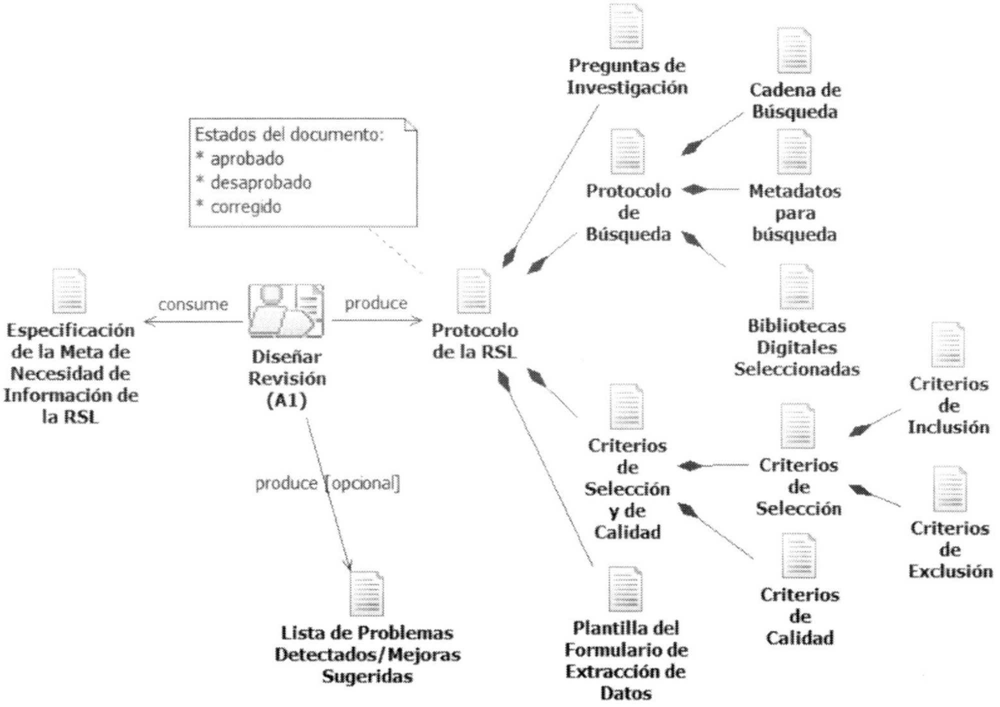

Fig. 4. Perspectiva Informacional para la actividad Diseñar Revisión (A1)

Cabe mencionar que el documento "Protocolo de la RSL" puede estar en estado *aprobado* o *desaprobado*. En caso de estar desaprobado, también se debe producir una "Lista de Problemas Detectados/Mejoras Sugeridas". Dicho artefacto será entrada a la actividad Mejorar Diseño de la RSL, la cual tiene como objetivo llevar adelante un conjunto de tareas que permitan introducir cambios, es decir corregir el "Protocolo de la RSL". Una vez que el protocolo ha sido corregido, se vuelve a realizar la actividad Validar Diseño de la RSL con la intención de controlar que el nuevo protocolo cumple con la "Especificación de la Meta de Necesidad de Información de la RSL". En definitiva, la actividad A1 finaliza cuando se da por aprobado al "Protocolo de la RSL".

3.2 Ejecutar Revisión (A2)

El principal objetivo de A2 es realizar la RSL. Además, para casos primerizos en donde no se repite o replica un estudio, se recomienda primero realizar una prueba piloto con la intención de ajustar el "Protocolo de la RSL" producido en A1. La Fig. 5 muestra las distintas sub-actividades y tareas de A2 junto con sus artefactos de entrada y salida.

En caso de considerarse necesario ejecutar una prueba piloto de la RSL, la primera tarea a realizar es Seleccionar Bibliotecas Digitales para Prueba Piloto. Esta consiste en escoger un subconjunto de bibliotecas (por lo general una o dos) a partir de las "Bibliotecas Digitales Seleccionadas" en A1. Luego se debe Ejecutar el Protocolo de Búsqueda sobre las bibliotecas previamente seleccionadas considerando la "Cadena de Búsqueda" y los "Metadatos para Búsqueda". Como salida se produce una lista de "Documentos Recuperados en Prueba Piloto". A partir de esta lista, en la actividad Aplicar Criterios de Selección se descargan los artículos y se filtran considerando los "Criterios de Inclusión" y los "Criterios de Exclusión". Como resultado se obtienen los "Documentos Seleccionados en Prueba Piloto".

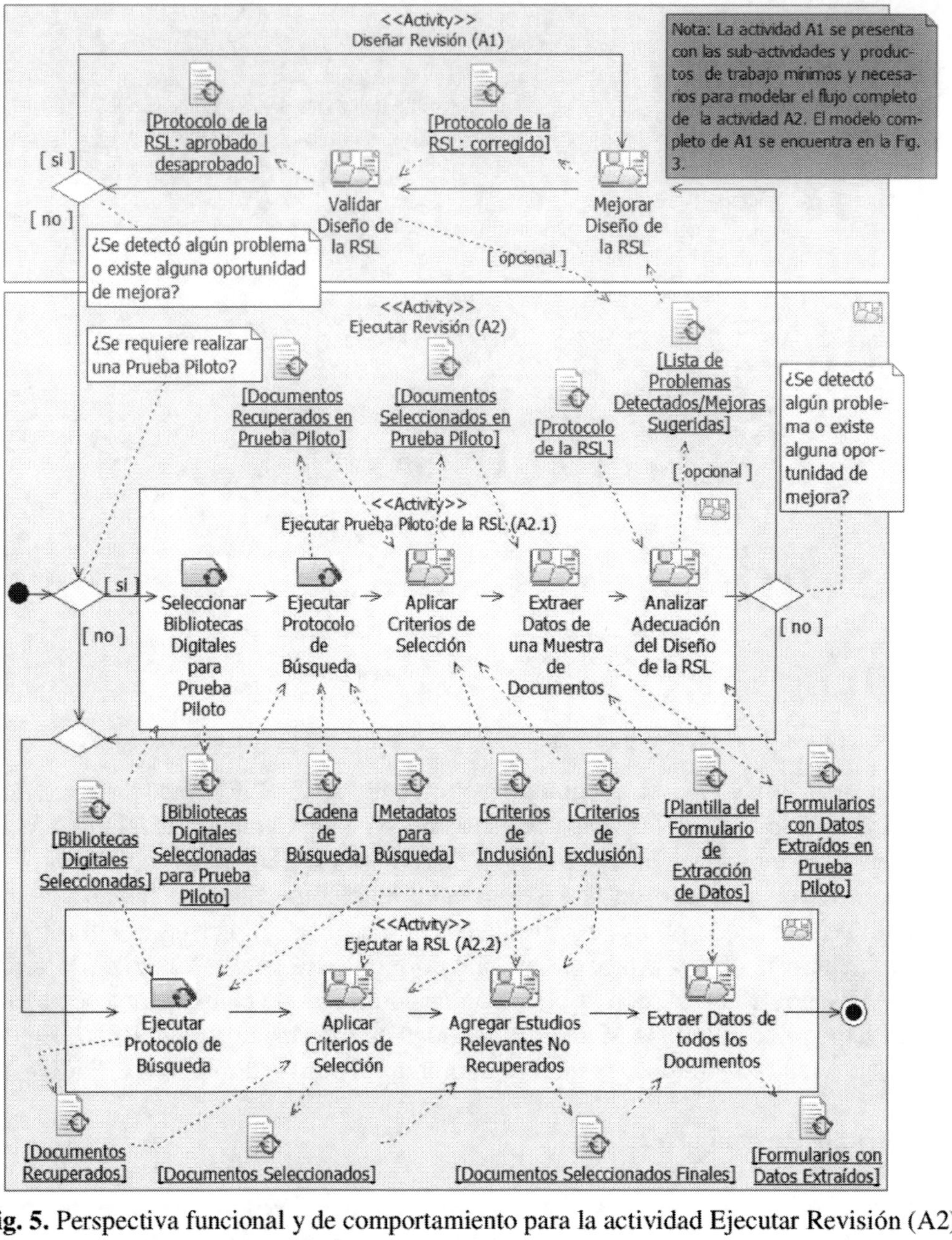

Fig. 5. Perspectiva funcional y de comportamiento para la actividad Ejecutar Revisión (A2)

A partir de este subconjunto de documentos de los inicialmente recuperados, se procede a Extraer Datos de una Muestra de Documentos. Como tareas de esta actividad está la selección de documentos de muestra, la cual puede realizarse de forma aleatoria [8], y la extracción de datos utilizando la "Plantilla del Formulario de Extracción de Datos" (estas tareas no se muestran en la Fig. 5). Notar que se extraen datos de solo una muestra ya que el fin de la prueba piloto es solo analizar qué tan adecuado es el protocolo que se está siguiendo. Si más de un investigador va a utilizar los formularios en la revisión final, entonces es recomendable que más de un investigador participe en la extracción de datos de la prueba piloto. El beneficio de que los formularios sean probados por distintos investigadores es facilitar el hallazgo de inconsistencias.

Finalmente, considerando todos los documentos que componen el "Protocolo de la

RSL" (ver Fig. 4) y los "Formularios con Datos Extraídos en Prueba Piloto" se debe Analizar Adecuación del Diseño de la RSL. Este análisis a partir de una prueba piloto permite refinar el formulario de extracción de datos y también ajustar otros aspectos del protocolo, tales como preguntas de investigación, estrategia de búsqueda y/o criterios de selección. En caso de que no fuera necesario realizar ajustes al protocolo, se debe llevar a cabo la actividad A2.2 (Ejecutar la RSL). Pero si se detectara algún problema o hubiera alguna oportunidad de mejora, tal como indica la Fig. 5, se deben realizar las actividades Mejorar Diseño de la RSL y Validar Diseño de la RSL ya descriptas en A1. Una vez hechos los cambios y que el Protocolo de la RSL pase a estado aprobado, se puede volver a realizar una nueva prueba piloto o directamente realizar A2.2.

Ejecutar la RSL (A2.2), implica Ejecutar Protocolo de Búsqueda teniendo en cuenta ahora a todas las "Bibliotecas Digitales Seleccionadas". Luego, se debe Aplicar Criterios de Selección sobre los "Documentos Recuperados" con el objetivo de descartar aquellos que no cumplen con los criterios definidos en A1. Como artefacto se produce "Documentos Seleccionados", el cual ingresa a Agregar Estudios Relevantes No Recuperados (actividad en la que se puede aplicar métodos de *snowballing*). Al final se debe realizar la actividad Extraer Datos de todos los Documentos haciendo uso de la "Plantilla del Formulario de Extracción de Datos". En los casos donde un mismo artículo sea revisado por varios investigadores, los datos extraídos deben compararse y los desacuerdos se pueden resolver por consenso entre los investigadores o por un investigador independiente adicional. Si cada uno de los investigadores revisa diferentes documentos porque las limitaciones de tiempo o recursos impiden que todos los documentos seleccionados sean evaluados por todos los investigadores, es importante asegurarse de emplear algún método para verificar que los investigadores extraigan los datos de manera consistente. Una vez concluida A2 se tendrá un conjunto de "Formularios con Datos Extraídos", los cuales son el insumo principal para la actividad A3.

3.3 Analizar y Documentar Revisión (A3)

Esta actividad tiene como objetivo principal analizar y comunicar los resultados de la revisión. Además, considerando que una RSL debe ser sistemática, reproducible y auditable, es por ende importante documentar el proceso seguido y los métodos aplicados.

La Fig. 2 muestra que la primera actividad a realizar es Analizar Resultados de la RSL. El análisis se realiza a partir de los "Formularios con Datos Extraídos". Se pueden tabular los datos y utilizar tablas que permitan encontrar similitudes y diferencias entre los distintos estudios. Como resultado se produce una "Síntesis de Datos" que permita dar respuesta a las preguntas de investigación. La síntesis por lo general es descriptiva. Sin embargo, es posible a veces complementar una síntesis descriptiva con un resumen cuantitativo a través de meta-análisis, usando técnicas estadísticas apropiadamente.

Finalmente se realiza la actividad Documentar/Informar Resultados. Para ello, inicialmente se establecen los mecanismos de difusión, por ejemplo, informes técnicos, artículos de revista, entre otros, y luego se producen los documentos que comunicarán los resultados a la comunidad interesada. De esta manera, finaliza el proceso de RSL.

3.4 Resaltando Aspectos del Proceso de RSL Propuesto

El proceso de RSL propuesto por Kitchenham *et al.* (Fig. 1) y adoptado o adaptado ligeramente por otros autores hasta el presente (como por ejemplo en [15, 16, 17]) sólo es representado (y débilmente) mediante la perspectiva de comportamiento desde el punto de vista de modelado de proceso. Si comparamos a la Fig. 1 con la Fig. 2 en donde ambas son una representación de la perspectiva de comportamiento, observamos, por un lado, una mayor riqueza de expresividad en secuencias y flujos de decisión en la Fig. 2 y, por otro lado, la posibilidad de representar diferentes niveles de granularidad en las definiciones de trabajo, como actividad, sub-actividad y tarea. (Notar que, por una cuestión de mantener el diagrama simple y del espacio que disponemos en este artículo, no hemos especificado otros aspectos como iteraciones y paralelismos –como por ejemplo el paralelismo que se puede modelar entre las tareas Definir Criterios de Calidad y Definir Criterios de Inclusión/Exclusión, dentro de la sub-actividad Definir Criterios de Selección y de Calidad en Fig. 2).

Si bien la perspectiva de comportamiento es sin dudas necesaria, es insuficiente por no representar entradas y salidas de las diferentes actividades y tareas. Por tal razón, la perspectiva funcional junto con la de comportamiento, enriquece la expresividad del modelo tal como se observa en las figuras 3 y 5. Aún más, la perspectiva informacional también enriquece y favorece la comprensión y rigor del proceso de RSL, al mostrar la estructura de un artefacto dado, tal como se ilustra para el artefacto "Protocolo de la RSL" (Fig. 4) el cual es producido por la actividad A1.

Por otra parte, un aspecto a resaltar de la presente propuesta, es la modelización de la sub-actividad A2.1 (Ejecutar Prueba Piloto de la RSL) la cual retroalimenta a la actividad A1 (Diseñar Revisión). Con frecuencia, esta actividad no se considera en los procesos adaptados, o si se menciona o considera [4, 15] está débilmente especificada. Por ejemplo, en [15] la actividad (paso) Selección y Extracción Piloto, se encuentra representada en la actividad (fase) A2, pero no retroalimenta a la actividad (fase) A1, lo cual podría ayudar a mejorar aspectos del diseño de la RSL, tal como proponemos en la Fig. 5, y veremos su utilidad en la sección 4. Notar que en nuestra propuesta se modela a la sub-actividad Validar Diseño de RSL en A1, y a la sub-actividad Ejecutar Prueba Piloto de la RSL, la cual claramente debe llevarse a cabo en A2 por contener tareas propias de la ejecución de la misma.

En definitiva, la principal contribución del presente trabajo consiste en robustecer al proceso de RSL actualmente utilizado por las comunidades científicas considerando, por una parte, los principios y beneficios de modelado de proceso con mayor rigor al usar en este caso tres perspectivas a saber funcional, informacional y de comportamiento conjuntamente. Y, por otra parte, la visión de desacoplar "el qué" hacer, lo cual se modeliza mediante procesos, actividades, tareas y artefactos, de "el cómo" llevar a cabo la descripción de la definición de trabajo, lo cual se modeliza mediante especificaciones de métodos (no tratado en este artículo). A menudo se observa en la literatura citada (y en general) una falta de separación de preocupaciones entre qué hacer (proceso) y cómo hacerlo (métodos).

4 Aplicación del Proceso a un Estudio de RSL

En [13] se presenta una familia de estrategias de evaluación. Toda estrategia, independientemente que sea de evaluación, desarrollo, testing, etc., debería integrar una base conceptual de dominio bien establecida, especificaciones de proceso y métodos. A fin de ampliar estas familias, se consideró desarrollar estrategias de testing. Por ende, el objetivo inicial es contar con un vocabulario para el dominio de testing. En esta dirección, en [14] se diseñó una RSL sobre ontologías de testing de software, es decir, se llevaron a cabo las actividades A1 y A2.1 de la Fig. 2. Al presente se ha completado la actividad A2 y se está realizando A3. El resultado de esta RSL permitirá establecer las bases para adoptar, adaptar o desarrollar una ontología de testing que pueda ser integrada al marco conceptual ya desarrollado para las estrategias de evaluación existentes.

Para ilustrar el proceso propuesto con sus perspectivas, a seguir se comentan algunos aspectos de la prueba piloto llevada a cabo en [14] que permitieron evaluar y refinar el diseño de la RSL. Como muestra la Fig. 4, para llevar a cabo A1 se requiere la "Especificación de la Meta de Necesidad de Información de la RSL". En este caso, la meta de necesidad de información establece que se deben analizar sistemáticamente los artículos de las fuentes bibliográficas digitales que documenten ontologías de testing de software. Como resultado de A1 se obtuvo el "Protocolo de la RSL". La Tabla 1 muestra los diferentes artefactos que componen dicho documento, los cuales se corresponden con aquellos especificados en la perspectiva informacional de la Fig. 4. Cabe aclarar que este protocolo es el resultado de haber llevado a cabo la sub-actividad Mejorar Diseño de la RSL luego de considerar la "Lista de Problemas Detectados/Mejoras Sugeridas" al ser validado por investigadores externos con experiencia en revisiones.

Tabla 1. "Protocolo de la RSL" para el estudio de ontologías de testing, producido en A1.

Preguntas de Investigación (PT 1.1 –Producto de Trabajo)	
PI_1: ¿Cuáles son las ontologías existentes del dominio de testing de software? PI_2: ¿Cuáles son los conceptos relevantes, sus relaciones, atributos y restricciones o axiomas necesarios para describir el dominio de testing de software?	
Protocolo de Búsqueda (PT 1.2)	
Cadena de Búsqueda (PT 1.2.1)	"Software Testing" AND ("Ontology" OR "Conceptual Base")
Metadatos para Búsqueda (PT 1.2.2)	Título; Resumen; Palabras Clave
Bibliotecas Digitales Seleccionadas (PT 1.2.3)	Scopus, IEEE Xplore, ACM Digital Library, Springer Link y Science Direct
Criterios de Selección y de Calidad (PT 1.3)	
Criterios de Inclusión (PT 1.3.1)	1) Que el trabajo esté publicado en los últimos 15 años; 2) Que el trabajo pertenezca al área de las Ciencias de la Computación; 3) Que el trabajo documente una ontología de testing de software; 4) Que el documento esté basado en investigación (no sea simplemente una "lección aprendida" o una opinión de experto).
Criterios de Exclusión (PT 1.3.2)	1) Que el trabajo sea un prólogo, resumen de artículo, entrevista, noticia, discusión, comentario, carta de lector, o poster; 2) Que el trabajo no sea un estudio primario; 3) Que el trabajo no esté escrito en inglés.
Criterios de Calidad (PT 1.3.3)	1) ¿El/los objetivo/s de la investigación está/n claramente identificado/s? 2) ¿Se encuentra presente la definición del contexto en el que la investigación se realizó? 3) ¿La ontología propuesta fue desarrollada siguiendo una metodología rigurosa y/o formal? 4) ¿La ontología propuesta fue desarrollada considerando además su vinculación con conceptos de Requisitos Funcionales y Requisitos No Funcionales?
Plantilla del Formulario de Extracción de Datos (PT 1.4)	
Investigador; Título del artículo; Autores del artículo; *Journal*/Congreso; Año de publicación; Biblioteca Digital; Nombre de la ontología presentada; Conceptos relevantes utilizados para describir el dominio de testing de software; Metodología utilizada para el desarrollo de la ontología; Contexto de la investigación; Objetivos de la investigación; ¿La ontología propuesta considera su vinculación con conceptos de Requisitos Funcionales y Requisitos No Funcionales?; Notas adicionales.	

Tabla 2. "Protocolo de la RSL" para el estudio de ontologías de testing corregido luego de A2.1 (en azul y subrayado se indican los cambios respecto del protocolo mostrado en Tabla 1).

Preguntas de Investigación (PT 1.1 –Producto de Trabajo)	
PI_1: ¿Cuáles son las ontologías con conceptualización del dominio de testing de software? PI_2: Considerando al conjunto de ontologías documentadas en los estudios seleccionados: ¿Cuáles son los términos más frecuentemente incluidos, sus atributos, relaciones y axiomas necesarios para describir el dominio de testing de software? PI_3: ¿Cómo se clasifican las ontologías de testing de software existentes?	
Protocolo de Búsqueda (PT 1.2)	
Cadena de Búsqueda (PT 1.2.1)	("Software Testing" OR "Software Test") AND ("Ontology" OR "Ontologies")
Metadatos para Búsqueda (PT 1.2.2)	Título; Resumen; Palabras Clave
Bibliotecas Digitales Seleccionadas (PT 1.2.3)	Scopus, IEEE Xplore, ACM Digital Library, Springer Link y Science Direct
Criterios de Selección y de Calidad (PT 1.3)	
Criterios de Inclusión (PT 1.3.1)	1) Que el trabajo esté publicado en los últimos 15 años (desde inicio del 2003 hasta el 12 de noviembre de 2018); 2) Que el trabajo pertenezca al área de las Ciencias de la Computación o al área de Ingeniería de Información / Sistema / Software; 3) Que el documento cuente con la conceptualización ontológica del dominio de testing (que no sea simplemente una "lección aprendida o una opinión de experto" o sólo una implementación).
Criterios de Exclusión (PT 1.3.2)	1) Que el trabajo sea un prólogo, resumen de artículo, entrevista, noticia, discusión, comentario, carta de lector, poster, tabla de contenidos o short paper (se considera short paper al que tiene hasta 4 pág.); 2) Que el trabajo no sea un estudio primario; 3) Que el trabajo no esté escrito en inglés; 4) Que el trabajo no documente una ontología de testing de software; 5) Que la ontología presentada en el documento sea una versión anterior a la versión más reciente y completa publicada en otro documento recuperado; 6) Que un mismo documento sea resultado de más de una fuente bibliográfica (en otras palabras, eliminar duplicados); 7) Que la ontología conceptualizada en el documento sea un fragmento de una ontología conceptualizada en otro documento recuperado.
Criterios de Calidad (PT 1.3.3)	1) ¿El/los objetivo/s de la investigación está/n claramente identificado/s? 2) ¿Se encuentra presente la definición del contexto en el que la investigación se realizó? 3) ¿La ontología propuesta fue desarrollada siguiendo una metodología rigurosa y/o formal? 4) ¿La ontología propuesta fue desarrollada considerando además su vinculación con conceptos de Requisitos Funcionales y Requisitos No Funcionales? 5) ¿Qué otras terminologías del dominio de testing de software se tuvieron en cuenta para desarrollar la ontología propuesta?
Plantilla del Formulario de Extracción de Datos (PT 1.4)	
Investigador; Título del artículo; Autores del artículo; *Journal*/Congreso; Año de publicación; Biblioteca Digital; Nombre de la ontología presentada; Conceptos especificados para describir el dominio de testing de software; Metodología utilizada para el desarrollo de la ontología; Terminologías o Vocabularios tenidos en cuenta para desarrollar la ontología propuesta; Clasificación de la ontología propuesta; Contexto de la investigación; Objetivos de investigación relacionados con ontologías de testing de software; ¿La ontología propuesta considera su vinculación con conceptos de Requisitos Funcionales y Requisitos No Funcionales?; Notas adicionales.	

Siguiendo el flujo de actividades modelado en la vista de comportamiento de la Fig. 2, se consideró importante realizar una prueba piloto para analizar la adecuación del protocolo. Como parte de la ejecución de A2.1, a partir de las "Bibliotecas Digitales Seleccionadas" en A1 (ver PT1.2.3 en Tabla 1) para esta prueba piloto se seleccionó Scopus ya que contiene recursos digitales de diversas fuentes, como Elsevier, IEEE Xplore y ACM Digital Library, entre otras. Luego de Ejecutar Protocolo de Búsqueda y Aplicar Criterios de Selección se obtuvieron 19 documentos los cuales fueron revisados por 3 investigadores para Extraer datos de una Muestra de Documentos. Finalizada A2.1 se obtuvo una "Lista de Problemas Detectados/Mejoras Sugeridas", por lo cual se volvió a ejecutar la actividad Mejorar Diseño de la RSL (tal como se prescribe en la Fig. 5 mediante las perspectivas funcional y de comportamiento).

Los cambios realizados en el protocolo se resaltan (en azul y subrayado) en la Tabla 2. A seguir se indican algunas correcciones realizadas gracias a la ejecución de la prueba piloto. El término "relevantes" en la pregunta de investigación PI_2 de Tabla 1 influyó en la cantidad de términos extraídos por cada investigador. A raíz de ello se propuso reformular la pregunta tal como se observa en el PT1.1 de Tabla 2 y el campo "Conceptos relevantes utilizados [...]" del formulario se cambió por "Conceptos especificados [...]". Se consideró este cambio ya que de esta manera resulta más objetivo y fácil de interpretar que con el diseño inicial. Además, la lectura de artículos durante la prueba piloto permitió detectar que se presentaban ontologías de diversos tipos como por ej., fundacional, de dominio de alto nivel, de dominio, y de aplicación o instancias. Ya que el objetivo final luego de ejecutar la RSL es adoptar, adaptar o construir una ontología de dominio, esta información resulta de suma importancia. Por lo tanto, se agregó una nueva pregunta de investigación (PI_3 en PT1.1 en Tabla 2) y el campo "Clasificación de la ontología propuesta" en el formulario (ver PT1.4 en Tabla 2).

Se modificó la cadena de búsqueda (comparar PT1.2.1 de tablas 1 y 2) porque no todos los motores de búsqueda tienen en cuenta variaciones o sinónimos de las palabras utilizadas. El criterio de inclusión 1 en PT1.3.1 (ver Tabla 1) es poco específico, por lo tanto, se modificó como se observa en PT1.3.1 de Tabla 2. La lectura de artículos también permitió detectar que algunos de ellos hacían mención a diferentes versiones de la misma ontología. Así, se agregó el criterio de exclusión 5 (ver PT1.3.2 en Tabla 2). Dado que las búsquedas en Scopus devuelven artículos que pertenecen a otras bibliotecas digitales se agregó el criterio de exclusión 6 del PT1.3.2 para eliminar duplicados.

Tras la lectura también se observó que algunas ontologías fueron construidas teniendo en cuenta a otras bases conceptuales, lo cual aporta cierto grado de calidad a las nuevas ontologías. Por ello, se agregó el criterio de calidad 5 en PT1.3.3 (ver Tabla 2) y el campo "Terminologías o Vocabularios tenidos en cuenta [...]" en el formulario PT1.4. Con este nuevo criterio de calidad se intenta recuperar información útil para la construcción de la nueva ontología (si fuera necesario construir una nueva).

5 Consideraciones Finales

En este trabajo, empleando perspectivas de modelado de proceso, hemos documentado la especificación del proceso de RSL usando principalmente el lenguaje SPEM. Adicionalmente, hemos resaltado los beneficios y fortalezas del modelo de proceso de RSL propuesto, y hemos ilustrado aspectos del mismo ejemplificando una RSL piloto sobre ontologías de testing de software.

El proceso especificado contribuye a un pilar de una estrategia de RSL bien establecida, sabiendo que además debería integrar las especificaciones de métodos. (Notar que, para una misma tarea, diferentes especificaciones de métodos se podrían aplicar). En consecuencia, el ciclo de vida de un proyecto de RSL debiera organizar las actividades y tareas considerando no sólo el proceso prescripto sino también la asignación apropiada de recursos tales como métodos, entre otros recursos, con el fin de alcanzar la meta propuesta. Existen actividades adicionales a las especificadas en la Fig. 2, que la planificación de un proyecto debería tomar en cuenta tales como documentar artefactos en todas las actividades y controlar cambios y versiones. La documentación continua y el versionado de artefactos es un factor clave para garantizar consistencia, repetitividad y auditabilidad de proyectos de RSL.

Como trabajo en marcha, luego de la prueba piloto, se está llevando a cabo la RSL de ontologías de testing de la cual ahora también participa un grupo de I+D de la Universidad ORT, Uruguay. La culminación de este proyecto se prevé para marzo de 2019. Como resultado de A3, se redactará un artículo de revista como informe de conclusión.

Referencias

1. Becker P., Lew P., Olsina L.: Specifying Process Views for a Measurement, Evaluation, and Improvement Strategy, In: Advances in Software Engineering Journal, Academic Editor: Osamu Mizuno, Hindawi Publishing Corporation, USA, V.2012, 27 pgs., (2012).
2. Becker P., Papa F., Olsina L.: Process Ontology Specification for Enhancing the Process Compliance of a Measurement and Evaluation Strategy, CLEI eJnal., 18:(1), pp. 1-26, (2015).
3. Biolchini J., Mian P.G., Natali A.C.C., Travassos G.: Systematic Review in Software Engineering. Technical Report RT-ES 679-05. PESC, COPPE/UFRJ, (2005).
4. Brereton P., Kitchenham B., Budgen D., Turner M., Khalil M.: Lessons from applying the systematic literature review process within the software engineering domain, Journal of Systems and Software, 80:(4), pp. 571–583, (2007).
5. Curtis B., Kellner M., Over J.: Process Modelling. Com. of ACM, 35:(9), pp. 75-90, (1992).
6. Garousi V., Mäntylä M.: A systematic literature review of literature reviews in software testing, Information and Software Technology, V.80, pp. 195-216, (2016).
7. Irshad M., Petersen K., Poulding S.: A systematic literature review of software requirements reuse approaches, Information and Software Technology, V.93, pp. 223-245, (2018).
8. Kitchenham B.: Procedures for Undertaking Systematic Reviews, Joint TR, Comp. Science Dep., Keele University (TR/SE-0401) and National ICT Australia Ltd. (0400011T.1), (2004).
9. Kitchenham B., Brereton P.: A systematic review of systematic review process research in software engineering, Information and Software Technology, 55:(12), pp. 2049-2075, (2013).
10. Kitchenham B., Charters S.: Procedures for Performing Systematic Reviews, EBSE Technical Report, Software Engineering Group, School of Computer Science and Mathematics Keele University and Department of Computer Science University of Durham, UK, v. 2.3., (2007).
11. Kitchenham B., Pretorius R., Budgen D., Brereton P., Turner M., Niazi M., Linkman S.: Systematic literature reviews in software engineering –A tertiary study, Information and Software Technology, 52:(8), pp. 792–805, (2010).
12. Olsina, L.: Functional View of the Hypermedia Process Model, 5th International Workshop on Engineering Hypertext Functionality, at ICSE'98, Kyoto, Japan, pp. 1-10, (1998).
13. Olsina L., Becker, P.: Family of Strategies for different Evaluation Purposes. XX CIbSE'17, CABA, Argentina, Published by Curran Associates, pp. 221-234, (2017)
14. Peppino D., Tebes G., Dameno J., Becker P., Olsina L.: Diseñando una Revisión Sistemática de Literatura sobre Ontologías de Testing de Software, 6to Congreso Nacional de Ingeniería Informática/Sistemas de Información (CoNaIISI), Mar del Plata, pp. 1-13, (2018).
15. Sepúlveda S., Cravero A., Cachero C.: Requirements modeling languages for software product lines: A systematic literature review, Inf. and Soft. Technology, V.69, pp. 16-36, (2016).
16. Tahir T., Rasool G., Gencel C.: A systematic literature review on software measurement programs, Information and Software Technology, V.73, pp. 101-121, (2016).
17. Torrecilla-S. C.J., Sedeño J., Escalona M.J., Mejías M.: Agile, Web Engineering and Capability Maturity Model Integration: A SLR, Inform. and Soft. Tech., V.71, pp. 92-107, (2016).

RET Keynote 2019
The Road to Data-driven Requirements Engineering

Xavier Franch[1]

[1] GESSI research group
Universitat Politècnica de Catalunya (UPC-BarcelonaTech)
Spain

Abstract. In the last years, we are witnessing the advent of data-driven approaches in almost every single software engineering activity, and requirements engineering is not the exception to the rule. The exploitation of data coming from several sources may indeed become an extremely useful input to requirements elicitation and management but it does not come for free. Techniques such as natural language processing and machine learning are difficult to master and require high-quality data, whilst their generalization remains as a challenge. In this keynote, I introduce the main concepts behind data-driven requirements engineering, then I provide an overview of the state of the art and report on results from some collaborative projects in which I'm participating, and last recapitulate lessons learned and open challenges. The research reported has been possible thanks to the support of the OpenReq (contract 732463) and Q-Rapids (contract 732253) H2020 projects supported by the European Union.

Proceso de Ingeniería de requisitos para un modelo de la calidad en Cuba

MSc. Yoandy Lazo Alvarado[1*], Ing. Leanet Tamayo Oro[1], MSc. Odannis Enamorado Pérez[1]

[1] Centro Nacional de Calidad de Software (CALISOFT). Calle 17, # 506, entre D y E, Plaza de la Revolución, La Habana, Cuba. yoandy.lazo, leanet.tamayo, odannis.enamorado@calisoft.cu

[*] Autor para correspondencia: yoandy.lazo@calisoft.cu

Resumen. Un elevado porciento de proyectos a nivel mundial, fracasan o son cancelados por una incorrecta ingeniería de requisitos. Incorporar buenas prácticas en este proceso proporciona el mecanismo apropiado para entender y analizar lo que desean y necesitan las partes interesadas. También permite evaluar y negociar una solución razonable, especificar, validar y gestionar los requisitos a medida que se transforman en un sistema funcional. La presente investigación tiene como objetivo elaborar un proceso de Ingeniería de requisitos para el Modelo de la Calidad para el Desarrollo de Aplicaciones Informáticas que contribuya a elevar los porcientos de proyectos exitosos, en las organizaciones desarrolladora de software en Cuba, respecto al cumplimiento de los requisitos pactados. La propuesta de solución contiene requisitos específicos y elementos de apoyo (descripción gráfica y textual del proceso), divididos por los tres niveles de madurez que plantea el modelo. Para alcanzar la meta propuesta se realizó una revisión bibliográfica sobre la disciplina ingeniería de requisitos, así como entrevistas y encuestas a los roles a fines a esta actividad en las organizaciones desarrolladoras de software de Cuba. La solución fue evaluada por expertos en un grupo focal y puesta en práctica, como un piloto, en tres organizaciones, también fue medida la satisfacción de los usuarios que la consumieron utilizando la técnica de Iadov.

Palabras clave: requisito, ingeniería de requisitos, software, proceso.

1. Introducción

Un porciento significativo de los proyectos de desarrollo de software, a nivel mundial, se cancelan o fracasan según estudios realizados; entre los años 2011 y 2015 los cancelados significaron el 39%, 46%, 40%, 47% y 45%, respectivamente, y los fracasados representaron el 22%, 17%, 19%, 17% y 19%, respectivamente [1, 2]. Una investigación realizada por Lehtinen et al. plantea que las causas de las fallas en los proyectos ocurren en varios procesos que incluyen la gestión, ventas y requisitos, e implementación. También plantea que las fallas están relacionadas con el entorno del proyecto, las personas, los métodos y las tareas [3, 4].

Un análisis de la publicación del Standish Group en el 2014 sobre un estudio de más de 2000 proyectos en 1000 empresas permitió conocer que, a pesar que el proyecto sea considerado exitoso respecto al cumplimiento de los plazos de entrega, presupuesto y requisitos acordados, los porcientos de utilización de las funcionalidades que componen los sistemas son: el 7% siempre, 13% a menudo, 16% algunas veces, 19% raras veces, 45% nunca [5]. Según plantea del Toro, esto se debe a que: 1) el cliente no la solicitó, pero pudo surgir de una mala interpretación de un requisito o los desarrolladores consideraron que podría ser de utilidad o interesante; o 2) el cliente lo solicitó, pero posteriormente se dio cuenta que no lo describió correctamente y ya no lo quiere; lo describió correctamente pero cuando lo vio implementado se dio cuenta que solicitó algo incorrecto; o lo describió correctamente pero ahora quiere algo diferente [6].

Los autores de esta investigación concuerdan con del Toro sobre la importancia de mantener una adecuada retroalimentación con las partes interesadas durante el ciclo de vida del desarrollo de software para disminuir los efectos de la volatilidad de los requisitos. Para garantizar esa retroalimentación, un puente indispensable que transita entre las necesidades de las partes interesadas, el diseño y el desarrollo del producto lo constituye el proceso de Ingeniería de requisitos (IR), el mismo proporciona el mecanismo apropiado para entender lo que desean las partes interesadas, analizar las necesidades, evaluar la factibilidad, negociar una solución razonable, especificar la solución sin ambigüedades, validar la especificación y gestionar los requisitos a medida de que se transforman en un sistema funcional [7].

Un diagnóstico realizado en el año 2014 por el Centro Nacional de Calidad de Software (CALISOFT) a una muestra del 43,75% de las organizaciones desarrolladoras de software en Cuba, donde se le realizaron entrevistas y encuentras a los roles involucrados, permitió caracterizar a dichas entidades [8]. Entre los aspectos evaluados estuvo el cumplimiento de las actividades que componen el proceso de IR planteadas por Pressman [7]. Un análisis de los resultados arrojados, permitió a los autores de esta investigación conocer que el 7,14% no identifica los requisitos de las partes interesadas, 14,26% no los específica, 21,43% no los valida, 28,57% no controla sus cambios y el 57,14% no mantiene la trazabilidad con los requisitos. Otro de los resultados obtenidos fue el de los proyectos terminados en el período 2011-2014 [9], donde se recogió que el 16,42% no cumplieron la totalidad de los requisitos pactados con el cliente; 11,94% fueron entregados fuera de tiempo y no cumplieron la totalidad de los requisitos y el 1,49% además de no cumplir la totalidad de los requisitos pactados fueron entregados fuera de costo [8].

En el 2017 se realizó otro diagnóstico a una muestra del 28,13% donde se conoció que el 48% de los proyectos culminados lo hicieron exitosamente, el 20% fueron cancelados y el 32% fueron fallidos. También se identificó que el porciento de implementación del proceso de IR alcanzaba el 48% [10].

Por todo lo descrito anteriormente se puede afirmar que el proceso en cuestión no es maduro y se reconoce la necesidad de establecer actividades que brinden una mayor retroalimentación con el cliente.

Las organizaciones desarrolladoras de software en Cuba han utilizado la NC-ISO 9001 y CMMI para alcanzar niveles de madurez en sus procesos de desarrollo [11], a la par se trabaja en la elaboración de un Modelo de la Calidad para el Desarrollo de Aplicaciones Informáticas (MCDAI) por CALISOFT con el fin brindar a la industria un modelo sustentado en las mejores prácticas internacionales que tenga en cuenta las características nacionales y se base en los siguientes principios: fácil de entender, fácil de aplicar y sirva de base para alcanzar evaluaciones en otros modelos reconocidos internacionalmente [12].

Teniendo en cuenta lo planteado anteriormente el objetivo de esta investigación es elaborar un proceso de Ingeniería de requisitos para el MCDAI que contribuya a elevar los porcientos de proyectos exitosos, en las organizaciones desarrolladora de software en Cuba, respecto al cumplimiento de los requisitos pactados.

2. Materiales y métodos

Como parte de la construcción del marco teórico de la investigación se realizó una revisión bibliográfica [13-18], lo que permitió conceptualizar el término *requisitos* como: necesidad o expectativa establecida, generalmente implícita u obligatoria, que expresa una condición o capacidad demandada por las partes interesadas o la organización, que debe cumplir o poseer un proceso, producto o componente de producto para solucionar un problema o lograr un objetivo y para satisfacer un contrato, norma, especificación u otro documento impuesto formalmente.

Para garantizar el correcto tratamiento de los requisitos durante el proceso de desarrollo de software surge la disciplina IR. En la tabla 1 se muestra las buenas prácticas según la bibliografía revisada [7, 13, 15, 16, 19-23].

Tabla 1. Buenas prácticas en el proceso de IR (elaboración propia).

No.	**Buenas prácticas**	**Pressman**	**Sommerville**	**NC ISO 9001**	**ISO/IEC/IEEE 12207 y 15288**	**CMMI – DEV y MPS. Br**	**MoProSoft y COMPETISOF**	**SWEBOK**
1	Concepción o creación de las bases para la ingeniería de requisitos	x	x	x	x	x	x	x
2	Desarrollo de requisitos	x	x	x	x	x	x	x
3	Recabación de requisitos	x	x	x	x	x	x	x
4	Especificación de requisitos	x	x		x	x	x	x
5	Elaboración del modelo de los requisitos	x			x	x	x	x
6	Identificar los requisitos de interfaz				x	x		
7	Establecer los conceptos y los escenarios de operación				x	x		x
8	Establecer una definición de la funcionalidad y de los atributos de calidad requeridos.				x	x		
9	Análisis y negociación	x	x		x	x	x	x
10	Validación de los requisitos	x	x	x	x	x	x	x
11	Gestión de requisitos	x	x	x		x	x	x
12	Identificación de manera única cada requisito	x	x	x				
13	Comprender los requisitos				x	x		

14	Obtener el compromiso sobre los requisitos				x	x	x	
15	Control de los cambios de los requisitos	x	x	x		x	x	x
16	Mantener trazabilidad de los requisitos	x	x	x	x	x	x	x
17	Asegurar el alineamiento entre el trabajo del proyecto y los requisitos					x	x	

Durante la revisión de las Normas Internacionales ISO/IEC/IEEE 12207 y 15288 se identificó que las actividades que proponen para IR son similares, en el caso de los modelos CMMI y MPS. Br también tienen enfoques análogos. Vale resaltar que como parte de la actividad de recabación de los requisitos se educen las necesidades de las partes interesadas y se trasforman en los requisitos de estos. Posteriormente esos requisitos evolucionan como parte de la especificación en los requisitos del producto a desarrollar. También se identificó la tendencia en estos modelos de referencia la inclusión del enfoque de gestión de reutilización de software como proceso de crear sistemas de software a partir de software existente, aplicando ingeniería de dominio, ya que este enfoque ha dotado a muchas organizaciones de ventajas competitivas en el mercado en cuando a calidad del producto, tiempo de desarrollo, costos de producción, entre otros [24-27].

El principal resultado del análisis de los sistemas aplicando ingeniería de dominio es el modelo de dominio, el cual describe a un alto nivel de abstracción las diversas familias de aplicaciones de un dominio específico, como objetivo además de captar los elementos comunes y variantes de la familia para una correcta gestión de la variabilidad de los productos resultantes [23].

2.1. Representación de los resultados de la investigación

La capacidad de adaptación de los procesos al mercado o a los clientes hace que los modelos de gestión, orientados a la calidad, centren su atención en los procesos como la palanca más potente para actuar sobre los resultados, de forma efectiva y sostenida a lo largo del tiempo [28, 29]. La investigadora Pérez plantea que el MCDAI tiene un enfoque a proceso, que se estructura en procesos bases y que estos a su vez están compuestos por un propósito; requisitos divididos por los niveles Básico, Intermedio y Avanzado; y elementos sugeridos entre los que se encuentra la descripción gráfica y textual del proceso ejemplo que dé cumplimiento a los requisitos [12].

Los resultados de esta investigación se elaboraron con la premisa que estuvieran alineados a la estructura del MCDAI. Para modelar el proceso de IR fue necesario analizar las técnicas de representación gráfica o textual: diagrama de flujo, carriles de notación, IDEF, ETVX, notación de modelado de proceso de negocio (BPMN, por sus siglas en inglés) y descripción textual [30-35]. Esto permitió, a los autores de esta investigación, identificar que la combinación BPMN y descripción textual son la variante más óptima porque: permiten una notación gráfica que describe la lógica de los pasos de un proceso de negocio; coordina la secuencia de los procesos y los mensajes que fluyen entre los participantes de las diferentes actividades; permite modelar los procesos de una manera unificada y estandarizada lo que facilita un entendimiento a todas las personas en la organización; explica las actividades y abarca la información sobre las necesidades del proceso, cuándo comienza, cuánto dura, las personas involucradas, la duración, cómo se ejecutan las actividades, cuándo termina y los diferentes escenarios que se pueden presentar [11].

3. Resultados

3.1. Modelo de la calidad

Como resultado de la investigación se definió un proceso de IR con el **propósito** de identificar los requisitos de las partes interesadas para un producto de software con el fin de que pueda proporcionar las capacidades necesitadas por estos, en un entorno determinado y transformar la visión orientada hacia las partes interesadas en una visión técnica que satisfaga las necesidades operativas de los usuarios.

Para darle complimiento a este propósito y basados en las buenas prácticas identificadas en la IR como parte de la construcción del marco teórico se propuso un conjunto de requisitos específicos (ver tabla 2[1]) divididos por los tres niveles de madurez que plantea el MCDAI (básico, intermedio y avanzado) [12] con el fin de facilitar que las organizaciones que lo adopten puedan realizar la mejora de proceso de manera escalonada con pequeños cambios.

Tabla 2. Requisitos específicos del proceso IR.

Nivel Avanzado
IR 2.1 Homologar requisitos técnicos.
IR 5.1 Modelar requisitos en función de la reutilización.
IR 6 Establecer la trazabilidad bidireccional. (15)
Aseguramiento de la Calidad (AC) 6 Ejecutar revisiones de inconsistencias. (17)
Nivel Intermedio
IR 2.2 Priorizar requisitos. (4)
IR 5 Modelar los requisitos técnicos. (5 y 7)
Nivel Básico
IR 1 Definir los requisitos de las partes interesadas pertinentes. (1 y 3)
IR 2 Analizar y especificar los requisitos. (4, 6 y 8)
IR 3 Lograr entendimiento y compromiso de los requisitos. (9, 13, 14)
IR 4 validar los requisitos técnicos. (10)
Gestión de la Configuración (GCf) 4 Controlar los cambios. (15)

3.2. Proceso y actividades

Como parte de la solución se propone la descripción gráfica (ver Fig. 1) y textual del proceso IR como ejemplo de cómo poner en práctica los requisitos específicos.

[1] En la tabla se pueden los enunciados de los requisitos, distribuidos por los niveles y entre paréntesis se relaciona a las buenas prácticas identificadas en la tabla 1.

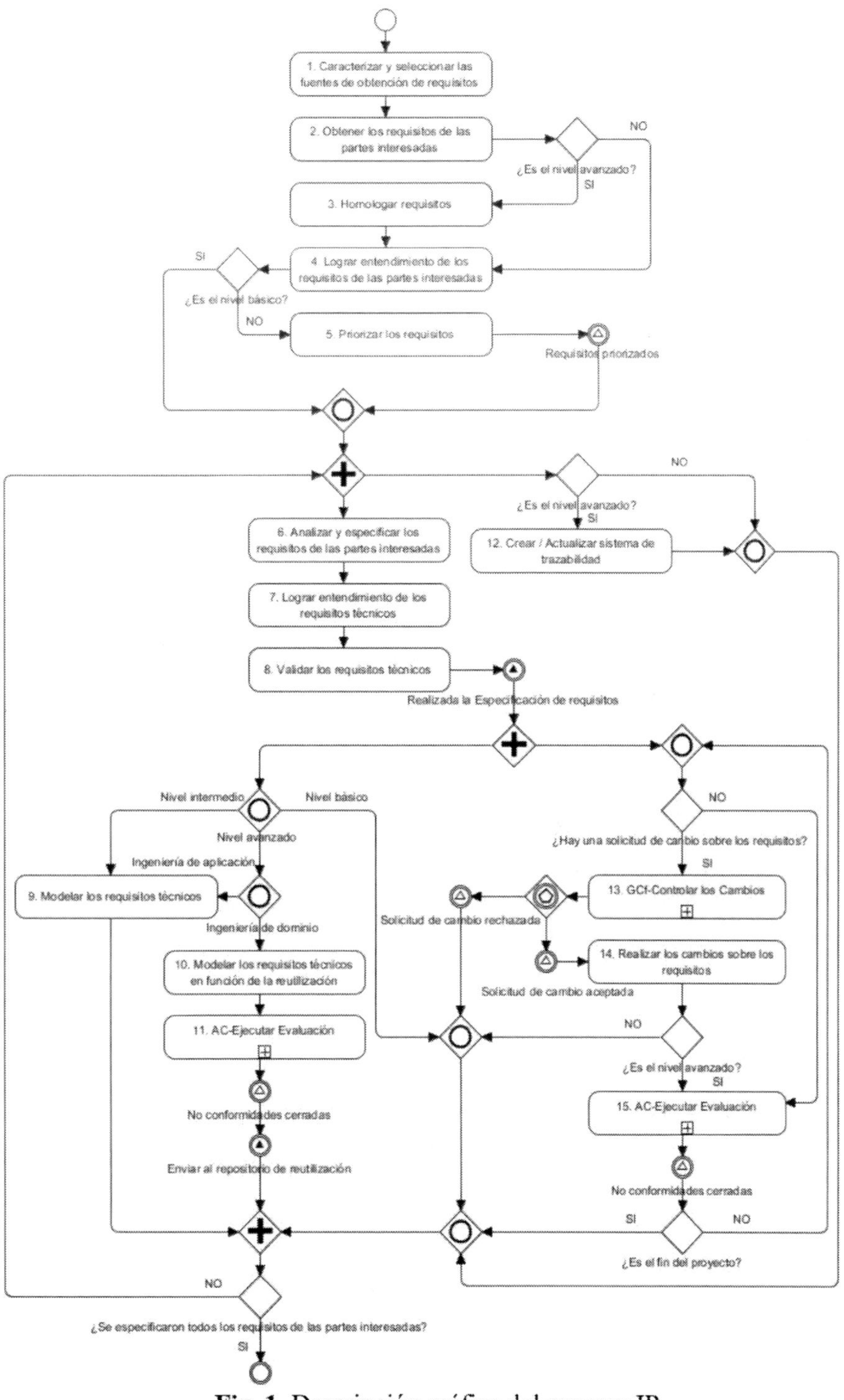

Fig. 1. Descripción gráfica del proceso IR.

A continuación, la descripción textual.

1. Caracterizar y seleccionar las fuentes de obtención de requisitos.

El Analista y el Cliente teniendo en cuenta las partes interesadas que fueron identificadas en GP – Gestión de Proyecto [36], determinan las fuentes de obtención de requisitos y las caracterizan. Para el nivel Avanzado, cuando se aplique ingeniería de dominio, el desarrollo va dirigido a una familia de aplicaciones, por lo tanto, la fuente de obtención de requisitos varía de clientes específicos a estudios de mercados y de negocios; cuando se aplique ingeniería de aplicaciones las fuentes están dadas por los activos de dominios definidos y el cliente específico.

El Analista, Jefe de Proyecto y Cliente seleccionan las fuentes de obtención de requisitos teniendo en cuenta su caracterización y el (los) proveedor(es) que representan los intereses de los clientes, en caso que aplique, y se responsabilice con brindar los requisitos necesarios.

Se obtiene como resultado de la ejecución de esta actividad la "Lista de fuentes de obtención de requisitos".

2. Obtener los requisitos de las partes interesadas.

El Analista teniendo en cuenta la "Lista de fuentes de obtención de requisitos", la "Oferta" y/o "Proyecto técnico" elaboradas cuando se concibió el proyecto: analiza los requisitos que se necesitarían para dar cumplimiento a los objetivos del proyecto; entrevista a los proveedores de requisitos para identificar sus necesidades y expectativas; caracteriza los entornos de operación de la organización; elabora un listado de requisitos y restricciones a partir de las necesidades y expectativas identificadas; refina el listado de requisitos como resultado del entendimiento con los proveedores; muestra la Lista de requisitos y restricciones a los proveedores, en caso de no estar satisfechos vuelve a identificar/mejorar los requisitos auxiliándose de técnicas (ejemplo; prototipo, grupo focal, casos de uso del negocio, modelo de procesos del negocio, entre otros).

Para el nivel Avanzado, cuando se aplique ingeniería de dominio, la obtención de los requisitos se realiza a través de estudios de mercado y de negocios, y el análisis de proyectos pasados. En estos casos, por lo general el proyecto no tiene un cliente específico, ya que se trabaja en la elaboración de un producto genérico; por tal motivo el análisis para resolver los conflictos entre requisitos se realiza con los expertos funcionales. Cuando se aplique ingeniería de aplicaciones, la obtención se realiza analizando los activos de dominio existentes con el cliente específico, para ello se tiene en cuenta los elementos comunes y variantes, opcionales u obligatorios, en caso de ser necesario, adoptarlos o diseñar nuevos requisitos.

Se obtiene como resultado de la ejecución de esta actividad la "Lista de requisitos y restricciones".

3. Homologar requisitos.

A partir del nivel Avanzado, el Analista teniendo en cuenta la "Lista de requisitos y restricciones": realiza un estudio de mercado en el dominio de aplicación correspondiente con el objetivo de identificar productos similares; homologa los requisitos de las partes interesadas con las funcionalidades de los productos similares con el objetivo de definir requisitos adicionales y comprobar que las necesidades funcionales identificadas corresponden a este tipo de producto.

Se obtiene como resultado de la ejecución de esta actividad el "Estudio de mercado" con nuevos requisitos en los casos que aplique.

4. Lograr entendimiento de los requisitos de las partes interesadas.

El Analista y las Partes interesadas, teniendo en cuenta el "Estudio de mercado", identifican nuevos requisitos.

El Analista teniendo en cuenta la "Lista de requisitos y restricciones", identifica los conflictos entre los requisitos y realiza propuestas de cómo eliminarlos auxiliándose de expertos funcionales.

El Analista y las Partes interesadas se reúnen para llegar a un consenso sobre la resolución de los conflictos identificados teniendo en cuenta la propuesta realizada.

El Equipo de proyecto y los proveedores de requisitos logran un entendimiento común de la "Lista de requisitos y restricciones".

Se obtiene como resultado de la ejecución de esta actividad la "Lista de requisitos y restricciones" (Actualizada).

5. Priorizar los requisitos.

A partir del nivel Intermedio el Analista teniendo en cuenta la "Lista de requisitos y restricciones": identifica el método apropiado para la priorización de requisitos de las partes interesadas (Ejemplos: análisis jerárquico, voto acumulativo, asignación numérica, priorización basada en valor, costo y riesgos, entre otras); prioriza los requisitos utilizando el método apropiado.

Se obtiene como resultado de la ejecución de esta actividad la "Lista de requisitos y restricciones" con los requisitos priorizados.

6. Analizar y especificar los requisitos de las partes interesadas.

El Analista teniendo en cuenta la "Lista de requisitos y restricciones" con la priorización: agrupa los requisitos funcionales y no funcionales que se correspondan a la iteración; analiza si existen requisitos de proyectos anteriores que puedan reutilizarse; identifica si los requisitos son necesarios o suficientes para desarrollar el producto que satisfaga a las partes interesadas y en caso de requerirlo, identifica nuevos requisitos derivados (requisitos funcionales); refina los requisitos funcionales en cuanto a su descripción y detalles de la funcionalidad; analiza la "Lista de requisitos y restricciones" teniendo en cuenta el Modelo de la calidad del producto de software definido en la NC-ISO/IEC 25010, con el objetivo de identificar requisitos implícitos (requisitos no funcionales); refina los requisitos no funcionales al asignar valores permisibles a los atributos de la calidad que el producto debería tener; revisa la viabilidad de los requisitos funcionales y no funcionales para determinar si son completos, factibles, realizables y verificables. A partir del nivel Intermedio, especifica los requisitos de las interfaces internas y externas del sistema.

Se obtiene como resultado de la ejecución de esta actividad la "Especificación de requisitos"; en lo adelante se tratará como requisitos técnicos.

7. Lograr entendimiento de los requisitos técnicos.

El Analista y las Partes interesadas teniendo en cuenta la “Especificación de requisitos” se reúnen para llegar a un entendimiento común de los requisitos técnicos descritos.

Se obtiene como resultado de la ejecución de esta actividad la “Especificación de requisitos” (Actualizada).

8. Validar los requisitos técnicos.

El Jefe de proyecto, Analista y Cliente, teniendo en cuenta la “Especificación de requisitos”, validan los requisitos técnicos utilizando la técnica de prototipos donde se muestran las posibles interfaces del sistema, y los elementos de entrada y de salida que se van a mostrar al usuario final.

El Analista en caso de surgir algún señalamiento u observación por parte del cliente actualiza la “Especificación de requisitos”.

Se obtiene como resultado de la ejecución de esta actividad la “Especificación de requisitos” (Firmada).

9. Modelar los requisitos técnicos.

A partir del nivel Intermedio el Analista: define el modelo conceptual, estableciendo las relaciones de las entidades del sistema o subsistema y sus atributos fundamentales, futuras clases persistentes y candidatas al modelo de datos; modela los requisitos realizando una descripción técnica (Modelo de Casos de Uso, Escenarios de operación, Modelo de Clases e Historias de Usuarios, en los casos que aplique);

El Jefe de proyecto y el Arquitecto distribuyen los requisitos en los módulos o subsistemas del proyecto.

A partir del nivel Avanzado se tiene en cuenta para la definición del Modelo de análisis del producto que se va a desarrollar a un cliente específico, el Modelo de dominio correspondiente a la familia de aplicaciones al que pertenece.

Se obtiene como resultado de la ejecución de esta actividad el “Modelo de análisis”.

10. Modelar los requisitos técnicos en función de la reutilización.

A partir del nivel Avanzado el Analista: define el modelo de dominio donde se describen sus fronteras con otros dominios y se especifica las características, capacidades, elementos comunes y variantes, opcionales u obligatorios; define el modelo conceptual, estableciendo las relaciones de las entidades que forman parte del dominio y sus atributos fundamentales, futuras clases persistentes y candidatas al modelo de datos estándar para la familia de aplicaciones; modela los requisitos realizando una descripción técnica para la familia de aplicaciones (Modelo de Casos de Uso, Escenarios de operación, Modelo de Clases e Historias de Usuarios; en los casos que aplique)

El Jefe de proyecto y el Arquitecto distribuyen los requisitos en los módulos o subsistemas del proyecto.

Se obtiene como resultado de la ejecución de esta actividad el “Modelo de dominio”.

11. AC-Ejecutar evaluación.

El Equipo de evaluación verifica que el "Modelo de dominio" se encuentre técnicamente correcto guiado por el subproceso AC-Ejecutar Evaluación [11].

Se obtiene como resultado de la ejecución de esta actividad el "Expediente de evaluación".

12. Crear / Actualizar sistema de trazabilidad.

En el nivel Avanzado el Analista teniendo en cuenta la Guía de trazabilidad: inserta en la herramienta seleccionada, a medida que se van elaborando: los objetivos del proyecto, los requisitos de las partes interesadas, los requisitos técnicos, los productos de trabajo y las tareas que le darán cumplimiento a los requisitos pactados; establece las relaciones bidireccionales correspondientes entre los elementos insertados en la herramienta; actualiza la herramienta, en caso de ser necesario, si surge un cambio a los requisitos o productos de trabajo.

Se obtiene como resultado de la ejecución de esta actividad la herramienta de trazabilidad con sus relaciones establecidas.

13. GCf-Controlar los Cambios.

El Comité de control de cambio analiza la petición de cambio sobre los requisitos como establece el subproceso GCf-Controlar los Cambios [37].

Se obtiene como resultado de la ejecución de esta actividad la "Solicitud de cambio" (aceptada).

14. Realizar los cambios sobre los requisitos.

El Analista teniendo en cuenta la "Solicitud de cambio" aceptada, en el nivel Básico e Intermedio, realiza los cambios correspondientes sobre los requisitos y los productos de trabajo relacionados; en el nivel Avanzado, los cambios se realizan auxiliándose de la herramienta de trazabilidad.

Se obtiene como resultado de la ejecución de esta actividad la "Especificación de requisitos" y los artefactos relacionados (actualizados).

15. AC-Ejecutar evaluación.

En el nivel Avanzado el Equipo evaluador ejecuta la revisión de inconsistencia entre los requisitos y los productos de trabajo asociados, teniendo en cuenta la herramienta y la guía de trazabilidad, como establece el subproceso AC-Ejecutar evaluación [11].

Se obtiene como resultado de la ejecución de esta actividad el "Expediente de la evaluación".

3.3. Índice de cumplimiento de requisito

Para medir la influencia del proceso en el éxito de los proyectos de desarrollo de software se propone el indicador **índice de cumplimiento de los requisitos (ICR)**. El mismo tiene como objetivo evaluar el cumplimiento de los requisitos pactados con los clientes. Se considera un requisito incumplido aquel que no haya sido desarrollado o que los resultados que se obtienen después de implementados no son los pactados. Para ello se identifican las siguientes medidas bases (CRP: Cantidad de requisitos pactados; CRI: Cantidad de requisitos implementados). Para calcular el ICR se utiliza la siguiente función de medición $ICR = \frac{CRI}{CRP}$. Los proyectos se consideran exitoso si $ICR > 0{,}95$.

4. Validación

4.1. Análisis de la propuesta teniendo en cuenta grupo focal

Los autores de la presente investigación consideran que los grupos focales constituyen una técnica valiosa y muy utilizada para obtener información. Por tal motivo decidieron su uso para conocer si la propuesta de solución emplea la terminología correcta y es técnicamente viable. Para su conformación se tuvo en cuenta los criterios emitidos por Aigneren y Méndez [38, 39], los que plantean que el tamaño del grupo debe oscilar entre 4 y 12 participantes; que todos los participantes tenga la posibilidad de emitir sus criterios; y que el grupo debe ser homogéneo con el fin de asegurar la diversidad de ideas. Para cumplir con lo antes expuesto se convocaron a 12 especialistas, con más de 5 años de experiencia en los roles de analista y arquitecto. Los seleccionados representaban las organizaciones CALISOFT, DESOFT, XETID, ETECSA, TRANSOFT, EICMA, AICROS y SEGURMÁTICA [40]. El resultado final fue un proceso de IR enriquecido con las experiencias de cada participante y el criterio unánime de que es una propuesta aceptada que se ajusta a las necesidades de las organizaciones desarrolladoras de software en Cuba.

4.2. Análisis de la implementación del proceso en proyectos pilotos

Después se dispuso a evaluar, mediante un pre-experimento, que al introducir el proceso de IR en proyectos de desarrollo de software se aumenta el éxito de los proyectos de un 48%, respecto a la dimensión de la variable índice de cumplimiento de los requisitos pactados.

Sampieri plantea que el preexperimento se puede hacer mediante un estudio de casos con una sola medición o a través del diseño de preprueba - postprueba con un solo grupo [41]. Al analizar las 2 opciones, se constató que en la primera no hay manipulación de las variables independientes y no se cuenta con una referencia previa de cuál era la situación antes de realizar el estímulo. En la segunda hay un punto de referencia inicial para ver qué nivel tenía el grupo en las variables dependientes antes del estímulo, permitiendo un seguimiento.

Teniendo en cuenta lo antes expuesto, el autor de esta investigación seleccionó la segunda variante, sabiendo que los 2 diseños preexperimentales no son adecuados para el establecimiento de relaciones entre las variables independientes y dependientes. Pero los considera importantes porque pueden arrojar resultados que al compararlos con los de otros métodos ayudan a llegar a conclusiones finales.

Para poner en práctica el preexperimento se seleccionaron 6 proyectos de 3 organizaciones diferentes (DATYS, AICROS y TRANSOFT). Para ellos se tuvieron en cuenta los siguientes aspectos: que esté finalizada la etapa de levantamiento de requisitos; que el cierre del proyecto esté establecido antes de los 6 meses y que el equipo de trabajo no exceda los 6 especialistas.

Al finalizar el piloto en los proyectos como parte del preexperimento se alcanzó un 83,33% en los proyectos exitoso teniendo en cuenta el índice de cumplimiento de los requisitos (ICR) pactados. Según la tabla 2 el proyecto 2 fue el que no cumplió el indicador.

Tabla 3. ICP por proyecto.

Proyectos	ICR	Proyectos	ICR
P1	1	P4	1
P2	0.90	P5	1
P3	0.99	P6	0.97

Los resultados permitieron a los autores de la investigación apreciar una mejoría en el éxito de los proyectos teniendo en cuenta la dimensión de la variable ICR, después de introducir el proceso propuesto.

4.3. Satisfacción de los usuarios finales

La técnica de V.A. Iadov fue creada por N. V. Kuzmina en 1970 para el estudio de la satisfacción por las carreras pedagógicas. Posteriormente ha sido utilizada en varias investigaciones para evaluar la satisfacción en disimiles contextos. La misma está conformada por 5 preguntas: 3 cerradas y 2 abiertas. Iadov constituye una vía indirecta para el estudio de la satisfacción, ya que los criterios que se utilizan se fundamentan en las relaciones que se establecen entre 3 preguntas cerradas que se relacionan a través de lo que se denomina el "Cuadro Lógico de Iadov". En la presente investigación se utiliza para evaluar la satisfacción de los proyectos pilotos (usuarios) respecto al proceso IR.

Luego de aplicar la encuesta a los 6 analistas y 6 arquitectos relacionados con los proyectos en piloto. Se calculó el índice de satisfacción grupal (ISG).

$$ISG = \frac{A(+1)+B(+2)+C(0)+D(-0.5)+E(-1)}{N} = \frac{12(+1)+0(+2)+0(0)+0(-0.5)+0(-1)}{12} = 1$$

El ISG = 1 significa el máximo de satisfacción por la propuesta del proceso base propuesto. Lo cual se corrobora en las respuestas de las preguntas 6 y 7, donde los encuestados expresaron que no cambiarían nada del proceso porque se ajusta a sus necesidades.

5. Conclusiones

Como parte de la revisión bibliográfica se obtuvo las principales buenas prácticas para la IR agrupadas en: 1) desarrollo de requisitos, donde se identifican las partes interesadas, sus necesidades y se especifican los requisitos y 2) gestión de requisitos, donde se identifican de forma única los requisitos, se controlan sus cambios y se mantiene la trazabilidad.

La descripción gráfica y textual del proceso IR constituye una guía para adoptar los requisitos del MCDAI divididos por los tres niveles de madurez y facilitar su adopción.

Incorporar actividades de retroalimentación con los clientes en el proceso de IR es un factor que influye en el éxito del proyecto, porque permite identificar los cambios necesarios a los requisitos, en el momento oportuno, con el fin de que el producto responda a sus necesidades y expectativas.

La validación de la propuesta, contribuyó a constatar que existe conformidad con el proceso propuesto por parte de usuarios, y que la ejecución del proceso puede contribuir al éxito de los mismos.

Se recomienda medir el impacto del proceso en la volatilidad de los requisitos con el fin de contribuir a que se cumpla la planificación del proyecto.

6. Referencias

1. The Standish Group International, *Chaos Report 2015*. 2015.
2. Rosato, M., *Go Small for Project Success*. PM World Journal, 2018. **VII**(V).
3. Lehtinen, T.O., et al., *Perceived causes of software project failures–An analysis of their relationships*. Information and Software Technology, 2014. **56**(6): p. 623-643.
4. McLeod, L. and S.G. MacDonell, *Factors that affect software systems development project outcomes: A survey of research*. ACM Computing Surveys (CSUR), 2011. **43**(4): p. 24.
5. The Standish Group International, *The Standish Group Report*. 2014.
6. del Toro, A.A., *Una mirada desde el desarrollo ágil a los Requisitos de Software. Experiencias en Datys Villa Clara*, in *Taller 2 - Ingeniería de Requisitos*, S.-I.d.S.y. Sistemas, Editor. 2018.
7. Pressman, R.S., *Ingeniería de software. Un enfoque práctico*. Séptima edición ed, ed. S.A.D.C.V. McGRAW-HILL Interamericana Editores. 2010, México. 102.
8. CALISOFT, C.N.d.C.d.S., *CS-03-D (14-001) Libro de diagnóstico*. 2014.
9. Pérez, D.M. and D.Q. Aveleira, *Evolución del Modelo de la Calidad para el Desarrollo de Aplicaciones Informáticas*, in *XVI Convención y Feria Internacional Informática 2016*. 2016: La Habana.
10. CALISOFT, C.N.d.C.d.S., *CS-03-D (17-001) Libro de Diagnóstico*. 2017.
11. Lazo, Y.A., *Proceso Base de Aseguramiento de la Calidad para el Desarrollo de Software en Cuba*. 2016, Universidad de las Ciencias Informáticas.
12. Pérez, D.M., *Guía general para un Modelo Cubano de Desarrollo de Aplicaciones Informáticas*. 2014, Universidad de las Ciencias Informáticas.
13. Sommerville, I., *Ingeniería de software*. Novena Edición ed, ed. P. Educación. 2011, México. 85.
14. Goguen, J.A., *Requirements engineering as the reconciliation of social and technical issues*. San Diego: Academic Press Professional ed. 1994.
15. IEEE, *SWEBOK. Guide to the Software Engineering Body of Knowledge*. Versión 3 ed. 2014. 3.
16. Team, C.P., *CMMI® for Development, Version 1.3, Improving processes for developing better products and services*. no. CMU/SEI-2010-TR-033. Software Engineering Institute, 2010.
17. Oficina Nacional de Normalización, *NC ISO 9000 Sistema de Gestión de la Calidad - Fundamentos y Vocabulario*. 2015.
18. ISO, I.O.f.S., I.E.C. IEC, and IEEE, *ISO/IEC/IEEE 12207, Systems and software engineering — Software life cycle processes*. 2017.

19. Oficina Nacional de Normalización, *NC ISO 9001 Sistema de Gestión de la Calidad — Requisitos*. 2015.
20. ISO, O.I.d.E., *ISO/IEC/IEEE 15288 Systems and software engineering — System life cycle processes*. 2015.
21. COMPETISOFT, P., *COMPETISOFT-Mejora de Procesos para Fomentar la Competitividad de la Pequeña y Mediana Industria del Software de Iberoamérica. Versión 0.2*. Diciembre, 2006.
22. Oktaba, H., *Modelo de Procesos para la Industria de Software-MoproSoft-Versión 1.3, Agosto de 2005*. 2005, NMX-059/01-NYCE-2005.
23. Montoni, M.A., A.R. Rocha, and K.C. Weber, *MPS. BR: a successful program for software process improvement in Brazil*. Software Process: Improvement and Practice, 2009. **14**(5): p. 289-300.
24. Bastarrica, C., *Productividad en la Industria TIC*. Bits, 2011.
25. Salazar, L.L., *Desarrollo del proceso Solución Técnica para los proyectos de desarrollo de la Universidad de la Ciencias Informáticas*. 2017, Universidad de las Ciencias Informáticas (UCI).
26. Northrop, L., et al., *A framework for software product line practice, version 5.0*. SEI.–2007–http://www. sei. cmu. edu/productlines/index. html, 2007.
27. Manso Martínez, M. and F.J. García Peñalvo, *Medición en la Reutilización Orientada a Objetos*. 2013.
28. Concepción, M.R., *De la Gestión de Procesos a la Gestión por Procesos*. Ciencias Holguín, 2010. **10**(2).
29. Zaratiegui, J.R., *La gestión por procesos: su papel e importancia en la empresa*. Economía industrial, 1999(330): p. 81-88.
30. Suárez, B.A., *Marco de procesos para las Entidades de Servicios de Tecnología de la Información de la Universidad de las Ciencias Informáticas*. 2013, Universidad de las Ciencias Informáticas (UCI).
31. Silega, M.N., *Método para la Transformación Automatizada de Modelos de Procesos de Negocio a Modelos de Componentes para Sistemas de Gestión Empresarial*. 2014, Universidad de las Ciencias Informáticas (UCI).
32. MANENE, L.M., *Los diagramas de flujo: su definición, objetivo, ventajas, elaboración, fases, reglas y ejemplos de aplicaciones*. Los diagramas de flujo, 2013.
33. Medina, Y.T., *Modelado de procesos con IDEF en la metodología RUP*. Serie Científica-Universidad de las Ciencias Informáticas, 2012. **5**(2).
34. Murcia-Oeste–Arrixaca, Á.I., *Manual para el diseño de procesos*. 2013.
35. Losavio, F., J.C. Guzmán, and A. Matteo, *Correspondencia Semántica entre los lenguajes BPMN y GRL*. Enl@ ce, 2011. **8**(1).
36. Suárez, B.A., et al., *Modelo de Calidad para el Desarrollo de Aplicaciones Informáticas: categoría de Gestión de Proyecto*, in *XVI Convención y Feria Internacional Informática 2016*. 2016: La Habana.
37. García, Y.G., *Proceso Base Gestión de la Configuración para un Modelo de Calidad en Cuba*. 2017, Universidad de las Ciencias Informáticas.
38. Aigneren, M., *La técnica de recolección de información mediante grupos focales. La Sociología en sus escenarios*. 2009.
39. Méndez, A.L.d., *La entrevista y los grupos focales*. 2007.
40. Lazo, A.Y., et al., *Apuntes sobre el Modelo de la Calidad para el Desarrollo de Aplicaciones Informáticas (MCDAI)*, in *XVII Convención y Feria Internacional Informática 2018*. 2018: La Habana.
41. Hernández, S.R., C.C. Fernández, and L.P. Baptista, *Metodología de la investigación*, ed. S. edición. 1991.

Padrão de Requisitos no Ciclo de Vida de Software: Um Mapeamento Sistemático

Taciana N. Kudo[1,3], Renato F. Bulcão-Neto[1], Alessandra A. Macedo[2], and Auri M. R. Vincenzi[3]

[1] Instituto de Informática, Universidade Federal de Goiás, Goiânia-GO, Brasil
{taciana,renato}@inf.ufg.br
[2] Depto. de Computação e Matemática, FFCLRP-USP, Ribeirão Preto-SP, Brasil
ale.alaniz@usp.br
[3] Depto. de Computação, UFSCAR, São Carlos-SP, Brasil
auri@dc.ufscar.br

Resumo Pesquisas demonstram que a prática de reúso por meio de padrões de requisitos é uma alternativa eficaz para tratar problemas de qualidade de especificação, com o benefício adicional de economia de tempo. Acredita-se que, em função das interações existentes entre a engenharia de requisitos e demais fases do ciclo de vida de software, esses benefícios se estenderão para todo o processo de desenvolvimento. Este artigo descreve um estudo secundário que identifica e analisa pesquisas que evidenciam tais benefícios com o uso de padrões de requisitos nas fases de projeto, construção, teste e manutenção. Realizou-se um mapeamento sistemático, cujo protocolo inclui busca automática em 4 bases de dados e a aplicação de critérios de inclusão e exclusão sobre 218 estudos, dos quais selecionaram-se 9 estudos primários para análise e síntese. Identificou-se uma carência de estudos relacionados ao objeto desta pesquisa, sendo a maioria relacionada a projeto de software, e nenhum a manutenção. Além disso, apenas um dos estudos analisados caracteriza-se como pesquisa de validação com estudo de caso, enquanto que os demais são propostas de solução, sem avaliação empírica, ou prática. Portanto, existe um campo aberto para pesquisas que explorem e comprovem, com avaliações empíricas e uso na prática, os benefícios de reúso com padrões de requisitos no ciclo de vida de software.

Keywords: Padrão de requisito · ciclo de vida de software · mapeamento sistemático

1 Introdução

Embora seja consenso que a Engenharia de Requisitos é uma atividade de extrema importância, na qual as funcionalidades e restrições do software devem ser bem identificadas e compreendidas, uma alta porcentagem de projetos de software não cumpre prazos e orçamento planejados, devido à documentação incompleta, com requisitos mal interpretados, conflitantes ou omitidos [21,17].

O reúso por meio de padrão de requisitos é uma abordagem que tem sido bastante explorada com o objetivo de melhorar a qualidade da documentação de requisitos de software [7,17]. Um padrão de requisito é uma abstração que reúne comportamentos e serviços de aplicações com características semelhantes, os quais podem ser replicados em documentações futuras. Um padrão de requisito serve também como um modelo para especificação de um novo requisito [24].

Por exemplo, para escrever um requisito de autenticação de usuário, é possível utilizar um padrão de requisito para esse fim, fazendo as devidas adaptações no requisito, se necessário. Na literatura são encontradas várias propostas de padrões de requisitos, por exemplo, para sistemas embarcados [14], sistemas gerenciadores de conteúdo [18] e sistemas de computação em nuvem [3]. Dentre os benefícios obtidos com a adoção de padrões de requisitos, têm-se: maior eficiência na elicitação, pois os requisitos não são identificados do zero; melhoria na qualidade e consistência no documento de especificação; e melhoria no gerenciamento dos requisitos [24].

Devido à interação inerente entre a engenharia de requisitos e as demais fases do ciclo de vida de software, pressupõe-se que os benefícios advindos do uso de padrões de requisitos podem alcançar as outras atividades de desenvolvimento. Embora existam estudos secundários sobre engenharia de software [19], engenharia de requisitos [15] e padrões de requisitos [7,2], não existem evidências em estudos dessa natureza que analisem o uso de padrões de requisitos nas demais fases do processo de desenvolvimento de software. Em suma, os estudos secundários existentes restringem-se a analisar a adoção de padrões de requisitos particularmente na fase de engenharia de requisitos.

Sendo assim, o objetivo deste artigo consiste em apresentar um estudo secundário na forma de um mapeamento sistemático, que identifica e analisa estudos primários que evidenciam o uso de padrões de requisitos nas fases de projeto, construção, teste e manutenção de software[4].

A metodologia definida apóia-se em trabalhos clássicos de estudos secundários em Engenharia de Software [12,19,8] com suporte da ferramenta *StArt*[5] para o planejamento e a condução do protocolo do mapeamento sistemático. Buscas automáticas foram realizadas em 4 bases de dados [9] e critérios de inclusão e exclusão foram aplicados para identificar os estudos relevantes.

Como resultado da aplicação do protocolo, foram identificados e analisados 9 estudos relevantes, classificados segundo o tipo de pesquisa realizado e o tipo de contribuição do padrão de requisito nas fases citadas, resultando no mapeamento de lacunas relacionadas a padrões de requisitos no ciclo de vida de software.

Este artigo está organizado como segue: a Seção 2 detalha o protocolo do mapeamento sistemático; a Seção 3 reporta a extração de dados dos estudos relevantes. As respostas às questões de pesquisa deste estudo e as lacunas de pesquisa estão sintetizadas na Seção 4. Por fim, a Seção 5 expõe as ameaças à validade deste estudo sistemático, bem como nossas considerações finais.

---

[4] Neste artigo, adotar-se-á a terminologia das fases do ciclo de vida de software proposta no SWEBOK (*Software Engineering Body of Knowledge*) [4].

[5] Disponível para download em `http://lapes.dc.ufscar.br/tools/start_tool`.

2 Protocolo do Mapeamento Sistemático

Um processo de estudo sistemático pode ser dividido em três fases principais [9]: planejamento, condução e publicação dos resultados. No planejamento, define-se um protocolo de modo que o estudo possa ser replicado futuramente. São integrantes desse protocolo: questões de pesquisa, estratégia de busca, *string* de busca, fontes de pesquisa e critérios de inclusão e exclusão dos estudos.

Na fase de condução, faz-se a identificação e seleção dos estudos relevantes, segundo os critérios definidos no protocolo. Desses estudos são extraídos dados, a partir dos quais faz-se uma síntese para responder às questões de pesquisa do protocolo. O mapeamento sistemático aqui apresentado seguiu essas fases.

2.1 Questões de Pesquisa e Palavras-chave

O principal objetivo deste mapeamento sistemático é identificar propostas de uso de padrões de requisitos e o seu impacto nas demais fases do ciclo de vida de software, além da engenharia de requisitos. Para atender a esse objetivo, as questões de pesquisa (**QP**) que se deseja responder são:

QP1. Em quais fases do ciclo de vida de software são usados padrões de requisitos: projeto, construção, teste e/ou manutenção?

QP2. Há evidências de uso prático de padrões de requisitos nessas fases do ciclo de vida de software?

QP3. Há benefícios relatados do uso de padrão de requisitos nessas fases? Se sim, quais métricas são utilizadas para medir esses benefícios?

Para responder adequadamente às questões de pesquisa, é necessário seguir uma estratégia de busca apropriada [9]. Para fundamentar a definição de termos padronizados da Engenharia de Software, os termos de pesquisa foram definido de acordo com o SEVOCAB[6]. Como resultado, chegou-se ao seguinte conjunto de palavras-chave em inglês: *requirement pattern, development process, software development, life cycle, design, construction, coding, implementation, test, integration* e *maintenance*.

2.2 Estratégia de Busca

Com base nas palavras-chave, e em busca de equilíbrio entre abrangência[7] e relevância dos resultados, foi definida a seguinte *string* de busca:

(“*requirement pattern*” OR “*requirement patterns*” OR
“*requirements pattern*” OR “*requirements patterns*”)
AND ((“*software development*” OR “*development process*”) OR
(“*life cycle*” OR *design* OR *construction* OR *coding* OR
implementation OR *test* OR *integration* OR *maintenance*))

[6] *Software and Systems Engineering Vocabulary* é uma iniciativa da ISO/IEEE de padronizar os termos utilizados na área de Engenharia de Software [11]

[7] Variações em inglês do termo “padrão de requisito” foram usadas em função das capacidades das máquinas de busca das fontes de pesquisa escolhidas.

Foram escolhidas 4 fontes de pesquisa relevantes (*ACM DL*, *Engineering Village*, *IEEE Xplorer* e *Scopus*) sobre as quais foram realizadas buscas sobre os metadados dos estudos. Como resultado, foram identificados 218 estudos[8], assim distribuídos: *ACM Digital Library* (24), *Engineering Village* (100), *IEEE Xplorer* (23) e *Scopus* (71). No caso da *ACM DL*, a busca foi expandida para *The ACM Guide to Computing Literature* por incluir uma coleção maior de artigos.

2.3 Identificação e Seleção dos Estudos Primários

Esta seção descreve o método utilizado para selecionar, dentre os 218 estudos identificados, quais são relevantes para responder às questões de pesquisa deste mapeamento sistemático. Um conjunto de 7 (sete) critérios de exclusão foi definido e aplicado a esses estudos. Os critérios de exclusão (CE) são:

CE1 - Não é um estudo primário.
CE2 - Não é um artigo (p.ex. prefácio/sumário de periódicos/anais de eventos).
CE3 - Não é relacionado com padrões de requisitos de software.
CE4 - Aborda padrões de requisitos apenas na fase de engenharia de requisitos.
CE5 - O texto completo do estudo não está em inglês.
CE6 - Não foi possível acessar o texto completo do estudo.
CE7 - É uma versão preliminar ou reduzida de outro estudo (não adiciona informação relevante).

Quando um estudo se encaixa em pelo menos um critério de exclusão, ele está automaticamente excluído do mapeamento. Caso contrário, o estudo deverá ser categorizado em um critério de inclusão (CI):

CI1 - Aborda padrões de requisitos na fase de projeto de software.
CI2 - Aborda padrões de requisitos na fase de construção de software.
CI3 - Aborda padrões de requisitos na fase de teste de software.
CI4 - Aborda padrões de requisitos na fase de manutenção de software.

O processo completo de seleção dos estudos primários pode ser visualizado na Figura 1, na qual são descritas também as quantidades de estudos selecionados em cada uma das atividades da fase de condução deste mapeamento sistemático.

Após a atividade de busca sobre as fontes de pesquisa, foi realizada a identificação e eliminação de 111 estudos duplicados. Em seguida, iniciou-se a leitura do título, resumo e palavras-chave de cada um dos 117 estudos restantes, sobre os quais foram aplicados os critérios de exclusão e inclusão. Como resultado, foram selecionados 39 estudos potencialmente relevantes, pois esta seleção baseou-se apenas na leitura e interpretação do conteúdo dos respectivos metadados.

Na atividade de extração dos dados, descrita na próxima seção, foi realizada a leitura na íntegra de cada um desses 39 estudos e constatou-se que apenas 9 deles realmente investigam o uso de padrões de requisitos em projeto, construção, teste ou manutenção de software.

[8] A atividade de busca foi realizada no período de 24 de abril a 5 de maio de 2018.

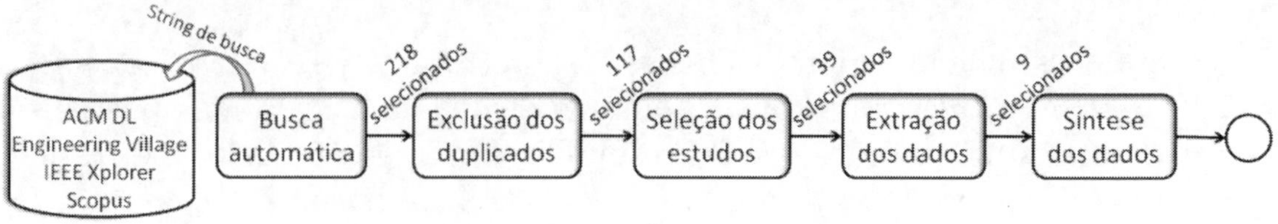

Figura 1. Atividades da fase de condução do Mapeamento Sistemático.

A lista a seguir consiste dos 9 estudos relevantes para extração e síntese (vide Seções 3 e 4), segundo o protocolo definido para este mapeamento sistemático. Esses estudos serão identificados ao longo deste artigo como A1 a A9:

A1 - Adaptive requirement-driven architecture for integrated healthcare systems [25]
A2 - Analysing security requirements patterns based on problems decomposition and composition [23]
A3 - An architectural framework of the integrated transportation information service system [5]
A4 - Application of ontologies in identifying requirements patterns in use cases [6]
A5 - Effective security impact analysis with patterns for software enhancement [16]
A6 - From requirement to design patterns for ubiquitous computing applications [13]
A7 - Modeling design patterns with description logics: A case study [1]
A8 - Mutation patterns for temporal requirements of reactive systems [22]
A9 - SACS: A pattern language for Safe Adaptive Control Software [10]

Quanto à aplicação dos critérios de exclusão, dos 117 artigos não-duplicados, 108 foram excluídos da seguinte maneira: 48% dos artigos (52) foram excluídos por abordarem padrões de requisitos apenas na engenharia de requisitos (**CE4**); 31,5% deles (34) por tratarem de padrões de requisitos, porém não relacionados a software (**CE3**); e os 20,5% restantes (22) pelos demais critérios.

3 Extração dos Dados

Esta seção descreve o processo de extração de dados baseado na leitura completa dos 9 artigos relevantes (A1 a A9) deste estudo. Apresenta-se uma análise comparativa dos tipos de contribuição, bem como o seguinte conteúdo extraído de cada um desses artigos:

1. o tipo de pesquisa apresentado no estudo;
2. o tipo de requisito para o qual o padrão de requisito é proposto;
3. a fase do ciclo de vida a qual o padrão de requisito está relacionado; e
4. o tipo de contribuição apresentada no estudo.

Dado o primeiro critério, os 9 estudos foram classificados pelo tipo de pesquisa desenvolvida, usando para este critério a definição de Petersen et al. [20], em que um conjunto de condições atendidas por uma pesquisa conduzem a uma classificação da mesma. Por exemplo, um artigo de opinião reporta o ponto de vista do autor sobre um assunto, porém sem nenhuma descrição de uso na prática, nem avaliação empírica, relato de experiência do autor, ou proposta de arcabouço conceitual ou de uma nova solução.

Conforme apresenta a Tabela 1, a maioria dos artigos (8 de 9) enquadra-se, pelos critérios de Petersen et al. [20], como "proposta de solução", pois não apresentam avaliação empírica da solução proposta em suas pesquisas. Dessas 8 propostas de solução, 3 apresentam uma prova de conceito informal como validação, sem descrever um estudo de caso, nem um experimento; os outros 5 não validam a solução proposta. Por fim, dentre os 9 artigos relevantes, apenas um foi classificado como "pesquisa de validação" (A7), por apresentar um estudo de caso, embora realizado em ambiente acadêmico.

Tabela 1. Tipos de pesquisa e validação dos artigos relevantes.

Tipo da pesquisa	Tipo de Validação
Proposta de solução	Prova de conceito informal: A2, A5, A9
	Sem validação: A1, A3, A4, A6, A8
Pesquisa de validação	Estudo de caso: A7

Em seguida, foi analisado se havia algum tipo específico de requisito tratado pelos padrões de requisitos propostos. Dos 9 artigos relevantes, 4 deles definem padrão para requisitos de adaptabilidade, 4 para requisitos de segurança e 1 define padrão para requisitos de propósito geral. A Tabela 2 mostra os artigos de acordo com os tipos de requisitos.

Tabela 2. Tipo de requisito considerado no padrão proposto.

Tipo do requisito	Artigos
Requisito de adaptabilidade	A1, A3, A6, A8
Requisito de segurança	A2, A5, A7, A9
Requisito de propósito geral	A4

Foi realizada uma análise comparativa detalhada entre as contribuições propostas em cada um dos trabalhos, a partir da qual pode-se notar algumas similaridades apresentadas a seguir.

Os artigos A1 e A3 propõem uma *arquitetura conceitual* semelhante para sistemas desenvolvidos a partir de padrões de requisitos. A comparação realizada entre essas propostas está representada na Figura 2: as linhas tracejadas A, B, C e D demonstram os pontos em comum entre as arquiteturas propostas por A1 (à esquerda) e A3 (à direita). Nas duas arquiteturas, a camada de requisitos (A) identifica, analisa e modela os possíveis requisitos como padrões de requisitos de usuário (URP). A camada de serviço (B) interage com a camada de requisitos e fornece serviços para satisfazer o URP. O mecanismo de segurança e compartilhamento de informação (C) garante um processo de troca de informação confiável entre os sistemas do mesmo domínio. A base de conhecimento (D) agrupa padrões, normas e ontologias do domínio do sistema. A motivação de ambas as pesquisas é a necessidade de compartilhamento de informações entre sistemas de um mesmo domínio: A1, para sistemas da área médica, e A3, para sistemas de transporte.

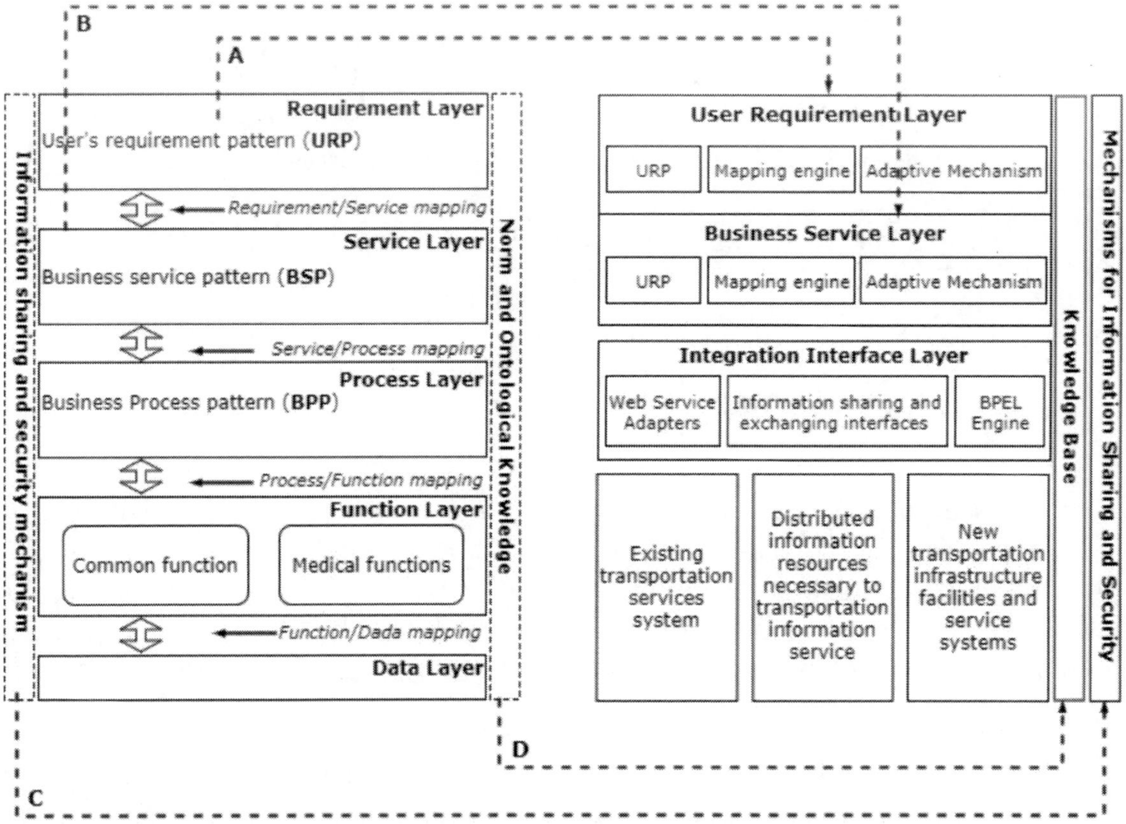

Figura 2. Análise comparativa entre as arquiteturas baseadas em padrões de requisitos propostas em A1 (à esquerda) e A3 (à direita).

Com relação ao objeto de estudo deste mapeamento sistemático, observa-se que os trabalhos apresentados em A1 e A3 estão diretamente relacionados à fase de *projeto de software*, pois os padrões de requisitos do usuário (URP) da camada de requisitos servem de base para a seleção eficiente dos serviços (BSP) na camada de serviços. Os URPs são os principais elementos na camada de requisitos que correspondem aos requisitos do usuário e orientam o funcionamento de todo o sistema.

Semelhanças também foram identificadas nos artigos A2 e A5 sobre como *representar requisitos de segurança na forma de padrão de requisito*. Foi possível observar que ambas as pesquisas tratam os mesmos conceitos de segurança (i.e.

contexto, ativos e ameaças) como padrões de requisitos, e as medidas de proteção são tratadas nos padrões de projeto. As semelhanças identificadas entre os estudos de A2 (à esquerda) e A5 (à direita) estão ilustradas na Figura 3 como linhas tracejadas. Os passos descritos na abordagem do estudo A2 — a identificação de interessados e objetivos, de ativos essenciais de informação, e de fontes de ameaças usando padrões — correspondem, respectivamente, aos seguintes itens do padrão de requisito de segurança do estudo A5: a definição do formato do padrão (contexto, problema, solução e estrutura), dos ativos, e das ameaças. A atividade "adicionar medidas de proteção no projeto do sistema" do estudo A2 é tratada como padrão de projeto de segurança no estudo A5.

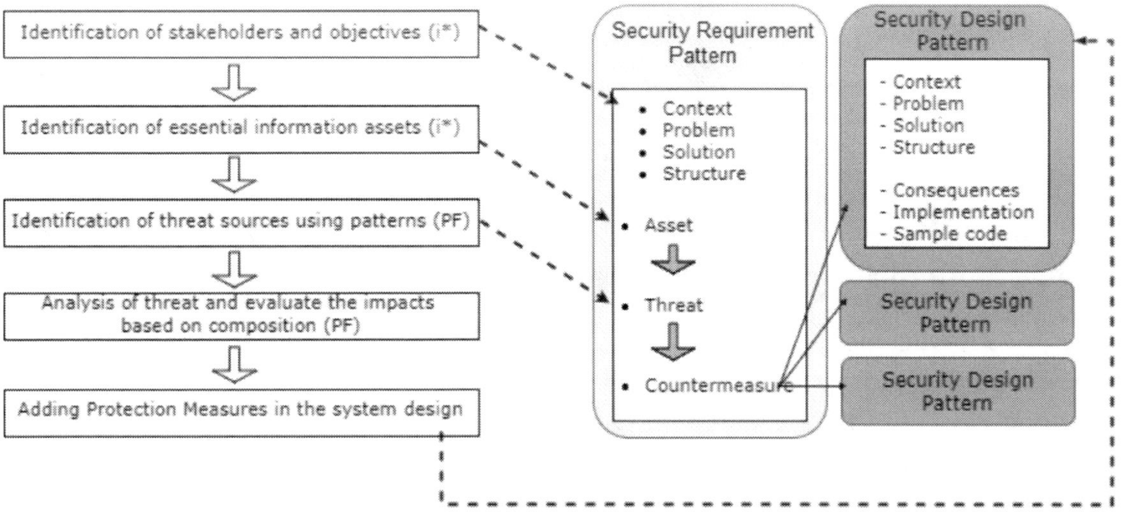

Figura 3. Análise comparativa entre as abordagens de segurança apresentadas em A2 (à esquerda) e A5 (à direita).

Conclui-se que os trabalhos A2 e A5 também estão relacionados com a fase de *projeto de software*, uma vez que ambos definem padrões de requisitos de segurança, de forma a impactar diretamente na definição de medidas de proteção por meio de padrões de projeto.

Foi também identificado que os artigos A8 e A9 apresentam propostas relacionadas ao formato de representação de padrões de requisitos. No artigo A8, associa-se uma fórmula em linguagem temporal linear para cada requisito escrito em linguagem natural, utilizando mutações para amenizar os problemas que podem surgir nessa associação. Para cada tipo de padrão de requisito, as falhas potenciais são identificadas e mutações apropriadas são introduzidas. As fórmulas que acompanham os mutantes podem ser usadas para a geração de testes, a adequação de conjuntos de testes, ou a construção automática de monitores para a verificação em tempo de execução do comportamento do sistema. Sendo assim, as mutações incluídas na transformação dos padrões de requisitos contribuem para a *fase de teste* no ciclo de vida de software. Já no artigo A9 é apresentada uma proposta de padrão de software que integra três tipos de padrão (de requisito, projeto e segurança), o qual nomeia como padrão composto. Baseado na ideia de *problem frames*, o padrão composto utiliza parâmetros extraídos do seu padrão de requisito. Cada conjunto de funções do padrão de requisito corresponde a soluções no padrão de projeto e a elementos contextuais no padrão de segurança. Portanto, essa proposta está também relacionada à *fase de projeto* de software.

Os artigos A4 e A7 utilizam o formalismo da lógica de descrição (LD) de ontologias para representar padrões de requisitos. No estudo A4, requisitos escritos em LD permitem a geração automática de código fonte; portanto, refere-se à *fase de construção* de software. Na proposta A7, foi implementado um mecanismo que, dado um padrão de requisito de segurança descrito em LD, consegue encontrar uma solução correspondente na forma de padrão de projeto. Daí também relaciona-se à *fase de projeto* de software.

Por fim, o estudo A6 tem como objetivo mapear a dependência entre padrões de projeto e padrões de requisitos de aplicações de computação ubíqua, cuja característica recorrente é a adaptabilidade. Uma abordagem que integra esses padrões tem como objetivo transpor as lacunas da fase inicial do desenvolvimento de software, em que os requisitos recorrentes exigem soluções semelhantes. Em suma, a principal contribuição do artigo A6 é para a fase de *projeto de software*.

As informações extraídas e a análise comparativa realizada na fase de extração desse mapeamento estão sintetizadas na Tabela 3 de acordo com 4 tipos de contribuições identificadas nos artigos: arquitetura conceitual para sistemas que usam padrão de requisito; processo para descoberta e uso de padrão de requisito; definição de formato de representação de padrão de requisito; e proposta de catálogo de padrões de requisitos.

Tabela 3. Informações extraídas dos artigos relevantes.

Tipo de contribuição do estudo	**Fase do ciclo de vida**	**Tipo de requisito**	**Artigos**
Arquitetura conceitual baseada em padrão de requisito	Projeto	Adaptabilidade	A1, A3
Formato de representação de padrão de requisito	Projeto	Segurança	A2, A5, A9
	Teste	Adaptabilidade	A8
Processo para descoberta e uso de padrão de requisito	Projeto	Segurança	A7
	Construção	Propósito Geral	A4
Catálogo de padrão de requisito	Projeto	Adaptabilidade	A6

4 Síntese dos dados

Esta seção apresenta uma síntese dos dados obtidos na fase de extração com o objetivo de responder às questões de pesquisa deste estudo secundário.

4.1 Sobre a Questão de Pesquisa 1

Em resposta à questão de pesquisa "*Em quais fases do ciclo de vida de software são usados padrões de requisitos: projeto, construção, teste e/ou manutenção?*", 7 estudos utilizam padrões de requisitos na fase de projeto de software, 1 na construção, 1 em testes de software e não houve nenhum para manutenção.

Dentre os 7 estudos que abordam padrões de requisitos em projeto de software (A1–A3, A5–A7 e A9), não existem autores de mais de um estudo, logo não se trata de uma iniciativa de um ou mais grupos de pesquisa. Duas hipóteses podem ser pensadas para a alta concentração dos estudos relacionados à fase de projeto: primeiro é o fato desta ser subsequente à engenharia de requisitos no processo de desenvolvimento tradicional, segundo a disseminação crescente do uso de padrões de projeto no desenvolvimento de software.

Além disso, embora tenham sido identificados 9 estudos que relacionam padrões de requisitos a alguma fase do ciclo de vida, 52 artigos foram excluídos na atividade de seleção pelo critério **CE4**, i.e. tratavam de padrão de requisito apenas na engenharia de requisitos. Essa diferença na quantidade de pesquisas relacionadas à engenharia de requisitos e aquelas que expandem padrões de requisitos para as demais fases do ciclo de vida deixa evidente uma oportunidade de pesquisa sobre padrão de requisito nas fases de construção, teste e manutenção.

Outra evidência é a inexistência de pesquisas sobre o uso de padrão de requisito que permeie o processo de desenvolvimento ao longo do ciclo de vida, i.e. partindo da engenharia de requisitos, passando pelo projeto, construção, teste, e sendo refinado na manutenção de software. Um desafio de estudo é pensar em como propor o uso de padrões de requisitos de forma que estes impactem na melhoria do processo de desenvolvimento como um todo, além dos conhecidos benefícios de qualidade de documentação e de economia de tempo.

4.2 Sobre a Questão de Pesquisa 2

Com relação à questão de pesquisa: "*Há evidências de uso prático de padrões de requisitos nessas fases do ciclo de vida de software?*", em nenhum dos artigos foi reportada evidência do uso de padrão de requisitos em ambiente de produção de software. Um total de 8 dos 9 artigos encontra-se no estágio de propostas de solução, sem validação, e apenas 1 artigo (A7) é validado com estudo de caso. Esta análise sugere que futuros trabalhos no tema em questão atenham-se cada vez mais à aplicação prática de padrão de requisito na indústria de software em todo o ciclo de desenvolvimento.

4.3 Sobre a Questão de Pesquisa 3

Referente à questão de pesquisa *"Há benefícios relatados do uso de padrão de requisitos nessas fases? Se sim, quais métricas são utilizadas para medir esses benefícios?"*, identificou-se que nenhum dos artigos relatou explicitamente qualquer benefício oriundo da prática de padrão de requisito.

Essa ausência de preocupação com métricas para analisar os benefícios do uso de padrões de requisitos se deve ao fato da maioria dos artigos estar no nível de propostas, sem uso prático dos mesmos.

4.4 Discussão

Ao interligar as informações da fase do ciclo de vida, do tipo de padrão de requisito proposto e o tipo de pesquisa de cada artigo, foi possível elaborar o gráfico de bolhas da Figura 4. Ao analisar o gráfico, observa-se que 4 estudos (A2, A5, A7 e A9) propõem padrão de requisito de *segurança* com uso na fase de *projeto*. Supomos que usar padrão de requisito para segurança deve-se ao fato desta característica ser recorrente em muitos sistemas, contando também com o apoio de padrões internacionais, como a família de padrões ISO/IEC 27000. Entretanto, esses estudos com segurança ainda carecem de maior validação com avaliações empíricas e uso na indústria de software.

Dos 9 estudos relevantes, 4 estudos (A1, A3, A6 e A8) utilizam padrão de requisito para *adaptabilidade*, sendo o último na fase de *testes* e os demais na fase de *projeto*. Além disso, nenhum desses 4 estudos apresenta validação de seus padrões, i.e., caracterizam-se como pesquisas de proposta conceitual de solução. Por fim, o estudo A4 é voltado para padrão de requisito de *propósito geral* com uso na fase de *construção* de software, mas também não apresentou validação.

Considerando ainda a Figura 4, tão importante quanto mapear as propostas de pesquisa é analisar as lacunas existentes:

1. existe uma carência geral de pesquisas de adoção de padrão de requisito em outras fases do ciclo de vida (9 estudos), excetuando a engenharia de requisitos (52 estudos).
2. ao analisar o lado esquerdo da figura, conclui-se que requisitos não funcionais (adaptabilidade e segurança) são os mais estudados quando do uso de padrão de requisito para as fases de projeto e testes. Porém, outros tipos de requisitos não funcionais podem ser explorados com padrão de requisito envolvendo outras fases do ciclo de vida como, por exemplo, aspectos de usabilidade com a geração automática de código e de casos de teste.
3. ao considerar o lado direito da figura, identificamos uma lacuna quanto à aplicação, na indústria de software, dos resultados das pesquisas de padrões de requisitos nas fases de projeto, construção, testes e manutenção — quase todas as propostas encontram-se em estágio de prova de conceito.

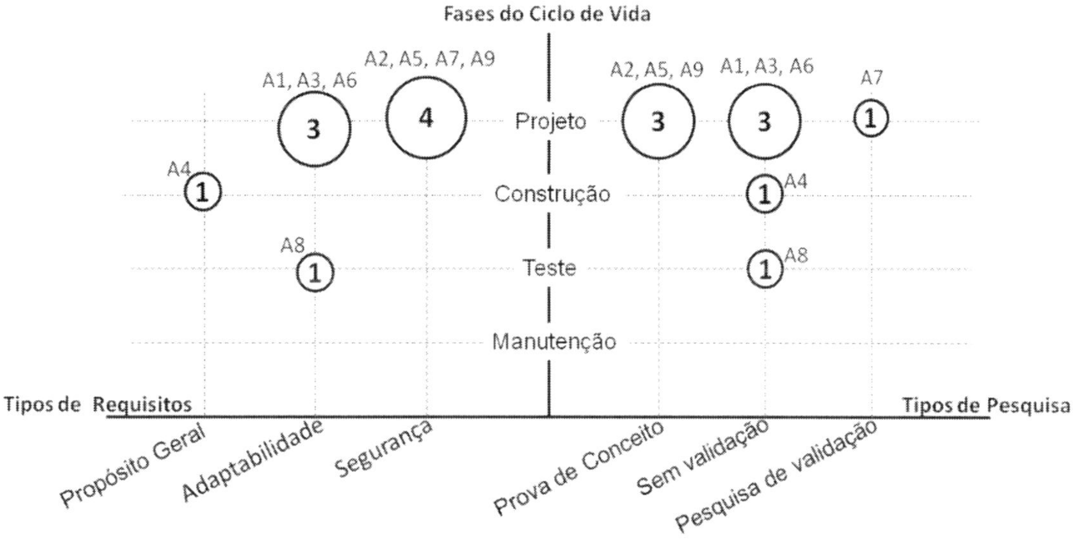

Figura 4. Mapeamento dos tipos de requisitos e de pesquisas sobre padrões de requisitos mapeados nas fases do ciclo de vida de software.

5 Considerações Finais

Os maiores problemas enfrentados em estudos sistemáticos são encontrar todos os estudos relevantes sobre um tema e, a partir dos estudos relevantes, selecionar evidências de qualidade. Por isso, ameaças foram mitigadas com 2 ações ao longo do planejamento e da condução deste mapeamento sistemático.

Primeiro, adotou-se uma estratégia de busca automática que combina fontes de informação consideradas relevantes para a Engenharia de Software com termos da *string* de busca baseados no vocabulário padrão SEVOCAB. Busca na literatura cinzenta não fez parte do protocolo, mais especificamente teses e relatórios técnicos, pois supõe-se que esse tipo de literatura, quando de boa qualidade, está publicada como artigo em periódicos ou conferências.

Segundo, três pesquisadores elaboraram o protocolo deste mapeamento sistemático e na condução do mapeamento, cada pesquisador exerceu seu papel: o pesquisador A, especialista em Engenharia de Requisitos, realizou a identificação e a extração de dados dos estudos relevantes; o pesquisador B, especialista em Engenharia de Software, verificou os resultados da fase de extração para mitigar a possibilidade de vieses ao longo do processo; e o pesquisador C, líder da equipe e com vasta experiência em Engenharia de Software, juntamente com A e B, realizou a análise, síntese e escrita dos resultados. No caso de divergências, A, B e C resolveram os conflitos em conjunto.

Apesar dos resultados obtidos neste mapeamento sistemático, de poucos estudos sobre o tema e com baixo índice de validação das propostas, os autores reforçam a reconhecida importância de padrões de requisitos no meio acadêmico [17,2]. Para impulsionar o desenvolvimento das pesquisas em padrões de requisitos no processo de desenvolvimento de software, sugerimos que a comunidade acadêmica aproxime-se da indústria de software para identificar as reais expectativas do setor. A comunidade deve também estabelecer métricas que evidenciem as vantagens do uso de padrões de requisitos em todas as fases do ciclo de vida como, por exemplo, a redução no tempo de projeto e na geração automática de código-fonte, a execução padronizada de testes e a melhoria na qualidade das especificações de software. Complementar a essas ações, a comunidade deve propor novas ferramentas de suporte ao desenvolvimento de aplicações com o uso de padrões de requisitos. Por fim, os pesquisadores devem elaborar metodologias de desenvolvimento que demonstrem como usar padrões de requisitos ao longo das fases do ciclo de vida de forma integrada às demais ações propostas.

Agradecimentos

Taciana Kudo agradece o auxílio financeiro concedido pelo Programa de Apoio à Pós-graduação (PROAP/CAPES). Renato Bulcão-Neto agradece a bolsa concedida pela CAPES/FAPEG (proc. n. 88887.305511/2018-00), vinculada ao estágio pós-doutoral realizado no Depto. de Computação e Matemática da FFCLRP-USP. Alessandra Macedo agradece o apoio financeiro da FAPESP (proc. n. 16/13206-4) e do CNPq (proc. n. 302031/2016-2 e 442533/2016-0).

Referências

1. Asnar, Y., Paja, E., Mylopoulos, J.: Modeling design patterns with description logics: A case study. In: Lecture Notes in Computer Science (including subseries Lecture Notes in Artificial Intelligence and Lecture Notes in Bioinformatics). vol. 6741 LNCS, pp. 169 – 183. London, United kingdom (2011)
2. Barros-Justo, J.L., Benitti, F.B.V., Leal, A.C.: Software patterns and requirements engineering activities in real-world settings:a systematic mapping study. Comp. Standards & Interfaces **58**, 23–42 (2018)
3. Beckers, K., Côté, I., Goeke, L.: A catalog of security requirements patterns for the domain of cloud computing systems. In: Proceedings of the ACM Symposium on Applied Computing. pp. 337–342 (2014)
4. Bourque, P., Fairley, R.E. (eds.): SWEBOK: Guide to the Software Engineering Body of Knowledge. IEEE Computer Society, Los Alamitos, CA, version 3.0 edn. (2014)
5. Chang, F., Gan, R.: An architectural framework of the integrated transportation information service system. In: 2009 IEEE International Conference on Grey Systems and Intelligent Services, GSIS 2009. pp. 1342 – 1346. Nanjing, China (2009)
6. Couto, R., Ribeiro, A.N., Campos, J.C.: Application of ontologies in identifying requirements patterns in use cases. In: Electronic Proceedings in Theoretical Computer Science, EPTCS. vol. 147, pp. 62 – 76. Grenoble, France (2014)
7. Da Silva, R., Benitti, F.: Standards writing requirements: A mapping systematic literature [Padrões de escrita de requisitos: Um mapeamento sistemático da literatura]. In: 14th Ibero-American Conference on Software Engineering and 14th Workshop on Requirements Engineering, CIbSE 2011. pp. 259–270 (2011)
8. Fabbri, S.C.P.F., Felizardo, K.R., Ferrari, F.C., Hernandes, E.C.M., Octaviano, F.R., Nakagawa, E.Y., Maldonado, J.C.: Externalising tacit knowledge of the systematic review process. IET Software **7**(6), 298–307 (2013)

9. Felizardo, K.R., Nakagawa, E.Y., Fabbri, S.C.P.F., Ferrari, F.C.: Revisão sistemática da literatura em Engenharia de Software: Teoria e Prática. Elsevier, first edn. (2017)
10. Hauge, A.A., Stølen, K.: SACS: A pattern language for safe adaptive control software. In: Proceedings of the 18th Conference on Pattern Languages of Programs. pp. 7:1–7:22. PLoP '11, ACM, New York, NY, USA (2011)
11. ISO/IEC/IEEE: IEEE software and systems engineering vocabulary. IEEE Computer Society pp. 1 – 437 (2016)
12. Kitchenham, B., Pearl Brereton, O., Budgen, D., Turner, M., Bailey, J., Linkman, S.: Systematic literature reviews in software engineering - a systematic literature review. Inf. Softw. Technol. **51**(1), 7–15 (Jan 2009)
13. Knote, R., Baraki, H., Söllner, M., Geihs, K., Leimeister, J.M.: From requirement to design patterns for ubiquitous computing applications. In: Proceedings of the 21st European Conference on Pattern Languages of Programs (Jul 2016)
14. Konrad, S., Cheng, B.H.C.: Requirements patterns for embedded systems. In: Proceedings IEEE Joint International Conference on Requirements Engineering. pp. 127–136 (2002)
15. Nicolas, J., Toval, A.: On the generation of requirements specifications from software engineering models: A systematic literature review. Inf. Softw. Technol. **51**(9), 1291–1307 (Sep 2009)
16. Okubo, T., Kaiya, H., Yoshioka, N.: Effective security impact analysis with patterns for software enhancement. In: 2011 Sixth International Conference on Availability, Reliability and Security. pp. 527–534 (Aug 2011)
17. Palomares, C., Quer, C., Franch, X.: Requirements reuse and requirement patterns: a state of the practice survey. Empirical Software Engineering **22**(6), 2719–2762 (2017)
18. Palomares, C., Quer, C., Franch, X., Renault, S., Guerlain, C.: A catalogue of functional software requirement patterns for the domain of content management systems. In: Proceedings of the 28th Annual ACM Symposium on Applied Computing, SAC '13, Coimbra, Portugal, March 18-22, 2013. pp. 1260–1265 (2013)
19. Petersen, K., Feldt, R., Mujtaba, S., Mattsson, M.: Systematic mapping studies in software engineering. In: Proceedings of the 12th International Conference on Evaluation and Assessment in Software Engineering. pp. 68–77. EASE'08, BCS Learning & Development Ltd., Swindon, UK (2008)
20. Petersen, K., Vakkalanka, S., Kuzniarz, L.: Guidelines for conducting systematic mapping studies in software engineering: An update. Information and Software Technology **64**, 1–18 (2015)
21. Tockey, S.: Insanity, hiring, and the software industry. Computer **48**(11), 96–101 (Nov 2015)
22. Trakhtenbrot, M.: Mutation patterns for temporal requirements of reactive systems. In: Proceedings - 10th IEEE International Conference on Software Testing, Verification and Validation Workshops, ICSTW 2017. pp. 116–121 (2017)
23. Wen, Y., Zhao, H., Liu, L.: Analysing security requirements patterns based on problems decomposition and composition. In: 2011 1st International Workshop on Requirements Patterns, RePa'11. pp. 11 – 20. Trento, Italy (2011)
24. Withall, S.: Software Requirement Patterns. Best practices, Microsoft Press, Redmond, Washington (2007)
25. Yang, H., Liu, K., Li, W.: Adaptive requirement-driven architecture for integrated healthcare systems. Journal of Computers **5**(2) (2010)

iPlus Methodology for Requirements Elicitation for Serious Games

Mayra Carrión[12], Marco Santorum[12], Jose Aguilar[3], María Peréz[1]

[1] Escuela Politécnica Nacional (National Polytechnic School), Quito, Ecuador
[2]Grupo de Investigación de Sistemas de Información, Gestión de la Tecnología e Innovación
[3] Centro de Estudios en Microelectrónica y Sistemas (CEMISID), Universidad de los Andes (Study Center in Microelectronics and Systems, University of the Andes), Mérida, Venezuela

Abstract. Serious Games (SGs) are used in various areas, such as training, advertising, medical fields and communications. In an educational context, a SG aims to enhance learning by means of a game. In order to ensure that a SG meets user's expectations, it must be designed using an appropriate methodology based on the next properties: user-centered, include experts in pedagogy and game design, among other things. The objective of this work is to present iPlus, a methodology for the design of SGs, which is based on the previous properties. iPlus allows the conception of educational SGs, based on a participative and user-centered approach.

Keywords: Serious Games, User-Centered Design, Serious Games Methodologies, Participative Approach.

1 Introduction

Nowadays, Information and Communications Technology (ICT) is one of the most important global industries that contributes to the quality of human life. ICT contributes to various aspects of living, including health, government, safety, and education. Within the educational field, ICT is seen as a tool that enables learning and the development of student skills [18]. It offers an alternative approach to traditional learning. One can see many examples of the use of ICT in educational platforms and virtual learning environments. However, despite new implementations, one also sees a rising level of school drop-outs, perhaps due to students' decreasing motivation to learn.

This problem has generated the necessity to define innovative learning strategies that help to revert this trend. In this context, serious games (SGs) are now widely used as a tool to support learning in different fields of study, such as medicine, military training, etc. SGs are seen as a useful pedagogical resource in the teaching-learning process, which takes advantage of the motivational factors used in video games, to make significant contributions in a student's learning process.

Chipia [7] states that SGs help provide an entertaining and self-empowering that motivates students. They also allow the development of the creativity, intellectual competence, emotional strength and personal stability.

Due to the high level of interest and social impact that SGs generate, it is necessary to examine the value they offer to education. For example, researchers have found that games that are not well designed [16] lose both their attraction and their game-like essence. Even more, they no longer fulfill serious teaching objectives.

In addition, not all the SGs that have been developed have applied design methodologies that incorporate both entertainment and pedagogy. The goal of our research is to propose a reference methodology for SG design that incorporates a participatory and user-centered approach, adaptable to users with non-standard cognitive abilities.

The rest of this research is divided into four sections: Section 2 presents related research on methodologies used to design SGs. Section 3 describes our methodological proposal, presenting phases and resources. In section 4, we illustrate the application of iPlus, and finally, section 5 presents the conclusions and perspectives of our research.

2 Related research

In this section, we describe research regarding SG design methodologies.

2.1 Methodologies for SG design

Standard video games are information-oriented applications, which development process often follows a traditional software development approach. Many methodologies for leisure game development already exist; however, SG design demands a specific methodology for its design.

Nadolski et al. [15] propose a methodology for the development of SGs in higher education, oriented towards professionals and composed of five phases (see Fig. 1), but the same author explains that the development of effective, attractive and efficient learning materials is not guaranteed. The SGs that are designed with this methodology are intended for the acquisition of complex cognitive skills in higher education.

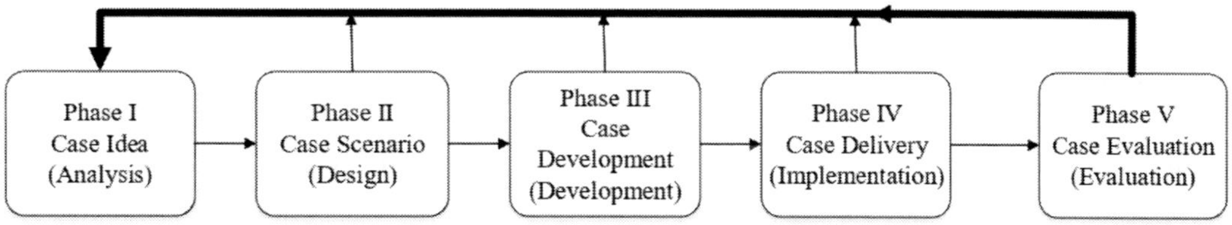

Fig. 1. Phases of the Nadolski et al. methodology [15].

Padilla [16] proposes a methodology for the design of educational video games (see Fig. 2), based on activities, models and generated documents. This methodology is independent of further implementation. The methodology is composed of four phases, and each of them is divided into activities, which define one or more design documents as a result. This methodology is oriented to design SGs for college students.

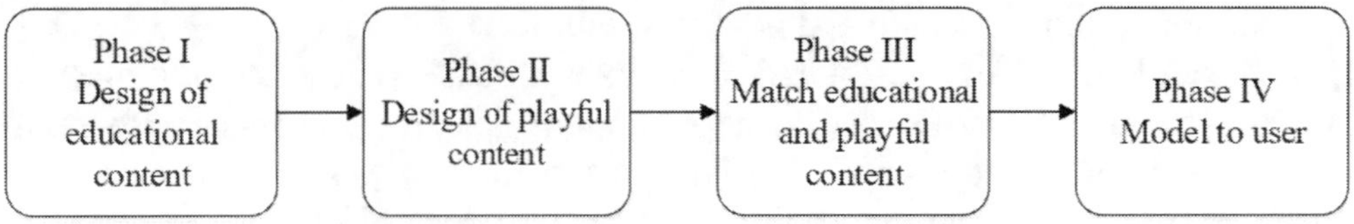

Fig. 2. Phases of the Padilla methodology [16].

López-Martínez et al.[13] have created a methodology that describes the process for the analysis and design of SGs, angled at combating childhood obesity (see Fig. 3). It comprises the understanding of children with respect to their eating habits. This methodology proposes to create video games within this specific context, where the performance of the SGs is measured using school students.

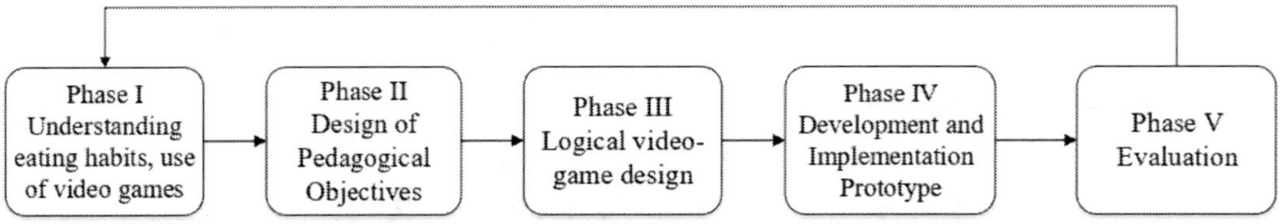

Fig. 3. Phases of the López-Martínez et al. methodology [13].

Another methodology is proposed by Marfisi-Schottmann [14], which is aimed towards the conception of learning games, based on seven phases, in which logic sequences can be either forward-backward or parallel (see Fig. 4). Phase three describes the complete scenario of the learning game and is considered one of the most delicate phases. This methodology is too extensive, and oriented towards higher education.

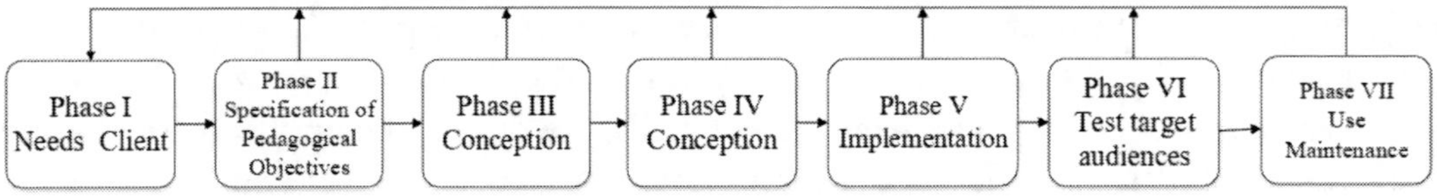

Fig. 4. Phases of the Marfisi-Schottmann methodology [14].

The methodology proposed by Prieto et al. [17] is directed towards the design of educational SGs based on adventure, where the story plays an important role. This methodology is composed of three pre-phases and six phases. In pre-phase one, the educational objectives are defined; pre-phase two explains the narrative of the game and its different elements; in pre-phase three the initial design of the game is specified. Subsequently, the following six phases are defined (see Fig. 5). This is not a user-centered approach. It is methodology-oriented for the design of SGs for college students.

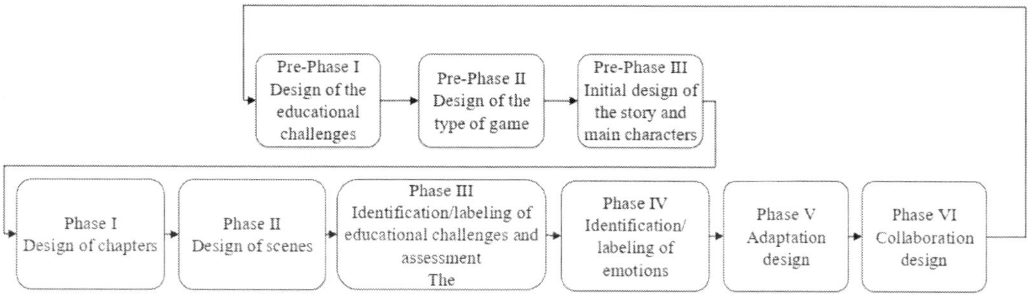

Fig. 5. Phases of the Prieto et al. methodology [17].

None of the methodologies described above contemplate the active participation of users. These methodologies are used in an educational context. The next proposal is one of the first methodologies proposed in a different context of use, oriented towards students with hearing disabilities.

Cano et al. [5] have defined a methodology, called MECONESIS (Methodology for Designing Serious Games for Children with Auditory Disabilities). It is based on a unified software development process. MECONESIS uses CTT language to model human-machine interactions, as well as UML to specify class diagrams. The goal of this methodology is to design SGs for people with auditory disabilities, following a user-centered design approach (see Fig. 6).

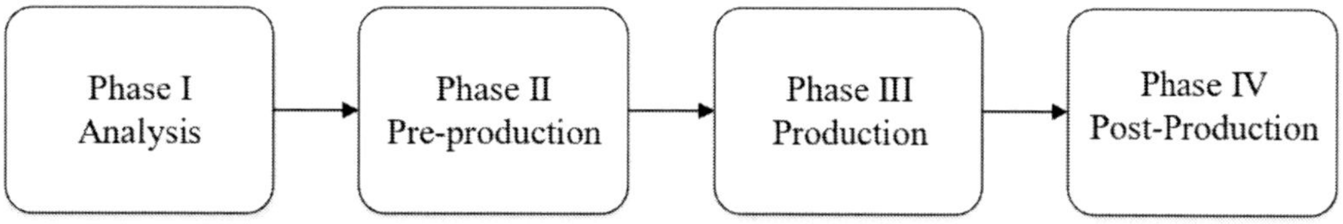

Fig. 6. Phases of the Cano et al. methodology [4].

2.2 Discussion

Table 1 presents a comparison between the previous methodologies and our methodology, based on the characteristics of iPlus. A first conclusion is that players are not very much involved in the game design processes, especially in their early stages.

On the other hand, there are several papers based on the development of SGs using methodologies for the development of software, of which some are oriented to the video game design, and very few are oriented to the design of SGs.

From an SG for education point of view, not many methodologies contemplate the development of educational SGs in a participative way, and none involves players and experts in the game design processes.

Our methodology is set apart from the others due to the participation of experts, such as pedagogists, educational psychologists, experts in the treatment of disabilities, software engineers and game designers who create and design SGs adapted to the specific needs of people who, in our case, have non-standard cognitive abilities.

Our proposal is built using a Design Science approach [10], where the product is designed through experimental protocols carried out in a participatory manner, thereby allowing for the consensus of the users and experts to obtain a product through stages, which are validated and adapted progressively, until a final product that is closer to the user's expectations is produced.

In our methodology, the pedagogical objectives, the story and the game mechanics, are an integral part of the game. Players create and share experiences with experts, and the user's skills and real needs are therefore taken into account. The product is adapted to his/her specific needs and not the other way around.

Table 1. Comparison between methodologies.

iPlus Characteristics	[15]	[16]	[13]	[14]	[17]	[4]
SGs for education	higher education	secondary education	regarding childhood obesity	higher education	educational adventure games	children with hearing impairment
User-centered design	N/A	N/A	N/A	N/A	N/A	focused on the context of use
Participatory approach	N/A	N/A	N/A	N/A	N/A	N/A
Oriented to people with non-standard cognitive abilities	N/A	N/A	N/A	N/A	N/A	people with hearing impairment

3 Methodological proposal

This section describes our proposal, called iPlus, which is a methodology created to design SGs for educational purposes [6]. iPlus presents a participatory approach , offering a phase for the ascertainment of consensual requirements through the participation of various experts, such as, for example, pedagogical experts, experts on the subject, or experts in the treatment of disabilities. iPlus methodology can be used in the requirements phase of any software development methodology, integrating easily.

3.1 iPlus phases

The methodology consists of five phases, as is described in Fig. 7.

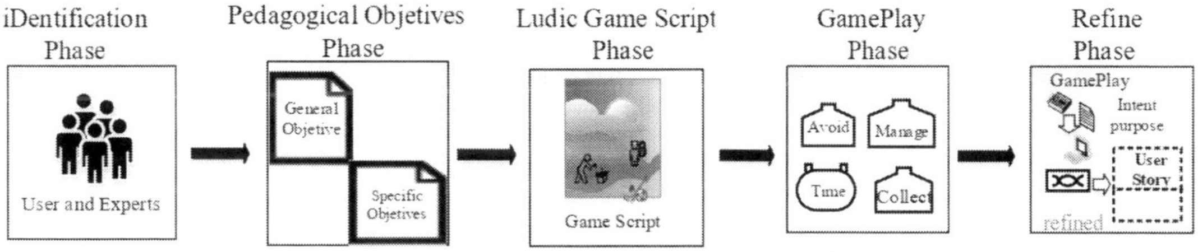

Fig. 7. iPlus methodology phases.

Phase 1: Identification. This is the initial phase of the methodology, where the general problem is defined by the sponsor or the interested party, and, depending on the problem, the participants of the methodology are identified. The objective of this phase is to ascertain which experts need to be involved in the initial conception of the serious educational game. In the conception of the game, there must be an expert in pedagogy who must ensure the correct definition of objectives, a subject expert who knows about the problem to be solved, an expert designer for the game, and developers.

Phase 2: Pedagogical Objectives. The second phase of the methodology is to define the main educational objective, as well as the general and specific pedagogica objectives, which involves the participation. Here, the critical thinking and creativity of the experts intervene, using techniques to promote the creativity, such as "brainstorming" and "affinity diagrams", and to unify ideas to formulate consensuated requirements. In particular, the requirements of the subject expert (product owner) must be met. The result of this phase is a format containing the definition of the general and specific pedagogical objectives.

Phase 3: Ludic Game Script. In this phase, the game script is created based on the requirement of subject expert (Product Owner). The participation of each expert is important, because each can conceptualize the different possible scenarios of the SG, whilst maintaining the general objective raised in the previous phase. The subject expert selects the best ideas proposed for the game script, using green stickers and red stickers for ideas that may present some difficulty. Then, with the selected ideas, the participants and the subject expert create the game script that contains the narrative, characters, and gamification elements [19][12], such as badges, points, prizes, which will be implemented in the SG. The result of this phase is the game script format.

Phase 4: GamePlay. The GamePlay phase aims to identify the functions/actions that are going to be developed for the game script. In addition, the genre of the game is identified in this phase. It can be a role play, adventure, simulation, reasoning, strategy, and/or action game [11]. This is done with the help of the experts and the game designer. Everyone participates in the creation of the GamePlay script, which refers to the description of the different actions that are going to be developed in the video game scenario. The GamePlay blocks [1][2][8] refer to the design of the functions that are part of the SG, for example, functions such as picking up, triggering, managing, creating, etc. The results of this phase are the full Game-Play script templates, the SG genre and the key description terms.

Phase 5: Refine. In this stage, the documents that were made previously are filtered, i.e. the purposes and scripts, to eliminate aspects that are repetitive or are not possible to create. To do this, a modified questionnaire for the evaluation of requirements is used [3]. The responsibles for these activities are the expert developer and the subject expert. The results of this phase are the epic user stories, which were defined according to the specific objectives elicited in the second phase.

3.2 iPlus Metamodel

iPlus methodology has been formalized through a metamodel (see Fig. 8) that describes the concepts that are used in the process of obtaining of requirements for SGs, with their relationships. Our metamodel was designed based on [20], where Michael Zyda says that an SG is composed of a story, art, and software, and involves a pedagogical component, adding other concepts like gamification, gameplay, genre and experts.

The iPlus metamodel is subdivided into the next parts. First, it starts from the SG base concept (class Serious Game), then a SG is composed of Gameplay elements (class GamePlay), which are the combination of five components: Rules, Input methods, Space-related setup, Time-related setup, and Drama-related setup. This is the software component, according to Michael Zyda. A SG is also composed of a story script for the game; this is the Ludic Game Script (Game Script class). Experts in different areas of knowledge participate in the elicitation of requirements (Class Experts) of a SG. The game genre (Genre class) is related to the Ludic Game Script.

The Game script of a SG can contain elements of gamification (Gamification class), and the Game Play is specified in the Refined GamePlay (Refined GamePlay), after a validation questionnaire. The refined Game Play elements are related to user stories.

Finally, a SG follows pedagogical objectives (Pedagogical Objective class). These pedagogical objectives are classified into general (General objective class) and specific objectives (specific objective class). The general objective contains the purposes or ideas proposed by the experts (purpose class). These purposes are discussed, in order to find a consensus (Agreed purpose class); they are validated trough a validation questionnaire (Refined purpose). The refined purposes are related to the user stories.

In this way, our iPlus metamodel describes the entire process of elicitation of requirements for SGs, followed by the methodology.

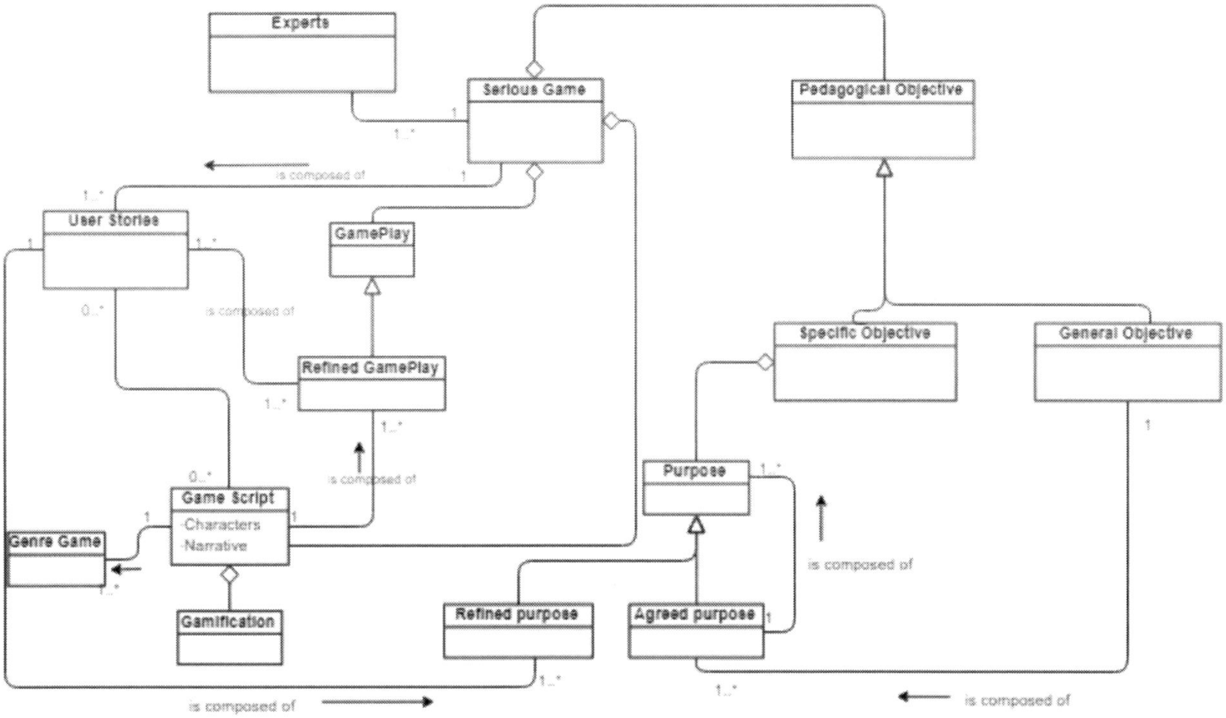

Fig. 8. iPlus Metamodel.

4 Application of iPlus

In this section, we present the application of the iPlus methodology, with the description of the results obtained in each phase, in a example that consists of a serious virtual reality game to carry out recreational therapy, or *Snoezelen,* for people with intellectual disabilities and low mobility. Recreational therapy is a form of treatment that uses recreational activities to work on rehabilitation goals. Through the use of recreational interests, recreational therapy helps improve physical abilities, such as increasing muscle strength, mobility and range of motion. It also promotes a greater self-confidence and the stress management, among other things. On the other hand, some studies have shown that virtual reality applications help in the rehabilitation of patients suffering of physical paralysis, spinal injuries, strokes, etc., because they increase motivation to reach a higher level of functional motor improvement [9].

In our case, the SG using images, augmented reality, and body movements, allow evoking and visiting places like a beach, the countryside, or a city. The SG allows working with emotions, generating states of relaxation, well-being, peace and quiet, with appropriate music. The SG allows working with cognitive abilities and influencing a cognitive psycholinguistic reality, because it provides more vocabulary. It affects the attention, memory, memory evocation and emotional control functions, which are all essentials for life. The phases of the methodology in the design of this game are described below.

Result of the Identification Phase. As a result of this phase, each expert that will participate in the conception of this SG is identified. Accordingly, an expert in people with disabilities is required. This is the same person responsible for the subject. An educational psychologist, an expert in pedagogy, an expert in video game designer, and expert developers will also participate, as is detailed in the Fig. 9.

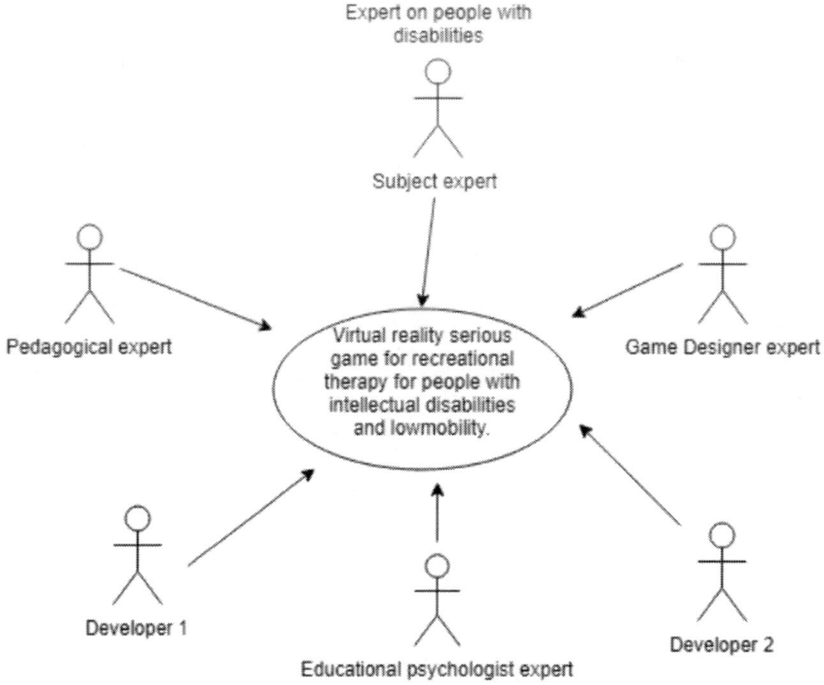

Fig. 9. Identified experts.

Result of the Pedagogical Objectives Phase. In this phase are defined the pedagogical objectives, the general objective, and the specific objectives, with the participation of all the experts, under the responsibility of the educational psychologist and pedagogical expert. To define the pedagogical objectives, the elements described below were used.
Materials. The materials used in this phase are: requirement questionnaire, multi colored pens, orange and pink post-its, a flipchart, and the general objective and specific objective formats.
Protocol. 1. Interview a subject expert in order to understand the needs of the client, 2. Write down the desired purposes, with the help of orange post-its. 3. Group individual purposes within general purposes, 4. Establish the general and specific objectives.
Result. Fig. 10 shows part of the interview questionnaire carried out with the subject expert, and shows some of the desired purposes written on orange post-its, and the general purpose on the pink post-it.

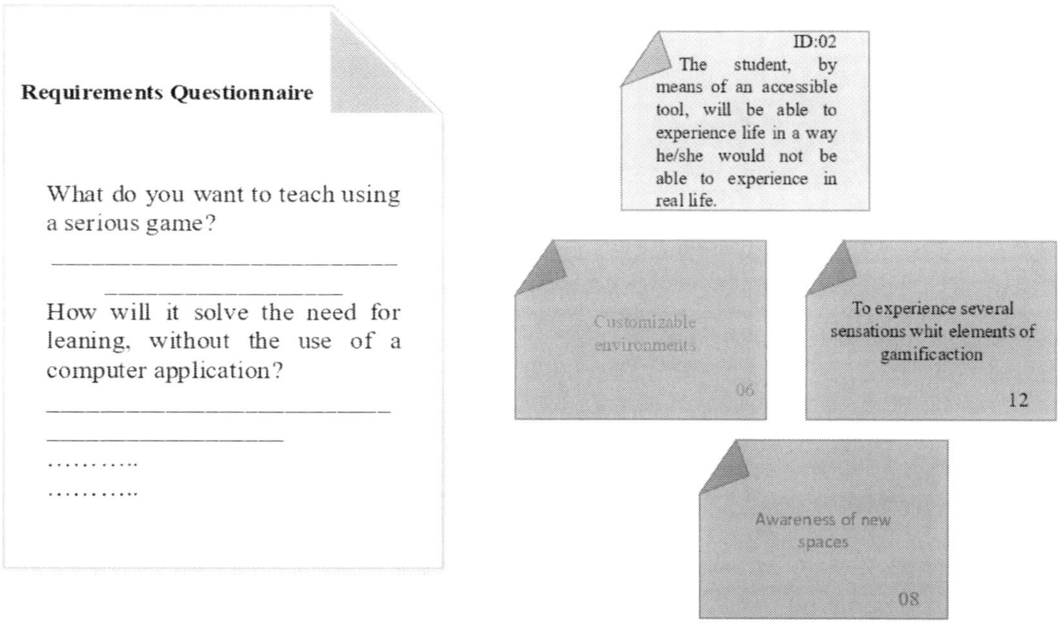

Fig. 10. Requirements questionnaire and desired purposes and general purposes.

With the help of the general purposes, the team of experts describes the general objective and the specific objectives (see Fig. 11), under the guidance of the pedagogical expert.

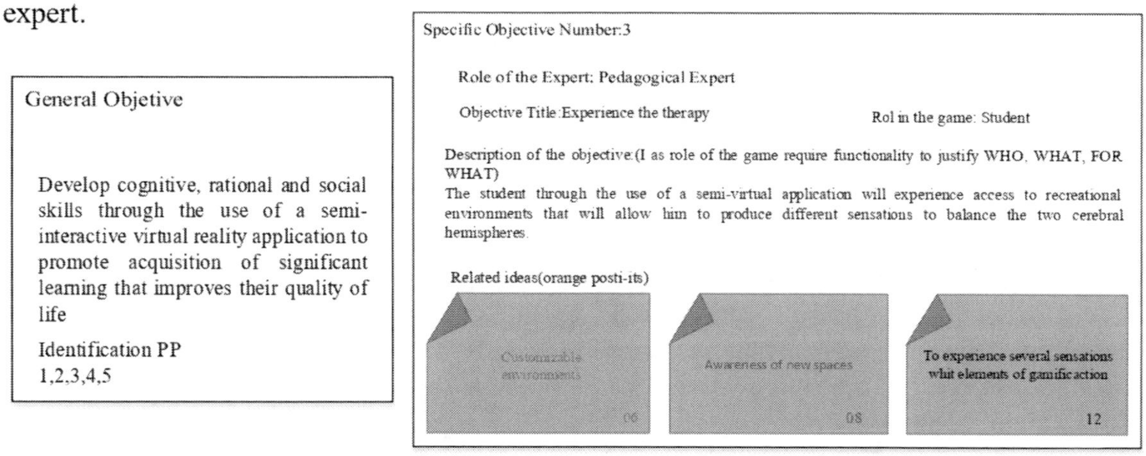

Fig. 11. Description of the general objective and the specific objectives.

Results of the Ludic Game Script Phase. In this phase, the game script or story of the SG is obtained.

Materials. The materials used in this phase are: multi colored pens, gamification blocks, story format, story selection format, green and red stickers.

Protocol. 1. Narrate possible game scripts for the SG, 2. Subject expert evaluates game scripts and label them with a red or green sticker, 3. Create the SG story in the game script selection format, along with all the participants.

Result: As result of this phase, a game script is defined with the help of all the experts, (see Fig. 12).

Consensual Story

Story

An explorer who visits different spaces, collecting basic objects accompanied by a pet and at the end of the visit receives a badge.

Characters

- Explorer
- Pet

How is the game won?
living immersion

Gamification elements

Start Assistant:
Appears when involved dressed according to the environment

Challenges and Missions
Answer questions

Levels:
Division within two levels of difficulty

- Recreational level

France, beach, mountain

- Ordinary level

Tracks, challenges, fly, space,etc

Fig. 12. Game script.

Result of the GamePlay Phase. In this phase are defined some of the functions, actions, and rules that are going to be implemented in the SG (see Fig. 13). The genre and the keywords for the project are obtained.

Materials. The materials for this phase are: multi colored pens, GamePlay blocks, GamePlay template, star stickers, green post-its, video game genres.

Protocol. 1. Describe functions to be developed using GamePlay blocks, keeping in mind the game script of the SG; carried out with the participation of all the experts, 2. Select the genre of the SG, with the help of the game designer, 3. Describe the key words of the SG.

Result. The results obtained in this phase are shown in Fig. 13. On the left, the expert, using GamePlay blocks, defines the actions that are going to be implemented in the SG within the game script. On the right, the figure shows the function description at the top, and the blocks to be used for such function at the bottom.

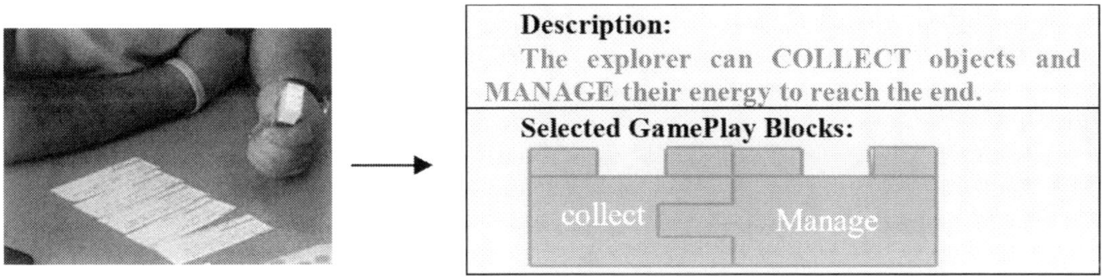

Fig. 13. Function description with GamePlay blocks.

Afterwards, with the participation of all the experts, the genre of the SG is identified, in this case being classified as Adventure. This process is carried out by voting, using Star stickers. Finally, in Fig. 14, the keywords identified by all the participants in the project, are shown within green post-its.

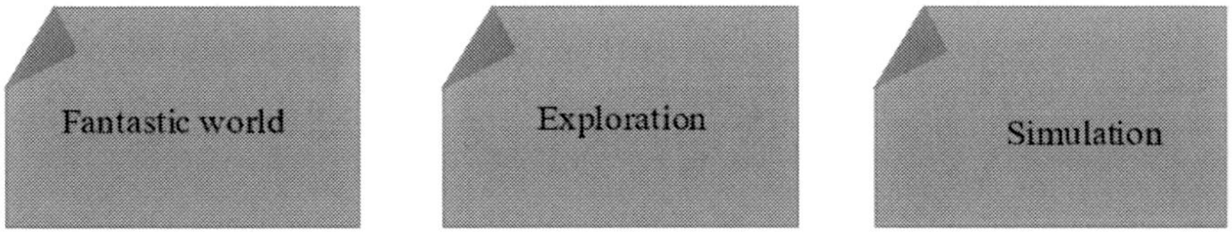

Fig. 14. Keywords.

Results of the Refinement Phase. This is the last phase of the methodology, during which the user story is obtained. The person responsible is the expert designer.
Materials. The materials to be used in this phase are: requirement evaluation questionnaire and user story template.
Protocol. 1. Verify the desired purposes, described in Phase 2; 2. Verify the GamePlay template and ensure that it is possible to execute it; 3. Set a meeting with the subject expert, to validate that all that has been obtained is what is necessary for the implementation, and with that, finally, develop a user story.
Result. Table 2 is an example of the result obtained in this phase, i.e. a user story that contains a description of the activities the designer must fulfill. Furthermore, the priority and the role to be carried out are specified in this user story.

Table 2. Result user story.

User story
Identifier: H001 Role: TUTOR User story Name: Offer support during therapy Priority: H (High) Description: The tutor with select the environment and configure the parameters to carry out the therapy (Time, Scenery, Sound, Image, Scene Elements) User Activities: - Tutor must be present the whole time the therapy is underway - Tutor chooses the environment to be used by the student/patient - Tutor selects the level of difficulty (recreational or normal) for the student/patient

Thus, using our methodology, user story can be obtained and then used by any expert from the development side, which can use any software development methodology (agile, etc.). Our methodology specifies the entry to any methodology for the development phase.

5 Conclusions and Perspectives

iPlus is a new methodological proposal that has been conceived with the help of experimental protocols and experts from different areas of knowledge that have validated its different phases. It has become a methodology with a multidisciplinary approach. This iPlus methodology can be added to other software development methodologies with an agile or traditional approach, in order to design SGs.

The iPlus methodology takes into account the basic concepts of a SG as proposed by Zyda. Likewise, it adds two elements to be taken into consideration in video games, such as GamePlay and Gamification, as is shown in the metamodel built for the methodology. In particular, the metamodel proposed in this work can be used in future works, for the development of a formal method of verification of the requirements obtained by the iPlus methodology for a SG, based on the process described by him.

This methodology considers the integration of different experts during the design of the SGs, in order to take into account the opinion of all, and respect the characteristics so who the SG is directed. The methodology considers both the pedagogical elements and scenarios, in order to develop a SG that allows the end user to be hooked.

Future works will be about the design and development of other SGs, in order to exhaustively validate the proposed methodology, and thus verify its robustness in the definition of SGs for non-standard cognition users, people with intellectual disabilities and/or gifted people.

Acknowledgements. We thank Continuing Education Centre (CEC-EPN) for its support.

References

1. Alvarez, J.: Du jeu vidéo au serious game. Université TOULOUSE II - Toulouse le Mirail Université (2007).
2. Alvarez, J. et al.: Introduction au Serious Game. , France (2012).
3. Bejarano, K. et al.: Especificación de Requerimientos Criterio de Calidad, http://pegasus.javeriana.edu.co/~CIS1310IS09/Anexos/Especificación de requerimientos Criterio de Calidad.pdf.
4. Cano, S. et al.: Towards a Methodology for Serious Games Design for Children with Auditory Impairments. IEEE Lat. Am. Trans. 14, 5, 1–11 (2016).
5. Cano, S.P.: Propuesta Metodológica para el Diseño de Juegos Serios para Niños con Implante Coclear TESIS DOCTORAL. Universidad del Cauca (2016).
6. Carrión, M. et al.: A Participatory Methodology for the Design of Serious Games in the Educational Environment. Congr. Int. Innov. y Tendencias en Ing. 2–6 (2017).
7. Chipia Lobo, J.F.: Juegos Serios: Alternativa Innovadora. In: Conocimiento Libre y Educación (CLED). pp. 1–18 (2011).

8. Djaouti, D. et al.: Classifying Serious Games. Handb. Res. Improv. Learn. Motiv. through Educ. Games. January 2016, 2–21 (2011).
9. Elizabeth Vela Martínez, D.: "Realidad Virtual En El Tratamiento Del Paciente Con Ictus Post-Isquémico". Revisión Bibiográfica Narrativa. Universidad de Valladolid (2017).
10. Hevner, A. et al.: Design Science in Information Systems Research. MIS Q. 28, 1, 75–105 (2004).
11. Jolivalt, B.: Les jeux vidéo. Presses universitaires de France, France (1994).
12. Kiryakova, G. et al.: Gamification in Education. Asbbs Am. Soc. Bus. Behav. Sci. 21, 1, 32–39 (2014).
13. López-Martínez, J.L. et al.: Una metodología para el análisis y diseño de un videojuego serio para combatir la obesidad infantil en el Estado de Yucatán, (2013).
14. Marfisi-Schottman, I.: Méthodologie, modèles et outils pour la conception de Learning Games. L'institut national des sciences appliquées de Lyon (2012).
15. Nadolski, R.J. et al.: EMERGO: A methodology and toolkit for developing serious games in higher education. Simul. Gaming. 39, 3, 338–352 (2008).
16. Padilla, N.: Metodología Para El Diseño De Videojuegos Educativos Sobre Una Arquitectura Para El Análisis Del Aprendizaje Colaborativo. Universidad de Granada (2011).
17. Prieto, R. et al.: Design methodology for educational games based on graphical notations: Designing Urano, http://dx.doi.org/10.1016/j.entcom.2016.08.005, (2017).
18. Schell, J.: The art of game design. Elsevier, USA (2008).
19. Zichermann, G., Cunningham, C.: Gamification by Design Implementing Game Mechanics in Web and Mobile Apps. Published by O'Reilly Media, Inc., 1005 Gravenstein Highway North, Sebastopol, CA 95472. O'Reilly, Canada (2011).
20. Zyda, M.: From Visual Simulation to Virtual Reality to Games, (2005).

A User-Centred Requirements Language for Conceptual Modelling in Information Systems

Fernando Wanderley, João Araujo, António Silva

NOVA-LINCS, FCT, Universidade Nova de Lisboa
Caparica, Portugal.
{f.wanderley, joao.araujo, ap.silva}@fct.unl.pt

Abstract. Conceptual Modelling is an indispensable part of information system design and development. The main purpose of conceptual modelling is to improve communication between the parties involved in the development process. Current conceptual modelling tools are not end-user centric and their main foci are on technical aspects. Thus, this paper aims to propose a user-centered and cognitive requirements language for conceptual modelling based on mind maps, through model-driven and domain specific language techniques. Besides, to speed up the whole (agile) development process, this cognitive language also provides code and database schema generation and support for validation of conceptual modelling using model animation. Finally, we describe an industrial case applied to our cognitive requirements language.

Keywords: Cognitive Requirements Language, Conceptual Modelling, Mind Map, Model-Driven Engineering, Domain-Specific Language.

1 Introduction

One of the main goals of requirements engineering is "conveying and promoting the understanding of the application domain" [1]. Consequently, models can improve the requirements engineering process and facilitate common understanding of domains and processes between end-users and system engineers [2]. The user perception (cognitive effectiveness) of a modelling language is likely to have an impact on whether or not users (i.e., part of system's stakeholders) perceive a language as useful and become interested in using it [3, 4]. This is highly relevant in areas where there is no de-facto standard modelling language. Prior research showed that perceived ontological deficiencies in a modelling language negatively influence usefulness and ease of use [5], and design aesthetics positively influence usage perceptions [6]. Visual models (i.e., diagrams) can support practitioners and their community to conceptualize problem spaces by providing a workbench and toolkit for problem solving in exploring, creating, refining and restructuring design solutions. Recent empirical results reported by Caire et al. [3] reinforced the importance of effective communication of requirements models with naïve users. According to their study, visual notations used by requirements models must improve the semantic transparency, semiotic clarity, and meaning of traditional notations adopted, reducing the cognitive load. In this sense, we have been investigating how cognitive models such as mind maps can be used in requirements engineering [7, 8, 9, 10] to facilitate communication among stakeholders.

Here we focus on conceptual modelling [13], in the context of system information development. Conceptual models are known to support the analysis, design, development and documentation of software in information systems. In particular, they are used for defining stakeholders' requirements and for conceptualizing diffuse knowledge in the domain. Thus, this paper presents an approach that incorporates user-centered visual notations, using a domain specific modeling language for end-user requirements modeling. The main goal is to improve the stakeholder's engagement in the conceptual modelling phase. To accomplish this, we propose a framework (UMMA - User Mind do-Main Analysis) that consists of a mind map user centered conceptual modelling language and a systematic process designed to gather domain knowledge, validate its consistency, generate code and database artifacts through Model-Driven Engineering (MDE) techniques. Our framework was applied to the Audiobus industrial case study, a bus commercial broadcast system.

This paper is organized as follows. Section 2 gives background theory on Mind Map Modelling, Model-Driven Engineering and Domain-Specific Modelling Language. Section 3 presents the UMMA framework (language and process). Section 4 shows the application of the framework to an industrial case study. Section 5 shows a discussion about our framework proposed in relation to other conceptual models qualities' approaches. Section 6 describes some related work. Finally, Section 7 draws some conclusions and points out directions for future work.

2 Background Theory

Mind Map Modelling. A mind map is a cognitive diagram used to view, classify and organize concepts and to generate new ideas in a simple and intuitive way. It is used to connect words, ideas and concepts to a central idea or concept [17]. It is similar to a semantic network, or a cognitive map, but without restrictions on the types of connections used. A mind map is a radial diagram that, through a vocabulary (i.e., a set of keywords), may cognitively represent and model a concept or a specific domain. According to Buzan [17], the main benefits of using mind maps are: the organization of the ideas and concepts, emphasis on the relevant keywords, association between the elements in the branches, grouping of ideas support for visual memory and creativity, and to trigger innovation. Both academy and industry have been considering techniques and mind map based tools for managing requirements elicitation. Mahmud reported [18] interesting results collected during an experiment with experts and non-experts using mind maps. Kof et al. [19] used the concept of map visualization for requirements tracing. Laplante [20] mentioned that mind maps could be used during elicitation discussions with stakeholders aiming to capture the essential parts (business terms) of problem space. Village et al. [21] reports the learnability characteristic of use map visualization in early software engineering design. Alexander et al. [22] reports that mind maps can help requirements engineers to remember and make good holistic visualizations about all system details, using a mixing of words, pictures and other rich resources. Sutcliffe et al. [23] discuss their experience about user-centred requirements engineering, where mind maps were used to encourage epidemiologists (domain experts) to make more use of visualization tools.

Model-Driven Engineering (MDE). It is an approach that focuses on models as first class entities for software development [35]. The use of models in the construction of complex systems is one way to solve the limited cognitive capacity of human beings, as it is "not possible to understand a complex system in its entirety" [36]. What MDE proposes is to reduce the software engineer need to manually interact with all the source code, allowing him to concentrate on higher level models, where he can abstract from the complexity involved in development using different platforms. Domain specialists have a more active role in the process, and can directly use models to more easily identify business concepts, while computer specialists can identify technical elements. In the context of MDE, metamodels are used to construct a formal definition of models. Based on this definition of a metamodel, it is possible to implement transformations of models that automatically refine, comprise, refactor or reengineer models. Metamodels and automatic transformations of models are key concepts in MDE [35, 38].

Domain Specific Modelling Language (DSML). Some of the recently proposed Model-Driven Engineering approaches are based on DSLs [24]. A DSL is a language offering expressive power focused on a particular problem domain, such as a specific class of a particular application aspect [24,25]. A DSML directly represents the problem space by mapping modelling concepts to domain concepts [25]. It matches vocabularies and mental representations of the domain experts and therefore can be a powerful and easy-to-use tool in a particular domain. DSM has enabled both end-users and software developers in describing key characteristics of a system from the perspective of the problem space, without getting overwhelmed by the accidental complexities of the solution space [24,25]. The DSL anatomy is essentially composed by: (i) abstract syntax, (ii) concrete syntax and (iii) the semantics definition [25]. The abstract syntax describes the structure of the language, the way that the different primitives can be combined together, independently of any particular representation or encoding. The concrete syntax describes specific representation of modelling language, covering encoding and visualization. The semantics definition describes the meaning of the elements defined in the language and the meaning of the different ways of combining them. The abstract syntax is designed by metamodeling techniques and well-formed rules. Regarding the concrete syntax of our visual language the Eugenia framework was used. Eugenia is a tool to facilitate the use of the GMF framework. GMF is a valid choice for concrete syntax development of graphical DSL(s) [25].

3 The UMMA Framework

The UMMA framework contains two main components: (i) the language for conceptual modelling and (ii) a process to use the language. The process is characterized by having domain gathering, validation and generation activities, executed by different stakeholders (A short video shows[1] the complete operationalization of the UMMA Framework). The next sections will explain these components in detail. The user-centred requirements language was designed following the main pillars of frameworks of quality for conceptual modelling: (i) LSS Framework [12], (ii) Krogstie [15] and (iii) the Moody "Physics of Notations" theory [16]. The language includes a set of graphical symbols, a set of compositional rules for building valid visual sentences, and definitions of their meanings, to improve the stakeholder involvement in conceptual modelling process.

Therefore, the user-centred requirements language proposed may improve communication, e.g., in design team meetings with fewer misunderstandings between experts and stakeholders due to the existence of a consistent terminology. The visual language also helps to bridge the gap between design and implementation of an information system. The provision of a detailed and unambiguous model can then be transformed into a working application. Thus, this framework aims to design a visual requirements language based on pillars of frameworks of quality for conceptual modelling. Besides these theoretical foundations, the approach was systematically built through the synergy among the model-driven engineering, domain-specific modelling language techniques and the cognitive properties of mind maps model.

3.1 Users-Centered Requirements Language

Abstract Syntax. The first activity of the development of the conceptual modelling editor was the metamodel definition. The metamodel was defined by specializing the mind map metamodel. The design of the metamodels was defined using Ecore language. We extend the mind map metamodel through inheritance strategy aiming to improve the modularity. As we can observe in Figure 1, the mind map metamodel consists of nodes (Node), connections (Edge) and graphical connectors (GraphicalConnectors). A graphical connector is used to represent a link between nodes not associated by connections (Edge). The nodes and connections correspond to the structure of a graph.

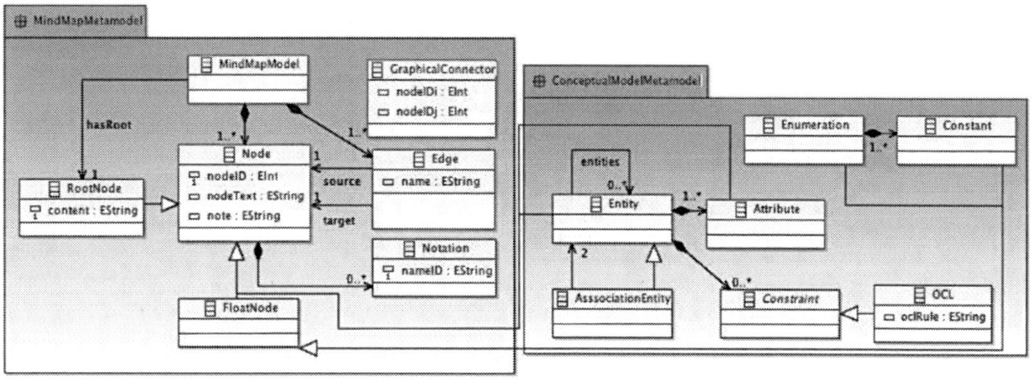

Fig. 1. Mind Map Metamodel.

[1] The UMMA Framework video - https://youtu.be/g6L9h3c5C-w

Furthermore, there are two important nodes for a mind map model: a root node (RootNode) and float nodes (FloatNodes). A root node is the center node of the mind map; therefore it must exist and be unique. It is the starting element of the mind map and other nodes must have a direct or indirect connection to it. Float nodes (such as constants and enumerations) are nodes that can float around the mind map with no connection with the root node. To design our conceptual language, without losing the cognitive properties that mind maps provide, an extension was created.

As we can observe in the metamodel also in Figure 1 the conceptual model elements {Entity, Attribute, AssociationEntity, Enumeration, Constant} extend the Node element, therefore inheriting the cognitive notations. The element entity (Entity) is one of the main elements in conceptual modelling, representing a part of a domain. Each entity is characterized by having multiple attributes (Attribute) or other entities. Association entities (AssociationEntity) can also be created, representing concepts regarding a pair of entities. Therefore, each association entity must be associated with 2 entities. Since there can be constants relating to a specific domain, our metamodel definition supports enumerations (Enumeration). This is characterized for having multiple constants and for being a float node. In order to further enhance the domain knowledge gathering, each entity can have multiple domain business rules associated to them. An entity can have several constraints (Constraint) concretely OCL rules. Note that there is no validation for the inserted rules, leaving that responsibility to the user using our tool.

Well-Formed Rules. A metamodel is a description of the language's abstract syntax since it defines: (i) a set of constructs pragmatically selected for the purpose of performing a specific (set of) task(s) and, (ii) a set of well-formedness rules for combining these constructs in order to create valid models in the language. In either case, context conditions are intended to constrain the language syntax by defining the set of correct (well-formed) sentences of the language. Some of these constraints are motivated by semantic considerations (laws of the domain being modeled) while pragmatic issues motivate others. Aiming to improve the semantics of our language, and adding constraints not covered by the metamodel, well-formed rules were defined. These rules were implemented using EVL from Epsilon tools. Figure 2 gives an example.

Rule #1: An entity must only be connected with attributes, other entities or the root node.

```
constraint EntityMustPointToRootNodeOrEntities{
check { var n = Node;
n = self.nodes.select(n : Node | isEntity(n.type()) and self.edges.select(c: Edge
| (isCenter(c.source.type()) or isEntity(c.source.type()) or
isAssociativeEntity(c.source.type())) and c.target = n).isEmpty());
return n.isEmpty();}
message : 'Entities must point to Domain or Entities Node"s: ' + toReadable(n+"")}
```

Fig. 2. Constraint of Entity construct.

Concrete Syntax. According to [24, 25] the success of the development of a graphical language depends on how the visual notation fits the domain. Our approach of a visual requirements language for conceptual modelling adopted the Moody's "Physics of Notations" theory [16].We specified default visual notations to represent specific elements for the Audiobus domain (Table 1). Thus, our visual language was built taking into account adaptability, where the notation was defined with end-user collaboration through GMF extensions. We use the participatory design activity [3, 27] to collaboratively define the symbols related to the domain concepts (Table 1) from an industrial case study, the Audiobus system, detailed later. After the initial model is built, refinements can occur (1.2 Refine Conceptual Model - see Section 3.2, Figure 3). These refinements are related to specializing and detailing entities (e.g., changing visual notation: for each domain concept, adding association entities, enumerations and add domain constraints by OCL rules).

Since the requirements engineer makes the refinements and specializations, they need to be validated by the domain expert to ensure that there is no consistency loss of domain knowledge. If the domain expert agrees that the refined domain model still maps the domain knowledge previously created, the process moves on, otherwise more refinement is needed. In the second activity, (2.1 Validate Conceptual Model - see Section 3.2, Figure 3) the software engineer will check if domain constraints are consistent in the conceptual model, designed in previous phase. This static analysis will be performed through model animation (by snapshots execution) using the USE tool [28].

Table 1. Visual Notation for Conceptual Modelling

Domain Model Concepts	Default Visual Notations	Audiobus Concepts	Domain-aware Visual Notations
RootNode		AudioBus *(extends Entity)*	
Entity		Broadcast *(extends Entity)*	
AssociationEntity		BusStop *(extends Entity)*	
Enum	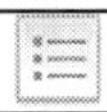	MobileDevice *(extends Entity)*	
Attribute and Constant	*<<no icons>>*	Coordinates *(extends Entity)*	

3.2 The UMMA Process

The BPM diagram shown in Figure 3 describes the UMMA process. Its main characteristic is to improve the communication among all stakeholders involved in the context of development of an Information System: the domain expert, the requirements engineer and the software engineer. Also the process aims to define a set of artifacts (Code and Database schema), from conceptual model, that must be validated by the active collaboration of the domain expert. The UMMA Process is essentially composed of three activities: (i) Domain Analysis, (ii) Conceptual Model Validation and (iii) IS Artifact Generation. The Domain Analysis is composed of 3 sub-activities. These sub-activities focus on the communication process between domain experts and requirements engineers aiming to capture the essential information of the domain [26] that can be reused [14].

The sub-activity (Gathering Knowledge Domain) aims to identify the main concepts of the domain represented through the information model by entities and their attributes. After validation, the process moves to the next activity. Otherwise, further refinement is needed to correct the inconsistencies found through snapshots. Once the domain model is validated, essential artifacts are generated (code and database schema).

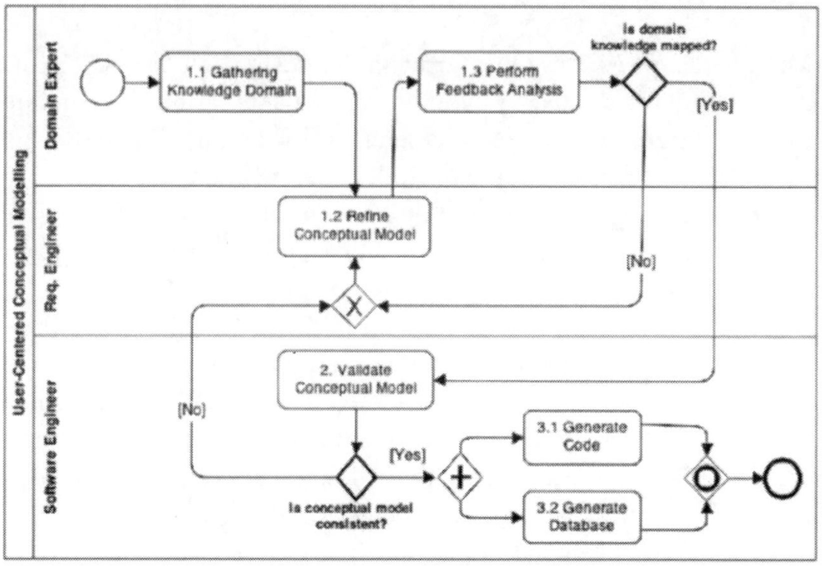

Fig. 3. The UMMA process

4 Industrial Case Study

The industrial case study we use here refers to the Audiobus system (Figure 4), an application developed by Mobciti. This is a startup company from Brazil that deals with innovation products which link informative, cultural and advertising contents for passengers using public transports. The Audiobus system (the flagship system of the Mobciti) has as a main goal to provide target customers and citizens (used to take a bus in their main destinations) with audio advertising an image (2), with adequate resolution. The bus receiver (3) communicates with the server (1).

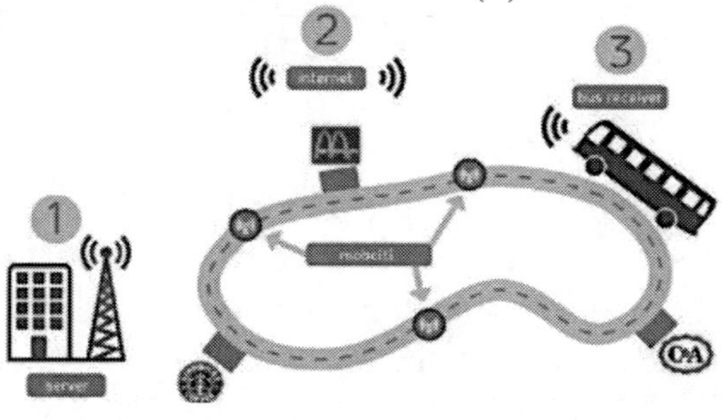

Fig. 4. Audiobus system

Gathering Knowledge Domain. The requirements engineer (one of the paper authors) interviewed the Audiobus Domain Expert. The Audiobus is an intelligent system that uses geographic information systems, which broadcasts digital surround sound for urban transports; customizes messages and contents exclusively developed for the surrounding area, and provides personalized advertising in each vehicle. A Broadcast has different types (Advertising or Music) and can be set to play by location (Georeferencing) or scheduling (Schedule). Also the broadcast can assume different status (Active, Inactive and Blocked) that is important information for Audiobus Domain Expert. The first artefact is an early conceptual model of the Audiobus system. The system distributes (through Broadcast) interaction contents through a mobile device installed in a Bus as a content receiver and service provider integrated with the bus audio system.

Refine Conceptual Model. After the first conceptual model is created, which captures the main concepts of the Audiobus domain knowledge, the requirements engineer identifies some refinements. These are: the BroadcastType, ContentType and Status. Initially defined as entities, these were recognized as Enumeration properties. This refinement happened because a finite set of constants, each one with a specific meaning could represent the information of these three concepts. Regarding the Status, besides changing it to enumeration, the requirements engineer, also changed his parent node.

This happened because the Status information had been managed by the *MobileDevice*, instead of *Broadcast* (domain expert viewpoint). Furthermore, the requirements engineer realizes that the entity "*Route*" can be represented as an association between two other entities, "*Bus*" and "*BusStop*" – see Figure 5. Also from the initial interaction with the domain expert (Gathering Knowledge Domain) the requirements engineer specifies some Audiobus domain constraints, which are related to the *MobileDevice*, *Bus* and *Route* entities. In the context of the *MobileDevice* the sound volume attribute has to be between 0.0 and 1.0db. Regarding the entity *Bus* the constraints states that the attribute *licensePlate* is unique. Finally, the constraints related to the entity *Route* says that the *totalKM* attribute must be below 10000 Km. As part of the refinement activity, the requirements engineer sets the specific visual notations (Table 1) to the conceptual model aiming to fit the Audiobus domain and to improve the cognitive comprehension for Domain Expert, through the participatory design techniques [3, 27].

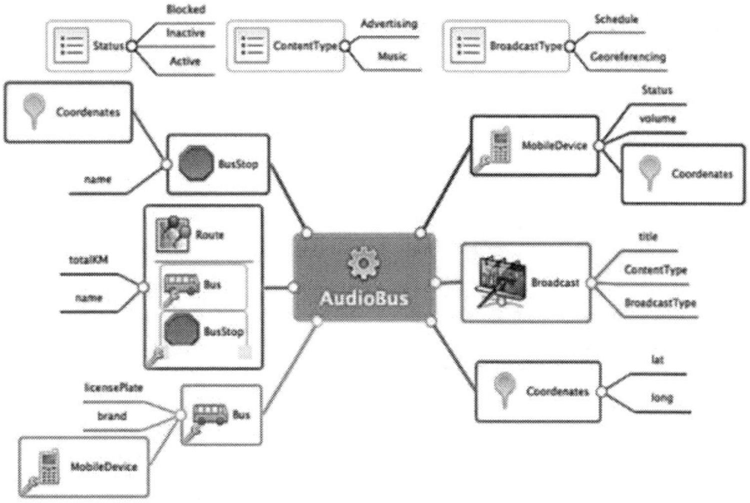

Fig. 5. The Audiobus Conceptual Model.

Conceptual Model Validation. After a positive feedback from the Audiobus domain experts about the mapping of the domain knowledge, the software engineer started the validation activity. This validation activity is concerned with checking if the domain constraints (business rules) designed in the conceptual model are still consistent according to the Audiobus domain expert expectation, to check after transformation. The software engineer generated the USE domain model (Figure 6B) through model transformation using our visual editor. We plan to derive Cardinalities in future work. To check the OCL, the software engineer created a set of USE commands (Figure 6A), to check domain properties existent in the conceptual model. Then, the software engineer created a MobileDevice object and set volume to 1.5db, violating the Audiobus domain constraint. The USE tool reported this constraint failed (MobileDevice::deviceVolume - Figure 6C) and the software engineer could check if the result was as intended.

Code Generation. This generation takes each entity and their attributes and maps them to a class and variable, respectively. In addition to the Java Code, this generation creates a set of inputs for the tool DresdenOCL[2]. As from the USE validation, the DresdenOCL tool can evaluate a set of OCL expressions for a given system state. The differences between the two tools shows that the DresdenOCL evaluates OCL expressions at the coding level, while USE does that at a modelling level. From Figure 7A, you can see the refined conceptual model and Figure 7B shows the MobileDevice generated Java class. Figures 7C and 7E show the system state where the OCL rules are going to be evaluated. The OCL rules representation are shown in Figure 7D and their result in Figure 7F, showing a positive result and a negative result.

Database Generation. As the crucial artifact of the information systems, the database schema is also generated. As the Java code generation, this generation takes the elements in the conceptual model and maps them into SQL database schema. For each **table**, an ID is generated by lowering the table' name and appending the string "ID". Each ID has the type int. IDs that are primary keys also have "Auto Increment" and "Not Null" specifications. If an entity is composed by other entities a foreign key is created for each one. In case of Association Entities, their associations are also foreign keys. All attributes (with exception of IDs) have the type "varchar (255)" by default, but can suffer from OCL inference like the other transformations (Figure 8).

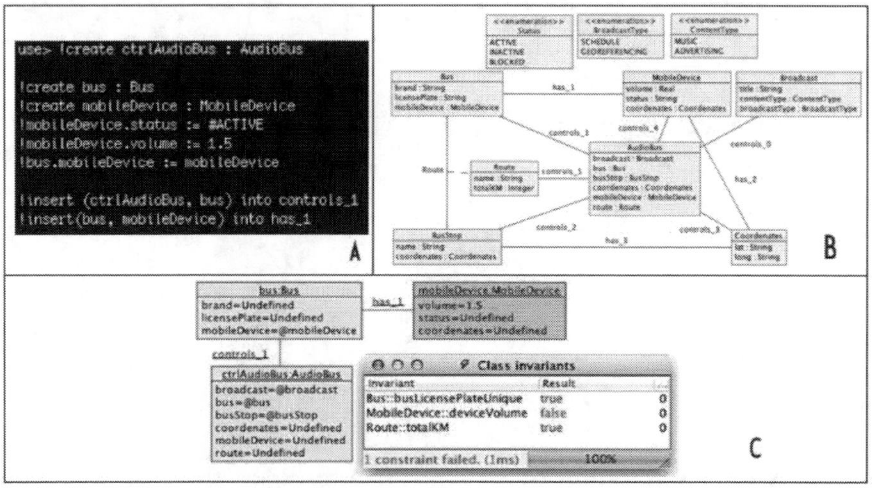

Fig. 6. The USE Environment.

[2] DresdenOCL - https://github.com/dresden-ocl

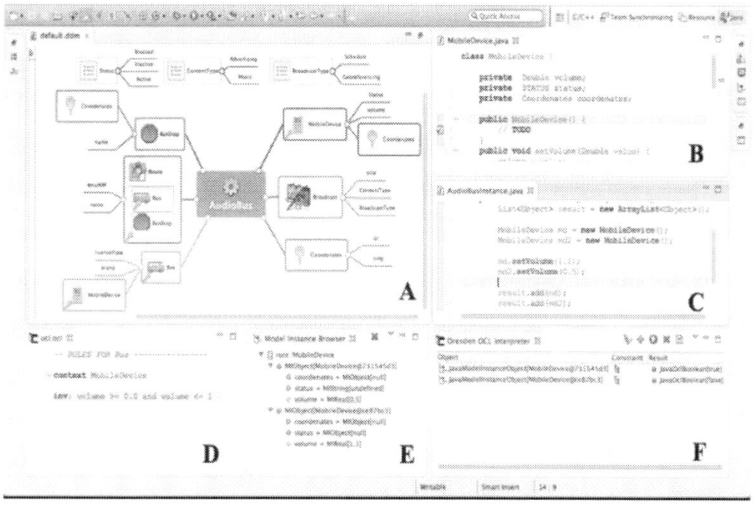

Fig. 7. The UMMA Environment.

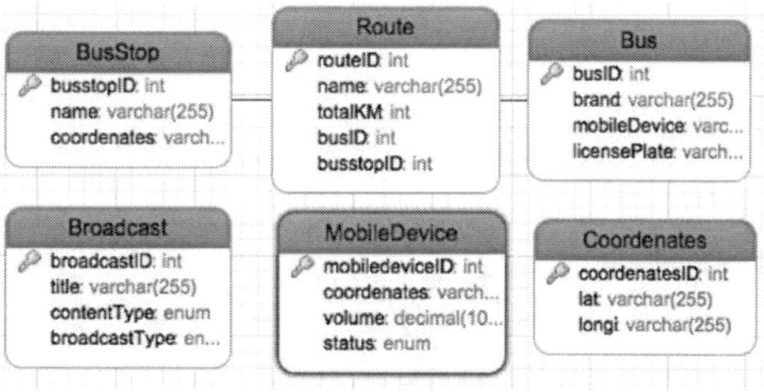

Fig. 8. MySQL Database Schema.

Besides the SQL relational schema, there is the possibility of creating a MongoDB template. That is, since the MongoDB is used to transfer sets of data, we create a template that represents the conceptual model. The transformation is straightforward, by showing each entity in a tree-like manner. Automatic integration between models, databases is important and has been addressed for quite some time [11].

4.1 Transformation Rules

All the transformations performed by our tool are made using EGL[3]. It starts from the created conceptual model and then the transformation itself is performed. For each entity created in the conceptual model, their name is taken and capitalized (e.g., "mobileDevice" → "MobileDevice") and their attributes and their attributes minimalized (e.g. "Volume" → "volume"). The attribute type is String by default, however since OCL rules can be inserted, we developed a little inference system. It works by analyzing the invariant lookup for OCL relational operators (<, <=, >, >=, <>, =) and the element the proceeds and precedes it. For determining the type we use regular expressions to

[3] EGL Language - http://www.eclipse.org/proposals/egl/

analyze if the expression if Numeric (Integer), Decimal (Double) or Boolean value, if no match is found than the type is String. To check the variable mentioned in the rule, we parse the expression that precedes the relation operator for "." and take the last element. That element is the variable affected by the restriction. That pair is then inserted in a map and checked for each attribute definition for the respective entity.

Note that, our tool does **not validate** the OCL rules, which is a concern for the user responsible for editing the diagram. This method does not cover all invariants specifications (a point for future work). Another inference made by our transformation regards the enumerations. When an attribute has its name equals to an enumeration in the conceptual model the transformation infers that the attribute type is the enumeration.

5 Discussion

The UMMA framework proposed was built based on the background theories of frameworks for quality of conceptual models [12, 15] and the recent Moody's theory of Physics of Notation [16]. The Lindland Framework (LSS) [12] propose three quality attributes for conceptual models. (i) **Syntactic Quality** refers to the consistency between the language and a model that was created by using the language. This consistency can be controlled via a comparison with the corresponding language grammar that is the modeling language's metamodel. We presented the definition of abstract syntax and well-formed rules (EVL) through the Metamodel Definition (using Ecore). (ii) The second pillar of LSS Framework is the **Pragmatic quality**; it describes a model's ability to help users in understanding the domain. In doing so, pragmatic quality connects the dimensions "model" and "user interpretation" through the orientation form of the model. To achieve these pragmatic properties our visual requirements language was defined based on native cognitive dimensions [29] of the **Mind Map Model.** (iii) The third quality attribute of LSS Framework is the **Semantic Quality**, which captures the relationship between the domain and a model and determines how well a model, conveys the intended meaning. The semantic quality is not trivial assessment as it depends on the empirical and iterative analysis of the users. Thus, to contribute to this capability, our approach, besides the visual language, defined a user-centered process (**User Feedback**) to engage the user.

Krogstie et al. [15] extended Lindland's framework (LSS) with a fourth dimension: **the Perceived Semantic Quality.** This dimension refers to the correspondence between the user interpretation (what a user thinks a model depicts) and the domain knowledge (what a user thinks a model should include). The Krogstie dimension refers directly to the cognitive properties of a visual language. So, the "Physics of Notation" can be considered as grounded theory, which refines the Krogstie's dimension. According to Moody et al. [37], visual notations play a critical role in requirements engineering (RE), and have dominated RE practice from its earliest beginnings. Visual notations play a critical role in communicating with end users and customers, as diagrams are believed to convey information more effectively to non-technical people than text. In this context, the UMMA framework was defined based on the **Visual Notation** techniques through the **GMF Extensions** providing the adaptability property of the concrete syntax of the visual language defined collaboratively with the domain expert.

6 Related Works

The increase of recent works points out the importance of the relationship between user perception of the quality of a conceptual modeling language from a cognitive point of view and its perceived usefulness. The recent empirical results of Figl and Derntl [30] reinforce the Moody's framework of quality characteristics of visual modeling languages, through a study with 198 use ratings of diagrams drawn with different modeling languages used in the e-learning domain. Barn and Clark [31] proposed a domain specific language for contextual design by support of the MetaEdit+ platform, focusing on improving the Cultural and Flow models. Diprose et al. [32] proposed the Ruru language, a visual language, which improves the usefulness and user friendliness for teaching novices in the robotic programming context. Almorsy et al. [33] presented the SecDSVL Language (Security Domain Specific Visual Language), which enables capturing of key security details to support enterprise systems security management process. Teixeira et al., [34] presented a user-centered requirements process in health information systems. The author tries to engage the end-user (e.g., clinical users) to define their expectation in Hierarchical Trees Activities. However, compared to our approach, both techniques have a shortcoming: the cost of learning a new modelling language and need to have proper automatic integration with other requirements approaches.

Jaafar [39] proposes the use of mind maps in the elicitation process and with tool support that promotes collaboration, aiming to study the impact of the mind map and groupware in facilitating requirements elicitation. A prototype based on PowerMeeting is developed to illustrate the idea of mind map groupware called Collaborative Mind Map Tool (CMMT). Integration to other requirements models is not really addressed.

Siau et al. [40] looks at the use of cognitive mapping techniques to improve the quality of conceptual modeling and discusses how human cognition is related to quality in conceptual modeling, the various cognitive mapping techniques, and how these cognitive mapping techniques can be used in conceptual modeling. Here they promote some integration with conceptual modeling only (in our case we want to integrate with other requirements models), but it is not clear how automatic integration is achieved.

Besides reinforcing the importance of development of user-centered languages improving the cognitive perceptions like in those related works, the present work differ from the others in two main aspects: (i) the use of a systematic language design based on essential pillars of quality for conceptual modelling and the synergy among the cognitive properties of mind maps, DSL techniques and the "Physics of Notations" theory of Moody; and (ii) the user-centered process defined, which guarantees conceptual model validation and generation of code and database schema in the context of IS. So, the novel approach of UMMA Framework is on the integration of code and database schema generation with the user active collaboration in the conceptual model process.

7 Conclusions

Gathering accurate domain knowledge is a difficult task, since different domain experts can have multiple backgrounds and use different mechanisms to communicate. The UMMA framework proposes a solution to tackle this issue by creating a visual language inspired by the cognitive and visual properties of mind maps, without forgetting relevant aspects of software development. By providing the ability to adapt its concrete syntax according to a specific domain, using visual notations to represent the domain entities and mapping them into various programming artifacts, we provide a set of contributions.: (i) promoting stakeholders engagement in domain analysis process; (ii) facilitating stakeholders validation of the artifacts produced; (iii) providing multiple validated programming artifacts (Java Code; SQL; USE) by the stakeholders' direct interaction. For future work we intend to apply the framework to other industrial case studies and evaluate the effectiveness of the approach in terms of usability and quality of the generated artifacts by defining and applying a set of relevant metrics.

Acknowledgments. The authors would like to thank FCT/UNL and NOVA LINCS UID/CEC/04516/2013, for the financial support for this work.

References

1. A. Gemino, Y. Wand, A framework for empirical evaluation of conceptual modeling techniques. IEEE Requirements Engineering Conference. 2004.
2. D. Moody, Theoretical and practical issues in evaluating the quality of conceptual models: Current state and future directions. Data and Knowledge Engineering. 2005.
3. P. Caire, N. Genon, P. Heymans, D. L. Moody, "Visual notation design 2.0: towards user comprehensible requirements engineering notations," IEEE RE 2013.
4. D. L. Moody, P. Heymans, R. Matulevicius, "Improving the effectiveness of visual representations in requirements engineering: An evaluation of i* visual syntax." 2009.
5. J. Recker, M. Rosemann, P. Green, M. Indulska, "Do ontological deficiencies in modeling grammars matter?", Management Information Systems. 2011.
6. A. Sonderegger, J. Sauer, The influence of design aesthetics in usability testing: Effects on user performance and perceived usability. Applied Ergonomics. 2010.
7. F. Wanderley, D. Silveira; "A Framework to Diminish the Gap between the Business Specialist and the Software Designer", QUATIC 2012, Lisbon, Portugal, 2012.
8. F. Wanderley, D. Silveira, J. Araujo, and Maria Lencastre. "Generating Feature Model from Creative Requirements using Model Driven Design", (SPLC '12), 2012.
9. F. Wanderley, D. Silveira, J. Araujo and A. Moreira. "Transforming Creative Requirements into Conceptual Models", RCIS, France, Paris, 2013.
10. F. Wanderley, and J. Araujo. "Generating Goal-Oriented Models from Creative Requirements using Model Driven Engineering", (MoDRE) @ RE, 2013.
11. P. Loucopoulos, R. and Zicari, Conceptual Modeling, Databases and CASE: An Integrated View of Information System Development, Wiley, 1992.
12. O. Lindland, G. Sindre, A. Solvberg, "Understanding quality in conceptual modelling", IEEE Software, 1994.
13. A. Olivé, "Conceptual Modeling of Information Systems", Springer, 2007.
14. M. Fowler, "Analysis Patterns: Reusable Object Models", Addison-Wesley. 1997.

15. J. Krogstie, G. Sindre, H. Jorgensen, "Process models representing knowledge for action: a revised quality framework", European Journal of Information Systems. 2006.
16. D. L. Moody, "The 'Physics' of Notations: Toward a Scientific Basis for Constructing Visual Notations in Software Engineering", IEEE Transactions on Software Engineering, 2009.
17. T. Buzan, "The Mind Map Book", BBC Active, 2003.
18. I. Mahmud "Mind-mapping: An Effective Technique to Facilitate Requirements Engineering in Agile Software Development" (ICCIT) 2011.
19. L. Kof., R. Gacitua, M. Rouncefield, P. & Sawyer. "Concept mapping as a means of requirements tracing" , MARK, 2010.
20. P. Laplante. "What Every Engineer Should Know about Soft. Engineering". 2007
21. J. Village, F. Salustri, P. Neumann. "Cognitive mapping: Revealing the links between human factors and strategic goals in organizations" Journal Ergonomics. 2013.
22. I. Alexander and N. Maiden, "Scenarios, Stories and Use Cases: Through the Systems Development Life Cycle", John Wiley & Sons - ISBN 0-470-86194-0, 2004.
23. A. Sutcliffe, S. Thew, P. Jarvis. "Experience with user-centred requirements engineering". Requirements Engineering Journal vol. 16 - Springer Editions. 2011.
24. M. Fowler "Domain-Specific Languages" Addison Wiley, 2010.
25. M. Voelter "DSL Engineering" (http://dslbook.org/), 2013.
26. K. Kang, S. Cohen, J. Hess, J. Feature-Oriented Domain Analysis (FODA) Feasibility Study, CMU/SEI 90-TR-021, Software Engineering Institute. 1990.
27. K. Bødker, F. Kensing, J. Simonsen, "Participatory IT design: Designing for business and workplace realities." Cambridge, USA: MIT Press. 2004
28. M. Gogolla, J. Bohling, and M. Richters, "Validating UML and OCL models in USE by automatic snapshot generation," Software & Systems Modeling, vol. 4. 2005.
29. T. R. Green, A. E. Blandford, L. Church, C. R. Roast, and S. Clarke, "Cognitive dimensions: Achievements, new directions, and open questions," J. of Vis. Lang. & Comp, 2006.
30. K. Figl and M. Derntl, "The impact of perceived cognitive effectiveness on perceived usefulness of visual conceptual modeling languages," ER. 2011.
31. B. S. Barn and T. Clark, "A domain specific language for contextual design." 2010.
32. J. P. Diprose, B. A. MacDonald, and J. G. Hosking, "Ruru: A spatial and interactive visual programming language for novice robot programming," (VL/HCC), 2011.
33. M. Almorsy and J. Grundy, "SecDSVL: A Domain-Specific Visual Language To Support Enterprise Security Modelling," ASWEC 2014.
34. L. Teixeira, C. Ferreira, and B. S. Santos, "User-centered requirements engineering in health information systems: A study in the hemophilia field", Computer programs in biomedicine, Elsevier, 2012.
35. Pressman, R. S., Software Engineering: a Practitioner's Approach, 6ª Edition, McGraw-Hill.
36. A. Kleppe, J. Warmer, W. Bast, "MDA Explained - The Model Driven Architecture: Practice and Promise", Addison-Wesley, 2003. (Object Technology Series).
37. D. Moody, P. Heymans, R. Matulevičius, "Visual syntax does matter: Improving the cognitive effectiveness of the i* visual notation, REJ 15(2):141-175, 2010.
38. M. Mernik, J. Heering, A. Sloanne, "When and how to develop domain-specific languages", ACM Computing Surveys, v. 37, n. 4, p. 316–344, Dec. 2005. ISSN 0360-0300.
39. J. Jaafar, M. Atan, and N. HAMID, "Collaborative mind map tool to facilitate requirement elicitation," 3rd Intl Conf, 2011.
40. K. Siau, X. Tan, "Improving the quality of conceptual modeling using cognitive mapping techniques", Data Knowl. Eng. 55(3): 343-365, 2005.

Hacia una nueva plantilla para la especificación de requisitos en lenguaje natural semi-estructurado

Raúl Mazo[1,2], Carlos Andrés Jaramillo[3]
[1]CRI, Universidad Panthéon Sorbonne, Paris, Francia,
[2] GiDITIC, Universidad Eafit, Medellín, Colombia
[3] Gerencia de innovación, SQA S.A., Medellín, Colombia
[1,2] raul.mazo@univ-paris1.fr, [3]carlos.jaramillo@sqasa.com

Resumen. La Ingeniería de requisitos es un enfoque sistemático y disciplinado para la especificación y gestión de requisitos de software; uno de sus objetivos es transformar las necesidades de los interesados en especificaciones formales con el fin de implementar un sistema. Estas necesidades por lo general se manifiestan y articulan en lenguaje natural, esto debido a la universalidad y facilidad que presenta el lenguaje natural para la comunicación de los requisitos. Para facilitar los procesos de transformación y para mejorar la calidad de los requisitos resultantes, varios autores han propuesto plantillas para la escritura de requisitos en lenguaje natural estructurado. Sin embargo, esas plantillas no permiten escribir ciertos requisitos funcionales, no funcionales y restricciones, y no se adaptan correctamente a ciertos tipos de sistemas como los adaptativos, los basados en líneas de productos y los embebidos. Este artículo (i) presenta algunas evidencias de las debilidades de la plantilla recomendada por el IREB® (International Requirements Engineering Institute) conocida como plantilla Rupp, y (ii) sienta las bases para la construcción de una mejor plantilla que facilite el trabajo de los ingenieros de requisitos y que a la larga mejore la calidad de los nuevos productos. Para ello, la plantilla Rupp fue empleada en la especificación de requisitos de un producto de software para la gestión de recursos humanos de una compañía de tecnología en la ciudad de Medellín-Colombia. En esta experiencia encontramos que algunos requisitos no podrían ser escritos correctamente usando dicha plantilla. Basados en la evidencia recolectada en este caso, este artículo presenta una versión mejorada de la plantilla Rupp que permite escribir correctamente todos los requisitos analizados. A pesar de los resultados prometedores de la validación de esta nueva plantilla, es aún un trabajo preliminar y no concluyente con respecto a su cobertura o al nivel de calidad de los requisitos que se pueden escribir con ella.

Palabras Clave: Requisitos, Ingeniería de requisitos, lenguaje natural, plantilla.

1. Introducción

Los requisitos son quizás la base más importante en la construcción de productos de software porque a través de éstos se puede lograr un entendimiento común entre las partes interesadas sobre el sistema que se va a implementar. Según Wiegers & Beatty [1], los dos objetivos más importantes en la especificación de un requisito son (i) que cuando varias personas lean el requisito lleguen a la misma interpretación; y (ii) la interpretación de cada lector coincida con lo que el autor del requisito intentaba comunicar.

En este sentido, Pohl [2] sostiene que el Lenguaje Natural (LN) es la forma más común de comunicar y documentar los requisitos de un sistema, puesto que el LN es universal y está al alcance de cualquier individuo en cualquier ámbito; además, no requiere ningún tipo de entrenamiento especial en la interpretación de notaciones o símbolos como ocurre cuando se utiliza un lenguaje de ingeniería como el UML (*Unified Modeling Language*). Sin embargo, estas ventajas se ven opacadas por las desventajas mismas del lenguaje natural [3]. De acuerdo con Mavin et al. [4] algunos de los problemas que pueden aparecer en la especificación de requisitos en LN son: (i) **ambigüedad**: una palabra o frase tiene dos o más significados diferentes; (ii) **vaguedad**: falta de precisión, estructura o detalle; (iii) **complejidad**: requisitos compuestos que contienen sub-cláusulas complejas o varias declaraciones interrelacionadas; (iv) **omisión**: requisitos faltantes, particularmente los requisitos para manejar el comportamiento no deseado; (v) **duplicación**: repetición de requisitos que definen la misma necesidad; (vi) **verbosidad**: uso de un número innecesario de palabras; (vii) **implementación**: declaraciones de cómo debe construirse el sistema, en lugar de qué debería hacer el sistema; y (viii) **falta de capacidad de ser probado**: requisitos que no se pueden probar (verdaderos o falsos) cuando se implementa el sistema

Para reducir la ocurrencia de esos problemas en las especificaciones de los requisitos de un sistema, varios autores han definido lo que se conoce como plantillas, moldes o patrones[1] [3]. Estas plantillas definen la estructura que deben tener los requisitos escritos en LN; esa estructura es flexible para que los requisitos resultantes tengan la ventaja de estar en LN y la ventaja de seguir una estructura bien definida. A este LN acotado por las posibilidades y las restricciones de la plantilla se le conoce como lenguaje natural semi-estructurado.

Las notaciones en lenguaje semi-estructurado, hacen posible construir requisitos siguiendo una plantilla y asignando una estructura similar a cada requisito. Este enfoque ayuda a evitar errores en las primeras etapas del proceso de desarrollo al especificar requisitos de alta calidad que son eficientes en tiempo y costo [5].

La plantilla propuesta por Rupp [3] también conocida MASTeR (*Mustergultige Anforderungen - die SOPHIST Templates fur Requirements*) [5], ha sido aceptada como un estándar[2] para la especificación sintáctica de requisitos de un sistema. Además, el uso de esta plantilla ha sido reconocido como una valiosa herramienta de ayuda para que los requisitos sean más precisos y tengan una estructura sintáctica estándar que facilite su comprensión [3]. Sin embargo, toda persona que haya usado la plantilla de Rupp en proyectos reales se ha podido dar cuenta de que algunos requisitos no pueden ser expresados con esa estructura sin que quede algún grado de ambigüedad o inconsistencia. Es por eso que este artículo se enfoca en investigar la siguiente pregunta: **¿Cuáles son los vacíos de la plantilla usada como estándar para la escritura de requisitos y cómo llenar esos vacíos?**

Para buscar respuesta a esta pregunta de investigación, hemos diseñado un experimento inspirado en el método de investigación *action science* o *action research* [6] que llamaremos en español: investigación-acción. Este método fue usado para analizar los requisitos de un proyecto industrial en una compañía colombiana. Por lo tanto, esta investigación pretende ***analizar*** la plantilla de Rupp ***con el fin de*** (i) evaluar su capacidad para representar requisitos de productos industriales de manera semi-estructurada, y (ii) proponer eventuales mejoras a la plantilla; ***desde el punto de vista de*** un académico y un experimentado ingeniero de requisitos ***en el contexto de*** una empresa de tecnología.

2. Estructura sintáctica de la plantilla de Rupp

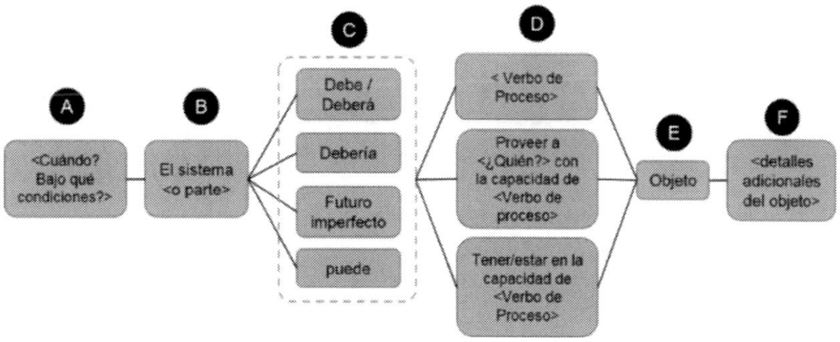

Figura 1. Plantilla de Rupp

[1] En ingles el término utilizado es template o boilerplate

[2] La plantilla ha sido estandarizada por el IREB® (International Requirements Engineering Institute) en el plan de certificación de ingenieros de requisitos IREB CPRE (Certified Professional for Requirements Engineering).

Como se muestra en la Figura 1 la plantilla está formada por 6 espacios para ir componiendo la sintaxis de un requisito. El resto de esta sección describe brevemente cada una de las partes que componen esta plantilla.

A. Condiciones

El primer espacio es una condición, por lo general opcional, que va al inicio del requisito, esta condición puede ser de dos tipos: condiciones lógicas compuesta por la conjunción "Si", y condiciones temporales compuesta por la conjunción "tan pronto como" o "después que".

B. El sistema

El segundo espacio es el nombre del sistema, el subsistema o componente del sistema que se especifica para el requisito.

C. Grado de obligatoriedad

El tercer espacio establece el grado de obligatoriedad[3] que puede adquirir el requisito.

D. Actividad funcional

El cuarto espacio caracteriza la actividad funcional que puede asumir el sistema, que incluye el verbo de proceso objeto del requisito.

E. Objeto

El quinto espacio es el objeto para el cual recae el comportamiento especificado en el requisito.

F. Detalles del Objeto

El sexto y último espacio son los detalles adicionales (opcionales) sobre el objeto, los adjetivos que lo califican o las características que el objeto puede poseer.

3. Método de Investigación

El caso industrial estudiado en esta investigación se ejecutó a través del método de investigación llamado investigación-acción [6]. Investigación-acción se define como "la intervención en una situación social con el fin de mejorar esta situación y aprender de ella" [7] [8]. El método investigación-acción tiene como objetivo mejorar la práctica mediante la solución de problemas reales y es conducida con el fin de investigar los fenómenos actuales en su contexto natural [9]. Hemos elegido este método porque nos permite responder a la pregunta de investigación y lograr el objetivo de esta investigación a partir de un experimento empírico en un caso industrial. Además, (i) este método de investigación se puede ejecutar a bajo costo ya que en él los investigadores juegan un rol activo, a diferencia de los estudios de caso (*case study*) en los cuales los investigadores juegan un rol meramente observacional y eso aumenta el riesgo y el costo del experimento puesto que solo se pueden ejecutar en ambientes reales; y (ii) el rigor del método investigación-acción permite reducir las amenazas a la validez del experimento.

Susman [10] ha desarrollado un modelo detallado del método investigación-acción con las diferentes etapas que se deben llevar a cabo en cada ciclo del proceso. La implementación del método investigación-acción se hace en varios ciclos y cinco etapas para cada ciclo, como se muestra en la Figura 2.

[3] El grado de obligatoriedad también se puede definir como un atributo del requisito y por eso sólo se puede emplear el verbo "deberá (shall)"[3]

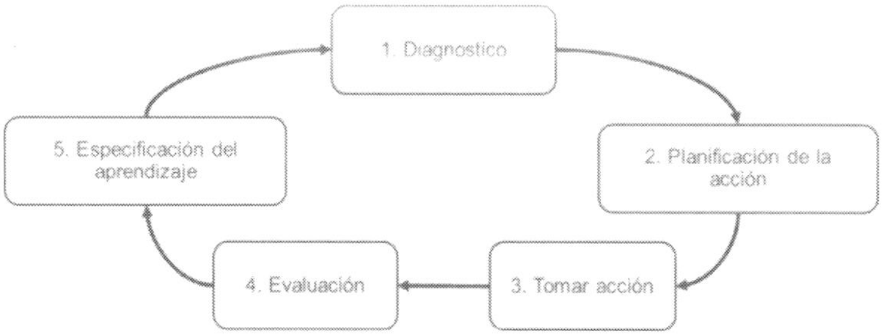

Figura 2. Proceso correspondiente a un ciclo en el método investigación-acción

A continuación resumimos las cinco etapas de cada ciclo del método investigación-acción:

1. **Diagnóstico**: identificar el problema y recopilar los datos requeridos para llevar a cabo un diagnóstico detallado.
2. **Planificación de la acción**: definir las diferentes soluciones posibles que abordan el problema definido en el primer paso.
3. **Tomar acción**: elegir una solución para implementar.
4. **Evaluación**: analizar los datos que corresponden a los resultados del plan de acción elegido.
5. **Especificación del aprendizaje**: interpretar los resultados de este plan de acción aprendiendo de acuerdo con el éxito de la solución o no. Por lo tanto, el problema se vuelve a evaluar y comienza un nuevo ciclo hasta que se resuelva el problema y todos los interesados estén satisfechos con el resultado obtenido.

Para realizar el análisis se tomó como referencia la especificación de requisitos de un proyecto de software para la compañía de tecnología SQA S.A. y se llevaron a cabo 3 ciclos para identificar las carencias, proponer las mejoras y evaluar la aplicabilidad de la plantilla mejorada en dicho proyecto. En este experimento, cada ciclo corresponde al análisis de una forma de especificación de los requisitos para el proyecto industrial. El experimento se llevó a cabo de la siguiente manera: en el **primer ciclo** se especificaron los requisitos sin utilizar ningún tipo de plantilla, estos fueron expresados en forma de prosa, tal como los interesados los manifestaron; en el **segundo ciclo** se especificaron los requisitos utilizando exclusivamente la plantilla Rupp; y en el **tercer ciclo** se especificaron los mismos requisitos utilizando la plantilla mejorada. En cada uno de ellos se ejecutaron las siguientes etapas:

1. **Diagnóstico**: al usar la plantilla de Rupp para representar los requisitos de cada uno de los sistemas que fueron usados del experimento, se identificaron algunos problemas. Esto permitió plantear en primera instancia la pregunta de investigación: ¿Cuáles son los vacíos de la plantilla usada como estándar para la escritura de requisitos y cómo llenar esos vacíos? Esta fase fue conducida a través de varios mini ciclos de especificación de los requisitos a fin de lograr tener un número de requisitos apropiados para lograr responder de forma sistemática a la pregunta de investigación.
2. **Planificación de la acción**: los autores de este artículo consideraron otras propuestas de plantillas de requisitos de otros autores. En particular, se tomó la plantilla de Rupp como referencia y en cada ciclo se evaluaba que la plantilla mejorada (resultante de cada ciclo) fuera consistente con otras plantillas encontradas en la literatura (p.e., EARS [4], Adv-EARS [11][12] e ISO/IEC/IEEE 29148-2011 [13]). Para garantizar que la plantilla mejorada seguía siendo consistente con la plantilla de Rupp y con las otras encontradas en la literatura se planeaba la siguiente estrategia: al principio de cada ciclo de escritura de los requisitos del caso industrial usando la nueva plantilla se usaban las plantillas encontradas en la literatura (no todas fueron encontradas desde el primer ciclo) con el fin de incorporar en la nueva plantilla los elementos de las otras que permitieran mejorar las situaciones en donde la plantilla de Rupp no fuese adecuada.
3. **Tomar acción**: se consideraron, en primer lugar, aquellos requisitos que no se pudieron especificar completamente utilizando la plantilla de referencia (de Rupp). Para estos

requisitos se evaluó en qué forma se podían especificar sintácticamente utilizando el lenguaje natural y las construcciones de otras planillas de especificación sintáctica de requisitos, con el fin de encontrar un patrón repetible en esta especificación. Si se identificaba un patrón repetible en al menos tres requisitos con condiciones similares, entonces se adicionaba este patrón a la nueva plantilla con el fin de enriquecerla.

4. **Evaluación**: al final de cada ciclo se evaluó si la plantilla propuesta permitía especificar por lo menos el 98% de los requisitos del proyecto correspondiente al ciclo en curso y a los requisitos de los proyectos de los ciclos precedentes sin que se presenten problemas de ambigüedad, vaguedad, complejidad, omisión, duplicidad, verbosidad, implementación o falta de capacidad de ser probado.

5. **Especificación del aprendizaje**: al final de cada ciclo los autores realizaron una interpretación de los resultados obtenidos y con base en esos resultados determinaron las fortalezas y limitaciones de la plantilla mejorada en el ciclo correspondiente.

Las diversas fases y la sucesión de ciclos son colaborativos dado que el proceso de investigación y objetivo se han llevado a cabo en colaboración entre los dos autores. Esta es otra característica que nos llevó a elegir la investigación-acción como método de investigación para este trabajo.

4. Problemas identificados en la plantilla de Rupp

Luego de realizar una evaluación sistemática de la plantilla de Rupp, usándola en diferentes en los requisitos del caso industrial de la empresa SQA S.A, se identificaron problemas que generan potenciales ambigüedades. Esos problemas se registraron en un documento, disponible en línea[4], que contiene cada uno de los requisitos utilizando en el caso industrial y cada uno de los problemas encontrados durante la investigación. En particular, la primera hoja presenta los requisitos utilizando lenguaje natural sin apoyo de ninguna plantilla, la segunda hoja presenta los requisitos utilizando la plantilla Rupp, la tercera hoja presenta los problemas que se identifican al utilizar la plantilla Rupp y la cuarta y última hoja presenta los requisitos utilizando la plantilla mejorada.

A continuación, se describen las dificultades y barreras que se han detectado al trabajar con la plantilla de Rupp. Para cada uno de este tipo de problemas hemos definido un nombre descriptivo, una breve descripción y un ejemplo que permita entender mejor el problema.

4.1. Motivos Faltantes

Algunas veces es necesario expresar el motivo o razón de un requisito. Por ejemplo, en los marcos de desarrollo ágil uno de los aspectos más importantes en la especificación de requisitos por medio de historias de usuarios es especificar el "por qué" o el "para qué" del requisito [14] [15]. Esto le da un mejor contexto a quien implemente la funcionalidad o comportamiento que describa el requisito y le permitirá entender mejor el nivel de importancia o prioridad del requisito. En la plantilla de Rupp no hay un espacio para definir, aunque sea de forma opcional, la razón de un requisito. Por ejemplo, los requisitos "El sistema SMV debe tener la capacidad de interactuar con otros dispositivos de personas cercanas para conocer su actividad vital" y "Si algún sensor sobrepasa los límites tolerables definidos, el sistema de domótica debe encender una sirena para prevenir al dueño de casa" tienen un "para qué" de importancia vital por tratarse de sistemas críticos. Si una plantilla de especificación de requisitos permitiera definir la razón de los requisitos, los desarrolladores podrán entender fácilmente, porque está consignado de manera explicita, lo importante que es implementar esos requisitos con altos niveles de calidad.

[4] https://docs.google.com/spreadsheets/d/1_xDK1A4JObOsOKDYW3NoT8q5_3BpOyJH-vl1w10OpUs/edit?usp=sharing

4.2. Omisión de cantidades y rangos

En ocasiones los requisitos hacen alusión no solo a un objeto específico, sino a varios objetos o a un rango de objetivos de la misma naturaleza. La plantilla de Rupp no permite explícitamente la posibilidad de especificar rangos o cantidades de objetos en los requisitos. Como lo podemos ver en el siguiente ejemplo de requisito, la omisión de esta cantidad puede dar lugar a ambigüedades o imprecisiones: "El subsistema de punto de venta debe proveer al administrador POS con la habilidad de vincular entre una y 10 bodegas máximo a un punto de venta"

El objeto bodega no hace alusión a una única bodega, sino que deja abierta la posibilidad de vincular un rango de bodegas a un punto de venta. De acuerdo con lo anterior, una plantilla de escritura de requisitos debería ofrecer explícitamente la posibilidad de cuantificar el número de objetos y objetivos.

4.3. Omisión de bicondicionales

Algunos requisitos exigen que ciertos comportamientos se lleven a cabo sólo si se cumplen ciertas condiciones; de otra manera el comportamiento no se podrá realizar. Llamamos a esto "bicondicional" para expresar que el comportamiento A se realice "si y solo si" se cumple B y viceversa. Por ejemplo, en el requisito "El subsistema de punto de venta debe mostrar las cajas si y solo si se encuentran en estado activo", un comportamiento se llevará a cabo solo para los objetos que se encuentren en cierto estado y no para todos los objetos dentro del dominio. Aquí hay una condición explicita que el requisito debe efectuar a través del verbo de proceso "mostrar", por medio del condicional "si y solo si". Consideremos otro ejemplo de requisito: "Después de que se ha encendido la aspiradora, el sistema Ivaccum debe iniciar el ciclo de limpieza si y solo si la carga de la batería de la aspiradora se encuentra en el 90% o más". En este caso el comportamiento del objeto depende de una condición sobre la carga de la batería.

Como se puede observar, este tipo de condiciones son comunes al momento de especificar requisitos en casos industriales; sin embargo, la plantilla de Rupp no facilita, explícitamente, su especificación.

4.4. Condicionalidad inapropiada para el requisito

En los requisitos los comportamientos se encuentran condicionados por diferentes factores, que implican interpretaciones diferentes dependiendo de estas condiciones. Por ejemplo, un requisito que especifica "Mientras el control de temperatura esté encendido, el sistema debe balancear la temperatura del ambiente" puede tener una interpretación diferente a la del requisito que específica "Si el control de temperatura está encendido, el sistema debe balancear la temperatura del ambiente" y también ambos pueden diferenciarse de un requisito que especifique "Tan pronto como el control de temperatura sea encendido, el sistema debe balancear la temperatura del ambiente". En los tres casos, aunque se utiliza una condición similar, la interpretación es diferente. En la plantilla de Rupp se emplean únicamente dos tipos de condicionales, los cuales son: los condicionales lógicos y los condicionales temporales [3]. Sin embargo, existen otros tipos de condiciones que no están cubiertos por la planilla Rupp, por ejemplo, comportamientos que son desencadenados por eventos y comportamientos que se llevan a cabo mientras el sistema se encuentra en un estado determinado.

4.5. Falta de verificabilidad de los requisitos no funcionales

La plantilla de Rupp fue creada con el objetivo de especificar requisitos funcionales [3]; sin embargo, no fue diseñada propiamente para la especificación de requisitos no funcionales (requisitos de calidad y restricciones). Por ejemplo, estos dos requisitos de calidad "El sistema deberá estar disponible para los usuarios 7x24x364" y "El rendimiento del sistema debe ser óptimo, procurando dar respuesta a los usuarios en menos de 2 segundos" tienen un factor medible y finito para determinar que el requisito satisfará o no la necesidad de los interesados. Sin embargo, la plantilla de Rupp no tiene una estructura explicita para la escritura adecuada de factores medibles y finitos de satisfacción de requisitos no funcionales.

4.6. Falta de referencia a sistemas o dispositivos externos

En caso de que el tipo de actividad del sistema sea un requisito de interfaz, la estructura sintáctica de la plantilla de Rupp no hace referencia explícita a sistemas o dispositivos externos. Por ejemplo, los requisitos "El subsistema de punto de venta debe ser capaz de leer códigos de barras en etiquetas de artículos" y "El sistema deberá ser capaz de obtener la información de un cliente" siguen la estructura sintáctica que propone la plantilla de Rupp; sin embargo, en ninguno de esos requisitos se menciona el nombre del sistema o dispositivo con el cual se intercambia información, ni se establece si la información va desde o hacia el dispositivo/sistema.

4.7. Falta de conceptos para escribir requisitos de líneas o familias de productos

En algunos casos, los requisitos no hacen referencia a un producto sino a varios productos de una misma familia [16]. Las líneas de productos se basan en el concepto de la gestión de la variabilidad para especificar, diseñar y desarrollar de manera intensiva los productos de una misma familia de manera prescrita. Aunque la plantilla de Rupp puede ser usada para especificar requisitos, con diferentes niveles de prioridad, de líneas de productos únicamente cambiando en la plantilla "El sistema" por "La línea de productos", no es posible definir con ella la variabilidad de los requisitos que pueden cambiar de un producto de la línea a otro. Por ejemplo, en los requisitos "La línea de productos de tiendas virtuales deberá calcular el valor del IVA de cada compra" o "La línea de productos de tiendas virtuales podría calcular el valor del IVA de cada compra" se especifican dos niveles de prioridad, pero no se considera la variabilidad de los requisitos, es decir, no se dice si es para todos los productos de la línea (obligatorio para todos los productos de la línea) o solo para algunos (opcional). Además, restricciones típicas en una línea de productos como por ejemplo "El usuario administrador de cada tienda virtual debe estar validado antes de poder gestionar los productos de la tienda virtual correspondiente" y "Los productos de la línea de tiendas virtuales que tengan la función A no pueden tener la función B", tampoco pueden ser especificadas con la plantilla de Rupp.

5. Propuesta de una nueva plantilla de especificación de requisitos

Considerando cada uno de los problemas encontrados durante la ejecución del método investigación-acción y ejemplificados en la Sección 4, los autores han mejorado la plantilla de Rupp [3] inspirándose en conceptos de otros trabajos relacionados encontrados en la literatura (p.ej., la plantilla EARS [4]). La nueva plantilla, ver Figura 3, está compuesta de ocho espacios y cada uno se estructuró pensando en una especificación sintáctica simple y a la vez robusta para abarcar la mayor cantidad de tipos de requisitos en varios tipos de sistemas. Los rectángulos en color *amarillo* representan condicionales; los rectángulos color *gris* se usan para representar la familia de sistemas, el sistema o una parte de éste; los rectángulos de color *naranja* representan el grado de obligación; los de color *verde* son las actividades que caracterizan el sistema; los rectángulos color *azul* representan los objetos (sustantivos), con sus respectivas cantidades y complementos; y el rectángulo de color *purpura* describe el criterio medible de verificación del requisito. Este último es de carácter opcional y por ese la unión con el resto de la plantilla se hace a través de una línea punteada.

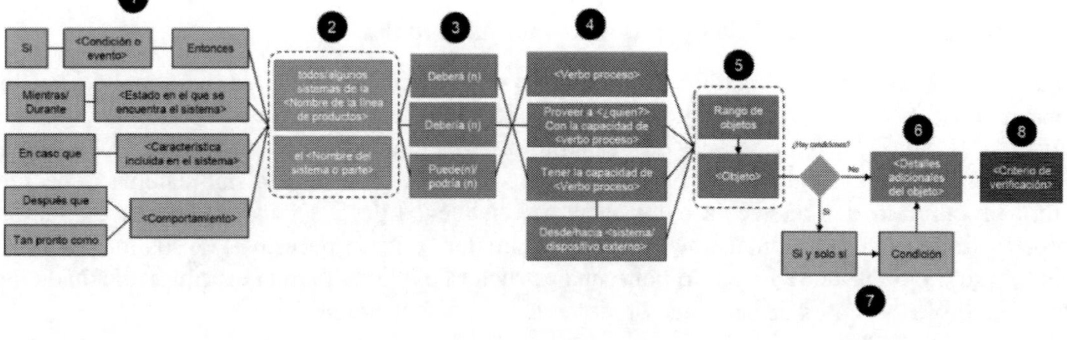

Figura 2. Nueva plantilla propuesta

A continuación, describiremos cada uno de los componentes de la plantilla resultante al final de los tres ciclos de investigación-acción en el caso del sistema PeopleQA de la empresa SQA S.A.

5.1. (1) Condiciones bajo las cuales se presenta un comportamiento

Algunos requisitos no describen comportamientos continuos sino comportamientos que se realizan o proporcionan solo bajo ciertas condiciones; por ejemplo, lógicas o temporales, como lo mostramos a continuación.

a. Requisitos con condiciones lógicas. Se utilizan para describir comportamientos que se desencadenan únicamente cuando se cumple una condición lógica [3] o cuando ocurre un evento inesperado [4]. La forma de esta especificación es: **SI** <condición o evento> **ENTONCES,** [(todos/algunos sistemas de la <Nombre de la línea de productos>)|(el <Nombre del sistema o parte>)] deberá(n)/debería(n)/podría(n).

b. Requisitos guiados por estado. Se utilizan para describir un comportamiento que se debe dar en el sistema mientras el sistema se encuentra en un estado específico. Esta condición fue propuesta por [4]. La forma de esta especificación es: **MIENTRAS (o DURANTE)** <Estado de activación> [(todos/ algunos sistemas de la <Nombre de la línea de productos>)|(el <Nombre del sistema o parte>)] deberá(n)/ debería(n)/podría(n).

c. Requisitos con característica opcional. Se utilizan para describir un comportamiento que se debe dar únicamente si se incluye una característica particular [4]. La forma de esta es especificación es: **EN CASO QUE** <la característica incluida>, [(todos/ algunos sistemas de la <Nombre de la línea de productos>)|(el <Nombre del sistema o parte>)] debe(n)/ debería(n)/podría(n)

d. Requisitos con condiciones temporales. Se utilizan para describir un comportamiento que se debe dar después que ocurre otro comportamiento y se da de forma secuencial, es decir el comportamiento A se efectúa después de B. Esta condición fue propuesta por [3]. La forma de esta especificación es:

   DESPUÉS QUE (o **TAN PRONTO COMO**) <comportamiento>, [(todos/algunos sistemas de la <Nombre de la línea de productos>)|(el <Nombre del sistema o parte>)]debe/debería/podría.
   La palabra "**DESPUÉS QUE**" significa que el sistema debe haber terminado un comportamiento en ejecución antes de iniciar otro comportamiento. La palabra "**TAN PRONTO COMO**" significa que el sistema no necesariamente tiene que haber terminado un comportamiento en ejecución antes de iniciar otro comportamiento.

   Los requisitos guiados por estado, requisitos con característica opcional fueron tomados de EARS [4]; los requisitos con condiciones lógicas y temporales fueron tomados de la plantilla de Rupp [3].

   A continuación, presentamos un ejemplo de requisito con condicionales, utilizando la plantilla mejorada:

   "Mientras no se haya confirmado el pago de una factura de un cliente, el subsistema deberá enviar un mensaje de texto diario al número celular que tenga registrado el cliente".

5.2. (2) Familia de sistemas, sistema o parte del sistema

Este espacio en la plantilla está reservado para el nombre de la línea de productos, o del sistema, subsistema o componente del sistema. En el caso de que se trate de un requisito de una línea de productos, se debe especificar si el requisito es válido para todos o solo para algunos sistemas. La estructura de esta segunda parte de la nueva plantilla es la siguiente: `(todos/algunos sistemas de la <Nombre de la línea de productos>)|(el <Nombre del sistema o parte>)`. El símbolo | significa que en un mismo requisito se debe usar sólo una de las dos partes entre paréntesis.

Completamos la segunda parte de la plantilla de Rupp con la posibilidad de especificar requisitos de líneas de productos puesto que dicha plantilla no se adaptaba correctamente para poderlos escribir en LN semi-estructurado.

A continuación, un ejemplo de requisito para líneas de productos de software, utilizando la plantilla mejorada:

"Si la aplicación de automatización es de tipo web, algunos sistemas de la línea de productos Automatización de pruebas deberán proveer al tester con la habilidad de seleccionar el tipo de navegador donde se ejecutará la prueba (ya sea Chrome, Firefox o Safari)".

5.3. (3) El grado de prioridad

En la plantilla de Rupp, este espacio tradicionalmente está reservado para especificar el grado de obligatoriedad del requisito; sin embargo, el concepto de "obligatoriedad" lo hemos tenido que cambiar por el de "prioridad" para no confundirlo con el concepto de "obligatoriedad" de las líneas de productos. El concepto de "obligatoriedad" usado para especificar ciertos requisitos de las líneas de productos como lo presentamos en el componente 2 de la nueva plantilla. La prioridad de los requisitos hemos usado la técnica MoSCoW [17], en la cual se establecen tres grados de prioridad: esenciales, recomendados y deseables.

a. Requisitos esenciales. Son requisitos que se deben implementar para lograr el éxito del producto o de la línea de productos. Se utiliza la palabra "deberá(n)".

b. Requisitos recomendados; es decir, que son importantes, pero no necesarios para alcanzar el éxito del producto o de la línea de productos. Se emplea la palabra "debería(n)".

c. Requisitos deseables (pero no necesarios) porque podrían mejorar la experiencia del usuario y la satisfacción del cliente. Se emplea la palabra "puede(n)" o "podría(n)". El plural se usa para requisitos de líneas de productos.

5.4. (4) La actividad

El cuarto espacio, el mismo de la plantilla de Rupp, especifica la caracterización de la actividad que es conducida por el sistema o por los sistemas de la línea correspondiente. Existen tres tipos de actividades que se pueden llevar a cabo:

a. Actividad autónoma. En esta actividad el(los) sistema(s) inicia(n) y ejecuta(n) el comportamiento de forma autónoma, no hay ningún usuario involucrado. La forma de esta este tipo de actividad es: …`[(todos los/algunos sistemas de la <Nombre de la línea de productos>)|(el <Nombre del sistema o parte>)] deberá(n)/debería(n) /podría(n) <Verbo de proceso>`

b. Interacción de usuario. En esta actividad el (los) sistema(s) provee(n) a un usuario con la capacidad o habilidad de usar cierto comportamiento que es iniciado o estimulado por un usuario (actor) que interactúa con el sistema. La forma de este tipo de actividad es: …`[(todos los/algunos sistemas de la <Nombre de la línea de productos>)|(el <Nombre del sistema o parte>)] deberá(n)/ debería(n)/podría(n) Proveer a <¿quién?> con la capacidad de <verbo proceso>`. Donde "quién" es el actor o usuario que debe tener la capacidad de usar la funcionalidad. Dicho usuario debe estar caracterizado correctamente y no incurrir en el uso indebido de sustantivos sin índice de referencia [3]; es decir, indicar "el usuario" sería un error que conduciría a una ambigüedad en la especificación.

c. Requisito de interfaz. En esta actividad, el sistema lleva a cabo un comportamiento con dependencia de otra entidad (que puede ser otro sistema o un dispositivo físico). Este espacio fue mejorado en la nueva plantilla adicionando explícitamente el nombre de la entidad externa con la cual interactúa el sistema y la dirección de la relación. La forma de este tipo de actividad es: ...[(todos los/algunos sistemas de la <Nombre de la línea de productos>)|(el <Nombre del sistema o parte>)] debe(n)/ debería(n)/podría(n) Tener la capacidad de <Verbo proceso>. Además, esta estructura se completa con la entidad con la cual interactúa el sistema:

- Si el comportamiento es ejecutado por el sistema externo que transmite datos a la interfaz del sistema receptor, entonces se complementará la especificación agregando: **Desde** <nombre del sistema o dispositivo externo>.

- Si el comportamiento es efectuado por el sistema e interactúa o afecta a otro sistema o dispositivo externo entonces se complementará la especificación agregando: **Hacia** <nombre del sistema o dispositivo externo>

5.5. (5) El objeto o los objetos

Este espacio está reservado para el objeto o los objetos que componen al sistema. En la nueva plantilla hemos incorporado el concepto de "rango", puesto que los objetos se pueden afectar en distintos rangos. Los rangos en la nueva plantilla se especifican de la siguiente manera:

a. Un único objeto: Un (uno, una) <objeto>

b. Un objeto específico: el (la) <objeto>

c. Cada objeto de un conjunto: cada <Objeto>

d. Varios objetos: X <objetos>, siendo X el número de objetos

e. Rango de objetos: Entre A y B <objetos>, siendo A el rango inferior y B el rango superior de objetos

f. Todos los objetos de un conjunto: Todos los (Todas las) <objetos>.

A continuación, un ejemplo de requisito con rango de objetos, utilizando la plantilla mejorada:

"El subsistema de inventario debe proveer al administrador de inventario con la capacidad de asociar a una caja registradora entre 1 y 3 pistolas lectoras de código de barras".

5.6. (6) Los detalles complementarios al objeto

En el sexto espacio de la plantilla se especifican de forma opcional los detalles complementarios del objeto, que pueden ser uno o varios adjetivos, así como una descripción más enriquecida sobre el objeto, sin el riesgo de llegar a alterar el significado propio de la especificación del requisito y centrándose únicamente en describir los detalles relacionados al objeto en cuestión. Este espacio de la plantilla se conservó de la plantilla de Rupp y no fue modificado por los autores.

5.7. (7) Condicionalidad en el objeto

Es posible que en algunos casos el comportamiento del requisito sea condicionado por el estado en el cual se encuentre un objeto. En la nueva plantilla hemos reservado el séptimo espacio para especificar un comportamiento que el sistema debe llevar cabo si y solo si, el objeto cumple cierta condición, en este caso el requisito se completa adicionando la siguiente expresión: **SI Y SOLO SI** <condición>. Es importante aclarar que esta condición es opcional y solo se da de forma explícita si el objeto puntual del requisito requiere especificar la condición, por lo tanto, no es obligatoria en la especificación del requisito.

A continuación, presentamos un ejemplo de requisito con condicionalidad en el objeto, utilizando la plantilla mejorada:

"El subsistema de inventarios podría proveer al administrador de bodega con la capacidad de eliminar una orden de compra, si y solo si, la orden de compra no ha sido despachada".

5.8. (8) El criterio de verificación (ajuste) del requisito

En algunos tipos de requisitos, especialmente en los requisitos no funcionales, es necesario establecer el grado en el cual el requisito se debe alcanzar. Robertson & Robertson [18] recomiendan incluir criterios de ajuste; es decir, incluir "una cuantificación del requisito que demuestre el estándar que debe alcanzar el producto" como parte de la especificación de cada requisito, funcional y no funcional. Los criterios de ajuste describen una forma medible de evaluar si cada requisito se ha logrado satisfacer correctamente.

Para tal fin, en la nueva plantilla, hemos agregado en el último espacio la opción de establecer un criterio medible u observable para determinar el grado de verificabilidad del requisito, esto con el fin de asegurar que el requisito se puede comprobar ya sea por una persona o una máquina. Este criterio se define a discreción del autor del requisito y es de carácter opcional, aunque se recomienda emplearlo siempre en los requisitos de calidad.

A continuación, un ejemplo de requisito no funcional, utilizando la plantilla mejorada:

"Si ocurre una falla que produce que el sistema se detenga, el sistema Oktupus deberá reiniciar todos los sensores en un tiempo inferior a 20 segundos".

6. Evaluación preliminar de la plantilla propuesta

Para la evaluación preliminar de la plantilla propuesta en este artículo se establecieron 2 grupos; cada uno compuesto por un analista de negocios con experiencias similares (esto es, mismo número de años en la empresa y participación en proyectos comparables en tema, duración y tamaño) en ingeniería de requisitos y con un entrenamiento previo del uso de la plantilla Rupp; y un revisor técnico de requisitos. El analista de cada grupo debía especificar los requisitos en la plantilla Rupp (para el caso del primer grupo) o en la plantilla mejorada (para el caso del segundo grupo) y el segundo rol inspeccionaba el trabajo del primero.

Como se mencionó en la Sección 3, se hicieron 3 ciclos para esta investigación. En el primer ciclo se especificaron los requisitos en prosa tal como los manifestaron los interesados. De esta actividad fueron especificados 46 requisitos. En el segundo ciclo, el primer grupo reescribió los requisitos utilizando para ello la plantilla Rupp y con un acompañamiento de los autores para apoyarlos en la resolución de dudas. Para este ciclo se obtuvieron 138 requisitos. Una vez concluida la especificación, el revisor técnico del primer grupo identificó 48 requisitos con problemas de especificación que no se adhieren al estándar propuesto por Rupp es decir que el 34.8% de los requisitos tuvieron problemas de adherencia con la plantilla de Rupp. Estos problemas fueron categorizados según siete tipos de criterios como se muestra en la Tabla 1 (para una explicación más detallada sobre cada uno de estos tipos de problemas y algunos ejemplos que se puedan presentar en una especificación de requisitos basada en la plantilla Rupp ver la Sección 4).

Problema identificado	Cantidad de requisitos usando la plantilla de Rupp	Cantidad de requisitos usando la plantilla propuesta
Condicionalidad inapropiada	6	0
Falta de referencia a sistemas o dispositivos externos	4	0
Omisión de bicondicionales	7	0

Omisión de cantidades y rangos	18	0
Falta de verificabilidad de requisitos No funcionales	3	0
Motivos Faltantes	3	0
Otros	7	3

Tabla 1 problemas identificados en la especificación de requisitos con las plantillas comparadas

Para el tercer y último ciclo, el segundo grupo se enfocó en especificar los mismos requisitos del ciclo número 2 utilizando la plantilla mejorada en este ciclo. Los resultados fueron interesantes. En este ciclo fue posible especificar satisfactoriamente el 98% de los requisitos utilizando la plantilla propuesta en este artículo. Solo 3 requisitos no lograron ser especificados completamente utilizando la plantilla mejorada, pero es de resaltar que 135 lograron una especificación que se adhiere a la plantilla mejorada, sin ningún tipo de observación por parte del revisor técnico.

El factor principal por el cual algunos requisitos continúan con algunos problemas cuando se utiliza la plantilla mejorada es porque se detectó durante el ciclo 3 que algunos requisitos cuando tienen un comportamiento restrictivo, es decir, cuando el requisito especifica lo que no debe hacer el sistema, en lugar de lo que debe hacer, la plantilla no se adhiere apropiadamente. De acuerdo con [1] este tipo de requisitos se conocen como **requisitos negativos** y serán parte de una investigación posterior sobre como especificar este tipo de requisitos.

La plantilla mejorada ha sido implementada para ser usada en la herramienta VariaMos[5] con el fin de facilitar la escritura de requisitos de dominio, de aplicaciones y de (auto) adaptación (para, por ejemplo, sistemas ciberfísicos auto-adaptables).

7. Trabajos relacionados

Aparte de la plantilla de Rupp hay otras propuestas de plantillas para la especificación de requisitos en LN semi-estructurado. Por ejemplo, EARS (*Easy Approach to Requirements Syntax*) [4] es una plantilla que considera varios patrones condicionales a partir de los cuales se tipifican varios requisitos. Por ejemplo, **requisitos ubicuos** (no tienen una condición previa que desencadenen comportamientos, pero siempre está activo), **requisitos guiados por eventos** (describen un comportamiento que se da en el sistema cuando se desencadena un evento) y **guiados por estados** (describen un comportamiento que se encuentra activo mientras el sistema está en un estado definido). La plantilla EARS se enfoca en una sintaxis orientada a patrones condicionales bajo los cuales se presentan los requisitos; adicionalmente la investigación en EARS se centra en la industria aeronáutica. A diferencia de ésta, nuestra propuesta pretende ser independiente del dominio de aplicación (ver Sección 4) y pretende soportar la escritura de requisitos no sólo funcionales sino también no funcionales y restricciones.

Alexander & Stevens [19] proponen una plantilla para escribir requisitos funcionales desde la perspectiva del usuario; ya que es más natural formular los requisitos en términos de la acción de un usuario, no desde la perspectiva del sistema [1]. La estructura de la plantilla es la siguiente:

```
El [Tipo de usuario o Nombre de actor] tiene la capacidad de [Verbo de
proceso] [para algún objeto] [Criterio de medición o calificación, tiempo
de respuesta o declaración de calidad]
```

A diferencia del trabajo propuesto por Alexander & Stevens, nuestro enfoque está orientado a la especificación de los requisitos desde la perspectiva del comportamiento de los sistemas y no de las necesidades propias de los interesados.

[5] https://variamos.com/variamosweb

Adv-EARS [11] [12] (*Advanced EARS*) propone una sintaxis en lenguaje semi-estructurado para especificar requisitos funcionales, de manera tal que se da un soporte automatizado para la derivación de casos de uso y actores en modelos de casos de uso. A diferencia de Adv-EARS nuestra plantilla se enfoca en requisitos funcionales y no funcionales, mientras que Adv-EARS se enfoca únicamente en requisitos funcionales. Esta sintaxis es una versión avanzada de [EARS], por lo cual se podría incorporar a futuro algunos elementos de Adv-EARS en nuestro trabajo.

Algunos artículos complementan nuestro trabajo; por ejemplo, Tjong et al. [20] y Denger et al. [21] presentan dos propuestas para reducir la ambigüedad de los requisitos por medio de patrones y reglas lingüísticas; aunque parte de nuestro trabajo también es reducir la ambigüedad del LN, nuestro trabajo se enfoca en mejorar las plantillas de especificación de requisitos, partiendo de una plantilla estándar. Arora et al. [22], [23] proveen una visión adicional al apoyar la conformidad automática de los requisitos usando técnicas de procesamiento de LN para la comprobación de requisitos, algo que nuestro trabajo no plantea y que será parte de un trabajo posterior sobre la comprobación automática de los requisitos. Además, [22] presenta también una plantilla flexible para especificar requisitos que se puede adaptar a diferentes estilos de escritura de requisitos y otras propuestas como la de Souag et al. [24] van aún más lejos permitiendo la generación automática de requisitos no funcionales (de seguridad en particular) en LN semi-estructurado gracias al uso de una ontología de seguridad [25] y a una propia a cada dominio. En contraste, nuestra propuesta es agnóstico al tipo de requisitos no funcionales, pero deberá a futuro inspirarse de los trabajos relacionados y de las ontologías de requisitos y dominios, para facilitar la escritura de requisitos.

8. Conclusiones y Trabajos Futuros

La plantilla de Rupp ha sido establecida como un estándar de facto para la especificación de requisitos individuales por parte del IREB, sin embargo, al momento de representar ciertos requisitos a nivel industrial esta plantilla se ve limitada. Es por eso que decidimos estudiar la pregunta de investigación relacionada con (i) los vacíos de la plantilla usada como estándar para la escritura de requisitos y (ii) cómo llenar esos vacíos. Este estudio lo fundamentamos en el método experimental de investigación llamado investigación-acción. Este método nos permitió usar de manera coherente la experiencia propia de los autores en el ámbito de la ingeniería de requisitos, y la información disponible a nivel industrial y en la literatura (otras plantillas y trabajos relacionados). Como resultado de este experimento logramos identificar los vacíos de la plantilla de Rupp y basados en esos vacíos propusimos una plantilla más robusta que, a diferencia de la otra, permitió representar en LN semi-estructurado la cuasi-totalidad de los requisitos y las restricciones del caso industrial.

A través de esta investigación pudimos observar que la plantilla de referencia debe ser mejorada y que es posible mejorarla. También constatamos que la nueva plantilla puede ser utilizada en casos industriales; sin embargo, nuestra investigación aún no es concluyente considerando que solo experimentamos con un solo caso industrial.

Algunos aspectos que quedan pendientes y requieren aún más trabajo, tanto teórico como experimental, son por ejemplo: recomenzar el experimento partiendo de una plantilla diferente a la de Rupp y comparar la plantilla resultante con la reportada en esta artículo; e implementar una herramienta de software que permita la comprobación automática de requisitos con base en la plantilla mejorada resultado de este trabajo de investigación, ya que otras herramientas se basan en la plantilla de Rupp y otras plantillas para realizar esta comprobación automática. También es necesario estudiar la plantilla mejorada en otros casos y en otros tipos de proyectos, p. ej., para sistemas complejos, sistemas pervasivos, líneas de productos dinámicos, sistemas autoadaptables, y sistemas inteligentes y de analítica. Adicionalmente se podrían definir patrones de lenguaje natural, verbos de proceso estandarizados y modelos que complementen la plantilla mejorada.

Adicional a lo anterior esperamos fortalecer la evidencia empírica respecto a las ventajas que tiene la plantilla mejorada, realizando por lo menos otros dos experimentos en empresas de sectores de actividad diferentes con el fin de tener observaciones más concluyentes sobre la facilidad de uso, la completitud y la precisión de la plantilla propuesta en otros contextos. Otro trabajo futuro consiste en complementar la plantilla propuesta en este artículo para el tratamiento de requisitos negativos, ubicuos, entre otros.

Referencias

[1] Wiegers K., Beatty J. Software Requirements, Third Edition. Microsoft Press, 2013.

[2] Pohl K. Requirements Engineering - Fundamentals, Principles, and Techniques Springer, 2010.

[3] Rupp C. Requirements-Engineering und -Management Hanser, 2007.

[4] Mavin A., Wilkinson P., Harwood A., Novak M. EARS: Easy Approach to Requirements Syntax. Requirements Engineering Conference, 2009.

[5] Rupp C. Requirements Templates - The Blueprint of your Requirement. SOPHIST GmbH, 2014.

[6] O'Brien R. An Overview of the Methodological Approach of Action Research. In Roberto Richardson (Ed.), Theory and Practice of Action Research. Brazil: Universidade Federal da Paraíba, 2001.

[7] Wieringa R., Morali A. Technical action research as a validation method in information systems design science. Design science research in information systems. Advances in theory and practice, 7286, 220-238. Springer Berlin Heidelberg, 2012.

[8] Susman G.I., Evered R.D. An Assessment of the Scientific Merits of Action Research. *Administrative Science Quaterly*: Vol. 23 (pp. 582-603), 1978.

[9] Koshy E., Koshy V., Waterman H. Action research in healthcare, Thousand Oaks, CA: Sage, 2011.

[10] Susman G. I. Action Research: A Sociotechnical Systems Perspective, Ed. G. Morgan. London: Sage Publications, 1983

[11] Majumdar D., Sengupta A., Kanjilal A., Bhattacharya S., Adv-EARS: A Formal Requirements Syntax for Derivation of Use Case Models, First International Conference on Advances in Computing and Information Technology, pp 40-48, 2011.

[12] Dipankar Majumdar, Sabnam Sengupta, Ananya Kanjilal, Swapan Bhattacharya, Automated Requirements Modeling with Adv-EARS. International Journal of Information Technology Convergence and Services, pp 57-67, 2011.

[13] ISO/IEC/IEEE 29148, Systems and software engineering — Life cycle processes — Requirements engineering, 2011.

[14] Cohn M. User Stories Applied for Agile Software Development, Adisson Wesley, 2004.

[15] Beck K. Embracing change with extreme programming, IEEE Computer. 32 (10): 70–77, 1999

[16] Mazo R. Guía para la adopción industrial de líneas de productos de software. Editorial Eafit, Medellín-Colombia, 2018.

[17] Clegg D., Barker R. Case Method Fast-Track: A Rad Approach, Addison-Wesley, 1994.

[18] Robertson S., Robertson J. Mastering the Requirements Process: Getting Requirements Right, 3rd ed. Addison-Wesley, 2013.

[19] Alexander I., Stevens R. Writing Better Requierements, Addison-Wesley, 2002.

[20] Tjong S. F., Hallam N., Hartley M. Improving the quality of natural language requirements specifications through natural language requirements patterns. In CIT'06, pp 199-205, 2006.

[21] Denger C., Berry D, Kamsties E. Higher quality requirements specifications through natural language patterns. In SwSTE'03, pp. 80-90, 2003.

[22] Arora C., Sabetzadeh M., Briand L. C., Zimmer F., Gnaga R. Automatic checking of conformance to requirement boilerplates via text chunking: An industrial case study, ACM / IEEE International Symposium on Empirical Software Engineering and Measurement, pp. 35-44, 2013.

[23] Arora C., Sabetzadeh M., Briand L., Zimmer F. Automated checking of conformance to requirements templates using natural language processing, TSE, vol. 41, no. 10, pp. 944-968, 2015.

[24] Souag A, Mazo R, Salinesi C, Comyn-Wattiau I. Using the AMAN-DA method to generate security requirements: a case study in the maritime domain. Requirements Engineering. 2018.

[25] Souag A, Salinesi C, Mazo R, Comyn-Wattiau I. A security ontology for security requirements elicitation. InInternational symposium on engineering secure software and systems (pp. 157-177). Springer, Cham, 2015.

Do We Preach What We Practice?

Investigating the Practical Relevance of Requirements Engineering Syllabi – The IREB Case

Daniel Méndez Fernández[1], Xavier Franch[2], Norbert Seyff[3], Michael Felderer[4], Martin Glinz[5], Marcos Kalinowski[6], Andreas Vogelsang[7], Stefan Wagner[8], Stan Bühne[9], Kim Lauenroth[10]

[1] Technical University of Munich, Germany
[2] Universitat Politècnica de Catalunya, Spain
[3] University of Applied Sciences and Arts Northwestern Switzerland
[4] University of Innsbruck, Austria
[5] University of Zurich, Switzerland
[6] Pontifical Catholic University of Rio de Janeiro, Brazil
[7] Technical University of Berlin, Germany
[8] University of Stuttgart, Germany
[9] Seven Principles AG, Germany
[10] adesso AG, Germany

Abstract. Nowadays, there exist a plethora of different educational syllabi for Requirements Engineering (RE), all aiming at incorporating practically relevant educational units (EUs). Many of these syllabi are based, in one way or the other, on the syllabi provided by the International Requirements Engineering Board (IREB), a non-profit organisation devoted to standardised certification programs for RE. IREB syllabi are developed by RE experts and are, thus, based on the assumption that they address topics of practical relevance. However, little is known about to what extent practitioners actually perceive those contents as useful. We have started a study to investigate the relevance of the EUs included in the IREB Foundation Level certification programme. In the first phase reported in this paper, we have surveyed practitioners mainly from DACH countries (Germany, Austria and Switzerland) who participated in the IREB certification. Later phases will widen the scope both by including other countries and by not requiring IREB-certified participants. The results shall foster a critical reflection on the practical relevance of EUs built upon the de-facto standard syllabus of IREB.

Keywords: Survey Research, Requirements Engineering Education, Certification Programs.

1 Introduction

Requirements Engineering (RE) plays a vital role for successful software and systems development projects [1] and, thus, training and teaching relevant RE knowledge to practitioners is of utmost importance. The non-profit organisation IREB (International

Requirements Engineering Board, www.ireb.org) has developed standardised syllabi at different levels for the individual certification of professionals in RE. These syllabi are created by RE representatives from academia, industry, and consulting. The Foundation Level (FL) syllabus includes different RE educational units (EUs), which, according to IREB, cover essential knowledge areas and are used as a baseline for the certification to become a certified professional for RE. IREB training providers rely on the IREB syllabus to develop course material to train candidates for the certification exams.

As of today, more than 40,000 candidates all over the world have passed the IREB FL exam. IREB is thus becoming the de-facto standard when it comes to standardised education for RE. However, the IREB certification programme, same as other educational RE curricula built upon the IREB syllabi, are all based on the core assumption that the IREB FL syllabus covers practically relevant topics. Yet, there is limited knowledge about the extent to which practitioners actually perceive the content as useful and relevant in their work.

In order to better understand the relevance of the topics included in the IREB FL syllabus, we have designed a study with three different goals: (1) *how useful* practitioners consider its content for their daily work, (2) *how relevant* they perceive it for their personal knowledge and interest, and (3) what do they *miss*. This paper reports on a first iteration of this study, in which we present results gathered from practitioners in the DACH area (Germany, Austria and Switzerland) taking the IREB FL exam. We plan future iterations in which other regions (e.g., Latin America, Asia, ...) are targeted, as well as RE practitioners in general, regardless whether they are certified by IREB or not. One hope we associate with this article is to motivate other researchers to join our endeavour. As an ultimate goal, this investigation allows us to critically reflect on the IREB FL syllabus, but also on other syllabi which are built upon it.

2 Fundamentals and Related Work

The IREB Foundation Level aims at providing the core knowledge of RE. The syllabus consists of nine educational units, see Table 1. The first version of the syllabus was developed by a group of RE researchers and practitioners in 2007 and since then, it has been revisited and extended. This paper is based on the current version of the syllabus 3 (Version 2.2). The goal of the syllabus has always been to define a basic RE body of knowledge that each RE practitioner should know. Therefore, it is important to assess the syllabus' content against the needs and demands of RE practitioners.

Besides our own work, there are other studies that aim at increasing the practical relevance of academic RE contributions in the long run. The NaPiRE initiative [1], for instance, constitutes a family of surveys on contemporary problems, causes, and effects in practice. Franch et al. [4] report on an ongoing survey-based study where practitioners assess the perceived relevance of RE research papers. Fricker et al. [5] surveyed several industrial RE projects to assess the current state of methods, tools, and techniques in RE practice. To the best of our knowledge, our research is the first aiming at the direct evaluation of current RE teaching syllabi from the perspective of practitioners' needs and expectations.

Table 1. Educational Units (EU) in IREB FL.

EU1	Introduction and Foundations
EU2	System and System Context
EU3	Requirements Elicitation
EU4	Requirements Documentation
EU5	Documentation of Requirements using Natural Language
EU6	Model-based Documentation of Requirements
EU7	Requirements Validation and Negotiation
EU8	Requirements Management
EU9	Tool Support

3 Study Design

In the following, we describe the overall design of our survey conducted in the IREB context. Details can also be taken from the disclosed replication package [2] that includes the export of raw data and analysis material as well as the full questionnaire.

3.1 Research Objectives and Questions

Our overall goal of the study is to critically reflect on the practical relevance of today's teaching material in Requirements Engineering and the extent to which it reflects practical needs. To this end, in this paper we aim at investigating what the perception of practitioners is on the usefulness and relevance of the IREB Foundation Level training material, i.e. the EUs of the syllabus, considering the perspective of practitioners taking part in the certification. We formulate the following research questions:

RQ1. How *useful* do practitioners perceive the content of RE educational material for their RE-related daily work?

RQ2 How *relevant* is the content of RE educational material with respect to practitioners' knowledge and interests?

RQ3 What topics do practitioners *miss*?

3.2 Instruments

To survey RE practitioners in the IREB certification programme context, we designed an instrument that captures various questions along two major parts:

- Demographics such as background and experience.
- Opinions, such as on relevance, on the educational units of the IREB FL syllabus.

Table 2 summarises the most relevant questions presented to practitioners in the survey as per selection with respect to our research questions. The full questionnaire, including details on the responses, can be found in our replication package [2].

Table 2. Summary of the questionnaire.

Block *General questions*	
Q2.1	What is your age?
Q2.2	What is your educational background?
Q2.3	What is your practical experience in requirements engineering?
Q2.4	What kind of certification do you already have?
Q2.5	How did you become aware of the IREB certification program?
Q2.6	What kind of tools and methods do you use in your daily work?
Q2.8	Do you have a CPRE FL certification?
Q2.9	Are you interested in CPRE certifications?
Q2.11	In which certifications are you interested?
Block *About the FL certification*	
Q3.1	Since when (year) do you have your CPRE Foundation Level certification?
Q3.2	Why did you choose CPRE Foundation Level?
Q3.4	In which country did you get your CPRE Foundation Level certification?
Block *Assessment of FL syllabus*	
Q5.1	Rate the different Educational Units (EUs) of the syllabus regarding their content (Note: for each of the 9 EUs, respondents rated: too generic – detailed enough – too many details – don't remember)
Q5.2	How do you rate the overall structure of the syllabus? (Note: respondents rated from 1 –extremely good– to 7 –extremely bad–)
Q5.3	How relevant are the following EUs for your personal knowledge and interest? (Note: for each of the 9 EUs, respondents rated from 1 –extremely interesting– to 5 –not interesting at all–)
Q5.4	How useful are the following EUs in your requirements engineering related daily work? (Note: for each of the 9 EUs, respondents rated from 1 –extremely important– to 5 –not important at all–)
Q5.5	What do you miss in the CPRE Foundation certification for your practical work? (Note: respondents rated four concepts –guidance in specific domains, methods and tools for the daily work, templates for my work, process focus rather than just providing a tool set– with either 1 –I want more–, 2 –It is okay as it is– or 3 –I want less–)

3.3 Data Collection

We aim at answering our research questions via survey research. The IREB environment provides the context for the survey. IREB EUs for the FL certification represent the study object. The practitioners asked to participate in the study also stem from the same IREB environment.

The survey was implemented using Qualtrics Survey Software and invitations have been sent out as an newsletter sent via email to approximately 40.000 registered IREB practitioners with the overall purpose of receiving feedback for a revision of the handbook (still ongoing). The data collection was conducted from April to August 2017. Prior to the survey, a pilot has been performed with 5 practitioners. To increase the motivation of the participants, a fitness smartwatch worth 250€ was raffled among all participants who completed the survey. Our respondents come mainly from the DACH area, i.e. Germany (D), Austria (A), and Switzerland (CH).

3.4 Data Analysis

Given the scope of the questions, we reduce the data analysis to basic descriptive statistics, including blocking of results according to chosen context factors such as experience. Qualitative data was analysed manually without an elaborate coding procedure due to the small number of answers.

4 Study Results

The theoretical population for the survey consists of practitioners taking the IREB FL exam (hereafter, "practitioners" for short). The survey received in total 137 responses. We analysed them and filtered out those that were incomplete leaving us with 108 practitioners' responses. Please note that not all survey questions were mandatory and the number of responses for single research questions varies slightly.

Looking at the age of the practitioners who participated in the survey, the majority of the respondents are fairly distributed between the ages 25-34 years (41), 35-44 years (33), and 45-54 years (26). Half of the sample (54) holds a professional degree. We measure the professional work experience of the respondents in a simplified manner via working years: 53 of the respondents have less than five years of experience, 39 between 5 and 15 years, and 16 have more than 15 years of experience. The certifications of our respondents are primarily in Requirements Engineering, Project Management, and Testing with 82, 50, and 27 respondents, respectively.

In the following, we report on the study results structured according to the research questions.

4.1 Usefulness for practitioners' daily work (RQ 1)

To analyse the usefulness of RE educational material, we asked our respondents to rate the individual IREB EUs according to their importance for their daily work using a Likert scale.

Table 3 gives an overview of the ratings our respondents gave to the individual EUs. All EUs in the list, except for EU1 (*Introduction and Foundations*) and EU9 (*Tool Support*), have been perceived as extremely important, very important or moderately important by more than 75% of the practitioners participating in the survey. For EU9, this percentage dropped to 53.41% and it dropped even to 50% for EU1.

We blocked those results by the respondents' working experience (see also the spreadsheets in the replication package [2] for a more detailed view) and we observed a trend in the perception: more experienced respondents seem to value the foundations more than less experienced ones. Indeed, 66.67% of the most experienced respondents (more than 15 years of experience) consider this EU extremely or very important, while for the least experienced ones (less than 5 years of experience) this number drops to 33.33%, while 40% of them still consider the EU to be moderately important. Our interpretation to these results is that experienced practitioners are aware of the complexities of RE and recognize the value of having an initial EU providing solid foundations for the rest of the syllabus.

As for EU9 (*Tool Support*), we couldn't find any trend in relation to the experience. One explanation might be that the content of this EU might not match the reality that practitioners face in their projects. To corroborate this argument, we point to our observation that the survey question rating the actually trained contents of these EUs (Q5.1) informs that 30% of the respondents rate EU9's content as too generic, being the worst ranked EU at this respect.

It is also worth pointing to the documentation of requirements, which spreads along three EUs: *Requirements Documentation* (EU4), *Documentation of Requirements in Natural Language* (EU5), and *Model-based Documentation* (EU6). We consider two of our observations to be relevant. First, the general EU4 is perceived as more useful than the two detailed ones (EU5 and EU6). As a slight nuance to this result, blocking the results by the degree of experience shows that more experienced practitioners tend to rank the two detailed EUs more important and the percentage of practitioners who rate the EU on natural language requirements as extremely important raises from 37.78% for less experienced respondents up to 67.74% for medium and even to 75% for very experienced ones. The model-based EU follows a very similar trend (increasing in the agreement from 35.55% to 56.25% and then to 58.33%). Our only explanation for that phenomenon is that the more experienced practitioners are, the more they tend to get specialised and to value more advanced techniques.

We have also analysed possible trends when blocking the results according to other factors. We observed, for instance, that respondents with a *Project Management* certificate tend to generally give a higher rating on the usefulness of the EUs than those with a different RE certificate (like REQB) or a testing certificate (e.g., ISTQB), with *Architecture* and especially *Business Process* certificates yielding the lowest ratings. The differences are even higher if we focus on the core EUs that deal with specific RE phases (EU3 to EU8). As the only but rather clear exception, the usefulness of model-based documentation (EU6) was rated higher by those having these last two certificates, being, in fact, the only core EU in which this higher rating was given. One explanation we have for this is that both software architects and process modellers value the use of models more. Concerning the other EUs, the rating of tooling (EU9) does again not align well with the rating of the core EUs. Respondents with architecture or testing certifications rate this EU with higher usefulness than the rest of certifications. We argue that the technical nature of such certifications provide respondents with a higher perception on the importance of tool support.

Finally, we found a potential relationship among the perceived usefulness and the motivations our respondents have for obtaining their certificates. Practitioners who stated to participating in the certification for personal interest give a higher rating than those participating because it was requested by their employers. This difference gets clearer if we consider the three highest ratings: in each EU, individuals who participated in the course motivated by personal interest, tend to rate the EU better than the others.

Table 3. Perceived usefulness of the IREB Educational Units (EUs) from a practitioners' perspective

#	Field	Extremely important		Very important		Moderately important		Slightly important		Not at all important		Total
1	EU1 - Introduction and Foundations	5.68%	5	15.91%	14	28.41%	25	28.41%	25	21.59%	19	88
2	EU2 - System and System Context	15.73%	14	29.21%	26	32.58%	29	15.73%	14	6.74%	6	89
3	EU3 - Requirements Elicitation	19.10%	17	39.33%	35	26.97%	24	10.11%	9	4.49%	4	89
4	EU4 - Requirements Documentation	24.72%	22	43.82%	39	21.35%	19	8.99%	8	1.12%	1	89
5	EU5 - Documentation of Requirements in Natural Language	21.59%	19	31.82%	28	27.27%	24	14.77%	13	4.55%	4	88
6	EU6 - Model-based Documentation	14.61%	13	31.46%	28	30.34%	27	20.22%	18	3.37%	3	89
7	EU7 - Requirements validation and negotiation	12.36%	11	25.84%	23	39.33%	35	17.98%	16	4.49%	4	89
8	EU8 - Requirements Management	20.22%	18	26.97%	24	30.34%	27	14.61%	13	7.87%	7	89
9	EU9 - Tool Support	6.82%	6	14.77%	13	31.82%	28	30.68%	27	15.91%	14	88

Table 4. Relevance to Practitioners' Interest of the IREB Educational Units (EUs)

#	Field	Extremely interesting		Very interesting		Moderately interesting		Slightly interesting		Not interesting at all		Total
1	EU1 - Introduction and Foundations	3.41%	3	28.41%	25	37.50%	33	22.73%	20	7.95%	7	88
2	EU2 - System and System Context	21.11%	19	45.56%	41	25.56%	23	4.44%	4	3.33%	3	90
3	EU3 - Requirements Elicitation	20.22%	18	52.81%	47	19.10%	17	6.74%	6	1.12%	1	89
4	EU4 - Requirements Documentation	25.56%	23	37.78%	34	30.00%	27	5.56%	5	1.11%	1	90
5	EU5 - Documentation of Requirements in Natural Language	22.22%	20	26.67%	24	30.00%	27	15.56%	14	5.56%	5	90
6	EU6 - Model-based Documentation	27.78%	25	43.33%	39	22.22%	20	5.56%	5	1.11%	1	90
7	EU7 - Requirements validation and negotiation	18.89%	17	46.67%	42	24.44%	22	7.78%	7	2.22%	2	90
8	EU8 - Requirements Management	22.22%	20	45.56%	41	24.44%	22	4.44%	4	3.33%	3	90
9	EU9 - Tool Support	10.00%	9	20.00%	18	35.56%	32	28.89%	26	5.56%	5	90

4.2 Relevance to practitioners' personal interests (RQ 2)

We asked the participants to rate the relevance of the individual EUs according to their personal knowledge and interest (see Table 4). The relevance of the 9 EUs composing the IREB FL syllabus was rated overall high. This means that for 6 out of the 9 EUs, more than 90% of the respondents gave a positive rating (at least moderately interesting). *Requirements Elicitation* (EU3) and *Model-based Documentation* (EU6) excel with more than 70% finding the topics at least highly interesting. Three EUs were reported with lower relevance. For *Documentation of Requirements in Natural Language* (EU5), 48.89% reported an extremely high or high relevance which went down to 31,82% for *Introduction and Foundations* (EU1) and 30.00% for *Tool Support* (EU9). For EU5, 21,1% reported a slight or no relevance at all, which raised to 30.68% for EU1 and even to 34.44% for EU9. The relatively low interest in these two last EUs is in tune with the results investigating their usefulness. In contrast, we observed a low interest in EU5, although it was ranked the 3rd most useful topic for practitioners' daily work (see Section 4.1).

When blocking our results again according to the experience of our respondents, the ones having an experience of between 5 and 10 years (32 participants) seemed to be more positive than the ones having less or more experience. On average, 25.72% of practitioners having between 5 and 15 years of experience rated the EUs as extremely relevant. This percentage drops to 16.33% for participants with an experience of less than 5 years (45 subjects), and down to 11.96% for practitioners having more than 15 years (12 respondents). Again, highly experienced participants rated EU9 lower. We couldn't find any trends when blocking the results according to any other criteria.

4.3 Missing Topics

To identify potentially missing topics, we asked the participants directly for 4 different categories: (1) guidance for specific domains, (2), methods and tools for their daily work, (3) templates for the work, and (4) overall process and approaches. The responses provided a rather mixed picture, in general seeming happy with the current extent of the content or wanting more, in particular for methods and tools and templates for their work (i.e. apparently a more practical focus). We blocked the results again according to the experience. The only trend that was apparent to us was that the less experienced our respondents are, the less they seem to be interested in guidance for specific domains. To investigate this topic further, we formulated also an open free text question. We received in total 42 answers and blocked the results again according to the practical experience. Very experienced practitioners with more than 15 years of experience (but with a rather low N=9) asked for more consideration of RE in the larger software engineering context as well as for advanced techniques to face specific project situations. This is reflected in statements like "[...] interview techniques (like minimum 7 W's for journalists), no grammar lectures as this is ground school stuff and does not help with reasonable content.", or "The syllabus should put a strong emphasis on creative finding and designing of solutions. In daily work it is expected from a requirements engineer to find and suggest innovative solutions not just to elicit and document requirements [...]."

The remaining respondents (N=33) stated either that nothing would be missing (12) or that they would miss more practical yet domain-independent guidance: "I miss a concrete approach, how the process might look in a real project [...]"; "Where to start? How to plan the process of RE? [...]"; "Templates, tools, practices"; "More real-life examples".

5 Discussion

Both the usefulness (RQ1) and the relevance (RQ2) of EU1 (Introduction and Foundations) and EU9 (Tool Support) are rated considerably lower than the other seven EUs. For EU9, this result is not surprising: 30 percent of the respondents consider this EU to be too generic (cf. Sect. 4.1). An analysis of the contents of EU9 confirms this finding. We were surprised, however, by the low rating of EU1, which covers foundational material. It seems that particularly the inexperienced respondents rated this EU low. Due to its introductory nature, the direct impact of EU1 on daily work might be difficult to perceive for inexperienced practitioners. Training providers should take this into account when deciding how to teach the material of EU1.

With respect to usefulness in practitioners' daily work, the EUs on requirements elicitation, documentation, and documentation in natural language are ranked highest. This is in line with the particular importance of these topics in today's industrial practice. Interestingly, the relevance of EU5 on documentation in natural language is rated lower than its usefulness. It seems that practitioners acknowledge the importance of natural language for expressing requirements, but do not find particular interest in the topic.

Concerning RQ3, our respondents did not identify major gaps in the syllabus. Experienced respondents seem to miss advanced techniques for dealing with specific project situations. However, this might go beyond the scope of a FL syllabus. Less experienced respondents tend to favour general-purpose processes rather than domain-specific or advanced techniques. We suggest to investigate whether inexperienced people would benefit if the syllabus had a stronger focus on general concepts, terms, and activities of requirements documentation and elicitation.

With respect to improvement potential of the syllabus, EUs 9 and 1 should be looked at first. The next candidates that could be better aligned with practical needs are (in this order) EUs 2, 7, 6, and 8. EU5 should be examined with respect to its rather low perceived relevance.

A final conclusion we can draw is that, in general, RE educational material could be better aligned with practical needs when it comes to specialised topics. Especially rather inexperienced students need to understand the characteristics of real-life RE situations and the high sensitivity of the various approaches and practices we have so far in RE to their context. In other words: a key take-away in the foundation of RE is that there is no such thing as a universal process. To especially drive home the complexity of real-life RE settings, educators thus need to rely on real-life examples while still aiming to provide a big picture (RQ3).

Our results indicate that the current IREB Foundation Level syllabus actually addresses the needs of its target audience, i.e., professionals having a limited amount of experience. Furthermore, experienced professionals also see value in such foundational topics. We believe that experienced professionals benefit from receiving holistic views on general, foundational terminology and practices which go beyond their daily work and provide them a broad perspective on the state of the art in RE.

6 Conclusions

In this paper, we report on a survey to explore the perceived usefulness and relevance of RE educational material, which we exemplarily analysed based on the educational units provided in the IREB Foundation Level syllabus. This survey has addressed the population of RE practitioners certified by IREB in DACH countries. Our findings indicate that this syllabus fits the needs of both inexperienced and experienced professionals. However, the results also provide indicators on how to increase the practical usefulness and relevance. At the same time, we postulate that usefulness for practice should not be the only quality criterion of a syllabus, especially in university or college-level education. This is also known as the RE education dilemma [7]).

Furthermore, there are still several limitations inherent to our study. First, some respondents might still have had problems distinguishing between the relevance for their personal knowledge and interest and the usefulness to their daily work. A richer investigation of such a differentiation would need, however, different forms of investigation that allows to better understand their preferences, motivations, and working context. Yet, the picture our results depict already shows some differences in the ratings which strengthens our confidence in the suitability of the used instrument. Hence, we believe that our survey provides already a first useful basis for an investigation of relevance and usefulness. Second, the response rate is very low. Therefore, our next step is to conduct other iterations using additional channels other than IREB. Generalising from our findings in the context of IREB to further educational material is dependent on the exact contents educators decide to deliver, and it also depends on the (pedagogical) way the content is exactly taught, which is out of the scope of the IREB syllabus. To provide richer conclusions, we also need further analyses. These are in scope of current work. We are currently analysing more context factors and we are working on a more elaborate statistical analysis considering also a complementary survey that captures the perspective of IREB training providers. The latter shall help grasping the perspective of practitioners and IREB training providers alike on the same aspects, thus allowing to delineate potential misconceptions. One hope we associate with this paper is also to motivate other researchers and educators to critically reflect on the practical relevance of RE educational material and to join us in the endeavour of exploring this highly diverse and sensitive topic.

References

1. D. Méndez Fernández, S. Wagner, M. Kalinowski, M. Felderer, P. Mafra, A. Vetrò, T. Conte, M.-T. Christiansson, D. Greer, C. Lassenius, T. Männistö, M. Nayebi, M. Oivo, B. Penzenstadler, D. Pfahl, R. Prikladnicki, G. Ruhe, A. Schekelmann, S. Sen, R. Spinola, A. Tuzcu, J. L. de la Vara, R. Wieringa. Naming the Pain in Requirements Engineering: Contemporary Problems, Causes, and Effects in Practice. In: Empirical Software Engineering Journal, 2016.
2. Daniel Mendez Fernandez, Xavier Franch, Norbert Seyff, Michael Felderer, Martin Glinz, Marcos Kalinowski, Andreas Vogelsang, Stefan Wagner, Stan Bühne, Kim Lauenroth: Do We Preach What We Practice? On Investigating the Practical Relevance of Requirements Engineering Syllabi. Replication Package. https://figshare.com/articles/Do_We_Preach_What_We_Practice_On_Investigating_the_Practical_Relevance_of_Requirements_Engineering_Syllabi_/7150805
3. K. Frühauf, E. Fuchs, M. Glinz, R. Grau, C. Hood, F. Houdek, P. Hruschka, B. Paech, K. Pohl, and C. Rupp. IREB Certified Professional for Requirements Engineering – Foundation Level – Syllabus, Version 2.2, 2015. https://www.ireb.org/en/downloads/#syllabus-foundation-level, visited 2018-12-09.
4. X. Franch, D. Méndez Fernández, M. Oriol, A. Vogelsang, R. Heldal, E. Knauss, G.H. Travassos, J. C. Carver, O. Dieste Tubío, T. Zimmermann. How do Practitioners Perceive the Relevance of Requirements Engineering Research? An Ongoing Study. In: Proc. International Requirements Engineering Conference, 2017.
5. S. A. Fricker, R. Grau, A. Zwingli. Requirements Engineering: Best Practice. In: Fricker S., Thümmler C., Gavras A. (eds) Requirements Engineering for Digital Health. Springer, 2015.
6. E. Bjarnason, P. Runeson, M. Borg, M. Unterkalmsteiner, E. Engström, B. Regnell, G. Sabaliauskaite, A. Loconsole, T. Gorschek, R. Feldt. Challenges and Practices in Aligning Requirements with Verification and Validation: A Case Study of Six Companies. In: Empirical Software Engineering Journal, 2014.
7. L. Macaulay, J. Mylopoulos. Requirements Engineering: An Education Dilemma. In: Autom Software Engineering, 1995.

ESELAW Keynote 2019

Empirical Software Engineering: Where do we come from and where are we going?

Marcela Genero[1]

[1] Department of Technologies and Information Systems
University of Castilla-La Mancha (UCLM)
Spain

Abstract. In this invited conference, a tour will be made about the evolution of Empirical Software Engineering to show its relevance in the present and the importance of this discipline to improve both the research and the practice of Software Engineering. With a look at the future, special emphasis will be placed on how to promote the University-Industry collaboration as the main challenge to face.

Identifying approaches to generate test cases in model-based testing: a systematic mapping

Matheus Monteiro Mariano[1], Érica Ferreira de Souza[2], André Takeshi Endo[2], and Nandamudi L. Vijaykumar[1]

Lab. of Comp. and Applied Math., National Institute for Space Research – INPE[1]
São José dos Campos/SP - Brazil
matheus.mariano@inpe.br, vijay.nl@inpe.br
Department of Computer, Federal University of Technology Paraná – UTFPR[2]
Cornélio Procópio/PR - Brazil
ericasouza@utfpr.edu.br, andreendo@utfpr.edu.br

Abstract. Context: Model-Based Testing (MBT) has attracted a lot of attention from software testing researchers, since it has been efficient in employing formal models to represent the reactive systems behavior in order to guide test case generation. **Objective:** This paper investigates approaches to automatically generate test cases in MBT, such as methods, criteria, formal models, and evaluation strategies of the generated test cases. **Method:** A systematic mapping was conducted in order to summarize the main approaches used in the MBT context. **Results:** From the mapping, we identified 97 studies addressing approaches to generate test cases in MBT. **Conclusion:** Several pointers to some approaches have been identified which will help practitioners and researchers to identify future research from existing research efforts in MBT. Among the indicators that most caught the attention is that there is a great effort spent in developing new test methods (32 methods), test criteria (29 criteria), formal models (24 models) and evaluations conducted in the selected studies (145 types).

1 Introduction

In order to assure software quality, several efforts in academia and industry have been dedicated to more refined test strategies [1]. Moreover, several products and services depend on developing systems considered critical and complex. A software system is considered critical when a fault (even simple ones) can lead to serious damage or loss both financially and socially. For example, if a software embedded in a satellite fails, the ground stations may not receive proper information to be used in several applications, causing financial losses.

In such scenarios, activities related with Verification, Validation and Testing (VV&T) have been employed throughout the software development process. These activities analyze the compliance of the developed software with the specification [2]. Among such activities, software testing can be defined as an execution process of a program with intention of finding errors.

During the testing activity, a model can be created to guide the test process in order to verify whether the behavior of implemented software is in conformance with its specification. Therefore, it is necessary to observe whether the software implementation is behaving in accordance with the specified model. According to El-Far and Whittaker [3], software testing requires the use of a model to guide efforts on generation and selection of test cases. In this context, *Model-Based Testing* (MBT) has attracted a lot of attention since there are several advantages in using models to represent the system's behavior and to guide the generation of test cases [4]. MBT can bring some benefits, such as high rate of failure detection, reduction of cost and time, traceability, and ease of updating software requirements [4].

One of the main features of MBT is the automated generation of test cases from a formal test model. In this respect, several formal techniques have been adopted to specify the system behavior as a test model, such as *Statecharts* [5], Finite State Machines (FSMs) [6], *Specification and Description Language* (SDL) [7] and *Labelled Transition Systems* (LTSs) [8]. Each modeling technique has specific methods and criteria to traverse a model and automatically generate test cases. However, depending on the nature of system, the number of test sequences generated can be potentially infinite or even very large, exceeding the capacity of exercising the test cases on the implementation.

The main objective of this paper is to investigate elements involved in automatic test case generation in MBT, focusing on studies that addressed, mainly, algorithms for test case generation, such as methods, criteria, formal models for generating test cases and evaluation strategies of the generated test cases and shows the main approaches used for each of these elements in the MBT context. To achieve this, we conducted a systematic mapping to summarize the main approaches used in such a context. A systematic mapping provides a broad overview of an area of research, determining whether there is research evidence on a particular topic [9]. We believe that the results of this mapping will help to identify areas for future research and also provide a map that appropriately allows placing new research activities.

The remainder of this paper is structured as follows. Section 2 presents the main underlying concepts of this work. Section 3 formally introduces the methods and procedures used to conduct the systematic mapping. Section 4 shows how the systematic mapping was conducted. Results are presented in Section 5. Section 6 reports a general discussion to highlight some points of our research. Lastly, conclusions, remarks and future directions are described in Section 7.

2 Background

Software Testing can be defined as as an execution process of a program with intention of finding errors [2]. Several activities that help in finding errors before the systems are finalized can avoid this problem, such as VV&T activities. VV&T dedicate(s) efforts to make a software specification cohesive with implementation and an approach to make this is to check if the system will behave as expected from a finite set of test cases [10].

Test activity can be applied in different levels of software. The three main levels are [2]: *(i)* unit testing, that focuses in identifying faults in small and independent components of software; *(ii)* integration testing, responsible in testing the integration of small units of software; and *(iii)* system testing, that verifies if the behavior of software is in conformance with requirements, analyzing the internal flow of a program. Each level analyzes a specific behavior of the program and for each level a specific technique can be applied. Two main testing techniques are: Structural testing which has the objective of analyzing the software based on the program code; and Functional testing which generates tests from a formal model without the code, analyzing if the behavior of software is in accordance with specification. Functional testing might employ an abstraction of the software, based on its specification, that represents the behavior of system. This approach is well-known as Model-Based Testing (MBT).

MBT is an approach that represents the behavior of system as a formal model [11], using an abstraction. Software modeling is important to conduct test activities because it enables to identify the behavior and its expected result. In MBT, model can be designed using a formal model technique without ambiguity [4]. Some of the most well-known techniques to represent test models for a system under test are Finite State Machine (FSM) [6], Statecharts [5], Specification and Description Language (SDL) [7], and Labelled Transition Systems (LTS) [8].

With a model, it is possible to employ test criteria and methods to generate test cases. The selection of criteria and methods is important because depending on the model size or the input range set it becomes impracticable to analyze all the possible combinations. A test criterion defines which elements of a model must be covered to generate a test sequence (test case). The main test criteria mentioned in literature are [12]: all nodes, all edges, all transition-pairs and fault model coverage. A method is an approach used to find a set of test cases implemented by an algorithm. In general, a method aims to achieve a test criterion by covering a model. Some known methods are: Distinguished Sequence (DS) [13], W-method [14], Transition Tour (TT) [15], Unique Input/Output (UIO) [16], Breadth First Search (BFS) [17] and Depth First Search (DFS) [17]. These methods differ with respect to cost of generated test suites and adopted criteria complexity.

2.1 Related Work

Before accomplishing the mapping, we adopted concepts of a tertiary study to look for secondary studies that already investigated MBT. Tertiary studies are reviews that focus only on secondary studies; i.e., it is a review about other secondary studies [9]. In this study, we used the following search string:

("MBT" OR "model based test" OR "model based testing" OR "model based tests" OR "MDT" OR "model driven test" OR "model driven testing" OR "model driven tests") AND ("Systematic Literature Review" OR "Systematic Review" OR "Systematic Mapping" OR "Mapping Study" OR "Mapping Studies" OR "Systematic Literature Mapping").

The search string was applied in the Scopus electronic database: 86 documents were returned and we found ten complete studies that are reviews on MBT. Some related studies are briefly described as follows.

Barmi et al. [18] conducted a systematic mapping with respect to the alignment of specification and testing of functional and non-functional requirements to identify gaps in the literature. The map summarizes studies and discusses them within sub categories with MBT and traceability. The main results showed that the papers that have linked the specification with test requirements focused on model-centric approaches, code-centric approaches, traceability, formal approaches and test cases, with focus on problems of MBT and traceability.

Siavashi and Truscan [19] conducted a systematic review in order to understand how an environment model can be used in MBT and challenges. Environment modeling is an activity that specifies a part of the real world, in which the system is integrated. From the characteristics and advantages, the authors conclude that using environment models can be helpful in robustness testing, safety testing and regression testing. However, methodological aspects of creating environment models are only discussed in a limited number of studies.

Gurbuz and Tekinerdogan [20] presented a systematic mapping to describe the advances in MBT for software safety. The results show that the safety area of MBT is broad and applicable to several domains with focus on reducing costs and increasing test coverage. Nevertheless, the solutions proposed are focused on specific domains, making the solution less generic and less reusable. More recently, Khan et al. [21] showed a systematic review in order to analyze the quality of empirical studies with MBT. The results identified that the community of MBT needs to provide more details in reporting guidelines, and few papers were applied in industry artifacts.

Each presented study conducted some kind of secondary study on MBT, but with different purposes. Other related studies have focused on mobile applications [22], search based techniques [23], aspect-oriented software [24], MBT tools [25, 26] and MBT approaches [27]. In the same way as related works, we also conducted a secondary study on MBT, however, our focus was to systematically map the methods, criteria, formal models for generating test cases and the evaluation strategies of the generated test cases.

3 Research Protocol

The research method was defined based on the guidelines given in Kitchenham and Charters [9]. The method involves three main phases: *(i)* **Planning:** refers to the pre-review activities, and establishes a protocol, defining the research questions, inclusion and exclusion criteria, sources of studies, search string, and mapping procedures; *(ii)* **Conducting:** focuses on searching and selecting the studies in order to extract and synthesize data from included ones; and *(iii)* **Reporting:** is the final phase and it writes up the results and circulates them to potentially interested parties. Following, the main parts of the mapping protocol used in this work are presented.

Research Questions. This mapping study aims at answering the following Research Questions (RQs):

- RQ1. When and where have the studies been published?
- RQ2. What are the methods used in the generation of test cases?
- RQ3. What are the test criteria used in the generation of test cases?
- RQ4. What formal modeling technique is presented for generating test cases?
- RQ5. What evaluation strategy is carried out in the selected study?

Inclusion and Exclusion Criteria. The selection criteria are organized in one Inclusion Criterion (IC) and seven Exclusion Criteria (EC). The inclusion criterion is: (IC1) The study must present an empirical approach for test case generation in MBT. The exclusion criteria are: (EC1) The study is published as a short paper or extended abstract; (EC2) The study is not written in English; (EC3) The study is an older version (less updated) of another study already considered; (EC4) The study is not a primary study, such as editorials, summaries of keynotes, workshops, and tutorials; (EC5) The study does not present an empirical approach to generate test cases; (EC6) The full paper is not available; and (EC7) Studies published before the year 2000. The EC7 was defined based on Offurt and Abdurazik's [28] study published in 1999. This study is referred to as one of the first MBT approaches. Thus, in this mapping we consider only studies published after that date.

Keywords and Search String. We defined the search string in this way to focus only in papers that use methods for test case generation. So, the search string considered two areas, MBT and test case generation (see Table 1), and it was applied in three metadata fields (namely, title, abstract and keywords). The search string was modified to be adapted to particularities of each source.

Table 1: Keywords for the search string

Areas	Keywords
MBT	"MBT", "model based test", "model based testing", "model based tests", "MDT", "model driven test", "model driven testing", "model driven tests"
Test Case	"test criteria", "test criterion", "testing criteria", "testing criterion", "generation method", "generation algorithm", "test cases generation"
Search String: ("MBT" OR "model based test" OR "model based testing" OR "model based tests" OR "MDT" OR "model driven test" OR "model driven testing" OR "model driven tests") AND ("test criteria" OR "test criterion" OR "testing criteria" OR "testing criterion" OR "generation method" OR "generation algorithm" OR "test cases generation")	

Source. We chose to work with Scopus[1] database, since this source is considered the largest abstract and citation database of peer-reviewed literature, with more than 60 million records. In addition, Scopus attaches papers of other international publishers, including Cambridge University Press, Institute of Electrical and Electronics Engineers (IEEE), Nature Publishing Group, Springer, Wiley-Blackwell, and Elsevier.

[1] *https://www.scopus.com/home.uri*

The studies returned from sources in the searching phase were cataloged and stored appropriately. This catalog helped us in the classification and analysis procedures. With the studies remained after applying IC and EC, the snowballing process was conducted. First, referring to papers cited in these remaining studies (backward snowballing) and second, referring to those studies that cited these remaining studies (forward snowballing).

Assessment. Before conducting the mapping study, we tested the mapping protocol. This test was conducted in order to verify its feasibility and adequacy, based on a pre-selected set of studies considered relevant to our investigation. First, the review process was conducted by the first author of this paper, and, only then, the other three authors carried out the review validation. The authors analyzed the studies using three different samples (approximately 30% each).

4 Conducting the mapping study

The main steps performed in this mapping study are shown in Figure 1.

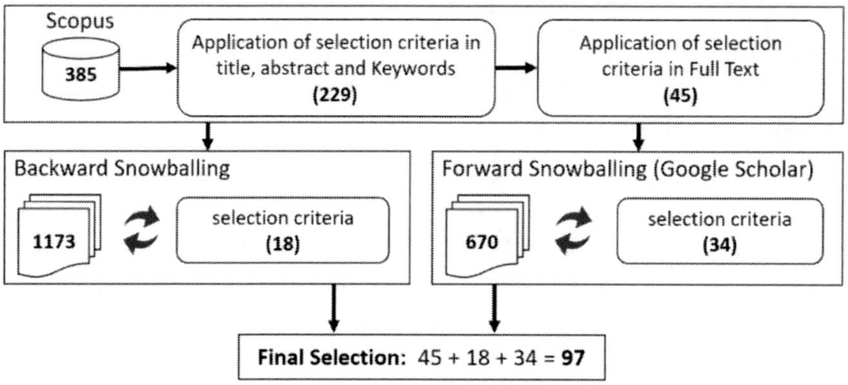

Fig. 1: Selection process

We considered the studies published until March 2018. As a result, 385 publications were returned by Scopus. The selection process was divided into two stages. In the 1st stage, inclusion and exclusion criteria were applied considering the title, abstract and keywords, so 156 publications (approximately 41%) were eliminated. In the 2nd stage, the exclusion criteria were applied considering the entire text, resulting in 45 studies (approximately 12% of total articles). Over these 45 studies considered relevant, we performed backward and forward snowballing. The backward snowballing resulted in 1173 studies. From these 1173 studies, the selection criteria were applied considering the title, abstract and keywords. Next, the selection criteria were applied considering the full text. This stage was carried in an iterative form. Three iterations were conducted and 18 new studies were selected. The forward snowballing returned 670 studies. Four iterations were conducted, resulting in 34 new studies. As a result, we got a final set of 97 studies[2].

[2] The references of the 97 selected studies can be accessed at: *https://goo.gl/i9QTiz*.

5 Data Extraction and Synthesis

After selecting the primary studies, we analyzed each one in order to answer the RQs. The studies classification was made from the RQs answers. The same answers were grouped and consequently a category was defined. Next, we present the main findings from data extraction and synthesis. The complete mapping of individual studies and its categories can be accessed at: *https://goo.gl/i9QTiz*.

In data extraction and synthesis, notice that for some RQs the sum of all classifications might be greater than the total number of papers in the systematic mapping. This occurs because a given paper can answer a RQ with more than one target (e.g. models, methods) of our investigation. In addition, in some RQs, elements that were mentioned only once were grouped into "Others" category.

RQ1. When and where have the studies been published?

Figure 2 shows the distribution of the studies by years. The results suggest that research on MBT has been growing, with a significant increase from 2014 to 2017. In fact, the period between 2011-March 2018 represents 72.2% of all publications of this mapping. That indicates the increased interest in MBT recently. In addition, in relation to the publication vehicle, Conferences are the sources with most publications representing 54.6% and Journals 41.2%. For 4.1% of the papers we do not identified the source of publication.

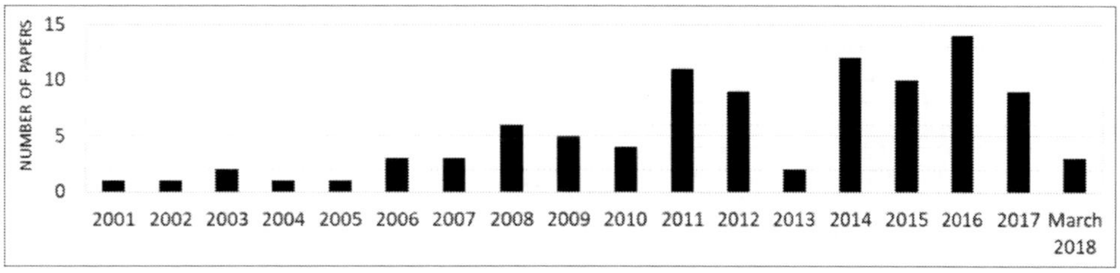

Fig. 2: Distribution of studies by year

RQ2. What are the methods used to generate test cases?

This RQ led us to identify the methods that have been used in MBT. Figure 3 shows the main methods identified. A total of 32 types were identified. Most of the papers propose a new method (24.1%), always to improve an existing method in terms of efficiency and coverage. For example, Hessel and Pettersson [29] proposed a new global algorithm that uses less memory and time to generate a test suite. In Dorofeeva and Koufareva [30], a modification in the classic W-method was proposed. Despite based on a classic method, it is considered as a new method, according to authors. The same occurs in Souza et al. [1] by proposing a new method called H-Switch Cover based on a classic algorithm n-switch set cover.

Optimal-path algorithms have also been used in the generation of test cases (13.5%), as shown in Figure 3. These algorithms are very useful to generate test cases with maximum coverage of a system model, while optimizing the number of test cases. Different types of algorithms were selected in this group. For example, Belli and Hollmann [31] employed the k-transition coverage to generate a test

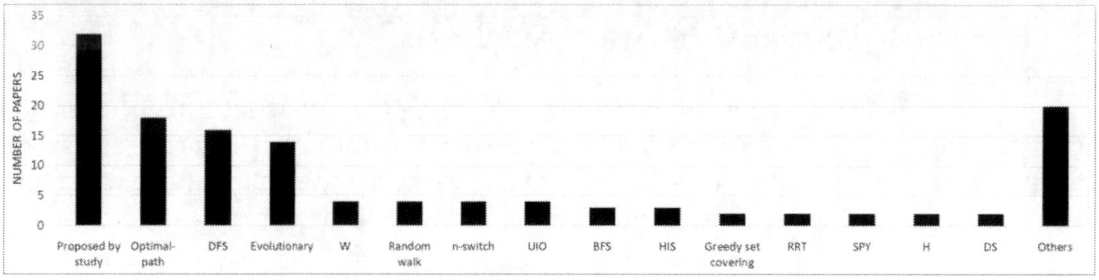

Fig. 3: Methods identified in the selected studies

case for each transition sequence of length k. Then, it is minimized using the Floyd-Warshall algorithm to generate the shortest path. In Julliand et al. [32], a method was proposed to generate test cases from a predicate abstraction of a system specified as an event-based system. This method uses the Chinese Postman Problem (CPP) to cover the transitions of the given model.

We also identified that the well-known classic algorithms continue to be used in MBT. Depth-First Search (DFS) algorithm, for instance, was the most mentioned (12%). This algorithm was used to generate a complete and fast coverage of the model, since it is well-known and very simple to implement. Many studies used the DFS concurrently with another criterion or method, such as Takagi et al. [33] that uses DFS to satisfy the n-switch coverage criterion or applied in a tool to automate all the MBT process like [34].

RQ3. What are the criteria used in the generation of test cases? RQ3 focuses on verifying the criteria used in the identified studies. Figure 4 shows the main criteria found in the selected studies. We identified 29 types of criteria, and the three most mentioned criteria are related to graph coverage: *All-edges* or equivalent (e.g., all-transitions in an FSM) with 36.5%, followed by *all-states* (13.9%), and *all-paths* (12.4%).

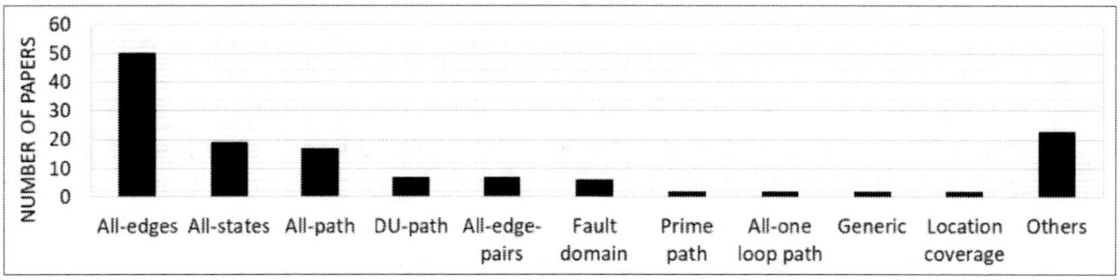

Fig. 4: Criteria identified in the selected studies

Many methods or algorithms identified in RQ2 use a single criterion to generate test cases. For instance, Belli et al. [35] propose a method that use an optimal-path finding algorithm to generate test cases covering *all transitions*. Devroey et al. [36] proposed an approach to generate a suite of abstract test cases that satisfies *all-states* criterion. Other studies adopt a method to cover two or more criteria. For instance, Hessel and Pettersson [29] apply both *all-transitions* and *all-states* to generate test cases using the global algorithm. Belli et al. [37] introduce an event-oriented approach to MBT of Web Service Compositions. In order to do this, their algorithm uses three different criteria to generate test cases: 2-length sequences (*all edges*), 3-length sequences (*all edge-pairs*), and 4-length sequences.

RQ4. What formal modeling technique is presented for generating test cases?

A large number of formal models for generating test cases were observed. However, several Unified Modeling Language (UML) models used in the studies drew our attention. So, we analyzed this RQ in two steps. First, we analyzed only UML models, in order to identify which UML diagram was the most used. Then, all other formal modeling techniques were analyzed.

Figure 5 shows the distribution of UML models. State diagram are the most used. Some studies convert a UML diagram to another formal model to generate test cases. For example, in Anbunathan and Basu [38], a state diagram is converted into Extended FSM (EFSM), and then to Control Flow Graph (CFG), to generate test cases applying some criteria like transition coverage, path coverage, or dataflow coverage. In other studies, the authors use state diagrams to generate test cases directly. For instance, Li and Offutt [39] analyze the ability of test oracles in revealing failures. To do so, test suites are generated from UML state diagrams applying ten elicited test oracle strategies.

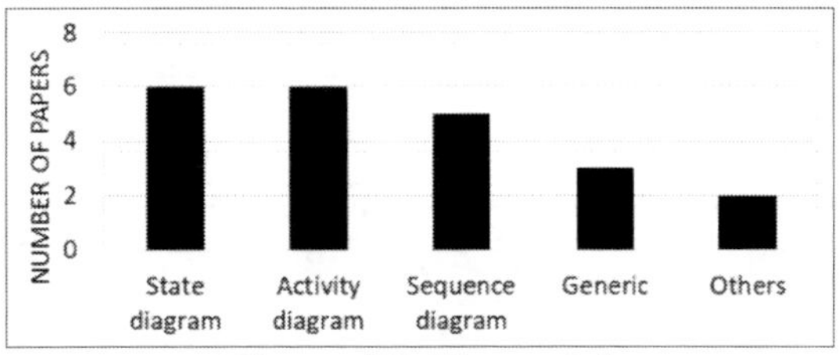

Fig. 5: UML models

Figure 6 presents the main identified formal models. In general, similarly to UML diagrams, state-based models are widely employed in the literature, with FSM being the most used. In Majeed and Ryu [40], for instance, a novel testing approach is proposed to combine OS-level replay mechanism with MBT and generate test cases applying the n-switch set cover in an FSM. Other studies proposed an extended version of FSM for a specific problem, as in Yao et al. [41]. In addition, despite state diagram representation in general can be considered as a graph representation, other formal models based on graphs (like event-driven models) are also popular in the literature.

RQ5. What evaluation strategy is carried out in the selected study?

Finally, RQ5 verifies what are the most used evaluation strategies in the literature. This evaluation strategy is related to the test cases generated and models used. We separated the evaluations into two categories (test case and model) since we observed that these were the most used in the selected studies.

Evaluations related to test cases were more commonly used in the selected studies. Some evaluations are: number of test cases (18.2%), fault detection

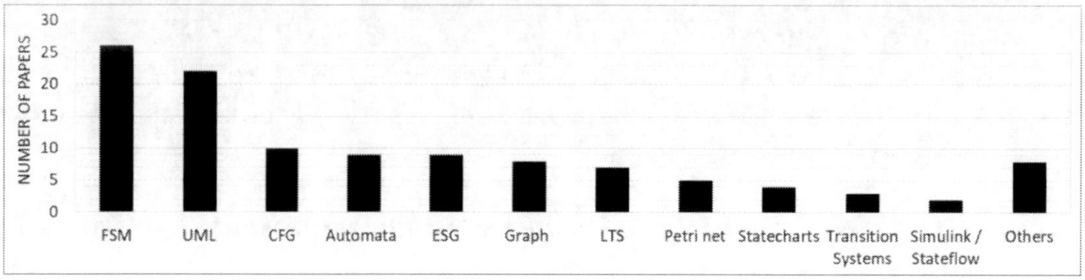

Fig. 6: Formal models used

(11.5%) and mutants analysis (7.4%). In Belli et al. [42], the authors propose a framework that uses pushdown automata (PDA) related to context-free languages to generate a small test set. The framework evaluation was based on the analysis of the number of test cases generated, as well as their average length, number of events executed, number of faults and the performance of fault detection. Ali et al. [43] introduce a technique to combine UML diagrams and Statecharts as an intermediate model (SCOTEM) to generate test paths, also defining coverage criteria to be used in the model. The validation of this technique analyzes fault detection capability, generating mutant programs.

With respect to model evaluations, they were based mainly on number of edges (7.4%), number of states (6.8%) and fault coverage (4.1%) in a model. For example, in Satpathy et al. [44], a method to cover parallel and hierarchical stateflow model was proposed, without flattening the components of the model, and generate test cases. The approach is evaluated considering the coverage of states and transitions. Cartaxo et al. [45] proposed to use a similarity function to generate less redundant test suite. The approach is compared with a random selection and uses the transition coverage to evaluate it.

Finally, we identified evaluations for both test cases and models, such as time (24.3%) and memory used (2.7%). The time is the most mentioned evaluation in the selected studies. Some studies use the time as a performance metric of computation time. For example, Dang and Nahhal [46] proposed a framework to use conformance testing in continuous and hybrid systems and a method based on Rapidly-exploring Random Tree, called RRT, to generate test cases. The time is used to analyze the efficiency of method in linear systems, comparing both the methods. In Wang et al. [47] time is used in an empirical evaluation of a tool, Tansuo, that uses a proposed approach to generate navigations graphs for dynamic web applications using combinatorial testing. The paper also analyzes how much time is needed to generate a navigation graph and to generate test cases using the t-way coverage criterion.

6 Discussion

In this work, directions to several approaches associated to MBT have been identified. Some relevant points are discussed as follows.

MBT is a research topic that shows itself in a constant growth, as can be seen in RQ1. This can also be confirmed by the number of secondary studies that have been conducted. We have identified ten secondary studies with different purposes and each with a considerable number of primary studies returned, which we believe are in the strong interest in this research area.

Another result that makes us infer the constant growth of interest in this area of research is the number of contributions on new methods proposed for the generation of test cases. As can be observed in RQ2, there is a great effort spent in developing new test methods; out of the 97 selected studies, 32 proposed a new method for generating test cases from formal models. We also identified 29 test criteria in RQ3. The formal models used were also quite varied with more than 24. And, with respect to RQ5 we identified 145 types of evaluations conducted in the selected studies considering the test cases generated and models used.

One of the main features of MBT is the automated generation of test cases usually based on a formal representation of the software specification. We noted by the systematic mapping that the industry has an inclination in employing UML models (22 UML models), due to the approximation with user and focus on systems that need the user control. On the other hand, in the case of academy, models like FSM (26) and Statecharts (4) are more used. In particular, FSMs have been heavily adopted to generate test cases for different kinds of applications, such as Web applications and embedded systems, specially reactive systems. FSM is commonly used for testing due to its rigor and simplicity. Great effort has been spent on the development of methods and criteria for FSM that select or generate effective test sets capable of revealing all faults from a given domain, as can be seen in RQ4. In general, these models (FSM and Statecharts) apply graph algorithms to generate test cases, either to obtain the best path or high coverage.

With respect to the evaluation strategy carried out in the selected studies, we have identified that the researchers usually divide the evaluations into two main categories: test cases and formal models. Evaluations related to test cases are more commonly used (39 different type of evaluations). Different analyses in the test cases are conducted to understand the behavior of the test methods. A tester can identify the trade-offs between test case characteristics, such as test suite length, and fault detection ratio, as shown in RQ5, and consequently choosing the best method to fit for a given project.

6.1 Threats to validity

The study selection and data extraction stages were initially performed by the first author. In order to reduce some subjectivity, the other authors performed these same stages over a sample of studies. The samples were compared in order to detect possible bias.

Our review was limited by the search terms used in the Scopus database. Although Scopus is considered the largest abstract and citation database, we tried to overcome possible limitations by using backward and forward snowballing. We also considered papers from a control group to calibrate the string. The categorization of papers was based on research questions (method, criterion, formal model and evaluation strategies). Even so, we are possibly leaving some valuable studies out of our analysis, since we considered papers indexed just by the Scopus database, and those obtained from snowballing. However, the studies discussed in this mapping provide an overview of empirical research on outcomes of existing research on MBT.

7 Conclusions

In this paper, we have reported the results of a systematic mapping on approaches to generate test cases in MBT. It is important to emphasize that our focus was on studies that addressed, mainly, algorithms for test case generation. We identified 97 studies addressing methods, algorithms, formal models and evaluation strategies on MBT. The major contribution of this study was to summarize and highlight the main aspects associated to MBT, but focused on the methods, formal models and evaluation strategies most used in the existing literature. These results could be of interest to several researchers involved with MBT. We believe that our summarization can help to direct researchers in their future research providing a pointer to appropriately position new activities in this research topic.

Future directions include conducting research on the behavior of the main methods and criteria returned in this mapping, considering FSMs with different configurations to represent different applications. In addition, as evaluation methods, the main evaluation strategies identified in this systematic mapping will be considered.

Acknowledgment

M.M. Mariano is financially supported by CAPES/Brazil. A.T. Endo and E.F. Souza are partially financially supported by CNPq/Brazil (grant number 420363/2018-1 and 432247/2018-1).

References

1. Souza, É.F., de Santiago Júnior, V.A., Vijaykumar, N.L.: H-switch cover: a new test criterion to generate test case from finite state machines. Software Quality Journal **25**(2) (2017) 373–405
2. Myers, G.J., Sandler, C., et al.: The art of software testing (2004)
3. El-Far, I.K., Whittaker, J.A.: Model-based software testing. Encyclopedia of Software Engineering (2001) 825–837
4. Utting, M., Legeard, B.: Practical model-based testing: a tools approach. Morgan Kaufmann Publishers Inc, San Francisco, CA, USA (2010)
5. Harel, D.: Statecharts: A visual formalism for complex systems. Science of computer programming **8**(3) (1987) 231–274
6. Lee, D., Yannakakis, M.: Principles and methods of testing finite state machines-a survey. Proceedings of the IEEE **84**(8) (1996) 1090–1123
7. Ellsberger, J., Hogrefe, D., Sarma, A.: SDL: formal object-oriented language for communicating systems. Prentice Hall (1997)
8. Tretmans, J.: Model based testing with labelled transition systems. In: Formal methods and testing. (2008) 1–38

9. Kitchenham, B.A., Charters, S.: Guidelines for performing systematic literature reviews in software engineering. Technical Report EBSE 2007-001, Keele University and Durham University, UK (2007)
10. IEEE: THE INSTITUTE OF ELECTRIC AND ELECTRONIC ENGINEERS (IEEE): standard for software verification and validation. Standard 1012 (2004)
11. Dalal, S.R., Jain, A., Karunanithi, N., Leaton, J., Lott, C.M., Patton, G.C., Horowitz, B.M.: Model-based testing in practice. In: International conference on Software engineering. (1999) 285–294
12. Ammann, P., Offutt, J.: Introduction to software testing. Cambridge University Press (2008)
13. Gonenc, G.: A method for the design of fault detection experiments. IEEE transactions on Computers **100**(6) (1970) 551–558
14. Chow, T.S.: Testing software design modeled by finite-state machines. IEEE transactions on software engineering (3) (1978) 178–187
15. Naito, S.: Fault detection for sequential machines by transition-tours. Proc. FTCS (Fault Tolerant Comput. Syst.), 1981 (1981)
16. Sidhu, D.P., Leung, T.K.: Formal methods for protocol testing: A detailed study. IEEE transactions on software engineering **15**(4) (1989) 413–426
17. Bondy, J., Murty, U.: Graduate Texts in Mathematics: Graph Theory. Springer, USA (2008)
18. Barmi, Z.A., Ebrahimi, A.H., Feldt, R.: Alignment of requirements specification and testing: A systematic mapping study. In: Software Testing, Verification and Validation Workshops (ICSTW). (2011) 476–485
19. Siavashi, F., Truscan, D.: Environment modeling in model-based testing: Concepts, prospects and research challenges: A systematic literature review. In: International Conference on Evaluation and Assessment in Software Engineering. (2015) 1–6
20. Gurbuz, H.G., Tekinerdogan, B.: Model-based testing for software safety: a systematic mapping study. Software Quality Journal (2017) 1–46
21. Khan, M.U., Iftikhar, S., Iqbal, M.Z., Sherin, S.: Empirical studies omit reporting necessary details: A systematic literature review of reporting quality in model based testing. Computer Standards & Interfaces (2017)
22. Ascate, M.S., Oliveira, K., Mendes, I., Fontão, A., Villanes, I., Dias-Neto, A.: Model-based testing for mobile applications: A systematic mapping study. In: Ibero-America Conference on Software Engineering (CIbSE). (2017)
23. Saeed, A., Ab Hamid, S.H., Mustafa, M.B.: The experimental applications of search-based techniques for model-based testing: Taxonomy and systematic literature review. Applied Soft Computing **49** (2016) 1094–1117
24. Hooda, S., Dalai, S., Solanki, K.: A systematic review of model-based testing in aspect-oriented software systems. In: Computing for Sustainable Global Development (INDIACom), 2016 3rd International Conference on. (2016) 2944–2949
25. Shafique, M., Labiche, Y.: A systematic review of state-based test tools. International Journal on Software Tools for Technology Transfer **17**(1) (2015) 59–76
26. Bernardino, M., Rodrigues, E.M., Zorzo, A.F., Marchezan, L.: Systematic mapping study on mbt: tools and models. IET Software **11**(4) (2017) 141–155
27. Dias, N.A.C., Subramanyan, R., Vieira, M., Travassos, G.H.: A survey on model-based testing approaches: a systematic review. In: International Conference on Automated Software Engineering (ASE). (2007) 31–36
28. Offutt, J., Abdurazik, A.: Generating tests from uml specifications. In: International Conference on the Unified Modeling Language (UML'99). 416–429
29. Hessel, A., Pettersson, P.: A global algorithm for model-based test suite generation. Electronic Notes in Theoretical Computer Science **190**(2) (2007) 47–59

30. Dorofeeva, M., Koufareva, I.: Novel modification of the w-method. Bulletin of the Novosibirsk Computing Center. Series: Computer Science (18) (2002) 69–80
31. Belli, F., Hollmann, A.: Test generation and minimization with basic statecharts. In: ACM symposium on Applied computing. (2008) 718–723
32. Julliand, J., Kouchnarenko, O., Masson, P.A., Voiron, G.: Test generation from event system abstractions to cover their states and transitions. Programming and Computer Software **44**(1) (2018) 1–14
33. Takagi, T., Oyaizu, N., Furukawa, Z.: Concurrent n-switch coverage criterion for generating test cases from place/transition nets. In: Computer and Information Science (ICIS), 2010 IEEE/ACIS 9th International Conference on. (2010) 782–787
34. Cartaxo, E.G., Andrade, W.L., Neto, F.G.O., Machado, P.D.: Lts-bt: a tool to generate and select functional test cases for embedded systems. In: ACM symposium on Applied computing. (2008) 1540–1544
35. Belli, F., Hollmann, A., Kleinselbeck, M.: A graph-model-based testing method compared with the classification tree method for test case generation. In: Secure Software Integration and Reliability Improvement. (2009) 193–200
36. Devroey, X., Perrouin, G., Schobbens, P.Y.: Abstract test case generation for behavioural testing of software product lines. In: International Software Product Line Conference: Companion Volume for Workshops, Demonstrations and Tools-Volume 2. (2014) 86–93
37. Belli, F., Endo, A.T., Linschulte, M., Simao, A.: A holistic approach to model-based testing of web service compositions. Software: Practice and Experience **44**(2) (2014) 201–234
38. Anbunathan, R., Basu, A.: Dataflow test case generation from uml class diagrams. In: IEEE International Conference on Computational Intelligence and Computing Research (ICCIC). (2013) 1–9
39. Li, N., Offutt, J.: Test oracle strategies for model-based testing. IEEE Transactions on Software Engineering **43**(4) (2017) 372–395
40. Majeed, S., Ryu, M.: Model-based replay testing for event-driven software. In: 31st Annual ACM Symposium on Applied Computing. (2016) 1527–1533
41. Yao, J., Wang, Z., Yin, X., Shiyz, X., Wu, J.: Formal modeling and systematic black-box testing of sdn data plane. In: Network Protocols (ICNP), 2014 IEEE 22nd International Conference on. (2014) 179–190
42. Belli, F., Beyazit, M., Takagi, T., Furukawa, Z.: Model-based mutation testing using pushdown automata. TRANSACTIONS on Information and Systems **95**(9) (2012) 2211–2218
43. Ali, S., Briand, L.C., Rehman, M.J.u., Asghar, H., Iqbal, M.Z.Z., Nadeem, A.: A state-based approach to integration testing based on uml models. Information and Software Technology **49**(11-12) (2007) 1087–1106
44. Satpathy, M., Yeolekar, A., Peranandam, P., Ramesh, S.: Efficient coverage of parallel and hierarchical stateflow models for test case generation. Software Testing, Verification and Reliability **22**(7) (2012) 457–479
45. Cartaxo, E.G., Machado, P.D., Neto, F.G.O.: On the use of a similarity function for test case selection in the context of model-based testing. Software Testing, Verification and Reliability **21**(2) (2011) 75–100
46. Dang, T., Nahhal, T.: Coverage-guided test generation for continuous and hybrid systems. Formal Methods in System Design **34**(2) (2009) 183–213
47. Wang, W., Sampath, S., Lei, Y., Kacker, R., Kuhn, R., Lawrence, J.: Using combinatorial testing to build navigation graphs for dynamic web applications. Software Testing, Verification and Reliability **26**(4) (2016) 318–346

A survey of software testing practices in Costa Rica

Christian Quesada-López[1,2], Erika Hernandez-Agüero[2], Marcelo Jenkins[1]

Universidad de Costa Rica, San Pedro, Costa Rica[1]
Universidad Estatal a Distancia, San Pedro, Costa Rica[2]
cristian.quesadalopez@ucr.ac.cr, ehernandez@uned.ac.cr,
marcelo.jenkins@ucr.ac.cr

Abstract. Software testing is an essential activity in software development projects for delivering high quality products. In a previous study, we reported the results of a survey of software engineering practices in the Costa Rican industry. To analyze more in depth the specific software testing practices among practitioners, we replicated a previous survey conducted in South America. Our objective was to characterize the state of the practice based on practitioners use and perceived importance of software testing practices. This survey evaluated 42 testing practices grouped in three categories: processes, activities and tools. A total of 92 practitioners responded to the survey. The participants indicated that: (1) task for recording of the results of tests, documentation of test procedures and cases, and re-execution of tests when the software is modified are useful and important for software testing practitioners. (2) Acceptance and system testing are the two most useful and important testing types. (3) Tools for recording defects and the effort to fix them (bug tracking) and the availability of a test database for reuse are useful and important. Regarding the use of practices, the participants stated that (4) Planning and designing of software testing before coding and evaluating the quality of test artifacts are not a regular practice. (5) There is a lack of measurement of defect density and test coverage in the industry; and (6) tools for automatic generation of test cases and for estimating testing effort are rarely used. This study gave us a first glance at the state of the practice in software testing in a thriving and very dynamic industry that currently employs most of our computer science professionals. The benefits are twofold: for academia, it provides us with a road map to revise our academic offer, and for practitioners it provides them with a first set of data to benchmark their practices.

Keywords. Software Testing, Industry Practices, Survey, Costa Rica, Replication, Empirical Software Engineering.

1 Introduction

Software testing is an essential activity in software development projects, for delivering high quality products. Software testing is a costly activity in the software development life cycle [1] and represents, on average, around 35% of the total budget of a development project [2]. Currently, there is a gap between knowledge in academia and the software testing practices used in industry [2]. Furthermore, there is a wide spectrum of testing practices conducted by different software teams [1] and a little evidence in the literature regarding the use and importance of such practices in industry [2]. The characterization of testing practices used in industry can help professionals, researchers, and academics in general to better understand the challenges faced by the software engineering profession [1].

To characterize testing practices in the software industry, a large number of surveys have been conducted in different countries. Garousi and Zhi [1], and Dias-Neto et al. [2] summarized previous surveys on software testing practices. In particular, Dias-Neto et al. [2] identified surveys conducted to characterize the adoption of software testing practices, tools, and methods. For example, a set of replications surveying testing practices in Canada was conducted from 2004 to 2013 [3, 4, 1] and a number of studies surveying testing practices in South America was conducted from 2006 to 2017 [5, 6, 2, 7]. Two more surveys were conducted in Australia and New Zealand between 2004 and 2012 [8, 9]. Finally, several studies surveying different aspects related to testing practices were conducted in other countries from 2010 to 2016 [10-18]. Further replications in different countries are still needed to allow the comparison of industrial trends in software testing practices [1, 2]. The results of these surveys can support evidence on testing practices in the software engineering community [1].

In Costa Rica, previous surveys had been conducted to characterize software engineering practices. In our previous work [19, 20], we replicated a survey based on [21, 22] where we identify the most common practices, methods and tools in professional practice and their related challenges. Moreover, we conducted a cross-factor correlation analysis of development and testing engineering practices versus practitioner demographics. In [23], the authors conducted a survey on development practices based on the HELENA study [24]. They studied development approaches, practices, and methods in industry. To analyze the specific software testing practices among practitioners in our country, we replicated previous surveys conducted in South America [5, 6, 2, 7].

The objective of our study was to characterize a set of software testing practices with respect to their use and importance from the point of view of practitioners of software organizations in Costa Rica. In this work, we replicated the previously surveys in [5, 6, 2, 7] with 92 practitioners from our country. As stated in [2], we were interested understanding the testing practitioners use and perceived importance of software testing practices. In addition, we wanted to compare the results of our study with the results of the previous surveys.

This study gave us a first glance at the state of the practice in software testing in a thriving and very dynamic industry that currently employs most of our computer science professionals. The benefits are twofold: for academia, it provides us with a road map to revise our academic offering, and for practitioners it provides a baseline to benchmark their current practices.

The paper is structured as follows: Section 2 describes the survey replication process. Section 3 analysis the results of the survey. Finally, Section 4 outlines our conclusions.

2 Replication process

Our study is an external replication of four previously conducted surveys in South America [5, 6, 2, 7]. Dias-Neto et al. [5] analyze the answers of 36 practitioners from 13 Brazilian organizations to identify the software testing practices used by the organizations and its importance. Greca et al. [6] replicated the original survey with 18 practitioners in Argentina. Dias-Neto et al. [2] conducted the same survey in Brazil and Uruguay with 150 practitioners. They surveyed different companies from Southern/Brazil (56 participants), Northern/Brazil (50 participants) and Uruguay (44 participants). Robiolo et al. [7] surveyed 25 practitioners from 25 organizations of the public sector.

In this study, we reported the responses from 92 practitioners from Costa Rica. The study includes a detailed analysis of the data collected, and its comparison with previous studies, in accordance with the recommendations and guidelines of [25, 26]. This study is descriptive [27] and is intended to compare and extend previous results [26], highlighting the similarities and differences in the use and importance of testing practices in different countries. We reused the survey goal, research questions, questionnaire, and analysis procedure reported in [7, 2] in our replication.

2.1 Goal and research questions

The goal of the study was to characterize testing practices based on the practitioners use and perceived importance in the context of software organizations in Costa Rica. The survey evaluated 42 testing practices grouped in three categories: processes, activities, and tools. Based on the objective, the following research questions are stated:

- RQ1: What are the testing practices used by practitioners?
- RQ2: What are the most important software testing practices?

2.2 Survey design

Target population and sampling. The target population are the practitioners applying testing practices in software organizations in Costa Rica. The practitioners were sampled by convenience. They were contacted through the University of Costa Rica and the State Distance University, two of the most important public universities in our country. E-mail distribution lists were used to support the recruitment of participants.

Instruments. We applied the questionnaire designed in [2] to collect the information. The instrument was divided into three parts: (1) profile and demographics, (2) the use of testing processes, activities and tools; and (3) perceived importance of testing processes, activities and tools. The instrument evaluated 42 testing practices grouped in three categories: testing processes (practices related to the adopted test processes in the software organization), testing activities (practices concerned with the procedures performed during the software testing), and testing tools (practices concerned with tools supporting the software testing). We used the Spanish version of the instrument. In order to validate the questionnaire (concepts and language), we conducted five survey pilots. Table 1 details the list of questions of the instrument.

Table 1 Survey questions. Based on [2].

Id	Question	Id	Question
D01	Job position	*A05*	Application of acceptance tests
D02	Experience in software testing	*A06*	Application of regression tests
D03	Academic degree	*A07*	Application of exploratory tests
D04	Certifications in testing	*A08*	Application of performance tests
D05	Development methodology	*A09*	Application of security tests
D06	Programming language expertise	*A10*	Registration of the time spent on testing
D07	Software platform used for development	*A11*	Measurement of the effort/cost of testing
D08	Company size	*A12*	Storage of records (log) of the executed tests
P01	Documentation of test plan	*A13*	Measurement of the defect density
P02	Documentation of test procedures and cases	*A14*	Conducting training on software testing
P03	Recording the results of test execution	*A15*	Separation of testing and dev activities
P04	Measurement and analysis of the test coverage	*A16*	Storage of test data for future use
P05	Use of methodology or process	*A17*	Analysis of faults patterns (trend)
P06	Analysis of identified defects	*A18*	Availability of human resources allocated full time for testing
P07	Identification and use of risks for planning and executing software tests	*A19*	Selection of test techniques according to the project's features
P08	Planning/Designing of testing before coding	*T01*	Availability of a test database for reuse
P09	Monitoring adherence to the test process	*T02*	Use of tools for automatic execution of test procedures or cases
P10	Re-execution of tests when the software is modified	*T03*	Use of tools for automatic generation of test procedures or cases
P11	Evaluation of the quality of test artifacts	*T04*	Use of test management tools to track and record
P12	Setting a priori criteria to stop the testing	*T05*	Use of tools to estimate test effort and/or schedule
P13	Reporting evaluation of a test round	*T06*	Use of test management tools to enact activities and artifacts
A01	Definition of a responsible professional or team	*T07*	Use of tools for recording defects and the effort to fix them (bug tracking)
A02	Application of unit tests	*T08*	Use of coverage measurement tools
A03	Application of integration tests	*T09*	Continuous integration tools for automated tests
A04	Application of system tests	*T10*	Selection of test tools according to project charcs.

D: Demographics. P: Testing processes. A: Testing activities. T: Testing tools.

Participants were asked to fill the entire questionnaire with the 42 testing practices according to the use level in their current organization and the perceived importance of a testing practice. Dias-Neto et al. [2, 5] defined a five point Likert scale to express the gradual increase in the level of use and importance of a testing practice, as shown in Table 2. As in previous study, each practitioner answer only one option for the level of use and importance for each software testing practice.

Data analysis. For each testing practice, we collected the use and importance level based on the opinions of the professionals. As recommended in [2, 5], we obtained the level of use and importance according to the characteristics of each participant.

Table 2 Level of use and importance. Based on [2].

L	Level of use	L	Level of importance
1	Not Applied: the practice is outside the scope of the organization's software projects.	1	Not important: the practice is not necessary for software projects.
2	Not used: the practice is within the scope of the organization, but it is not used in any software project.	2	Low value: the practice has low importance to use in software projects.
3	Infrequent use: the practice is not frequently used in the organization's software projects.	3	Limited value: the practice can be adequate to use in software projects.
4	Habitual use: the practice is used in most of the organization's software projects.	4	Significant value: the practice is recommended to use in software projects.
5	Standard use: the practice is used in all organization's software projects.	5	Essential value: the practice must be used in all software projects.

L: Likert Scale.

First, the responses of the professionals were differentiated by assigning a weight for each participant according to their experience, academic degree, and certifications on testing (Eq. 1). Second, we multiplied each answer by the weight of the participant and computed the total value for a testing practice (Eq. 2). Finally, we obtained a normalized value for the levels of use and importance that oscillates between 0% and 100% (Eq. 3). We applied the following formulas:

$$W(i) = DT(i) \div MdDT + TT(i) \div MdTT + f(i) + g(i) + h(i) \qquad (1)$$

Where: $W(i)$ is the total weight for participant i. $DT(i)$ is the number of years of experience for participant i in software development. $TT(i)$ is the number of years of experience for participant i in software testing. $MdDT$ and $MdTT$ are the median of DT and TT. $f(i)$ is the highest academic degree for participant i (0-High school, 1-Undergraduate, 2-Specialization, 3-Master, 4-Ph.D). $g(i)$ is the self-assigned expertise level by the participant i (0-None, 1-Low, 2-Medium, 3-High, 4-Excellent). $h(i)$ is the number of testing certifications reported by the participant i.

$$T(j) = \sum_{i=1}^{N}(Answer(i,j) * W(i)) \qquad (2)$$

Where: $T(j)$ is the total value obtained for use and importance regarding the testing practice j. $Answer(i,j)$ is the answer value (1–5) relating to the use and importance by the participant i for the testing practice j.

$$N(j) = T(j) \div (\sum_{i=1}^{N} W(i) * 5) \qquad (3)$$

Where: $N(j)$ is the normalized value for use and importance of testing practice j and $(\sum_{i=1}^{N} W(i) * 5)$ is the maximum possible value for testing practice j.

For each testing practice, the use and importance were analyzed and compared with previous studies, and the correlation between use and importance perceived was evaluated. For this study, we replicated the analysis proposed in [2].

2.3 Survey execution

The electronic questionnaire was implemented using *LimeSurvey* (www.limesurvey.org) and was available in a Survey Server at the University of Costa Rica for a period of two months, from September to October 2018. Participants were asked to complete the survey online. All participants were invited to participate anonymously and voluntarily by email. Practitioners could withdraw at any time, and only summarized and aggregated information were published. Similar to experiences in previous studies [19, 20], some participants leave questions unanswered and others leave the questionnaire without completing it. Only the completed answers were considered for the analysis of results. After data pre-processing, the responses of 92 professionals were analyzed.

2.4 Threats to Validity

This work is subject to the threats to the validity reported for this type of studies including previous replications and the results must be interpreted carefully. The main threats to validity are related to the quantity and representativeness of the sample. The survey does not necessarily represent all the Costa Rican industry. Moreover, the survey reflects the practitioners interpretation of importance and use. The answers could not necessarily represent the reality of testing practices.

3 Analysis of results

3.1 Demographics of the participants

In total, we received 92 complete answers. Our participants could indicate more than one job position. The 54% (50) of the practitioners reported one position, 23% (21) two positions, 8% (14) reported 3 and 4 positions, and 7% (7) reported up to 7 positions. Participants claimed to be mostly project managers (18%), analysts (17%), developers (16%), and quality managers (14%). Furthermore, participants reported to be software engineers (9%), test analysts (8%), testers (8%), quality engineers (6%), and software architects (3%). Around 36% of participants are working on quality/testing. However, 32% (29) of the participants reported that both development and quality teams perform testing activities, 34% (31) reported that only quality teams perform testing, and 26% (24) reported that the development teams perform testing activities.

Participants reported on average, 11.5 years of experience in the software industry, and 5.5 years of experience in software quality and testing. Only 20% (18) of the participants hold a software testing certification. Some 15% (14) of practitioners are ISTQB Certified Testers, 3% (3) are Certified Test Manager (CTM), and 1% (1) is a

Certified Software Quality Engineer (CSQE). Finally, participants reported their academic degree, 49% (45) hold an university degree, 36 (33%) a master degree, 14% (13) has a technical specialization, and only 1% (1) holds a Ph.D.

With respect to organizations size, 50% (46) of participants work in organizations with more than 100 employees, 16% (15) in organizations with 50-99 employees, 22% (20) work in organizations with 10-49 employees, and 12% (11) in organizations with less than 10 employees. In total, 59% (54) of the practitioners claim to apply agile methodologies, 26% (24) traditional methodologies and 15% (14) use a hybrid development methodology. The most used programming languages are.Net in C# and Visual Basic (35%), Java (24%), C/C++ (11%), PHP (9%), and Python (9%).

3.2 Analysis of the use and perceived importance of testing practices

We used the answers of all participants for this part of the analysis. The p-value for the Shapiro-Wilk test indicates that the values representing the influence (weight) of the participants were normally distributed. Table 3 presents a heat map with the results of the use and importance of software testing practices in five studies. The most used and perceived important (P. I.) testing practices in process (P), activities (A), and tools (T) were marked in green, and the least used and important ones were marked in red. The greener color means the practice is deemed useful and/or important, the redder mean the practice is not considered important or not implemented. We present the results of Costa Rica (CR), Argentina (AR) [7], Northern Brazil (NBR), Southern Brazil (SBR), and Uruguay (UY) [2].

Use of testing practices in Costa Rica. By analyzing the green patterns in Table 3, we can conclude that the three most used testing processes reported were: the recording of test cases results (*P03*), the documentation of test procedures and cases (*P02*), and the re-execution of tests when the software is modified (*P10*). In the case of testing activities, the three most used were the application of acceptance testing (*A05*) and system testing (*A04*), and the definition of a responsible professional or team (*A01*). Finally, the three most used testing tools were: tools for recording defects and the effort to fix them - bug tracking (*T07*), a test database for reuse (*T01*), and management tools to track and record the results (*T04*).

On the other hand, the processes for planning/designing of testing before coding (*P08*), the evaluation of the quality of test artifacts (*P11*), and the measurement and analysis of the test coverage (*P04*) were reported as the three least used. The measurement of the defect density (*A13*), the analysis of faults patterns – trends (*A17*), and the registration of the time spent on testing (*A10*) were reported as the three least used activities. Finally, the three least used tools were the tools for automatic generation of test procedures or cases (*T03*), coverage measurement tools (*T08*), and tools to estimate test effort and/or schedule (*T05*).

Importance of testing practices in Costa Rica. By observing the green patterns in Table 3, we can conclude that the three most perceived important testing processes were: the task of recording the results of tests cases (*P03*), the documentation of test procedures and cases (*P02*), and the re-execution of tests when the software is modified (*P10*). These processes were also the most used by practitioners. In the case of testing activities, the three perceived as most important were the application of acceptance testing (*A05*), the application of integration tests (*A03*), and the storage of records (logs) of the executed tests (*A12*). Besides, system testing (*A04*), and a definition of a responsible professional or team (*A01*) were perceived important. Finally, the three most important testing tools were: tools for recording defects and the effort to fix them - bug tracking (*T07*), tools for automatic execution of test procedures or cases (*T02*), and a test database for reuse (*T01*). The management tools to track and record the results (*T04*) were also perceived as important.

Likewise, the processes for test artifacts quality (*P11*), for planning/designing of testing before coding (*P08*), and for reporting evaluation of a test round (*P13*) were perceived as the three least important. The measurement of the defect density (*A13*), the application of exploratory tests (*A07*), and the analysis of faults patterns – trends (*A17*) were perceived as the three least important activities. The perceived as the three least important tools were the tools to estimate test effort and/or schedule (*T05*), coverage measurement tools (*T08*), and tools for automatic generation of test procedures or cases (*T03*).

Finally, some trends across replications could be observed. There is a set of used and important practices (*P02, P03, P10, A01, A03, A04, A05, T01, T07*) and a set of less used and considered less important practices (*P08, A10, A11, A13, A14, A17*).

3.3 Analysis of correlation between use and perceived importance

Table 4 presents the Spearman's rho correlation coefficient between the use and perceived importance of each testing practice (two-tail test with $p < 0.01$). In this case, there was a positive correlation between the use and perceived importance, and all correlations were statistically significant. The values above 0.5 were considered as highly correlated and are marked in bold. A high correlation means that the participants either: (1) deemed the practice useful and important, or (2) they deemed the practice not useful and not important.

Our results show that although there is a correlation between the values of use and perceived importance, only 18 of 42 practices are highly correlated (*P01, P02, P03, P09, P12, P13, A01, A04, A06, A07, A10, A11, A12, A13, T01, T05, T06, T07*). We agreed with [2] when they state that practitioners can find the practices they use daily to be important and therefore, either they cannot distinguish between use and important or they do not see value in the distinction. In the following section, we compare the relation between use and importance.

3.4 Analysis between use and perceived importance

Table 5 presents the "More used" and "More important", and the "Less used" and "Less important" testing practices. To classify the practices, the top 21 most used practices and the top 21 most perceived as important practices were selected. The set of "most used most used, most important" practices represents the good practices in testing per-

Table 3 Comparison on the use and perceived importance of testing practices.

	2018		2017 [7]		2017 [2]		2017 [2]		2017 [2]		
	CR (n=92)		AR (n=25)		NBR (n=50)		SBR (n=56)		UY (n=44)		
	Use	**P. I.**	**Use**	**P. I.**	**Use**	**P. I.**	**Use**	**P. I.**	**Use**	**P. I.**	
P01	76%	86%	67%	76%	78%	85%	69%	75%	79%	85%	*P01*
P02	84%	95%	72%	80%	86%	87%	81%	84%	83%	89%	*P02*
P03	85%	96%	76%	83%	91%	94%	86%	90%	90%	94%	*P03*
P04	64%	87%	57%	70%	65%	75%	65%	79%	66%	76%	*P04*
P05	77%	93%	58%	76%	75%	81%	73%	78%	74%	80%	*P05*
P06	72%	90%	59%	78%	71%	77%	73%	79%	71%	76%	*P06*
P07	66%	85%	53%	76%	68%	75%	63%	74%	65%	77%	*P07*
P08	55%	79%	52%	72%	62%	68%	59%	70%	58%	67%	*P08*
P09	67%	85%	47%	64%	64%	75%	58%	66%	61%	72%	*P09*
P10	83%	95%	74%	85%	90%	92%	87%	91%	86%	90%	*P10*
P11	58%	76%	48%	71%	63%	71%	60%	69%	62%	75%	*P11*
P12	72%	87%	50%	73%	65%	77%	63%	73%	64%	74%	*P12*
P13	68%	84%	58%	78%	72%	80%	62%	67%	74%	86%	*P13*
A01	82%	93%	79%	89%	90%	94%	84%	86%	89%	92%	*A01*
A02	79%	92%	79%	93%	71%	81%	79%	88%	78%	86%	*A02*
A03	81%	95%	77%	88%	79%	87%	83%	90%	86%	92%	*A03*
A04	83%	93%	81%	89%	88%	92%	89%	94%	88%	93%	*A04*
A05	88%	97%	82%	87%	83%	88%	82%	89%	85%	92%	*A05*
A06	79%	91%	74%	82%	84%	90%	83%	91%	84%	90%	*A06*
A07	69%	76%	60%	69%	85%	82%	77%	81%	82%	75%	*A07*
A08	71%	89%	73%	80%	70%	81%	68%	77%	71%	81%	*A08*
A09	71%	89%	80%	88%	70%	88%	68%	79%	74%	85%	*A09*
A10	63%	78%	52%	60%	66%	75%	71%	75%	70%	78%	*A10*
A11	64%	81%	45%	51%	62%	78%	69%	76%	65%	78%	*A11*
A12	81%	94%	76%	80%	78%	84%	79%	78%	83%	87%	*A12*
A13	56%	74%	47%	57%	47%	63%	56%	65%	49%	60%	*A13*
A14	65%	84%	55%	65%	64%	80%	62%	80%	66%	80%	*A14*
A15	77%	89%	81%	90%	82%	80%	82%	84%	85%	85%	*A15*
A16	78%	88%	71%	82%	78%	81%	70%	77%	77%	78%	*A16*
A17	58%	78%	67%	77%	63%	73%	57%	72%	60%	71%	*A17*
A18	78%	92%	75%	82%	78%	84%	77%	89%	83%	85%	*A18*
A19	70%	89%	71%	79%	80%	84%	70%	80%	84%	85%	*A19*
T01	77%	91%	79%	87%	80%	81%	78%	88%	85%	91%	*T01*
T02	71%	94%	54%	74%	68%	78%	69%	81%	66%	81%	*T02*
T03	58%	83%	53%	69%	58%	69%	62%	71%	62%	73%	*T03*
T04	74%	90%	66%	83%	82%	83%	75%	84%	84%	88%	*T04*
T05	62%	81%	50%	69%	64%	73%	65%	75%	63%	74%	*T05*
T06	73%	89%	56%	77%	71%	78%	68%	80%	71%	76%	*T06*
T07	82%	95%	65%	83%	86%	89%	84%	89%	88%	92%	*T07*
T08	61%	82%	48%	73%	57%	71%	62%	78%	54%	68%	*T08*
T09	66%	87%	48%	75%	59%	75%	70%	82%	61%	70%	*T09*
T10	67%	83%	56%	73%	69%	83%	66%	78%	71%	83%	*T10*

Table 4 Spearman's correlation between use and importance.

Id	Testing practice	r_s	Id	Testing practice	r_s
P01	Documentation of test plan	**.585**	*A09*	Application of security tests	.323
P02	Documentation of test proc. and cases	**.644**	*A10*	Registration of the time spent on testing	**.565**
P03	Recording the results of test execution	**.556**	*A11*	Measurement of the effort/cost of testing	**.561**
P04	Measurement, analysis of test coverage	.393	*A12*	Storage of records (log) of the executed tests	**.585**
P05	Use of methodology or process	.492	*A13*	Measurement of the defect density	**.532**
P06	Analysis of identified defects	.400	*A14*	Conducting training on software testing	.459
P07	Identification and use of risks	.447	*A15*	Separation of testing and dev activities	.468
P08	Plan/Design tests before coding	.372	*A16*	Storage of test data for future use	.482
P09	Monitoring adherence to the test process	**.602**	*A17*	Analysis of faults patterns (trend)	.411
P10	Re-execution of tests when modified	.467	*A18*	Availability of human resources full time	.476
P11	Evaluation of the quality of test artifacts	.395	*A19*	Selection of test techniques based on features	.450
P12	Setting a priori criteria to stop testing	**.712**	*T01*	Availability of a test database for reuse	**.548**
P13	Reporting evaluation of a test round	**.537**	*T02*	Automatic execution of test proc. or cases	.360
A01	Def. of a professional or team	**.516**	*T03*	Automatic generation of test proc. or cases	.355
A02	Application of unit tests	.448	*T04*	Test management tools to track and record	.453
A03	Application of integration tests	.456	*T05*	To estimate test effort and/or schedule	**.542**
A04	Application of system tests	**.605**	*T06*	Test management tools to enact artifacts	**.545**
A05	Application of acceptance tests	.472	*T07*	Recording defects and the effort to fix them	**.518**
A06	Application of regression tests	**.562**	*T08*	Use of coverage measurement tools	.479
A07	Application of exploratory tests	**.587**	*T09*	Continuous integration for automated tests	.424
A08	Application of performance tests	.306	*T10*	Selection of test tools based on proj. charcs.	.450

Table 5 Use and importance similarities between testing practices.

Id	"More used" and "More important"	Id	"Less used" and "Less important"
P02	Documentation of test procedures and cases	*P04*	Measurement and analysis of the test coverage
P03	Recording the results of test execution	*P07*	Identification and use of risks
P05	Use of methodology or process	*P08*	Planning/Designing of testing before coding
P06	Analysis of identified defects	*P09*	Monitoring adherence to the test process
P10	Re-execution of tests when modified	*P11*	Evaluation of the quality of test artifacts
A01	Definition of a responsible professional or team	*P13*	Reporting evaluation of a test round
A02	Application of unit tests	*A07*	Application of exploratory tests
A03	Application of integration tests	*A10*	Registration of the time spent on testing
A04	Application of system tests	*A11*	Measurement of the effort/cost of testing
A05	Application of acceptance tests	*A13*	Measurement of the defect density
A06	Application of regression tests	*A14*	Conducting training on software testing
A12	Storage of records (log) of the executed tests	*A17*	Analysis of faults patterns (trend)
A15	Separation of testing and dev activities	*A19*	Selection of test techniques based on features
A18	Availability of human resources full time	*T03*	Tools for automatic generation of test cases
T01	Availability of a test database for reuse	*T05*	Use of tools to estimate test effort and/or schedule
T04	Test management tools to track and record	*T08*	Use of coverage measurement tools
T06	Test management tools to enact artifacts	*T09*	Use of continuous integration tools for tests
T07	Tools for bug tracking and effort to fix them	*T10*	Selection of test tools according to project charcs.

formed by Cost Rican practitioners. The set of "least used, least important" testing practices represent those that seem to be not relevant in the context of these organizations. Furthermore, these practices could represent gaps in knowledge about their benefits or simply a lack of organizational resources to put them into practice. These practices may point out the gaps between the academia and industry and, for example, have to be addressed through practitioners' training courses and software process improvement plans in order to show the benefits of their application. Table 6 presents the "More used" and "Less important", and the "Less used" and "More important" testing practices. The set of "most used, least important" testing practices includes the practices used by software practitioners, but considered not as important as other practices. In this case, other used practices could generate more value in supporting testing activities. The set of "least used, most important" testing practices are those not used by practitioners in their software organizations, but perceived as important for their professional practice. They can be complex or expensive to implement, they may have considerable training needs, or these organizations may not have the necessary tools to perform them.

Table 6 Use and importance differences between testing practices.

Id "More used" and "Less important"	Id "Less used" and "More important"
P01 Documentation of test plan	*A08* Application of performance tests
P12 Setting a priori criteria to stop testing	*A09* Application of security tests
A16 Storage of test data for future use	*T02* Automatic execution of test procedures or cases

3.5 Comparing the results among replications

To compare the results of this survey with previous studies, the "More used" and "More important" testing practices, and the "Less used" and "Less important" testing practices were analyzed. Table 7 presents the "More used" and "More important" testing practices for each replication. Five testing practices are common in all surveys (*P03, A01, A03, A04, A05*) and four practices are common in four surveys (*P2, P10, A15, A18*). Table 8 presents the "Less used" and "Less important" testing practices for each replication. Six testing practices are reported in four surveys (*P07, P09, A11, T03, T05, T08*). In [6], no practices were classified as less used and less important. In Table 7 and Table 8, we only include practices of our survey, and practices with more than three occurrences across replications. We found no significant differences on practice perceived usefulness and importance between our survey and previous surveys. As in other countries, important practices are not being used in our software industry. This opens an interesting line of research to find out why they are not being used.

4 Conclusions

This paper reported a survey study of software testing practices in the Costa Rican software industry and compared the results with previous studies conducted in South America. We characterized a set of testing practices with respect to their use and perceived importance from the point of view of 92 practitioners.

Table 7 Comparison of "More used" and "More important" testing practices.

Id	"More used" and "More important"	CR	[7]	[2]	[6]	[5]
P02	Documentation of test procedures and cases	✓	✓	✓		✓
P03	Recording the results of test execution	✓	✓	✓	✓	✓
P05	Use of methodology or process	✓				✓
P06	Analysis of identified defects	✓				
P10	Re-execution of tests when the software is modified	✓	✓	✓		✓
A01	Definition of a responsible professional or team	✓	✓	✓	✓	✓
A02	Application of unit tests	✓	✓		✓	
A03	Application of integration tests	✓	✓	✓	✓	✓
A04	Application of system tests	✓	✓	✓	✓	✓
A05	Application of acceptance tests	✓	✓	✓	✓	✓
A06	Application of regression tests	✓	✓	✓		
A12	Storage of records (log) of the executed tests	✓	✓			
A15	Separation of testing and dev activities	✓	✓		✓	✓
A16	Storage of test data for future use		✓		✓	✓
A18	Availability of human resources allocated full time for testing	✓	✓	✓	✓	
T01	Availability of a test database for reuse	✓	✓			
T04	Test management tools to track and record	✓	✓			
T06	Test management tools to enact activities and artifacts	✓				
T07	Tools for recording defects and the effort to fix them (tracking)	✓	✓			

The main software testing practices reported in this survey were the recording of the results of tests, documentation of test procedures and cases, and re-execution of tests when the software is modified. The acceptance and system testing were the two most useful and important testing types. The tools for recording defects and the effort to fix them (bug tracking) and the availability of a test database for reuse were reported useful and important. In contrast, the planning and designing of software testing before coding and evaluating the quality of test artifacts were not a regular practice. Finally, there is a lack of measurement of defect density and test coverage in the industry; and tools for automatic generation of test cases and for estimating testing effort are rarely used.

A set of testing practices were common across different countries: the application of integration, system and acceptance tests, the recording of test execution results and the definition of a responsible professional or team for testing. In contrast, our results confirm that the main testing limitations are related to the monitoring and measurement of tests and defects, the automatic generation of test cases and procedures and the management of test coverage and effort.

Further studies in different countries and regions should be conducted to compare industrial trends in software testing practices. We believe this work could be used by organizations, practitioners and academics to improve the state of the practice in our software industry. It could be interesting to make a comparison about some data of demographics of the participants (such as years of experience, academic degree) between this survey and previous ones and to find out if different demographics could influence the results by country.

Table 8 Comparison of "Less used" and "Less important" testing practices.

Id	"Less used" and "Less important"	CR	[7]	[2]	[6]	[5]
P04	Measurement and analysis of the test coverage	✓	✓	✓		
P07	Identification and use of risks	✓	✓	✓		✓
P08	Planning/Designing of testing before coding	✓	✓	✓		
P09	Monitoring adherence to the test process	✓	✓	✓		✓
P11	Evaluation of the quality of test artifacts	✓	✓	✓		
P13	Reporting evaluation of a test round	✓				
A07	Application of exploratory tests	✓	✓			
A10	Registration of the time spent on testing	✓	✓			
A11	Measurement of the effort/cost of testing	✓	✓	✓		✓
A13	Measurement of the defect density	✓	✓	✓		
A14	Conducting training on software testing	✓	✓			
A17	Analysis of faults patterns (trend)	✓		✓		✓
A19	Selection of test techniques based on features	✓				
T03	Use of tools for automatic generation of test procedures or cases	✓	✓	✓		✓
T05	Use of tools to estimate test effort and/or schedule	✓	✓	✓		✓
T08	Use of coverage measurement tools	✓	✓	✓		✓
T09	Use of continuous integration tools for automated tests	✓	✓			
T10	Selection of test tools according to project characteristics	✓	✓			

Acknowledgments. This work was partially supported by Universidad Estatal a Distancia Comiex-19-2017 and Universidad de Costa Rica project No. 834-B7-749. We would like to thank Guilherme Travassos, Santiago Matalonga, Martín Solari, Arilo Dias-Neto and Gabriela Robiolo for providing earlier version of the questionnaire. We thank all practitioners of the survey for their participation.

References

1. Garousi, V. & Zhi, J. (2013). A survey of software testing practices in Canada. Journal of Systems and Software, 86(5), 1354-1376.
2. Dias-Neto, A., Matalonga, S., Solari, M., Robiolo, G. & Travassos, G. (2017). Toward the characterization of software testing practices in South America: looking at Brazil and Uruguay. Software Quality Journal, 25(4), 1145-1183.
3. Geras, A., Smith, M. & Miller, J. (2004). A survey of software testing practices in Alberta. Canadian Journal of Electrical and Computer Engineering, 29(3), 183-191.
4. Garousi, V. & Varma, T. (2010). A replicated survey of software testing practices in the Canadian province of Alberta: What has changed from 2004 to 2009? Systems and Software, 83(11), 2251-2262.
5. Dias-Neto, A., Natali, A., Rocha, A. & Travassos, G. (2006). Caracterizacao do estado da pratica das atividades de teste em um cenario de desenvolvimento de software brasileiro. In Simposio Brasileiro de Qualidade de Software, Vila Velha, ES. http://www.lbd.dcc.ufmg.br/colecoes/sbqs/2006/002.pdf.
6. Greca, F., Rossi, B., Robiolo, G. & Travassos, G. (2015). Aplicación y Valoración de la Verificación y Validación de Software: una Encuesta Realizada en Buenos Aires. In ASSE/SADIO 2015 (pp. 26–40). ISSN: 2451-7593.

7. Robiolo, G., Melani, M., Rossi, B. & Travassos, G. (2017). Aplicación e Importancia de las Pruebas de Software: una Encuesta Realizada en Buenos Aires en el Ámbito Público. XX Ibero-American Conference on Software Engineering (CibSE 2017). Argentina, 22-23 May 2017.
8. Ng, S., Murnane, T., Reed, K., Grant, D. & Chen, T. (2004). A preliminary survey on software testing practices in Australia. In Australian Software Engineering Conference (pp. 116-125). IEEE.
9. Kirk, D. & Tempero, E. (2012). Software development practices in New Zealand. In 2012 19th Asia-Pacific Software Engineering Conference (Vol. 1, pp. 386-395). IEEE.
10. Causevic, A., Sundmark, D. & Punnekkat, S. (2010). An industrial survey on contemporary aspects of software testing. In Software Testing, Verification and Validation (ICST), 2010 Third International Conference on (pp. 393-401). IEEE.
11. Engström, E. & Runeson, P. (2010). A qualitative survey of regression testing practices. In International Conference on Product Focused Software Process Improvement (pp. 3-16). Springer, Berlin.
12. Kasurinen, J., Taipale, O. & Smolander, K. (2010). Software test automation in practice: empirical observations. Advances in Software Engineering, 2010.
13. Greiler, M., Deursen, A., & Storey, M. A. (2012). Test confessions: a study of testing practices for plug-in systems. In Proceedings of the 34th International Conference on Software Engineering (pp. 244-254).
14. Rafi, D., Moses, K., Petersen, K., & Mäntylä, M. (2012). Benefits and limitations of automated software testing: Systematic literature review and practitioner survey. In Proceedings of the 7th International Workshop on Automation of Software Test (pp. 36-42). IEEE Press.
15. Lee, J., Kang, S. & Lee, D. (2012). Survey on software testing practices. IET software, 6(3), 275-282.
16. Daka, E. & Fraser, G. (2014). A survey on unit testing practices and problems. In Software Reliability Engineering (ISSRE), 2014 IEEE 25th International Symposium on (pp. 201-211). IEEE.
17. Pfahl, D., Yin, H., Mäntylä, M. & Münch, J. (2014). How is exploratory testing used? A state-of-the-practice survey. In Proceedings of the 8th ACM/IEEE international symposium on empirical software engineering and measurement (p. 5). ACM.
18. Smolander, K., Taipale, O. & Kasurinen, J. (2016). Software Test Automation in Practice: Empirical Observations. In Data Structure and Software Engineering (pp. 107-145). Apple Academic Press.
19. Quesada-López, C. & Jenkins, M. (2017). Un estudio sobre las prácticas de la ingeniería del software en Costa Rica: Resultados preliminares. Proceedings of the XX Ibero-American Conference on Software Engineering (CibSE 2017). Buenos Aires, Argentina, 22-23 May 2017.
20. Quesada-López, C. & Jenkins, M. (2018). Factores asociados a prácticas de desarrollo y pruebas de software en Costa Rica: Un estudio exploratorio. Proceedings of the XXI Ibero-American Conference on Software Engineering (CibSE 2018). Bogotá, Colombia, 23-27 Abril 2018.
21. Garousi, V., Coşkunçay, A., Betin, A. & Demirörs, O. (2015). A survey of software engineering practices in Turkey. Journal of Systems and Software, 108, 148-177.
22. Garousi, V., Coşkunçay, A., Demirörs, O. & Yazici, A. (2016). Cross-factor analysis of software engineering practices versus practitioner demographics: An exploratory study in Turkey. Journal of Systems and Software, 111, 49-73.
23. Aymerich, B., Díaz, I., Guzmán, J., López, G. & Garbanzo, D. (2018). Software Development Practices in Costa Rica: A Survey. In International Conference on Applied Human Factors and Ergonomics (pp. 122-132). Springer, Cham.
24. Kuhrmann, M., Diebold, P., Münch, J., Tell, P., Garousi, V., Felderer, M.,& Prause, C. R. (2018). Hybrid Software and System Development in Practice. Software Engineering und Software Management.
25. Carver, J. C. (2010). Towards reporting guidelines for experimental replications: A proposal. In 1st international workshop on replication in empirical software engineering.
26. Carver, J., Juristo, N., Baldassarre, M., & Vegas, S. (2014). Replications of software engineering experiments. Empirical Software Engineering, 19(2), 267-276.
27. Linaker, J., Sulaman, S. M., de Mello, R. M., H˜st, M., & Runeson, P. (2015). Guidelines for conducting surveys in software engineering. Technical report.

A model approach to ISO-29110 for very small enterprises

Hugo Ordoñez[1], Manuel Pastrana[2], Claudia Castiblanco[1], Orlando Rincón[3], Armando Ordonez[4]
[1]Research Laboratory in Development of Software Engineering – Universidad San Buenavetura – Cali, Colombia
[2]GrintTic– Universidad Antonio José Camacho - Cali, Colombia
Parque Soft, Cali, Colombia
[4]Intelligent Managemet Systems – Fundación Universitaria de Popayán - Popayán, Colombia

haordonez@usbcali.edu.co, mapastrana@admon.uniajc.edu, ccastiblan73@gmail.com, orincon@parquesoft.com, jaordonez@unicauca.edu.co

Abstract: In today's globalized world, very small entities (VSE) are forced to guarantee process quality. This implies complying with international standards that offer guidelines for improving software processes and products. However, requirements of these standards are difficult to comply with for VSE. Previous works have described ISO 29110 implementations. However, few approaches describe guidelines for implementing these standards in specific environments. This paper describes a model approach for the implementation of good practices to the specific context of the Valle del Cauca region in Colombia.

Keywords: ISO 29110, very Small enterprises, software development.

1 Introduction

In today's competitive world, multinational companies are forced to seek alternatives to reduce costs. Thus, many software development tasks are being outsourced to smaller companies located in different countries [1]. In this process, quality of processes and products must be guaranteed [2]. Most commonly outsourced services are coding, infrastructure maintenance, and custom application development [3].

To access this global market, very small entities (VSE) must guarantee the quality of their processes. This implies complying with standards such as ISO / IEC 12207, ISO / IEC 15504 and CMMI that provide guidelines for improving software processes and products [4].

Despite its importance, standards adoption by VSE has been slow. This is firstly because requirements of models such as CMMI are difficult to comply with, and require effort, time, and financial resources not easily assumable by this sort of companies. Secondly, some guidelines are not applicable to small projects, which are the most common in VSE. Thirdly, standards require a different way of thinking, so that company staff carries out new tasks regarding process quality. Finally, some robust models such as CMMI propose an administrative structure that hardly coincides with that of small organizations, in which members share functions of various roles. Such is the case of the administrator who in many cases may have both technical and administrative responsibilities in various projects [5].

Aware of the importance of VSE for the global economy, the ISO and the Joint Technical Committee for Standards of T.I (JTC1), define the ISO / IEC 29110 standard (Hereafter ISO 29110) [6]. ISO 29110 defines a set of good practices to be followed by the VSEs to guarantee a quality development process. This standard describes the processes, the life cycle, and standardizes some concepts. [7].

Based on the above, this article described a model approach for the implementation of good practices based on the ISO 29110 standard. The model is based on elements that make up the standard: requirements engineering, configuration management, functional and physical architecture, verification and validation, integration, product deployment, interface management, self-assessment and Project management.

The rest of this paper is organized as follows, Section 2 presents the motivating scenario, section 3 presents the background, section 4 describes the proposed model, Section 5 describes the application of the model in a set of selected companies, section 6 presents the conclusions and future work.

2 Motivating scenario

According to the software industry report of SeniSoft and Fedesoft (2017), 95% of companies in the department of Valle del Cauca (Colombia) are VSE (Figure 1). Most of the customers of these companies came from United States, Mexico, Costa Rica, and Ecuador. Nearly 80% of applications developed belong to financial, resource management, and development fields, and the remaining (20%) are related to digital content (animation, video games and television).

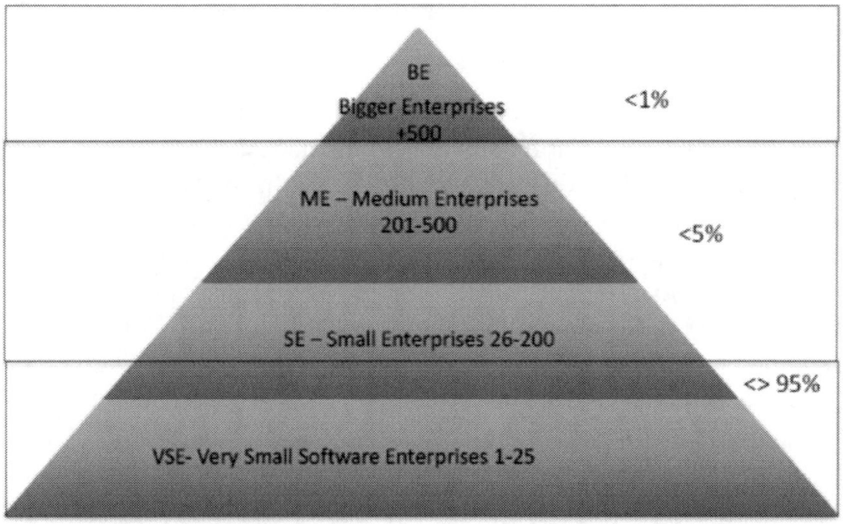

Figure 1. Characterization of the software industry in Valle del Cauca

At the national level, the situation is very similar, 6 cities concentrate around 6,600 software companies, and among them, 90% are micro and small businesses.

The model approach described here aims at guiding VSE towards the implementations of ISO 29110, and other standards according to organization needs.

3 Background

The International Organization for Standardization (ISO), and the International Electrotechnical Commission have been working on the development of an adaptable model for small size companies. To do so, standards for software development were carefully reviewed. In [8], a set of recommendations to achieve high-quality software process is detailed. Diverse standards have been considered for documenting each stage of the development process, specifically the analysis and design phase [9]. Equally, other standards are proposed for evaluating company maturity based on models such as CMMI [10]. This review allows identifying specific work areas: requirements engineering, configuration management, functional and physical architecture, verification and validation, integration, product deployment, interface management, self-assessment and Project management.

Additionally, a set of profiles was defined to classify companies according to their implementation level (initial, basic, intermediate and advanced) of the previously listed areas.

Once the critical areas and the classification profiles have been identified, the ISO 29110 standard was defined. This standard promotes software processes involving a clear elicitation stage, a design based on solid decisions (non-empirical), version control, continuous integration, continuous deployment, unit testing, validation, and a light but effective documentation that guarantee continuous delivery.

Some works [6] [11] describe ISO 29110 implementations. However, few approaches describe guidelines for implementing these standards in specific environments. This paper describes a model approach for the implementation of good practices to the specific context of the Valle del Cauca region in Colombia

4 Proposed model

The empirical design of the model is composed of 5 parts: firstly, the work is separated into categories based on ISO 29110. Secondly generic profiles to classify companies' categories are defined, based on the same normative. Thirdly, companies' categories are classified according to these generic profiles. Fourthly, according to the third part (Generic Profiles), the companies are trained in areas with more deficiencies. Finally, a set of strategies to reach a higher profile is carried out. The model is explain in more detail from here:

First part: the work is divided into categories.

The ISO / IEC 29110 standard describes 9 categories which will be use for the design of the proposal model (See **Figure 2**). Coming up will be describe them shortly:

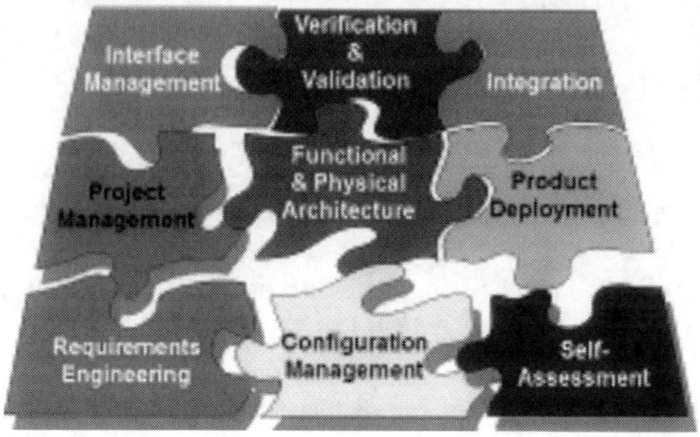

Figure 2. Categories in ISO 29110

Project management.

Project management is a key area for organizations success [12]. Here, company's effort is devoted to make a projection of budget and time required to meet customers' requirements, manage legal documentation, and generate all the products on time and on budget [13]. Project management allows monitoring the project, and mitigating risks adequately [12]. So, the design of the model should consider for all the companies how they are doing the planning of the project (time and cost estimation, plus priorization of development activities) and the traceability of the planning.

Requirements engineering.

In this stage, project requirements are elicited, interpreted and refined [14]. It is perhaps one of the most critical stages [15]. However, sometimes importance is not given to formally describe requirements through formal artifacts such as use cases (UC) [16] and user stories (US) [17] [18]. This lack of documentation is due to the fact that some companies consider these formats very wasteful. Short time for delivery and inadequate project management may also cause this inadequate documentation. Here, the design of the model should consider how the companies are actually doing the requirements elicitation and guide them to accepted artifacts like UC or US.

Functional & physical architecture

Architectural design should not be an empirical product based solely on experience [14] [19]. It should include a clear knowledge of the quality attributes needed to achieve the proper system behavior. These attributes may be solved appropriately using design patterns, which are already created and tested solutions to common problems. Patterns can vary depending on the application (desktop, web, web responsive, mobile or integration). Despite of its importance, this stage is one of the most neglected ones due to the amount of experience required [15]. In this way, the model should focused in the use of software development patterns for improve the architectural design and the quality attributes.

Construction and unit test

Construction is commonly the most time consuming phase [19]. The final result of this phase is the final product. Two possible approaches exist in this area: traditional and agile [14]. Agile approach has shown more positive results compared to traditional, due to its variety of ceremonies, techniques and dynamics that facilitate communication between the project team and clients [15]. One of the good practices in this category is the Unit test, a minimum seal of quality at code level that each programmer implements before delivering the code [17]. The proposal model design should consider if this practice exist or not inside the companies and how guide them to implement it.

Version control

In a centralized repository of code, all the changes of the product under construction or finished are shared. This repository allows tracing changes, preventing loss of information and recovering from failures. Versioning tools support collective ownership of the code as source code is available at any time for the entire team [17]. Even though most of the companies have this implemented, the design of the model should consider how well they are using it and how they can get all the benefits this, for example DevOps practices based on version control.

Integration and test

Continuous integration is a good practice that enables the development team to be prepared to deploy in a final environment or in test environment at any time [17]. In this way, configuration problems are avoided. This practice goes hand in hand with continuous deployment and version control [17] which will be consider in the proposal model.

Verification and validation.

Every software development company should have a coding standard that guides programming syntax. Additionally, malpractices such as excessive use of nested conditions, variables defined without use, etc. should be identified. The work team must perform frequent code inspections either manually or through static code analyzers [17]. The above seeks to identify all the possible bugs prior to the functional tests. On the other hand, functional tests must be implemented to identify if the product complies with requirements from the analysis stage. These tests can be carried out manually or with automation software. This will be consider in the proposal model through the implementation of a static code analyzer.

Product delivery

Proper planning of product delivery to the client depends on the quality of its development process. The higher the quality and the more parts of the process are automated for inspection, the higher the quality of the result and greater guarantee of product delivery. This part of the design of the model depends from all the other categories describe above.

Self-assessment.

The success of agile frameworks such as XP and SCRUM lies in the fact a retrospective reflection is carried out after every iteration. Therefore, this stage becomes critical. While there are formats called lessons learned [13], in most of the VSEs documentation is made only at the end of the project, without learning from the process, and leaving this highly valuable information aside. The model here lead the companies to the implementation of retrospective analysis, so they can learn about they experiences and give some information to the company about what are they doing well to keep doing and what not to stop it.

Second Part: Categorize the generic profiles

ISO/IEC 29110 defines 4 profiles to classify implementation level of good practices, these are: *Initial*: when organizations work empirically, without development standard, project management, and development stages don't follow any guidelines. *Basic*: organizations have formalisms for some stages, but do not implement international standards or good practices. *Intermediate*: companies know and use some standards and good practices. *Advanced*: this is the ideal status, the internal software development process is well known due to its standardization, all the artifacts are based on accepted and internationally recognized models, and good practices are part of the organizational culture.

Third part: Classify the organizations

A classification is made according to the 4 profiles (Initial, basic, Intermediate, advances) for each of the 9 categories described in the standard. Here a google form questionnaire is used to identify the current status of each organization, weaker categories, and possible strategies to improve. The questionnaire can be found on the next link https://docs.google.com/forms/d/e/1FAIpQLSfJdP-wKdMtg0rd4PskC7PjuVDrRnBEG3zbBrrilNHo3jVfig/viewform?vc=0&c=0&w=1. Some of the questions are just to know general aspects of the companies like the experience of the developers of each companies. Other questions point to how many activities are doing simultaneously? Or in how many projects are they at time? To know is there overload.

Other questions try matters like development and software quality assurance asking for example: if it is known in the project who will do a specific activity? The activities are choose by the team or assigned by a team leader? Is there any retrospective analysis? Is there any improve from the things learning during the retrospective analysis? Are there some guides for the software development like standards o procedures? Unit test is used in the development process? Version control is applied in the process? For mention some of them.

Part of the questionnaire is focused too on the planning with questions like: is there any plan follow during the development? Is it verify? Is it management? Are there metrics implemented in the process to measure if the goals of the delivery are been achieved or not? Is there any documentation during the process?

Fourth part: Training

Based on the results of the questionnaire and after the classification, the proposal model identify in which categories is necessary to carry out a training. These concepts are exposed to companies and those already present within their organizational culture are strengthened [20].

Fifth part: Define strategies within each category

In this las part, the proposal model suggest that after the training, some strategies must be generated together with the organization members to define good practices, artifacts, techniques and tools to use. These strategies must be executed and evaluated to measure the impact of the strategies. Depending on the results, organizations can be categorized in a higher profile.

5 Action Research

The proposed model was used to support the implementation of good practices in software development in VSE in the southwestern region of Colombia. To this end, a consultant group with extensive experience in software engineering was formed (3 Ph.D. degree, 3 MSC, and 4 professionals).

A call for companies in the sector was made, 19 companies participated and 4 were selected (EMP1, EMP2, EMP3, EMP4). The selection requirement follow the next criteria:

- Recent certificate of existence and legal representation.
- Resume of the team members (according to a predefined format of pacific).
- Data authorization form for each company and the people involved in the project.
- Be one of the first four companies to full fill the above requirements.

ISO 29110 categories and profiles were used to generate an evaluation instrument (survey) on the implementation of good practices (First and second stage of the proposed model). Some elements were evaluated such as the use of coding standards, architectural models, design patterns used, requirements elicitation methods and quality control. Thus, the initial status of each company was determined. Besides they were classified by category and profile (third stage of the model), which allowed identifying areas requiring training and topics. Evaluation results can be seen in Table 1.

Table 1 Evaluation results of the initial state.

Categories	**EMP1**	**EMP2**	**EMP3**	**EMP4**
Requirements engineering	Basic	Basic	Basic	Basic
Functional and physical architecture	Basic	Basic	Intermediate	Basic
Construction and unit test	Basic	Basic	Intermediate	Intermediate
Versions control	Intermediate	Basic	Intermediate	Basic
Integration and test	Basic	Initial	Intermediate	Basic
Verification and validation	Basic	Basic	Intermediate	Intermediate
Product delivery	Basic	Initial	Basic	Basic

Self-assessment	Initial	Initial	Initial	Initial

Based on the above classification, the initial state of each company is determined. The objective is to take companies to the next profile. To this purpose, topics to be reinforced in each of the categories are selected as follows:

Requirements engineering

Light and effective documentation is a priority for the VSEs. Most of these companies recognize the virtues of user stories (US) versus traditional use cases (UC). Although, in some cases, companies use poorly structured UC that do not comply with the guidelines described in [21]. In other cases, in the absence of an international standard that regulates US different models like the one proposed by [17] and [22], The companies do not know which is the most appropriate model (US, UC) to their needs, and how to formally implement it. Additionally, they are unaware of alternatives to facilitate fluid dialogue with clients [23]. In this category, the topics to be reinforced in all the companies were:

- Identification of elicitation techniques used by the companies (interviews, surveys, observation, etc.) based on [24].
- User stories as elicitation artifacts.
- Model for a proper description of user stories [22].
- Business process models (BP, under BPMN notation) to complement elicitation artifacts. Based on [25].
- Estimation based on poker scrum, and MoSCoW technical prioritization based on [26].
- Creation of a product backlog based on [26].

Functional and physical architecture.

Software architecture is one of the most recognized problems in the software industry [27]. In the VSE, this topic is often left aside, specifically because most problems are solved in the same way and particular restrictions of each project are ignored. Therefore, it is necessary to socialize the importance of restrictions identification, quality attributes of architectural models, and design patterns. Equally, it is necessary to highlight the most proper way to document architectures, describing decisions in a clear and simple way, and including only the most relevant information. The selected topics are:

- Acceptance criteria for software restrictions.
- Agile practices to be used.
- Software Architecture Document (SAD)

Configuration management

Configuration management includes a set of good practices proposed by [17] focusing on preventive quality. Good practices are defined for software construction, unit testing, version control, continuous integration, continuous deployment, testing, verification, product validation, and delivery. The topics selected for all the companies are detailed below.

- **Construction and unit test**, for each company, the analysis, development and architect teams were involved. The topics selected were:
    - Introduction to agile software development with SCRUM and XP.
    - SCRUM board Planning
    - Sprints planning
    - Short iterations
    - Good practices for software development

- **Version control,** a person from each company with the configuration manager role was involved. The topics selected were:
    - Selection of a version control system. GitLab was selected for the study.
    - Demo of the versioning tool and workshop
- **Integration and test,** a person from each company with the configuration manager role was involved. The topics selected were:
    - Selection of a continuous integration tool. Jenkins was proposed to support this task.
    - Continuous integration workshop and Jenkins Demonstration
- **Verification and validation,** analysis and development team of each company was involved. The topics selected were:
    - Daily meeting
    - Iteration review
- **Product delivery,** a person from each company with the configuration manager role was involved. The topics selected were:
    - Selection of a continuous deployment tool. Jenkins was proposed
    - Continuous deployment workshop and Jenkins Demo.
- **Self-assessment,** analysis and development team of each company was involved. The topics selected were:
    - Retrospective project analysis
    - Retrospective techniques and workshop on retrospective techniques.

Thus, all companies received information on methods and tools necessary for implementing good practices.

After the training phase, companies applied good practices in pilot projects, and the impact of these practices in the development process was evaluated. Results obtained are detailed below by category:

Requirements engineering

In EMP1 use cases artifact is replaced by user stories following the model described in [22]. In EMP2, EMP3 and EMP4, HU have been used, however, these documents didn't follow a standard, therefore the model described in [22] was selected.

Additionally, all companies adopt the estimation and prioritization model according to [26]. Thus all the companies can correctly create and use the product backlog within their process. On the other hand, business processes (BP) were used according to [23] as a complement to the product backlog. In particular, EMP1 was unaware of the potential of this technique, and that its main client implemented BP in its daily operation. Through dialogue with EMP1 client, it was possible to unify efforts in requirements elicitation using BP models.

Functional and physical architecture

In all the companies, restrictions identification was included in user stories acceptance criteria. This identification allows defining the drivers in the architecture document that guide the solution through the use of design patterns. Additionally, all companies manage to define a standardized Software Architecture Document (SAD) format, adapted to their specific process.

Construction and unit test

Through the use of user stories and the product backlog, the configuration of the SCRUM board was achieved in each project. This board allows monitoring and controlling projects, and also evaluating the overload of activities to a person. Likewise, this board enables managers to estimate personnel availability for other projects, and implement an integral risk management. Finally, this board facilitates the possibility of dividing the work into Sprints both for planning and for cost evaluation. This practice is adopted to support the commercial area of the companies. In addition to the above, it is determined that all development iterations must be short, that is, they must not take more than 1 to 4 weeks to be complete.

On the other hand, all the bad practices in the development process were identified. This allows defining with each company, development standard required. To this purpose, Sonar was implemented as a static code analysis tool.

Version control

EMP1 and EMP4 used GitLab as version system. The advantages of working with this version system and the appropriate implementation were explained. These sort of systems supports good practices suggested by [17] to guarantee collective code ownership and quick failure recovery. EMP2 used SVN as its version systems, however, after the training it was decided to change the version system to GitLab. By its part, EMP3 used TFS (Team Foundation Services) and it was not necessary to change the tool, as TFS supports all the requirements of the ISO standard.

Integration and Test

Jenkins was selected as it could be used with the programming languages used by the 4 companies. Besides, Jenkins can also easily integrated with versioning tools and supports continuous deployment.

With the exception of EMP3, all other companies were unfamiliar with continuous integration tools; therefore Jenkins was adopted within the process. Currently, all 4 companies use this tool to verify integration and deployment. This tool allows deploying the solution at any time (from the first sprint). Additionally, the team can also react quickly to syntactic errors uploaded to the repository, preventing thus that bugs identification and correction takes too long.

Verification and validation

The four companies were made aware of the importance of collaborative work and constant communication. Thus, based on [26], daily meetings (SCRUM ceremony) were carried out. In this meeting, teams identify in front of the scrum board, progress achieved through the question "what did I

do yesterday? Identify work to be done during the day with the question" What will I do today? and finally, socialize problems through the question: what problems or difficulties have I had?. In addition, iteration revision was successfully implemented. From this point, each company is aware that a set of activities must be included in the planning Sprints, for deliverable preparation, quality evaluation, and at least an internal review where of sprint objectives fulfillment is evaluated.

Product delivery

Through the use of Jenkins, a continuous delivery model adapted to the specific needs of each company was implemented. In all cases, the final version was not delivered to the production server, but to a test server to be validated through acceptance tests. This strategy was adopted because most of the companies offer services and not customized developments. In addition, incremental functional demonstrations can be made to clients, which allows showing progress achieved during the development process.

Self-assessment.

None of the companies had used retrospective models, and therefore they had no capacity to learn from previous projects. After training, companies became aware of retrospective techniques and decided to evaluate the impact of learning about the successes and failures of each sprint.

It is important to highlight that the success of the proposed approach to depends on the support of the company managers, and also on the dedication of the staff to these activities [28].

After the training and adoption of the model, the implementation of good practices was measured again through a liker-based survey. Table 3 shows the results of this reclassification.

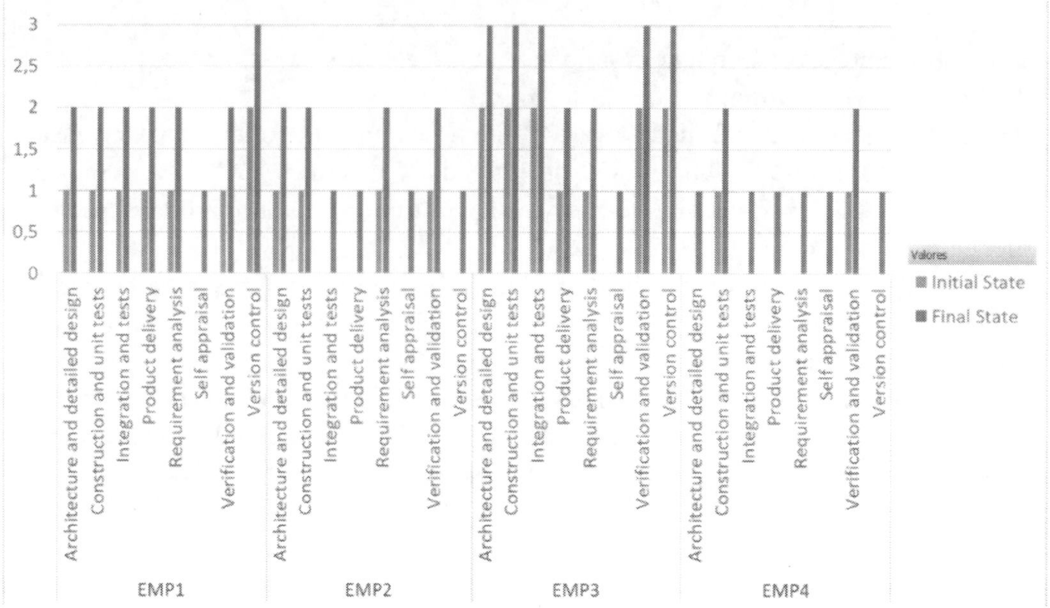

Figure 3 Results or the reclassification by category

As can be seen in Figure 3, the application of the model approach proposed in this paper makes a positive impact on companies, as they improved good practices in software development. For example, regarding the requirements analysis, all the companies reached an intermediate profile. Whereas regarding version control, 2 of the 4 companies manage to reach an advanced profile. Likewise, the 4 companies achieved an intermediate profile in the construction and unit tests.

These results allow us to infer that the proposed model approach enhance the good practices in software development of VSE based on 29110 standard.

6 Conclusions and future work

The model approach to ISO 29110 is a highly relevant contribution for companies in the ICT sector in the region. In the case study, the model contributed to improving VSE productivity, by promoting the use of good practices. During the application of the model, the adoption of business process models (BP) was carried out as a complement to requirements analysis, improving communication between client and team. In addition, companies achieved a better understanding of estimation, as more activities were considered regarding internal quality, meetings and formal deliveries to the client.

On the other hand, code revision and refinement standards were implemented along with continuous integration. It is important to highlight that the above goes hand in hand with the generation of strategies to reduce "technical debt" through continuous improvement.

Besides, companies adopted short iterations (sprint) and continuous deliveries, and became aware of the need to integrate Project Management and development team to jointly coordinate commitments with clients. Equally, companies become aware of the direct relationship between commercial quotation, planning, and billing.

In future, it is expected to apply the model to diverse companies to refine the approach and adapt it to other organizations. The project management area is also expected to be included, as it was left out of the scope of the present research.

7 References

[1] S. Beecham and J. Noll, "Who are we doing Global Software Engineering research for ?," 2013.

[2] H. Annous, L. Livadas, and G. Miles, "OffshoreQA: A Framework for Helping Software Development Outsourcing Companies Comply with ISO 9001:2008," in *2010 5th IEEE International Conference on Global Software Engineering*, 2010, pp. 313–315.

[3] I. Technologies, I. Business, A. Informatics, and N. Faculty, "Aspects of Software System Development with Respect to IT Outsourcing," pp. 52–55, 2015.

[4] Y. Kryuchkova and D. Pavlov, "Implementing Usability Methods into CMMI-Compliant Software Development Process Внедрение практик юзабилити в процесс разработки ПО в соответствии с С MMI Юлия Крючкова," pp. 111–116, 2010.

[5] N. Ehsan, A. Perwaiz, J. Arif, E. Mirza, and A. Ishaque, "CMMI / SPICE based Process Improvement," pp. 859–862, 2010.

[6] C. Y. Laporte and R. V. O. Connor, "Implementing Process Improvement in Very Small Enterprises with ISO / IEC 29110 A Multiple Case Study Analysis," 2016.

[7] M. Muñoz, J. Mejía, A. Lagunas, C. De Investigación, and A. C. U. Zacatecas, "Implementación del estándar ISO / IEC 29110 en entornos ágiles : Una revisión sistemática de literatura Implementation of the ISO / IEC 29110 standard in agile environments : A systematic literature review."

[8] IEEE, "INTERNATIONAL STANDARD ISO / IEC / IEEE Systems and software engineering — engineering," *ISO/IEC/ IEEE 12207*, vol. 2011, pp. 1–94, 2011.

[9] I. Standard, "Systems and software engineering — Content of life-cycle information items (documentation)," *ISO/IEC/ IEEE 15289*, vol. 2015, 2015.

[10] ISO, "An exemplar Process Assessment Model," *ISO/IEC 15504*, vol. 2006, 2006.

[11] M. Muñoz, J. Mejía, A. Lagunas, C. De Investigación, and A. C. U. Zacatecas, "Implementación del estándar ISO / IEC 29110 en entornos ágiles : Una revisión sistemática de literatura Implementation of the ISO / IEC 29110 standard in agile environments : A systematic literature review," *13th Iber. Conf. Inf. Syst. Technol.*, 2018.

[12] Project Management Institute, *Guía de los fundamentos para la dirección de proyectos*, vol. 87, no. 11. 2013.

[13] PMI, *PMI FUNDAMENTOS PARA LA DIRECCIÓN DE PROYECTOS (GUÍA DEL PMBOK)*. 2004.

[14] R. Pressman and B. Maxim, *SOFTWARE ENGINEERING: A PRACTITIONER'S APPROACH*. 2007.

[15] S. Hastie and S. Wojewoda, "Standish Group 2015 Chaos Report - Q&A with Jennifer Lynch," *http://www.infoq.com/articles/standish-chaos-2015*, 2015. [Online]. Available: http://www.infoq.com/articles/standish-chaos-2015.

[16] IEEE 1998, "IEEE Std 830-1998," *Especificación Requisitos Softw. según el estándar IEEE 830*, p. 19, 2000.

[17] K. Beck, *Extreme Programming Explained: Embrace Change*, no. c. 1999.

[18] M. Cohn, *User Stories Applied: For Agile Software Development (Addison Wesley Signature Series)*, vol. 1, no. 0. 2004.

[19] I. Sommerville, *Ingeniería del Software*. 2011.

[20] Carlos Alberto Molina Gómez, *Yes, I Can. Reflexiones en torno al subjetivar-se*, Primera, 2. Cali, Colombia, 2018.

[21] I. of E. and E. Engineers, "Especificacion de Requisitos segun el estandar de IEEE 830," p. 27, 2008.

[22] M. Cohn, *User Stories Applied: For Agile Software Development (Addison Wesley Signature Series)*, vol. 1, no. 0. 2004.

[23] M. Pastrana, H. Ordóñez, A. Ordóñez, and L. Merchan, "Requirements elicitation based on

inception deck and business processes models in scrum," *Commun. Comput. Inf. Sci.*, vol. 735, pp. 327–339, 2017.
[24] R. S. Pressman and D. Ph, *Ingeniería del software.* .
[25] M. Pastrana, H. Ordóñez, A. Ordonez, L. H. Thom, and L. Merchan, "Optimization of the inception deck technique for eliciting requirements in SCRUM through business process models," *Lect. Notes Bus. Inf. Process.*, vol. 308, pp. 649–655, 2018.
[26] K. Schwaber and J. Sutherland, "La Guía de Scrum," *Scrumguides.Org*, vol. 1, p. 21, 2013.
[27] S. Hastie and S. Wojewoda, "Standish Group 2015 Chaos Report - Q&A with Jennifer Lynch," *http://www.infoq.com/articles/standish-chaos-2015*, 2015. .
[28] C. A. M. Gómez, *Entre ovejas anda el lobo*, Primera, 2. Cali, Colombia: Universidad de San Buenaventura Cali, 2016.

Resultados preliminares de un estudio de casos sobre el impacto del uso de un framework en el código generado

Anaisa Hernández González[1], Vanessa Muñoz Castillo[1], David Santana Ballate[1], Fernando Arteaga Céspedes[2],

[1] Universidad Tecnológica de La Habana "José Antonio Echeverría", CUJAE, La Habana, Cuba
[2] AXES Network, Québec, Canadá
{anaisa, vmunoz, dsantana}@ceis.cujae.edu.cu, fernadoarteaga.personal@gmail.com

Abstract. Uno de los retos de la Industria de Software es la medición del esfuerzo requerido para producir el software. Los framework pueden considerarse como herramientas concebidas para agilizar el desarrollo. Sin embargo, este factor no se toma en cuenta cuando se realizan estimaciones, obteniéndose resultados inexactos. El objetivo de este estudio exploratorio es investigar cómo el uso de un framework puede influir en el esfuerzo de desarrollo, a partir del análisis del código fuente que se genera de forma automática y aquellas líneas que los programadores modifican o crean. En este trabajo se incluye el diseño del estudio y los resultados preliminares para un caso y cinco unidades de análisis. Los hallazgos obtenidos hasta el momento, evidencian que puede existir una relación entre la complejidad del producto y el código generado automáticamente, pero que sí hay un por ciento no despreciable del código que se obtiene automáticamente.

Keywords: Framework, Marco de trabajo, Líneas de Código Fuente (LOC), Métodos de estimación

1 Introducción

La estimación en el mundo de la Industria de software, se ha convertido en uno de los principales retos para la gestión de proyectos. Dentro de este proceso se estudian un grupo de variables e indicadores que proporcionan un grado de riesgo aceptable, aunque los resultados no son exactos,

La medición del esfuerzo, tradicionalmente se realiza por alguno de estos tipos de medición: directas (por ejemplo, líneas de código fuente) e indirectas (por ejemplo, funcionalidad y complejidad) [1]. Por lo que hay diversidad de métodos que se basan en alguno de estos elementos.

En la investigación publicada en el trabajo "Influence Analysis of Select Factors in the Function Point Work Effort Estimation" [2], se describen los resultados de un experimento donde se analizan los datos de 1333 proyectos contenidos en el repositorio de proyectos ISBSG versión 13 (International Software Benchmarking Standards Group), observándose que el tamaño relativo del proyecto y la productividad son factores importantes para estimar el esfuerzo de desarrollo utilizando el método de puntos de función.

Los métodos de estimación parten de conocer el tamaño del proyecto y en la etapa inicial, esta es una tarea difícil porque solo están disponibles los requisitos de alto nivel [3]. Los métodos contemplan siempre su ajuste a partir de diferentes factores que pueden afectar su desarrollo.

La Ingeniería de Software es una tecnología en capas (métodos, procesos y herramientas), y en la capa de herramientas se incluyen aquellos que hacen el proceso de desarrollo de software más rápido, entre ellas, los generadores de código.

En la actualidad, el desarrollo de software se ha visto favorecido por el empleo de herramientas que generan parte del código fuente de la aplicación. Entre estas herramientas se encuentran los Entornos de Desarrollo Integrado (IDE, por sus siglas en inglés, Integrated Development Enviroment) y los marcos de trabajo o framework.

En muchas ocasiones, cuando se realizan estimaciones no se toma en cuenta dicho factor, obteniéndose resultados incorrectos. Las estimaciones de esfuerzo inexactas pueden llevar a cronogramas y presupuestos poco realistas y, por tanto, pueden constituir un riesgo comercial significativo [4].

Pobres estimaciones del esfuerzo requerido para desarrollar el software conducen a presiones de tiempo en la ingeniería de software [5]. En esta revisión sistemática a la literatura se identifica a la falta de datos históricos como causa de las estimaciones deficientes.

Para comprender en profundidad el fenómeno en su contexto real, en este trabajo se describe el diseño de un estudio de casos que se propone responder a la pregunta de cómo el uso de un framework puede influir en la estimación del esfuerzo y el tiempo de desarrollo, a partir del análisis del por ciento de líneas de código fuente de una aplicación informática que se generan automáticamente usando un framework y fueron o no modificadas por el equipo de desarrollo, y las creadas nuevas. Se incluye, además, los resultados preliminares del estudio para un caso y cinco unidades de análisis.

La precisión de la medición depende del instrumento o de las métricas que son medidas [6], por lo que esta investigación conllevó al desarrollo de un software para la recolección de datos, cuyos elementos esenciales se describen en el trabajo.

El artículo está estructurado en tres acápites. Primeramente se analizan varias investigaciones que profundizan en el estudio de los framework y de los métodos de estimación, para esclarecer sobre las necesidades de este trabajo. En el segundo acápite, se justifica la selección del método de estudio de caso y se describe el protocolo diseñado que servirá de guía para el trabajo. Por último, se presentan los resultados obtenidos hasta el momento de la publicación de esta memoria.

2 Contexto

En la literatura se encuentran algunos ejemplos que profundizan en el estudio de los framework.

En el año 2015 se publicó un trabajo donde se recogen los resultados de un estudio empírico sobre la evaluación del desempeño de los framework PHP con el objetivo de sugerir cuál utilizar en el futuro para la tecnología web en proyectos grandes [7]. Para el estudio seleccionaron CodeIgniter, CakePHP, Symfony y Laravel y como proyecto el desarrollo de una aplicación sencilla que muestra el mensaje "Hello Word".

En [8] se pretendió demostrar que se puede usar Vagrant con cualquier lenguaje y framework, por lo que seleccionaron framework que dan soporte a diferentes lenguajes de programación para construir aplicaciones web: Angular JS (Java script), Django (Python), Rails (Ruby) y Symfony (PHP). Como proyecto seleccionaron una aplicación que muestra el texto de la canción "Song for Kids".

El trabajo que se describe en [9], evalúa varios framework de código abierto con el fin de encontrar el más adecuado para el desarrollo de un sistema de apoyo a la toma de decisiones. Los framework seleccionados fueron: Rails (Ruby), Django (Python), Grails (Java) y Play (Java).

Los criterios de selección de los framework en estos estudios, por lo general, estaban asociados a que trabajan con un lenguaje de programación popular, que las tendencias de búsqueda evidencian que los usuarios están interesados en usarlo y el nivel de adopción por la industria de acuerdo al volumen de escenarios reales donde se han usado, entre otros.

Estos estudios empíricos resultan de interés pues seleccionaron a los framework como objetivo. Aunque la finalidad de estas investigaciones no aporta información científica vinculada con el objeto de este estudio, sí demuestran que es de interés de la comunidad científica investigar sobre el potencial de estas herramientas.

El proceso de estimación de tiempo y esfuerzo de un proyecto informático actual se realiza de dos maneras diferentes, siguiendo el criterio de expertos en el tema o basando la estimación en modelos matemáticos, conocidos como métodos de estimación.

La jerarquía de modelos de estimación de software, bajo el nombre de COCOMO (COnstructive Cost MOdel) propuesto por Barry Boehm [10], se ha convertido en uno de los modelos de estimación más utilizados por los grupos de desarrollo de software. Entre los modelos más utilizados dentro de esta jerarquía se encuentran: Puntos de Función, Puntos de Casos de Uso y Puntos de Objetos.

Estos métodos de estimación definen un conjunto de factores que evalúan el impacto de la tecnología, las particularidades de la solución a desarrollar y la capacidad, experticia y otras cualidades de los implicados en el proyecto. Estos factores pueden ser aceleradores o retardadores en el tiempo y esfuerzo de desarrollo.

Los framework pueden considerarse como herramientas concebidas para agilizar el desarrollo del producto de software.

De todos estos métodos, el de Puntos de Objetos es el único que da importancia a la plataforma de forma explícita [11]. Sin embargo, no dejan claro cómo otorgar valor al indicador. Todos los framework no tienen el mismo impacto en la generación automática de código ni todos los proyectos tienen la misma complejidad.

En [12] se describen los hallazgos encontrados en una revisión sistemática de la literatura, que investiga sobre los métodos de estimación en el desarrollo ágil de software. En cuanto a las técnicas de estimación más utilizadas, se destaca el criterio de expertos, el método de puntos de casos de uso y la modificación del método de puntos de casos de uso. Las métricas de tamaño empleadas con mayor frecuencia son los puntos de casos de uso y los puntos de historia. En este estudio no se formuló ninguna pregunta que permitiera profundizar si las organizaciones que investigan los trabajos seleccionados, utilizan framework de desarrollo para acelerar el proceso.

Un importante prerrequisito para la aplicación profesional de técnicas de estimación, es contar con datos históricos relevantes, lo que constituye una paradoja pues en el momento que se estima (al inicio del proyecto) no se dispone de información suficiente [1]. Estos autores consideran que son varios los factores que deben tomarse en cuenta para ajustar la estimación y los clasifican en cuatro grupos: de las tecnologías, del producto, del proceso de desarrollo y de recursos. Dentro de la primera clasificación mencionan a los lenguajes de programación, pero no la utilización de herramientas de generación de código.

En la investigación que se describe en [13], se define un nuevo modelo de estimación de esfuerzo destinado a proyectos que reutilizan artefactos desarrollados en proyectos anteriores con un alcance similar (requisitos funcionales similares), para lo cual desarrollan un modelo matemático que toma como base el método de puntos de casos de uso.

Al usar como base este método, los autores comparten su utilidad por ser un método que no le interesa ni la arquitectura del software ni el lenguaje que se utiliza en la construcción; lo que le permite una amplia aplicabilidad. Aunque proponen modificaciones a algunos factores técnicos y ambientales ampliando su alcance o adicionando otros factores (por ejemplo, el de reutilización), no valoran explícitamente el impacto del uso de herramientas de generación de código en la construcción del software.

En [4] se realiza un estudio sobre los factores que afectan la precisión de las estimaciones de esfuerzo sobre todo en proyectos ágiles y distribuidos globalmente. Los autores revisan estudios empíricos y revisiones sistemáticas a la literatura vinculadas con el tema y encuentran que factores como las habilidades del equipo, la complejidad de los cambios, el conocimiento y la experiencia de los desarrolladores son factores que afectan la estimación de esfuerzo. Como resultado de su investigación, identifican cuatro factores que afectan estas estimaciones: el tamaño de las personalizaciones del producto, la prioridad del cliente, la madurez del equipo y el desarrollo en sitios múltiples. Los resultados indican que tiene una fuerte influencia el tamaño de las personalizaciones del producto en la precisión (directa) y el sesgo de las estimaciones de esfuerzo (indirecta).

En la revisión a la literatura y la encuesta aplicada a organizaciones de software, cuyos resultados se presentan en [14], se aborda la estimación del esfuerzo de desarrollo desde una perspectiva industrial profundizando en las habilidades de las organizaciones para aplicar ciertos métodos de estimación y las prácticas aplicadas durante este proceso. En este trabajo se identifica que la estimación se realiza principalmente para planificar y dar seguimiento al proyecto de software, la mejora de procesos y la reducción de gastos generales de gestión del proyecto. Además, detectan que el juicio de expertos es el método que prevalece en la estimación. Entre las razones que se reconocen para usar otros métodos está, la desconfianza con los métodos basados en datos por la falta de evidencia sustancial a favor de ellos.

3 Método de estudio de casos

Un estudio de casos es una investigación empírica que hace uso de múltiples fuentes de evidencias para investigar una instancia (o un pequeño número de instancias) de un fenómeno contemporáneo relacionado con la ingeniería de software dentro de su contexto real, específicamente cuando las fronteras entre el fenómeno y su contexto no se pueden definir claramente. Es decir, brinda resultados de investigación a partir de proyectos del mundo real [15].

El uso del método requiere una consideración cuidadosa para la selección de los casos, las fuentes de datos y la recopilación, el análisis y la calidad [16].

Varios autores han hecho referencia a las situaciones en las cuales puede ser conveniente utilizar el estudio de casos como método cualitativo [15-18].

Entre los elementos que se mencionan están:

- El fenómeno objeto de estudio es amplio y complejo, de tal manera que el planteamiento de una pregunta causal no es posible debido a un insuficiente cuerpo de conocimiento.
- Cuando el tipo de pregunta de investigación da respuesta a preguntas como: "cómo" o "por qué" y, tradicionalmente, se ha utilizado con fines de exploración o para definir las preguntas, construcciones, propósitos o hipótesis.
- El investigador tiene poca o ninguna posibilidad de controlar los eventos.
- El fenómeno u objeto de estudio es contemporáneo dentro de un contexto de vida real, especialmente cuando los límites entre el fenómeno y el contexto no son evidentes claramente.
- Poner a prueba o desarrollar una teoría.
- Aumentar los conocimientos sobre un fenómeno o cómo este cambia.

El estudio de casos cuyo diseño y resultados preliminares se describen en este trabajo, es el resultado de una investigación aplicada que busca responder a preguntas concretas que se presentan con el objetivo de encontrar respuestas que pueden tomarse en cuenta de manera inmediata en contextos o situaciones específicas. Dentro de ella se evalúa como exploratoria por cuanto es una primera aproximación para detectar variables, relaciones y condiciones en las que se da el fenómeno en el que estamos interesados.

La finalidad es definir con mayor certeza un fenómeno o evento no estudiado con esta perspectiva para derivar hipótesis y conocer las variables relevantes. Además, se satisfacen los dos requerimientos previos para el desarrollo de una investigación exploratoria: usarla cuando aparece un fenómeno nuevo que por su novedad no admite todavía una descripción sistemática y/o cuando el tema ha sido poco explotado y reconocido.

Se hará una percepción directa del objeto de investigación para investigar el fenómeno directamente. En esta observación se usa un software para recopilar los datos, lo que es propio de una observación encubierta en la que las personas objeto de investigación no saben que son observados. En el epígrafe siguiente se describen los elementos de esenciales de este software.

3.1 Protocolo del estudio de caso

Para la aplicación de este método hay que seguir un protocolo formal que servirá de guía para garantizar la coherencia y repetitividad de la investigación. Un protocolo contiene el instrumento para investigar y los procedimientos y las reglas que se deben seguir usando el instrumento [16].

Los elementos que se tomaron en consideración en el diseño del estudio de caso parten de la síntesis presentada en [15] y se refieren a:

1. **Justificación del caso**

   La principal motivación del estudio en este momento es desde el punto de vista académico, pues al profundizar en los métodos de estimación del esfuerzo y el tiempo de desarrollo de un producto de software, se ha identificado que, por lo general, no toman en consideración el impacto del uso de un framework durante la construcción de la aplicación informática.

   Como resultado secundario del estudio, se puede obtener un criterio para seleccionar un framework de desarrollo, basado en el código generado de forma automática y el que se requiere modificar y/o crear. Para la industria, esta podría ser una justificación válida.

2. **Objetivo de estudio**

   El objetivo del estudio es investigar cómo el uso de un framework puede influir en el esfuerzo de desarrollo a partir del análisis del código fuente que se genera de forma automática y aquel que los programadores modifican o crean, para lo cual se hará un estudio exploratorio.

3. **Casos y unidades de análisis**

   Los casos representan temas de interés del estudio empírico, por lo que en esta investigación consideramos el marco de desarrollo o framework. No es suficiente un caso único para arribar a conclusiones pues cada framework de desarrollo tiene una arquitectura propia. Los framework PHP implementan el patrón MVC y resuelven varios de los problemas frecuentes de diseño de forma distinta, todo en una única herramienta. Sin embargo, para otros entornos (por, ejemplo, .NET y Java), se requieren de varias herramientas para construir una aplicación. Esto podría producir resultados diferentes.

   La complejidad de un proyecto puede ser diferente y requiere de un esfuerzo diferente. Por tal motivo, como fuente real de información (unidad de análisis) se propone utilizar varios productos de software que difieren en cuanto a su complejidad.

   En [16] utilizan datos de la Compañía Seamrush para sugerir los cinco framework PHP que deben usar en 2018 de acuerdo a las facilidades que proporcionan. Los resultados muestran que el 78.6% de los proyectos web desplegados en el momento del estudio estaban desarrollados en PHP, el 20.3% en ASP.NET, el 4% en Java, el 1.1% en ColdFusion, el 0.8% en Perl, el 0.5% en Ruby y el 0.2% en Python. Existe gran variedad de framework para cada uno de estos lenguajes, pero estas estadísticas evidencias que para el estudio puede resultar conveniente centrarnos en los framework PHP por su frecuencia de uso.

   De acuerdo a la distinción de Yin en [16], estamos en presencia de un estudio de casos embebido porque se estudiarán múltiples unidades de análisis dentro de un caso y un estudio de caso múltiple (Figura 1).

Figura 1. Estudio de casos múltiple y embebido

El número de casos viene determinado por la cantidad operativa de recolección y análisis (cantidad que se puede manejar realísticamente de acuerdo a los recursos disponibles), el entendimiento del fenómeno (cantidad que permiten responder a las preguntas de investigación) y la naturaleza del fenómeno objeto de análisis.

4. Pregunta de investigación

¿Cómo el uso de un framework o marco de trabajo puede influir en la estimación del esfuerzo y tiempo de desarrollo, tomando como base la cantidad de líneas de código fuente generadas automáticamente que no cambian, modificadas a partir de la generadas y nuevas que tiene el producto de software?

5. Proposiciones o hipótesis

Según [16], cuando se trata de un estudio exploratorio para el cual es poco o no existe un marco teórico, se puede justificar la existencia de proposiciones que podrán derivarse de los resultados del estudio. En este caso consideramos que la investigación podría estar comprobando que:

- la complejidad de un proyecto, expresada en la cantidad de líneas de código fuente que lo implementan, guarda relación con la utilidad de usar un framework en su construcción, y
- es posible reducir en un por ciento el esfuerzo de desarrollo obtenido aplicando un método de estimación cuando para su construcción se utilice un framework.

6. Recolección y análisis de datos

La medición del código fuente es una acción bastante compleja para ser realizada de forma manual. Esto se debe, fundamentalmente, al elevado número de líneas de código que posee cualquier producto de software. Por tal razón, es recomendable realizar dicha medición de forma automatizada logrando minimizar el esfuerzo humano [19].

Tomando esto en consideración, se decidió recolectar los datos de forma automática con el uso de un software.

Como resultado práctico de la investigación realizada hasta el momento, se obtuvo una aplicación (CodeCompare) que, a partir de la carga de un script que contenga la estructura de la base de datos del proyecto (unidad de análisis) a estudiar y del código fuente final del mismo, es capaz de determinar el por ciento de la aplicación que se generó automáticamente y el equipo de desarrollo no modificó (%LCFA), el por ciento de la aplicación que se generó automáticamente y el equipo de desarrollo modificó (%LCFAM) y el porciento que fue creado completamente (%LCFN). Las fórmulas siguientes permiten obtener estos indicadores:

$$\%LCFA = (LCFA/LCF) * 100 \quad (1)$$

$$\%LCFAM = (LCFAM/LCF) * 100 \quad (2)$$

$$\%LCFN = (LCFN/LCF) * 100 \quad (3)$$

donde: LCF: Total de líneas de código fuente del proyecto.

LCFA: Total de líneas de código fuente que se generaron automáticamente y el equipo de desarrollo no modificó.

LCFAM: Total de líneas de código fuente que se generaron automáticamente y el equipo de desarrollo modificó.

LCFN: Total de líneas de código fuente nuevas.

Las ventajas de CodeCompare fueron resaltadas en [11] y se refieren a la posibilidad de identificar cuánto trabajó un equipo de desarrollo en un proyecto en aras de evaluar el desempeño de sus miembros y cuánto apoyó el framework en la construcción.

La versión desarrollada hasta el momento evalúa el impacto del framework Yii 2 y debe incluir en el futuro la valoración de los otros marcos de desarrollo.

La aplicación recopila estos datos y los del proyecto que se estudie, lo que permitirá tener una clara cadena de pruebas cuando estos sean analizados para comprobar las hipótesis y responder a las preguntas de investigación. En la Figura 2 se presenta la salida de la aplicación CodeCompare con los datos recopilados para un proyecto específico.

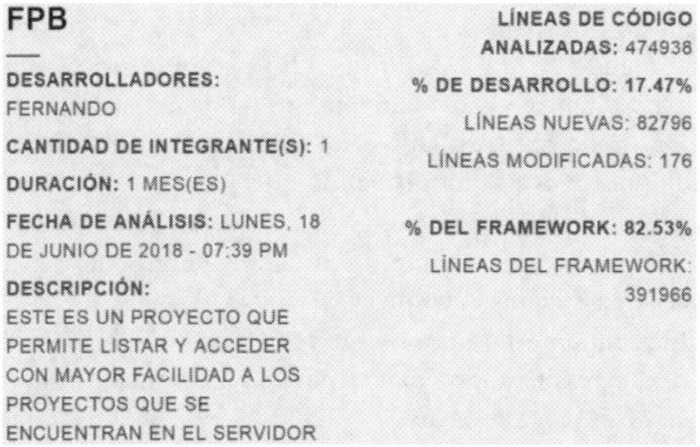

Figura 2. Resultados de la comparación utilizando la aplicación CodeCompare.

Cuando se realiza una investigación cualitativa, la recolección y el análisis ocurrirán prácticamente en paralelo, por lo que durante el desarrollo del estudio se puede decidir incorporar nuevos datos a recolectar, incrementar o decrementar la cantidad de casos de estudio o las unidades de análisis o modificar algún otro elemento planificado.

En el análisis de los datos se usarán los métodos estadísticos (medidas de dispersión, dependencia), que permitan analizar los resultados obtenidos.

3.2 Estrategia de selección de casos y datos

Tanto los casos como las unidades de análisis son seleccionados intencionalmente de acuerdo al objetivo del estudio y para tener la variación de las propiedades que el estudio tiene intención de comparar.

En cuanto a las unidades de análisis, se seleccionaron cinco que responden a proyectos para el desarrollo de aplicaciones web de complejidad diferente, de acuerdo a la clasificación descrita en [6] (Tabla 1).

Tabla 1 Descripción de los proyectos analizados.

Proyecto	Descripción	Complejidad
Forgas (FBP)	Aplicación para la gestión de la información de un centro gastronómico, que además provee un cuadro de mando.	Pequeña
CodeCompare	Aplicación para calcular el % de desarrollo por parte del equipo y por parte del framework Yii2.	Pequeña
Inforzine	Aplicación para la gestión de la información de una revista virtual.	Media
Rentas	Aplicación que permite la gestión de la información de una casa de renta.	Media
MisCasasRenta	Aplicación que permite la gestión de varias casas de renta a la vez.	Grande

3.3 Validez

Para establecer la validez del estudio, se toman en cuenta los factores propuestos por Yin [16]:

- **Validez de constructo:** con este objetivo se hizo el estudio piloto cuyos resultados preliminares se describen en este trabajo. Al estudiar las unidades de análisis en un caso, se pretendió evaluar si las medidas que se analizan daban respuesta a la pregunta de investigación, evaluándose que son pertinentes y adecuadas al objetivo del estudio de casos.
- **Validez interna:** se considera que la ejecución completa del estudio al resto de los casos en las cinco unidades de análisis, requerirá la incorporación de otros participantes para el desarrollo de los productos a medir. La experiencia de los nuevos participantes en el framework puede influir en el producto final que se obtenga. Por lo que, para un mismo framework se

deben desarrollar las cinco unidades de análisis por el mismo participante, empezando por los proyectos de menor alcance.

- **Validez externa:** la selección de los casos tomó en cuenta las tendencias del uso de los framework y, en el caso de las unidades de análisis, contar con proyectos de diferentes niveles de complejidad.
- **Fiabilidad:** los datos recopilados se obtienen de forma automática sin influencia de un investigador específico, y se grafican para su análisis usando una herramienta clásica de tabulación electrónica (Microsoft Excel).

El elemento principal que puede considerarse como amenaza a la investigación está asociado con la experticia de los participantes que se incorporen al desarrollo de las unidades de análisis. Además, resultan insuficientes las investigaciones que se publican sobre el impacto del uso de herramientas acelerados en la construcción del software, en la estimación del esfuerzo,

4 Resultados preliminares

Los resultados que se presentan son preliminares y se corresponden con el estudio piloto que se hizo utilizando un caso y cinco unidades de análisis.

Existen más de 40 framework PHP, pero según [21], los más utilizados en 2017 en la construcción de proyectos web fueron: Laravel (22.7%), Symfony (15.1%), Codelgniter (14.4%), CakePHP (8.6%), Zend (7.8%), Phalcon (7,7%), Slim (7.1%) y Yii (6.7%). Después aparecen otros siete (7) con por cientos que van desde 2.3% a 0.2%.

Para el estudio piloto se escogió Yii pues todos los investigadores lo dominaban y resultaba menos complejo validar el trabajo. Además, en el transcurso de la última década, el por ciento de proyectos web que usan este framework se ha ido incrementando mientras que otros frameworks se han mantenido o disminuido [18]. Estas tendencias hacen inclinar la selección del resto de los casos en Laravel, Symfony, Codelgniter y CakePHP.

Los resultados obtenidos hasta el momento se presentan en la Tabla 2, y se corresponden con la cantidad total de líneas de código fuente, las generadas por el framework y no sufrieron modificaciones, las generadas por el framework que el equipo de desarrollo cambió y las implementadas por los desarrolladores.

Tabla 2 Resultados preliminares.

Proyecto	Total	Implementadas por los desarrolladores (%)	Generadas por el framework que el equipo de desarrollo cambió (%)	Generadas por el framework y no sufrieron modificaciones (%)
Forgas	474938	82796 (17.43%)	176 (0.04%)	391966 (82.53%)
CodeCompare	891537	497286 (55.78%)	201 (0.02%)	394050 (44.20%)
Inforzine	1744340	1352161 (77.52%)	117 (0.01%)	392062 (22.48%)
Rentas	2175952	1758881 (80.83%)	2962 (0.14%)	414109 (19.03%)
MisCasasRenta	3217105	2820264 (87.66%)	761 (0.02%)	396080 (12.31%)

En la medida que el proyecto se complejiza, el por ciento de cantidad de líneas de código nuevas aumenta y disminuye el por ciento de líneas de código que son generadas por el framework sin ser modificadas. Sin embargo, las generadas que sufren cambios no tienen variaciones significativas.

En proyectos pequeños, la utilización de herramientas tiene mayor significación que los métodos y el proceso; por lo tanto, tienden a desarrollarse en un entorno automatizado [5]. Los resultados obtenidos hasta el momento con el estudio de casos, tienden a reforzar los alcanzados en este estudio ya que para proyectos pequeños los desarrolladores cuando evalúan lo que genera el framework, lo asumen sin realizar modificaciones prácticamente; sin embargo, en proyectos grandes la situación es al revés, el equipo de desarrollo prefiere crear su propio código sobre el que puede generar el framework.

5 Conclusiones

La utilización de los IDEs y framework ha revolucionado la industria del software, disminuyendo considerablemente el tiempo de desarrollo de las aplicaciones. Esto provoca que la fase de desarrollo es menor que la de planeación y de análisis y diseño, aspecto que no es sopesado de forma apropiada, a nuestro juicio, en los métodos de estimación.

La idea no es utilizar las líneas de código fuente para estimar, si no analizar los productos de software construidos para estimar cuánto contribuyó el uso del framework en la aplicación obtenida.

Para atender el problema que persigue explorar el impacto del uso de un framework de desarrollo; se decidió realizar una investigación cualitativa que, usando el método de estudio de casos, realice un estudio exploratorio que permita generar ideas e hipótesis para nuevas investigaciones.

La pregunta de investigación definida busca evaluar cómo el uso de los framework se relaciona con los métodos de estimación de software, a partir de comprobar si la complejidad de un proyecto expresada en la cantidad de líneas de código fuente guarda relación con la utilidad de usar un framework y si es posible reducir en un por ciento el esfuerzo de desarrollo obtenido aplicando un método de estimación usando este tipo de herramientas.

Si efectivamente puede impactar, podría definirse un factor técnico que pondere este impacto y que pueda incorporarse en los métodos de estimación. Otras preguntas de investigación podrían derivarse de estos resultados, por ejemplo, ¿el efecto del uso de un framework es el mismo si se utilizan diferentes predictores de tiempo?

Una vez analizados los datos obtenidos hasta el momento, se aprecia que puede existir una relación asociada a la complejidad del proyecto y a la generación de código automáticamente, mientras mayor complejidad tenga el proyecto, mayor posibilidad de que se implementen el código por los desarrolladores sin usar el framework.

Referencias

1. Bundschuh, M., Dekkers, C.: The IT Measurement Compendium Estimating and Benchmarking Sucess with Functional Size Measurement. Springer Science & Business Media, Heidelberg (2008).
2. Prokopova, Z., Silhavy, P., Silhavy, R.: Influence Analysis of Select Factors in the Function Point Work Effort Estimation. In: Silhavy, R., Silhavy, P., Prokopova, Z. (eds.). Intellingent Systems in Cybernetics and Automation Control Theory. CoMeSySo 2018, Advances in Intelligent Systems and Computing. pp. 112-124, Springer, Heidelberg (2019).
3. Kwon, D., Jeon, I. Yoon, G. Bakr, B.A. Kim, K.P.; A Study on Probabilistic Schedule Estimation and Refinement of the Small and Medium-Sized Software Development Projects. Journal Software. 13(3), 201-210 (March 2018).
4. Usman, H., Brito, R., Börstler, J.: Effort Estimation in Large-Scale Software Development: An Industrial Case Study. Information and Software Technology. 99, 21-40 (2018).
5. Usman, M., Mendes, E., Weidt, F, Britto, R.: Effort estimation in agile software development: A systematic literature review. In Proceedings of the 10th International Conference on Predictive Models in Software Engineering pp. 82-91. ACM. (2018)
6. Reddy, J. M., Prasad, S. V. A. V., Murthy, B. R.: Significance of Software Layered Technology on Size of Projects. Journal of Science and Technology. 2(1), 46-58 (2017).
7. Olanrewaju, R. F., Islam, T., Ali, N.: Chapter 40 Empirical study of the evolution of PHP MVC Framework. In: Advanced Computers and Communication Engineering Technology: Lectures Notes in Electrical Engineering 315. pp. 399-410 (2015).
8. Gajda, W., Chapter 2 Four Web Framework in four minutes, in ProVagrant. 21-40 (2015).
9. Teixeira, L., Xambre, A. R., Alvelos, H., Filipe, N., & Ramos, A.: Selecting an Open-Source framework: a practical case based on software development for sensory analysis. Procedia Computer Science. 64, 1057-1064 (2015).
10. Boehm, B.: Software Engineering Economics. IEEE transactions on Software Engineering. **1**, 4-21 (1984).
11. Santana, D., Arteaga, F, Muñoz, V, Hernández, A.: Evaluación del impacto del uso del framework Yii2 en la estimación del esfuerzo de desarrollo de software. In: CCIA2018 XIX Convención Internacional de Ingeniería y Arquitectura, IV Congreso Internacional de Ingeniería Informática y Sistemas de Información. La Habana, Cuba (2018).
12. Kuutila, M., Mäntylä, M. Farooq, U., Claes, M.: Time presure in software engineering: A systematic literature review. arXiv preprint arXiv: 1901.05771 (2019).
13. Rak, K., Car, Ž., Lovrek, I.: Effort estimation model for software development projects based on use case reuse. Journal Software: Evolution and Process. p. e2119. (2018).

14. Trendowicz, A. Münch, J. Jeffery, R.: State of the practice in software effort estimation: A survey and literature review. In Z. Huzar et al. (eds.). IFIP International Federation for Information Processing CEE-SET 2008, LNCS4 4980. pp. 232-245 (2011).
15. Runeson, P., Host, M., Rainer, A., Regnell, B.: Case study research in software engineering: guidelines and examples. John & Sons, New Jersey (2012).
16. Yin, R.K.: Case study research: design and methods. 5th Edition. Sage Publications (2014).
17. Dubé, L., Paré, G.: Case Research in informatic systems: current practices, trends and recommendations. Ecole des Hautes Etudes Commerciales de Montréal. 1-36 (2001).
18. Fenton, N., Bieman, J.: Software metric: a rigorous and practical approach. 3rd Edition. CRC Press (2015).
19. Rathore, D.: PHP framework 2018 - Tops 5 PHP frameworks to use in 2018, https://www.dunebook.com/php-framework-2018.
20. Dapozo, G. N., Greiner, C. L., Ferraro, M. D. L. A., Medina, Y., Pedrozo Petrazzini, G., & Lencina, B.: Medición y estimación del software: métodos y herramientas para mejorar la calidad del software. In WICC2014. XVII Workshop de Investigadores en Ciencias de la Computación. pp. 575-579 (2014).
21. Google. Symfony, Laravel, Yii, CakePHP, Codelgniter - Explorer - Tendencias de Google 2017, https://www.trends.google.com/trends/.

Semantic Enterprise Application Integration at Service Layer: A Systematic Mapping

Gabriel dos A. C. V. Real[1], Julio C. Nardi[2], Monalessa P. Barcellos[1], Ricardo de A. Falbo[1]

[1] Ontology and Conceptual Modeling Research Group (NEMO),
Department of Computer Science, Federal University of Espírito Santo - Vitória - ES - Brazil
[2] Informatics Department, Federal Institute of Espírito Santo, Colatina - ES, Brazil.

Abstract. Organizations use several applications to support their business processes and activities. These applications should be integrated to provide a better support and meet the organizations' needs. Moreover, to properly support the processes, Enterprise Application Integration (EAI) should address the service integration layer. EAI must cope with semantic conflicts that often arise when integrating applications due to the heterogeneity of the applications. In this paper, we present a systematic mapping that investigated EAI initiatives that address semantic aspects and cover the service integration layer. Our main interest is to investigate the approaches adopted to integrate services and the use of ontologies in this context. The results provide a panorama of research in this area.

Keywords: Enterprise Application Integration, Service Integration, Semantic Integration, Ontology, Systematic Mapping.

1 Introduction

There are a lot of information systems to support the business processes of companies, non-profit organizations, and governmental organizations [14]. Enterprise Application Integration (EAI) is one of the solutions which provide the ability to integrate many applications running in an enterprise [2], and a promising way for unhindered information flow, resolving the problem of "islands of information" [7]. However, EAI has been one of the main challenges faced by organizations [6].

The applications[1] to be integrated are usually developed by different groups that, many times, do not have any concern with integration. As a result, these applications, almost all, are heterogeneous, autonomous and distributed [11]. Thus, multiple technical, syntactical and semantic conflicts can arise when integrating applications [11]. Nowadays, technical and syntactical aspects of application integration are relatively well-established, but semantic aspects have still been challenging [12].

Semantic integration, which is based on meaning, is more reliable than syntactical integration, which is based only on the processing of strings and union of schemes [21]. In semantic EAI, a common understanding of the handled terms and services exchanged

[1] In this paper, *application* and *system* are used as synonymous.

by applications is shared [4]. In this context, ontologies can be used to establish a common understanding about the domain of interest, serving as an interlingua to provide communication between applications [4] and promoting integration at different layers (data, message/service, and process) [16]. In other words, ontologies can be used as a reference model to map concepts and services used by the different enterprise applications [4]. In Computer Science, ontology is considered an explicit concrete artifact representing a model of consensus within a community and a universe of discourse, aimed at supporting semantic interoperability in its various forms (e.g., model integration, service interoperability, knowledge harmonization, and taxonomy alignment) [10].

Among the reasons for interest in service layer integration, we found that enterprises are getting away from tight application-to-application interfaces and are adopting more service-oriented, loosely coupled, message-based, and asynchronous techniques [19]. The notion of business services and Service Oriented Architecture (SOA) provides a view of integrated components to be dealt with as encapsulated and reusable high-level services. Also, an integration scenario is composed of one or more processes, and processes consist of services, links connecting services and rules defining operations on process data or service execution order [15]. Services can then address integration problems and also create new capabilities on existing application services. A composed process can, e.g., offer a reusable complex functionality which can be adopted in further composed processes as a single service [15].

Considering the relevance of service integration and the challenges of semantic integration, we decided to investigate semantic EAI initiatives with focus on the service layer. By that, we aim to provide an overview of this research topic by means of a mapping study. A mapping study is a secondary study designed to give a panorama of a research area/topic through a systematic method and, using a well-defined classification for selecting and analyzing the works focus of interest. From that, it also aims to identify available evidence about the interest topic contributing for pointing out issues to be addressed in future researches [13] [17].

This mapping study refines and updates two studies previously performed by some of the authors of this paper. First, [16] investigated semantic EAI initiatives in general, analyzing aspects such as business application domain, addressed integration layers (data, message/service, process) and ontology use. Next, [6] updated the study by [16] and, after that, analyzed in deep the semantic EAI initiatives addressing the process layer. In [6], Cerqueira et al. investigated how semantic integration has been performed at the process layer and the use of ontologies in this context. In our study, we updated the study by [6] with regard to the semantic EAI initiatives in general. Thus, we investigated in deep the semantic EAI initiatives addressing the service layer, by analyzing how semantics has been assigned to services and the use of ontologies in these service integration initiatives.

It is important to clarify some terminological aspects used along this paper. Despite the definitional differences/interrelations between *integration* (as the act of incorporating components into a complete set in a way to form a new system constituting a whole and creating synergy [11]), and *interoperability* (as the ability of applications/components to exchange data and services preserving the constituent parts as they are [19]), these terms are often used indistinctively [16]. In this paper, therefore, the term "integration" is adopted in a broader sense, covering both integration and interoperability meanings.

We present our mapping study in this paper, which is organized as follows: Section 2 provides the background for the paper, talking briefly about EAI, services and ontologies; Section 3 presents the research protocol used in the study; Section 4 presents the obtained results; Section 5 discusses the findings that emerge from the results; Section 6 describes the limitations of this work; and, finally, Section 7 presents our final considerations.

2 Background

EAI is crucial for organizations, since applications increasingly need to work together to support business processes. According to [7], EAI is the integration of applications enabling information sharing to efficient operations and flexible delivery of business services to the customer, considering current or legacy applications.

To integrate enterprise applications, it is necessary to create a coherent information system architecture in which the various business processes, information storages and systems are integrated so that they appear seamless for the user. It is necessary, thus, to define an integrated system as a collection of subsystems that interact to form a whole, and whose properties emerge due to the interaction of its subsystems [19] [22].

Nonetheless, enterprise applications many times have trouble to interoperate with others because their structure and design did not consider interoperability needs. According to [11], these are HAD (heterogeneous, autonomous, and distributed) applications. Heterogeneous means that each enterprise application implements its own data and process model. Autonomous means that enterprise applications may run independently of any other application. Distributed means that applications locally implement their data model, which they generally do not share with other enterprise applications. This, therefore, contributes to make EAI a difficult and complex task.

EAI can cover different layers [11]: data, message/service, and process. Data integration deals with moving or federating data between multiple data stores. Integration at this layer assumes bypassing the application logic and manipulating data directly in the database, through its native interface. Message (or service) integration addresses messages exchange between the integrated applications. Process integration views enterprises as a set of interrelated processes and it is responsible for handling message flows, implementing rules and defining the overall process execution [11]. In this paper, we are particularly interested in service integration.

According to [11] a service is defined as the realization of a business functionality via software that anyone can use to compose new applications by using these services in the context of new or modified processes. Service integration provides loosely coupled integration and has played an important role in EAI. Moreover, there is a strong connection between process integration and service integration, since process integration may occur from connections among services [6].

Semantic conflicts can arise in any of the integration layers, whenever applications are built with different conceptualizations. To avoid them, the meaning of the interchanged information and shared functionalities/tasks has to be understood across the applications. Ontologies have been employed for the establishment of common understanding to explain implicit and hidden knowledge, contributing to solving semantic conflicts [16].

Considering their generality level, ontologies can be classified as: top-level ontologies (so-called foundational ontologies), which describe general concepts like, time, space, event, object, etc., and are independent of particular domains or tasks; domain ontologies, which describe concepts related to a generic domain (e.g., Electrocardiogram); task ontologies, which describe the conceptualization related to a generic task or process (e.g., Diagnosis); and application ontologies, which deal with concepts related to a particular application (e.g., a medical ontology for heart diseases built on Diagnosis and Electrocardiogram ontologies). Ideally, domain and task ontologies should be defined from top-level ontologies and application ontologies should be based on domain and task ontologies [9].

3 The Research Protocol

The study was conducted following the approach defined in [13][17], which involves: planning, when the research protocol is defined; conducting, when occurs the execution of the protocol, data extraction, analyze and record; and reporting, when the results are recorded and made available to possible interested parties. Next, we present the main parts of the protocol used in the study.

The study **goal** was to investigate EAI initiatives that address semantic aspects and the service layer. By "address the service layer" we mean that the integration occurs by the exchange of information through messages. For achieving the goal, we defined nine **research questions,** which are shown bellow with their rationale:

RQ1. *When and in which type of vehicle (journal/ conference/ symposium/ workshop) have the studies been published?*: Aims at giving an understanding on when and where publications about semantic EAI initiatives addressing the service layer have been published.

RQ2. *Which types of research (considering the classification defined by [20]), have been done?:* Investigates which type of research is reported in each selected publication. This question is useful to evaluate the maturity stage of the research topic.

RQ3. *What are the business application domains addressed in the EAI initiatives?:* Identifies the business applications domains that have been supported by semantic EAI initiatives addressing the service layer and verifies if there is predominance of any of them.

RQ4. *Have ontologies been adopted in the EAI initiatives? If so, what the purpose of using them?:* Verifies if ontologies have been used in semantic EAI initiatives and the identifies the purpose of using them.

RQ5. *What kinds of ontologies (considering their generality level) have been used?:* Identifies the kinds of ontologies used in semantic EAI initiatives addressing the service layer and verifies if there is a predominance of some kind.

RQ6. *Which languages/formalisms have been used to create the ontologies?:* Identifies how ontologies have been represented in semantic EAI initiatives.

RQ7. *How has service integration been addressed in the EAI initiatives?:* Investigates the technological strategies and integration approaches used to perform semantic integration at the service layer.

RQ8. *How is semantics assigned to services?:* Investigates which techniques and methods have been used to assign semantics to services in semantic EAI initiatives addressing the service layer.

RQ9. *Have systematic approaches been used to conduct the EAI initiatives?:* Verifies whether the initiatives have been followed by systematic approaches to performing semantic integration at service layer. This question helps identify if there has been a concern with providing clear guidance for users to perform semantic EAI addressing the service layer.

Since this study updates previous studies, we applied the same **search string** used in [16] and [6]. The search string has two groups of terms joined in conjunction with the AND operator. The first group includes terms to capture studies related to integration/interoperability of enterprise applications. The second aims at capturing studies that deal with semantic aspects. Within each group, the OR operator was used to allow for synonyms. The search string used in this study is: *("application integration" OR "application interoperability" OR "enterprise system integration" OR "enterprise system interoperability" OR "integration of information system" OR "interoperability of information system" OR "integration of application" OR "interoperability of application" OR "interoperability of enterprise application" OR "interoperability of enterprise system" OR "integration of enterprise application" OR "integration of enterprise system" OR "interoperability of business application" OR "interoperability of business system" OR "integration of business application" OR "integration of business system" OR "integration of heterogeneous system" OR "integration of heterogeneous application" OR "interoperability of heterogeneous system" OR "interoperability of heterogeneous application" OR "interoperability of information system" OR "integrated application" OR "interoperable application" OR "integrated enterprise system" OR "interoperable enterprise system" OR "information system integration" OR "information system interoperability" OR "enterprise system integration" OR "enterprise system interoperability" OR "business system integration" OR "business system interoperability") AND (semantic OR semantics OR semantically).*

The search was performed in the following six **sources**: IEEE Xplore), ACM Digital Library, Scopus, Science Direct, Engineering Village, and Web of Science. These sources are the same searched in [16] and [6]. They were selected based systematic reviews in the Software Engineering area and on other studies conducted by members of our research group.

Publication selection was performed in four steps: *In Preliminary Selection and Cataloging (S1)*, the search string was applied in the search mechanism of each digital library (we limited the search scope to the title, abstract and keywords metadata fields).

After that, we identified publications indexed by more than one digital library and removed the duplications. *In Selection of Relevant Publications – 1st filter (S2)*, the abstracts of the selected publications were analyzed considering the following inclusion (IC) and exclusion (EC) criteria: (IC1) the study addresses an EAI initiative that considers semantic aspects; (EC1) the publication does not have an abstract; (EC2) the publication is an abstract only; (EC3) The publication is not written in English; (EC4) the publication is an older version or a publication already selected; (EC5) the publication is a secondary study, a tertiary study, an editorial or a summary. In *Selection of Relevant Publications – 2nd filter (S3)*, the full text of the publications selected in S2 was read and analyzed considering the cited inclusion and exclusion criteria. Publications whose full text was not available were also excluded (EC6). With the publications selected in S3 we updated the study reported in [16] and [6]. Then, to focus on publications presenting EAI initiatives addressing the service layer, in *Selection of Relevant Publications – 3rd filter (S4)*, we applied an additional inclusion criterion: (IC2) the publication presents a semantic EAI initiative addressing the service layer, to the publications selected in S3 and also to all the publications addressing semantic EAI initiatives selected in [16] and [6]. As a result, we obtained the publications object of the study described in this paper.

The publications returned in the publication selection steps were cataloged and stored in spreadsheets. We defined an id for each publication and recorded the publication title, authors, year, and vehicle of publication. Data from the publications returned in S4 were extracted and organized into a data extraction form oriented to the research questions. The spreadsheets and form produced during the study can be found in http://bit.ly/SEIA-SLM-Spreadsheet. Publication selection and data extraction were performed by the first author and reviewed by the second, third and fourth authors. Discordances and possible biases were discussed in meetings.

4 Data Synthesis

This study considered publications until December 31st, 2017. In S1, we searched for studies published from 2016, since [6] selected studies published until December 31st, 2015. We obtained 140 publications as result of S1. After duplications removal 113 publications remained. 32 of them were selected in S2. In S3, five publications were selected. In S4 we applied IC2 to the five publications selected in S3. All of them were also selected in S4. Moreover, we applied IC2 to the publications selected in [16], resulting in 40 publications, and to publications selected in [6], which resulted in five publications. After all these steps, we have selected 50 publications presenting semantic EAI initiatives that address the service layer. Figure 1 illustrates the process followed and the number of publications selected in each step. Due to space limitation, we do not provide in this paper the list of selected publications. It can be found in http://bit.ly/SEIA-SLM-Publications.

Analyzing the 50 publications selected in the final selection stage, we noticed that some of them refer to a same work and report different parts of that work. In these cases, we decided to analyze together the set of publications referring to a same work and count them as only one study, since they refer to the same work. As a result, we identified 45 different approaches (instead of 50). Next, we present the data synthesis for each research question.

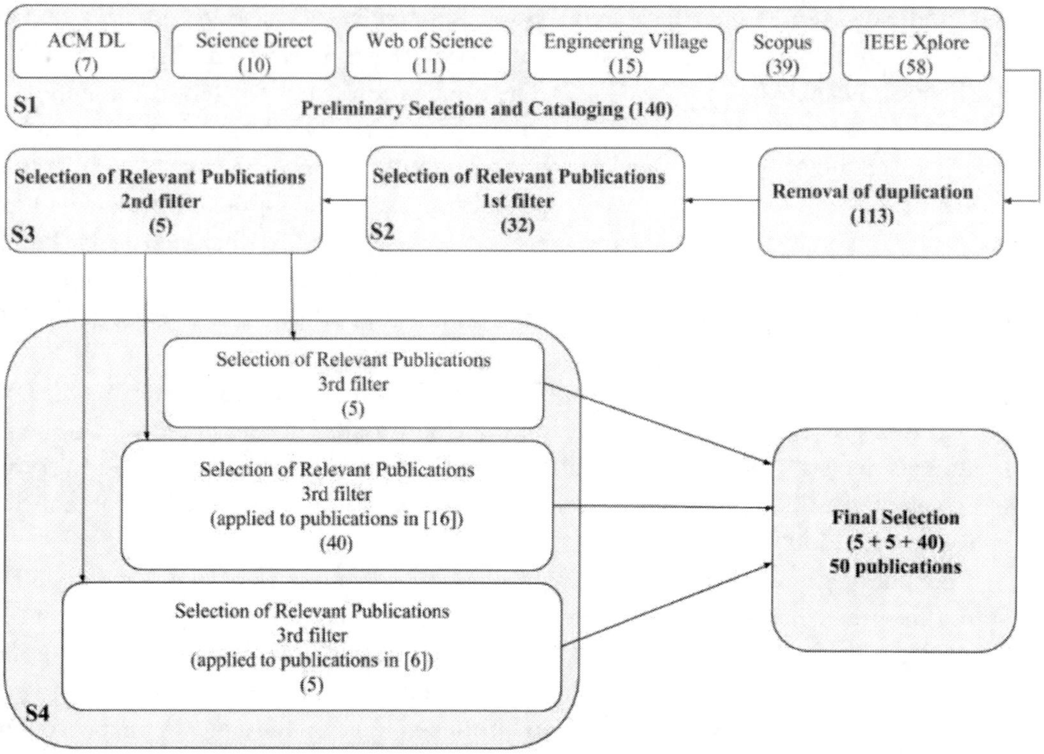

Fig. 1. – Publication Selection Process

RQ1 - When and in which type of vehicle have the studies been published?

Figure 2 shows the distribution of studies per year. Regarding the type of vehicle, twenty-one studies (47%) were published in conferences, sixteen studies (36%) in journals, six (13%) studies in symposiums, one study (2%) in workshop, and one study (2%) was published as a book chapter. The years of 2015 and 2016 have no publications of studies about semantic EAI addressing the service layer.

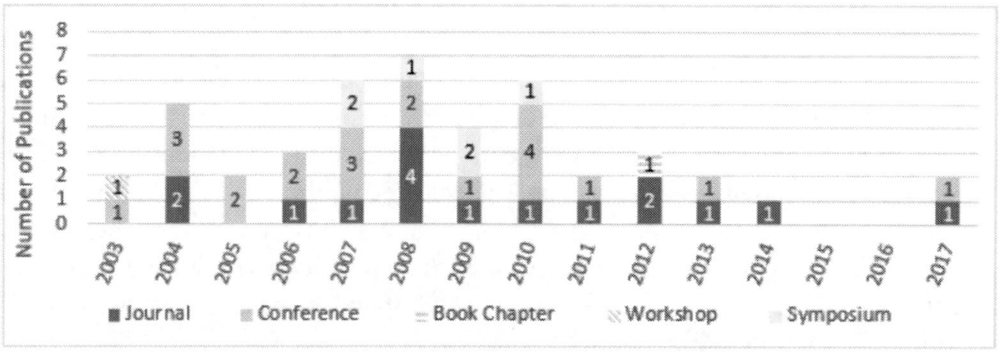

Fig. 2. – Distribution of selected studies over the years

RQ2 - Which types of research have been done?

Following the classification by [20], thirty-three (73%) of the analyzed studies are *Proposal of Solution*. From these, ten (22%) are also *Validation Research* (i.e., they use a proof of concept, experiment, prototype or similar to evaluate the proposal) and two (4%) are also *Evaluation Research* (i.e., the proposal was evaluated in practice). Nine proposals (20%) do not propose a solution, but address some kind of evaluation. Three (7%) of them are *Validation Research* and six (13%) are *Evaluation Research*. Three (7%) studies were classified as *Experience Paper*.

RQ3 - What are the business application domains addressed in the EAI initiatives?

Most of the investigated semantic EAI initiatives (ten studies, 22%) are independent of the application domain. Nine studies (20%) concern E-Business and E-Commerce domains. Three studies (7%) regard Educational and Medical domains each. Financial, Manufacturing, Product Development, and Supply Chain were application domains addressed in two studies (4% per domain) each. Accounting, Construction Industry, Digital Asset Management, E-Gov, Emergency Management and Geographical Information, Management and Maintenance Decision of Electric Equipment, Multimedia Content, Oil Industry, Power Marketing, Process Management, Production Process Simulation, Software Engineering are application domains in only one study (2%) each.

RQ4 - Have ontologies been adopted in the EAI initiatives? If so, what is the purpose of using them?

Ontologies are adopted in thirty-seven studies (82%). Eleven studies (24%) use ontologies to *Data Description*, one study (2%) to *Service Description*, seventeen studies (38%) to *Data and Service Description*, one study (2%) to *Data and Process Description*, and four studies (9%) to *Data, Service and Process Description*. Two studies (4%) use ontologies as *Reference Model* and one study (2%) use to *Framework Description*. Eight studies (18%) do not use ontologies.

RQ5 - What kinds of ontologies (considering their generality level) have been used?

Table 1 presents the quantity and percentage of studies per kind of ontologies. "Unspecified" refers to studies that use ontologies, but they do not specify their kinds, and it was not possible to identify them.

Table 1. – Kinds of Ontologies used in the Studies

Kind of Ontologies	Quantity of Studies	Percent of Studies (%)
Domain Ontology	26	58%
Domain Ontology and Application Ontology	5	11%
Domain Ontology and Foundational Ontology	1	2%
Domain Ontology, Application Ontology and Foundational Ontology	1	2%
Unspecified	4	9%
Do not use Ontology	8	18%

RQ6 - Which languages/formalisms have been used to create the ontologies?

The studies adopt several languages/formalisms to represent ontologies, ranging from Semantic Web languages to simpler data representation techniques. The following languages/formalisms were identified: OWL (six studies, 13%), RDF (four studies, 9%), OWL-DL (one study, 2%), OWL-S (three studies, 7%), XML (three studies, 7%) and WSMO (two studies, 4%). Considering studies that adopt more than one language/formalism, there are six studies (13%) using OWL, four (9%) using XML, five (11%) using OWL-S, and one (2%) using RDF. Finally, two studies (4%) use a language proposed in the own study, and seven studies (16%) propose the use of ontologies, but do not make commitment to any specific language/formalism.

RQ7 - How service integration is addressed in the EAI initiatives?

The studies use diverse technologies for integration. With the focus on just one technology, we found eleven studies (24%) using *Web Services*, eleven studies (24%) using *Semantic Web Services*, ten (20%) using *Mediators*, three (7%) using *Workflow*, two studies (4%) using *Model-Driven Architecture*, one study (2%) using *Agent-Based Paradigm*, one study (2%) using *Middleware*, one study (2%) using *Event-Based-Paradigm*, and one study (2%) applying *Dictionary Inference Rules*. Among studies that combine technologies for service integration, two studies (4%) use *Mediator and Web Services*, one study (2%) use *SOA and Workflow*, and one study use *Mediator and Semantic Web Services*.

RQ8 - How is semantics assigned to services?

As pointed out in RQ4, most of the studies (82%) use ontologies. In the service context, ontologies are used to assign semantics to structural aspects of the services, describing the types of inputs, outputs, preconditions, and postconditions. The semantic descriptions of services are used to ease the search in the services registers architecture, where agents can search for descriptions using the same concepts of the services announced. Transformations from the types of messages to be exchanged are performed using ontologies to stablish semantic to existing data in the messages and make them compatible among the integrated services. The use of Domain Ontologies is predominant for assigning semantics to services. Semantic Web strategies and standard web technologies (OWL-S, OWL, WSMO, WSDL, RDF, RDFS, XML) are predominant among strategies to implement semantics in services. The eight (18%) studies that do not use ontologies have some common vocabulary defining involved data, except for two studies that do not focus on data description.

RQ9 - Have systematic approaches been used to conduct the EAI initiatives?

Forty-one studies (91%) do not follow a systematic approach or method to guide the semantic EAI initiative. Thus, only four studies (9%) use approaches guiding the steps to be followed in the integration.

5 Discussion

Considering the distribution of studies along the years, as shown in Fig. 2, we point out the period between 2006 and 2010. In 2006, we notice the start point in the increase number of the published studies, achieving the peak in 2008. From that, the number of published studies decreases gradually, passing through 2010 until 2017. This tendency seems to correspond, in terms of Gartner Hype Cycle, to the "Technology Trigger" phase (specially by adoption and standardization of semantic web technologies), achieving the "Peak of Inflated Expectations" until the "Trough of Disillusionment" and some level of stability.

Looking at the vehicles where the analyzed studies have been published (RQ1), 64% of these studies were published in scientific events (conferences, symposiums and workshops), whereas 36% were published in journals. Considering that journals usually require more mature works, we can say that the topic addressed in this mapping has been explored and discussed with relative degree of maturity by the research community. By the analysis of RQ3, we can see that the analyzed studies have taken place in diverse business domains, which points out that semantic EAI initiatives at service layer runs through several business domains. This indicates its applicability. On the other hand, analyzing the types of research (RQ2), only 8 studies (18%) reported evaluations in real scenarios (Evaluation Research). This indicates that, despite the (supposed) maturity degree presented by published studies, the research area lacks in reporting of real experiences.

Data obtained from RQ4, RQ5, and RQ6 reveal a predominance of the use of *Domain Ontologies* to *Data and Service description*. The use of domain ontologies to semantically describe service information is used in the analyzed publications to establish a common understanding of the service inputs, outputs, preconditions, and postconditions. The service description is then mapped to ontology concepts, which provides the common vocabulary for message exchanging among the integrated applications. As an example, in [14], a domain ontology is used to describe services inputs and outputs, creating a mapping between process and service information. OWL and XML are used as formalism to create ontologies, down-cast and up-cast transformations. In [3], in turn, domain ontology is used in mediation services to translate output information of one business activity into input information of another. The translation is made based on the semantic mapping between service parameters. All studies using *Domain Ontology* or *Service Ontology* use the ontology to *Data and Service description*. This is aligned to the necessity of data description to turn possible service description. Most of these studies use semantic web technologies (such as OWL, OWL-S, WMSO) to describe services. Also, all the studies that use ontologies to address semantics at service layer focus on structural aspects of service (services inputs and outputs). Only in [4] behavioral aspects are considered in the semantic service integration. The authors suggest mapping the applications structural aspects to a structural integration model and then looking for services and tasks (i.e., behavioral aspects) with the same semantics.

As for assigning semantics to services (RQ8), as we mentioned above, there is a predominance of assigning semantics to data that constitute the services (i.e., service structural aspects), mainly using domain ontologies for data description (inputs, outputs, preconditions, postconditions). Service ontologies (such as OWL-S) are used in some studies. OWL-S contemplates a service composition in the form of a process model composed of atomic and composite processes that have control constructs to define the interaction between client and services.

Concerning how semantic service integration has been addressed (RQ7), (*Semantic*) *Web Services* (24%), together with *Mediator* (22%) have been the most used approaches (46%). Web services, by principle, play an important role in many analyzed studies in providing a loosely coupled integration implementation. Semantic web services, in turn, are used towards filling semantic issues in web services, providing descriptions of services capabilities in a way to turn viable automatic or semi-automatic identification of services, for use in compositions. The use of Service Oriented Architecture (SOA) or the use of service register is common in studies involving (semantic) web services. They use service matching to find necessary services, usually to support business process and some choreographic or orchestration. Approaches that use a Mediator need more complex logic for semantic data conversions, service interconnection, services matching or technological compatibilizations. A common characteristic to the three cited categories is to take the business processes into account to organize the services. This is an important aspect to integrate services and there is still a gap between business process models and information system deployment [3].

Finally, just a few studies (9%) followed a systematic approach to carry out EAI (RQ9). In [18], the used approach focuses on creating associations between the conceptual models and the application logic using ontologies to create conceptual models and associate these models to the system resources. [4], in turn, uses a semantic integration approach independent of how the integration will be designed and implemented. The focus is on using ontologies to assign semantics at the conceptual level. The approach used in [1] uses an upper ontology to assign semantics to data, service and process. All these approaches have in common the use of conceptual models to assign semantics. By doing that, semantic aspects also addressed as independent of technological issues. Although a massive use of technologies is usually necessary to implement (semantic) service integration, it seems to exist a tendency towards a separation of concerns regarding conceptual and technological aspects. As such, as in Software Engineering research area, semantic EAI approaches should define semantic service integration at conceptual level and then devote to aspects such as platform, programming language and architectural design definitions.

6 Limitations of the Study

In general, researchers conducting mapping studies have to make a lot of decisions and exercise a lot of judgment. Depending on that, different sets of publications can be obtained and different conclusions can be reached [23].

Some of the challenges we experienced in this study regard to how to apply the inclusion/exclusion criteria in a consistent way, how to classify data, and how to interpret them. We carried out some actions aiming at minimizing the influence of these challenges on the results. Thus, publication selection and data extraction were initially performed by only one of the authors, which followed the procedures established in the research protocol. To reduce the subjectivity, the other three authors performed the same procedures over the previous analyzed publications. As such, each publication was analyzed by at least two researchers. Discordances and possible biases were discussed and addressed by the researchers.

The study considered six digital libraries as sources. Although this set of digital libraries represents a comprehensive source of publications, the exclusion of other sources and the fact that we did not perform snowballing may have left some valuable publications out of our analysis.

Another limitation is related to the classifications we made for categorizing data. We defined a classification schema for each research question. Some categories were based on classifications previously proposed in the literature (e.g., in RQ2 we followed the categorization defined by [20]). Others were established during data extraction, based on data provided by the analyzed studies (e.g., in RQ4 we created a categorization regarding the purpose of using ontologies). Determining the categories and how studies fit them involves a lot of judgment. For achieving a more consistent analysis, some studies classifications were discussed in meetings. Anyway, we cannot ensure that all results concerning the studies classification are fully repeatable.

7 Final Considerations

Organizations use several applications to support business processes. The execution of services of these applications supports implementing the business processes functions. Thus, to better support the business processes, applications should be integrated through the integration of their services, in a way that the integration scenario implements the supported business processes. The integration scenario consists of services, links connecting services and rules defining operations on process data or service execution order [15].

Integration at service layer can provide a loosely coupled way of application collaboration, and a semantic layer can improve service architectures like SOA for describing the services announced. Semantic issues arise in EAI integration whenever applications use different conceptualizations. In this context, ontologies can be used as an effective tool to conceptualization alignment and to cope with heterogeneity problems. At the service layer, ontologies can provide a shared understanding of data services and processes in the integration scenario and facilitate communication between the applications [4].

In this paper, we presented a mapping study that investigated semantic EAI initiatives addressing the service layer. The results of the mapping provide a panorama of research related to services integration in semantic EAI initiatives.

Considering the study results, we identified the following gaps in the investigated research topic: (i) lack of systematic approaches for guiding integration at the service layer; (ii) task ontologies have not been used to support service integration; and (iii) lack of a general conceptualization about enterprise application services. As for (i) only few EAI initiatives followed a systematic approach and systematic approaches are necessary to provide feasible methods to perform semantic EIA. With respect to (ii), we noticed a lack of concern with behavioral aspects of services. Most of the studies focus on structural aspects of service (input and output parameters) to assign semantics. However, behavioral aspects should also be taken into account. In this context, task ontologies can be useful to assign semantics to services, functionalities, activities, and their related information [5]. Concerning (iii), none of the analyzed publications provide a conceptualization about enterprise application service. Understanding what an enterprise application service is, as well as the concepts related to it is important to properly address semantic service integration. Moreover, it is necessary to understand the semantic relations among application services and business process activities [8] in order to provide integrated solution to better support the business processes.

Apart from the studies reported in [16] and in [6], which served as a starting point to our study, we did not find any other related work. There are similarities and differences between the studies performed by [16] and [6] and ours. As for similarities, the three studies investigated semantic EAI initiatives and the use of ontologies in this context. Concerning differences, we can highlight the study focus and the investigated aspects. [16] aimed to provide a panorama concerning semantic EAI in general. [6], in turn, focused on semantic EAI addressing the process layer. Our study is more interested in semantic EAI addressing the service layer. Thus, in our study, we analyzed in depth how integration initiatives have been addressing semantic integration at service layer, and how semantics has been assigned to services. Moreover, we extended the coverage of the studies by [16] and [6] until 2017.

Acknowledgment

This research is funded in part by the Brazilian Research Funding Agency CNPq (Process 407235/2017-5), FAPES (Process 69382549/2014) and CAPES (Process 23038.028816/2016-41 and Finance Code 001).

References

1. Alazeib A, Balogh A, Bauer M, Bouras A, Friesen A, Gouvas P, Mentzas G, Pace A (2007) Towards Semantically-Assisted Design of Collaborative Business Processes in EAI Scenarios. In IEEE (eds), 5th IEEE Int. Conf. on Industrial Informatics; Vienna, p. 779-784.
2. Al-Ghamdi AA, Saleem F (2014). Enterprise Application Integration as a Middleware: Modification in Data & Process Layer. In Science and Information Conf., pp. 698-701.
3. Benaben F, Boissel-Dallier N, Pingaud H, Lorre JPL (2013) Semantic issues in model-driven management of information system interoperability. Int J Comput Integrated Manuf 26:11, 1042-1053.
4. Calhau RF, Falbo RA (2010) An Ontology-Based Approach for Semantic Integration. In IEEE (eds), 14th IEEE Int. Enterprise Distributed Object Computing Conf., pp. 111-120.
5. Calhau RF, Falbo RA (2012) A Configuration Management Task Ontology for Semantic Integration. In 27th Annual ACM Symposium on Applied Computing, New York, p. 348.

6. Cerqueira LD, Nardi JC, Barcellos MP, Falbo RA (2016) Process Integration in Semantic Enterprise Application Integration: A Systematic Mapping. In Ontobras - CEUR Workshop Proceedings, pp. 95-106.
7. Erasala N, Yen DC, Rajkumar TM (2003) Enterprise Application Integration in the electronic commerce world. Computer Standards & Interfaces, 25:2, 69-82.
8. Fonseca VS, Barcellos MP, Falbo RA (2017) An ontology-based approach for integrating tools supporting the software measurement process. Science of Computer Programming, 135: 20-44.
9. Guarino N (1998) Formal Ontology and Information Systems. In IOS Press (eds), The 1st International Conference on Formal Ontology in Information Systems, Trento, pp. 6-8.
10. Guizzardi G, Lopes M, Baião F, Falbo R (2009) On the Importance of Truly Ontological Distinctions for Ontology Representation Languages: An Industrial Case Study in the Domain of Oil and Gas. In BPMDS 2009 and EMMSAD 2009, LNBIP, 29, pp. 224–236.
11. Izza S (2009) Integration of industrial information systems: from syntactic to semantic integration approaches. Enterprise Information Systems, 3:1, 1-57.
12. Izza S, Vincent L, Burlat P (2008) Exploiting semantic web services in achieving flexible application integration in the microelectronics field. Computers in Industry, 59:7, pp. 722-740.
13. Kitchenham BA, Charters S, Budgen D, Brereton P, Turner M, Linkman S, Jørgensen M, Mendes E, Visaggio G (2007) Guidelines for performing Systematic Literature Reviews in Software Engineering - EBSE Technical Report.
14. Martinek P, Tóthfalussy B, Szikora B (2008a) Execution of Semantically Enriched Business Processes. In IEEE International Technology Management Conference, Lisbon, pp. 1-8.
15. Martinek P, Tothfalussy B, Szikora B (2008b) Implementation of semantic services in Enterprise Application Integration. WSEAS TRANSACTIONS on COMPUTERS, 7:10, 1658–1668.
16. Nardi JC, Falbo RA, Almeida JPA (2013) A Panorama of the Semantic EAI Initiatives and the Adoption of Ontologies by these Initiatives. In LNBIP, 5th International IFIP Working Conference, Enschede 1:44, pp. 198-211.
17. Petersen K, Vakkalanka S, Kuzniarz L (2015) Guidelines for conducting systematic mapping studies in software engineering: An update. Information and Software Technology, 64, 1-18. DOI 10.1016/j.infsof.2015.03.007.
18. Tektonidis D, Bokma A, Oatley G, Salampasis M (2006) ONAR: An Ontologies-based Service Oriented Application Integration Framework. In: Interoperability of Enterprise Software and Applications, Springer, London.
19. Vernadat FB, (2007) Interoperable enterprise systems: Principles, concepts, and methods. Annual Reviews in Control 31:, 137-145.
20. Wieringa R, Maiden N, Mead N, Rolland C (2005) Requirements engineering paper classification and evaluation criteria: a proposal and a discussion. Requirements Engineering, 11:1, 102-107. DOI 10.1007/s00766-005-0021-6.
21. Muthaiyah S, Kerschberg L (2008) Achieving interoperability in e-government services with two modes of semantic bridging: SRS and SWRL. Journal of Theoretical and Applied Electronic Commerce Research, 3:3, 52-63.
22. Pokraev S (2009) Model-driven semantic integration of service-oriented applications. PhD Thesis, University of Twente, Enschede, The Netherlands.
23. Wohlin C, Runeson P, Höst M, Ohlsson MC, Regnell B, Wesslén A, (2012) Experimentation in Software Engineering. 1st ed. Springer Science & Business Media.

Towards code reviewer recommendation: a systematic review and mapping of the literature

Vinicius Schettino[1], Marco Antônio P. Araújo[1,2], and José Maria N. David[1], Regina Braga[1]

[1] Federal University of Juiz de Fora - Juiz de Fora, Brazil
[2] Federal Institute of Education, Science and Technology of Southeast Minas Gerais - Juiz de Fora, Brazil
vinicius.schettino@ice.ufjf.br

Abstract. (Context) Code review is a well-established practice for early detecting and reducing software defects. Researchers have shown that reviewer reputation and experience applied on the evolving component are important factors for review efficiency. In global software development, manual and human based methods for choosing a reviewer for a certain patch can be even more inefficient, due the developer's lack of knowledge about their teammate's expertise and physical contact with their peers. **(Objective)** This paper aims to present a review of Information Technology (IT) based tools and methods for code reviewer recommendation, with emphasis on application contexts, input data and empirical validations. **(Method)** To reach this goal, we conduct a systematic mapping and review compliant with existing evidence-based Software Engineering literature. **(Results)** Our results show that many authors seek real and open source datasets to validate their work, especially from GitHub. Also, previous works propose development and revision expertise and social relationships as inputs for recommendation methods, evaluating them with metrics such as Top-k and review activeness. **(Conclusion)** We classified these methods and conclude that new research should consider focusing on open/real datasets, and propose new validation approaches and method inputs especially for global software development.

Keywords: code review, code reviewer recommendation, global software development.

1 Introduction

Code reviewing is considered as an important technique for defect control and detection in software based systems [1]. The practice consists of a developer analyzing a colleague's code searching for defects, based on a pre-agreed checklist. Morales et al. [2] report lower incidence of anti-patterns through active participation and coverage of reviewed code. Kemerer and Paulk [3] show results where code reviewing is responsible for avoiding bad design practices.

The firt reports about code reviewing are from the 80s. Fagan et al. [4] describe a well-defined process, based on checklists, review meetings and auditing. These activities were designed for waterfall development approach, focusing on code quality and early bug detection.

As software development evolved, code review followed its path. The development of agile methods, concerns about software quality, and the increasing demand for higher levels maintainability are among the main factors that have led its evolution. Collaboration between authors and reviewers have become more important, and tools have emerged to support such interaction, e.g. Gerrit. This recent version of code review is called Modern Code Review (MCR) [5].

Pull-based development is a growing distributed development flavor [6], supported by tools such as GitHub and Gitlab. In this approach, the developer who wants to contribute create a pull request (PR). It contains the changeset and further explanations about its motivation and operation that will be analyzed and may be approved by a core contributor with sufficient permissions [7]. Code review plays a key role in this method, taking advantage of decentralized and branch based version control systems. The revision is conducted on the software platform, usually supported by features such as reviewer assignment, pull request search, tags and snippet-specific comments.

Previous works show that reviewer characteristics might impact code review efficiency. Baysal et al. [8] and Bosu [9] report that reviewer experience is important for code review. The number of reviewers and amount of interaction are analyzed by Kononenko et al. [10]. Thongtanunam et al. [11] show when a unsuitable reviwer is assigned, the review can last 12 days longer. Xia et al. [12] show that reviewer experience on the changed component is also significant on code review efficiency. In particular in a pull-based development context, Jiang et al. [13] show that activeness is the most important attribute sought in a suitable reviewer.

In distributed development context, manual reviewer assignment can be even harder than in collocated teams [14]. In global development there are more reviewers, submitters and different aspects such as timezone, availability, culture, experience and knowledge. It gets harder for a human to take all these factors into consideration. Since previous studies show that the choice of a reviewer who turns out to be unfit affects process efficiency, tools that support the code reviewer search and assignment are important.

In the Free/Open Source Software domain (FOSS), there is a special attention to code review. Major projects incorporate this practice as a mandatory step in order to accept contributions [15, 16].

Given the difficulty and the importance of code reviewer recommendation methods in association with the broad range of methods already proposed in several contexts, we present a systematic review [17] of the literature towards code reviewer recommendation. After reviewing existing evidence-based Software Engineering literature, we aim to present the state-of-the-art of code reviewer recommendation tools, methods and relevant features observed on the choice of potential reviewers. We seek to present how this research has grown, and who the top contributors are. We also aim to show the contexts in which this kind of technique is often used, and how these works evaluate and compare their results. These analysis may help to settle grounds on code review future recommendation approaches, evaluate the efficiency of existent tools and aid future reseachers on this field.

Previous works have attempted to gather and evaluate different methods of code reviewer recommendation, though none of them have proposed a systematic approach to find them. Furthermore, no clear classification model of the methods, nor the context where they best fit in have been presented.

Yang et al. [18] present several studies and apply a popular method for a large pull request dataset, drawing conclusions about the importance of activeness of reviewers and inactive reviewers in the process. They also provide an in-depth analysis about this pull request dataset, helping evaluate the relevance of review behaviors on recommendations. Hannebauer et al. [19] recognize the difficulty of assigning suitable reviewers and compare empirically eight algorithms with different approaches in four major FLOSS projects, finding that those based on review expertise yield better recommendations. Consentino et al. [20] conduct a broader systematic mapping of the pull-based development in GitHub, addressing code review and other development processes.

Although we praise the efforts of previous works, we find that a systematic approach is more suitable in order to bring evidence in this research field. The formalism and scientific rigor of the systematic review and mapping make the process and the results reproducible and adaptable, avoiding researcher bias and fostering evidence-based conclusions [21].

Besides this Introduction, this paper is structured as follows: Section 2 explains the sytematic review and mapping protocol. The reports for review and mapping are presented on Section 3 and 4. A clousure of this research and continuation possibilities are provided on Section 5 and 6.

2 Systematic review and mapping

The main goals of a systematic review and mapping can be condensed as "give a complete, comprehensive and valid picture of the existing evidence" [21]. Thus, it is necessary to carry out both identification, analysis and interpretation in a scientific and rigorous way [21].

A systematic approach to scientific computer science research has been proposed by Kitchenham [17], adapting systematic review guidelines from other fields, medicine in particular. A mapping study may be applied for an overview of the state-of-the-art, whereas a review focuses on a specific research question related to the outcomes of the studies [21]. Both may follow the same protocol, but differ when they might deal with inclusion/exclusion criteria and the scope. In this work, both approaches can be helpful, given the sought goals. We need both a general view of the research field and a narrow outcome/efficiency and context analysis to present the desirable objectives.

This review was conducted based on the steps suggested by Wholin et al. [21]: planning, conducting and reporting the related studies.

All evaluation steps were carried out by four different experts, in independent analysis. The research questions, inclusion/exclusion criteria and any other significant divergence were widely discussed before taking the next step.

2.1 Review and mapping planning

The planning phase includes the identification of the need for a review, the development of a review protocol and the specification of research questions [17]. The need is grounded as no recent systematic review of this field was found. As we defined our objective as "find evidence of IT based tools and methods for code reviewer recommendation, with emphasis on application contexts, input data and empirical validations", we propose a compatible goal to the systematic review and mapping. According to the Goal/Question/Metric (GQM) approach [22], we aim to "**analyze** the metrics, measures, criteria and aspects used in the code reviewer recommendation, **in order to** classify them regarding code review efficiency **from the point of view** of software team members **in relation to** their colleagues in the context of software maintenance and evolution."

Mapping questions: In order to characterize the research field, we gathered a set of questions towards code reviewer recommendation. These are the research questions of the systematic mapping:

MQ1: Who are the most active authors in the area? We identify the main authors in the field, offering a comprehensive start point to future researchers.

MQ2: Which publication vehicles are the main targets for research production in the area? The publication type and weight can provide evidence of field maturity and attention from the academic community.

MQ3: In which context code review recommendation solutions are used? (Global Software Development, Industry, Open Source) We want to understand the context that nourishes code review recommendation research, as we hypothesize that this technique is important in Global Software Development.

Review Questions: For a more specific and in-depth review, we propose the following questions to be answered in the systematic review:

RQ1: How is the code review efficiency measured? In order to propose new recommendation methods and tools, it is important to have ways to compare new results with previous works.

RQ2: What information from software repositories are used to recommend code reviewers? In order to propose new recommendation methods and tools, it is important to understand which variables were used so that newcomers can discuss and extend their applications.

PICOC: Through the PICOC approach, proposed by Petticrew and Roberts [23], the research questions in this study were described by the five elements of a researchable question:

- Population (P): software developers
- Intervention (I): code reviewer recommendation
- Comparison (C): -
- Outcomes (O): methods and tools that support code reviewer recommendation
- Context(C): code review

Inclusion/Exclusion Criteria: We submitted the results to an inclusion/exclusion criteria checklist to get a fine adjustment of the search and to evaluate the relevance of the papers found. To be considered, a paper must meet all the criteria shown below:

- IC1: The paper proposed a code reviewer recommendation method AND
- IC2: The algorithm inputs are clear AND
- IC3: The efficiency measurement approach is clear AND
- IC4: There is empirical evidence of the method efficiency AND
- IC5: The paper are written in English language AND
- IC6: The paper are reported at a peer reviewed Workshop or Conference or in a Journal.

Sources: After we defined the research questions, we chose the sources of papers to execute our search string. This process was conducted based on the following: Capacity for executing using logical expressions; capacity for full-length or specific paper topic searches; available in the researcher's institution; papers on Computer Science. Four sources met these characteristics: Scopus, IEEExplore, ScienceDirect, Compendex

Query String: Based on the research goals defined by GQM approach [22] and the chosen terms on PICOC [23], the string was generated by gathering the terms with Boolean OR/AND operators. Similar terms and synonymous where also included in order to obtain a broader spectrum of papers. Terms such as "pull-request" were added to be sure we would find papers about new developments in Modern Code Review in the context of pull-based software development. The following query string was chosen:

("software developer" AND developer) AND ("reviewer recommendation" OR "commenter recommendation") AND (method OR tool OR solution OR framework) AND ("code review" OR "pull-request" OR "pull request")

The proposed query string was reviewed by all the authors separately, as well by an external researcher in order to validate its composition and synonyms. All terms were found in related works to ensure they are well known and usual on this research field.

2.2 Review and mapping conduction

In this phase we executed the query string in each database, with slight modifications in order to comply with each engine syntax. The results were imported to Parsifal (http://parsif.al), a useful open source tool to support the systematic framework proposed by [17]. This tool was used to remove duplicated papers and classify the remaining as relevant or not to this research, based on the inclusion/exclusion criteria presented above.

Overall, 106 papers were found. Of those, 29 were duplicated and 60 were rejected based on the exclusion criteria above, during the abstract reading. The main reason of rejection was not presenting a recommendation system with efficiency empirical evidence (IC1 and IC4). The remaining 17 papers were classified for complete reading, fulfilling all the inclusion criteria.

3 Systematic mapping report

The 17 selected papers were analyzed in order to answer the mapping questions (MQ). MQ1 (Who are the most active authors in the area?) is included in order to reveal the main contributors, leading newcomers to have good starting points in this research field. Table 1 summarizes the distribution of works by author. Raula Gaikovina Kula appeared in three of the selected papers, while Jing Jiang appeared in 2 of them as well as in related works [13].

Name	Count
Raula Gaikovina Kula	3
Norihiro Yoshida, Hajimu Lida, Xin Yang, Jing Jiang, Jia-Huan He, Ken-ichi Matsumoto	2
Patanamon Thongtanunam, Chakkrit Tantithamthavorn, Mohammad Masudur Rahman, Chanchal Roy, Jason Collins, Yue Yu, Huaimin Wang, Gang Yin, Charles Ling, Vipin Balachandran, Catarina Costa, Jair Figueredo, Leonardo Murta, Anita Sarma, Motahareh Zanjani, Huzefa Kagdi, Christian Bird, Haochao Ying, Liang Chen, Jian Wu, Tingting Liang, Xin Xia, Xinyu Wang, David Lo, Xiaohu Wang, Xue-Yuan Chen	1

Table 1. Author names and number of publications

Another way to visualize how mature a research field is is to look at the main channels of research publication, such as workshops, conferences and journals. To answer MQ2 (Which publication vehicles are the main targets for research production in the area?) we found that 23% of the selected articles came from journals, and 59% of them were published at conferences. The rest (18%) were presented at workshops. Although in Computer Science the number of conferences is significantly higher compared with journals, this ratio may indicate that this is not yet a mature field, with a relevant proportion of in-progress research.

As well as the channel category, its weight is more evidence of field maturity. In table 2 we show the distribution of papers in the respective channels and their h5-indexes, found on Google Scholar[3]. This table is sorted by highest h5-index.

[3] https://scholar.google.com/citations?view_op=top_venues&hl=en

Reference	Channel	h5-index
[24][25]	ICSE - IEEE/ACM International Conference on Software Engineering	68
[26]	IEEE Transactions on Software Engineering	52
[27]	GLOBECOM - IEEE Global Communications Conference	48
[28]	SIGSOFT - ACM International Symposium on Foundations of Software Engineering	43
[29]	Journal of Intelligent Information Systems	22
[30]	Journal of Computer Science and Technology	22
[31]	IEICE Transactions on Information and Systems	17
[32]	SANER - IEEE International Conference on Software Analysis, Evolution and Reengineering	13
[33, 34]	APSEC Asia-Pacific Software Engineering Conference	12
[35]	IEEE/ACM International Workshop on Software Mining	*
[36]	International Workshop on CrowdSourcing in Software Engineering	*
[37][38][39]	ICSME - IEEE International Conference on Software Maintenance and Evolution	*
[40]	IWCSN - International Workshop on Complex Systems and Networks	*

Table 2. Papers per channel and their respective H-indexes

In order to seek answers to MQ3, we classified each paper using one or many categories, based on the context in which the study was conducted. We only took into consideration direct mentions to some terms, for example "Open Source" or "Distributed Development". Even if the study used open software repositories or distributed development tools (such as GitHub), we looked for direct mentions of this information being relevant to their conclusions.

Code review recommendation may be harder in some contexts, such as in global and open source software development. Thus, it might be that some of them need more sophisticated recommendation techniques than others. MQ3 (In which context code review recommendation solutions are used?) was formulated to provide evidence for this hypothesis. Table 3 shows the distribution we found, sorted by highest publication year. The contexts used in the categorization were found in related works and accepted papers.

Reference	Pull Based	Open Source	Distributed Development	Modern Code Review	General Development
[29]					[X]
[40]		[X]	[X]		
[27]	[X]	[X]	[X]		
[35]				[X]	
[28]			[X]		
[26]			[X]	[X]	
[36]	[X]		[X]		
[24]	[X]		[X]		
[31]		[X]			
[39]				[X]	
[30]	[X]	[X]			
[32]				[X]	
[38]	[X]		[X]		
[37]	[X]		[X]		
[33]	[X]		[X]		
[25]					[X]
[34]		[X]			

Table 3. Context related keywords

Code reviewer recommendation seems to be tightly related with distributed development and the pull-based approach, although there are some occurrences of general development and Modern Code Review. This special attention seems to be tied to the inherent challenges of global software development. Ying et al. [36] cite the greater number of reviews (through pull requests) of this method as motivation to automatic code reviewer recommendation. Yu et al. [33] say that finding the right reviewer to a PR in an open source project is a typical crowdsourcing job. Thus, it needs to solicit opinions of the community. Also in this context, reliable and rich information that helps to identify an appropriate code reviewer is often hard to find and aggregate, especially manually [24].

Almost every paper used known Open Source projects in order to evaluate their proposals, but some of them used specific data of this kind of development in order to motivate and execute code reviewer recommendation. In this context, a rapid online collaboration encourages more and more developers to join in OSS projects, while on the other hand, integrating new developers with teams is challenging and pivotal to the success of a project [40]. While the amount of contribution is high, experienced developers who are responsible for ensuring that only high quality changesets will be merged can get swamped with a large number of patches to review [34]. This scenario can delay the PR merge and discourage new contributions [30].

Open Source codebases are important to ensure a given experiment is auditable and reproducible. Thus, we suggest that new method proposals should be evaluated also in real situations, especially with already used open codebases, in order to make their contribution value clear.

4 Systematic review report

The two Review Questions (RQs) were planned in order to give a narrow perspective of how the selected works handle the recommendation and assert their efficiency. With RQ1 (How the code review efficiency is measured?) we seek to understand how past authors discovered how good their methods are, giving newcomers a entry point on how new methods may be evaluated. In Table 4, papers are categorized by their efficiency measurement methods and sorted by latest publication year.

Reference	Top-K	Precision/Recall	MRR	Activeness	Fostering	Performance
[29]		[X]				[X]
[40]	[X]	[X]	[X]			
[27]		[X]				
[35]	[X]	[X]				
[28]	[X]					
[26]	[X]					
[36]	[X]	[X]				
[24]	[X]	[X]	[X]			
[31]				[X]		
[39]	[X]	[X]				
[30]	[X]					
[32]	[X]		[X]			
[38]	[X]		[X]			
[37]	[X]	[X]				
[33]	[X]	[X]				
[25]	[X]					
[34]	[X]	[X]				

Table 4. Efficiency Methods

The most used efficiency assertion method is the Top-K ranking, with Precision and Recall analysis. Top-K is the similarity percentage between a K-sized set the algorithm recommended in comparison with a same sized standard set. In the presented cases the comparison default group consist of actual humans: by comparing the recommendation with the posteriori choice or with a manual analysis and classification of "good" and "bad" reviews. So these methods are evaluated by how close to a human recommendation they are. Precision is the percentage of relevant items (thus, among human recommendation set) out of all recommended items, and recall is the measure of how many relevant items were left out of the method recommendation.

Beside Top-K ranking, Thongtanunam et al. [32] also proposed an analysis based on the Mean Reciprocal Rank (MRR). This approach takes in consideration not only the set but also the position of the recommendations. So if the first recommendation is inside the user recommendation set, the method gets a higher MRR.

Yang et al. [31] applies a social network approach, with different evaluation methods. They measure how the recommended reviewers could affect the activeness of the code review process.

Comparisons with previous works are important to show the contribution of new approaches, and this is simpler when the same efficiency metrics are used. Hence, new researchers might want to address the main metrics presented here to evaluate new methods. However, some metrics might be more suitable in certain contexts. As shown in MQ3 response, aspects of Global Software Development make code reviewer recommendation a non-trivial task for a human, which might not have all the information needed [24]. Challenges such as culture and timezone conflicts, language and lack of personal contact also make this task harder.

Since traditional metrics such as Top-k are based on how close a set of recommendations is to a human recommendation, they might not be enough to evaluate a recommendation method in this context. Yang et al. [31] use an approach which takes into consideration how the recommended reviewer impacted the process observing the activeness of a review. Previous works also discussed the positive traits of a code review, focused on comment usefulness, changeset configuration and reviewer profile [9, 41].

Addressing RQ2 (What information from software repositories are used to recommend code reviewers?), we define categories of code reviewer recommendation methods, based on the main inputs they use and extending previous classifications [19]. The next subsections describe these categories, using some of the papers to exemplify. Table 5 summarizes the results of this classification. Four categories were identified: review expertise, development expertise, social relationships and hybrid approaches.

4.1 Review Expertise

Methods in this category recommend a reviewer based on their experience in similar changesets. The similarity can be measured by file/code or by PR text proximity, or even a blend of both. While Fejzer et al. [29] propose a reviewer

Category	Articles
Review Expertise	[29, 27, 26, 39, 32, 38]
Development Expertise	[28, 24, 25, 34]
Social Relationships	[40, 35, 31, 33, 37]
Hybrid Approaches	[36, 30]

Table 5. Method classification summary

profile and similarity function between such profiles and change proposals to be reviewed, Liao et al. [27] define a set of topics to describe the expertise of a reviewer and the expertise needed for a given review. Thongtanunam et al. [32] leverage the similarity of a previously reviewed file path to recommend an appropriate code reviewer.

4.2 Development Expertise

Some authors used expertise in development to infer that a subject might be a good reviewer. To recommend an expert to merge two branches, Costa et al. [28] analyse their past changes in the project, especially dependencies of the current changeset. Rahman et al. [24] presented CORRECT, a method that leverages cross project development expertise in order to find suitable reviewers.

4.3 Social Relationships

Another approach is to use the social relationships of past revisions and collaborations in order to find a suitable reviewer. The links are usually designed as graphs that are built with help of textual analysis looking for similarity of the given pull request and project history. Fu et al. [40] propose recommendations based on a graph mapping work status and the social relationships of developers. Xia et al. [35] use latent factor models and neighborhood methods to capture implicit relations seeking higher recommendation efficiency. Yu et al. [33, 37] extend traditional Machine Learning methods of bug triaging to reviewer recommendation, mining comment networks of pull request discussions on global software development. Yang et al. [31] employ social network analysis (SNA) techniques based on reviewer contribution and activeness. Much of the research that focuses on this kind of approach is new, leading us to believe that it is an interesting matter to be analyzed and discussed in depth.

4.4 Hybrid Approaches

These methods bring together different inputs in order to take the best of both worlds. Through a graph, Ying et al. [36] simultaneously considers developer expertise and authority to recommend. With CoreDevRec, Jiang et al. [30] propose to taking into account file paths of modified codes, relationships between contributors and core members, and activeness of core members.

In order to summarize and make the contributions of this work clear, Table 6 briefly lists responses to our Mapping and Review Questions.

Question	Answer
MQ1	Raula Gaikovina Kula.
MQ2	Mainly Conferences (58%).
MQ3	Specially in Global Software Development.
RQ1	Mainly Top-k Rank with precision and recall.
RQ2	Review and Development Expertise, Social Relationships and Hybrid Approaches

Table 6. Review and Mapping Responses Summary

5 Conclusions

Code review is a well-established practice, with effects which have been studied and supported by many authors over the years. From the traditional process that included review meetings and a rigid workflow born in the 70s, the technique has evolved to a lightweight flexible workflow that values knowledge transfer and interpersonal relationships.

Recent studies have shown the impact of reviewer adequacy on code review efficiency, leading to meaningfully discussions and early defect detection. These results motivate researchers to find new methods to recommend suitable reviewers given the context of a revision, such as changeset composition, author and technology involved and textual composition of the review request.

This paper provides evidence on IT based tools and methods for code reviewer recommendation, with emphasis on application contexts, input data and empirical validations. Through a systematic mapping and review complying with existing evidence-based Software Engineering literature, we presented the state of the art of this research field, supporting new research to fill the gaps left by previous works. Although there are some initiatives to provide empirical evidence in this research field, this is the first systematic rigorous attempt to reach this goal.

This is a growing search field, with several ongoing works. Many contexts, inputs and results have been shown, and there is still no silver bullet method to find the best reviewer for a code review process.

Many works argue that in global software development, especially in Open Source and Pull-based contexts, automatic reviewer recommendation becomes more valuable: different cultures, schedules, availability, activeness and knowledge can influence the choice, and it is hard for a human to gather all this information and select a suitable reviewer.

The analyzed papers employ different inputs, such as reviewing expertise, development expertise and social relationships on one or many projects. Historical data are compared with information of the given review, and the methods recommend a set of reviewers that might be suitable in each case.

In order to evaluate their method's efficiency, most authors evaluate how close their recommendations to a real human choice, through Top-k with precision and recall analysis. There are approaches that measure how efficient the review of a reviewer they recommended was, in order to evaluate the quality of the method. Using standard top-k analysis it is important to compare with previous works, and we encourage new research to also evaluate results with review efficiency metrics that have already been discussed in mature literature.

6 Future work

In future research, we aim to further investigate the assertions and hypothesis based on the evidence identified in this systematic mapping and review. In depth studies can be made in order to understand the impacts of good reviewers on Open Source ecosystems. Also, besides using the main metrics found to address RQ1 to evaluate new methods, we intend to explore new ways of evaluating methods for global software development, measuring how good a review done by a recommended reviewer was. This approach is still mostly under explored and may be relevant for distributed contexts. Recent studies have shown that social relationships are growing in relevance in code reviewer recommendation, so this is an aspect that we would like to investigate as well.

References

1. Boehm, B., Basili, V.R.: Software defect reduction top 10 list. Computer **34**(1) (12 2001) 135–137
2. Morales, R., McIntosh, S., Khomh, F.: Do code review practices impact design quality? a case study of the qt, vtk, and itk projects. 2015 IEEE 22nd International Conference on Software Analysis, Evolution and Reengineering (SANER) **00** (2015) 171–180
3. Kemerer, C.F., Paulk, M.C.: The impact of design and code reviews on software quality: An empirical study based on psp data. IEEE Transactions on Software Engineering **35**(4) (07 2009) 534–550
4. Fagan, M.E.: Design and code inspections to reduce errors in program development. IBM Syst. J. **15**(3) (09 1976) 182–211
5. Bacchelli, A., Bird, C.: Expectations, outcomes, and challenges of modern code review. In: Proceedings of the 2013 International Conference on Software Engineering. ICSE '13, IEEE Press (2013) 712–721
6. Gousios, G., Storey, M.A., Bacchelli, A.: Work practices and challenges in pull-based development: The contributor's perspective. In: Software Engineering (ICSE), 2016 IEEE/ACM 38th International Conference on, IEEE (2016) 285–296
7. Gousios, G., Pinzger, M., Deursen, A.v.: An exploratory study of the pull-based software development model. In: Proceedings of the 36th International Conference on Software Engineering, ACM (2014) 345–355
8. Baysal, O., Kononenko, O., Holmes, R., Godfrey, M.: The influence of non-technical factors on code review. (2013) 122–131
9. Bosu, A., Greiler, M., Bird, C.: Characteristics of useful code reviews: An empirical study at microsoft. In: Proceedings of the 12th Working Conference on Mining Software Repositories. MSR '15, Piscataway, NJ, USA, IEEE Press (2015) 146–156
10. Kononenko, O., Baysal, O., Guerrouj, L., Cao, Y., Godfrey, M.: Investigating code review quality: Do people and participation matter? (2015) 111–120
11. Thongtanunam, P., Kula, R., Cruz, A., Yoshida, N., Iida, H.: Improving code review effectiveness through reviewer recommendations. (2014) 119–122

12. Xia, X., Lo, D., Wang, X.b., Yang, X.: Who should review this change?: Putting text and file location analyses together for more accurate recommendations. In: IEEE 23rd International Conference on Software Analysis, Evolution, and Reengineering (SANER 2016). (2015) 261–270
13. Jiang, J., Yang, Y., He, J., Blanc, X., Zhang, L.: Who should comment on this pull request? analyzing attributes for more accurate commenter recommendation in pull-based development. Information and Software Technology **84** (2017) 48–62
14. Yu, Y., Wang, H., Yin, G., Wang, T.: Reviewer recommendation for pull-requests in github. Inf. Softw. Technol. **74**(C) (June 2016) 204–218
15. Asundi, J., Jayant, R.: Patch review processes in open source software development communities: A comparative case study. In: System Sciences, 2007. HICSS 2007. 40th Annual Hawaii International Conference on. (2007) 166c–166c
16. Baysal, O., Kononenko, O., Holmes, R., Godfrey, M.W.: The secret life of patches: A firefox case study. In: 2012 19th Working Conference on Reverse Engineering. (2012) 447–455
17. Kitchenham, B.: Procedures for performing systematic reviews. Keele, UK, Keele University **33**(2004) (2004) 1–26
18. Yang, C., Zhang, X., Zeng, L., Fan, Q., Yin, G., Wang, H.: An empirical study of reviewer recommendation in pull-based development model. In: Proceedings of the 9th Asia-Pacific Symposium on Internetware. Internetware'17, New York, NY, USA, ACM (2017) 14:1–14:6
19. Hannebauer, C., Patalas, M., Stünkel, S., Gruhn, V.: Automatically recommending code reviewers based on their expertise: An empirical comparison. In: Proceedings of the 31st IEEE/ACM International Conference on Automated Software Engineering. ASE 2016, New York, NY, USA, ACM (2016) 99–110
20. Cosentino, V., Izquierdo, J.L.C., Cabot, J.: A systematic mapping study of software development with github. IEEE Access **5** (2017) 7173–7192
21. Wohlin, C., Runeson, P., Höst, M., Ohlsson, M.C., Regnell, B., Wesslén, A.: Experimentation in software engineering. Springer Science & Business Media (2012)
22. Basili, V.R., Weiss, D.M.: A methodology for collecting valid software engineering data. IEEE Trans. Softw. Eng **SE-10, no. 6** (1984) 728–738
23. Petticrew, M., Roberts, H.: Systematic reviews in the social sciences: A practical guide. John Wiley and Sons (2008)
24. Rahman, M.M., Roy, C.K., Collins, J.A.: Correct: code reviewer recommendation in github based on cross-project and technology experience. In: Software Engineering Companion (ICSE-C), IEEE/ACM International Conference on, IEEE (2016) 222–231
25. Balachandran, V.: Reducing human effort and improving quality in peer code reviews using automatic static analysis and reviewer recommendation. In: Software Engineering (ICSE), 2013 35th International Conference on, IEEE (2013) 931–940
26. Zanjani, M.B., Kagdi, H., Bird, C.: Automatically recommending peer reviewers in modern code review. IEEE Transactions on Software Engineering **42**(6) (2016) 530–543
27. Liao, Z., Li, Y., He, D., Wu, J., Zhang, Y., Fan, X.: Topic-based integrator matching for pull request. GLOBECOM 2017 - 2017 IEEE Global Communications Conference (2017) 1–6
28. Costa, C., Figueiredo, J., Murta, L., Sarma, A.: Tipmerge: recommending experts for integrating changes across branches. In: Proceedings of the 2016 24th ACM SIGSOFT International Symposium on Foundations of Software Engineering, ACM (2016) 523–534

29. Fejzer, M., Przymus, P., Stencel, K.: Profile based recommendation of code reviewers. Journal of Intelligent Information Systems (Aug 2017)
30. Jiang, J., He, J.H., Chen, X.Y.: Coredevrec: Automatic core member recommendation for contribution evaluation. Journal of Computer Science and Technology **30**(5) (2015) 998–1016
31. Yang, X., Yoshida, N., Kula, R.G., Iida, H.: Peer review social network (person) in open source projects. IEICE TRANSACTIONS on Information and Systems **99**(3) (2016) 661–670
32. Thongtanunam, P., Tantithamthavorn, C., Kula, R., Yoshida, N., Iida, H., Matsumoto, K.I.: Who should review my code? a file location-based code-reviewer recommendation approach for modern code review. (2015) 141–150
33. Yu, Y., Wang, H., Yin, G., Ling, C.X.: Who should review this pull-request: Reviewer recommendation to expedite crowd collaboration. In: Software Engineering Conference (APSEC), 2014 21st Asia-Pacific. Volume 1., IEEE (2014) 335–342
34. Lee, J.B., Ihara, A., Monden, A., i. Matsumoto, K.: Patch reviewer recommendation in oss projects. In: 2013 20th Asia-Pacific Software Engineering Conference (APSEC). Volume 2. (Dec 2013) 1–6
35. Xia, Z., Sun, H., Jiang, J., Wang, X., Liu, X.: A hybrid approach to code reviewer recommendation with collaborative filtering. In: 2017 6th International Workshop on Software Mining (SoftwareMining). (Nov 2017) 24–31
36. Ying, H., Chen, L., Liang, T., Wu, J.: Earec: leveraging expertise and authority for pull-request reviewer recommendation in github. In: Proceedings of the 3rd International Workshop on CrowdSourcing in Software Engineering, ACM (2016) 29–35
37. Yu, Y., Wang, H., Yin, G., Ling, C.X.: Reviewer recommender of pull-requests in github. In: 2014 IEEE International Conference on Software Maintenance and Evolution. (Sept 2014) 609–612
38. Xia, X., Lo, D., Wang, X., Yang, X.: Who should review this change?: Putting text and file location analyses together for more accurate recommendations. In: Software Maintenance and Evolution (ICSME), 2015 IEEE International Conference on, IEEE (2015) 261–270
39. Ouni, A., Kula, R.G., Inoue, K.: Search-based peer reviewers recommendation in modern code review. In: 2016 IEEE International Conference on Software Maintenance and Evolution (ICSME). (Oct 2016) 367–377
40. Fu, C., Zhou, M., Xuan, Q., Hu, H.X.: Expert recommendation in oss projects based on knowledge embedding. (12 2017) 149–155
41. Rahman, M.M., Roy, C.K., Kula, R.G.: Predicting usefulness of code review comments using textual features and developer experience. In: Proceedings of the 14th International Conference on Mining Software Repositories. MSR '17, Piscataway, NJ, USA, IEEE Press (2017) 215–226

Towards A Proposal To Decrease Road Accidents In Ecuador: Requirements Derived From A Secondary Study

Efraín R. Fonseca C.[1], John W. Castro[2], Mary Carmen López[1], and Franklin Onofa[1]

[1]Departamento de Ciencias de la Computación, Universidad de las Fuerzas Armadas ESPE, Sangolquí, Ecuador
[2]Departamento de Ingeniería Informática y Ciencias de la Computación, Universidad de Atacama, Copiapó, Chile
erfonseca@espe.edu.ec
john.castro@uda.cl
carmen121987@hotmail.com
frank_saske@hotmail.com

Abstract. *Context:* 1.2 million people die around the world due to road traffic accidents (RTA) every year. This situation is particularly critical in Ecuador, because of the number of people died is 28 for every 100,000 inhabitants, a higher number than 18, the overall average around the world. This situation ranked Ecuador second in Latin-America RTA. There are nowadays different technological solutions to control RTA, which is not consistent with the Ecuadorian reality, possibly because of (among other causes) funds are not allocated to research in this field. *Aim:* To gather requirements to structure a current, compact, generic and low-cost technological model to reduce the road accident rate in Ecuador. *Method:* We carried out a Systematic Mapping Study (SMS) on Scopus, Springer, IEEE, ACM, and Science Direct digital databases. *Results:* The SMS process obtained 16 primary studies as of April 2018. *Conclusions:* There are many technological proposals that have covered the requirements to reduce RTA, many of which are low cost and can be combined.

Keywords: systematic mapping study, requirements, technological factors, road accidents

1 Introducción

Los accidentes de tránsito (AT) son una de las principales causas de muerte y lesiones a nivel mundial [5]. De acuerdo con el "Reporte del Estado Global Sobre la Seguridad de las Vías" de la Organización Mundial de la Salud, Ecuador ocupa el segundo lugar en mortalidad por AT en América Latina, dado que mueren 28 personas por cada 100.000 habitantes, una cantidad mayor a la media global que es de 18 [3].

De hecho, los AT son la primera causa de muerte en Ecuador, llegando incluso a ser catalogados como un problema social por el daño físico y psicológico que representa para la familia de los occisos y para los lesionados al momento de su reincorporación a la sociedad; así mismo, por las pérdidas económicas que resultan de estos eventos, que también son muy significativas [2]. Por ejemplo, del 2011 al 2018 se registraron 22 víctimas en promedio por accidentes de tránsito y se calcula una pérdida de 600 millones de dólares por año [2].

La Agencia Nacional de Tránsito de Ecuador (ANT) indica que el 50,09% de los AT se produjeron por impericia o imprudencia del conductor, el 13,2% por irrespeto a las normas de tránsito, el 12,31% por exceso de velocidad, el 9,73% por embriaguez, el 7,69% por condiciones externas sin determinar y el 6,99% por imprudencia de otros involucrados [1]. Así mismo, indican que en el primer semestre del año 2015 el número de siniestros alcanzó los 14.322, 7,44% menos que en igual periodo del 2016. De estos, los occisos más frecuentes son los peatones, motociclistas y ciclistas [1].

El avance tecnológico actual está permitiendo disminuir la accidentabilidad vial a nivel mundial, considerando cada una de las causas y circunstancias mencionadas. No obstante, en Ecuador existe muy poca investigación por escasez de fondos de inversión. Por ello, creemos que la innovación tecnológica, especialmente la de bajo costo, podría incidir positivamente en la reducción de los AT en este país [13]. Por lo tanto, llevamos a cabo un Mapeo Sistemático de Literatura (SMS de las siglas del inglés Systematic Mapping Study) con el propósito de *elicitar los requisitos, elementos y especificaciones necesarios para estructurar un modelo tecnológico actual, compacto, genérico y de bajo costo, que permita disminuir la accidentabilidad vial en Ecuador.*

Los resultados obtenidos de la elicitación permitieron estructurar un modelo híbrido de diferentes tecnologías utilizadas para reducir los niveles de accidentabilidad vial. Más específicamente, el modelo propuesto se caracteriza por tener una:

- Red de sensores inalámbricos para intercambiar mensajes entre los vehículos cercanos en la carretera.
- Repositorio público centralizado para almacenar información de la accidentabilidad vial.
- Manilla inteligente para sensar los signos vitales y el comportamiento del conductor.
- Modulo inteligente de control de accidentabilidad vial.

Estamos convencidos que la aproximación de modelo obtenida podría constituirse en la base de una implementación futura que aporte significativamente a la disminución de la accidentabilidad vial en Ecuador.

Lo que resta del artículo está organizado como sigue. En la Sección 2 se analizan trabajos relacionados con la accidentalidad vial, a modo de motivación de la investigación. La Sección 3 detalla el proceso de revisión de literatura realizado. A paso seguido, la Sección 4 presenta los resultados obtenidos tras la investigación, lo cuales dan respuesta a las preguntas de investigación. La

Sección 5 detalla el modelo obtenido tras la síntesis de resultados. Finalmente, la Sección 6 reporta una discusión final seguida de las conclusiones.

2 Trabajos Relacionados

La Comisión de Tránsito de Ecuador realiza diferentes campañas de educación vial destinadas a peatones y conductores, con el propósito de aplacar el creciente índice de accidentes de tránsito [19]. No obstante, al tratarse únicamente de campañas de concientización, no se han obtenido resultados alentadores. Es preciso el planteamiento de soluciones que den soporte a los conductores en diferentes situaciones para evitar los accidentes de tránsito.

A continuación se realiza un análisis de la tendencia de soluciones tecnológicas para prevenir los accidentes de tránsito, con el propósito de motivar la investigación sobre la base de diferentes alternativas existentes.

Penizzotto & otros [15], Seo & otros [19] y Singh [20] presentan soluciones que integran tecnologías Wireless, GPS y sensores de movimiento, con el propósito de alertar al conductor sobre la proximidad de objetos que podrían representar peligros inminentes (persona, autos, bicicletas, etc.) y prevenir así posibles colisiones.

Lenard & otros [11] proponen una aplicación que emite señales de alerta al detectar probabilidades de ocurrencia de una colisión entre un conductor y un ciclista. La aplicación incluye elementos tanto para el vehículo como para el ciclista, de tal modo que el sistema emita una señal en el parabrisas del vehículo para avisar sobre la presencia de un ciclista en cualquier lugar de las cercanías; de igual manera el ciclista es alertado para que evite ser atropellado.

La propuesta de Kumar & Toshniwal [9] determina comportamientos inusuales en los conductores, sobre la base de algoritmos, inteligencia artificial y reconocimiento facial. Los autores indican que su propuesta de fundamenta en el almacenamiento de patrones de comportamiento del conductor, a partir de los cuáles se determina un comportamiento anómalo que puede corresponder a que el conductor este experimentando una condición de salud anormal o que se esté durmiendo.

Autores como Hassinger [6], proponen la utilización de técnicas de minería de datos para identificar factores que influyen en la ocurrencia de los accidentes de tránsito. El autor indica que en ciertos lugares de las carreteras son más frecuentes los accidentes de tránsito que en otras; así mismo, indica que un análisis al respecto podría ayudar a identificar la causa de la relación frecuencia de los accidentes - lugar específico. El autor menciona que la regla de asociación es una de las técnicas más populares de minería de datos, la cual permite identificar la correlación de varios atributos de los accidentes de carretera, generando información útil que puede utilizarse para coadyuvar esfuerzos preventivos.

Thompson & otros [21] proponen un sistema para el monitoreo de avance, salida de carril, advertencias de colisión frontal y colisión peatonal, utilizando alertas sonoras y visuales, en los vehículos.

Como se puede apreciar las propuestas actuales se enfocan en el uso de tecnologías de la información y la comunicación para reducir los accidentes de tránsito, con énfasis en el vehículo, el conductor y los obstáculos que podrían representar un potencial peligro en la carretera. Esto nos ha motivado a realizar una SMS con el propósito de *elicitar los requisitos, elementos y especificaciones necesarios para estructurar un modelo tecnológico actual, compacto, genérico y de bajo costo, que permita disminuir la accidentabilidad vial en Ecuador.*

El cumplimiento del objetivo planteado en este estudio se fundamentó en la respuesta dada a las preguntas de investigación planteadas a continuación.

RQ1: ¿Qué tipos de sistemas son utilizados para el control de los accidentes de tránsito?

RQ2: ¿Cuáles son las estrategias aplicadas para el control de los accidentes de tránsito?

RQ3: ¿Bajo qué criterios se puede diseñar una plataforma tecnológica que permita controlar los accidentes de tránsito?

RQ4: ¿Cuál es la frecuencia de creación de aplicaciones para controlar los accidentes de tránsito?

3 Método de Investigación

El presente estudio consistió en una SMS basada en un protocolo riguroso que permitió analizar e interpretar estudios fiables relacionados con el objetivo de la búsqueda [7]. Como resultado se obtuvo los requisitos, elementos y especificaciones necesarios que permitieron estructurar la arquitectura de un modelo tecnológico actual, compacto, genérico y de bajo costo, que podría disminuir la accidentabilidad vial en Ecuador. Es preciso mencionar que el proceso de revisión se realizó en el mes de abril de 2018.

El protocolo aplicado fue basado (con ciertas modificaciones orientadas a la mejora) en las guías de revisión sistemática de literatura propuestas por Kitchenham et al. [8]. Las fases consideradas en esta revisión son: (1) Aproximación a la revisión, (2) planeación de la revisión, (3) selección de estudios, (4) extracción de información, y (5) síntesis de resultados. Cada una de estas fases son descritas a continuación, a excepción de las fases 4 y 5 que serán detalladas en Secciones por separado dada su magnitud y particularidad. En esta Sección se incluirá una sub Sección de amenazas a la validez inherentes a cada fase.

3.1 Aproximación a la revisión

El proceso de revisión fue contextualizado en base a la motivación, objetivo y preguntas de investigación que se detallaron en las Secciones 1 y 2. Cabe mencionar que habitualmente las preguntas de investigación tienden a expresarse en formato PICOC [16], lo que puede resultar en mayor o menor grado una complicación, dependiendo del enfoque de las preguntas de investigación. En este caso en particular expresar en formato PICOC las preguntas de investigación es completamente irrealizable. PICOC ha sido definido en el contexto de una revisión sistemática de literatura en la que típicamente se realiza la comparación de dos tratamientos versus una salida, como por ejemplo en el tratamiento de la penicilina contra placebo, para el tratamiento de una infección. En nuestro caso lo que estamos buscando es una información específica en ciertos artículos, por lo tanto plantear preguntas PICOC no parece tener mayor acierto.

3.2 Planeación de la revisión

La revisión fue planificada en base a una estrategia de búsqueda que considera: (1) Establecer los criterios de inclusión y exclusión, (2) conformar un grupo de control, y (3) estructurar la cadena de búsqueda.

Criterios de inclusión y exclusión Consideramos necesario establecer los criterios de inclusión y exclusión de estudios en este punto, ya que es preciso hacer explícitas las características de los estudios que deseamos identificar (así como las de los que no), las cuales serán utilizadas incluso para la conformación del grupo de control. Es preciso aclarar que para establecer los criterios de inclusión y exclusión, así como para lo que resta del proceso de revisión, fue necesario contar con un grupo de al menos dos investigadores para evitar sesgo al momento de la toma de decisiones; en este caso, se conformó un *grupo de 4 investigadores* (dos estudiantes de master y dos profesores doctores titulares).

Criterios de inclusión: Estudios cuyo propósito sea mejorar el control de accidentes de tránsito basados en el uso de elementos tecnológicos; Estudios enfocados en mejorar la seguridad vial controlando los accidentes de tránsito, en base a la adquisición y/o tratamiento de datos y Propuestas de modelos o marcos tecnológicos de bajo coste y de fácil implementación, enfocados en el control de accidentes de tránsito.
Criterios de exclusión: Estudios que hagan referencia únicamente a aspectos meramente tecnológicos orientados a la implementación, mas no a la mejora del control de accidentes de tránsito; Estudios cuyo propósito sea mejorar el control del tráfico de vehículos, mas no el control de accidentes de tránsito y Estudios escritos en idiomas diferentes al inglés.

Grupo de control El grupo de control (GC) consiste en un conjunto de estudios cuyas características están íntimamente relacionadas con el objetivo de la revisión y respondan estrictamente a los criterios de inclusión. El GC tiene como propósito ser la fuente de las palabras con las que se conforma la cadena de búsqueda.

La conformación del GC inicia con una revisión básica de literatura realizada por los investigadores involucrados, en donde cada uno selecciona y propone artículos de fuentes fiables. A paso seguido se realiza un grupo de discusión para validar las propuestas de los investigadores y en consenso conformar el GC. En este caso el GC se conformó con *5 estudios*.

Cadena de búsqueda La cadena de búsqueda fue estructurada a partir de una revisión detallada de los artículos del GC, la cual fue realizada por cada investigador. Con esta actividad se pretendió identificar y extraer los términos más relevantes relacionados con el objetivo de la revisión. A paso seguido, se realizó un grupo de discusión con el propósito de categorizar los términos por su relevancia y frecuencia en cada estudio y entre los estudios; de la mano de la utilización de la herramienta NVIVO que permitió identificar las veces que se repiten los términos en los estudios del GC.

Del proceso anterior se determinaron los términos más relevantes dentro de *3 categorías*: Contexto de operación, tecnología y propósito. Luego de un pilotaje iterativo de prueba - error en una base digital con los términos más relevantes de cada categoría, se seleccionó como cadena de búsqueda definitiva:

((“accident control” OR “accident”) AND (“mobile phone application” OR “technical platforms” OR “web application” OR “web platforms”) AND (“monitoring” OR “control system”)).

Esta cadena fue adaptada al formato de las diferentes bases digitales utilizadas, para iniciar el proceso de selección de estudios.

3.3 Selección de Estudios

El proceso de selección incluye la búsqueda de: (1) Estudios candidatos, (2) Estudios seleccionados, y (3) Estudios primarios.

Estudios candidatos La búsqueda de estudios candidatos (EC) tiene como punto de partida la cadena de búsqueda, la cual se adaptó en las bases digitales: IEEE, SCOPUS, ACM, Springer y Science Direct. Estas bases indexan y/o almacenan (entre otras cosas) conferencias y revistas internacionales de alto impacto, son de fácil acceso y con algunas de ellas la Universidad de las fuerzas Armadas ESPE tiene suscripción, razón por la cual fueron seleccionadas.

Como resultado de la búsqueda se obtuvieron un total de *674 estudios candidatos* distribuidos así: 10 en ACM, 137 en Science Direct, 417 en SCOPUS, 91 en Springer y 19 en IEEE.

Estudios seleccionados El proceso de identificación de estudios seleccionados (ES) se basa en la aplican de los criterios de inclusión y exclusión en los estudios candidatos a nivel de título, resumen, palabras claves e introducción.

No obstante, previo a este proceso fue necesario hacer una depuración de estudios candidatos, dado que se detectaron estudios duplicados dentro de la misma base y entre las diferentes bases digitales.

Tras la identificación de ES realizada por cada investigador, se instauró un grupo de discusión para validar la selección en base del número de coincidencias y discrepancias. En los 674 estudios candidatos se tuvo únicamente una *discrepancia del 9.05%*. Tras la discusión se llegó a un consenso y se obtuvo como resultado *61 artículos seleccionados*.

Estudios primarios El proceso de selección de estudios primarios (EP) en base a los ES consistió en la unificación de los ES, descarga de los ES y selección de EP.

Más en detalle, en primer lugar se unificaron los ES de las diferentes bases digitales. A paso seguido, se procedió a descargar los ficheros con el texto completo de los ES. Finalmente, los ES fueron analizados minuciosamente y filtrados en base a los criterios de inclusión y exclusión, obteniéndose un total de *16 estudios primarios*.

Es preciso mencionar que por falta de espacio, hemos omitido gráficos de procesos y tablas de resumen de los hallazgos, en caso de requerirse mayor detalle, se puede visitar el siguiente *enlace*.

3.4 Amenazas a la validez

Identificamos como posibles amenazas a la validez: (i) Cobertura de las RQ, (ii) sesgo hacia ciertas publicaciones, (iii) calidad de la evaluación, y (iv) desconocimiento del área. Es probable que las RQ planteadas podrían cubrir parcialmente la temática de estudio, lo que intentamos mitigar definiendo un objetivo de trabajo y planteando varias RQ en consenso, con el propósito de hacer alcanzable el objetivo. Es posible que en un SMS se tienda a encaminar el proceso hacia un grupo específico de estudios, lo cual evitamos conformando un GC de literatura y planteando en consenso una cadena de búsqueda con términos explícitos sacados del GC. Es probable que la calidad de la evaluación de los estudios no haya sido la adecuada por desconocimiento del área de investigación, lo que mitigamos incluyendo en el equipo a dos investigadores con experiencia en temas de internet de las cosas, Wireless Sensor Networks y realización de SLR.

4 Extracción de información

En esta sección damos respuesta a las preguntas de investigación, a partir del análisis de los estudios primarios identificados en la literatura.

RQ1: ¿Qué tipos de sistemas son utilizados para el control de los accidentes de tránsito?
Fueron identificadas diferentes categorías de elementos en torno a los cuales se presentan las causas de los AT. A partir de estos elementos se identificaron los requisitos de un sistema para el control y la reducción de los AT. *El factor más importante para evitar los AT es el conductor*. Además, se deben considerar *las condiciones meteorológicas, el cumplimiento de las normas de tránsito*

y por supuesto *las limitaciones propias del ser humano para reaccionar ante situaciones de riesgo*. Los sistemas estructurados en torno a estos requisitos pretenden *hacer que la conducción sea más cómoda y segura*, incluso pueden *evitar o corregir descuidos y errores que como humanos se pueden cometer*. En torno a estos requisitos genéricos abstraídos, a continuación se exponen diferentes alternativas propuestas en los estudios primarios para disminuir la accidentabilidad vehicular.

- *Detección de sueño o falta de atención al volante [15]*. Consiste en un sistema electrónico que tiene un sensor en el volante que cuenta cuántas veces por minuto el conductor realiza correcciones en la dirección. Para mantenerse en un carril, los conductores mueven o corrigen la posición del volante constantemente, para intentar ir lo más centrados posible en él. Si el sistema cuenta menos correcciones por minuto de lo que se considera normal, interpreta que el conductor puede estar distraído, cansado o incluso estar durmiéndose al volante. A paso seguido, el sistema genera alertas de esta situación al conductor (cartel en la pantalla digital del cuadro de instrumentos, una alarma sonora, o una vibración en el volante).
- *Advertencia de ángulo muerto en el espejo retrovisor [10]*. Durante la conducción no se tiene una visión completa de todo lo que sucede alrededor del coche, incluso con la ayuda de los retrovisores existe un ángulo muerto al que solo se tiene acceso si se gira la cabeza para cerciorarse de que no existe ningún en ese espacio. Este sistema informa la presencia de objetos en el ángulo muerto, mediante una señal visual sobre el espejo retrovisor, o en el marco del espejo. El sistema emplea radares, en las esquinas del paragolpes trasero orientado hacia el área que queda oculta.
- *Reconocimiento de señales de velocidad y adelantamiento [18]*. Este sistema implementa una cámara ubicada en la parte alta del parabrisas, centrada delante del espejo retrovisor, la misma que vigila los márgenes de la calzada y reconoce las señales circulares de velocidad máxima. En la pantalla digital del cuadro de instrumentos se muestra de manera permanente la velocidad límite en el tramo en el que se encuentra el conductor, y se va actualizando en tiempo real según cambien las señales.
- *Reconocimiento de objetos [9]*. Este sistema cuenta con dos cámaras de alta resolución colocadas en la parte alta del parabrisas para tener una visión clara y evitar colisiones con peatones o ciclistas. Este sistema es capaz de: distinguir entre peatones, ciclistas, coches y otros objetos; medir la distancia hasta los objetos mencionados; predecir la trayectoria de los objetos versus la que lleva el coche; determinar si existe riesgo de colisión entre los objetos y el vehículo; tomar las medidas preventivas para evitar el accidente o aminorar las posibilidades de ocurrencia. El sistema advierte al conductor e incluso puede accionar automáticamente los frenos del vehículo.
- *Sistemas anti colisión [12]*. Este estudio indica de la existencia de varios tipos de sistemas de frenado automático. Algunos reducen la velocidad excedida del vehículo hasta incluso llegar a detenerlo por completo; mientras que otros, informan al conductor para que este realice una acción. Adicional-

mente, existen propuestas de sistemas de anticipación de curvas, los cuales en combinación con el GPS del vehículo, reconocen cuándo éste está llegando a una curva, la dificultad de la misma y estiman la velocidad óptima para tomar la curva con seguridad. Si la velocidad está fuera de los parámetros de seguridad, los frenos en conjunto con el diferencial del vehículo actúan automáticamente para reducir la velocidad.

- *Sistemas de comunicación entre coches para aviso y alerta [14].* Consiste en un sistema de comunicación local inalámbrica, con un alcance de unos 500 o 600 metros, de modo que sea posible transmitir mensajes entre los vehículos, por proximidad, e ir retransmitiendo el mensaje unos a otros. El conductor visualiza el mensaje de alerta en la pantalla digital del cuadro o de la consola central, el cual le advierte de que hay problemas unos metros más adelante, para que aminore la marcha y pueda evitar cualquier peligro; por ejemplo, chocar por alcance a un vehículo que está detenido. El sistema se interconecta con otros sistemas de seguridad que estén alertas, y actúen de manera automática, antes incluso de que el conductor asimile el mensaje de alerta y reaccione.
- *Minería de datos para caracterizar geográficamente los accidentes [22].* La minería de datos es una técnica de análisis de datos que emplea procedimientos estadísticos. Con la minería de datos se realiza una caracterización geográfica de los accidentes de tránsito mediante el análisis de conglomerados (k-medias) y reglas de asociación (correlación). Esta caracterización busca identificar patrones recurrentes de accidentabilidad en zonas geográficas específicas, con el objetivo de que la autoridad u organismo competente adopte medidas preventivas enfocadas a la particularidad de los patrones de accidentabilidad identificados en cada área geográfica.

Los sistemas descritos utilizan diferentes tipos de hardware y software para: (i) Capturar las señales procedentes de los sensores, (ii) filtrar las señales, (iii) procesar cada una de ellas, y (iv) analizar los resultados de forma conjunta para detectar los primeros síntomas de colisión. Los costos asociados con la implementación de los diferentes componentes no se han logrado establecer, porque no han sido descritos en los estudios primarios identificados; no obstante, en función del conocimiento de los investigadores se puede indicar que las soluciones que incluyen sensores y localización geográfica son consideradas de costo moderado.

RQ2: ¿Cuáles son las estrategias aplicadas para el control de los accidentes de tránsito?

Identificamos 4 estrategias para el control de los AT. En primer lugar, se plantean *planes integrales de movilidad*, basados en estudios de diagnóstico sobre los problemas predominantes en cada ciudad [17]. En segundo lugar, se propone incrementar *la educación vial* en todos los niveles de formación dando a conocer todas las tecnologías disponibles que pueden ser usadas para disminuir los AT [17]. En tercer lugar, responder a la demanda creciente de movilidad con una amplia y eficiente *red de transporte equipada con diferentes tecnologías*, como el uso de

GPS, cámaras de seguridad, etc. [17]. Finalmente, realizar un *monitoreo permanente de la siniestralidad vial*, para desarrollar *políticas que tiendan a mitigarla o evitarla.* Este monitoreo también puede fortalecerse a partir de la instalación de cámaras de registro en los puntos más conflictivos de la ciudad y analizando los datos de las estadísticas de accidentalidad vial [17].

RQ3: ¿Bajo qué criterios se puede diseñar una plataforma tecnológica que permita controlar los accidentes de tránsito?
Identificamos que el diseño de un proceso tecnológico que permita reducir los accidentes de tránsito debe contemplar tecnología en 3 ámbitos. El primero, es la tecnología de hardware que permita la recolección y monitoreo de datos (como *Wireless Sensor Network*, Cámaras, GPS). El segundo, corresponde a la tecnología empleada en el diseño y construcción de máquinas (robots) que desarrolle actividades pre-configuradas. Finalmente, tecnologías de la información y comunicación para capturar, procesar, almacenar, analizar y comunicar la información recolectada para la adecuada toma de decisiones.

RQ4: ¿Cuál es la frecuencia de creación de aplicaciones para controlar los accidentes de tránsito?
La Figura 1 presenta una visión sintética de los estudios primarios identificados.

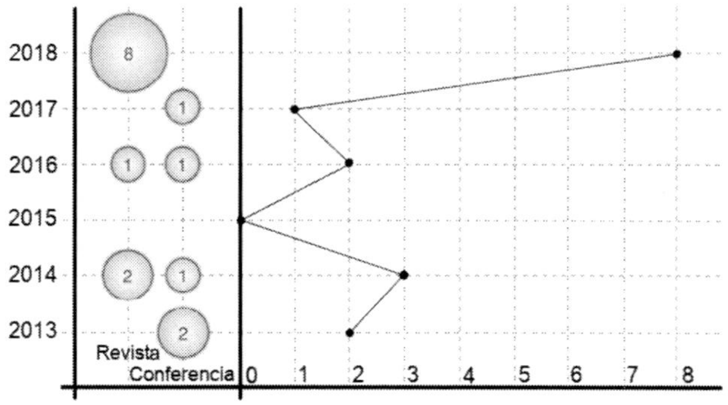

Fig. 1: Mapeo con la distribución de estudios primarios por tipo y año de publicación

En esta figura, los resultados han sido divididos en dos partes. La primera (lado izquierdo), consiste en un gráfico de dispersión XY con burbujas en las intersecciones de las categorías tipo-año de publicación. Los tipos de publicación son conferencias y revistas. El tamaño de cada burbuja está determinado por el número de estudios primarios que se clasificaron como pertenecientes a cada categoría. La segunda (lado derecho), presenta el número de estudios primarios por año de publicación. En los estudios primarios encontramos trabajos que principalmente reportan el uso de aplicaciones y métodos para mejorar la prevención de accidentes de tránsito. Estos trabajos han sido publicados a partir del 2013 y han tenido un incremento notable en el último año.

5 Síntesis de Resultados

Los estudios primarios destacaron al conductor como el factor más importante a considerar al momento de proponer soluciones para la accidentabilidad vial. En este contexto los estudios primarios indican que *las causan más comunes de los accidentes son el sueño, la distracción, el cansancio, el ángulo muerto de la visión y la impericia al volante.* Para contrarrestar estas causas y evitar accidentes de tránsito se han propuesto varios mecanismos tecnológicos basados principalmente en sensores inalámbricos, GPS, cámaras y radares; a través de los cuales, *se alertan a los conductores con pantallazos, sonidos, vibración e incluso frenado automático.*

Los estudios primarios también mencionan *otros causales de la accidentabilidad vial que tienen que ver con la vía y con el vehículo, tales como objetos que están en la vía, obscuridad, eventos de la carretera y desperfectos del vehículo.* Para abordar estas causas también se han propuesto *mecanismos tecnológicos basados principalmente en cámaras de reconocimiento, GPS y redes de comunicación inalámbrica.* Sobre la base de estos elementos tecnológicos se *detectan objetos en las vías como ciclistas, vehículos estacionados, dificultad de las curvas.* Las soluciones implementadas *alertan al conductor a través del panel, frenado automático, recomendación de velocidad para tomar las curvas, mensajería entre vehículos sobre eventos de la carretera.*

A modo de síntesis se propone el modelo indicado en la Figura 2, al cual fue estructurado en torno a los requerimientos identificados referentes al conductor, a la vía y al vehículo.

El principio fundamental del modelo propuesto es el bajo costo, para cumplir con esto se deberían seleccionar preferentemente elementos de hardware libre.

La propuesta contempla una red inalámbrica de sensores (WSN de las siglas del inglés Wireless Sensors Network) que se establece temporalmente entre los vehículos que estén a una distancia mínima. Una vez establecida la red, se intercambia información de algún evento que suceda en la vía e incluso en el vehículo. El vehículo que divulga el evento, lo registra en Internet en un repositorio público de información y también en la WSN, creando una información en cadena.

La solución integra dos módulos: (1) manilla para la muñeca del conductor, y (2) Modulo de Control de Accidentabilidad Vial (MCAV) que se conecta al vehículo. La manilla incluye un conjunto de sensores para monitorear los signos vitales del conductor y el patrón de movimiento del volante. Estas señales pasan al Micro Computador (MC) de para ser filtradas, procesadas y pasadas al MCAV para su procesamiento y detección de síntomas comparando con patrones del repositorio público. Los resultados de la comparación activan alertas para el conductor.

El MCAV por su parte detecta la severidad de las curvas por medio de GPS y recomienda al conductor la velocidad adecuada para cada curva. Por otra parte

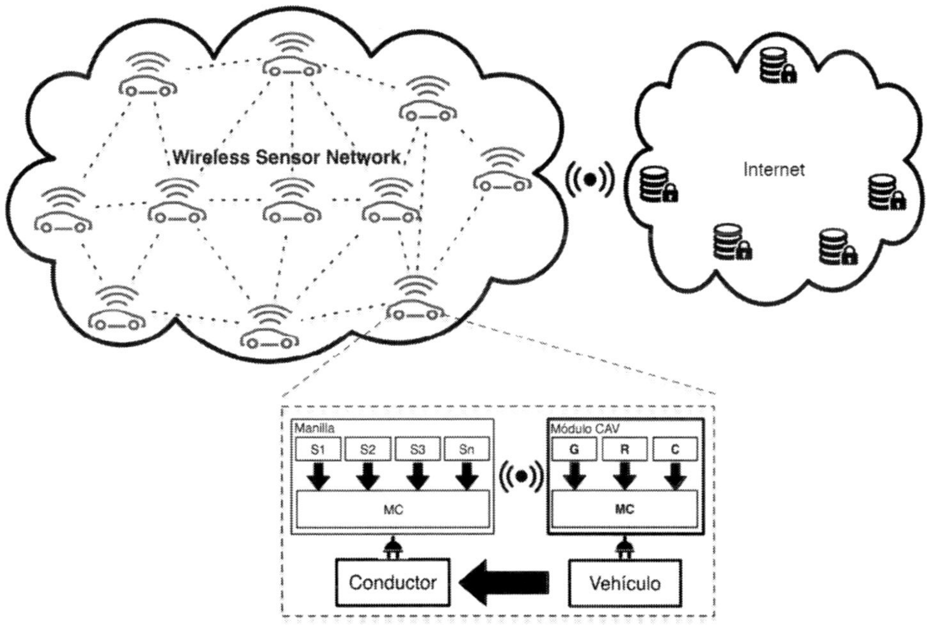

Fig. 2: Modelo Para Mitigar Accidentes de Tránsito en Ecuador

se incluye un radar que da aviso al conductor sobre objetos que podrían estar en el ángulo muerto de su visión. La cámara del MCAV sirve para, en conjunto con la manilla del conductor, monitorear el ritmo de movimientos del volante y detectar patrones inadecuados; o en su defecto puede interactuar con el radar para la detección de objetos en la carretera.

6 Discusión, Conclusiones y Trabajos Futuros

Este trabajo describe un SMS realizado para identificar y sintetizar los requerimientos de las propuestas más recientes y representativas que se están implementando a nivel mundial, para disminuir los AT. Como resultado se obtuvieron 16 estudios primarios publicados en conferencias y revistas de alto impacto. El uso de aplicaciones tecnológicas para la reducción de accidentes de tránsito no posee hasta al momento una solución única, es decir no existe tecnología alguna que logre abarcar todas las causas de los AT [22].

En los estudios primarios se identificó diferentes tipos de tecnología utilizada y similitud en la aplicación de sistemas, equipos, procesos y desarrollo tecnológico. Otros estudios, destacan el uso de nueva tecnología aún en desarrollo, así como también el análisis y prevención de AT mediante la aplicación de técnicas de gestión de datos. Además, se evidenció la existencia de diferentes aplicaciones tecnológicas, estudios de trayectorias, y análisis de patrones de comportamiento que pretenden predecir y evitar que ocurran AT, mediante la emisión de alertas hacia el conductor.

Considerando que los países que usaron tecnología han logrado reducir los niveles de siniestralidad, como trabajo futuro se propone: (i) El desarrollo de un sistema que emita advertencias al conductor, (ii) creación de un *Data Warehouse* y (iii) la implantación de un centro de vigilancia tecnológica. El objetivo del sistema sería evitar que un conductor cometa imprudencias frente al volante sin darse cuenta. Si recibe un aviso (por ejemplo, un breve movimiento en el asiento del conductor) debería parar, tomar algo que le despeje y despierte, o mejor todavía descansar. Si a pesar de las advertencias del sistema, el conductor no se detiene e insiste en seguir conduciendo, de nada habrá servido la tecnología; por lo tanto, también es necesario educar a los conductores. No obstante, debido a la magnitud de este problema, se prevé también la posibilidad de construir un almacén de datos que aporte las estadísticas de accidentabilidad vial, por ejemplo, un *Data Warehouse* que permita el análisis de los datos e identificación de patrones de siniestralidad para la toma de decisiones.

En vista de que el desarrollo tecnológico avanza cada día brindando nuevas posibilidades de prevención de accidentes de tránsito, es importante contemplar la implantación de un centro de vigilancia tecnológica enfocado en la investigación sobre la aplicación de tecnología reciente para mejorar los índices de accidentabilidad vial. Dicho centro, debería ser una iniciativa conjunta entre la academia, la industria automotriz y el estado. Es importante mencionar que el uso de la tecnología por sí sola no es la solución definitiva a la disminución de la siniestralidad vial de las naciones; sino tambien, es una herramienta adicional dentro del conjunto de estrategias adoptadas por la sociedad y el estado para mejorar los índices de accidentes de tránsito [4].

Agradecimientos

Esta investigación fue posible gracias al financiamiento que da la *Corporación Ecuatoriana para el Desarrollo de la Investigación y la Academia (CEDIA)* al Grupo de Trabajo: "Internet de las Cosas y Ciudades Inteligentes".

Referencias

1. Autores, V.: Ecuador es el segundo país en muertes por accidentes de tránsito. https://lahora.com.ec/noticia/1101523310/ecuador-segundo-pac3ads-en-muertes-por-accidentes (Junio 2013)
2. Autores, V.: Policía busca soluciones a la problemática de los accidentes de tránsito. www.policiaecuador.gob.ec/policia-buscar-soluciones-a-la-problematica-de-los-accidentes-de-transito/ (Noviembre 2014)
3. Autores, V.: Informe sobre la situación mundial de la seguridad vial. Tech. Rep. WHO/NMH/NVI/15.6, Organización Mundial de la Salud (2015)
4. Blömacher, K., Nöcker, G., Huff, M.: The role of system description for conditionally automated vehicles. Transportation Research Part F: Traffic Psychology and Behaviour 54, 159 – 170 (2018)

5. Ernstberger, A., Joeris, A., Daigl, M., Kiss, M., Angerpointner, K., Nerlich, M., Schmucker, U.: Decrease of morbidity in road traffic accidents in a high income country - an analysis of 24,405 accidents in a 21 year period. IJ 46, 135–143 (2015)
6. Hassinger, M.: Aplicación de Técnicas de Minería de Datos en Accidentes de Tránsito. Master's thesis, Universidad Politécnica de Valencia (2015)
7. Kitchenham, B., Charters, S.: Tech. Rep. EBSE 2007-001, Keele University and Durham University Joint Report (2007)
8. Kitchenham, B.A., Budgen, D., Brereton, P.: Evidence-Based Software Engineering and Systematic Reviews. Taylor & Francis Group (2015)
9. Kumar, S., Toshniwal, D.: A data mining approach to characterize road accident locations. JMT 24(1), 62–72 (Mar 2016)
10. Lee, M., Sunwoo, M., Jo, K.: Collision risk assessment of occluded vehicle based on the motion predictions using the precise road map. Robotics and Autonomous Systems 106, 179 – 191 (2018)
11. Lenard, J., Welsh, R., Danton, R.: Time-to-collision analysis of pedestrian and pedal-cycle accidents for the development of autonomous emergency braking systems. Accident Analysis & Prevention 115, 128 – 136 (2018)
12. Lower, M., Magott, J., Skorupski, J.: A system-theoretic accident model and process with human factors analysis and classification system taxonomy. Safety Science 110, 393 – 410 (2018)
13. Montalvo, K.: Efectos de la política seccional sobre la congestión vehicular del Distrito Metropolitano de Quito durante el período 1985-2008: un análisis de la inversión municipal y el costo de la congestión. Master's thesis, Pontificia Universidad Católica del Ecuador (2009)
14. Nelli, L., Langbein, J., Watson, P., Putman, R.: Mapping risk: Quantifying and predicting the risk of deer-vehicle collisions on major roads in england. Mammalian Biology 91, 71 – 78 (2018)
15. Penizzotto, F., Vicente, A., Slawiñski, E.: Method to estimate human inattention in teleoperation of mobile robots. Journal of Control Engineering and Applied Informatics 16(3), 94 – 105 (2014)
16. Petticrew, M., Roberts, H.: Systematic Reviews in the Social Sciences: A Practical Guide. Wiley-Blackwell (2008)
17. Rea, R.V., Johnson, C.J., Aitken, D.A., Child, K.N., Hesse, G.: Dash cam videos on youtube offer insights into factors related to moose-vehicle collisions. Accident Analysis & Prevention 118, 207 – 213 (2018)
18. Rodríguez, M.D., Roa, R.R., Ibarra, J.E., Curlango, C.M.: In-car ambient displays for safety driving gamification. In: Proceedings of the 5th Mexican Conference on HCI. pp. 26:26–26:29. MexIHC'14, ACM, New York, NY, USA (2014)
19. Seo, H.S., Lee, C.J., Kim, H.U., Noh, D.G., Lee, S.S.: A left turn assist application using wireless vehicle-to-vehicle communications at unsignalized intersections. In: Proceedings of International Conference on Advances in MC & M. pp. 374:374–374:377. MoMM '13, ACM, New York, NY, USA (2013)
20. Singh, P., Juneja, N., Kapoor, S.: Using mobile phone sensors to detect driving behavior. In: Proceedings of the 3rd ACM Symposium on Computing for Development. pp. 53:1–53:2. ACM DEV '13, ACM, New York, NY, USA (2013)
21. Thompson, J.P., Mackenzie, J.R., Dutschke, J.K., Baldock, M.R., Raftery, S.J., Wall, J.: A trial of retrofitted advisory collision avoidance technology in government fleet vehicles. Accident Analysis & Prevention 115, 34 – 40 (2018)
22. Visintin, C., Golding, N., van der Ree, R., McCarthy, M.A.: Managing the timing and speed of vehicles reduces wildlife-transport collision risk. Transportation Research Part D: Transport and Environment 59, 86 – 95 (2018)

Sobre la Viabilidad de un Componente para Especificar Requisitos No Funcionales: Un Estudio de Síntesis Estructurada

Sandra L. Buitrón[1][0000-0001-6127-1849], Cecilia Apa[2][0000-0003-1588-709X], Francisco J.Pino[1][0000-0003-0668-4485] and Guilherme Horta Travassos[3][0000-0002-4258-0424]

[1] Grupo IDIS, Universidad del Cauca, Popayán, Colombia

[2] Universidad de la República, Montevideo, Uruguay

[3] PESC/COPPE/UFRJ, Rio de Janeiro, Brasil

{sandrabr@unicauca.edu.co, ceapa@fing.edu.uy, fjpino@unicauca.edu.co, ght@cos.ufrj.br}

Abstract. Contexto: La elicitación de los requisitos no funcionales (RNF) influencia la calidad de los productos de software. Sin embargo, no se encuentra evidencia de propuestas que definan cómo elicitarlos utilizando aspectos específicos de gestión de conocimiento, logrando una participación activa de los stakeholders. Como solución a este problema, en el 2016 propusimos el Framework MERliNN para apoyar la elicitación de RNF, el cual cuenta con MERliNN-CE, un componente para la especificación de RNF. Objetivo: Fortalecer los resultados obtenidos a partir de la realización de los estudios primarios de MERliNN-CE en organizaciones de la industria software en Colombia a través de un estudio secundario de síntesis de evidencia. Método: Se utiliza el método SSM (*Structured Synthesis Method*) para representar y agregar los resultados obtenidos de los estudios primarios de MERliNN-CE. Resultados: Se identifican 3 aspectos contextuales y 10 relaciones causa-efecto en los estudios primarios. Se identifican aspectos inexplorados o desconocidos de los estudios, así como, niveles bajos de confianza de los resultados y amenazas a la validez durante la agregación realizada. Por último, se establece una línea base de conocimiento sobre la aplicabilidad de MERliNN-CE. Conclusiones: El componente presuntamente es viable para la especificación de RNF en proyectos de desarrollo de software web que estén en etapas iniciales de construcción y que no cuenten con un proceso de elicitación de RNF. Entretanto, los niveles bajos de confianza obtenidos indican la necesidad de organizar una familia de estudios para aumentar la confianza en los resultados y evaluar la evolución de MERliNN-CE.

Keywords: Ingeniería de Software, Ingeniería de Software Experimental, Representación de Evidencia, Agregación de Evidencia, Síntesis Estructurada

1 Introducción

En la etapa de elicitación de requisitos se deben considerar dos elementos principales: los requisitos funcionales y los no funcionales [1]. Estos dos tipos de requisitos permiten entender las necesidades de los interesados del proyecto [2], con el objetivo de que en las etapas siguientes del ciclo de desarrollo se puedan plasmar de manera adecuada y completa las alternativas de solución mediante un producto software [3].

Considerando: (i) que un RNF se define como "un atributo de" o "una restricción del sistema" [4], (ii) la importancia que tienen los RNF para el desarrollo de un producto software [5], (iii) que no existe un consenso adecuado con respecto a las técnicas de obtención de estos requisitos [6], y (iv) que uno de los factores que contribuyen al éxito de la Elicitación de Requisitos No funcionales (ERNF) es la participación de los usuarios [7], en el año 2016 se propuso el Marco de trabajo para la ERNF basado en gestión de conocimiento [8], denominado Framework MERliNN. Este *Framework* cuenta actualmente con tres elementos desarrollados: las dimensiones de contexto, un marco conceptual, un método para la ERNF y un componente en desarrollo que busca abordar a futuro la representación de estos requisitos. El método para la ERNF incluye, entre otros, un instrumento denominado MERliNN-CE para la especificación de RNF.

Con el objetivo de realizar una validación preliminar de MERliNN-CE se llevaron a cabo dos estudios primarios en algunas empresas Colombianas desarrolladoras de software. A partir de estos estudios y con el objetivo de fortalecer la estrategia de investigación, se hace necesario realizar un análisis integral de estos resultados preliminares, con el fin de poder determinar la viabilidad de este componente. En ese sentido, en este artículo se presentan los resultados de una síntesis de evidencia de estos estudios primarios sobre MERliNN-CE utilizando el método SSM [9].

El resto del documento se estructura de la siguiente manera: en la sección 2 se presenta de forma general el Framework MERliNN, estudios relacionados con la ERNF y el conjunto de estudios primarios de MERliNN-CE. La sección 3 detalla el método SSM en términos de su aplicación sobre los estudios de MERliNN-CE. La sección 4 reporta las amenazas a la validez del estudio. La sección 5 muestra la discusión de los resultados de la síntesis estructurada y finalmente en la sección 6 se presenta las conclusiones.

2 Contexto

2.1 El Framework MERliNN

El Framework MERliNN nace de un proceso de investigación que busca aportar con una alternativa de solución al problema de la ausencia de mecanismos concretos para realizar el proceso de ERNF en proyectos de desarrollo software [10], dado que estos requisitos son omitidos debido a razones como su desconocimiento y dificultad para identificarlos [11] [12] [13] [14] [15]. El Framework MERliNN fundamenta su construcción en la Gestión del Conocimiento (GC) dado que ésta ha sido reconocida como disciplina esencial para la industria del software [16] [17] [18] [19].

El Framework MERliNN se presenta de manera detallada en [20] junto a sus tres elementos ya construidos: dimensiones, marco conceptual y método de ERNF. El método contiene el componente MERliNN-CE para la especificación de RNF (objeto de este estudio) y contará a futuro con un nuevo componente MERliNN-REP que busca representar los RNF durante la ERNF para visibilizarlos en los proyectos software.

2.2 El Componente MERliNN-CE

Para definir la estructura del componente para la ERNF (MERliNN-CE), se realizó un mapeo sistemático [21], para un periodo entre 2005-2014, frente a cómo era abordado el conocimiento acerca de los RNF en la elicitación de requisitos (ER) y los fundamentos usados en las propuestas. En la Tabla 1 se presenta una síntesis de estos resultados:

Tabla 1. Propuestas frente a elicitación de requisitos no funcionales

Cómo se aborda el conocimiento acerca de los RNF	Fundamentación
Niveles de conocimiento, que se combina en intercambia en un contexto. [22]	Intercambio de conocimiento.
Reutilización de RNF definidos aumentan las alternativas de requisitos a implementar. [23]	Ontología y reutilización del conocimiento.
Dimensiones de calidad que se relacionan para afinar el conocimiento. [24]	Jerarquía y capas relacionadas.
Enfoques del proceso de ERNF desde las dimensiones: contexto, proceso y aplicación. [25]	Análisis multidimensional de enfoques existentes.
Dominio del conocimiento permite inferir requerimientos que no son explícitos. [26]	Entendimiento de las necesidades de los interesados.
Cualidades externas e internas del software. ¿Quién decide cuáles y qué tipos de RNF importan? [27]	Perspectiva de los arquitectos y cualidades del software.
Conocimiento intercambiado al momento de la obtención de los requisitos. [28]	Facilitadores de flujos de conocimiento y artefactos.
Definición de RNF calidad. [29]	Categorías - Norma ISO 9126.
Conocimiento de los stakeholders para iniciar el proceso de ER. [30]	Trazabilidad de requisitos tempranos y modelado visual.
Conocimiento sobre los RNF existente en el documento de especificación. [31]	Representación bajo metodología UML.
Conocimiento transferido entre estados. [32]	Perspectiva de la colaboración.

Los resultados del mapeo sistemático evidenciaron aspectos los siguientes aspectos: (i) que el componente pudiera ser utilizado en colaboración y, (ii) que se pudieran tener en cuenta los procesos de del proceso de negocio, (ii) procesos de negocio y, (iii) atributos de calidad. Un ejemplo del componente MERliNN-CE diligenciado se muestra en la Tabla 2.

Tabla 2. Componente MERliNN-CE diligenciado

Número de proceso		**1**		**Detalle de característica de calidad**	
Interfaz (1)	**Entradas**	**Salidas**	**Requisitos Legales**	***Seguridad (S)***	***Compatibilidad (C)***
Manual ***Semi automática*** ***Automático***	Información general del paciente (nombre, apellidos, edad)	Información cargada en el formulario de consultas	1751 de 2015, art 8, sobre integralidad de la tecnología en el servicio de salud	Los datos deben ser fieles y pertenecer inequívocamente a cada paciente	El intercambio de información no es permanente

2.3 Estudios Previos para Evaluar la Viabilidad de MERliNN-CE

Una *primera evaluación* de MERliNN-CE se realizó a través de un estudio de caso (**E_CE**) [20], a partir del cual se obtienen resultados positivos acerca de su viabilidad en términos de idoneidad y adaptabilidad para el apoyo a procesos de ERNF. Este estudio fue llevado a cabo durante mes y medio, en una organización desarrolladora de software a la medida, en Colombia, con 3 años de trayectoria. Se seleccionaron tres proyectos con un total de 5 participantes (gerente de la organización y analistas de requisitos) y los resultados se registraron a través de una encuesta al final del estudio. Algunos de los comentarios obtenidos fueron: (i) el conocimiento manejado es fácil de entender, (ii) el uso del componente requiere mayor conocimiento de RNF, y (iii) la metodología implementada en el componente permite un buen uso del mismo.

Posteriormente, se ejecutó una *segunda evaluación* de MERliNN-CE, a través de un estudio no sistemático basado en lecciones aprendidas (**E_NS**) [33], utilizándolo en 9 proyectos reales durante 3 meses [34] para 4 organizaciones Colombianas interesadas, dedicadas al desarrollo software a la medida. Los proyectos se encontraban en proceso de levantamiento de requisitos, participaron activamente un total de 21 analistas de requisitos con conocimientos básicos de RNF y los gerentes de las organizaciones. Como resultado se obtuvo un consolidado de lecciones aprendidas (LA).

Estos dos estudios primarios han sido analizados individualmente y para lograr una vista unificada frente a la viabilidad de MERliNN-CE, se decide realizar un estudio secundario que refuerce los resultados ya obtenidos, con el fin de observar oportunidades de investigación para las futuras evaluaciones.

3 Agregación de Evidencia

La agregación o síntesis de evidencia puede definirse como cualquier método o procedimiento que sea utilizado para crear generalizaciones o responder a preguntas de investigación científicas a través de la integración e interpretación de resultados de investigación [35]. La síntesis o agregación de evidencia es una parte fundamental de los estudios secundarios para interpretar de forma agregada la evidencia obtenida a partir de estudios primarios. De acuerdo con [36], los métodos de agregación de evidencia pueden clasificarse en métodos integrativos e interpretativos. Los métodos integrativos buscan interpretar lo que un conjunto de evidencias relacionadas, respecto del mismo fenómeno, nos enseña como un todo, dando una descripción cualitativa o un indicador cuantitativo (p.e. tamaño y efecto de una relación causa efecto).

Los métodos interpretativos tienen como objetivo la descripción o desarrollo de los conceptos que forman parte del fenómeno, organizando el marco teórico de conocimiento a través de un modelo, taxonomía o similar. En [37] se pueden encontrar los diferentes métodos de síntesis existentes en la literatura técnica clasificados según si son interpretativos, integrativos y si poseen representaciones gráficas. De los diferentes métodos de agregación de evidencia disponibles se decidió utilizar el método SSM ya que permite la agregación de evidencia cualitativa y cuantitativa a través de modelos esquemáticos, ha sido utilizado en múltiples síntesis de evidencia con resultados exitosos [38] [39] [9] y además dispone de un soporte computacional para su uso [40]. A su vez, provee un interesante balance de síntesis integrativa e interpretativa [41].

SSM propone la siguiente secuencia de pasos para llevar a cabo la síntesis de resultados: (1) *Identificación y selección de estudios primarios.* Se seleccionan los estudios primarios de una forma sistemática, de acuerdo a la teoría pre-seleccionada y a los objetivos y preguntas de investigación. Posteriormente se realiza una evaluación de calidad de dichos estudios, estimando la confianza de la evidencia presentada; (2) *Análisis y representación de la evidencia.* Para cada estudio seleccionado se modela la teoría subyacente, definiendo los constructos importantes, proposiciones y valores de las proposiciones; y (3) *Consolidación y síntesis de la evidencia.* Se agrega la evidencia extraída de los estudios primarios, basándose en los modelos de evidencia construidos en el paso anterior. Para esto último, es necesario definir la compatibilidad de las estructuras teóricas, lo cual permite la agregación de evidencia.

Los elementos que componen SSM son presentados en la siguiente sección de forma intercalada con la descripción de su aplicación sobre los estudios primarios de MERliNN-CE. Al finalizar se obtiene la explicación del método y su aplicación.

3.1 Síntesis y Agregación de Resultados de MERliNN-CE

1. Identificación y Selección de Estudios Primarios. Los estudios primarios seleccionados para la síntesis fueron los estudios E_CE y E_NS, presentados en la sección 2.3, ya que: observan el mismo objeto de estudio, comparten la misma teoría y cuentan con resultados cualitativos suficientes para cubrir los pasos del método SSM. Estos conforman la evidencia empírica reportada hasta el momento del uso de MERliNN-CE.

2. Análisis y Representación de la Evidencia. En este paso se extrae la información de los estudios primarios seleccionados para representar y modelar la evidencia. Para esto, SSM se basa en [42] que sugiere 4 elementos principales para el modelado de las teorías en Ingeniería de Software (IS): **constructos** (elementos básicos), **proposiciones** (cómo los constructos se relacionan), **explicaciones** (por qué las proposiciones fueron especificadas) y **alcance** (cuál es el universo del discurso aplicable a la teoría). Dada la similitud de los estudios E_CE y E_NS, los conceptos identificados y su modelado es equivalente. En la Tabla 3 se presentan los elementos principales (constructos) que componen el modelo de la evidencia para los dos estudios.

Tabla 3. Elementos que componen el modelo de la evidencia de los estudios E_CE y E_NS

Constructo		Descripción
C1	MERliNN-CE	Instrumento de especificación de RNF (Tecnología)
C2	Capacity	Percepción de la capacidad de uso de MERliNN-CE por parte del analista de sistema y del gerente de proyecto
C3	Convenience	Percepción de la conveniencia de uso de MERliNN-CE por parte del analista de sistema y del gerente de proyecto
C4	Flexibility	Percepción de la flexibilidad de uso MERliNN-CE por parte del analista de sistema y del gerente de proyecto

C5	Sufficiency	Percepción de la suficiencia de uso MERliNN-CE por parte del analista de sistema y del gerente de proyecto
C6	Usefulness	Percepción de la utilidad de uso de MERliNN-CE por parte del analista de sistema y del gerente de proyecto
C7	Web System	Sistema que utiliza internet para operar

Los elementos que modelan la evidencia pueden ser del tipo: arquetipo, aspecto contextual, causa, efecto y moderador. Los primeros tres representan un tipo particular de valor para una variable (conceptos de valor), usualmente las variables independientes del estudio. Los arquetipos son la raíz de la jerarquía y están fijos en 4 conceptos (*activity*, *actor*, *technology* y *system*), los cuales intentan capturar la situación típica en IS descrita como "un actor aplicando una tecnología para realizar una determinada actividad en un sistema de software".

Los **aspectos contextuales** son usados para describir el contexto y condiciones en donde se espera que ocurran las proposiciones establecidas (p.e Web System). Las **causas** son aquellos aspectos contextuales que son directamente responsables de las proposiciones. Los **efectos y moderadores** son denominados conceptos variables y se relacionan a las variaciones asociadas con las variables dependientes. Para éstos, es necesario identificar la intensidad de los efectos (implementada con una escala de *Likert* de hasta 7 puntos en la herramienta de SSM) y la dirección de los moderadores. Para los estudios sobre MERliNN-CE se tienen efectos cuya intensidad es medida de acuerdo a: (i) los resultados obtenidos de la aplicación de una encuesta a los participantes en el estudio E_EC y, (ii) la consolidación y análisis sobre las lecciones aprendidas reportadas por los participantes para el estudio E_NS.

Análisis de Información y Extracción de Datos de la Evidencia 1 - Estudio E_EC: se extraen los resultados del *survey* presentados en el artículo fuente frente a las siguientes 5 características cualitativas de viabilidad de MERliNN-CE: Flexibilidad (FX), Conveniencia de uso para el proceso de ERNF (CV), Capacidad de ajustarse a las dinámicas del proyecto (CP), Suficiencia para lograr la especificación de RNF (SF) y Utilidad para el proceso de ERNF (UT). Para mejorar la interpretación estadística de estos resultados, se calcula la moda para cada uno de los roles involucrados (gerente de proyecto y analista de sistema), los cuales se mapean posteriormente a una escala de *Likert* de 3 puntos (Positivo (P), Negativo (N) e Indiferente (I)). De acuerdo a esta escala: 1 o 2 se interpretó como "Negativo", 4 o 5 se interpretó como "Positivo" y, 3 se interpretó como "Indiferente". El resultado final de esta interpretación para cada característica evaluada, para los dos roles del estudio de caso, fue P (positiva).

Análisis de Información y Extracción de Datos de la Evidencia 2 - Estudio E_NS: para este estudio se requirió un proceso de transformación de datos para cada grupo de lecciones aprendidas (LA), tanto de analistas como de gerentes, de manera que pudieran ser homogeneizadas semánticamente al primer estudio E_EC. Las LA fueron mapeadas frente a las 5 características codificadas y evaluadas en el estudio E_EC, tomando como criterio de mapeo la ocurrencia de alguno de los siguientes sinónimos[1] : FX: (ajustable, adaptable), CP: (competente, preparado, apto), CV: (interés,

[1] De acuerdo a la Real Academia de Lengua Española (RAE)

comodidad, oportunidad, ventajoso), SF:(Capacitado, capaz, apto, hábil, idóneo, competente), UT: (Provecho, beneficio, rendimiento, interés, aplicación). Estos resultados intermedios fueron llevados a la misma escala de *Likert* de 3 puntos utilizada por el estudio E_EC para cada característica, en donde el valor "Indiferente" indica la ausencia de LA relacionadas a esa característica.

Para obtener un resultado final de cada característica se realizó un conteo de votos de las lecciones aprendidas clasificadas usando las siguientes reglas: (i) para resultados de interpretación que tuvieron el mismo valor P, N o I su resultado final de interpretación fue ese mismo valor P, N o I, (ii) si entre 2 resultados uno era I y el otro P o N, el resultado del conteo es el valor P o N, (iii) si entre 2 resultados uno era P y el otro N, el resultado final es I. En la Tabla 4 se presentan los resultados finales de E_NS.

Tabla 4. Resultado final de la transformación de LA para el estudio E_NS

Característica	FX	CP	CV	SF
Analistas	I	N	P	I
Gerentes	P	I	I	P

Como siguiente paso, se debe estimar el valor de confianza, en un rango de 0% a 100%, de los conceptos variables (moderadores y efectos), lo cual determina el grado de fiabilidad de los mismos. El método SSM propone que dicha estimación se realice a través de dos actividades: (i) clasificación del tipo de estudio (experimento controlado, *quasi*-experimento, observacional y no sistemático) y, (ii) evaluación de la calidad del mismo a través de un *checklist*. El estudio E_EC fue clasificado como observacional y E_NS como no sistemático, obteniendo un valor de confianza de 37% y 14% respectivamente. Para los elementos presentados en la Tabla 3 se desarrolla un esquema teórico utilizando la notación dada por [42], presentado parcialmente (por temas de legibilidad) en la Fig. 1 (evidencia de E_EC desde la perspectiva del gerente del proyecto). Un constructo es representado como una clase o un atributo de una clase, pudiendo tener subclases (utilizando la misma notación de UML) o componentes. Usualmente si el constructo representa un valor de variable particular (p.e. *Web System*), entonces es modelado como una subclase o componente. Sin embargo, si el foco está en la variación de las variables, entonces el constructo es modelado como una propiedad de la clase.

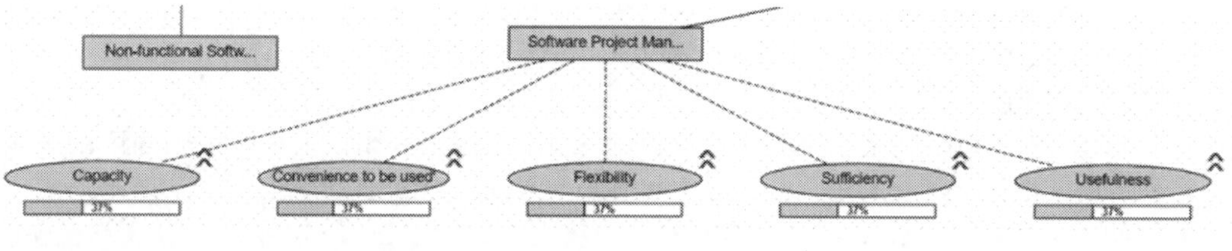

Fig. 1. - Diagrama esquemático del modelo del estudio E_EC para el gerente de proyecto

Como se puede observar, los conceptos variables son representados como elipses para los **efectos observados** (p.e. *Flexibility*), y en caso de tener **moderadores** se representarían con paralelogramas (no presentes en este modelo).

La lectura que se puede realizar del diagrama de la Fig. 1 es la siguiente: "El gerente de proyecto (actor/aspecto contextual) percibe la Conveniencia, Capacidad, Flexibilidad, Suficiencia y Utilidad (efectos) del instrumento MERliNN-CE (causa) para la elicitación de requisitos no funcionales (actividad) de sistemas de información del tipo web (aspecto contextual)". Además, se puede visualizar que todos los efectos identificados del uso de MERliNN-CE, por el gerente de proyecto, son positivos (representados con una doble flecha verde en la parte superior derecha de cada elemento) y un nivel de confianza del 37% (representado con una barra debajo de cada elemento). Si bien esto indica resultados positivos, un nivel de confianza menor al 50% es considerado muy bajo como para denotar causalidad.

Para el estudio E_NS, el nivel de confianza es aún más bajo (14%) y frente a los efectos se tiene que: en el caso del analista, los efectos son positivos para FX, SF y UT e indiferentes para CP y CV; en el caso del gerente del proyecto los efectos positivos son para CV, indiferentes para FC y SF y negativos para CP y UT. Esto último particularmente presenta las diferencias de efectos entre los modelos E_EC y E_NS.

3. Consolidación y Síntesis de las Evidencias. En este paso se agrega la evidencia extraída de los estudios primarios, basándose en los modelos de evidencia construidos en el paso anterior. Para esto es necesario definir la compatibilidad de las estructuras teóricas. Esta compatibilidad puede estar dada bajo una de las siguientes formas: (i) cuando los conceptos de valor son los mismos, o (ii) cuando los conceptos de valor tienen el mismo significado, lo cual incluye causa, arquetipos y aspectos contextuales.

Para el caso de las evidencias E_EC y E_NS la forma de compatibilidad se da a través de que los conceptos son los mismos, y la herramienta los mapea automáticamente, al poseer el mismo nombre. Luego de definir la compatibilidad de los conceptos de valor, al momento de agregar la evidencia haciendo uso de la herramienta provista por SSM se extraen y agrupan los conceptos variables (efectos y moderadores), intensidad (positiva, indiferente o negativa) e incertidumbre (valor de confianza). Se experimentan conflictos (diferencias en la dirección de la intensidad) para los efectos de CP y CV para el rol de gerente de proyecto, los cuales fueron positivos en E_EC e indiferentes en E_NS. Y también para los efectos CP, FX, SF y UT para el rol de analista de sistemas, los cuales fueron positivos en E_EC e indiferentes (FX y SF) o negativos (CP y US) en E_NS. La intensidad final obtenida se refleja en el modelo de la Fig. 2.

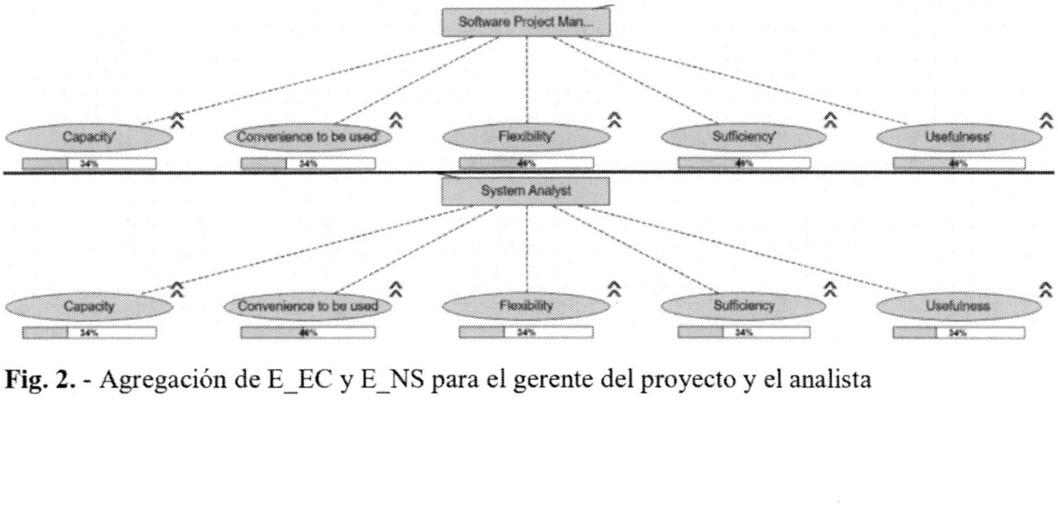

Fig. 2. - Agregación de E_EC y E_NS para el gerente del proyecto y el analista

El método SSM utiliza el *Mathematical Theory of Evidence [43]* (también conocida como Dempster-Shafer theory, DST) como formalismo matemático para obtener los resultados agrupados. A través de DST se calcula la intensidad del efecto de los resultados agregados, así como su nivel de confianza. Los mismos se presentan en la Tabla 5, nombrados como "Int" y "Conf" respectivamente.

Tabla 5. Efectos agregados para el componente MERliNN-CE

Efectos	E_EC		E_NS		Agregación	
	Analista	Gerente	Analista	Gerente	Analista	Gerente
	Int, Conf	Int, Conf	Int, Conf	Int, Conf	Int, Conf	Int, Conf
FX	P, 37%	P, 37%	I, 14%	P, 14%	P, 34%	P, 46%
CP	P, 37%	P, 37%	N, 14%	I, 14%	P, 34%	P, 34%
CV	P, 37%	P, 37%	P, 14%	I, 14%	P, 46%	P, 34%
SF	P, 37%	P, 37%	I, 14%	P, 14%	P, 34%	P, 46%
UT	P, 37%	P, 37%	N, 14%	P, 14%	P, 34%	P, 46%

De la Tabla 5, se puede observar que la intensidad de los efectos de los resultados agregados se mantiene positiva para todos los efectos (tanto analista como gerente) variando el nivel de confianza de cada uno, habiéndose incrementado para aquellos resultados que mostraron la misma intensidad en ambos estudios (46%) y disminuido para aquellos que presentaron conflictos (34%).

De forma general se puede observar que la evidencia agregada presenta efectos positivos de la percepción del uso de MERliNN-CS, respecto de las 5 características evaluadas (FX, CP, CV, SF y UT). Claramente el nivel de confianza de la evidencia E_EC es más fuerte, por ser un estudio observacional, en comparación con E_NS al ser no sistemático. En la Tabla 6 se muestran las proposiciones y explicaciones que surgen del resultado de la agregación, respecto de los constructos mencionados en la Tabla 3.

Es importante destacar que los datos utilizados para el modelado de la evidencia y agregación de la misma son los que al momento se encontraban disponibles de ambos estudios, siendo la moda de los resultados del *survey* en el caso de E_EC y el resumen de las lecciones aprendidas en el caso del estudio E_NS. Para E_EC queda pendiente el análisis de las lecciones aprendidas resultantes de este estudio. En relación a E_NS se toma el resumen de las lecciones aprendidas (reportado), no pudiendo acceder al conjunto de datos original. La implicancia e interpretación de estos resultados se presentan en la sección 5.

Tabla 6. Proposiciones y explicaciones de la evidencia agregada

Proposiciones	
P1	El gerente de proyecto percibe alguna flexibilidad de MERliNN-CE para la ERNF.
P2	Existe alguna posibilidad de que MERliNN-CE sea capaz de adaptarse a los proyectos de desarrollo en etapas iniciales.
P3	El analista de sistemas percibe algún grado de conveniencia de MERliNN-CE en relación a beneficios de su uso y comodidad.

P4	El gerente de proyecto percibe cierto grado de suficiencia de MERliNN-CE en empresas emergentes.
P5	Existe alguna percepción de utilidad de MERliNN-CE, pero la misma varía de acuerdo a la perspectiva del rol.
Explicaciones	
E1	Algunos gerentes percibieron la *flexibilidad* del uso de MERliNN-CE al incluir el instrumento para complementar el proceso existente en la organización o comenzar un proceso nuevo en los casos de que no existiera.
E2	El analista percibe poca *capacidad de ajuste* de MERliNN-CE en proyectos que se encuentran en etapas finales de desarrollo.
E3	Los analistas perciben la *conveniencia* en relación a la reutilización de MERliNN-CE para los procesos de verificación de requisitos, especificación y priorización de características de calidad. También perciben *beneficios* en relación a: trazabilidad con procesos de negocio, posibilidad de trabajo distribuido de elicitación, claridad en el proyecto y apoyo en la definición del alcance.
E4	El gerente de proyecto de una empresa registra que para sus procesos de ingeniería fue *suficiente* dado el reciente nacimiento como organización.
E5	El gerente de proyecto percibe un *uso adecuado* de MERliNN-CE debido a que su empresa ya estaba teniendo un acercamiento a la ERNF. Sin embargo el analista no percibe la utilidad de MERliNN-CE debido a un mal uso del instrumento por falta de tiempo o en casos que no reportaban utilidad.
Alcance	
El componente MERliNN-CE presuntamente es viable para la especificación de RNF en proyectos de desarrollo de software web que estén en etapas iniciales de construcción y que no cuenten con un proceso de ERNF.	

4 Amenazas a la Validez

La agregación de evidencia de diferentes estudios posee diversos riesgos [9], en esta sección discutimos las posibles amenazas a la validez, enfatizando en las acciones de mitigación utilizadas. La amenaza al omitir estudios primarios importantes no afecta en nuestro caso, ya que los estudios agregados eran todos los disponibles al momento. En relación a la representación de la evidencia, los investigadores pueden reflejar su opinión y, por tanto, sesgar la representación. En nuestro caso, el modelo fue generado por un investigador no participante en los estudios primarios y luego validado con un grupo externo de investigadores con experiencia en el uso de SSM.

Cada estudio, por su parte posee sus propias amenazas a la validez, por lo que fuimos cuidadosos al interpretar los resultados tomando en cuenta: (1) los datos de ambos estudios son de diferente naturaleza (sufrieron transformaciones a través de un proceso subjetivo para poder ser agregados, perdiendo precisión en el tamaño del efecto), (2) varios efectos son percibidos como positivos tanto por analistas como por gerentes en base a la falta de procesos de ER en las organizaciones. Este tipo de contexto es probable que haya influenciado positivamente en la viabilidad del uso de MERliNN-CE.

La implementación del método en la herramienta computacional utilizada tiene diversas limitaciones. En particular, se identificó que algunos aspectos importantes de los estudios primarios no eran tomados en cuenta en la evaluación de calidad o bien existía alguna limitación al evaluarlos, por ejemplo: cantidad de sujetos/unidades experimentales del estudio no eran tenidos en cuenta, muchos aspectos eran clasificados de forma binaria (Si/No) no permitiendo una escala más precisa, entre otros.

5 Discusión de los Resultados

Los resultados obtenidos de la síntesis de los estudios primarios realizados sobre la viabilidad de MERliNN-CE son positivos con baja confianza (menor al 50%). Esto indica la necesidad de realizar más estudios para aumentar dicha confianza, sobre todo en aquellas características que denotaron una confianza más baja (las cuales experimentaron conflictos en la agregación) como son: la *Flexibilidad, Capacidad, Suficiencia y Utilidad* para el caso del analista de sistemas; y la *Capacidad y Conveniencia* para el gerente de proyecto, buscando obtener proposiciones más fuertes y explicaciones más detalladas de las mismas. Por otro lado, es imperante que para los estudios futuros y con el fin de aumentar la precisión en las intensidades de los efectos definidos se diseñen previamente los instrumentos necesarios y suficientes para la recolección de los datos, de manera tal que soporten adecuadamente los resultados de validación.

El modelo de agregación denota la carencia de variables moderadoras en los estudios y cómo éstas influencian en la percepción de los participantes, por ejemplo: experiencia de los participantes, tipo de software a construir, tipo de RNF a especificar, entre otras. En esa misma línea, medir el esfuerzo, tiempo y costo invertido en la realización de la actividad nos brinda información más rica acerca del uso de MERliNN-CE.

Solamente la perspectiva de percepción de uso de MERliNN-CE fue observada en los estudios. Otras perspectivas interesantes no presentes en la agregación que podrían enriquecer el modelo (y a su vez apoyar la triangulación de los resultados de viabilidad obtenidos) podrían ser: calidad del RNF especificado usando MERliNN-CE, percepción de los desarrolladores que utilizan esos requisitos para construir el producto de software, calidad del producto de software construido, entre otras. El aspecto de calidad del RNF es muy importante y merece especial atención, debido a la diversidad de RNF y particularidades de cada uno [13]; en este sentido, considerar tipos de tecnologías adecuadas para cada tipo de RNF resulta necesario. Por último, mejoras en la implementación del método SSM a través de la herramienta serían beneficiosas. En particular, en lo que refiere a la evaluación de la calidad de los estudios primarios.

6 Conclusiones

En este artículo se presentó la síntesis de resultados de la agregación de evidencia de dos estudios primarios realizados para evaluar la viabilidad del componente MERliNN-CE del Framework MERliNN a través del uso del método SSM. Los resultados obtenidos muestran que, si bien se perciben efectos positivos del uso del componente, los mismos presentan baja confianza (menor a 50%), identificando los de más baja confianza a ser foco de atención en futuros estudios. Del resultado de la agregación se identificaron diversas amenazas a la validez relacionadas a: (i) carencia de datos de mayor calidad y necesidad de transformación de los mismos al ser agregados, (ii) posible influencia positiva del contexto de las organizaciones al no contar con ninguna tecnología para la ERNF, (iii) falta de triangulación de resultados y (iv) limitantes del uso de la herramienta computacional para realizar la agregación. A su vez, se identificaron potenciales variables moderadoras de interés no presentes en el modelo (experiencia, tipo de software, tipo de RNF), así como otras perspectivas de evaluación de la viabilidad del componente (calidad del RNF construido, percepción de utilidad por parte del desarrollador del RNF especificado, calidad del producto de software construido).

Para finalizar, concluimos que la realización de la síntesis de resultados nos llevó a identificar oportunidades de mejora para futuros estudios, con relación a aumentar la confianza obtenida hasta el momento, mitigar las amenazas a la validez identificadas y a incluir aspectos no conocidos que enriquezcan el cuerpo de conocimiento actual sobre MERliNN-CE. Esta síntesis constituye una línea base de conocimiento a partir de la cual se diseñará una familia de estudios a realizar a futuro en el Framework MERliNN.

Referencias

1. Chung, L., et al., *Non-functional requirements in software engineering*. Vol. 5. 2012: Springer Science & Business Media.
2. Zowghi, D. and C. Coulin, *Requirements elicitation: A survey of techniques, approaches, and tools*, in *Engineering and managing software requirements* 2005, Springer. p. 19-46.
3. Pandey, D., U. Suman, and A. Ramani. *An effective requirement engineering process model for software development and requirements management*. in *2010 International Conference on Advances in Recent Technologies in Communication and Computing*. 2010. IEEE.p. 287-291.
4. Glinz, M. *On non-functional requirements*. in *Requirements Engineering Conference, 2007. RE'07. 15th IEEE International*. 2007. IEEE.p. 21-26.
5. Cysneiros, L.M. and J.C. Sampaio do Prado Leite, *Non-functional requirements: From elicitation to modelling languages*. Proceedings-International Conference on Software Engineering, 2002: p. 699-700.
6. Rahman, M. and S. Ripon, *Elicitation and modeling non-functional requirements-a POS case study*. arXiv preprint arXiv:1403.1936, 2014.
7. El Emam, K. and N.H. Madhavji. *A field study of requirements engineering practices in information systems development*. in *Requirements Engineering, 1995., Proceedings of the Second IEEE International Symposium on*. 1995. IEEE.p. 68-80.
8. Buitrón, S.L., B.L. Flores-Rios, and F.J. Pino, *Elicitación de requisitos no funcionales basada en la gestión de conocimiento de los stakeholders*. Ingeniare. Revista chilena de ingeniería, 2018. 26(1): p. 142-156.
9. Dos Santos, P.S.M. and G.H. Travassos, *On the representation and aggregation of evidence in software engineering: A theory and belief-based perspective*. Electronic Notes in Theoretical Computer Science, 2013. 292: p. 95-118.
10. Serna-Montoya, É., *Estado actual de la investigación en requisitos no funcionales*. Ingeniería y Universidad, 2012. 16(1): p. 225-246.

11. Mijanur Rahman, M. and S. Ripon, *Elicitation and Modeling Non-Functional Requirements – A POS Case Study*. International Journal of Future Computer and Communication, 2013: p. 485-489.
12. Silva, A., et al., *A process for creating the elicitation guide of non-functional requirements*, in *Software Engineering Perspectives and Application in Intelligent Systems* 2016, Springer. p. 293-302.
13. Silva, A., P. Pinheiro Adriano Albuquerque, and J. Barroso. *A survey about the situation of the elicitation of non-functional requirements*. in *Iberian Conference on Information Systems and Technologies, CISTI*. 2016.
14. Maiti, R.R. and F.J. Mitropoulos. *Capturing, eliciting, predicting and prioritizing (CEPP) non-functional requirements metadata during the early stages of agile software development*. in *Conference Proceedings - IEEE SOUTHEASTCON*. 2015.
15. Fernández, D.M., *Supporting Requirements Engineering Research That Industry Needs*.
16. Dingsøyr, T., F.O. Bjørnson, and F. Shull, *What do we know about knowledge management? Practical implications for software engineering*. IEEE Software, 2009. 26(3): p. 100-103.
17. Aurum, A., F. Daneshgar, and J. Ward, *Investigating Knowledge Management practices in software development organisations–An Australian experience*. Information and Software Technology, 2008. 50(6): p. 511-533.
18. Mathiassen, L. and P. Pourkomeylian, *Managing knowledge in a software organization*. Journal of Knowledge Management, 2003. **7**(2): p. 63-80.
19. Rodríguez-Elías, O. and A. Martínez García, *Diseño de sistemas y estrategias de gestión del conocimiento: Un enfoque metodológico orientado a procesos y flujos de conocimiento*. Editorial Académica Española, 2011.
20. Buitrón, S.L., Pino, Francisco J. (in press), *Elicitación de requisitos no funcionales basada en la gestión de conocimiento: El marco de trabajo MERliNN*. Revista Ingenierias Universidad de Medellín, 2018. 17 No. 32.
21. Petersen, K., et al. *Systematic Mapping Studies in Software Engineering*. in *EASE*. 2008.p. 68-77.
22. Teixeira, L., et al. *Requirements engineering using mockups and prototyping tools: developing a healthcare web-application*. in *International Conference on Human Interface and the Management of Information*. 2014. Springer.p. 652-663.
23. de Araújo, A.L., L.M. Cysneiros, and V.M.B. Werneck. *NDR-Tool: Uma Ferramenta de Apoio ao Reuso de Conhecimento em Requisitos Não Funcionais*. in *WER*. 2014.
24. Larburu, N., R.G. Bults, and H.J. Hermens. *Making medical treatments resilient to technological disruptions in telemedicine systems*. in *Biomedical and Health Informatics (BHI), 2014 IEEE-EMBS International Conference on*. 2014. IEEE.p. 285-288.
25. Loucopoulos, P., et al. *A systematic classification and analysis of NFRs*. 2013.p. 208-217.
26. Hadar, I., P. Soffer, and K. Kenzi, *The role of domain knowledge in requirements elicitation via interviews: an exploratory study*. Requirements Engineering, 2014. 19(2): p. 143-159.
27. Ameller, D., et al. *How do software architects consider non-functional requirements: An exploratory study*. 2012.p. 41-50.
28. Rosenkranz, C., H. Vranesic, and R. Holten, *Boundary interactions and motors of change in requirements elicitation: A dynamic perspective on knowledge sharing*. Journal of the Association for Information Systems, 2014. 15(6): p. 306.

29. Smith, M.J. and G. Salvendy, *Human Interface and the Management of Information. Interacting with Information: Symposium on Human Interface 2011, Held as Part of HCI International 2011, Orlando, FL, USA, July 9-14, 2011. Proceedings*. Vol. 6771. 2011: Springer.
30. Helming, J., et al. *Towards a unified requirements modeling language*. in *Requirements Engineering Visualization (REV), 2010 Fifth International Workshop on*. 2010. IEEE.p. 53-57.
31. Song, X., Z. Duan, and C. Tian. *Non-functional requirements elicitation and incorporation into class diagrams*. in *International Conference on Intelligent Information Processing*. 2010. Springer.p. 72-81.
32. Chakraborty, S., S. Sarker, and S. Sarker, *An exploration into the process of requirements elicitation: A grounded approach*. Journal of the Association for Information Systems, 2010. 11(4): p. 1.
33. Montesi, M. and P. Lago, *Software engineering article types: An analysis of the literature*. Journal of Systems and Software, 2008. 81(10): p. 1694-1714.
34. Buitrón, S.L. and F.J. Pino. *Non-Functional Requirements Elicitation in the Context of Software Industry: An Experiences Report*. in *21st Conferencia Iberoamericana en Software Engineering* 2018. Bogotá: CIbSE - IberoAmerican Conference on Software Engineering Steering Committee.p. 523-536.
35. Cooper, H., L.V. Hedges, and J.C. Valentine, *The handbook of research synthesis and meta-analysis*2009: Russell Sage Foundation.
36. Noblit, G.W., R.D. Hare, and R. Hare, *Meta-ethnography: Synthesizing qualitative studies*. Vol. 11. 1988: sage.
37. Dos Santos, P.S.M. and G.H. Travassos, *Scientific Knowledge Engineering: a conceptual delineation and overview of the state of the art*. The Knowledge Engineering Review, 2016. 31(2): p. 167-199.
38. Martínez Fernández, S.J., et al. *Aggregating empirical evidence about the benefits and drawbacks of software reference architectures*. in *Empirical Software Engineering and Measurement (ESEM), 2015 ACM/IEEE International Symposium on*. 2015.p. 154-163.
39. Dos Santos, P.S.M., et al., *On the benefits and challenges of using kanban in software engineering: a structured synthesis study*. Journal of Software Engineering Research and Development, 2018. 6(1): p. 13.
40. Dos Santos, P.S.M., I.E. do Nascimento, and G.H. Travassos. *A computational infrastructure for research synthesis in software engineering*. in *Workshop en Ingeniería del Software Experimental (ESELAW)*. 2015.p. 309-322.
41. Cruzes, D.S. and T. Dybå, *Research synthesis in software engineering: A tertiary study*. Information and Software Technology, 2011. 53(5): p. 440-455.
42. Sjøberg, D.I., et al., *Building theories in software engineering*, in *Guide to advanced empirical software engineering*2008, Springer. p. 312-336.
43. Shafer, G., *A mathematical theory of evidence*. Vol. 42. 1976: Princeton university press.

DS Keynote 2019

Design Science for PhD Research in the Software Engineering Domain

Oscar Pastor[1]

[1] R & D Center for Methods of Software Production (PROS)
Universitat Politecnica de Valencia (UPV)
Spain

Abstract. The conference will introduce the principles of Design Science with the perspective developed by Prof. Roel Wieringa in his book "Design Science", clearly distinguishing between questions of knowledge and engineering problems, and introducing the research cycles corresponding to each case. A rigorous framework for the structuring and development of Doctoral Thesis work will be presented from a methodological point of view and with concrete examples, which participants will be able to apply to their Doctoral Thesis work. The final objective is that doctoral students know how to apply the principles of Design Science to the development and management of their scientific work and can use an effective research methodology, well supported by clear concepts and efficient in their application.

Marco de trabajo para el desarrollo web de software de gestión de información, con integración de enfoques, basado en tecnologías semánticas.

Carlos Alberto Pereira Marín[1]

[1] Departamento de Ciencias de la Computación

Universidad Central "Marta Abreu" de Las Villas (Cuba)

carlosap@uclv.edu.cu

Resumen. Los constantes cambios del desarrollo tecnológico y organizacional han provocado el fracaso de muchos proyectos informáticos hacia una óptima alineación con el negocio, por falta de acierto en la adopción de tecnologías para la gestión desde la perspectiva del desarrollo de software. Una de las dificultades radica en acertar con el enfoque adecuado, dentro de la gran diversidad existente. Algunas soluciones se plantean mediante integraciones, para ganar en adaptabilidad, eficiencia, agilidad, etc., pero estas adolecen de debilidades heredadas y otras originadas en el proceso. Por su parte, las tecnologías semánticas han disparado la creación de modelos y herramientas que combinan el modelado y ejecución de procesos de desarrollo de software; es un área situada en la confluencia varias tecnologías y uno de los movimientos tecnológicos dominantes de hoy en día. Esta investigación propone un marco de desarrollo de software, basado en una arquitectura multicapa, que logra integrar varios enfoques de gestión con tecnologías semánticas. Se combinan el útil desarrollo dirigido por modelos, basado en ontologías y el conveniente desarrollo adaptativo, logrando un proceso ágil en las actuales exigencias de rápida adaptabilidad. Se establece un ciclo de vida iterativo, donde su tiempo de vida se acorta y el conocimiento del dominio se consolida, a partir de la interacción de todos los participantes en el proceso. La capacidad de desarrollo, el grado de madurez y la alineación con el negocio de las tecnologías adoptadas son evaluadas a partir de modelos *ISO* establecidos para determinar la factibilidad de la aplicación del marco propuesto.

Palabras clave: Software, Desarrollo Ágil, BPM, SOA, BRM, Integración, Ontologías, Semántica.

1. Introducción

El ambiente organizacional o de negocio se ha caracterizado en los últimos tiempos por las inestabilidades, y por consiguiente, en derivaciones de reevaluaciones sobre las perspectivas de crecimiento de organizaciones enteras, así como en reposicionamientos y consolidaciones de diversos mercados. Según Oltra_Badenes [1] y Martins [2], las tecnologías de información (TI) tienen una relevante influencia en las organizaciones, debido a la masiva adopción de sistemas de información por el ambiente corporativo. El término genérico de sistemas de información, en el área de la gestión de organizacional, hace referencia al concepto de un sistema o software de gestión (en lo adelante SG), el cual es un programa o una aplicación informática enfocada en brindar soporte a la gestión diaria y continúa de los diferentes escenarios y procesos, con el objetivo de controlar los aspectos administrativos y de las acciones (planeación, organización, dirección, control) de gestión organizacional en general.

La evolución del rol de las TI, desde el plano operativo al plano estratégico, ha exigido de las entidades investigadoras y desarrolladoras de software constantes resultados sobre procedimientos, métodos y modelos de mejora para implementar los SG. Las principales líneas de investigación están centradas sobre plataformas móviles y aplicaciones web, encaminadas, desde mediados de la década del 2000, hacia una variedad de enfoques y tecnologías de gestión (ETG), entre las cuales se encuentran la gestión de procesos de negocios (*BPM*), la arquitectura orientada a servicios (*SOA*), los modelos de decisión y reglas de negocio (*BRM*), el procesamiento de grandes cantidades de datos (*BigData*), la inteligencia de negocios (*BI*), la aplicación de ontologías y la reutilización del conocimiento, la web semántica (WS), entre otros. Además, se han establecido estándares que respaldan estos paradigmas y cuyas pautas están dadas en su mayoría por organizaciones y consorcios como *OMG*, *W3C*, *BRG*, *BPMI*, *IBM*, *ORACLE*, etc.

El raudal de perspectivas de uso y la diversidad de ETG hacen muy fecunda el área de desarrollo de SG, pero a la vez constituyen una disyuntiva para los decisores de estrategias TI, ya que casi siempre va a aparecer la necesidad de personalización del SG, y en este sentido los ETG proporcionan soluciones aisladas a problemas relacionados [3]. La integración de varios ETG ha sido asumida como una vía de solución a esta necesidad, para adjudicarle al desarrollo y a los propios sistemas características de mejoras.

En este disruptivo panorama tecnológico para la gestión organizacional se presentan otras dificultades que entorpecen cualquier tipo de proceso de desarrollo SG. En primer lugar, según Buschle, Johnson [4], la integración de ETG plantea retos difíciles en el análisis y la interpretación de la detallada y compleja información contenida en modelos combinados, donde estos últimos son inadecuados para un procesamiento automático con las limitadas capacidades de análisis de las herramientas de soporte que existen actualmente. También se presenta la situación de que cada enfoque tiene sus propios principios de desarrollo, establecidos en los manifiestos de sus respectivas comunidades [5-7], y no siempre estos principios y valores se cumplen cabalmente en un proceso de integración. También concurre el aumento de la complejidad inherente de un SG, lo cual limita la comprensión de todas las sutilidades de su diseño por lo que su construcción exige de modelos y procesos de desarrollo con alto nivel de abstracción [8-12]; además, la rápida evolución de las tecnologías demanda eficiencia, agilidad y adaptabilidad en estos procesos. También es ineludible la incorporación de la organización a la WS, por medio de la interoperabilidad semántica, pero para ello es necesario un cambio de formato en la codificación de la información, ya que la misma debe ser entendida además, por las propias computadoras.

Teniendo en cuenta todos estos planteamientos anteriormente descritos se expone el siguiente, **problema científico**: ¿Cómo facilitar un proceso de construcción y despliegue de un SG para entornos Web, cuya arquitectura tecnológica permita un oportuno desarrollo adaptativo a los entornos, donde las políticas, los procedimientos y la lógica de negocio evolucionen demasiado rápido, como para que los enfoques y tecnologías tradicionales puedan asimilar los cambios, y así facilitar una adecuada alineación TI/Negocio?.

Justificación: La web semántica es un área prolífera, situada en la confluencia varias tecnologías y uno de los movimientos tecnológicos dominantes de hoy en día, donde la generalización en la aplicación de las tecnologías semánticas ha sido muy marcada en las áreas de la ingeniería de software.

Considerando la necesidad de moderar la dispersión de direcciones en el desarrollo de SG, hacia un enfoque más integrador, la motivación esencial y punto de partida de esta investigación está en la utilidad que implica adoptar cierto enfoque de desarrollo que permita manejar la complejidad, a través de métodos apropiados de abstracción, sin renunciar a las buenas prácticas del desarrollo ágil de software y que explote las posibles sinergias entre los diferentes enfoques de gestión, a partir de modelos ontológicos, para mejorar la personalización del SG y la capacidad de respuesta de la organización de manera sostenible.

Luego, se plantea como **objetivo general:** Proponer un marco de trabajo para facilitar la construcción y despliegue de SG en entornos web, donde se sistematicen varios enfoques de desarrollo, mediante el uso de las tecnologías semánticas y la definición de aspectos metodológicos, que permitan un desarrollo adaptativo a los objetivos del negocio.

Objetivos específicos:

1. Identificar y definir los enfoques y las tendencias integracionistas en el desarrollo de SG y sus características más relevantes, para determinar aportaciones y limitaciones respecto de la alineación TI/Negocio.
2. Diseñar un modelo semántico que permita la incorporación estructural de los conceptos de arquitectura y de enfoque desde una perspectiva de innovación tecnológica, donde la composición de ontologías y su transformación en bases persistentes son los puentes en una arquitectura de integración.
3. Establecer, con el apoyo de este modelo de sistema, un marco de trabajo metodológico que ofrezca indicaciones para la construcción de aplicaciones web semánticas basadas, en cualquiera de los enfoques definidos o integrados y se facilite el desarrollo adaptativo de software.
4. Evaluar el marco de trabajo propuesto en un escenario de pruebas, a partir de los procedimientos establecidos en la investigación

Se deslinda por tanto como objeto de estudio el desarrollo de software de gestión, así como el campo de acción la integración de enfoques tecnológicos y finalmente como **hipótesis de la investigación:** La aplicación del marco de trabajo propuesto por equipos de desarrollo de SG, permitirá la construcción y despliegue de un sistema de gestión para entornos web, donde la integración de varios enfoques de gestión mediante tecnologías semánticas, en particular con el uso de varias ontologías, facilitará el desarrollo adaptativo.

2. Resumen sobre el dominio del problema y estado del arte

En la investigación se puntualizan conceptos y aspectos importantes sobre la alineación de los objetivos de las TI y del negocio, así como la exposición de algunos modelos para la evaluación del grado de madurez de dicha alineación [13-17]. También se caracterizan varios enfoques de desarrollo de software empresarial, entre ellos el *BPM*, el *SOA*, el *BRM* [5-7, 18] y la WS, sus perspectivas de alineación respecto de los objetivos del negocio, así como las principales ventajas y desventajas para su adopción [3, 19, 20]. Se analizan algunos marcos de integración de estos enfoques y la utilización de las tecnologías semánticas en el mejoramiento del desarrollo y de los propios SG, teniendo a las ontologías y sus especificaciones como núcleo del mismo. Para manejar

la complejidad de los actuales SG se describen, de manera resumida, el desarrollo SG basado en modelos orientado por las tecnologías semánticas y también la necesidad del desarrollo adaptativo.
Sobre el estado del arte se puede sintetizar, que tanto en el discurso investigativo como en el práctico del desarrollo SG, se observa una tendencia a la adopción del enfoque integrado *BPM-SOA*, en cuya sinergia se define la dirección del consumo de los servicios por parte de los procesos. En la literatura consultada no se encontró un método o modelo con enfoque integrador, en cuyo proceso se mantuvieran intacto los preceptos de las tecnologías involucradas en este estudio. En estas integraciones las RN fueron tratadas o adoptadas como parte integrante y no como un enfoque en sí. Varios de sus principios para el desarrollo SG son vulnerables a irregularidades en su cumplimiento, quizás por la insolvencia de un lenguaje estandarizado para modelar y codificar los diferentes tipos de RN tratados en la literatura.
Los principales resultados sobre el enriquecimiento semántico de los enfoques BPM, SOA y BRM, permiten cambiar el enfoque hacia metodologías que toman como punto de partida la información relevante para determinar el flujo y la estructura de los procesos, las decisiones y los servicios en una AE.
Para manejar la complejidad de la construcción de un SG se proyecta al ODD como progreso en la comunidad MDD para un desarrollo eficiente, pero sin perder de vista el desarrollo ágil como vía de respuestas rápidas. La WS constituye un espacio idóneo para la integración de enfoques en soluciones SG, pues sus tecnologías dan libertad para las operaciones de datos estructuradas y poco estructuradas [15, 19, 21-23].

3. Metodología de la investigación

Se actúa según los siguientes retos metodológicos, técnicos y de implementación.

- La investigación está basada en la revisión bibliográfica sobre el estado del arte en los diferentes ETG y tendencias del desarrollo de SG y de la integración.
- Las estructuras de la información en el modelo y su procesamiento no deben quedar obsoletas a los cambios y deben ser fácilmente exportables a otras formas de representación simbólica.
- La dependencia de plataforma física y lógica está dirigida a las aplicaciones web, con la intención de ganar en disponibilidad e incrementar posibilidades de mercados.
- La orientación a la composición ontológica y reutilización como forma de integrar tecnologías será parte de la garantía de la interoperabilidad.
- El cumplimiento de estándares y buenas prácticas es característica primordial en una arquitectura escalable.
- Las tecnologías propuestas se basan en los principios de software libre y código abierto.
- La validación de los resultados se hace mediante modelos y procedimientos establecidos para el área de resultados de innovación tecnológica.

4. Solución propuesta y los resultados logrados hasta el momento

La propuesta de solución aborda el problema de la siguiente manera: Se define el marco de trabajo y sus funcionalidades. Se definen aspectos conceptuales y metodológicos para el modelado e integración de las ontologías propuestas y se diseña un modelo arquitectónico a partir de estas. Los principios de desarrollo del marco preceden a la definición de las actividades y roles en el desarrollo. Finalmente se describe el ciclo de vida del proceso y se proponen las métricas para la evaluación del proceso desde varias perspectivas. A continuación los principales resultados

4.1. Aspectos metodológicos para el modelado e integración de ontologías.

Las ontologías son gestionadas, en tiempo de diseño y modelado, por los analistas y/o ingenieros ontológicos, así como todas las partes interesadas de cada uno de los dominios involucrados; en tanto los lenguajes *OWL* y *SWRL* son los estándares de implementación ontológica en este contexto. Se proponen 4 ontologías, las cuales son integradas mediante una ontología base diseñada a partir del modelo CANVAS para modelos de negocio [24].

4.2. Diseño del modelo arquitectónico

Los modelos multiniveles surgen principalmente para plataformas de integración, debido a las mejoras logradas en la tecnología de redes y al hecho de contar con servidores con *APIs* públicas y estables. Aquí se diseña un modelo arquitectónico multicapa basado en tecnologías semánticas que va a encauzar las diferentes etapas de desarrollo del marco. Su estructura modular está definida por tres principales capas, donde dos de ellas se descomponen en varios subniveles, para lograr cumplir con el principal reto en una arquitectura de integración de varios paradigmas tecnológicos. Debido a la complejidad de la estructura para ser mostrado en detalle en este documento, se mostrará la captura de pantalla del modelo en la figura 1, para lograr una visión general de los distintos niveles y sus componentes. En esta arquitectura, las ontologías de domino, de sistema, de reglas de negocio, de servicios y de procesos conforman el núcleo informacional del modelo, para luego ser integradas a partir de una ontología base que será el punto de partida del marco de desarrollo. Luego de la instanciación de la ontología resultante de la integración comienza la etapa de transformación hacia niveles de menor nivel de abstracción, hasta llegar al nivel de generación de código.

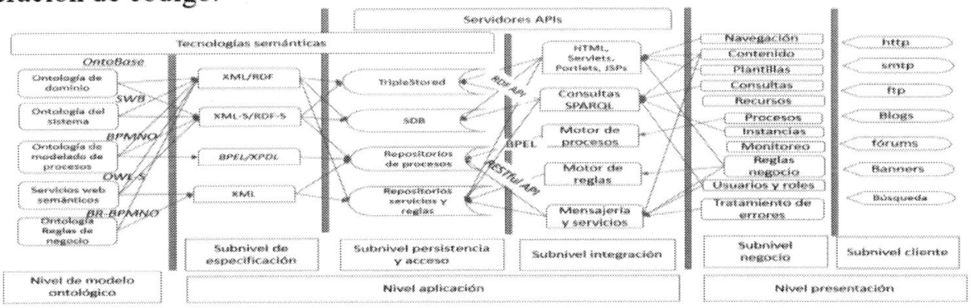

Fig. 1: Modelo multicapa para una arquitectura web semántica como espacio integrador de paradigmas tecnológicos (elaboración propia)

4.3. Actividades y etapas del marco de desarrollo y ciclo de vida

Se establecen algunos principios de desarrollo para que puedan resolverse los principales problemas que se plantean, por ejemplo, el usuario es actor central de las pruebas intermedias dentro del ciclo de vida; los paradigmas involucrados mantienen sus preceptos básicos; las transformaciones hacia las tecnologías semánticas no pueden actuar en deterioro de los mismos; las ontologías constituyen el núcleo para la representación de todos los requerimientos del sistema y del negocio; para esto último, la necesaria completitud modular es imperativa para el desarrollo, despliegue y evolución de cada nivel, entre otros. Luego se definen las actividades y los roles las cuales se reflejan de manera resumida en el esquema de la figura 2.

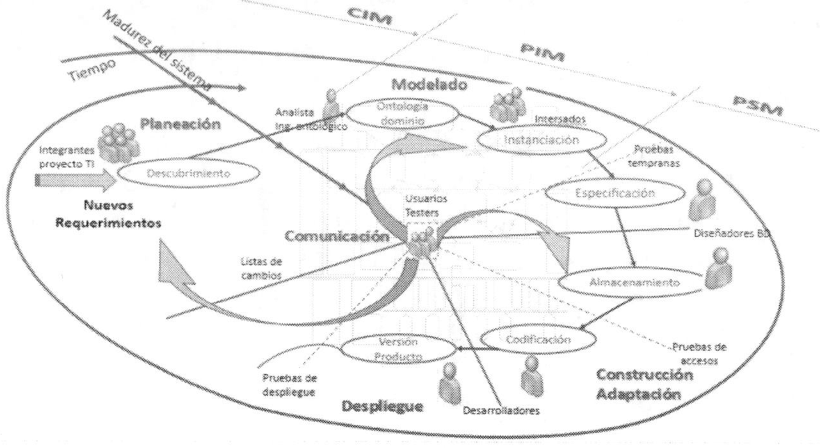

Fig. 2: Esquema del ciclo de vida del marco propuesto.

La descripción de las etapas del marco metodológico garantiza un desarrollo con consistencia entre las iteraciones del ciclo de vida, de manera que el esfuerzo realizado por usuarios, analistas y programadores en la creación de contenido para una iteración, no se pierda en una nueva iteración. La ejecución de las actividades, si bien conlleva una lectura secuencial, fomenta una permanente retroalimentación entre ellas e incluso desde las etapas tempranas. Este modelo combina métodos de desarrollo, si se tienen en cuenta, por un lado, las ontologías son bases para una metodología de desarrollo orientado a la semántica [25] y basado en modelos; mientras que las diferentes etapas de pruebas insertadas antes y después de la generación de código propician la retroalimentación entre las partes interesadas para un desarrollo adaptativo. En cada iteración del marco, su tiempo de vida se acorta y el conocimiento del dominio se consolida, a partir de la interacción de todos los participantes en el proceso. El sistema madura a medida que el conocimiento lo hace y ambos convergen hacia el dominio de la solución, es decir, hacia el sistema de gestión con los requerimientos cumplidos.

4.4. Novedad de la propuesta

El *valor teórico* consiste en la definición de un marco de trabajo que sirve como modelo de desarrollo para la construcción y despliegue de sistemas web de gestión de información, donde se contextualizan e integran varios enfoques de gestión y se orienta un desarrollo integrado de varios métodos basado en su ciclo de vida y en una arquitectura multicapa con tecnologías semánticas. Las ontologías aquí, son además de artefactos durante la implementación, componentes de software y utilizadas en tiempo de ejecución, mejorando la gestión de entornos de alto dinamismo conceptual y permitiendo a la vez la incorporación de la organización al entorno de la web semántica.

En el *valor práctico* se impone la prerrogativa de utilizar el marco de trabajo para la gestión del conocimiento y como medio de entendimiento, lo cual genera mayor productividad al identificar el conocimiento válido y socializarlo entre las partes interesadas, dotándoles de mayor capacidad de innovación y conformando un modelo integral colaborativo, debido al entorno de trabajo que se genera entre los participantes del proyecto TI. Además, esta utilización junto a varios métodos de desarrollo que se permite aplicar, ayuda a reducir los tiempos de respuesta y crear software organizacional con alta capacidad de adaptabilidad a los cambios trazados en las estrategias de negocio, lo que facilita una rápida y adecuada alineación con las TI, determinado también por la reutilización de recursos y la minimización del coste de despliegue de nuevas aplicaciones o versiones.

En su *valor metodológico* se busca desarrollar mejores prácticas de desarrollo, con ventajas tales como, organización por niveles, almacenamiento de la información generada en todos los niveles, fácil entendimiento de los procesos, y la integración del desarrollo a través de modelos.

5. Principales aspectos pendientes

Para determinar el grado de capacidad y madurez del marco de desarrollo se adaptará el modelo de la norma *ISO* 15504:2008 SPICE de 5 niveles, con modelo de referencia la norma *ISO* 12207:2008 para procesos de ciclos de vida de software. Para medir el grado de alineación a partir de la aplicación de este modelo, se utilizará el modelo SAMM de 5 niveles, alineados con CMMI y adaptados al contexto [2, 10, 26]. En estos modelos intervienen importantes factores como los ejecutivos, las estrategias, los recursos humanos, los procesos, la infraestructura, arquitecturas, aplicaciones, etc. Esta última evaluación permitirá trazar estrategias TI que permitan una mejor alineación.

6. Referencias.

1. Oltra_Badenes, R., *Sistemas integrados de gestión empresarial. Evolución histórica y tendencias de futuro.* Primera edición. ed, ed. U.P.d. Valencia. 2012, Valencia, España: Unión nacional de editoriales. pp. 110.
2. Martins, A. *Alineamiento entre las estrategias de las tecnologías de la información y del negocio.* Managment, 2013. url: https://mba.americaeconomia.com/articulos/columnas/alineamiento-entre-las-estrategias-de-ti-y-del-negocio.
3. Malorny, M., et al. *Herausforderungen der Integration von SOA, BPM und BRM* in *Multikonferenz Wirtschaftsinformatik 2018*. 2018. Lüneburg, Germany: Institut für Wirtschaftsinformatik.
4. Buschle, M., P. Johnson, and K. Shahzad. *The Enterprise Architecture Analysis Tool - Support for the Predictive, Probabilistic Architecture Modeling Framework.* in *19th Americas Conference on Information Systems.* 2013. Chicago, Illinois.
5. Ross, R.G., *Business Rules Manifesto. Principles of the Business Rule Approach.*, B.R. Group, Editor. 2003, Business Rule Solutions, LLC: EEUU.
6. Erl, T., *The Annotated SOA Manifesto*, S.M.W. Group, Editor. 2011.
7. Burlton, R., *Manifiesto de Procesos de Negocio*, BPTrends, Editor. 2012.
8. Morales_Arias, J.J. and C.J. Pardo_Calvache, *Revisión sistemática de la integración de modelos de desarrollo de software dirigido por modelos y metodologías ágiles.* Revista Informador Técnico 2016. **Vol. 80**(Nro. 1): p. pp. 13.
9. Bousetta, B., O. El_Beggar, and T. Gadi, *A methodology for CIM modelling and its transformation to PIM.* Journal of Information Engineering and Applications, 2013. **Vol. 3**(Nro. 2): p. pp. 22.

10. Fengel, J., *Semantic Model Alignment for Business Process Integration.*, in *College of Engineering and Built Environment*. 2014, Dublin Institute of Technology: Dublin, Belgium. p. pp. 230.
11. Vallecillo, A., *On the Industrial Adoption of Model Driven Engineering. Is your company ready for MDE?* International Journal of Information Systems and Software Engineering for Big Companies (IJISEBC). 2014. **Vol. 1**(Nro. 1): p. pp. 52-68.
12. Gutierrez_Guerrero, J.M., *Desarrollo de sistemas software industriales dirigidos por modelo: Aplicación a OPC UA e IEC 61131-3* in *Departamento de Lenguajes y Sistemas Informáticos*. 2018, Universidad de Granada: Granada, España. p. pp. 512.
13. Stark, K. *Arquitectura empresarial ¿qué es y para que sirve?* Evaluando software, 2016. url: http://www.evaluandosoftware.com/arquitectura-empresarial/.
14. Chen, W., et al., *Semantic Enterprise Architecture Management*, in *ICEIS-SEAM 2013*. 2013, University of Augsburg: Germany. p. pp. 8.
15. Hitpass_Heyl, B. *Hacia una ontología de arquitectura de negocio y de procesos basada en un modelo de negocio.* in *XLI Latin American Computing Conference (CLEI)*. 2015. Arequipa, Peru.: IEEE.
16. Arango_Serna, M.D., J.E. Londoño_Salazar, and J.A. Zapata_Cortés, *Arquitectura empresarial, una visión general.* Revista Ingenierías Universidad de Medellín,, 2010. **Vol. 9**(Nro. 16): p. pp. 101-111.
17. Garzón, C.A. and J.I. Peña, *Coevolución de las tecnologías de la información con la estrategia del negocio* Revista Ciencias Estratégicas, 2015. **Vol. 23**(Nro. 33): p. pp. 17-29.
18. Gomes_Figueiredo, J. and C.A. Pereira_Marín, *Extensión del BPMNO para el enfoque de reglas de negocio en el desa-rrollo de sistemas.* Revista Ciencia y Técnica Administrativa., 2017. **Vol. 16**(Nro. 4): p. ISSN: 1666-1680.
19. López_Paz, C.R., *Metodología para la sistematización de los servicios de consultoría TI.*, in *Departamento de Tecnología Informática y Computación*. 2011, Univresidad de Alicante: España. p. pp. 204.
20. Londoño_Salazar, J.E., *Modelo funcional de Integración de la Arquitectura Empresarial de 'N' entidades alrededor de un grupo empresarial. Un enfoque de orientación a servicios y modelado de capacidades de negocio.*, in *Facultad de Minas*. 2014, Universidad Nacional de Colombia.: Medellin, Colombia. p. pp. 237.
21. González_Pérez, S.J., *Arquitectura de eGoverment basada en modelos de información interoperables.*, in *Departamento de Informática*. 2015, Universidad de Oviedo: Oviedo, España. p. pp. 327.
22. Belalcázar, A., *Arquitectura de un Data Center con herramientas DEVOPS*, in *Facultad de Informática*. 2017, Universidad Nacional de la Plata: La Plata, Argentina. p. pp. 200.
23. Bhatia, M.P.S., A. Kumar, and R. Beniwal, *Ontologies for Software Engineering: Past, Present and Future.* Indian Journal of Science and Technology., 2016. **Vol. 9**(Nro. 9): p. pp 16.
24. Osterwalder, A. and Y. Pigneur, *Generación de modelos de negocio* Business Model Generation, ed. C.L.P. Deusto, S. L. U. 2011, Barcelon, España: Grupo Planeta.
25. Normas_ISO. *ISO/IEC 15504 SPICE. El Estándar internacional ISO/IEC 15504.* 2011 [cited 2019 En. 2019]; Available from: https://www.normas-iso.com/iso-iec-15504-spice/.
26. Derriks, T., *A Business Process & Rules Management Maturity Model for the Dutch governmental sector.*, in *Informatic Department*. 2012, University Utrecht: Utrecht, Netherland.

Traceability in Software Product Lines

Yenisei Delgado Verdecia

Computer Science Department, University of Chile
ydelgado@dcc.uchile.cl

Abstract Software Product Lines (SPL) have been established as one of the best ways to promote massive reuse of software assets. The relationship between assets in a SPL is called traceability, and its definition is essential for obtaining consistent products. If this definition is formal, it can also be used for deriving new products. Nevertheless, it is a difficult task due to the diversity of artifacts involved, the difficulty of formalizing variability and the variety of relationships that may exist between different artifacts. In this sense, Model-driven engineering (MDE) is a promising paradigm to model various concerns and artifacts. The purpose of this thesis is twofold. First, it attempts to identify and define the traceability among SPL artifacts applying MDE. Second, it purports to define an SPL traceability metamodel that can be applied as a basis for SPL configuration, customization and evolution.

Keywords: Software Product Line, Model-drive engineering, SPL traceability metamodel

1 Introduction

Software Product Line (SPL) is an approach to developing *"a set of software-intensive systems sharing a common, managed set of features that satisfy the specific needs of a particular market segment or mission and that are developed from a common set of core assets in a prescribed way"* [5]. An asset is a reusable software artifact and so it can be used in the development of more than one product. The set of products generated using an SPL is known as a product family, *i.e.*, those that can be developed from the set of common assets [25]. Variability is a key concept in SPL. Assets can be defined as common or variable, where the former are those that must be part of every product and the latter refers to those assets that may or may not be part of a product [22]. The SPL approach has been successfully used in various domains, to optimize the product development process, through the identification and systematic reuse of common elements that are shared by several products. Consequently, this approach is applied to managing and building multiple software products from a set of already developed and tested assets [18].

SPL defines two major processes: *Domain Engineering* (DE) and *Application Engineering* (AE). DE refers to the development of core assets including both, commonalities and variabilities while AE refers to the development of individual products by reusing the existing core assets. AE may also need to add assets that have not yet been developed or to modify some of the existing ones in order to meet the requirements of a specific product [14]. Each of these processes is composed by sub-processes *i.e.*, DE consists of the *Domain analysis*, *Domain design* and *Domain realization* and AE consists of the *Application analysis*, *Application design*, and *Application realization* sub-processes. Each of these sub-processes implies the execution of certain activities and the generation of particular artifacts, as shown in Figure 1.

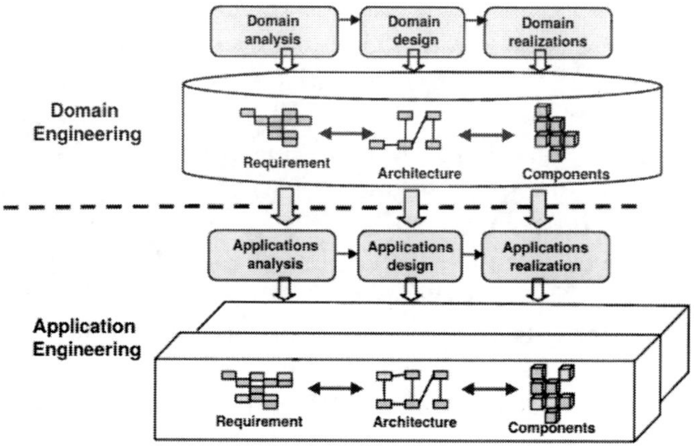

Figure 1. Software Product Line (Adapted from [14])

The artifacts developed in the DE include requirements models, architectural models, software components, test plans and test designs, among others. These artifacts refer to the whole SPL and not just to one product, and therefore, they include the expected variability in all potential products within the scope. Similarly, the artifacts developed in the AE encompass the same artifacts but now for specific products, and therefore they do not include variability.

Software traceability is the ability to establish links between requirements, design, and implementation of a system [1] with the purpose of enhancing the quality of a software system. According to CoEST[1], traceability is defined as "*the ability to interrelate any uniquely identifiable software engineering artifact to any other, maintain required links over time, and use the resulting network to answer questions of both the software product and its development process*" [6]. Then, the traceability enables: (i) to support the analysis of implications and integration of changes in a software system as well as its maintenance and evolution, (ii) to test software system components by indicating alternatives and compromises made during its development and (iii) to reuse software system components by identifying and comparing requirements of new and existing systems [21].

[1] Center of Excellence for Software and Systems Traceability. See `http://www.coest.org/`

Traceability relations can be classified into *vertical* and *horizontal* relations, depending on whether the relations are among elements of the same artifact or elements of different artifacts, respectively [11]. Nonetheless, SPL introduces two new dimensions into the field of traceability [14]. The first dimension is traceability among artifacts of the domain engineering that include variability and those at the application engineering level that involve no variability. The second dimension introduces the notion of traceability in time and involves configuration management and software evolution.

Achieving traceability in SPL is difficult due to: (i) the need to have a deep understanding of the impact of variability in all development phases, (ii) the diversity of existing artifacts and (iii) the need to establish different kinds of relationships between diverse artifacts [8]. Additionally, managing variability within SPLs implies a particularly complex issue when dealing with traceability [7, 13]. Traceability between variation points in different artifacts of the DE should be explicitly captured taking into account the relationship and consistency between commonalities and variabilities between each pair of artifacts. Though simpler, traceability between artifacts in the AE is not only horizontal, *i.e.,* between different artifacts of the AE, but also vertical, *i.e.,* artifacts in the AE must be consistent with those corresponding to the same stage in the DE. For example, the *Requirements* artifact of the AE should consider all commonalities defined in the *Requirements* artifact of the DE, and possibly some of the variable elements; in exceptional cases, it can also include new elements.

In general terms, *SPL traceability* shows which and how many artifacts perform each product feature and which and how many artifacts implement each design decision [10]. Therefore, having a clear vision of SPL artifacts traceability is essential to derive consistent products (configuration). Moreover, explicitly defining traceability, makes it easier to introduce modifications required for particular products (customization), and for evolving the SPL as a whole.

Based on this, SPL traceability should be based on the models used in the SPL process, should be customized to capture relevant trace types, and should be capable to handle variability. In this sense, Model-driven engineering (MDE) can be used to model the various concerns and artifacts of a product line [15]. It provides unified formalisms for models and transformations for dealing with software artifacts and processes within the SPL. Therefore, the purpose of this proposal is to propose an SPL traceability metamodel in order to support the configuration, customization and evolution of SPLs.

2 Problem Statement and Motivation

As previously mentioned, establishing the traceability in a SPL allows us to verify the consistency of a member of the family with the definition of all stages, *e.g.,* a product's features are consistent with all other artifacts defined for the SPL, or that the product architecture follows the same architectural pattern and includes the components prescribed in the Domain design. Formally defining traceability also requires the formal definition of each artifact and relationship involved in the SPL. There are few works that focus on SPL traceability and even fewer address product line architecture.

The software architecture is the artifact that defines the organization of the software components so that both, functional and non functional requirements are taken into account [4]. In this sense, there are a series of proposals for defining the software architecture, but only some of them propose a way to formalize this definition, and almost none of them for formalizing the definition of the product line architecture (PLA), *i.e.,* the artifact built in the Domain design that defines the architecture including its variability.

In addition, to defining traceability it is not clear what are the core assets that are required in each SPL phase and the relationship between them, neither which models help to separate concerns or viewpoints involved in product line development. Even though traceability has been recognized as relevant, there are very few proposals that formalize it, so, in its current state, cannot be used to automate or assist product configuration, customization or SPL evolution.

3 Research Proposal

In this section, we present the hypotheses, objective and research questions.

3.1 Hypotheses

Considering the problem described, we state the following hypotheses:

- The formal definition of the traceability metamodel in an SPL supports:
  H1: *the derivation of products within the scope of the SPL (configuration).*
  H2: *the derivation of products beyond the the original scope of the SPL (customization).*
  H3: *the evolution of any of the artifacts defined for the SPL (evolution).*

3.2 Objectives

To address these hypotheses, the main objective of this proposal is the following:

- Propose a metamodel for SPLs that defines all horizontal and vertical traceability links between artifacts to assist product configuration, customization and SPL evolution.

Taking into account the main objective, the following specific objectives are defined:

(i) Identify and formally define the artifacts built in each phase of the SPL.
(ii) Define the conceptual relationship between artifacts.
(iii) Formalize the whole traceability metamodel.
(iv) Define how this metamodel can be applied for SPL configuration, customization and evolution.

4 Related work

Based on our purpose, we focus our discussion of related work on model-driven engineering and SPL and traceability definition and formalization.

4.1 MDE and SPL

Model-driven engineering (MDE) arises due to the need for more abstract software description, and to increase software productivity and quality [3]. As SPL and MDE have common concerns *e.g.*, improving productivity, making software development cost-effective, capturing domain and technological knowledge in separate artifacts, increasing software quality, enforcing architecture, and automating the construction of software products as much as possible, MDE is a promising technique for SPL [15]. In this context, several approaches have emerged to create SPL [12,16,23,24], in view of conceiving the whole software development cycle as a process of creation, iterative refinement, and the integration of models.

4.2 Traceability definition and formalization

SPL traceability refers to the relations between artifacts in different phases of SPL processes development [1]. Accordingly to Kim *et al.* [9], five traceability dimensions are necessary to relate artifacts of DE and AE processes: i) Domain refinement: trace links between artifacts in different phases of the DE process, ii) Application refinement: trace links among artifacts in different phases of the AE process, iii) Instantiation: traceability space for relating artifacts of the same DE and AE processes, iv) Domain similarity: trace links between artifacts in the same phase of the DE process, and v) Application similarity: traceability space for trace links among artifacts in the same phase of the AE process.

Several approaches use some of the traceability dimensions mentioned above, to relate artifacts of SPL phases. Satyannanda *et al.* [17] define an approach to identify the traceability between a feature model and the component and connector view of a software architecture using Formal Concept Analysis (FCA) technique. In this work, the authors use functional decomposition of a feature and functional decomposition of an architecture to find matching elements. This approach provides trace links between the functional requirements and a component and connector design model as a part of refinement traceability.

Sousa *et al.* [20] present a model-driven framework to traceability in SPL. This approach is based on the work by Pohl *et al.* in [14], that consists of establishing trace links between variability elements and software artifacts. The framework allows the user to select which models to use during development, without being imposed with a specific metamodel.

Shen *et al.* [19] propose a feature-oriented traceability metamodel for SPL development based on four hierarchical layers with different stakeholder concerns, including domain requirement goals, feature model, feature implementation model and program implementations. The authors focus on the visual representation of the traceability in a SPL, trying to represent artifacts in different abstraction levels and explicit/implicit traceability links among them.

Anquetil *et al.* [2] present a model-driven traceability framework for SPL. This metamodel is based in orthogonal traceability dimensions in SPL development defined by the authors. In this works is establishes trace links between features and artifacts of DE phases.

Related works show different approaches to defining traceability between SPL artifacts. However, the mentioned works do not specifically define the artifacts of the SPL to manage traceability in all development phases of the SPL. Additionally, they do not define horizontal and vertical trace links between SPL artifacts for configuring consistent products, introduce modifications required for a particular product or to support SPL evolution as a whole.

5 Research Development

In this section, we describe the methodology that will be followed for reaching the stated objectives. Afterwards, a work plan is presented.

5.1 Methodology

Figure 2 shows the phases and activities of the proposed methodology:

(i) Literature review about (survey)
  - SPL artifacts and traceability
  - Proposals for formalizing artifacts and traceability in the context of MDE

(ii) Formal definition (proposal)
  - Artifacts involved in an SPL applying MDE
  - Links between formally defined artifacts using weaving models
  - Traceability metamodel integrating the two previous activities

(iii) Empirical evaluation of the SPL traceability model proposed (H1, H2, H3).
  - Apply the traceability metamodel to configure, customize and evolve an SPL using an open source ERP (exploratory case study).
  - Adjust the SPL traceability metamodel according to the results of the previous step (proposal)
  - Apply the adjusted traceability metamodel to a commercial ERP (confirmatory case study)

5.2 Work plan

Figure 3 describes the planned timeline for the development of all activities defined as part of the methodology. It is worth noting that the dissertation will be written all along the doctoral work development.

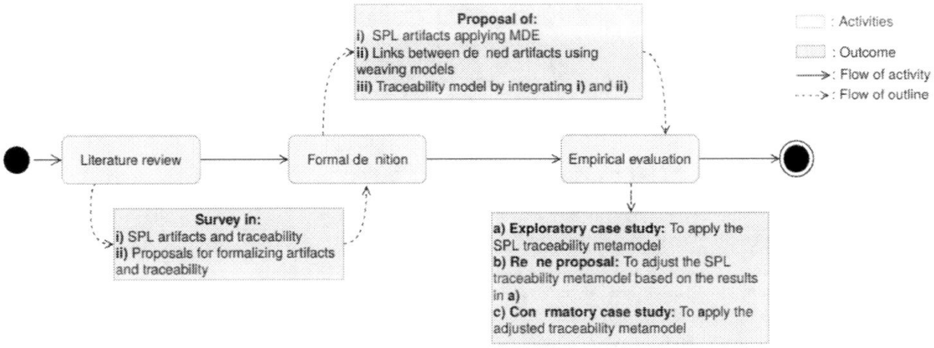

Figure 2. Activities of our research methodology

Figure 3. Overview of our work plan

References

1. I. Alexander. Towards automatic traceability in industrial practice. In *Proc. of the 1st Int. Workshop on Traceability*, pages 26–31, 2002.
2. N. Anquetil, U. Kulesza, R. Mitschke, A. Moreira, J.-C. Royer, A. Rummler, and A. Sousa. A model-driven traceability framework for software product lines. *Softw. Syst. Model.*, 9(4):427–451, 2010.
3. M. Brambilla, J. Cabot, and M. Wimmer. Model-driven software engineering in practice. *Synthesis Lectures on Software Engineering*, 1(1):1–182, 2012.
4. J. Cleland-Huang, O. Gotel, A. Zisman, et al. *Software and systems traceability*. Springer, 2012.
5. P. Clements and L. Northrop. *Software Product lines: practices and patterns*, volume 3. Addison-Wesley Reading, 2002.
6. CoEST. CoEST18: Center of excellence for software traceability. `http://www.coest.org.`, 2018. Online; accessed 21/09/2018.
7. J. Díaz, J. Pérez, and J. Garbajosa. A model for tracing variability from features to product-line architectures: A case study in smart grids. *Requir. Eng.*, 20(3):323–343, 2015.
8. W. Jirapanthong and A. Zisman. Supporting product line development through traceability. In *12th Asia-Pacific Software Engineering Conference (APSEC 2005),15-17 December 2005, Taipei, Taiwan*, pages 506–514, 2005.

9. J. Kim, S. Kang, and J. Lee. A comparison of software product line traceability approaches from end-to-end traceability perspectives. *International Journal of Software Engineering and Knowledge Engineering*, 24(04):677–714, 2014.
10. P. Lago, E. Niemela, and H. Van Vliet. Tool support for traceable product evolution. In *8th European Conference on Software Maintenance and Reengineering, 24-26 March 2004, Tampere, Finland, Proceedings*, pages 261–269. IEEE, 2004.
11. M. Lindvall and K. Sandahl. Practical implications of traceability. *Software: Practice & Experience*, 26(10):1161–1180, 1996.
12. N. Loughran, P. Sánchez, A. Garcia, and L. Fuentes. Language support for managing variability in architectural models. In *Software Composition*, pages 36–51, Berlin, Heidelberg, 2008. Springer Berlin Heidelberg.
13. M. Moon, H. S. Chae, T. Nam, and K. Yeom. A metamodeling approach to tracing variability between requirements and architecture in software product lines. In *7th IEEE International Conference on Computer and Information Technology (CIT 2007)*, pages 927–933, 2007.
14. K. Pohl, G. Böckle, and F. J. v. d. Linden. *Software Product Line Engineering: Foundations, Principles and Techniques*. Springer-Verlag, Berlin, Heidelberg, 2005.
15. J.-C. Royer and H. Arboleda. *Model-Driven and Software Product Line Engineering*. ISTE. Wiley, 2013.
16. P. Sánchez, N. Loughran, L. Fuentes, and A. Garcia. Engineering languages for specifying product-derivation processes in software product lines. In *Software Language Engineering*, pages 188–207, Berlin, Heidelberg, 2009. Springer.
17. T. K. Satyananda, D. Lee, S. Kang, and S. I. Hashmi. Identifying traceability between feature model and software architecture in software product line using formal concept analysis. In *2007 International Conference on Computational Science and its Applications (ICCSA 2007)*, pages 380–388, 2007.
18. SEI. Arcade Game Maker pedagogical product line. `http://www.sei.cmu.edu/productlines/ppl/`, 2018. Online; accessed 21/05/2018.
19. L. Shen, X. Peng, and W. Zhao. A comprehensive feature-oriented traceability model for software product line development. In *20th Australian Software Engineering Conference, 14-17 April 2009, Australia*, pages 210–219, 2009.
20. A. Sousa, U. Kulesza, A. Rummler, N. Anquetil, R. Mitschke, A. Moreira, V. Amaral, and J. Araujo. A model-driven traceability framework to software product line development. In *ECMDA Traceability Workshop (ECMDA-TW)*, pages 97–109, 2008.
21. G. Spanoudakis and A. Zisman. Software traceability: a roadmap. In *Handbook Of Software Engineering And Knowledge Engineering: Vol 3: Recent Advances*, pages 395–428. World Scientific, 2005.
22. J. van Gurp, J. Bosch, and M. Svahnberg. On the notion of variability in software product lines. In *Proceedings Working IEEE/IFIP Conference on Software Architecture*, pages 45–54, 2001.
23. M. Voelter and I. Groher. Product line implementation using aspect-oriented and model-driven software development. In *Proceedings of the 11th International Software Product Line Conference*, SPLC '07, pages 233–242, Washington, DC, USA, 2007. IEEE Computer Society.
24. D. Wagelaar. Context-driven model refinement. In *Model Driven Architecture*, pages 189–203, Berlin, Heidelberg, 2005. Springer.
25. J. Withey. Investment Analysis of Software Assets for Product Lines. Technical Report CMU/SEI-96-TR-010, Software Engineering Institute, Carnegie Mellon University, Pittsburgh, PA, 1996.

Propuesta de un Modelo de Proceso de Implantación de Sistemas Informáticos (MoProIMP)

Marisa Daniela Panizzi [1]

[1] Programa de Doctorado en Ciencias Informáticas. Facultad de Informática. Universidad Nacional de La Plata. Calle 50 y 120. La Plata, Buenos Aires. Argentina
marisapanizzi@outlook.com

Resumen. La implantación de sistemas informáticos es una de las fases genéricas de cualquier modelo de proceso de software. A partir de la construcción del estado del arte sobre el proceso de implantación, se evidencia que las propuestas metodológicas existentes no soportan al proceso de implantación o lo hacen débilmente. Se plantea y delimita el problema, los objetivos, las preguntas de investigación y la metodología seleccionada. Se presentan los avances de un Modelo de Proceso de Implantación de sistemas informáticos denominado MoProIMP. Luego, se resume un caso de estudio que sirvió como validación inicial al modelo propuesto. Por último, se enuncian conclusiones preliminares y describen los futuros pasos y aspectos abordar para la continuación de la tesis doctoral.

Palabras Clave: procesos de software, implantación de sistemas informáticos, modelo de proceso.

1 Introducción

En este contexto, se define implantación de sistemas informáticos al conjunto de actividades y tareas necesarias que permiten la transferencia del producto software finalizado a su ambiente de utilización, por parte de la comunidad usuaria. [1]. A este proceso se le resta importancia por tratarse del último eslabón de la cadena de procesos de software [2].

Las metodologías o estándares para el desarrollo de software conocidos en la actualidad acredita un desarrollo consolidado a lo largo de las últimas dos décadas. El proceso de implantación de sistemas informáticos, definido en las diferentes metodologías o estándares soportan algunos de los elementos de un proceso de software: actividades, artefactos o productos, técnicas/prácticas, herramientas y roles. Sin embargo, no existe una visión de proceso de implantación que custodie todos los elementos en su totalidad.

En esta Tesis Doctoral , se busca hacer frente a este problema mediante la formulación de una propuesta unificada de un modelo de proceso de implantación que integre las fases, actividades y tareas, técnicas y prácticas, herramientas, artefactos, roles y competencias. Para delimitar el problema a resolver esta tesis se enfoca en tres objetivos específicos:

- Desarrollar una taxonomía de los procesos de implantación de sistemas informáticos basada en el conjunto de metodologías y estándares existentes.
- Desarrollar un modelo de proceso de implantación de sistemas informáticos que identifique fases, actividades y tareas, técnicas y prácticas, herramientas, artefactos y roles que articule con las buenas prácticas que proponen los estándares de certificación de procesos de software.
- Desarrollar un modelo de competencias duras y blandas para el peopleware que participa en el proceso de implantación de sistemas informáticos.

Estos objetivos conducen a la formulación de la pregunta objeto de investigación:

¿Se puede cubrir la vacancia de un Modelo de Proceso para la implantación de sistemas informáticos que integre las fases, actividades y tareas, las técnicas y prácticas, las herramientas, los artefactos o productos, los roles incorporando las capacidades de peopleware?.

Para el desarrollo de este proyecto de investigación, se seguirá un enfoque de investigación clásico [3] con énfasis en la producción de tecnologías [4]; identificando métodos y materiales necesarios para desarrollar el proyecto:

- Métodos. Revisiones sistemáticas de la literatura propuestas por Kitchenham et al. [5] y Genero et al. [6]. Prototipado evolutivo experimental (método de la Ingeniería) propuesto por Basili [7]. Método DESMET propuesto por Kitchenham [8]
- Materiales. Formalismos de modelado conceptual usuales en la Ingeniería de Software [9] y en la Ingeniería del Conocimiento [10], [11]. Modelos de Proceso usuales en Ingeniería de Software [12][13].

A continuación se presenta el estado de arte, luego los avances realizados hasta el momento y por último, se enuncian conclusiones parciales y los aspectos pendientes a abordar.

2 Estado del arte

Se realizó un mapeo sistemático de la literatura[1] para identificar cuáles de las metodologías de desarrollo de software, son las más estudiadas por la comunidad científica y las más utilizadas en la industria del software. Para su desarrollo, se utilizó el proceso propuesto por Kitchenham et al. [5] y Genero et al. [6]. La Tabla 1 sintetiza las tareas realizadas en la "Actividad de Planificación de la revisión".

En la actividad "Realización de la revisión", se seleccionaron los estudios considerando algunos criterios utilizados por Sierra et al. [14].

Tabla 1. Planificación de la revisión

Tareas	Descripción
Identificar la necesidad del estudio	Identificar (determinar) cuáles de las metodologías de desarrollo de software son las más estudiadas por la comunidad científica, ya sea porque se las compara, se analizan sus aportes, se evalúa su aplicación en la industria del software, se experimenta con ellas, etc.
Formular las preguntas de investigación (PI)	PI1: ¿Qué metodologías permiten llevar adelante la construcción de un producto software? PI2: ¿En qué actividades de la construcción del producto software, gestión o procesos de

[1] En Inglés Systematic Mapping Studies o SMS.

	soporte se centra la investigación? PI3: ¿Qué aportes realizan los trabajos? PI4: ¿Cuáles son los tipos de investigación sobre las metodologías de desarrollo?
Términos de investigación	T1:desarrollo de software, T2:software development, T3:metodologías, T4:methodologies, T5:método, T6:methods, T7:software, T8: framework, T9:proceso, T10:development, T11:process
Cadenas de búsqueda (CB)	*CB1:((¨desarrollo de software)¨AND (¨proceso¨OR ¨metodologías¨OR ¨métodos¨))* *CB2:((¨software development¨) AND (¨process¨OR ¨methodologies¨OR ¨methods¨))* *CB3:((¨software)¨AND ((¨proceso¨OR ¨process¨OR ¨framework¨))* *CB4: ((developmentframework¨) OR ((framework¨AND ¨methodologies¨AND ¨¨software¨))* *CB5: ((¨development¨) AND (¨methodologies¨) AND (¨software¨))* *CB6: (¨development¨AND ¨methodology¨)* *Las cadenas de búsqueda definidas no contribuyen de manera lineal a la construcción del estado de arte de la tesis. No obstante se consideran pertinentes para el desarrollo del SMS cuyo propósito es identificar las metodologías o estándares más utilizados.*
Criterios de selección de estudios	Criterios de inclusión: ▪ Artículos que respondan a las preguntas de investigación ▪ Estudios duplicados: si hay varios artículos de un mismo autor que contemple la misma investigación, se considerara el más completo. ▪ Artículos publicados a partir del año 2008 ▪ Artículos en Español e Inglés Criterios de exclusión: ▪ Estudios a los que no se tiene acceso ▪ Artículos que no coincidan con los criterios de inclusión
Fuentes de Datos	Publicaciones de congresos y revistas de: IEEE Explore, ACM Digital Library, Springer, Elsevier Science (Science Direct), SEDICI[2], RELAIS[3], SISTEDES Biblioteca Digital[4]
Validación del protocolo	El protocolo de revisión ha sido validado con los Directores de la tesis doctoral.

La cantidad de artículos seleccionados se presenta en la Tabla 2:

Tabla 2. Fuentes de búsqueda y trabajos seleccionados para cada etapa.

Fuentes de búsqueda	Artículos relevantes[5]	Artículos no considerados	Artículos primarios
IEEE Explore	57	13	44
ACM Digital Library	15	6	9
Springer	4	3	1
Elsevier Science (Science Direct)	16	4	12
SEDICI	11	1	10
SISTEDES Biblioteca Digital	3	1	2
RELAIS	2	2	0

[2] SEDICI: Repositorio digital de la Universidad Nacional de La Plata, sitio: http://sedici.unlp.edu.ar/

[3] RELAIS: Revista Latinoamericana de Ingeniería de Software, Publicación Técnica de acceso abierto de la Red de Ingeniería de Software de Latinoamérica coordinada por la Universidad Nacional de Lanús, Argentina. ISSN: 2314-2642; sitio: http://revistas.unla.edu.ar/software/index

[4] Biblioteca Digital Sistedes. La Fundación Sistedes organiza las Jornadas Sistedes, que alberga las Jornadas de Ingeniería de Software y Base de Datos (JISBD) , sus actas se pueden encontrar en el sitio: https://biblioteca.sistedes.es/biblioteca/conferencias/

[5] Son los encontrados y seleccionados de los resultados de búsqueda iniciales que contienen los términos de búsqueda en el resumen, la introducción, las palabras clave o título.

El esquema de extracción, se presenta en la Tabla 3.

Tabla 3. Extracción de datos de los estudios primarios.

Datos extraídos	
Dimensión	**Categorías**
General:	ID (Identificador de registración del articulo), cadena de búsqueda, Año, titulo, autores, fuente de búsqueda, publicación, país, palabras clave, citas, problema y resultados.
Contexto:	*Procesos principales*: Requisitos, Desarrollo, Despliegue o Implantación, Arquitectura y Diseño, Mantenimiento, Pruebas. *Procesos de soporte y de la organización*: Verificación y validación, gestión de la configuración, gestión del proyecto, gestión del riesgo, gestión de la calidad [12].
Contribución:	Métrica, modelo, proceso, herramienta, artefacto, método/metodología, práctica/s, no contribuye.
Tipos de investigación:	Validación, evaluación, propuesta de solución, filosóficos, comunicar una experiencia, opinión [15].
Resultados preliminares	Los resultados de las metodologías, modelos, métodos presentados en los estudios.

Al analizar los artículos primarios, se concluyó que el desarrollo de software presenta una tendencia hacia las metodologías ágiles (Scrum, XP, FDD, la familia de las metodologías Crystal, DSDM) en el período considerado para este estudio. No obstante, se visualiza que la única metodología robusta que logra un porcentaje de representatividad equivalente al de algunas metodologías ágiles, es RUP.

Con base en los resultados del SMS realizado, se realiza un análisis comparativo de las metodologías de desarrollo con el propósito de determinar de qué manera se custodia el proceso de implantación de sistemas informáticos. Se consideran las metodologías de desarrollo cuya cota de representatividad, en los estudios primarios es igual o superior al 15 %. Además, se consideran Métrica V3 y MoProsoft, dado que el Grupo de Investigación de Ingeniería de Software del III-LIDI-UNLP realiza investigación conjunta con Universidades de España y de México.

Se utiliza del método DESMET, el método de evaluación cualitativa basada en el análisis de características [8], cuyo propósito es dar respuesta a la siguiente pregunta de investigación: ¿Todos los elementos del proceso de implantación de un sistema informático se encuentran cubiertos en las metodologías de desarrollo consideradas?.

Las características a utilizar en el análisis de los elementos de un proceso de software, son: ¨Fases/Actividades/Tareas¨, ¨Herramientas¨, ¨Técnicas/Prácticas¨, ¨Artefactos (Insumos/Productos)¨, ¨Roles¨ y ¨Competencias¨. En la Tabla 4, se presenta el grado de cumplimiento de las características consideradas para el proceso de implantación (en la Tabla, Implantación) y para los procesos de gestión de proyectos de software (en la Tabla, Gestión del Proyecto). El grado de cumplimiento se considera en tres niveles: total ("T"), parcial ("P") o nulo ("N").

Tabla 4. Resultados del grado de cumplimiento de las características.

	Metodologías/Procesos															
	SCRUM		Programación Extrema (XP)		Desarrollo basado en funcionalidades (FDD)		Metodologías Cristal		Desarrollo de Sistemas Dinámico (DSDM)		Proceso Unificado de Rational (RUP)		METRICA Versión 3		MoProSoft	
	Implantación	Gestión del Proyecto	Implantación	Gestión del Proyecto	Implantación	Gestión del Proyecto	Implantación	Gestión del Proyecto	Implantación	Gestión del Proyecto	Implantación	Gestión del Proyecto	Implantación	Gestión del Proyecto	Implantación	Gestión del Proyecto
Fases / Actividades/ Tareas	N	T	N	P	N	T	N	T	P	T	T	T	T	T	N	T
Herramientas	N	P	N	N	N	N	N	N	N	P	T	T	N	N	N	N
Técnicas/Prácticas	N	T	N	P	N	T	N	T	N	P	N	N	T	T	N	N
Artefactos (Insumos / Producto	N	T	N	P	N	T	P	T	P	T	T	T	T	T	N	T
Roles	N	T	N	P	P	T	P	T	N	T	T	T	T	T	N	T
Competencias	N	N	N	N	N	N	N	N	N	T	N	N	N	N	N	T

El reporte completo del establecimiento del estado del arte se encuentra en el repositorio SEDICI [16].

3. Propuesta de solución – Avances realizados

A partir de lograr identificar una serie de deficiencias y/o carencias para la ejecución exitosa del proceso de implantación de sistemas informáticos, se propone un **Mo**delo de **Pro**ceso de **IMP**lantación de sistemas informáticos, que se denomina MoProIMP. Su arquitectura presenta su modelo de ciclo de vida adoptando los 5 grupos de procesos de PMIBOK [17]. Su elección, se debe a que es un estándar reconocido a nivel mundial y de aplicación en la industria del software a nivel nacional. A cada uno de los procesos, en el modelo propuesto se lo denomina *fase.*

Para la aplicación del modelo en la industria nacional y que se realice de manera escalonada, se han adoptado tres de los niveles de capacidad propuestos en el estándar CMMI-DEV [18]. Estos son: *nivel 1= Realizado, nivel 2= Gestionado y nivel 3= Definido.* No se ha considerado el nivel *0= Incompleto* ya que significa la no realización o la realización parcial de ese proceso en la organización. Los tres niveles de capacidad considerados se analizaron a un nivel de granularidad de las tareas propuestas en MoProIMP. Se consideraron los niveles de capacidad en lugar de los niveles de madurez, porque en el contexto de la industria Argentina, son pocas las empresas que han alcanzado niveles de madurez 4 y 5, por lo tanto esto dificultaría llevar a cabo la validación de MoProIMP.

El modelo adopta un grupo de tareas de la metodología Métrica versión 3[19] por haberse analizado y considerado una de las metodologías más completas.

Se propusieron las fases, las actividades y sus objetivos, las tareas (identificando las vinculaciones) y los elementos de dependencia entre las mismas (los elementos de entradas y las salidas), se ilustran en la Figura 1. Para su representación se utilizó la técnica SADT[6] [20] con algunas adaptaciones.

Se presenta un extracto con la descripción de una de las fases de MoProIMP.

La **Fase 1: Iniciación**, se compone de: *Exploración del proyecto*, cuyo objetivo consiste en estudiar las características del proyecto y la documentación de los requisitos del mismo; *Exploración de los aspectos organizacionales*, que consiste en identificar los mecanismos de documentación, comunicación para la implantación en el contexto organizacional y la gestión de configuración; *Evaluación de los recursos,* que consiste en revisar los recursos necesarios para la implantación y *la Determinación de la factibilidad* para identificar los riesgos y definir la factibilidad.

La Tabla 5, presenta la **Fase 1: Iniciación,** las tareas de cada actividad, el nivel de capacidad para la tarea y las entradas y las salidas de cada una de las tareas.

[6] Structured Analysis and Design Technique

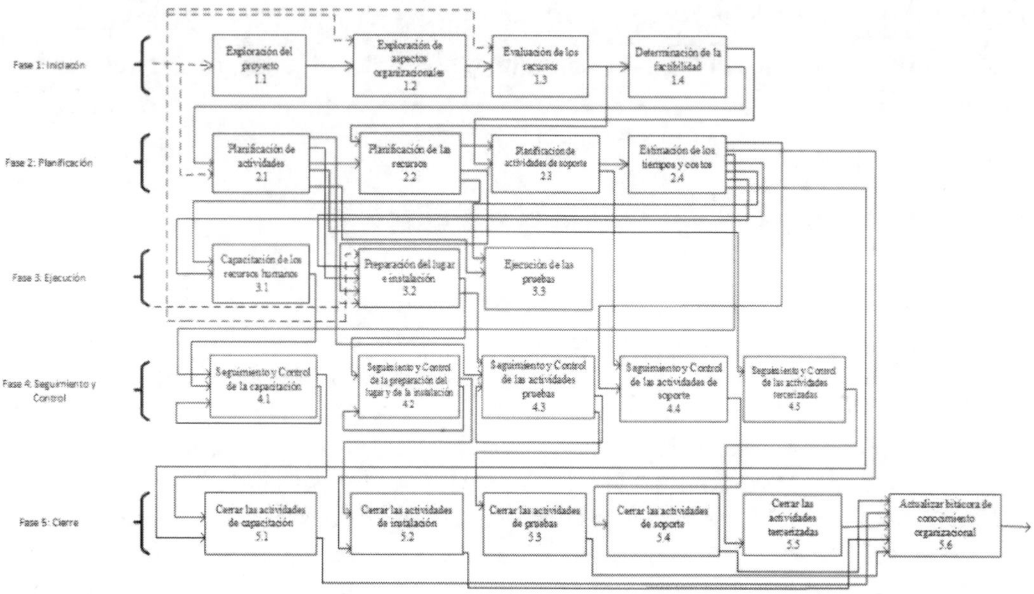

Figura 1. Proceso de Implantación (**MoProIMP**).

Tabla 5. Fase 1: Iniciación, actividades, tareas, nivel de capacidad, entradas y salidas

Fase	Actividades	Tareas	NC	Entradas	Salidas
1. Iniciación	1.1.	1.1.1.Revisar el plan del proyecto	2	Plan del proyecto	Reporte de situación de la implantación
		1.1.2. Revisar documento de requisitos	2	Documento de Requisitos	
		1.1.3. Revisar la arquitectura del producto software	2	Documento de arquitectura del software	
	1.2.	1.2.1. Revisar el protocolo de documentación de la organización	3	Protocolo de documentación Reporte de situación de la implantación	Reporte de situación de la implantación
		1.2.2. Revisar el protocolo de comunicación de la organización	3	Protocolo de comunicación Reporte de situación de la implantación	Reporte de situación de la implantación
		1.2.3. Revisar el protocolo de la gestión de la configuración	2	Protocolo de gestión de la configuración Reporte de situación de la implantación	Reporte de situación de la implantación
	1.3.	1.3.1. Determinar los recursos humanos existentes en la organización	2	Reporte de situación de la implantación Listado de usuarios Listado de recursos humanos de sistemas (técnicos)	Reporte de recursos humanos internos Reporte de situación de la implantación
		1.3.2.Determinar los recursos tecnológicos existentes en la organización	2	Reporte de situación de la implantación Documento de infraestructura	Reporte de recursos tecnológicos Reporte de situación de la implantación
	1.4.	1.4.1. Identificar los riesgos	2	Reporte de situación de la implantación	Reporte de analisis de riesgos Reporte de situación de la implantación
		1.4.2.Realizar el estudio de factibilidad	2	Reporte de situación de la implantación	Reporte de factibilidad Reporte de situación de la implantación

Se experimentó con el prototipo del modelo en un caso de estudio que corresponde a la implantación de un sistema de gestión de agencias de publicidad para Latinoamérica. Esto se realizó en una empresa multinacional que se encuentra en la República Argentina y ofrece servicios de consultoría. Se consideraron las tareas correspondientes a un nivel de capacidad 2 = gestionado de MoProIMP, dado que la organización se encuentra en un nivel de capacidad equivalente. El sistema de gestión es un ERP[7] desarrollado a medida del cliente; cuenta con los módulos convencionales

[7] En Inglés, Enterprise Resource Planning

de un ERP, entre ellos clientes, proveedores, etc. Los escenarios posibles para el proceso de implantación pueden ser: 1) Empresa nueva en un país nuevo (implica la apertura de una sucursal del grupo de agencias en un país nuevo y esto conlleva a la configuración de todos los aspectos impositivos del país), 2) Empresa nueva en un país existente (se cuenta con experiencia de los aspectos impositivos del país) o 3) Empresa nueva en instalación existente (implica la replicación de una instalación, se utiliza el mismo servidor de una sucursal existente sin compartir la base de datos). El primer escenario es el más complejo y es sobre el cual se aplicó el modelo propuesto.

En [21] se encuentra el detalle del modelo completo como así también la descripción completa del caso de estudio.

4 Conclusiones y Futuros trabajos

El desarrollo del SMS y luego la evaluación basada en características en base a los lineamientos del método DESMET, permitió identificar de qué manera las metodologías de desarrollo soportan el proceso de implantación de sistemas informáticos. Se logró evidenciar un conjunto de vacancias que presenta el proceso de implantación como proceso genérico dentro del proceso de desarrollo de software.

Se logró poner en práctica el modelo propuesto en una implantación de un sistema de gestión de agencias de publicidad para Latinoamérica.

La experimentación con el modelo permitió confirmar algunas debilidades que siguen persistiendo en el proceso de implantación; entre las que podemos mencionar métricas específicas, la gestión de riesgos, espacios institucionales para compartir conocimiento, roles con las competencias específicas para la realización del proceso.

Los próximos aspectos abordar son:

1) La construcción de los artefactos de entrada y salida para cada una de las tareas del modelo empleando los lineamientos propuestos por algún estándar.
2) Realizar un relevamiento y sistematización de las técnicas y prácticas, herramientas que se emplean en el desarrollo de las tareas del proceso y roles que participan.
3) Proponer una taxonomía de roles que participen en el proceso como así también un conjunto de competencias duras y blandas para los mismos.
4) Evolucionar el modelo, desarrollar validaciones parciales y una vez logrado el modelo completo validarlo en tres casos de estudio.

Referencias

1. Panizzi, M., Bertone, R., Hossian, A. (2017). Proceso de Implantación de Sistemas Informáticos – Identificación de vacancias en Metodologías Usuales. Libro de Actas de la V Conferencia Iberoamericana de Computación Aplicada CIACA 2017. Pág. 207 -215. ISBN 978-989-8533-70-8. Vilamoura, Algarve, Portugal.
2. Marisa Panizzi, Alejandro Hossian, Ramón García-Martínez. (2017). Implantation: A Comparative Study and Identification of Gaps in Usual Methodologies. The 29th International Conference on Software Engineering & Knowledge Engineering (SEKE

2017). Wyndham Pittsburgh University Center, Pittsburgh, USA, from July 5 to July 7, 2017. Pags 619-621. DOI reference number: 10.18293/SEKE2017-012

3. Riveros, H. y Rosas, L. (1985). El Método Científico Aplicado a las Ciencias Experimentales. Editorial Trillas. México. ISBN 96-8243-893-4.
4. Sábato, J. y Mackenzie, M. (1982). La Producción de Tecnología. Editorial Nueva Imagen. México. ISBN 968-429-348-8.
5. Kitchenham, B. and Charters, S. (2007). Guidelines for performing Systematic Literature Reviews in Software Engineering. Versión 2.3 EBSE-2007-01.
6. Genero Bocco M., Cruz-Lemus J. y Piattini Velthuis M. (2014). Métodos de investigación en ingeniería del software. Editorial Ra-Ma, 2014. ISBN 978-84-9964-507-0.
7. Basili (1993). The Experimental Paradigm in Software Engineering. En Experimental Software Engineering Issues: Critical Assessment and Future Directions (Ed. Rombach, H., Basili, V., Selby, R.). Lecture Notes in Computer Science, Vol. 706. ISBN 978-3-540-57092-9.
8. Kitchenham, B. A. (1996). "DESMET: A Method for Evaluating Software Engineering Methods and Tools," Department of Computer Science, University of Keele, Technical Report TR96-09, August 1996. ISSN:1353-7776
9. Rumbaugh, J., Jacobson, I., Booch, G. (1999). The Unified Modeling Language, Reference Manual. Addison Wesley, ISBN-10: 02-0130-998-X.
10. Gómez, A., Juristo, N., Montes, C. y Pazos, J. (1997). Ingeniería del Conocimiento. Editorial: Centro de Estudios Ramón Areces.
11. García-Martínez, R. y Britos, P. (2004). Ingeniería de Sistemas Expertos. Editorial Nueva Librería. ISBN 987-1104-15-4.
12. ISO/IEC/IEEE 12207:2017. (2017). Systems and software engineering- Software life cycle processes. International Organization for Standardization.
13. Oktaba, H., Garcia, F., Piattini, M., Ruiz, F., Pino, F., Alquicira, C. (2007). Software Process Improvement: The Competisoft Project. IEEE Computer, 40(10): 21-28. ISSN 0018-9162.
14. Sierra Jose Maria, Vizcaíno Aurora, Genero Marcela, Piattini Mario. (2017). A systematic mapping study about socio-technical congruence. Information and Software Technology http://dx.doi.org/10.1016/j.infsof.2017.10.004
15. Wieringa, R., Maiden, N.A.M, Mead, N.R. and Rolland, C. (2006) Requirements engineering paper classification and evaluation criteria: a proposal and a discussion. Requirements Engineering, 11(1), pp 102-107.
16. Panizzi Marisa. (2019). Establecimiento del estado sobre el proceso de implantación de sistemas informáticos. Reporte Técnico de Tesis Doctoral. RT-UNLP- III-LIDI. Publicado en: http://sedici.unlp.edu.ar/handle/10915/72633
17. A Guide to the Project Management Body of Knowledge. (PMBOK® Guide) – Fifth Edition. (2013). Project Management Institute. ISBN 978-1-935589-67-9.
18. CMMI® para Desarrollo, Versión 1.3 (2010). Mejora de los procesos para el desarrollo de mejores productos y servicios. TECHNICAL REPORT. Editorial Universitaria Ramón Areces.
19. PAe, Métrica versión.3. (2001). Portal de Administración Electrónica. Gobierno de España.
20. Marca David A. and McGowan, Clement L. “SADT: Structured Analysis and Design Techniques”. McGraw-Hill, New York, NY. (1988).
21. Panizzi, M., Bertone, R. Hossian, A., (2018). Propuesta de un Modelo de Proceso de Implantación de Sistemas Informáticos (MoProIMP). Libro de Actas del XXIV Congreso Argentino de Ciencias de la Computación. Universidad Nacional del Centro de la Provincia de Buenos Aires. ISBN: 978-950-658-472-6

Measuring Quality in Hybrid Software Processes

Jacqueline Marín Sánchez

Computer Science Department, Universidad de Chile, jamarin@dcc.uchile.cl

Abstract. Using hybrid processes is an international controversial trend as a means for adapting to fast technological and market changes without losing control over projects. Recent researches show that this approach is the result of a development evolution mainly grounded in experience and driven by pragmatism. A series of researchers propose a mix of traditional and agile processes in different development scenarios, but these processes are barely planned or defined in advance and are combined according to particular needs. Also, the nonexistence of specific process metrics for hybrid processes, make difficult to evaluate the quality of the mix of practices that make up the process, and threatens potential process improvement for that context. This research proposes a framework for evaluating the quality of hybrid software processes as a function of their context characteristics. In this way, the software process can take advantage of favorable factors, minimize the impact of those less favorable, and help achieve the project objectives.

1 Introduction

Software development has adopted different forms during its evolution. It has followed highly formalized or structured approaches with close management supervision, and also other more unstructured approaches. Many processes, models, methods, tools, techniques and concrete practices have been proposed to this end. However, evidence suggests that there is no unique best approach.

Traditional processes follow methods based on the quality of the artifacts, the predictability of their activities and on architectural designs that can adapt to change before it has an adverse impact on the system [4]. Despite the advantages of traditional processes these approaches have some difficulties such as: long development time, involvement of the client only at the beginning of the project, costly changes, difficulties for innovation, excessive documentation, and others.

As a consequence, around 1990 a community with a radically different perspective has emerged. This new way of addressing software development, called "agile", is ruled by 12 principles explained in the Agile Manifesto [3]. Agile methods and practices aim to simplify the software process by avoiding "bureaucracy" and advocate short time cycles, close involvement of the client and an adaptive rather than predictive strategy [1].

Many researchers plead that agile methods provide a better way to address people's needs, accelerate software development and improve quality and customer satisfaction. However, agile methods are also rarely used in their pure form [25] and can fail when they are applied in the wrong context [16].

The choice of a process is not a simple deterministic exercise but depends on the characteristics of individual development environments [6]. It is necessary to consider contextual factors such as the application domain, organizational, project and team characteristics, among others [26]. For that reason, a large number of researchers such as [4,17,25], advocate for a balance between discipline and agility in order to take advantage of the best of both worlds.

Currently, the term "hybrid software development approach" is used to refer to the balance between agility and discipline [18]. According to Kuhrmann et al. [17], a hybrid software development approach is any combination of agile and traditional approaches that an organizational unit adopts and customizes to its own context needs, e.g., application domain, culture, processes, project, organizational structure, techniques, technologies, etc.

1.1 Problem description

Clarke and O'Connor [6] proposed a comprehensive list of situational factors that characterize the context of a project to support the selection and/or optimization of the software process. However, as also argued in [9], their proposal gather too many factors (44 factors and 170 sub-factors) that yield an even higher number of combinations.

In [15], authors propose another framework to support the selection of appropriate practices according to some context factors [6]. Although this framework was successfully tested with a repository of traditional processes, there is no evidence of its applicability for agile methods nor that research had gone any further.

Boehm and Turner [5] propose a risk-based approach for structuring projects to incorporate both traditional and agile approaches according to a project's needs. This approach proposes to continuously monitor and evaluate the selected process performance considering five context factors: team size, criticality, dynamism, personnel and culture, but it does not explain how it should be done.

Recent results from surveys applied in software industry such as HELENA survey [17,19], indicate that the combination of traditional and agility development is a reality in practice for most organizations and projects. In [17], it is concluded that the use of hybrid approaches does not depend on external triggers, but this approach is the result of a natural process evolution, which is mainly driven by experience, learning, and pragmatism. Even so, it is not clear which contextual factors affect the applicability of a hybrid approach.

On the other hand, some works such as [7], propose a mix of traditional and agile processes in order to address deficiencies in different development scenarios. However, these proposals show mainly European and North American situation, and they survey both, small as well as large software companies. Most of these works present a poor characterization of the influence of contextual factors on their proposals. This lack of information makes it difficult to replicate or adapt these results.

There is a lot of literature about the measurement and improvement of traditional software development processes. To a lower extent, there are also some attempts to measure and improve agile software development processes. However, there is no evidence of mechanisms for evaluating hybrid processes. Küpper et al. [20], reported an ongoing research about developing a method to support the evidence-driven construction of hybrid development approaches, but it does not explain how to measure appropriateness for a particular context.

Therefore, this research intends to answer the following research questions:

RQ1: What are the context factors that influence the adoption of hybrid software development processes?

RQ2: How can one evaluate whether a hybrid software development approach is appropriate for a particular context?

2 Research Goals and Hypothesis

2.1 Goals

The **general goal** of this thesis is to define a set of metrics and indicators that allow the evaluation of the adequacy of a hybrid software development approach to its context characteristics and the project objectives. We expect that these metrics result will be useful to support decision making about hybrid software process improvement and/or optimization whenever necessary.

The **specific goals** defined to reach the general goal are the following:

- Identify context factors that affect the use of hybrid software processes.
- Define metrics and indicators for measuring hybrid software process quality.
- Propose a framework for evaluating the quality of hybrid software processes as a function of their context characteristics.

2.2 Hypothesis

There are metrics and indicators that allow us to evaluate and potentially improve the quality of a hybrid software development process, taking into account contextual factors and project objectives.

3 Background and Related Work

An appropriate software process must fit the needs of the project. These needs are based on the context of the situation in which it should work and therefore, the software process depends on the context [6].

According to Pressman [23], a software process can be seen as a guide for the activities, actions and tasks that are required to obtain high quality software. Additionally, Osterweil [21] emphasizes that software processes must be treated in the same way as software: they must be carefully designed, constructed, tested, executed, maintained and reused.

One of the most important and crucial issues in mastering any complex phenomenon is being able to understand and assess its state and behavior [11]. In software development, measuring processes would allow us to understand, control and improve the processes, products, projects and resources [10].

3.1 Contextual Factors

The scenarios in which the practice takes place are rarely the same. The size and maturity of the organization, types of customers, human factors, organizational culture, geographical location and others, impose different influences in unique ways [9].

According to Clarke and O'Connor [6], the contextual factors affecting the software development process can be classified as: personnel, requirements, application, technology, organization, operation, management and business. Each classification contains a set of factors that include different sub-factors. For example, *organization* takes into account maturity, management commitment, stability, structure, facilities and organization size. On the other hand, Boehm and Turner [4] propose five critical factors for deciding between following a traditional or agile approach depending on the particular project situation: size, criticality, dynamism, personnel and culture. According to this research, a project that adjusts to four of these agile or traditional factors, but does not satisfy the fifth, is a project that requires risk evaluation and probably a combination of both approaches is the most appropriate way to follow.

Therefore, a project's context is multidimensional and it is not always clear which factors are those that affect process quality the most. For the purpose of this thesis, research will be conducted in Chilean small companies. This reduces the context dimensions, but the whole methodology can still be applied in other contexts.

3.2 Hybrid Software Processes

Different aspects such as the benefits brought by the agile philosophy and its difficulties in domains where traditional processes still work fine, as well as the variable characteristics of different contexts, has led to defend the idea of combining both approaches [25]. According to Boehm and Turner [4], discipline without agility results in an inflexible hierarchy while agility without discipline leads to the heady, unencumbered enthusiasm of a start-up company-before it has to turn a profit.

In 2011, West et al. [27] stated that hybrid software development had become standard in practice. Recent studies such as [17,19], have confirmed this reality. However, the results of the HELENA Survey [17] report that hybrid development approaches are barely planned or defined in advance. They evolve with time guided by pragmatism and experience. Practices, methods, processes, etc, are selected and personalized on demand [20] and process optimization depends on the situational characteristics [6]. All these issues, and also the nonexistence of process metrics specific for hybrid processes, make difficult to evaluate the quality of the mix of practices that make up the process, and threatens potential process improvement for that context.

3.3 Process Measurement and Improvement

Fenton and Bieman [10] indicate that measurement is the process by which numbers or symbols are assigned to attributes of entities within a given domain, using clearly defined rules. Given the relevance of also measuring attributes that might be considered as non measurable, e.g. customer satisfaction, Hubbard [14] states that measurement is a quantitatively expressed reduction of uncertainty based on one or more observations. In [10] it is also argued that observations that can reduce uncertainty can quantitatively measure the risk of negative events or the likelihood of positive outcomes.

Within the software engineering context, a measure provides a quantitative indication of the extent, amount, dimension, capacity, or size of some attribute of a product or process [23]. A metric is a quantitative measure of the degree to which an entity possesses a given attribute [12]. An indicator is a metric or combination of metrics that provide insight into the software process, a project, or the product itself [23].

Every measurement action must be motivated by a particular goal or need that is clearly defined and easily understandable [10]. For example, if we would like to know "how much does a project cost?", we can measure the time and effort involved in all activities and processes performed during development. In this way, we obtain an understanding of the total cost of the project and the contribution of each activity to this total cost.

According to Pressman [23], the only rational way to improve any process is to measure specific attributes, develop a set meaningful metrics based on these attributes, and then use the metrics to provide indicators that will lead to a strategy for improvement. Process measurement in traditional software development seeks information about complying with the plan, adherence to the specified process, change prevention, minimizing errors before deployment, measuring productivity and effort, etc. [23]. There is a lot of research that propose metrics for traditional scenarios, such as those presented in [28]. This study presents a model of software process metrics based on CMMI as a means for evaluating, controlling and improving process maturity and capacity. With this goal, they define a set of metrics categorized as: Effort distribution, Defect distribution, Process efficiency, and some others for fulfilling the plan and the schedule.

But, what happens when changes in the requirements are frequent?, when the degree of uncertainty is high?, when there is little personnel and time is limited? According to Fuggetta and Di Nitto [11], metrics established for traditional processes, as they are defined, are not necessarily appropriate for evaluating a software process in an agile environment. Nevertheless, empirical investigation into metrics in agile development is scarce [24].

In their research, Oza and Korkala [22] classified metrics used in agile development as Code level, Productivity/effort level, and Economic metrics. Gustafsson [13], for its part, classified agile metrics into five categories as Quality, Predictability, Business value, Lean, and Cost. On the other hand, Downey and Sutherland [8] propose nine metrics for evaluating hyper-productive teams guided by Scrum, such as: Velocity, Work Capacity, Focus Factor, Percentage of

Adopted Work, Percentage of Found Work, Accuracy of Estimation, Accuracy of Forecast, Targeted Value Increase, Success at Scale, and the Win/Loss Record of the Team. The metrics mentioned in these and other works will be used as a starting point of our research.

In software development consistency is the exception and inconsistency is the most common state [2]. Thus, it is necessary to ensure that the process as a whole "converges" towards the desired outcome, tolerating, controlling, and exposing deviations as they occur [11]. In general, it is essential to identify and develop new methods to assess, represent, and communicate the state of a software process.

4 Methodology and Work Plan

Taking into account that there exist a large number of different context variables that influence the mix of practices, finding an appropriate mix can involve a lot of variables. Therefore, in order to limit the scope, this research will focus on small companies, where variables relating project and organization size will not be considered as constants. Also, in order to take advantage of the availability of Chilean companies, the research will focus on Chilean small companies.

The methodology to be applied along the whole research contains five steps: review, contextualize, propose, validation and conclusion. Figure 1 shows the work plan to be followed. Also, along with the whole research work we expect to publish conference and journal papers including partial results.

A. **Review**: This step is composed of three sub-steps where concepts are reviewed. The first two are finished and the third one in ongoing work.
   1. Review of context attributes favoring traditional and agile processes: A survey was conducted for understanding the factors that favor or prevent the successful adoption of traditional and agile software processes.
   2. Review the trends in software development approaches in Chile and the rest of the world: Data resulting form the HELENA Stage 2 [19] was analyzed for knowing the state of the practice of traditional and agile processes in industry. Results of this survey show that Chile, similarly to what happens in the rest of the world but to a lower extent, is more conservative in adopting agile practices for management and less conservative for engineering activities. This work also found a trends towards hybrid software development both, in Chile and the rest of the world.
   3. Systematic Literature Review on software process quality metrics: We conducted a systematic literature review for identifying metrics and indicators that have been applied for measuring traditional and agile software processes. This is a basis for studying the Chilean situation.

B. **Contextualize**: This step includes data collection and analysis.
   4. Data collection: Data about traditional and agile practices applied in small companies will be collected, along with the context situations when they are applied. Also, metrics and indicators commonly used for measuring quality will be collected. To this end, Ground Theory will be applied gathering information from semi-structured interviews.

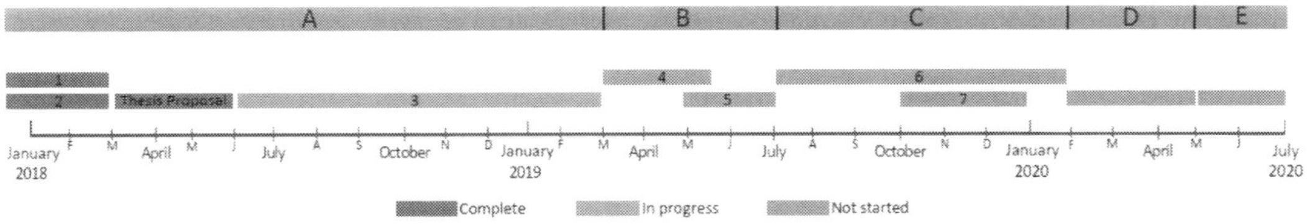

Fig. 1: Work plan.

5. Data analysis: Collected data will be organized according to their relationships using Affinity Diagrams so that it can be analyzed and used as an input for proposing the evaluation framework.

C. **Propose**: The main contribution of this thesis will be built in this step. It includes two sub-steps: framework proposal and its initial validation.

6. Proposal: In this stage, all data and knowledge about factors, practices and their relationships acquired in previous steps will be used for proposing a first version of a framework that allows for the evaluation of hybrid software process quality.
7. Initial validation: This first framework will be validated through a multi case study in two to four Chilean companies. Gathered information will be used for adjusting and improving the framework.

D. **Validation**: Here, the adjusted framework will be used in small companies that apply hybrid software development processes using action research. The goal is to be able to measure and improve the process quality. To this end, we will participate hands-on in project development in the company so that first-hand data can be collected.

E. **Conclusion**: In this step we will write the thesis document including the results of all the previous steps.

Acknowledgements

The work of Jacqueline Marín Sánchez was partly supported by CONICYT-PCHA/Doctorado Nacional/2016-21160112.

References

1. S. Augustine. *Managing agile projects.* Prentice Hall PTR, 2005.
2. R. Balzer. Tolerating inconsistency. In *ICSE 1991*, pages 158–165. IEEE.
3. K. Beck et al. Manifesto for Agile Software Development. [online]. 2001. Available at: http://www.agilemanifesto.org/.
4. B. Boehm and R. Turner. *Balancing Agility and Discipline: A Guide for the Perplexed.* Addison-Wesley Professional, 2003.
5. B. Boehm and R. Turner. Using risk to balance agile and plan-driven methods. *Computer*, 36(6):57–66, 2003.
6. P. Clarke and R. V. O'Connor. The situational factors that affect the software development process: Towards a comprehensive reference framework. *Information and Software Technology*, 54(5):433–447, 2012.

7. T. Dingsøyr, N. B. Moe, T. E. Fægri, and E. A. Seim. Exploring software development at the very large-scale: a revelatory case study and research agenda for agile method adaptation. *Empirical Software Engineering*, 23(1):490–520, 2018.
8. S. Downey and J. Sutherland. Scrum metrics for hyperproductive teams: how they fly like fighter aircraft. In *HICSS 2013*, pages 4870–4878. IEEE.
9. T. Dybå, D. I. Sjøberg, and D. S. Cruzes. What Works for Whom, Where, When, and Why? On the Role of Context in Empirical Software Engineering. In *ESEM 2012*, pages 19–28. IEEE.
10. N. Fenton and J. Bieman. *Software metrics: a rigorous and practical approach.* CRC Press, 2014.
11. A. Fuggetta and E. Di Nitto. Software process. In *FOSE 2014*, pages 1–12. ACM.
12. A. Geraci et al. *IEEE standard computer dictionary: Compilation of IEEE standard computer glossaries.* IEEE Press, 1991.
13. J. Gustafsson. Model of agile software measurement: A case study. 2011.
14. D. W. Hubbard. *How to measure anything: Finding the value of intangibles in business.* John Wiley & Sons, 2014.
15. S. Jeners, R. O'Connor, P. Clarke, H. Lichter, M. Lepmets, and L. Buglione. Harnessing Software Development Contexts to Inform Software Process Selection Decisions. *Software Quality Professional*, 16(1):35–36, 2013.
16. P. Kruchten. Contextualizing agile software development. *Journal of Software: Evolution and Process*, 25(4):351–361, 2013.
17. M. Kuhrmann, P. Diebold, J. Münch, P. Tell, V. Garousi, M. Felderer, K. Trektere, F. McCaffery, O. Linssen, E. Hanser, and C. R. Prause. Hybrid Software and System Development in Practice: Waterfall, Scrum, and Beyond. In *Proceedings of the 2017 International Conference on Software and System Process*, ICSSP 2017, pages 30–39. ACM, 2017.
18. M. Kuhrmann, J. Münch, P. Diebold, O. Linssen, and C. R. Prause. *On the Use of hybrid development approaches in software and systems development: Construction and test of the HELENA Survey.* Gesellschaft für Informatik eV, 2016.
19. M. Kuhrmann, P. Tell, J. Klnder, R. Hebig, S. Licorish, and S. MacDonell. Complementing Materials for the HELENA Study (Stage 2). Technical report, 11 2018.
20. S. Küpper, A. Rausch, and U. Andelfinger. Towards the Systematic Development of Hybrid Software Development Processes. In *ICSSP 2018*, pages 157–161. ACM.
21. L. Osterweil. Software processes are software too. In *ICSE 1987*, pages 2–13. IEEE.
22. N. Oza and M. Korkala. Lessons learned in implementing agile software development metrics. In *UKAIS*, page 38, 2012.
23. R. S. Pressman. *Software Engineering: A Practitioner's Approach.* McGraw-Hill Education, 2010.
24. P. Ram, P. Rodriguez, and M. Oivo. Software process measurement and related challenges in agile software development: A multiple case study. In *PROFES 2018*, pages 272–287. Springer.
25. G. Theocharis, M. Kuhrmann, J. Münch, and P. Diebold. Is Water-Scrum-Fall Reality? On the Use of Agile and Traditional Development Practices. In *PROFES 2015*, pages 149–166. Springer.
26. L. R. Vijayasarathy and C. W. Butler. Choice of software development methodologies: Do organizational, project, and team characteristics matter? *IEEE Software*, 33(5):86–94, 2016.
27. D. West, M. Gilpin, T. Grant, and A. Anderson. Water-Scrum-Fall Is The Reality Of Agile For Most Organizations Today. *Forrester Research*, 26, 2011.
28. R. Xu, Y. Xue, P. Nie, Y. Zhang, and D. Li. Research on cmmi-based software process metrics. In *IMSCCS (2) 2006*, volume 2, pages 391–397. IEEE.

Algoritmos para la sumarización lingüística de datos, ayuda a la toma de decisiones en organizaciones orientadas a proyectos

Iliana Pérez Pupo[1], Osvaldo Santos Acosta[1], Rafael E. Bello Pérez[2], Pedro Y. Piñero Pérez[1]

[1] Grupo de Investigación en Gestión de Proyectos, Universidad de las Ciencias Informáticas, Carretera a San Antonio Km 2 ½, La Habana, 54830, Cuba.

[2] Centro de Estudios Informáticos, Universidad Central "Marta Abreu" de Las Villas, Cuba

[1] {iperez, osantos, ppp}@uci.cu, [2]rbellop@uclv.edu.cu

Resumen. El desarrollo vertiginoso de productos y servicios de software, genera información diversa en las empresas y organizaciones que lo utilizan, especialmente en las orientadas a proyectos, donde intervienen numerosos especialistas de disímiles áreas de conocimiento. La interpretación de la información almacenada en estos escenarios podría influir en la toma de decisiones, que impactan a su vez en la producción. Para facilitar la comprensión y uso de esos datos se han creado técnicas que ayudan a extraer conocimiento potencial descubriendo relaciones intrínsecas entre ellos. Las técnicas de soft computing es un ejemplo de ello, pero en particular, la sumarización lingüística de datos, es recomendable si se desea facilitar la interpretación de los datos a los especialistas. Otro elemento importante de la sumarización lingüística de datos son los indicadores (T) de evaluación de calidad de los resúmenes generados, propuestos por Zadeh. En este trabajo se generan algoritmos de sumarización lingüística de datos combinando técnicas de soft computing y para su evaluación se aplican indicadores de evaluación de la calidad inspirados en los T de Zadeh. Para la validación se utilizan datos relacionados con la información histórica registrada en organizaciones orientadas a proyectos y se aplican métodos de análisis de evaluación cuantitativa y tests de ranking.

Palabras Clave: Sumarización Lingüística de Datos, Toma de Decisiones, Gestión de Proyectos, Soft Computing.

1 Introducción

Actualmente en las organizaciones orientadas a proyectos se manifiesta un incremento considerable de la cantidad de datos que se generan y que influyen en la toma de decisiones. En este escenario se realizan grandes esfuerzos por mejorar la eficiencia y la eficacia en la gestión, pero persisten numerosas dificultades en los procesos de toma de decisiones como muestran diferentes estudios.

Los estudios continuos realizados por el Standish Group International [1] [2], en 50.000 proyectos de todo el mundo, desde pequeños hasta grandes proyectos muestran el comportamiento histórico de esta problemática, ver Fig. 1. Se observa que el número de proyectos renegociados se ha mantenido siempre por encima de los satisfactorios que no superan el 35% de los proyectos. Por otra parte, el porciento de proyectos cancelados se mantiene en un número elevado [3].

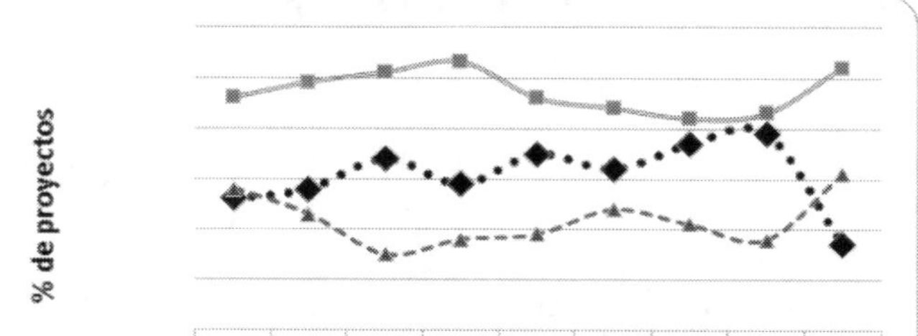

	1998	2000	2002	2004	2006	2008	2010	2012	2014
Satisfactorios	26	28	34	29	35	32	37	39	17
Renegociados	46	49	51	53	46	44	42	43	52
Cancelados	28	23	15	18	19	24	21	18	31

Fig. 1. Comportamiento de proyectos, según Standish Group, *Datos tomados de [4].

En estos reportes se señalan causas fundamentales del fracaso de los proyectos: la mala gerencia, errores en la planificación, e insuficiencias en la toma de decisiones durante el control y seguimiento, entre otras [5] [6] [7]. Para ayudar a resolver esta situación es importante el desarrollo de nuevas tecnologías que contribuyan a la toma de decisiones y conocer que estos escenarios están caracterizados por:

- Los datos que se manejan son heterogéneos y están afectados en gran medida por la percepción de los especialistas que los generan. Este fenómeno provoca la incertidumbre de la información expresada en: la ambigüedad en los conceptos, imprecisión por errores de medición o percepción de los especialistas, la veracidad de los datos que se recogen y la incompletitud de la información.
- Las decisiones se toman fundamentalmente durante los cortes de proyectos, que tienen lugar con frecuencia semanal o quincenal y se necesita agilidad en las decisiones.
- Generalmente estas organizaciones tienen que tomar decisiones no en un proyecto específico, sino en programas de proyectos, donde la complejidad y cantidad de información aumenta, lo que dificulta la interpretabilidad de los factores que influyen en el éxito o fracaso de los proyectos.
- Generalmente los especialistas que toman decisiones en los proyectos no son expertos en análisis de datos, por lo que requieren que los sistemas de información prevean información clara, fácilmente interpretable y de ser posible, cercana al lenguaje natural.

Estas dificultades podrían ser mitigadas aplicando técnicas para el descubrimiento de conocimiento y el análisis de resúmenes históricos de los datos en forma lingüística, facilitando su interpretación para los decisores [8]. Las técnicas de descubrimiento de conocimiento se han clasificado principalmente en dos clases: predictivo y descriptivo. El objetivo de las técnicas descriptivas es explorar patrones (correlaciones, tendencias, grupos, trayectorias y anomalías) que resumen las relaciones subyacentes en los datos [9]. En este contexto surge la sumarización lingüística de datos (SLD, también conocido como LDS del inglés: *linguistic data summarization*) [10] como una de las técnicas de descubrimiento de conocimiento descriptivo con un enfoque interesante y prometedor para producir resúmenes a partir de datos numéricos utilizando lenguaje natural.

El trabajo se organizada por secciones de la siguiente forma: En la sección 2 se resume el diseño de la investigación y un breve estudio del estado del arte asociado al tema. En la sección 3 se presentan algoritmos para la construcción de resúmenes lingüísticos. En la sección 4 se comparan los resultados generados por los algoritmos. Finalmente, en la sección 5 se presentan las conclusiones del trabajo.

2 Diseño de investigación

A partir de la situación problemática analizada en la investigación y resumida en la introducción de este artículo, se identificó el siguiente problema de investigación: ¿Cómo descubrir conocimiento en forma de resúmenes lingüísticos que sinteticen las problemáticas existentes, para la ayuda a la toma de decisiones, en organizaciones orientadas a proyectos? A partir de este problema se identifica como objeto de investigación es: "Descubrir conocimiento en forma de resúmenes lingüísticos".

Para resolver este problema los autores se plantean el siguiente objetivo general: "Desarrollar nuevos algoritmos para la sumarización lingüística de datos que sirvan de ayuda a la toma de decisiones en organizaciones orientadas a proyectos, combinando diferentes técnicas de soft computing". Siendo el campo de investigación: "Algoritmos de sumarización lingüística de datos".

Los objetivos específicos son:

- Construir un marco teórico referencial asociado a los métodos relacionados con la sumarización lingüística de datos, tendencias, y aplicaciones en la gestión de proyectos.
- Desarrollar algoritmos para la generación de resúmenes lingüísticos de datos a partir de la información histórica generada en organizaciones orientadas a proyectos, combinando diferentes técnicas de soft computing, considerando las particularidades de los proyectos.
- Validar los algoritmos propuestos a partir de la aplicación de diferentes técnicas de triangulación metodológica.

La hipótesis definida es la siguiente: "El desarrollo de nuevos algoritmos para sumarización lingüística de datos y su aplicación en organizaciones orientadas a proyectos, ayudará a los procesos de toma de decisiones en estas organizaciones".

Se define como variable dependiente: "Descubrir conocimiento, en forma de resúmenes lingüísticos, que sintetice las problemáticas existentes en organizaciones orientadas a proyectos". Mientras que la variable independiente es: "Algoritmos para la sumarización lingüística de datos".

A partir del diseño de investigación se siguió la siguiente metodología de trabajo. Primero se procede a construir un marco teórico referencial asociado a las técnicas existentes de sumarización lingüística de datos y su aplicación en organizaciones orientadas a proyectos. Es este primer paso se aplican los métodos teóricos: histórico-lógico y el hipotético deductivo. En un segundo momento se proponen nuevos algoritmos para la sumarización lingüística de datos. Luego, en un tercer momento se procede a la comparación de los algoritmos propuestos con otras técnicas identificadas en la bibliografía. Para este último paso se aplican métodos empíricos tales como el método experimental aplicado sobre el Repositorio de datos para investigaciones en gestión de proyectos [11] de la Universidad de las Ciencias Informáticas y las encuestas a especialistas en gestión de proyectos para evaluar los resúmenes generados de acuerdo al criterio de los expertos.

Yager trata la sumarización de datos en [12] y un año después Zadeh introduce los cuantificadores difusos *Q* [13], lo cual representa el grado de satisfacción de una cualidad por un conjunto de objetos. Para ello se cuenta con un sumarizador *S*, un filtro *R* y los valores de verdad *T*, que representan indicadores para medir la calidad de los resúmenes. El objetivo de este trabajo es generar resúmenes que cumplan las protoformas declaradas en la Tabla 1, siendo el objeto de análisis los "proyectos".

Tabla 1. Tipos de resúmenes objeto de esta investigación.

Tipo	Ejemplo
Qy´are S	La mayoría de los proyectos están evaluados de mal.
Qy´R are S	La mayoría de los proyectos con mal rendimiento están evaluados de mal

Para un mejor análisis de las investigaciones en este campo y su aplicación en las organizaciones orientadas a proyectos se realizó una búsqueda bibliográfica en las bases de datos bibliográficas bajo el término "linguistic data summarization".

Como resultado, entre las técnicas más conocidas de sumarización lingüística de datos se encuentran: las propuestas por Kacprzyk y Zadrożny, quienes en [14] [15] utilizan consultas difusas en la construcción de resúmenes con protoformas básicas, y en [16] usan reglas de asociación. Luego en [17] se propone el uso reglas IF-THEN para la generación de resúmenes lingüísticos. Posteriormente Donis-Díaz y otros autores proponen el uso de algoritmos genéticos [10] y su hibridación con búsqueda local [18], pero en estos enfoques los autores no consideran las relaciones presentes entre las variables, elemento que puede ser mejorado con otras técnicas.

En la búsqueda realizada no se encuentran aplicaciones de las técnicas de sumarización lingüística de datos en las organizaciones orientadas a proyectos.

3 Algoritmos para la sumarización lingüística de datos

En el presente artículo se presentan dos nuevos algoritmos para la generación de resúmenes. El primero es un algoritmo que combina el análisis de componentes principales (PCA) con el algoritmo Apriori ver el algoritmo *LDS_PCA*. El segundo algoritmo propuesto combina el PCA con el algoritmo de estimación de distribuciones UMDA ver el algoritmo LDS_PUMDA.

Algoritmo *LDS_PCA*

D: conjunto de datos y A_{LV}: variables lingüísticas describen los datos

Q: cuantificador

percentil: para determinar la pertenencia de una variable a una componente

Paso 1. components = do_pca(D)
Paso 2. u = calculate_umbral (components, percentil)
Paso 3. DB = transform_fuzzy(D, A_{LV})
Paso 4. Rules = generate_rules_from_components(component)
Paso 5. Summaries = generate_lds_rules(D, Rules, A_{LV}, Q)
Paso 6. T = evaluate_summaries(Summaries)
Paso 7. Summaries_ordered = best_summaries(Summaries, T)
Paso 8. Generate output(Summaries_ordered)

En el algoritmo *LDS_PCA* se aplica el algoritmo PCA [19] para construir los componentes principales. Por cada componente se recuperan las variables con mayor relación en el contexto de la componente, las que tengan valor de pertenencia mayor al umbral *u*. Luego se aplica el algoritmo Apriori por cada conjunto de variables seleccionadas por componente, este enfoque disminuye el espacio de búsqueda de los resúmenes. Se refinan las reglas de asociación generadas por Apriori y se generan resúmenes lingüísticos a partir de dichas reglas. Finalmente se calculan los valores de T que permiten evaluar los resúmenes lingüísticos generados.

Algoritmo *LDS_PUMDA*

Máster

Paso 1. components = do_pca(D)
Paso 2. u = calculate_umbral(components, percentil)
Paso 3. DB = transform_fuzzy(D, A_{LV})
Paso 4. For each component,
Paso 5. Execute UMDA(D, Q, $components_i$, u) in slave number *i*
Paso 6. $summaries_i$ = receive_summaries_from slave number *i*
Paso 7. Summaries = Merge($summaries_i$)
Paso 8. T = evaluate_summaries($summaries_i$)
Paso 9. Summaries_ordered = best_summaries(Summaries, T)
Paso 10. Generate output(Summaries_ordered)

Esclavo

Paso 1. Recibir los datos de entrada y a partir de los en la componente i-ésima
Paso 2. $t = 1$
Paso 3. Generar población *P(t)* con *N* individuos de la forma QRy´s are S
Paso 4. Evaluar la población *P* con la función objetivo
Paso 5. Mientras no se cumpla condición de parada
Paso 6. Seleccionar los mejores individuos de la población P_{se}
Paso 7. Estimar la distribución $ps(P_{se}, t)$ a partir del conjunto P_{se}
Paso 8. Generar $P'(t)$ nuevos puntos según la distribución $ps(P_{se})$
Paso 9. Construcción de la nueva población P(t+1) = replacement(P(t), P´(t))
Paso 10. t = t +1
Paso 11. Enviar al master la población final *P(t)*

Este algoritmo persigue dos objetivos en la búsqueda de resúmenes: el primer objetivo está asociado a la obtención de resúmenes con buenos valores de *T* y el segundo asociado a lograr diversidad en los resúmenes encontrados. Para lograr el primer objetivo la función objetivo se centra en el cálculo de los valores *T* para cada uno de los resúmenes. Para lograr elevar la diversidad, que es el 2do objetivo, se concibe el algoritmo con múltiples subpoblaciones, que evolucionan de forma independiente en las estaciones esclavas, donde cada subpoblación evoluciona a partir de una de las componentes principales obtenidas con PCA y sus atributos asociados. Finalmente se generan resúmenes por cada subpoblación, es decir, por cada esclavo.

Este segundo algoritmo está propuesto en una variante paralela con el objetivo de lograr un mejor rendimiento de ejecución del algoritmo.

4 Validación de los resultados

Para el diseño de experimentos se emplean técnicas de triangulación metodológica:

- Triangulación de datos, donde se comparan los algoritmos propuestos usando dos bases de datos, del repositorio de datos sobre gestión de proyectos [11].
- Triangulación de expertos, donde se evalúa la calidad de los resúmenes en escenarios reales con cinco expertos, doctores del claustro de la Maestría en Gestión de Proyectos.
- Triangulación de métodos, donde se comparan los algoritmos propuestos con un algoritmo basado en reglas de asociación reportado en la bibliografía.

Las bases de datos empleadas relacionan las siguientes variables: la evaluación de proyectos, las competencias de los recursos humanos, el tiempo planificado y el tiempo real empleado en el desarrollo del proyecto, así como la eficiencia y la eficacia de los recursos humanos.

En la tabla 2 se muestra la comparación realizada a los algoritmos respecto a la cantidad de los resúmenes generados y a los indicadores de calidad de los resúmenes [20]. Para la comparación de los indicadores se aplica agregación promediando los valores T de los resúmenes, y para una mejor interpretación se muestra este valor en 2-tuplas, empleando el siguiente conjunto de términos: LBTL = {Bajísimo, Muy bajo, Bajo, Medio, Alto, Muy alto, Altísimo}.

Tabla 2. Comparación de resultados en un conjunto de datos de 24 atributos y 8430 registros.

Criterios de comparación	Algoritmo basado en reglas de asociación		Algoritmo *LDS_PCA*	
Cantidad de resúmenes	167		150	
	Promedio	2-tuplas	Promedio	2-tuplas
Certidumbre (T1)	0,78	(Muy alto, -0,04)	0,78	(Muy alto, -0,04)
Imprecisión (T2)	0,46	(Medio, -0,04)	0,47	(Medio, -0.03)
Cobertura (T3)	0,58	(Medio, 0.08)	0,55	(Medio, 0.05)
Adecuación (T4)	0,08	(Bajísimo, 0.07)	0,08	(Bajísimo, 0.07)
Longitud (T5)	0,98	(Altísimo, -0,01)	0,94	(Altísimo, -0.06)

Como se puede apreciar, a modo general con el algoritmo LDS_PCA se obtienen mejores resultados que con el algoritmo basado en reglas de asociación reportado en la bibliografía para el mismo juego de datos: generó 17 resúmenes menos y según el promedio de los valores de T, genera resúmenes de mejor grado de verdad, mejor precisión y menor longitud. Esto mejora el nivel de comprensión o interpretabilidad de los resúmenes.

Los resúmenes más relevantes obtenidos por los algoritmos propuestos fueron:

- Alrededor del 50% de los proyectos que tienen (el "índice de ejecución" mal) o (la "cantidad de RRHH evaluados de bien" es baja) o ("la evaluación del proyecto" es regular) o (la "cantidad de RRHH evaluados de regular" es baja) tienen la "ejecución en proceso del proyecto" mal.
- En pocos proyectos que tienen el "tiempo trabajado" perfecto tienen "el 50% de los RRHH tienen competencia baja".
- En la mayoría de los proyectos que tienen (la cantidad de RRHH con competencia media) es baja, se cumple que (la cantidad de RRHH evaluados de bien) es baja.

La valoración de los expertos sobre estos resúmenes es la siguiente: en el primero se interpreta que el 50 % de los proyectos que están mal presentan dificultades en su producción en proceso, lo cual acarreará mayores conflictos con los clientes sino se toman medidas rápidamente. El segundo indica la dependencia de las competencias laborales con la eficiencia en el trabajo, se reporta que existen pocos proyectos con una excelente gestión de tiempo que tienen el 50% del personal con bajas competencias. Con otros resúmenes se identifica que el indicador de índice de ejecución de las tareas influye significativamente en la evaluación del proyecto. Además, se permite detectar proyectos donde hay problema en la evaluación de recursos humanos y otros en los que hay una mala distribución de los recursos humanos a partir de sus competencias.

El tercer resumen evidencia que las competencias de los recursos humanos impactan en la calidad de su evaluación.

5 Conclusiones y trabajos futuros

Los expertos en gestión de proyectos consultados concluyen que es posible la aplicación de la sumarización lingüística de datos para la gestión de proyectos de software, permitiendo a los líderes de proyectos la toma de decisiones asociadas al control y seguimiento de los proyectos.

Los algoritmos propuestos generaron menor cantidad de resúmenes respecto a los algoritmos empleados en la comparación reportados en la bibliografía.

La introducción de técnicas paralelas en el algoritmo LDS_PUMDA permitió no solo mejorar la eficiencia sino también obtener mejor calidad de resúmenes.

Como trabajo futuro, los autores se proponen un mayor estudio de los valores de T de los resúmenes lingüísticos respecto a su extensión a la teoría neutrosófica para incluir el tratamiento no solo de los valores de certeza, sino también de falsedad y neutralidad en el momento de medir la calidad de los resúmenes lingüísticos en proyectos de gestión de software. También el desarrollo de nuevas variantes de algoritmos basados en metaheurística para la generación de resúmenes lingüísticos.

Referencias

[1] T. S. G. International, "The CHAOS Manifesto. The Standish Group International, Incorporated.," 2014.

[2] S. Group and others, "The chaos manifesto think big, act small," *Recuperado Em*, vol. 13, 2015.

[3] Standish Goup International, "The CHAOS Report," The Standish Group International, Inc., 2015.

[4] T. Clancy, "The standish group chaos report," *Proj. Smart*, 2014.

[5] M. Delgado, M. D. Ruiz, D. Sánchez, and M. A. Vila, "Fuzzy quantification: a state of the art," *Fuzzy Sets Syst.*, vol. 242, pp. 1–30, 2014.

[6] J. Á. Gimeno Alonso, "Fallos en proyectos: investigación sobre causas generales," *XVI Congr. Int. Ing. Proy.*, 2012.

[7] A. Bassi, S. Vigato, L. Buffoni, M. Bonetti, G. LuciaSwitzerland, and R. Vaccargiu, "Pmo and Project Success the Importance of a Project Management Structure Survey by Swiss Companies," *Manag. Knowl. Learn. Int. Conf. 2018*, vol. 16, p. 18, 2018.

[8] J. Gomes and M. Romão, "Improving project success: A case study using benefits and project management," *Procedia Comput. Sci.*, vol. 100, pp. 489–497, 2016.

[9] J. Kacprzyk and S. Zadrożny, "On a fuzzy querying and data mining interface," *Kybernetika*, vol. 36, no. 6, pp. 657–670, 2000.

[10] C. A. Donis-Diaz, R. Bello, J. Kacprzyk, and others, "Linguistic data summarization using an enhanced genetic algorithm," *Czas. Tech.*, vol. 2013, no. Automatyka Zeszyt 2 AC (10) 2013, pp. 3–12, 2014.

[11] P. P. Pérez, I. P. Pupo, C. C. Rivero Hechavarría, C. R. Lusardo, R. G. Sosa, and S. T. López, "Repositorio de datos para investigaciones en gestión de proyectos," *Rev. Cuba. Cienc. Informáticas*, vol. 13, no. 1, pp. 176–191, 2019.

[12] R. R. Yager, "A new approach to the summarization of data," *Inf. Sci.*, vol. 28, no. 1, pp. 69–86, 1982.

[13] L. A. Zadeh, "A computational approach to fuzzy quantifiers in natural languages," *Comput. Math. Appl.*, vol. 9, no. 1, pp. 149–184, 1983.

[14] J. Kacprzyk and S. Zadrożny, "On a fuzzy querying and data mining interface," *Kybernetika*, vol. 36, no. 6, pp. 657–670, 2000.

[15] J. Kacprzyk and S. Zadrożny, "Linguistic database summaries and their protoforms: towards natural language based knowledge discovery tools," *Inf. Sci.*, vol. 173, no. 4, pp. 281–304, 2005.

[16] J. Kacprzyk and S. Zadrozny, "Linguistic summarization of data sets using association rules," in *Fuzzy Systems, 2003. FUZZ'03. The 12th IEEE International Conference on*, 2003, vol. 1, pp. 702–707.

[17] D. Wu, J. M. Mendel, and J. Joo, "Linguistic summarization using if-then rules," in *Fuzzy Systems (FUZZ), 2010 IEEE International Conference on*, 2010, pp. 1–8.

[18] C. Donis-Diaz, A. Muro, R. Bello-Pérez, and E. V. Morales, "A hybrid model of genetic algorithm with local search to discover linguistic data summaries from creep data," *Expert Syst. Appl.*, vol. 41, no. 4, pp. 2035–2042, 2014.

[19] N. González García and A. Taborda Londoño, "Análisis de componentes principales Sparse: formulación, algoritmos e implicaciones en el análisis de datos," 2015.

[20] J. Kacprzyk and R. R. Yager, "Linguistic summaries of data using fuzzy logic," *Int. J. Gen. Syst.*, vol. 30, no. 2, pp. 133–154, 2001.

A Software Architecture for Integrating Augmented Reality to a Board Game for Water Source Care Awareness

Jefferson H. Iglesias and Andrés A. Navarro-Newball
{jehi0056,anavarro}@javerianacali.edu.co

Pontificia Universidad Javeriana, Cali, Colombia

Abstract. We present a way to integrate board games with augmented reality (AR). After analysing the state of AR, we propose an architecture integrating a user experience layer based on AR to a serious board game experience. We worked collaboratively with Rodacanto, a foundation working for heritage an natural preservation in a rural community nearby. Our testbed for the project was a board game promoting environment preservation, focusing on water issues related to this rural community. We implemented a first prototype using a mobile application. Validation with players shows potential of the proposed approach.

Keywords: Software Architecture, Augmented Reality, Tangible User Interfaces, Board Games, Serious Games, Cooperative Design

1 Introduction

Rodacanto is a foundation located in the Village of Potrerito in Colombia. Here, activities focus on the creation of a culture of peace through art. One of the projects under development within the foundation involves the generation of awareness about the care and use of water through games. With the help of Rodacanto, we explore the possibility of improving learning through techniques such as AR, this being one of the elements of innovation in pedagogy shown as a trend by the Open University in its reports of innovation in pedagogy [1]. AR is a technology that offers new ways of educating effectively and attractively and that can take advantage of the growing boom in the use of mobile devices as educational tools. Mobile devices can be used outdoors and indoors and allow displaying digital content superimposed on images from the real world, favouring interactions between the environment and the user [3]. Tobar-Muñoz [4] argues that AR games-based learning benefit the processes of learning and teaching. Tangible User Interfaces (TUIs) take advantage of the human capacity to manipulate objects and can be used in conjunction with AR. TUIs transport the digital component to tangible elements (e.g. objects belonging to a board game) that the user can manipulate to perform different activities, with specific devices and can be more enjoyable than traditional GUIs [5]. The goal of our project is to design and test an architecture that supports the integration of board games and AR for the generation of awareness in the use and care of water resources.

Lou, Maher and Lee [6] present two examples of interaction with TUIs. According to them [6], there are five distinguishable properties that differentiate TUIs from traditional GUIs. All of these features can be useful in our AR board game proposal where some physical elements relate to a virtual element of the system: (1) TUIs allow accessing multiple objects with independent functionalities; (2) TUIs enable interaction concurrency as the user can manipulate these several objects at the same time; (3) the objects used in the interaction can be designed for a specific function; (4) the system can determine the position and orientation of the physical objects with which it interacts; (5) TUIs allow the reconfiguration of elements in a simple way, adapting their workspace according to their needs. AR has been implemented with positive results with the objective of teaching or fun through games in multiple contexts [7, 8]. Architectures proposed for the implementation of systems that integrate AR have been varied [9–11]. A service-oriented architecture for an implementation of an e-business system that integrates AR. A client-server architecture for education control and automation. A system with a robust architecture that allows to adapt the learning content for children and adults according to the context. Hybrid systems integrating board games with video-games may improve the interaction, from the recreational point of view of the players [12]. However, we did not find any AR board game architecture that could support our project for the Rodacanto foundation.

2 Development

We used a cascade software engineering approach and included the Rodacanto Foundation's leaders and children to get requirements following a cooperative design process. We managed to understand users, tasks and environments to bring their fantasy and create artistic content for the game. All the interactions with children and Rodacanto personnel had an informed consent approved by the Rodacanto Foundation. We identified the elements related to water care and use and their potential in AR in order to obtain functional requirements. We interviewed project leaders from the Rodacanto foundation using open questions. This helped us identify what Rodacanto wanted to show, including water good practices, impact of careless water use and bad practices. We identified some issues (e.g. show children how to measure water sources health), which in terms of functional requirements could be summarised as: (1) input: marker on the board; (2) output: AR content rendered on the screen; (3) description: player must point the camera to the marker to display content (Figure 1H). Children were involved throughout design and development using an iterative process, including multidisciplinary skills and perspectives. With the help of one expert in the Waldorf pedagogy from Rodacanto, we made two surveys to take into account children's tastes and interests so we could include some in the game design. Table 1 summarises our findings and our proposal regarding those. Children drew most of the game visual elements (Figure 1A). We used as a reference the geographical distribution of the region where Rodacanto is located. We went to Rodacanto and started a fictional walk through the map in order to get narrative elements for the game from the children (Figures 1C and D). Additionally, we pre-defined some game mechanics. Then we developed an initial draft of the game board, including elements of the geography of the region (Figure 1B). We overlaid the images from the children (Figure 1A) on our proposed layout (Figure 1B) as shown in Figures 1E and F. The game consists of a tour of the area of Potrerito, while identifying the different concepts on the care and use of water and the environment, and at the same time overcoming the obstacles that stand in the way for recovering the nature and sources of water. Each player starts at a different point on the board and must walk all the path through the board until returning to the starting point. This route can be made with up to four characters (similar to parcheesi). All participants will see an introductory video at the beginning of the game (using AR), which shows the possible consequences of not taking care of the environment. In order to define the player who starts the game, the dice is thrown by each participant and the one who gets the highest number starts and the shift continues to this player's right. There special stops in the path (all of them using some form of AR). When the player is stopped by a goblin, he/she will observe an AR video related to water and/or environmental issues. Then he/she must answer a question. If the response is incorrect he/she must return to the previous goblin point. When the player reaches a live nature spot in the path, he/she can listen an AR audio playing the sounds of nature and throw the dices again. If the player is stopped by a witch, he/she has to go back to the previous witch in the path. Figure 1G shows the children playing the game.

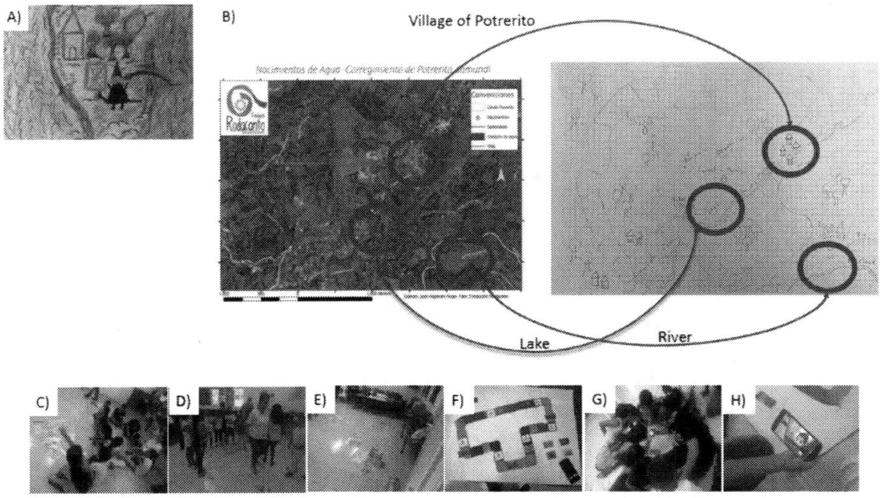

Fig. 1. Game board design and gameplay. A) Visual content from children. B) Matches between the GPS image and the board. C) Getting children's imaginary. D) First gameplay with prototype AR. E) Final board layout on the floor. F) Final board incorporating children's art. G) AR during game play. H) AR is used to display information, questions and characters.

2.1 Architecture Design

We identified non-functional requirements and proposed an architecture. We had to choose a design pattern and design a data base. We defined the design of the proposed architecture for the system, based on the non-functional requirements and main quality attributes that we had to achieve. According to the analysis performed, we defined two quality attributes that are of great relevance in the interaction of children with AR, usability and performance [13], given that the interaction between the users of the system is dramatically different to conventional AR systems as we are using the board game as a TUI. Usability refers to easiness to learn to use the system, adapting the system to user needs and user satisfaction. Usability is attribute of quality of great importance in the design of games for children, facilitating the interaction of these with new technologies such as AR. Learning how to use the system and the interaction with the physical game is of great importance to ensure a good user experience. Performance refers to the players' involvement in the game.

Next, we describe the scenarios of quality that we want to deal within the architecture proposed for the system, to meet the requirements of users, with the aim of facilitating the interaction of children with this new game. Scenarios 1 to 3 are usability scenarios. Scenario 4 is a performance scenario. An artefact is a component from the architecture (Figure 2C). (1) Scenario 1. The stimulus is: learn how to use the functionality of content added to the reality (AR). The artefact is: recognition of markers and interaction with the board module. The response is: show video content. The measure is: number of errors less than three. (2) Scenario 2. The stimulus is: learn how to use the functionality of content added to the reality (AR). The artefact is: recognition of markers and interaction with the board module. The response is: show 3D character. The measure is: number of errors less than three. (3) Scenario 3. The stimulus is: learn how to use the functionality. The artefact is: verication of answers module. The response is: question displayed and checked. The measure is: customised content. (4) Scenario 4. The stimulus is: request for verication of response of the player. The artefact is: Content management module. The response is: show response to the petition, with the verication of the response data. The measure is: 3 seconds per verication.

The relationship between software architecture and usability focuses not only on the user interface, but it has a high correlation with the components of the system (Figure 2A, [14]), which present different types of oriented patterns to achieve usability in the system, considering elements such as help systems, error management, etc. According to analysis of quality attributes defined for the application and the tactics or selected patterns, we propose the architecture shown in Figure 2C. In this diagram, we relate to the components proposed by Bass, Bonnie and Kates [14] and Bass, Kazman and Clements [15], in a way to facilitate the learning of the use of the system by children and provide a good experience for users. As mentioned, [15] the separation of the system using pattern model view controller (MVC), supports the usability of the system allowing to respond to different views of the data. Accordingly, we propose performing an

Table 1. Game Design

Finding	**Our approach**
The four subjects preferred by children are: mathematics, natural science, arts and physical education. They like the mathematical operations, physical activity, painting and animals.	The topic of the game is natural sciences. The player has to rescue the water sources by getting information and surpassing challenges that occur during his/her walk through the path
59% of the children like to play accompanied, and 35% prefer to play alone.	It is a board game that supports up to four players or four groups of players
Children's favourite games are traditional games (e.g. hide and seek) with 31.35% and video games with 25%; because they consider them fun.	The game can be taken from the table to the floor to make players be more active during gameplay
Characteristics of games that children like most are those dealing with changing the image of the characters and interacting caring for the characters.	Each character has an AR version that can be visualised with a mobile device. Characters are animals from the Potrerito region
The games that most children like are domino, parcheesi, and chess.	Our game is also a board game. The player incarnates an animal from the region that has to walk the path saving water sources. The player who arrives first wins
Most of the children like to receive awards.	The player who arrives first wins
Most of the children like to have sound effects and music in the games.	There is AR multimedia content adapted to the game
Half of the children like games that are challenging, other children are indifferent to them.	The game has challenges that children have to overcome in order to save the water sources
Most of the children are amused by technology-based games.	The games uses mobile AR to augment the content of the board with information and challenges

integration of the patterns from Bass, Bonnie and Kates [14] and Bass, Kazman and Clements [15], in reference to the adaptability of the system, considering the tasks carried out and their context to deliver aid to the user over the use of the system, as well as behaviour consistent with this. We propose to extend the use of the context to adapt the behaviour of the system and in turn manage these components adapted to the MVC pattern, so that it generates an excellent user experience (Figure 2B). For example, We can define tasks such as display AR or display questions and answers. Additionally, we can define a context such as range age 7 to 10, beginner. Then, the system behaves (e.g. too slow, displaying videos wrongly) in some way and reaches a status such as error, normal condition of operation, stable lightning.

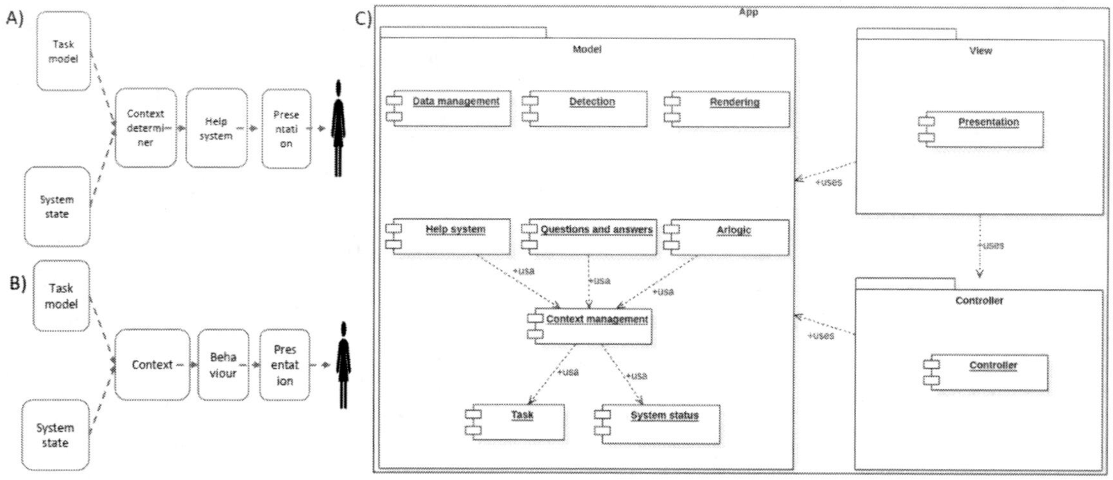

Fig. 2. Architecture. A) Usability pattern. B) Proposed extension. C) MVC base architecture.

3 Validation

We carried out functional tests of each of the components or processes implemented for the prototype, as well as integral tests of the main service of the application. Additionally, we iterated and tested the prototype with eleven children from the Rodacanto Foundation. Our game takes important elements from the parcheesi game (Table 1). For example, the player has to follow a path from the beginning to the end. The one who arrives first wins. The player can have more than one character in the path. We defined the 7-10 years old, beginner's context and the display content and question tasks and we evaluated the system, which reached the status normal operation. Regarding the quality assurance scenarios we found that: (1) Scenario 1: successful with only one mistake. (2) Scenario 2: Successful with no errors. (3) Scenario 3: successful with questions customised according to Rodancanto's interests. (4) Scenario 4: successful with

2 seconds per response. Additionally, with think aloud and observation, we captured some opinions from the users. For example, videos should be shorter and content should be provided by the children; the game should add challenges to be solved in the real world; there was knowledge appropriation; there should be funny characters and obstacles. And characters should be smaller. We tested the game with two groups of children. This helped children integrate as a group. This is evidenced that the game can be played in groups. However, it is desirable to have more mobile devices available.

4 Conclusion and Further Work

In general, through the interaction of children with AR and the board game, we evidenced a positive perception of these, through statements like "so cool", "very funny", "Where can I download it?", etc.; as well as the intention to continue participating in the game or the desire to participate from the children who were watching the game. Therefore, the game encourages the motivation of children for learning and raising awareness about the care of the water and the environment. Additionally, validation showed some basic learnig. However, some game features may be enhanced. Our contribution was to add a usability pattern to the MVC architecture. This extension allowed us implementing a working prototype and content flexibility for an AR biard game. For example, questions were customised and multimedia content could be updated. Overall, it was possible to adapt the architecture to the game required by the Rodacanto Foundation. It is possible to adapt it to other path following board games. We can work in the enhancements detected with think aloud. Additionally, other contents were identified that could be added in the dynamics of the game.

5 Acknowledgements

Authors acknowledge InfiValle as executing entity of the project: "Training and innovation for the strengthening of the competitiveness of the ICT sector in the western region: Formatic and Innovatic, Valle del Cauca", which is financed with resources from the General System of Royalties; the Government of the Valle del Cauca for having prioritized the project; PacifiTIC as operating entity; the Rodacanto Foundation for raising its necessities and to allocate human talent to work in the solution and/or improvement of the situation of the organization. The project allowed us to have the advice and scientific accompaniment of the Pontificia Universidad Javeriana Cali, which through this project tends to have a more competitive ICT sector in Valle del Cauca.

References

1. Sharples, M., Adams, A., Alozie, N., Ferguson, R., FitzGerald, E., Gaved, M., McAndrew, P., Means, B., Remold, J., Rienties, B., Roschelle, J., Vogt, K., Whitelock,

D. and Yarnall, L. (2015). Innovating Pedagogy 2015: Open University Innovation Report 4. Milton Keynes: The Open University.

2. Fuht, B. Handbook of augmented reality, Springer, 1 edition (2011). ISBN: 978-1-4939-0127-2. doi: 10.1007/978-1-4614-0064-6
3. Kysela, J. and Ŝtorková, P. Procedia - Social and Behavioral Sciences, 174, 926-931 (2015). Using Augmented Reality as a Medium for Teaching History and Tourism. ISSN 1877-0428. https://doi.org/10.1016/j.sbspro.2015.01.713.
4. Tobar-Muñoz, H., Baldiris, S. and Fabregat, R. Co Design of Augmented Reality Game-Based Learning Games with Teachers Using Co-CreaARGBL Method. In: 16th International Conference on Advanced Learning Technologies (ICALT), Austin, TX, pp. 120-122, IEEE(2016). doi: 10.1109/ICALT.2016.32
5. Sitdhisanguan, K., Dechaboon, A., Chotikakamthorn, N. and Out, P. Comparative study of WIMP and tangible user interfaces in training shape matching skill for autistic children. In: TENCON 2007 - 2007 IEEE Region 10 Conference, Taipei, pp. 1-4, IEEE(2007). doi: 10.1109/TENCON.2007.4428939
6. Maher, M.L. and Lee, L. Synthesis Lectures on Human-Centered Interaction, 10(2), i-111 (2017). Designing for Gesture and Tangible Interaction. doi:10.2200/S00758ED1V01Y201702HCI036
7. Sheng, L.Y. Modelling learning from Ingress (Google's augmented reality social game). In: 63rd Annual Conference International Council for Education Media (ICEM), Singapore, pp. 1-8, IEEE(2013). doi: 10.1109/CICEM.2013.6820152
8. Salazar, M., Gaviria,J., Laorden, C. and Bringas, P.G. Enhancing cybersecurity learning through an augmented reality-based serious game. In: Global Engineering Education Conference (EDUCON), Berlin, pp. 602-607, IEEE(2013). doi: 10.1109/EduCon.2013.6530167
9. Park, S., Lee, J., Kim, Y. and Ryu, J. A Preliminary System Framework for 'SilGam' Book. In: International Symposium on Ubiquitous Virtual Reality, Gwangju, pp. 64-67, IEEE(2009).doi: 10.1109/ISUVR.2009.20
10. Wang R. and Wang X. Applying Service-Oriented Architecture into an Augmented Reality E-business System. In: IEEE International Conference on e-Business Engineering, Xi'an, pp. 621-626, IEEE(2008). doi: 10.1109/ICEBE.2008.103
11. Doswell, J.T. Augmented Learning: Context-Aware Mobile Augmented Reality Architecture for Learning. In: Sixth IEEE International Conference on Advanced Learning Technologies (ICALT'06), Kerkrade, pp. 1182-1183, IEEE(2006). doi: 10.1109/ICALT.2006.1652683
12. Regan L. Mandryk and Diego S. Maranan. False prophets: exploring hybrid board/video games. In: CHI '02 Extended Abstracts on Human Factors in Computing Systems (CHI EA '02), pp. 640-641, ACM(2011). DOI=http://dx.doi.org/10.1145/506443.506523
13. Radu, L. Core (2017). Exploring the Usability of Augmented Reality Interaction Techniques During Children's Early Elementary-School Years. oai:smartech.gatech.edu:1853/56248
14. Bass, L., John, B. and Kates, J. Achieving Usability Through Software Architecture (CMU/SEI-2001-TR-005). Pittsburgh, PA: Software Engineering Institute, Carnegie Mellon University, (2001).
15. Bass, L. Clements, P. and Kazman, R. Software Architecture in Practice. Addison-Wesley Professional; 3 edition (2012). ISBN-10: 9780321815736

GeCodP: Herramienta para la generación de código de pruebas integrada en entornos productivos

Danay Larrosa Uribazo[1], Martha Dunia Delgado Dapena[1], Alejandro Miguel Güemes Esperón[1]
[1] Dpto. de Ingeniería de Software, Universidad Tecnológica de La Habana "José Antonio Echeverría",
Calle 114 % Ciclovía y Rotonda, Marianao, La Habana, Cuba
[1] {dlarrosau, marta, aguemes}@ceis.cujae.edu.cu

Resumen. En la actualidad existen herramientas para la generación de código de pruebas unitarias. Sin embargo, se centran en un leguaje específico. Esto trae como consecuencia, que siempre que se necesite generar pruebas para un nuevo lenguaje se tenga que realizar todo el producto desde cero. Este trabajo presenta un primer acercamiento a una herramienta para la generación de código de pruebas integrada en diferentes entornos productivos. La herramienta GeCodP se ha integrado al entorno de desarrollo Eclipse para generar código de pruebas, unitarias y funcionales, en lenguajes de la familia XUnit. Se describen, además, los mecanismos de extensión de la herramienta que permiten adicionar nuevos dominios de entrada y nuevos lenguajes de código de prueba, de forma tal que la herramienta pueda ser utilizada en otros entornos de desarrollo de software. Para ello, se parte de un modelo de generación automática de pruebas basado en búsquedas definido previamente.

Palabras Clave: Pruebas de Software, Pruebas Unitarias, Generación automática de Código de Pruebas, Herramientas de Ejecución de Pruebas.

1 Introducción

La realización de pruebas unitarias durante el proceso de desarrollo de software es de gran importancia para la detección temprana de defectos y de esta forma, contribuir a la calidad del producto de software en desarrollo [1]. Sin embargo, estas pruebas son costosas en tiempo y esfuerzo, por lo que se hace necesaria su automatización [2]. Otro aspecto importante a tener en cuenta durante la realización de las pruebas, es la realización de un buen diseño de los casos de pruebas debido a que permite encontrar más defectos [3].

Existen diversas herramientas de la familia XUnit para la ejecución automática de pruebas unitarias para diferentes lenguajes de programación, tales como: JUnit [4], NUnit [5] y PHPUnit [6]. Sin embargo, estas herramientas no cuentan con funcionalidades que contribuyan en el diseño de las pruebas. Esto trae como consecuencia, que los desarrolladores y probadores, en gran medida no cuenten con un buen diseño de los casos de pruebas.

Con respecto al diseño de los casos de pruebas, diferentes trabajos científicos se han dedicado a esta etapa del proceso de pruebas, como [2, 7-9]; y en [10-14] se centran en la generación de pruebas unitarias. Además, en [15-19] se encargan de la generación de valores de pruebas mediante la utilización de Inteligencia Artificial para evadir la explosión combinatoria de valores. Sin embargo, en su mayoría son propuestas teóricas o no tienen en cuenta técnicas de diseño de la Ingeniería del Software para lograr mayor detección defectos con menos casos de pruebas [1, 3].

En los últimos años, se han desarrollado herramientas que tienen en cuenta el diseño y ejecución de las pruebas unitarias a partir de código fuente, como [20-23]. Para ello, generan código de pruebas que puede ser ejecutado en una herramienta de la familia XUnit. Sin embargo, estas herramientas se centran en un solo lenguaje de programación. Esto trae como consecuencia, que siempre que se necesite generar pruebas para un nuevo lenguaje se tenga que realizar todo el producto desde cero.

En [24], se ha definido un modelo para la generación automática de pruebas basado en búsquedas, conocido como MTest.search. El modelo consta de Flujos de Trabajo para la ejecución de pruebas tempranas en el entorno de producción, Modelos de Optimización para reducción de casos de pruebas funcionales y unitarias, y Herramientas [25, 26] Automatizadas Integradas que dan soporte a la ejecución de los flujos de trabajo. Los Modelos de Optimización están compuestos por: un modelo de dominio de entrada, un modelo de pruebas, un modelo de pruebas reducido y un modelo de ejecución. La utilización de este modelo permite realizar extensiones en los modelos de dominio de entrada y de ejecución para la generación de pruebas en diferentes lenguajes sin modificar los modelos de pruebas.

Este trabajo presenta un primer acercamiento a una herramienta para la generación de código de pruebas integrada en diferentes entornos productivos. La herramienta GeCodP se ha integrado al entorno de desarrollo Eclipse para generar código de pruebas, unitarias y funcionales, en lenguajes de la familia XUnit. Se describen, además, los mecanismos de extensión de la herramienta que permiten adicionar nuevos dominios de entrada y nuevos lenguajes de código de prueba, de forma tal que la herramienta pueda ser utilizada en otros entornos de desarrollo de software. Para ello, se parte del modelo MTest.search.

2 Arquitectura de GeCodP

GeCodP es una herramienta para la generación de código de pruebas en diferentes lenguajes y a partir de diferentes dominios de entrada. Se sustenta en el Modelo de Generación automática de Pruebas basado en búsquedas (MTest.search) descrito en [24]. Aunque surge como un componente del Modelo se puede utilizar de forma independiente. Esto se hace posible a través de los mecanismos de extensión que ofrece y que permiten personalizarlo para ser utilizado en diferentes entornos de desarrollo tecnológico.

Como soporte al modelo se han desarrollado un conjunto de componentes y herramientas que cubren la generación de casos y código de pruebas en diferentes entornos y los mecanismos de extensión que permiten entenderlos y adaptarlos a las necesidades del entorno productivo.

Las herramientas están organizadas mediante el patrón Arquitectura basada en componentes y está orientado a la experticia del usuario de MTest.search. Se expresa a través de una arquitectura compuesta por tres capas: capa de generación de suit de pruebas, capa de extensión y capa de entorno usuario (ver Fig. 1). La herramienta GeCodP (paquete Generación de código) integra el resto de los componentes que dan soporte al modelo.

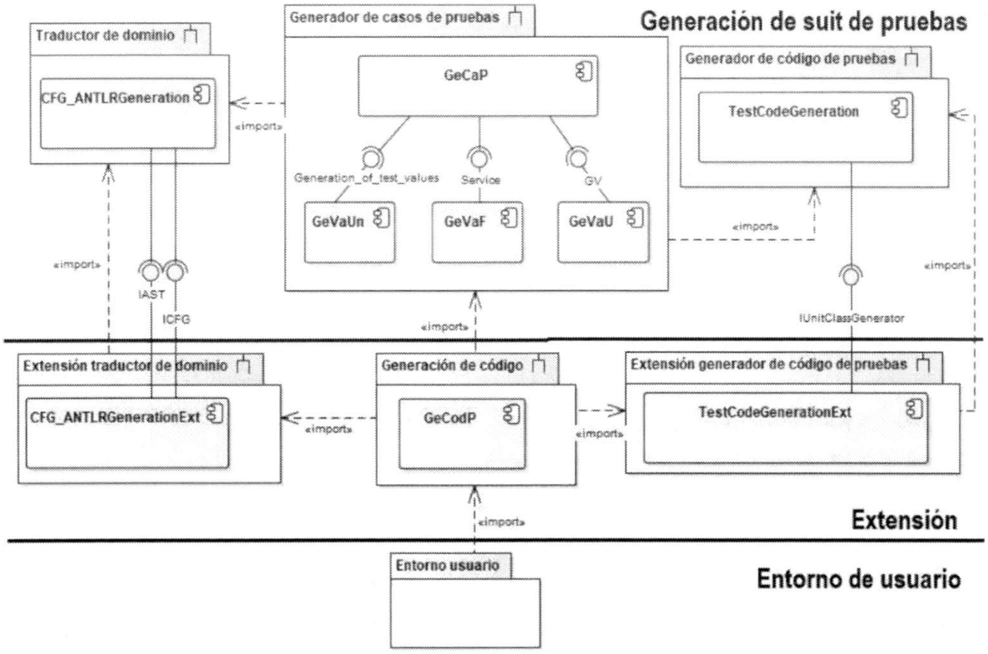

Fig. 1. Arquitectura basada en componentes de la herramienta GeCodP.

La primera capa, contiene el componente GeCaP que integra otros componentes que hacen posible la generación de la suit de pruebas reducida. A esta capa solo deben tener acceso los desarrolladores del equipo de proyecto de MTest.search, de forma tal que se garantice la consistencia y flexibilidad del modelo y sus mecanismos de extensión. La extensión del modelo de reducción basado en búsquedas es privativa de esta capa.

La segunda capa, contiene el componente GeCodP implementado en Java que permite a los usuarios avanzados utilizar los mecanismos de extensión previstos para el modelo de dominio, el modelo de pruebas y el modelo de ejecución.

Por último, la tercera capa está concebida para la personalización de MTest.search a los entornos productivos específicos del usuario. En ella se deben implementar aplicaciones clientes que capturan la información del dominio de entrada y que visualizan la suit de pruebas reducida en el lenguaje o artefacto de salida correspondiente.

Para la inserción de estas herramientas en los entornos productivos debe tenerse en cuenta que en el mercado existen diversas herramientas para la ejecución automática de pruebas, una vez que los desarrolladores o probadores han diseñado adecuadamente los casos de prueba. Por tal motivo, estas herramientas de ejecución de pruebas del mercado, que hayan sido seleccionadas por la empresa, y las herramientas que automatizan la generación de los casos de prueba propias de MTest.search, serán integradas en el entorno productivo.

3 Propuesta de solución

Los mecanismos de extensión de la propuesta permiten dos tipos de extensiones que serán descritas a continuación.

Extender a nuevos dominios de entrada. Procedimiento a seguir:

1 Crear un nuevo componente que importe el componente CFG_ANTLRGeneration del paquete Traductor de dominio y el componente GeCaP_Classes para el trabajo con el grafo de control de flujo.

2 Implementar una clase CFGGenerator que implemente la interfaz ICFG. Para ello, redefinir el método que genera el grafo de control de flujo a partir del código fuente en el nuevo dominio.

En caso de utilizar la herramienta ANTLR para analizar el código del nuevo dominio:

3 Crear un nuevo componente que importe ANTLR (versión 4.1.1).

4 Implementar la gramática del nuevo dominio de entrada, de modo que se genere un AST (Árbol de sintaxis abstracta) en lenguaje Java.

5 Importar el componente creado en 3 en el componente creado en 1.

6 Implementar una clase GeneradorAST que implemente la interfaz IAST en el componente creado en 1. Para ello, redefinir el método que genera el AST a partir del código fuente en el nuevo dominio, mediante la utilización del componente creado en 3.

7 Utilizar el método que genera el AST al principio del método que genera el grafo de control de flujo.

Extender a nuevos códigos de prueba. Procedimiento a seguir:

1 Crear un nuevo componente que importe el componente TestCodeGeneration.

2 Implementar una clase XUnitClassGenerator que implemente la interfaz IXUnitClassGenerator. Para ello, redefinir los métodos para crear la clase de prueba a partir de los casos de pruebas generados, la clase bajo prueba y el método bajo prueba; y para crear los métodos de pruebas teniendo en cuenta el framework de XUnit a utilizar para la ejecución de las pruebas.

Una vez creadas las extensiones descritas previamente, en la capa de extensión, el usuario avanzado debe importar el componente GeCodP y redefinir el método que genera el código de prueba teniendo en cuenta el nuevo dominio de entrada y el nuevo código de salida.

En el caso de la capa de entorno del usuario, es necesario importar el componente GeCodP, para la generación de código de pruebas en un lenguaje específico. Para ello, el usuario debe especificar el código a probar y el lenguaje de programación asociado a dicho código.

4 Resultados y discusión

Con el objetivo de evaluar la introducción de GeCodP en diferentes entornos se diseñaron dos casos de estudio que fueron conducidos por las preguntas siguientes:

1. ¿Es posible extender a nuevos dominios de entrada y a nuevos códigos de pruebas?
2. ¿Es posible generar código de pruebas prueba para diferentes lenguajes de la familia XUnit, a partir de métodos codificados en diferentes lenguajes de programación?

Para ello, se implementaron los mecanismos de extensión descritos previamente para Java y C#. Además, se personalizó el modelo para el entorno de desarrollo Eclipse 4.5.2 o inferior, que permite el trabajo con código Java y C#.

La generación de código de pruebas se realizó en una PC con las siguientes características: Procesador Intel Core i3-4160 de 3.60 GHz y, Memoria RAM de 4 GB. Se utilizó el formato de xUnit 4, en Eclipse 4.5.2.

Pregunta 1. ¿Es posible extender a nuevos dominios de entrada y a nuevos códigos de pruebas?

Para ello, se crearon los componentes necesarios que implementan las interfaces del subsistema Traductor de dominio, teniendo en cuenta el procedimiento descrito en el epígrafe anterior para a extender a nuevos dominios de entrada.

Para la creación del componente con la gramática de ANTLR para un nuevo dominio de entrada, ver Fig. 2 a. Para la creación del componente que genera el grafo de control de flujo a partir del código fuente del nuevo dominio de entrada, ver Fig. 2 b. Luego, para extender a nuevos códigos de pruebas, también se tuvo en cuenta el procedimiento descrito en el epígrafe anterior. Para ello, se crearon los componentes necesarios que implementan las interfaces del subsistema Generador de código de pruebas (ver Fig. 2 c).

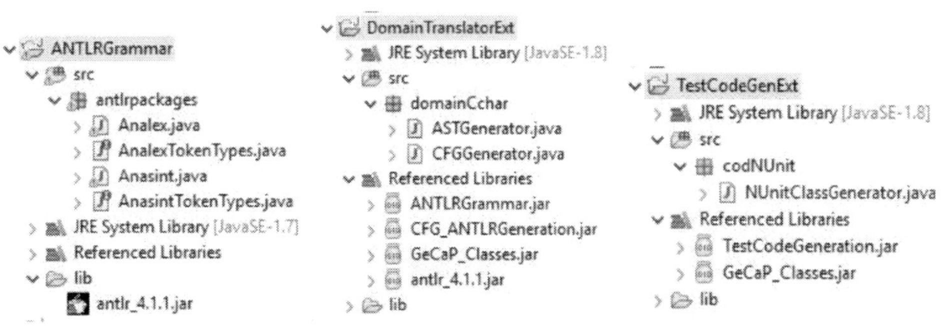

Fig. 2. Vista de implementación de los componentes a) ANTLRGrammar, b) DomainTranslatorExt y, c) TestCodeGenExt.

Pregunta 2. ¿Es posible generar código de pruebas prueba para diferentes lenguajes de la familia XUnit, a partir de métodos codificados en diferentes lenguajes de programación?

Para la generación de los casos de pruebas se utilizó el código fuente del algoritmo de clasificación de triángulos definido en [1], en lenguaje de programación Java y C#. Para ello, se crearon los componentes de extensión necesarios, como se mostró en la respuesta de la pregunta anterior. Además, se generó el código de pruebas para su posterior ejecución en JUnit y NUnit, para la ejecución de pruebas unitarias en Java y C# respectivamente.

Para la visualización del trabajo de la herramienta se utilizó el plugin desarrollado para el entorno de desarrollo Eclipse. Partiendo del código fuente en ambos lenguajes se obtuvo el código de pruebas que se muestra en Fig. 5 y Fig. 6 respectivamente.

```java
import triangleClassification.TriangleClassification;
import org.junit.Assert;
import org.junit.Test;

public class TestTriangleClassification {

    @Test
    public void test_triangleClassification_CP1() {
        TriangleClassification triangleClassification = new TriangleClassification();
        String expected = "Los lados -1, 0 y 0 no forman un triángulo.";
        Assert.assertEquals(expected, triangleClassification.triangleClassification(-1, 0, 0));
    }

    @Test
    public void test_triangleClassification_CP2() {
        TriangleClassification triangleClassification = new TriangleClassification();
        String expected = "Los lados 17, 0 y 0 no forman un triángulo.";
        Assert.assertEquals(expected, triangleClassification.triangleClassification(17, 0, 0));
    }

    @Test
    public void test_triangleClassification_CP3() {
        TriangleClassification triangleClassification = new TriangleClassification();
        String expected = "Los lados 10, 9 y -1 no forman un triángulo.";
        Assert.assertEquals(expected, triangleClassification.triangleClassification(10, 9, -1));
    }

    @Test
    public void test_triangleClassification_CP4() {
        TriangleClassification triangleClassification = new TriangleClassification();
        String expected = "Los lados 27, 16 y 10 no forman un triángulo.";
        Assert.assertEquals(expected, triangleClassification.triangleClassification(27, 16, 10));
    }

    @Test
    public void test_triangleClassification_CP5() {
```

Fig. 3. Fragmento de código de prueba a partir de lenguaje Java.

```csharp
using System;
using NUnit.Framework;
using System.Text;

namespace UNitTesting
{
[TestFixture]
public class TriangleClassificationCSTestClass1 {

    [Test]
    public void test_triangleClassification_CP1() {
        TriangleClassificationCS triangleClassification = new TriangleClassificationCS();
        String expected = "Los lados -1, 0 y 0 no forman un triángulo.";
        Assert.assertEquals(expected, triangleClassification.triangleClassification(-1, -1, -1));
    }

    [Test]
    public void test_triangleClassification_CP2() {
        TriangleClassificationCS triangleClassification = new TriangleClassificationCS();
        String expected = "Los lados 17, 0 y 0 no forman un triángulo.";
        Assert.assertEquals(expected, triangleClassification.triangleClassification(1, -1, -1));
    }

    [Test]
    public void test_triangleClassification_CP3() {
        TriangleClassificationCS triangleClassification = new TriangleClassificationCS();
        String expected = "Los lados 10, 9 y -1 no forman un triángulo.";
        Assert.assertEquals(expected, triangleClassification.triangleClassification(21, 20, 0));
    }

    [Test]
    public void test_triangleClassification_CP4() {
        TriangleClassificationCS triangleClassification = new TriangleClassificationCS();
        String expected = "Los lados 27, 16 y 10 no forman un triángulo.";
        Assert.assertEquals(expected, triangleClassification.triangleClassification(27, 16, 10));
    }
```

Fig. 4. Fragmento de código de prueba a partir de lenguaje C#.

Como se puede observar en las figuras anteriores, la utilización del modelo MTest.search permite la generación de código de pruebas, sin modificar la generación de los casos de pruebas. Solo es necesario implementar los mecanismos de extensión descritos previamente para agregar un nuevo lenguaje, lo cual evita comenzar a automatizar desde cero todo el proceso de generación de pruebas unitarias.

5 Conclusiones y trabajos futuros

El presente trabajo facilita el proceso de pruebas durante el desarrollo de productos de software, debido a que permite automatizar el diseño de casos de pruebas y generar código de pruebas funcionales y unitarias. Además, se ofrecen mecanismos de extensión para permitir la inclusión de nuevos dominios de entrada y lenguajes de codificación de las pruebas a ejecutar. Como trabajos futuros, se hace necesario optimizar la generación de los casos de pruebas a través del componente GeCaP. Para ello, es necesario combinar diferentes técnicas de diseño de casos de pruebas y la comparación de diferentes algoritmos de optimización para analizar su comportamiento en el problema en cuestión.

Referencias

1. Myers, G.J., Badgett, T., Sandler, C.: The art of software testing. John Wiley & Sons, Inc., New Jersey, USA (2012)
2. Anand, S., Burke, E.K., Chenc, T.Y., Clark, J., Cohen, M.B., Grieskamp, W., Harman, M., Harrold, M.J., McMinn, P.: An orchestrated survey of methodologies for automated software test case generation. The Journal of Systems and Software 86, 1978– 2001 (2013)
3. Pressman, R.S., Maxim, B.R.: Software Engineering. A Practitioner's Approach. McGraw-Hill Education, New York, USA (2015)
4. JUnit, Sitio oficial JUnit, www.junit.org, Access date: 2018-07-18, Last update date: 2018-04-13
5. NUnit, Sitio oficial NUnit, www.nunit.org, Access date: 2018-07-13, Last update date: 2017
6. Bergmann, S., Sitio oficial PHPUnit, http://phpunit.de/, Access date: 2018-07-18, Last update date: 2018-06-05
7. Bregieiro, J.C.: Search-based test case generation for object-oriented java software using strongly-typed genetic programming. In: Proceedings of the 10th annual conference companion on Genetic and evolutionary computation, pp. 1819-1822. ACM, (2008)
8. Carvalho, G., Falcão, D., Barros, F., Sampaio, A., AlexandreMota, LeonardoMotta, Blackburn, M.: NAT2TESTSCR: Test case generation from natural language requirements based on SCR specifications. Science of Computer Programming 95, 275-297 (2014)
9. Polo, M., Ruiz, F., Rodríguez-Bobada, R., García, I.: Test Case Generation with Regular Expressions and Combinatorial Techniques. In: 10th IEEE International Conference on Software Testing, Verification and Validation Workshops, pp. 189-198. IEEE, (2017)
10. Díaz, E., Tuya, J., Blanco, R., Dolado, J.J.: A tabu search algorithm for structural software testing. Computers & Operations Research 35, 3052–3072 (2008)
11. Gambi, A., Kappler, S., Lampel, J., Zeller, A.: CUT: automatic unit testing in the cloud. In: ISSTA 2017 Proceedings of the 26th ACM SIGSOFT

International Symposium on Software Testing and Analysis pp. 364-367. ACM, (2017)
12. Havrikov, N., Gambi, A., Zeller, A., Arcuri, A., Galeotti, J.P.: Generating unit tests with structured system interactions. In: AST '17 Proceedings of the 12th International Workshop on Automation of Software Testing, pp. 30-33. IEEE, (2017)
13. Jones, B.F., Sthamer, H.-H., Eyres, D.E.: Automatic structural testing using genetic algorithms. Software Engineering Journal 11, 299-306 (1996)
14. Sekhara, S., Hari, M.L., Kiran, U., Ch, S., Ranjan, P.: Automated Generation of Independent Paths and Test Suite Optimization Using Artificial Bee Colony. Procedia Engineering 30, 191-200 (2012)
15. Han, X., Lei, H., Wang, Y.-s.: Multiple paths test data generation based on particle swarm optimisation. IET Software 11, 41-47 (2016)
16. Hermadi, I., Lokan, C., Sarker, R.: Dynamic stopping criteria for search-based test data generation for path testing. Information and Software Technology 56, 395-407 (2014)
17. Khari, M., Kumar, P.: A Novel Approach for Software Test Data Generation using Cuckoo Algorithm. In: ICTCS '16 Proceedings of the Second International Conference on Information and Communication Technology for Competitive Strategies ACM, (2016)
18. Moadab, S., Rashidi, H.: Automatic path-oriented test data generation by boundary hypercuboids. Journal of King Saud University - Computer and Information Sciences 28, 82-97 (2016)
19. Varshney, S., Mehrotra, M.: Search based software test data generation for structural testing: a perspective. ACM SIGSOFT Software Engineering Notes 38, 1-6 (2013)
20. Mirshokraie, S., Mesbah, A., Pattabiraman, K.: JSEFT: Automated Javascript Unit Test Generation. In: 2015 IEEE 8th International Conference on Software Testing, Verification and Validation (ICST), pp. 1-10. IEEE, (2015)
21. Prasetya, I.S.W.B.: T3: Benchmarking at Third Unit Testing Tool Contest. In: 2015 IEEE/ACM 8th International Workshop on Search-Based Software Testing, pp. 44-47. IEEE, (2015)
22. Panichella, A., Molina, U.R.: Java unit testing tool competition: fifth round. In: SBST '17 Proceedings of the 10th International Workshop on Search-Based Software Testing pp. 32-38. IEEE, (2017)
23. Sakti, A., Pesant, G., Guéhéneuc, Y.-G.: JTeXpert at the SBST 2017 Tool Competition. In: SBST '17 Proceedings of the 10th International Workshop on Search-Based Software Testing pp. 43-46. IEEE, (2017)
24. Delgado, M.D., Macias, A., Larrosa, D., Verona, S., Fernández, P.B.: Model for Automatic Generation of Search-Based Early Test. Computación y Sistemas 21, 503-513 (2017)
25. Fernández, P.B., Cantillo, W., Delgado, M.D., Rosete, A., Yáñez, C.: Generación de combinaciones de valores de pruebas utilizando metaheurística. Ingeniería Industrial 37, 200-207 (2016)
26. Macías, A., Delgado, M.D., Fajardo, J., Larrosa, D.: Generador de valores de casos de pruebas funcionales. Lámpsakos 51-58 (2016)

Sistemas de Información para una Medicina de Precisión: Identificación de Variaciones Genómicas para el Diagnóstico del Cáncer de Mama

Alba Escalera Balsera[1[0000-0003-1027-8594]], Ana León Palacio[1[0000-0003-1027-8594]] y Oscar Pastor López[1]

[1] Centro de Investigación en Métodos de Producción de Software (PROS), Universitat Politècnica de València, Valencia, España

albaescalera7@gmail.com, {aleon, opastor}@pros.upv.es

Abstract. El cáncer de mama es el cáncer que más afecta y mata a mujeres tanto a nivel mundial como en España. El análisis de las características genéticas de cada paciente hace posible el estudio de variaciones significativas del ADN para facilitar un diagnóstico precoz, el cual es esencial para tratar el desarrollo del tumor. El problema se debe a la gran cantidad de información disponible, lo que hace necesario el uso de un método para almacenar y administrar adecuadamente estos datos de un modo óptimo para su explotación. En este contexto, la Ingeniería de Sistemas de Información y las técnicas de modelado conceptual, proporcionan una solución adecuada para determinar qué datos son relevantes y cómo gestionar la información correspondiente. Con estos fundamentos, en este trabajo se ha escogido el método SILE (Search, Identification, Load and Exploitation) para la búsqueda, identificación, carga y explotación de variaciones genómicas relacionadas con el cáncer de mama, con el fin de una posterior explotación en el ámbito del diagnóstico clínico.

Keywords: Cáncer de mama, Medicina de Precisión, método SILE, Sistemas de Información.

1 Introducción

La Medicina de Precisión es un enfoque emergente que se basa en predecir cuáles son las estrategias, tanto de tratamiento como de prevención, que funcionarán correctamente para una determinada enfermedad en un grupo característico de personas [1]. Uno de los criterios en los que se basa es en la variabilidad del genoma, por ello se estudian las variaciones genómicas. Para ello es necesario secuenciar los genomas de numerosos individuos y compararlos. En la última década se han realizado muchos estudios gracias a la evolución de las tecnologías de secuenciación, como por ejemplo las Next Generation Sequencing (NGS) o la proliferación de estudios del genoma completo (GWAS).

Las variaciones encontradas en estos estudios han de ser anotadas para evaluar su impacto clínico y, también, ser almacenadas de forma que puedan ser accesible al público. Con este objetivo se utilizan las bases de datos, en este caso las bases de datos genómicas [2].

La búsqueda de variaciones genómicas se hace generalmente asociada a un fenotipo, en este caso al cáncer de mama. La importancia de su estudio es que es la neoplasia maligna que afecta y mata a más mujeres en el mundo y en España [3]. Se calcula que 1 de cada 8 mujeres lo padecerá a lo largo de su vida [4].

El reto de la medicina personalizada es encontrar objetivos moleculares concretos de cada tipo de tumor donde poder actuar, de modo que es imprescindible identificar qué variaciones en el ADN se corresponden con cada tipo, esto se hace a partir de la información disponible en las bases de datos genómicas. Sin embargo, esto no es una tarea trivial y surgen problemas a la hora de utilizarlas [5]: Debido a la naturaleza experimental del dominio genómico y a la diversidad de tecnologías de secuenciación existentes se pueden generar asignaciones de patogenicidad o riesgo engañosas, lo cual conlleva a diagnósticos genéticos equivocados; existen miles de bases de datos con gran cantidad de información desconectada y estructurada de forma diferente, lo que hace difícil la búsqueda y comprensión de ella; y la falta de controles a la hora de publicar la información disponible hace que se den situaciones de redundancia de datos.

Para afrontar los problemas mencionados es necesario contar con un método que guíe de forma sistemática la búsqueda de fuentes de información adecuadas y la identificación de la información relevante para su posterior carga y explotación por un sistema de información que de soporte a la medicina de precisión.

Con todo esto en mente, en la próxima sección se presenta el método SILE. En el apartado 3 se introduce el caso concreto de la aplicación del método para el cáncer de mama, diferenciándose los cuatro pasos del método. Finalmente, las conclusiones a las que se ha llegado y los trabajos futuros que se pretenden realizar se muestran en la última sección.

2 Método SILE

En el presente trabajo se utiliza el método SILE [6] desarrollado por el Centro de Investigación PROS[1], de la Universidad Politécnica de Valencia. El método está compuesto por las cuatro fases siguientes: Búsqueda, Identificación, Carga y Explotación (por sus siglas en inglés Search, Identification, Load, Exploitation). El objetivo de SILE es la búsqueda, identificación, carga y explotación de la información genética relevante, en este caso las variaciones con significado clínico para el cáncer de mama [6]. A continuación, se describe cada uno de los cuatro pasos de SILE:

- **Búsqueda:** Consiste en la búsqueda y selección de las bases de datos que proporcionan información relevante para la enfermedad en cuestión. De este modo se conoce cuáles son las más adecuadas para dicha tarea.

[1] http://www.pros.webs.upv.es/

- **Identificación:** Es el proceso por el cual se identifica la información relevante, según el cumplimiento de determinados criterios de calidad, que serán explicados posteriormente. Además, en este proceso de identificación se detectan problemas de datos tales como inconsistencias, que puedan afectar al proceso de carga y explotación de la información.
- **Carga:** El grupo ha desarrollado una base de datos específica, llamada Human Genome Database (HGDB), con el fin de gestionar de un modo eficiente los datos genómicos. Esta base de datos se basa en el Modelo Conceptual del Genoma Humano (CMHG), el cual se va a explicar en el siguiente apartado. Tanto la HGDB como el CMHG se desarrollaron con el objetivo de definir todas las características que forman el genoma humano y, así, crear una estructura sólida sobre la que construir un Sistema de Información Genómica (SIG).
- **Explotación:** La creación de conocimiento como resultado de la correcta gestión de datos es el objetivo principal de la última etapa de la metodología SILE. La fase de explotación consiste en señalar las variaciones genómicas presentes en una muestra de una paciente y compararlas con las contenidas en el conjunto de datos almacenado en la HGDB. La explotación del conjunto de datos finalmente conduce a una evaluación de riesgo genético basada en evidencias validadas disponibles en fuentes de datos públicos.

Tanto la búsqueda como la identificación (incluyendo la detección y, posterior eliminación, de información redundante) son procesos que están en fase de automatización por su complejidad, mientras que las fases de carga y explotación ya están completamente automatizadas.

2.1 Modelo Conceptual del Genoma Humano

Según [7], el ámbito del genoma humano posee una gran cantidad de información biológica, la cual ha de ser capturada, manipulada y controlada de manera eficaz; por lo que son necesarios enfoques avanzados en Ingeniería de Sistemas de Información. Para ello es necesaria la aplicación del modelado conceptual para poder comprender la información relevante en el dominio. De este modo, es más sencillo representarla con claridad, lo que permite desarrollar una estrategia de gestión de datos eficaz.

El objetivo principal del Modelo Conceptual del Genoma Humano (MCGH) es comprender los conceptos básicos que explican cómo la estructura genotípica se manifiesta en un fenotipo. Además, las bases de datos que se basan en el MCGH se desarrollan y diseñan desde una perspectiva holística, de modo que posibilitan la integración de diferentes fuentes de datos que representan diferentes perspectivas del conocimiento genómico.

A continuación, se detallan los criterios de calidad utilizados para la selección de las variaciones relevantes.

2.2 Criterios de Calidad

Los criterios de calidad se establecen con el objetivo de identificar qué información es relevante de entre toda la que está disponible y, de este modo validar los resultados. Los escogidos para este estudio han surgido a partir de la colaboración con expertos en diagnóstico genético.

A continuación, se van a explicar los tres criterios de calidad que se siguen para cada una de las variaciones:

1. Cada variación debe tener asociada al menos una publicación, la cual sustente la relación genotipo-fenotipo.
2. El significado clínico de la variación ha de ser distinto de benigno, probablemente benigno, probablemente patogénico, no provisto, incierto o conflicto en la interpretación.
3. Se ha de hacer una revisión de lo que dice cada publicación sobre la variación estudiada. En dicha revisión se han de confirmar los siguientes parámetros:
   a. El estudio ha tenido que ser realizado en humanos.
   b. En él han debido de participar más de 500 personas, tanto muestras como controles.
   c. La evidencia estadística ha de ser la siguiente:
      (1) Para las variaciones patogénicas: Odds Ratio (OR) > 1 y límite inferior del Intervalo de Confianza (IC) > 1.
      (2) Para las variaciones protectoras: Odds Ratio (OR) < 1 y límite superior del Intervalo de Confianza (IC) < 1.
      (3) Son deseables estudios que hayan sido reproducidos.

El OR indica la presencia de un factor aumenta la probabilidad de que un suceso ocurra siendo 1 la no existencia de asociación, > 1 la existencia de asociación positiva (la presencia del factor aumenta la probabilidad de que ocurra el suceso) y < 1 la existencia de asociación negativa (la presencia del factor disminuye la probabilidad de que ocurra el suceso). Además, se ha de presentar el intervalo de confianza (IC) para dicho OR, el cual será del 95%.

3 El Caso del Cáncer de Mama

Una vez explicado el método que se va a seguir se ha de evaluar cómo funciona en la práctica cuando es aplicado a un caso en concreto, el cáncer de mama. Con ello se persiguen dos objetivos principales: Verificar el valor del método en el caso seleccionado y crear un conjunto de experiencias prácticas del método SILE en enfermedades en particular, con el fin de poder comparar en el futuro los puntos comunes y las diferencias en la aplicación de dicho método en distintas enfermedades.

Este trabajo se centra en el primer punto, para que pueda ser viable la realización del segundo en posteriores estudios. El objetivo, como se ha dicho, es la determinación de variaciones relevantes relacionadas con la enfermedad para que puedan ser utilizadas en un diagnóstico genómico efectivo. A continuación, se detallan los pasos seguidos en cada una de las fases.

3.1 Búsqueda

El primer paso en este trabajo fue buscar información sobre las diferentes bases de datos genómicas para escoger las más adecuadas. Una vez contrastada se decidió utilizar ClinVar, Ensembl, GWAS Catalog y SNPedia. Un motivo común a todas ellas es que son públicas, por lo que cualquier usuario puede consultar datos. Además, otras de las razones son:

En el caso de ClinVar, esta almacena informes de las relaciones entre variaciones humanas y fenotipos proporcionando como respaldo referencias a las evidencias bibliográficas de ello (PubMed). De este modo, ayuda a conocer la relación que existe entre la variación genómica y el fenotipo observado [8].

Ensembl se creó con el objetivo de anotar el genoma humano e integrar dicha anotación con otros datos biológicos. Además, se ha incluido genómica comparativa, variaciones y datos regulatorios, lo cual la hace una base de datos idónea para la búsqueda de variaciones y el efecto que estas tienen en el ser humano [9]. Posee una herramienta llamada BioMart que permite la descarga de los datos almacenados.

GWAS Catalog almacena información sobre estudios de asociaciones genómicas (GWAS), los cuales permiten investigar el impacto de las variaciones comunes en una enfermedad compleja. Además, se encarga de extraer el fenotipo y las asociaciones significativas con las variaciones y de los metadatos de la muestra poblacional [10].

Para finalizar, SNPedia es una página de libre acceso que se basa en un modelo wiki, en la que los usuarios pueden editar y añadir su información. En ella se almacenan datos de polimorfismos de un único nucleótido (SNP) obtenidos de otras fuentes de información, principalmente de otras bases de datos [11].

Una vez seleccionadas las bases de datos, se descargó de ellas la información de las variaciones genómicas asociadas al fenotipo de interés. Estas variaciones se buscan filtrando por "breast cancer", pueden ser variaciones bien que lo causen, que protejan de él, etc., es decir, que estén relacionadas con el cáncer de mama. Junto con cada una de las variaciones se obtiene el identificador de la publicación o publicaciones en las cuales se ha estudiado. En estos artículos se da, además, información sobre las siguientes características: cromosoma, gen, significado clínico y fenotipo. También se explica la población sobre la que se ha realizado el estudio y los parámetros estadísticos resultantes.

3.2 Identificación

El proceso de identificación tiene el objetivo de determinar cuáles son las variaciones obtenidas con significancia clínica del total de variaciones que se pueden encontrar con la búsqueda realizada en las bases de datos explicadas. Este consiste en una revisión manual, analizando el artículo en el cual se ha estudiado dicha variación con el objetivo de comprobar si cumple los criterios de calidad propuestos anteriormente (apartado 2.2) y, de esta manera se realiza la validación de los resultados obtenidos.

Las variaciones genómicas para el cáncer de mama obtenidas, aplicando la metodología explicada, son 125, partiéndose de 16.240. Todas las variaciones encontradas son SNPs. Como se observa, una vez aplicados los criterios explicados en el apartado 2.2. disminuyó considerablemente el número de variaciones asociadas al cáncer de mama. Con ello se confirma la dificultad supuesta en la búsqueda en bases de datos.

Cuando se descargan las variaciones asociadas a un fenotipo determinado, en este caso "breast cancer", se obtiene la información por publicaciones. Es decir, las variaciones pueden tener asociadas a ella desde una a numerosas publicaciones, lo que indica que se han confirmado en base a más de un estudio; y en cada publicación también se puede estudiar una o muchas variaciones. Finalmente se obtuvo 161 publicaciones, habiendo partido de 46.128.

Una vez aplicados todos los filtros de calidad se llegó a la obtención de las variaciones significativas para la enfermedad. De ellas, ninguna se encuentra en todas las bases de datos. Solamente 6 de ellas pertenecen a Ensembl, GWAS Catalog y SNPedia; y una de ellas a Ensembl, GWAS Catalog y ClinVar. La mayor parte de ellas, es decir 136 de las 161, aparecen tanto en Ensembl como en GWAS Catalog.

Al estudiar en qué cromosomas aparecen cada una de las variaciones se observa que no se encuentran en ninguno de los dos cromosomas sexuales (X e Y) y, sin embargo, sí que aparecen en todos los demás al menos una vez. En cuanto a los genes que afectan, bien porque se encuentren en ellos o porque estén cerca y afecten a su regulación, hay un total de 59 genes en los que se han encontrado variaciones y 37 variaciones que no están relacionadas con ningún gen debido a que se encuentran en ADN intergénico. Del conjunto de variaciones obtenidas, 122 tienen como significado clínico asociación, 2 factor de riesgo y solo una es protectora frente al cáncer de mama. Por último, el 68% de las variaciones están relacionadas con el cáncer de mama en general, sin especificar un tipo concreto de este; el 12% provocan cáncer de mama temprano, el cual ocurre en mujeres más jóvenes que la media; el 11% causa cáncer de mama con receptor de estrógeno negativo; el 3% cáncer de mama con receptor de estrógeno positivo y, finalmente, el 2% cáncer de mama triple negativo.

3.3 Carga y Explotación

Durante la fase de carga se transforma la información extraída de las bases de datos a un formato que permita su almacenamiento y explotación bajo una estructura común. En este caso, la proporcionada por el CSHG. Para ello es necesario identificar las discrepancias que puedan surgir en la representación del mismo concepto, como por ejemplo el tipo de variación. En el caso de Ensembl se consideran 8 tipos de variaciones[2] mientras que ClinVar considera 31[3]. Para ello se realizó un mapping entre los distintos tipos de acuerdo con el CSHG. Además de las discrepancias, también se trabajó en la detección de redundancias de información y en la implementación de sistemas de control de restricciones como "orphan foreign keys" propias de la tecnología de almacenamiento utilizada (en este caso una base de datos relacional implementada en MySQL).

[2] https://www.ensembl.org/info/genome/variation/prediction/classification.html

[3] https://www.ncbi.nlm.nih.gov/variation/docs/glossary/

Una vez integrada y representada la información bajo una estructura común, se procedió a su posterior explotación. Para ello se utilizó una herramienta desarrollada por el equipo de investigación llamada VarSearch [12]. El objetivo de esta herramienta es realizar un diagnóstico genético a partir de la muestra de un paciente. La información sobre la información genética de un paciente, proveniente de la secuenciación de su ADN, se almacena en ficheros VCF (Variant Call Format) [13] que son procesados por VarSeach con el objetivo de identificar qué variaciones de ADN presentes en la muestra están relacionada con el riesgo de sufrir una determinada enfermedad. En este caso, la herramienta contrasta la información de la muestra con la información sobre las variaciones asociada al cáncer de mama detectadas durante la fase de identificación. Una vez finalizado el procesado de la muestra, se genera un informe genético que indica el riesgo del paciente a padecer la enfermedad en función de sus características genéticas (siempre en términos de probabilidad).

El uso de esta herramienta da soporte a la ya mencionada Medicina de Precisión, mejorando el proceso de diagnóstico genético que actualmente es lento y costoso debido a la gran cantidad de fuentes de datos e información que es necesario manejar.

4 Conclusiones y Trabajos Futuros

En el ámbito de la Medicina de Precisión basada en la genómica, es necesaria la existencia de una estrategia de desarrollo de sistemas de información eficaz y eficiente. En este artículo se ha mostrado cómo enfrentar este problema para un dominio clínico concreto, el cáncer de mama. Esto se ha hecho utilizando un modelo conceptual centrado en cómo se han de seleccionar las fuentes de datos relevantes, cómo obtener de ellas un conjunto de variaciones candidatas que son significativas en términos clínicos para la enfermedad de estudio y, por último, cómo filtrarlas para reducir dicho conjunto de variaciones con el fin de obtener un listado de variaciones válidas según los criterios aplicados.

En el presente trabajo se informa sobre cómo se aplicó el método para el caso del cáncer de mama. Uno de los resultados más relevantes es el conjunto de variaciones genómicas seleccionadas como significativas para la enfermedad, las cuales se han cargado en una base de datos que es utilizada por una plataforma de software de diagnóstico genómico (GenesLove.Me [14]).

Los resultados del método han sido validados por un equipo de expertos en diagnóstico genómico. Así mismo, éste está siendo utilizado en varios proyectos en desarrollo en el entorno hospitalario, con el objetivo de incorporar el conocimiento genético a la historia clínica del paciente y mejorar así el proceso diagnóstico.

Debido a que la aplicación del método SILE puede tener diferentes propiedades en las distintas enfermedades, los próximos trabajos se van a centrar en aplicar dicho método a nuevas enfermedades, además de las que ya se ha aplicado como son cáncer de colón y la enfermedad del Alzheimer, de este modo se podrá comparar los resultados obtenidos. Analizando así las similitudes y las diferencias del proceso y, adaptar los criterios de calidad utilizados por el método para la información particular en cada estudio determinado. El propósito final es proponer un método holístico y universal que pueda aplicarse con el objetivo de gestionar correctamente los sistemas de información genómica para la desafiante Medicina de Precisión.

Agradecimientos

Este trabajo ha sido financiado por la Agencia Estatal de Investigación, la Generalitat Valenciana y por el Fondo Europeo de Desarrollo Regional (FEDER) en el marco de los Proyectos de Investigación de referencia TIN2016-80811-P y PROMETEO/2018/176, así como por la Universitat Politècnica de València en el marco de la beca FPI 2137.

Referencias

1. Fradkin, J., Hanlon, M., Rodgers, G.: NIH Precision Medicine Initiative: implications for diabetes research. Diabetes Care, 39(7), 1080-1084 (2016). doi: 10.2337/dc16-0541
2. Brookes, A., Robinson, P.: Human genotype–phenotype databases: aims, challenges and opportunities. Nature Reviews Genetics 16(12), 702-715 (2015). doi: 10.1038/nrg3932
3. Global Cancer Observatory, http://gco.iarc.fr/today/online-analysis-multi-bars?mode=cancer&mode_population=continents&population=900&sex=2&cancer=29&type=0&statistic=0&prevalence=0&color_palette=default, último acceso 02/07/2018.
4. Asociación Española Contra el Cáncer, https://www.aecc.es/es/todo-sobre-cancer/tipos-cancer/cancer-mama, último acceso 02/07/2018.
5. León, A. et al.: Data Quality Problems When Integrating Genomic Information. Lecture Notes in Computer Science 173-182 (2016). doi:10.1007/978-3-319-47717-6_15
6. León, A. et al.: A Method to Identify Relevant Genome Data: Conceptual Modeling for the Medicine of Precision. Conceptual Modeling 597-609 (2018). doi: 10.1007/978-3-030-00847-5_44
7. Reyes, J.: Diseño y Desarrollo de un Sistema de Información Genómica Basado en un Modelo Conceptual Holístico del Genoma Humano. Tesis doctoral, Universitat Politècnica de València, Valencia (2018).
8. National Center for Biotechnology Information, https://www.ncbi.nlm.nih.gov/clinvar/intro/, último acceso 28/06/2018.
9. Ensembl, https://www.ensembl.org/info/about/index.html, último acceso 28/06/2018.
10. European Bioinformatics Institute, https://www.ebi.ac.uk/gwas/docs/about, último acceso 28/06/2018.
11. SNPedia, https://www.snpedia.com/index.php/SNPedia:About, último acceso 28/06/2018.
12. Reyes Román, J. et al.: VarSearch: Annotating Variations using an e-Genomics Framework. In: Proceedings of the 13th International Conference on Evaluation of Novel Approaches to Software Engineering, pp.328-334. Funchal, Portugal (2018). doi: 10.5220/0006781103280334
13. Danecek, P.: The variant call format and VCFtools. Bioinformatics 27(15), .2156-2158 (2011). doi: 10.1093/bioinformatics/btr330
14. Reyes Román, J., Iñiguez-Jarrín, C., Pastor López, Ó.: GenesLove.Me: A Model-based Web-application for Direct-to-consumer Genetic Tests. In: Proceedings of the 12th International Conference on Evaluation of Novel Approaches to Software Engineering, pp.133-143. Porto, Portugal (2017). doi: 10.5220/0006340201330143

ParticipaAware: Fomentando la participación ciudadana por medio de notificaciones móviles vinculadas a lugares de interés del ciudadano *

[1]Rebeca Arteta,[1]Jorge Saldivar,[1]Cristhian Parra, and[1]Luca Cernuzzi

Universidad Católica Nuestra Señora de la Asunción, Asunción, Paraguay

Resumen Las nuevas tecnologías han permitido la creación de nuevos espacios de participación cívica. Investigaciones anteriores sugieren que para maximizar la tasa de participación las plataformas ciudadanas deben funcionar integradas con la vida cotidiana del ciudadano. Por esto, el presente trabajo introduce un modelo de participación cívica basado en tecnología y propone ParticipaAware, una aplicación móvil de participación que permite al ciudadano involucrarse en procesos de ideación orientados a resolver problemáticas de su entorno cotidiano. ParticipaAware incluye un sistema automático de notificaciones entorno a los lugares de interés del ciudadano. Se presenta también una validación experimental de la propuesta a través del caso de estudio "Revitalizando Asunción".

Keywords: Participación ciudadana · Compromiso cívico · Tecnología Móvil.

1. Introducción y Motivación

La irrupción de las nuevas tecnologías han permitido la creación de nuevos espacios de participación cívica. Sin embargo, se requiere motivar a los ciudadanos a utilizarlas. Una limitación importante de muchas de las plataformas de participación ciudadana—sean éstas digitales o no—es operar desconectadas de la fuente o del origen del problema que desean abordar o resolver. Es por esto que investigaciones anteriores sugieren que para maximizar la tasa de participación las plataformas ciudadanas deben funcionar integradas con la vida cotidiana del ciudadano.

Una limitación importante de muchos de los espacios de participación ciudadana es que operan desconectados de la fuente o del origen del problema que desean abordar o resolver. El ciudadano, entonces, se ve obligado a realizar esfuerzos adicionales al tener que salir de su entorno cotidiano para asistir a una reunión o debate en un determinado lugar y horario, o para acceder a foros en línea que lo obligan a tener que recordar constantemente la dirección web o sus credenciales de acceso. A partir de esto, investigaciones anteriores sugieren que para incrementar la participación en las plataformas ciudadanas–sean

* Financiado por el CONACYT Paraguay en el marco de su programa PROCIENCIA con fondos del FEEI.

físicas o digitales—estas deben funcionar integradas con la vida cotidiana del ciudadano [6].

Los dispositivos móviles constituyen una gran oportunidad para fomentar el involucramiento y el compromiso cívico [1, 2, 6].

Varios son los autores que han aprovechado estas ventajas de los dispositivos móviles para crear espacios de participación ciudadana ya sea para ofrecer mejoras en las tomas de decisiones [12], [5]; ofrecer canales de comunicación entre ciudadanos y gobiernos [11], [9]; proveer información local a los ciudadanos [7], [13]; utilizar herramientas que consideran tiempo y contexto para el compromiso con la comunidad [4]. Algunas de las buenas prácticas de diseño sugeridas fueron tenidas en cuenta para la propuesta de nuestro modelo; sin embargo, nosotros buscamos proveer información local de manera más personalizada a través de notificaciones teniendo en cuenta los puntos de interés declarados por el usuario. Además, buscando facilitar aún más la experiencia del usuario y su acceso a información relevante, hemos decidido incluir el envío de notificaciones automáticas y, de cierto modo, personalizadas.

Teniendo en cuenta estas consideraciones este trabajo propone ParticipaAware, una plataforma digital móvil de participación cívica que permite al ciudadano involucrarse en discusiones que buscan resolver problemáticas de su entorno cotidiano. Para lograrlo, el desarrollo de ParticipaAware abordó dos desafíos de diseño principales: i) el diseño e implementación de un sistema de notificaciones que permita al ciudadano recibir avisos automáticos acerca de las conversaciones entorno a sus lugares de interés, como pueden ser el barrio de residencia, el barrio de la universidad o el barrio del lugar de trabajo; ii) el diseño e implementación de una interfaz que permita una experiencia positiva de uso de la tecnología para cada ciudadanos. La solución propuesta fue evaluada a través de un caso real de participación cuyos resultados son analizados en el afán de fomentar e incentivar la participación ciudadana.

2. El modelo ParticipaAware

En este estudio proponemos un modelo de participación que consta de los siguientes componentes (ver figura 1): **Organizadores:** Instituciones públicas o privadas o simplemente un grupo de personas que proponen una iniciativa para recolectar ideas sobre como resolver una problemática; **Iniciativa:** el proceso de recolección de las contribuciones propuestas por los ciudadanos afectados por una determinada necesidad; **Solución:** Idea o conjunto de ideas que han sido seleccionadas para resolver el problema planteado; **Ciudadanos:** Constituyen el elemento principal de este modelo, ya que con sus contribuciones estarían colaborando con la búsqueda de la solución a los problemas que afectan a su entorno cotidiano; **Contribuciones:** Se distinguen tres tipos: ideas que representan las propuestas de los ciudadanos, comentarios o opiniones de los ciudadanos sobre las ideas de otros, y votos que constituyen evaluaciones positivas o negativas a las ideas; **AppCivist**[1]**:** Plataforma tecnológica de participación ciudadana [8].

[1] http://pb.appcivist.org/#/v2/assembly/participapy/home

Sus funcionalidades de administración de usuarios, ideas, comentarios y votos, disponibles a través de un API REST pública[2], fueron utilizados como parte de la solución; **Lugares de Interés:** Lugares a los que los ciudadanos acuden con mayor frecuencia o que forman parte de su día a día. Nos limitamos, a modo experimental, a tres lugares que podrían ser del interés del ciudadano, su casa, donde estudia/trabaja y donde realiza actividades de ocio o distracción; **Notificaciones:** Se utilizan para notificar al ciudadano sobre ideas y opiniones relacionadas a sus lugares de interés.

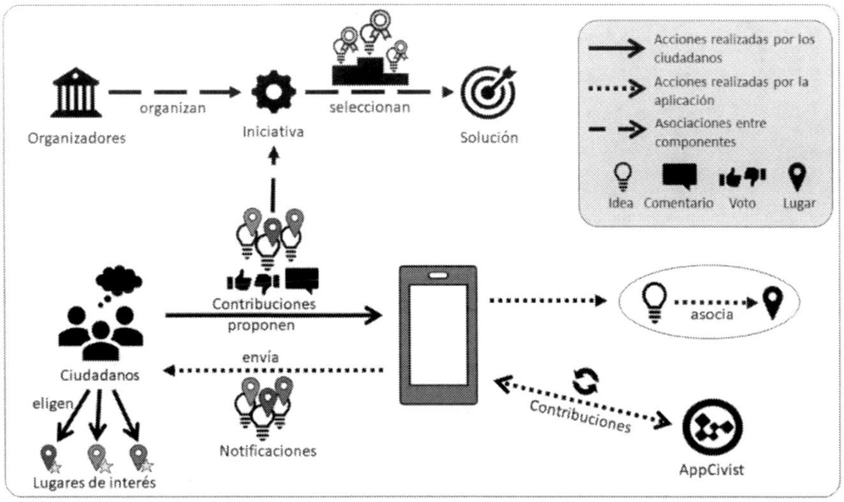

Figura 1: Modelo de ParticipaAware

ParticipaAware implementa un sistema de notificaciones push que consiste en mensajes que aparecen o emergen en los dispositivos que hayan instalado la aplicación y que además hayan autorizado la recepción de las mismas. La recepción de una notificación no requiere que el usuario esté utilizando activamente la aplicación o su dispositivo.

Las notificaciones ayudan a promover el uso de la aplicación móvil y, a su vez, incentivan la participación. Con el objetivo de personalizar las notificaciones a ser enviadas a cada usuario, se diseñó un sistema de notificaciones basado en las siguientes reglas: **Regla 1:** A cada usuario se le envía notificaciones de aquellas ideas que estén asociadas a sus lugares de interés. Previo al envío de la notificación se asegura que el usuario no sea el autor de la idea a ser enviada, que no haya emitido su valoración, positiva o negativa, sobre la idea a ser enviada, y que la idea aún no le haya sido enviada; **Regla 2:** En caso de no haber o de que ya hayan sido enviadas todas las ideas asociadas a los lugares de interés del usuario, se le enviará notificaciones que contengan comentarios pertenecientes a las ideas asociadas a sus lugares de interés. Por cada comentario a ser enviado se validará que el usuario no sea el autor del mismo y que aún no se le haya sido enviado; **Regla 3:** En caso de no haber o de que ya hayan sido enviadas

[2] https://platform.appcivist.org/api/doc

todas las ideas o comentarios asociados a los lugares de interés del usuario, se le enviarán notificaciones que contengan ideas asociadas a otros lugares. Previo al envío se validarán los criterios mencionados en la Regla 1; **Regla 4:** En caso de no haber o de que ya hayan sido enviadas todas las ideas o comentarios asociados a los lugares de interés del usuario y las ideas asociadas a otros lugares, se le enviarán notificaciones que contengan comentarios que pertenezcan a ideas que no estén asociadas a sus lugares de interés. Por cada comentario a enviar se verificarán los criterios mencionados en la Regla 2; **Regla 5:** Finalmente, en caso de no existir aún ideas y comentarios en el sistema, se le enviará al usuario notificaciones que contengan mensajes que lo motiven a participar, ya sea creando ideas, comentarios o votos.

El modelo fue implementado en una aplicación móvil para el sistema operativo Android y se encuentra disponible para su descargar en el Play Store[3]. ParticipaAware dispone de una interfaz a través de la cual el usuario puede indicar sus lugares de interés seleccionando los barrios donde reside, donde trabaja o estudia, y donde realiza actividades de ocio. Así mismo, la aplicación dispone de las funcionalidades de ideación, votación y de generación de comentarios.

3. Caso de Estudio: Revitalizando Asunción

El modelo de ParticipaAware fue evaluado a través de un caso real de participación ciudadana, denominado *Revitalizando Asunción*, en soluciones para sus lugares de interés en la ciudad de Asunción (Paraguay), es decir sus barrios de residencia, trabajo o estudio, y esparcimiento.

En particular, en el estudio nos enfocamos en entender el efecto del sistema de notificaciones en la dinámica de participación de los ciudadanos. En ese sentido, intentamos comprobar si el momento del día en que el ciudadano recibe la notificación afecta su nivel de participación. El envío de notificaciones se ha realizado: *CN1:* Cada tres días a las 9 a.m., *CN2:* Cada tres días a la 13 p.m.; y *CN3:* Cada tres días a las 19 p.m. El nivel de participación de los participantes fue medido de acuerdo a la cantidad de contenido generado, i.e., ideas, votos, comentarios, a partir de las notificaciones recibidas.

Se decidió diseñar el experimento siguiendo un enfoque *Between-Group* [10] con tres grupos de participantes, cada uno asociado a una de las condiciones de notificación definidas anteriormente. Los participantes del estudio fueron asignados a los grupos aleatoriamente intentando una composición homogénea de grupos en cuanto a edad, sexo y experiencia en el uso de dispositivos móviles.

Previo al inicio del experimento se difundió a través de la red social Facebook un cuestionario que invitaba a la gente a participar del proceso Revitalizando Asunción. Se solicitó a los interesados datos de contacto (teléfono móvil y correo electrónico) además de información sobre su edad, sexo, tipo sistema operativo, (Android, iOS, Windows Mobile, etc.) y experiencia utilizando dispositivos móviles y descargando aplicaciones.

---

[3] Enlace de descarga en el Play Store:
https://play.google.com/store/apps/details?id=com.participa.py

Un total de 113 persona completaron el cuestionario. De esos 87 (77 %) comentaron que contaban con dispositivos Android; el restó manifestó utilizar iPhone. A los 87 usuarios de Android se les envío por correo electrónico las instrucciones de cómo y dónde descargar ParticipaAware. Las 21 personas que descargaron la aplicación fueron asignadas a los tres grupos del experimento.

Posterior al experimento hemos llevado a cabo entrevistas semi-estructuradas con 9 participantes—3 de cada grupo—con la finalidad de tener un mayor conocimiento sobre su experiencia usando ParticipaAware. Los entrevistados tuvieron una participación de forma voluntaria, sin retribución económica. Las entrevistas fueron grabadas en audio, con una duración promedio de 20 minutos.

Durante las entrevistas se preguntó a los participantes como se habían enterado de esta iniciativa y si habían comprendido el propósito de la misma. Además, indagamos sobre las notificaciones para saber si los participantes las recibían, si las consideraban molestas o no y si las veían como un factor que les impulse a participar. Les preguntamos también sobre la valoración de los participantes respecto a iniciativas de participación ciudadana mediadas por la tecnología y orientadas a la innovación del sector público.

Para finalizar conversamos con los entrevistados sobre ParticipaAware buscando profundizar sobre la experiencia de los participantes en el uso de nuestra aplicación y plataformas tecnológicas similares.

4. Resultados

De las 21 personas que descargaron la aplicación móvil, se tiene que un 76 % de ellas son de sexo Masculino y un 24 % son de sexo Femenino. Además, las edades varían en un rango de 19-64 años, como se puede visualizar en la Tabla 1. A continuación se presentan los resultados del caso de estudio.

Con la finalidad de verificar el cumplimiento o no de la hipótesis planteada, se ha llevado a cabo un Análisis de Varianza de un Factor (o *One-way ANOVA* en inglés) [10]. La finalidad de este método es comprobar el cumplimiento de la hipótesis nula, la cual sostiene que la media, o el valor promedio, de todos los grupos es la misma. En contra partida, la hipótesis alternativa sostiene que al menos uno de los grupos presenta una diferencia estadísticamente significativa con respecto a los demás grupos [3].

Como se observa en la Tabla 1 las contribuciones más comunes fueron los votos. Este resultado es de algún modo esperable considerando que la acción de votar es la menos demandante en cuanto a esfuerzo y tiempo en comparación a la creación de ideas o comentarios. La Tabla 1 presenta también estadísticas descriptivas de los tres grupos experimentales, entre los cuales resalta el G1 por ser el grupo que en promedio generó más contenido (62), seguido por el G2 (17) y G3 (9). En G1 se destaca la participación del participante 875 quién fue el más activo no solo en su grupo sino en general.

ANOVA retorna como resultado *F-statistic*, el cual es utilizado para calcular la probabilidad de que sea verdadera la hipótesis nula. Si la probabilidad es menor a 0.05, para los fines de este estudio, decimos que no se puede comprobar

Tabla 1: Contribuciones por grupos y participantes

Grupo	*Participante*	*Sexo*	*Edad*	*Ideas*	*Comentarios*	*Votos*	*Total*
G1 (7)	875	Masculino	31	3	8	39	50
	880	Masculino	59	0	0	4	4
	890	Femenino	32	0	0	4	4
	907	Masculino	21	0	0	2	2
	906	Masculino	20	0	0	1	1
	899	Femenino	26	0	0	1	1
	897	Masculino	27	0	0	0	0
Total				3	8	51	62
Promedio							8.86
Varianza							331.48
G2 (7)	908	Masculino	19	0	0	11	11
	873	Masculino	20	0	0	3	3
	900	Masculino	54	2	0	0	2
	909	Masculino	19	1	0	0	1
	879	Masculino	25	0	0	0	0
	871	Masculino	27	0	0	0	0
	872	Masculino	24	0	0	0	0
Total				3	0	14	17
Promedio							2.43
Varianza							15.62
G3 (7)	905	Femenino	21	0	0	3	3
	904	Masculino	20	0	1	1	2
	878	Femenino	37	0	0	1	1
	881	Femenino	46	0	0	1	1
	920	Masculino	48	1	0	0	1
	1063	Masculino	30	0	0	1	1
	802	Masculino	23	0	0	0	0
Total				1	1	7	9
Promedio							1.28
Varianza							0.90

la hipótesis alternativa aceptándose la hipótesis nula. En nuestro caso la hipótesis alternativa indica que el momento del día en el cual se envían las notificaciones tiene un efecto en el nivel de participación.

En la Tabla 2, resultados del análisis ANOVA, se puede apreciar que la probabilidad de la hipótesis nula es casi del 40 %, muy superior al límite definido. Esto nos lleva a concluir que el momento del día en el cual las notificaciones son enviadas no tiene un efecto en el nivel de participación. Sin embargo, las estadísticas descriptivas indican una diferencia en el número de contribuciones de los grupos, destacándose el G1 por sobre el resto. Quizás una nueva evaluación con un mayor volumen de datos permita identificar esta diferencia.

Tabla 2: Análisis de Varianza (ANOVA)

Origen de las variaciones	*Suma de cuadrados*	*Grados de libertad*	*Promedio de los cuadrados*	*F*	*Probabilidad*
Entre grupos	233.24	2	116.62	1.00	0.39
Dentro de los grupos	2088	18	116		
Total	2321.24	20			

En las entrevistas con los participantes estos señalaron no haber utilizado previamente una aplicación móvil de participación ciudadana y que el motivo principal que los ha impulsado a formar parte de esta iniciativa fue la curiosidad por probar la herramienta propuesta. En general, todos los participantes indicaron que la aplicación les pareció intuitiva y fácil de usar. Específicamente dos de los participantes mencionaron no haber recibido notificaciones, 881 por haber desinstalado la aplicación y 906 por tener la aplicación instalada pero sin haber iniciado sesión. Los usuarios que sí recibían notificaciones, las han considerado útiles y no molestas.

Uno de los entrevistados fue el participante 875 (G1), el más activo en general. Este participante mencionó que el poder hacer uso de las TIC para este tipo de propósitos le resultó interesante y lo motivó a formar parte de esta iniciativa. Así mismo, ante la pregunta de cómo se podría involucrar a más personas, respondió que:

"Las personas tienen buenas ideas y pueden contribuir con aportes muy interesantes, pero, me parece, que no están acostumbradas a hacer este tipo de colaboraciones. Entonces, capaz haya que hacer un trabajo antes, de presentar la iniciativa dando algunos ejemplos de cómo participar. Quizás hay que enseñar primero a participar haciendo uso de las TICs." (Participante 875)

Por otro lado, la participante 905 (G3) tuvo un total de tres contribuciones del tipo voto. Esta participante afirmó tener un nivel de participación más bien de observación, mencionando dos razones principales: i) las ideas asociadas a su lugar de interés ya cubrían todas las necesidades (no tenía otras ideas de solución); ii) no disponía de mucho tiempo para usar la aplicación móvil, ya que el crear ideas o comentarios requieren de un mayor esfuerzo y tiempo. Falta de tiempo y evitar duplicaciones pudieron haber sido también las razones por las que otros participantes siguieron el proceso desde una perspectiva más de observadores.

5. Discusión y Trabajos Futuros

Este trabajo ha propuesto, primeramente, un modelo de participación que busca promover la participación de los ciudadanos intentando involucrar a los mismos en discusiones alrededor de sus lugares de interés. Como segunda contribución, este modelo fue implementado en una aplicación móvil para el sistema operativo Android que ofrece espacios de ideación y discusión para la búsqueda de soluciones a problemas identificados como relevantes para los ciudadanos. La aplicación móvil cuenta con un sistema de notificaciones que permite no solo incentivar la participación por medio de recordatorios sino además permite personalizar los mensajes de alerta con información relacionada a lugares cotidianos y de interés del ciudadano participante en procesos deliberativos y de discusión.

Los resultados estadísticos del experimento demuestran que el momento en el día en que se reciben estas notificaciones no influye directamente en el nivel de contribución del participante. Creemos, sin embargo, que la experiencia se vio afectada y limitada primeramente por la cantidad reducida de participantes involucrados y también por los desafíos propios que conlleva realizar experimentos con tecnologías móviles en las manos de los ciudadanos y no en laboratorios o ambientes más controlados.

De los resultados obtenidos y de las sugerencias hechas por los participantes durante las entrevistas, se propone extender la aplicación con algunas funcionalidades y haciendo uso del GPS para rastrear las ubicaciones más frecuentadas por el usuario, y posteriormente, sugerirle posibles lugares que sean de su interés. Así mismo, se pretende extender el grupo de potenciales usuarios implementando una versión de ParticiaAwere para el sistema operativo iOS.

Con respecto al proceso participativo un aspecto a cuidar en futuras ocasiones es tener el respaldo de alguna autoridad competente que garantice el cumplimiento y puesta en marcha de las ideas propuestas. Esto, a priori, motivaría la participación de una ciudadanía que está dispuesta a colaborar pero que demanda que al menos se estudien y evalúen sus propuestas.

Referencias

1. Al-Nuaim, H.: Context-aware mobile interface design for m-government. In: User-Centric Technology Design for Nonprofit and Civic Engagements, pp. 171–186. Springer (2014)
2. Campbell, S.W., Kwak, N.: Mobile communication and civic life: Linking patterns of use to civic and political engagement. Journal of communication **60**(3), 536–555 (2010)
3. Creech, S.: Anova, https://www.statisticallysignificantconsulting.com/Anova.htm
4. Ganoe, C.H., Robinson, H.R., Horning, M.A., Xie, X., Carroll, J.M.: Mobile awareness and participation in community-oriented activities. In: Proceedings of the 1st international conference and exhibition on computing for geospatial research & application. p. 10. ACM (2010)
5. Garcia, A.C.B., Vivacqua, A.S., Tavares, T.C.: Enabling crowd participation in governmental decision-making. J. UCS **17**(14), 1931–1950 (2011)
6. Graeff, E.: Crowdsourcing as reflective political practice: Building a location-based tool for civic learning and engagement (2014)
7. Han, K., Shih, P.C., Carroll, J.M.: Local news chatter: augmenting community news by aggregating hyperlocal microblog content in a tag cloud. International Journal of Human-Computer Interaction **30**(12), 1003–1014 (2014)
8. Holston, J., Issarny, V., Parra, C.: Engineering software assemblies for participatory democracy: The participatory budgeting use case. In: Proceedings of the 38th International Conference on Software Engineering Companion. pp. 573–582. ACM (2016)
9. Hosio, S., Goncalves, J., Kostakos, V., Riekki, J.: Crowdsourcing public opinion using urban pervasive technologies: Lessons from real-life experiments in oulu. Policy & Internet **7**(2), 203–222 (2015)
10. Lazar, J., Feng, J.H., Hochheiser, H.: Research Methods in Human-Computer Interaction. Wiley Publishing (2010)
11. Thiel, S.K., Lehner, U., Stürmer, T., Gospodarek, J.: Insights from a m-participation prototype in the wild. In: Pervasive Computing and Communication Workshops (PerCom Workshops), 2015 IEEE International Conference on. pp. 166–171. IEEE (2015)
12. Thome, J., Li, A., Sivaraman, V., Bridge, C.: Mobile crowdsourcing older people's opinions to enhance liveability in regional city centres. In: Intelligent Sensors, Sensor Networks and Information Processing (ISSNIP), 2014 IEEE Ninth International Conference on. pp. 1–7. IEEE (2014)
13. Woodcock, A., Frankova, K., Garton, L.: Voiceyourview: anytime, anyplace, anywhere user participation. Work **41**(Supplement 1), 997–1003 (2012)

Mecanismo de Selección Automática de Firmas en Ficheros ELF Maliciosos para un Motor Antivirus

Ing. Yolanda de los A. Varela Paez[1], Ing. Ernesto Mario Padrón Avila[1], MSc. Victoria Isabel Pérez Plana[1]

[1]Segurmática. Zanja No.651, esquina a Soledad, Centro Habana, La Habana. {yavarela, empadron, victoria}@segurmatica.cu

Resumen. Con el auge de la industria del malware es común encontrar malware camuflado en diferentes tipos de archivos. Ejecutables, scripts, imágenes, entre otros, han sido utilizados como portadores de código malicioso en diferentes sistemas operativos. En los últimos años se ha incrementado la cantidad de malware recibido en Segurmática que tiene como objetivo los Sistemas Operativos tipo UNIX. El procesamiento de forma manual de las muestras dificulta su rápida incorporación a las bases del antivirus. La selección automática de firmas de los programas malignos es un método que permite agilizar la detección de los mismos por el antivirus, permitiendo que los analistas de malware se enfoquen en los de mayor complejidad. El presente trabajo describe el desarrollo de un mecanismo de selección automática de firmas en ficheros con formato ELF.

Palabras Clave: ELF, Antivirus, Programa Maligno, Firma, Procesamiento Automático.

1 Introducción

La industria del malware[1] se ha desarrollado en los últimos años, con actividad maligna que se manifiesta como el ataque a entidades bancarias, el uso de ransomware y el minado de criptomonedas.

Con el desarrollo de Internet de las cosas (IoT) ha crecido exponencialmente la cantidad de dispositivos conectados a internet que implementan software libre y sistema operativo Gnu/Linux. Como consecuencia, este se ha convertido en un objetivo para los creadores de programas malignos. [1] En 2014 la operación Windigo orquestada por ESET sacó a la luz un informe sobre códigos maliciosos con más de 25000 servidores afectados en el mundo, gran parte de ellos Linux [2] lo que demuestra que este sistema operativo tampoco escapa a la amenaza del malware.

Uno de los componentes más importantes de un antivirus, en especial del motor antivirus, es la identificación, que permite la detección de patrones malignos en flujos de datos que pueden ser ficheros, conexiones de red, entre otros. [3] Una de las formas de identificación de malware es mediante firmas. Las clásicas firmas de virus son una secuencia continua de bytes comunes en cierta muestra de malware, lo que significa que se contiene dentro de este o del archivo infectado y no en archivos no afectados [4]

[1] Malware es un término genérico para denotar todo tipo de software no deseado [19]

El malware puede esconderse en diversos tipos de ficheros, desde empaquetados, ejecutables, textos hasta imágenes, por lo que el motor antivirus debe ser capaz de analizar los distintos tipos de ficheros en sus diversos formatos. El formato ejecutable usado mayormente en los sistemas operativos tipo Unix, es el ELF (Executable and Linking Format) que fue originalmente desarrollado y publicado por UNIX System Laboratories (USL) como parte de la Application Binary Interface (ABI). [5]

En los últimos años se ha incrementado la cantidad de malware en formato ELF recibido en Segurmática que tiene como objetivo los sistemas operativos tipo UNIX. Actualmente el procesamiento de los mismos es realizado por los analistas de malware de forma manual, lo cual no es suficiente para dar respuesta a las amenazas. Por ello es necesario implementar el mecanismo para la selección automática de firmas en ficheros ELF maliciosos.

1.1 Estado del arte

Muchos proyectos de investigación han abordado el tema de la detección de malware en Linux. En [6] y [7] se presenta un método de detección de malware que, utilizando inteligencia artificial, mina la información de las llamadas al sistema extraídas de la tabla de símbolos de los ejecutables de Linux. El método propuesto en estos trabajos es muy efectivo contra malware ofuscado o empaquetado.

El algoritmo propuesto en [8] desensambla el programa binario, construye los gráficos de flujo de control por cada función del programa y produce una representación intermedia. La representación intermedia se genera utilizando una biblioteca de transformadores de instrucción x86, de manera que sea independiente de la arquitectura. Dicha representación intermedia puede contener bibliotecas y llamadas al sistema que, por definición, son específicas de la plataforma. Esta última dependencia se elimina con el uso de funciones resumen expresadas en forma de representación intermedia. Este algoritmo probó ser muy eficaz en la detección de malware ofuscado con tamaño menor que 5 Mb; pero no lo suficientemente rápido para lo que necesita un antivirus.

Si bien en los últimos años la identificación por firmas se ha ido complementando con algoritmos como los anteriormente mencionados, que permiten la identificación de familias y variantes de malware conocido y desconocido con características similares, generalmente estos realizan un mayor uso del procesador. Las firmas son una forma rápida de identificar malware desconocido, que luego puede agruparse por su similitud para desarrollar algoritmos genéricos. De aquí que las firmas tradicionales ocupen una parte importante de la actualización de los antivirus.

La selección automática de firmas de malware es un método que permite reducir el tiempo transcurrido entre la recepción de un fichero infectado o malicioso y la incorporación de su detección a la base de firmas del antivirus. Esto permite que los analistas de malware se enfoquen en las amenazas de mayor complejidad.

Usualmente este proceso se apoya en métodos de análisis estático y/o dinámico. Un archivo entrante se clasifica teniendo en cuenta una clasificación de malware particular y se genera una firma de malware para dicho archivo. [9]

En [10] se describe el sistema Autosig desarrollado en Ikarus Software GmbH en el cual solo es automática la generación real de firmas. Estas no se agregan automáticamente a las actualizaciones que se distribuyen a los usuarios. Además, solo genera firmas genéricas. Para el malware del que existe una sola muestra en la colección de malware de Ikarus, se calcula el CRC del archivo completo. Por otra parte el sistema Hancock desarrollado en Symantec Research Lab [11] genera automáticamente firmas con la mínima probabilidad de falsos positivos. Al mismo tiempo, maximiza la capacidad de detección de cada firma. Si bien este sistema muestra resultados prometedores, consume gran cantidad de recursos y tiempo para su ejecución.

En la empresa Segurmática también se ha automatizado el proceso de selección de firmas. Para ello se cuenta con la herramienta Signgen que procesa muestras de diferentes formatos; pero actualmente no cuenta con el mecanismo necesario para procesar muestras de tipo ELF.

2 Contenido

En el presente trabajo se describe la implementación del mecanismo de selección de firmas en ficheros con formato ELF para un Motor Antivirus.

2.1 Características de los ELF

Existen varios tipos de ELF, los más comunes: reubicables, ejecutables y objetos compartidos. Los reubicables contienen código y datos adecuados para ser enlazados con otros archivos objeto para crear un archivo ejecutable u objeto compartido. Los ejecutables poseen un programa adecuado para su ejecución y los objetos compartidos contienen código y datos adecuados para enlazar en dos contextos: primero, el editor de enlaces puede procesarlos con otros archivos reubicables y compartidos para crear otro archivo objeto; segundo, el enlazador dinámico lo combina con un archivo ejecutable y otros objetos compartidos para crear una imagen de proceso. [5]

Además, los ELF pueden estar comprimidos con UPX (Ultimate Packer for Executables), BurnEye, Elfe entre otros métodos de protección de binarios. UPX es usado por intrusos con un nivel de conocimientos bajo como una herramienta de protección de sus aplicaciones maliciosas. Este software tiene soporte para reducir el tamaño de binarios diferentes tipos incluido ELF. [12] BurnEye es utilizado por los intrusos con nivel de conocimientos medio, medio-alto, que conocen la estructura de binarios ELF. BurnEye ofrece tres niveles de protección de binarios ELF, por capas: ofuscación de código, cifrado de aplicación a través de contraseñas y técnicas de OS fingerprinting. [12] Elfe es utilizado por los intrusos con nivel de conocimientos medio, medio-alto, que conocen la estructura ELF. Por medio de esta herramienta se puede especificar cuál de las secciones del binario (.text, .data, .rodata) se quiere proteger. [12] En este trabajo no se tendrán en cuenta los ELF comprimidos, solo los ejecutables y objetos compartidos de 32 bits

Un archivo con formato ELF consta de un encabezado ELF, seguido de una tabla de encabezado de programa y uno o varios segmentos, o de varias secciones y una tabla de encabezado de secciones, o ambas cosas. El encabezado ELF siempre está en el desplazamiento cero del archivo. La ubicación de la tabla de encabezado de programa y de la tabla de encabezado de secciones en el archivo se definen en el encabezado ELF. Las dos tablas describen el resto de las particularidades del archivo. [5]

En la siguiente figura se muestra la salida de la herramienta Readelf que ilustra la estructura de un ELF:

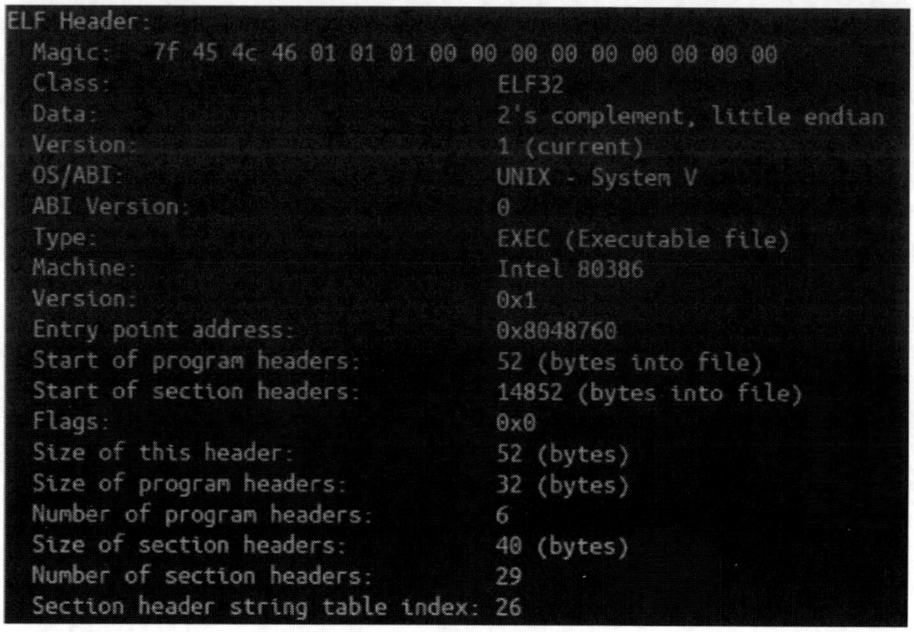

```
ELF Header:
  Magic:   7f 45 4c 46 01 01 01 00 00 00 00 00 00 00 00 00
  Class:                             ELF32
  Data:                              2's complement, little endian
  Version:                           1 (current)
  OS/ABI:                            UNIX - System V
  ABI Version:                       0
  Type:                              EXEC (Executable file)
  Machine:                           Intel 80386
  Version:                           0x1
  Entry point address:               0x8048760
  Start of program headers:          52 (bytes into file)
  Start of section headers:          14852 (bytes into file)
  Flags:                             0x0
  Size of this header:               52 (bytes)
  Size of program headers:           32 (bytes)
  Number of program headers:         6
  Size of section headers:           40 (bytes)
  Number of section headers:         29
  Section header string table index: 26
```

Fig. 1. Estructura del ELF Header.

Cada una desempeña un papel diferente en el proceso de enlace/carga de los ejecutables ELF. Para comprender la relación entre las secciones y los segmentos, podemos visualizar los segmentos como una herramienta que facilita el trabajo del cargador (loader) de Linux, ya que agrupan las secciones por atributos en segmentos individuales para hacer que el proceso de carga del ejecutable sea más eficiente, en lugar de cargar cada sección individual en la memoria. [13] La siguiente figura intenta ilustrar este concepto:

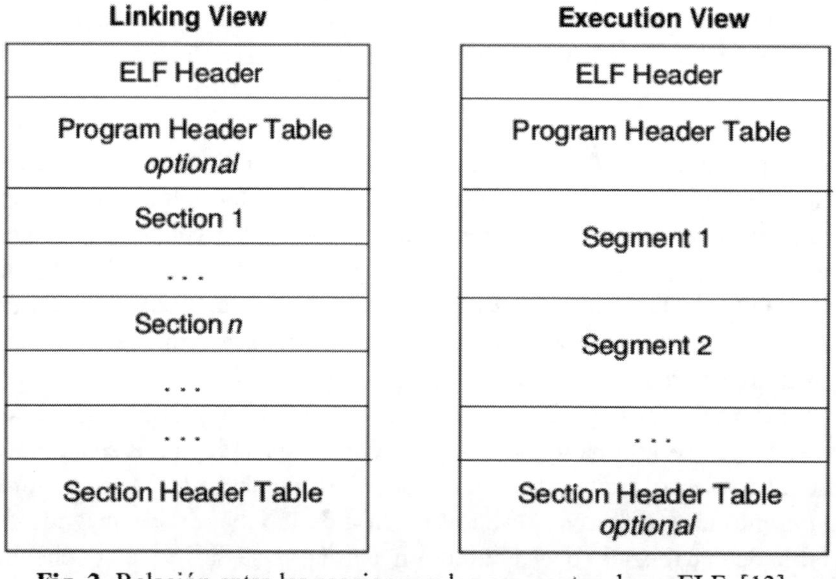

Fig. 2. Relación entre las secciones y los segmentos de un ELF. [13]

2.2 Selección de firmas

La selección de las firmas se debe realizar en el área más propensa a contener el código malicioso para reducir la probabilidad de ocurrencia de falsos positivos. Generalmente se seleccionan en la sección o segmento que contiene el código ejecutable del fichero, o sea, el que contenga el punto de entrada.

En los ELF ejecutables y objetos compartidos debe aparecer información de los segmentos (Program Header Table, detrás del ELF Header) y opcionalmente de las secciones (Section Header Table, casi al final del fichero).

Si el fichero es reubicable, opcionalmente aparece información de los segmentos y debe aparecer información de las secciones.

Para obtener el punto de entrada de un fichero ELF lo primero que se hace es chequear que en el ELF_Header estén los "números mágicos" los 4 primeros bytes corresponden a 7fh,'E','L','F'. Después se chequea si es de 32 o 64 bits en el campo EI_CLASS donde 1 significa que es de 32 bits y 2 de 64 bits. Este campo EI_CLASS no es chequeado por el loader. Puede estar modificado y aun así ser un fichero válido. Sin embargo, el campo e_ehsize (tamaño del encabezamiento ELF) que está en la posición 28h para 32 bits ó 34h para 64 bits si se chequea. Para los ELF de 32 bits es 52 ó 0x34h y 64 ó 0x40h para los de 64 bits. [14]

Se chequea qué tipo de fichero es, en la posición 10h en el campo e_type. El valor 1 significa que es relocable, 2 ejecutable y 3 objeto compartido. Puede adoptar otros valores igualmente válidos.

Los datos necesarios para calcular el punto de entrada son:

- e_entry, dirección virtual del punto de entrada (0 si no tiene punto de entrada)
- e_phoff, desplazamiento de la tabla de encabezado de programa (0 si no tiene segmentos)
- e_shoff, desplazamiento de la tabla de encabezado de secciones (0 si no tiene secciones)
- e_phentsize, tamaño de una entrada en la tabla del encabezado de programa.
- e_phnum número de entradas en la tabla del encabezado de programa.
- e_shentsize, tamaño de una entrada en la tabla del encabezado de sección.
- e_shunum, número de entradas en la tabla del encabezado de sección.
- e_shstrndx, número de entradas en sección de cadenas de nombres.

El segmento donde está el punto de entrada debe cumplir las siguientes condiciones:

- Ser cargable, o sea, p_type = 0x1h = PT_LOAD.
- Tener permisos de lectura y ejecución (p_flags)
- El intervalo de memoria del segmento debe contener el punto de entrada.
  `p_vaddr <= e_entry < (p_vaddr + p_memsz - 1)`

La sección donde aparece el punto de entrada debe cumplir las condiciones siguientes:

- El tipo de sección debe ser de información de programa (sh_type=0x1h=SHT_PROGBITS)
- Las banderas deben indicar que la sección ocupa memoria y contiene instrucciones ejecutables por la máquina (sh_flags=0x6h)
- El nombre de la sección es .text (instrucciones ejecutables de un programa)
- El intervalo de memoria de la sección debe contener el punto de entrada.

```
s_addr <= e_entry < (s_addr + s_size - 1)
```

La firma que se selecciona se compone de dos secuencias de bytes contenidas en la sección o el segmento que contiene el punto de entrada. La primera secuencia será de 48 bytes siempre que sea posible y se obtendrá a partir del punto de entrada de ejecución del fichero. Si no existen suficientes bytes de información entre el punto de entrada y el final de los datos válidos de no cavidad[2], se ejecutan pasos de desplazamientos de menos un byte respecto al punto de entrada, siempre y cuando no sea un área de información redundante[3], en cuyo caso no se considerará absolutamente ningún byte previo al punto de entrada y se conformará la firma con la secuencia de bytes a partir del punto de entrada que pueda obtenerse siempre que no sea menor que 16 bytes. La segunda secuencia se busca dentro de la sección o segmento del punto de entrada también, dentro del área de no cavidad, procesando bloques de 64 bytes y comenzando por aquel bloque de mayor desplazamiento físico respecto al punto de entrada.

La selección de dos secuencias de bytes en posiciones diferentes persigue el objetivo de reducir la probabilidad de falsos positivos. Por otro lado, al seleccionar secuencias no muy largas se agiliza el proceso de escaneo del motor al no tener que chequear un buffer muy extenso.

2.3 Selección y procesamiento de ficheros

Para poner a prueba el algoritmo desarrollado se conformaron dos grupos de ficheros. El primer grupo compuesto por 7 746 programas malignos que serán procesados para seleccionarle firmas. Todos son binarios de 32 bits, sin comprimir y con codificación Little Endian, de ellos 915 objetos compartidos y el resto ejecutables. Está compuesto por una representación de varios tipos de malware: troyanos, gusanos y rootkits.

El segundo grupo se conformó con 31 962 binarios originales o goodware, obtenidos a partir de diferentes distribuciones de sistemas operativos, para comprobar que las firmas seleccionadas no detecten falsos positivos. Este grupo contiene ejecutables, objetos compartidos y reubicables en similar proporción.

3 Resultados

El procesamiento de los ficheros concluyó satisfactoriamente. Se le seleccionaron cadenas al 96% de los ficheros sin detectarse falsas alarmas. Al 3% no se le pudo seleccionar firmas debido a que las áreas de código eran muy pequeñas y el restante 1% pertenecían a una clasificación de malware más complejo que necesita intervención manual. Como resultado se seleccionaron firmas que detectan malware de las familias coinminer, ransomware y banker. El procesamiento demoró menos de 10 minutos logrando una reducción significativa del tiempo de análisis e incorporación de las identificaciones a la base de firmas del motor antivirus que de haberse hecho manualmente hubiese tardado semanas.

[2] Se entiende por área de cavidad aquella área comprendida al final de la sección que comienza con al menos ocho ceros y contiene solo ceros. El área de la cavidad no incluye los primeros ocho ceros.

[3] Área de información redundante aquella con al menos 5 bytes nulos u 8 bytes no nulos iguales.

4 Conclusiones y trabajos futuros

Como resultado de la investigación y desarrollo del proyecto se obtuvo una solución capaz de seleccionar firmas de ficheros ELF ejecutables y objetos compartidos de 32 bits sin comprimir. Como continuidad de este trabajo se planea desarrollar el mecanismo que permita procesar también ficheros de 64 bits.

Referencias

1. Shahzad, F.; Farooq, M.: ELF-Miner: using structural knowledge and data mining methods to detect new (Linux) malicious executables, vol. 30, Londres: *Springer-Verlag*, 2012.
2. López, A.: Malware en Linux: Rootkits, introducción y clasificación. *Incibe-Cert.* https://www.certsi.es/blog/malware-linux. 2015. Accedido el 20 de junio de 2018.
3. Rivero Pérez, A.; Lodos Vigil, J.: Motor Antivirus de Segurmática: para el presente y el futuro. *Tecnomática,* vol. 13, nº 1, 2014.
4. Malanov, A.: Los principios fundamentales de los antivirus: virus, firmas, desinfección. *Kaspersky Lab.* https://www.kaspersky.es/blog/signature-virus-disinfection/9298. 2016. Accedido el 14 de junio 2018.
5. Committee, TIS.: Executable and Linkable Format (ELF). 1995.
6. Asmitha, K. A.; Vinod, P.: A machine learning approach for Linux malware detection. *International Conference on Issues and Challenges in Intelligent Computing Techniques (ICICT)*, 2014.
7. Bai, J.; Yang,Y.; Mu, S.; Ma, Y.: Malware detection through mining symbol table of Linux executables. *Information Technology Journal,* vol. 12, nº 2, 2013. pp. 380-383
8. Christodorescu, M.; Jha, S.; Seshia, S. A.: Semantics-aware malware detection*, 2005 IEEE Symposium on Security and Privacy (S&P'05)* Oakland, 2005. pp. 32-46. http://ieeexplore.ieee.org/stamp/stamp.jsp?tp=&arnumber=1425057&isnumber=30765.
9. Sun, N.; Winkler, P.; Chu, C.; Jia, H.; Geffner, J.: Automated malware signature generation, U.S. Patent No 8, 201, 244, 12 de junio de 2012.
10. Ask, K.: Automatic Malware Signature Generation. *International workshop on recent advances in intrusion detection,* Springer, Berlin, Heidelberg, pp. 101-120. (2019)
11. Griffin, K.; Schneider, S.; Hu, X.; Chiueh, T.-c.: Automatic Generation of String Signatures for Malware Detection. *Recent Advances in Intrusion Detection. RAID 2009. Lecture Notes in Computer Science*, vol. 5758. Springer, Berlin, Heidelberg. (2009)
12. Sarkisov, E.; Dittrich, D.: Análisis Forense de Sistemas GNU/Linux, Unix. https://s3.amazonaws.com/academia.edu.documents/38522062/Analisis_Forense_Linux.pdf?AWSAccessKeyId=AKIAIWOWYYGZ2Y53UL3A&Expires=1544826968&Signature=xPrfydIhfevpS3cg%2FPqczQcyER8%3D&response-content-disposition=inline%3B%20filename%3DAnalisis_Forense_de_S. (2002). Accedido el 30 de noviembre de 2018.
13. Sanmillan, I.: Executable and Linkable Format 101 - Part 1 Sections and Segments, 2018.

14. Barry, D.: A Whirlwind Tutorial on Creating Really Teensy ELF Executables for Linux . muppetlabs.com. http://www.muppetlabs.com/~breadbox/software/tiny/teensy.html. Accedido el 4 de diciembre de 2018.

15. Labs, P.: Panda Mediacenter. https://www.pandasecurity.com/spain/mediacenter/malware/2017-en-cifras/.2018. Accedido el 18 junio 2018].

16. Bortnik, S. ¡Cumplimos 10.000! FAQ sobre las firmas antivirus. *Eset.* https://www.welivesecurity.com/la-es/2014/06/26/cumplimos-10000-faq-firmas-antivirus/. 2014. Accedido el 14 junio 2018.

17. Bayer, U.; Moser, A.; Kruegel, C.; Kirda, E.: Dynamic Analysis of Malicious Code. *Journal in Computer Virology.* vol. 2, pp. 67-77, 2006.

19. Lab, K. *Kaspersky Lab Daily*. https://www.kaspersky.es/blog/. 2018. Accedido el 19 junio 2018.

20. Specification, Workgroup.: 64-bit ELF v2 ABI Specification. Power Arquitecture. 2017.

Ingeniería de requerimientos de un software para soportar el entorno personal de aprendizaje de estudiantes de la UCI

Taire Faife Rodríguez[1], Dunia Ma. Colomé Cedeño[1], Gustavo García González[1],

[1] Universidaad de las Ciencias Informáticas, Departamento Ingeniería de Software, La Habana, Cuba
{tfaife, dcolome, ggarcia}@uci.cu

Resumen. El número de aplicaciones informáticas disponibles en Internet crece exponencialmente. Este fenómeno posibilita el enriquecimiento de los entornos de aprendizaje, pero a la vez provoca incertidumbre en la selección de cuáles herramientas incorporar a estos espacios. Existen software que posibilitan gestionar los entornos de aprendizaje de los individuos en la red, los que, a pesar de sus múltiples potencialidades, presentan limitaciones que afectan su empleo, entre ellas se encuentran la insuficiente interoperabilidad entre sus componentes; la deficiente sincronización de sus contenidos y las dificultades en las recomendaciones que realizan. El objetivo de esta investigación es establecer los requisitos de un producto de software que apoye el proceso personal de aprendizaje, para lo cual se sigue un proceso de ingeniería de requisitos. La ingeniería de requisitos que se presenta en este trabajo se desarrolló según las etapas: Estudio de factibilidad, Adquisición y Análisis, Especificación y Validación. En la concepción del estudio de factibilidad se aplicó una encuesta, empleando la escala de Likert, y el análisis de sistemas similares para identificar la posibilidad de continuar con el desarrollo de esta ingeniería. La especificación de requerimientos del sistema se detalló con la técnica de historias de usuario, la cual es propuesta por el escenario cuatro de la metodología de desarrollo de software AUP-UCI, para encapsular los requerimientos identificados. Los requerimientos fueron validados con prototipos de alta fidelidad y con el método de Kano, el cual arrojó la concentración de la clasificación de los requerimientos en los tres tipos ideales de atributos.

Palabras clave: ingeniería de requerimientos, entorno personal de aprendizaje, aprendizaje.

1 Introducción

El continuo desarrollo de las Tecnologías de la Información y la Comunicación (TIC) y su creciente incorporación a los procesos formativos en centros educacionales, hace cada vez más necesario encontrar alternativas que apoyen y enriquezcan estos procesos. Esta evolución de las TIC y la emergencia de nuevos paradigmas en la web, con sus consiguientes aplicaciones en el campo de la educación, permiten poner a disposición de los individuos una gran diversidad de recursos educativos y herramientas informáticas. Así mismo, facilita el acceso a nuevos y variados entornos de formación virtuales y la realización de un conjunto de actividades formativas desde cualquier lugar, desde cualquier dispositivo y en cualquier momento. El desarrollo exponencial de nuevas aplicaciones de software, brindan crecientes posibilidades a los individuos para enriquecer sus ambientes personales de formación. En el año 2001, en el marco del proyecto NIMLE (Northern Ireland Integrated Managed Learning Environment), se comenzó a desarrollar la idea de un entorno personal de aprendizaje centrado en el alumno, como evolución de los entornos virtuales de enseñanza aprendizaje, centrados en la institución. En el 2004, el JISC (Joint Information System Commitee de la Gran Bretaña) incluyó una sesión específica en su congreso anual dedicada a entornos telemáticos centrados en el alumno a los que llamaron Personal Learning Environment (PLE). Esta fue la primera vez que se empleó oficialmente dicho concepto, que posteriormente evolucionó y se ha generalizado con el acrónimo PLE.

Los PLE "son una colección de instrumentos, materiales y recursos humanos que el estudiante emplea en un determinado momento en el contexto de un proyecto educativo" (G Atwell, 2007). El PLE es "el conjunto de herramientas, fuentes de información, conexiones y actividades utilizadas habitualmente por el individuo, suponiendo esto un cambio en la práctica pedagógica hacia un aprendizaje abierto, social y centrado en el estudiante" (Jordi Adell & Linda Castañeda, 2010). El concepto de PLE necesita ser desarrollado de forma práctica, de manera que los individuos comprendan la contribución de la tecnología a la eficiencia del proceso de aprendizaje. (Linda Castañeda & Jordi Adell, 2013)

En la actualidad existen software para gestionar los PLE, los cuales brindan páginas de inicio que permiten la integración de diferentes herramientas de la Web 2.0 así como la disposición de información de manera ordenada y fácil de localizar. La similitud técnica entre estas herramientas es elevada: poseen una variedad considerable de características relacionadas con la usabilidad y los aspectos estéticos; sin embargo, poseen limitaciones que dificultan su empleo, entre las que se pueden enunciar las siguientes: no facilitan la comunicación entre los widgets que proporcionan; las recomendaciones a canales de noticias no tienen en cuenta la región del usuario; no son totalmente gratuitas; no admiten la configuración de correos electrónicos ni la de los clientes de mensajería institucionales y presentan dificultades con la sincronización de los widgets. En la Universidad de las Ciencias Informáticas (UCI) los estudiantes emplean habitualmente diferentes herramientas informáticas, que sin estar ellos totalmente conscientes, forman parte de sus PLE, al constituir componentes del entorno donde aprenden. Entre estas herramientas se encuentran redes sociales (ej. Facebook y Twitter), herramientas de mensajería instantánea (ej.: Pidgin, Pandion y Trillian), sistemas de gestión del aprendizaje (ej. Zera y Moodle), sitios para la descarga y la visualización de materiales audiovisuales (Internos), entre otras. Estas herramientas se emplean de forma dispersa y no están totalmente integradas por lo que no se aprovechan todas sus potencialidades tecnológicas para conformar un PLE en la UCI.

A partir de la situación problemática descrita anteriormente el problema a resolver con el desarrollo de esta investigación es el siguiente: ¿Cómo establecer una base para el diseño y la construcción de un software que soporte el entorno personal de aprendizaje de los estudiantes de la UCI? El objetivo de esta investigación es establecer los requisitos de un producto de software que apoye el proceso personal de aprendizaje, para lo cual se sigue un proceso de ingeniería de requisitos. Existen diversas etapas para la ingeniería de software (Ian Sommerville, 2011), (Karol Frühauf, et al., 2015), (Roger S. Pressman, 2010), que aunque se diferencien por los nombres que cada autor le ha dado, en su esencia se asemejan por las actividades que se realizan en cada una de ellas. En este trabajo se presentan primeramente los materiales y métodos utilizados para el desarrollo de la investigación. Luego se exponen los principales resultados de las fases ejecutadas: Estudio de factibilidad, Adquisición y Análisis y, Especificación. Finalmente, se presentan los resultados de la validación de los requerimientos especificados.

2 Materiales y métodos

Con el propósito de alcanzar el objetivo propuesto, el trabajo se desarrolló en las siguientes etapas, propuestas por [6] para desarrollar una ingeniería de requerimientos: Estudio de factibilidad, Adquisición y Análisis, Especificación y Validación. En la concepción del estudio de factibilidad se determinó la aplicación de una encuesta, la cual fue aplicada a especialistas en Ciencias Informáticas y profesores con experiencia en el desarrollo de software para el e-learning y otros temas relacionados con tecnología educativa. Se encuestaron un total de catorce expertos, de ellos dos Dr.C., tres MSc. y nueve Ingenieros en Ciencias Informáticas.

En la elaboración de la encuesta se empleó la escala de Likert para facilitar el procesamiento de los datos aportados por los encuestados, lo cual se realizó con el empleo del software SPSS. También durante el estudio de factibilidad se realizó el análisis de sistemas similares y que presentan relación con el sistema a desarrollar; en este caso se realizó el análisis de Symbaloo, iGoogle y Netvibes. El análisis de las diferentes funcionalidades que brindan estos sistemas permitió establecer las bases para lograr un mejor diseño del PLE. También se realizó el estudio de las interfaces, motivando al surgimiento de nuevas ideas que se utilizaron con el fin de lograr el diseño de los prototipos del sistema, de forma que le permita al estudiante gestionar su PLE en un ambiente cómodo y agradable.

La etapa Análisis de requerimientos tomó como base de partida la información extraída de la encuesta aplicada a los especialistas y el análisis a los sistemas similares, técnicas detalladas anteriormente. La información obtenida con el empleo de estas técnicas se transformó en los requerimientos apropiados para el diseño del sistema que dará soporte al PLE de los estudiantes de la UCI. Como técnicas de observación complementarias se utilizaron escenarios, técnica que permite a través de descripciones en la que un usuario realiza cierta actividad, identificar requerimientos, así como la etnografía para estudiar el entorno del usuario y observar sus hábitos cotidianos. A partir de estas técnicas se infirieron requerimientos para el soporte del software que gestionará el PLE de los estudiantes de la UCI.

La especificación de requerimientos del sistema se detalló con la técnica de historias de usuario, la cual es propuesta por el escenario cuatro de la metodología de desarrollo de software AUP-UCI, para encapsular los requerimientos funcionales del sistema. Con el empleo de esta técnica se describió lo que se espera como salida de la implementación, y cómo se ve beneficiado el usuario final.

Como técnica para validar los requerimientos del sistema se diseñaron prototipos de alta fidelidad, con el objetivo de proporcionar un entorno visual sencillo que permita al cliente adaptarse al trabajo con los requerimientos especificados. Esta técnica permitió detectar posibles errores en la descripción de la especificación que no habían sido identificados, al permitir representar aspectos más precisos del sistema. También como parte de la validación, se aplicó el método de Kano, el cual incluyó la aplicación de un cuestionario a una muestra de estudiantes de la UCI y permitió medir el grado de satisfacción del cliente.

3 Estudio de factibilidad

El desarrollo del estudio de factibilidad y sus principales resultados, con el objetivo de valorar si el sistema que gestionará el PLE de los estudiantes de la UCI es útil para la UCI, se presenta a continuación. Previo a la aplicación de los instrumentos seleccionados para esta etapa se realizó un estudio de los conceptos relacionados con los PLE y los softwares que existen actualmente para gestionarlos, permitiendo de esta forma un mejor entendimiento de las necesidades del cliente y la confección de algunas interrogantes o ideas que se utilizarían como guía para lograr una mejor comunicación durante el proceso.

En la concepción del estudio de factibilidad se determinó la aplicación de una encuesta a especialistas en Ciencias Informáticas y profesores con experiencia en el desarrollo de software para el e-learning y otros temas relacionados con tecnología educativa; procedentes todos de la UCI. Se encuestaron un total de catorce expertos, de ellos dos Dr.C., tres MSc. y nueve Ingenieros en Ciencias Informáticas.

El procesamiento de los datos se desarrolló con el empleo del asistente matemático SPSS, arrojando como principales resultados los que se muestran a continuación. Los encuestados respondieron lo siguiente relacionado con la necesidad de integrar todas las herramientas que emplean los estudiantes de la UCI de manera cotidiana, en un software que gestiona el PLE. (Fig. 1)

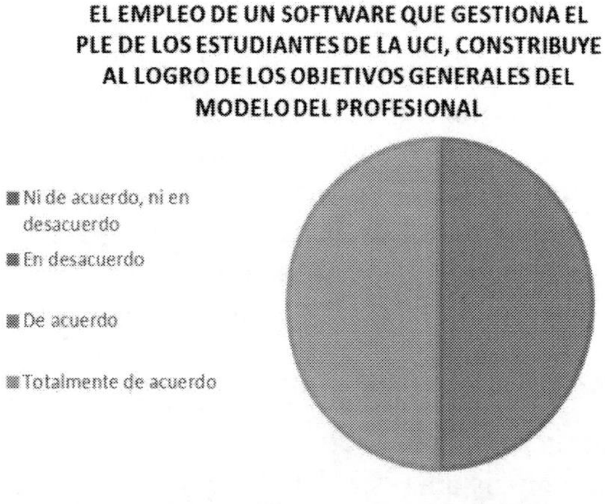

	Frecuencia	Por ciento
Ni de acuerdo, ni en desacuerdo	0	0
En desacuerdo	0	0
De acuerdo	7	50
Totalmente de acuerdo	7	50

Fig. 1. Necesidad de la integración de todas las herramientas en un software PLE.

Relacionado con la afirmación presentada a los encuestados sobre la forma en que los estudiantes de la UCI gestionan sus PLE, los resultados se muestran en la Fig. 2, lo cual confirma la necesidad de ofrecer recursos a los estudiantes para apoyarlos en la gestión de sus PLE.

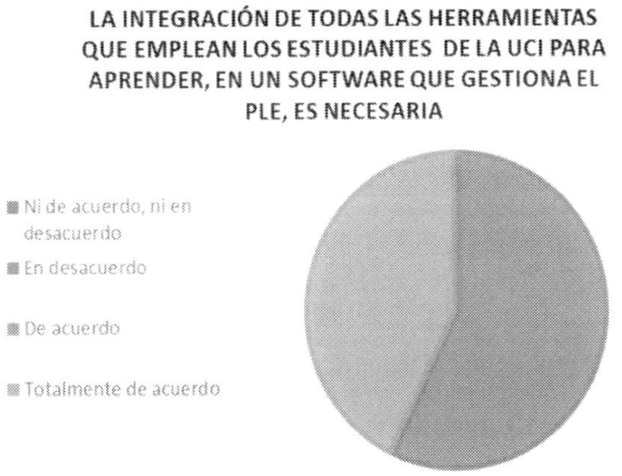

	Frecuencia	Por ciento
Ni de acuerdo, ni en desacuerdo	0	0
En desacuerdo	0	0
De acuerdo	8	57.1
Totalmente de acuerdo	6	42.9

Fig. 2. Forma en que los alumnos gestionan sus PLE

Relacionado con la afirmación presentada a los encuestados sobre la forma en que los estudiantes de la UCI gestionan sus PLE, los resultados se muestran en la Fig.3, lo cual confirma la necesidad de ofrecer recursos a los estudiantes para apoyarlos en la gestión de sus PLE.

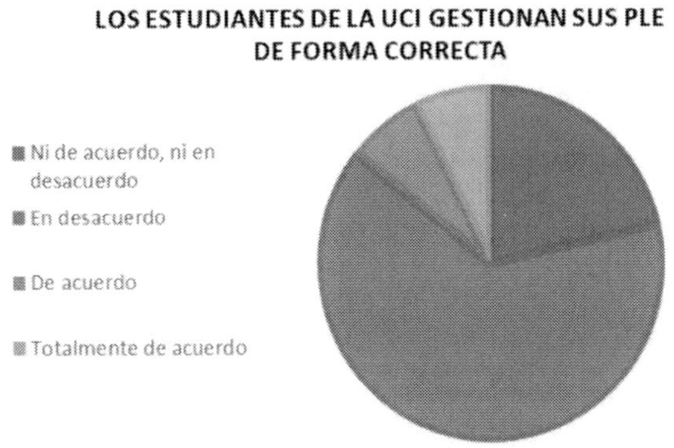

	Frecuencia	Por ciento
Ni de acuerdo, ni en desacuerdo	3	21.4
En desacuerdo	9	64.3
De acuerdo	1	7.1
Totalmente de acuerdo	1	7.1

Fig.3. Forma en que los alumnos gestionan sus PLE.

Ante la siguiente pregunta formulada a los encuestados: ¿Cuáles de las siguientes herramientas Ud. considera que deben formar parte del PLE de los estudiantes de la UCI?, estos coincidieron en su mayoría en algunas de ellas, entre las que se pueden mencionar, por orden de interés para ellos las siguientes: Plataforma educativa Zera (13 interesados), Google (12), Akademos (12), cliente de correo electrónico (11), cliente de mensajería instantánea (10), Twitter (8) y Facebook (7). Lo anterior, refuerza la necesidad de desarrollar un software que gestione sus PLE, como parte del estudio de factibilidad. El estudio de factibilidad arrojó la utilidad de un software personalizado que gestione el PLE de los estudiantes de la UCI, lo cual valida la continuidad del proceso Ingeniería de Requerimientos. Como parte del estudio de factibilidad se realizó un análisis de los sistemas similares Symbaloo, iGoogle y

Netvibes. El análisis de las diferentes funcionalidades que brindan estos sistemas permitió establecer las bases para lograr un mejor diseño del sistema a desarrollar. También se realizó el estudio de las interfaces, motivando al surgimiento de nuevas ideas que se utilizaron con el fin de lograr el diseño de los prototipos del sistema, de forma que le permita al estudiante gestionar su PLE en un ambiente cómodo y agradable.

4 Adquisición y análisis de requerimientos

Empleando como técnicas la encuesta cerrada y el análisis a los sistemas similares, detalladas en la sección anterior, se realizó el análisis de los requerimientos. La información obtenida con su empleo se transformó en los requerimientos apropiados para el diseño del sistema de soporte al PLE de los estudiantes de la UCI. Como técnicas de observación complementarias se utilizaron escenarios y la etnografía para estudiar el entorno del usuario y observar sus hábitos cotidianos. A partir de estas técnicas se infirieron requerimientos para soportar el software de gestión del PLE de los estudiantes de la UCI. Los requerimientos identificados se clasificaron en funcionales y no funcionales, determinando su prioridad a partir del factor Importancia. A continuación, se presentan los principales requerimientos funcionales con prioridad Alta, especificando su descripción en la Tabla 1.

Tabla 1. Requerimientos funcionales del sistema que soporta el PLE de los estudiantes de la UCI.

No	Requerimiento	Descripción
RF1.	Añadir widget	El sistema debe permitir añadir un widget.
RF2.	Eliminar widget	El sistema debe permitir eliminar el widget.
RF3.	Compartir widget	El sistema debe permitir compartir el widget.
RF4.	Intercambiar información con ZERA	El sistema debe permitir intercambiar información con el LMS ZERA de la UCI.
RF5.	Establecer un ecosistema de widget	El sistema debe adoptar normas de widgets que ayuden a establecer un ecosistema de widgets que se pueden ejecutar en diferentes plataformas.
RF6.	Añadir escritorio	El sistema debe permitir añadir un escritorio.
RF7.	Comunicar con redes sociales	El sistema debe permitir la interacción con las redes sociales Facebook y Twitter.

5 Especificación de requerimientos

La especificación de requerimientos del sistema que dará soporte al PLE de los estudiantes de la UCI se realizó empleando Historias de Usuario, técnica que propone el escenario cuatro de la metodología AUP-UCI, para encapsular los requerimientos funcionales del sistema. El empleo de esta técnica permitió describir la salida de la implementación y el beneficio del usuario final.

6 Validación de requerimientos

Como técnica para validar los requerimientos del sistema se realiza el diseño de un prototipo de alta fidelidad, con el objetivo de proporcionar un entorno visual sencillo que permita al cliente adaptarse al trabajo con los requerimientos especificados.

Los prototipos de alta fidelidad permiten representar aspectos más precisos del sistema, estos son útiles para detallar el proceso interactivo de una o varias tareas concretas. La propuesta se basa en obtener los prototipos a partir de la especificación de requerimientos que, sin tener la totalidad de las funcionalidades, permitan al usuario hacerse una idea de la estructura y las opciones de navegabilidad del sistema. En la Fig.4 se muestra una captura de pantalla de la vista Listar RSS, correspondiente al requerimiento funcional de igual nombre.

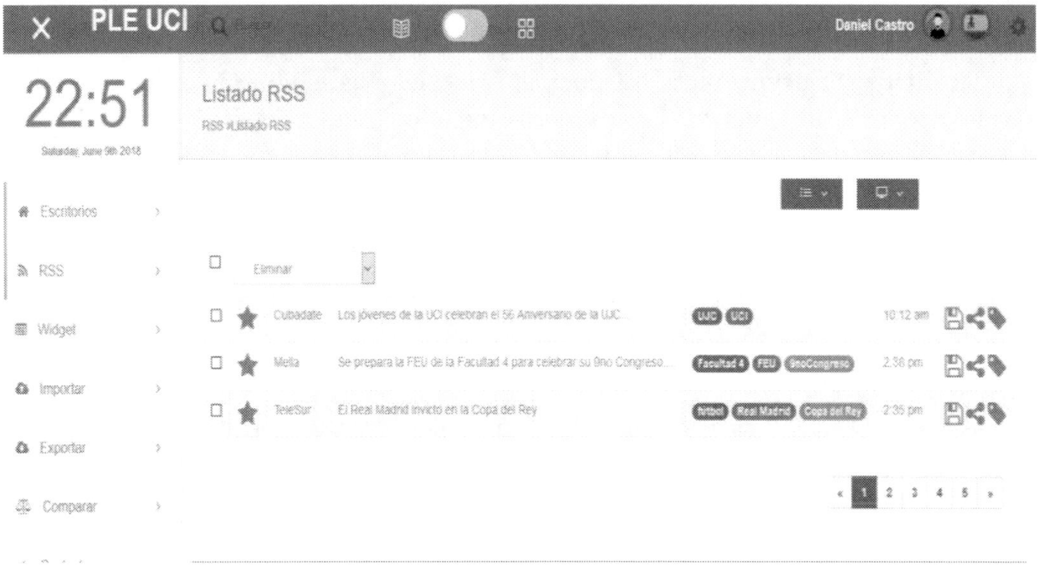

Fig.4. Requerimiento funcional Listar RSS.

6.2 Aplicación del método Kano

La aplicación del método Kano, requirió la selección de una muestra de requerimientos que permitieran realizar acciones importantes en el sistema. Esta selección arrojó los siguientes requerimientos 1) Añadir widget, 2) Listar RSS, 3) Compartir widget, 4) Eliminar widget, 5) Importar OPML, 6) Exportar OPML, 7) Intercambiar información entre widgets, 8) Intercambiar información con ZERA, 9) Añadir escritorio. El instrumento fue aplicado a una muestra de 15 estudiantes de la Facultad 4 de la UCI; tres de segundo año, tres de tercer año, cuatro de cuarto año y cinco de quinto año, de la carrera Ingeniería en Ciencias Informáticas. Para cada requerimiento se mostraron tres preguntas: una para medir cómo se siente si la característica está presente en el sistema, otra para medir cómo se siente si la característica no está presente en el sistema y la otra para medir el grado de importancia que le atribuye al requerimiento especificado; para cada pregunta el usuario respondió una de cinco opciones. La clasificaron de los requerimientos arrojó seis factores de entusiasmo (Compartir widget, Importar OPML, Exportar OPML, Intercambiar información entre widgets, Intercambiar información con ZERA), dos de desempeño (Añadir widget, Añadir escritorio) y tres básicos (Listar RSS, Eliminar widget).

7 Conclusiones

Con los elementos teóricos y prácticos más actuales de las ciencias informáticas en lo referido a tecnología educativa, se establecieron las bases para el diseño y la construcción de un sistema que soporte el PLE de los estudiantes de la UCI, a través del desarrollo de una ingeniería de requerimientos, validada con métodos científicos. La ingeniería de requerimientos presentada constituye una base para la ejecución de las posteriores fases del desarrollo de software, dado que se encuentra totalmente desarrollada y documentada. El conjunto de métodos científicos utilizados para la validación de los requerimientos (prototipos de alta fidelidad y método Kano) permitió comprobar que: los requerimientos propuestos responden a las necesidades de los estudiantes de la UCI y que existe una alta satisfacción de los usuarios actuales y potenciales con respecto a la necesidad, utilidad y actualidad del sistema propuesto.

Referencias

1. Atwell, G.: Personal learning environments-the future of elearning?, http://www.elearningeuropa.info/files/media/media11561.pdf (2007)
2. Sommerville, I.: Ingeniería de Software. Pearson Educación de México, S.A. de C.V. (2011)
3. Adell, J., Castañeda, L.: Los Entornos Personales de Aprendizaje (PLEs): una nueva manera de entender el aprendizaje. Alcoy: Marfil. (2010)
4. Frhauf, K., Fuchs, E., Paech, B., Glinz, M., Grau, R., Colin, H., Rupp, C.: Profesional Certificado en Ingeniería de Requisitos de IREB - Nivel Básico (2015)
5. Castañeda, L., Adell, J.: Entornos Personales de Aprendizaje: Claves para el eco- sistema educativo en la red. Marfil. (2013)
6. Pressman, R.: Ingeniería del Software. Un enfoque práctico. Séptima edición. (2010)

Semantic enrichment over words vector space in short texts generated by Project Management tools

Laynier Piedra Diéguez [1[0000-0001-8699-7718]] José E. Medina Pagola[2[0000-0001-7344-0945]]
Surayne Torres López[1[0000-0002-6037-6603]]

[1] Laboratorio de Investigaciones en Gestión de Proyectos, Universidad de las Ciencias Informáticas, Cuba, Carretera a San Antonio de Baños Km 2 1/2, Boyeros, La Habana, Cuba.
[2] Senior Researcher, Universidad de las Ciencias Informáticas, Cuba, Carretera a San Antonio de Baños Km 2 1/2, Torrens, La Lisa, La Habana, Cuba.

Abstract. The short texts analysis has been a problem to deal with, during the automatic decision support processes due to the limited information they contain. The project management tools generate this type of texts and it is necessary to give them the most appropriate treatment to obtain valid and reliable results. A strong case is the Xedro-GESPRO tool, in which an evaluation model of labor competencies in projects is generated based on the analysis of the evidence of human resources' performance. This model was implemented without a text comparison technique to consider semantic or contextual, even when those mentioned evidences and labor competencies, are very short texts. This induce system to erroneous competence-evidence matching, and later, to wrong values in labor performance metrics. At the end, an imprecise evaluation of competence is suggested. To deal with this problem, we used a model based on artificial neural networks (ANN). This model was used to capture semantic information from a textual corpus specialized in project management and so to improve the analysis of the indicators that are used for the evaluation of labor competencies. The used model significantly improved the effectiveness of the process compared to previous techniques. It was also able to capture relationship between bad written terms or English words.

Keywords: knowledge discovery, project management, information recovery, short texts, text similarity, NLP, Word2Vec, skip-gram.

1 Introduction

The complexity that organizations acquire as they grow, needs a competence management that allows having a qualified staff to guarantee the successful development of each one of the tasks. The need for a competence management is manifested in more than one moment of the human resources management, both in the selection (Garcés Hernández, 2017), as in the formation of teams and authors have considered it essential to achieve the objectives of the mission of the organization (Cuesta Santos A. , 2016).

Business management in Cuba needs an approach in line with international dynamics, which is closer each time due to foreign investment opportunities, new companies established in the Mariel Special Development Zone, and business agreements established with several countries (Martínez García , 2018). From this need arise the sections related to labor competencies in the Guidelines for the Economic and Social Policy of the Party and Revolution, established in 2011, updated in 2017 and in constant analysis and monitoring (Martínez Hernández & Puig Meneses, 2018).

One of the characteristics mentioned as fundamental for the competencies, is that they must be perceptible (Torres López, 2015), and this supposes the possibility of measuring them. These measurements can be made using different methods related to tests, analysis of interview results (Garcés Hernández, 2017), and analysis of the evidence gathered from the processes in which the worker intervenes (Torres López, 2015).

A more complete investigation was presented in 2015. The result of that investigation automated the evaluation process based on competencies, and formalized the evaluation within a model, taking into consideration the definition of the competences and dimensions that constitute these competences. Model also included the performance evidences, and the relationship of both elements with work performance (Torres López, 2015). The name is "Model of competency evaluation based on evidence during project management", hereinafter MEC-GP, and it is implemented on the project management tool Xedro-GESPRO. MEC-GP constitutes a fundamental reference for the present investigation.

Inside, this model of competency evaluation uses the cosine similarity of the vector representation of texts approach, to determine the correspondence between evidence and competences. However, cosine uses the frequency of appearance of the terms by means of the TF-IDF scheme (Sparck Jones, 1972) (Zimniewicz, Kurowski, & Węglarz, 2018) (Slamet, et al., 2018) as a basis for subsequent calculations of the procedure; then calculate several indicators. A previously trained neural network receives these indicators and proposes an evaluation. This evaluation of the system not only supports the evaluation of performance but also the decision-making in terms of training or personnel training (Torres López, 2015).

The moment in which the cosine distance is applied to determine what evidence will be used to evaluate which competences in MEC-GP, is a critical moment with a high impact on the system because it is the starting point for the further calculations. Because of the nature of the analyzed data, the use of this measure of similarity is not the best alternative, considering that the dimensions and evidences are short texts (Torres López, Aldana Cuza, Piñero Perez, & Piedra Diéguez, 2016). That´s why the TF-IDF or other frequency based text vector representations would lead to erroneous calculation, affecting all further processes. In this case, several metrics and final evaluation recommendation of the system were being negatively affected.

In this paper, a new measure is proposed, based on the semantic enrichment of short texts, using a specific data set of project management and a trained neural network to generate contexts for each term to be compared by cosine. The structure of the document is made as follows: next, the theoretical basis related to the method is mentioned, as well as the conceptualization of the proposed measure. Then the experimentation is mentioned and, based on the results, the efficiency is analyzed by making a comparison with the results of the step corresponding to the cosine in MEC-GP. For last, conclusions of the investigation are listed, prior to the bibliographic references for the investigation.

2 Theoretical framework

The application of techniques based on counting or morphology of words is not enough to perform short text analysis. Semantics should also be considered. Semantic is determined by the context in which every analyzed word is found. It is agreed that similar contexts will have - in addition to similar words - semantically related terms (Altszyler & Brusco, 2015). The way in which human beings use natural language is analyzing the words in relation to their own closest words, that is: their context (Carrasco Gómez, 2017).

Based on the above, some works have been developed to exploit the possibilities of Artificial Neural Networks (ANN) to improve numerous Natural Language Processing (NLP) techniques, among which are the classification and vector representation of texts, framed in the paradigm that has been released as Word embedding (Bengio, Schwenk, & Senecal, 2006). One of the most popular models of this paradigm is Word2Vec (Mikolov, Yih, & Zweig, Linguistic Regularities in Continuous Space Word Representations, 2013), which allows to capture both syntactic and semantic information of words. One of the models that contains Word2Vec allows to obtain the context from a word (skip-gram model) (Mikolov, Le, & Sutskever, Exploiting Similarities among Languages for Machine Translation, 2013). Within Word2Vec models, their authors recommend Skip-gram for its "best word representations when monolingual data is small" (Mikolov, Le, & Sutskever, Exploiting Similarities among Languages for Machine Translation, 2013).

3 Proposed method

For this research, the used model contains an evolution of Skip-gram, which is based on it, but also recognizes the morphology of the words by representing each word as a bag of n-grams texts, and so, being a word a summation of these n-grams (Bojanowski, Grave, Joulin, & Mikolov, 2017). This approach also allows recognizing similarities between misspelled words and words in other languages that share similar morphology; example: "instalador" and "installer". The authors also recommend skip-gram for other PLN tasks, such as translation, automatic answering systems, information retrieval and others (Mikolov, Yih, & Zweig, Linguistic Regularities in Continuous Space Word Representations, 2013) (Mikolov, Le, & Sutskever, 2013). In this case, it has been used for its original purpose: the similarity of texts.

The textual basis for training the model in this case, are specific terms of project management, related to job skills and evidence of performance in the production and development of software, scientific investigations and training of several software development centers. Six million of terms are used for model training.

As for MEC-GP, cosine was used, but it was modified to include the semantic enrichment of texts. The value of similarity between the texts of the dimension and the evidence of MEC-GP is replaced by the value obtained by the sCC function, which is defined as follows:

$$\mathrm{sCC}(X,Y) = sim\,\cos((X + Cx),(Y + Cy))$$

Where X and Y are short texts to calculate their similarity; Cx and Cy are the concatenations of the contexts of each term from X and Y respectively generated by the model. The sCC measure is the resulting cosine similarity from: the concatenation of the short text X with the contexts of its terms, and the concatenation of the short text Y with the contexts of its terms. Further, in this document, this proposed similarity measure is called a contextual cosine (sCC). Figure 1 shows the operation scheme of the proposed measure.

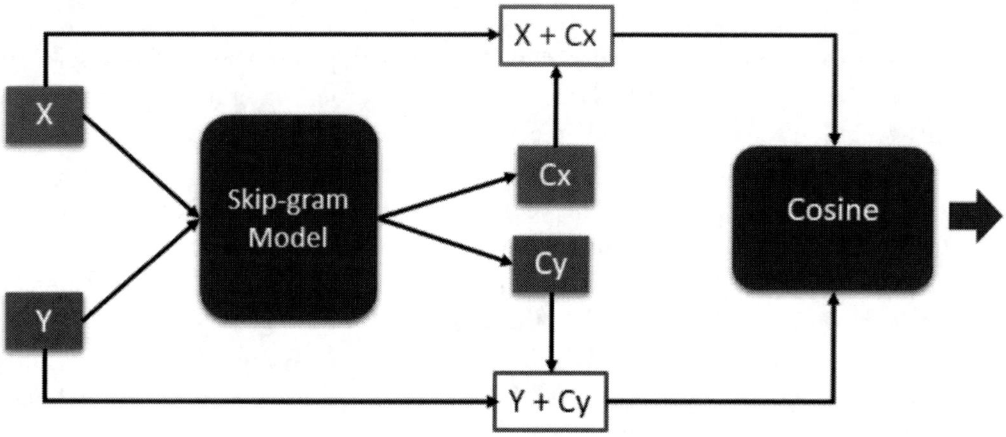

Fig. 1. Diagram of the Contextual Cosine (sCC) similarity calculations.

4 Experimental evaluation

The experimental process was carried out on the framework R, with the tool RStudio to automate the processing. Both the creation of the skip-gram type RNA model and the final similarity, were prepared in this language, usually used for statistical processing, but extendable through a system of packages to other functions such as machine learning and data mining, and to other languages such as C ++, Java, Python, and others (Rahlf, 2017).

The preparing process of the model was carried out using one corpus specialized in project management and freed from stopwords. It was used an implementation of word embedding from the R package "fastrtext" (Benesty, 2018), which implements the vector representation of the words published by Bojanowski, Mikolov and others in 2016 (Bojanowski, Grave, Joulin, & Mikolov, 2017). Some additional packages were used to process the text automatically, and assist the calculation of the sCC; however, all of these secondary operations can be performed with the basic commands of the tool.

The next table shows generated contexts for some common tasks retrieved from the mentioned software management tool. These are not simulations but real performed tasks executed during recent years by Spanish-speaking software development teams. Texts are tokenized to avoid prepositions, pronouns, and other stopwords that might interfere the correct context generation. The retrieved information contains words with several miswriting errors and other misspellings. This reinforces the need of a more efficacious method to deal with variety of writing and thinking during task assignations, and more important: to detect similarity in short texts despite of errors, distinguishing true correspondence between competencies and tasks performed.

Table 1. Contexts generated.

Short text	Generated context
revision adherencia procesos productos ppqa	revisiones vision revisadas division mision gerencia ejecucion precesos trasferencia productos loteproductos producen producto adherencia produce pmc 3520 cm sam pp
revision calisoft elementos cliente pertenecen linea base	revisiones vision revisadas division mision gespro13 lips pertenecen albet fiscalia elemento elmentos talentos madurez fcliente client clientenp ente ambiente pertenecia integridad madurez jee lineas línea pertenecen minima jee mssql subiendo linea tcp permitiendo
crear repositorio proyecto	aglutinar embebida deshabilta repositorios repomine desee reubicar dispositivo proyecto. deproyecto poyecto preproyecto proyector
desarrollar reporte hito	Desarroll desarrollo desarrllar desarrollar desarrollado report reportes filtro haya alta gema fase lavandero hi
diseña casos prueba flujo caso uso requisito basico alterno	diseñar diseñada diseñador diseños diseño textual etc foros digitales pruebar pueba parcial junit pruebas flujos flex respectivo grafo seguir carretera retenidos arquitectonicamente subeclipse configuacion jdom lanzamiento alarmas textual requisitos encolarse viene autoservicio relacionado basicos incluya durante 3ero interno alternativa alternativo dijistra economica
documenta modelo logico base datos	Documenta documentar documentacion documental documento metamodelo ddl modelos madurez modelio lógico tecnologico metodologico metodolgogico on-

	tologicos mssql subiendo linea tcp permitiendo datos. Metadatos mssql corrida backups

In order to test the proposed method, same evidences that MEC-GP had previously compared using the simple cosine, were used in experimentation. This was done also to determine if sCC was able to obtain better and more reliable results, including ability to find a relationship between the texts where MEC-GP had obtained a poor relationship or cero.

To check the validity of the results, 831 evidence-dimension pairs were randomly selected. They were presented to two experts with more than 10 years of project management experience to establish if they were related or not, and from this and on, to verify the effectiveness of the sCC.

Figure 2 shows how sCC is more effective than simple cosine of MEC-GP. The efficacy of this measure was analyzed by calculating the Three Values threshold formula proposed in MEC-GP (Torres López, 2015). To analyze the efficacy of sCC against the similarity component of MEC-GP, the similarities offered by both measures were compared according to the pattern defined by the experts.

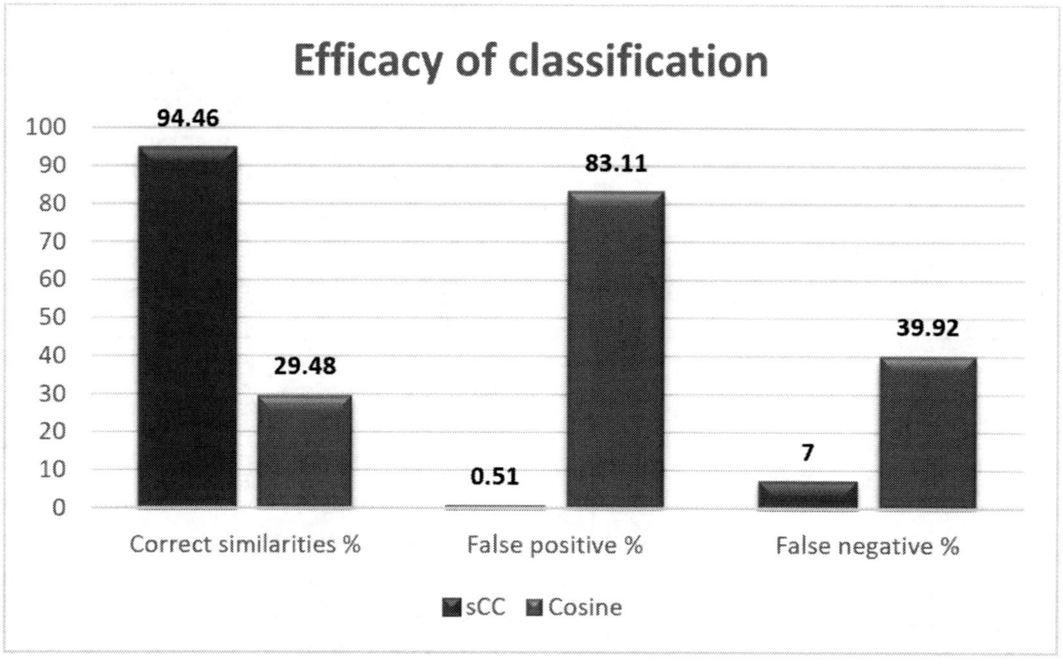

Fig. 2. Comparison between results.

For this case, efficacy was defined as the percentage of correct classifications, understanding by correct classification the finding of dimension-evidence similarity values above the defined threshold, coinciding with the pattern defined by the experts. Figure 2 shows that sCC obtains 64.98% more of correct classifications than MEC-GP when verified, failing in only 0.51% when detecting correspondences where there was none.

In addition, SCC only failed to detect 7% of the correspondences, while the simple cosine of MEC-GP didn´t detect them in more than 39% of the cases.

Even when sCC depends on the semantic enrichment that is made of the texts to be compared, in this case a small enrichment was chosen with the objective of not obtaining excessively optimistic results; however, it is possible to add a greater context for each term in order to raise the semantic quality of text strings. The debate will be about how many terms brain needs to find meaning to a central word within them. That would be the optimal size for context but it may depends on the area of knowledge that is analyzed and the idiom or language in which the texts are found.

5 Conclusions

A measure of similarity was created and it made possible to detect in greater depth the similarity between two short texts. The processing of short texts could be improved with the addition of semantic information to the measure of similarity used, resulting in a better measurement, which takes into account the characteristics of the language and the area of application of the procedure.

In the context of project management, this measure of similarity allowed to locate more effectively the correspondence between evidence of work performance and expected competencies of project members.

Not only was it possible to detect semantic relationships between the terms from the model, but also to extract others with lexicographic errors, or in other languages, such as English. This also improves the internal validity of the model since during the dynamics of using project management tools, writing errors occur, or English terms are commonly used.

References

1. Altszyler, E., & Brusco, P. (2015). Análisis de la dinámica del contenido semántico de textos. *Argentine Symposium on Artificial Intelligence (ASAI 2015).* Rosario: Sociedad Argentina de Informática e Investigación Operativa (SADIO). Retrieved from http://hdl.handle.net/10915/52169
2. Benesty, M. (2018, Enero). fastRtext. *R wrapper for fastText C++ code from Facebook.* The Comprehensive R Archive Network. Retrieved from https://CRAN.R-project.org/package=fastrtext
3. Bengio, Y., Schwenk, H., & Senecal, J. (2006). Neural probabilistic language models. *Innovations in Machine Learning*, 137–186.
4. Bojanowski, P., Grave, E., Joulin, A., & Mikolov, T. (2017). Enriching Word Vectors with Subword Information. (H. Schutze, Ed.) *Transactions of the Association for Computational Linguistic, 5*, 135–146.
5. Carrasco Gómez, P. A. (2017). *Uso de representaciones vectoriales de las palabras para la detección de dobles sentidos.* Valencia: Universidad Politécnica de Valencia.

6. Cuesta Santos, A. (2016). Contribución a la evaluación del desempeño, el sentido de compromiso y el accionar de la gestión del capital humano en la empresa. *Anales de la Academia de Ciencias de Cuba, 6*(3). Retrieved 2018, from http://www.revistaccuba.cu/index.php/acc/article/view/564
7. Garcés Hernández, S. C. (2017). *DISEÑO DE PROTOCOLO DE PROCEDIMIENTO DE SELECCIÓN ORIENTADO EN COMPETENCIAS LABORALES.* Bogotá: UNIVERSIDAD DE CUNDINAMARCA.
8. Martínez García , Y. (2018, Marzo 9). De la inversión extranjera y sus avances. *Periódico Granma.* Retrieved from http://www.granma.cu/cuba/2018-03-09/de-la-inversion-extranjera-y-sus-avances-09-03-2018-14-03-02
9. Martínez Hernández, L., & Puig Meneses, Y. (2018, Marzo 26). Analizó V Pleno del Comité Central del Partido importantes temas de la actualización del modelo económico y social. *Periódico Granma.* Retrieved Abril 2018, from http://www.granma.cu/cuba/2018-03-26/analizo-v-pleno-del-comite-central-del-partido-importantes-temas-de-la-actualizacion-del-modelo-economico-y-social-cubano-26-03-2018-22-03-07
10. Mikolov, T., Le, Q. v., & Sutskever, I. (2013). *Exploiting Similarities among Languages for Machine Translation.* Santa Clara, California.
11. Mikolov, T., Yih, W. T., & Zweig, G. (2013). Linguistic Regularities in Continuous Space Word Representations. *Proceedings of the 2013 Conference of the North American Chapter of the Association for Computational Linguistics: Human Language Technologies*, (pp. 746-751). Retrieved from arXiv preprint arXiv:1301.3781.
12. Rahlf, T. (2017). *Data Visualisation with R.* Nueva York: Springer International Publishing.
13. Slamet, C., Atmadja, A. R., Maylawati, D. S., Lestari1, R. S., Darmalaksana, W., & Ramdhani, M. A. (2018). Automated Text Summarization for Indonesian Article Using Vector Space Model. *The 2nd Annual Applied Science and Engineering Conference (AASEC 2017). 345.* Pekanbaru-Riau, Indonesia: IOP Publishing. doi:doi:10.1088/1757-899X/288/1/012037
14. Sparck Jones, K. (1972). A statistical interpretation of term specificity and its application in retrieval. *Journal of documentation*, 11-21.
15. Torres López, S. (2015). *Modelo de evaluación de competencias a partir de evidencias durante la gestión de proyectos.* Tesis Doctoral, Universidad de las Ciencias Informáticas, Laboratorio de Investigaciones de Gestión de Proyectos, La Habana. Retrieved 2018
16. Torres López, S., Aldana Cuza, M. L., Piñero Perez, P. Y., & Piedra Diéguez, L. A. (2016, Noviembre). Red neuronal multicapa para la evaluación de competencias laborales. *Revista Cubana de Ciencias Informáticas, 10*(Especial UCIENCIA), 210-223. Retrieved 2018, from https://rcci.uci.cu/?journal=rcci&page=article&op=view&path%5B%5D=1466
17. Zimniewicz, M., Kurowski, K., & Węglarz, J. (2018). Scheduling aspects in keyword extraction problem. *International Transactions in Operational Research*, 507–522. doi:https://doi.org/10.1111/itor.12368

Towards integrating BPMN 2.0 with CMMN and DMN standards for flexible business process modeling

Andrea Delgado[1] and Daniel Calegari[1]

Instituto de Computación, Facultad de Ingeniería, Universidad de la República, Julio Herrera y Reissig 565, Uruguay
adelgado,dcalegar@fing.edu.uy

Abstract. Business Process Model and Notation (BPMN 2.0) is a standard widely used in organizations to support requirements elicitation of their operational processes. However, the language targets fully structured processes, i.e. processes for which most exceptional paths and variants are previously known, providing little room for flexibility. On the other hand, the Case Management Model and Notation (CMMN) is designed to support the modeling of processes which cannot be predicted in advanced, at least not completely. Also, the Decision Model and Notation (DMN) helps decoupling business rules from both languages. In this paper, we present an analysis of the level of support for the integration of these standards for flexible business process modeling.

Keywords: Requirements elicitation of business processes · Modeling languages:BPMN 2.0, CMMN, DMN · Business process flexibility

1 Introduction

In the last two decades the Business Process Management (BPM) paradigm [1] has been adopted as the main approach to support organization's improvement. Business Processes (BPs) modeling has gained great importance in the software requirements field since they provide the main input for the development of Process Aware Information Systems (PAIS) [6] to support BPs operation. In fact, Business Process Management Systems (BPMS) [2] allows BPs enactment based on the same models captured in the requirements phase.

Modeling challenges arise, e.g.: when defining all possible execution paths for BPs regarding decisions based on different type of clients, contexts for instances, occurrence of events, messages received, among others. Also arise when the BP cannot be completely defined in design time (i.e.: loosely specified BPs), since decisions will be taken based on specific data or events during BP execution.

To deal with these and other flexibility issues in BPs, a taxonomy of flexibility needs for PAIS is defined in [10]: variability focuses on defining variants of a process family at design time; looseness deals with processes that cannot be completely prespecified prior to execution; adaptation deals with both planned and unplanned exceptions in design and runtime; and evolution refers to the ability of implemented BPs to evolve as the process evolves. Several approaches exists to deal with flexibility [10], but only few of them provide support for modeling and executing BPs in a flexible way.

The Business Process Model and Notation (BPMN 2.0) [7] provides constructions addressing most of the modeling and execution needs, mostly for structured process with predefined execution options. On the other hand, the Case Management (CM) approach deals with process that are data driven in which although the activities are well defined, the control flow between them is loosely specified. The Case Management Model and Notation (CMMN) [8] standard provides support for modeling case management loosely specified processes.

Another aspect that can be difficult to express in BP models are business rules of the organization, e.g.: the combination of values regarding the execution of selected variables or data managed by the process. To tackle with this complexity, the Decision Modeling Notation (DMN) [9] supports the definition of business rules that can be connected with BPMN 2.0 and CMMN concrete constructors (business rule tasks and decision tasks, respectively). This simplifies maintenance and evolution of business rules without impacting the BP implementation.

In previous work we have dealt with process variability [3] in BPMN 2.0 at design time. In this paper, we present an analysis of the integration of three standards: BPMN 2.0, CMMN and CMN, and the existing tool support for their combined use. The aim of the work is to analyze how the combination of these languages provide support for flexible BPs modeling, with focus on both prespecified and loosely specified processes.

The rest of the document is organized as follows. Section 2 discusses the integration of the three languages and Section 3 presents an example of such integration in two selected tools. Section 4 presents a discussion on the analysis and tools. Finally, Section 5 presents some conclusions.

2 Flexible business process modeling

From a modeling perspective, the three languages can be connected, by design, for flexible business process modeling, integrating both structured and loosely specified processes. For space reasons we do not delve into details on the definition of the languages nor on a comparison of them. Instead, we focus on how their integration is supported in practice.

BPMN - CMMN If the process is mostly structured with some flexible parts, the model should be BPMN 2.0-based, invoking a CMNN process for the flexible parts. One construction that can be used to integrate CMMN into the BPMN process is the Call Activity, which is provided in BPMN 2.0 to define reusable sub-process that can be invoked from several processes.

CMMN – BPMN If the process is mostly non-structured with some structured parts, the model should be CMMN-based, invoking a BPMN sub-processes when needed. CMMN already provide a construction for this, the Process Task, which reference a sub-process in BPMN.

BPMN – DMN / CMMN - DMN In both cases, the integration with DMN specifications of business rules, defined as decision tables, will ease the understanding, execution and maintenance of business rules. In BPMN 2.0 the business rule task, and in CMMN the decision task, are the constructors linked with DMN decision tables.

2.1 Tool support

We carried out a survey of tools with support for the modeling and execution of BPMN, CMMN and DMN, which is summarized in Table 1. The list is not intended to be exhaustive, but expressive enough to overview the maturity level of support for the languages. Nevertheless, as far as we know, there is no other BPMN tool supporting the other two languages.

It can be seen that, after BPMN, the DMN language is the most supported at both modeling and execution level. The latter is justified by the existence of many business rules management system (BRMS) solutions, e.g.: Drools[1], which just adapted their operation to the new language. This is in fact the case of Activiti, jBPMN and Signavio, which use Drools as its BRMS.

Although there are also many case management systems, they have different execution models that do not make it easy to adapt to the CMMN language, and thus, its support is defined from scratch by conforming to the corresponding BPMN engine execution model. As far as we know, only Camunda and Flowable integrates the three languages in a unified way, for both modeling and execution. However, there is no complete support, since there are some aspects under development. We discuss them in the case study presented in the next section.

3 Example of integration

We have modeled a simple business process integrating a BPMN-based structured workflow together with DMN-based rule driven decisions, and CMMN-based unstructured case handling. We also implemented it in both Camunda and Flowable in order to compare them as a validation of the maturity level of support for these standards. Complete code can be found online[2].

We used the "Car Insurance Application" BPMN-based business process provided by Camunda, which is depicted in Figure 1.

The process starts when someone requests a car insurance. The first step is a business rule task (Determine risks) that automatically determines whether the insurance can be provided right away (green risk), the application need to be checked in detail (yellow risk) or the insurance will be refused (red risk). This business rule task is a fully automated DMN decision table shown in Figure 2.

[1] Drools: https://www.drools.org/

[2] Case study source code: https://gitlab.fing.edu.uy/open-coal/bpmnstandards2018

Table 1. BPMN, DMN & CMMN tool support (last update: jun'18)

	BPMN		DMN		CMMN	
	Modeling	Execution	Modeling	Execution	Modeling	Execution
Business Process Management Systems (BPMS)						
Activiti[1]	✓	✓	✓	✓	✗	✗
Adoxx[2]	✓	✗	✓	✗	✗	✗
bpmn.io[3]	✓	✗	✓	✗	✓	✗
Camunda[4]	✓	✓	✓	✓	✓	✓
Flowable[5]	✓	✓	✓	✓	✓	✓
jBPM[6]	✓	✓	✓	✓	✗	✓
Oracle BPM[7]	✓	✓	✓	✗	✗	✗
Signavio[8]	✓	✓	✓	✓	✓	✗
Trisotech[9]	✓	✗	✓	✗	✓	✗
Visual Paradigm[10]	✓	✗	✗	✗	✓	✗
Business Rules Management Systems (BRMS)						
Drools[11]	✗	✗	✓	✓	✗	✗
Fico[12]	✗	✗	✓	✓	✗	✗
Ground Lion[13]	✗	✗	✓	✓	✗	✗
Open Rules[14]	✗	✗	✓	✓	✗	✗

[1] Activiti: https://www.activiti.org/
[2] Adoox: https://www.adoxx.org
[3] bpmn.io: http://bpmn.io/
[4] Camunda: https://camunda.com/
[5] Flowable: https://www.flowable.org
[6] jBPM: https://www.jbpm.org/
[7] Oracle BPM: http://www.oracle.com/us/technologies/bpm
[8] Signavio: https://www.signavio.com
[9] Trisotech: http://www.trisotech.com
[10] Visual Paradigm: https://www.visual-paradigm.com/
[11] Drools: https://www.drools.org/
[12] FICO: http://www.fico.com
[13] Ground Lion: https://www.groundlion.be
[14] Open Rules: http://openrules.com/

If the application is denied (red risk) or it is approved (green risk), the process ends by first registering the denial or issuing the policy, respectively, using specific service tasks. We have adapted the BPMN model by removing two final send message tasks since they did not contribute to our purposes. If the application must be manually checked (yellow risk), it goes to a task connecting with the CMMN-based unstructured case handling depicted in Figure 3.

This case handling has different possible actions for approving or denying the application, and it is performed by a knowledge worker. If the application is approved by the worker, it can also be approved/rejected by a worker in a high hierarchy. The task has a non-interrupting timer event set in two days in order to speed up the application check if it takes longer than that.

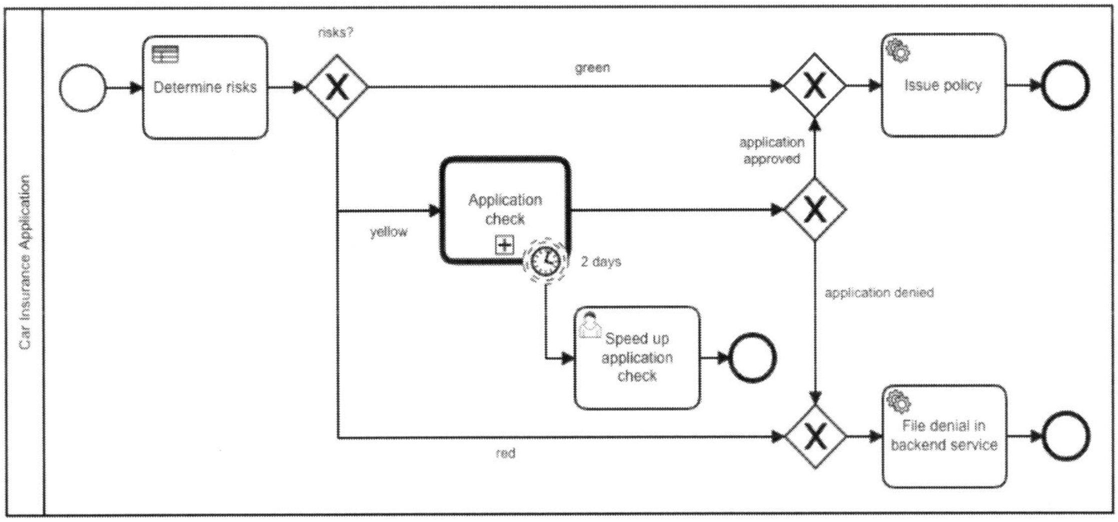

Fig. 1. BPMN example: car insurance application

C	Input			Output	
	Age	Car Manufacturer	Type of Car	Risk	Risk Evaluation
1	<= 21	–	–	"beginner"	"yellow"
2	<= 30	"BMW"	–	"young and fast"	"yellow"
3	–	"Porsche"	"911"	"careless speeding"	"yellow"
4	–	"BMW"	"X3"	"premium car"	"yellow"
5	<= 25	"Porsche"	"911"	"young and too fast"	"red"

Fig. 2. DMN example: determine risks. Default output = green risk

3.1 Camunda

We have modeled the case study using Camunda Modeler, which is based on the bpmn.io modeler, and Camunda for Windows for its execution. We configured Camunda to be used together with Tomcat, as the application server, and PostgreSQL, as the database management system.

We have built a set of test cases covering every possible flow, based on the DMN and CMMN-based tasks output criteria:

- **Case 1**. Age: 28, Manufacturer: Fiat, Type: Uno.
  DMN Output: Risk evaluation = green
- **Case 2**. Age: 22, Manufacturer: Porsche, Type: 911.
  DMN Output: Risk evaluation = red (Risk = "young and too fast")
- **Case 3**. Age: 28, Manufacturer: BMW, Type: X3.
  DMN Output: Risk evaluation = yellow (Risk = "premium car")

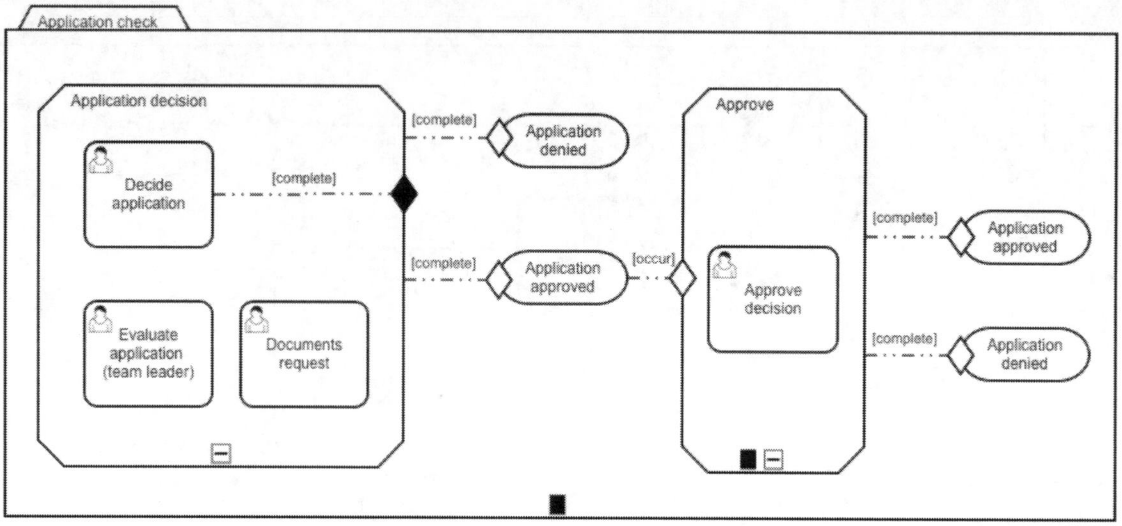

Fig. 3. CMMN example: application check

- ◇ **Case 3.1**. CMMN Decide application: application denied.
- ◇ **Case 3.2**. CMMN Decide application: application approved; but CMMN Approve decision: application denied.
- ◇ **Case 3.3**. CMMN Decide application: application approved; and CMMN Approve decision: application approved.

We evidence a seamless integration of DMN and BPMN. The process engine and the rules engine are connected through the configuration of process variables corresponding with the inputs and outputs of the business rule.

With respect to the integration of CMMN and BPMN, it is important to note that the case study provided by Camunda does not execute on the platform as it is modeled. We changed the CMMN model completion criteria, and added a stage to the last task, so that the model could be executed. This happens because CMMN tasks have a different lifecycle which must be know in detail so that the BPMN process can finish. In particular, the Aplication decision stage was configured to be automatically completed in such a way that if any additional tasks, which are not part of the output criteria, were not completed, the stage changed status and thus the CMMN process could continue. We also added another stage for the same purpose.

3.2 Flowable

We have used Flowable v6.3.0, together with Tomcat and PostgreSQL, as with Camunda. We also used the same set of test cases as before.

We first performed an interoperability check by importing the case study models from Camunda. We did not have any problem with respect to BPMN and DMN models. In the case of CMMN we faced some problems until we tried v6.3.0 (released during the study).

For integrating BPMN and DMN we needed to change rule selection policy (from C:collect to F:first) since it is not possible to handle the type of the output returned by the DMN engine. Nevertheless, after this change, the execution of the different DMN scenarios was done without problems.

In the case of the integration of BPMN and CMMN, we needed to define input variables from Java code since it was not possible to link them from the model editor. Moreover, it was possible to call the CMMN case handling using the call activity and execute the different CMMN scenarios, but it was not possible to return control to the BPMN process. We think this will be addressed soon since the integration is still under development.

4 Analysis and discussion

From a modeling perspective, the three standards can be easily integrated by design, and, as depicted in Table 1, there are tools available to do so.

These tools allow to fully represent BPMN and CMMN models. However, as far as we can validate, DMN modeling tools only support the decision logic level, i.e.: business knowledge models in the form of decision tables specifying how an output is determined from a set of inputs. The decision requirements level, also defined in the standard, is not supported, i.e.: a Decision Requirements Diagram (DRD) showing how a set of decisions depend on each other, on input data, and on business knowledge models. In this sense, DMN is not yet fully supported.

The fact of using existing modeling elements for different purposes might be confusing when integrating languages, in particular, using a Call Activity within a BPMN model for both: the integration of a CMMN fragment, and a BPMN reusable subprocess call. It could be clearer for modelers to use different elements in order to state different semantics. In the same line, there are some cases in which a CMMN model could be replaced by a BPMN ad hoc sub-process, to represent those activities whose execution flow is flexible. In this sense, some complimentary works must be considered, e.g.: [11], in order to have a bigger picture on the comparison of the languages from a modeling perspective.

From a process enactment perspective, CMMN does not have the same support as BPMN or DMN. There are few options for executing CMMN models, being a standard not already adopted by most of the BPMS since it requires to unify different execution models in one process engine. On the contrary, since business rules management systems (BRMS) are a central component, and there exist BRMS that can be easily integrated on any BPMS by using a service layer, e.g.: Drools, the absence of native support for DMN does not represent a problem. Nevertheless, in these cases the integration could not be done seamless, requiring to adapt the BPMN models to be connected to some external BRMS.

Since the three languages are standards whose support is expected to increase in the following years, they must be considered when selecting a BPMS. In previous works [5, 4] we have proposed a methodology for the systematic evaluation of BPMS, considering both functional and non-functional aspects. In this methodology, there is a category named "Process Design and Modeling" which considers BPMN as the language for business process modeling. This category must be updated in order to consider the integration of the three languages.

5 Conclusions

We present an analysis of the integration of three standards: BPMN 2.0, CMMN and DMN, and the existing tool support for their combined use. Besides the three languages can be connected, by design, for flexible business process modeling, there are some open issues, as discussed in Section 4.

The integration of BPMN 2.0 and CMMN languages becomes a key element in process modeling and execution when both structured and loosely specified paths exist. Moreover, the separation of concerns between business rules specification and their implementation, as decision tables supported by the DMN standard, helps in providing more flexible process models.

We focused on how the integration of the languages is supported in practice. Based on our analysis and proof of concepts using Camunda and Flowable, we can conclude that the integration of the three standards has great potential to support the complexity of nowadays processes.

6 Acknowledgements

This work was partially funded by Comisión Sectorial de Investigación Científica (CSIC), Uruguay. We would like to thank undergraduate student Fabricio Agretti who worked in the project regarding the prototype implementation.

References

1. van der Aalst, W.M.P., ter Hofstede, A.H.M., Weske, M.: Business process management: a survey. In: Business Process Management, International Conference, BPM 2003. LNCS, vol. 2678, pp. 1–12. Springer (2003)
2. Chang, J.: Business Process Management Systems: Strategy and Implementation. CRC Press (2016)
3. Delgado, A., Calegari, D.: BPMN 2.0 based modeling and customization of variants in business process families. In: XLIII CLEI. pp. 1–9. IEEE (2017)
4. Delgado, A., Calegari, D.: Evaluating non-functional aspects of business process management systems. In: XLIII CLEI. pp. 1–10. IEEE (2017)
5. Delgado, A., Calegari, D., Milanese, P., Falcon, R., Garcia, E.: A systematic approach for evaluating BPM systems: Case studies on open source and proprietary tools. In: Open Source Systems: Adoption and Impact - 11th IFIP WG 2.13 Intl.Conf., OSS 2015. IFIP, vol. 451, pp. 81–90. Springer (2015)
6. Dumas, M., van der Aalst, W.M., ter Hofstede, A.H.: Process-aware Information Systems: Bridging People and Software Through Process Technology. John Wiley & Sons, Inc. (2005)
7. OMG: Business process model and notation (BPMN) v2.0. Tech. rep., OMG (2011)
8. OMG: Case mgmt model and notation (CMMN) v1.1. Tech. rep., OMG (2016)
9. OMG: Decision model and notation (DMN) v1.1. Tech. rep., OMG (2016)
10. Reichert, M., Weber, B.: Enabling Flexibility in Process-Aware Information Systems - Challenges, Methods, Technologies. Springer (2012)
11. Zensen, A., Küster, J.: A comparison of flexible BPMN and CMMN in practice: A case study on component release processes. In: EDOC. pp. 105–114. IEEE (2018)

Riscos de Engenharia de Requisitos com a utilização de Metodologias Ágeis

Marcelo Ferreira de Almeida Araújo[1], Angélica Toffano Seidel Calazans[1], Roberto Ávila Paldês[1], Kiane Fialho Rezende[1], Fábio de Souza Gonçalves[1], Fernando de Albuquerque Guimarães[1], Eloisa Toffano Seidel Calazans[1], Emeli Braosi[1], and Edna Dias Canedo[2]

[1] Centro Universitário de Brasília, UniCEUB, Brasil
contato@rederequisitos.com.br
[2] Universidade de Brasília, UnB, Brasil
ednacanedo@unb.br

Resumo Os métodos ágeis têm agregado maior valor à Engenharia de Requisitos, mas alguns riscos podem comprometer esse esforço. O objetivo da pesquisa foi de identificar quais riscos são mais impactantes em projetos ágeis e quais são as ações adotadas para tratá-los. Analisaram-se 21 artigos para identificação dos riscos mais citados, sendo classificados em 5 categorias. Para obter a percepção de líderes de projetos ágeis, foram entrevistados 6 gerentes de organizações diversas. A percepção de 53 desenvolvedores foi obtida por um questionário. Constataram-se riscos como: não entendimento dos requisitos pelo desenvolvedor; falta de disponibilidade do cliente; falhas na gerência das mudanças. O risco com menor impacto, segundo os desenvolvedores, foi a mudança dos requisitos não funcionais e, segundo os líderes, foi a mudança em requisitos funcionais. Encontraram-se alguns riscos não citados pela literatura e, finalmente, foram apontadas estratégias para a sua mitigação ou eliminação.

Keywords: Engenharia · Requisitos · Riscos · Ágil · Software

1 Introdução

O Manifesto Ágil [1] trouxe ideias como valorizar a interação entre pessoas, a comunicação com o cliente, aceitar e reagir rapidamente à mudanças. Esse enfoque, entretanto, pode representar a admissão e a ampliação de riscos relativos ao processo de definição dos requisitos do software.

Um risco é entendido como a probabilidade de ocorrer perda, dano ou atraso, no presente ou futuro, durante a construção de um produto de software [2], [3]. No processo de gerenciamento de riscos [4], existe a necessidade de definir os impactos dos riscos no desenvolvimento do produto de software, além de definir a probabilidade, o planejamento das respostas aos riscos como forma de eliminar, mitigar ou contingenciar esses riscos [5].

Nesse contexto, o objetivo do estudo é de identificar quais riscos relacionados a requisitos são mais impactantes em projetos que utilizem os métodos ágeis e quais as ferramentas adotadas para mitigar ou eliminar esses riscos, na percepção de desenvolvedores e líderes. Os objetivos específicos são: identificar os riscos relacionados a requisitos e ao contexto ágil, descobrir os níveis de impacto de cada risco relacionado a requisitos e evidenciar as estratégias de eliminação e mitigação desses riscos.

A justificativa e motivação para a elaboração do estudo é a crescente utilização das metodologias ágeis em projetos de desenvolvimento e manutenção de software [6], [7].

2 Riscos de requisitos em métodos ágeis

O foco principal dos métodos ágeis de desenvolvimento de software é a simplicidade e a velocidade [21]. Os riscos presentes no modelo podem ser classificados em 6 grupos: risco de requisitos, riscos técnicos, riscos de cronograma, riscos de projeto, riscos de fornecedores e riscos de pessoas [9].

Com base nessa classificação e em estudo [10] com três metodologias ágeis (XP, SCRUM e DSDM) foiram identificados os seguintes riscos de requisitos: User Stories alteradas em função do Test Driven Development e integração continua para validar e detectar erros regressivos e efeitos colaterais (XP); o uso de User Stories possibilitam um alto grau de clareza em uma linguagem que o cliente entende. A inclusão do cliente no planejamento e revisão das reuniões também ajudam a manter esse risco controlado (SCRUM); entre outros aspectos. Também foram identificados [11] os seguintes fatores de riscos relacionados a requisitos: conflito de requisitos, falta de clareza de requisitos, mudanças de requisitos, falhas de documentação, falha de comunicação.

São ainda destacados como riscos em relação ao modelo ágil [12]: requisitos insuficientes e ambíguos, compreensão insuficiente de negócios, domínio e contexto, negligência das partes interessadas com relação aos requisitos não-funcionais, falta de comunicação, planejamento inadequado e insuficiente, documentação.

No contexto de requisitos, o SCRUM [13] incorpora os seguintes tipos de riscos: desenvolver as funções erradas do software, desenvolver a interface do usuário errada, alterações tardias nos requisitos, falta de requisitos congelados, incompreensão dos requisitos. Na dimensão do planejamento e controle são apontados [13] riscos como: comunicação ineficaz, alteração de escopo, gestão de mudanças inadequada. requisitos).

Não focando no contexto ágil, mais identificando riscos com relação a requisitos no desenvolvimento de software [14] identificam vários tipos de riscos relacionados a requisitos, entre eles: excessivo número de requisitos, clientes não representativos com relação ao contexto do software a ser desenvolvido; requisitos incorretos, requisitos complexos, requisitos incompletos, requisitos que não atendem totalmente às necessidades dos clientes, requisitos com conflitos, requisitos não rastreáveis, requisitos não estáveis, baixa qualidade dos requisitos.

Considerando que a maioria dos modelos ágeis trabalha com requisitos representados em forma de User Stories, foi sugerido [15] um framework com 13 critérios de qualidade de User Stories como forma de melhorar os requisitos ágeis.

Esse framework visa a melhoria de qualidade, atomicidade, orientação ao problema, estimativa, completude, entre outros quesitos relativos às User Stories.

3 Metodologia

Para levantamento dos riscos relacionados a requisitos considerando o contexto de desenvolvimento ágil, foram analisadas as seguintes fontes de artigos científicos: Google Scholar, SCRUM Alliance e SCRUM.Org.

Foram utilizadas as seguintes strings de busca: (requisitos or requirements) and (software) and (riscos or risks) and (ágil or agile or scrum or xp); (requirements) and (software) and (risks) and (agile or scrum or xp); requisitos and software and riscos and ágil e foram obtidos 1000 resultados.

Foram eliminados os artigos e fontes de informação que não estavam disponíveis integralmente e os que não eram aderentes ao tema. Após isso, os artigos e e fontes de informação foram classificados por quantidade de citações e aderência ao tema. Chegou-se ao universo final de 21 artigos e fontes de informação. As fontes foram lidas integralmente e selecionados 8 artigos aderentes ao contexto da pesquisa. os riscos contidos nesses artigos foram listados e classificados .

Para obter a percepção dos líderes e desenvolvedores, os seguintes instrumentos de coleta de dados foram aplicados: entrevistas semi-estruturadas (líderes), questionários (desenvolvedores). A construção do instrumento de coleta de dados para o roteiro de entrevista semiaberta teve o objetivo de obter a percepção dos líderes de projetos. Para identificar riscos que existem, mas não estavam listados no material analisado pela pesquisa, o instrumento tinha uma questão aberta com a possibilidade do líder se posicionar sobre outros riscos que identificava no contexto de requisitos ágeis e que não tinham sido citados. Foi realizado também, o relacionamento dos riscos com algumas etapas do Gerenciamento de Riscos [13]. Assim, no instrumento de coleta de dados, foram adicionados questionamentos para cada risco: 'Qual o impacto?' (Alto, médio ou baixo), 'Qual a probabilidade?' (Alta, média ou baixa), 'Qual a estratégia para eliminar?', 'Qual a estratégia para mitigar?'.

Na construção do questionário [16], onde aplicável, utilizou-se a escala de Likert adaptada para avaliação dos achados. Para análise dos dados coletados, utilizaram-se técnicas estatísticas (questionários) e análise de conteúdo (entrevista). Nas entrevistas qualitativas utilizou-se o método Condensação de Significados [17] com o objetivo de identificar pontos em comum da percepção dos participantes e também para classificar os riscos identificados nos artigos.

4 Resultados e discussão

Considerando os artigos selecionados, foi construída a lista de riscos relacionados a requisitos em métodos ágeis (Tabela 1). Os riscos foram divididos em 5 categorias realcionados: aos negócios e a barreiras de comunicação, aos requisitos funcionais e não funcionais, às mudanças de requisitos, ao cliente e à qualidade.

Tabela 1. Riscos de requisitos identificados versus fontes de informação.

Tipos de riscos relacionados a requisitos	Descrição do Risco	[18]	[19]	[9] [10]	[13]	[12]	[11]	[20]	[21]
Relacionados aos negócios e a barreiras de comunicação	Negócio / Escopo / objetivos não-claros		X		X	X			
	Não entendimento dos requisitos pelo cliente e/ou desenvolvedor (falhas na comunicação)	X	X	X	X	X	X	X	
Requisitos funcionais e não funcionais	Falta de definição ou definição insuficiente dos Requisitos funcionais, user story			X		X			
	Indefinição dos Requisitos não funcionais		X	X		X			
	Falha na priorização de requisitos								X
Mudanças de requisitos	Mudanças (instabilidade) nos requisitos funcionais ou user stories	X	X	X		X	X		
	Mudança dos requisitos não funcionais (instabilidade) ou user stories				X				
	Mudanças nos requisitos de negócios, mercado ou tecnologia	X		X					
	Falhas na gerência de mudança				X				
Cliente	Pouca ou não aceitação do usuário final			X				X	
	Falta de disponibilidade do cliente		X						
	Falta de conhecimento do cliente		X						
	Diferentes expectativas sobre o sistema entre distintos usuários.	X							X
Qualidade user story e documentação	Problemas de qualidade com relação as user stories (não ambiguidade, não conflito, insuficientes, independência, correta, clara etc)			X		X	X		
	Problemas na documentação (insuficiência, erros)	X				X	X	X	

A percepção dos desenvolvedores foi obtida em 23 organizações que trabalham com Métodos Ágeis, no período de 26/10/2018 a 29/11/2018.

Foi construída pela análise de 53 questionários respondidos por especialistas usando o Google Forms. Para obter a percepção de líderes e desenvolvedores, foram selecionados 6 gerentes de projetos de organizações para aplicação de entrevistas semiabertas, realizadas no período de 26/10/2018 a 29/11/2018.

Em ambas as coletas, foram tomadas informações relativas ao perfil do respondente, como o cargo do respondente, empresa, tempo total de experiência com métodos ágeis (em anos), tipo de projeto (manutenção ou desenvolvimento de um novo software). O cuidado foi para interpretar o cenário dos resultados.

4.1 Análise do perfil dos participantes

Com relação a experiência do líder com desenvolvimento ágeis, 2 líderes possuíam mais de 10 anos nesse contexto (33%). Dois líderes tinham menos de 2 anos e 2 líderes de 4 a 5 anos.

A análise dos dados com relação a especialidade da equipe, 64% dos líderes identificou que trabalha com perfil de colaboradores de sênior/especialistas o que mostra uma equipe madura no desenvolvimento de projetos de software. A maioria dos líderes classificou a experiência da equipe entre 6 e 8, considerando a escala de 1 a 10.

Com relação ao prazo dos projetos, 50% dos líderes trabalha com projetos de 6 meses a 1 ano. O restante ficou distribuído entre 33% em projetos abaixo de 3 meses (inclusive) e somente um líder com projetos superiores a 1 ano.

Considerando o foco dos projetos, 66% dos líderes citou a automação do processo de negócio. Com relação ao tipo de desenvolvimento, 83% trabalham com novo desenvolvimento e manutenção de sistemas. Com relação a quantidade de participantes da equipe, 50% dos líderes informou que cada equipe tem de 8 a 12 pessoas.

4.2 Análise de conteúdo dos questionários aplicados

Foi realizada a análise de conteúdo das entrevistas e questionários aplicados. A Figura 1 apresenta os resultados comparativos da análise de conteúdo das entrevistas e dos questionários. É interessante ressaltar que existiram respostas dos líderes, com relação aos impactos dos riscos, em que não houve consenso, tais como, negócio/ nscopo/ objetivos não-claros onde os graus variaram de 1 a 5 (com 2 líderes optando por 3), mudança de requisitos não funcionais, pouca ou não aceitação do usuário final, diferentes expectativas sobre o sistema. Assim , optou-se por não representar os valores da média da percepção dos lideres para esses riscos. A Análise de Variância e Desvio Padrão das respostas obtidas dos desenvolvedores demonstrou que os dados variaram em média abaixo de 1,23 ao redor de médias que ficaram no máximo em 4,11.

Na percepção dos líderes, foram identificados os 5 riscos com fator de impacto maior: falta de disponibilidade do cliente (4,5); falta de (ou pouco) conhecimento do sistema atual pelo cliente (4,16); falha na gerência de mudanças (4,0); não entendimento dos requisitos pelo desenvolvedor (falhas na comunicação) (4,0); falha na priorização de requisitos (3,83). Esse resultado ratifica achados de outros pesquisadores [21], [19], [9], [10]. A percepção de desenvolvedores e líderes identifica riscos em comum com maior impacto: não entendimento dos requisitos pelo desenvolvedor (falhas na comunicação); falta de disponibilidade do cliente; falhas na gerência das mudanças.

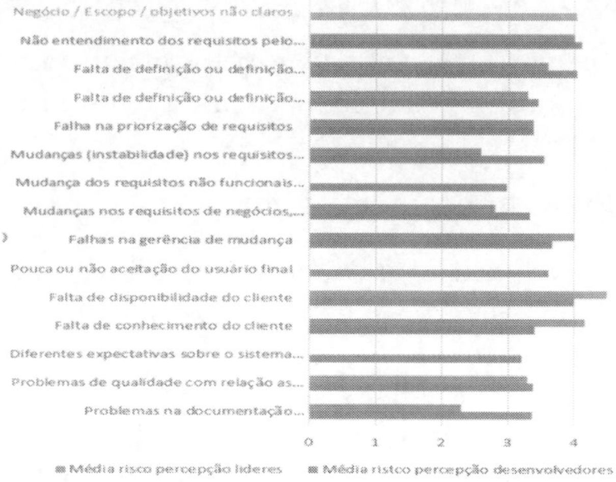

Figura 1. Média das respostas dos Desenvolvedores e Líderessobre impacto por risco

Pode-se notar que na escala de 1 a 5, na percepção do desenvolvedor, apenas um risco obteve média abaixo de 3. Esse risco estava relacionado ao impacto na mudança dos requisitos não funcionais. Na percepção dos líderes, o risco impacto na mudança dos requisitos funcionais é o risco de menor impacto. A justificativa pode se dar pelas observações dos líderes quando citam que: "o desenvolvimento de software assume desde o início a incidência de mudanças", "metodologia ágil proporciona amadurecimento gradual da solução", "aceitar a instabilidade".

Outra descoberta foi a identificação de três riscos, não citados pela literatura, mas que foram identificados pelos líderes:

- Mudança da equipe de desenvolvimento, mudar sua configuração da equipe. O líder deu grau 4 para esse risco.
- Equipes grandes com mais de 7 pessoas é um risco para o projeto. O líder identificou para esse risco o grau 4.
- Cultura da organização não aderir aos métodos ágeis. Segundo o líder não se consegue implantar a metodologia ágil sem uma cultura organizacional ampla. Foi identificado o grau 4 de risco.

Com relação à identificação de estratégias de eliminação e mitigação de todos esses riscos, foram identificados para os riscos relacionados:

- Aos negócios e a barreiras de comunicação: comunicação com o cliente (50%), participação ativa do PO (33%), aproximação do cliente (33%), trabalhar a comunicação (33%);
- Aos requisitos funcionais e não funcionais: investir na comunicação, proximidade e feedback com o cliente (50%), Design Thinking, brainstorming para validar a avaliação dos stakeholders, a partir da avaliação das personas construídas (33%), a proximidade com o cliente (33%), o envolvimento do PO é essencial para mitigar ou eliminar esse risco (83%);
- As mudanças de requisitos: Participação do PO (50%) ,springs curtos (33%), comunicação, priorização, reuniões de planejamento;

- Ao Cliente: solicitar mudança PO e do cliente (33%), promover a conscientização do PO e do cliente (33%), envolver a equipe (33%), usar técnicas de brainstorming, técnicas de levantamento, reuniões de todos os usuários daquele sistema e envolvê-los no levantamento, alinhando expectativas (66%);
- A qualidade User Story e documentação: participação de especialistas (50%), as ferramentas de qualidade (reunião por pares, checklist) (50%). O Scrum Master deve atuar nesse contexto (33%), ter um processo de qualidade (revisão por pares, documentação reversa, cheklist (50%),

Com relação aos novos riscos identificados pela pesquisa, foram identificadas as seguintes ações de mitigação ou eliminação: mudança da equipe de desenvolvimento: evitar o máximo as alterações na equipe e dar condições favoráveis para a pessoa se sentir motivada e não sair da equipe. Caso haja saída de pessoas, para mitigar esse risco pode-se dividir a equipe. Equipes grandes com mais de 7 pessoas: pode-se criar mecanismos de comunicação. Utilizar o conceito de Squads que são equipes que trabalham no mesmo projeto (2/3/10 equipes trabalhando no mesmo projeto). Cultura da organização: a realização de várias atividades para difundir a cultura de métodos ágeis, tais como workshops, eventos tipo Hackathon e vários treinamentos sobre agilidade.

5 Conclusão e trabalhos futuros

O objetivo deste trabalho foi identificar quais riscos relacionados a requisitos são mais impactantes em projetos que utilizem os Métodos Ágeis e quais as ferramentas adotadas para mitigar ou eliminar esses riscos, na percepção de desenvolvedores e líderes. Com a análise das respostas foi constatado a existência de riscos mais impactantes na percepção de líderes e desenvolvedores: não entendimento dos requisitos pelo desenvolvedor (falhas na comunicação); falta de disponibilidade do cliente; falhas na gerência das mudanças. Foram identificados também, riscos não citados pela literatura pesquisada, tais como, mudança da equipe de desenvolvimento, equipes grandes com mais de 7 pessoas e a cultura da organização não aderente aos Métodos Ágeis. Foram identificadas também, as estratégias para mitigar ou eliminar esses riscos. As que apareceram na maior parte das estratégias: participação do PO e aproximação com o cliente. Foram citadas ferramentas de Design Thinking, brains-torming, Canvas de negócio ou Canvas de projetos, benchmark, alinhamento de expectativas (grooming), treinamento. Cabe ressaltar que a aproximação com o cliente faz parte dos valores do modelo ágil, o que nos permite questionar se isso está sendo realizado. Como trabalhos futuros, sugere-se identificar os motivos pelos quais as percepções de desenvolvedores e líderes não estão totalmente alinhadas.

Referências

1. Manifesto for Agile Software Development. http://agilemanifesto.org/
2. Charette, R.: Why software fails. IEEE Spectrum, Vol. 42.N.9, pp 89-94 (2005)

3. Zamith, J.: Gestão de riscos e prevenção de perdas: um novo paradigma para a segurança das organizações. 1 ed. Rio de Janeiro: FGV (2007)
4. PMI.: Um guia do conhecimento em gerenciamento de projetos. Guia PMBOK, 5a. ed, Project Management Institute (2013)
5. Macedo, M.H.B., Salgado, E.G.: Gerenciamento de risco aplicado ao desenvolvimento de software. Sistemas & Gestão 10, pp 158-170 (2015)
6. Almeida, G.A.M.de.: Fatores de escolha entre metodologias de desenvolvimento de software tradicionais e ágeis. Dissertação. Escola Politécnica da Universidade de São Paulo, USP (2017)
7. Santos, A. C. C. dos et al.: Experiência Acadêmica de uma Fábrica de Software utilizando Scrum no Desenvolvimento de Software In: Wokshop Brasileiro de Métodos Ágeis, p. 86- 96 (2010)
8. Vicente, A. A: Definição e gerenciamento de métricas de teste no contexto de métodos ágeis. Dissertação. Instituto de ciências matemáticas e computação, Universidade São Paulo, USP (2010)
9. Moran, A.: Agile Risk Management. In: Agile Risk Management. Springer Briefs in Computer Science. Springer, DOI: 10.1007/978-3-319-05008-9-3, (2014)
10. Moran, A.:Applying Agile Risk Management. In: Agile Risk Management. Springer Briefs in Computer Science. Springer, DOI: 10.1007/978-3-319-05008-9-4 (2014)
11. Ancveire, I., Gailite, I., Gailite, M., Grabis, J.: Software Delivery Risk Management: Application of Bayesian Networks in Agile Software Development. Information Technology and Management Science, 18 (2015)
12. Ghobadi, S., Mathiassen, L.: Risks to Effective Knowledge Sharing in Agile Software Teams: A Model for Assessing and Mitigating Risks. John Wiley & Sons Ltd, Information Systems Journal 27, 699–731 (2016)
13. Rech, P.J.: Gerenciamento de riscos em projetos de desenvolvimento de software com SCRUM. Dissertação. Programa de Pós-Graduação em Ciências da Computação da Faculdade de Informática da Pontifícia Universidade Católica do Rio Grande do Sul, Porto Alegre (2013)
14. Siqueira, D.L., Fontoura, L: Argumentation Schemes for Collaborative Debate of Requirement Risks in Software Projects. International Journal of Software Engineering and Knowledge Engineering Vol. 27, Nos. 9&10 pp1613–1635 (2017)
15. Lucassen, G., Dalpiaz, F., Van Der Werf, J.M.E.M. et al.: Improving Agile Requirements: The Quality User Story Framework and Tool Requirements Eng. 21: 383. https://doi.org/10.1007/s00766-016-0250-x. (2016)
16. Martins, G.A.: Estudo de Caso – uma estratégia de pesquisa. São Paulo: Atlas, (2006)
17. Kvale, Steinar.: Interviews: an introduction to qualitative research interviewing. California: Sage publications (1996)
18. Schwaber, K. Suttheland, J.: Um guia definitivo para o Scrum: As regras do Jogo. www.scrumguides.org/docs/scrumguide/v2017/2017-Scrum-Guide-Portuguese-Brazilian.pdf (2017)
19. Curcio, K. - Requirements engineering: A systematic mapping study in agile software development, The Journal Systems and Software (2018)
20. Sundararajan, S., Bhasi, M., Vijayaraghavan,P.K.: Case study on risk management practice in large offshore-outsourced Agile software projects. IET Softw., Vol. 8, Iss. 6, pp. 245–257 doi: 10.1049/iet-sen.2013.0190 (2014)
21. Shrivastava, S.V., Rathod, U. A Risk Management Framework for Distributed Agile Projects January. Information and Software Technology, v. 85. DOI: 10.1016/j.infsof.2016.12.005 (2017)

CIbSE - IberoAmerican Conference on Software Engineering
c/o Luca Cernuzzi
Universidad Católica "Nuestra Seóra de la Asunción",
Campus Universitario, Asunción
Barrio Santa Ana, C.C.1683, C.P. 1364
Asunción - Paraguay

ISBN 978-1-5108-8795-4

CURRAN ASSOCIATES INC.
proceedings.com